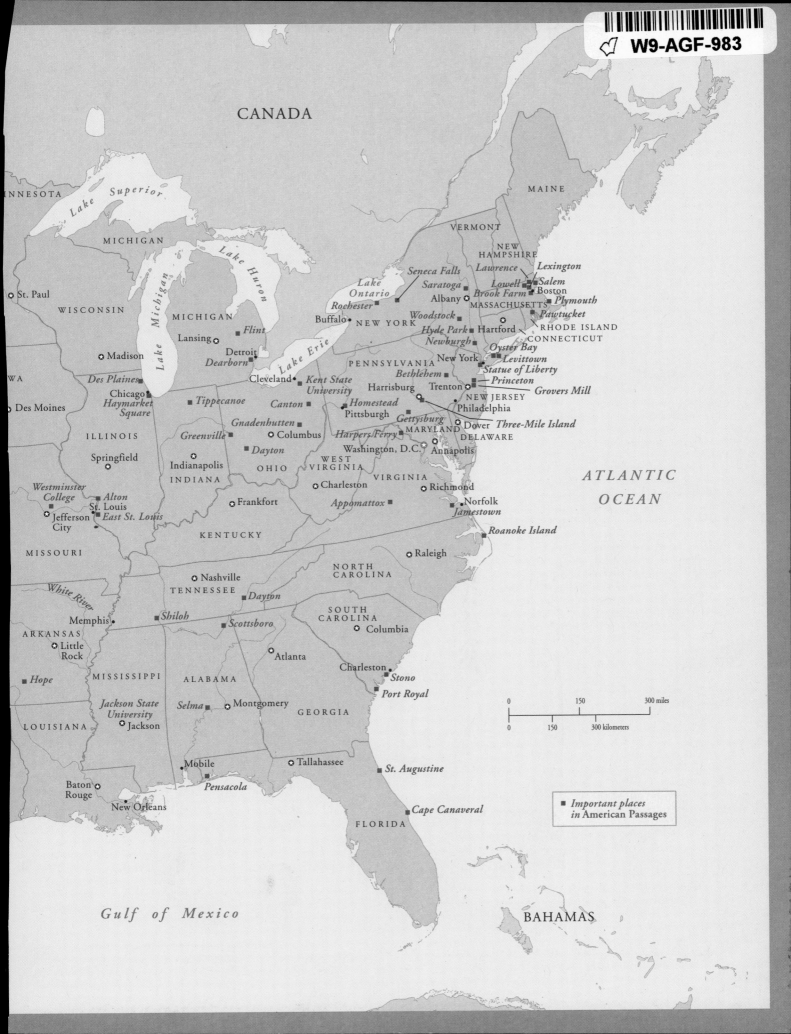

CANADA

MINNESOTA

MAINE

Lake Superior

MICHIGAN

Lake Huron

VERMONT

NEW HAMPSHIRE

St. Paul

WISCONSIN

MICHIGAN

Lake Michigan

Flint

Lansing

Madison

Detroit
Dearborn

Lake Erie

Des Plaines

Chicago
Haymarket Square

Tippecanoe

Cleveland

Kent State University

Canton

ILLINOIS

IOWA

Des Moines

Springfield

Greenville

Gnadenhutten

Columbus

Dayton

Indianapolis

INDIANA

OHIO

Homestead
Pittsburgh

WEST VIRGINIA

Seneca Falls

Lake Ontario

Saratoga

Rochester

Buffalo

NEW YORK

Albany

Woodstock

Hyde Park

Newburgh

PENNSYLVANIA

Bethlehem

Harrisburg

Harpers Ferry

Gettysburg

MARYLAND

Lawrence   *Lexington*

Lowell   *Salem*
Brook Farm   Boston

MASSACHUSETTS   *Plymouth*

Hartford   *Pawtucket*

RHODE ISLAND

CONNECTICUT

Oyster Bay

New York   *Levittown*

Statue of Liberty

Trenton   *Princeton*

Grovers Mill

NEW JERSEY

Philadelphia

Dover   *Three-Mile Island*

DELAWARE

ATLANTIC OCEAN

Washington, D.C.   Annapolis

Westminster College

Alton

St. Louis

Jefferson City   *East St. Louis*

MISSOURI

Frankfort

KENTUCKY

Charleston

VIRGINIA

Appomattox

Richmond

Norfolk

Jamestown

Roanoke Island

Nashville

TENNESSEE

Dayton

NORTH CAROLINA

Raleigh

Memphis

Shiloh

Scottsboro

ARKANSAS

Little Rock

Hope

MISSISSIPPI

ALABAMA

SOUTH CAROLINA

Columbia

Atlanta

Charleston

Stono

Jackson State University

Selma

Montgomery

GEORGIA

Jackson

LOUISIANA

Port Royal

Mobile

Tallahassee

Pensacola

Baton Rouge

New Orleans

St. Augustine

Cape Canaveral

FLORIDA

Gulf of Mexico

BAHAMAS

| 0 | | 150 | | 300 miles |
| 0 | 150 | | 300 kilometers | |

■ *Important places in American Passages*

Connecting the themes and issues that stretch across the American timeline

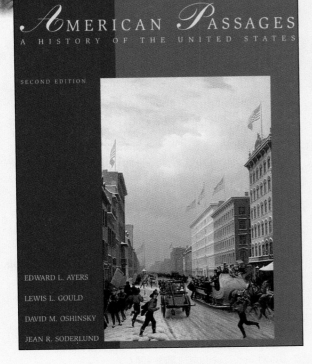

Through its evocative, highly readable discussion of U.S. History, *American Passages* reveals the vital story of an ever-growing, ever-evolving nation. Within the book's chronological framework, the authors deftly weave their crisp, up-to-date coverage of key events, movements, and groups of people into one interrelated narrative that offers clear analysis of the nation's history. In this edition, the authors have strengthened the thematic connections among chapters, which further emphasizes the commonalities that can be found as we examine the American timeline. This unifying structure allows students to draw connections between these themes and issues and leaves them with a deeper, more sophisticated understanding of the past. The book's online and print resources—fully integrated with the text—encourage students to use their critical thinking skills and extend their exploration of history into an interactive learning environment.

An award-winning team of highly respected authors

The authors of *American Passages* are outstanding scholars in their respective areas of history. These authors' work provides the text with a current and accurate narrative history of America.

Edward L. Ayers, Hugh P. Kelly Professor of History and Dean of the College and Graduate School of Arts and Sciences, University of Virginia, has won numerous teaching awards. His Web site "The Valley of the Shadow: Two Communities in the American Civil War" won the first eLincoln prize, and his book *The Promise of the New South: Life After Reconstruction* was a finalist for the National Book Award. His newest publication, *In the Presence of Mine Enemies: War in the Heart of America, 1859–1863*, will be available in Fall of 2004.

Lewis L. Gould, Eugene C. Barker Centennial Professor Emeritus in American History, University of Texas at Austin, is a nationally recognized authority on First Ladies and the Presidency. He has won numerous teaching awards, including the University Continuing Education Association's 2003 Distance Learning College Course Award. His book *The Modern American Presidency* explores the transformations of the White House over the past century.

David M. Oshinsky, George W. Littlefield Professor in American History, University of Texas at Austin, teaches courses in twentieth-century U.S. History. He is author of such noted titles as *A Conspiracy So Immense: The World of Joe McCarthy* and has won, among other awards, the American Bar Association's Scribes Award for distinguished legal writing.

Jean R. Soderlund, Professor and Chair of the Department of History, Lehigh University, has written articles and chapters in books on the history of women, African Americans, Native Americans, Quakers, and the development of abolition in the British North American colonies and early United States.

American Passages, **Second Edition is available in the following volume options. Choose the version that's right for your course!**
- ■ **Comprehensive Volume**
  Chapters 1-32 ★ 1008 pages
  Casebound ★ 0-534-60741-1
- ■ **Volume I:** To 1877
  Chapters 1-16 ★ 560 pages
  Paperbound ★ 0-534-60742-X
- ■ **Volume II:** Since 1863
  Chapters 15-32 ★ 576 pages
  Paperbound ★ 0-534-60743-8

Packaged with free access to American Journey Online and InfoTrac® College Edition!

Preview

Detailed table of contents

Examples of new content in Chapters 1–9

■ Colonial period includes new information on North America before Columbus's arrival, the Spanish empire, and Native Americans who lived within British settlements.

■ Perspectives on the American Revolution and the new United States place greater emphasis on the young republic's achievements within an international context.

Examples of new content in Chapters 9–15

■ For the period between 1815 and Reconstruction, the authors consolidated material on Andrew Jackson, antebellum reform, and the War with Mexico so that these chapters work more effectively as a narrative. Memorable quotations and surprising facts have been woven in throughout these chapters.

Examples of new content in Chapters 16–24

■ For the late nineteenth century, the authors reduced the amount of text devoted to national politics and also pared down the coverage that farm problems and Populism receive so that students can better understand this complex period.

■ The approach to progressivism and then the 1920s has been streamlined to provide better access to the significance of these decades rather than to a detailed recounting of what occurred.

Examples of new content in Chapters 31–32
■ *For the final chapters the authors integrated the events of September 11, the unfolding of the war on terrorism, and the war with Iraq into the narrative in a way that helps students grasp how the nation's present situation grew out of the political and diplomatic decisions of the 1980s and 1990s.*

Examples of new content in Chapters 25–30
■ *For the mid-twentieth century, the authors tightened the narrative, focusing again on events of major political, diplomatic, and economic significance, while expanding coverage of cultural and technological change, from rock music and television to the polio vaccine and the computer. There is more on the way that Americans of different backgrounds lived their everyday lives in times of economic depression, world war, unprecedented prosperity, and social unrest.*

A panoramic view of the nation's progress

4

P
A S S A G E S
— 1855
TO 1877 —

Americans of the 1850s had no idea that the Civil War awaited them. They could not imagine that a vast war, larger than any Europe had known, could overwhelm the new republic. New farms and plantations, after all, spread rapidly in expectation of more boom years like the 1850s. Villages and workshops spread throughout the

enemies who quickly turned to violence, as well as white northerners who supported or tolerated the violence. The years of 1866 and 1867 were full of a promise and a terror no one could have imagined ten years before. In many ways, the Civil War had not yet ended; its consequences had hardly begun.

For the next decade, Reconstruction in the South gradually receded. The process left blacks with greater political rights in law because of the Fourteenth and Fifteenth Amendments, but a more limited role in the day-to-day process of governing. The presidency of Ulysses S. Grant was a disappointment because the hero of the war proved unable to provide effective leadership, sectional reconciliation, or honest government. An economic collapse in 1873 helped the Democrats restore the national political balance and hasten the end of Reconstruction. The disputed election between Rutherford B. Hayes and Samual J. Tilden in 1876 saw the abandonment of black southerners to the rule of those who believed in white supremacy. The Civil War had preserved the Union and abolished slavery, but the unsettled problem of race cast a long shadow into the future.

Sunday Morning in Virginia. This painting by Winslow Homer chronicled the great hunger of former slaves and their children for the blessings of literacy.
Winslow Homer, "Sunday Morning in Virginia," 1877 Cincinnati Art Museum, John M. Emerey Funds Acc. 1924. 247.

Innovative **Passages** sections provide students with a unique vantage point on history, serving as both a summation of previous events and as a preview of what is to come. The **Passages** essays appear every fourth chapter, introducing the coming material with photos, maps, charts, and a comprehensive timeline. These essays give students a comparative look at key events, people, and movements and are organized into three themes—**Politics and Diplomacy, Social and Cultural Events**, and **Economics and Technology**. When students read the **Passages** sections in conjunction with the chapter introductions and conclusions, they can visualize the progression of history and see people, events, and movements within the context of the whole story.

1868: Louisa May Alcott publishes *Little Women*
1869: Licensing of women lawyers begins
First intercollegiate football game played between Princeton and Rutgers

1870: First Greek letter sorority, Kappa Alpha Theta, founded
1871: Cable car invented
1872: American Public Health Association starts
1873: Mark Twain and Charles Dudley Warner publish *The Gilded Age*

1867: Patrons of Husbandry (Grange) founded
1868: First 8-hour day for federal workers
1869: Gold Corner scheme of Jay Gould and Jim Fisk
Transcontinental railroad completed

1870: Standard Oil Company of Ohio organized
1871: Chicago fire burns center of city
1872: Adding machine invented
1873: Panic of 1873 starts depression

Politics & Diplomacy

1855

1855: Proslavery and free-soil forces clash in Kansas
Massachusetts desegregates public schools
1856: John Brown's raid in Kansas
James Buchanan elected president
Congressman Preston Brooks canes Senator Charles Sumner
1857: *Dred Scott* decision
Lecompton Constitution
Hinton R. Helper, *The Impending Crisis of the South*
1858: Lincoln-Douglas debates
1859: John Brown's raid on Harpers Ferry
Vicksburg convention calls for reopening of African slave trade
Kansas ratifies free-soil constitution
1860: Democratic convention divides
Abraham Lincoln elected president
South Carolina secedes from the Union

1861

1861: Mississippi, Florida, Alabama, Georgia, Louisiana, and Texas secede
Montgomery Convention creates Confederate States of America
Lincoln inaugurated
Firing on and surrender of Fort Sumter
Arkansas, Tennessee, Virginia, and North Carolina secede
Confederate victory at Bull Run (Manassas)
Jefferson Davis elected president of Confederacy with six-year term
Union navy seizes Confederate commisioners Mason and Slidell from British ship *Trent*
1862: Confederates surrender Fort Donelson to Grant
Virginia v. Monitor in Hampton Roads, Virginia
Grant wins dramatic victory at Shiloh
New Orleans surrenders to Admiral Farragut

1863

1862: *(continued)* Jackson's Shenandoah Valley Campaign
Lee takes command of Army of Northern Virginia
Lee drives McClellan from Richmond in Seven Days' Battles
Confederate victory at Second Bull Run (Manassas)
Battle of Antietam (Sharpsburg)
First Emancipation Proclamation
Burnside replaces McClellan as commander of Army of Potomac
Lee overwhelms Burnside at Fredericksburg
1863: Second Emancipation Proclamation
Culmination of Lee's victory over Hooker at Chancellorsville
Grant's successful campaign in Mississippi
Death of Stonewall Jackson
Union victory at Gettysburg
Vicksburg surrenders to Grant

NEW!

The extended captions in the exciting new **Picturing the Past** features echo the themes presented in the **Passages** timelines, thus reinforcing the connections students make across chapters and across periods of time. To provide visual cues that further emphasize the thematic connections, the **Picturing the Past** features are color-coordinated with the **Passages** timelines. This new feature also serves the valuable pedagogical function of helping students learn to "read" visual materials, such as photos and maps, and extract those materials' historical significance.

P
ICTURING THE PAST ◆ SOCIAL & CULTURAL EVENTS
A. YEOMAN FARM

Non-slaveholding whites in the antebellum South, living on farms such as this one in Texas, comprised approximately 75 percent of the white population. Most owned small plots of land they farmed themselves with the aid of their family and local networks of kin and community for access to market goods. They are frequently referred to as yeomen farmers, an ideal of the self-sufficient farm household as one of the cornerstones of American democracy.

Access to arable land and the prospects to purchase slaves became issues of increasing concern through the 1850s. Land

Painting of a block house in New Braunfels, by Carl G. von Iwonski. Courtesy of the Daughters of the Republic of Texas Library

exhausted by tobacco or cotton or that was tied up in large holdings of wealthier farmers raised the stakes of access to western lands. In many areas back east in Virginia and the Carolinas, poorer white families and younger sons found themselves unable to move from laborers and farm tenants to land ownership. While many southern yeomen families migrated to southern Illinois, Indiana, and Missouri to break ground in areas without slavery, many others considered the opportunity to own slaves part of their political birthright and supported slavery's expansion even if they owned no slaves themselves.

$\mathscr{P}$rimary source documents echo true voices of the past

In each chapter, students will find one to two enlightening primary source documents, ranging from speeches to diary entries (such as the journals of Lewis and Clark), poems, and ordinary citizens' eyewitness accounts of historical events. They incorporate social, political, and economic history and represent many areas of history, including Native Americans, minorities, and women. Additional documents are available at the *American Passages* Book Companion Web Site.

Documents included in this Second Edition:

Chapter 1
★ Admiral Christopher Columbus's Diary Account of Reaching America, October 12, 1492
★ An Aztec Report of the Fall of Tenochtitlán, 1521

Chapter 2
★ Richard Frethorne, a Virginia Colonist, Writes Home, 1623
★ The Mayflower Compact, 1620

Chapter 3
★ Mary Rowlandson's Narrative of Her Capture by Narragansett Indians, 1676
★ The Trial of Bridget Bishop, an Accused Witch, Salem, 1692

Chapter 4
★ Venture Smith Resists Slavery
★ David Brainerd's Mission to the Conoy and Lenape Indians, 1745

Chapter 5
★ Virginia Resolves against the Stamp Act, 1765
★ The Narrative of Mary Jemison, 1775–1779

Chapter 6
★ Petition of Philadelphia Jews for Equal Rights, 1783
★ Patrick Henry Opposes the Constitution, 1788

Chapter 7
★ The Bill of Rights, 1791
★ U.S. Federal Census of 1790

Chapter 8
★ Thomas Jefferson's First Inaugural Address, March 4, 1801
★ The Journals of Meriwether Lewis and William Clark, 1805

Chapter 9
★ American Society for Improving Indian Tribes, The Blessings of Civilization, 1824
★ Ohio Board of Canal Commissioners, Annual Report, 1828

Chapter 10
★ David Walker, Appeal . . . to the Colored Citizens of the World, 1829
★ Memorial and Protest of the Cherokee Nation, 1836

Chapter 11
★ Alexis de Tocqueville, *Democracy in America*, 1840
★ Horace Mann, Absolute Right to an Education, 1846

Chapter 12
★ "Declaration of Sentiments" of the Woman Suffrage Movement, 1848
★ Harriet Beecher Stowe, *Uncle Tom's Cabin*, 1852

Chapter 13
★ Hinton Helper, *The Impending Crisis of the South*, 1857
★ James D. B. DeBow, "The Interest in Slavery of the Southern Non-Slaveholder," 1860

Chapter 14
★ Louisa May Alcott, "Journal," April 1861
★ Sarah Morgan, "Diary," March 1864

Chapter 15
★ Abraham Lincoln "The Gettysburg Address," 1863
★ "Letter to the Union Convention, 1865," Black Citizens of Tennessee

Chapter 16
★ The Fifteenth Amendment, 1870
★ *Minor v. Happersett* 21 Wallace, 162, 1875

Chapter 17
★ Howard Ruede, Sod-House Days, 1877

Chapter 18
★ "The Indian Situation," 1891
★ Populist Party Platform, 1892

Chapter 19
★ Petition from the Citizens of New Jersey to the U. S. Congress Praying for Congress to Make the Act of Lynching a Crime in the United States, 1900
★ William McKinley: Reciprocal Trade Agreements, 1901

Chapter 20
★ W. E. B. Du Bois on what Blacks Felt during the Age of Roosevelt, 1903
★ The Roosevelt Corollary to the Monroe Doctrine 1904, 1905

Chapter 21
★ The New York Tribune Reports the Triangle Fire, March 26, 1911
★ The Social Cost Of Industrialism: An Excerpt From Woodrow Wilson's First Inaugural Address, March 4, 1913

Chapter 22
★ Wilson's War Message To Congress, April 2, 1917
★ President Wilson's Appeal To The Voters To Return a Democratic Congress, October 24, 1918

Chapter 23
★ Claude McKay *If We Must Die!*, 1922
★ Elsie Hill on Why Women Should Have Full Legal Equality, 1922

Chapter 24
★ Franklin D. Roosevelt, Commonwealth Club Address

Chapter 25
★ Huey P. Long Condemns FDR and the New Deal
★ An Automobile Worker's Recollection of the GM Sit-Down Strike

Chapter 26
★ An American Soldier Remembers the Bataan Death March
★ Japanese Relocation Order, February 19, 1942

Chapter 27
★ The Truman Doctrine March 12, 1947

Chapter 28
★ Chief Justice Earl Warren, Opinion of the Court in *Brown* v. *Board of Education*, May 17, 1954
★ President Eisenhower's Farewell Address, January 17, 1961

Chapter 29
★ An Open Letter to the Grape Industry by Cesar Chavez

Chapter 30
★ *Roe v. Wade*, 1973
★ The Nixon Tapes, 1973

Chapter 31
★ Ronald Reagan's Second Inaugural Address, January 1985

Chapter 32
★ President George W. Bush Responds to Terrorism, September 2001

Over 100 full-color maps that plot the course of America's development

Map 8.2 *Western Exploration, 1803–1807*
At about the same time Meriwether Lewis and William Clark led the Corps of Discovery along the northern route to treat with Native Americans, explore the natural resources, and locate a northwest passage, Zebulon Pike traveled north along the Mississippi River and west to the Rocky Mountains.

6.4 *Ratification of the Constitution*
The pattern of support by relatively small states is visible in the votes of Delaware, New Jersey, Georgia, and Connecticut. In Pennsylvania, Massachusetts, and New York, the more populated urban areas supported ratification.

American Passages' solid full-color mapping program includes more than 100 maps that place battles, election results, transportation systems, population shifts, and other events, movements, and developments in the context of the national and global geographical boundaries.

At the *American Passages* Book Companion Web Site, students will find maps from the text—many of which are animated and are accompanied by map exercises.

Map 15.1 *Vicksburg*
After months of frustration, Ulysses S. Grant and William T. Sherman found a way to attack Vicksburg south and east. Following great struggle, the Union generals were able to take the city on July 4, 1863.

New **map captions,** written by the authors, highlight the major points conveyed in the maps and help students learn to look for key geographic features and cause-and-effect relationships.

Colorful features that frame and add dimension to the story

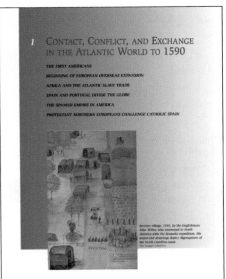

New **chapter outlines** give students a sense of what to expect in the coming chapter.

The solid, **full-color illustration program** includes numerous photos, reproductions of works of fine art, political cartoons, posters, architectural plans, book covers, contemporary advertisements, graphs, and tables.

Ulysses S. Grant distinguished himself in key battles in Tennessee and Mississippi in 1862. Many months and battles would pass, however, before Grant would assume command in the East.
The Granger Collection, New York

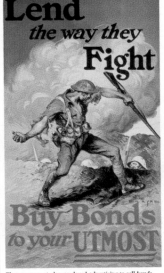

The government also employed advertising to sell bonds. This poster showing an American soldier at the front was one of the ways that Washington sought to awaken public opinion to the need for bond sales.
Gift of Henry Colgate, Picker Art Gallery, Colgate University

The spread of industrialism brought new products into the home that were advertised as laborsaving devices for women. The reality was that the amount of work women did expanded as a result of the new machinery for domestic use.
From the Collections of the Library of Congress

Obtaining a degree was not a guarantee of access to professions that males controlled. Myra Bradwell tried to become a lawyer in Illinois, but the state bar association rejected her application. She sued in federal court, and in 1873, the U.S. Supreme Court ruled that the law did not grant her the right to be admitted to the bar. One justice said that "the paramount destiny and mission of woman are to fulfill the noble and benign offices of wife and mother." That decision gave the Illinois legislature the authority to deny women the chance to practice law. In 1870, there were only five female lawyers in the nation.

The Supreme Court also rebuffed efforts to secure woman suffrage through the courts. Virginia Minor, president of the Woman Suffrage Association in Missouri, tried to vote during the 1872 election, but

In this conjectural view of Jamestown c. 1614, the fortified wall shows concerns for defense against the Powhatan confederacy.
Colonial Williamsburg Foundation

Enhanced art and **photo captions** allow students to see these images through a trained historian's eyes, identifying historically significant and noteworthy details.

The Cotton Club in Harlem was the nightly center of the social scene of the Harlem Renaissance. The Cotton Club orchestra in 1925 entertained the white patrons who came up from Manhattan to sample the excitement of black music and culture.
© Frank Driggs/Corbis

Young people devoured the work of the acidic essayist and social critic Henry L. Mencken, who wrote for the *American Mercury.* Mencken was a Baltimore newspaperman who had little time for the sacred cows

tocracy of the Long Island shore. In Gatsby's failure to win his dream, Fitzgerald saw the inability of Americans to escape the burdens of their own pasts.

This book comes to life at the *American Passages* Book Companion Web Site
http://history.wadsworth.com/passages2e

Designed by Edward Ayers, Gregg Michel, and Will Thomas, the *American Passages* Book Companion Web Site offers numerous features that will reinforce students' learning. Completely integrated with the text, this exciting resource allows you and your students to move back and forth among maps, chapter-related subject matter, and links to other sites on the Web.

Browse and search by chapter
Because the organization of the *American Passages* Book Companion Web Site mirrors that of the text, students can easily find the material that corresponds to the chapter they're currently studying.

Examine hundreds of primary source documents
Sources include book excerpts, government and legal documents, magazine and newspaper articles, diaries, letters, audio and video clips, images, maps, speeches, and more.

Explore a myriad of maps

At the site, students have access to the text's maps—many of which are animated, dramatically illustrating major developments and changes over a period of time.

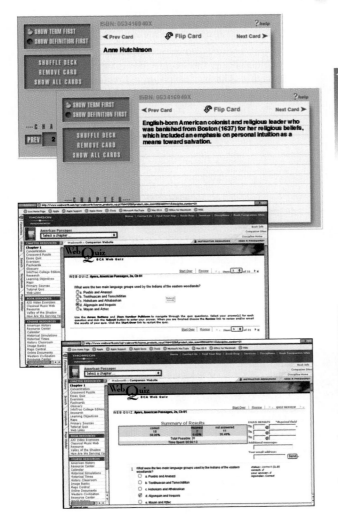

Students get hands-on practice with study questions

Study questions with answers follow a variety of strategies. Some focus on a single document. Others concentrate on several documents within one chapter. Still others address themes and issues that connect to other chapters and across time periods. From the exercise page, students can also connect to self-quizzes keyed to chapters, flashcards, a glossary, and crossword puzzles.

Find additional resources on the Web

Organized by chapter, an annotated list of links directs students outside the *American Passages* Book Companion Web Site to other useful, reliable, content-rich Internet sites.

Plus—resources for you

The *American Passages* Book Companion Web Site also offers you password-protected access to such resources as:

★ Microsoft® *PowerPoint*® presentations
★ *Instructor's Manual* (with *Resource Integration Guide*)
★ *Test Bank*
★ *American Journey Online Instructor's Guide*
★ *NewsEdge,* an authoritative online news service that delivers customized news feeds daily

There's even more to explore at the Wadsworth American History Resource Center http://history.wadsworth.com

This newly enhanced resource center features numerous resources for you and your students, including a direct link to the *American Passages* Book Companion Web Site!

You'll find such resources as:

★ The Wadsworth **U.S. Image Bank,** which contains over 400 images and 150 maps from U.S. history that can be incorporated into multimedia presentations and used as lecture enrichment tools.

★ Interactive **You are There** simulations, which include detailed accounts of key events, along with critical thinking exercises that put students in the historical setting and multiple-choice quizzes that test their knowledge of the subject.

★ An **At the Movies** feature that provides descriptions, critical thinking questions, and Web links for major films throughout American history.

★ **American Journey Online** activities.

★ A link to the "Today in U.S. History" Web site, which shares the events that occurred on a specific date in the nation's development.

★ And much more!

FREE access with every new copy of the text... exclusively from Wadsworth!

American Journey Online
http://ajaccess.wadsworth.com

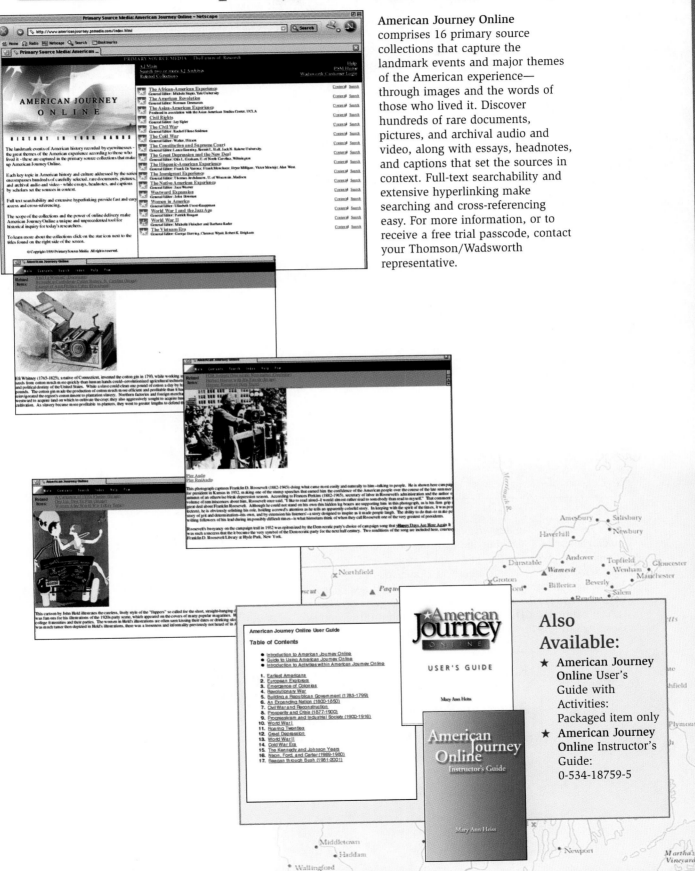

American Journey Online comprises 16 primary source collections that capture the landmark events and major themes of the American experience—through images and the words of those who lived it. Discover hundreds of rare documents, pictures, and archival audio and video, along with essays, headnotes, and captions that set the sources in context. Full-text searchability and extensive hyperlinking make searching and cross-referencing easy. For more information, or to receive a free trial passcode, contact your Thomson/Wadsworth representative.

Also Available:

★ American Journey Online User's Guide with Activities: Packaged item only

★ American Journey Online Instructor's Guide: 0-534-18759-5

$\mathcal{C}$reating a personalized suite of teaching and learning tools is easy with the **Resource Integration Guide**

CHAPTER 1 – CONTACT, CONFLICT AND EXCHANGE IN THE ATLANTIC WORLD

Chapter Outline	Ideas for Instruction	Print Resources	Media & Internet Supplements
The First Americans p. 9	**Lecture/Discussion** Topic: 1 **"Making It Real"** Student Projects: 1,2 **Transparency Acetates** 1, 4, 5, 6	**Test Bank** MC: 1-6 Chronology: 1-5 Identification: 1-2 Essay: 1 **Study Guide** Chapter 1	**WebTutor™** Chapter 1 **Multimedia Manager for U.S. History** **American Journey Online and InfoTrac® College Edition search terms:** Maya Aztecs Atlantic slave trade Spanish empire Iroquois Algonquian Anasazi Christopher Columbus Protestant Reformation Martin Luther Hernán Cortés Francis Drake
Beginning of European Overseas Expansion p. 15		**Test Bank** MC: 7-10 Identification: 3-4	**American Passages Book Companion Web Site** http://history.wadsworth.com/passages2e Filled with outstanding, chapter-specific features that reinforce students' learning, such as primary source documents, animated maps, study questions, self quizzes, and more.
Africa & the Atlantic Slave Trade p. 19	**Transparency Acetates** 25, 2	**Test Bank** MC: 11-13 True-False: 1 Essay: 2	
Spain & Portugal Divide the Globe p. 21	**Primary Source** *Admiral Christopher Columbus's Diary Account of Reaching America, October 12, 1492* **Transparency Acetates** 3, 9	**Test Bank** MC: 14-16 True-False: 2 Identification: 5-6 Essay: 3	**Wadsworth American History Resource Center** http://history.wadsworth.com Numerous resources for you and your students, including a U.S. image bank, interactive simulations, and more.
The Spanish Empire in America p. 25	**Primary Source** *An Aztec Report of the Fall of Tenochtitlán* **Lecture/Discussion Topic** 2 **Transparency Acetates** 7, 8	**Test Bank** MC: 17-25 True-False: 3-8 Identification: 7-10 Essay: 4-5	
Protestant Northern Europeans Challenge Catholic Spain p. 31		**Test Bank:** MC: 26-30 True-False: 9-10 Identification: 11-15 Essay: 6	

Instructor's Manual

for American Passages, Second Edition

With the easy-to-use *Resource Integration Guide,* you can quickly compile a teaching and learning program that complements both the text and your personal teaching style. The *Resource Integration Guide,* which appears in the *Instructor's Manual for American Passages,* features chapter-by-chapter ideas for instruction, as well as suggestions for incorporating the CD-ROMs, video, Web, and print resources described in this Preview into your course.

Keep exploring this Preview to learn more about the extensive selection of supplements that accompanies *American Passages,* Second Edition!

Classroom presentation tools

Multimedia Manager for U.S. History
Cross-platform CD-ROM
0-534-64164-4
Wadsworth's digital library and presentation tool—featuring photos, art, video, Web links, and more—on one cross-platform CD-ROM! With its easy-to-use interface, you can take advantage of Wadsworth's ready-made presentations, or customize your own presentation by importing lecture slides or other material. The result is an interactive and fluid lecture that truly engages your students.

CNN® Today Video: United States History
0-534-17510-4
Launch your lectures with riveting footage from CNN, the world's leading 24-hour global news television network. This new CNN Today Video allows you to integrate the newsgathering and programming power of CNN into the classroom to show students the relevance of course topics to their everyday lives. Video segments cover topics such as Jamestown, slavery reparations, school desegregation, and D-Day. Organized by topics covered in a typical course, the video is divided into short segments—perfect for introducing key concepts. Each video clip is followed by questions for discussion. A Thomson/Wadsworth exclusive. *(Available to qualified adopters in North America only).*

U.S. History Video Library
This selection of videos, from **Films for the Humanities and Sciences** and other sources, includes titles such as Colonialism, Nationalism, and Migration; From Workshops to Factory: Revolution; and Progress: Politics, Technology, and Science. Available to qualified adopters; contact your Thomson/Wadsworth representative for more information.

Transparency Acetates for U.S. History
0-534-17434-5
Contains more than 150 four-color map images from all of Wadsworth's U.S. history texts. A correlation guide for *American Passages* is included.

ℛesources for presentation, testing, and classroom management

Instructor's Manual
0-534-60748-9

The *Instructor's Manual* includes chapter outlines, chapter objectives, a "Making it Real" section that provides recommendations for assignments, writing assignments, class starter and lecture topic suggestions, and a "Further Resources" section that lists additional readings and audio/visual resources. The *Instructor's Manual* also includes a *Resource Integration Guide* that links each chapter of the text to instructional ideas and corresponding supplemental resources. At a glance, you can see which selections from the text's teaching and learning ancillaries are appropriate for each key chapter topic.

ExamView® Computerized Testing
0-534-60750-0

Create, deliver, and customize tests and study guides (both print and online) in minutes with this easy-to-use assessment and tutorial system. *ExamView's Quick Test Wizard* guides you step-by-step through the process of creating and printing a test in minutes. The *Online Test Wizard* allows you to format a test for delivery over a local area network (LAN) or stand-alone computer. And *ExamView* is the only test generator that allows you to see the test you are creating on the screen exactly as it will print!

ExamView and ExamView Pro are registered trademarks of FSCreations, Inc. Used herein under license.

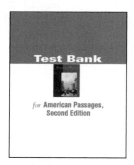

Test Bank
0-534-60749-7

Completely revised, this *Test Bank* provides a variety of question styles to emphasize critical thinking skills. In addition to multiple choice questions, it offers identification, true/false, chronology and essay questions.

WebTUTOR Advantage

Enhance your course with the course management capabilities of WebTutor™ Advantage on WebCT and Blackboard!
See the next page for details.

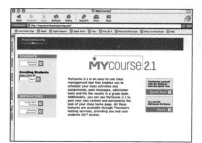

MyCourse 2.1

Ready for you to populate with your own content, this course management system gives you a convenient way to create a simple course Web site. *MyCourse 2.1* is easy to set up and use—no pincodes are necessary. With it, you can attach or load your syllabus, import class rosters and gradebooks, assign your own materials, track and report on student progress, and more. Contact your Thomson/Wadsworth representative if you are interested in using *MyCourse 2.1*.

Online resources—thought-provoking teaching and learning tools for you and your students

FREE with your adoption of the text!
InfoTrac® College Edition

With your adoption, you and your students receive four months of free access to *InfoTrac College Edition's* online database of continuously updated, full-length articles from thousands of journals and periodicals dating back over twenty years, including *American History, Antiquity, Biography, History Today, Past & Present,* and *Smithsonian.* **NEW!** Students now have instant access to critical thinking and paper writing tools through InfoWrite.
Journals subject to change.

New features now included!
WebTutor™ Advantage for WebCT and Blackboard

WebCT: 0-534-60747-0
Blackboard: 0-534-60746-2
WebTutor Advantage's flexible format allows you to assign pre-formatted, text-specific content that is available as soon as you log on or customize its environment in any way you choose—from uploading images and other resources, to adding Web links, to creating your own practice materials. **New** in *WebTutor Advantage*—a seamless link to *InfoTrac College Edition* that allows you and your students instant access with no additional passcodes. Also new: a daily news feed from **NewsEdge,** an authoritative source of late-breaking local, national, and international news of interest to you and your students. *WebTutor Advantage* is now available on *eCollege!* Ask your local Thomson/Wadsworth representative for more information or visit
http://webtutor.thomsonlearning.com and click on *eCollege.*

Exclusively from Thomson/Wadsworth and the Gale Group!
Opposing Viewpoints Resource Center

Expose your students to all sides of today's most compelling issues! The *Opposing Viewpoints Resource Center* draws on Greenhaven Press' acclaimed social issues series, as well as core reference content from other Gale and Macmillan Reference USA sources. The result is a dynamic online library of current event topics—the facts as well as the arguments of each topic's proponents and detractors. For a demonstration, please visit **http://www.gale.com/opposingviewpoints,** or contact your Thomson/Wadsworth representative for more information.

Also available for students

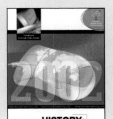

History: HITS on the Web
0-7593-0708-3
HITS on the Web is an exciting, class-tested product specially designed to help history students utilize the Internet for studying, conducting research, and completing assignments. *HITS on the Web* can be bundled with any Wadsworth history textbook at a very affordable price. Please contact your local Thomson/Wadsworth sales representative for information.

*A*lso available to enhance your students' learning

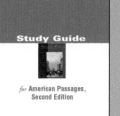

Study Guide
Volume I: 0-534-60744-6
Volume II: 0-534-60745-4
This student resource guide is organized by chapter and contains chapter outlines, chapter summaries, *American Journey Online* and *InfoTrac College Edition* exercises, essay questions, identification items, objective questions, and Internet exercises that are intended to aid in the student's understanding of the material. Available in two volumes.

United States History Atlas
0-534-61895-2
This invaluable collection of more than 50 clear and colorful historical maps covering all major periods in American history is available only as a package item. Please contact your local Thomson/Wadsworth sales representative for information.

U.S. History Series
Even the most familiar story can take on a new vitality when told by the right authors. That's why Wadsworth is proud to present three unique series that will stimulate fresh interest in people and events that have become as familiar as America itself. Each series features uncommon books that make great core or supplemental texts—providing you with flexibility in making reading assignments. They're the perfect way to give your course unique depth!

Wadsworth's U.S. History Series includes:

To learn more about the titles in these series, please visit the History page on **http://www.newtexts.com** and click on the link.

Readers

Speaking of America
Laura A. Belmonte
Volume I: To 1877
ISBN: 0-15-506355-3; Volume II: Since 1865
ISBN: 0-15-506363-4
The *Speaking of America* readers expose college students to a variety of sources on United States history. Each book includes a wide array of primary documents, poems, short stories, song lyrics, monograph and article excerpts, and news accounts encompassing multicultural and regional perspectives. The selected readings feature both famous and ordinary Americans, and they address important episodes in politics, economics, and foreign policy, as well as social and cultural changes.

Those United States: International Perspectives on American History
Gerald Michael Greenfield and John D. Buenker
Volume I ISBN: 0-15-508258-2
Volume II ISBN: 0-15-508259-0
Organized chronologically, these books' nontraditional approach presents American history in an international context, from the viewpoints of international (as well as American) writers. The text includes the voices of people who lived during the time periods covered, as well as the work of some present-day international scholars.

Voices of the American Past: Documents in U.S. History
Raymond M. Hyser and J. Christopher Arndt
Volume I ISBN: 0-15-507508-X
Volume II ISBN: 0-15-507509-8
Voices of the American Past presents a variety of diverse voices by providing more than 230 selections. Excerpts from speeches, letters, journals, books, magazine articles, hearings, and government documents raise issues from public and private aspects of American life throughout history.

Additional Resources

0-534-63737-X

www.wadsworth.com

www.wadsworth.com is the World Wide Web site for Wadsworth and is your direct source to dozens of online resources.

At www.*wadsworth.com* you can find out about supplements, demonstration software, and student resources. You can also send e-mail to many of our authors and preview new publications and exciting new technologies.

www.wadsworth.com
Changing the way the world learns®

Free study resources for your American History course—*available online!*

Primary source documents, video and audio clips, activities, and self-quizzing—all FREE to you when you purchase this text!

American Passages Book Companion Web Site

http://history.wadsworth.com/passages2e

Filled with exclusive resources designed specifically to accompany this text!

This Web site adds interest and interactivity through a rich collection of maps, audio clips, photographs, cartoons, and documents. Every chapter in the textbook includes elements that are linked to material found exclusively on the Web site. Carefully coordinated with the text and following the book's chronology, 400 items are available to enhance the student's learning experience, including 100 new documents with accompanying introductions, 65 new images, 65 new links, and 20 new animated maps with exercises that encourage student interactivity. This site also offers, for each chapter, new "Opposing Voices" features, which present a series of documents that are related around key points relevant to the chapter. These features stimulate discussion and allow students to compare and contrast sets of relevant documents.

Look for this icon throughout the text! It directs you to related material on the American Passages Book Companion Web Site.

The Wadsworth American History Resource Center

http://history.wadsworth.com

At this Web site, you'll find: An *At the Movies* feature, which provides descriptions, critical thinking questions, and Web links for major films throughout American history; the Wadsworth U.S. Image Bank, which contains hundreds of images and maps that can be incorporated into multimedia presentations; *American Journey Online* activities; interactive "You Are There" simulations, which give you the opportunity to "virtually" experience life in another place and time; a link to the "Today in U.S. History" Web site, which shares the events that occurred on a specific date in the nation's development; a link to the *American Passages* Book Companion Web Site; and more!

American Journey Online

http://ajaccess.wadsworth.com

FREE access with every new copy of the text!

American Journey Online comprises 16 primary source collections that capture the landmark events and major themes of the American experience—through images and the words of those who lived it. Discover hundreds of rare documents, pictures, and archival audio and video, along with essays, headnotes, and captions that set the sources in context. Full-text searchability and extensive hyperlinking make searching and cross-referencing easy.

Also Available:

American Journey Online **User's Guide with Activities**

Available on the home page of **http://ajaccess.wadsworth.com**, at the Book Companion Web Site (**http://history.wadsworth.com/passages2e**), or as a print resource (ISBN 0-534-17433-7).

AMERICAN PASSAGES

A History of the United States

Second Edition

Edward L. Ayers
University of Virginia

Lewis L. Gould
University of Texas at Austin, Emeritus

David M. Oshinsky
University of Texas at Austin

Jean R. Soderlund
Lehigh University

THOMSON
WADSWORTH

Australia • Canada • Mexico • Singapore • Spain
United Kingdom • United States

THOMSON

WADSWORTH

Publisher: **Clark Baxter**
Senior Development Editor:
  Margaret McAndrew Beasley
Assistant Editor: **Julie Yardley**
Editorial Assistant: **Eno Sarris**
Technology Project Manager: **Jennifer Ellis**
Executive Marketing Manager: **Caroline Croley**
Marketing Assistant: **Mary Ho**
Advertising Project Manager: **Tami Strang**
Project Manager, Editorial Production: **Kimberly Adams**
Print/Media Buyer: **Karen Hunt**

Permissions Editor: **Joohee Lee**
Production Service: **Carlisle Communications, Ltd.**
Text Designer: **Garry Harman, the ArtWorks**
Photo Researcher: **Lili Weiner**
Copy Editor: **Sarah Greer Bush**
Cover Image: Hippolyte Sebron. *Street Scene in New York,* 1855. Photo: Gérard Blot. Réunion des Musées Nationaux/Art Resource, NY.
Compositor: **Carlisle Communications, Ltd.**
Printer: **Transcontinental Printing/Interglobe**

For more information about our products, contact us at:
Thomson Learning Academic Resource Center
1-800-423-0563
For permission to use material from this text,
contact us by: **Phone:** 1-800-730-2214
Fax: 1-800-730-2215
Web: http://www.thomsonrights.com

Wadsworth/Thomson Learning
Belmont, CA 94002-3098
USA

Asia
Thomson Learning
5 Shenton Way #01-01
UIC Building
Singapore 068808

Australia/New Zealand
Thomson Learning
102 Dodds Street
Southbank, Victoria 3006
Australia

Canada
Nelson
1120 Birchmount Road
Toronto, Ontario M1K 5G4
Canada

Europe/Middle East/Africa
Thomson Learning
High Holborn House
50/51 Bedford Row
London WC1R 4LR
United Kingdom

Latin America
Thomson Learning
Seneca, 53
Colonia Polanco
11560 Mexico D. F.
Mexico

Spain/Portugal
Paraninfo
Calle/Magallanes, 25
28015 Madrid, Spain

Library of Congress Control Number: 2003101459

Student Edition: ISBN 0-534-60741-1

Instructor's Edition: ISBN 0-534-60751-9

ABOUT THE AUTHORS

EDWARD L. AYERS Edward Ayers is the Hugh P. Kelly Professor of History at the University of Virginia. He was educated at the University of Tennessee and Yale University, where he received his Ph.D. in American Studies. He has written and edited several books. His most recent book, *In the Presence of Mine Enemies: War in the Heart of America, 1859–1863,* is forthcoming (fall, 2003). *The Promise of the New South: Life After Reconstruction* (1992) won prizes for the best book on the history of American race relations and on the history of the American South. It was a finalist for both the National Book Award and the Pulitzer Prize. He is the co-editor of *The Oxford Book of the American South* (1997) and *All Over the Map: Rethinking American Regions* (1996). Ayers has won a number of

teaching awards, including the Outstanding Faculty Award from the State Council of Higher Education and the Distinguished Young Teacher Award from the Alumni Board of Trustees.

The World Wide Web version of Ayers's work, "The Valley of the Shadow: Two Communities in the American Civil War," has been ranked as one of the top four education sites in the world by the *Encyclopedia Britannica* and named as the best Civil War site by Yahoo!. Ayers is Executive Director of the Center for Digital History, an institute at the University of Virginia dedicated to crafting and teaching history in new media, and is currently serving as Dean of the College and Graduate School of Arts and Sciences. Ayers is the author of Chapters 9–15.

LEWIS L. GOULD Lewis Gould is the Eugene C. Barker Centennial Professor Emeritus at the University of Texas at Austin. After receiving his Ph.D. from Yale University, he began a teaching career in which he had more than ten thousand students. He was recognized for outstanding undergraduate teaching in large lecture sections of the American History survey and for his excellent graduate teaching.

Gould is a nationally recognized authority on first ladies and the presidency. His comments have appeared in numerous press accounts about presidential wives, including The *New York Times,* the *Washington Post,* and the *Los Angeles Times.* He has appeared on C-Span, *The CBS*

Morning News, Nightline, The ABC Evening News, and a large number of nationally syndicated radio programs. He also participated in the PBS program on Lyndon Johnson and the A&E biography of Lady Bird Johnson. Among his important publications are *American First Ladies: Their Lives and Their Legacy* (2001); *1968: The Election That Changed America* (1993); *The Presidency of Theodore Roosevelt* (1991); *Lady Bird Johnson: Our Environmental First Lady* (1999); *The Modern American Presidency* (2003), and *Grand Old Party: A History of the Republicans* (2003). Gould is the author of Chapters 16–24, 31, and 32.

DAVID M. OSHINSKY David Oshinsky received his undergraduate degree from Cornell University and his doctorate from Brandeis. He is currently Littlefield Professor of History at the University of Texas at Austin. Prior to that he taught for twenty-six years at Rutgers University, where he held the Board of Governors Chair as well as chairman of the History Department. Oshinsky is the author of four books, including *A Conspiracy So Immense: The World of Joe McCarthy* (1983), which was voted one of the year's "best books" by the *New York Sunday Times Book Review,* and won the Hardeman Prize for the best work about the U.S. Congress. His latest book, *Worse than Slavery: Parchman Farm and the Or-*

deal of Jim Crow Justice (1996), won both the Robert Kennedy Book Award for the year's most distinguished contribution to the field of human rights and the American Bar Association's Scribes Award for distinguished legal writing.

Oshinsky is a regular contributor to scholarly journals, the *Washington Post Book World, New York Sunday Times Book Review, New York Times* Op-Ed page, and *New York Times Sunday Magazine.* He was awarded a senior fellowship by the National Endowment for the Humanities and spent 1999–2000 as a Phi Beta Kappa Visiting Scholar. Oshinsky is the author of Chapters 25–30.

JEAN R. SODERLUND Jean Soderlund is Professor and Chair of the Department of History at Lehigh University and Co-Director of the Lawrence Henry Gipson Institute for Eighteenth-Century Studies. She received her Ph.D. from Temple University and was a post-doctoral fellow at the McNeil Center for Early American Studies at the University of Pennsylvania. Her book *Quakers and Slavery: A Divided Spirit* won the Alfred E. Driscoll Publication Prize of the New Jersey Historical Commission. Soderlund was an editor of three volumes of the *Papers of William Penn* (1981–1983) and co-authored *Freedom by De-*

grees: Emancipation in Pennsylvania and Its Aftermath (1991).

She has written articles and chapters in books on the history of women, African Americans, Native Americans, Quakers, and the development of abolition in the British North American colonies and early United States. She is currently working on a study of the Lenape people within colonial New Jersey society. She is a council member of the McNeil Center for Early American Studies, and she served as a committee chair for the American Historical Association. Soderlund is the author of Chapters 1–8.

BRIEF TABLE OF CONTENTS

TABLE OF CONTENTS

3 CRISIS AND CHANGE, 1675–1720 *64*

4 THE EXPANSION OF COLONIAL BRITISH AMERICA, 1720–1763 *93*

$\mathcal{P}$assages
1764 TO 1814 . . . .*122*

5   WARS FOR INDEPENDENCE, 1764–1783   *128*

6   TOWARD A MORE PERFECT UNION, 1783–1788   *160*

Passages
1855 to 1877 354

*P*assages
1909 to 1933 578

𝒫assages
1933 to 1960 . . . . *684*

25 THE NEW DEAL, 1933–1939 *688*

26 THE SECOND WORLD WAR, 1940–1945 *715*

Passages
1960 to 2003 790

LIST OF DOCUMENTS

LIST OF MAPS

For animated versions of selected American Passages maps, please visit the companion web site at http://history.wadsworth.com/passages2e.

PREFACE

Hippolyte Sebron. Street Scene in New York, 1855.
Photo: Gérard Blot. Réunion des Musées Nationaux/Art Resource, NY.

A "NOVEL" APPROACH: TELLING THE STORY OF THE AMERICAN PAST

In the first edition of *American Passages* we introduced a tight narrative organization that places readers directly into the story of the past, experiencing events as they unfolded for the people of that era—whether simultaneously or in a sequential chain. Judging by the responses from instructors and students who are using the text and web resources, this approach has proven both engaging and valuable in making history make sense.

WHY STORY IS AT THE CENTER OF OUR HISTORY

History textbooks often focus on one topic at a time—politics, culture, reform, or the economy, for example. That kind of presentation, logical as it may seem, comes with a cost: it turns textbooks simply into gathered information rather than compelling stories.

People do not live one topic at a time. We experience many facets of history every day, all in the flow of time. Things happen simultaneously and in connection. We are used to the idea that our lives combine a mixture of major and minor events, of fads and movies and TV shows as well as elections, wars, and laws. The past was like that as well.

People confront surprise every day, for history seldom follows a straight line. No one could have predicted Bacon's Rebellion, John Brown's Raid, the Haymarket Riot, or the Watergate break-in. Nor could Americans have foreseen the emergence of Thomas Paine, Harriet Beecher Stowe, Henry Ford, or Martin Luther King, Jr. And who could have known on the morning of September 11, 2001, how different life would seem just that afternoon and in the days, weeks, and months that followed?

FEATURES OF *AMERICAN PASSAGES*

American Passages is written to convey the excitement and uncertainty of this nation's past—to see it whole. Eight "Passages "sections, appearing regularly throughout the text, provide broad overviews that connect ideas and themes across chapters. In addition to a textual outline, the "Passages" sections weave in photographs, posters, graphs, and maps illustrative of the period. Two-page "Passages" timelines help students place smaller stories into context and to understand interrelationships of people, ideas, movements, and events.

This edition of *American Passages* also adds a new feature, Picturing the Past, which uses extended captions to link illustrations in each chapter to the larger themes explored in the "Passages" sections. Since photos, cartoons, maps, and other visual materials are so important in our understanding of the past, we have paused a little longer over three images in each chapter to call students' attention to the detail and meaning those images convey. These extended captions are labeled corresponding to the three major organizing principles of the book—Politics and Diplomacy, Social and Cultural Events, and Economics and Technology—and are color-coordinated to the timelines in the "Passages" sections. This visual and thematic association will help students understand how people and events connected across time. And the exercise of looking at images through a historian's eye will also help them learn to evaluate images on their own.

We have added map captions that explain the significance of specific features and relationships. By highlighting the important information in various types of maps, these captions will help students develop their own map-reading and critical thinking skills. Also new to this edition are Web icons throughout the text that alert students to the remarkable resources available on the Web site custom-built for *American Passages*. Far more than any traditional ancillary or generic Web site, the site for this book amplifies and deepens the specific topics students are reading about, offering hundreds of documents, maps, illustrations, and multimedia selections—all organized to match up with the text's table of contents. Its dynamic maps and expanded entries make the *American Passages* site the most helpful and engaging resource of its kind. Visit the companion site at http://history.wadsworth.com/passages2e.

CONTENT REVISIONS

The second edition works to tell the stories of the American past as effectively as possible. The authors have trimmed the text so that it is even tighter and more efficient, making room for colorful and telling details. Each section of *American Passages* has been substantially improved. Throughout, we have consulted the latest scholarship and integrated the nuances, additions, and corrections that current literature offers.

Chapters on the colonial period include new information on North America before Columbus's arrival, the Spanish empire, and Native Americans who lived within British settlements. Perspectives on the American Revolution and the new United States place greater emphasis on the young republic's achievements within an international context.

In the chapters that cover the decades between 1815 and Reconstruction, we have consolidated material on Andrew Jackson, antebellum reform, and the War with Mexico so that these chapters work more effectively as a narrative. Memorable quotations and surprising facts have been woven in throughout these chapters.

For the late nineteenth century, we have reduced the amount of the text devoted to national politics and have also pared down some detail on farm problems and Populism so that students can better understand this complex period. The approach to progressivism and then to the 1920s reflects this same intention to provide better access to the significance of these decades rather than to a detailed recounting of events. For the mid-twentieth century—the chapters from the 1930s through the 1970s—we have tightened the narrative, focusing again on events of major political, diplomatic, and economic significance, while expanding our coverage of cultural and technological change, from rock music and television to the polio vaccine and

the computer. There is more information on the way that Americans of different backgrounds lived their everyday lives in times of economic depression, world war, unprecedented prosperity, and social unrest. For the final chapters we have integrated the events of September 11 and the unfolding of the war on terrorism into the narrative in a way that helps students grasp how the nation's present situation grew out of the political and diplomatic decisions of the 1980s and 1990s.

The second edition of *American Passages*, in short, remains true to its original vision of history as interwoven stories and now tells those stories even more effectively.

ACKNOWLEDGMENTS

I would like to thank my students and colleagues at the University of Virginia who have helped me struggle with the tough questions of American history. I am grateful, too, to Katherine Pierce and Margaret Beasley for their imagination, hard work, and good advice in the creation of this book. Finally, I am very appreciative of my co-authors, who have been engaged scholars, thoughtful critics, devoted teachers, and good friends throughout the years it took us to write *American Passages*.
Edward L. Ayers

I would like to acknowledge the help of the following former students who contributed in constructive ways to the completion of the textbook: Martin Ansell, Christie Bourgeois, Thomas Clarkin, Stacy Cordery, Debbie Cottrell, Patrick Cox, Scott Harris, Byron Hulsey, Jonathan Lee, John Leffler, Mark Young, and Nancy Beck Young. Karen Gould gave indispensable support and encouragement throughout the process of writing the text. Margaret Beasley supplied patient, informed, and thorough editorial guidance for the second edition, and the authors are all in her debt for that significant contribution. I am grateful as well to the readers of my chapters who made so many useful and timely criticisms.
Lewis L. Gould

I would like to thank my colleagues and students at Rutgers for allowing me to test out an endless stream of ideas and issues relating to modern American history, and also for their thoughts on how a good college textbook should "read" and what it should contain. As always, the support and love of my

family—Matt, Efrem, Ari, and Jane—was unshakable. Above all, I must commend my co-authors and my editors for their remarkable patience and professionalism during this long collaborative process.
David M. Oshinsky

I am grateful to my husband, Rudolf Soderlund, and my family for their support throughout this project. They have provided valuable feedback on the text. Many scholars in the colonial and early national periods shared their ideas orally and through publications. I received very helpful comments from James S. Saeger, Roger D. Simon, Marianne S. Wokeck, my co-authors of this text, and the anonymous readers for the press.
Jean R. Soderlund

Reviewers
The authors wish to thank the following professors who have provided useful feedback and suggestions at various stages in the writing and revising of *American Passages*.

Joseph Adams, St. Louis Community College at Meramec
Dawn Alexander, Abilene Christian University
Charles Allbee, Burlington Community College
Julius Amin, University of Dayton
Melodie Andrews, Mankato State University
Richard Baquera, El Paso Community College–Valle Verde
Robert Becker, Louisiana State University
Peter Bergstrom, Illinois State University
Blanche Brick, Blinn College
John Brooke, Tufts University
Neil Brooks, Essex Community College
Linda D. Brown, Odessa College
Colin Calloway, Dartmouth University
Milton Cantor, University of Massachusetts
Kay Carr, Southern Illinois University
Paul Chardoul, Grand Rapids Junior College
Thomas Clarkin, University of Texas, Austin
Myles Clowers, San Diego City College
William Cobb, Utah Valley State College
David Coon, Washington State University
Stacey Cordery, Monmouth College
Debbie Cottrell, Smith College
A. Glenn Crothers, Indiana University Southeast
David Cullen, Collin County Community College
Christine Daniels, Michigan State University

Amy E. Davis, University of California, Los Angeles
Ronnie Day, East Tennessee State University
Matthew Dennis, University of Oregon
Robert Downtain, Tarrant County Junior College, Northeast Campus
Robert Elam, Modesto Junior College
Rob Fink, Texas Tech University
Monte S. Finkelstein, Tallahassee Community College
Linda Foutch, Walter State Community College
Robert G. Fricke, West Valley College
Michael P. Gabriel, Kutztown University
David Hamilton, University of Kentucky
Beatriz Hardy, Coastal Carolina University
Peter M. G. Harris, Temple University
Thomas Hartshorne, Cleveland State University
Gordon E. Harvey, University of Louisiana at Monroe
Ron Hatzenbuehler, Idaho State University
Robert Hawkes, George Mason University
William L. Hewitt, West Chester University
James Houston, Oklahoma State University
Raymond Hyser, James Madison University
Lillian Jones, Santa Monica College
Jim Kluger, Pima Community College
Timothy Koerner, Oakland Community College
James Lacy, Contra Costa College
Alton Lee, University of South Dakota
Liston Leyendecker, Colorado State University
Robert Marcom, San Antonio College
Greg Massey, Freed-Hardeman
Michael Mayer, University of Montana
Randy McBee, Texas Tech University
Loyce B. Miles, Hinds Community College
Kimberly Morse, University of Texas, Austin
Augustine Nigro, Kutztown University
Elsa Nystrom, Kennesaw State
David O'Neill, Rutgers University
Elizabeth R. Osborn, Indiana University–Purdue University, Indianapolis
Betty Owens, Greenville Technical College
Mark Parillo, Kansas State University
J'Nell Pate, Tarrant County Junior College, Northeast Campus
Louis Potts, University of Missouri at Kansas City
Noel Pugach, University of New Mexico
Alice Reagan, Northern Virginia Community College
Marlette Rebhorn Austin Community College, Rio Grande Campus
David Reimers, New York University
Hal Rothman, Wichita State University
Erik S. Schmeller, Tennessee State University
John G. Selby, Roanoke College

Ralph Shaffer, California Polytechnic University
Kenneth Smemo, Moorhead State University
Jack Smith, Great Basin College
Thaddeus Smith, Middle Tennessee State University
Phillip E. Stebbins, Pennsylvania State University
Marshall Stevenson, Ohio State University
William Stockton, Johnson County Community
    College
Suzanne Summers, Austin Community College
Frank Towers, Clarion University

Steve Tripp, Grand Valley State University
Daniel Usner, Cornell University
Daniel Vogt, Jackson State University
Stephen Webre, Louisiana Technical College
John C. Willis, University of the South
Harold Wilson, Old Dominion University
Nan Woodruff, Pennsylvania State University
Bertram Wyatt-Brown, University of Florida
Sherri Yeager, Chabot College
Robert Zeidel, University of Wisconsin

AMERICAN PASSAGES
A History of the United States

Second Edition

PASSAGES

PREHISTORY
TO 1763

And so we journeyed for seventeen days, at the end of which we crossed the river [Rio Grande] and traveled for seventeen more. At sunset, on plains between some very tall mountains, we found some people who eat nothing but powdered straw for a third of the year. Since it was that season of the year, we had to eat it too. At the end of our journey we found a permanent settlement where there was abundant corn. The people gave us a large quantity of it and of cornmeal, squash, beans and cotton blankets. . . . From here we traveled [to where people] gave me five emeralds made into arrowheads. . . . Since they seemed very fine to me, I asked them where they had gotten them. They told me that they brought them from some very high mountains to the North.

—Cabeza de Vaca, 1542*

FROM 1534 TO 1536, the Spanish explorer Álvar Núñez Cabeza de Vaca and three others traveled through Texas and northern Mexico, trying to reach Mexico City. They had been part of an expedition to Florida that ran afoul of Apalachee Indians, escaped across the Gulf of Mexico in makeshift boats, then were enslaved in Texas by Karankawa Indians. In his *Relación,* Cabeza de Vaca described their adventures, including the harrowing passage across the gulf, long journeys without food, and sojourns among Texas Indians.

Warpaths, ocean voyages, hunting trails, trade routes, death, communication and exchange among people—creating societies in America embodied passages of every kind. Asians migrated across the

Indians in Florida transporting crops in a dugout canoe for storage in a large granary. Engraving by Theodor de Bry.
Colonial Williamsburg Foundation

*Martin A. Farata and José B. Fernandez, *The Account: Álvar Núñez Cabeza de Vaca's Relación* (1993), p. 103.

Bering land bridge and along the Pacific coast more than 10,000 years ago, settling throughout North and South America. Over time, they created distinct cultures in every part of the hemisphere, from the Aztecs of Mexico to the Algonquians of eastern North America. Over thousands of years, American civilizations rose and fell, as empires built pyramids and temple mounds, developed cities and cultures, and competed for territory and trade.

In the fifteenth century A.D., Western Europeans came to America to fish, trade, and establish colonies, bringing new technology, lust for wealth, and destructive microbes that spelled death for millions of Native Americans. The Europeans adapted their traditions and goals to exploit the abundant, yet often unfamiliar, resources of the New World. The Spanish struck it rich with the Potosí and Zacatecas silver mines that financed their religious wars in Europe and became the envy of other nations. Privateers from France, England, and the Netherlands attacked the Spanish silver fleets, while explorers searched unsuccessfully for mines in North America. Instead, they found treasures in furs, sugar, tobacco, and rice.

To reap fortunes from the earth, the colonizers first exploited Native Americans, who died in such numbers from disease and harsh treatment that Europeans

Bartholomew Gosnold in New England. The engraver, Theodor de Bry, suggests a larger fleet than Gosnold's single ship, the Concord.
The Granger Collection

Indigo Culture, from Henry Mouzon's map of Saint Stephen Parish. South Carolina slaves processed blue indigo dye, which required special skills and was dangerous because the offensive odor drew swarms of disease-bearing flies.
Duke University Special Collections

turned to another continent, Africa, for laborers. Portugal developed the Atlantic slave trade during the fifteenth century, initially buying slaves to toil on sugar islands near Africa. With the development of sugar, and later tobacco, rice, and indigo in America, the Portuguese and other Europeans purchased millions of people from African merchants for transport across the Atlantic. For more than 350 years, the cultures, sweat, and blood of enslaved Africans enriched the New World societies.

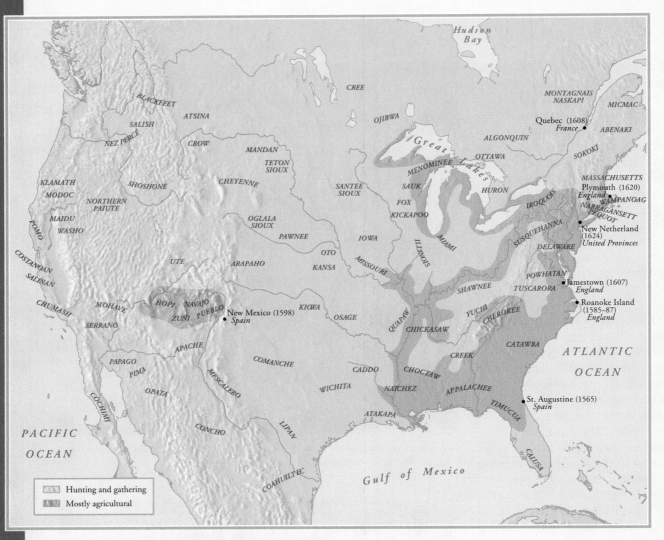

North America in the Early Seventeenth Century
This map shows the location of some of the Native American groups in North America, indicating the areas in which Indians of the eastern woodlands and American Southwest grew Indian corn, beans, squash, and other crops. The map also includes the earliest European settlements, from St. Augustine in 1565 to New Netherland in 1624.

From the sixteenth century on, Europeans battled for North America with Native Americans and among themselves. The French settled Canada and the Mississippi Valley, primarily for furs. Spain held Florida, Texas, and New Mexico as outposts to protect its silver mines and fleets. The English founded colonies in New England, the Chesapeake, and Carolinas for economic opportunity and religious freedom. In 1664, they pushed the Dutch out of New Netherland, thus connecting their chain of colonies along the Atlantic. Throughout America, Europeans hoped for a new chance in the New World.

Population Growth of the Thirteen British Mainland Colonies, 1630–1760

1630	1640	1650	1660	1670	1680	1690
4,646	26,634	50,368	75,058	111,935	151,507	210,372

The thirteen mainland British colonies had various beginnings, charters, provincial governments, economic bases, peoples, and religions. Yet they all had ties with England, in language, imperial government and laws, culture, and commerce. During the eighteenth century, the colonies forged closer bonds with the English—with greater participation in imperial wars, increased trade, and better communication. At the same time, the British provinces also became more distinctly American, as people from Africa, Ireland, and the European continent diversified the population and its culture. With natural population growth and swelling immigration, the British colonies expanded across the continent.

Native Americans responded to depopulation, defeat, and white expansion by creating new worlds of their own. Despite some military successes, they ultimately reshaped their communities and cultures, as disease worked its tragic course and European-American societies grew. The surviving members of Indian nations often merged to forge new ethnic identities, or lived together in multi-ethnic communities, often with whites and escaped slaves. Some retained remnants of their land within white settlements, while the majority moved to the frontier for political autonomy.

Tishcohan was one of the Lenape leaders who lost their land in eastern Pennsylvania with the infamous Walking Purchase of 1737. Portrait by Gustavus Hesselius, 1735. Courtesy of the Historical Society of Pennsylvania Collection, Atwater Kent Museum of Philadelphia

Three centuries passed from the time Western European fishermen first camped on North American shores until Great Britain and its colonies expelled France from the continent with the Seven Years' War. By 1763, the land and people of America had permanently changed.

1700	1710	1720	1730	1740	1750	1760
250,888	331,711	466,185	629,445	905,563	1,170,760	1,593,625

	38,000 B.C.	A.D. 1502	1602
Politics & Diplomacy	**38,000–12,000 B.C.:** Ancient hunters migrate to America **A.D. 300–1600:** Ghana, Mali, and Songhay empires in West Africa **A.D. 700–1450:** Cahokia and other Mississippian centers in North America **A.D. c. 1000:** Leif Eriksson's colony on Newfoundland **A.D. c. 1300:** Aztecs settle in Valley of Mexico **1420:** Prince Henry of Portugal begins exploration **1492:** Christopher Columbus crosses Atlantic Ocean	**1513:** Juan Ponce de León explores Florida for Spain **1519:** Magellan's expedition to circumnavigate world **1521:** Hernán Cortés defeats Aztecs **1528:** Cabeza de Vaca to Florida and Texas **1540:** Coronado explores American Southwest **c. 1550:** Iroquois form confederacy **1565:** Spanish found St. Augustine, Florida **1585:** English colony at Roanoke Island **1599:** Spanish destroy Ácoma	**1607:** English colony at Jamestown **1608:** French establish Quebec **1620:** Separatists found Plymouth **1630:** Puritans establish Massachusetts Bay colony **1634:** The *Ark* and the *Dove* arrive in Maryland **1642:** English Civil War begins **1643:** New England Confederation **1663:** Carolina proprietors receive charter **1664:** English forces conquer New Netherland
Social & Cultural Events	**1324:** Gonga-Mussa's pilgrimage to Mecca	**1507:** Martin Waldseemüller names New World after Amerigo Vespucci **1517:** Martin Luther challenges the Church of Rome **1534:** English Act of Supremacy **1536:** John Calvin's *Institutes of the Christian Religion* **1542:** Bartolomé de las Casas's *A Short Account of the Destruction of the Indies* **1585:** John White's drawings of Roanoke **1590:** Theodor de Bry's *America*	**1636:** Harvard College established Roger Williams's exile to Rhode Island **1637:** Anne Hutchinson tried for heresy **1638:** First printing press in the English colonies **1639:** French establish first hospital in North America **1647:** Massachusetts requires town schools **1649:** Maryland's act for religious toleration **1650:** Anne Bradstreet's *The Tenth Muse Lately Sprung Up in America* **c.1661:** Henri Couturier's portrait of Peter Stuyvesant **1662:** Halfway Covenant **1663:** John Eliot's Bible in Massachusetts Indian language
Economics & Technology	**Pre-2500 B.C.:** Corn developed as staple crop in central Mexico **c. 1200 B.C.:** Corn produced in American Southwest **1440s:** Portuguese mariners take Africans as slaves **c. 1450:** European fishermen at Grand Banks off Newfoundland **c. 1452:** Portugal begins sugar production on Madeira **c. 1460:** European improvements in navigation and ships **1478:** Abraham Zacuto calculates latitude using sun	**1502:** Enslaved Africans imported in Spanish America **1503:** Spanish Casa de Contratación to supervise trade **1540s:** Silver mines at Zacatecas and Potosí **1562:** John Hawkins interlopes in slave trade **c. 1585:** Growth of Amsterdam as mercantile center	**1602:** Dutch East India Company **1617:** Tobacco successful staple crop in Virginia **c. 1619:** Africans arrive in Virginia **1621:** Dutch West India Company **1640s:** Sugar production in English West Indies **1642:** French found Montreal for fur trade **1651:** First English Navigation Act

1675: King Philip's War Bacon's Rebellion **1680**: Pueblo Revolt **1681**: William Penn receives Pennsylvania charter **1688**: Glorious Revolution in England **1689**: Massachusetts, New York, and Maryland revolutions **1691**: Salem witchcraft hysteria **1699**: French establish Louisiana	**1712**: Slave revolt in New York City **1732**: Founding of Georgia **1739**: Stono Uprising in South Carolina	**1754**: Albany Congress **1754–1763**: Seven Years' War **1763**: Pan-Indian War in Ohio Valley and Great Lakes region
c.1674: *Mrs. Freake with Baby Mary* by unknown artist **1682**: Publication of *The Narrative of the Captivity and Restoration of Mrs. Mary Rowlandson* **1687**: Isaac Newton's *Principia Mathematica* **1688**: Germantown, Pennsylvania, Quakers issue antislavery protest **1690**: John Locke's *Essay Concerning Human Understanding* **1693**: College of William and Mary founded	**1695**: Jews worship openly in New York **1704**: First regular newspaper in Anglo-America, *The Boston News-Letter* **1716**: Theater built in Williamsburg, Virginia **1720**: Theodore Jacob Frelinghuysen's revivals in New Jersey **1721**: Smallpox inoculation in Boston **1731**: Benjamin Franklin's circulating library in Philadelphia **1739**: George Whitefield tours northern colonies	**1751**: Benjamin Franklin's reports on electricity **1752**: Adoption of Gregorian Calendar in Anglo-America **1761**: John Winthrop observes the transit of Venus **1763**: Rise of Delaware prophet Neolin
1672: Royal African Company **1673**: Regular postal route between Boston and New York **1670s**: Shift to slaves in Chesapeake **1698**: Royal African Company loses slave trade monopoly **1699**: Woolen Act	**1700s**: Adoption of rice in South Carolina **1720s**: Expansion of German and Scots-Irish immigration **1732**: Hat Act **1733**: Molasses Act **1740s**: Eliza Pinckney cultivates indigo in South Carolina	**1750**: Iron Act, Georgia legalizes slavery **1750s**: British colonial trade expands with Southern Europe "Consumer revolution" in British colonies early 1760s: Economic slump in British colonies

1 CONTACT, CONFLICT, AND EXCHANGE IN THE ATLANTIC WORLD TO 1590

THE FIRST AMERICANS

BEGINNING OF EUROPEAN OVERSEAS EXPANSION

AFRICA AND THE ATLANTIC SLAVE TRADE

SPAIN AND PORTUGAL DIVIDE THE GLOBE

THE SPANISH EMPIRE IN AMERICA

PROTESTANT NORTHERN EUROPEANS CHALLENGE CATHOLIC SPAIN

Secotan Village, *1585, by the Englishman John White, who journeyed to North America with the Roanoke expedition. His watercolor drawings depict Algonquians of the North Carolina coast.*
The Granger Collection

When the Italian navigator Christopher Columbus sighted San Salvador on October 12, 1492, Native Americans lived in cities and towns throughout North and South America. Their numbers had already begun to decline from disease as a result of contact with Europeans who fished off the North American coast in the late fifteenth century. Columbus called the Native Americans *Indios,* or Indians, because he thought he had reached islands in the Far East. Though not the first European to arrive, his landfall initiated the conquest and settlement of two continents, whose vast extent and wealth were previously unknown to Europeans.

For Native Americans, white men and sailing ships spelled demographic catastrophe. Within 150 years, the Indian population was reduced by 90 percent, their cities defeated and destroyed, and, for many, their lands appropriated for farming and grazing livestock. For Europeans, Columbus's unexpected "discovery" represented new challenges and opportunities. For sub-Saharan Africans, European colonization of America would stimulate the slave trade, which over the next four centuries transported at least 10 million Africans across the Atlantic. To exploit the riches of America, Europeans used the labor of both Native Americans and Africans.

Yet contact among Native Americans, Europeans, and Africans involved more than conquest, enslavement, and death. Together the three major cultural groups created new traditions and societies in the New World. Although the Europeans must be declared winners in the contest for power, the American colonies were shaped by exchange of knowledge, culture, and work among all participants. Three major cultural traditions came together in the Western Hemisphere. This chapter explores Native American, European, and African societies at the time of contact; European exploration; and Spanish colonization in Central and South America. The Spanish empire subsequently extended into New Mexico and California, serving as an important model for English settlement in North America.

THE FIRST AMERICANS

Estimates of the number of Native Americans in 1492 vary widely, from 8 million to more than 100 million. They possessed widely divergent cultures, ranging from the Inuit who hunted seal and walrus along the shores of the Arctic Ocean, to the Aztecs of central Mexico and Incas of the Peruvian Andes who lived in state-level agricultural societies. In the geographic area that now encompasses the United States, they included mound-building farmers of the Mississippi valley, the pueblo-dwelling Hopi and Zuñi Indians and nomadic Apaches of the southwest, and the Iroquois and Algonquians of the eastern woodlands.

Native American Societies Before Contact

Archeological evidence from various sites in North and South America suggests these diverse peoples were descendants of Asians who migrated by boat along the Pacific coast or who crossed the Bering land bridge from Siberia to Alaska more than 10,000 years ago. As glaciers from the last Ice Age receded, groups migrated throughout the hemisphere. Their cultures and languages diverged as they adapted to their environments. Initially, they hunted game, fished, and collected berries, seeds, and nuts.

When ancient Americans began cultivating crops, they laid the foundation for more densely populated societies. Of greatest importance to Indians of North America was the development of maize, or Indian corn, probably from the grass *teosinte,* which grew in dry areas of Mexico and Guatemala. In addition to maize, early Mexicans domesticated beans, squash, chili peppers, and avocado. Agriculture proved revolutionary for some ancient American societies, as higher yields spurred population growth and a greater division of labor.

Between 1500 B.C. and Columbus's arrival, civilizations rose and declined throughout the Americas. Ancient Americans built empires, much like their counterparts in Egypt, Greece, and Rome, with cities, extensive trade networks, systems of religion and knowledge, art, architecture, and hierarchical social classes. Two of the best-known civilizations of precontact America were the Mayan, located on the Yucatán peninsula, and the Mexican. The Maya, at their height from 300 to 900 A.D., built cities of stone pyramids, temples, and palaces, with populations ranging to more than 60,000. Mayan kings, considered divine, extended their empire to over fifty different states and maintained trade with distant peoples. The Maya had a numeral system based on units of twenty, hieroglyphics, knowledge of astronomy, and several calendars.

The Mexicans, who lived in the Valley of Mexico, built the city of Teotihuacán east of Lake Texcoco. Its population of about 200,000 depended on intensive farming of nearby irrigated lands. The grid-patterned Teotihuacán held at its core the Pyramid of the Sun and the Pyramid of the Moon. Even after the city's decline it retained religious significance for later Mexicans.

CHRONOLOGY

38,000–12,000 B.C.   Migration of ancient hunters to the Americas

300–900 A.D.   Height of Mayan civilization in Yucatan

300–1600 A.D.   Succession of empires, Ghana, Mali, and Songhay, in West Africa

700–1450 A.D.   Mississippian people build Cahokia and other urban centers in North America

c. 1000 A.D.   Leif Eriksson establishes Viking colony on Newfoundland

c. 1300 A.D.   Aztecs settle in Valley of Mexico

1420   Prince Henry of Portugal initiates search for ocean route to Asia

1440s   Portuguese mariners take Africans as slaves

c. 1452   Portugal begins sugar production on Madeira

c. 1460–1500   European improvements in navigation and ships

1487   Bartholomeu Dias of Portugal rounds Cape of Good Hope

1492   Christopher Columbus crosses Atlantic Ocean

1494   Treaty of Tordesillas establishes Line of Demarcation

1497–1498   Vasco da Gama reaches India for Portugal

1517   Martin Luther challenges the Church of Rome

1519–1521   Hernán Cortés conquers the Aztecs

1519–1522   Magellan's expedition circumnavigates the world

1528–1536   Cabeza de Vaca's adventures in Florida and Texas

1534   Act of Supremacy separates England from the Church of Rome

1539–1542   Hernando de Soto explores the region from Florida to the Mississippi River

1540–1542   Coronado explores the American Southwest

1541   Cartier establishes Charlesbourg-Royal in Canada

1556   Philip II of Spain takes the throne

1558   Elizabeth I becomes queen of England

1564   French Huguenots build Fort Caroline in northern Florida

1577–1580   Francis Drake circumnavigates the globe

1585   English attempt colonization at Roanoke Island

1588   English defeat the Spanish Armada

The Aztecs settled in the Valley of Mexico in the fourteenth century, building their capital, Tenochtitlán, on an island in Lake Texcoco, which they connected to the shore by causeways. They cultivated intensively the marshlands surrounding their island and built a militaristic state. By the time the Spanish *conquistadores* arrived in 1519, the Aztecs controlled territory from the Pacific to the Gulf Coast. The Aztecs required tribute from the people they conquered—gold, feathers, turquoise, food, cotton, and human beings for sacrifice. They believed that every day they had to feed human hearts to the sun god, Huitzilpochtli, to prevent the world from coming to an end.

To the north of the Valley of Mexico, the Hohokam occupied desert lands in Arizona and northern Sonora, where, with irrigation, they cultivated Indian

Map 1.1 *America Before Columbus*

The first inhabitants of North America probably migrated from Asia by boat and across the Bering land bridge (Beringia), which was created when sea levels dropped during the last Ice Age. Archaeological evidence along the Pacific coast and from sites such as Cahokia and Mesa Verde provide important information about Native American societies before 1492.

*Hohokam pottery decorated with bird motif, c. 700–900
A.D. found at Snaketown, Arizona.*
ASM specimen A-26556, Santa Cruz on puff plate from Snaketown, Arizona.
State Museum, University of Arizona. Helgatweis, photographer.

corn, cotton, squash, and beans. Their canals, up to
ten miles long, diverted water from nearby rivers.
When Athabaskan raiders from the north attacked
Hohokam towns, they tried to protect themselves by
building high adobe walls, then after 1400 A.D. simply
abandoned many of their villages.

Enemy attacks and crop failures from lack of rain
forced other Indians of the southwest to leave their
towns. The Anasazi farmers of northern Arizona and
New Mexico, Colorado, and Utah relied on rain and
floods to water their crops. One of their settlements
was Pueblo Bonito in Chaco Canyon, which housed
perhaps 1,000 people in 800 rooms surrounded by
high walls; another was the complex of rock dwellings
built high in the canyon cliffs at Mesa Verde. Descendants of the Anasazi—the Hopi and Zuñi Indians—
were called "Pueblo" Indians by the Spanish for the
adobe villages with large apartment dwellings in
which they lived.

Farther east, in a large area drained by the Mississippi River, by 1000 B.C. early Americans developed civilizations characterized by large earthen burial mounds, some sixty feet high. These mounds
entombed corpses and such grave goods as copper
spoons and beads made from seashells. The Adena-
Hopewell people, who built the Great Serpent Mound
located in southern Ohio, lived in small villages
along rivers, hunted game, fished, and raised squash,

Indian corn, sunflowers, and gourds. As evidenced
by the grave goods, their trading network extended
from the Gulf Coast (shells) to Lake Superior (copper). By 800 A.D., people in the Mississippi Valley
constructed large towns, including Cahokia, which
was located near present-day St. Louis. At the center
of these towns stood large rectangular mounds
topped by temples and mortuaries in which members
of the upper class were buried. By 1450, the region's
population declined, perhaps as a result of illness
spread by urban crowding.

People of the Eastern Woodlands

Along the Atlantic seaboard extending inland to the
Appalachian Mountains lived Native Americans of
two major language groups, the Algonquian and the
Iroquois. The eastern woodlands incorporated a wide
variety of habitats. In most parts, decent soil and
moderate rainfall and temperatures supported agriculture and many kinds of game, fish, and wild
plants. Algonquian-speaking people dominated the
Atlantic coast from Canada to Florida; they included
the Pokanokets, Narragansetts, and Pequots in New
England; the Lenapes of the middle Atlantic region;
and members of the Powhatan confederacy in what
became Virginia. Many of the Iroquois lived in the

*The Anasazis established agricultural towns in the area
extending from the Grand Canyon in Arizona into
southern Utah and Colorado. At Mesa Verde, by 1150 A.D.,
they built large multiroomed houses in caves near the top
of canyon walls, probably for protection against enemies.*
© Craig Aurness/Corbis

Finger Lakes area of central New York. They belonged to five tribes: the Mohawks, Oneidas, Onondagas, Cayugas, and Senecas, from east to west, who banded together in the Iroquois confederacy.

Although important cultural differences existed between the two language groups and even among bands within each group, Indians of the eastern woodlands had much in common. They held land cooperatively: the tribe as a whole claimed ownership rights, not individual members or families. Except in far northern New England, Indians had a mixed economy of agriculture, gathering, fishing, and hunting. Women were responsible for raising corn, squash, beans, and (where possible) tobacco. They also gathered nuts and fruit, built houses, made clothing, took care of the children, and prepared meals, while men cleared land, hunted, fished, and protected the village from enemies. The combination of corn, squash, and beans enriched the soil, providing high yields from small plots of land; eaten together these foods were high in protein. The Native Americans cleared land by girdling the large trees (removing a strip of bark around the trees about three feet from the ground). When the trees died, the Indians removed them, burned the underbrush, and sowed crops among the stumps. Eastern woodlands people used nets and weirs to catch fish and, to assure good hunting, they periodically burned underbrush from sections of forest. The burning stimulated the growth of lush grass, providing fodder for deer and other game. The fires allowed some sunlight to penetrate the forest, promoting the growth of strawberries, raspberries, and blackberries.

Indian religions, though widely diverse in many ways, incorporated a common worldview. The people of the eastern woodlands believed that the earth and sky formed a spiritual realm of which they were a part, not the masters. Spirits inhabited the earth and could be found in plants, animals, rocks, or clouds. Each spirit, or *manitou*, could become the guardian of a young Indian man (less often a young woman), who, in search of a manitou, went into the woods alone, without eating or sleeping perhaps for days. If the spirit made itself known, it would provide help and counsel to the individual for the rest of his or her life. These Native Americans also believed in a Master Spirit or Creator, who was all-powerful and all-knowing, but whose presence was rarely felt. Religious leaders were *shamans* who performed rituals to influence weather conditions or ward off danger. They were usually men, but in some communities were women. Indians believed that shamans could cure illness, interpret dreams, bring good weather, and predict the future.

Prehistoric Cahokia Mounds, c. 1100–1150 A.D., Drawing by William R. Iseminger based on archeological evidence. Monks Mound dominated the palisaded area, which had at its center a rectangular ball court with two poles.
Depiction of Cahokia Mounds—AD 1150 by William R. Ieminger. Courtesy of Cahokia Mounds State Historic Site

PICTURING THE PAST ✦ SOCIAL & CULTURAL EVENTS

GREAT SERPENT MOUND

Courtesy, National Museum of the American Indian, Smithsonain Institute #P18523

This is an aerial photograph of the Great Serpent Mound in southern Ohio, which was probably built by the Adena or Hopewell people sometime between 500 B.C. and 500 A.D. The Hopewell people had trade networks extending to the Gulf Coast, Rocky Mountains, and Lake Superior. Archeologists digging at Hopewell sites have recovered copper, quartz, shark and grizzly bear teeth, and silver from distant areas. Artisans created jewelry, smoking pipes, musical panpipes, and other art from these materials.

The Great Serpent Mound, more that one-quarter mile long from the triangular tip to the tail, demonstrates the knowledge of astronomy of these ancient people. According to anthropologist William F. Romain in *Mysteries of the Hopewell* (2000), the mound is oriented to true astronomical north and its measurements conform to the standard Hopewell 1,053-foot unit of length. The large oval and serpent's head almost perfectly face the setting sun on June 21, the summer solstice; the serpent's body is aligned to the rising and setting moon.

The kinship group, or extended family, formed the basis of Native American society. The heads of kinship groups chose the band's chief leaders, called *sachems,* who with advice assigned fields for planting, decided where and when to hunt, managed trade and diplomacy with other Indians and Europeans, and judged whether or not to go to war. Among Algonquian-speaking natives, the heads of extended families were men, as were the sachems they chose. But in Iroquois culture, women served as clan leaders, taking a share of political power. Iroquois society was matrilineal, with family membership passing from mother to children; and matrilocal, as the husband left his family to live with his wife's. Women elders could not speak publicly at tribal councils or serve as sachems, but they chose these political leaders and advised them on such matters as waging war.

Thus, in 1492, highly complex and differentiated societies existed in North and South America. Dense populations inhabited parts of South, Central, and North America. Throughout the hemisphere, Indian people had distinctive cultures tied to the resources of their environment. Despite this wide variety of languages and cultures, most Europeans adopted the single name that Columbus mistakenly employed—Indians. An alternative the colonists used was "savages." The view of many Europeans—that Native Americans had undifferentiated, uncivilized societies—justified conquest and expropriation of their lands.

Man with Body Paint *by John White, 1585. Men were the political leaders, warriors, and hunters in Algonquian society.*
© British Museum

BEGINNING OF EUROPEAN OVERSEAS EXPANSION

Europeans had more in common with Native Americans than they liked to admit; nevertheless, in important ways, their cultures were distinct. Like the people of America, Europeans spent most of their energy producing or gathering food. They farmed, raised livestock, and gathered nuts and berries. In the south and west of England, for example, farmers engaged in intensive cultivation of wheat, rye, and other crops. In most of England and Wales, however, farmers planted just an acre or two and spent more time gathering. In contrast to Native Americans, Europeans believed that individuals could own land and thus had the right to sell, fence, plant, erect buildings, hunt, cut lumber, and exclude others from use.

The societies from which most colonizers came were patriarchal, meaning that descent followed the father's line and political power was nearly always in the hands of men. Though women occasionally took the throne, for instance, Isabella of Spain and Elizabeth I of England, men controlled government, the church, and the military. Married women were considered subordinate to their husbands. Under English common law, a married woman was a *feme covert*, or covered woman, who could not own or manage property, make a contract, write a will, take custody of her children, own a business, or sue in court, without her husband's permission. An unmarried woman or widow, in legal terms a *feme sole*, was not subject to these restrictions.

In the fifteenth century, the pope headed a united Christian church in western and central Europe. At the same time, monarchs consolidated power in Portugal, Spain, France, and England, providing financial support and a greater sense of national identity to fuel European expansion. In turn, wealth from distant empires and trade funded wars among these emerging nations.

Trade with the East

When Columbus sailed out into the Atlantic Ocean in 1492, he expected to establish a new trade route with Asia. In the fifteenth century, eastern trade was a chief source of riches, for affluent Europeans wanted spices that would not grow in Europe such as black pepper, cinnamon, and cloves for preserving and flavoring their food. Merchants commanded high prices for transporting spices, silk, cotton cloth, and jewels from India, the East Indies, and other parts of East Asia.

Before 1500, Arab and Italian merchants dominated the eastern trade. Arabs controlled eastern trading centers and carried goods to the Red Sea and Persian Gulf. From there, caravans took cargoes to Mediterranean ports for purchase by Italian merchants. The Italians then distributed the spices and other goods throughout Europe by way of pack train and coastal shipping. European cities developed to handle the exchange of valued eastern products in return for silver, gold, woolen and linen cloth, furs, and leather. Centers of trade and banking included Paris, Lyons, Amsterdam, London, Hamburg, Danzig, Barcelona, Cadiz,

*P*ICTURING THE PAST ✦ SOCIAL & CULTURAL EVENTS

WOMAN AND GIRL OF POMEIOC

A cheife Heroroans wyfe of Pomeoc. and her daughter of the age of 8. or. 10. yeares.

The Englishman John White painted this watercolor in 1585, during his stay in the Roanoke colony on the coast of what is now North Carolina. It is one of a series of illustrations, also including *Secotan Village* and *Man with Body Paint* in this chapter, that provide some of the best evidence about the Algonquians of eastern North America in the late sixteenth century.

The label at the top states that this is the wife of a chief of Pomeioc and her daughter aged 8 or 10 years. White tried to present the Indians' appearance faithfully, including their hairstyles, jewelry, and clothing. The chief's wife is dressed like other women of the Eastern Woodlands during the summer and is carrying a container for liquids. The girl has an English doll that Thomas Harriot, another colonist, said Indian children enjoyed. Algonquian women in North Carolina and Virginia cared for children and raised crops including corn and tobacco.

© British Museum

Lisbon, Venice, and Genoa. The rise of great cities accompanied the growth of unified political states. Merchants provided funding for kings to consolidate small feudal states into nations. In Portugal, Spain, France, and England, commercial interests supported unification to obtain social order, monopolistic privileges, and standardized codes of law.

Portugal Explores the West African Coast

Early in the fifteenth century, Prince Henry of Portugal, called "the Navigator," decided to challenge the Arab and Italian hold on eastern commerce. Henry brought together men interested in overseas trade and exploration. Beginning in 1420, he sent ships down the western coast of Africa. He had four goals: to increase the

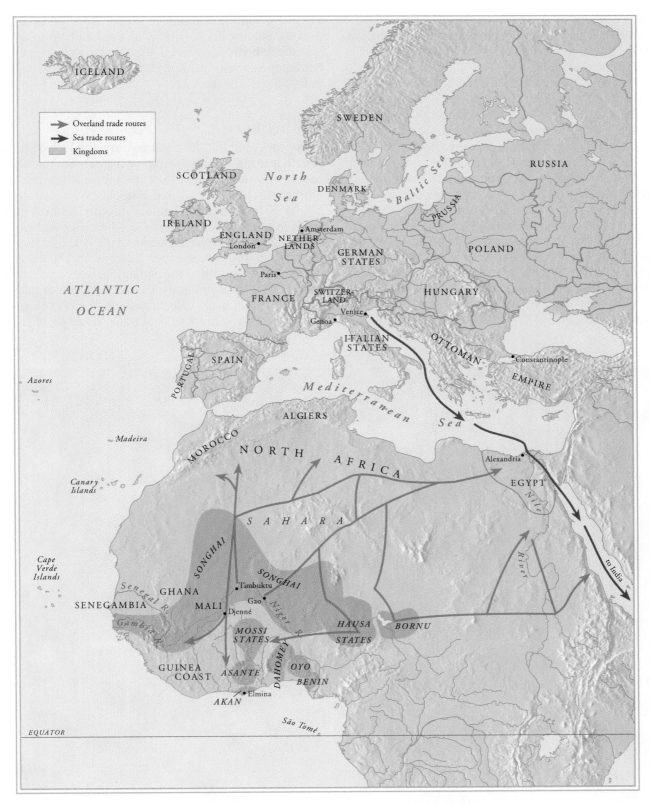

Map 1.2 *Europe and West Africa in the Fifteenth Century*

Exploration of North and South America was an outgrowth of trade in the Eastern Hemisphere. Europeans delivered cloth and other manufactures to northern Africa; then camels carried the cargoes across the Sahara to cities such as Timbuktu, Gao, and Djenné. There they loaded gold, ivory, and kola nuts for return to the Mediterranean. Africans also traded with Asia to obtain cloth, porcelain, and spices.

power of Portugal by adding territorial possessions; to benefit economically from commerce with the African coast; to reach Asia and take a share of that trade; and to spread Christianity.

Headway down the African coast was slow because European sailors knew nothing of the ocean beyond Cape Bojador. In 1420, cartographers knew a great deal about the Mediterranean Sea and constructed highly accurate charts, called *portolano,* of its shorelines and harbors. Such maps did not exist for the West African coast, so one task of Prince Henry's explorers was to chart their progress. Seamen had heard that monsters and perhaps even Satan swelled in the waters beyond Cape Bojador, while other stories told that the ocean boiled at the equator. In fact, strong southward ocean currents facilitated outbound progress, but made return to the Mediterranean difficult. From ancient mathematicians and geographers, most notably Ptolemy, mapmakers knew that the world was round, but they also adopted Ptolemy's be-

lief that a southern continent joined Africa to China, thus eliminating the possibility of a sea route from the Atlantic to the Indian Ocean. Prince Henry challenged current wisdom by sending ships down Africa's coast to find a route to the east.

New Technology

In the early and mid-fifteenth century, the lack of adequate instruments hampered navigation. Compasses had been in use since at least the thirteenth century, but not until about 1460 did Europeans develop the means of determining latitude (distance north or south from the equator). In the Northern Hemisphere, sea captains calculated the height of the Pole Star from the horizon to determine their latitude. The Pole Star cannot be seen south of the equator, however, so navigators there measured the altitude of the sun at midday. In making these calculations, they used the astrolabe or the quadrant to determine the angle of the

Engraving of an early sixteenth-century cosmographer working in his study with contemporary instruments, including dividers, rule, compass, quadrant, and sand glass.
National Maritime Museum

sun from the horizon, then consulted astronomical tables that Abraham Zacuto, a Jewish astronomer, compiled in 1478. A method for determining longitude remained unknown until the eighteenth century.

Improvements in ships and gunnery during the fifteenth century also aided exploration and conquest. By 1400 it had become clear that Mediterranean galleys, powered by oarsmen, were impractical in the high waves of the Atlantic. The first European oceangoing ships were square-rigged. Their broad sails could power large vessels, but they required a favorable tailwind to proceed from one point to another. To increase maneuverability along jagged coastlines, Portuguese seafarers designed the caravel with lateen (triangular) sails. The most successful Portuguese ship for long voyages was the *caravela redondo*, the square-rigged caravel, developed late in the fifteenth century, and adopted by other European nations. This ship combined the speed of square rigging with the agility of lateen sails. For protection from privateers and in time of war, the Portuguese mounted artillery on the caravels and by 1500 introduced the practice of broadside fire. They changed nautical warfare by sinking enemy vessels with gunfire instead of boarding them with foot soldiers.

Despite these improvements in the design of ships, they remained uncomfortable places in which to live on voyages of months and years. Except for senior officers, none of the seamen had regular sleeping quarters—they slept on deck, or below in bad weather. Their shipmates included rats and cockroaches. When it rained, everything got wet, including the cooking fire built in a sandbox on deck. The mariners ate ship's hardtack, beans, salt pork, and beef, and drank mostly wine, since their casked water quickly became foul.

AFRICA AND THE ATLANTIC SLAVE TRADE

Despite their limited technology, the Portuguese explorers ventured farther and farther down the West African coast. In 1434, Gil Eannes sailed past Cape Bojador. Subsequent voyages established a lucrative coastal trade in slaves, gold, and malaguetta pepper in the Senegal region and farther south and east to the Gold Coast and Benin. Merchants now began investing in expeditions. Between the 1440s and 1505, Portuguese traders transported 40,000 Africans to perform domestic labor in Portugal and Spain and to work on the sugar plantations of the Azores, Madeira, and Canary Islands.

West African Cultures

From before 300 A.D. to 1600, a succession of empires—Ghana, Mali, and Songhay—dominated western Africa. They had large armies, collected tribute over vast distances, and traded with Europeans and Arabs. West Africans were predominantly agricultural people. Ghana declined by 1100 as a result of droughts that dried up several rivers. Mali then took control, as its monarchs regulated the gold trade. The Mali kings were followers of Islam: one of the most famous, Gonga-Mussa, made a pilgrimage to Mecca in 1324 to fulfill his religious duty as a Muslim. His caravan is said to have included 60,000 people and 80 camels carrying over 24,000 pounds of gold.

Mali provided stable government over a wide area until the fifteenth century, when Songhay successfully challenged its dominance. Songhay was centered at Gao. Under Sonni Ali, who ruled from 1468 to 1492, Songhay captured Timbuktu, an important trading and cultural center of Mali. Askia Mohammed, who ruled from 1493 to 1528, expanded the empire even farther. He strengthened ties with other Muslims and reformed government, banking, and education. He adopted Islamic law and encouraged intellectual growth at Timbuktu and Gao. After his reign, Songhay declined; Moroccans conquered Timbuktu in 1593.

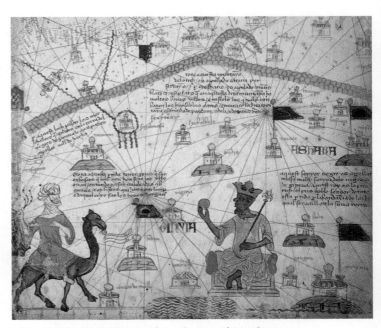

This 1375 European map of northwest Africa shows an Arab trader approaching Mansa Musa of Mali, who is holding a large nugget of gold.
The Granger Collection

A bronze relief of Benin, a powerful kingdom when the Portuguese began trading along the African coast in the late fifteenth century.
The Granger Collection

Beyond these empires, along the West African coast lay smaller states with highly developed cultures. Although influenced by Islam, they retained much of their traditional religions. Divine kings governed many of the coastal states. Like Native Americans and Europeans, the people of Africa kept religion central to their lives and endowed their leaders with both political and religious authority.

Most important in traditional African religions was a single all-powerful God, the Creator. The Creator provided lesser gods, including gods of rain, thunder, and lightning; of rivers and lakes; of animals, trees, and hills. These gods could be benevolent or harmful, so people had to seek positive relationships through rituals, sacrifice, and prayer. Africans also believed that their ancestors watched over the extended family, with power over fertility, health, and even life. When the eldest father, or patriarch, of a kinship group died, his spirit became a god. Elaborate funeral rites demonstrated the importance of the dead to the living. All family members paid respect to the deceased, whose internment was delayed until distant relatives could arrive. Before his death, the patriarch had been the extended family's priest; he communicated with its ancestors through prayer and the sacrifice of animals such as chickens and sheep. The patriarch also served as political leader. Thus in many African societies, the state, religion, and family united under a single hierarchical structure.

Kinship in West Africa varied from one culture to another, as extended families could be either patrilineal or matrilineal. In all cases, however, a child belonged to only one kin group. If the system was patrilineal, then descent flowed from father to child. If it was matrilineal, descent proceeded from mother to child, but the mother's brother, not the mother, assumed responsibility. When a woman married, she usually went to live with her husband's family. The husband compensated her family for the loss of her services with a payment called bridewealth. *Polygyny,* or having more than one wife, was generally reserved to men of high status. When men had more than one wife, each woman lived with her children in a separate house.

The extended family held land in common and assigned plots to individual families. Women and men worked in fields growing crops such as rice, cassava, wheat, millet, cotton, fruits, and vegetables. They had livestock, including cattle, sheep, goats, and chickens. Families produced food for their own use and for the market, where women were the primary traders. Artisans were skilled in textile weaving, pottery, basketry, and woodwork. They also made tools and art objects of copper, bronze, iron, silver, and gold. As in the case of Native Americans, West Africans had experienced the rise and fall of empires and possessed diverse, complex cultures at the time Europeans arrived on their shores in the mid-fifteenth century.

The Atlantic Slave Trade Begins

Over the course of four centuries, Africa lost more than 10 million people to the Atlantic slave trade. Slavery had existed in Africa and throughout the Mediterranean for centuries before the Portuguese arrived on the West African coast. African slavery was different, however, from the institution that developed in America. Most African slaves were prisoners of war; others had committed some offense that caused their kinfolk to banish them. All were considered "outsiders." The primary function of slavery in West Africa was social rather than economic—to provide a place in society for people cut off from their families. Trans-Saharan traders transported some African slaves for sale to wealthy European households. Because this trade was limited, most slaves remained in West Africa, where they achieved status as a member of a household, married, and had children. Enslaved Africans could be transferred from one owner to another at will, but their children could not be sold and were frequently emancipated.

The plantation slave system that became dominant in America began near Africa. Portugal began growing sugar as early as 1452 on the island of Madeira, off West

Africa. Sugar cane required large amounts of menial, unpleasant labor in a hot climate. To supply Madeira, Portuguese merchants purchased black slaves from Muslim trans-Saharan traders and from Africans along the coast. When sugar production could expand no further in Madeira, the Portuguese colonized the small islands in the Gulf of Guinea: São Tomé, Príncipe, and Fernando Po. Sugar production was successful, but mortality was high and the demand for laborers great, spurring growth of the slave trade on the Gold Coast. By the end of the fifteenth century, before European settlement in America, Portugal developed both the plantation system and the commercial mechanism for purchasing human beings from African traders. The growth of slavery and the slave trade in America after 1500 represented an expansion of these earlier developments.

SPAIN AND PORTUGAL DIVIDE THE GLOBE

Once Portugal had established trade on the West African coast, Spanish merchants tried to participate. Prince Henry appealed to the pope, who in 1455 gave Portugal sole possession of lands to the south and east toward India. The pope's decision gave Portugal a monopoly on the Atlantic slave trade. Spain and Portugal affirmed the decision with the Treaty of Alcaçovas (1479), in which Spain recognized Portugal's sphere of interest in Africa, and Portugal acknowledged Spain's claim to the Canary Islands.

As the Portuguese sailed south, they came to recognize the vastness of the African continent. They made rapid progress only after 1482, when King John II of Portugal stepped-up the program of discovery. In 1483, Diogo Cão reached the Congo River and in 1487 Bartholomeu Dias rounded the Cape of Good Hope. The Portuguese now knew that a sea route to India existed.

Columbus Sails West

The Spanish had to find another course if they were going to trade with the Far East. Thus, Isabella funded Christopher Columbus, despite skepticism of his calculation of the distance to Asia. In August 1492, Columbus sailed west from the Canaries, taking advantage of the favorable current and trade winds. The ships reached San Salvador in October, but Columbus thought they had located the East Indies. Hoping to establish trade, Columbus sailed southward to Cuba,

A Fula town in West Africa, drawn by a European. West Africans, like Europeans but not Native Americans, kept domestic livestock. The village raised Indian corn, which had been brought from America.

Reproduced from the Collections of the Library of Congress

Columbus's arrival in the West Indies, as imagined by the Flemish engraver Theodor de Bry, who published a series of volumes on "America" in the late sixteenth and early seventeenth centuries.
Courtesy of the John Carter Brown Library at Brown University

then touched Hispaniola, where Native Americans offered gold in return for the trade goods he brought. When the Spanish lost their flagship *Santa Maria* on a coral reef, they built a small fort with its timbers.

Leaving a small contingent of men, Columbus set out for home in January 1493, again found favorable winds, but encountered a violent storm and sought shelter in Portugal. King John II, whose explorers had not yet reached India by sailing around Africa, refused to believe that Columbus had located Asia. The lands he had found, the king claimed, lay within Portugal's sphere.

Spanish and Portuguese "Spheres"

Isabella and Ferdinand rejected Portugal's argument, petitioning Pope Alexander VI, who was Spanish, to grant them dominion over the newly discovered lands. After negotiations with John II, the pope established a Line of Demarcation, giving all lands "discovered or to be discovered" west of the line to Spain and all lands east of the line to Portugal. The Treaty of Tordesillas (1494) located the line 370 leagues (about 1,000 miles) west of the Azores and expanded the principle of

"spheres of influence" by which European nations sought to dominate most of the world. Portugal retained its rights to the Atlantic slave trade and the sea route around Africa to India. Spain received permission to explore, conquer, and Christianize all lands and people to the west. The question of where Portuguese and Spanish spheres should be divided in the Far East was left unresolved until 1529, when the Treaty of Saragossa established a line seventeen degrees to the east of the Moluccas (Spice Islands), thus placing most of Asia within Portugal's sphere.

Between 1494 and 1529, Portugal and Spain sent out expeditions to explore their spheres. Columbus made three more voyages to the west: in November 1493 he sailed with seventeen ships to the Lesser Antilles, Puerto Rico, and Hispaniola. Later he explored the shores of South and Central America. Meanwhile, Columbus's claim that he had found a passage to the East by sailing west prodded the Portuguese to complete their efforts to reach India. In 1497–1498, Vasco da Gama rounded the Cape of Good Hope and sailed across the Indian Ocean, returning to Portugal with a cargo of pepper and cinnamon. The voyage to India was much more difficult than Columbus's Atlantic crossing. During the two-year journey that took at least 300 days at sea, more than one-third of the crew died. In 1500, Portugal instructed Pedro Álvares Cabral to find the Cape of Good Hope by sailing west. Instead, he touched the coast of Brazil, further convincing the Portuguese that this was not Asia. On the basis of Cabral's expedition and because a section of Brazil lay east of the Line of Demarcation, Portugal claimed that part of South America. Amerigo Vespucci made two separate voyages, in 1499 and 1501, for Spain and Portugal respectively. He explored much of the Atlantic coast of South America, demonstrating that it was a huge land mass that had to be circumnavigated to reach Asia. In reward for his insights, many Europeans associated his name—not that of Columbus—with the newly "discovered" continents.

An Expanding World

Europeans continued to search for a western sea route to Asia. Ferdinand Magellan convinced King Charles I of Spain that he could sail around the cape of South America and claim the Molucca Islands. Magellan was Portuguese, but his country gave him no support since it already had a profitable sea route to the East. With five ships, in 1519 Magellan set out on an expedition that would take three years. The voyagers faced shipwreck, a harrowing passage through the straits subsequently named for Magellan, and starvation. The Pacific was so much wider than anticipated that the mariners had to

Admiral Christopher Columbus's Diary Account of Reaching America, October 12, 1492

This document is from an abstract of Columbus's diary made by the Spanish missionary Bartolomé de las Casas. The admiral's original diary no longer exists. This selection begins as the Europeans sight land and describes their first contact with the Native Americans. Because Columbus thought his expedition had reached the East Indies, he called the people Indians.

At two hours after midnight the land appeared, from which they were about two leagues distant. They hauled down all the sails . . . passing time until daylight Friday, when they reached an islet of the Lucayas, which was called Guanahani in the language of the Indians. Soon they saw naked people; and the Admiral [Columbus] went ashore in the armed launch, and Martín Alonso Pinzón and his brother Vicente Anes, who was captain of the *Niña*. The Admiral brought out the royal banner and the captains' two flags with the green cross. . . . Thus put ashore they saw very green trees and many ponds and fruits of various kinds. The Admiral called to the two captains and to the others who had jumped ashore and to Rodrigo Descobedo, the recorder of the whole fleet, and to Rodrigo Sánchez de Segovia; and he said that they should be witnesses that, in the presence of all, he would take, as in fact he did take, possession of the said island for the king and for the queen his lords, making the declarations that were required, and which at more length are contained in the testimonials made there in writing. Soon many people of the island gathered there. What follows are the very words of the Admiral in his book about his first voyage to, and discovery of, these Indies.

I, he says, in order that they would be friendly to us—because I recognized that they were people who would be better freed [from error] and converted to our Holy Faith by love than by force—to some of them I gave red caps, and glass beads which they put on their chests, and many other things of small value, in which they took so much pleasure and became so much our friends that it was a marvel. Later they came swimming to the ships' launches where we were and brought us parrots and cotton thread in balls and javelins and many other things, and they traded them to us for other things which we gave them, such as small glass beads and bells. In sum, they took everything and gave of what they had very willingly.

But it seemed to me that they were a people very poor in everything. All of them go around as naked as their mothers bore them; and the women also, although I did not see more than one quite young girl. And all those that I saw were young people, for none did I see of more than 30 years of age. They are very well formed, with handsome bodies and good faces. Their hair [is] coarse—almost like the tail of a horse—and short. They wear their hair down over their eyebrows except for a little in the back which they wear long and never cut. Some of them paint themselves with black, and they are of the color of the Canarians, neither black nor white; and some of them paint themselves with white, and some of them with red, and some of them with whatever they find. And some of them paint their faces, and some of them the whole body, and some of them only the eyes, and some of them only the nose.

They do not carry arms nor are they acquainted with them, because I showed them swords and they took them by the edge and through ignorance cut themselves. They have no iron. Their javelins are shafts without iron and some of them have at the end a fish tooth and others of other things. All of them alike are of good-sized stature and carry themselves well. . . . They should be good and intelligent servants, for I see that they say very quickly everything that is said to them; and I believe that they would become Christians very easily, for it seemed to me that they had no religion. Our Lord pleasing, at the time of my departure I will take six of them from here to Your Highnesses in order that they may learn to speak. No animal of any kind did I see on this island except parrots. All are the Admiral's words.

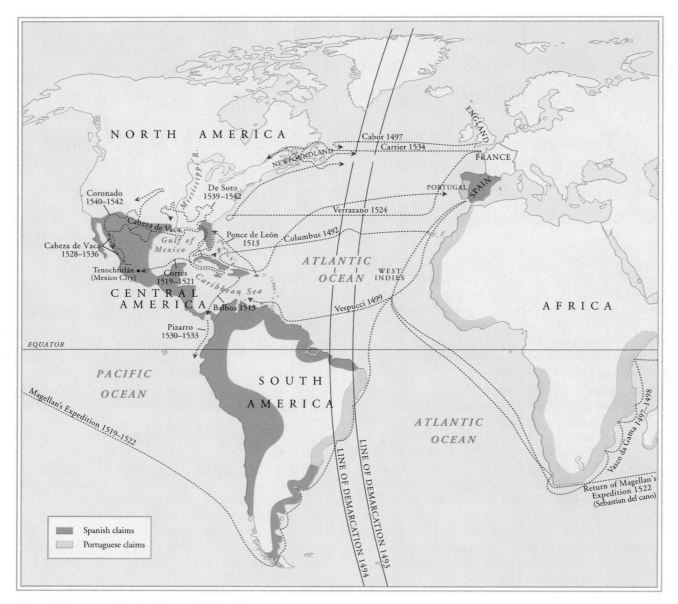

Map 1.3 *European Explorations, 1492–1542*

Before 1542, Spain and Portugal dominated European exploration. Generally conforming to the 1494 Line of Demarcation, Portugal's "sphere of influence" included Brazil (in eastern South America), Africa, and South Asia. Spain claimed the rest of South and Central America. France and England sent out explorers but did not establish permanent colonies in North America until the early seventeenth century.

View an animated version of this map or related maps at http://history.wadsworth.com/passages2e.

eat ship rats and leather. When inhabitants of the Philippines killed Magellan, Sebastian del Cano took command, returning to Spain with one surviving ship, laden with cloves. Together, Magellan and del Cano commanded the first circumnavigation of the globe. In doing so, however, they demonstrated that the southwest passage through the Straits of Magellan was much more difficult than envisioned.

England and France ignored the pope's division of the world between Spain and Portugal. With their more northerly location and some knowledge of the coast of North America, they sought a northwest passage to the East. During the fifteenth century (before Columbus's landfall), seafarers from England and France had caught fish in the Newfoundland Banks. Some sailors had camped ashore, where they traded with Native Americans. When King Henry VII of England sent John Cabot, an Italian whose name was really Giovanni Caboto, in search of a northwest passage in 1497, the expedition reached Newfoundland. Cabot sailed again the next year, but most of his ships were lost and he died at sea. Although the English were discouraged by Cabot's failure to find a passage, his efforts supported England's later claim to land in North America.

A generation after Cabot, the French entered the search for a route to Asia. In 1524, King Francis I sent another Italian sea captain, Giovanni da Verrazano, to look for the elusive passage. Landing at Cape Fear (now North Carolina), Verrazano sailed north along the Atlantic seaboard to Newfoundland, finding no evidence of a waterway through the continent. In expeditions dating 1534 and 1535, Jacques Cartier hoped to find the route by way of the gulf and river of St. Lawrence. Although neither Verrazano nor Cartier found a northwest passage, they supported France's claim to part of the continent.

THE SPANISH EMPIRE IN AMERICA

Because England and France showed only occasional interest in America before 1560, and Portugal focused on the eastern trade and Brazil, the Spanish had little interference from other Europeans in exploring and settling the rest of the New World. By 1543, their colonies extended south to Chile and north through Mexico; they had explored from Florida to California in what is now the United States. Spanish conquistadores advanced from island to island in the West Indies, then moved through Mexico and Central America. The conquistadores expected to make their fortune in America and retire to Spain. In contrast, the Spanish Crown had a more complicated set of goals in colonizing America: to enhance its power among European nations; to exploit the wealth of the New World; and to convert the Native Americans to Christianity. While in many ways the goals of the Spanish monarchy and its settlers overlapped, sometimes their interests diverged, especially when it came to the welfare of Native Americans.

Spanish Invasion

When the Spanish found little gold on Hispaniola, they enslaved its inhabitants and expropriated the land. The natives died when forced to work on plantations and tend livestock. European diseases and cruel treatment took their toll. As a result, the colonists sent slave-raiding parties to other islands and to the mainland. The conquistadores who explored Cuba and Puerto Rico were seeking slaves and gold. Juan Ponce de León, known for his search in 1513 for the legendary "fountain of

youth" in Florida and Yucatan, sought Indian slaves. The same year Vasco Núñez de Balboa led explorers across the Isthmus of Panama, becoming the first Europeans to see the Pacific Ocean. Alonso Álvarez de Pineda, in 1519–1520, sailed the coastline of the Gulf of Mexico from Florida to Mexico.

As Spanish explorers became aware of the vastness of the Americas, they organized militarily to subdue the Americans. Despite the small size of their armies, the Spanish prevailed over large empires, aided significantly by diseases such as smallpox. They also made alliances with the enemies of the Indian emperors and took advantage of metal weaponry and horses. The most famous of the conquerors is Hernán Cortés who, in 1519, launched an expedition against the Aztecs of Mexico. With an army of only 500 troops, Cortés persuaded the Totonacs of Cempoala, who were dominated by the Aztecs, to join him. Then defeating the Tlaxcalans and gaining their support as well, he marched to Tenochtitlán, the Aztec capital. He entered the city without opposition and seized Moctezuma, the emperor. When Cortés outlawed human sacrifice and made incessant demands for gold, the Aztecs rebelled. In the heat of battle, they killed Moctezuma and forced the Spanish and their allies to retreat, slaying many as they tried to escape across the causeways linking Tenochtitlán with the shore of Lake Texcoco.

Cortés returned in 1521, however, after smallpox ravaged the Aztec capital. With thousands of Indian allies, the Spanish built small ships to cross Lake Texcoco, took control of the causeways, and after a long

Portrait medal of Hernán Cortés produced when he visited Spain in 1529.
Staatliche Museen zu Berlin Preubischer Kulturrbesitz Mutoz Kabinett

An Aztec Report of the Fall of Tenochtitlán 1521

The Aztecs fought the Spanish and their Indian allies for months before the invaders, led by Hernán Cortés, prevailed. This document gives an Aztec view of the surrender and shows the immediate impact of the defeat on ordinary men, women, and children.

And when night had fallen, then it rained and sprinkled at intervals. Late at night the flame became visible; just so was it seen, just so it emerged as if it came from the heavens. Like a whirlwind it went spinning around and revolving; it was as if embers burst out of it—some very large, some very small, some like sparks. Like a coppery wind it arose, crackling, snapping, and exploding loudly. Then it circled the dike and traveled toward Coyonacazco; then it went into the middle of the lake there to be lost.

None shouted; none spoke aloud.

And on the next day, nothing more happened. All remained quiet, and also our foes [so] remained.

But the Captain [Cortés] was watching from a roof-top at Amaxac—from the roof-top of [the house of] Aztauatzin—under a canopy. It was a many-colored canopy. He looked toward [us] common folk; the Spaniards crowded about him and took counsel among themselves.

And [on our side] were Quauhtemoc and the other noblemen—the vice ruler Tlacotzin, the lords' judge Petlauhtzin, the captain of the armies Motelchiuhtzin. . . . All of these noblemen were assembled at Tolmayecan; they appeared to consult among themselves how to do that which we were to undertake and how we should yield to [the Spaniards].

Thereafter only two [men] took Quauhtemoc in a boat. . . .

And when they carried Quauhtemoc off, then there was weeping among all the common folk. They said: "Now goeth the young lord Quauhtemoc; now he goeth to deliver himself to the gods, the Spaniards!"

And when they had betaken themselves to bring and disembark him thereupon all the Spaniards came to see. They drew him along; the Spaniards took him by the hand. After that they took him up to the roof-top, where they went to stand him before the Captain, the war leader. And when they had proceeded to stand him before [Cortés], they looked at Quauhtemoc, made much of him, and stroked his hair. Then they seated him with [Cortés] and fired the guns. They hit no one with them, but only made them go off above, [so that] they passed over the heads of the common folk. Then [some Mexicans] only fled. With this the war reached its end.

Then there was shouting; they said: "Enough! Let it end! Eat greens!" When they heard this, the common folk thereupon issued forth. On this, they went, even into the lagoon.

And as they departed, leaving by the great road, once more they there slew some, wherefore the Spaniards were wroth that still some again had taken up their obsidian-bladed swords and their shields. Those who dwelt in house clusters went straightway to Amaxac; they went direct to where the ways divide. There the common folk separated. So many went toward Tepeyacac, so many toward Xoxouiltitlan, so many toward Nonoalco. . . .

And everywhere the Spaniards were seizing and robbing the people. They sought gold; as nothing did they value the green stone, quetzal feathers and turquoise [which] was everywhere in the bosoms or in the skirts of the women. And as for us men, it was everywhere in [our] breech clouts and in [our] mouths.

And [the Spaniards] seized and set apart the pretty women—those of light bodies, the fair[-skinned] ones. And some women, when they were robbed, covered their face with mud and put on old, mended shirts and rags for their shifts. They put all rags on themselves.

And also some of us men were singled out—those who were strong, grown to manhood, and next the young boys, of whom they would make messengers, who would be their runners, and who were known as their servers. And on some they burned [brand marks] on their cheeks; on some they put paint on their cheeks; on some they put paint on their lips.

And when the shield was laid down, when we gave way, it was the year count Three House and the day count was One Serpent.

siege and bitter fighting destroyed Tenochtitlán building by building. They rebuilt the city as Mexico City, the capital of New Spain. Cortés then sent troops to take Guatemala; rival conquistadores seized Honduras. Francisco Pizarro advanced to the south, preceded by smallpox, defeating the Incas of Peru after a difficult struggle. Others expanded into Argentina and Chile.

Exploration of Florida and the American Southwest

In 1528, Pánfilo de Narváez led an expedition to Florida. His venture led to later exploration of territories that became the southern United States. Narváez and his men landed at Tampa Bay where they met Native Americans who warned them to return to the sea. When the Europeans refused, and spoke of their search for silver and gold, the Indians directed them to "Apalachen," near the present site of Tallahassee. The Spanish marched northward through insect- and snake-infested terrain. Soon discouraged, they made the mistake of kidnapping a chief of the Apalachees. The Indians attacked, convincing the Spanish to return to New Spain immediately. The soldiers constructed barges to carry them across the Gulf of Mexico. When storms separated the craft, most of the explorers, including Narváez, were lost at sea.

Two barges crossed the gulf intact, beaching their occupants on the Texas coast. The native Karankawas captured the survivors. After several years, one of the Spaniards, Álvar Núñez Cabeza de Vaca, who had become an Indian priest and healer, escaped with three others, including Alonso del Castillo, Andrés Dorantes, and a slave Esteban. They hoped to reach New Spain, but lacked maps or instruments to find their way. For several years they sojourned with a series of Native American peoples, learning their languages and customs. The Spanish earned the Indians' friendship and respect with seemingly miraculous cures. When they finally reached Mexico City in 1536, Cabeza de Vaca told the Spanish viceroy about their journey.

Cabeza de Vaca's report excited interest in exploring lands north of Mexico. When Cabeza de Vaca refused to head an expedition, the viceroy sent Esteban with a Franciscan missionary, Fray Marcos de Niza, along with several Indians. When Esteban was killed by Zuñis, Fray Marcos returned to Mexico City with extravagant claims that the land flowed with riches.

In 1540, an army of 336 Spanish and about 1,000 Indians marched north under command of Francisco Vásquez de Coronado, with Fray Marcos as their guide. The explorers intended to conquer the cities of gold (the so-called "Seven Cities of Cibola") but were disappointed. The "golden" city that Fray Marcos had spotted was actually a Zuñi Indian pueblo, Hawikúh, made of adobe. The Zuñis unsuccessfully resisted the intruders, then informed the Spanish that the cities of gold lay to the west. Another Indian told stories about great wealth in the country to the east. Over the next year, Coronado's troops explored in both directions. They encountered the Hopi of northeastern Arizona and buffalo-hunting Indians of the Great Plains, saw the Grand Canyon, and traveled as far east as Kansas. They found no gold or silver but left descriptions of a substantial part of the American Southwest.

To reinforce Coronado's army, the viceroy in 1540 sent Hernando de Alarcón by ship up the western coast of Mexico. Though the two explorers failed to make contact, Alarcón sailed into the Colorado River. Two years later, Juan Rodríguez Cabrillo sailed with two ships up the coast of Baja California. They were the first Europeans to visit what is now California. After Cabrillo died in January 1543, his deputy Bartolomé Ferrelo sailed almost as far north as Oregon.

Unknown to Coronado, an expedition led by Hernando de Soto, governor of Cuba, came within a few hundred miles of his own company at about the same time. In 1539, De Soto and about 600 troops landed in Tampa Bay. Over the next three years they trekked through the southeast, exploring lands hitherto unknown to the Spanish. They plundered the towns of the Apalachees and other Florida Indians who were part of the Mississippian cultures, with temple mounds and long-range trading networks. Stealing food, taking Indians as slaves, and killing those who resisted, De Soto's men marched north from the Florida peninsula, through central Georgia to the Carolinas, then west across the Appalachians into the Tennessee River valley. They followed the river south into Alabama, then traveled west toward the Mississippi. Despite heavy losses when Chickasaws burned their camp and supplies, De Soto crossed into Arkansas. After he died of a fever in 1542, the 300 survivors of his expedition safely reached New Spain by boat.

In 1542, the initial period of Spanish expansion came to a close throughout America. Without discovery of precious metals, they had little immediate reason to push farther into North America. During the half century since Columbus sailed west, contact and exchange among Native Americans, Europeans, and Africans created new social and political systems. Although the Spanish expected to create a society much like the one at home, the results of colonization proved different than planned.

Demographic Catastrophe and Cultural Exchange

Contact among Europeans, Native Americans, and Africans after 1492 changed societies in both hemispheres. This process, called the *Columbian exchange,* included transmission of disease, knowledge about food and technology, and culture.

Disease was the chief ally of the Spanish in their drive through Central and South America. Smallpox was most lethal; other killers included measles, bubonic plague, chicken pox, influenza, whooping cough, and diphtheria. These diseases were particularly deadly because the microbes were new to America, and the Indians lacked immunity. Populations declined by an estimated 90 percent, as whole tribes were eliminated and others weakened severely. Illness spread from one native population to another, infecting the people of North America even before the English and French established colonies along the Atlantic coast. Some regions of the continent seemed uninhabited to European latecomers because of prior contact with disease.

The Columbian exchange also included livestock and crops that diversified cultures across continents. European settlers imported horses, sheep, cattle, pigs, and chickens for transportation, clothing, and food. While Europeans and Africans raised livestock as part of their agricultural economies, Native Americans depended on hunting and fishing to supplement crops. Af-

Sixteenth-century drawings of Aztecs suffering from smallpox when the Spanish invaded. An Aztec description stated that "first an epidemic broke out, a sickness of pustules . . . . They spread everywhere, on the face, the head, the chest, etc. [and] brought great desolation" as people could neither "move nor stir" and many died.
Reproduced from Collections of Library of Congress

ter European settlement, some Indians adopted horses and became skilled riders; others raised pigs and fowl. Problems resulted, however, because Europeans often allowed their animals to roam. Cattle and pigs trampled native fields, and helped spread disease and the seeds of aggressive European plants that changed the American landscape by forcing out native species.

Indians introduced the Europeans and Africans to crops that soon circled the globe and had a major impact on the growth of world populations: Indian corn (or maize), tomatoes, potatoes, peppers, beans, chocolate, pumpkins, and tobacco. The white potato of South America became a major staple in northern Europe; the sweet potato and Indian corn were important throughout the world. New crops also came to America from Europe and Africa, including cultivated rice, wheat, oats, sugarcane, bananas, onions, peaches, and watermelon. And while Europeans brought firearms and iron tools, Native Americans showed them how to build canoes and catch fish with weirs.

Native Americans generally resisted assimilation to Spanish culture. They retained their languages, clothing, housing, agricultural methods, and, to a considerable extent, religion. The degree to which they blocked acculturation depended largely on class. The Spanish focused much attention on the local Indian leaders (*caciques*) and their sons, with whom they interacted more frequently than with ordinary Indians. Many caciques learned to speak Spanish, converted to Christianity, and adopted Hispanic clothing. Their sons attended schools where they learned Latin and other advanced subjects. The common Indians avoided some Spanish ways of living and accepted others. They raised and ate chickens, but grew wheat primarily to pay as tribute. They abhorred cattle, but groups like the Apaches quickly accepted the horse. Natives favored their digging-sticks over the European plow, which would have required the use of draft animals and alteration in the assignment of fields.

Religion

The complexity of interaction between the Spanish and Native Americans can be seen most vividly in religion. The Europeans had a mandate from the pope to convert the "pagans" of America to Christianity. The missionaries believed that it was an act of humanity to introduce the Indians to Catholicism. The Spanish eliminated human sacrifice and destroyed temples and relics, but for the most part avoided forced conversion. At first, the missionaries expected most Native Americans to accept Spanish religious practice without change, as many Indians consented to baptism and voluntarily built churches in every town. But most Indians merged the European faith with rituals and beliefs of their traditional religions, resulting in *syncretism,* the blending of two faiths. For example, some natives added the Christian God to their polytheistic system; others focused on the saints or the Trinity rather than the supreme God. Indians organized *cofradías,* which were societies to raise money for church functions and festivals. The natives controlled the cofradías and at times asserted independence from the Spanish church authority.

The retention of native beliefs and practices disappointed many Spanish priests, who would accept nothing less than complete submission to their form of Catholicism. Nevertheless, missionaries worked for humane treatment of Indians. Colonists often justified enslaving Indians because they had "inferior" cultures and religion. A number of priests, of whom Bartolomé de las Casas is best known, condemned the cruelty and enslavement. In his *Short Account of the Destruction of the Indies,* written in 1542, las Casas argued for more enlightened policies. Describing atrocities and slaughter in one colony after another, he informed the king of "the excesses which this New World has witnessed, all of them surpassing anything that men hitherto have imagined even in their wildest dreams."

Spanish Imperial Government

As conquest of the Americas progressed, Spain established a colonial government whose purposes were to convert Native Americans and bring them under control of the Spanish monarchy, and to exploit their labor and the wealth of the New World. The Spanish were only partly successful in imposing their rule over the Indians. The colonial government was most effective in central Mexico and the Andes, where the Europeans substituted their own imperial rule for that of the Aztecs and Incas. Native Americans in northern Mexico, Florida, Arizona, New Mexico, and central Chile, who had never been subject to empires, evaded Spanish rule. Many in the fringe areas, such as the Apaches, avoided Spanish domination altogether because their bands were highly mobile and autonomous.

The Spanish colonial administration was hierarchical and tied closely to Spain. Sovereignty, or supreme political power, rested in the monarch. The Spanish, like other Europeans at the time, believed that God vested such power in the Crown. Neither Spanish colonists nor Indians had much say in making and enforcing laws. The right of subjects to appeal official decisions to the king, however—along with delays caused by distance, corruption, and inefficiency—introduced flexibility into the governmental structure.

Directly below the monarch was the Council of the Indies, located in Spain and composed of men who knew little about the New World. The council regulated trade, appointed officials, made laws, and determined who should be allowed to emigrate. The highest officials residing in America were the viceroys. In the sixteenth and seventeenth centuries, the Spanish empire consisted of two viceroyalties: New Spain, with its capital in Mexico City, and Peru, with its capital in Lima. The viceroyalties were divided into provinces, ruled by governors and *audiencias,* which advised the governors and functioned as courts. The audiencias could appeal all decisions to the king, thus limiting the wide powers of the viceroys and governors. So did the *residencia,* which investigated these officials at the end of their terms and reported any corruption to Spain.

In central Mexico and Peru, the Spanish viceroys, governors, and audiencias took the place of the ruling native elite. At the local level, however, native leaders often retained their positions. Called caciques, they headed the Indian towns, collected tribute from households, and recruited forced laborers upon demand of the colonial authorities.

Spanish Mercantilism

The Crown regulated commerce through the *Casa de la Contratación,* a trading house founded in 1503 in Seville. Thus Spain elaborated its economic policy of mercantilism, which held that nations had monopolistic rights to trade with their colonies. With tight governmental control, the primary goal of economic activity under mercantilism was to achieve a favorable balance of trade. Colonies were expected to serve as markets for goods from the home country and provide raw materials, gold, and silver to increase its wealth. All merchants desiring to send ships to Spanish America needed permission from the Casa, as did anyone wishing to emigrate. The Casa denied leave to persons of Jewish ancestry, for example, though in fact many found passage to America without official permission. To the monarch, a crucial function of the Casa was registration of precious metals, because the king received one-fifth, called the "royal fifth," of all silver and gold. Colonists had to obtain permission to build plantations and mines. In return they paid taxes to the king and, if they found precious metals, the royal fifth.

When Columbus obtained gold from the inhabitants of Hispaniola, he raised expectations of great wealth. However, the explorers at first met disappointment. Even the Aztecs failed to satisfy the Spanish thirst for gold, so most colonists turned to agriculture to make their fortunes. Then, in the 1540s, the Europeans located two immensely rich silver mines, one at Potosí in present-day Bolivia and the other at Zacatecas in Mexico. Between 1500 and 1650 about 181 tons of gold and 16,000 tons of silver officially reached Europe from America. Production of silver expanded greatly in the 1570s with the introduction of mercury to the refining process.

The Spanish organized their silver trade to outwit privateers of other nations, especially France and England. In 1565, the Spanish founded St. Augustine in Florida as a base to fight the buccaneers and reinforce Spain's claim to North America. They devised a convoy system to protect their fleets. Two convoys left Seville each year, carrying goods such as wine, books, oil, grain, clothing, and other luxuries: one left in May headed for Mexico, and the other departed in August for the Isthmus of Panama, from which mules carried the goods to Peru. Both convoys stayed the winter with the intention of meeting in Cuba by early summer so they could return to Spain before the onset of hurricanes. The Panama fleet sometimes ran into trouble when the mule train carrying Potosí silver arrived late.

For the Spanish monarchy, the discovery of rich mines fulfilled their dreams in the New World. The king used the bullion to pay for his European wars. American silver and gold helped to create inflation throughout Europe, as the immense supply depressed their value and the prices of other goods increased. Merchants depended on the bullion to pay for luxuries from the East. Goods worth about one-half the value of the metals were returned to the colonies.

Forced Labor Systems

Because Spanish immigrants were few in number and had no intention of working in the mines or fields, they adopted ways to compel Native Americans to work. In the mid-sixteenth century, the white colonists remained a small percentage of New World inhabitants, with a population of about 100,000 in New Spain compared with an estimated 2.6 million Native Americans in central Mexico. But if some European settlers hoped to have millions of Christianized Indian workers do their bidding, they were disappointed. The catastrophic level of native deaths and resistance of Indians to conversion created New World societies unlike those the Spanish and Native Americans had previously known.

When the first explorers on Hispaniola tried to consign the native Arawaks to slavery, most of the Indians died. In 1500, the Spanish Crown ruled that only Indians captured in a "just war" could be forced into perpetual bondage. This judgment had little impact because conquistadores could define as hostile any natives who resisted capture. In 1513, the government drew up a document called the *Requerimiento* (or Requirement), which explorers read when they entered an Indian town for the first time. The requerimiento informed the natives that they must accept the sovereignty of the Catholic church and the Spanish monarchy. If they did, they would become Spanish subjects in peace; if they did not, the soldiers would "make war against you . . . take you and your wives and your children and . . . make slaves of them . . . and shall do to you all the harm and damage that we can." By the time the king outlawed most Native American slavery in 1542, the Arawaks of the West Indies had been destroyed. The Spanish had expropriated their lands for sugar plantations, replacing the Indians with enslaved Africans. On the mainland, the Spanish government established two forms of forced Indian labor. With the *encomienda,* Indians living on specified lands had to pay tribute to individual colonists and sometimes provide labor for which they received minimal wages. At first, the encomienda system included no transfer of land to the colonists, but as the numbers of Native Americans declined and Spanish increased, the colonists took Indian property for farms and ranches. By the seventeenth century, grazing livestock replaced Indian farms on vast stretches of Spanish America.

In 1600, about 1 million Indians survived in central Mexico, a significant decrease from a generation earlier, when the population was 2.6 million. This severe decline caused problems for the Spanish who depended upon the natives for food and labor. Thus, the government devised the *repartimiento* system. Indians could be forced to work in mines, agriculture, or public works for several weeks, months, or even a year. For example, natives labored for yearlong stints at the Potosí silver mines in Bolivia. At Potosí, workers assigned as carriers climbed some 600 feet through tunnels about as wide as a man's body with heavy loads of silver ore on their backs. Those who worked in refining were exposed to mercury poisoning because part of the process involved walking with bare legs through the slurry of mercury, water, and ore. As the Indian population declined, the Spanish had difficulty in finding enough workers. When they attempted to increase the length and frequency of work periods, Indians resisted the changes, sometimes successfully.

As early as 1502, on West Indies plantations, the Spanish turned to the people of Africa to meet their insatiable labor demands. They had already purchased Africans from Portuguese traders to work in Spain and on the sugar plantations of the Canary Islands. The

An exterior view of Potosí, the Spanish silver mine in what is now Bolivia. The mine yielded immense wealth, but with a dreadful toll as laborers worked in harsh conditions deep underground.
The John Carter Brown Library at Brown University

government set up a system of licenses, or *asientos,* for merchants to supply certain numbers of slaves. During the sixteenth century, ships transported approximately 75,000 Africans to Spanish America, with perhaps an equal number dying en route, either in Africa or at sea. The Spanish imported Africans to work on sugar plantations in the West Indies and coastal areas of the mainland where most Native Americans had died. Severe work regimes and rampant disease also resulted in high death rates among imported blacks.

PROTESTANT NORTHERN EUROPEANS CHALLENGE CATHOLIC SPAIN

Until 1560, French and English activity in America remained much more tentative and sporadic than Spain's. Although fishing expeditions regularly visited the North American coast, initiatives for permanent colonies gained little support. But religious and political change in Northern Europe provided the impetus to test Spain's domination of the New World. In the age of Reformation and religious wars, America became both a refuge for religious dissidents and a bat-

tlefield on which European nations fought for wealth, glory, and national sovereignty.

The Protestant Reformation

When the German priest Martin Luther in 1517 issued his ninety-five theses against the sale of indulgences, the Church of Rome was the sovereign faith of western and central Europe. Luther believed the church was corrupt. The sale of indulgences, which were supposed to reduce the amount of time a deceased person spent in purgatory, was an example of its decline. Luther believed that people received salvation as a gift from God in return for faith ("justification by faith") rather than for good works. They could not earn salvation by taking pilgrimages, giving money to the church, hearing masses, or going on crusades against the Muslims. Luther also challenged the authority of priests, arguing for a "priesthood of all believers." Christians should seek the word of God in the Bible, which he translated into German to make it more available to laypeople. Luther contended that the Bible recognized only two sacraments, baptism and communion, not the seven authorized by the Catholic church. He also opposed the requirement of celibacy for priests, marrying Katharina von Bora, a former nun.

*P*ICTURING THE PAST ✦ POLITICS & DIPLOMACY

QUEEN ELIZABETH I

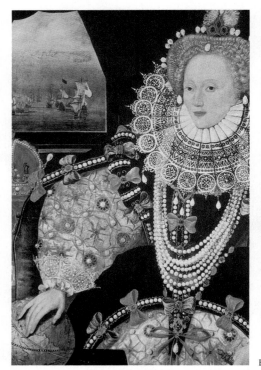

The queen sat for this portrait at about the time of the defeat of the Spanish Armada in 1588, as suggested by the naval scene in the upper left. The artist depicted her interest in exploration, particularly in North America, by resting her hand on that part of the globe. Under Elizabeth, sea captains such as John Hawkins and Francis Drake interloped in Spanish trade and attacked Spain's colonies and ships. Roanoke was intended to compete with Spain in the New World and to serve as a base to plunder its settlements.

As in the portraits of James I and Charles II in Chapter 2, the English monarch is portrayed as a powerful figure in luxurious clothing and jewelry. In 1588, Elizabeth was fifty-five years old and never married. She had ruled for thirty years, bringing England into the forefront of European nations and reestablishing the Anglican church.

By courtesy of the National Portrait Gallery, London

Luther's teachings led to many divisions in western Christianity, as common people and princes alike adopted his beliefs. In Germany, which was composed of many individual states, some princes accepted Lutheranism and others remained Catholic, requiring their subjects to follow their example. Lutheranism spread through northern Germany and into Scandinavia. Luther inspired other critics of Catholicism to offer variant Protestant doctrines, including the Mennonites, Hutterites, and Swiss Brethren, all called Anabaptists because they required adult baptism.

The most influential of the systems of belief that Lutheranism spawned was that of John Calvin, a native of France, who attempted to create a model society at Geneva, Switzerland. Followers of Calvin established churches in the Reformed tradition: they were known variously as French Huguenots, English Puritans, Scottish Presbyterians, and Dutch and German Reformed. Calvin went further than Luther in arguing that humans could do nothing to save themselves. This concept of predestination meant that God alone determined who would be saved (the "elect"). Through communion with God, the elect learned that they were saved; they strove to live blamelessly to reflect their status.

Calvin and his followers convinced the city council and churches of Geneva to adopt many Reformed doctrines, stripping the churches of decoration, images, and colorful rituals. The Bible, as interpreted by Calvin, became the basis for law. The civil government punished moral offenders and nonbelievers identified by the church elders. The Calvinists disciplined individuals for dancing, wearing fancy clothes, and insubordination. They forced one man to walk through the city wearing only a shirt because he criticized Calvin, and burned another at the stake for heresy. Although Calvin failed to obtain all of his demands from the Geneva council, he came close to establishing a theocracy, in which the church fathers ruled in the name of God.

Protestant ideas spread to France and England quickly. In France, Calvin attracted many adherents, called Huguenots, among the nobles and prosperous commoners. The French monarchy considered Protestants a threat to its monopoly of power. Even after the Edict of Nantes of 1598, which offered freedom to worship, Huguenots faced serious discrimination.

In England, years before Luther, opposition had existed to the Catholic hierarchy, its taxes, monasteries, and the use of images in church. Thus Henry VIII found sympathy for his break with Rome when the pope refused to allow an annulment of his marriage to Catherine of Aragon. Henry wanted to marry Anne Boleyn, who he hoped would provide a male heir. Parliament passed the Act of Supremacy (1534), mandating that the king be "taken, accepted, and reputed the only supreme head on earth of the Church of England." The Crown dissolved the monasteries and confiscated their property. Henry was no Lutheran, however, for the Six Articles (1539) that formed the theological basis of Anglicanism confirmed Catholic beliefs on priestly celibacy, the mass, confession, and sacraments. But because the Six Articles were ambiguous on many points, the Church of England from its inception allowed a fairly wide range of doctrine. In 1552, the revised Anglican prayer book incorporated many Protestant beliefs. Soon after, Henry's daughter Mary I attempted to force England back to the Church of Rome. Her persecution of Protestants earned her the name "Bloody Mary"; her marriage to the staunch Catholic Philip II of Spain inspired an English nationalism that fused loyalty to church and state. When Mary died in 1558, her half-sister, Elizabeth I, became queen, ending the immediate threat that England would return to Catholicism. The new English monarch and a large proportion of her subjects identified Spain as a threat to their national church, now Protestant, and their independence as a nation.

Under Elizabeth, the English confronted Spain on a number of fronts, leading to a showdown in 1588. In the religious struggles of the late sixteenth century, England became a dominant Protestant power, supported the Dutch revolt against Philip II, and challenged Spain's monopolistic claims to the New World. Though pragmatic and more interested in power than theology, Elizabeth confirmed England's break with the pope and approved earlier moderate Protestant reforms. The Act of Uniformity (1559) required adherence to the Anglican Book of Prayer. The queen suppressed resistance from both Calvinists, who wanted further reforms, and the supporters of Rome. Some Catholics turned to Elizabeth's cousin, Mary, Queen of Scots, a Roman Catholic and heir to the English throne. In 1587, after several unsuccessful plots on Elizabeth's life, Mary was tried as a conspirator and beheaded.

One of Mary, Queen of Scots's most fervent supporters was Philip II of Spain. Throughout Europe he strove to wipe out the Protestant heresy. He considered Elizabeth a dangerous foe, not least for her support of the revolt in the Netherlands. When many Dutch adopted Calvinism, Philip retaliated with his Inquisition, executing thousands. The Dutch rebelled. In 1581, the northern part of the Netherlands, composed of seven provinces, including Holland, declared its independence as the United Provinces. The southern region, called the Spanish Netherlands (now Belgium), remained under Philip's control. When Elizabeth sent aid to the United Provinces in 1585, she in effect declared war on Spain. The most important battle occurred in 1588, when Philip sent his mighty Armada of 130 ships and 30,000 men to invade England. The English defeated the Armada, thus preserving their national sovereignty and religion.

French Huguenots and English Sea Dogs

In France, persecution led some Protestant Huguenots to look to America as a refuge. In 1555, a group of wealthy Frenchmen sent Huguenot settlers to Brazil. When disputes occurred among the colonists, some returned to France; the Portuguese, who claimed Brazil, killed or enslaved the majority who remained. In 1562, Huguenots tried again, establishing Charlesfort on the South Carolina coast, in part to attack the Spanish silver fleet as it headed home. When the Spanish moved against the small French colony in 1564, they found it already abandoned. But the Huguenots attempted another settlement that year, this one at Fort Caroline on the St. Johns River in northern Florida. The Spanish quickly destroyed it, murdering most of the settlers.

The English "sea dogs" learned a great deal about the New World from the Huguenots. With Elizabeth I's ascension to the throne in 1558, seafarers and colonizers like John Hawkins, Francis Drake, Humphrey Gilbert, and Walter Raleigh gained favor and support. Hawkins visited Fort Caroline in 1565; other Englishmen gained knowledge of the North American coast from the French. The English also acquired a taste for conquest in Ireland, where their brutal subjugation of the native Irish presaged later actions against the Indians.

The English took their time before attempting an American colony. The Spanish remained a serious threat. Thus for two decades, until the 1580s, English adventurers sought wealth by sea. In 1562, John Hawkins took 300 Africans to Hispaniola without a license. The local Spanish officials allowed him to exchange the slaves for sugar and hides because the colony needed labor. Hawkins made a second voyage, earning another handsome profit, this time mostly in silver. When the Spanish authorities protested, Elizabeth forbade further expeditions, but reversed her decision in 1567. On his third voyage, Hawkins was conducting business in the harbor of San Juan de Ulúa, Mexico, when the annual fleet arrived from Spain several weeks early, destroying three of his ships. Hawkins and his cousin Francis Drake escaped with two badly damaged vessels. Their crews nearly starved on the return to England.

Hawkins stopped interloping in Spanish trade, but other English privateers followed. The most famous was Francis Drake, who in 1572 intercepted the mule train carrying Potosí silver across Panama with the help of Native Americans and runaway African slaves. Five years later he set out to circumnavigate the globe. Following Magellan's route through the straits, he attacked Spanish towns along the Pacific coast, explored the North American coast for evidence of a northwest passage, and returned to England in 1580 by way of Asia and the Cape of Good Hope. Six years later, when England and Spain were formally at war, Drake attacked Spanish ports in America, including St. Augustine in Florida, which he looted and burned.

While Drake was making his fortune through piracy, other sea dogs hoped to make their mark by starting colonies. With experience in Ireland, they decided to ignore Spain's claim to North America. On the basis of Cabot's voyage of 1497, Elizabeth granted a charter to Humphrey Gilbert, who sailed to Newfoundland in 1583. He assumed ownership for the English Crown. Nothing came of Gilbert's colony, however, as he was lost at sea on his return to England.

Walter Raleigh then attempted a settlement farther south, in the land named for the "virgin" Queen Elizabeth. In 1585, the first group of settlers arrived at Roanoke Island, in what is now North Carolina. After their ships returned home leaving them with short supplies, the colonists tried to force neighboring Indians to provide food. Quickly a pattern of hostility emerged between the English and Native Americans. Francis Drake saved the Roanoke colonists from starvation, carrying them home in 1586. A year later, Raleigh sent out another expedition. This time the war with Spain prevented ships from returning to Roanoke until 1590, when all that was left of the colony was the word "Croatoan" carved on a tree. The colonists may have moved to nearby Croatoan Island, or farther inland to live with Native Americans, but the fate of the "Lost Colony" has never been determined. The English did not colonize successfully in North America until the founding of Jamestown in 1607.

CONCLUSION

By 1590, the Spanish had created an empire that extended from South America through the West Indies and Mexico. They funded their European wars to extinguish Protestantism with American silver and gold. The Portuguese, united under the Spanish Crown in 1580, had developed the Atlantic slave trading system that sent enslaved Africans to Brazil and New Spain.

The irony of colonization in America was that European nations at war in the Old World emulated one another in the New. The Spanish and Portuguese provided the model for later colonizers in expropriating land and labor from Indians and Africans. Europeans justified their behavior toward the people of America and Africa by emphasizing religious and cultural differences, ignoring much that they had in common. Although European nations organized colonization in various ways, all sought mercantilistic ends. In the early seventeenth century, when the English, French, and Dutch settled in North America, their goals were very similar to those of Spain. They hoped to locate precious metals, find the elusive northwest passage, exploit Indian labor, extend Christianity to America, and expand the power of the state.

Recommended Readings

Bethell, Leslie, ed. *Colonial Spanish America* (1987). Essays provide useful syntheses on the development of the Spanish colonies.

Casas, Bartolomé de las. *A Short Account of the Destruction of the Indies.* Ed. and trans., Nigel Griffin (1992). A priest's sharp denunciation of Spanish colonization, written in 1542.

Davidson, Basil. *The Search for Africa: History, Culture, Politics* (1994). A readable history by a veteran historian of the continent.

Dixon, E. James. *Bones, Boats, and Bison: Archeology and the First Colonization of Western North America* (1999). Clear review of archeological evidence of first Americans.

Klein, Herbert S. *The Atlantic Slave Trade* (1999). Surveys the growing literature about the international slave trade.

Kupperman, Karen Ordahl. *Roanoke: The Abandoned Colony* (1984). A lively account of the early English attempt to settle in North America.

Lockhart, James. *The Nahuas After the Conquest: A Social and Cultural History of the Indians of Central Mexico, Sixteenth Through Eighteenth Centuries* (1992). Explores the development of Nahua society and culture, including chapters on households, social structure, land tenure, religion, language, and the arts.

Nash, Gary B. *Red, White, and Black: The Peoples of Early North America,* 4th ed. (2002). An excellent introduction to the meeting of cultures in the New World.

Schwartz, Stuart B. *Victors and Vanquished: Spanish and Nahua Views of the Conquest of Mexico* (2000). A very good collection of documentary sources on Mexican society and the Spanish invasion.

Weber, David J. *The Spanish Frontier in North America* (1992). The best synthesis on Spanish exploration and colonization north of Mexico.

American Journey Online and InfoTrac College Edition

Visit the source collections at http://ajaccess. wadsworth.com and infotrac.thomsonlearning.com and use the Search function with the following key terms to explore documents, images, audio and video clips, articles, and commentary related to the material in this chapter.

Maya
Aztecs
Atlantic slave trade
Spanish empire
Iroquois
Algonquian
Anasazi

Christopher Columbus
Protestant Reformation
Martin Luther
Hernán Cortés
Francis Drake

🌐   **Additional resources, exercises, and Internet links related to this chapter are available on the American Passages Web site: http://history.wadsworth.com/passages2e**

2 COLONIZATION OF NORTH AMERICA 1590–1675

THE SPANISH IN NORTH AMERICA

THE ENGLISH INVADE VIRGINIA

FISHING, FURS, AND SETTLEMENTS IN THE NORTH

RELIGIOUS EXILES FROM ENGLAND

ENGLISH COLONIZATION AFTER 1660

Navajo wall art in the Canyon del Muerto, Arizona, showing the arrival of a Spanish missionary and soldiers in the late sixteenth or early seventeenth century.
© Jerry Jacka

In 1590, the only permanent European settlement in what is now the United States was St. Augustine, the struggling Spanish town in Florida that the English privateer Francis Drake had burned four years earlier. Spain was much more concerned with its silver mines and West Indies plantations than in colonizing along the Atlantic coast, yet wanted to prevent intrusion by other nations, for good reason. In the late sixteenth century, buccaneers from France and England thought the best way to get rich was by looting the Spanish silver fleet and ports.

Though Spain expanded in Florida and New Mexico in the 1600s, the English defeat of the Armada and Dutch surge in overseas trade eroded Spanish control of the New World. France, England, the Netherlands, and Sweden all established colonies in North America by 1638, hoping to duplicate Spain's success. While none found gold or an easy route to Asia—and the Swedes and Dutch soon lost their toeholds in the Delaware and Hudson valleys altogether—Europeans prospered from the West Indies sugar boom, Canadian fur trade, and Chesapeake tobacco. New England offered a haven for Puritan dissenters.

By 1675, the English held a string of settlements along the Atlantic coast. Unlike the Spanish, England's colonization proceeded with little regulation from the Crown, resulting in a variety of social, economic, and political structures. The English government helped to create the diversity by granting different kinds of charters to individuals and groups.

The expansion of European settlement in North America changed the countryside forever. Cheap, even free, land and developing commerce offered opportunity to men and women of all economic classes who were willing to risk their lives by crossing the Atlantic. Their farms eliminated Indian hunting lands, altering the ecological balance of plants and animals. Though many Native Americans resisted the European invasions, disease seriously undermined their power. The fur trade also changed the cultural values of many Indians, drawing them into Atlantic commerce and tempting them to overhunt. For Native Americans from New Mexico to Canada, European colonization was a disaster.

THE SPANISH IN NORTH AMERICA

After Coronado and de Soto failed to locate cities of gold, Spain abandoned further exploration in North America. Then, Francis Drake's voyage along the Pa-

cific coast raised alarms of foreign interest in the region north of Mexico. In 1581, the viceroy of New Spain gave Franciscan priests permission to establish missions among the Pueblo Indians of the Rio Grande Valley. The friars named the area San Felipe del Nuevo México. The missionaries described the Pueblos as friendly and numerous: thousands could be converted to Christianity and forced to labor for Hispanic colonists. But by the time a party arrived in 1582 to escort the Franciscans back to Mexico, the missionaries had been killed by the Native Americans.

Settlement of New Mexico

Despite this setback, the Spanish remained interested in the region. Conquistadores needed permission from the Crown to invade new lands, however, for the king had issued Orders for New Discoveries (1573), which more strictly regulated colonization, in part to protect Native Americans from the atrocities Bartolomé de las Casas had described decades before. When one would-be conqueror led an illegal expedition into New Mexico in 1590, he was arrested and returned to Mexico City in chains.

The Spanish government delayed appointing a governor of New Mexico until 1595, when the viceroy authorized Juan de Oñate to undertake settlement with his own funds. Oñate, a native of Mexico, inherited great wealth and obtained even more by marrying Isabel Tolosa Cortés Moctezuma, a descendant of both Cortés and the Aztec emperor. The expedition proved expensive as delays increased costs. Finally, in 1598, 129 soldiers, their families, servants, and slaves, and 7,000 livestock headed north. Ten Franciscan missionaries accompanied the colonists. Oñate expected his investment to yield an empire. As he wrote King Philip II, "I shall give your majesty a new world, greater than New Spain." The governor envisioned mines of silver and gold and a water passage through the continent. He believed his province would extend from the Atlantic to the Pacific.

Upon arrival in New Mexico, Oñate declared Spanish sovereignty over Pueblo lands. In a ritual complete with trumpets and High Mass, he promised peace and prosperity to those who cooperated. According to the Spanish, the Pueblos acquiesced "of their own accord." The Franciscans founded missions in the largest pueblos and supervised construction of a church in the Tewa pueblo, Yungé, which the Spanish designated as their capital, San Gabriel.

For some months, the Spanish and the Indians coexisted without serious incident. The colonists moved into the Pueblos's apartments in San Gabriel,

CHRONOLOGY

1598 Spanish expedition into New Mexico

1599 Destruction of Ácoma by the Spanish

1603 James I takes the English throne

1605 French establish Port Royal

1607 English found colony at Jamestown

1608 French establish Quebec

1609 Henry Hudson explores for the Dutch East India Company

1609–1614 Anglo-Powhatan War in Virginia

1616–1618 Plague epidemic decimates eastern New England natives

1619 Africans arrive in Virginia

Virginia Company establishes a representative assembly

1620 Separatists found the Plymouth colony

1622 Native Americans attack the Virginia colony

1624 Virginia Company loses charter • Virginia becomes a royal colony • Dutch West India Company establishes New Netherland

1625 Charles I becomes king of England

1630 Massachusetts Bay colony founded by Puritans

1634 The *Ark* and the *Dove* arrive in Maryland

1636 Founding of Connecticut and Rhode Island

1637 Massachusetts and Connecticut troops destroy the Pequots

Anne Hutchinson is tried for heresy

1642–1648 English Civil War

1649 Charles I of England is beheaded

1651 English Parliament passes first Navigation Act

1660 Charles II of England becomes king

1663 Carolina proprietors receive charter

1664 English forces conquer New Netherland • New York and New Jersey are founded

1673 Dutch recapture New York, then return the colony to England with the Treaty of Westminster (1674)

forcing the inhabitants to depart. Soon the Indians tired of providing food, which they had intended as gifts but the Spanish considered tribute. The soldiers resorted to murder and rape to obtain supplies. The crisis came in December 1598, when a Spanish troop demanded provisions from the people of Ácoma, a pueblo high atop a mesa west of the Rio Grande. One of Coronado's party had described Ácoma as "the greatest stronghold ever seen in the world." The Pueblos refused to give flour to the soldiers and killed eleven men when they attempted to take the food by

force. Oñate moved swiftly, his small army laying siege to Ácoma with several cannons, as men and women defended the town with arrows and stones. The Spanish killed approximately 500 men and 300 women and children; they captured the survivors. The town was leveled. Everyone was sentenced to servitude, and each man over age twenty-five had one foot cut off. The Ácomas would not rebuild their town until the late 1640s.

With this harsh action, Oñate only temporarily prevented further opposition among the Pueblos, for

THE ENGLISH INVADE VIRGINIA

The Pueblo town of Ácoma, located on a mesa in New Mexico, strongly resisted the Spanish in 1598.
© Kevin Fleming/Corbis

another town resisted the following year. The colonists also complained of food shortages and the governor's mismanagement; many returned to Mexico. The Franciscans charged that Oñate's cruelty to the Indians made conversion difficult. Oñate was removed as governor, tried, and found guilty of mistreating the Native Americans and some of his settlers. He was banished from New Mexico, but sailed to Spain, where he received a knighthood and position as the Crown's chief inspector of mines.

After Oñate's departure, New Mexico became a royal province. Pedro de Peralta, the next governor, established a new capital at Santa Fe in 1610. As late as 1670 only 2,800 Spanish colonists inhabited the Rio Grande Valley. The Hispanics lived on farms and ranches along the river, exploiting the Pueblos's labor through the encomienda system to produce hides, blankets, sheep, wool, and pine nuts for sale in Mexico.

Spanish Missions in New Mexico and Florida

The Franciscan missionaries, who assumed a major role in colonizing the Spanish borderlands, were members of the Catholic religious order that Francis Bernardone of Assisi had founded (in Italy) in 1209. The friars vowed not to engage in sexual relations or acquire property, living on the gifts of others. Unlike other religious brotherhoods, which remained in seclusion, the Franciscans operated in the world among ordinary Christians. The Orders for New Discoveries of 1573 gave primary responsibility to the friars for "pacifying" the Indians of New Mexico and Florida.

During the first part of the seventeenth century, many Pueblos seemed to accept the Franciscans'

message. The friars initially offered gifts of food, metal tools, beads, and clothing. Placing some confidence in the priests, the natives agreed to build convents and churches. Women built the walls, while men did carpentry. The priests decorated the sanctuaries with paintings, statues, and silver chalices. They created missions by imposing their influence over existing Indian towns, backed by threat of military force. In New Mexico, the Spanish started more than fifty churches by 1629; in Florida, missions extended west from St. Augustine to the Gulf Coast and north into Georgia (or Guale, as the region was called).

The Native Americans who came under Spanish control could, in theory, choose whether or not to accept Christian baptism, but recognized that soldiers supported the priests. The Franciscans expected the natives to learn the catechism and enough of the Castilian (Spanish) language to communicate, and to adopt European dress, food, and farming methods. Many Indians embraced Catholicism, but in doing so, modified the religion. Even in the twentieth century, the Pueblos preserved both native and Catholic religious practices. Christian Indians in Florida continued to play a ball game during the 1600s until the missionaries realized it had religious significance and abolished the game, calling the pole used as a target the "ballpost of the devil."

In merging Indian gods with the Christian Trinity and adding Catholic holidays to native celebrations, Native Americans altered Spanish Catholicism. With the "Lady in Blue," they created a religious tradition that both the Indians and Spanish accepted. In the 1620s, Plains Indians reported that a nun appeared to them, telling them in their language to become Christians. Though the woman remained invisible to the missionaries, they believed the stories. On a trip to Spain, one priest discovered that a Franciscan nun, María de Jesús de Agreda, claimed to have made flights to America with the help of angels. María de Agreda's claims and the Indians' visions together created the resilient legend of the Lady in Blue.

THE ENGLISH INVADE VIRGINIA

New Mexico and Florida remained marginal outposts in the Spanish empire. Spanish control was tenuous because their military forces were small and cultural influence weak. After the defeat of the Spanish Armada, Philip II's government could not keep other European nations out of North America. During the first decade of the seventeenth century, the English, French, and Dutch sent expeditions to fish, search for a northern passage to the East, trade for furs, and establish colonies.

English Context of Colonization

Seventeenth-century England was an intensely hierarchical society, in which the king claimed divine right, or God-given authority, and the nobility and gentry dominated Parliament. But it was a society undergoing turmoil and change. Elizabeth I's successor was her cousin, James I, who governed from 1603 until 1625, when he died and his son, Charles I, took the throne. Both James and Charles had strife-torn reigns marked by power struggles with Parliament, culminating in Charles's loss of the English Civil War and his beheading in 1649. Parliament was composed of two houses: the House of Lords, made up of nobles and high church officials; and the House of Commons, who were elected representatives from the counties and boroughs. The Commons normally comprised country gentry, government officials, and lawyers; the electorate included male landowners, or an estimated 15 to 30 percent of all Englishmen. By imposing levies without Parliament's consent, James I and Charles I challenged its prerogative to approve or reject new taxes. For their part, the legislators tried to whittle away at royal powers. The fundamental issue concerning the balance of power between the king and property holders, as represented in Parliament, remained unsettled until the Glorious Revolution of 1688.

Economic developments loosened English society, giving individuals greater opportunity to change from one social class or occupation to another. Many found it necessary to move geographically as the woolen industry expanded, causing landowners to raise more sheep. In what has been called the "enclosure movement," landlords ended leases for tenant farmers living on their lands, confiscating common fields that peasant communities had shared for grazing their livestock and raising crops. The landowners enclosed the commons with fences and hedges. In 1500, peasants had farmed 70 percent of arable land in England, but by 1650, they farmed only 50 percent. Thus many tenants were forced from the land. Some went to London, where the population expanded from 55,000 in 1520 to 475,000 in 1670. Others were among the colonists who signed for America.

A developing economy meant dislocation for poor tenants; it spelled opportunity for merchants. They found it first in the woolen trade with Antwerp, in what is now Belgium. When this trade declined after 1550,

James I of England, who chartered the Virginia and Plymouth companies to colonize North America. Portrait by Daniel Mytens, 1621.
By courtesy of the National Portrait Gallery, London

they looked for alternative investments, which they found as war with Spain brought demand for coal, lead, glass, ships, salt, iron, and steel. Investors formed joint-stock companies to explore trade routes and establish new markets. The companies obtained capital by selling stocks. These investments were risky, for shareholders were liable for all company debts. The stocks could also be immensely profitable, as in the case of Francis Drake's circumnavigation of the globe, which brought a 4,600 percent profit.

Joint-stock companies provided capital for the first permanent English colonies in America. Unlike the Spanish monarchy, the English Crown had little role in funding, or even governing, its first New World settlements. In 1606, James I granted a charter to the Virginia Company with rights to settle colonies in North America. The Virginia Company included two groups, one in London and the other in Plymouth, in

PICTURING THE PAST ✦ ECONOMICS & TECHNOLOGY

LONDON IN 1616

The Granger Collection

In this painting of London in 1616, London Bridge crosses the Thames River. On the northern bank was the core of the city, which grew impressively during the late sixteenth and seventeenth centuries. Many of the buildings shown here were destroyed in the great fire of 1666. On the southern bank is Southwark, the suburb that attracted taverns, cockfights, and theaters— including Shakespeare's Globe Theatre—because it lay outside London's laws.

London became one of the world's largest cities, as its industry and port drew rural English people seeking work. Many impoverished migrants found employment, but others continued to move, signing up for transport as indentured servants to America. Forty percent of English immigrants to North America came from London in the seventeenth century, and an additional 11 percent came from adjacent counties.

---

the west of England. The groups received overlapping claims, with the Plymouth group obtaining lands from what is now Maine to Virginia and the London group receiving Connecticut to the Carolinas. Either could settle in the overlapping area, but initial colonies had to be at least one hundred miles apart.

Jamestown

In 1607, the Virginia Company of London funded the first permanent English colony at Jamestown. When the first 104 settlers arrived in May 1607, they had endured a long winter crossing. The native inhabitants watched them select a site on the James River, chosen for safety from Spanish attack, but next to malarial swamps. The Native Americans called their territory Tsenacommacah, or "densely inhabited land." They were Algonquian-speaking Indians; most belonged to

a confederacy that Powhatan, head sachem of the Pamunkey tribe, had forged in eastern Virginia. Before the arrival of the English, the chief unifying force among the bands of the Powhatan confederacy was the threat from powerful enemies, the Manahoacs and the Monacans, who controlled lands to the west. The leaders of tribes subject to Powhatan were supposed to pay tribute and provide military assistance, but they sometimes refused.

One of Powhatan's brothers was Opechancanough, described as having "large Stature, noble Presence, and extraordinary Parts" and being "perfectly skill'd in the Art of Governing." Historical evidence suggests that he was born around 1544 and, at about age sixteen, was taken by a Spanish ship to Spain, where he received instruction in the Castilian language and adopted the name Don Luis de Velasco after the viceroy of New Spain. The new Don Luis stayed with the Spanish until

In this conjectural view of Jamestown c. 1614, the fortified wall shows concerns for defense against the Spanish and the Powhatan confederacy.
Colonial Williamburg Foundation

1570, when he accompanied several missionaries to his homeland on Chesapeake Bay. He broke with the priests when they criticized him for taking several wives and murdered the priests the next year. If Opechancanough and Don Luis were the same man, as seems likely, he was well prepared with knowledge of Europeans when the Jamestown settlers arrived.

The English colony's first decade was a struggle. The company ran Virginia as a business enterprise, keeping control of government, land, and trade. Settlers were company employees, not landholders. To satisfy investors, the company instructed the colonists to search for gold and silver mines, find a passage to Asia, and establish industries and trade that would offer handsome returns. The company had chosen individuals for these purposes, not people who were willing to grow crops. Among the first Jamestown settlers were many gentlemen, who by definition avoided manual labor. They were adventurers who expected to strike it rich and return to England. The rest of the first colonists, who were nearly all men, included the gentlemen's personal servants, a jeweler, goldsmith, perfumer, carpenters, blacksmiths, and some laborers. No one described himself as a farmer.

When the colonists failed to locate mines or a passage to the East, their lives became aimless. Rather than plant crops or even hunt and fish, they expected the company and neighboring Indians to provide food. When sufficient provisions failed to arrive, the settlers starved. One of the leaders, a young officer named John Smith, took control in 1608, stabilizing the colony briefly by making everyone work. When criticism of his strict discipline reached company officials the next year, they removed him from command. During the particularly bitter winter of 1609–1610, one man killed his pregnant wife and chopped her up, planning to eat her body. Some of the colonists dug up graves to eat the corpses. By spring 1610, only sixty colonists remained of at least 600 who had come to Jamestown in three years. Though some had returned to England or escaped to live with the Indians, the majority died of starvation and disease.

In 1609, without gold mines or a trade route to Asia, the Virginia Company hoped to salvage its investment by exploiting the land. To recruit farmers, the company offered each emigrant one share of stock and a parcel of land after seven years of service. The settlers remained employees of the company in the meantime, with assigned tasks and the obligation to buy all supplies and ship all products through the company store.

Still, the Jamestown settlers refused to work. When Sir Thomas Dale arrived as governor in May 1611, he found nothing but a few gardens planted and the inhabitants at "their daily and usual work, bowling in the streets." He established his *Laws Divine, Morall and Martiall,* which were mostly martial. The men received military ranks, were divided into work gangs, and proceeded from home to work—and to church twice daily—at the beat of a drum. Laws prescribed death for a variety of crimes, including rape, adultery, theft, lying, slander against the company, blasphemy, and stealing an ear of corn. For taking two or three pints of oatmeal, one man had a large needle thrust through his tongue, then was chained to a tree until he starved. For the first offense of failing to work regular hours, an idler was tied neck to heels all night. The punishment for a second offense was whipping and for a third offense, death. Though the required hours of work were reasonable—five to eight hours per day in the summer and three to six in the winter—the punishments specified in "Dale's Laws" became a scandal in England, discouraging prospective emigrants. In the words of John Smith, "no man will go from [England] to have less liberty there."

The Struggle for Virginia

The Jamestown adventurers had expected to put the Indians to work in silver mines and fields, as in New Spain, but the inhabitants proved too few in number for an adequate workforce, yet too powerful for the wretched gang of settlers to conquer. During the early years at Jamestown, the English seemed irrational in their dealings with the Native Americans. To many colonists, the natives were barbarians. While some settlers attempted to trade for food, others burned Indian villages and crops.

In 1608–1609, Captain John Smith tried to force the sachems to provide food. The Indians had spared his life several times; nevertheless, he kidnapped two men, obligating Opechancanough to beg for their release. Next, he entered the Pamunkey village with soldiers demanding food, which the Indi-

John Smith threatening Opechancanough in 1608, with images in the background of skirmishes between colonists and Indians that took place at other times, not on this occasion. From Smith's Generall Historie of Virginia.
North Wind Photo Archives

ans refused to give, and again humiliated the tall sachem: in Smith's words, he did "take this murdering Opechancanough . . . by the long lock of his head; and with my pistol at his breast, I led him [out of his house] amongst his greatest forces, and before we parted made him [agree to] fill our bark with twenty tuns of corn." Otherwise, Smith warned, he would load the ship with their "dead carkases." Opechancanough probably never forgot this scene. Between 1609 and 1614, full-scale war existed between the Virginia colonists and the Powhatan confederacy. The English, with reinforcements from the Virginia Company, defeated Powhatan, taking control of the James River.

In contrast to Spain, the English Crown failed to take responsibility for protecting any rights of Native Americans. When colonists had sufficient power, they enslaved Indians, sending them away from their homelands to prevent escape. The English justified expropriation of native lands with the belief that the king of England, as the Christian monarch, received sovereignty over North America from God. Thus, the Virginia Company obtained rights to land from the Crown, not the Indians. Another basis for taking native territory was the legal concept, *vacuum domicilium,* which meant that lands not occupied could be taken. To the English, "occupation" meant improving the land with buildings, fences, and crops; they did not recognize Indian sovereignty over the vast stretches of hunting lands that extended beyond small villages and fields. Even when the English purchased land from the Indians, their contrasting concepts of ownership caused grave misunderstanding. Whereas the colonists believed in private property, the natives thought they were selling the rights to use lands for hunting, fishing, and communal farming. They expected to continue using the territory they had "sold" for these purposes. Conflicts resulted when, for example, a settler's cattle trampled Indian crops, or when a native killed a colonist's cow, mistaking it for a deer.

Tobacco Boom

Demand for land became paramount in Virginia after 1617, when the colonists discovered tobacco as a staple crop. Though James I called smoking "a custom loathsome to the eye, hateful to the nose, harmful to the brain, dangerous to the lungs, and in the black stinking fumes thereof, nearest resembling the horrible stygian smoke of the pit that is bottomless," the habit consumed England. The mercantilist advantages were clear. With production in Virginia, the English could acquire tobacco from its own colony, rather than pay premium prices to foreign countries, and could generate an industry to process the leaves. For Virginians, the tobacco trade meant capital to purchase manufactures from home. Tobacco became the first staple crop in England's colonial mercantilist system, followed by sugar, after 1640, in the West Indies.

In 1619, the Virginia Company updated the land policy, granting "headrights" of one hundred acres of land to those who came before 1616 and fifty acres to those who came after. Settlers who paid their own way received land immediately; those who immigrated at the company's expense received land after seven years of service. Virginia settlers thus fell into two categories: freeholders who paid for their own transportation; and servants, whose way the Virginia Company or someone else financed. Recipients of headrights did not pay for the land, but owed quitrents, annual pay-

To cure tobacco for sale, workers hung leaves from rafters in a tobacco house until sufficiently dry. The laborers then cut the leaves from the plant stalks, removed the largest fibers from the leaves, and "prized" or packed the leaves into hogsheads.
© Bettmann/Corbis

ments to the company, of one shilling per year for each fifty acres. Also in 1619, the Virginia Company relaxed its hold on the government of Virginia by establishing an assembly of elected delegates. The governor, who was appointed by the company, retained the right to veto all laws; the company's General Court in London could also disallow any decision. The Virginia Company also adopted English common law to replace the martial law under which the colony had operated.

While the revised land policy and the assembly gave settlers a greater stake in society, the adoption of tobacco assured Virginia's ultimate success. During the 1620s, tobacco drew high prices, as much as three shillings per pound. Virginia became the first North American "boom town," as settlers threw all of their energies into growing tobacco. Between 1617 and 1623, approximately 5,000 new immigrants arrived. Because the amount of the crop a planter could grow depended largely on the number of workers, those with capital eagerly paid to transport servants. The Virginia Company imported workers too, but still failed to show a profit, partly because company officials diverted many servants to their own plantations.

Africans in Early Virginia

English servants provided most of the labor in the colony until late in the seventeenth century. But Virginia planters needed as much labor as they could afford to strike it rich from tobacco, so they also purchased Africans, probably even before 1619 when a Dutch ship brought about twenty blacks. Though some Africans became servants with terms shorter than lifetime bondage, others probably were slaves. Little is known of their status during the early decades. In 1625, Africans numbered twenty-three of 1,200 Virginia colonists. Fifteen were the property of two men: Abraham Peirsey, the wealthiest man in the colony, and George Yeardley, who had served as governor. In 1660, about 900 blacks and 24,000 Europeans lived in the Chesapeake Bay area.

In contrast, by 1660, Africans outnumbered whites in Barbados, the richest of the English West Indies. Founded in 1627, Barbados quickly turned to sugar production, importing Africans to raise and process the crop. The white islanders created a harsh slave regime to prevent organized rebellion and to force the rapidly growing black population to perform hard, repetitive labor.

Until the 1660s, conditions for Africans remained less rigid in Virginia than in the West Indies. Some Virginia blacks achieved freedom, married, and a few acquired land. For example, by the 1650s, free blacks Anthony and Mary Johnson owned a 250-acre plantation on Virginia's eastern shore and, like neighboring whites, protected their property by going to court. Even so, other Africans remained in bondage, as Virginians adopted the practice by example from the Portuguese, Spanish, and Dutch. In purchasing people from slave traders, the white colonists bought into the Atlantic slave system.

Early Virginia documents distinguished consistently between white servants and blacks, always with the suggestion that Africans were subordinate. In a 1627 will, Governor Yeardley bequeathed his "goode debts, chattels, servants, negars, cattle or any other thing" to his heirs. Censuses of the 1620s also point to the lower regard for Africans: English settlers were listed with full names while most Africans were enumerated simply with a first name or designated as "negar" or "Negro." For example, Anthony and Mary Johnson were called "Antonio a Negro" and "Mary a Negro Woman" in early records. The Virginia tax law of 1643 further demonstrated that the colonists viewed Africans as different from themselves. Everyone who worked in the field was to be taxed—all men and black women. White women apparently were not expected to tend tobacco. Virginia also excepted blacks, but not white servants, from the obligation to bear arms.

The Colony Expands

The colonists had found the way to success—by growing tobacco—but Virginia faced difficulty for many years. Because mortality remained high and settlers had few children, the population grew slowly despite immigration that averaged about 1,000 people per year. From 1619 to 1640, the population rose from 700 to about 8,000, though approximately 20,000 immigrants had arrived during that time. Young men and women who left England to become servants in Virginia gambled with their lives to obtain land, which they could not gain at home. Dysentery, typhoid fever, and malaria took their toll on new settlers who suffered a period of "seasoning" after their arrival in Virginia. Men were much more likely to migrate to the colonies than women. A 1625 census indicated that more than three-quarters of the Virginia colonists were male and less than one-fifth were children. Many people came as servants, which meant that they could not legally marry and have children for years, until their terms expired. The census also provided ample evidence of mortality and disrupted families, as many of the married couples were childless, in part because of high infant and childhood mortality. And with short life expectancy for adults, more than one-half of the colony's children had lost one parent, and one-fifth apparently had no relatives in Virginia at all.

By 1621, Opechancanough and a prophet named Nemattanew, whom the colonists called "Jack of the Feathers" because he wore clothes covered with plumes, recognized the threat of increased immigration. Now that the English had tobacco, they were not going to leave. Nemattanew inspired a nativist religious revival among the Powhatans, rejecting Christianity and European customs. Opechancanough organized a military offensive to push the English back

Richard Frethorne, a Virginia Colonist, Writes Home, 1623

Conditions in Virginia remained dreadful for immigrants in the 1620s, as Richard Frethorne tells his parents at home in England. A year after the 1622 massacre by the Powhatan confederacy, the Englishman reports ongoing hostilities and the settlers' constant fear of "the Enimy."

Loving and kind father and mother, my most humble duty remembered to you, hoping in God of your good health, as I myself am at the making hereof. This is to let you understand that I your Child am in a most heavy Case by reason of the nature of the Country, [which] is such that it causeth much sickness, as the scurvy and the bloody flux and divers other diseases, which maketh the body very poor, and weak. And when we are sick there is nothing to Comfort us; for since I came out of the ship, I never ate anything but peas, and loblollie (that is, water gruel). As for deer or venison I never saw any since I came into this land. There is indeed some fowl, but We are not allowed to go and get it, but must Work hard both early and late for a mess of water gruel and a mouthful of bread, and beef. A mouthful of bread, for a penny loaf must serve for 4 men which is most pitiful. . . .

[P]eople cry out day and night, Oh that they were in England without their limbs and would not care to lose any limb to be in England again, yea though they beg from door to door. For we live in fear of the Enimy every hour, yet we have had a Combat with them on the Sunday before Shrovetide, and we took two alive and make slaves of them. But it was by policy, for we are in great danger, for our Plantation is very weak by reason of the dearth, and sickness, of our company. For we came but Twenty for the merchants, and they are half dead Just; and we look every hour When two more should go. Yet there came some four other men yet to live with us, of which there is but one alive; and our Lieutenant is dead, and his father and his brother. . . . [A]nd yet we are but 32 to fight against 3000 if they should come. And the nighest help that We have is ten miles of us, and when the rogues overcame this place last, they slew 80 Persons. How then shall we do, for we lie even in their teeth. They may easily take us but that God is merciful and can save with few as well as with many; as he showed to Gilead. And like Gilead's soldiers, if they lapped water, we drink water which is but Weak.

And I have nothing to comfort me, nor there is nothing to be gotten here but sickness, and death, except that one had money to lay out in some things for profit. But I have nothing at all—no, not a shirt to my back but two rags (2), nor no clothes but one poor suit, nor but one pair of shoes, but one pair of stockings, but one cap, [and] but two bands. My Cloak is stolen by one of my own fellows, and to his dying hour [he] would not tell me what he did with it; but some of my fellows saw him have butter and beef out of a ship, which my cloak, I doubt [not], paid for. So that I have not a penny, nor a penny Worth, to help me to either spice or sugar or strong Waters, without the which one cannot live here. For as strong beer in England doth fatten and strengthen them, so water here doth wash and weaken these here [and] only keeps life and soul together. But I am not half a quarter so strong as I was in England, and all is for want of victuals; for I do protest unto you that I have eaten more in [a] day at home then I have allowed me here for a Week. . . .

Good Father, do not forget me, but have mercy and pity my miserable case. I know if you did but see me you would weep to see me, for I have but one suit. But it is a strange one, it is very well guarded. Wherefore, for God's sake, pity me. I pray you to remember my love to all my Friends and kindred. I hope all my Brothers and Sisters are in good health, and as for my part I have set down my resolution that certainly Will be, that is, that the answer of this letter will be life or death to me. Therefore, good father, send as soon as you can, and if you send me any thing let this be the mark. ROT

Richard Frethorne,
Martin's Hundred

into the sea. At the same time, he used diplomacy to convince the settlers to lower their guard. When several whites killed Nemattanew in 1622, Opechancanough rallied his troops, slaying one-fourth of the settlers before the colony could react. A ten-year war followed, in which each side tried to annihilate the other, but failed, and in 1632 agreed to peace.

Though the bankrupt Virginia Company lost its charter in 1624, immigration to the colony continued. Its economic promise helped convince the English Crown to claim it as a royal colony. Desire for new tobacco lands placed constant pressure on the Powhatans, so in 1644, Opechancanough launched another attack. After two years of war, the Powhatans submitted and Opechancanough was captured and murdered by a guard. The 1646 treaty required the Native Americans to live on lands north of the York River and, to symbolize their subordination, pay an annual tribute of twenty beaver skins. Colonists expanded rapidly north and south of the James River and to the eastern shore.

FISHING, FURS, AND SETTLEMENTS IN THE NORTH

While settlers and Native Americans struggled for Virginia, French, Dutch, and English adventurers explored and colonized the region to the north. French and English sailors had fished the Newfoundland Banks since the fifteenth century. By 1600, groups monopolized specific waters, such as the French who caught walrus in the Gulf of St. Lawrence. The beaver furs that Europeans obtained in petty trade with Native Americans became popular in Europe for making felt hats, exciting merchants in France, the Netherlands, and England to seek more permanent arrangements. All three nations claimed the northern territories as their own, ignoring of course the prior ownership of the Indians.

New France

In North America, French traders focused on furs. When a ship sent to North America in 1582 returned to France with a cargo of furs earning a 1,500 percent profit, merchants enthusiastically organized more voyages. Samuel de Champlain established the first successful French colony in the New World. Working for Pierre du Gua de Monts, who had received a charter from the king of France, in 1605 Champlain planted a temporary base at Port Royal on the Bay of Fundy in

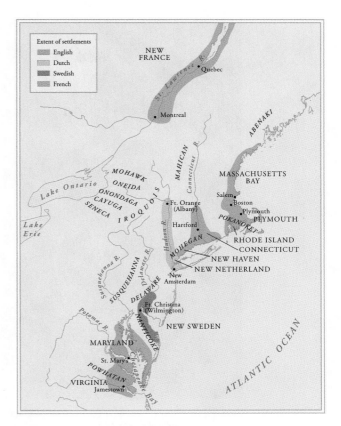

Map 2.1 *Eastern North America*
By the mid-seventeenth century, northern European nations established colonies along the Atlantic coast from French Quebec and Montreal in the St. Lawrence Valley to the English settlements on Chesapeake Bay. Although at this date all of the colonies were relatively small, New England and the Chesapeake were expanding agricultural societies while the French, Dutch, and Swedes concentrated on trade.

Canada. He sailed south to Cape Cod looking for a permanent site, but decided in 1608 to retain Port Royal and establish a main settlement on the St. Lawrence River. The French chose Quebec, which meant "the place where the river narrows" in Algonquian, an ideal location for controlling the Canadian interior.

For two decades, both Port Royal and Quebec remained little more than trading posts. The French had already traded with the Micmacs of the coastal region and Algonquins of the St. Lawrence Valley. Champlain strengthened these ties, and made new alliances with several groups: the Montagnais, who lived in the region north of the St. Lawrence River and like the Algonquins and Micmacs were Algonquian; and the Hurons, who were Iroquoian and lived north of Lake Ontario. This

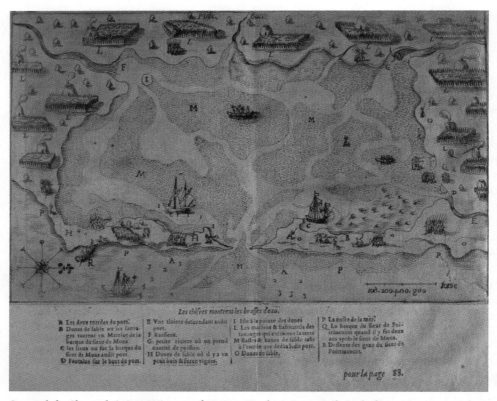

Samuel de Champlain's 1605 map of Nauset Harbor, Cape Cod, including wigwams and adjacent cornfields. "B" indicates a skirmish in which a sailor was killed; "G" depicts an Indian fish trap.
Courtesy of Osher Map Library and Smith Center for Cartographic Education

location enabled the Hurons to link French outposts with the interior, the source of the most valuable furs. In 1609, to demonstrate allegiance to his allies, Champlain helped them fight a group of Iroquois from what is now New York, thus making the Five Nations enemies of New France. He also explored the watershed of the St. Lawrence River and lands as far west as Lake Huron.

In 1627, Quebec was still essentially a trading post with about 100 French inhabitants, including a few women. Cardinal Richelieu, who for all practical purposes ruled France, organized the Company of One Hundred Associates to spur colonization. The company received a charter for territory from the Arctic Circle to Florida and from the Atlantic to the Pacific, with a monopoly on the fur trade. The company also pledged to send missionaries to the Indians and grant them the status of "natural French" when they were baptized. The priests established missions in Indian villages and learned their languages, looking for similarities between the two cultures in an effort to make the Indians part of French society.

Because the company focused on the fur trade and considered transporting settlers too expensive, in 1663 just 3,000 French settlers lived in the colony. The Crown revoked the company's charter, making New France a royal province. Nevertheless, population growth remained slow. From the beginning, the government refused to allow Protestants, who were the most likely immigrants, to settle there; it wanted to maintain control of the society through the Catholic church. Further, New France developed under feudal land tenure, in which wealthy lords received large manors, or *seigniories,* along the St. Lawrence River. Ordinary settlers on these manors became tenants rather than independent farmers. Lacking the opportunity to improve their status in the New World, French peasants were reluctant to make the dangerous transatlantic voyage.

The fur trade and small population made French relations with the Native Americans different from those of New Spain and Virginia where labor demands and white expansion put greater pressure on the Indians. The most efficient way to obtain furs was to offer desirable products from Europe, including textiles, guns, metal tools, pots, and alcohol, not to drive trading partners from the land or to exploit their labor. One French priest reported that, at least for a while, the Montagnais thought they were getting the better deal.

"I heard my [Indian] host say one day, jokingly, *Missi picoutau amiscou,* 'The Beaver does everything perfectly well, it makes kettles, hatchets, swords, knives, bread; and in short, it makes everything.' He was making sport of us Europeans . . . [and said], showing me a beautiful knife, 'The English have no sense; they give us twenty knives like this for one Beaver skin.' "

Nevertheless, the French arrival had tragic effects for the Indians of Canada, who succumbed to disease in large numbers. The demand for furs altered cultural attitudes and intensified hostility among nations. In keeping with their religion, Indians had taken only what they needed from nature and little more; they generally used entire animals, the meat as well as the skins. With the fur trade, natives killed animals just for their furs and in numbers far greater than before. As a result, the balance of nature that the Native Americans had maintained was broken. They had to reach farther and farther back into the continent as they exterminated the deer, beaver, and other fur-bearing animals.

New Netherland

In the first decade of the seventeenth century, the Dutch, too, challenged the dominance of Spain in the New World. The seven northern United Provinces had declared independence from Spain in 1581 and remained at war until 1609, when they signed a twelve-year truce. With its expiration, the war resumed and continued as part of the Thirty Years' War, which ended in 1648 with the Treaty of Münster, recognizing Dutch independence.

Despite this ongoing struggle, Dutch commerce flourished. Because land was scarce and high-priced in the Netherlands, and agriculture insufficient, affluent individuals put their capital into trade. In 1602, merchants formed the United East India Company, which six years later had 160 ships around the globe. In 1609, the company sent out Henry Hudson, an Englishman, to search for the long-sought northwest passage through North America. He sailed up the river that later bore his name, trading for furs with the Native Americans. The pelts brought a good return in Holland, so the company dispatched traders who set up a post near the present site of Albany and explored Long Island Sound and the Connecticut River. In 1621, the Dutch government chartered another group, the West India Company, to establish commerce and colonies in America. Like the East India Company, it received broad powers, including the rights to make war and sign treaties. During the seventeenth century, the Dutch muscled their way to control a large part of

The Seal of the Province of New Netherland, 1623, with an image of a beaver in center, evokes the Dutch focus on trade.
© Museum of The City of New York

international commerce, including the Atlantic slave trade and routes to Asia.

To provide a base for trade in the Hudson River region, in 1624 the Dutch West India Company appointed Cornelius Jacobsen May to found New Netherland; the first colonists were mostly Protestant refugees from the Spanish Netherlands. They established their primary settlement, called New Amsterdam, on Manhattan Island, and maintained trading posts at Fort Orange (near Albany), and on the Delaware and Connecticut Rivers. As in Jamestown, the first settlers were employees of the company who received no land of their own. The company paid for their transportation, tools, livestock, and two years' worth of supplies, assigning them company land on which to plant. The colonists were expected to trade only with the company. The government consisted of appointed company officers headed by a director-general, or governor, with wide powers. The colonists could not elect an assembly or any of their officials.

With good soil, the lucrative fur trade, and lumbering, the colony prospered economically, though its population grew slowly. Brewing became the second most important industry; in 1638, New Amsterdam residents complained that they were losing sleep from the singing of drunken sailors. People of many nationalities and religions arrived to take advantage of the Dutch policy of religious freedom, but few Dutch could be convinced to emigrate. In 1629, the company attempted to spur population growth by offering huge manors, called patroonships, to any member of the company who transported fifty persons to work his land. On the Hudson River, each patroonship extended for miles along one bank or both banks. Similar to New France, the settlers were tenants of the manor. This arrangement attracted few settlers: in fact it discouraged immigration because the manors tied up large tracts that might otherwise go to small farmers.

At first, New Netherland had good relations with the Indians because the colony grew slowly and depended on the fur trade. In the famous 1626 purchase, Director-general Peter Minuit exchanged goods worth about sixty guilders for Manhattan Island. Upriver, the Dutch bought furs from the Iroquois, the enemies of the Algonquians and Hurons who supplied the French, thus contributing to the devastating warfare among tribes. By the late 1640s, the Iroquois, with help from epidemics, destroyed the Hurons, a nation of about 20,000 people. At the same time, constant warfare and disease seriously debilitated the Iroquois as well.

In the region surrounding New Amsterdam, relations deteriorated between the whites and the Indians after 1638. As with the English, the Dutch and natives had different conceptions of land ownership. Although the Indians understood that they had sold rights to share the land and intended to continue using it themselves, the Dutch believed they had bought exclusive rights. Violence erupted as the settlers' cattle destroyed the Indians' corn, and dogs belonging to Native Americans attacked Dutch livestock. Beginning in 1640, the Dutch and Indians of the lower Hudson Valley fought a series of damaging wars that ended only in 1664, when the English took control of New Netherland and made peace with the Native Americans.

New England Before the Pilgrims

Along the coast of New England, relations between the Indians and English were rocky from the start. Before the Pilgrims established Plymouth in 1620, a number of expeditions explored the region, traded, and tried to colonize. In 1602, Bartholomew Gosnold and thirty-two men sailed the *Concord* to Maine and continued south to Martha's Vineyard, where they traded for furs. When they alienated the natives and one of their men was wounded, Gosnold and his crew returned to England. In 1607, the Plymouth group of the Virginia Company sent an expedition to the Kennebec River in Maine, but the colony lasted only one year. The company abandoned efforts to establish a permanent base, instead funding voyages for fish and furs. Like the Dutch and French, the English set up commercial networks with tribes who had contested land and resources before the Europeans arrived, thereby intensifying these rivalries.

Even before the founding of Plymouth, then, the natives of New England had considerable experience with the English. This contact had catastrophic effects on the Indian population. A plague epidemic brought by Europeans swept eastern New England during 1616–1618, killing thousands. Large areas along the coast were depopulated. The Massachusetts natives were initially friendly and interested in trade, but good relations proved elusive. The English shot some Native Americans and set dogs on others. A few they kidnapped, then expected them to serve as diplomats to their people. The English also made trade agreements, then failed to honor them. By the time the Pilgrims arrived in 1620, the surviving Indians along the coast had been severely weakened by disease and were understandably wary of the newcomers.

RELIGIOUS EXILES FROM ENGLAND

While the colonizers of Virginia, New France, and New Netherland had primarily economic motives, the English founders of Plymouth, Massachusetts Bay, and Maryland sought a place where they could practice their religion free from persecution and at the same time earn a decent living. Seventeenth-century England was rife with religious controversy. The government required attendance at Anglican worship and financial support of ministers. When dissenters refused to obey, holding separate services, they could be imprisoned and fined. Roman Catholics could also be stripped of their property and jailed for life if they refused to take the oath of supremacy to the king, which denied the authority of the pope. The search for freedom of worship became a major impetus for crossing the Atlantic.

English Calvinists

By 1603, when James I took the throne, two strains of English Calvinism, or Puritanism, had developed. One group included the Separatists, or Pilgrims, who founded Plymouth in 1620; the others, known as Puritans, established the Massachusetts Bay colony ten years later. Both groups charged that the Anglican church needed to be "purified" of its rituals, vestments, statues, and bishops. They rejected the church hierarchy, believing each congregation should govern itself. The Separatists started their own congregations, abandoning all hope that the church could be reformed. The Pilgrims' decision to begin a colony in America was the ultimate expression of this separatism. The Puritans, on the other hand, hoped to reform the Church of England from within. Their purpose in founding Massachusetts Bay was to develop a moral government that they hoped the people of England would someday make their own.

The Mayflower Compact, 1620

When the *Mayflower* reached land at Cape Cod (in what is now Massachusetts) and the colonists decided to settle there instead of prolonging their difficult journey, they lacked the legal basis (a charter) to establish a government. Thus, the adult males of the colony signed a mutual agreement for ordering their society, what John Locke called, decades later, a "social compact."

In the name of God Amen. We whose names are underwriten, the loyall subjects of our dread soveraigne Lord King James by the grace of God, of great Britaine, Franc, & Ireland king, defender of the faith, &c.

Haveing undertaken, for the glorie of God, and advancements of the Christian faith and honour of our king & countrie, a voyage to plant the first colonie in the Northerne parts of Virginia, doe by these presents solemnly & mutualy in the presence of God, and one of another, covenant & combine our selves togeather into a civill body politick; for our better ordering, & preservation & furtherance of the ends aforesaid; and by vertue hearof to enacte, constitute, and frame shuch just & equall lawes, ordinances, Acts, constitutions, & offices, from time to time, as shall be thought most meete & convenient for the generall good of the Colonie: unto which we promise all due submission and obedience.

In witnes whereof we have hereunder subscribed our names at Cap-Codd the •11• of November, in the year the raigne of our soveraigne Lord King James of England, France, & Ireland the eighteenth and of Scotland the fiftie fourth. An°: Dom. 1620.

John Carver
William Bradford
Edward Winslow
William Brewster
Isaac Allerton
Myles Standish
John Alden
Samuel Fuller
Christopher Martin
William Mullins
William White
Richard Warren
John Howland
Stephen Hopkins
Edward Tilley
John Tilley
Francis Cooke
Thomas Rogers
Thomas Tinker
John Rigdale
Edward Fuller

John Turner
Francis Eaton
James Chilton
John Crakston
John Billington
Moses Fletcher
John Goodman
Degory Priest
Thomas Williams
Gilbert Winslow
Edmund Margeson
Peter Brown
Richard Britterige
George Soule
Richard Clarke
Richard Gardiner
John Allerton
Thomas English
Edward Doty
Edward Leister

The Plymouth Colony

The Pilgrims were a small band who had originated in Scrooby, England, where they established a separate congregation. In 1607, when some were jailed as nonconformists, they decided to leave England for the Netherlands, which offered freedom of worship. The Pilgrims settled in Leyden, but were unhappy there, so made an agreement with a group of London merchants who obtained a patent for land from the Virginia Company. In exchange for funding to go to America, the Pilgrims promised to send back fish, furs, and lumber for seven years.

Thirty-five of the Leyden congregation chose to emigrate. Sailing first to England, they joined sixty-seven others, of whom many were not Separatists. In September 1620, the *Mayflower* departed Plymouth, England, crowded with 102 passengers, about twenty crew members, and assorted pigs, chickens, and goats. Headed for Virginia, the ship reached Cape Cod on November 9th. In shallow waters, fearing shipwreck, the exhausted travelers built their colony at Plymouth, even though they were outside the jurisdiction of the Virginia Company. They now lacked a legal basis for governing themselves or for claiming land. The first problem was most urgent because some of the colonists questioned the authority of the Pilgrim leaders. The group avoided a revolt by drafting and signing the "Mayflower Compact," a social compact by which they agreed to form a government and obey its laws. The London merchants eventually solved the second problem by obtaining title to the land.

Plymouth's first years were difficult, though the settlers found unused supplies of corn left by Indians struck recently by epidemic disease, and chose the site of a deserted Patuxet village with relatively clear fields. Over the first winter they built houses, but one-half of the colonists died of illness and exposure to the cold. In the spring of 1621, they planted corn with the help of Squanto, perhaps the lone surviving Patuxet, and other crops. Squanto and neighboring Pokanokets helped the Plymouth colony despite earlier problems with Englishmen. In 1614, Squanto and about twenty other Patuxets had been kidnapped by an English sea captain, who intended to sell them as slaves in Spain. Saved from bondage by Spanish priests, Squanto made his way to England, where he learned the language, then to Newfoundland, and finally back to Patuxet in 1619. There he found unburied bodies of many of his people who had perished in the epidemic. One Englishman described the scene: "[T]heir bones and skulls made such a spectacle . . . . it seemed to me a new found Golgotha."

At harvest in 1621, the Indians and colonists celebrated together for three days. Soon after their feast, the ship *Fortune* arrived with thirty-five new settlers, for whom no food was available until the next year's crop. When the colonists filled the *Fortune* with furs and lumber in hopes of starting to repay their debt to the London merchants, the French captured the ship.

The seal of the Massachusetts Bay Company, 1629, shows an Indian calling to the English, "Come over and help us."
Courtesy of the Massachusetts Historical Society

By 1623, though, the Plymouth colony was well established and growing, as new immigrants arrived. The community solved the problem of food supply by assigning individual plots to families. Still, the hard-working colonists had trouble fulfilling their bargain with the merchants. During a trading voyage, the crew mutinied. On one fishing trip, the ship sank; when it was raised and sent out again, the Spanish captured it. The London merchants gave up and in 1626 agreed to sell the land to the colonists for a large sum, which they paid by 1645, receiving a patent of ownership. Although Plymouth's economic fortunes improved, the colony remained small and self-consciously separate from the larger group of English dissenters who streamed into New England.

Massachusetts Bay

The Puritan migration to Massachusetts Bay was much larger and more tightly organized than the Plymouth settlement. During 1630, the first year, 700 women, men, and children arrived in eleven ships. Though at least 200 died during the first winter, the colony grew quickly as about 12,000 people went to Massachusetts during the 1630s. From King Charles I, the Massachusetts Bay Company obtained a charter specifying its government and the colony's boundaries. When most of the company officials emigrated, taking the charter with them, they greatly enhanced the colony's independence from the Crown and the Anglican church.

Thus the Massachusetts Bay colonists did not answer to London merchants who expected handsome profits. The Puritans themselves financed coloniza-

Reconstructed village at Plymouth, with fences to protect gardens from roaming livestock.
Plimoth Plantation, Inc., Photographer, Gary Andrashko

tion; they included wealthy investors as well as many middling families who could pay their own way. As a result, the founders devoted much of their energy to creating a model society. In the words of leader John Winthrop, the colony would be "as a Citty upon a Hill, the Eyes of all people are uppon us; soe that if wee shall deale falsely with our god in this worke wee have undertaken and soe cause him to withdrawe this present help from us, wee shall be made a story and a byword through the world." The Puritans believed that in addition to their charter from the king they had a covenant with God that bound them to create a moral community. As Calvinists, they held that individuals were saved from eternal damnation by faith, rather than by good works. Men and women could seek to avoid sin and work hard throughout their lives, but unless they were among God's chosen, or the "elect," they would go to hell. Under the covenant, the elect were responsible for the behavior of unsaved members of their community. The Puritan leaders were responsible to God. They thought that if they maintained a moral society, the Lord would help it prosper.

In Massachusetts, the Puritans restructured the company government to create their version of a godly commonwealth. According to the Massachusetts Bay charter, the company officials included a governor, deputy governor, and executive board of eighteen "assistants," to be elected by "freemen" (stockholders) who would meet in a general assembly, called the General Court. These officers could make laws and regulations, appoint lower officials, grant lands, and punish lawbreakers. The colony's leaders changed the rules to allow all male church members (the male elect), not just stockholders in the company, to become freemen. In theory, every freeman would be a member of the General Court, or colonial legislature. But as the population grew and towns formed quickly, freemen voted in town meetings for representatives to the assembly.

With the governor and assistants, the General Court drew up a law code for the colony, which after several revisions was published as the *Laws and Liberties of Massachusetts* (1648). The code was a combination of biblical law, English common law, and statutes tailored specifically to colonial needs. It protected the liberties of individuals by upholding trial by jury and due process of law, including the rights of the accused to a prompt public trial and to call witnesses. It also prohibited feudal tenure of lands and outlawed slavery, "unless it be lawfull captives, taken in just warrs, and such strangers as willingly sell themselves or are solde to us." This provision limited the possibility that whites would be enslaved, but had little effect on black bondage. The *Laws and Liberties* pre-

Unlike most English colonists, John Winthrop came from a well-to-do background. He helped finance the Massachusetts Bay colony and served as governor.
Courtesy of the Massachusetts Historical Society

scribed the death penalty for fewer crimes than in England, but included as capital offenses blasphemy and adultery (in cases where the woman was married), which under the English common law were lesser crimes. Children could be put to death for failing to respect their parents, while fornicators were required to marry and be whipped or fined. The code enabled judges to extend the terms of negligent servants and send back to England any married persons who arrived in Massachusetts without their spouses. Although these terms may seem harsh, the colony did not actually impose the death penalty for blasphemy or abuse of parents by children, and executed only two people for adultery. The magistrates evidently wanted to instill fear in the hearts of potential offenders rather than to exact harsh punishments.

The Puritans attempted to create a theocracy, a government operated according to God's will, as determined by the colony's leaders. The Puritan government was composed of members of the elect; ministers advised the magistrates but could not serve officially. The government required all inhabitants to attend Puritan churches. Persons who disagreed with orthodox doctrines could be expelled, whipped, fined, and even executed. The church was the center of each town, with all property owners paying taxes for its support. Though the Puritans had suffered persecution for their beliefs in England, they refused to allow freedom of worship in Massachusetts. Instead, they replaced one established church for another.

New England Society

Unlike the Jamestown settlers, a large proportion of Puritan immigrants came in families. Many originated from Norfolk, Suffolk, and Essex (together called East Anglia). Located directly across the North Sea from the Netherlands, East Anglia was the center of both the wool trade and Puritanism. By 1630, its residents had kept contact with European Calvinists for almost a century; entire congregations, ostensibly part of the Church of England, adopted Puritan ways. For decades they had worshipped freely, protected by the local Puritan gentry. Then during the 1620s and 1630s, the Puritans faced a series of hardships, including a depressed market for woolen cloth, poor harvests, and bubonic plague. Charles I and the Anglican church hierarchy, notably Archbishop William Laud, enforced laws against nonconformists, removing Puritan ministers from their pulpits. Many families migrated to Massachusetts, where they could make a new start under a congenial government. Some entire communities accompanied their minister.

In Massachusetts, the migrants created towns that often resembled the ones they had left. When a group arrived, its leaders petitioned the General Court for a place to settle and permission to establish a church and town government. The town meeting elected a board of selectmen who administered town business, including road building, maintenance of schools, and law enforcement. The town meeting also divided the town lands. The amount of land a family received depended upon its wealth and social status. Typically, a town followed one of two patterns of land distribution according to the kind of land tenure its founders knew in England. Emigrants from East Anglia generally chose the *closed field* system, in which families received individual farms, with house lot and land for planting, grazing livestock, and cutting lumber. These settlers also created commercial towns. In contrast, emigrants from Yorkshire, in northern England, chose the *open field* system, designating town lands for different purposes—house lots lined up in compact rows, fields, meadows, and wood lots. In Rowley, Massachusetts, for example, families received strips in the fields, where they grew crops in coopera-

Mrs. Elizabeth Freake and Baby Mary, *painted c. 1674 by an unknown artist, illustrates one of the many roles of seventeenth-century women, that of mother. The wife and child of a successful merchant, their clothing depicts the family's wealth.*
Worcester Art Museum, Worcester, Massachusetts, Gift of Mr. & Mrs. Albert W. Rice

tion with their neighbors. Together they made many decisions, including which fields to plant and which to leave fallow. Families also received "stinting rights," or permission to pasture animals on common lands. The number of cattle and sheep a family could pasture depended upon the size of their lands.

The Puritan notion of an ideal community defined the ways in which the Puritans acted toward one another and toward outsiders. If the model society were to succeed, everyone had to have a place in the family, church, and commonwealth. Like other English, the Puritans kept a hierarchical social order. In the family, the husband was superior to the wife, but together they ruled the children and servants. In the church, the minister and elders dominated the congregation. In the commonwealth, the officials led the people. Ideally, this hierarchy required little coercion, when people saw themselves as part of the community and worked for the common good, or "weal" (hence "commonwealth"), rather than for their own benefit. They understood that all humans were equal spiritually but accepted social inequality as the will of God.

Most Puritan women accepted a subordinate place in their society without complaint. They viewed themselves as part of a community and a family, with duties determined by their sex and age, not as individuals with equal rights. Women raised children; kept the house and garden; preserved fruits and vegetables; made beer, cider, cheese, and butter; tended livestock and poultry; spun and wove cloth; sewed clothing; cared for the sick; and supervised the training of daughters and servants. Women often specialized in certain trades, such as spinning, weaving, poultry raising, or medicine; they conducted trade among themselves, separate from the commercial networks of their husbands. Men had responsibility for raising grain such as wheat, Indian corn, and rye; cutting firewood; and maintaining the fences, buildings, and fields. In addition to farming, many followed a trade or profession such as fishing, carpentry, shopkeeping, overseas trade, medicine, or the ministry. Only men could vote in church and town meetings, serve as government officials, or become ministers. Only when a man became incapacitated, or was away from home, was his wife expected to take his place at work or to represent the family in legal matters or disputes. She temporarily assumed the role of "deputy husband," then yielded it when he became well or returned. Puritans recognized women's ability in public matters, but expected them normally to confine themselves to accepted women's tasks.

The role of Puritan women in the church was indicative of their place in society. On the one hand, women were the spiritual equals of men and held responsibility for the religious education of their children. On the other hand, the Puritans emphasized the inheritance of Eve, who they believed led Adam to sin in the Garden of Eden. Women were expected to keep quiet in the church. They could not preach or vote on church business, though they could exert informal influence on their husbands. The Puritans, like other Christians of the time, embraced Saint Paul's instruction to the Corinthians: "Let your women keep silence in the Churches. . . . And if they will learn anything, let them ask their husbands at home." The Puritans believed that by nature women were morally and intellectually weak. The pain of childbirth was God's punishment of all women for Eve's seduction of Adam. Although a few rebelled against the injunction to keep quiet, most Puritan women and girls accepted their subordination to men.

In this patriarchal society, children deferred to their fathers, assuming a subservient role until they were able to establish households of their own.

Though some New England colonists held servants and a few owned enslaved Africans, sons and daughters comprised the majority of the workforce. Families on average had five children who reached adulthood. They worked for their parents until marriage—longer in the case of sons who inherited the family farm. Unlike seventeenth-century Virginia, living conditions in Massachusetts promoted patriarchy, for life expectancy was long. Persons who survived childhood diseases often lived past age sixty or even seventy. Thus, eldest sons could be middle-aged before their fathers died and willed them control of the family homestead. On the other hand, younger sons who had little hope of receiving the farm often moved away from their parents, settling in the new towns that developed throughout New England. Parents usually attempted to give all of their children a start in life, with a farm, apprenticeship, money, or college tuition to sons, and personal property or cash to daughters.

Connecticut and New Haven

An early destination for emigrants looking for good land was Connecticut. The first Puritans went there to trade with Native Americans, but when news of attractive land in the Connecticut Valley arrived in Massachusetts, many settlers decided to move. The Earl of Warwick owned the rights to the land at the mouth of the Connecticut River, which he ceded to a group of Puritan noblemen. To build a trading post and settlement they sent John Winthrop, Jr., who convinced Thomas Hooker, the minister of Newtown, Massachusetts, to lead some of his congregation there. With another group that left from Dorchester, they founded Connecticut in 1636. Lacking a charter from the king, the founders agreed upon the *Fundamental Orders of Connecticut,* which created a General Assembly of representatives from each town. In most respects, the Connecticut government resembled that of Massachusetts, with the exception that freemen, or voters, did not have to be church members. The assembly elected a governor, who could serve only one year at a time, and a group of magistrates who functioned as the upper house of the assembly. As in Massachusetts, Puritanism was the only recognized religion and received tax support.

As white settlement expanded, relations between the Puritans and Native Americans deteriorated. Like other English, the Puritans believed that the Indians worshipped the devil and had barbarous customs. The settlers justified expropriation of native lands on the basis of *vacuum domicilium.* Even more, the Puritans considered the Indians "strangers," who

PICTURING THE PAST ✦ POLITICS & DIPLOMACY

PEQUOT WAR DIAGRAM

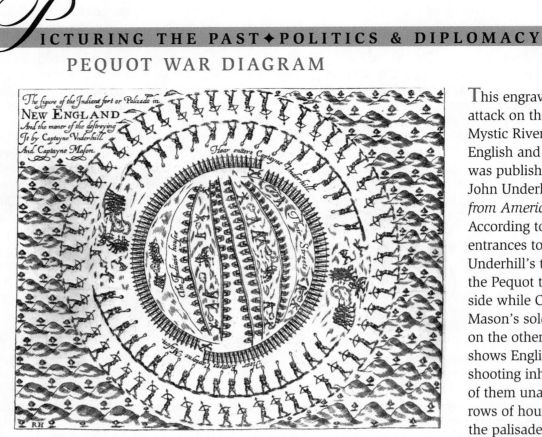

The Granger Collection

This engraving of the attack on the Pequots at Mystic River in 1637 by the English and Narragansetts was published in Captain John Underhill's *News from America* (1638). According to labels on the entrances to the palisade, Underhill's troops entered the Pequot town on one side while Captain John Mason's soldiers entered on the other. The engraver shows English warriors shooting inhabitants, some of them unarmed, between rows of houses. Outside the palisade are rings of soldiers with muskets and Narragansetts with bows and arrows.

The English killed the Pequots and burned the town to the ground. The Narragansetts, who had nearly ended their long-standing conflict with the Pequots before the attack, were shocked by the slaughter. According to Underhill, the Narragansetts were pleased with the conquest but cried "mach it, mach it; that is, it is naught, it is naught, because it is too furious, and slaies too many men."

could have no role in building the model society. They were dispensable and dangerous, presenting a dual threat because their customs could corrupt the holy commonwealth and they resented their loss of lands.

The 1637 war against the Pequots of eastern Connecticut showed the lengths to which the New England settlers could go. The Pequots, a powerful tribe, attempted to unite New England Indians against the English. In May 1637, troops from Massachusetts and Connecticut, with their Indian allies, the Narragansetts, attacked a Pequot village on the Mystic River before dawn, killing hundreds of sleeping women, children, and old men. The Pequots who escaped this

massacre, mostly young men absent from the town, were later executed or enslaved. The Treaty of Hartford (1638) declared their nation dissolved.

Shortly after the Pequot War, in 1638, a group of staunch Puritans established New Haven, on the Long Island Sound west of the Connecticut colony. Persecuted in England, Reverend John Davenport took his flock first to Boston, but decided to move on. They had no charter for New Haven, so the freemen made the Bible their law, eliminating trial by jury, for example, because it had no scriptural basis. Only male church members could vote. The colony grew as the settlers built towns farther west along the sound and on Long

Island. Together, the towns agreed upon a government comprised of a governor, magistrates, and a representative assembly.

Exiles to Rhode Island

The founding of Rhode Island resulted from another kind of emigration from Massachusetts, that of people who refused to submit to the Puritan magistrates. The first was Roger Williams, a likeable but stubborn, independent-minded minister who challenged Massachusetts Bay's policy toward the Indians and its theocratic laws. Williams had studied divinity at Cambridge University, where he became a vocal Separatist. He immigrated to Massachusetts Bay in 1631, arousing the colony when he refused the pulpit in Boston's church because its members had not renounced the Church of England.

Williams then accused Massachusetts of holding fraudulent title to its territory because the king had no authority to give away Indian lands. The colony should send the charter back to the king for correction; the settlers should return to England if they could not obtain rights from the true owners of the land. Williams raised a troublesome issue that the Puritan officials refused to recognize, so they ordered him to be still. He would not be quiet, soon broaching the issues of religious freedom and separation of church and state. "Forced worship stinks in God's nostrils," he proclaimed. "There is no other prudent, Christian way of preserving peace in the world, but by permission of differing consciences." He attacked the laws requiring church attendance and tax support of Puritan churches. Williams feared that government would pollute the church, not that giving legal preference to one religion was unfair. He opposed laws regulating religion to protect the church from state interference.

The General Court banished Williams from Massachusetts for challenging the government; in 1636 he went to Narragansett Bay. There he purchased land from the Narragansett Indians, establishing Providence Plantation at the Great Salt River. With the sympathizers who joined him, he created a society based on religious toleration, separation of church and state, and participation in government by all male property owners. Williams welcomed people of all religions to Providence Plantation, as long as they accepted the right of others to worship freely. Williams himself became wealthy through trade with the Native Americans and the Dutch. In 1638, he transferred ownership of Providence to a group of thirteen associates, of whom he was one.

Another exile from Massachusetts was Anne Hutchinson, a midwife and nurse, who in 1634 arrived in Boston with her husband, merchant William Hutchinson, and children. As Hutchinson assisted women in childbirth and sickness, she became convinced that Bostonians placed too much emphasis on good works and not enough on faith. She was a follower of one of Boston's ministers, the influential John Cotton, who stressed the importance of the individual's relationship with God over the obligation to obey laws. Hutchinson went further than Cotton, nearly saying that if a person were saved it did not matter how she or he behaved, a belief known as the Antinomian heresy.

To the orthodox Puritan faction led by Governor John Winthrop, Hutchinson was a threat for several reasons. She emphasized individual judgment over communal authority, thus questioning the rule of colonial leaders. She told the Puritan patriarchs that God spoke to her directly, that she did not need the assistance of magistrates and ministers in interpreting God's will. Further, Hutchinson went outside the accepted role of women by taking a public stand on religion. But most seriously, she became the standard bearer for a group who contested power with the Winthrop faction. In 1637, Winthrop's government put Hutchinson on trial for defaming ministers and exiled her from the colony. With her family and supporters she founded a colony at Portsmouth on Narragansett Bay.

Following the settlement of Williams and Hutchinson on Narragansett Bay, several other dissenters established colonies there. William Coddington, a supporter of Hutchinson, started the town of Newport; and Samuel Gorton founded Warwick. The four leaders had trouble cooperating, but knew they needed a charter from the English government to avoid annexation by Massachusetts. Roger Williams went to England for that purpose during the Civil War. The 1644 Rhode Island charter, which Parliament granted, united the four settlements under one representative assembly, which could pass statutes consistent with the laws of England. The Rhode Island colonists based their government on Williams's principles of freedom of worship, separation of church and state, and wide participation in government.

The Proprietary Colony of Maryland

In 1632, Charles I granted a charter for Maryland to George Calvert, the first Lord Baltimore, who had served in high office until he converted to Catholicism. Forced to resign, but still a royal favorite, Calvert requested a grant in America to build a haven for Catholics. He also expected to support his family by selling the land. He died before actually obtaining the charter, so his son, Cecilius Calvert, the second Lord Baltimore, became lord proprietor of Maryland. The colony was carved out of the northern part of Virginia. Calvert received ownership of the soil and was sovereign in government, subject only to the king.

Calvert spent £40,000 for two ships, the *Ark* and the *Dove,* with supplies to send the first settlers, who arrived in Maryland in 1634. The proprietor planned a feudal system in which manorial lords received large tracts depending on the number of tenants they transported. For example, a person who brought five laborers to Maryland at a total cost of £20 received a manor of 2,000 acres.

Though Maryland settlers suffered no "starving time" as in Virginia and had a cash crop in tobacco, the colony grew slowly. Mortality was high and immigration sluggish. By 1642, Calvert had granted rights for only sixteen manors, mostly to wealthy Catholic friends. To improve his income, Calvert distributed farms to more ordinary immigrants, who had to pay annual quitrents. Over the seventeenth century, rich investors acquired sixty manors but by far most settlers were small landowners.

The extension of land ownership beyond Calvert's circle of loyal supporters created problems for the lord proprietor. Under the charter, he was obligated to call together an assembly of freemen, or landowners, to enact laws. Calvert interpreted this to mean that they should approve legislation he prepared, while the freemen, meeting first in 1635, claimed the right to draft the code of laws. Calvert refused to accept their draft, so for three years the colony operated without a code. In 1638, they reached a compromise, with the proprietor and assembly each drafting some of the bills. The colony finally had a legal basis for governing and punishing crime.

But the struggle for power between the proprietor and freemen continued. The ordinary planters, who formed the majority of freemen and were mostly Protestant, resented the power of the Catholic elite and had little sympathy for Calvert's vision of a society in which all Christians could worship freely. Religious and political strife became most acute in Maryland during the English Civil War and the Puritan Commonwealth, from 1642 to 1660.

The Impact of the English Civil War

For two decades, the English Civil War altered the political situation in England. The war resulted from a contest for power between Parliament and Charles I. Charles imprisoned opponents without due process, and launched a crusade to force all his subjects, even those in Presbyterian Scotland and Catholic Ireland, to conform to the Anglican church. In 1642, war broke out between the "Cavaliers," or royalists, and the "Roundheads," or parliamentary forces, of whom many were Puritans. Oliver Cromwell led the Roundheads to victory in 1648; the following year they beheaded the king.

The revolutionaries attempted to rule through an elected Parliament, but conflicting factions of Puritans and radical sects undermined their plans. Some radical theorists wanted an entire restructuring of society—in the words of one contemporary, "a world turned upside down." They called for extension of the vote to all men and redistribution of land. The gentry and wealthy merchants who had led Parliament to victory utterly rejected these ideas. In 1653 they

Cecilius Calvert, proprietor of Maryland until 1675, with his grandson and a young enslaved African standing to the side. The Calverts are holding a map of the Chesapeake.
Courtesy Enoch Pratt Free Library, Baltimore

named Cromwell the Lord Protector of the Commonwealth of England, Scotland, and Ireland. He ruled alone, backed by the army, until his death in 1658. An attempt failed to make his son Richard the successor, and two years later, the monarchy was restored. The accession of Charles II did not mean a complete reversal to the time of his father. The king confirmed Parliament's right to approve taxes and abolished the royal courts that had punished opponents of the Crown. But the Restoration brought the Cavaliers back into power, making the Anglican church the state religion once again.

The struggle for power during the Civil War and its aftermath had repercussions in the colonies. Initially, the rebellion of English Puritans against the king raised hopes among New Englanders that English society would be reformed. Of more practical importance to the colonies was the lack of military protection from England. Plymouth, Massachusetts, Connecticut, and New Haven counted among their enemies the French, Dutch, Native Americans, and Rhode Island. In 1643, they formed the New England Confederation, agreeing to share the cost of war, provide soldiers in proportion to population, and make no treaties without each colony's consent. The New England Confederation was the first league of colonies in English North America and the only successful one before the Revolutionary War. In assuming power to conduct war and make treaties, it went beyond colonial rights. The English government, in the midst of Civil War, was too preoccupied to react.

In the Chesapeake colonies, the Civil War and its aftermath were more disruptive. In 1652, the English Commonwealth removed the royalist Virginia governor, William Berkeley, because he had proclaimed Charles II the king upon his father's execution. In Maryland, the parliamentary revolt weakened the position of Lord Baltimore, whose authority came directly from the king. Protestants, especially Puritans, constituted an antiproprietary force. Ironically, the proprietor had encouraged Puritans to migrate from Virginia, where they had suffered Governor Berkeley's persecution. Calvert had approved the "Act Concerning Religion" (1649), which guaranteed freedom of religion to all Christians. Nevertheless, in 1654, the Maryland Puritans established a commonwealth. Their assembly deposed the proprietor's government, restricted the right of Catholics to worship, and created a Puritan code of behavior, including laws against swearing, drunkenness, and breaking the Sabbath. Calvert appealed to Oliver Cromwell, who confirmed his proprietorship, but Lord Baltimore regained control of the colony only in 1657, after a period of local civil war.

Charles II, who became king upon the Restoration of the English monarchy in 1660, fostered colonization in North America, in part, to pay his debts.
The Granger Collection

ENGLISH COLONIZATION AFTER 1660

The accession of Charles II in 1660 initiated a new phase of colonization, in which the English government paid more attention to its colonies than it had before the Civil War. In 1662, the Crown granted Connecticut a charter, and the following year confirmed the charter Rhode Island had received from Parliament. To tighten colonial administration, the king and Parliament approved a series of navigation acts that formed the basis of a mercantilist colonial policy.

Navigation Acts

The English Commonwealth, recognizing the growing economic value of the colonies, had passed the Navigation Act of 1651. The law required that goods brought to England or its colonies from Asia, Africa, or America be carried on English ships (including those of English colonies). Goods from European nations had to be transported on either English ships or those of the country of origin. The chief purposes of the act were to encourage growth of England's merchant marine and to challenge Dutch ascendancy on the seas and in colonial ports. The Commonwealth went further in 1652–1654, with the first Anglo-Dutch War, by attacking Dutch vessels in the English Channel and North Sea.

The Navigation Acts of 1660, 1663, and 1673 confirmed the 1651 restrictions on transport and created a list of "enumerated articles"—major colonial products including tobacco, sugar, indigo, cotton, ginger, and dyewoods—that could be shipped only to England or another English colony. The colonists could not sell these goods directly to other nations. The "articles" first went to England, where they were taxed and reexported by English merchants, who benefited from the business. Conversely, with some exceptions, goods shipped from other nations to the English colonies had to go to England first. The colonists considered these laws detrimental because English middlemen added charges to products going in both directions. The English government created a colonial administration to enforce the acts, but the results were complicated and inefficient. Colonial governors lacked the resources (and in many cases the will) to eliminate smuggling.

Carolina

Charles II was penniless when he ascended the throne and owed substantial debts to his supporters. Expansion of the colonial empire permitted him to repay these creditors and at the same time advance England's commerce and national power. Carolina was the first post-Restoration colony on the North American mainland. In 1663, the area between Virginia and Spanish Florida was unoccupied by Europeans, but Spain had better title to the land than England had. With the Treaty of Madrid (1670), the English obtained Spain's concession of lands north of present-day Charleston. The chief promoters of Carolina were Anthony Ashley Cooper, Governor William Berkeley of Virginia, and John Colleton, a West Indies planter. They obtained help from five men who were close to the king; together the eight associates became proprietors of Carolina. They obtained a charter like Maryland's and received wide latitude in matters of religion. They drew up the "Fundamental Constitutions of Carolina," creating a complicated feudal society with nobles and lords, a scheme the ordinary settlers of Carolina refused to accept.

Two colonies developed in Carolina. Small planters from Virginia built the first, which later became North Carolina. As early as 1653, people had settled on the shores of Albemarle Sound, where they raised tobacco, corn, and livestock. In 1664, Berkeley

sent William Drummond to organize a council and assembly. The Albemarle settlement remained poor, a haven for pirates, and difficult to govern. In 1691, the Carolina proprietors effectively established North Carolina by appointing a separate governor.

The second Carolina colony was located at Charles Town, in the future South Carolina. After two unsuccessful attempts, Anthony Ashley Cooper in 1670 organized a permanent settlement. Many of its early settlers came from the West Indies island of Barbados, which had run out of vacant land. The Barbadian planters had money to develop plantations in Carolina and owned African slaves to do the work. The proprietors offered generous acreages to household heads for each person brought to the colony. A planter, with his own family and several enslaved blacks, could qualify for hundreds of acres. From the colony's founding, a large proportion of South Carolinians were African slaves. They produced food, livestock, firewood, and barrel staves for Barbados.

New York and New Jersey

To control eastern North America, the English next had to seize New Netherland. With a series of outposts, the Dutch held the region between Connecticut and Maryland, including lands on the Delaware River that Sweden had settled in 1638 and the Dutch captured in 1655. The English justified their attack in 1664 against New Netherland on several grounds, including John Cabot's 1497 voyage to the region and Dutch illegal trade with English colonies. Settlers from New England living under Dutch jurisdiction reported that Dutch military defenses were weak. James, the duke of York, Lord High Admiral of the Navy, urged his brother, Charles II, to send a fleet. The king granted James a proprietary charter for lands between the Connecticut and Delaware Rivers, as well as Long Island, Nantucket, Martha's Vineyard, and part of present-day Maine. The charter gave the duke wide governmental powers, even dispensing with an assembly. The duke could write his own legal code as long as it conformed to the laws of England.

With charter in hand, James quickly forced out the Dutch. In 1664, his deputy governor, Richard Nicolls, took New Amsterdam without a fight. The second Anglo-Dutch War (1665–1667) in part resulted from this action. Assuming ownership, James called his colony New York, but granted the land between the Delaware and lower Hudson Rivers to John Lord Berkeley and Sir George Carteret, who named the area New Jersey.

PICTURING THE PAST◆SOCIAL & CULTURAL EVENTS

NEW AMSTERDAM IN 1643

Rare Books Division, The New York Public Library. Astor, Lenox and Tilden Foundations

This view of New Amsterdam suggests a bustling trading port with two successful Dutch inhabitants. Note at the bottom, behind the woman, four African laborers. The illustration reflects both the economic focus and ethnic diversity of New Netherland. The colony welcomed immigrants from many European countries, including France, Germany, and Sweden. Despite official recognition of the established Dutch Reformed Church, people of other religions, including Jews, Quakers, Lutherans, and Puritans, could practice their beliefs.

The West Indian Company imported enslaved Africans into New Netherland to provide much needed labor. By the English takeover in 1664, about 500 slaves lived in the colony, the majority in New Amsterdam. The WIC, which owned many of the Africans, began a policy of offering land and freedom to some individuals. Some others received a status of "half-freedom" in which they owned independent farms but had to provide waged labor to the company when needed. In 1664, about seventy-five free blacks lived in the city.

Despite his extensive powers, James realized that he had to make New York attractive to inhabitants if his colony was to prosper. He gave residents the choice of keeping their Dutch citizenship or becoming naturalized as English subjects. In 1665, he issued a legal code, called the "Duke's Laws," which guaranteed freedom of religion, recognized preexisting titles to land, and allowed New Englanders living in towns on Long Island to choose selectmen. The New York government consisted of a governor and council appointed by the duke, but no legislature.

When England and the Netherlands continued their rivalry in the third Anglo-Dutch War (1672–1674), the Dutch easily recaptured New York. After sixteen months they returned the colony to England as part of the Treaty of Westminster (1674). Receiving a new charter, James resumed possession of New York and reconfirmed his grants to New Jersey. The territory had by then been divided into two colonies, West New Jersey and East New Jersey. Berkeley had sold West New Jersey to a Quaker, Edward Byllinge, who then transferred title to a group of coreligionists, including William

Penn. The duke confirmed Carteret's right to East New Jersey immediately, but waited until 1680 to approve the Quaker proprietorship of West New Jersey.

CONCLUSION

During the first three-quarters of the seventeenth century, the English, French, and Dutch ended Spain's mastery of the New World. By 1675, the English held colonies along the Atlantic coast from New England to the Carolinas. The French controlled Canada and had explored the Great Lakes and the upper Mississippi Valley. The Dutch established, but lost, New Netherland. Spain retained its borderland outposts in New Mexico and Florida. Everywhere the Europeans colonized, the Indians died from epidemic disease. Their relations with the white invaders depended a great deal on the numbers of Europeans who arrived, their attitudes, and goals of settlement.

From the beginning, the English colonies were diverse—in their form of government, degree of stability, relations with Native Americans, and economic base. The Crown fostered this variety by granting charters to an assortment of companies and individuals, including Puritan and Catholic opponents of the established church. Virginia and Maryland prospered from tobacco, but battled persistent high mortality. Still, in the mid-seventeenth century, the Chesapeake was "the best poor man's country" for English people willing to take risks. Most New Englanders came primarily to start a model society based on their Calvinist beliefs. They enjoyed a healthier climate than the people of the Chesapeake, but inferior soil. They supported themselves modestly by fishing and mixed farming, developing trade with the West Indies to pay for English imports. In New Mexico, Hispanic colonists exploited the Pueblos' labor to support their trade with Mexico, while Catholic missionaries tried to claim the Indians's souls. In all three areas—New England, the Chesapeake, and New Mexico—pressures between Europeans and Native Americans, and within the colonial societies, would soon erupt in war.

Recommended Readings

Anderson, Virginia D. *New England's Generation: The Great Migration and the Formation of Society and Culture in the Seventeenth Century.* (1991). Compares the motivations and experiences of Puritan settlers with succeeding generations.

Berlin, Ira. *Many Thousands Gone: The First Two Centuries of Slavery in North America* (1998). An important synthesis of stages in the rise of slavery in the British colonies and Louisiana.

Cronon, William. *Changes in the Land: Indians, Colonists, and the Ecology of New England* (1983). Contrasts Native American and settler use of the environment.

Dunn, Richard S. *Sugar and Slaves: The Rise of the Planter Class in the English West Indies, 1624–1713* (1972). An insightful history of the creation of slave regimes in the English Caribbean.

Greene, Jack P. *Pursuits of Happiness: The Social Development of Early Modern British Colonies and the Formation of American Culture* (1988). Provides a useful framework for understanding the various ways in which British settlements evolved.

Gutiérrez, Ramón A. *When Jesus Came, the Corn Mothers Went Away: Marriage, Sexuality, and Power in New Mexico, 1500–1846* (1991). Provocative evaluation of Spanish settlement, focusing particularly on women's status.

Kupperman, Karen Ordahl. *Indians and English: Facing Off in Early America* (2000). A perceptive analysis of the complexity of Native-European encounters during the early seventeenth century.

Mancall, Peter C. and Merrell, James H., eds. *American Encounters: Natives and Newcomers from European Contact to Indian Removal, 1500–1850* (2000). A collection of path-breaking articles.

Morgan, Edmund S. *American Slavery, American Freedom: The Ordeal of Colonial Virginia* (1975). A detailed, stimulating account of English settlement and the transition to slavery.

Ulrich, Laurel Thatcher. *Good Wives: Image and Reality in the Lives of Women in Northern New England, 1650–1750* (1982). A thoughtful study of the various roles of colonial women.

American Journey Online and InfoTrac College Edition

Visit the source collections at http://ajaccess. wadsworth.com and infotrac.thomsonlearning.com and use the Search function with the following key terms to explore documents, images, audio and video clips, arti-

cles, and commentary related to the material in this chapter.

Jamestown
Plymouth colony
Puritans
Massachusetts Bay colony

Spanish missions
Virginia Company
Anne Hutchinson

Additional resources, exercises, and Internet links related to this chapter are available on the American Passages Web site: http://history.wadsworth.com/passages2e

3 CRISIS AND CHANGE 1675–1720

REBELLIONS AND WAR

WILLIAM PENN'S "HOLY EXPERIMENT"

THE GLORIOUS REVOLUTION AND ITS AFTERMATH

WARS AND RIVALRY FOR NORTH AMERICA

THE ENTRENCHMENT OF SLAVERY IN BRITISH AMERICA

ECONOMIC DEVELOPMENT IN THE BRITISH COLONIES

A 1730 depiction of the slave market in New York Harbor. In Northern port cities, slaveholding was common at this time among upper class and middling families.
Picture Collection, The Branch Libraries, The New York Public Library, Astor, Lenox & Tildon Foundation

I n February 1676, Narragansett Indians burned Lancaster, Massachusetts, killing many of the English settlers and taking others prisoner, including Mary White Rowlandson, a minister's wife, and her three children. The Narragansetts had joined the Wampanoags and other New England Algonquians to destroy the European settlements. Their leader was the Wampanoag sachem, Metacom, called King Philip by the colonists. In the Indians' words, according to Rowlandson, "they would knock all the Rogues in the head, or drive them into the Sea, or make them flie the Country."

Though Rowlandson began her captivity with hatred toward the Indians, whom she called "Barbarous Creatures," she came to respect some as individuals and to appreciate aspects of their culture. She was most impressed, she said, that while the Algonquians had little corn, "I did not see (all the time I was among them) one Man, or Woman, or Child, die with Hunger." They ate "Ground-nuts . . . also Nuts and Acorns, Hartychoaks, Lilly-roots, Ground-beans, and several other weeds and roots that I know not." Desperately hungry, Rowlandson ate unfamiliar foods too, surviving to rejoin her husband in Boston.

King Philip's War, as the English settlers called it, was just one of the crises that afflicted colonial America in the last quarter of the seventeenth century. In Virginia, a comparatively minor skirmish between Indians

CHRONOLOGY

1675 Appointment of English Lords of Trade	**1690** Spanish settlements in Texas
1675–1676 King Philip's War • Bacon's Rebellion	**1691** Massachusetts receives its new charter
1678 Charles II demands renegotiation of Massachusetts charter	**1691–1692** Salem witchcraft hysteria
1680 Popé's Rebellion	**1693** Spanish regain control of New Mexico
1681 William Penn receives Pennsylvania charter	**1696** Board of Trade and Plantations replaces Lords of Trade
1682 La Salle claims the Mississippi Valley for France	**1698** Royal African Company loses slave trade monopoly
1683 Iroquois of New York defeat New France	**1699** French establish Louisiana
1684 Revocation of Massachusetts charter	**1701** Iroquois treaty of neutrality
1685 James II becomes king of England • Dominion of New England created	**1702–1713** Queen Anne's War
1688–1689 Glorious Revolution in England • William and Mary ascend throne	**1704** South Carolina defeats Spanish Florida
1689 Revolutions in Massachusetts, New York, and Maryland	**1712** Slave revolt in New York City
1689–1697 King William's War	**1715** Calverts regain Maryland government • Yamassee War in South Carolina

and whites escalated into Bacon's Rebellion, a civil war among the English settlers. In New Mexico, the Pueblos expelled the Spanish for thirteen years. Following closely upon King Philip's War and Bacon's Rebellion, William Penn intended to avoid conflict with the Indians in founding Pennsylvania. An unstable English government disrupted politics in the colonies when James II, a Roman Catholic, succeeded his brother King Charles II in 1685. James's attempt to make sweeping changes in both the home and colonial governments met strong resistance. The Glorious Revolution quickly ended his reign. In 1689, settlers in Massachusetts, New York, and Maryland overthrew his provincial governments, declaring allegiance to the new king and queen, William and Mary. In Massachusetts, the impact of years of political uncertainty helped spread witchcraft hysteria from Salem to other towns.

Metacom, the Wampanoag leader, who in 1676 tried to drive the New England settlers back "into the Sea."
Courtesy American Antiquarian Society

From 1689 to 1713, European wars spilled into North America, fueling hostilities in Florida and Canada among Native Americans, English, French, and Spanish. The French moved south through the Mississippi Valley and founded Louisiana, while the English pushed south into Florida, west across the Appalachian Mountains, and north into Maine. As the English colonies expanded and matured, their economies and labor systems diverged, particularly with the entrenchment of slavery. Despite revolutions and wars, planters built successful staple crop economies in the southern colonies, while northerners profited from networks of trade with England, Europe, and the West Indies.

REBELLIONS AND WAR

The wars of 1675 to 1680 in New England, Virginia, and New Mexico resulted from pressures that had been building for decades. In Massachusetts, the spread of settlement forced Native Americans to defend their homes. In Virginia, demands of ex-servants for good land precipitated a civil war, while in New Mexico, severe droughts deepened opposition to forced labor, impelling the Pueblos to rid themselves of Spanish overlords. After the upheavals, elites in each settlement made changes that avoided further serious revolt.

Decline of New England Orthodoxy

In 1675, Massachusetts seemed to have lost sight of the goals of its first settlers. When the Indians attacked, Puritan ministers warned the sons and daughters of the founding generation that God was punishing them for their faithlessness and sin.

In fact, Puritan church membership had declined since 1650, especially among men. After midcentury, women became a large proportion of the "elect," comprising 60 percent, and in some congregations 75 percent, of newly admitted members. The ministers believed that men were becoming more worldly, thus undermining the church's social and political authority. A related problem was that the children of nonchurch members could not be baptized. In 1662, the clergy devised an alternative to full church membership, the Half-Way Covenant, which permitted adults who had been baptized but who were not yet saved to be "half-way" members. In congregations that accepted this innovation (not all churches did), people could assume partial status by showing that they understood Christian principles

The Hingham, Massachusetts, church was originally built in 1681, when ship carpenters framed the interior of the roof as a ship's keel in reverse (left). The exterior view (right) reflects renovations completed in the eighteenth century.
The Structure of Praise by Arthur Mazmarian © 1970 by Beacon Press. Reprinted by permission of Beacon Press, Boston

and would strive to obey God. As unconverted members, they were not entitled to take communion, but could have their children baptized.

The growth of competing religions in New England also proved to Puritan ministers that the model society had failed. Believing theirs to be the only true religion, Puritans rooted out dissent. After 1650, the Quakers and Baptists threatened religious unity. The Society of Friends, or Quakers, was a radical Protestant sect born in the turmoil of the English Civil War. Like the Puritans, they were reformers who believed that the Church of England was corrupt and should be purified of its rituals, decorations, and hierarchy. But the Quakers went even further. They claimed that the Puritans also practiced false doctrine by paying ministers to preach, relying too much on the Bible as the word of God, and retaining the sacraments of baptism and communion. The Friends believed that God communicated directly with individuals through the "Spirit" or "Light." They worshipped by gathering in plain meetinghouses to "wait upon the Lord." In worship services, they had no Bible reading, prepared sermon, music, or ritual. Rather, they waited in silence for the Spirit to inspire one or several of the congregation to communicate God's message. Ministers, who included women as well as men, regularly re-

ceived inspiration to speak. They required no advanced learning because their words were supposed to come straight from God, not from a prepared text.

Appalled by these Quaker teachings, Puritan leaders tried to prevent their spread by deporting the traveling missionaries. The Friends were stubborn, however, repeatedly returning to Massachusetts. They interrupted Puritan church services, preached in the streets, and made some converts among the people. The Puritan magistrates arrested and whipped them, even cropping their ears. In 1658, the General Court prescribed the death penalty for Quakers who returned after banishment.

The hangings of several Quaker missionaries caused consternation on both sides of the Atlantic. When Charles II demanded an explanation, the Puritans ended the executions. The magistrates continued to persecute nonconformers, but over the decades following 1660 realized that their policy of intolerance had failed. Rhode Island served as a base for Quaker missionaries to evangelize in the Puritan colonies, further supporting its reputation among Puritans as "the sewer of New England." The Baptists, whose objection to infant baptism was their chief disagreement with orthodox Puritans, increased in numbers after approval of the Half-Way Covenant, which they vehemently opposed. They believed that a church should

A QUAKER WOMAN PREACHING

QUAQUERESSE qui preche.

Courtesy of Special Collections, University Research Library, University of California at Los Angeles

The Quakers were unique among English religions in the seventeenth century in recognizing women as ministers. Women were among the earliest followers of George Fox of England, considered the founder of Quakerism around 1650. Female missionaries then traveled through the British Isles, Europe, and America. They believed that God spoke through them, and they hoped to convince others of the "Light."

In New England, the women ministers challenged both the Puritan faith and expectations of female subordination. When Quaker missionaries interrupted church services and gained followers, Massachusetts leaders banished them and threatened to execute those who returned to the colony. Several were hanged, including Mary Dyer in 1660, who had determined to "look their bloody laws in the face." This illustration was published somewhat later, in (J. F. Bernard), *The Ceremonies and Religious Customs of the Various Nations of the Known World . . .* (1733–1739), when Quakers had become less controversial and worshipped openly in Massachusetts.

---

include only the saved, indeed that only the saved should be baptized. Despite persecution, dissenters successfully formed congregations throughout New England.

King Philip's War

The unceasing expansion of white settlers into the frontier destroyed the relative peace between the Algonquians and the settlers of New England. By 1675, more than 50,000 whites inhabited the region. The colonists had large families of sons and daughters who desired farms of their own. These settlers occupied more and more of the hunting, fishing, and agricultural lands of the Indians.

Since the massacre of the Pequots in 1637, the Puritans and Native Americans of New England had managed an uneasy peace. The colonists traded for furs with local nations and with the Mohawks, the closest nation of Iroquois in New York. Some Puritan ministers, of whom John Eliot is best known, convinced several local tribes who were greatly diminished by disease and

loss of lands to dwell in "praying towns." In these villages, adjacent to but separate from the towns of white settlers, the Indians were supposed to adopt English customs and learn the fundamentals of Puritan religion. By 1674, Eliot had organized fourteen praying towns of Native Americans who took the first steps toward giving up their traditional ways.

Many New England Indians, including Wampanoags and Narragansetts, did not form praying towns, but even so remained allies of the Puritan governments for many years. Trouble began in 1671, when the Plymouth government attempted to force the Wampanoags to surrender their firearms and obtain permission to sell land. Metacom (or King Philip) built a league with neighboring tribes. When John Sassamon, an Indian educated at Harvard College, informed the Plymouth government of impending attack and was murdered, the white authorities hanged three Wampanoags for the deed.

In 1675, Metacom mobilized Algonquians throughout New England, attacking fifty-two English towns. White refugees fled to Boston. But by the end of

Mary Rowlandson's Narrative of Her Capture by Narragansett Indians, 1676

Mary Rowlandson was the wife of the minister of Lancaster, Massachusetts, which the Narragansetts assaulted in 1676 during King Philip's War. The following account of the attack, taken from the published narrative of her captivity, illustrates the religious framework in which she cast her experiences.

At length they came and beset our own House, and quickly it was the dolefullest day that ever mine eyes saw. The House stood upon the edge of a Hill; some of the *Indians* got behind the Hill, others into the Barn, and others behind any thing that would shelter them; from all which Places they shot against the House, so that the Bullets seemed to fly like Hail; and quickly they wounded one Man among us, then another, and then a third. About two Hours (according to my observation in that amazing time) they had been about the House before they could prevail to fire it. . . . They fired it once, and one [colonist] ventured out and quenched it; but they quickly fired it again, and that took.

Now is that dreadful Hour come that I have often heard of, (in the time of the War, as it was the Case of others,) but now mine Eyes see it. Some in our House were fighting for their Lives, others wallowing in their Blood; the House on fire over our Heads, and the bloody Heathen ready to knock us on the Head if we stirred out. Now might we hear Mothers and Children crying out for themselves and one another, *Lord, what shall we do?* Then I took my Children (and one of my Sisters, hers) to go forth and leave the House; but as soon as we came to the Door and appeared, the *Indians* shot so thick that the Bullets rattled against the House as if one had taken an handful of Stones and threw them; so that we were fain to give back. We had six stout Dogs belonging to our Garrison, but none of them would stir, though another time, if an *Indian* had come to the Door, they were ready to fly upon him, and tear him down. The Lord hereby would make us the more to acknowledge his Hand, and to see that our Help is always in him. But out we must go, the Fire increasing and coming along behind us roaring, and the *Indians* gaping before us with their Guns, Spears, and Hatchets to devour us. . . .

The Bullets flying thick, one went thorow my side, and the same (as would seem) thorow the Bowels and Hand of my dear Child in my Arms. One of my eldest Sister's Children (named William) had then his Leg broken, which the *Indians* perceiving, they knock'd him on the head. Thus were we butchered by those merciless Heathen, standing amazed, with the Blood running down to our Heels. My elder sister, being yet in the House, and seeing those woful Sights, the Infidels hauling Mothers one way and Children another, and some wallowing in their Blood, and her elder son telling her that (her Son) William was dead, and myself was wounded; she said, *And, Lord, let me die with them!* which was no sooner said but she was struck with a Bullet, and fell down dead over the Threshold. I hope she is reaping the Fruit of her good Labours, being faithful to the Service of God in her Place. In her younger years she lay under much trouble upon Spiritual accounts, till it pleased God to make that precious Scripture take hold of her Heart, *2 Cor.* xii. 9, *And he said unto me, My grace is sufficient for thee.* More than twenty years after, I have heard her tell how sweet and comfortable that Place was to her. But to return: the *Indians* laid hold of us, pulling me one way and the Children another, and said, *Come, go along with us.* I told them they would kill me. They answered, *If I were willing to go along with them, they would not hurt me.* . . .

I had often before this said, that if the *Indians* should come, I should chuse rather to be killed by them than taken alive; but when it came to the trial my mind changed; their glittering Weapons so daunted my Spirit, that I chose rather to go along with those (as I may say) ravenous Bears, than that moment to end my daies.

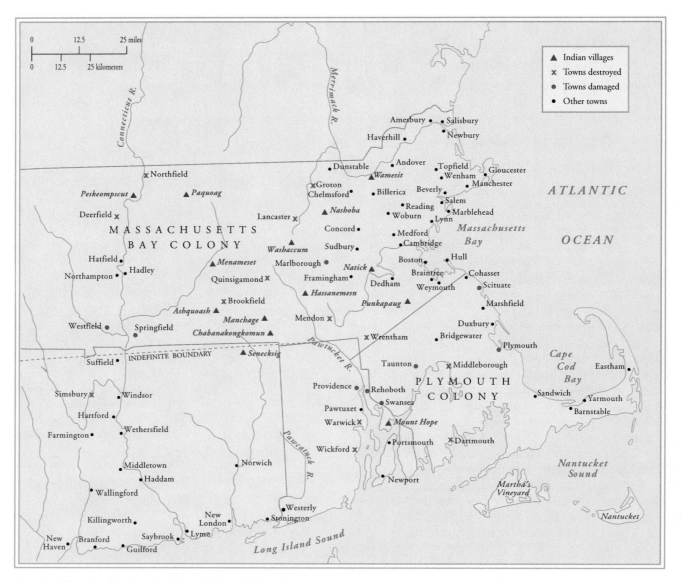

Map 3.1 *New England at the Time of King Philip's War, 1675–1676*
The Indians and English destroyed and damaged each other's towns throughout Plymouth, Rhode Island, and Massachusetts. The Narragansetts, who lived in Rhode Island and had assisted the Puritan governments against the Pequots in 1637, entered King Philip's War after an English army invaded their territory.

summer 1676, with the help of the Mohawks, the colonial governments turned back the attack, as disease, hunger, and a weapons shortage weakened Metacom's troops. The war took a heavy toll on both sides, for the Algonquians destroyed twelve towns and killed many colonists. White frontier settlement would not reach its 1675 limits for another forty years.

For the Indians of southern New England, the war was calamitous. Thousands died and many others were enslaved. Even bands who supported the English

lost autonomy. At the outbreak of war, the colonists had forced residents of the praying towns to live on desolate Deer Island in Boston Harbor, where they suffered from lack of food and shelter. Some of the Indian men later fought in the colonial militia against Metacom, but when the war was over, all Native Americans in southern New England had to live in praying towns, where they worked as servants or tenant farmers for neighboring whites. Metacom was killed, his head paraded before the white settlements and kept on a pole in Plymouth for twenty years; his wife and son were sold as slaves.

War in the Chesapeake

Just as New England struggled over land in King Philip's War, Virginia faced a similar crisis in Bacon's Rebellion. The Chesapeake uprising involved civil war among the English as well as Indian-white conflict. But at its root, the chief issue was land: how could the competing interests of landless immigrants and dispossessed natives be resolved? Since the 1640s, the white population of Virginia and Maryland had grown quickly. By 1670, approximately 40,000 colonists lived in the Chesapeake, including native-born sons and daughters of early settlers as well as more recent arrivals. Among the new immigrants were servants who expected to obtain land upon completing their terms. In the 1670s, however, many Virginians discovered that the combination of low tobacco prices and high land prices blocked their dream of obtaining plantations. They received headrights, but could find no good vacant tobacco land to claim.

Part of the problem, these landless freemen believed, was that the Indians held too much territory. Specifically, the 1646 treaty between the Virginia government and the Powhatans designated the area north of the York River for Native Americans. This agreement had been acceptable to whites in the 1640s when space south of the York seemed ample, but was unsatisfactory thirty years later, when white settlement was pushing north. It was also true, many freemen recognized, that wealthy planters, powerful in govern-

ment, speculated in large acreages that they left empty while others starved for land.

The first flames of war occurred in July 1675, when some Doeg Indians attempted to take hogs as payment for a settler's unpaid debt. After people on both sides were killed, the Susquehannocks got involved. When they attacked frontier settlements, a thousand-man army of Virginia and Maryland colonists marched against their village on the Potomac River. Vastly outnumbered, several Susquehannock sachems agreed to negotiate, but when they left their stockade, the colonists murdered them. During the winter of 1675–1676, the Susquehannocks retaliated, raising fears that King Philip's War had spread south. Discontented and vengeful colonists responded indiscriminately, killing friendly neighboring Indians rather than those who were actually attacking the frontier.

The landless freemen found a leader in Nathaniel Bacon. Only twenty-nine years old, Bacon had come to Virginia with enough money to purchase a large plantation. Governor Berkeley nominated him to the Virginia council, despite his youth. Nevertheless, Bacon evidently saw his opportunity to challenge Berkeley for leadership of the colony by mobilizing freemen and small planters against the Indians. While Berkeley wanted peace with the Susquehannocks, Bacon's forces intended to annihilate all of the natives. The settlers knew that the natives were weak, with just a fraction of their pre-1607 population. Bacon's supporters also demanded a greater voice in the Virginia government.

Governor Berkeley declared Bacon a traitor and sent troops to end his forays against the Indians. He

Metacom's war club, inlaid with wampum beads. This club was stolen in 1970 from the Fruitlands Museum in Harvard, Massachusetts.
Department of Special Collections, Charles E. Young Research Library, UCLA

*P*ICTURING THE PAST✦ECONOMICS & TECHNOLOGY

MARYLAND PLANTER'S HOUSE

Courtesy of Historic St. Mary's City

This is a reconstruction of a typical Chesapeake colonist's house at the Godiah Spray tobacco plantation at historic St. Mary's City, Maryland. Most dwellings in the seventeenth-century Chesapeake were impermanent structures of wood. Many had only one room, without glass windows or wooden floors. They decayed quickly from the hot, humid climate and insects. Scholars have used archeological evidence and historical documents to determine the size and construction of these cabins.

Despite the growth of large plantations in Virginia and Maryland between 1675 and 1720, more than one-third of white families lived in small cabins and rented rather than owned land. The men who supported Nathaniel Bacon came from this group. They rarely owned servants or slaves to help grow tobacco. They possessed some livestock and agricultural tools, but most used wooden rather than pottery dishes, and lacked bed and table linens, knives, forks, spices, and books.

---

also called new elections that brought many Bacon supporters into the House of Burgesses. The delegates passed measures that extended suffrage to landless freemen, taxed provincial councilors, and placed limits on the terms and fees of local officials. These efforts failed to end the rebellion, as Bacon's army burned Jamestown. For months, Virginians plundered the plantations of neighbors who took the other side. Few white fatalities occurred, however, as rebels vented most of their frustration by killing Indians. The rebellion finally ceased with Bacon's death, probably of dysentery, in October 1676. The war marked a serious defeat for the Indians of the Chesapeake, who lost the protection of the 1646 treaty and gradually surrendered their lands.

Bacon's Rebellion awakened the Virginia elites to the dangers of a large class of landless freemen, but resulted in no substantive political change. A new assembly in 1677 reversed the reform acts of the 1676

House of Burgesses, including the law extending the vote to landless freemen. A commission appointed by the Crown to end the rebellion also opposed expanding popular power, stating that to grant suffrage to unpropertied men was "repugnant to the Lawes of England and to the Lawes and Peace of the Colony." The commission did call for taxing "the great Ingrossers of Lands" who caused "misery and mischiefs" by "occasioning the Planters to stragle to such remote distances when they cannot find land neerer to seat themselves but by being Tenants which in a Continent they think hard," but nothing was done. Rather than create a society in which power and wealth were distributed more evenly, in which Virginia once again would offer opportunity to poor Englishmen, the planter elite began importing more enslaved Africans. Bound for life and restricted by laws, black slaves could not demand farms or a voice in government. With settlement in New Jersey, Carolina, and Penn-

Sir William Berkeley was governor of Virginia for more than a quarter century. He alienated landless Virginians by ignoring their grievances and by attempting to keep peace with the Indians.
Courtesy of R.J.G. Berkeley-Berkeley Castle, and Jamestown-Yorktown Foundation

sylvania during the 1670s and 1680s, immigrants had better options than Virginia.

The Pueblo Revolt

Four years after Bacon's Rebellion, across the continent in New Mexico, the Pueblos drove out the Spanish—and kept them out for thirteen years. The Pueblos had the advantage of a much smaller white population in New Mexico—2,800—than in New England or the Chesapeake. The Spanish hold over the missions was tenuous, for native fighting men greatly outnumbered Spanish troops. Nevertheless, the Hispanic settlers and priests demanded forced labor and strict adherence to Christianity. A number of Indian towns had rebelled during the previous half century, but most failed to win autonomy.

The Pueblos became more desperate during the 1670s, when New Mexico endured severe drought. As famine persisted, they faced Apache and Navajo attacks. The Pueblos became convinced that the root of their troubles lay in their rejection of ancient gods, the *katsina*. To bring rain and renewed prosperity, some presented gifts to the katsina and performed dances that the Spanish had outlawed. When punished for abandoning Catholicism, the Indians felt even greater resentment, leading to revolt.

The leader of the 1680 rebellion was Popé, a medicine man of the village of San Juan, north of Santa Fe. When the katsina told him that the Spanish must be driven from the land, he organized a general insurrection, sending knotted ropes to allied villages, indicating when the uprising should start. On August 10, 1680, the Pueblos launched a full-scale attack, killing 400 colonists and twenty-one priests. Strategically, the Indians confiscated or destroyed the settlers' chief means of transportation, their horses and mules. When Santa Fe fell to the rebels on September 21, the whites escaped south, settling in the area of present-day Ciudad Juárez, Mexico. Some Spaniards explained the revolt as God's punishment for their sins, whereas others blamed the harsh labor and efforts to repress native religions. As Popé supervised, the Pueblos destroyed churches, broke up church bells, and burned images of Christ and the saints. According to one witness, "in order to take away their baptismal names, the water, and the holy oils, [the Indians] were to plunge into the rivers and wash themselves."

Several times during the next few years, the Spanish attempted unsuccessfully to retake New Mexico. The rebellion spread south into northern Mexico, where Native Americans demolished settlements and missions. But by 1692, as famine continued, the Pueblo alliance fell into disarray. The new Spanish governor of New Mexico, Don Diego de Vargas, marched north to Santa Fe with 160 troops. Though many Indians resisted, the Spanish reestablished control over the province. In December 1693, after a three-day siege, Vargas's troops took Santa Fe, killing all of the Indian men and making slaves of the women and children. The Spanish subsequently retained a foothold in New Mexico, but not without further struggle. The Pueblos rejected the Franciscan missionaries, revolting once again in 1696. Some Pueblos fled from New Mexico while others submitted as Vargas systematically conquered the Indian towns once again. After 1696, the Spanish and Pueblos lived together in relative peace, but only because

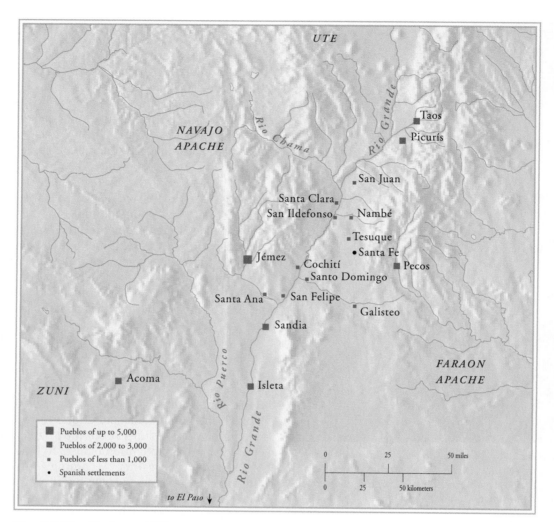

Map 3.2 *New Mexico, c. 1680*
The Spanish had established their colony in 1598 by sending soldiers, their families, and Franciscan missionaries north through the Rio Grande Valley. In 1680, the Spanish population remained small and centered in the capital, Santa Fe.

the Hispanics eased requirements for tribute, forced labor, and adherence to Christianity.

WILLIAM PENN'S "HOLY EXPERIMENT"

In England, the Quaker leader William Penn approached Charles II with a petition to establish a new colony in America, one that would avoid bloodshed by dealing justly with the Indians. While the Pueblos had not yet driven out the Spanish, Penn knew of King Philip's War and Bacon's Rebellion. He was determined to do things differently in Pennsylvania.

Plans for Pennsylvania

Penn had inherited a £16,000 debt owed to his father by the king, but had little hope for repayment in cash, so he requested a colony on the west bank of the Delaware River. The king approved Penn's request in 1681, granting him a charter for Pennsylvania that was more restrictive than Lord Baltimore's, in part because the English government was attempting to assert greater control over its colonies, in part because Penn was a Quaker. The new proprietor received the right to enact laws and impose taxes with the consent of the freemen, but was required to submit all laws for approval to the home government within five years of passage. And to protect the status of the Church of England, the charter stipulated that twenty Anglican inhabitants could request a minister from the bishop of London.

In establishing Pennsylvania, Penn hoped to provide a haven for Quakers, who faced persecution in England because they would not pay tithes for church support or attend Anglican services. Friends also refused to give oaths, so they could not legally pledge allegiance to the king. A Quaker ideal was to live according to the doctrine that all were equal in the eyes of God; thus they rejected certain customs, such as removing one's hat in the presence of superiors. For practicing their faith, they were jailed and fined, and when they refused to pay, local English officials took their property.

William Penn conceived of his colony as a "holy experiment," a place where Quakers could exercise their beliefs without interference and the government would operate like a Quaker meeting, acting in unison as it followed God's will. Penn also intended to pay the Lenape Indians for tracts of land and to set up arbitration panels of Native Americans and colonists to resolve conflicts peacefully. He paid the Lenapes a much lower price than he in turn charged the settlers, however, and assumed the Indians would leave after they sold their land.

Like Lord Baltimore, Penn intended to make a fortune from Pennsylvania, summing up his goals: "the service of God first, the honor and advantage of the king, with our own profit." Despite Penn's strong Quaker convictions, which for some suggested a simple life, he appreciated fine food, drink, and accommodations. He possessed large landholdings in southern England and Ireland, retained many servants, and enjoyed such delicacies as salmon, partridges, saffron, and chocolate. Urgently needing money, he thought the sale of millions of acres in America would solve his financial problems.

Penn spent a great deal of time planning the colony. His scheme of government established an assembly with two houses, both elected by the freemen. Freemen included adult males who owned at least fifty acres of land or paid taxes on other property. During the early decades, when servants received fifty acres at the end of their terms, nearly every man in Pennsylvania could vote. Penn did not extend that right to women, nor did he alter the common law restrictions on married women. Though women Friends took an active role in their meetings as ministers, missionaries, and supervisors of discipline, their legal status in the Quaker commonwealth was similar to that in other colonies. Penn's laws stood out in another respect, however, requiring capital punishment for just two offenses, treason and murder.

Drawing of William Penn, by Francis Place. A wealthy Quaker, Penn sought to create a model society in Pennsylvania.
The Historical Society of Pennsylvania

The proprietor's planning went beyond politics, for he also drew up specifications for his capital city. In designing Philadelphia, in taking on the role of city planner, Penn was unique among early English colonizers. He conceived the city as a large "green country town," with wide streets in a grid pattern, public parks, ample lots, and brick houses. He failed to fulfill his plan completely because he could not obtain enough acreage to build Philadelphia as he wanted. Dutch and Swedish residents already owned the land along the Delaware River, so Penn decided to buy a site of just 1,200 acres between the Delaware and Schuylkill Rivers. His plan remained orderly, with the grid design and parks, but with lots of one-half to one acre instead of one hundred acres for those who purchased "proprietary shares" of 5,000 acres. To maintain a constant income from the colony, landowners would pay annual quitrents.

A Diverse Society

Penn sold land briskly, as 600 people bought 700,000 acres within four years. Most of the buyers were Quaker farmers, merchants, artisans, and shopkeepers from England, though many also originated from

P

DUTCH EDITION OF SOME ACCOUNT

Een kort Bericht
Van de Provintie ofte Landfchap
PENN-SYLVANIA
genaemt, leggende in
AMERICA;
Nu onlangs onder het groote Zegel van Engeland
gegeven aan
WILLIAM PENN, &c.
MITSGADERS
Van de Privilegien, ende Macht om
het felve wel te Regeeren.
Uyt het Engels overgefet na de Copye tot London gedrukt by *Benja-min Clark*, Boekverkooper in George Yard Lombardftreet, 1681.
Waer by nu gevoegt is de Notificatie van s'Konings Placcaet/
in date van den 2 April 1681. waar inne de tegenwoordige
Inwoonders van PENN-SYLVANIA, belaft word
WILLEM PENN en zijn Erfgenamen, als volkomene
Epgenaars en Gouverneurs, te gehoorfamen.
Als mede,
De Copye van een Brief by den felven W.P. gefchreven aan
zekere Regeeringe Anno 1675. tegens de Vervolginge
en voor de Vryheyt van Confcientie, aan alle &c.

Tot ROTTERDAM,
Gedrukt by PIETER VAN WYNBRUGGE, Boek-Drukker in de
Leeuweftraat, in de Wereld Vol-Druk. *Anno* 1681.

The Historical Society of Pennsylvania

William Penn had his promotional pamphlet, *Some Account of the Province of Pennsylvania in America; Lately Granted under the Great Seal of England to William Penn, &c. Together with Privileges and Powers necessary to the well-governing thereof,* translated into Dutch and German. He had traveled in Holland and Germany in 1677 and now made use of contacts to generate sales of land in his colony. Penn wrote to Quakers throughout England, Scotland, Ireland, and Wales and sent promotional tracts.

Some Account discussed the benefits of colonies to prospective settlers and to England, described the climate and natural resources of Pennsylvania, outlined Penn's proposed government, and set the terms for buying land. Penn offered useful advice on what to pack, including "all sorts of apparel and utensils" for farming, construction, and domestic use. He added, for those who had heard of harsh conditions in early Virginia and Massachusetts, that America had advanced by 1681, "for there is better accommodation, and English provisions are to be had at easier rates."

Scotland, Ireland, Wales, Europe, the West Indies, Maryland, and New York.

Penn's settlers moved into an area inhabited by the Lenapes, who welcomed the newcomers, and by Swedes, Finns, and Dutch, who served as intermediaries with the Indians. The Lenapes, or Delawares as the colonists later called them, had conducted trade with the Dutch as early as 1610 and yielded land to the whites. Because Dutch and Swedish settlements remained small, relatively few violent incidents occurred. By the time Penn arrived with thousands of colonists, the Lenapes had declined significantly from disease. As they sold their lands, some moved to northern or western Pennsylvania, while others remained on marginal tracts in the Delaware Valley.

The European "old residents" integrated with the new arrivals, though not without friction. Some earned money by selling land and provisions, or serv-

ing as guides and interpreters. One local Swede, Captain Lasse Cock, in 1682 translated for the Indians and English, and traveled to the Susquehanna and Lehigh Rivers as Penn's emissary. The Swedes, Dutch, and Finns continued to worship in their own congregations, but became naturalized as English subjects and some served in the assembly and local government. The old residents made up a large part of the population in the Lower Counties (later Delaware), leading to conflict as the different interests of the Lower Counties and Pennsylvania became clear. In 1704, after two decades of wrangling, the three southern counties obtained their own separate Delaware assembly.

Pennsylvania got a boost from its late arrival on the colonial scene because its merchants could tap existing networks in the Atlantic economy. Substantial traders came from New York, the Chesapeake, and the West Indies, bringing their connections and capital to

Wampum belt, which, according to legend, the Lenape gave to William Penn in 1682. It has become a symbol of Penn's efforts to preserve peace with the Indians of Pennsylvania.
The Historical Society of Pennsylvania

build breweries, tanneries, warehouses, wharves, and ships. Farmers found a market for wheat, livestock, and lumber in the West Indies. By 1700, Philadelphia became a thriving port town, with 700 houses and more than 3,000 people.

But for William Penn, his colony was deeply disappointing, as land sales reaped smaller profits than he had hoped and the costs of administering the colony soared. When purchasers refused to send him quitrents, he went more seriously into debt. Penn traveled to his colony twice, but stayed a total of only four years. Although the province became prosperous and quite successful as a tolerant, diverse society, he reckoned it a failure.

THE GLORIOUS REVOLUTION AND ITS AFTERMATH

The founding of Pennsylvania coincided with the Crown's effort to tighten colonial government. Compared with the Spanish empire, English administration was a hodgepodge. The Privy Council at first appointed temporary committees to address colonial concerns, then in 1675 formed a permanent committee, the Lords of Trade, which met sporadically. Even after 1696, when the more formalized Board of Trade and Plantations was established, this body could gather information and give advice, but lacked authority to appoint colonial officials or enforce laws. These powers belonged to a host of governmental offices, including the secretary of state, the Treasury, and the War Office.

Dominion of New England

While experimenting with these committees, the Crown made other efforts to rein in the colonies. Most vulnerable was the Massachusetts Bay colony, both for its unrestrictive charter and the perceived intransigence of Puritan leaders. In 1678, Charles II required Massachusetts to send agents empowered to renegotiate the charter. He specifically wanted the New Englanders to comply with the Navigation Acts and apologize for having coined their own money. The colonists delayed action, though they sent regrets for having passed laws contrary to the laws of England. They offered to renounce any "except such as the repealling whereof will make us to renounce the professed cause of our first coming hither."

Impressed by neither the Puritans' arguments nor the speed of their response, the English government brought legal proceedings against the Massachusetts Bay Company for "usurping to be a body Politick," and revoked the charter in 1684. The colony's assembly, the General Court, was prohibited from meeting. In February 1685, before a royal governor could be appointed, Charles died and his brother James became king. James II quickly took advantage of events to move toward centralizing the colonies. With the Privy Council's consent, in 1685, he combined Massachusetts, New Hampshire, and Maine under the Dominion of New England, added Plymouth, Rhode Island, and Connecticut in 1686, and New York and New Jersey in 1688. Apparently, James's plan for the colonies was to create two large dominions, one north of the fortieth degree of latitude (the approximate location of Philadelphia) and one to the south. These dominions would supersede colonial charters, eliminating the confusing diversity of laws and political structures. Representative government would end.

For Massachusetts Puritans, the Dominion of New England was a disaster. James's governor-general, Sir Edmund Andros, made sweeping changes that undercut the Puritan notion of a covenanted community. He levied taxes without the approval of a representative assembly, restricted the power of town

Roman Catholic, he installed his friends in office and defied Parliament. Protestants feared James would make England a Catholic nation under authoritarian rule. Thus, parliamentary leaders forced him into exile in France, inviting his Protestant daughter Mary and her husband William of Orange, the leader of the Dutch, to take the throne. The Glorious Revolution, though bloodless, had long-lasting results in England: it permanently limited the king's power by establishing parliamentary control of taxation, supremacy of law, and autonomy of the courts.

In the morning of April 18, 1689, many of Boston's populace formed companies with the militia. Numbering more than one thousand by afternoon, the insurgents, who included several Puritan ministers and some wealthy merchants, deposed the dominion government. They interpreted the revocation of the charter and James's illegal taxation and expropriation of lands as part of a "popish plot" that Protestant New England must help destroy.

With the dominion gone, Plymouth, Rhode Island, and Connecticut reactivated their charters, but

James II at the time of his accession in 1685, by Godfrey Kneller. An opponent of representative government, James was quickly deposed in the Glorious Revolution of 1688.
By Courtesy of the National Portrait Gallary, London

meetings, mandated religious toleration, and confiscated a Boston church for use by Anglicans. Andros enforced the Navigation Acts, favored his own cronies over the Puritan elite in distributing patronage, required landowners to obtain new land titles from the Crown, demanded payment of quitrents, and took control of common lands. A number of colonists rebelled, refusing to pay taxes without a voice in their passage, but were jailed and fined.

Revolutions of 1689

Governor Andros managed to avoid serious revolt until the spring of 1689, when news of James's removal from the throne reached Massachusetts. The king's rule had been as heavy-handed in England as in the colonies. A

A nineteenth-century rendering of Sir Edmund Andros's unpopularity in Boston, by Howard Pyle. Through Andros, James II disbanded colonial governments in New England and New York, creating his Dominion of New England.
The Granger Collection

Massachusetts, which had lost its charter under Charles II, had to negotiate a new one. The colonists' arguments for the charter were based less on the old covenant theory than on the fundamentals of the Glorious Revolution, especially the right of English people to representative government. The resulting 1691 Massachusetts charter, which annexed Plymouth to the Bay colony, established a royal province with an elected assembly and a governor appointed by the king. The charter required freedom of worship and forbade religious restrictions on voting.

Revolutions also took place in New York and Maryland in the wake of James II's loss of power. New York fell into turmoil with news of William and Mary's ascent to the throne in England and the revolt in Boston. The reports unleashed opposition to Lieutenant Governor Francis Nicholson, who headed the dominion's government in New York. Again the struggle was defined in religious terms, as a crusade to destroy the "papist" threat.

In the city of New York, insurgents included merchants and artisans who had been denied economic privileges to trade and mill flour under James's government. In 1689, led by Jacob Leisler, a German-born merchant and militia captain, they forced Nicholson back to England and elected a Committee of Safety to replace James's council. When Henry Sloughter, the new governor appointed by William and Mary, arrived in 1691, however, he reinstalled James's councilors and executed Leisler for treason. Despite Leisler's early proclamation of the new monarchs in 1689, his enemies had better connections in London.

In Maryland, simmering resentment of Protestants against the Roman Catholic proprietor, Charles, Lord Baltimore, erupted in the summer of 1689. Baltimore's troubles intensified when his nephew, George Talbot, president of the provincial council, murdered the king's customs collector "with a dagger newly prepared and sharpened" aboard a royal ship. This event rocked the colony, so Baltimore sent a man he thought would provide strong leadership as governor, William Joseph, a Roman Catholic and adherent of James II. Upon arrival in 1688, Joseph proceeded to alienate Maryland's assemblymen, calling them adulterers and drunks. When he required them to renew their oaths of fidelity to the proprietor, they refused.

In July 1689, a handful of Maryland leaders formed the Protestant Association. Aroused by rumors that Catholics were plotting with the Indians to destroy the Protestants, the Association raised troops, defeating the proprietary government without a shot. The rebels obtained articles of surrender that banned Catholics from provincial offices; sent a message to William and Mary informing them of the takeover and requesting a Protestant government; and elected an assembly—the "Associators' Convention"—that ruled Maryland for the next two and one-half years.

The three provincial revolutions of 1689, in Massachusetts, New York, and Maryland, had similarities to England's Glorious Revolution in the relative absence of bloodshed and the recurring theme of "popish plots." They failed, however, to bring about permanent change in the constitutional relationship between England and its colonies. The provincials, lacking delegates in Parliament, continued to endure taxation and mercantilist regulation without their assent. The colonial revolts of 1689 resembled Bacon's Rebellion of 1676, as they mobilized out-of-power elites against those who controlled the colonial governments. In 1676, in Virginia, the insurgents had manipulated landless discontents by appealing to hatred against Native Americans as well as grievances against Berkeley's government. In 1689, the leading rebels employed the twin specters of authoritarianism and Catholicism, with rumors of impending French and Indian attack, to gain support from the populace.

Witchcraft in New England

In May 1692, Governor William Phips arrived in Boston Harbor with the new Massachusetts charter. He found the colony in disarray. Symptomatic of the Massachusetts state of affairs was the witchcraft hysteria that had erupted months earlier in Salem Village, a farming community north of Boston. Since 1675, the Bay colony had one crisis after another— King Philip's War, loss of the charter, Andros's dominion, the Revolution of 1689. Accompanying this turmoil were structural changes in the society, as traditional religious authority yielded to elites whose power rested on mercantile wealth. The Salem witch mania was a tragic holdover from a passing culture. Its fury was aggravated by the psychological reaction of traditionally minded folk to the new, more commercial, secular society of turn-of-century New England.

Belief in witchcraft was embedded in European and Anglo-American culture, though, ironically, it was losing force by the time of the Salem outbreak. The colonists, like their contemporaries in the Old World, believed that both God and Satan influenced everyday events. When something bad happened that they could not explain, people turned to supernatural

⊕ The Trial of Bridget Bishop, an Accused Witch, Salem, 1692

This report of Bridget Bishop's trial, published by Cotton Mather in *Wonders of the Invisible World*, shows the grounds, including spectral evidence, on which Massachusetts courts convicted women and men of practicing witchcraft. In Goody Bishop's case, her accusers said her "shape" had attacked them. They also testified that Bishop's specter had tried to compel them to sign the devil's "book."

I. She was indicted for bewitching of several persons in the neighborhood, the indictment being drawn up, according to the form in such cases usual. And pleading, not guilty, there were brought in several persons, who had long undergone many kinds of miseries, which were preternaturally inflicted, and generally ascribed unto a horrible witchcraft. There was little occasion to prove the witchcraft; it being evident and notorious to all beholders. Now to fix the witchcraft on the prisoner at the bar, the first thing used was, the testimony of the bewitched; whereof, several testified, that the shape of the prisoner did oftentimes very grievously pinch them, choke them, bite them, and afflict them; urging them to write their names in a book, which the said specter called, ours. One of them did further testify, that it was the shape of this prisoner, with another, which one day took her from her wheel, and carrying her to the riverside, threatened there to drown her, if she did not sign to the book mentioned; which yet she refused. Others of them did also testify, that the said shape, did in her threats, brag to them, that she had been the death of sundry persons, then by her named; that she had ridden a man, then likewise named. Another testified, the apparition of ghosts unto the specter of Bishop, crying out, you murdered us! About the truth whereof, there was in the matter of fact, but too much suspicion.

II. It was testified, that at the examination of the prisoner, before the magistrates, the bewitched were extremely tortured. If she did but cast her eyes on them, they were presently struck down; and this in such a manner as there could be no collusion in the business. But upon the touch of her hand upon them, when they lay in their swoons, they would immediately revive; and not upon the touch of anyone's else. Moreover, upon some special actions of her body, as the shaking of her head, or the turning of her eyes, they presently and painfully fell into the like postures. And many of the like accidents now fell out, while she was at the bar. One at the same time testifying, that she said, she could not be troubled to see the afflicted thus tormented.

III. There was testimony likewise brought in, that a man striking once at the place, where a bewitched person said, the shape of this Bishop stood, the bewitched cried out, that he had tore her coat, in the place then particularly specified; and the woman's coat, was found to be torn in that very place.

IV. One Deliverance Hobbs, who had confessed her being a witch, was now tormented by the specters, for her confession. And she now testified, that this Bishop, tempted her to sign the book again, and to deny what she had confessed. She affirmed, that it was the shape of this prisoner, which whipped her with iron rods, to compel her thereunto. And she affirmed, that this Bishop was at a general meeting of the witches, in a field at Salem Village and there partook of a diabolical sacrament, in bread and wine then administered!

explanations, including the possibility that an individual had compacted with the devil to do evil deeds. In England, witchcraft had been a capital offense since the time of Henry VIII in the early sixteenth century; colonial governments followed suit in condemning those who gave "entertainment to Satan." Over the seventeenth century, the Puritan governments charged many more men and women with witchcraft than did other English colonies: three hundred and fifty New Englanders were accused during the years 1620 to 1725. Of this number, the Salem episode accounted for almost 200. The southern and middle colonies tried few accused witches and executed none.

The witchcraft cases of Salem in 1691–1692 at first resembled those in other places and times. Several girls experimented with magic, aided by a slave woman Tituba and her husband John, who together baked a "witch cake" of rye meal and urine, feeding it to a dog. The girls, who included nine-year-old Betty Parris, the daughter of Salem Village's minister, started having fits, presumably caused by witches. According to one report, the girls began "getting into holes, and creeping under chairs and stools, and to use sundry odd postures and antic gestures, uttering foolish, ridiculous speeches." Possession spread to other village girls, leading to the arrest of three women as witches—Tituba; a poor beggar, Sarah Good; and an ailing elderly woman, Sarah Osborne.

These three alleged witches were the sort of people traditionally prosecuted for the crime. Generally, in witchcraft cases, the accused were women past menopause, who in various ways deviated from expected roles. They had fewer children than the average woman their age. Lacking sons, a significant percentage of accused witches were heirs or potential heirs of estates, with greater economic autonomy than most New England women. Some claimed the power of a "cunning woman" to heal and foretell the future; many had been convicted of assaultive speech; and they were often involved in conflict within their families and neighborhoods. Revealingly, men of the same age group and troublesome character were much less likely to be identified as witches. These assertive old women went beyond the accepted bounds of female behavior and, as a result, became vulnerable to prosecution as witches.

While the Salem craze commenced in the time-worn pattern, it soon engulfed people of all social levels. Accusations descended upon prosperous church members, a minister, a wealthy shipowner, and several town officials. Hysteria spread from Salem to adjacent towns. Over three-quarters of the alleged witches were women; half of the accused men were their relations. Of those executed, fourteen women and five men were hanged on "Witches Hill" and another man was crushed to death with stones. Only one of the dead was of high status—the Puritan minister George Burroughs. Governor Phips, supported by influential clergymen, had allowed the prosecutions to proceed after his arrival, but put a stop to them when the accusers pointed to people at the highest levels of society, most significantly, to his own wife, Mary Phips. It had become clear, to many besides the governor, that the situation was out of control, that the evidence presented by the possessed was unreliable and quite likely the work of the devil. After Salem, witchcraft no longer assumed its earlier importance in New England society.

WARS AND RIVALRY FOR NORTH AMERICA

From 1680 to 1713, the Spanish, English, French, and many Indian nations battled for territory in North America. Despite the political and social turmoil of the 1680s and early 1690s, the English settlements were the largest and most dynamic European colonies on the continent. By the mid-1680s, New France had approximately 10,000 settlers, compared with more than 70,000 in New England alone. Spanish Florida was comprised chiefly of missions, run by forty Franciscan priests, and the fortified town of St. Augustine, which held about 1,400 Hispanic, African, and Indian residents. Despite declining populations, many Native American peoples remained powerful in eastern North America, in particular the Five Nations of the Iroquois in New York.

In the late seventeenth century, the three primary areas of dispute on the continent were Florida and Guale (later Georgia), Louisiana and Texas, and Canada. Conflict occurred against the backdrop of two

Hanging of witches in England c. 1650. No similar image exists of the Salem hangings.
Courtesy, Peabody Essex Museum, Salem, Mass.

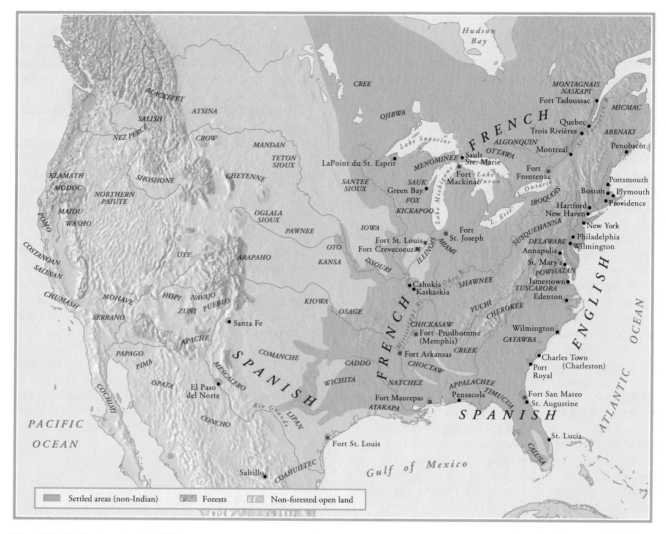

Map 3.3 *North America in 1700*

Significant change had occurred in North America since the early 1600s. Along the Atlantic coast, the English now had settlements from Maine (part of Massachusetts) to South Carolina. As the English population expanded, Native Americans declined, with many groups absorbed into other nations, such as the Catawbas of South Carolina.

long European wars, the War of the League of Augsburg, 1689–1697, and the War of the Spanish Succession, 1702–1713 (respectively known as King William's War and Queen Anne's War to the English colonists).

Florida and Guale

Beginning in 1680, the English colonists of South Carolina decided to take advantage of smoldering unrest among the mission Indians of Guale and Florida to attack the Spanish colony. The Native Americans had rebelled against forced labor and efforts to stamp out their traditional religions. They killed Spanish mis-

sionaries and destroyed property, but had not closed the missions altogether. The Carolinians raided Guale and Florida with no humanitarian motives to assist the Indians. In fact, a chief reason for attacking the Spanish missions was to capture Native Americans to sell as slaves in the West Indies. The English also wanted to control the deerskin trade in the southeast.

By 1686, the Carolinians thrust the missionaries out of Guale. Then in 1704, during Queen Anne's War, an army under former Carolina governor James Moore crushed the missions in Apalachee. The Carolinians obtained help from their trading partners, the Yamassees, and from many of the mission Indians, who

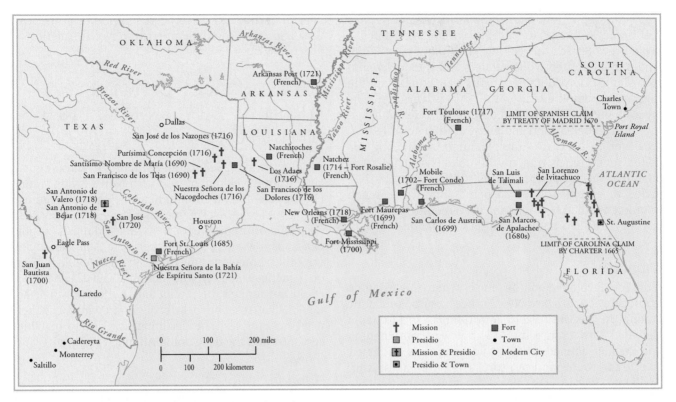

Map 3.4 *Southeastern North America in the Early 18th Century*
French colonies along the Mississippi River and Gulf Coast challenged Spanish dominance in the region. The Spanish settlements in Texas and Florida included missions and provided a defensive buffer for Mexican silver mines and shipping lanes off the Florida coast.

resented Spanish oppression. Moore's troops inflicted brutal torture, burning people alive. The surviving Apalachees dispersed, losing their identity as a nation. The Spanish retained St. Augustine and a fort they built at Pensacola in 1698, but lost control of Guale and most of Florida.

Louisiana and Texas

The Spanish erected their fort at Pensacola Bay in response to French efforts to establish a colony in Louisiana. At risk, the Spanish knew, were their silver mines in Mexico and domination of the Gulf of Mexico. In 1682, René Robert Cavelier, Sieur de La Salle, had explored the Mississippi River from New France to the gulf, naming the territory Louisiana in honor of King Louis XIV. La Salle sailed to France, then returned to set up a colony. However, he miscalculated the location of the Mississippi, instead building Fort St. Louis in Texas, near Matagorda Bay. The colony quickly dissolved from disease, loss of ships, and at-

tacks by Karankawa Indians; in 1687, La Salle was murdered by his men.

The French incursion in the Gulf of Mexico inspired the Spanish to expand their settlements in the borderlands. In 1690, they founded missions among the Caddo people of eastern Texas and western Louisiana, from whom they took the Caddo word, Tejas or Texas, meaning "friends." Three years later, when the Caddos blamed the friars for bringing smallpox, they escaped. The Spanish abandoned Texas until the French once again entered the area.

In 1699, Pierre LeMoyne, Sieur d'Iberville, resumed the French search for an opening to the Mississippi River, which was difficult to locate in the muddy Mississippi Delta. Iberville found the river's mouth by accident, then built forts at Biloxi Bay and on the Mississippi to establish French possession. Spain might have forced the French out of Louisiana with quick action, but in 1700, the grandson of French King Louis XIV took the Spanish throne; the two nations became allies against the English, Dutch, and Austrians in the War of the Spanish Succession.

Although the French-Spanish alliance gave Louisiana a chance to develop without interference from New Spain, the colony grew slowly. In 1708, about one hundred white soldiers and settlers lived in Louisiana. They obtained food, deerskins, and the right to occupy the land from local Native Americans by exchanging firearms and other goods. Relations between the French and Indians were not trouble-free, however. In 1715, for example, after Natchez Indians killed four French traders, the colonists literally demanded the assassins' heads. When the Natchez failed to execute all of the perpetrators, the French murdered Indian hostages and required the Natchez to accept a fortified trading post on their land.

Canada

Conflict developed in the north when the Iroquois confederation attacked New France to stop French fur trading in the Ohio Valley and Illinois. The Iroquois defeated New France in 1683, but war continued as the English, French, and Native Americans struggled over trade routes and territory. The outbreak of King William's War in 1689 fueled the contest, as the Five Nations attacked settlements in Canada, while the French and their Indian allies destroyed English frontier outposts from New York to Maine. New England troops took Port Royal in Acadia, but failed to conquer Quebec. Though the European belligerents agreed in the Peace of Ryswick (1697) to return to prewar status in North America, the Canadians won an important victory over the Iroquois and their English allies. The Five Nations signed a neutrality treaty in 1701. Frustrated by New York's failure to provide reinforcements, they ended their alliance with the English. New France then developed trade, religious missions, and agricultural settlements in the Great Lakes and Illinois Territory.

The renewal of hostilities between the English and French in 1702, with Queen Anne's War, again brought raids on the New England frontier. In 1704, the Canadians and Native Americans attacked Deerfield, Massachusetts, burning houses and barns, killing inhabitants, and taking many captives. The English once again took Port Royal, but called off an attack on Quebec when they lost 900 men in storms on the St. Lawrence River. This time, however, the peace treaty gave the victory to England (which had joined with Scotland in 1707 to form Great Britain). In North America, the Treaty of Utrecht (1713) ceded Nova Scotia (formerly Acadia), Newfoundland, and control of the Hudson Bay territory to the British. Yet they had failed to oust France from North America.

THE ENTRENCHMENT OF SLAVERY IN BRITISH AMERICA

Despite wars, rebellions, and witch hysteria, the most significant development in British North America during the late seventeenth and early eighteenth century was large-scale investment in enslaved Africans. The decisions of thousands of individual colonists to purchase men, women, and children who had been seized from their homelands in Africa left an indelible imprint on American society and culture. The slave buyers could not foretell the monumental effects of their actions. They responded to economic conditions: their need for workers, the declining availability of white servants, and the developing Atlantic slave trade.

Adopting Slavery

How could people who increasingly prized their own freedom—who had braved a treacherous ocean voyage to find opportunity in a new land—deprive other human beings of liberty, and often life itself? The answer lies in traditional English culture and the colonists' perceived economic needs.

The English, like other Europeans, believed that hierarchies existed in human society and, indeed, all of nature. Humans were superior to animals; Christians superior to "heathens." English language and culture also differentiated sharply between white and black, with whiteness suggesting purity and good, blackness imbued with filth and sin. The English compared their light skin with the Africans' darker brown color, judging the latter to be inferior. In African religion, social customs, dress, and political organization, the Europeans found serious deficiencies, just as they had found deficiencies among Native Americans. The people of sub-Saharan Africa, the English thought, were lower on the scale of humanity and could justifiably be enslaved. The example of the Portuguese, Spanish, and—most recently—the Dutch, who had fabricated the Atlantic slave trade over the previous two centuries, made the decision to buy Africans seem natural. The mainland English colonists could also look to their countrymen in the West Indies, where thousands of African slaves toiled in sugar fields, outnumbering whites.

Despite this cultural context, colonists viewed their investment in slaves as an economic decision. In Virginia and Maryland, planters purchased Africans because they needed large numbers of workers to grow tobacco. Chesapeake settlers had learned that Native Americans, who easily escaped enslavement and died in catastrophic numbers, would not fill their labor needs. White servants filled the gap until about 1675. Many young Englishmen, and fewer women, had willingly signed up to work for three or more years in return for passage and rights to fifty acres of land. In the last quarter of the century, however, the supply of English servants declined in Maryland and Virginia. Economic conditions improved in England, while good tobacco land became scarce. Bacon's Rebellion taught Chesapeake elites the danger of importing thousands of white servants under these circumstances. With the founding of the Carolinas, New Jersey, and Pennsylvania, where land was plentiful, servants had a wider range of options.

Theodor de Bry's illustration of a Dutch ship trading on the coast of West Africa. The people in the canoe, indicated with "B," represent African merchants who traded human beings to the Europeans for goods such as cloth, rum, and firearms.
Rare Books Division, The New York Public Library. Astor, Lenox, and Tilden Foundations

Chesapeake planters searching for an alternative labor supply turned to African slaves. Population figures for Virginia and Maryland demonstrate graphically the result of individual decisions. In 1660, only 900 blacks resided in the Chesapeake, some of whom had come as servants and were free. Two decades later, their number had grown to 4,300; by 1720, blacks comprised one-fifth of the population. A similar increase occurred in the Carolinas (primarily South Carolina), where 38 percent of the residents in 1720 were African slaves. The situation was different in New England, where only 2 percent of the population was enslaved, and in the Middle Colonies (New York, New Jersey, Pennsylvania, and Delaware), where about one resident in ten suffered perpetual bondage.

The Slave Trade

English entry into the Atlantic slave trade helped spur the transition to an African workforce. Though smugglers like John Hawkins had interloped earlier in the Spanish trade, England officially became involved in selling human beings in 1663. Charles II granted a monopoly to supply captives to the English colonies first to the Company of Royal Adventurers, then in 1672 to the Royal African Company. When the companies could not meet the demand of labor-hungry colonists, smugglers got involved, so in 1698, the Crown abandoned the monopoly, opening the slave trade to any English merchant who wanted to participate. As a result, the supply of Africans in the English colonies soared and slave prices declined, thus encouraging colonists to invest in even more black labor.

The experience of enslavement and transit across the Atlantic Ocean was dehumanizing and perilous. Probably one-half of the persons sold into slavery died while still in Africa before transport or during the Atlantic passage. Approximately three-quarters of those taken to English North America came from the area of West Africa between Senegambia and the Bight of Biafra, with the remainder coming mostly from Angola. As European sea captains made successive trips to the coast, African traders had to reach farther and farther into the continent to find enough people to enslave. Some captives marched 500 miles or more to the sea in "coffles," the term given to the files of shackled prisoners. On the coast, they were confined in enclosures called barracoons, often exposed to the sun for long periods without adequate food and drink. When a ship arrived, according to a Dutch trader, Willem Bosman, in 1700, the Africans were lined up on shore,

> where, by our surgeons . . . they are thoroughly examined, even to the smallest member, and that naked both men and women, without the least distinction or modesty. Those that are approved as good, are set on one side; and the lame or faulty are set by as invalids, which are here called *mackrons:* these are such as are above five and thirty years old, or are maimed in the arms, legs or feet; have lost a tooth, are grey-haired, or have films over their eyes; as well as all those which are affected with any venereal distemper, or several other diseases.

For the Africans chosen for transport, the horror had only begun. The Europeans branded them with the insignia of the company—for example, slaves of the Royal African Company had their skins burned with the letters "DY," for James, duke of York. Then followed the voyage across the Atlantic, called the "middle passage," which could take from three weeks to more than three months, depending upon the weather and destination. Ships normally carried rations for three months, so bad storms could mean starvation. Weather permitting, the captives spent their days on deck, the men in chains, the women and children unrestrained. At night, and around the clock if weather was bad, slaves occupied spaces about the size of coffins in the hold of the ship, where temperatures could reach extremely high levels. Disease was often rampant. Some slaves attempted suicide by jumping overboard or refusing to eat: the latter was so common that traders invested in a tool called the *speculum oris* to force open a person's mouth.

Africans also rebelled violently, attacking the white captain and crew, occasionally taking over the ship. Because they were unfamiliar with ocean navigation, mutineers had the best hope of success when the ship was still in African waters and large numbers could carry out the revolt, escaping to shore. When rebels failed, punishment was swift and brutal. The slave trader Bosman described an incident when a sea captain placed an extra anchor in the ship's hold. The enslaved Africans,

> unknown to any of the ship's crew, possessed themselves of a hammer, with which, in a short time

they broke all their fetters in pieces upon the anchor: After this, they came above deck, and fell upon our men, some of whom they grievously wounded, and would certainly have mastered the ship, if a French and English ship had not very fortunately happened to lie by us; who perceiving by our firing a distressed-gun, that something was in disorder on board, immediately came to our assistance with shallops and men, and drove the slaves under deck: notwithstanding which, before all was appeased, about twenty of them were killed. The Portuguese have been more unlucky in this particular than we; for in four years they lost four ships in this manner.

Upon arrival in America, the Africans faced the ordeal of sale by auction or prearranged contract. They were stripped naked once again and examined for disease and physical defects. Because the greatest need was for strong field hands who would provide years of labor, plantation owners paid the highest prices for healthy young men in their prime. Buyers paid less for women, children, and older men. For both the Africans and their owners, the year following debarkation was most critical. During this period of seasoning, Africans endured serious illness and high mortality from the new disease environment.

Systems of Slavery in British North America

As more and more Africans arrived, colonial assemblies instituted black codes to define slavery and to control the black population. Before 1660, Maryland had officially sanctioned perpetual bondage, but Virginia moved more slowly. Enough flexibility existed in Virginia society to allow black servants to gain freedom, earn their livelihoods, and in some cases acquire land. In the 1660s, however, Virginia joined Maryland in enacting laws that recognized differences in the terms of white servants and African slaves. By law, slavery lasted a person's entire lifetime, descended from mother to child, and was the normal status of blacks, but never whites.

In the late seventeenth and early eighteenth century, both Virginia and Maryland created clearly articulated caste systems based on perceptions of race. A person's skin color denoted status: all Africans and their descendants encountered severe discrimination, whether enslaved or free. The Virginia assembly ruled that any master who killed a slave during punishment was not guilty of a felony. Conversely, no black person, slave or free, could strike a white, even in self-defense. Virginia lawmakers made emancipation difficult to obtain. Evolving black codes banned interracial marriage, forbade owners from releasing their slaves except in special cases, and restricted enslaved blacks from traveling without permission, marrying legally, holding property, testifying against whites, or congregating in groups. Over the course of the eighteenth century, other British colonies passed similar codes that ranged from fairly moderate New England laws to a harsh regime in Carolina, keyed in large part to the density of the black population.

In the life of an African slave, these laws had force, but more direct was the power of the master over work and family. To be a slave meant that someone else possessed your body and could command your daily activities. The owner chose your job; he or she decided whether your children would stay with you or be sold away. During off-hours, Africans generally maintained autonomy in religion, social customs, and family life.

The work Africans and native-born African Americans performed varied from one region to another. In the Chesapeake and the Carolinas, most slaves spent long hours planting, weeding, and harvesting tobacco, corn, and rice. A farm's production depended largely upon the number of workers tending the crop. Over time, as the southern black population increased naturally and importation continued, the supply of labor became more plentiful. Plantation owners assigned slaves to different tasks, though most still raised the staple crop. Some men became drivers and artisans; some women served as nurses, cooks, and spinners. Both women and men performed domestic service. At the same time, female slaves were responsible for the household needs of their own families, including food preparation, laundry, and sewing.

Agricultural production in the Middle Colonies and New England centered on grains and livestock, which demanded less labor than tobacco or rice, so most parts of the northern countryside had relatively few slaves. Exceptions included New York and neighboring eastern New Jersey, which had difficulty attracting European immigrants; thus, well-to-do farmers purchased large numbers of Africans to work their land. The largest slaveholder in New Jersey was probably Colonel Lewis Morris of Shrewsbury, who employed more than sixty slaves at his plantation and ironworks. In Rhode Island's Narragansett region, some plantation owners held as many as fifty blacks. Most northern slaves lived in the port towns, however, where women worked as cooks and household servants, and men labored at crafts, domestic service, and as shipbuilders and sailors. Boston, New York, and Philadelphia merchants imported Africans as part of the West Indies trade. In New York City, blacks were

about one-fifth of the population; in Boston and Philadelphia they comprised about one-tenth.

A source of comfort to slaves who had lost their African homelands and kin was to establish new families in America. Slaves achieved some autonomy from their masters by creating families and kinship networks. All knew, however, that owners could destroy loving relationships by selling away spouses, children, brothers, and sisters. The ability of blacks to form families changed over time and varied from one region to another. High mortality and a skewed sex ratio prevented many African-born men from marrying and having children. In the disease-ridden West Indies and northern cities like Philadelphia, mortality was so high that colonists had to keep importing Africans to avoid population decline. In the Chesapeake colonies, however, natural population growth began with the first generation of native-born slaves. African American women had more children than their African mothers, creating communities of slaves on large plantations. Whereas most of the first Africans dwelled in white households with just a few blacks, their offspring, known as "country-born" slaves, lived with parents, brothers, and sisters. The third generation lived with grandparents and cousins as well.

Resistance and Rebellion

For many slaves, family and kin helped to reduce their feelings of despair; for others nothing relieved the pain of lifetime bondage. Many resisted their masters' power by staging slowdowns, pretending illness, destroying crops and tools, committing theft, arson, assault, and murder. Newly arrived Africans were especially likely to rebel against their new status, often running away. Slaves who were sold away from their families frequently escaped to join them again. Men ran away in greater numbers than women, who, as mothers, found it difficult to escape with children in tow.

Although slaves in the English West Indies often rebelled, blacks in the mainland colonies rarely took the ultimate step of armed insurgency, primarily because they were so outnumbered by whites. Before 1713, West Indian blacks staged seven full-scale revolts; their large population made success seem possible. In Barbados, in 1675, for example, conspirators planned to take over the island, installing an elderly slave Cuffee as king. When whites got wind of the plot, they burned alive or beheaded thirty-five blacks. On the mainland, just one slave revolt occurred by the early 1700s. In New York City, in 1712, about twenty slaves set fire to a building, attacking the white men who came to extinguish it. Nine whites were killed;

terror spread up and down the Atlantic coast. As in the case of later slave revolts and conspiracies, the revenge wreaked upon the black community surpassed any violence the rebels had committed. In the wake of the New York revolt, thirteen slaves were hanged, three burned at the stake, one tortured on the wheel (an instrument used to stretch and disjoint its victims), and another starved to death in chains; six committed suicide to avoid such treatment.

Early Abolitionists

As slavery became entrenched in North America, a few white colonists questioned its morality. They feared slave rebellions and abhorred the violence needed to enslave Africans, transport them to the colonies, and keep them in bondage. Slavery was morally repugnant, they believed, because all humans are equal in the eyes of God. One of the American opponents of perpetual bondage was Samuel Sewall, a Boston judge, who wrote in 1700, "It is most certain that all Men, as they are the Sons of Adam . . . have equal Right unto Liberty, and all other outward Comforts of Life."

Quakers also spoke out publicly against the institution. Certainly not all Friends were abolitionists— in Pennsylvania and New Jersey before 1720 a large proportion of the Quaker elite owned slaves—but a few interpreted Quaker ideals to mean that human bondage reeked with sin. According to John Hepburn of New Jersey, for example, slavery violated the Golden Rule to do unto others as you wish others to do unto you. Whereas owners got rich without physical labor, wore fine-powdered wigs and greatcoats, and their wives and children similarly lived well, slaves endured beatings, wore rags, and slept in the ashes of the fire. In the context of rising importation throughout the colonies, however, the protests of Sewall, Hepburn, and a few other critics had little effect.

ECONOMIC DEVELOPMENT IN THE BRITISH COLONIES

Despite differences in agriculture, labor, and commerce from one region to another, the mainland colonies were all part of the Atlantic economy, dominated by the staple crops of sugar, tobacco, and rice. The developing mercantile economies of New England and the mid-Atlantic region depended heavily upon the slave system, because their chief market was pro-viding food for the multitudes of blacks laboring on West Indies sugar plantations.

Northern Economies

Family farms and dependence on the sea characterized New England's economy. When its agriculture failed to provide a lucrative staple crop, traders turned to fishing and shipping. With rocky, generally poor soil and a cool climate, the region could not grow a profitable commercial crop like tobacco or sugar, so rural New England families raised livestock, wheat, rye, Indian corn, peas, other vegetables, and fruit. They ate most of what they produced—a fairly monotonous diet of brown bread, boiled or baked peas, boiled meat and vegetables, and dark beer or apple cider—within their families and communities.

Fishing and shipping developed as important industries during the seventeenth century. The New England fishers initially sold their catch, in return for manufactured goods such as shoes, textiles, glass, and metal products, to London merchants, who sent the fish to Spain, Portugal, and the Wine Islands, off the coast of Africa.

The fishing industry spurred the growth of maritime trade, as New England merchants recognized even greater profits to be made by trading directly with the Wine Islands and the West Indies. They formed partnerships among themselves and with English merchants, encouraging a local shipbuilding industry. The New Englanders exported fish, barrels, and other wood products. They imported wine, fruit, and salt from the Wine Islands, and rum, molasses, sugar, dyes, and other goods from the Caribbean. Soon, aided by the Navigation Acts, they were the chief carriers of goods along the North American coast, exchanging enslaved Africans and rum distilled from West Indies molasses for Pennsylvania wheat and livestock, Chesapeake tobacco, North Carolina tar and turpentine, and South Carolina rice. The credits they earned in shipping were as significant as the value of New England products sold in the trade.

The economy of the Middle Colonies resembled New England's in a number of ways, but was much more prosperous agriculturally. With plenty of good land, farmers raised wheat and livestock commercially, purchasing servants and some slaves to supplement family labor. The region had two ports: one at New York City and the other at Philadelphia. Though neither city matched Boston in population or commercial importance before 1750, both quickly surpassed the Massachusetts seaport after that date. New York merchants maintained links with Amsterdam, the Dutch West Indies, and New Spain even after the English takeover in 1664. Philadelphia Quakers exploited their connections with Friends in other ports, especially in England and the West Indies.

Life in the Seaports

Maritime trade encouraged the development of port cities in the British provinces: Boston, New York, Philadelphia, and Charleston. Until 1750, merchants of Boston and other seaport towns in Massachusetts and Rhode Island dominated colonial trade. The ports thrived because they forged commercial links between farmers and external dealers, housing the markets through which imports and exports flowed. The maritime industry itself created demand for shipbuilders, suppliers of provisions, rope and sailmakers, carters, dockworkers, and sailors.

Commercial growth brought social change, distinguishing an urban lifestyle from the countryside. Some merchants became fabulously wealthy from transatlantic and coastal trade. They spent their income conspicuously, building costly mansions, purchasing enslaved Africans as household servants, and wearing expensive clothes. They lived comfortably, with servants and slaves to do their menial chores. Other city dwellers were much less fortunate because they earned minimal wages or lacked employment. Port cities stimulated both affluence and dire poverty. They attracted many people who hoped to make their fortunes, or at least a decent living, but died with little more than the clothes on their backs. Maritime commerce frequently suffered disruption from war, bad weather, and economic downturns. Seamen and artisans, dependent on overseas trade, could expect little work during the winter, when few ships sailed. City folk were also at greater risk of death than those who lived in the country, as some arriving ships spread smallpox and other diseases to the dense urban populations. The towns lacked adequate sanitation facilities, so garbage and waste cluttered streets, polluting the water supply.

As trade expanded, sailors became an important segment of the labor force. They were a varied lot. Some went to sea only part-time, to supplement the income of their farms. Others chose seafaring as a career, joining a fraternity and dividing their time between shipboard and the taverns and boardinghouses of port towns throughout the Atlantic world. Some had no choice in the matter at all, for they were enslaved Africans whose masters purchased them to man the ships. Sailors led a difficult and dangerous life. Crews on ordinary merchant ships were small, so

Cod fishing was an early industry of Europeans in the North Atlantic. This illustration depicts a dry fishery on the Newfoundland coast in which cod were lightly salted and dried for sale in southern Europe
North Wind Picture Archives

seamen worked long hours loading and unloading the ship, maintaining the rigging and sails, and pumping water from the bilge, an especially backbreaking job. The organization of labor on board was hierarchical, with power descending from the captain to mate, to specialists like ship carpenter and surgeon, to seamen. Discipline could be harsh. The crewmen had little hope of moving up through the ranks, for captains were generally from affluent families, often merchants and part-owners of their ships. Instead, the more common fate of an ordinary "Jack Tar" was early death or disability from shipwreck, combat with enemies or pirates, and such occupational hazards as falling overboard, broken bones, scurvy, rheumatism, and hernias, or the "bursted belly" as they called it.

When conditions on ship became insufferable, the seamen rebelled, sometimes deserting the ship at the next port. Most radically, men mutinied and, if successful, sometimes became pirates. They plundered merchant vessels and port towns, sharing the proceeds evenly among themselves, electing officers, and recruiting much larger crews than could be found on merchant ships. With eighty or more men on a pirate ship of average size, compared with fifteen on a comparable merchant vessel, each had much less work to do. One pirate, Joseph Mansfield, admitted in 1722 that "the love of Drink and a Lazy Life" were "Stronger Motives with him than Gold."

Plantation Economies in the Chesapeake and South Carolina

From 1675 to 1720, tobacco remained king in Maryland and Virginia, as planters increasingly purchased enslaved Africans instead of white servants. The wealth of plantation owners grew with each child born to a slave mother. At the same time, the richest planters bought up the land of small farmers who found it difficult to compete with the slaveholders. The wealthiest man in early eighteenth-century Virginia was Robert Carter of Lancaster County, called "King" Carter. As a slave trader and land speculator, he parlayed his inheritance of £1,000 and 1,000 acres into an estate of £10,000 in cash, 300,000 acres of land, and over 700 slaves. Carter, with his relatives and friends, formed a tightly knit group of Chesapeake gentry.

In 1720, and throughout the eighteenth century, Chesapeake society was hierarchical. At the bottom of the social structure were African and country-born slaves, who owned no property and had little hope for freedom. Above them were the non-landholding whites, perhaps 40 to 50 percent of white families, who rented land, owned a horse or two, some cows, a few pigs, tools, and some household goods, but rarely held bound servants or slaves. They lived in shanties and ate from wooden dishes rather than from pottery. Their incomes from tobacco were so meager that they had trouble paying taxes and rent. Often they were in debt to the local merchant-planter for needed manufactured goods, such as ammunition, fabric, shoes, and tools. Next higher were small landholders whose incomes allowed them to live more comfortably, with pottery, more furniture, and nicer (though still quite small) homes. If they owned several slaves, which few did before 1720, they worked alongside them in the fields and house.

In the upper 5 percent were the gentry, who owned many slaves, large acreages, and usually acted as merchants as well. They served as intermediaries for smaller planters, selling tobacco abroad and importing manufactured goods. As such, they became creditors of their poorer neighbors, who often owed them substantial debts. In Maryland and Virginia, the merchant-planters conducted trade without the development of port cities. Ships docked at their plantations along the many tributaries of the Chesapeake Bay to load casks of tobacco and unload imported goods. Tobacco required relatively little processing: workers dried the leaves in sheds, removed large fibers, and packed the tobacco in casks made by local coopers. Merchant-planters and rural artisans, including slaves, provided goods and services for the community without centralizing their activities in towns. Even the two capitals, Williamsburg and Annapolis, remained small throughout the colonial period.

Situated in a semitropical climate, South Carolina developed a plantation economy that was linked to, and in many ways resembled, the West Indies. Most early settlers, both black and white, came from the English colony of Barbados, where land was in short supply and almost entirely devoted to sugar cultivation. White planters claimed Carolina headrights, then sold corn, salt beef, salt pork, barrel staves, firewood, and Native American slaves to the islands. South Carolinians enslaved the Indians they captured in raids throughout the American Southeast and obtained them from native traders in exchange for guns, ammunition, and cloth. Native Americans also supplied deerskins, which found a ready market in England, though they were not valued quite so highly as Canadian furs.

As with the northern fur trade between Europeans and Indians, the Carolinians used English trade goods to establish alliances with native groups. Such major trading partners as the Yamassees, however, quickly discovered that white merchants used theft, violence, rum, and false weights to gain unfair advantage. In 1715, in league with the Creeks, the Yamassees attacked white settlements, nearly destroying the colony. The whites saved themselves by getting help from the Cherokees. The Yamassees and Creeks were defeated, their people killed, enslaved, or forced to migrate from the coastal area. White South Carolinians then expropriated their lands.

The settlers wanted the new territory because they had found an export that became much more lucrative than provisions, enslaved Indians, or deerskins. Planters had experimented with a variety of crops—tobacco, cotton, sugar, silk, wine grapes, and ginger—but rice proved most successful in the wet lowlands of the Carolina coast. Also significant were the skills in rice production that many Africans brought to America. Rice exports expanded rapidly in South Carolina, reaching 1.5 million pounds per year by 1710 and nearly 20 million pounds by 1730. The chief markets for rice were Europe and the West Indies. Carolinians first sent their crop directly to Portugal, but in 1705 Parliament added rice to the list of enumerated products that had to be shipped to England first, taxes paid, and then reexported to Europe. The colonists argued that, in the case of southern Europe, this detour made their crop arrive too late for Lent, when much of it was consumed. In response, Parliament allowed South Carolina after 1731 to trade directly with Spain, Portugal, and Mediterranean Europe, but the larger share of the rice crop, which went to northern Europe, still required transit through Britain.

The conversion to rice transformed South Carolina society, affecting the black population with special force. Before planters adopted full-scale rice production, slaves had performed a variety of jobs in crafts, timber, livestock, and agriculture. Their workloads were moderate, especially in comparison with the West Indies. Rice monoculture changed this situation altogether, as planters imported thousands of Africans. In the coastal areas north and south of Charleston, blacks reached 70 percent of the population in the 1720s. With high importation and harsher working conditions, death rates surged. As in the Chesapeake, wealthy planters bought up neighboring farms while investing heavily in slaves. They created large rice plantations, worked by growing numbers of African slaves. Small planters moved to the periphery, where they raised grain and livestock for the rice district and the Caribbean. The rice planters found the Carolina lowlands isolated and unhealthy, so they left their plantations part of the year. However, the Carolinians supervised their plantations directly—unlike British West Indian sugar planters who fled to England, leaving management in the care of overseers.

Charleston, where the rice planters spent at least several weeks each year, was the fourth largest city in the British colonies. The port channeled the trade in provisions, deerskins, rice, slaves, and English manufactures. Charleston remained smaller than Boston, Philadelphia, and New York because British and New England shippers controlled its trade. Without a strong merchant community, the South Carolina seaport lacked the impetus for shipbuilding and associated crafts.

CONCLUSION

Between 1675 and 1720, the people of North America shed blood over territory, trade, and political autonomy. As English, French, and Spanish settlers expanded into new regions, they established commerce, but also spread smallpox and fostered conflict among the Indians. The Narragansetts and Wampanoags of New England waged a costly war in 1675–1676, while the Pueblos successfully, though temporarily, expelled the Spanish from New Mexico. Native Americans throughout the continent, weakened by disease and war, yielded to the Europeans. During Bacon's Rebel-

lion and the Revolutions of 1689, governments in Virginia, Massachusetts, New York, and Maryland faced challenges from rival elites and their discontented, lower class allies.

By the turn of the eighteenth century, the Spanish reconquered New Mexico and infiltrated Texas, France moved into the Great Lakes region and Louisiana, and the English pushed out in many directions. To develop their economies, the British colonists imported Africans in large numbers. With the growth of plantation slave economies in the South and maritime commerce in the North, British North America developed distinctive regional characteristics. Yet in 1720, the Atlantic seaboard colonies had much in common: their settlement by enterprising men and women, regard for English rights of property and representation, and governance within the British imperial system. During the next half century, the importance of these commonalities would become clear.

Recommended Readings

Demos, John. *The Unredeemed Captive: A Family Story from Early America* (1994). The evocative tale of a Puritan minister's daughter who was held captive by the Mohawks and refused to return home.

Hoffman, Ronald et al., eds., *Through a Glass Darkly: Reflections on Personal Identity in Early America* (1997). Interesting essays relating individual biography to colonial development.

Innes, Stephen, ed. *Work and Labor in Early America* (1988). Insightful essays that demonstrate the range of labor systems and working conditions in the British colonies.

Jordan, Winthrop D. *White Over Black: American Attitudes Toward the Negro 1550–1812* (1968). Basic source on the construction of ideas about race in Anglo-America.

Karlsen, Carol F. *The Devil in the Shape of a Woman: Witchcraft in Colonial New England* (1987). Convincing argument about the significance of gender in witchcraft trials.

Lovejoy, David S. *The Glorious Revolution in America* (1972). The best introduction to the colonial revolutions of 1689.

McCusker, John J., and Menard, Russell R. *The Economy of British America 1607–1789, with Supplementary Bibliography* (1991). An excellent survey of economic and demographic development.

Thornton, John. *Africa and Africans in the Making of the Atlantic World, 1400–1680* (1998). An influential work demonstrating the impact of Africa and Africans on the slave trade and the development of colonial American societies.

Tomlins, Christopher L., and Mann, Bruce H., eds. *The Many Legalities of Early America* (2001). Path-breaking essays that explore relationships among early Americans through the law.

Usner, Daniel H., Jr. *Indians, Settlers, and Slaves in a Frontier Exchange Economy: The Lower Mississippi Valley Before 1783* (1992). A history of colonial Louisiana and West Florida, focusing on relations between Europeans and Native Americans.

American Journey Online and InfoTrac College Edition

Visit the source collections at http://ajaccess.wadsworth.com and infotrac.thomsonlearning.com and use the Search function with the following key terms to explore documents, images, audio and video clips, articles, and commentary related to the material in this chapter.

Metacom	Bacon's Rebellion
King Philip's War	Glorious Revolution
William Penn	Salem witch trials

Additional resources, exercises, and Internet links related to this chapter are available on the American Passages Web site: http://history.wadsworth.com/passages2e

4 THE EXPANSION OF COLONIAL BRITISH AMERICA 1720–1763

INTELLECTUAL TRENDS IN THE EIGHTEENTH CENTURY

THE GREAT AWAKENING

CULTURAL DIVERSITY AND EXPANSION

WARS FOR EMPIRE

THE BRITISH PROVINCES IN 1763

Benjamin Franklin Drawing Electricity from the Sky, *by Benjamin West, c. 1805. Franklin's kite experiment demonstrating the electrical nature of lightning, along with his various activities promoting social welfare, placed him in the forefront of the American Enlightenment.*
Philadelphia Museum of Art: Mr. and Mrs. Wharton Sinkler Collection

In 1721, smallpox hit Boston viciously, infecting about 6,000 residents and killing 844. Business stopped for several months, as almost every family battled the contagion. In many respects, this epidemic was unremarkable in the British American colonies: settlers and Native Americans alike had previously experienced the ravages of disease. But this time, one Puritan minister took an unprecedented step. Cotton Mather, who thirty years earlier had helped aggravate the Salem witch hysteria, encouraged a Boston doctor, Zabdiel Boylston, to test inoculation. Mather had learned from Onesimus, his African slave, and from English scientific papers, that inoculation was used in Africa and Turkey to prevent smallpox epidemics. An experiment would be risky, for the procedure involved introducing the smallpox virus into the body, thereby giving the person what was usually (but not always) a mild case of the disease. Many doctors, as well as much of Boston's populace, condemned the proposal. Nevertheless, Dr. Boylston inoculated about 250 persons over the course of a year. Those who submitted to the procedure had a much lower death rate than Bostonians who contracted the disease naturally.

Mather was far ahead of his time in advancing the theory that disease was caused by an invasion of the body by viruses, which he called invisible "worms." Significantly, it was a minister, rather than a physician or scientist, who advanced this hypothesis. During the eighteenth century, science lacked the rigid boundaries of complexity and specialization that would later separate it from other fields of intellectual endeavor. American theologians and philosophers, as well as doctors, naturalists, and astronomers, read the latest scientific literature from England and Europe. The great divide between science and religion did not yet exist. Like many other theologians, Mather understood epidemics as God's punishment for sin. But he also believed inoculation was a divine gift, that people should use any means available to combat disease.

CHRONOLOGY

1720	Theodore Jacob Frelinghuysen begins revivals in New Jersey
1721–1722	Smallpox inoculation in Boston
1732	Founding of Georgia • Hat Act
1733	Molasses Act
1734	Jonathan Edwards starts revivals in Northampton, Massachusetts
1737	Walking Purchase in eastern Pennsylvania
1739	Stono Uprising in South Carolina
1739–1740	George Whitefield tours northern colonies
1739–1744	War of Jenkins' Ear
1740	James Oglethorpe leads invasion of Florida
1741	British attack on Cartagena
1744–1748	King George's War
1745	New Englanders conquer Louisbourg
1747	Boston riot against impressment
1750	Iron Act
1754	Defeat of Virginia militia at Fort Necessity • Albany Congress proposes plan for colonial unity
1754–1763	Seven Years' War
1755	Braddock's defeat near Fort Duquesne
1758	British capture Louisbourg
1760	British conquer Montreal, seizing control of Canada
1763	Pan-Indian war begins in Ohio Valley and Great Lakes region • Proclamation of 1763 outlaws white settlement west of the Appalachians • Paxton Boys revolt in Pennsylvania

Mather's support for inoculation has been called the greatest contribution to medicine by an American during the colonial period. Certainly it represented change, as the Enlightenment, a new intellectual movement, spread from Britain to the colonies. During the years 1720 to 1763, the British provinces experienced intellectual, religious, and social ferment as they continued to expand through North America. As new knowledge, beliefs, and consumer goods arrived from Europe, colonists from Maine to Georgia (founded in 1732) increasingly lived within a common cultural framework. With rising wealth, colonial elites supported colleges and purchased books and luxury goods. This common culture had important ties to England, yet was not altogether English, for immigrants from Scotland, Ireland, and the continent of Europe, and slaves from Africa brought ideas and practices from their native lands. Immigration into the British colonies also promoted regional diversity, as the newcomers from Europe settled on the frontier from Pennsylvania to Georgia, and the numbers of enslaved Africans grew to 40 percent of the southern population. The Europeans came looking for land: when they set up farms in contested territory, they provoked conflicts with the Native Americans, French, and Spanish, resulting in a series of wars that lasted a quarter century. When the Seven Years' War ended in 1763, the British colonies took a great deal of pride in their contribution to the victory, offering it as evidence of their economic and political maturity within the empire.

INTELLECTUAL TRENDS IN THE EIGHTEENTH CENTURY

The willingness of Mather and Boylston to try inoculation showed important changes in the way people viewed their world. The Puritan clergyman's personal journey from witch hunter in 1692 to medical investigator in 1721 reflected the growing inclination to find natural rather than supernatural causes for unexplained events. The Enlightenment blossomed first in Europe and then in America, encompassing political theory and philosophy as well as science. Though primarily intellectual, the Enlightenment had far-reaching effects, inspiring new technology as well as concepts of human freedom. For Americans, its greatest significance lay in the acceptance of natural rights philosophy, which paved the way for independence and republican government.

Newton and Locke

In the late seventeenth century, two English theorists, Sir Isaac Newton and John Locke, had challenged traditional notions that humans had no role in determining their fate, that they could only trust in God to rule the universe. They confronted this older view without denying the existence of God. Newton discovered universal laws that predictably govern the motion of planets, moons, and comets, the motion of falling bodies on earth (gravity), and the ebb and flow of tides. His work demonstrated that the universe operated according to fixed principles, which humans are capable of detecting and understanding. Locke built upon Newton's breakthrough in his *Essay Concerning Human Understanding* (1690). Locke argued against the accepted belief in innate knowledge, that infants are born with ideas implanted by God in their minds. He contended that all knowledge is gained by experience, not preordained at birth. Humans are born with the ability to learn, to use their acquired knowledge to benefit society.

Locke, and the Enlightenment thinkers he inspired, believed in freedom and the possibility of human progress, in the right of people to improve the conditions in which they live. Science, of course, was an important means of such improvement. The English philosopher also had a major impact upon eighteenth-century politics, in particular providing a theoretical basis for the American Revolution and the Constitution. In *Two Treatises on Civil Government* (1690), he argued that humans, according to natural law, had rights to life, liberty, and property. By social contract, they formed governments to guarantee those rights. If a state failed in its obligation, the people had the duty to rebel and establish a new government.

Education in the British Colonies

Throughout British North America, formal education beyond basic reading, writing, and arithmetic was rare, so few read the works of Locke and Newton directly. After 1720, however, as newspapers became more available and reprinted articles from London, provincial readers gained greater familiarity with Enlightenment thought. Many colonists learned to read, though boys and girls spent much of their time learning the occupations they would pursue as adults. The availability of formal schooling varied widely by region, class, and gender. Nowhere did a system of universal, free, public education exist, though New England had some tax-supported schools. Everywhere, schools emphasized moral behavior and used religious texts.

New England made the greatest effort of the British colonies to educate its populace. In 1642, the Massachusetts legislature required parents and ministers to teach all children to read so they could obtain direct understanding of the Bible and the colony's laws. In 1647, the assemblymen ordered towns with at least fifty families to establish petty (elementary) schools, and those with one hundred families to maintain Latin grammar (secondary) schools. Connecticut and Plymouth passed similar legislation. Though some towns ignored the laws, most New England children learned to read, whether from their parents, at the town school, or at dame schools, where women in their homes taught young girls and boys for a fee. Writing was considered a separate skill, and was less crucial for girls to learn. The percentage of New England females who could write and do arithmetic was significantly lower than for males. Girls, on the other hand, commonly learned sewing and knitting. Boys who planned to enter college attended grammar school from about age seven to fourteen, studying Latin, elementary Greek, and sometimes Hebrew. Latin was necessary for the professions, including law, medicine, and the ministry.

South of New England, colonial governments did not require town schools. In the Middle Colonies, churches and private teachers offered instruction. Affluent Quaker and Anglican boys were most likely to obtain formal education, though after 1750 girls and poor boys, including African Americans, had better access to schools. As in Massachusetts, females were much less likely to learn to write than males. In the Chesapeake, with dispersed settlement, neither Maryland nor Virginia had many schools. Upper-class boys

In colonial America, children—especially girls—were less likely to learn to write than to read. Many people could not write their signatures so they made a mark on legal documents; then someone else wrote their name next to the mark.
Courtesy American Antiquarian Society

and girls had private tutors, while middling families in some localities pooled their resources to establish schools. Overall, sons received much more instruction than daughters, and large numbers of poor whites obtained no education at all. Very few slaves learned to read and write, for owners thought these skills would breed discontent and enable slaves to forge passes, facilitating escape.

New England also surpassed other regions in higher education, as the Puritans established Harvard College in Massachusetts in 1636 and Yale College in Connecticut in 1701. William and Mary, founded in Virginia in 1693, was the only other college in the British colonies before the 1740s. None of the colonial colleges admitted women. The Puritans intended Harvard to preserve classical learning and civilization, provide liberal education to the region's male elite, and ensure a supply of well-educated ministers. Harvard offered a curriculum of ethics, religion, logic, mathematics, Greek, Hebrew, rhetoric, and natural history (biology and geology). Most early graduates became clergymen, while others went into medicine, public service, teaching, commerce, and agriculture.

Harvard alumni in Connecticut established Yale to provide advanced education closer to home. Yale had a tentative beginning, but gained more stability by 1720, after receiving funds from Elihu Yale and about 800 volumes for its library, including the books of Locke, Newton, and other Enlightenment figures. The College of

The New England Primer, *first published in the 1680s, taught children moral lessons along with their alphabet and spelling.*
Courtesy, American Antiquarian Society

William and Mary also struggled at first. Chartered by the Crown to train Anglican clergy, educate young men in religion, and convert Native Americans, the school failed to offer college-level courses until the 1720s. Many elite families in the southern provinces continued to depend upon private tutors, trips to Britain, and northern colleges to educate their sons.

The Growth of Science

After 1720, influenced by Scottish universities that quickly absorbed Enlightenment thinking into their curricula, American colleges expanded their coursework to include French, English literature, philosophy, and science. They offered mathematics and what was then called natural philosophy—astronomy, physics, and chemistry. The colleges hired some of their faculty from Scotland and purchased scientific apparatus, including telescopes, sextants, clocks, and orreries, which demonstrate the motion of planets and moons within the solar system.

American professors of natural philosophy were part of a larger community of scholars centered in the prestigious Royal Society of London, which published a journal, *Philosophical Transactions,* of the latest scientific ideas and knowledge. This transatlantic community included academics like John Winthrop of Harvard College, as well as largely self-taught men like Benjamin Franklin and John Bartram. More than thirty colonists belonged to the Royal Society. Scientists took from the Enlightenment a commitment to experiment and observe natural phenomena to obtain information that would lead to human progress. John Winthrop was the most renowned professor of natural philosophy in British America, with research interests in such wide-ranging subjects as sunspots, mathematics, earthquakes, and the weather. In 1761, Winthrop participated in an important international scientific effort to calculate the distance between the Earth and sun, made possible by the transit of the planet Venus across the face of the sun. Venus had last crossed the sun in 1639, when no useful measurements had been made. Winthrop journeyed to Newfoundland to observe the transit. His data, combined with observations from the Cape of Good Hope, were inexact, but eight years later, scientists—including Winthrop—had another chance. This time, at least part of the transit could be viewed in the mainland British colonies. The stakes were high because another transit would not occur for 105 years. The data were again imprecise, but when combined with measurements from around the globe, yielded results very close to the accepted distance of 93 million miles between the Earth and sun.

Other colonists contributed to understanding the physical world. Perhaps best known for his diplomacy and political leadership during the Revolutionary era, Benjamin Franklin has become a symbol of the American Enlightenment for his efforts to improve society through science, inventions, and civic organizations. Franklin was born in Boston, ran away at age seventeen from an apprenticeship with his older brother, and arrived in Philadelphia nearly penniless. He built a highly successful printing business, publishing a newspaper, books, and *Poor Richard's Almanack,* which gained a wide readership. Throughout his life, Franklin put the Enlightenment ideal of human progress into action. He founded a debating club to discuss politics, morals, and natural philosophy, and helped establish the first American lending library, a hospital, and the College of Philadelphia. Franklin's experiments in electricity yielded information about its properties, including the basic concepts of "plus" and "minus." His inventions, which applied scientific principles to improving daily life, included bifocal eyeglasses, the lightning rod, and an iron stove that was more efficient than colonial fireplaces.

John Bartram, also of Pennsylvania, was the most energetic of American naturalists, whose chief contribution to science was collecting specimens of New World plant life. In return for a yearly pension from the king and payment for seeds he sent to wealthy collectors in England, Bartram traveled all over the eastern seaboard searching for new plants and animals. His efforts greatly expanded botanical knowledge of the Western Hemisphere, for he sent specimens to such scholars as Carl Linnaeus, the Swedish author of the modern classification system.

Another prominent American naturalist was Cadwallader Colden, a Scot who immigrated to the colonies after receiving his medical degree. Like many well-educated doctors, Colden had broad interests in science. While serving as surveyor-general and lieutenant-governor of New York, he collected and classified plants in the neighborhood of his estate. He corresponded with European botanists, sending them specimens and descriptions. As their demands became overwhelming, Colden taught his daughter, Jane, how to classify according to Linnaeus's scheme. Her accurate descriptions and drawings earned high praise from Linnaeus, Bartram, and other naturalists.

Changes in Medical Practice

Just as Colden and other university-trained doctors were interested in many scientific fields, the practice of medicine itself attracted people of widely different backgrounds. Medicine was beginning to develop as a profession. During the colonial period, men with formal medical education comprised a small proportion of the people who provided care for disease, physical injury, and childbirth. Having completed formal coursework abroad—the first medical school in the British colonies, located in Philadelphia, did not open until 1766—educated physicians were at the top of their profession and charged the highest fees. Consequently, they practiced primarily in the cities. Below them were men who learned their craft as apprentices; though they assumed the title of doctor in the colonies, they were actually akin to the surgeon-apothecaries of Great Britain. As surgeons, they performed emergency procedures such as setting bones, amputating limbs, and removing superficial tumors, but no major surgery. As apothecaries, they prepared and prescribed drugs for a variety of illnesses.

Female midwives traditionally attended childbirth, treated the ill, and prescribed herbal remedies. Having learned their skills through informal apprenticeships and from witnessing the childbirths of neighbors and relatives, they received payment for their services. During the colonial period, childbirth was the province of women. As an expectant mother's labor began, she called together a group of women, presided over by the midwife, who assisted in the birth. In the early stages of her labor, the woman provided special refreshments, called "groaning beer" and "groaning cakes." The attendants helped her walk around and offered herbal teas or liquor to relieve the pain. In normal deliveries, the mother squatted on a "midwife's stool" or remained standing while supported by several women. If complications occurred, the midwife manipulated the infant manually, but would not perform a Caesarean section. In the worst cases, the midwife had to kill the child; sometimes the mother died. Without modern antibiotics, women constantly faced the threat of infection during pregnancy and in the weeks following delivery.

In the last half of the eighteenth century, the practice of obstetrics changed. In 1762, Dr. William Shippen, Jr., returned from studying medicine in England and Scotland to give lectures in anatomy to Philadelphia midwives and doctors. Soon he accepted only male students. Shippen established an obstetrical practice of his own, quickly attracting well-to-do patients who expected a more elevated level of care than they received from midwives. Affluent urban women were convinced that the male physicians offered a better chance for a safe, less painful delivery. The doctors' obstetrical training, their use of opiates and instruments such as forceps, spelled progress to these women, in-

ducing them to abandon the traditional woman-dominated rituals of childbirth. That the new obstetrics brought improvement is doubtful. The male doctors, faced with taboos against observing the private parts of ladies, attended their clients in darkened rooms, with the woman lying in bed under covers. The physicians also lacked the means to prevent infection; their use of blood-letting and opium could impede safe delivery. In any case, midwives continued to attend the great majority of women, those who lived in rural areas and the poor who could not afford the doctors' fees.

THE GREAT AWAKENING

As Enlightenment ideas gained sway, many Protestant ministers embraced Christian rationalism, a theology that stressed moral, rational behavior and the free will of individuals to lead their lives and achieve salvation. Some rationalists spoke of an impersonal God who had long ago created the universe to operate according to natural laws, rather than a loving or angry God who controlled a person's daily life. For many, the rationalist religion was comforting, because it included in the church all who tried to live decent Christian lives, not just those who believed they were saved. To others, however, Christian rationalism was heretical, for it rejected the Calvinist belief that salvation came from grace, as the gift of God, and that people must be saved to be full members of the church.

From the 1720s to the 1760s, ministers from various denominations called for the renewal of these beliefs in a series of revivals, known as the Great Awakening. Several of the most important Awakeners brought the impetus for revival from Europe and Great Britain. Religious ferment convulsed British North America, spreading from the churches to threaten social and political authority.

Religious Diversity Before the Great Awakening

In 1720, the British provinces varied widely in religious and ethnic makeup. New England was the most homogeneous, for Massachusetts, New Hampshire, and Connecticut remained predominantly Puritan and of English descent. The established Puritan churches received tax support, but Anglicans, Baptists, and Quakers could also worship freely. Rhode Island, which still embraced the principles of religious liberty and separation of church and state, was home to various denominations, including Quakers, Baptists, and Separatists.

From their founding, the Middle Colonies offered an open door to people of various backgrounds. In the late seventeenth century, according to one report, residents of New York City spoke eighteen different languages. In eastern New Jersey, Scottish Presbyterians, Dutch Reformed, New England Puritans, Baptists, and Quakers settled towns and plantations, and farther south, on both sides of the Delaware River, Native Americans, Dutch, Swedes, and Finns met the Quakers who accompanied William Penn. Philadelphia and its environs in the 1720s boasted organized meetings of many denominations. Though disputes occasionally arose between churches, the Quaker government upheld liberty of conscience throughout the colonial period.

With few towns in the Chesapeake, the established Anglican church suffered from southern rural conditions, as ministers in Virginia faced serious obstacles in meeting the spiritual needs of their scattered congregations. Only half of the Anglican churches had regular preachers. Few planters were interested in converting their African slaves, who kept—and passed on to their children—many traditional African beliefs. The colony's laws against nonconformity prevented most dissent, so only a few Presbyterians and Quakers worshipped openly. In Maryland, many Quakers and Roman Catholics retained their faith, but suffered legal disabilities. The established Church of England in South Carolina was in better condition than in Virginia; some prosperous parishes could afford to pay their well-trained clergy adequately. Even so, Presbyterians, Baptists, Huguenots, and Quakers worshipped freely, for the proprietors had actively recruited dissenters to increase population and obtain their political support.

The Great Awakening shattered the existing church structure of the colonies, as congregations wakened to the teachings and vigorous preaching style of revivalist, or New Light, ministers. Religious diversity grew in provinces where established churches, with government support, dominated religious life—especially Puritan churches in Connecticut and Massachusetts, and the Anglican establishment in Virginia. As a result of the revivals, these colonies became more like Rhode Island, New York, and Pennsylvania.

Early Revivals in the Middle Colonies and New England

In 1720, New Jersey felt the first stirrings of the Great Awakening, when Theodore Jacob Frelinghuysen emigrated from Holland to serve four churches in the Raritan Valley. He had been educated in Dutch Reformed pietism, which emphasized the importance of conversion and personal religious experience (or piety). Using an emotional, revivalist preaching style, he led many people to experience salvation. But Frelinghuysen created a split in the Dutch Reformed churches of New Jersey between his followers, who believed a person must experience God's saving grace before participating in church sacraments, and his opponents, who thought that a commitment to living a godly life was sufficient.

Next, revivals engulfed Presbyterian churches in New Jersey, as they adopted doctrines preached by Gilbert and John Tennent, the sons of William Tennent, a Scots-Irish immigrant and Presbyterian minister. The younger Tennents took pulpits in New Brunswick and Freehold, close to Frelinghuysen's congregations. Impressed by the Dutch Reformed pastor's style of preaching, they inspired revivals of their own. Meanwhile, in Neshaminy, Pennsylvania, the elder Tennent established a seminary, called the "Log College" by his critics, where many New Light ministers received training.

In Massachusetts, revivals began in 1734, when minister Jonathan Edwards of Northampton preached a series of sermons on salvation, inclining many of his parishioners to believe they were saved. They went through the process of self-judgment—first feeling despair as sinners who were damned to hell, then rejoicing in the conviction that God rescued them from this fate. Edwards wrote to a colleague that "this town never was so full of Love, nor so full of Joy, nor so full of distress as it has lately been." Over the next few years, the revival spread to other towns along the Connecticut River.

Revivalism Takes Fire

Beginning in 1739, the Great Awakening spread throughout the British mainland colonies after a young Anglican minister, George Whitefield, arrived from England to tour the Middle Colonies. Called the Grand Itinerant, he had a magnificent voice, ranging from a whisper to a roar, that could be heard by large crowds in fields and city streets. Benjamin Franklin calculated that 25,000 people could easily hear the spectacular preacher at one time.

Whitefield found adherents across denominational lines and among native-born Americans and immigrants alike. In 1740, Jonathan Edwards invited Whitefield to Northampton, prompting the itinerant to travel through New England, where he attracted crowds as large as 8,000 in Boston. Other New Light ministers followed, including Gilbert Tennent and James Davenport, a Puritan preacher of Southold, Long Island.

George Whitefield, the itinerant English evangelist, had a spellbinding effect on his listeners, as portrayed here by John Wollaston.
The Granger Collection, New York

farm families and enslaved African Americans. Followers called each other "Sister" and "Brother," whether slave or free, affluent or poor. They refused to attend their local parish services and condemned many aspects of gentry culture, including horseracing, cockfights, elegant dress, and entertaining on Sunday. Lacking formal churches, Baptists met in fields and homes. The ministry was open to all, even women and slaves, with no requirement for college training.

The Awakening's Impact

The revivals proved to be socially divisive, as many communities split into two groups, the "New Lights" and the "Old Lights." The style of most New Light preachers was to give impassioned, extemporaneous sermons that contrasted dramatically with the closely reasoned sermons of their opponents, the rationalist Old Light ministers. New Lights believed that salvation was more important than religious training; they required a "saved" ministry, with a dynamic preaching style. Congregations responded by fainting, shrieking, and shedding tears. Old Light clergymen, who defended their advanced education in theology, Greek, Hebrew, and ethics, resented accusations that they were unsaved. In turn, they charged the revivalists with being unlearned.

As congregations broke apart, bitter disputes ensued over church property and tax support, spilling what had begun as a religious controversy into the courts and politics. Where strong established churches existed—as in Massachusetts, Connecticut, and Virginia—the New Lights challenged political as well as religious authority. In response, the Connecticut Assembly, for example, passed an Anti-Itinerancy Act, which made it illegal for a clergyman to preach in another's parish without his permission and repealed the 1708 law permitting religious dissent.

Higher education in the British colonies also felt the flames of revivalistic fervor. Yale College was at the center of the intense religious and political battles in Connecticut. When the New Haven church separated, a large number of students, many of them studying for the ministry, followed the New Lights. They skipped classes to attend revivals, challenged Yale's curriculum, and questioned whether their teachers were saved. To suppress the student rebellion, Thomas Clap, head of the college, obtained permission from the Connecticut Assembly to expel any student who attended New Light services. Clap's opposition to the Awakening was not permanent, however, for by 1753 he himself had become a New Light. As in many congregations, people eventually found

Davenport took the Awakening to extremes, harshly attacking other pastors as "unconverted." In 1743, he instigated the burning of books written by well-known clergymen; a year later he repented this excess.

The full force of the Awakening hit the south later than New England and the Middle Atlantic. During the 1740s, Presbyterian missionaries—men who received their education at Tennent's Log College—set up churches on the southern frontier. The new settlements were a fertile field for the revivalists because few regular clergy had migrated west. The more explosive Baptist revivals began in the 1750s, when itinerants traveled through Virginia and North Carolina making converts and forming churches. The Baptists believed that individuals should be saved before they were baptized. With their emotional religious style and challenge to the Anglican establishment in Virginia, they appealed particularly to ordinary white ways to heal the bitterness and division that the Great Awakening had caused.

A more lasting effect of the revivals was the founding of new colleges. Until the mid-1740s, only Harvard, William and Mary, and Yale—all with ties to established churches—existed in the British colonies. The revivals created a need for ministerial training. Between 1746 and 1769, the revivalists founded the College of New Jersey (now Princeton), the College of Rhode Island (Brown), Queen's College (Rutgers) in New Jersey, and Dartmouth College in New Hampshire. Anglicans established King's College (Columbia) in New York City, while a group of civic leaders, headed by Benjamin Franklin, started the College of Philadelphia (University of Pennsylvania) on a nonsectarian basis. Though each of these new schools except the College of Philadelphia was tied to a specific religious denomination, they all accepted young men of various faiths. These new colleges taught traditional subjects, but also adopted the new curricula in mathematics, science, and modern languages.

CULTURAL DIVERSITY AND EXPANSION

Between 1720 and 1760, the population of British North America grew from 472,000 to 1,600,000. Much of this growth came from natural increase, but new arrivals also spurred population growth, as thousands of Germans and Scots-Irish immigrated, and slave traders continued to import blacks.

The newcomers brought ideas, religious beliefs, skills, and ways of life that significantly altered the cultural mix of the British colonies. Some played important roles in spreading the Enlightenment, while others started the Great Awakening. The immigrants from the European continent and the British Isles sought a new beginning in "the best poor man's country": many disembarked in the Middle Colonies, traveling west to settle the backcountry from Pennsylvania south through the Shenandoah Valley to the Carolinas. Others went directly to Georgia, which reformers started in 1732 as a haven for the poor. The population explosion and demand for new lands brought the British colonists face to face with the Spanish in Florida, the French in Canada and the Ohio Valley, and Native Americans all along the frontier.

German and Scots-Irish Immigrants

More than 100,000 Germans left their homelands for America during the century after 1683; most of them

Map 4.1 *German and Scots-Irish Settlements in Colonial British America, c. 1760*
Germans and Scots-Irish were relative latecomers in colonial British America, so they established farms outside the first English settlements. Many entered ports on the Delaware River, moved north and west in Pennsylvania, then south through western Maryland, the Shenandoah Valley of Virginia, and North and South Carolina.

immigrated between 1727 and 1756. Some were forced out by religious persecution, oppressive regulations, and war; others sought economic opportunity. Promoters called "newlanders" told Germans of cheap fertile land and mild government in the British colonies. Many immigrants paid their own passage. Those who could not signed on as "redemptioners," the equivalent of indentured servants, whose labor would be sold for a number of years upon arrival. Immigrants went to ports from New York to Georgia, with most entering the Delaware Valley. Some Germans remained in Philadelphia, but the majority headed for the Pennsylvania hinterland and south through the backcountry of Maryland, Virginia, and the Carolinas.

German-speaking immigrants found the freedom they sought in North America, congregating in distinct communities, building separate churches and schools, and maintaining German language and culture. Pennsylvania was the heart of German America, as the colony's religious freedom allowed a multitude of sects and churches to flourish—the Mennonites, Amish, Brethren, Moravians, Schwenkfelders, Lutheran, and Reformed.

Cultural exchange between the Germans and English enriched American society. German churches installed organs and introduced the sophisticated choral music of their homelands. The printer Christopher Saur reprinted German hymnals along with his German-language newspaper and almanac. Congregations founded schools in which children learned both German and English. Immigrants retained the old tongue in their churches and homes, but used English in business, the courts, and politics. German American decorative arts proliferated by the 1740s, in house ornaments, furniture, and elaborately illustrated documents, such as marriage certificates, with gothic *Fraktur* lettering.

German farm women did much heavier fieldwork than most English wives, but otherwise played a similar role in maintaining domestic culture. Germans favored the more efficient European stoves over English fireplaces, and pewter over tinware. In diet, they ate relatively little meat and preferred coffee to tea.

The baptismal certificate is an example of German American Fraktur, *or documents illustrated with color designs and drawings.*
Courtesy, Winterthur Museum

But like their English neighbors, German women served as midwives and dispensed herbal remedies.

Though some German immigrants engaged in politics and law, most remained uninvolved in government during the colonial period. As non-British immigrants with little wealth, they needed time to become naturalized, learn the language and political culture, and establish themselves economically. As exiles from persecution, high taxes, and war, Germans were grateful for the high degree of freedom that they found in the new land.

Large numbers of Scots, Scots-Irish, and Irish Catholics also came during the eighteenth century, settling in New York, Pennsylvania, Delaware, western Maryland, and the southern backcountry. Most were Ulster Scots (or Scots-Irish as they were called in America), Presbyterians whose families had migrated during the 1600s from Scotland to northern Ireland in search of economic opportunity. There they had combined tenant farming and weaving until the early eighteenth century, when their leases expired. Because landlords raised rents exorbitantly, many Ulster Scots left with their families for the colonies. The first large wave of immigrants departed during 1717–1718; poor harvests and downturns in the linen industry impelled successive groups toward America.

In the colonies, the Scots-Irish achieved a reputation as tough defenders of the frontier. As relatively late arrivals, they had to stake out farms on the edges of existing white settlements. The combination of agriculture and linen manufacture was a distinctive contribution of the Ulster Scots to the colonial economy. As frontier inhabitants, the Scots-Irish came into frequent contact with Native Americans, often with tragic results. The new settlers often marked out their farms on Indian hunting lands without negotiating a sale. One Pennsylvania frontiersman, not recognizing the Indians' rights, echoed the early Puritans when he argued that it was contrary to "the laws of God and nature, that so much land should be idle, while so many Christians wanted it to labor on, and to raise their bread."

The Founding of Georgia

The last of the British mainland colonies, Georgia lured many German and Scots-Irish immigrants, as well as Scots and English. Animated by Enlightenment ideals of human progress and freedom, James Oglethorpe and John Viscount Percival, members of the Associates of the Late Doctor Bray, a philanthropic society, sought a charter for the colony. They were convinced that something had to be done to help the poor. They also argued that the settlement could serve as a buffer between Spanish Florida and South Carolina. The English had craved the region since the late seventeenth century when Carolinians destroyed the Spanish missions of Guale. George II granted the charter, placing control of the colony in the hands of trustees, or proprietors, who could neither receive financial benefits from the province nor own land within its bounds.

The double function of Georgia as a haven for the poor and a military outpost shaped the terms under which settlers immigrated. The trustees intended to create a peaceful, moral society of small farmers in which everyone, except indentured servants, worked for themselves. The proprietors wanted to avoid duplicating lowland South Carolina where large plantation owners lived off the toil of their slaves. The Georgia Trustees, led by Oglethorpe, set three significant policies: they prohibited importation of hard liquor, banned slaveholding, and limited land ownership to 500 acres or less. Each free male immigrant was granted land at no charge, but no one could buy or sell real estate, and only men could inherit land. The trustees hoped to keep Georgia as a refuge for small farmers who, coincidentally, would defend the southern frontier.

In February 1733, the ship *Anne* with approximately one hundred passengers arrived at a site on the Savannah River. Here they built the first town, Savannah, on a high bluff overlooking the river. Oglethorpe purchased land from the Native Americans and pledged to prevent price gouging in trade, a significant complaint of the Indians against South Carolina merchants. He established alliances with Lower Creeks, Cherokees, and Chickasaws against Spanish Florida, not least because English traders offered better merchandise than their rivals.

Many settlers in Georgia believed that the prohibitions on liquor, land sales, and slavery were unreasonable, but they could do little to change the colony's direction because they lacked a representative assembly. The embargo on rum, a major Caribbean commodity, prevented expansion of trade with the West Indies, a ready market for their abundant lumber. The bans on slavery and large landholdings were also unpopular with many settlers, who coveted the grander lifestyle of planters north of the Savannah River, in South Carolina.

In consequence, Georgia grew slowly, as some settlers left almost immediately. The trustees gradually recognized their failure, allowing the importation of rum in 1742, and land sales and slavery in 1750. Preparing to turn the colony over to the Crown, in 1751 they called together Georgia's first elected assembly,

A view of Savannah as it stood on the 29th of March 1734.

which obtained legislative powers three years later when the royal government took control. The Georgia population swelled as South Carolinians migrated across the Savannah River, transforming Georgia into a slave society. By 1773, the province had 33,000 inhabitants, of whom 45 percent were enslaved blacks.

Despite its halting start before 1750, Georgia attracted settlers of a variety of nationalities and religions. The colony tapped the eighteenth-century flow of European immigrants, including Spanish and German Jews and German-speaking Lutherans. One of the Lutheran ministers described their satisfaction with the new land: "Every year God gives them what they need. And since they have been able to earn something apart from agriculture, through the mills which have been built and in many other ways, they have managed rather well with God's blessing, and have led a calm and quiet life of blessedness and honesty." Another group of German Protestants, the Moravians, were less content in Georgia, where they hoped to convert the Native Americans. Led by Count Nikolaus Ludwig von Zinzendorf, they arrived in 1735 and were gone five years later, because as pacifists, Moravian men could not serve in the militia. When the threat of Spanish invasion intensified in the late 1730s, most of the Moravians departed for Pennsylvania, which required no military service.

The Growth of the African American Population

The failure of the trustees to create a free society in Georgia was symptomatic of the entrenchment of slavery in America. Like the Germans and Scots-Irish, Africans helped diversify the American population and shape its culture. Though the number of African Americans grew naturally in many places, slave traders imported over 200,000 people between 1720 and the Revolution, most from West and Central Africa. In 1750, blacks comprised one-fifth of the population of the mainland colonies, including about 40 percent in the Chesapeake and the Lower South.

As the number of African Americans increased and slave societies matured, blacks created patterns of community, work, and culture. Extended kinship networks structured community life on large plantations, and even in places where slaves lived in small households, such as in northern cities, family ties remained paramount. Blacks were most successful in perpetuating African language and customs in regions where they were most numerous, particularly the

Venture Smith Resists Slavery

Born in West Africa around 1729, Venture Smith was captured at age six by an enemy army. He was sold as a slave and taken to Rhode Island, then worked for his master carding wool and farming on Fisher's Island. His autobiography, published in 1798 after he had purchased freedom for himself and his family, graphically depicts his enslavement and resistance to slavery.

. . .After I had lived with my master thirteen years, being then about twenty-two years old, I married Meg, a slave of his who was about my own age. My master owned a certain Irishman, named Heddy, who about that time formed a plan of secretly leaving his master. After he had long had this plan in meditation, he suggested it to me. At first I cast a deaf ear to it, and rebuked Heddy for harboring in his mind such a rash undertaking. But after he had persuaded and much enchanted me with the prospect of gaining my freedom by such a method, I at length agreed to accompany him. Heddy next inveigled two of his fellow-servants to accompany us. The place to which we designed to go was the Mississippi. Our next business was to lay in a sufficient store of provisions for our voyage. We privately collected out of our master's store, six great old cheeses, two firkins of butter, and one batch of new bread. When we had gathered all our own clothes and some more, we took them all about midnight and went to the water side. We stole our master's boat, embarked, and then directed our course for the Mississippi River.

We mutually confederated not to betray or desert one another on pain of death. We first steered our course for Montauk Point, the east end of Long Island. After our arrival there, we landed, and Heddy and I made an incursion into the island after fresh water. . . . [Later, Heddy] went directly to the boat,

stole all the clothes in it, and then travelled away for East Hampton. . . . I advertised Heddy and sent two men in search of him. They pursued and overtook him at Southampton and returned him to the boat. I then thought it might afford some chance for my freedom, or at least be a palliation for my running away, to return Heddy immediately to his master, and inform him that I was induced to go away by Heddy's address. Accordingly, I set off with him and the rest of my companions for my master's, and arrived there without any difficulty. I informed my master that Heddy was the ringleader of our revolt, and that he had used us ill. He immediately put Heddy into custody, and myself and companions were well received and went to work as usual.

Not a long time passed after that before Heddy was sent by my master to New London jail. At the close of that year I was sold to a Thomas Stanton, and had to be separated from my wife and one daughter, who was about one month old. He resided at Stonington Point. To this place I brought with me from my late master's, two johannes, three old Spanish dollars, and two thousand of coppers, besides the five pounds of my wife's money. This money I got by cleaning gentlemen's shoes and drawing-boots, by catching muskrats and minks, raising potatoes and carrots, etc., and by fishing in the night, and at odd spells.

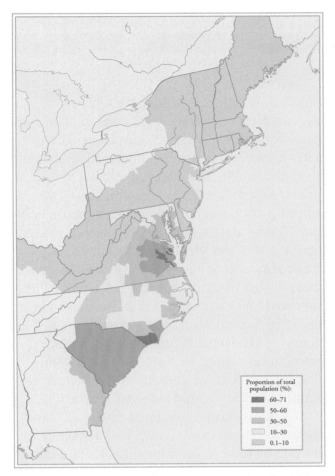

Map 4.2 *African American Population in Colonial British America, c. 1760*
A much higher concentration of enslaved African Americans lived in colonies south of Pennsylvania. Notice, however, that the percentage of slaves in parts of New York and New Jersey was as high as in portions of the Chesapeake region and North Carolina. Uniform data for South Carolina mask the fact that the population of African Americans was much larger along the seacoast than in the upcountry.

ceived a certain amount of work to perform each day—a field to hoe, thread to spin, a fence to build. Those who completed their assignments quickly had time to raise their own crops and livestock. Consequently, Carolina slaves participated in trade, selling their production at the "Negro market" in Charleston on Sundays. As in Africa, women were responsible for marketing the family's goods. In the Chesapeake, most slaves on plantations labored for a specified number of hours rather than by the task. They planted, weeded, or harvested in gangs until the overseer told them to stop. As a result, they had little time to work for themselves.

The persistence of African culture was conspicuous in language, food, music, dance, and religion. Some newly arrived Africans knew Dutch, Spanish, Portuguese, French, or English from former contacts in Africa or the West Indies, but to communicate with other slaves and with Europeans, most adopted Creole speech, a combination of English and African languages. In the Lower South, for instance, the Creole tongue known as Gullah evolved from English and various languages from southern Nigeria, the Gold Coast, Angola, and Senegambia. African Americans retained black dialect from Creole. For example, most blacks used the word *buckra*, from the African word meaning "he who governs," to refer to white men. Africans also influenced white

South Carolina low country and, later, Georgia. Because they came from hundreds of societies in Africa, with many different cultural attributes, they had difficulty keeping traditional ways intact. They melded African and European forms together, and in the process, influenced evolving mainstream cultures, especially in the South.

The opportunity of slaves to engage in independent activities varied with the amount of time they had to spend working for their master. In South Carolina, blacks labored by the task; each slave re-

This illustration on a 1751 map drawn by Joshua Fry and Peter Jefferson, father of Thomas, demonstrates the significance of enslaved Africans in the Chesapeake labor force.
Colonial Williamsburg Foundation

PICTURING THE PAST ◆ SOCIAL & CULTURAL EVENTS

SLAVE ADVERTISEMENTS

Courtesy, American Antiquarian Society

Colonial newspapers regularly published advertisements of enslaved Africans for sale and notices of escaped servants and slaves. These items often provide detailed information about the skills, health, and living conditions of African Americans. This excerpt includes, first, a notice for "A Parcel of likely young Negroes to be Sold." These slaves had probably been imported from Africa or the West Indies. Another advertisement is to sell "A Strong, healthy and handy Negro Woman, that has had the Small Pox and can do all sorts of Houshold Business, can speak English, and has been several years in the Country." This suggests qualities that were important to owners in cities such as Boston— ability to do all kinds of domestic work and familiarity with the language and region.

In the advertisement for the escaped slave Caesar, we learn about his age and appearance, and that he took some of his master's clothes. Like other owners who composed runaway advertisements, John Woods tried to guess the slave's motivation.

---

speech patterns, when white children and immigrants sometimes adopted African American dialect. One British traveler complained that plantation owners allowed "their children . . . . to prowl amongst the young Negroes, which insensibly causes them to imbibe their manners and broken speech." Some African words became part of American vocabulary, including cola, yam, goober (peanut), and toting (carrying) a package.

Blacks contributed to the food and material culture of British America, popularizing new foods such as okra, melons, and bananas. They made clay pipes, pottery, and baskets with African designs, and carved eating utensils, chairs, and other useful objects from wood. They built houses on African models rather than European. In music, they introduced the use of percussion instruments—cymbals, tambourines, and

drums—to British military bands. While masters discouraged Africans from drumming because of the potential to call others to revolt, whites enjoyed the music of black fiddlers. Slaves helped create the Virginia "jig," a fusion of African and European elements, accompanied by banjos and fiddles.

Along with whites, during the Great Awakening, Africans shaped the forms of worship in southern Baptist churches. Blacks retained traditional African concepts of the hereafter, where the deceased reunited with ancestors, combining these beliefs with European views of heaven. Funerals remained important to African Americans throughout the colonies, as mourners buried the dead facing Africa, with traditional rituals, music, and dance. In Philadelphia, for example, the blacks' burial ground was the focus of community activities where they gathered on Sundays and holidays, "dancing after the manner of their several nations in Africa, and speaking and singing in their native dialects." Blacks also passed down African medical practice, a combination of physical and psychological treatment including magic. More African American women than men were doctors, practicing midwifery as well as nursing and providing cures.

Despite cultural exchange and indications of human understanding, the antagonism and economic exploitation inherent in slavery poisoned relationships among whites and blacks. Whites believed that African Americans were an inferior race; masters used their power in the slave system to control their human property with harsh punishments. Nevertheless, blacks refused to accept their subordinate position, as increasing numbers ran away or were truant for weeks at a time.

Some enslaved Africans took more violent means, killing their masters or setting fire to fields and homes. In 1739, a group of more than fifty bondmen revolted near the Stono River in South Carolina. For most of a day, they marched with drums and banners from one plantation to another, killing about twenty whites. When armed planters defeated the rebels in battle, some of the slaves regrouped and headed for St. Augustine, Florida. But the South Carolina militia pursued the insurgents, putting to death everyone suspected of being involved. The Stono Uprising sent shock waves throughout the American colonies. The South Carolina legislature enacted a harsh slave code in an effort to prevent future revolts and limited slave importation for a decade. Most of the core group who planned the Stono Rebellion were African-born slaves, who hoped to escape to Florida, where Spanish authorities offered them religious sanctuary and freedom. By 1740, about one hundred former Carolina slaves had built the village of Gracia Real de Santa Teresa de Mose, called Mose, two miles north of St. Augustine.

During the eighteenth century, newly arrived Africans, often called "salt-water Negroes," were more likely to rebel or run away than Creole, or "country-born" slaves. With Native Americans and runaway white servants, escaped slaves created maroon societies in frontier areas. They farmed, raised livestock, hunted, and fished. In the Great Dismal Swamp, on the North Carolina-Virginia border, communities numbering perhaps 2,000 people took refuge from colonial authorities. The Dismal Swamp settlements grew from small groups of Native Americans from Virginia to include Indians and whites from the Carolinas and increasing numbers of escaped Africans.

Native American Worlds in the Mid-Eighteenth Century

As the British colonies grew, Native Americans chose strategies to maintain their communities and cultures. Those who remained within the British provinces were called by white Americans "Settlement Indians," "domestic Indians," or "little Tribes." Many lived among Euro-Americans and worked as servants, slaves, day laborers, mariners, artisans, and tenant farmers, assimilating some parts of English culture, but rejecting others. Others lived on remnants of traditional lands, such as the Mashpees in Massachusetts, Lenapes (or Delawares) in New Jersey, and Catawbas in South Carolina. They continued to hunt, fish, gather berries and wood, and raise corn while also trading with neighboring whites. Indians peddled venison and turkeys to the colonists or crafted baskets and brooms for sale. The Lenapes of central New Jersey farmed parcels of land through the eighteenth century: they pursued their traditional seasonal economy by hunting in Pennsylvania, fishing at the Jersey shore, and gathering berries and wood for baskets in the Pine Barrens.

Dr. Alexander Hamilton, a recent immigrant from Scotland, recorded many encounters with Indians in 1744 as he traveled through the settlements from Maryland to Maine. The Native Americans he met varied greatly in status, from an Indian sachem who had established himself as a wealthy planter to those on the margins, who tried to hold on to native traditions within an alien culture. In Rhode Island, he approached the large plantation of

> an Indian King named George . . . upon which he has many tennants and has, of his own, a good stock of horses and other cattle. The King lives after the English mode. His subjects have lost their own government policy and laws and are servants or vassals to the English here. His queen goes in a high modish dress in her silks, hoops, stays, and dresses like an English woman. He educates his children to the belles letters and is himself a very complaisant mannerly man. We pay'd him a visit, and he treated us with a glass of good wine.

During worship in a Boston church, Hamilton sat near several Native Americans. He met an Indian at Princeton who saluted him with "How' s't ni tap" and, in New York, watched "about ten Indians fishing for oysters . . . stark naked" near his tavern. While most native people who stayed in white settled areas had given up political autonomy, they had not surrendered all of their traditions. Many spoke English in addition to their native language, but did not learn to read and write.

David Brainerd's Mission to the Conoy and Lenape Indians, 1745

Rev. David Brainerd was born in Connecticut and attended Yale College, but became a New Light during the Great Awakening and was expelled for claiming his tutor was unsaved. Brainerd became a missionary to the Indians of Pennsylvania and New Jersey, and started a revival, with his Indian interpreter Moses (Tunda) Tatamy, among Lenapes at Crossweeksung in central New Jersey. As he describes in this excerpt from his published journal, however, Conoy Indians at Juneauta in the Susquehanna Valley were much less interested in his message.

September 19 [1745].—Visited an Indian town called Juneauta, situate on an island in Susquehannah. Was much discouraged with the temper and behaviour of the Indians here, although they appeared friendly when I was with them the last spring. . . .

September 20.—Visited the Indians again at Juneauta Island, and found them almost universally very busy in making preparations for a great sacrifice and dance. Had no opportunity to get them together in order to discourse with them about christianity, by reason of their being so much engaged about their sacrifice. . . .

In the evening they met together, near a hundred of them, and danced round a large fire, having prepared ten fat deer for the sacrifice; the fat of whose inwards they burned in the fire, while they were dancing, and sometimes raised the flame to a prodigious height, at the same time yelling and shouting in such a manner, that they might easily have been heard two miles or more.

They continued their sacred dance all night or near the matter; after which they ate the flesh of the sacrifice, and so retired each one to his lodging.

I enjoyed little satisfaction this night, being entirely alone on the island, as to any christian company, and in the midst of this idolatrous revel; . . . I at length crept into a little crib made for corn, and there slept on the poles.

Lord's Day, September 21.—Spent the day with the Indians on the island. As soon as they were well up in the morning, I attempted to instruct them, and laboured for that purpose to get them together, but quickly found they had something else to do; for near noon they gathered together all their powwows, or conjurers, and set about half a dozen of them to playing their juggling tricks, and acting their frantic distracted postures, in order to find out why they were then so sickly upon the island, numbers of them being at that time disordered with a fever and bloody flux. . . .

Their monstrous actions tended to excite ideas of horror, and seemed to have something in them, as I thought, peculiarly suited to raise the devil. . . . I sat at a small distance, not more than thirty feet from them, though undiscovered, with my Bible in my hand, resolving if possible to spoil their sport, and prevent their receiving any answers from the infernal world, and there viewed the whole scene. They continued their hideous charms and incantations for more than three hours, until they had all wearied themselves out, although they had in that space of time taken sundry intervals of rest, and at length broke up, I apprehended, without receiving any answer at all.

After they had done powwowing, I attempted to discourse with them about christianity; but they soon scattered, and gave me no opportunity for anything of that nature.

Crosweeksung, in New-Jersey, 1745. Preached to my people from John xiv, 1.–6. The divine presence seemed to be in the assembly. Numbers were affected with divine truths, and it was a season of comfort to some in particular.

O! what a difference is there between these and the Indians I had lately treated with upon Susquehannah! To be with those seemed like being banished from God and all his people: to be with these like being admitted into his family and to the enjoyment of his divine presence! How great is the change lately made upon numbers of these Indians, who not many months ago were many of them as thoughtless, and averse to christianity as those upon Susquehannah! And how astonishing is that grace that has made this change!

The Lenape leader Teedyuscung by William Sauts NetamuX'we Bock. In this drawing, Teedyuscung's combination of a Euro-American coat and vest and Indian hairstyle and jewelry reflects his attempt to bridge cultures.
By permission of Yale University Press

The Great Awakening made a significant impact on many Indians within colonial settlements who had long resisted Christianity. The dynamic preaching of New Light ministers, who welcomed enthusiastic response from their listeners, was attractive to Native Americans who had retained traditional rituals and dance. The Society in Scotland for Propagating Christian Knowledge, a group of Presbyterian ministers and laymen, supported missions in the Middle Colonies, particularly that of Reverend David Brainerd and, after his death in 1747, his brother Reverend John Brainerd. David Brainerd was expelled from Yale College because he had joined the New Lights and became a missionary to Indians in Pennsylvania and New Jersey. With crucial assistance from his Lenape interpreter, Moses (Tunda) Tatamy, he inspired a

revival at Crossweeksung in central New Jersey. The community soon outgrew its limited space, so Brainerd encouraged the Lenapes to move to another site, where he attempted to create a New England-style praying town. While the Indians attended the Presbyterian church and school, they did not give up their seasonal economy of hunting, fishing, and gathering as the Brainerds hoped. Other New Jersey Lenapes joined the Moravian missions near Bethlehem, Pennsylvania, while many continued to resist Christianity altogether.

Native Americans who intended to preserve their political independence moved west, a strategy that worked temporarily. From 1660 to the 1740s, for example, Iroquois, Shawnees, and Lenapes relocated in the eastern part of the Ohio Valley, from the Allegheny River in western Pennsylvania to west-central Ohio. Wyandots inhabited the lands to the west, at Sandusky and near the French fort at Detroit. Some Iroquois migrated from western New York, while Lenapes and Shawnees moved from eastern Pennsylvania under pressure from white settlers. Some of the Lenapes left the east as a result of the "Walking Purchase" of 1737, when two of William Penn's sons, the proprietors, used an alleged 1686 deed to cheat the Indians out of their territory on the Pennsylvania side of the Delaware River. The deed, of which only a copy survived, ceded lands as far as a man could walk in one and a half days. Coerced by an alliance between the Penns and the Iroquois, the Lenapes agreed to comply. The Penns sent runners in relay to cover more than sixty miles of land in a day and a half, a deception the Lenapes could not fail to remember; in 1754, with the outbreak of war on the Pennsylvania frontier, many sought revenge.

The Ohio Valley became the focus of conflict in the 1740s as the British and French competed for trade. Following the Lenapes and Shawnees west, some Pennsylvania traders took up residence in the multi-ethnic towns such as Chiningue (or Logstown), where Iroquois, Lenapes, Shawnees, Ottawas, and other Indians lived. The Ohio Valley, as one Indian leader said, was "a country in between" the English and the French, unfortunately a country that the Europeans craved. From 1754 to 1814, the Native Americans fought the British and Americans to keep their lands and native religions, forging pan-Indian alliances to meet the Anglo threat.

WARS FOR EMPIRE

For a quarter century beginning in 1739, the British colonies took part in conflicts between Great Britain and Spain, France, and Native Americans. The War of Jenkins' Ear (1739–1744) against Spain; King George's War (1744–1748) against France; the Seven

Years' War (1754–1763), also called the French and Indian War in the colonies; and the Indian war for autonomy in the Ohio Valley (1763–1765) all required British colonists to participate more actively in defending the empire.

The Southern Frontier

The colonies along the southern tier—British South Carolina and Georgia, Spanish Florida, French Louisiana, and Spanish Texas and New Mexico—competed for trade with Native Americans and control of territory. Except for war between Georgia and Florida in the early 1740s, the most important battles along the southern rim were commercial, a competition the British traders often won because they had more plentiful and cheaper goods. They exchanged tools, clothing, scissors, guns, ammunition, and rum, in return for slaves, deerskins, and furs from the Indians. In comparison with the English provinces, the Spanish and French colonies remained small and badly supplied by their parent nations. In 1760, Florida had approximately 3,000 Hispanic settlers, Texas had 1,200, and New Mexico about 9,000, while Louisiana counted 4,000 whites and 5,000 enslaved Africans. In contrast, in the same year, South Carolina and Georgia had a population of about 45,000 whites and 59,000 black slaves.

Governor James Oglethorpe of Georgia tried to use the outbreak of the War of Jenkins' Ear to eject the Spanish from Florida. As part of the 1713 Treaty of Utrecht, Britain had obtained the *asiento,* the right to sell a specified number of African slaves and commodities to the Spanish provinces. This opening led to British smuggling, which the Spanish countered with heavy-handed searches of British ships. Accounts of Spanish brutality inflamed the British public, especially when Captain Robert Jenkins displayed one of his ears, which he claimed the Spanish cut off when they caught him smuggling. In 1740, Oglethorpe attacked Florida with seven ships and 2,000 troops. They captured several Spanish forts and Mose, the village of escaped Carolina blacks, but failed to conquer Fort San Marcos, where the residents of St. Augustine and Mose took cover. A large percentage of Florida residents were soldiers to guard Atlantic shipping lanes. When Hispanic and black soldiers slipped out of the fort and recaptured Mose, and then the fort was resupplied by Cuba, Oglethorpe retreated.

In 1741, a force of 3,600 colonists participated in the British expedition against the Spanish fort at Cartagena, in what is now Colombia. The campaign ended bitterly, with heavy losses from battle and smallpox.

The following year, the Spanish took revenge for the invasion of Florida by attacking St. Simon's Island, Georgia, but withdrew before conquering it. After some minor skirmishes, both sides gave up, bringing calm to the Georgia-Florida border.

King George's War

The British avoided further conflict with Florida because, in 1744, they began hostilities with France in the War of the Austrian Succession, known to the colonists as King George's War. The war began in Europe, but spilled into North America when, provoked by French attacks on Nova Scotia, Governor William Shirley of Massachusetts launched an attack on Louisbourg, which controlled access to the St. Lawrence River. In April 1745, 4,000 New England farmers and fishermen assaulted the French garrison, which held out against the badly organized offensive until June, then surrendered. New Englanders considered Louisbourg a great victory, even after many of their troops succumbed to disease. The war degenerated into a series of debilitating border raids. The Canadians and their Indian allies ravaged Saratoga, New York, and northern New England. In spring 1746, a fleet of seventy-six ships left France to retake Louisbourg, but after fighting disease and Atlantic storms for three months they returned to France empty-handed.

Despite this reprieve, New Englanders had little to celebrate, for they faced another threat—from their own imperial navy. During the war, Parliament permitted naval officers to impress sailors without the permission of colonial authorities. The Royal Navy used impressment, or involuntary recruitment, because many seamen fled the harsh conditions on naval vessels. In 1747, several thousand Bostonians protested when a British press gang from the fleet of Admiral Charles Knowles swept up men along the waterfront. The mob surrounded the governor's house and burned a British barge in his courtyard. When the governor called up the militia, the troops refused to move. Knowles threatened to shell the town, but after negotiations lasting several days, he released the impressed men instead.

As the colonists became more involved in imperial politics, they learned that their interests held little sway. To their shock, the British government restored Louisbourg to the French in the Treaty of Aix-la-Chapelle (1748), as the combatants agreed to return all North American territories seized during the war. Despite heavy human and financial costs, the war brought no change in the power balance between Great Britain and France in North America.

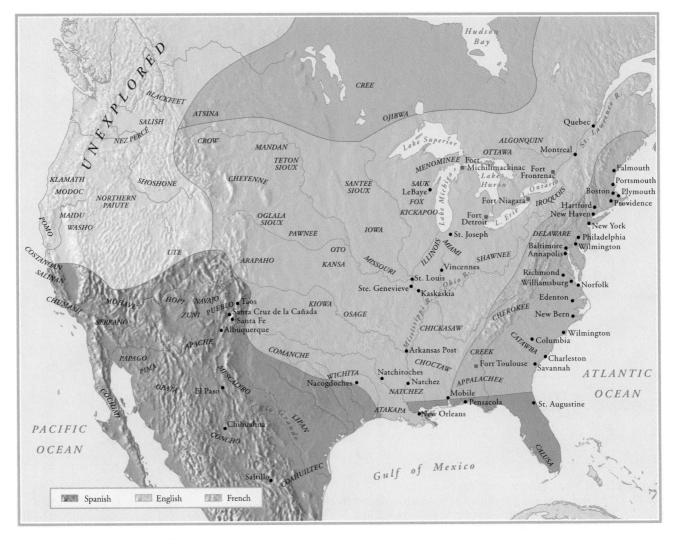

Map 4.3 *North America in 1750*

Great Britain, France, and Spain claimed the indicated areas just before the Seven Years' War. While waves of immigrants from Germany and the British Isles had expanded settlement in the British provinces since 1700 (see Map 3.3), the French colonies still consisted primarily of trading posts, forts, and relatively small agricultural areas. Native Americans controlled much of the territory claimed by France.

The Seven Years' War

During King George's War, the British and Iroquois had evicted French traders from the Ohio Valley. The Canadians returned, however, backed by a government that was determined to force out the British colonists who had stepped-up activity in the area. The Ohio Company of Virginia, which had received the rights to half a million acres from the British government, in 1749 made preparations to sell land in the region of present-day Pittsburgh, Pennsylvania, where the Monongahela and Allegheny rivers combine to form the Ohio River. Virginia's claim to the territory dated from its charter. In response, the French constructed forts to stop the incursion of Anglo-American traders and Virginia's land speculators. In 1754, the governor of Virginia sent a young militia officer, George Washington, with about 160 troops to erect a stronghold to defend the colony's interests. When hostilities resulted, the Virginians were defeated at the inadequate structure they had built, Fort Necessity, by a superior force of French and Indians.

Recognizing that war was imminent, seven colonies sent delegates to a congress at Albany, New York, where they negotiated unsuccessfully with the

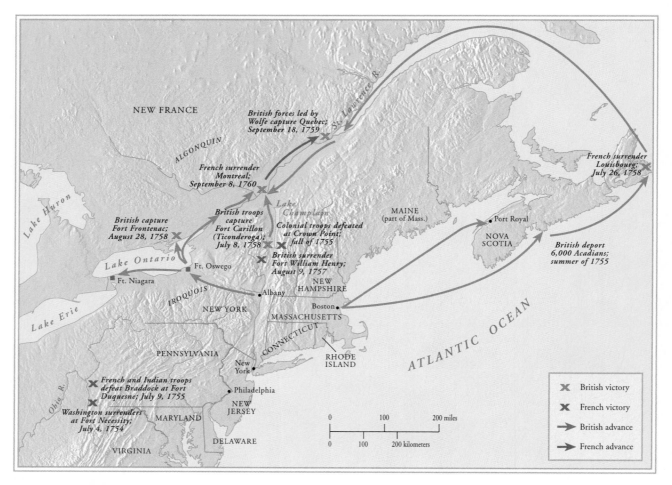

Map 4.4 *Seven Years' War in North America*
The war began in the Ohio Valley, an area Virginians claimed and hoped to sell to settlers. To do so, they had to force out the French, who sent troops to establish ownership; defeat the Delawares and Shawnees, who had built towns along the Allegheny and Ohio Rivers; and prevail over Pennsylvania's competing charter claims.

Iroquois for an alliance against the French. The Albany Congress also amended and adopted the Albany Plan devised by Benjamin Franklin to unite the colonies for common defense. The plan would have to be endorsed by each colony and the Crown. When the delegates returned home with the proposal for an intercolonial government empowered to tax, pass laws, and supervise military defense, not one of the assemblies approved.

The British decided to destroy French forts in what they considered their territory even before a formal declaration of war. In early 1755, Major General Edward Braddock landed in the colonies with two British regiments. Joined by hundreds of provincial soldiers, the army marched through the Virginia backcountry to capture Fort Duquesne (now Pittsburgh). The British troops were unprepared for frontier fighting, but thought their mission was easy because the garrison had only 250 French troops. Ten miles short

Benjamin Franklin published his "Snake Device" just before the Albany Congress in 1754. Considered the first political cartoon in the colonies, it later became an important symbol of American resistance to Britain.
The Historical Society of Pennsylvania

The Death of General Wolfe, *by Benjamin West. Though an inaccurate depiction of the British victory at Quebec, the painting has several interesting features: the Mohawk prominently represents the Iroquois-British alliance and the colonial ranger behind him wears Indian moccasins and leggings.*
National Gallery of Canada, Ottawa. Transfer from the Canada War Memorials, 1921 (Gift of the 2nd Duke of Westminster, Eaton Hall, Cheshire, 1918)

of Fort Duquesne, however, the French and allied Indians ambushed Braddock's army, killing or wounding two-thirds of the British force. The general himself was mortally wounded. George Washington, his uniform ripped by bullets, led the retreat.

The 650 Native Americans who fought with the French included their traditional allies and some Delawares and Iroquois of the Ohio Valley who had previously supported the British. By 1754, some Ohio Indians were convinced that Britain and its colonies posed the greatest threat to their lands; with the defeat of Braddock, many more joined the French. Between 1755 and 1757, Delawares, Shawnees, Iroquois, and many others attacked the white frontier from Pennsylvania to Virginia, burning settlements and killing or capturing thousands of colonists.

Help for the westerners was slow in coming. In 1756, the struggle in North America became part of the larger European conflict known as the Seven Years'

War, in which Great Britain supported Prussia against Austria, Russia, and France. The French penetrated into New York, seizing Fort William Henry and 2,000 soldiers at Lake George. The tide changed after the British statesman William Pitt took command of the war effort. He poured money and men into the American theater, expecting colonial legislatures to do the same. The new generals Jeffery Amherst and James Wolfe, with an army of almost 10,000 men, captured Louisbourg in July 1758. The French then pulled their troops out of the Ohio Valley to protect Quebec and Montreal, allowing the British to take control of the west. Without French supplies and devastated by smallpox, the Native Americans ended their war on the frontier.

In 1759, the British and provincial armies had even greater success, leading some of the Iroquois of New York to abandon neutrality to join their side. The British reestablished control of New York, while from Louisbourg, General Wolfe sailed up the St. Lawrence to Quebec, where after several months his forces pierced the defenses of the well-fortified city. The next year, Amherst's army seized Montreal, thus ending French control of Canada.

While the defeat of Canada marked the end of the war in North America, the Seven Years' War continued off the coast of France, in India, and in the West Indies. The British military took a number of French sugar islands, including the richest, Guadeloupe. When Spain entered the conflict as France's ally in 1762 in return for the promise of lands west of the Mississippi River, the British captured Manila in the Philippines and Havana, Cuba.

During the Seven Years' War, thousands of colonists joined the British army, and many more served in the provincial forces. The experience brought ordinary settlers into close contact with the imperial authorities—and many loathed the experience. The British army contained professional soldiers drilled rigorously in military tactics, cleanliness, and order. Women served in the field, generally soldiers' wives who cooked, washed, and nursed. British officers, from the upper classes, maintained discipline with punishments of death for major offenses such as desertion, and up to 1,000 lashes—which could also kill—for lesser crimes. The British officers disdained the colonial units, which submitted to much lighter discipline and sometimes elected their superiors. Because the provincials failed to keep their camps and clothing clean, many died from disease. For their part, some colonial soldiers thought the British regulars were immoral, profane men who needed to be controlled with brutal discipline.

The British colonists welcomed the Treaty of Paris in 1763, which finally ended the war. Under the treaty, France lost all of its territory in North America, but retrieved the valuable sugar islands of Guadeloupe and Martinique. Spain relinquished Florida to get back Cuba and the Philippines and, because the British lacked interest in the region, acquired French territory west of the Mississippi and New Orleans, located on the east side of the river. The Treaty of Paris gave the British colonists security from France and Spain, while the home government received two unprofitable colonies, Canada and Florida. The provincials celebrated the victory with patriotic fervor, as New York City raised a statue of George III, who had taken the throne in 1760 at age twenty-two. Many colonists, especially New England ministers, had interpreted the war as a fight against Catholicism and tyranny. They viewed the victory as a sign that God favored Britain and its colonies. One Massachusetts clergyman preached,

Safe from the Enemy of the Wilderness, safe from the gripping Hand of arbitrary Sway and cruel Superstition; Here shall be the late founded Seat of Peace and Freedom. Here shall our indulgent Mother [Britain], who has most generously rescued and protected us, be served and honoured by growing Numbers, with all Duty, Love and Gratitude, till Time shall be no more.

The Indians Renew War in the Ohio Valley

The Treaty of Paris seriously undermined the position of Native Americans east of the Mississippi whether they had fought for the British or French, or had remained neutral. The defeat of France worsened the situation of native people in the Ohio Valley, for they could no longer play one European nation off the other. The British alone supplied European goods, so they could set prices and the terms of trade. They ended the custom of giving annual presents, charged high prices, stopped selling rum, and reduced the amount of ammunition sold. Further, with the end of the Seven Years' War, white settlers streamed west into Indian lands, as wealthy land speculators and poor squatters alike ignored treaties that colonial governments had made with the Native Americans.

The altered British trade policies and land grabbing drove many Delawares, Shawnees, Iroquois, and others to renew the fighting. They gained spiritual unity from the Delaware prophet Neolin, one of a line of spiritual leaders among the Delawares and Shawnees, who preached that Indians must reject Christianity and European goods, particularly rum, and revitalize their ancient culture. Neolin called on Native Americans to drive the Europeans out, demanding: "Whereupon do you suffer the whites to dwell upon your lands? Drive them away; wage war against them. I love them not." He warned his followers, "if you suffer the English among you, you are dead men. Sickness, smallpox, and their poison will destroy you entirely."

Many Indians throughout the Ohio Valley adopted Neolin's strategy, boycotting the fur trade by hunting only for their own food and personal needs. The Delaware councils called for a gradual return to military skills with bow and arrow and adopted a ritual tea, which caused vomiting, to cleanse themselves of the "White people's ways and Nature." In 1763, Native Americans from western Pennsylvania through the Great Lakes region launched a pan-Indian assault on British garrisons, often called Pontiac's War. A follower of Neolin and leader of the Ottawas, Pontiac laid siege unsuccessfully to the British fort at Detroit. Other Indians defeated thirteen British outposts, though not

PICTURING THE PAST ✦ POLITICS & DIPLOMACY

TREATY NEGOTIATIONS

This engraving, *The Indians Giving a Talk to Colonel Bouquet . . . in Octr. 1764*, was based on a sketch by the artist Benjamin West. The illustration was first published in a 1766 account of Henry Bouquet's successful 1764 expedition against the Ohio Indians during Pontiac's War. Bouquet's troops left Fort Pitt on October 3rd, marching west toward the Muskingum River in what is now eastern Ohio. While en route they received a message that the Delaware and Shawnee leaders "were coming as soon as possible to treat of peace." After building fortifications, Bouquet and his aides met with the Indians October 17–20th. They struck a truce, and the Natives pledged to return white captives. When they delivered more than 200 captives by November 9th, the war ended east of the Muskingum but continued in the west. The engraving shows a typical treaty scene, with a Native leader using a wampum belt to speak, while a scribe took minutes.

Forts Niagara or Pittsburgh. While the British army established military dominance in the Ohio Valley by the end of 1763, after the Native Americans ran short of ammunition and succumbed to smallpox, fighting continued for two more years.

In addition to armed force, the British government tried to end the war by keeping white settlers out of the Ohio Valley. The king issued the Proclamation of 1763, which drew a line along the crest of the Appalachian Mountains from Maine to Georgia, requiring colonists to stay east of the line. Colonial governors were instructed to prohibit surveys or land grants west of the Proclamation line; only authorized agents of the Crown could buy lands from the Indians for future settlement. The Proclamation failed in its purpose, however, as land speculators continued their operations and immigrants demanded farms. The British government, weighed down by debt from the Seven Years' War, failed to supply manpower to enforce the law. The government withdrew troops from the Ohio Valley and Great Lakes

region, while provincial governments, dominated by speculators, ignored encroachment on Indian lands.

THE BRITISH PROVINCES IN 1763

The end of the Seven Years' War brought pivotal changes in British North America. For over a century and a half, Europeans had crossed the ocean to trade with the Native Americans, build farms and businesses, and develop networks of Atlantic commerce. The colonies had dealt with crises, from economic slumps to rebellions, becoming ever more confident of their position as semi-independent societies. During the last quarter century, with greater involvement in imperial affairs and rising importation of consumer goods, the provincials felt more a part of the British empire—more English—even as they created a separate identity as Americans. Most importantly, they believed that they were equal to the residents of Great Britain, that they possessed the rights of English people.

The Economy

In 1763, the mainland provinces still operated within the system of British mercantilism, which consisted of regulations on colonial trade and manufactures. For mercantilism to work to Britain's benefit, the colonies had to produce raw materials and agricultural staples needed by the home economy and serve as a market for its manufactured goods. Such colonial products as sugar, molasses, tobacco, cotton, certain wood products, copper, and furs were "enumerated," meaning that they could be shipped only to Britain or British colonial ports, not to foreign countries such as France and Spain. The basic laws establishing the British mercantilist system were the seventeenth-century Navigation Acts, which Parliament supplemented from time to time. Though most colonial trade conformed to the law by the eighteenth century, smuggling occurred often enough to prompt demands within the British government for strict enforcement. In particular, colonial shippers bribed customs officials to ignore the Molasses Act (1733), which levied prohibitive duties on foreign sugar products, including a tax of sixpence per gallon on molasses. The British West Indies planters had pushed for the act to create a monopoly for themselves, lowering the cost of provisions and raising the price of their exports. If the Molasses Act had been enforced, it would have severely damaged the economies of New England and the Middle Colonies, which traded with the French, Spanish, and Dutch West Indies as well as the British islands.

Other laws passed by Parliament prior to 1763 had a significant but uneven impact on colonial economic growth. British legislation, combined with lack of investment capital, limited the development of most manufactures. The Woolen Act (1699) and the Hat Act (1732) banned the export of American-produced woolen products and hats from one colony to another. Other laws prohibited the export of machinery and the migration of skilled craftsmen from Britain to America. The Iron Act (1750) allowed duty-free import of colonial bar iron into Britain, but forbade fabrication of iron goods in the colonies. Nevertheless, crude iron production received substantial investment, as did shipbuilding and rum distilling. Unhampered by mercantilist regulation, North American shipbuilders produced nearly 40 percent of vessels in the British-owned merchant fleet.

Despite these laws, the wealth of the British colonies increased between the 1720s and 1760, as trade flourished with the West Indies and, after 1750, with southern Europe, where crop failures and population growth swelled demand for wheat and flour. The Middle Colonies, already expanding with German and Irish immigration, were well situated to supply new markets. Philadelphia became the largest city in the British colonies: its wealthy merchants invested in ships, built mansions, purchased coaches and other luxuries, and speculated in western lands from the profits of trade. Artisans, shopkeepers, and farmers prospered. To the south, large planters in the Chesapeake and Carolinas accumulated great estates, while ordinary farmers more modestly improved their standard of living. All along the eastern seaboard, after 1750, white families indulged in what has been called a "consumer revolution." Not only could they purchase cloth, clothing, carpets, paper, gloves, mirrors, clocks, silverware, china tea sets, pottery, and books, but they had more choices in the specific kind of cloth or paper or gloves they could buy. In New York City in the 1750s, for instance, merchants advertised gloves of various colors—purple, orange, white, and flowered—as well as different sizes and materials, including chamois, silk, "Maid's Lamb Gloves," and "Men's Dog Skin Gloves." This is just one example of the wide variety of consumer goods that became available in mid-century.

The colonies became major markets for textiles, metalware, and other items, which under the Navigation Acts they could import only from Britain. The consumer revolution made the British more attentive to their North American provinces, while at the same time, the imports helped to create in America a more standardized English culture. Affluent colonists became aware of the latest fashions in England, and complained when they received out-of-date merchandise. The young George Washington groused in 1760, for example, "that instead of getting things good and fashionable in their several kinds we often have Articles sent Us that coud only have been usd by our Forefathers in the days of yore."

The economic upswing of the 1750s gave way to a depression after 1760, as the Seven Years' War moved to the Caribbean and military spending dropped. The seaport towns, having attracted workers during the wartime boom, faced deepening poverty and rising demands for relief. With depressed wages and long periods of unemployment, families found survival difficult. The resumption of immigration from Europe after the war intensified economic hardships and contributed to unrest on the frontier.

$\mathscr{P}$ICTURING THE PAST ✦ ECONOMICS & TECHNOLOGY

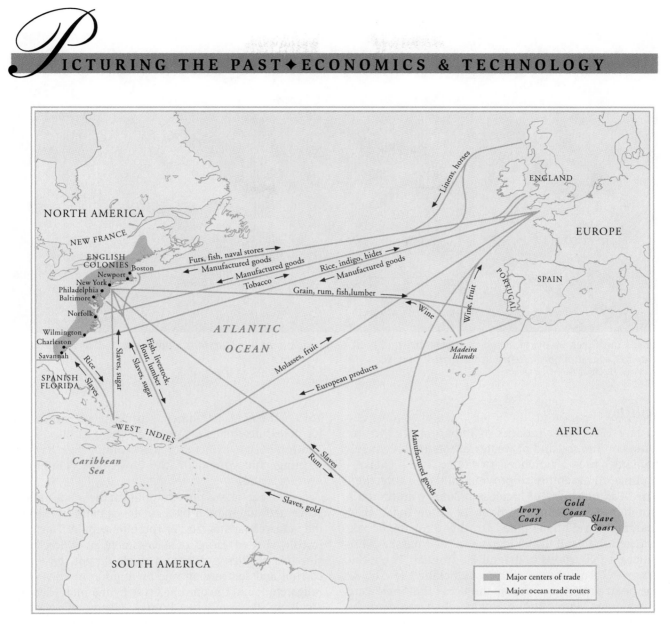

Map 4.5 *Colonial Overseas Trade*

By 1750, the Atlantic economy had matured, as each of the British mainland colonies developed products for sale in Great Britain, Europe, Africa, and the West Indies. Patterns of trade were much more complicated than the notion of a "triangular trade route" in which England sold manufactured goods in Africa in exchange for slaves who were sent to America where they produced sugar, tobacco, and rice destined for Europe. While this exchange was important, other trade patterns sustained colonial economies as well: shipment of fish and lumber from New England to the West Indies; and mid-Atlantic flour and meat to southern Europe and the West Indies. The fur trade linked Native Americans to the Atlantic economy. West Indies sugar—and the rum New England and Philadelphia distillers manufactured from it—found markets everywhere. Because the Navigation Acts allowed American ships to carry goods, the shipping trade itself became a significant source of income.

Grey's Inn Creek Shipyard, *by an unknown artist, c. 1760. Shipbuilding, at this Maryland shipyard as well as in northern seaports, was a major industry in the British colonies.*
Maryland Historical Society, Baltimore

Politics

In late 1763, after months of Indian attacks in the Ohio country, a band of western Scots-Irish Pennsylvanians used violence to force the Quaker-dominated assembly to provide military protection. The "Paxton Boys" of Lancaster County murdered a number of Christian Indians at Conestoga, then marched on Philadelphia. By the time the rebels reached the capital, the legislature had passed a bill raising 1,000 troops to defend the frontier. The westerners returned home without attacking the city. At the heart of their revolt was the belief that they were poorly represented in the provincial government. As the backcountry population exploded, eastern politicians guarded their power by allotting fewer assembly seats to outlying counties than they deserved.

The Paxton Boys revolt signaled the end of an era of political stability that had prevailed since the late 1720s in the British mainland provinces. As part of Britain's empire, the eighteenth-century colonists believed themselves among the most fortunate people on earth. The Glorious Revolution of 1688–1689, which removed James II, had ended the long, bitter contest between king and Parliament. The monarch's power was subsequently limited by the national legislature, comprised of the House of Lords, which represented the aristocracy, and the House of Commons, which in theory represented everyone else. As a result of the

1689 settlement, Parliament's consent was necessary for taxes, new courts, raising an army in peacetime, and foreign invasions. It gained control over its own meetings and, after 1707, the Crown lost veto power over legislation.

The balance of powers, political theorists argued, prevented domination by a single segment of society, the monarch, aristocracy, or common people. Thus, the British avoided forms of government considered destructive of liberty: rule by a single despot (tyranny); corrupt and self-serving rule by a group of aristocrats (oligarchy); and uncontrolled rule by the mob (democracy). In their provincial governments, the British colonists expected to find a similar balance, one that would protect their rights. Indeed, the prevailing structure of governor, appointed council, and elected lower house of assembly reflected the English model.

The British provinces were the only European settlements in North America where ordinary people could vote for representative legislatures. An estimated 50 to 75 percent of white men were qualified to vote in the British colonies, the result of much broader property ownership than in England, where about 15 to 30 percent of adult males had the franchise. According to English political theory, a person needed a "stake in society," a certain amount of property, to vote or hold office. Servants, slaves, children, and unpropertied men were beholden to someone else, so they could not make independent decisions. Giving them suffrage would award their owner, father, or employer another vote, the theorists claimed, especially in many places where people voted orally, in public. By tradition, women also lacked the franchise, whether or not they owned property or were married. Denial of the vote to all females arose from the belief that they were intellectually and morally inferior to men and thus should have no formal role in government.

The colonists favored direct representation, requiring their legislators to live in the area from which they were elected and to advocate the interests of their constituents, unlike England, where members of the House of Commons did not have to reside in their electoral districts. The British believed that Parliament represented all of the people of the empire whether they elected delegates or not, a concept known as virtual representation.

Beyond suffrage, English political theory also recognized the right of common people to resort to crowd action to withstand tyranny and require authorities to protect them from harm. The people had this right, theoretically, as long as violence was limited—directed at property rather than at persons. At various times, colonial mobs protested to prevent grain from being exported when food was in short supply, to destroy houses of prostitution, and to stop the British navy from impressing men into the king's service, as with the 1747 Knowles riot in Boston.

The Paxton Expedition, *by Henry Dawkins, depicts the threat by western "Paxton Boys" against Philadelphia, demanding frontier defense during Pontiac's War.*
The Library Company of Philadelphia

The most important and sustained political development in British America during the first half of the eighteenth century was the rise of the elected lower houses of assembly. The legislatures acquired greater power and assumed more functions, most significantly, the right to initiate bills to raise taxes and disburse public funds—the "power of the purse." They also gained the authority to initiate other legislation, choose their own leadership, and settle disputed elections.

King George III, at the time of his coronation in 1760, by Allan Ramsay.
Colonial Williamsburg Foundation

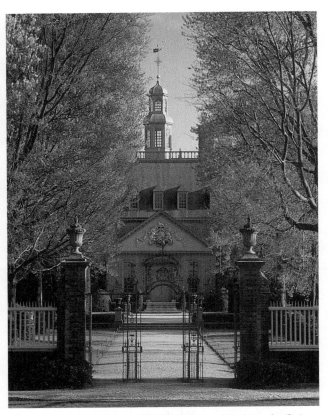

The Governor's Palace at Williamsburg, Virginia, built in the early eighteenth century. At a time when most Virginians lived in rough-hewn, one-room dwellings, the elegant mansion symbolized the king's authority in America.
Colonial Williamsburg Foundation

The political stability and rise of the assemblies that marked the mid-eighteenth century resulted from a number of factors, including the long period of economic growth that began in the 1720s. Prosperity supported the formation of cohesive elites—mostly second, third, and fourth generation Americans with inherited wealth and large estates, enslaved Africans or servants to meet their domestic needs, and (consequently) sufficient leisure time for politics. They formed a class of skilled politicians, men who learned from their fathers how to govern, then elaborated the art. Many studied the law: the growth of the colonial bar accompanied the professionalization of politics. Economic prosperity inclined ordinary whites to defer to the elites as long as opportunity was good and they had crops to tend or other work to do. Their deference to social and economic superiors became most visible after 1725, when participation at the polls declined among eligible voters, and incumbent assemblymen won reelection year after year.

The provincial elites also benefited after 1720 from the British decision to administer the colonies with a light touch, allowing royal governors to accommodate the assemblies. And while riots occurred during the 1740s and 1750s over land claims and impressment, none threatened social disorder on the level of the seventeenth-century rebellions. Indeed, most ordinary whites feared attacks by Native Americans and slave revolts more than misuse of governmental power by elites.

CONCLUSION

By the end of 1763, the British colonists of North America had reason to be optimistic about their future, despite the pan-Indian assaults in the Ohio Valley and postwar economic downturn. The British army had withstood the worst attacks in the west, and colonists could expect a return to prosperity. After a quarter century of war, they celebrated the withdrawal of Spain and France east of the Mississippi and looked forward to peace and semi-autonomy within the empire. Free colonists appreciated the benefits of being British—their liberties and right to participate in government as well as access to advanced learning and consumer goods. At the same time, the Americans were creating societies quite different from the English, with greater ethnic and religious diversity, dependence on enslaved labor, and wider opportunity to acquire land (even if it meant pushing out the Indians). After 1763, the London government shocked the American colonists with its effort to rein in the empire, to make them surrender some of their accumulated rights. In turn, the British were unprepared for the coordinated fury with which the thirteen mainland provinces greeted their "reforms."

Recommended Readings

Anderson, Fred. *Crucible of War: The Seven Years' War and the Fate of Empire in British North America, 1754–1766* (2000). A convincing analysis of the significance of the Seven Years' War.

Bailyn, Bernard, and Morgan, Philip D., eds. *Strangers within the Realm: Cultural Margins of the First British Empire* (1991). Important essays on specific groups, including Native Americans, Scots-Irish, African Americans, Germans, and Dutch.

Carson, Cary, et al., eds. *Of Consuming Interests: The Style of Life in the Eighteenth Century* (1994). Excellent essays on topics ranging from housing and art to consumer behavior.

Daunton, Martin, and Halpern, Rick, eds. *Empire and Others: British Encounters with Indigenous Peoples, 1600–1850* (1999). Significant essays on relations between Natives and English in eastern North America and elsewhere.

Isaac, Rhys. *The Transformation of Virginia, 1740–1790* (1982). Uses anthropological methods to explore cultural and political change in eighteenth-century Virginia.

Merrell, James H. *Into the American Woods: Negotiators on the Pennsylvania Frontier* (1999). Focuses on Indian and Euro-American go-betweens and their ultimate failure to preserve peace in the Ohio Valley.

Morgan, Philip D. *Slave Counterpoint: Black Culture in the Eighteenth-Century Chesapeake and Lowcountry* (1998). A comprehensive study of African American work and culture in the South.

Richter, Daniel K. *Facing East from Indian Country: A Native History of Early America* (2001). Approaches significant events in relations between Indians and settlers from Native perspectives.

Steele, Ian K. *Warpaths: Invasions of North America* (1994). Examines the Seven Years' War as one of a series of European invasions of Indian territory during the colonial period.

Ulrich, Laurel Thatcher. *A Midwife's Tale: The Life of Martha Ballard, Based on Her Diary, 1785–1812* (1990). The prize-winning account of a Maine midwife within the context of eighteenth-century society.

American Journey Online and InfoTrac College Edition

Visit the source collections at http://ajaccess.wadsworth.com and infotrac.thomsonlearning.com and use the Search function with the following key terms to explore documents, images, audio and video clips, articles, and commentary related to the material in this chapter.

Benjamin Franklin	Seven Years' War
Great Awakening	Proclamation of 1763
French and Indian War	

P ASSAGES

1764
TO 1814

DURING THE AMERICAN REVOLUTION, sixteen-year-old Dicey Langston of the South Carolina frontier left home in the middle of the night, by herself, to warn her brother's unit about Tory troop movements. As a historian later described Langston's journey,

> Many miles were to be traversed, and the road lay through woods, and crossed marshes and creeks where the conveniences of bridges and foot-logs were wanting. She walked rapidly on, heedless of slight difficulties; but her heart almost failed her when she came to the banks of the Tyger—a deep and rapid stream, rendered more dangerous by the rains that had lately fallen. . . . But the energy of a resolute will, under the care of Providence, sustained her.*

Dicey Langston's effort, like those of thousands of Americans, was emblematic of her country's passage from a collection of British provinces in 1764, to a stable republic with some international standing a half century later. The thirteen mainland colonies, proud of their contribution to victory in the Seven Years' War, were stunned by Britain's program to curtail their rights. Stretching from the mountains of northern New England to the rice fields of coastal Georgia, diverse in economics, religion, ethnicity, and politics, the colonies mustered enough unity to organize a revolutionary Congress, stop British imports, raise an army, obtain help from France, and win the war.

The Federal Pillars, from the Centinel *(Boston, Massachusetts), August 2, 1788, illustrates ratification of the Constitution of 1787.*
Courtesy, American Antiquarian Society

The states refused to create a unified nation, however, and instead established, under the Articles of Confederation, thirteen separate republics joined loosely by a representative Congress. Without power to tax or raise troops, the Congress faced severe postwar problems in demobilizing the army, paying the war debt, protecting

*Elizabeth F. Ellet, *Domestic History of the American Revolution* (1850), p. 234.

the frontiers, and unifying a populace divided by war. In the wake of bankruptcy and insurrection, in 1787 nationalists called together a constitutional convention. Through a series of compromises, the framers drafted the new Constitution, which gave more authority to the central government, yet retained considerable power in the states. Americans ratified the document with the understanding that amendments to protect individual liberties and states' rights would be approved.

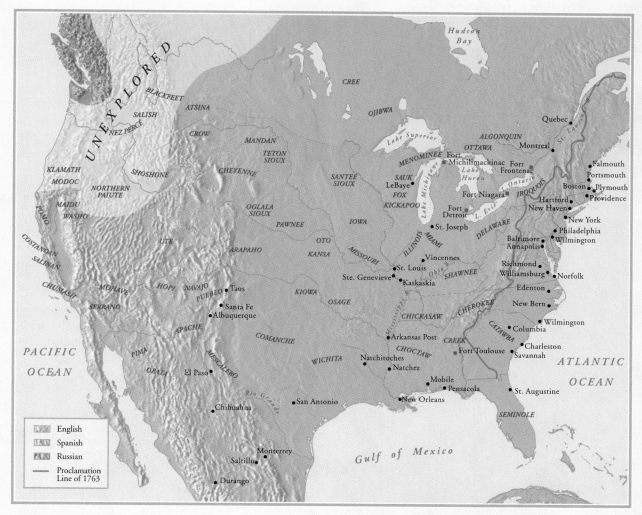

North America in 1764

Significant changes in European claims to regions in North America resulted from the Seven Years' War. The Treaty of Paris of 1763 divided former French territory between Great Britain to the east of the Mississippi River and Spain to the west. The British also gained Spanish Florida.

After the first national elections, the Constitution's proponents, the Federalists, controlled the new government, with George Washington as president. Having agreed upon the frame of government, they were unprepared for the bitter factionalism that forged political parties in the 1790s. Nor were they ready for the foreign entanglements that resulted from two decades of war between Great Britain and post-revolutionary France. Only after the United States declared war on the British in 1812 and held its own as the conflict ended in stalemate, did the nation

Constitution and the Guerriere, *by Thomas Birch, depicts an important victory of the USS* Constitution *early in the War of 1812.*
Courtesy of the U.S. Naval Academy Museum

finally demonstrate its independence. By 1814, most of the men who led the American Revolution had passed from power—though James Madison would remain president for several years—and a new generation was taking control.

The heroic story of the young nation surmounting difficulties—two wars against Great Britain, a constitutional crisis, several internal rebellions, an undeclared conflict with France, and constant fighting on the frontier—masks other narratives, those of women, African Americans, and Native Americans, who failed to achieve autonomy. Though Dicey Langston was just one of thousands of sisters, mothers, and wives who risked their lives during the Revolution, after the war women still lacked basic legal and political rights to hold property after marriage, vote, and take part in government. And while revolutionary rhetoric against slavery resulted in abolition in the North and many private manumissions in the Chesapeake region, most African Americans remained enslaved, a condition perpetuated by the new Constitution and development of cotton. Even most free blacks had little opportunity to acquire property and were denied suffrage and participation in government.

Negroes in Front of the Bank of Pennsylvania, Philadelphia *(1814) shows a group of black workers, the male sawyers laboring in a public space and a female domestic caring for a white child.*
The Metropolitan Museum of Art, Rogers Fund, 1942 (42.95.16) Photograph © 1989 The Metropolitan Museum of Art.

A Stockbridge Indian in the Continental army.
By permission of Yale University Press.

For Native Americans, the success and growth of the new nation meant their decline. Despite revitalization movements to restore traditional cultures led by Neolin, Handsome Lake, Tenskwatawa, and others, and destructive wars to defend their homelands in Alabama, Tennessee, Kentucky, and Ohio, by 1814 the United States dominated most of the territory east of the Mississippi River. Native Americans tried various routes to survive and retain as much of their autonomy as possible—adoption of white culture, cession of some lands for the promise they could keep others, alliances with Great Britain and Spain, and pan-Indian war. In the face of unremitting westward settlement and continuing disease, the Indian peoples of eastern North America became remnants of formerly powerful nations.

Trade Between Thirteen Colonies/United States and England, 1760–1791 (pounds sterling).
Though trade with England was only part of American commerce, this chart suggests the Revolution's impact. British imports spiked between 1769 and 1771, after Parliament partially repealed the Townshend Act. Imports and exports then plummeted during the Revolution, rising unevenly after 1782. The trade imbalance led to political unrest such as Shays's Rebellion.
Source of Data: Bureau of the Census, *Historical Statistics of the United States Colonial Times to 1970* Part 2 (Washington, D.C., 1975), p. 1176.

	1760	1775	1780
Politics & Diplomacy	**1765:** Stamp Act protest **1766–1771:** Regulator movements in North and South Carolina **1767:** John Dickinson's "Farmer" letters against Townshend Act **1768:** Non-importation movement **1769:** Spanish colonize California **1770:** Boston Massacre **1772:** Committees of Correspondence **1773:** Boston Tea Party **1774:** Coercive Acts; port of Boston closed First Continental Congress	**1775:** Battles of Lexington and Concord Lord Dunmore's proclamation to servants and slaves **1776:** Thomas Paine's *Common Sense* Declaration of Independence **1777:** Burgoyne surrenders to Americans at Saratoga **1778:** Alliance with France Iroquois attacks in New York and Pennsylvania	**1780:** Pennsylvania law for gradual abolition of slavery **1781:** Articles of Confederation ratified Surrender of Cornwallis at Yorktown **1783:** Treaty of Paris **1787:** Shaysites attack Springfield, Massachusetts, arsenal Northwest Ordinance Constitution sent to states for ratification **1789:** Inauguration of President George Washington
Social & Cultural Events	**1765:** First American medical school **1766:** Queens College (Rutgers) New Southwark Theatre in Philadelphia **1769:** *The American Magazine* (Philadelphia) published Benjamin West's *Death of General Wolfe* American scientists observe transit of Venus **1770:** Equestrian statue of George III installed in New York **1771:** Benjamin Franklin starts *Autobiography* c. **1772:** John Singleton Copley's portrait of Samuel Adams **1773:** Phillis Wheatley's *Poems on Various Subjects, Religious and Moral*	**1776:** Jemima Wilkinson becomes Public Universal Friend **1779:** John Murray's American Universalist Church	**1780s:** Northern black separate churches and societies **1783:** Noah Webster's American spelling book First daily newspaper, *Pennsylvania Evening Post* **1784:** Judith Sargent Murray begins essays on women's status **1786:** Virginia statute for religious liberty Gilbert Stuart's portrait of Joseph Brant
Economics & Technology	**1760s:** British American traders cross Mississippi River **1764:** Sugar and Currency Acts	**1776:** Adam Smith's *An Inquiry into the Nature and Causes of the Wealth of Nations* **1778:** Captain James Cook explores the Pacific Northwest **1779:** Continental money becomes nearly worthless	**1780s:** Rapid settlement of Kentucky and Tennessee Oliver Evans automates grist mills **1781:** Bank of North America in Philadelphia **1783:** Great Britain closes West Indies to American ships **1784:** Spain closes port of New Orleans to Americans **1784:** Debt crisis spurs protests in U.S. **1788:** Pennsylvania Society for the Encouragement of Manufactures and the Useful Arts introduces spinning jennies

1790	1796	1800

1791: Bill of Rights ratified
1794: Whiskey Rebellion
1795: Jay Treaty

1798: Alien and Sedition Acts
Quasi-War with France
1799: Fries Rebellion

1800: Washington, D.C., becomes national capital
Gabriel's rebellion
Jefferson elected president
1803: *Marbury v. Madison* case
Louisiana Purchase
1804: Lewis and Clark expedition
1809: Tecumseh organizes pan-Indian confederacy
1812: U.S. war with Great Britain
1814: Treaty of Ghent

1791: Charles Willson Peale's *Thomas Jefferson*
c.1793: Mary Wollstonecraft's *Vindication of the Rights of Women* circulates in the U.S.
1795: Philadelphia Quaker women establish first female benevolent society in U.S.

1797: Second Great Awakening begins in New England
1799: Rise of Handsome Lake as Seneca prophet
Charles Brockden Brown's *Wieland*

1800s: Tenskwatawa, the Shawnee Prophet, inspires following
1800: Library of Congress
1801: Cane Ridge, Kentucky, camp meeting
1805: Pennsylvania Academy of Fine Arts

1790: Samuel Slater builds first U.S. water-powered textile mill
Congress passes patent law
1791: Bank of the United States
Excise tax on whiskey
Alexander Hamilton's plan for promoting manufactures
1793: British blockade of French West Indies
Eli Whitney's cotton gin
1795: Great Britain opens West Indies to U.S. trade

1796: Spain opens navigation on Mississippi River
Alexander Hamilton's industrial town in New Jersey fails
1798: Eli Whitney attempts to manufacture guns with interchangeable parts
1790s: U.S. international trade soars with European conflict
Cotton expands southern slavery
Northern cities become magnets for African Americans

1802: Oliver Evans's high pressure steam engine
1806: Non-Importation Act
1807: Embargo Act
1808: Federal ban on international slave trade
1809: Giles's Enforcement Act
Embargo repealed; replaced with Non-Intercourse Act
1811: Charter of National Bank expires

5 WARS FOR INDEPENDENCE 1764–1783

REALIGNMENTS IN THE SPANISH BORDERLANDS

THE BRITISH COLONIES RESIST IMPERIAL REFORM

RESISTANCE BECOMES A WAR FOR INDEPENDENCE

WAR IN THE NORTH, 1776–1779

THE WAR MOVES WEST AND SOUTH

A woman and African American man are prominently portrayed in this illustration of the Stamp Act riots in Boston, 1765.
Reproduced from the Collections of the Library of Congress
#LC-US261-449

The treaty of 1763 forced Spain and Great Britain to reassess their North American colonies. Both nations had new kings, as Charles III took Spain's throne in 1759 and George III became the British monarch in 1760. For the Spanish, the borderlands in North America were of secondary importance, serving as a buffer to protect the Mexican silver mines. For Britain, however, the mainland provinces had become increasingly significant as a source of revenue and market for consumer goods. The Seven Years' War marked Britain's ascendancy to world power, but resulted in a national debt of £130 million. Annual interest payments alone amounted to £4.5 million, equal to more than half of the government's yearly expenditures prior to the war.

When Parliament imposed levies on the American colonies to help pay expenses, the colonists protested vehemently that they should not be taxed without their consent. They complained that they had no representatives in Parliament, that only their elected provincial assemblies could constitutionally tax them. Beginning in 1764, the Americans petitioned, rioted, boycotted British goods, destroyed tea, and ultimately defied George III and parliamentary leaders when they sent troops. The colonists' belief that they possessed the same rights as the English was something for which many were willing to fight. Nevertheless, the consensus to declare independence did not come quickly, nor was the war to defend independence easily won. Americans who disagreed that the British actions warranted insurrection remained loyal to the king. These loyalists, also called Tories after the pro-monarchy faction in England, tried to subvert the revolutionary governments and formed loyalist militia units to fight alongside British troops. They found allies in many Indians and African Americans who conducted wars of independence of their own. Other colonists remained neutral, whether from principled opposition to violence or from sheer indifference. The Revolution touched everyone, Native Americans, women, and enslaved blacks, as well as the white men who served as military and civilian leaders and comprised most of the armed forces. The cause of the patriots—or Whigs, as the American revolutionaries called themselves after the English party that had led opposition to the Crown—depended upon the efforts of many people, those who supplied and supported the troops, as well as those who fought.

REALIGNMENTS IN THE SPANISH BORDERLANDS

The peace of 1763 required Spain to withdraw from Florida, assume the government of Louisiana, and re-think its defenses in Texas and New Mexico. With Britain's enhanced power, safeguarding the Mexican silver mines took high priority. The Spanish also considered the soaring population of the British colonies a threat to their American empire.

Florida and Louisiana

Spain ordered all of its subjects to leave Florida when Britain took control. Though the British promised religious freedom to the Catholic Floridians, some 200 Christian Indians, 79 free African Americans, 350 slaves, and nearly all of the 3,000 Hispanics departed. They sold their property at a loss to British bargain hunters. The free blacks of Mose, near St. Augustine, could expect enslavement by the English, so took Spain's offer of homesteads in Cuba. They received some tools and money from the government, but faced hard times because they never received adequate compensation for their property in Florida.

Acquisition of Louisiana, including all French territory west of the Mississippi River and New Orleans, on the east bank, gave Spain an extensive region to administer. The Spanish needed to win the loyalties of French inhabitants and Native Americans and hoped to keep the British colonists out. The concern about British expansion became all too real as interlopers spanned the Mississippi River to trade with Indians on the Great Plains. Indeed, within a decade, 4,000 British colonists and their 1,500 African American slaves were living on the Gulf Coast and eastern shore of the Mississippi.

The more immediate challenge for Spanish authorities in Louisiana, however, was asserting political control of the province. For several years, French government remained; even after the first Spanish governor, Antonio de Ulloa, arrived in 1766, he tried to govern jointly with the last French governor. Adhering to Charles III's instructions, Ulloa left the French administration and legal system intact, even allowing the French flag to fly over the capital.

Ulloa did not extend this leniency to commerce, however. He tried to stop business with France and Great Britain and restricted the Native American trade to certain dealers. New Orleans merchants feared loss of markets and lower prices for their tobacco, indigo, sugar, deerskins, and lumber. Like the thirteen British provinces on the Atlantic coast, at about the same time, the merchants protested the new restrictions, then in October 1768 issued a declaration of loyalty to the king of France. With few Spanish troops at his disposal, Governor Ulloa left for Cuba. When the French refused to intervene, the colony became independent, but only for a year.

CHRONOLOGY

1764 Sugar and Currency Acts • St. Louis founded

1765 Stamp Act provokes widespread colonial protest • Stamp Act Congress

1766 Parliament repeals Stamp Act, passes Declaratory Act • Spanish governor arrives in Louisiana

1766–1771 North Carolina Regulator movement

1767 Passage of Townshend Act • John Dickinson publishes "Farmer" letters

1767–1769 South Carolina Regulator movement

1768 Massachusetts assembly sends "circular letter" • Non-importation movement against Townshend duties • British troops stationed in Boston • Louisianans expel Spanish governor

1769 Spanish reestablish control of Louisiana

1770 Boston Massacre • Partial repeal of Townshend Act

1772 Burning of *Gaspée*

1772–1773 Committees of Correspondence established

1773 Boston Tea Party

1774 Passage of Coercive Acts; port of Boston closed • Quebec Act • First Continental Congress • Congress organizes Continental Association

1775 Battles of Lexington and Concord • Second Continental Congress • Battle of Bunker Hill • Congress authorizes invasion of Canada • Lord Dunmore's proclamation to servants and slaves

1776 Thomas Paine publishes *Common Sense* • British evacuation of Boston • Declaration of Independence • Cherokee War on the southern frontier • Americans defeated on Long Island; British occupation of New York City • Battle of Trenton

1777 Battle of Princeton • British occupy Philadelphia after defeating Washington at Brandywine • Battle of Germantown • Burgoyne surrenders to Americans at Saratoga • Congress approves Articles of Confederation; sends document to states for ratification

1778 Alliance with France • Iroquois and loyalist attacks in New York and Pennsylvania • British withdraw from Philadelphia • Whig frontiersmen take settlements in the Illinois country • British invade Georgia

1780 Americans surrender at Charleston • Battle of Camden

1781 Battle of Cowpens • Articles of Confederation ratified • Battle of Guilford Courthouse • Southern army reconquers most of South Carolina and Georgia • Surrender of Cornwallis at Yorktown

1782 Massacre at Gnadenhutten

1783 Signing of Treaty of Paris

The Spanish regained Louisiana when General Alexander O'Reilly arrived in 1769 with more than 2,000 soldiers. An Irishman with a successful career in the Spanish army, O'Reilly arrested the rebels, put five of them to death, but pardoned most who had participated in the uprising. He raised the Spanish flag and within a year ended French government, changed the legal system, made Castilian the official language, and outlawed trade with other nations. Despite the merchants' fears, the economy flourished as smuggling continued with Britain, and Spanish markets welcomed their goods. St. Louis, established in 1764, became the thriving center of trade for beaver, buffalo, and deerskins with Native Americans of the Illinois and Missouri countries. Louisiana remained culturally French, as the numbers of French settlers far surpassed the Spanish.

Fortifying the Southwest

With ownership of Louisiana, the Spanish could alter their defenses along the frontier in Texas and New Mexico. They removed several forts from East Texas. By the 1760s, the most immediate danger in the southwest came from the Apaches and Comanches, who defended their freedom from Hispanic slave catchers and attempted to drive the Spanish back into Mexico. Skillfully adopting the European horse and gun, they refused to submit to Spanish rule or Christianity. Spain gave up trying to convert them through missions, emphasizing military defense instead. The Apaches and Comanches raided settlements and pack trains, stole horses, mules, cattle, and supplies, killing Pueblos and white settlers alike.

During the 1760s and 1770s, in the face of constant Indian assaults, Spain tried to reform administration and improve defense. From 1766 to 1768, the Marqués de Rubí, a high-level military official from Spain, inspected the fortifications and missions of the Southwest. He discovered badly located presidios (or forts) and soldiers suffering from lack of food and clothes because of their commanders' greed. At one Texas presidio, Rubí found sixty troops without shoes or uniforms and, among them, only two muskets that worked. He recommended building new presidios and relocating others to create an orderly cordon of military bases situated about a hundred miles apart. The presidios would extend from the Gulf of California to the Gulf of Mexico, along a line that was close to the present boundary between the United States and Mexico. Small numbers of Spanish troops would hold garrisons at Santa Fe and San Antonio, north of the cordon, to help defend Hispanics and allied Indians in New Mexico and Texas. The borderlands officials also received more autonomy to deal with local problems, but lacked sufficient troops to conquer the Apaches and Comanches.

THE BRITISH COLONIES RESIST IMPERIAL REFORM

In Britain's colonies, which experienced few restrictions before 1763, trouble began when George III appointed George Grenville as first minister, with responsibility for solving the debt crisis. Grenville decided that Americans should pay more taxes because they benefited from the Seven Years' War and continued to drain the government's budget for administrative and military costs. Because the British at home were highly taxed, Grenville's plan to make the colonies pay their way seemed reasonable to many. The Americans saw it differently, however, and quickly moved to the brink of revolt.

The Sugar and Currency Acts

Grenville began his program in 1764 with the Sugar Act, which initiated a new policy of charging duties primarily to raise revenue rather than to regulate trade. It reduced the duty on foreign molasses from sixpence (under the Molasses Act of 1733) to threepence per gallon, which was further reduced to one penny in 1766. Grenville assumed merchants would pay the lower tariff rather than go to the risk of smuggling and bribery. The law also added timber, iron, and hides to the list of enumerated goods. To make smuggling more hazardous, the act gave increased powers to the vice-admiralty courts. Because these courts lacked juries, the government expected easy convictions for smuggling. In addition, the law expanded the use of writs of assistance (search warrants), empowered the Royal Navy to inspect ships, and required endless bureaucratic paperwork from colonial shippers. Parliament also passed the Currency Act (1764), which had the potential to cause further hardship by forbidding colonies from issuing paper money, thus creating a shortage of currency.

Coming in the midst of an economic depression, this legislation stirred up colonial protest. Provincial assemblies sent petitions to England requesting relief. Most urgently, merchants feared that if imports of foreign molasses were cut off, their provision trade to the Spanish and French West Indies would be lost. Without foreign credits, they could not pay for British manufactures. The Americans slowed down their orders from Britain and encouraged home industry, arousing opposition to Grenville's policies from English businessmen. One colonial merchant wrote to associates in England that if the government deprived Americans of paper currency, "we shall not be able to export Provisions &c. in the same Degree as formerly, and if we are not on any Terms allow'd a Trade to get Money from abroad, we shall have none to pay you for Goods, and then unless you will send them Gratis our Dealings must end."

The Stamp Act

Passed by Parliament in 1765, the Stamp Act provoked an even greater storm of protest. The law departed entirely from the confines of mercantilist policy, for its purpose was to raise an internal revenue, which would be used to pay troops in the colonies. The act required individuals to purchase stamps for official documents and published papers, including deeds, liquor licenses, bills of lading, court documents, wills, passports, playing cards, newspapers, and pamphlets. All publications and official transactions were to be subject to this special tax, which increased with the value of a land sale or the size of a pamphlet. The tax could be paid only in specie, an onerous requirement because colonists generally used paper money and credit instead of the scarce gold and silver. The vice-admiralty courts would enforce the act, confiscating any land or property involved in transactions conducted without the stamps.

Colonists of all walks of life found the Stamp Act offensive. Everyone who engaged in public business, whether to buy a newspaper or sell property, would have to pay the tax. Because Parliament, not their provincial assemblies, passed the act, Americans considered it a violation of their rights as British subjects. As they understood the British constitution, the people must consent to taxes through their representatives. The provinces could not send delegates to Parliament, so that body should not tax them to raise revenue. As one Philadelphia merchant said succinctly, "the point in dispute is a very Important one, if the Americans are to be taxed by a Parliament where they are not nor can be Represented, they are no longer Englishmen but Slaves." Only tariffs to regulate trade such as the 1733 duty on molasses, many colonists believed, were constitutionally valid.

Recognizing Parliament's attack on their powers, provincial assemblies protested the Stamp Act. In the Virginia House of Burgesses, the newly elected Patrick Henry, only twenty-nine years old, introduced fourteen resolves against the tax. The Virginia assembly refused to accept all of Henry's proposals, but in June 1765, approved the more moderate resolutions that defended the colonists' right to tax themselves.

When newspapers spread word of Virginia's action, other provinces responded. Rhode Island instructed its officials to ignore the stamp tax; Massa-

Paul Revere's engraving of the hanging in effigy of an American-born member of Parliament, John Huske, an alleged Stamp Act supporter.
Courtesy, American Antiquarian Society

chusetts, Connecticut, New York, New Jersey, Pennsylvania, Maryland, and South Carolina passed resolves similar to Virginia's. In October 1765, representatives from nine colonies traveled to New York City to attend the Stamp Act Congress. In resolutions and petitions to Parliament, the congress upheld the power of representative assemblies, not Parliament, to tax the colonists. Further, the congress defended trial by jury, which the expanded authority of the vice-admiralty courts threatened. By issuing resolves and organizing the Stamp Act Congress, the colonial elite challenged British efforts to assert control.

Ordinary colonists joined the challenge. They drew upon the tradition of the mob to protest what they considered tyranny. The anti-Stamp Act riots began in Boston on August 14, 1765, when a group who called themselves the Loyal Nine organized a demonstration to hang in effigy the appointed stamp collector for Massachusetts, Andrew Oliver. The crowd destroyed a partially constructed building they thought

Virginia Resolves Against the Stamp Act, 1765

When news arrived in 1765 that Parliament had passed the Stamp Act, the colonists protested the internal tax. In the Virginia assembly, Patrick Henry introduced resolutions defending the right of "taxation of the people by themselves, or by persons chosen by themselves to represent them" and accusing Parliament of attempting to destroy "American freedom." Newspapers published seven resolutions, of which the Virginia legislators passed the first four listed below, which were more moderate than the rest.

Resolved, That the first adventurers and settlers of this His Majesty's Colony and Dominion of Virginia brought with them, and transmitted to their posterity, and all other of His Majesty's subjects since inhabiting this His Majesty's said Colony, all the liberties, privileges, franchises, and immunities, that have at any time been held, enjoyed, and possessed, by the people of Great Britain.

Resolved, That by two royal charters, granted by King James the First, the colonists aforesaid are declared entitled to all liberties, privileges, and immunities of denizens and natural subjects, to all intents and purposes, as if they had been abiding and born within the realm of England.

Resolved, That the taxation of the people by themselves, or by persons chosen by themselves to represent them, who can only know what taxes the people are able to bear, or the easiest method of raising them, and must themselves be affected by every tax laid on the people, is the only security against a burthensome taxation, and the distinguishing characteristick of British freedom, without which the ancient constitution cannot exist.

Resolved, That His Majesty's liege people of this his most ancient and loyal Colony have without interruption enjoyed the inestimable right of being governed by such laws, respecting their internal polity and taxation, as are derived from their own consent, with the approbation of their sovereign, or his substitute; and that the same hath never been forfeited or yielded up, but hath been constantly recognized by the kings and people of Great Britain.

Resolved therefore, That the General Assembly of this Colony have the only and sole exclusive right and power to lay taxes and impositions upon the inhabitants of this Colony, and that every attempt to vest such power in any person or persons whatsoever other than the General Assembly aforesaid has a manifest tendency to destroy British as well as American freedom.

Resolved, That His Majesty's liege people, the inhabitants of this Colony are not bound to yield obedience to any law or ordinance whatever, designed to impose any taxation whatsoever upon them other than the laws or ordinances of the General Assembly aforesaid.

Resolved, That any person who shall, by speaking or writing, assert or maintain that any person or persons other than the General Assembly of this Colony, have any right or power to impose or lay any taxation on the people here, shall be deemed an enemy to His Majesty's Colony.

---

he intended as his stamp office, then damaged his home. Oliver resigned his commission. Twelve days later, a Boston mob attacked the houses of several other officials, gutting the mansion of Lieutenant Governor Thomas Hutchinson.

Protesters all along the Atlantic seaboard mobilized to prevent stamp distribution, scheduled to begin November 1. News of Oliver's resignation prompted anti-Stamp Act mobs in other cities to demand the same from their appointed stampmen. In some colonies, rioters forced stamp officials to relinquish their commissions. In others, just the threat of disorder was effective. By the end of 1765, distributors in every colony except Georgia had resigned.

The men who led the crowds called themselves Sons of Liberty. They were mostly propertied men—small merchants, shopkeepers, and craftsmen. The activists were people who needed documents to conduct business, who would regularly feel the pinch of the stamp tax. The Sons of Liberty also established networks to organize boycotts of British goods. Merchants and retailers in New York City, Philadelphia, and Boston signed pacts to stop imports until Parliament repealed the act. By early 1766, the Sons of Liberty coerced customs officials and judges to open the ports and resume court business without stamps. To Thomas Hutchinson, it appeared "the authority of every colony is in the hands of the sons of liberty." In truth, the American resistance aimed to expunge the stamp tax, not end British authority. The movement achieved success in 1766, when Parliament repealed the Stamp Act, after British businessmen from more than twenty cities petitioned for relief. Suffering from postwar economic depression and unemployment, the British textile industry faced even worse times with an American boycott. British merchants clearly understood the growing significance of the colonial market.

Protest Widens in the Lower South

In the Carolinas, the Stamp Act resistance spawned revolts against colonial elites. To blacks, the radicals' oft-spoken argument that the English government intended to deprive white Americans of freedom—to make them slaves—seemed ironic. Yet such statements also gave hope, for the revolutionary movement spotlighted the institution of slavery and its immorality and injustice. In January 1766, in Charleston, 1,400 seamen and a group of black slaves threatened serious disorder. The sailors became restless because the customs agents refused to release ships from port without stamped documents. The people of Charleston were even more concerned, however, when a group of enslaved men marched through the town shouting "Liberty!" The city armed itself against a slave revolt, while the South Carolina assembly became so frightened that it restricted slave imports for three years.

The North Carolina Regulator movement also began in 1766, inspired by the uproar against the Stamp Act, but targeted the colonial elite, not Britain. Six thousand western farmers demanded confirmation of land titles and the end of speculators' monopoly of the best land. The Regulators also protested corrupt local officials, excessive court fees and taxes, and lack of adequate representation for ordinary backcountry farmers in the North Carolina legislature. They called for a secret ballot to reduce the influence of wealthy planters in assembly elections. The North Carolina Regulators refused to pay taxes and closed several courts. In 1771, when the government sent the eastern militia, 2,000 Regulators met them at Alamance Creek but were dispersed.

Most of the grievances of the South Carolina Regulators were different, except that they too lacked fair representation in the provincial government. They were planters who wanted to bring order, "to regulate" the backcountry. The South Carolina legislature had failed to create local government for the westerners, so they had no courts or jails. Everyone had to travel to Charleston to conduct legal business, but even worse, bandits roamed freely, stealing horses and cattle, destroying property, and sometimes torturing and killing their victims. The frontier robbers were mostly propertyless whites and some free blacks and escaped slaves; one report in the *South-Carolina Gazette* noted "a Gang of Banditti, consisting of Mulattoes—Free Negroes, and notorious Harbourers of run away Slaves." The Regulators resorted to vigilante "justice," capturing and whipping suspected felons, taking some to jail in Charleston, and evicting others from the colony. They finally ceased their activities in 1769 when the legislature established a circuit court system for the entire province.

The Townshend Revenue Act

In other British mainland colonies, attention focused on imperial tensions rather than on regional disputes. The British government and American radicals emerged from the Stamp Act crisis with conflicting views: while the Americans celebrated the Stamp Act's repeal, the British yielded no authority. In the Declaratory Act, passed with the repeal in March 1766, Parliament affirmed its power "to make laws and statutes of sufficient force and validity to bind the colonies and people of America, subjects of the crown of Great Britain, in all cases whatsoever." The act generated little response in the colonies, but should have, for it laid the basis for subsequent restrictions.

In June 1767, Parliament passed three more laws affecting the Americans: an act establishing the American Board of Customs Commissioners to enforce legislation against illegal trade, the New York Restraining Act, and the Townshend Revenue Act. The Restraining Act would have dissolved the New York Assembly for refusing adequate supplies to British soldiers stationed in the province. Instead, the New York legislators gave in, pledging additional funds for the troops. The Townshend Revenue Act was conceived by Charles Townshend, the British chancellor of the exchequer, who wanted the Americans to contribute, over time, an increasing percentage of imperial expenses in North America. The Townshend Act, which placed duties on tea, glass, paper, lead, and paint would be just the beginning, for they would raise less than one-tenth of the colonial administrative and military costs. The revenues would pay the salaries of governors and judges, thus removing their dependence upon the provincial legislatures. The act also required colonial courts to provide customs officials with writs of assistance to search houses and businesses for smuggled merchandise.

To American Whigs, the Townshend Act was dangerous for two reasons: It raised revenue without the approval of colonial assemblies and it removed royal officials from the lawmakers' control. If the king rather than the legislatures paid provincial governors, the colonies lost a powerful negotiating tool for obtaining consent to the laws they wanted. While the British saw the Townshend Act as an appropriate way to force the Americans to begin paying their share, the colonists believed it was a step toward tyranny.

At first, colonial reaction to the Townshend Act was restrained. Then, in December 1767, a few weeks after the Townshend Act went into effect, John Dickinson, a Philadelphia lawyer and owner of a Delaware plantation, began publishing a series of twelve letters signed "A Farmer." Soon reprinted by newspapers throughout the thirteen colonies and published in pamphlet form as *Letters from a Farmer in Pennsylvania* (1768), Dickinson's arguments galvanized opposition to the Townshend duties. He rejected the position that the colonists should accept external taxes (duties) but not internal taxes (like the stamp tax), stating that only elected representatives could legally impose *any* revenue tax. He believed that Parliament could collect duties in the colonies if the purpose was to regulate trade (as with the Molasses Act of 1733), but not to raise revenue. Further, the purpose of the funds collected under the Townshend Act was oppressive, for it eliminated the power of the colonial legislatures over Crown officials. Dickinson predicted: "If we can find no relief from this infamous situation . . . we may bow down our necks, with all the stupid serenity of servitude, to any drudgery which our lords and masters shall please to command." Dickinson urged the thirteen colonies to petition for repeal; if that failed, they should once again boycott British goods.

Massachusetts responded first. In early 1768, its assembly petitioned George III for redress, then dispatched a "circular letter" to the other twelve colonies suggesting they do the same. The new English secretary of state for the colonies, Lord Hillsborough, realized that the circular letter was a call to unified resistance.

John Dickinson inspired opposition to the Townshend Act with his Letters from a Farmer in Pennsylvania. *This engraving shows the right arm of Dickinson's "Patriotic American Farmer" resting on the English Magna Charta.* The Library Company of Philadelphia

Denouncing Dickinson's pamphlet as "extremely wild," he ordered the Massachusetts assemblymen to rescind their circular letter. They refused. When he directed colonial governors to dissolve assemblies that responded to the letter, most legislatures sent petitions and were disbanded.

Simultaneously, Hillsborough reassigned military units from the Ohio Valley to Florida, Nova Scotia, Quebec, and the mid-Atlantic region where they could be called upon to control the defiant provinces. In June 1768, he sent British regiments to Boston when the customs commissioners demanded protection against rioters. As the troops disembarked in October, they heard cries of protest but met no armed resistance.

During 1768, Boston residents signed a non-importation agreement, using the same strategy against the Townshend Act that had proved successful against the Stamp Act. Most of the city's merchants pledged to stop importing goods from Great Britain after January 1, 1769, unless the Townshend duties were repealed. The non-importation movement soon spread to New York City, where artisans supported the merchants by

The Occupation of Boston, *1768, engraving by Paul Revere(?), illustrates the arrival of British troops on the Long Wharf (center).*
Courtesy, American Antiquarian Society

agreeing to boycott any retailer who imported British goods. Traders in Philadelphia, New Haven, and other northern ports delayed action, however, because they would face economic loss. They waited until 1769 for the imperial government to respond to their petitions, then approved non-importation. In Virginia, George Washington kindled the boycott. He wrote, "At a time when our lordly masters in Great Britain will be satisfied with nothing less than the deprivation of American freedom, it seems highly necessary that some thing should be done to avert the stroke and maintain the liberty which we have derived from our Ancestors."

The boycotts, which were unofficial agreements without the force of law, met uneven success. Between 1768 and 1769, American imports from England declined by 38 percent. As the months passed, however, importers wavered as their incomes fell. In contrast, craftspeople—beyond their concern for liberty—often benefited from the boycott because it created a demand for their products. Some artisans organized into street groups to threaten merchants and customs officials who tried to undermine the non-importation pacts.

Women participated both as purchasers of goods and as producers. Many "Daughters of Liberty" gave up imported tea and clothing, signing agreements to avoid the banned goods. The *Boston News-Letter* reported that "a large circle of very agreeable ladies in

this town . . . unanimously agreed" not to purchase ribbons and other imports. Instead, throughout New England, women organized spinning bees to produce woolen yarn. In Boston, some impoverished women profited from the temporary demand for American-made cloth, when William Molineaux, a merchant and radical Whig, contracted with local artisans to build 400 spinning wheels, which he distributed to women to spin yarn in their homes. With this "putting-out" system, Molineaux and the spinners responded to both their patriotism and economic needs.

Crisis in Boston

During the years 1769 to 1775, Boston became the powder keg of the Revolution. Violence broke out in the summer of 1769 between the Bostonians and British redcoats, whose chief responsibilities were to protect the despised customs commissioners and help them collect duties. The soldiers became even more unpopular when they took jobs at low pay during their off-duty hours, thus throwing city laborers out of work.

The first serious incident occurred in July 1769, when a redcoat, John Riley, was jailed for hitting a local butcher who had insulted him. A near riot followed as twenty of Riley's comrades tried to rescue him from jail. Such episodes continued into early

Burning of Gaspée, by Charles De Wolf Brownell. The seizure and burning of the British customs ship Gaspée *by Rhode Island merchants in June 1772 moved the colonies closer to revolution.*
Courtesy of the Rhode Island Historical Society, Neg. #RHi (×4)1

1770. On March 2, the violence escalated when soldiers seeking revenge for an insult attacked workers at John Gray's ropeworks. Street fights intensified over the next few days.

On March 5, the bloodiest incident occurred, the so-called Boston Massacre. A young apprentice taunted the British sentry at the Customs House, who hit the boy with his gun. When a crowd gathered, shouting at the sentry, "Kill him, kill him, knock him down," Captain Thomas Preston led seven soldiers in his defense. The crowd grew larger, throwing snowballs, ice, and sticks at the soldiers and threatening them with clubs. Then someone hit a redcoat with a club, knocking the gun out of his hands. Preston's men fired, killing five townspeople and wounding six. The dead became martyrs, with March 5 commemorated as "Massacre Day" in the years ahead. The incident crystallized the colonists' opposition to standing armies. Nevertheless, when Captain Preston and six soldiers were tried for murder, the jury found two soldiers guilty of manslaughter and cleared the others. The radical Whig lawyer John Adams defended them, saying that all Englishmen should have a fair trial.

Just as the crisis in Boston reached its head in spring 1770, the British government decided on partial repeal of the Townshend Act, removing its duties except tea. The duties had raised under £21,000 in revenues, but cost hundreds of thousands of pounds sterling in trade as a result of the non-importation movement. As in the case of the Stamp Act, British officials backed away from a specific revenue measure without abandoning their right to levy taxes. Following Parliament's action, merchants in New York City and other colonial ports, eager to resume trade, cancelled their boycotts except on tea. Imports into the thirteen colonies from England rebounded over the next several years, increasing from £1.3 million in 1769 to £4.2 million in 1771.

The Gaspée Incident

For two years, the conflict between Great Britain and the colonies abated, then flared again in 1772. Trouble

𝒫 ICTURING THE PAST ◆ POLITICS & DIPLOMACY

SAMUEL ADAMS

Courtesy of Museum of Fine Arts, Boston. Deposited by the City of Boston

John Singleton Copley painted this portrait of Sam Adams soon after the Boston Massacre. The artist shows Adams pointing at the Massachusetts charter, charging the British government with disregarding the colonists' rights. By 1770, Copley was considered by many the preeminent portraitist in British America. Unlike other painters of the time, his works were realistic, as in showing Adams's irritation with clenched lips, lined face, and coat somewhat askew. It is interesting to compare this image with Allan Ramsay's portrait of George III in Chapter 4. While both painters intended to show men of authority, Copley depicts Adams wearing a plain cloth coat.

Beginning with the Stamp Act, Sam Adams helped to make Boston the center of colonial resistance. Less is known about the details of his activity than of other revolutionaries because his papers have been lost (or he destroyed them before he died). He was a member of the Loyal Nine and the Sons of Liberty, helped draft the circular letter of 1768, and led events culminating in the Boston Tea Party.

---

began this time in Rhode Island, when more than one hundred men burned the British schooner *Gaspée,* wounding its commander, William Dudingston. Avidly enforcing the Sugar Act, the *Gaspée* had harassed merchant vessels sailing through Narragansett Bay. The Crown named a Commission of Inquiry to locate the perpetrators and send them to England to be tried for high treason. Though the Commission identified none of the *Gaspée*'s attackers, colonists viewed the policy of taking defendants to England for trial as a serious threat to their constitutional rights.

In response, the Virginia assembly appointed a Committee of Correspondence to monitor British policy and facilitate communication among the provinces. Within a year, Committees of Correspondence in all thirteen provinces coordinated opposition to Britain's restraints.

The Boston Tea Party

The final showdown began in 1773, when Parliament passed the Tea Act to bail out the nearly bankrupt East India Company. Though some colonists purchased British tea, the boycott on the product was still in effect and many purchased cheaper, smuggled Dutch tea. To sell the company's huge surplus, the government dropped a heavy import duty into England on tea headed for America, but retained the Townshend duty, which Lord North insisted on keeping to uphold Parliament's power to tax the colonies. The company also received a monopoly in the colonies, with the right to choose certain provincial merchants as agents. The company selected consignees in the ports of Charleston, Philadelphia, New York, and Boston, to whom it promptly dispatched nearly 600,000 pounds of tea.

The Tea Act was doubly offensive to American Whigs as it renewed opposition to the duty and caused outrage over favoritism and privilege. One radical called the act "a dirty trick" and accused Lord North of "low cunning" for trying to break American resistance by reducing the price of tea. Before the tea ships arrived in Charleston, Philadelphia, and New York, militants convinced the East India Company's agents to resign. In Boston, the consignees, two of them sons of pro-British Governor Thomas Hutchinson, declined to quit. When three ships arrived, members of the Boston Committee of Correspondence, led by Samuel Adams, prevented them from unloading. Adams, the cousin of John, had been the chief agitator in Boston since the Stamp Act. A skilled politician and writer, though failed businessman, he kept the pot simmering against British policies and Governor Hutchinson. Now, with the Boston committee, he brought matters to a head: in a series of meetings, thousands of residents of Boston and surrounding towns met to refuse the tea. On December 16, 1773, when customs officials and Hutchinson denied the ships clearance to leave port, radicals ill-disguised as Mohawks boarded the ships, broke open the tea chests, and dumped them overboard. The destruction cost nearly £10,000.

For the British, the Boston Tea Party required stern action. London decided that steps must "be taken to secure the Dependence of the Colonies," and in particular, "to mark out Boston and separate that Town from the rest of the Delinquents." George III believed that the Americans must be forced to submit, because they increasingly assumed the "independency which one state has of another, but which is quite subversive of the obedience which a colony owes to its Mother Country." In 1774, Parliament passed four Coercive Acts, which the colonists called the Intolerable Acts. They closed the port of Boston until residents paid for the destroyed tea and altered the provincial charter to limit the power of town meetings and create a Crown-appointed, instead of elected, provincial council. Further, the acts expanded the governor's control over the courts, allowed the removal of trials of royal officials to England or to another colony, and permitted quartering of troops in private buildings if a colony failed to provide suitable barracks. The Crown appointed General Thomas Gage, commander of the British army in North America, as Massachusetts governor, thus threatening the colonists with military force.

Americans also considered the Quebec Act (1774) intolerable, though London did not intend it to punish the Bostonians. The Quebec Act helped keep the loyalty of French Canadians by confirming religious freedom to Roman Catholics in the province, allowing

A British cartoon mocking American women who joined the boycott on tea, titled "A Society of Patriotic Ladies at Edenton in N.C."
Colonial Williamsburg Foundation

them to hold public office. It denied the Canadians an elected assembly, however, designating an appointed governor and council to make laws. Residents of the thirteen colonies abhorred the act because it extended rights to "papists" and undermined representative government. It also gave control of the Ohio Valley to the Quebec government, thus curbing the ambitions of speculators in other colonies.

The First Continental Congress

Though the British government expected the Coercive Acts to isolate Boston and convince other provinces to be obedient, the policies actually pushed Americans toward more unified resistance. After the port of Boston closed, residents faced severe unemployment and food shortages. Neighboring towns provided supplies and harbored refugees looking for work. Sam Adams and the Boston Committee of Correspondence called for an immediate boycott of British trade. Instead the other provinces favored a Continental Congress to consider what action to take. The Massachusetts assembly proposed a meeting in Philadelphia on September 1, 1774, to which all of the thirteen colonies except Georgia sent delegates. The fifty-five representatives included Richard Henry Lee, Patrick

Henry, and George Washington of Virginia; Sam and John Adams of Massachusetts; and John Dickinson and Joseph Galloway of Pennsylvania.

The primary purpose of the First Continental Congress was to obtain repeal of the Coercive Acts and other restrictions. The Congress wanted Parliament to recognize the rights of Americans, but was not ready to declare independence. Some of its leadership, notably Galloway (who later became a loyalist), argued for a moderate course, but the Congress was committed to action. It confirmed the Suffolk County Resolves forwarded to Philadelphia by a local Massachusetts convention. The Resolves blasted the Coercive Acts as "gross infractions of those rights to which we are justly entitled by the laws of nature, the British constitution and the charter of this province." The laws should "be rejected as the attempts of a wicked administration to enslave America." Everyone qualified to fight should learn "the art of war as soon as possible, and . . . appear under arms at least once a week." By endorsing these Resolves, the Congress took a militant stance.

Further, the Continental Congress passed non-importation, non-exportation, and non-consumption resolutions, ending all trade with Great Britain and Ireland, and exports to the West Indies. It also banned importation of slaves. If the British had hoped to divide the colonies by closing Boston, expecting other cities to pick up its trade, the plan backfired when all of the colonies closed their ports. The boycott would continue until repeal of the Coercive Acts. Congress set up the Continental Association to enforce the ban on trade through elected local committees, called Committees of Observation and Inspection, or Committees of Safety. The groups would expose violators of the boycott as "enemies of American liberty," publicizing their names and interrupting their business. Almost every town and county in the thirteen colonies elected these committees, which soon took on other functions of local government, including raising militias and collecting taxes. This transfer of authority from colonial governments to the Committees of Observation was revolutionary, for Americans were vesting sovereignty in themselves rather than in Parliament.

RESISTANCE BECOMES A WAR FOR INDEPENDENCE

Over the winter of 1774–1775, the rift widened between the thirteen colonies and Great Britain. George III and his ministers considered the colonies in rebellion, yet the colonists themselves were unprepared to declare independence.

Lexington and Concord

The British instructed General Gage to take forceful action. Headquartered in Boston, he decided to seize the patriots' stores of food and ammunition at Concord, which he had learned about from an informer. Militant Bostonians discovered Gage's plan from their own spies, so they were ready to spread the alarm on the night of April 18th, 1775, when 700 redcoats mustered on Boston Common. Paul Revere and William Dawes escaped the city to raise the colonial militia and alert leaders Sam Adams and John Hancock, who were staying at Lexington, on the route to Concord. The Massachusetts Provincial Council, just a few weeks before, had resolved to resist any advance by Gage's troops.

As the British marched the sixteen miles to Concord, they heard church bells and saw lights in windows. Soon after sunrise on April 19th they reached Lexington, where they met about seventy armed militia, nearly half of the town's adult males. The Lexington company, led by Captain John Parker, had formed only a few weeks earlier, so their training was incomplete. But they were willing to defend, in the words of their town meeting, their "natural, constitutional and chartered rights." In the face of six companies of British infantry, Captain Parker attempted to disperse his troops. The British officer, Major John Pitcairn, wanted to disarm the Americans, not engage in battle. As the British advanced, a shot rang out, then several shots, and a British volley. Pitcairn tried to stop his troops, but the carnage continued for fifteen to twenty minutes, leaving eight Lexington men dead and ten wounded. Only one British soldier was wounded and none killed.

The British reached Concord at about eight o'clock in the morning, long after the patriots had hidden most of their military stores. Following a brief skirmish in which the Americans inflicted more casualties than the British, the redcoats headed back to Boston. The march became a harrowing escape for their lives. Hundreds of colonial militia from throughout the Massachusetts countryside rushed to battle. These farmers used guerrilla tactics, shooting from behind trees, walls, rocks, and buildings. The British countered the guerrillas by sending advance parties to clear houses along the route. Using their famed skills with the bayonet, the redcoats killed the occupants and set fire to the homes. By the end of the day, British losses totaled seventy-three dead and 200 wounded or missing, while Massachusetts counted forty-nine killed and forty-three wounded and missing.

Map 5.1 *Battles in Eastern Massachusetts*
Paul Revere and William Dawes left Boston during the night of April 18th, 1775, to alert colonial leaders that the British troops were marching to destroy military supplies at Concord. The map also shows the location of the Battle of Bunker Hill two months later.

Battle of Lexington, *engraving by C. Tiebout after the drawing by E. Tisdale. The artist evokes the confusion and shock of the first battle of the Revolution.*
Collection of the New York Historical Society

In the days that followed the battles of April 19th, New England went to arms. Over 20,000 volunteers streamed to Cambridge. A large proportion of these soldiers soon returned home, but many stayed, expecting their wives, mothers, and sisters to work the family farms and defend the towns. One group of about thirty-five women, dressed in men's clothes and armed with muskets and pitchforks, guarded a bridge on the route British reinforcements might travel from Canada. As Abigail Adams, the wife of John Adams, later wrote, "We are in no wise dispirited here. If our men are all drawn off and we should be attacked, you would find a race of Amazons in America."

Troops from throughout New England besieged Gage's redcoats in Boston. Nathanael Greene, a young ex-Quaker, led 1,500 troops from Rhode Island. Connecticut promised 6,000 men and New Hampshire sent 2,000. From these earliest days of conflict, African American men served in the militia units. Without a unified army, each colony separately raised troops, selected officers, and secured provisions. By May 1775, the New England forces surrounding Boston numbered about 17,000. Ethan Allen and his Green Mountain Boys of Vermont captured Fort Ticonderoga, the British garrison on Lake Champlain in northern New York.

George Washington, *by James Peale. In choosing Washington as commander-in-chief, the Continental Congress selected a revolutionary dedicated to republican government. His perseverance and leadership kept the army together despite battlefield reverses and lack of supplies.*
Independence National Historical Park

The Second Continental Congress

On May 10, 1775, the Second Continental Congress met in Philadelphia. While the delegates remained unwilling to support independence, they were disappointed by Parliament's refusal to change its course. They faced the prospect of executing a war already in progress, convinced that British troops had fired the first shots and committed atrocities. To ensure that all of the colonies backed the war and to place the military under the control of Congress, they appointed George Washington of Virginia as commander-in-chief of the Continental army. Designating a southerner to head the military, which in June 1775 consisted of New Englanders, broadened the appeal of the Massachusetts cause. At the same time, Washington was himself a delegate to Congress and steadfastly committed to civilian control of the armed forces. Despite his limited military experience, Washington proved to be an excellent choice. His military bearing, determination, dignity, physical stamina, and ability to learn from his mistakes suited his role as commander-in-chief.

To serve under Washington, Congress appointed thirteen generals. Its four major generals were Artemas Ward of Massachusetts; Philip Schuyler of New York; Israel Putnam of Connecticut; and Charles Lee, a veteran officer of the British army and recent immigrant to Virginia. The adjutant general was Horatio Gates, also a veteran British officer and Virginia planter.

"An Open and Avowed Rebellion"

Before Washington could arrive in Massachusetts, his troops engaged in the Battle of Bunker Hill. Learning that the British planned to seize the hills overlooking Boston, a detachment of the patriot army began to fortify the Charlestown heights. By mistake, the men built defenses on Breed's Hill rather than on the higher and less exposed Bunker Hill. This lapse might have isolated the detachment from the rest of the army had the

British moved more quickly. Instead of attacking immediately, however, General Gage and the man who would soon replace him as commander of British forces, William Howe, foolishly allowed the Americans to complete their fortifications and obtain reinforcements. The British regulars lined up in proper European formation to storm Breed's Hill. Boston residents climbed to their roofs to watch. While the redcoats shot as they advanced up the hill—to little effect—the patriots waited until the enemy was within range of their guns. The redcoats failed on their first two assaults, losing many officers and troops, then with reinforcements took the hill when the Americans' ammunition gave out. The patriots retreated, pounded by artillery from British ships. While the British won the battle, their losses were staggering, as more than 40 percent of their combatants were killed or wounded.

During the year following Bunker Hill, many colonists became Whigs. The lives lost on battlefields in eastern Massachusetts undercut advocates of restraint. Still, given opposition from many delegates, the Continental Congress could not declare independence. During the summer of 1775, Congress asked the king for peace while preparing for war. In July, it approved a petition to George III, called the Olive Branch Petition, asking that he resolve their dispute with Parliament. Upon receipt of the petition in August, outraged by the colonists' armed resistance, the king proclaimed the thirteen provinces in "an open and avowed rebellion." In December, Parliament cut off all trade with the colonies, making American ships and any vessels engaging in commerce with the mutinous provinces subject to confiscation. For many Americans, these actions proved that the British government meant to crush the colonies militarily and economically.

The Continental Congress further alienated the British by ordering General Philip Schuyler to invade Canada. The congressmen hoped to make Canada the fourteenth British colony in rebellion. They expected to obtain help from French Canadians and perhaps even France itself, but even more, they wanted to prevent a northern attack. The American invasion of Canada was a failure from the start. Schuyler, suffering from illness and indecision, assembled troops and provisions too slowly, wasting valuable summer days. In September, much too late, Brigadier General Richard Montgomery took charge and moved the army north via Lake Champlain.

Concurrently, Washington dispatched a small army led by Benedict Arnold and Daniel Morgan over a rugged route through Maine. Their march took so much longer than predicted that the men had to eat their dogs and soap. When the combined American forces finally attacked Quebec in a blinding December snowstorm, they were defeated with heavy casualties, including Montgomery dead and Arnold wounded. The army remained in Canada until May 1776 when British reinforcements arrived, pushing the patriots back into New York. For Congress, the campaign was a tragic error. The thirteen colonies lost 5,000 troops to battle, desertion, and disease, and an enormous amount of supplies.

Taking Sides

The deepening conflict forced colonists to decide whether or not to support the revolutionary Whigs. Some people remained neutral, either because they cared little about the issues involved or because, like the pacifist Quakers, they were opposed to violence on religious grounds. Loyalists rejected the Revolution for a variety of motives. Some believed that the king and Parliament were right, or at least had reason to expect the colonists to pay their share toward imperial administration. During the course of the war, about 80,000 loyalists departed for Britain or other British colonies. Many more, numbering perhaps several hundred thousand, continued to live among their patriot neighbors. Tories included Crown officials, Anglican clergy, and merchants with close ties to Britain. Some of the best known loyalists were wealthy gentlemen and officeholders: Governor Thomas Hutchinson and Chief Justice Peter Oliver of Massachusetts; Joseph Galloway, speaker of the Pennsylvania Assembly; and Frederick Philipse, landlord of a 50,000-acre manor in New York.

Many Tories were not rich or intimately tied to Great Britain, for the Revolution became a power struggle within American society, not just one between the colonies and London. The tenants of New York manors, for example, took the opposite side of their landlords. Thus, residents of Frederick Philipse's manors became Whigs, while tenants of the patriot Livingstons and Schuylers supported the British. In Maryland, the loyalists gained widespread backing in Eastern Shore counties where farmers, suffering from economic decline and lack of political power, regarded the patriot elite as their enemies. The South Carolina backcountry divided along lines drawn during the 1760s, with the more affluent former Regulators supporting the Whigs, and their opponents, the "lower sort," casting their lot with the British.

Of considerable concern to white Americans were the loyalties of enslaved African Americans. Of the 2.5 million people in the thirteen colonies in 1775, about 500,000 were blacks. As the rhetoric of revolution

Antoine De Verger's sketch of American army uniforms reflects the military role of African Americans.
Anne S. K. Brown Military Collection, Brown University Library

reached African American slaves, increasing numbers escaped. On Maryland's Eastern Shore, loyalist whites made common cause with the bondpeople of Whig planters: in fall 1775, a Dorchester County committee reported that "the insolence of the Negroes in this county is come to such a height, that we are under a necessity of disarming them. . . . The malicious and imprudent speeches of some among the lower classes of whites have induced them to believe that their freedom depended on the success of the King's troops."

A chief source of unrest, the patriots believed, was the November 1775 proclamation of Lord Dunmore, royal governor of Virginia, declaring "all indented [sic] servants, Negroes, or others [owned by rebels] free, that are able and willing to bear arms, they joining His Majesty's Troops." Whigs considered this proclamation foul play, an attempt to start an insurrection. They increased slave patrols and warned of harsh punishments to those who ran away or took up arms against their masters. The penalty for slave rebellion, of course, was death. Nevertheless, African Americans aided the British by joining the army and employing their firsthand knowledge of the Chesapeake Bay. Some served as pilots along its tributaries,

while others delivered fresh provisions to the British ships by foraging plantations at night.

African Americans also supported the Revolution, but received little welcome from the Whigs. As the Americans created an army from volunteer forces besieging Boston, they excluded slaves and even free blacks from participating. From 1775 through much of 1776, when white enlistments seemed adequate, the patriot leaders, many of them slaveowners, were unwilling to exchange freedom for military service. By 1777, however, when recruiters found it difficult to fill their quotas, the states north of Virginia began accepting free blacks and slaves. Officially, Virginia took only free African Americans, but some masters sent slaves as substitutes for themselves. An estimated 5,000 African Americans served in the Continental army and state militias or at sea on American privateers. At the end of their service, many but not all of the enslaved African Americans who fought for independence received freedom. Some masters who had pledged liberty to their slaves if they served as substitutes broke the promises after the war.

Estimates of the total number of Americans who joined the Whig forces range from 100,000 to 250,000.

*P*ICTURING THE PAST✦POLITICS & DIPLOMACY

DEBORAH SAMPSON

Courtesy of the Rhode Island Historical Society, #RHi ✕5 32 Mas. 1900.6.1

Deborah Sampson, shown in this 1797 portrait by Joseph Stone, was the most famous of women who served as revolutionary soldiers. After the war she gave lectures about how she disguised herself as a man, using the name Robert Shurtleff. She fought at the battles of White Plains and Yorktown, was wounded, and later received back pay and a veteran's pension.

The role of women in combat during the Revolution—and later U.S. conflicts—is often ignored because it undermines gender beliefs that men are the defenders of family and nation. Female soldiers challenged the notion that men deserved to participate politically in the new nation—and women did not—because men had won independence on the battlefield. Approximately 20,000 women served in American units during the Revolutionary War, including several hundred who enlisted formally and many thousands who provided medical care, food, clothing, and military supplies. Others participated in local defense and served as spies.

Most signed up for tours of duty lasting several months or a year, not for the duration of the war. An ardent Boston patriot, for example, a poor shoemaker named George Robert Twelves Hewes, served at least six different stints for a total of twenty months. Ordinary people like Hewes did their best to support both the patriotic cause and their families. Thus, Washington and his generals constantly faced the problem of expiring enlistments, a condition that severely hampered execution of the war. The inability of Congress to pay soldiers adequately also hindered recruitment and retention of troops. As time went on, the American troops became better trained and disciplined, but originated from less privileged rungs of society. By 1778, most of the states had to adopt conscription to fill their quotas. Men were drafted by lottery, but could pay a fine or hire a substitute, loopholes that contributed to disproportionate service by the poor.

Women took part in the American war effort by operating farms and businesses in their husbands' absence, defending their homes and families against marauding enemy soldiers, supplying food and clothing for the troops, and joining the army. Perhaps several hundred women put on uniforms to become soldiers. These troops included Deborah Sampson of Massachusetts, who enlisted under the name Robert Shurtleff. She fought in battle, but was discovered when she received a wound; after the war she collected an army pension. Others performed unofficial short-term service as spies. The most substantial contribution of women to the American military was that of the Women of the Army, as George Washington called them. Numbering perhaps 20,000 over the course of the war, they served as nurses, cooks, laundresses, and water carriers. They were regular members of the army who drew rations and were subject to military discipline. Some saw action in battle, particularly women in artillery crews who carried water to swab out the cannon after each firing. The story of "Molly Pitcher" evolved from women like Mary Hayes of Carlisle, Pennsylvania, who took the place of fallen soldiers.

Independence and Confederation

During the winter and spring of 1776, fighting continued between Great Britain and the thirteen colonies. Though the Canada campaign was a disaster, the Americans gained success in their siege of Boston. They sledged the heavy guns from Fort Ticonderoga about 300 miles, installing them in March 1776 on the Dorchester Heights. Instead of storming the artillery, the British withdrew from the city, sailing to Nova Scotia in preparation for an invasion of New York City.

In 1776, London undertook a huge effort to put down the revolt. It sent across the Atlantic Ocean 370 transports with supplies and 32,000 troops, of whom many were German mercenaries (called Hessians because the largest proportion came from the principality of Hesse-Cassel). The British intended these soldiers to join General William Howe's 10,000 troops from Nova Scotia, take New York City, and destroy Washington's army. The British navy, with seventy-three warships and 13,000 sailors in American waters, would bombard seaports and wreak havoc on colonial shipping.

As the British military descended upon New York in midsummer 1776, the Continental Congress finally declared independence. The force of events propelled most moderate delegates to cast their vote for a complete break. In January 1776, Thomas Paine, a recent immigrant from England, had published *Common Sense*. Though his arguments were familiar to Congress and readers of political tracts, Paine convinced the American public of the need for independence. *Common Sense* sold more than 100,000 copies within a few months, reaching hundreds of thousands of people as copies changed hands and nonreaders listened to Paine's words read aloud. Paine used language that appealed to ordinary Protestant Americans, employing biblical arguments that churchgoing farmers and craftspeople could appreciate, and avoiding Latin phrases and classical references. He wanted to demonstrate that the time for compromise had passed, that the proper course was to shed the British monarchy and aristocracy to create an American republic. "We have it in our power to begin the world over again," he wrote. The bloodshed that began at Lexington justified rejection of the king: "No man was a warmer wisher for a reconciliation than myself, before

Thomas Paine, *by John Wesley Jarvis. A superb propagandist, the recent English immigrant convinced many Americans, "'tis time to part"—to declare independence.*
Independence National Historical Park

the fatal nineteenth of April, 1775, but the moment the event of that day was made known, I rejected the hardened, sullen-tempered Pharaoh of England for ever." Pragmatically, Paine argued that the colonists must break their ties with London if they expected aid from France and Spain. He pointed out the importance of American exports, which "will always have a market while eating is the custom in Europe." He exclaimed, "'TIS TIME TO PART . . . there is something very absurd, in supposing a continent to be perpetually governed by an island."

Through the spring of 1776, sentiment for independence increased. News that the British had engaged German mercenaries heated the debate. The provincial assemblies of Georgia, South Carolina, and North Carolina gave their delegates in Congress permission to support the break, while Rhode Island declared independence on its own. Virginia proposed that Congress separate from Britain, taking measures "for forming foreign alliances and a confederation of

In this painting, The Declaration of Independence, *by John Trumbull, the drafting committee stands at center: from left to right, John Adams, Roger Sherman, Robert Livingston, Thomas Jefferson, and Benjamin Franklin.*
Yale University Art Gallery, Trumbull Collection. Copyright Yale University Art Gallery

the colonies." But in June, the New York, Pennsylvania, Delaware, and Maryland assemblies, controlled by moderate factions, were still not ready to condone a split. Nevertheless, Congress appointed a committee to draft the Declaration of Independence, of which Thomas Jefferson, a wealthy thirty-three-year-old Virginia planter and lawyer, was the principal author. A graduate of the College of William and Mary and a serious intellectual, he had been an active opponent of British policies since first elected to the Virginia assembly in 1769.

The Declaration set forth Congress's reasons for separating from the government of George III; the revolutionaries focused on the king's offenses because they had already denied the sovereignty of Parliament. It held "these truths to be self-evident: That all men are created equal; that they are endowed by their Creator with certain unalienable rights; that among these are life, liberty, and the pursuit of happiness." (See the Appendix for full text.) Employing the philosophy of John Locke and other Enlightenment writers, Jefferson continued, "that, to secure these rights, governments are instituted among men, deriving their just powers from the consent of the governed; that whenever any

form of government becomes destructive of these ends, it is the right of the people to alter or to abolish it, and to institute new government." Congress placed the blame for the breach on the king, listing his misdeeds: refusing to approve necessary laws passed by the colonial assemblies, dissolving legislatures and courts, stationing a standing army, interrupting trade, and imposing taxes without colonial consent. Most recently, Congress announced to the world, George III had declared "us out of his protection and wag[ed] war against us. He has plundered our seas, ravaged our coasts, burned our towns, and destroyed the lives of our people. He is at this time transporting large armies of foreign mercenaries to complete the works of death, desolation, and tyranny already begun." In reference to Lord Dunmore's proclamation, the congressmen accused the king of exciting "domestic insurrection among us." For these reasons and more, Congress declared the thirteen colonies, now to be called the United States of America, "free and independent states" having "full power to levy war, conclude peace, contract alliances, establish commerce, and do all other acts and things which independent states may of right do."

On July 2, 1776, all delegations to Congress approved independence except New York's, which had not received new instructions so was forced to abstain. Completing revisions two days later, Congress adopted the Declaration. For many Americans, independence ended the problem of fighting a government that they continued to recognize as sovereign. When the Continental troops heard the Declaration read on July 9, they cheered, as did civilians throughout the states. However, the battles to defend this independence still lay ahead. General Washington cautioned "every officer and soldier . . . that now the peace and safety of his Country depends (under God) solely on the success of our arms."

To mount sufficient military force to win the war, the states needed unity. In mid-July 1776, Congress began debating the Articles of Confederation, a plan for permanent union, which it approved and sent to the states for ratification more than a year later. The chief disagreement among the congressmen was one that remained central to American politics for two centuries, the power of the national government versus that of individual states. The Articles permitted less centralized authority than would the Constitution, which was drafted a decade later. Under the Articles, Congress had responsibility to conduct foreign affairs, make war and peace, deal with Native Americans residing outside the states, coin and borrow money, supervise the post office, and negotiate boundary disputes between states. The "United States" meant thirteen sovereign states joined together by a Congress with specific functions. Article 1 established the "confederacy" to be called the United States of America, not a sovereign nation. Article 2 held that "each State retains its sovereignty, freedom and independence, and every power, jurisdiction, and right, which is not by this confederation expressly delegated to the United States, in Congress assembled." The Congress could neither tax nor raise troops, but could only assess quotas on the states, a serious disadvantage in time of war. Even so, the Articles failed ratification until 1781, when the last of the thirteen states finally approved. Conflict over state claims on western lands held up ratification. In the meantime, Congress attempted to govern within the limits of the unratified Articles, but its inability to raise revenue and draft troops obstructed the American war effort, creating huge shortages of supplies and men.

WAR IN THE NORTH, 1776-1779

For the American patriots, the Revolution was a defensive war. It lasted eight years, from 1775 to 1783, longer than any other in United States history until the Vietnam War. The Continental army was often outmatched, for it remained smaller than General Washington wanted; his troops constantly needed training as veterans left and new recruits arrived. But as the theater of war moved from one region to another, American generals obtained reinforcements from state militias and local volunteers. The British, despite considerable assistance from Tories, lacked enough reserves to subdue the rebellious North American seaboard. The sheer expanse of the thirteen states and the 3,000-mile distance from England made the British army's task extremely difficult, despite its formal training and Britain's larger population and wealth.

Invasions of New York

To conquer New York, and thus divide New England from the rest of the states, in July 1776, British troops landed on Staten Island. In August, they attacked Washington's army at Brooklyn Heights. The redcoats defeated the Americans badly, pushing them back to Manhattan Island, and then to White Plains. But they failed to take advantage of Washington's mistakes, which could have allowed them to surround his troops. In November, however, the British did hand Washington a humiliating defeat by capturing the 2,900 defenders of Manhattan's Fort Washington.

The Continental army retreated across New Jersey with the British and their German allies at its heels. The patriots crossed the Delaware River into Pennsylvania, allowing the British to occupy New

Pulling down the statue of George III in New York City, July 9, 1776.
From the Collections of the Library of Congress

Jersey towns. The British gathered Tory support by offering a pardon to anyone who would take a loyalty oath within sixty days. For the Whigs, as Thomas Paine wrote, these were "times that try men's souls." The army was in retreat, the New Jersey government had dispersed, and citizens who were skeptical of Washington's abilities rallied to the British.

Before the end of the year, however, fortunes changed. British plundering across New Jersey turned indifferent farmers into radical Whigs, who became guerrillas, ambushing the enemy and stealing supplies. Meanwhile, Washington devised a plan that bought him time, acting before the enlistments of a large proportion of his army would expire on December 31. He attacked 1,400 Hessians at Trenton on Christmas night, in the midst of a winter storm. Taking the enemy by surprise, the Americans captured more than 900 men. In early January, Washington took the offensive once again, having convinced many of his soldiers to extend their terms for six weeks. Pennsylvania and New Jersey militia, inspired by the victory at Trenton, reinforced his troops. Washington eluded a superior British army under Lord Cornwallis, then defeated a smaller force at Princeton. General William Howe withdrew most of his army to New York. In the words of one British officer, the Americans had "become a formidable enemy."

In 1777, as the British made plans to suppress the rebellion once and for all, their strategy for the upcoming campaign became confused. General Howe intended to take Philadelphia, not by crossing New Jersey, but by means of his brother Admiral Richard Howe's fleet. At the same time, London organized an invasion from Canada, to win back Fort Ticonderoga and divide the states. The campaigns were not coordinated and neither started before June, when British General "Gentleman Johnny" Burgoyne led his force of more than 7,000 British regulars, German mercenaries, Native Americans, and Canadians by boat down Lake Champlain. True to his reputation, Burgoyne overburdened his troops with baggage, including cartloads of personal clothing and champagne. Burgoyne easily took Fort Ticonderoga, then headed for Albany. The American forces under Philip Schuyler felled trees and rolled boulders into the path of Burgoyne's heavy column. Covering twenty-three miles of terrain that was difficult even without American sabotage took the British army twenty-four days. Short on supplies and horses, Burgoyne sent 800 troops to Bennington, Vermont, where General John Stark and his militia ambushed them by pretending to be Tories. Troops under British officer Barry St. Leger returned to

Battle of Princeton, 1777, *painted by William Mercer ten years later. The battles at Trenton and Princeton, New Jersey, renewed hope for the patriot cause.*
Princeton University Library

Canada when they heard that Benedict Arnold was headed west to intercept them. The rebel forces, on the other hand, burgeoned with volunteers as British soldiers pillaged the countryside. In September, near Saratoga, Burgoyne encountered the American army under General Horatio Gates, who had replaced Schuyler. The Americans surrounded the enemy, firing upon them day and night. Burgoyne sent for help from New York City, but Howe had long since sailed with most of his troops to Philadelphia. Burgoyne's 5,800-man army thus surrendered at Saratoga on October 17, 1777.

The British Occupy Philadelphia

As Burgoyne marched toward disaster in New York, General Howe more successfully reached Philadelphia. In July, his 13,000 soldiers departed from New York City aboard a fleet of 260 ships, but instead of disembarking within a week along the Delaware River, they sailed south to the Virginia capes then up the Chesapeake Bay to Head of Elk. Their voyage lasted over a month, costing Howe valuable time that might have permitted him to assist Burgoyne. Washington tried unsuccessfully, with an army of 11,000 at Brandywine, to block Howe's advance through southeastern Pennsylvania. The British occupied Philadelphia, dividing their forces between Germantown and the capital. On October 4, 1777, Washington attacked the British encampment at Germantown, inflicting serious damage though he was once

Map 5.2 *Northern Campaigns, 1776–1778*
The major revolutionary battles of these years took place in New York, New Jersey, and Pennsylvania. The inset indicates battles in 1776, when the British invaded Long Island and New York City, pushing Washington's troops across New Jersey until they won crucial battles at Trenton and Princeton. The larger map illustrates British offensives in 1777, while the 1778 battle at Monmouth Court House appears on the inset.

again defeated. Elizabeth Drinker, a Quaker resident of Philadelphia, in her diary reported significant losses on both sides. She wrote, "this has been a sorrowful day at Philadelphia and much more so at Germantown and thereabouts." She recorded news of the Continental army's movements, fearing that the troops would carry the battle to her city. "The apprehensions of their entering," she believed, "will render this night grievous to many." Washington did not attack Philadelphia, so the enemy retained control of the capital until they withdrew the next June.

Even so, in 1777, the British had failed to put down the American rebellion during yet another season of war. Upon hearing that Burgoyne's army had surrendered, the Howe brothers resigned. General Henry Clinton became the new commander of British forces in North America. The redcoats wintered in relative comfort at Philadelphia while Washington's troops nearly starved and froze to death at Valley Forge, to the west of the city. In February 1778, Continental soldiers lacked adequate clothing and received just three pounds of bread and three ounces of meat to last a week. Some ate only "fire cakes," baked from a paste of flour and water. Nevertheless, they became a disciplined army at Valley Forge, under the Prussian officer Baron von Steuben, who rigorously trained the Americans in the European art of war.

Alliance with France

While February 1778 brought despair to the Americans, it also brought hope—in the form of an alliance with France. Already supporting the United States with economic and military assistance, the French government hoped to recoup the international status it had lost during the Seven Years' War. Convinced by the victory at Saratoga that the former colonies could win the war, the French signed two pacts with the United States. The first was the Treaty of Amity and Commerce, in which France recognized American independence and both nations pledged "a firm, inviolable and universal peace." The second was the military Treaty of Alliance, in which they agreed to fight Great Britain jointly until the Americans had won independence, pledged not to negotiate a separate peace, and confirmed their defensive alliance "forever." France renounced claims to its former colonies in North America, but could retain any of the British West Indies that it conquered.

In supporting the Americans, the French renewed their long struggle with Great Britain that had been suspended in 1763. France's entry widened the war, placing greater focus on the West Indies, whose sugar production made them more valuable than the North American mainland to the British. The following year, Spain allied with France, but refused to recognize or assist the American insurgents beyond providing limited financial aid. Unlike France, which denied interest in North America, the Spanish viewed the Americans as potentially dangerous competitors.

The Wartime Economy

Despite significant economic assistance from France and a much smaller contribution from Spain, the United States had grave economic problems during the war. The loss of British markets devastated farmers, merchants, and fishermen, as the embargo closed crucial ports in the West Indies and British Isles. The Royal Navy attacked and blockaded American harbors and ravaged ships at sea. On land, the armies laid waste to farms and towns.

For Congress, the chief economic problem was paying for the war. Without the power to tax, it printed money, a total of almost $200 million in paper bills by 1779. The states printed a similar amount, despite their ability to tax, primarily because printing money was easier than trying to collect revenues from a financially strapped populace. Unfortunately, as the war continued year after year, the demand for military equipment, food, medical supplies, clothing, and soldiers' wages persisted. This extraordinary demand for provisions coupled with the continuing emission of paper money sent prices soaring. By 1779, the paper money was nearly worthless, inspiring the slogan "not worth a Continental."

The depreciation of currency resulted in popular unrest, as a group of Philadelphia militia in 1779 demanded a more equitable military draft and regulation of food prices. They were angry that the burden of militia service fell disproportionately on the poor because others could pay fines to avoid the draft. At the same time, the prices of food and firewood skyrocketed. In just two months, August and September 1779, the price of beef, flour, and molasses rose by more than 80 percent. The protesters, according to one broadside posted along the streets, blamed "a few overbearing Merchants, a swarm of Monopolizers and Speculators, an infernal gang of Tories" for the spiraling costs.

In the so-called "Fort Wilson Incident," armed members of the Philadelphia militia met at Burns's Tavern on October 4, planning to capture and exile from the city four suspected Tories. Several hundred militiamen marched their prisoners through the streets to the fife and drum of the Rogue's March, ordinarily played by the military when a soldier was discharged dishonorably.

ꝑICTURING THE PAST✦ECONOMICS & TECHNOLOGY

CONTINENTAL CURRENCY

Courtesy, American Antiquarian Society

The Continental Congress, which acted under the Articles of Confederation throughout the war, lacked the ability to tax. Because the states were reluctant to raise money through taxation to support the war, Congress funded military spending through loans and printed money. Before the Revolution, colonies had printed paper currency. For example, New York and Pennsylvania issued paper money as loans, thus putting needed money into circulation and obtaining public revenue from the interest.

Continental money, as noted in this example, promised the bearer the equivalent in Spanish dollars. Congress thus rejected the English system of pounds, shillings, and pence to adopt the Spanish denomination. This was a logical step because Spanish coins manufactured from Mexican and South American silver and gold had commonly circulated in colonial British America despite the official English currency. Unfortunately, Continental dollars quickly lost value as Congress printed millions to fund the war. By April 1781, $168 Continental was the equivalent of one silver dollar.

The militia was ridiculing the reputed Tories, all four of them wealthy citizens. When rumors raced through the capital that the militia planned to arrest others, about thirty gentlemen who thought they might be targets armed themselves and gathered at the house of lawyer James Wilson. Though a member of Congress, Wilson was suspect because he opposed price regulation. The militia marched past "Fort Wilson," gave three cheers, then shots rang out. Though it is unknown who shot first, both sides subsequently exchanged fire. After cavalry broke up the battle, six people lay dead and seventeen wounded, the majority of them militia.

The Fort Wilson Incident terrified many people because lower-class patriots had directed armed force against the Whig elite, protesting the policies of their own government. Henry Laurens, a wealthy South Carolina merchant and member of the Continental Congress, wrote, "we are at this moment on a precipice, and what I have long dreaded and often intimated to my friends, seems to be breaking forth—a convulsion among the people."

THE WAR MOVES WEST AND SOUTH

The failure of the British army to defeat Washington's troops and the entry of France into the war led the imperial government to rethink its military strategy. Protection of Caribbean sugar islands from the French navy gained top priority. With redeployment of forces to the West Indies, British General Clinton had to consolidate his army, so in June 1778, he pulled his occupation forces out of Philadelphia, marching across New Jersey toward New York. Washington's army caught up with Clinton at Monmouth Courthouse, where the battle, fought in traditional European style, was indecisive. The British escaped to New York.

The Frontier War

In the west, from New York to Georgia, fighting devastated the backcountry. When the Revolution broke out, many Indians supported the British, who still held garrisons in the west and had more gunpowder and provisions than the patriots. Yet Native Americans responded in various ways to "this dispute between two brothers," as neutral Iroquois called the Revolution in 1775. "The quarrel seems to be unnatural," they said; "you are two brothers of one blood." Just as colonists divided among radical Whigs, Tories, and neutrals, so did the Native Americans. Even within some tribes, factions separated those who favored the British or the Americans, or wanted to avoid any involvement. The militant Indians who sided with Great Britain considered the threat of white settlers crossing the Appalachians as most dangerous to their future. Many attempted to form pan-Indian alliances to fight their own wars of independence against land grabbers from the east.

Beginning in 1776, Indians attacked Anglo-Americans from the Georgia frontier to the Great Lakes. The Cherokees raided the southern backcountry and planned a major assault on Tennessee, but ran short of gunpowder and were defeated by Whig militia in fall 1776. Many Cherokees, Choctaws, Creeks, Shawnees, Iroquois, and others did not give up, however, but rather planned in 1779 "a general invasion of the Frontiers" coordinated by Henry Hamilton, the British lieutenant governor of the Illinois country. George Rogers Clark, a surveyor, heard of plans for the Indian and British offensive. To Patrick Henry, he wrote, "the Case is Desperate but Sir we must Either Quit the Country or attack Mr. Hamilton." In 1779, with a small force, Clark assaulted Fort Vincennes and obtained the British surrender, thus ending the pan-Indian campaign.

Despite Clark's victory at Vincennes, the Kentucky-Ohio frontier remained embattled throughout the war. The same was true of Pennsylvania and New York, where after 1777 most Iroquois and Delawares abandoned their neutrality to ally with the British. In 1778 and 1779, Major John Butler, his son Captain Walter Butler, and the Mohawk leader Theyendanegea, also known as Joseph Brant, led Tory and Native American forces against white settlements. The loyalists and Iroquois burned houses, barns, fields, and orchards, ran off livestock, and killed or captured settlers over a swath of frontier ranging from fifty to a hundred miles wide. In summer 1779, General Washington sent General John Sullivan with 4,000 troops, who retaliated by burning Iroquois villages, orchards, and fields of corn. At Newtown, New York, Sullivan defeated a contingent of about 700 loyalists and Indians. His scorched-earth policy seriously damaged most of the Iroquois towns; displaced Indians suffered through the winter of 1779–1780 on short rations. But the next spring they renewed their assaults.

Because many Anglo-Americans had trouble distinguishing between Indian friends and foes, Native Americans who allied with the United States or remained neutral throughout the war fared little better with the Whigs than those who sided with the British. In March 1782, frontier militia massacred ninety-six pacifist Indian men, women, and children at the Moravian mission of Gnadenhutten in Ohio. Another group, the Catawbas of South Carolina, performed extensive service for the patriots. They searched for loyalists and escaped slaves, supplied food to the rebels, fought the Cherokees in 1776, and battled the British, who destroyed their town in retaliation. After the war, the South Carolina assembly compensated the Catawbas for their loyalty and livestock, refusing to abet the governor's plan to lease out their reservation. The Mahicans of Stockbridge in western Massachusetts, who fought in the American army, returned home to find that whites had taken over their land.

The Southern Campaigns

While the Revolution ravaged the frontier, the main theater of war remained east of the Appalachians,

Joseph Brant, *by Gilbert Stuart. The Mohawk leader, who was educated among whites and traveled to Great Britain in 1775, convinced many Iroquois to ally with the British.*
New York State Historical Association, Cooperstown

The Narrative of Mary Jemison, 1775–1779

Mary Jemison was a white woman who had been captured by Indians and spent most of her life among the Senecas. Her journal provides the view of an Iroquois woman, as her adopted people first agreed with the revolutionaries to maintain neutrality, then allied with the British. The Iroquois lost their villages and stocks of food when the American general John Sullivan conducted his scorched earth policy.

Thus, at peace amongst themselves, and with the neighboring whites, though there were none at that time very near, our Indians lived quietly and peaceably at home, till a little before the breaking out of the revolutionary war, when they were sent for, together with the Chiefs and members of the Six Nations generally, by the people of the States, . . .

Our Indians obeyed the call, and the council was holden, at which the pipe of peace was smoked, and a treaty made, in which the Six Nations solemnly agreed that if a war should eventually break out, they would not take up arms on either side; but that they would observe a strict neutrality. . . .

About a year passed off, and we, as usual, were enjoying ourselves in the employments of peaceable times, when a messenger arrived from the British Commissioners, requesting all the Indians of our tribe to attend a general council. . . .to engage their assistance in subduing the rebels, . . .

The Chiefs then arose, and informed the Commissioners of the nature and extent of the treaty which they had entered into with the people of the states, the year before, and that they should not violate it by taking up the hatchet against them.

The Commissioners continued their entreaties without success, till they addressed their avarice, by telling our people that the people of the states were few in number, and easily subdued; . . . and added, that the King was rich and powerful, both in money and subjects: That his rum was as plenty as the water in lake Ontario: that his men were as numerous as the sands upon the lake shore:—and that the Indians, if they would assist in the war, and persevere in their friendship to the King, till it was closed, should never want for money or goods. Upon this the Chiefs concluded a treaty with the British Commissioners, in which they agreed to take up arms against the rebels, . . .

As soon as the treaty was finished, the Commissioners made a present to each Indian of a suit of clothes, a brass kettle, a gun and tomahawk, a scalping knife, a quantity of powder and lead, a piece of gold, and promised a bounty on every scalp that should be brought in. Thus richly clad and equipped, they returned home, after an absence of about two weeks, full of the fire of war, and anxious to encounter their enemies. . . .

Previous to the battle at Fort Stanwix, the British sent for the Indians to come and see them whip the rebels; and, at the same time stated that they did not wish to have them fight, but wanted to have them just sit down, smoke their pipes, and look on. Our Indians went, to a man; but contrary to their expectation, instead of smoking and looking on, they were obliged to fight for their lives, and in the end of the battle were completely beaten, with a great loss in killed and wounded. Our Indians alone had thirty-six killed, and a great number wounded. Our town exhibited a scene of real sorrow and distress, when our warriors returned and recounted their misfortunes, and stated the real loss they had sustained in the engagement. The mourning was excessive, and was expressed by the most doleful yells, shrieks, and howlings, and by inimitable gesticulations. . . .

In one or two days after the skirmish at Connissius lake, Sullivan and his army arrived at Genesee river, where they destroyed every article of the food kind that they could lay their hands on. A part of our corn they burnt, and threw the remainder into the river. They burnt our houses, killed what few cattle and horses they could find, destroyed our fruit trees, and left nothing but the bare soil and timber. But the Indians had eloped and were not to be found. . . .

THE WAR MOVES WEST AND SOUTH

where in 1778, the British inaugurated a new strategy. Retaining troops in New York City, they invaded the south, counting on loyalist support in Georgia, the Carolinas, and Virginia to restore colonial governments to the Crown. The British also expected the large numbers of enslaved African Americans in the south to weaken patriot defenses. In November 1778, General Clinton sent 3,500 troops under Lieutenant Colonel Archibald Campbell to Georgia, where they joined 2,000 soldiers from Florida. They captured Savannah and Augusta, but had trouble conquering the backcountry. Then, with 10,000 troops, the British turned to Charleston, where in May 1780 they compelled the American general Benjamin Lincoln to surrender 5,500 men. The British fanned out through South Carolina, as many residents pledged their loyalty to the king. In July 1780, General Horatio Gates arrived to build a new southern army. Disaster struck once again, when Gates placed too much responsibility on untrained militia in action against Lord Cornwallis at Camden. The battle was a rout; even the regular Continentals were dispersed, and Gates—the hero of Saratoga—was disgraced.

The tide turned after General Nathanael Greene replaced Gates as commander of the southern army. The British contributed to the turnaround, as they became more insistent in demanding oaths of allegiance from Carolinians who preferred to keep out of the fray. This provoked a backlash, particularly because the British army stretched itself so thin that it withdrew protection from the people who took the oaths, thus exposing them to punishment by the Whigs. The redcoats and Tories also plundered, outraging many southerners and pushing them into the American camp. Most notorious was Banastre Tarleton's Tory Legion, which executed prisoners of war and destroyed houses and fields, leaving many families homeless. "Bloody" Tarleton created new revolutionaries, who joined Greene's army or the smaller irregular brigades led by Thomas "The Gamecock" Sumter, Colonel Andrew Pickens, and Francis Marion, "the Swamp Fox." During 1780 and 1781, Greene rebuilt the southern army using both traditional and guerrilla forces.

While not welcome as soldiers in South Carolina and Georgia, African American slaves played an important role in the southern campaigns, acting as spies and counterspies for each side. One man, Antigua, received freedom by act of the South Carolina assembly for himself, his wife Hagar, and child in reward for "procuring information of the enemy's movements and designs." Throughout the South, African Americans provided much of the supporting labor for both armies, as they built fortifications, worked in lead mines, constructed and repaired roads, produced arms

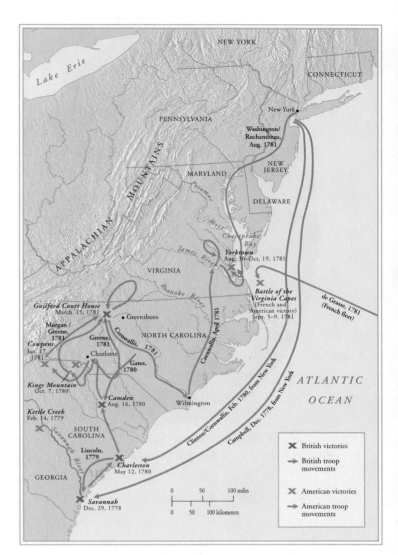

Map 5.3 *Southern Campaigns, 1778–1781*

In late 1778, the British decided to invade the South, where they were no more successful in ending the war. They agreed to peace after their defeat to the Americans and French at the Battle of Yorktown in Virginia.

View an animated version of this map or related maps at http://history.wadsworth.com/passages2e.

and ammunition, and drove wagons. American officers complained about the chronic shortage of black laborers, because Whig slaveowners jealously guarded their strongest and most talented slaves to work on their plantations. Further, thousands of African Americans took advantage of General Clinton's 1779 proclamation offering freedom to those who joined the king's service.

A practice of rebel leaders highlighting their ability to dissociate their own fight for liberty from the plight of enslaved African Americans was to offer

Nathanael Greene, *by Charles Willson Peale. A former Quaker, Greene used both guerrilla tactics and formal military methods to wage his successful southern campaign.*
Independence National Historical Park

recruits enlistment "bounties" in slaves, much as other states promised bounties in land. In South Carolina, Thomas Sumter offered one African American bondman or woman to each private who would enlist for ten months. A colonel would receive three mature blacks and one child. The practice was adopted by Andrew Pickens as well, and supported by General Greene, who expected to pay the bounties from slaves confiscated from loyalist estates. Because sufficient numbers of African Americans owned by Tories were lacking, regiments reported "pay" in arrears, some with grotesque precision. One payroll noted a deficit of 93 3/4 mature slaves and "Three Quarters of a Small Negro."

In fall 1780, Lord Cornwallis decided to head north, for while the British had destroyed two American armies and taken control of South Carolina and Georgia, the time had come to conquer the entire South. As his forces marched toward North Carolina, however, they met heavy resistance. In several battles,

the conflict became a civil war, as Americans fought on both sides. In October 1780, just to the south of the state line at King's Mountain, Whig frontier units defeated an enemy force, of which only Patrick Ferguson, the commander of the loyalists, was British. In January 1781, at Cowpens, General Daniel Morgan crushed Tarleton's Tory Legion by making the most of his sharpshooting frontiersmen. Morgan lined up the riflemen in front of his disciplined Continentals. The sharpshooters fired several volleys at Tarleton's troops then withdrew to back up the regulars, who took the brunt of the fighting.

When Cornwallis learned that Tarleton's legion was lost, he chased the Americans into North Carolina, abandoning most of his equipment and supplies to move quickly. In March, Cornwallis met Greene at the Guilford Courthouse, where the American general used Morgan's Cowpens tactics, though less effectively because his successive lines of irregulars and Continentals were spread too far apart. Though the battle ended indecisively, one-fourth of Cornwallis's troops lay wounded or dead. Having discarded tents, medical equipment, and food—and cut off from his base in South Carolina—the British general withdrew to the North Carolina coast where he sought naval support.

Meanwhile, Greene moved south to reconquer South Carolina and Georgia, where the British still had 8,000 men in arms. Because these troops were spread out in numerous towns and forts, Greene's 1,500 Continental soldiers and the guerrilla brigades of Sumter, Pickens, and Marion could pick off the garrisons one by one. Greene wrote to Washington in May 1781 that if the enemy "divide their force, they will fall by detachments, and if they operate collectively, they cannot command the country." By July, the Americans had pushed the redcoats and Tories back to a narrow strip of territory between Charleston and Savannah, which the British held until their evacuation the next year. Despite initial disastrous defeats, the Whigs prevailed in the Carolinas and Georgia by recruiting irregular forces and employing them strategically. The great sweep of territory controlled by the former thirteen colonies proved impossible for the British army to subdue.

The surrender of Cornwallis at Yorktown in October 1781 effectively ended the war. The general had moved into Virginia, replacing Benedict Arnold as commander of the British forces there. Arnold, the former American officer, had turned traitor, joined the British army, and most recently captured Richmond. With an army of about 8,000 men, Cornwallis intended to concentrate British military efforts in Virginia, so requested more troops from New York. General Clinton refused. Their squabbling and delay allowed the Americans and the French to surround Cornwallis's camp on the Virginia peninsula by land and sea. Several times before, the French forces had collaborated with the Americans, but their joint efforts had resulted in failure. This time, soldiers under the Comte de Rochambeau and French fleets commanded by the Comte de Grasse and Comte de Barras played a decisive role in defeating Cornwallis. Washington's army marched south from New York to join American and French troops assembled in Virginia. The operation was a marvel of military cooperation for the eighteenth century; it even included the construction of bake ovens outside New York City to camouflage Washington's departure. With 17,000 men and heavy artillery, the American and French forces won the British surrender, finally placing the seal on American independence.

The Peace Settlement

In negotiating the peace, the United States had to reckon with both its adversary Great Britain and its ally France, which in turn was beholden to Spain. American peace commissioners Benjamin Franklin, John Jay, and John Adams, whom Adams called "militia diplomats," shrewdly worked one European nation against the other to obtain a desirable settlement. They ignored Congress's instructions to take advice from France because they understood that French and Spanish goals were different from their own. France had little interest in a strong American nation; Spain particularly feared its territorial expansion. Thus, in violation of the 1778 treaty with France, the American diplomats negotiated separately with the British, obtaining recognition of independence and most other provisions they requested.

The British and American peacemakers approved preliminary articles of peace on November 30, 1782; the Treaty of Paris signed on September 3, 1783 was essentially unchanged. The new nation would extend from approximately the present United States–Canada boundary on the north, to the Mississippi River on the west, to the thirty-first parallel on the south. The American diplomats also secured fishing rights off Newfoundland and the St. Lawrence River, of particular interest to New Englanders. Further, the British agreed to evacuate their troops promptly from the United States "without causing any destruction or carrying away any Negroes or other property of the American inhabitants." For its part, Congress would urge state governments to return confiscated property to the loyalists. Prewar debts owed by citizens of each country to citizens of the other would be honored: they should "meet with no lawful impediment to the recovery of the full value in sterling money."

Surrender of Lord Cornwallis, *by John Trumbull. Their loss at the Battle of Yorktown convinced the British that retaining the thirteen rebellious colonies was not worth the cost.*
Yale University Art Gallery, Trumbull Collection. Copyright Yale University Art Gallery

Preliminary Peace Negotiations with Great Britain, *by Benjamin West. This unfinished portrait of the American diplomats includes, from left to right, John Jay, John Adams, Benjamin Franklin, Temple Franklin (Franklin's grandson who served as the commission's secretary), and Henry Laurens (who was not present to sign the final treaty).*
Courtesy, Winterthur Museum

The treaty was a success on paper for the United States, but left France and Spain dissatisfied and pro-British Native Americans "thunder struck." In coming decades, the Americans would struggle to enforce its provisions. The French gained little from the war except the separation of the mainland colonies from Great Britain. The Spanish had wanted to keep the Americans out of the Mississippi Valley and hoped to obtain the return of Gibraltar from the British. They instead accepted East and West Florida and the Mediterranean island of Minorca. Native Americans were furious that their British allies had signed away their lands.

While U.S. possession of the trans-Appalachian region remained disputed for decades, the provision that most immediately caused trouble was the one dealing with enslaved African Americans. Even before the final treaty was signed, American slaveowners claimed that the British military forces were taking their "property." The situation was complicated, for thousands of African Americans had fled behind British lines to find freedom and some had fought against their former masters. The British ruled that blacks who sought refuge before the signing of the provisional treaty in November 1782 could not be considered the property of Americans because they were already free, but slaves who escaped after that date would be returned to their masters. General Washington, Congress, and state governments tried but failed to convince the British to return all blacks to their former masters. At least 20,000 African Americans, including those who accompanied loyalist owners as well as the ex-slaves of Whigs, left with the British military. Some went to Nova Scotia, where they received a generally unfriendly welcome from white residents, while many others were transported to Florida and the West Indies. In the Sugar Islands most of the newly freed blacks were quickly re-enslaved.

CONCLUSION

The War of Independence was a success as American Whigs cast off a monarchy to create a new government in which many people, not a king and nobility, held power. They rejected as tyranny British efforts to impose revenue taxes without approval of representative assemblies and to curb rights such as trial by jury. The patriots used a variety of tactics including economic boycotts, riots, mass meetings, and petitions. Their local associations assumed governmental authority, providing the basis for republican rule.

Against many odds—including opposition from large numbers of loyalists—the thirteen British colonies won independence, created a confederation of sovereign states, and obtained claims to the vast trans-Appalachian territories. French financial aid and mili-

tary support were crucial to victory. The Whigs avoided military dictatorship, preserved individual rights for white Americans, and established the framework for a future democratic society. Yet not all Americans reaped immediate benefits. While wartime ideology challenged slavery in the North, the vast majority of African Americans remained enslaved. And though the Revolution offered women new, temporary roles in the economy and military—and more permanent educational opportunities after the peace—their political and legal status was essentially unchanged. The Treaty of Paris ignored the territorial rights of Native Americans.

Of immediate importance to the nation's leaders, however, was establishing a stable government. The 1780s presented a series of challenges to the new republic.

Recommended Readings

Calloway, Colin G. *The American Revolution in Indian Country: Crisis and Diversity in Native American Communities* (1995). Focuses on eight Indian communities to demonstrate the diversity of Native American experiences during the Revolutionary War.

Foner, Eric. *Tom Paine and Revolutionary America* (1976). A readable "life and times" of the author of *Common Sense.*

Gross, Robert A. *The Minutemen and Their World* (1976). An interesting study of how revolutionary fervor developed in Concord, Massachusetts.

Higginbotham, Don. *The War of American Independence: Military Attitudes, Policies, and Practice, 1763–1789* (1971). Straightforward military history of the Revolution.

Hoffman, Ronald, and Albert, Peter J., eds. *Women in the Age of the Revolution* (1989). Very good essays on women's status and contributions to the War of Independence.

In Search of Early America: The William and Mary Quarterly, 1943–1993, comp. Michael McGiffert (1993). Compilation of classic essays published in the foremost journal of early American history.

Morgan, Edmund S., and Morgan, Helen M. *The Stamp Act Crisis: Prologue to Revolution,* 2nd ed. (1996). A close examination of a crucial episode in the pre-revolutionary decade.

O'Shaughnessy, Andrew Jackson. *An Empire Divided: The American Revolution and the British*

Caribbean (2000). Evaluates the differences that led West Indies planters to stay within the empire while mainland colonists rebelled.

Quarles, Benjamin. *The Negro in the American Revolution*, 2nd ed. (1996). The classic text on African Americans during the war.

Young, Alfred F., ed. *The American Revolution: Explorations in the History of American Radicalism* (1976). Important essays on the role of ordinary Americans in the Revolution.

American Journey Online and InfoTrac College Edition

Visit the source collections at http://ajaccess. wadsworth.com and infotrac.thomsonlearning.com and use the Search function with the following key terms to explore documents, images, audio and video clips, articles, and commentary related to the material in this chapter.

Stamp Act	Boston Tea Party
Boston Massacre	Battle of Lexington
Battle of Concord	Declaration of Independence
Thomas Paine	

Additional resources, exercises, and Internet links related to this chapter are available on the American Passages Web site: http://history.wadsworth.com/passages2e

6 TOWARD A MORE PERFECT UNION 1783–1788

POLITICS AND CHANGE IN THE NEW REPUBLIC

CHALLENGES TO THE CONFEDERATION

POLITICAL AND ECONOMIC TURMOIL

THE MOVEMENT FOR CONSTITUTIONAL REFORM

The Great Seal of the United States, adopted by Congress in 1782, incorporated as symbols of the new nation the thirteen stars and stripes, the eagle with the olive branch of peace and arrows of war, and the motto E Pluribus Unum, Latin for "Out of Many, One."
© Bettmann/Corbis

The American Patriots had won victory on the battlefield and, at least on paper, in negotiating the peace. The new country soon discovered, though, that independence brought severe tests as well as opportunities. In 1786, Dr. Benjamin Rush of Philadelphia summarized in a pamphlet the tasks facing the United States:

> There is nothing more common than to confound the terms of *the American revolution* with those of *the late American war*. The American war is over: but this is far from being the case with the American revolution. On the contrary, nothing but the first act of the great drama is closed. It remains yet to establish and perfect our forms of government; and to prepare the principles, morals, and manners of our citizens, for those forms of government. . . .

Having fought for liberty and self-government, Americans now had to create an effective political framework to protect those rights. Their first government was a confederation of small republics in which property-holding white men elected representatives. But questions remained about how to avoid the opposite evils of tyranny and anarchy, questions that inspired fiery debates and even rebellion during the 1780s.

American leaders had understood since 1776 that the task of creating a workable government lay before them. They were less prepared for other problems that arose soon after the peace. With limited powers under the Articles of Confederation, the Congress faced challenges in demobilizing the army, conducting trade outside the confines of British mercantilism, paying the war debt, coexisting with Spanish colonies in Louisiana and Florida, dealing with Native Americans, and supervising white settlement in the West. Despite Congress's competent action on some of these issues, the need for a more powerful central government became clear. Just four years after the conclusion of peace, delegates from the states met in Philadelphia to draft the new Constitution, which became law upon ratification in 1788. This Constitution has endured, with relatively few amendments, for over two centuries.

CHRONOLOGY

1783   Protest of Continental army officers at Newburgh, New York • Great Britain closes British West Indies to American ships • Massachusetts Supreme Court finds slavery unconstitutional

1784   Rhode Island and Connecticut pass gradual abolition laws • Spain closes port of New Orleans to Americans • Spain signs treaty of alliance with the Creeks • United States forces Iroquois to cede rights in Northwest Territory with Treaty of Fort Stanwix

1785   Native Americans yield lands in Ohio with Treaty of Fort McIntosh • Congress passes land ordinance for the Northwest Territory

1786   Shawnees sign Treaty of Fort Finney • Country party takes control of Rhode Island assembly • Virginia statute for religious liberty • Annapolis convention fails • Western Confederacy rejects treaties ceding lands in the Northwest Territory • Massachusetts farmers close county courts

1787   Shaysites attack the federal arsenal at Springfield, Massachusetts • Constitutional Convention meets in Philadelphia • Congress passes Northwest Ordinance • Constitution signed and sent to the states for ratification

1787–1788   Publication of *The Federalist* essays • Ratification of the Constitution by eleven states

POLITICS AND CHANGE IN THE NEW REPUBLIC

In contrasting "the American revolution" with "the late American war," Rush made a distinction that many people have debated since the 1780s. Rush thought the revolution had to continue because the government was not yet "perfect"—the states had too much power, leading to disunity and inertia. Others have framed the question in a different way: to what extent did the War of Independence bring about basic changes in politics and society? The war was revolutionary for propertied white men, but less so for women, African Americans, religious minorities, and the poor.

Republican Politics

Under the Articles of Confederation, the United States consisted of thirteen sovereign states rather than one nation. In framing the Confederation, representatives from the states had refused to transfer sovereignty to a central government. Only state assemblies, elected by the voters, could impose taxes; the central government, or Congress, would be an agent of the states. This decision was based on republican theory, that only in a small republic could representatives act according to the will of its citizens. If the territory were large, the interests and desires of the people would be too diverse, making harmony impossible. State officials, guarding their power, feared that a strong national government would be dominated by factions with interests opposite their own. Each state had an equal vote in Congress and sent delegates "appointed in such manner as the legislature of each State shall direct." Congress had responsibility to conduct foreign affairs, declare war and peace, and coin money, but could not levy taxes or raise troops. During the 1780s, its dependence on the states for funds brought the Confederation to a standstill. For years, Congress sought an amendment of the Articles to permit a national tax, but failed to obtain the required unanimous consent of the states.

The structure of the state governments reflected their framers' concept of republicanism. Most of the state constitutions resembled the old colonial governments, but incorporated changes that made them more responsible to the people. Most had two-house legislatures and a governor, but gave the largest share of power to the lower house of assembly, elected annually by the voters. The radical Pennsylvania constitution of 1776, more democratic than others, included no governor or upper house of assembly (senate), which was designed to represent the wealthier segment of society. Georgia also excluded the upper house and denied its governor any power. Even states that retained the governor eliminated his veto over legislation or allowed the assembly to override with a two-thirds vote. All of the states produced written constitutions as a protection against the kind of changes they believed the British had made in their unwritten constitution before the Revolution.

During the late 1770s and 1780s, as Americans formulated and revised state constitutions, they also developed the method by which frames of government were written and approved, the constitutional convention. Pennsylvania radicals called the first state convention in 1776, explaining that its members would be "invested with powers to form a plan of government only, and not to execute it after it is framed." Then, in 1780, Massachusetts voters demanded a convention to write a new constitution rather than accept a document their assemblymen had prepared. The constitution was ratified by the people (voters), who thus claimed to be sovereign—the ultimate source of political power—because the frame of government originated with them. Within a few years, other states adopted the same process, recognizing that a constitution should not be written by a governmental body—the legislature—that the constitution created. As one theorist argued, "Conventions . . . are the only proper bodies to form a Constitution, and Assemblies are the proper bodies to make Laws agreeable to that Constitution." Remarkably, in Massachusetts in 1780, every free man, even those without property, could vote on the new constitution. The document they approved limited suffrage to propertied men.

State constitutions also provided some protection for the liberties many Americans had defended in the Revolution. Virginia included a model Declaration of Rights that other states copied loosely. Most state constitutions offered freedom of worship, required search warrants, and banned excessive fines and quartering of troops in private dwellings. Only some of the states, however, guaranteed trial by jury and the rights of free speech, press, and assembly. A few opposed monopolies and imprisonment for debt.

The state constitutions were radical in the context of eighteenth-century politics because they vested power in the voters and lower houses of assembly. Nevertheless, the definition of who was qualified to cast ballots and hold office remained traditional. John Adams spoke for most politicians of his time when he wrote that only property holders should be counted among the sovereign people who could choose and serve as magistrates because the purpose of government was to safeguard property. "It is dangerous," Adams wrote, ". . . to alter the qualifications of voters. There will be no end to it. New claims will arise. Women will demand a vote. Lads from 12 to 21 will think their rights not enough attended to, and every man, who has not a farthing, will demand an equal voice." Voters, according to republican theory, must have a stake in society. Wives, slaves, servants, and unpropertied laboring men were dependent on others and thus unqualified for suffrage. Yet in most places, women and free African Americans who owned property were also barred from voting, by law or by informal pressure. One exception was New Jersey, where the 1776 state constitution extended the vote to "all

PICTURING THE PAST ✦ POLITICS & DIPLOMACY

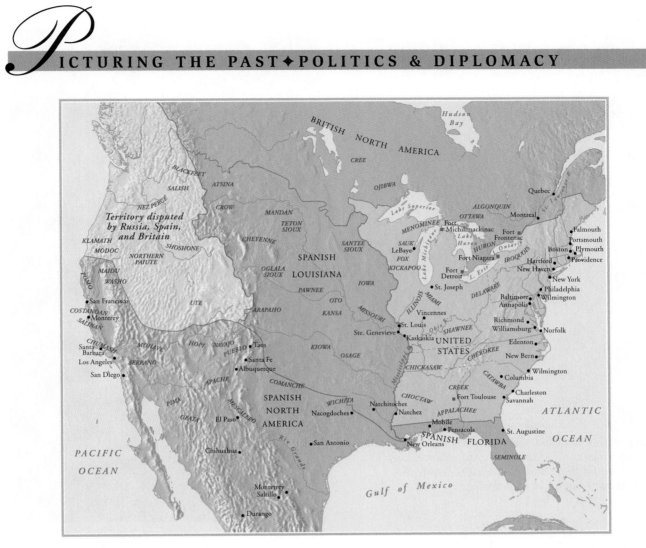

Map 6.1 *North America in 1783*

The peace treaty ending the American Revolution gave the United States most of the territory from the Atlantic Ocean to the Mississippi River, south of the St. Lawrence River and Great Lakes, and north of Spanish Florida. The new nation obtained claims to the region west of the Appalachians primarily because Great Britain, France, and Spain had more urgent goals. The treaty left several borders vague, however, and the United States had difficulty enforcing several provisions. Spain refused to recognize the 31st parallel as Florida's northern border and closed the Mississippi River to American trade. See Map 6.2 for the area Spain ceded to the United States in 1795. Problems with Britain were more long-lived. Until 1796, the British refused to evacuate nine military posts, including Michilimackinac, Detroit, and Niagara. Britain controlled the west through these forts, both militarily and through diplomatic alliances with the region's Native Americans. The imprecise border between Maine and Canada nearly caused war between the United States and Britain two generations later, when the boundary dispute was resolved diplomatically in 1842.

"Keep Within Compass," published during the era of the new republic (c. 1785–1805), warned young women to remain within traditional female roles despite the revolutionary change in government.
Courtesy, Winterthur Museum

Girl in Green, *by an unknown artist, c. 1790. While women's status remained circumscribed in many areas after the Revolution, their access to education improved, as suggested in this rare image of a girl reading a book.*
Abby Aldrich Rockefeller Folk Art Center, Williamsburg

free inhabitants" who held sufficient property; in 1807, the legislature fell into line with other states by disenfranchising all women and blacks.

Women's Rights

Republican politics brought little change to women's lives. A married woman was still subject to the English common law that gave control of her property and earnings to her husband and denied her the right, without his permission, to make a will, sign contracts, sue in court, or act as a guardian. Despite independence, the American lawmakers refused to cast off this English tradition. Women were also barred from positions of high status. They could serve as ministers among Quakers and some Baptists but in no other churches; they taught school only at the primary level. None were lawyers or wealthy merchants, though some became successful shopkeepers. Women also lost ground in medicine. As medical courses at the college level became available to men, doctors with formal training

displaced lay practitioners, including some midwives. Change occurred most noticeably in Boston, New York, and Philadelphia, where affluent clients demanded the new college-trained obstetricians.

In the post-revolutionary years, increased support for female education marked the most positive alteration in women's lives. This change accompanied the more general perception that a republic needed an educated people. Though women were denied entrance to all colleges, a number of academies opened their doors to provide secondary-level education to well-to-do girls. The school curricula included the three R's, English composition and grammar, geography, music, dancing, and needlework. The young

Judith Sargent, *by John Singleton Copley, before her marriage to John Murray. She became a proponent of advanced education for women.*
Frick Art Reference Library

women did not receive instruction in Latin, Greek, or advanced science and mathematics, the courses their brothers took to prepare for college.

Discussion of the need for better female education became intertwined with ideas about women's roles in the new nation. Beginning in 1784, Massachusetts writer Judith Sargent Murray published a series of essays, later compiled in a book titled *The Gleaner,* in which she argued that young women should prepare to support themselves in case they found no suitable husband or their spouse died. "Our girls," she wrote, "are bred up with one particular view: . . . an establishment by marriage." Murray believed that young women should learn a vocation for independence, but also justified advanced female education on the grounds that girls with developed minds would become better wives and mothers. Dr. Benjamin Rush pointed out that improved schooling would help women fulfill their duties in running households and preparing sons to be virtuous, wise leaders of the republic. He wrote, "our ladies should be qualified to a certain degree, by a peculiar and suitable education, to concur in instructing their sons in the principles of liberty and government." Nurturing incorruptible future leaders, or "republican motherhood," was women's principal responsibility under the new government, not voting or holding office.

The Question of Abolishing Slavery

The revolutionary rhetoric of freedom and self-determination unleashed a public debate over the legitimacy of slavery. African Americans fueled the discussion by escaping to the British and serving in the American army. In doing so, African Americans made whites more aware of the hypocrisy of fighting a war of independence while they kept other human beings in chains.

In the north, the first significant opposition to slavery had developed among Pennsylvania and New Jersey Quakers well before the Revolution. Since the seventeenth century, individual members of the Society of Friends had argued that black bondage violated basic Christian concepts, particularly the belief that all humans are equal in the eyes of God. For decades, these Quaker abolitionists failed to convince their meetings that slavery was wrong because many wealthy, powerful Friends held slaves. But after 1750, the Society of Friends became the first American religion to denounce perpetual bondage as a sin and to prohibit members from holding slaves. The Quakers then spearheaded an emancipation movement that gained strength among other whites in the 1770s and 1780s, contributing, along with escapes by African Americans, to the growth of free black communities in Philadelphia, New York, and other northern towns. In addition, by the 1780s, slavery was less important economically in northern states than in the south, thus the combination of religious conviction, natural rights concepts of liberty and equality, and pressure by African Americans could undercut its viability. Prospective owners, already sensitized by guilt, grew wary of purchasing slaves, who were likely to demand emancipation or run away. Instead, northern employers hired workers from among the growing numbers of free laborers, including many African Americans.

In Pennsylvania and New England, state governments acted against slavery by the mid-1780s. The Pennsylvania assembly passed the first abolition law in 1780, its preamble reflecting the ideas that inspired many abolitionists of the revolutionary era:

> When we contemplate our abhorrence of that condition to which the arms and tyranny of Great Britain were exerted to reduce us, when we look back on the variety of dangers to which we have been exposed, [we are grateful for] the manifold blessings which we have undeservedly received. . . . We conceive that it is our duty, and we rejoice that it is in our power, to extend a portion of that freedom to others.

*P*ICTURING THE PAST ✦ SOCIAL & CULTURAL EVENTS

PENNSYLVANIA ABOLITION SOCIETY BROADSIDE

The Library Company at Philadelphia

In 1775, ten Philadelphia men founded the first abolition society in America. They were mostly Quaker craftsmen and shopkeepers who were determined to sway public opinion against slavery and liberate enslaved people through legal and political action. Interrupted by the American Revolution, they reorganized in 1784, after Pennsylvania passed its gradual abolition act of 1780. PAS members then focused on enforcing its provisions, in particular making sure that free African Americans were not re-enslaved.

The abolition society distributed this diagram of a slave ship as part of a broadside against the international slave trade. The illustration shows the lower deck, with compartments (starting from the left) for men, boys, women, and girls. The text of the 1789 tract described the situation of the enslaved Africans, "packed, side by side, almost like herrings in a barrel, and reduced nearly to the state of being buried alive."

The act was less comprehensive than its heartiest supporters wished. As a result of compromises required for passage, the Pennsylvania act abolished slavery gradually—so gradually that under its provisions no black Pennsylvanian would achieve freedom until 1808. The law provided that children born to slave mothers after March 1780 would be freed when they reached age twenty-eight. Slaves who had been born before that date would remain in bondage.

The Pennsylvania act was more effective than expected, as many enslaved blacks, exasperated that the law failed to free them, escaped their masters. Hundreds of slaveholders conformed to the spirit of the law by manumitting their slaves, regardless of birth date, at about age twenty-eight. Though these owners benefited from the labor of African Americans during their prime years, still, the manumissions helped to bring about the early end of slavery in the state. Also significant was the work of the Pennsylvania Abolition Society, which tested the limits of the 1780 abolition act by providing legal counsel to African Americans to defend their liberty. The number

of slaves in Pennsylvania declined from almost 7,000 in 1780, to 795 in 1810.

Elsewhere in the north, the Massachusetts supreme court in 1783 decided that slavery was incompatible with the state's 1780 constitution, which said all men are free and equal, though it did not specifically outlaw perpetual bondage. As blacks sued for freedom, the courts ruled on their behalf, and so by 1790, Massachusetts reported no slaves on the federal census. The Connecticut and Rhode Island legislatures in 1784 followed Pennsylvania's example by passing gradual abolition laws, and Vermont and New Hampshire also banned the institution. New York and New Jersey passed gradual abolition acts in 1799 and 1804 respectively.

During the 1780s, considerable support for abolition also developed in the Chesapeake region, though enslaved African Americans comprised almost 40 percent of the population. Southern states, like their northern counterparts, continued the First Continental Congress's prohibition of the slave trade. Some people expected cessation of the trade to result in the gradual death of slavery in Virginia and Maryland—a mistake because the African American population there grew naturally by reproduction. Involuntary bondage would persist without positive action for abolition.

Thomas Jefferson exemplified the troubled and confused state of mind of many white Americans about slavery. Though he remained a slaveholder throughout his life and held racist beliefs, Jefferson claimed to support a strategy for gradual abolition in Virginia. The plan, never considered by the assembly, would have freed and educated African American children born after the law went into effect and, when adults, removed them to a separate territory. Relocation of blacks would ensure that whites would keep political power after emancipation.

Efforts for general abolition failed south of Pennsylvania, yet some progress occurred when Virginia (in 1782), Delaware (in 1787), and Maryland (in 1790) made private manumission easier. New laws permitted slaveholders who were inspired by antislavery beliefs to free their slaves. A private abolition movement took fire in areas of the Upper South where Quakers and Methodists were numerous and planters were changing from tobacco to wheat as their chief crop, thus requiring fewer field hands. Though declining demand for labor played a role in their decision, still, slaveholders had the choice of whether to emancipate or sell their bondpeople. A market for slaves existed in the Carolinas and Georgia, where abolitionist sentiment had little impact.

The rise in the number of free African Americans in the Upper South was a measure of opposition to slavery. The free black population in Delaware rose to more than 8,000 by the end of the century; in Maryland to 20,000, and in Virginia to nearly 13,000. Even with impressive numbers of manumissions, however, in 1800 emancipated blacks were just 8 percent of all African Americans in the region.

Defining Religious Liberty

The issue of religious freedom also confronted the architects of the new state governments. Revolutionary ideals led many to challenge laws that forced people to attend and financially support an established church. Before the Revolution, the colonies had varied widely in the relationship of church and state. Congregational churches were tax-supported in Massachusetts, New Hampshire, and Connecticut, while the Church of England (Anglican) was established in the Carolinas, Virginia, Maryland, and New York. In contrast, Rhode Island, New Jersey, and Pennsylvania protected a great diversity of religions, giving none of them public

funds. All of the colonies, however, placed limits on who could serve in political office.

The break with Great Britain had the greatest impact on the established Church of England, called the Protestant Episcopal church in the United States after the Revolution. With independence, some of its parishes dissolved, as missionaries departed because the church hierarchy in England stopped paying their salaries. Many Anglican clergymen and laypeople in New England and the Mid-Atlantic region became loyalists, helping to fuel the Whig movement for disestablishment. All of the states in which the Anglican church was established promptly ended government support except Virginia, which finally acted in 1786. Its assembly passed Thomas Jefferson's statute for religious liberty, stating, "no man shall be compelled to frequent or support any religious worship, place or ministry whatsoever, nor shall be enforced, restrained, molested, or burthened in his body or goods, nor shall otherwise suffer on account of his religious opinions or belief."

Nevertheless, the movement to end discrimination stalled, and in the 1780s, religious tests for political office remained common. Most Americans, who were overwhelmingly Protestant, thought that only Christian men, preferably Protestants, should

The Residence of David Twining, *by Edward Hicks. While northern Quakers had emancipated their slaves by the late 1780s, most free African Americans, like the man at the plow, continued to work for others as indentured servants because, as former slaves, they lacked funds to establish their own shops and farms.*
Abby Aldrich Rockefeller Folk Art Center, Williamsburg

Petition of Philadelphia Jews for Equal Rights, 1783

Though Pennsylvania was renowned for religious liberty, its constitution limited election to the state assembly to Christians. As other states broadened religious liberty during the revolutionary era, Philadelphia Jews called for redress of this inequity. The new Pennsylvania constitution adopted in 1790 removed this religious test.

To the honourable the Council of Censors, assembled agreeable to the Constitution of the State of Pennsylvania. The Memorial of . . . the Synagogue of the Jews at Philadelphia, . . .

That by the tenth section of the Frame of Government of this Commonwealth, it is ordered that each member of the general assembly of representatives of the freemen of Pennsylvania, before he takes his seat, shall make and subscribe a declaration, which ends in these words, "I do acknowledge the Scriptures of the old and new Testament to be given by divine inspiration," . . .

Your memorialists beg leave to observe, that this clause seems to limit the civil rights of your citizens to one very special article of the creed; whereas by the second paragraph of the declaration of the rights of the inhabitants, it is asserted without any other limitation than the professing the existence of God, in plain words, "that no man who acknowledges the being of a God can be justly deprived or abridged of any civil rights as a citizen on account of his religious sentiments." But certainly this religious test deprives the Jews of the most eminent rights of freemen, solemnly ascertained to all men who are not professed Atheists.

May it please your Honors, . . .

—Your memorialists cannot say that the Jews are particularly fond of being representatives of the people in assembly or civil officers and magistrates in the State; but with great submission they apprehend that a clause in the constitution, which disables them to be elected by their fellow citizens to represent them in assembly, is a stigma upon their nation and religion, . . .

The Jews of Pennsylvania in proportion to the number of their members, can count with any religious society whatsoever, the Whigs among either of them; they have served some of them in the Continental army; some went out in the militia to fight the common enemy; all of them have cheerfully contributed to the support of the militia, and of the government of this State; they have no inconsiderable property in lands and tenements, but particularly in the way of trade, some more, some less, for which they pay taxes; they have, upon every plan formed for public utility, been forward to contribute as much as their circumstances would admit of; and as a nation or a religious society, they stand unimpeached of any matter whatsoever, against the safety and happiness of the people.

And your memorialists humbly pray, that if your honours, from any consideration than the subject of this address, should think proper to call a convention for revising the constitution, you would be pleased to recommend this to the notice of that convention.

govern. State and local laws required observance of the Sabbath, outlawed gambling and other entertainments, and proclaimed days of thanksgiving and prayer. The states most resistant to disestablishment were the old Puritan strongholds in New England. Massachusetts, New Hampshire, and Connecticut required tax support for Protestant churches well into the nineteenth century.

CHALLENGES TO THE CONFEDERATION

Despite the dominance of the states, the Confederation Congress had important functions that required far more unity and power than it possessed. Of all Congress's difficulties, the inability to tax was most damaging, resulting in the Confederation's quick demise.

Military Demobilization

One of the most remarkable aspects of the American revolutionary experience—in light of revolutions since that time—was the absence of a serious military challenge to civilian control. George Washington was committed to popularly elected government and thus ignored suggestions that he become a military ruler. Even so, the United States faced two problems concerning the armed forces. During the war, Congress failed to pay or supply the army properly, but had promised generous pensions and bounties to entice men to sign up for the duration of the war. The second question confronting Congress was whether to establish a peacetime army, an issue that had both ideological and financial significance.

For two years after the Battle of Yorktown in 1781, the Continental army continued to exist, with Washington encamped at Newburgh, New York, where his troops monitored the British army still in New York City. American officers and enlisted men voiced grievances because they needed food, clothing, and wages. Soldiers rioted and insulted their officers, while many simply went home with no compensation except their weapons. Officers at Newburgh drew up a list of complaints for Congress, demanding as much of their back pay as possible and a full reckoning of the entire sum they were owed. The officers suggested that they receive lump sums instead of the promised pensions of half-pay for life. They seemed so disgruntled that Washington remained at Newburgh instead of going home to Mount Vernon as he had planned.

The officers' discontent became more threatening when several politicians, who favored a strong central government, recognized an opportunity to pressure the states into giving Congress the power to tax. In what became known as the Newburgh conspiracy, Robert Morris of Philadelphia and Gouverneur Morris and Alexander Hamilton of New York hatched a plan to use the officers' protests to strengthen the Confederation. Washington would not cooperate, stating that the army was a "most dangerous instrument to play with," even to obtain a national tax. In early 1783, rumors spread that the officers were ready to take "manly" action against the government unless their demands were met. The crisis ended when Washington pledged to negotiate for their back pay and pensions and the officers swore their loyalty to Congress. For its part, Congress agreed to pay troops three months' wages at discharge, while officers would receive pensions of five years' full pay in government bonds. A group of eighty enlisted men stationed at Lancaster, Pennsylvania, found the offer unacceptable, so they mutinied and marched on Philadelphia, barricading the State House where Congress met. Though the soldiers backed down without violence, the frightened congressmen fled to Princeton.

Restitution of military pensions, back wages, and bounties took until the 1790s because Congress lacked the funds to discharge its debts. Soldiers who had been promised land bounties in the west had to wait fifteen years for surveys, in large part because Native Americans refused to give up the territory. By the 1790s, most veterans had long since sold their rights to speculators for a fraction of their worth.

The issue of a standing army squared revolutionary ideology against the need for defense. One of the chief causes of the Revolution had been the peacetime quartering in New York and Boston of the British army, which patriots called a "MONSTER of a standing ARMY." But now the United States faced threats from the Spanish in Florida and Louisiana, the British in Canada, and Native Americans everywhere along the frontier. In April 1783, Congress appointed a committee to consult Washington and other generals on military requirements. The commander-in-chief argued that the United States had to be prepared against its enemies. He suggested retaining 2,600 Continentals in one artillery and four infantry regiments. He also advised Congress to organize a national citizens' militia that would stay in training for ready defense. In 1784, Congress dismissed Washington's plan, stationing a total of eighty men at two forts in New York and Pennsylvania. For reasons of principle and finances, the Confederation government virtually disbanded the army during an interval of peace, a pattern the nation would follow well into the twentieth century.

Economic Troubles

The Confederation Congress failed to solve the problem of its war debt, which by 1790 amounted to an estimated $10 million owed to other countries and $40 million owed to Americans. During the war, the government had issued paper currency to pay for goods and services. It abandoned this policy because of rampant inflation. Congress turned to the states, which refused to contribute sufficient funds, then borrowed from France and from American merchants and farmers for military provisions. It also deferred payment on soldiers' wages. As the principal and interest mounted on these promissory notes and bonds, Congress requested an amendment to the Articles to permit a national duty of 5 percent on all imports. The legislators

*P*ICTURING THE PAST◆POLITICS & DIPLOMACY

ROBERT MORRIS AND GOUVERNEUR MORRIS

Courtesy of the Museum of American Art of the Pennsylvania Academy of Fine Arts, Philadelphia.
Bequest of Richard Ashhurst

In 1783, Charles Willson Peale painted this portrait of Robert Morris (right) and Gouverneur Morris, the superintendent of finance and his assistant, who were unrelated. Robert Morris, born in Liverpool, England, was a wealthy Philadelphia merchant who supervised procurement of military supplies during the Revolution. He was one of the founders of the Bank of North America, the country's first bank, which was modeled after the Bank of England and was intended to help relieve the wartime economic crisis. Gouverneur Morris, who came from a wealthy New York family, excelled as Robert Morris's assistant in the finance office.

Both men became frustrated by Congress's weakness and the repeated failure to gain approval of a national tax. They joined with other nationalists in the Newburgh conspiracy to use the army's discontent over unpaid wages to force adoption of a more centralized government. When Alexander Hamilton became the first secretary of the treasury, he adopted a number of Robert Morris's ideas, including the national bank and federal assumption of state debts.

---

tried for five years to obtain the necessary unanimous agreement of the states, but failed on each attempt.

One long-lasting consequence of the war's inflationary crisis was conflict between urban and rural interests over public finance. The spiraling cost of food and fuel in the late 1770s had hurt city residents much more than farmers. In public debate over currency and credit, farmers wanted access to government loans based on the value of their land and its production, similar to the colonial land banks that had allowed them to use real estate as collateral for loans. Though the provincial currency issued by the land banks had

been fairly stable, in the 1780s, merchants and urban artisans recalled the more recent inflation of the Revolution. They believed that paper currency based on real estate would send prices sky-high. At the same time, merchants knew that the economy would stagnate if specie (gold and silver) were required for every transaction, so they embraced an alternative method of generating paper currency, the bank.

The first bank in the United States was the Bank of North America, created in 1781 in Philadelphia. Robert Morris proposed the institution, based on the Bank of England, as a way to help solve the wartime fiscal crisis. Morris obtained support from Alexander Hamilton, Thomas Paine, and a committee of Congress for his plan; both the Congress and state of Pennsylvania chartered the institution. Instead of issuing paper currency through a land office, as farmers wanted, the bank issued currency in the form of short-term loans to merchants. These bank notes were backed by gold and silver plate and coins that investors deposited in return for a share of the bank's profits. The attraction for stockholders was that formerly idle gold and silver assets could now earn interest. The Bank of North America earned regular profits during its first two decades, beginning with an 8.74 percent dividend to investors in 1782. If people doubted the security of the bank, they could redeem their bank notes. Bank advocates believed that once a few people tested its soundness and received specie, others would trust the bank and accept the bank notes as currency.

In fact, the Bank of North America followed a conservative course that kept it solvent financially but made it unpopular with many people. The bank's manager, Thomas Willing, lent money only to good credit risks in the mercantile community, thus angering artisans and farmers who viewed the bank as a monopoly created by Congress to benefit the commercial elite. Also, Willing refused to liberalize the bank's loan policy by taking advantage of confidence in the bank's strength. Instead of expanding the money supply as later banks did, the Bank of North America made loans only up to the amount of specie in its vaults.

The Bank of North America helped the mercantile community through a time of uncertainty. Commerce had suffered during the Revolution as merchants lost connections with trading partners in Great Britain and the British West Indies. In 1783, Americans expected to reestablish those ties as well as enter new markets in Europe and the French and Spanish colonies. With their newly won independence, they gained release from the restrictions of British mercantilism.

But being part of the mercantilist system had brought advantages as well as constraints. The British closed the ports of the British West Indies to American ships, a sharp blow for New England and the Middle Atlantic states, which before the war had found a major market in the islands for exports of fish, grain, flour, lumber, and livestock. To Great Britain and its colonies, the United States was now a foreign country. Americans could sell provisions in the islands and purchase rum, sugar, and molasses, but everything had to be carried on British ships. West Indies planters complained because this resulted in higher prices; American shipowners had to find new routes. On the

America Triumphant and Britannia in Distress, *from Weatherwise's* Town and Country Almanack *(1782) illustrates the hopes of Americans for prosperity now that they were free from British mercantilism.*
Colonial Williamsburg Foundation

other hand, Britain was eager to purchase tobacco from the Chesapeake and to sell to Americans all the manufactures they would buy. U.S. merchants had access by treaty to ports in France and the French colonies, but were barred from trading in New Spain. Gradually, Americans developed trade with Germany, the Netherlands, Scandinavia, and even China. By the end of the 1780s, U.S. exports recovered to approximately their prerevolutionary level.

The road to recovery was rocky, however, because in the immediate postwar years American demand for British manufactures far outstripped exports. During the Revolution, American artisans had attempted to supply metal goods and textiles, but had been unable to match British quality and prices. With peace, British manufacturers extended generous credit to American consumers for clocks, watches, furniture, textiles, clothing, mirrors, and other goods. When depression hit in fall 1783 because of the loss of the West Indies market, American farmers, merchants, and shopkeepers found themselves seriously in debt. In New England, for example, the balance of trade with Great Britain was so uneven that exports covered only 13 percent of imports. While the economy improved after mid-1785, many farmers had difficulty escaping from debt.

Indeed, estimates of the gross national product suggest that the Revolution had an extended negative impact on the American economy. Data available for 1774 and 1790 indicate that income declined by over 40 percent, close to the decrease Americans experienced during the Great Depression of the 1930s.

Foreign Affairs

Though the United States had won both the war and the peace, its leaders soon learned that they received little respect among European nations. Despite the boundary provisions of the Treaty of 1783, Spain and Great Britain took advantage of the Confederation's weakness to trespass on territory in the west. The Spanish and English gained allies among Native Americans who were losing their lands to the steady stream of white settlers crossing the Appalachians.

During the 1780s, Spain tried to restrict expansion of the United States. The Spanish government had refused to accept the treaty boundaries granting the region between the Appalachians and the Mississippi River to the United States. With settlers rapidly filling the area, Spain feared for its control of Louisiana and East and West Florida; it wanted to extend its territory north from West Florida to the Ohio River. The Spanish pursued this objective in a number of ways. They retained forts north of the 31st parallel, which the United States claimed as its southern border. Then, in 1784, the Spanish government closed the port of New Orleans to Americans, apparently hoping to detach from the United States the region that later became Kentucky and Tennessee. Settlers in the trans-Appalachian region protested vigorously because they needed access to the New Orleans market for their goods. Some threatened to secede from the United States unless Congress convinced Spain to reverse its decision; a few, including James Wilkinson, a former Continental army officer, actually negotiated with the Spanish. Reporting on a journey in the west, George Washington wrote, "the western settlers (I speak now from my own observation) stand as it were upon a pivot; the touch of a feather would turn them any way."

Congress directed John Jay, the secretary of foreign affairs and a New Yorker, to negotiate with Spain to reopen the port. The Spanish diplomat, Diego de Gardoqui, refused to budge, instead offering to open other Spanish ports to U.S. commerce if Americans would relinquish demands for free navigation on the lower Mississippi. With the permission of Congress, Jay agreed to a treaty that provided commercial advantages for eastern merchants but closed New Orleans to westerners for a generation. The west and south erupted in opposition, blocking approval of the Jay-Gardoqui Treaty. The lower Mississippi River remained closed until 1788

when the Spanish permitted Americans to use New Orleans upon payment of duties.

The Spanish government also cooperated with Native Americans to slow the influx of Anglo-American settlers into contested territory. Spanish colonists in the Floridas remained few, so they depended upon good relations with the Creeks, Choctaws, and Chickasaws who controlled the region. Groups of Creeks who had migrated to Florida, and were called Seminoles by the British, could mobilize at least twice as many soldiers as the Spanish. Contrary to Spain's traditional policy of considering Native Americans as subjects to the Crown, its colonial officials in 1784 signed written treaties of alliance with the Indians.

Most threatening of these pacts to the United States was the one with the Creeks, which their leader Alexander McGillivray arranged. The son of a Scottish trader and a French-Creek woman, and educated in Charleston, McGillivray could negotiate his way in both European and Indian societies. To protect Creek lands from settlers streaming in from Georgia, he offered the Spanish "a powerful barrier in these parts against the ambitious and encroaching Americans" in return for an alliance and weapons. The Creeks called the invading Georgians "Ecunnaunuxulgee," or "people greedily grasping after the lands of the red people." With Cherokees and Shawnees to the north, the Creeks battled Anglo-Americans through the 1780s, thus slowing settlement on the southwest frontier.

The Confederation government also had difficulty establishing its claims against the British and the Indians of the Ohio Valley. In the treaty of 1783, the British had promised to remove their troops from forts in the Great Lakes region. Through the 1780s, however, they refused to withdraw, hoping for return of the territory. They barred American ships from the Great Lakes and allied with Native Americans who wanted to halt white settlement. British diplomats justified these actions with the excuse that Americans had failed to pay prewar debts to British creditors and return confiscated loyalist property.

Great Britain's neglect of its Indian allies in negotiating the peace led the U.S. government to treat them as a conquered people. With great bravado, considering the Confederation's small army, American commissioners said to the Ohio Indians, "You are mistaken in supposing that . . . you are to become a free and independent nation, and may make what terms you please. . . . You are a subdued people." Other officials announced, "We claim the country by conquest." Under threat of arms, a group of Iroquois yielded rights in the Northwest with the Treaty of Fort

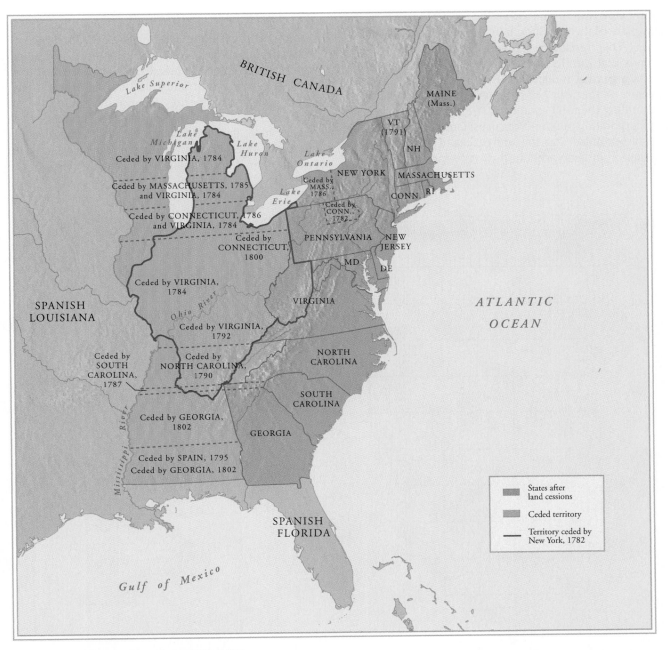

Map 6.2 *Western Land Cessions, 1782–1802*
A number of states claimed territory west of the Appalachians based on their colonial charters. For example, under Connecticut's charter, which defined the Pacific Ocean as its western boundary, residents claimed part of Pennsylvania as well as western lands.

Stanwix (1784); Wyandots, Delawares, and others ceded Ohio lands in the Treaty of Fort McIntosh (1785); and Shawnees gave up territory in the Treaty of Fort Finney (1786). Many Native Americans refused to recognize these treaties because the Indian negotiators lacked authority and had been forced to sign.

Soon, frontier warfare made U.S. officials realize that they were the ones who were "mistaken" in presuming that the Indians had been "subdued." Theyendanegea (Joseph Brant), the pro-British Mohawk leader, rallied Indians against white settlement in the Northwest. In 1786, he urged potential allies, "the Interests of

Any One Nation Should be the Interests of us all, the Welfare of the one Should be the Welfare of all the others." Their resistance convinced Secretary of War Henry Knox that the United States must change its tactics or risk a general Indian war. He suggested that Congress return to the policy of purchasing lands, instead of demanding them by conquest. The congressmen agreed, incorporating into the Northwest Ordinance of 1787 the futile promise that the Indians' land "shall never be taken from them without their consent."

The Northwest Ordinances

Despite war with the Indians and the presence of British troops, the Confederation Congress moved forward with legislation to create the Northwest Territory. The issue of western lands had divided the thirteen states even during the Revolution. Some states claimed territories from their colonial charters, while others, such as Maryland and New Jersey, had never possessed such claims. Titles stood in conflict with one another, as in the case of the region north of the

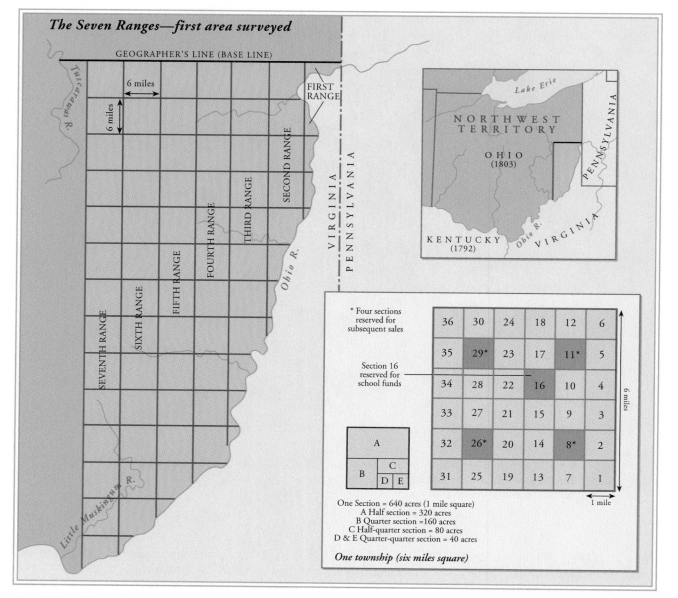

Map 6.3 *Land Ordinance of 1785*
This map shows the plans for dividing land in eastern Ohio into townships and lots. The minimum price was $1 per acre.

Ohio River, which Virginia claimed in its entirety and Connecticut and Massachusetts claimed in part. States lacking rights to western lands believed that all should be ceded to the Confederation because together the states had won the trans-Appalachian territory in the Revolution. Virginia, whose charter rights were oldest, resolved the issue in 1781 by agreeing to transfer to the United States the region north and west of the Ohio River, the area that later became the states of Ohio, Indiana, Illinois, Michigan, and Wisconsin. Virginia offered cession on the condition that the territory eventually be divided into states that would join the Confederation on an equal basis with the original thirteen. The trans-Appalachian lands south of the Ohio River remained temporarily under the control of Virginia, North Carolina, and Georgia.

Congress passed three ordinances to establish guidelines for distributing land and governing the Northwest Territory. Wealthy speculators who had purchased rights from Native Americans had significant influence over the shape these ordinances took. Thomas Jefferson was principal author of the first ordinance, which passed Congress in 1784. This law gave settlers a great deal of autonomy in establishing a territorial government. The Northwest would be divided into seven districts, with the settlers of each to govern themselves by choosing a constitution and laws from any of the existing states. When any district reached the population of the smallest of the original thirteen states, it would be admitted as a state to the Confederation on equal terms. Congress retained responsibility for selling the public lands.

The second ordinance, passed in 1785, set the rules for distributing lands. The influence of speculators was apparent, for the minimum price of a lot was $640, payable in specie or its equivalent, a sum far beyond the means of many potential settlers. All property would be surveyed before sale, laid out in townships six miles square. Each lot would contain 640 acres sold at a minimum of one dollar per acre, with better land offered at a higher price. The government retained lots for public schools and for distribution to Revolutionary War veterans. Because of the relatively high cost, Congress found few individual buyers. In fact, many land-hungry squatters simply set up their farms without government approval, sometimes purchasing rights from neighboring Indians, sometimes not. So Congress accepted a deal offered by a group of New England speculators, the Ohio Company, agreeing to sell them 1.5 million acres for $500,000 in depreciated bonds, or less than ten cents per acre in hard money. Given the Confederation's debt, the sale was welcome.

Congress further cooperated with the Ohio Company in drafting the Northwest Ordinance of 1787. In response to speculators' demands, the law established firmer congressional control over the territory, providing settlers less self-government than under the 1784 ordinance. Initially, a governor, secretary, and three judges appointed by Congress would administer the government. When 5,000 adult males resided in the territory, they could elect an assembly, but the governor held a veto over its actions. Men were eligible to vote if they owned at least fifty acres of land. Three to five states would be created from the Northwest Territory, with each state qualified to enter the union when its population reached 60,000. New states would have equal status with the original thirteen. The ordinance of 1787 also included provisions for individual rights that the Congress and the Ohio Company hoped would attract purchasers. They expected many settlers to come from New England. The ordinance protected private contracts, religious liberty, trial by jury, and habeas corpus (protection against illegal imprisonment). It prohibited slavery from the region forever. Thus, while catering to the interests of speculators, the Northwest Ordinance also extended rights won during the Revolution to new settlers in the west. Further, it limited the spread of slavery and determined that western territories would achieve the status of states rather than remain colonies.

POLITICAL AND ECONOMIC TURMOIL

Political strife under the Articles of Confederation disappointed Americans who had high hopes for their republic. Instead of harmony, economic interests clashed; the states failed to satisfy everybody. Many elites thought the United States was becoming too democratic and anarchic—as farmers revolted, government failed to control the violence, and some legislatures approved the insurgents' demands.

Creditors Versus Debtors

As a result of the postwar depression, farmers throughout the United States faced economic hardship. Many had eagerly purchased British manufactures, expecting to pay for the new clothes and consumer goods by selling their grain and livestock to the West Indies. British merchants offered easy credit to stimulate sales; American merchants and shopkeepers passed the credit on to farm families who would pay with the fall crop.

The house of cards collapsed when the British government closed the West Indies to American ships. English mercantile houses called in their debts in specie only, starting a chain of default that extended from London to the frontier. Americans lacked the gold and silver that the British demanded, but merchants refused to accept payment in farm products because they had no market for the goods. So they took farmers to court: in many places, the number of debt cases rose dramatically. For example, in Hampshire County, Massachusetts, from 1784 to 1786, the court heard 3,000 debt cases. Almost one-third of the county's adult males were prosecuted for insolvency.

State governments aggravated the situation by imposing taxes to repay war bonds in full, a policy that worked to the advantage of wealthy speculators who had bought up the bonds from farmers and artisans at a large discount. The Massachusetts government particularly favored mercantile interests, levying on farmers high taxes that also had to be paid in specie. When farmers defaulted, the courts sold their land and cattle, often at only one-third to one-half value. If their assets failed to cover the debts and back taxes, the farmers were imprisoned until they or someone else paid the sum. Often men sat in crowded jails with insufficient ventilation, heat, or food because they owed small debts. Ordinary folk became angry as they feared imprisonment and the loss of their farms.

Farmers Demand Reform

Protesters mobilized as they had in the prerevolutionary period, at first meeting in county conventions to draw up petitions to the state assembly. In Massachusetts, they demanded changes in the state constitution to make the government more responsive to their needs and less costly to run. They wanted abolition of the state senate, which represented the commercial elite; lowering of property qualifications to hold office; and transfer of the capital from Boston to a more central location. Inland towns found it difficult to send representatives to the assembly because expenses were so high. The farmers also demanded paper money and tender laws, the latter enabling them to settle debts and taxes with goods rather than specie. Both would ease the credit crisis. During the Revolution, the yeomen had benefited from inflation and were able to pay off prewar debts with cheap dollars. While they stopped short of demanding a return to high inflation, they hoped for a gentle upswing in prices and a larger money supply to help them settle their debts.

When state legislatures emitted paper money or passed tender laws, as in Rhode Island, North Carolina, New York, and Georgia, little unrest ensued. In Rhode Island, political parties channeled conflict, for after the Country party ousted the Mercantile party in spring 1786, the new assembly issued paper money with stiff fines for creditors who refused to accept it. Elites elsewhere referred to "Rogue Island," even suggesting that the state be abolished and divided between Massachusetts and Connecticut. In other states, mercantile factions maintained control of the government. They detested paper money because debtors would pay in depreciated bills; they opposed tender laws because of the lack of a market for grain and livestock. Merchants argued that paper currency issued as loans on farm property (rather than as notes based on gold and silver deposited in banks) was immoral because it would lose value, allowing debtors to violate contracts by paying back less than they had borrowed. Creditors asserted that their property rights were at risk.

Shays's Rebellion

When state governments failed to help, debtors in New England, New Jersey, Pennsylvania, Maryland, Virginia, and South Carolina protested militantly. Events moved furthest in Massachusetts. In fall 1786, armed Massachusetts farmers closed down county courts to prevent further hearings for debt. Perhaps one-fourth of potential soldiers in the state were involved, calling themselves the "Regulators," after the Carolina insurgents of the 1760s. Their opponents first labeled the rebels "Green Bushers" because they wore a sprig of evergreen—the Massachusetts symbol for liberty—then called them Shaysites when Daniel Shays, a forty-year-old veteran of Bunker Hill and Saratoga, emerged as leader. The government frantically requested aid from Congress, which complied by requisitioning $530,000 and 1,340 soldiers from the states. When the states failed to cooperate, the powerlessness of the Confederation was clear.

The Massachusetts government acted on its own, taking measures that further alienated angry farmers. The assembly passed the Riot Act, which prohibited armed groups from gathering in public and permitted sheriffs to kill rioters who refused to disband. The legislature also suspended habeas corpus, allowing officials to jail suspected insurgents without showing cause. The farmers refused to back down, as one warned, "I am determined to fight and spill my blood and leave my bones at the courthouse till Resurrection." They protested that the suspension of habeas corpus was "dangerous if not absolutely

Daniel Shays and Job Shattuck, *from the cover of a pamphlet supporting Shays's Rebellion.*
The Granger Collection, New York

destructive to a Republican government." Nevertheless, in November 1786, the state government sent 300 soldiers to arrest rebel leaders; when that failed to stop the farmers from closing the courts, Boston merchants raised private funds to outfit 4,400 troops. Residents of Boston and coastal towns who feared the inflationary consequences of paper money filled the ranks. Revolutionary general Benjamin Lincoln commanded the army; in January 1787, they marched to Worcester to protect the county court.

Lincoln's army forced the Shaysites to choose between submission and armed rebellion, for a middle ground of petitions and court closings was no longer viable. The farmers amassed their own troops, estimated at 2,500 men, with Shays in charge of one regiment. They unsuccessfully attacked the federal arsenal at Springfield for weapons to assault Boston, then regrouped to await the merchants' army. Shays was convinced that their cause was just; in a newspaper interview he confidently stated that he "knew General Lincoln was coming against him, but as he would bring with him nobody but shopkeepers, lawyers, and doctors, he could easily defeat him." Lincoln attacked Shays by surprise in a blizzard, dispersing the rebels within half an hour.

The aftermath of Shays's defeat was more divisive and bloody than the engagements between the armies. The assembly declared a state of "open, unnatural, unprovoked, and wicked rebellion," giving the governor the power to treat the Shaysites as enemies of the state. The legislators passed the Disqualification Act, which barred people implicated in the revolt from voting and holding office for three years,

teaching school, or keeping inns and taverns. Many of the insurgents escaped to New York and Vermont. Others, including individuals who had not been involved, were imprisoned. Militant Shaysites prolonged the conflict by raiding homes and kidnapping people who had sided with the government. As a result of the uprising and repression, voter turnout skyrocketed in the April 1787 election. A much greater number of western Massachusetts towns sent delegates to the legislature than they had in previous years, making the new assembly somewhat more responsive to rural debtors. While refusing to approve paper money, it enacted a tender law and quickly restored the civil rights of the insurgents.

THE MOVEMENT FOR CONSTITUTIONAL REFORM

The Confederation's helplessness in response to spreading armed rebellion strengthened the hand of nationalists like Robert Morris and Alexander Hamilton, who had been arguing for a more powerful central government. By 1787, Congress had lost much of its authority, and representatives stopped attending, often preventing action for lack of a quorum. Because it had failed to obtain a national tax and could not force the states to send requisitioned funds, the Confederation was broke. In 1785, Congress stopped interest payments on the French debt and in 1787 ended those on the principal. Nor could it reimburse American creditors. In 1787, Congress transferred responsibility for the national debt to the states.

The Philadelphia Convention

In September 1786, when Shays's Rebellion was still gathering steam, representatives gathered for a convention in Annapolis, Maryland, to discuss amending the Articles to give Congress power to regulate trade. The convention failed when only five state delegations arrived on time. Several of the delegates, including Alexander Hamilton, James Madison, and John Dickinson, called for another convention to meet in May 1787 at Philadelphia to consider a more thorough revision of the Articles. By early 1787, the disorder in Massachusetts and the growing concern about state emission of paper money built support for constitutional reform. In February, Congress endorsed a change. Twelve states—all but Rhode Island where farmers controlled the legislature—sent delegates to Philadelphia.

James Madison, *1783, by Charles Willson Peale. Like most of his fellow delegates, Madison was relatively young when he helped frame the Constitution.*
The Granger Collection, New York

Though the appointed day was May 14, 1787, the convention failed to start until May 25 when enough representatives finally arrived. State legislatures had delayed choosing their delegations and travel was slow. Among the first were Virginia's representatives, who used the extra time for planning. James Madison, a thirty-six-year-old planter, slaveholder, and intellectual who had served in the Virginia assembly and Congress, came to the convention well prepared. A shy man who avoided public speaking, Madison nevertheless took a dominant role in the proceedings, for which he has been called the father of the Constitution. Propelled by the breakdown of Congress and the problems he witnessed in state government, Madison wanted to reform the Confederation to create a stronger central government. He believed that state constitutions with powerful assemblies were too democratic, giving too much influence to the common people. As a consequence, these legislatures collaborated with debtors by circulating paper money, which Madison considered an attack on property. The people should be represented adequately, Madison thought, but their power must be constrained. The United States needed a new constitution that would place authority in the hands of well-educated, propertied men. Another Virginia delegate was George Washington, whose popularity and prestige made his support for

the convention crucial. He presided over the proceedings, but participated little in the debates.

A total of fifty-five men served at the Constitutional Convention between opening day and adjournment four months later. Twenty-one were practicing lawyers, another thirteen had been educated in the law, seven were merchants, and eighteen were farmers or planters; nineteen owned African American slaves. Most were relatively young men under the age of fifty, and many had served in the Revolution and had held political office. Benjamin Franklin, now eighty-one years old and ailing, was a member of the Pennsylvania delegation. Several heroes of the Revolution were absent, including Thomas Jefferson and John Adams, who served as ministers to France and Great Britain, respectively. Samuel Adams was not chosen as a delegate and Patrick Henry refused to participate because he "smelt a rat." Most of the delegates supported a plan to place more power in the national government.

The Great Compromise

The convention can be divided into two periods. During the first seven weeks, the matter overshadowing all discussion was the power of "large" versus "small" states. After this issue was resolved, delegations formed blocs in new ways, according to concerns about the executive, slavery, and commerce. The basic question that the convention avoided debating at length was whether to amend the Articles of Confederation or write an entirely new constitution. Madison, who thought the Confederation beyond repair, moved the convention along with a document he had drafted in advance, called the Virginia Plan, which scrapped the Articles. Madison was able to set the convention's agenda because at the outset no other delegate had prepared an alternate design.

The Virginia Plan proposed a powerful central government, dominated by a National Legislature of two houses (bicameral). The lower house would be elected by qualified voters and would choose the members of the upper house from nominations by state legislatures. The number of delegates from each state depended upon population. This bicameral National Legislature was empowered to appoint the executive and judicial branches of the central government and to veto state laws.

Several states opposed the Virginia Plan because it gave greater representation in the National Legislature to states with large populations. Delaware, Maryland, New Jersey, and Connecticut feared the power of Virginia, Pennsylvania, and Massachusetts, which together comprised almost one-half of the American

This painting of the Constitutional Convention of 1787 by an unknown artist shows George Washington presiding. Because the convention met in secrecy, the artist used his imagination to paint the scene.
Independence National Historical Park

people. If the Virginia Plan were adopted, just four states could dominate the legislature. In dividing on this issue, states considered the possibility of future population expansion as well as present size. Thus states with unsettled territories mostly sided with the large states, while those without room for growth chose the opposite camp.

The small states preferred a constitution that retained the structure of the Confederation Congress, but expanded its powers. In mid-June, William Paterson introduced the New Jersey Plan, which proposed a one-house, or unicameral, Congress in which the states had equal representation. Congress would appoint an executive council which in turn would choose a supreme court. As in the Virginia Plan, the authority of Congress was much enlarged, with powers to tax, regulate commerce, and compel states to obey its laws. The large states objected to this plan, arguing that Delaware (population 59,000) should not have as much power as Virginia (population 748,000).

The debate over representation in Congress brought the convention to an impasse. It made little progress toward a new constitution until the issue of state representation was resolved. The large states had the votes in the convention but knew that ratification would be impossible if the Virginia Plan prevailed. The Delaware delegation threatened to walk out until Con-

necticut formally proposed what has become known as the "great compromise." The plan established a bicameral Congress, with representation in the lower house based upon population. This body, called the House of Representatives, would be elected directly by the voters every two years and have the sole right to initiate revenue bills. Thus, the idea that people with a stake in society should elect the representatives who taxed them was incorporated into the document. In the upper house, called the Senate, states would have equal representation; each state legislature would choose two senators for six-year terms. The bicameral Congress resolved the division between the small and large states and also satisfied those who wanted to limit the influence of ordinary voters. Senators were expected to come from the wealthier, more established segments of society; their long terms and appointment by state legislators would shield them from public opinion. Both houses of Congress had to approve legislation.

The compromise between the large and small states created a government that was both national and federal. It was *national* because the House of Representatives was popularly elected, with not more than one representative per 30,000 people. Upon ratification, the United States would become a single nation rather than a confederacy of states. By expanding legislative powers, the sovereign people vested more authority in the central government. Congress received the powers to tax, coin and borrow money, regulate commerce, establish courts, declare war, and raise armed forces. States were specifically forbidden from keeping troops without the permission of Congress, making treaties, coining money, and issuing paper currency. At the same time, the new Constitution established a *federal* government, one in which the states retained rights, including equal representation in the Senate. Congress was forbidden from giving one state preference over another when levying taxes and regulating trade, nor could it impose export duties, prohibit the slave trade until 1808, or carve a new state from any state's territory without permission. Approval by three-fourths of the states would be necessary to amend the Constitution. But despite these provisions, many Americans believed that the states—the small republics—had lost too much power. The struggle for ratification revolved in large part around this issue.

The Executive, Slavery, and Commerce

Once the question of state representation was solved with the "great compromise," the convention made greater headway. Factions within the convention shifted from one debate to the next.

The power of the executive was a concern to people living in a world dominated by kings and princes. Delegates wanted to ensure that their government remained a republic, that it would not become a monarchy or dictatorship. At the same time, they believed that the executive branch should serve as a check on the legislature. The convention debated several questions affecting the executive's power. Should there be a single president or an executive board? While some argued that a plural executive could prevent one person from usurping power, the convention chose a single president, expecting to limit his authority in other ways. Length of term also stimulated discussion, for the longer the term the greater a president's autonomy. The convention reached agreement on a four-year term, without specifying the number of times he could be reelected.

The question of how the president would be chosen was divisive, between those who preferred direct election by the people and those who wanted Congress or the state legislatures to make the choice. Once again, the issue of states' rights reared its head. A committee appointed by the convention devised an ingenious but complicated formula to satisfy all sides: an "electoral college" was empowered to elect the president and vice president, with each state allotted as many votes as it had representatives and senators. Thus, even the smallest state received three votes and the large states were represented according to population. The state legislatures could determine how to choose the electors. The electoral college would never meet together as a group. The electors of each state gathered within their states to cast votes, which they sent to Congress for counting. If no candidate received a majority, the House of Representatives made the selection from among the five candidates with the most votes.

Of the Philadelphia convention's decisions on the executive, most crucial to the endurance of the Constitution was the balance of power between the executive and legislative branches. The convention gave the president a veto power over laws passed by Congress. The legislators could override the veto if two-thirds of both houses approved. Congress also had authority to remove the president by impeachment and trial for treason, bribery, and "other high Crimes and Misdemeanors." While Congress received power to declare war and raise troops, the president served as commander-in-chief. Only with the "advice and consent" of the Senate could the chief executive negotiate treaties and appoint ambassadors, Supreme Court justices, and other officials.

Slavery was a major factor in the convention's deliberations, though the words "slavery," "slave," and "slave trade" appeared nowhere in the 1787 Constitution. African American bondage affected the debates on representation in Congress, the election of the president, and the regulation of commerce. The southern states wanted to include slaves in a state's population when computing delegates to the House of Representatives and votes in the electoral college. Northerners protested that this gave white southerners an unfair advantage (illustrated in Table 6.1) because enslaved people could not vote. As part of the "great compromise," the convention decided that five enslaved Americans would count as three free persons for apportioning representation and direct taxes among the states. Since three-fifths of slaves living in the Chesapeake and Lower South numbered 380,000 people, the power of white voters south of Pennsylvania was significantly magnified.

Table 6.1	Enslaved Population in the United States, 1790	
	Total	**Slaves**
New England	1,009,206	3,763
Middle Atlantic	1,017,087	45,210
Maryland and Virginia	1,067,338	395,663
Lower South	726,626	237,141

First page of the United States Constitution of 1787.
Eastern National Park & Monument Association

Political bargaining resulted in additional provisions that upheld slavery. The convention approved a fugitive slave clause, which prevented free states from emancipating slaves who had escaped from masters in other states. The delegates also adopted a provision that forbade Congress from prohibiting slave importation for twenty years (with no requirement that it ban the slave trade after that time). North and South Carolina and Georgia demanded the option of importing people from Africa because they expected settlement to continue into western Georgia and the present states of Alabama, Mississippi, and Tennessee. Northern delegates, who might have pushed the convention toward the abolition of slavery, did almost nothing to promote that end.

Instead of trying to eliminate slavery under the new government, the northerners made the regulation of commerce their priority. The Lower South obtained the twenty-year protection of the slave trade when New England delegates promised their support in return for a compromise on international trade. The southern states suspected that the national government, if dominated by northerners in the future, would place heavy taxes on tobacco, rice, and indigo—the South's main exports. Southerners thought that navigation laws could also work to their detriment, be-cause northern merchants owned most American shipping. If Congress passed legislation requiring that all exports be transported in American ships, southerners would lose the choice of using a foreign, perhaps cheaper, carrier. Northerners, on the other hand, wanted Congress to have the authority to negotiate trade agreements on an equal basis with other nations. Congress could then retaliate if a country imposed restrictions such as closing ports. The convention settled these matters, first by forbidding Congress from imposing export duties, then with a deal that empowered Congress to regulate commerce. In return for South Carolina's vote for the latter provision, New England agreed to extend the slave trade for twenty years.

The Philadelphia convention created a Constitution that shifted important powers to a national government, but still vested a great deal of authority in the states. The framers painstakingly created checks and balances among the branches of government. They required direct popular election of only the House of Representatives, giving that body the right to initiate taxes. The convention incorporated flexibility into the document, which had been absent in the Articles of Confederation, by permitting amendment with approval of two-thirds of both houses of Congress and three-fourths of the states.

Patrick Henry Opposes the Constitution, 1788

Patrick Henry, who had drafted the Virginia resolves against the Stamp Act in 1765, vigorously opposed the Constitution. By June 2, 1788, when the Virginia convention began debate, eight states had ratified the document. In these excerpts from his June 5 speech, Henry voiced Antifederalist arguments that the Constitution offered insufficient safeguards against abuse of power by the new central government and lacked a bill of rights.

. . . I rose yesterday to ask a question which arose in my own mind. When I asked that question, I thought the meaning of my interrogation was obvious. The fate of this question and of America may depend on this. Have they said, We, the states? Have they made a proposal of a compact between states? If they had, this would be a confederation. It is otherwise most clearly a consolidated government. The question turns, sir, on that poor little thing—the expression, We, the *people*, instead of the *states*, of America. I need not take much pains to show that the principles of this system are extremely pernicious, impolitic, and dangerous. Is this a monarchy, like England—a compact between prince and people, with checks on the former to secure the liberty of the latter? Is this a confederacy, like Holland—an association of a number of independent states, each of which retains its individual sovereignty? . . .

Here is a resolution as radical as that which separated us from Great Britain. It is radical in this transition; our rights and privileges are endangered, and the sovereignty of the states will be relinquished: and cannot we plainly see that this is actually the case? The rights of conscience, trial by jury, liberty of the press, all your immunities and franchises, all pretensions to human rights and privileges, are rendered insecure, if not lost, by this change, so loudly talked of by some, and inconsiderately by others. Is this tame relinquishment of rights worthy of freemen? Is it worthy of that manly fortitude that ought to characterize republicans? It is said eight states have adopted this plan. I declare that if twelve states and a half had adopted it, I would, with manly firmness, and in spite of an erring world, reject it. You are not to inquire how your trade may be increased, nor how you are to become a great and powerful people, but how your liberties can be secured; for liberty ought to be the direct end of your government. . . .

Liberty, the greatest of all early blessings—give us that precious jewel, and you may take every thing else! . . . The confederation, this same despised government, merits, in my opinion, the highest encomium: it carried us through a long and dangerous war; it rendered us victorious in that bloody conflict with a powerful nation; it has secured us a territory greater than any European monarch possesses: and shall a government which has been thus strong and vigorous, be accused of imbecility, and abandoned for want of energy? Consider what you are about to do before you part with the government. Take longer time in reckoning things; revolutions like this have happened in almost every country in Europe; similar examples are to be found in ancient Greece and ancient Rome—instances of the people losing their liberty by their own carelessness and the ambition of a few.

The document shielded some individual rights, though critics argued that many were omitted. The Constitution protected trial by jury in criminal cases and habeas corpus. It banned religious tests for holding office under the United States, ex post facto (retroactive) laws, and bills of attainder, which extinguished a person's civil rights upon sentence of death or as an outlaw. While codifying the principles of self-government and individual liberties, however, the convention denied them to almost one-fifth of the

American population by embedding slavery within the fabric of the new government.

Ratification

After the delegates to the Philadelphia convention signed the Constitution on September 17, 1787, they quickly sent it to the Confederation Congress, which forwarded it to the states after little debate. One congressman from Virginia, Richard Henry Lee, tried to bury the document by adding amendments, but was overruled. Article 7 of the document required ratification by nine state conventions. States refusing to ratify could remain independent or unite together under another frame of government. Advocates of ratification knew that prompt action was necessary to forestall an effective opposition movement.

The group favoring ratification was not particularly well organized but had two advantages over its opponents. One advantage came from the choice of a name, the Federalists, for it undercut the ground on which their adversaries stood. James Madison, Alexander Hamilton, John Jay, and other supporters of the Constitution argued in favor of the federalist provisions that reserved powers to the states as well as the nationalist elements of the prospective government. While others denounced the Constitution because it transferred too much power to the national government from the states, the Federalists claimed the document provided balance. The critics were obliged to take the negative name of Antifederalists, which misrepresented their position in favor of states' rights.

The second advantage of those favoring ratification was that many advocates of a strong central government resided in the coastal cities and towns, where public opinion was easier to mobilize than in outlying areas. Most newspapers supported the Constitution. For example, in New York, where the ratification battle became intense, Hamilton, Madison, and Jay published in the newspapers a series of eighty-five essays that provided a detailed argument in favor of the Constitution. The essays also gained wide attention outside New York, and in spring 1788, the authors published them in book form as *The Federalist,* which is considered a major work in American political theory.

Most Federalists gained their livelihoods as merchants, shopkeepers, professionals, artisans, and commercial farmers. As creditors and consumers, many favored the Constitution because it stopped state emission of paper currency. Federalists desired a government that would foster the growth of a market

The Federal Procession in New York, *1788, artist unknown. Residents of New York City celebrated the new Constitution, applauding their representative Alexander Hamilton's efforts for ratification.*
The Granger Collection, New York

economy and facilitate trade with other countries. They believed a national government would provide the stability and strength that were lacking under the Confederation, enabling the United States to gain stature among the nations of Europe. Some frontier settlers, seeking military defense against Native Americans, also supported the Constitution.

The Federalists, who viewed commercial development more favorably than the Antifederalists, thought the purpose of government was to arbitrate among opposing interests. Federalists believed that society benefited when people pursued individual goals. They considered elusive the republican ideal of a community in which everyone could reach consensus because they had similar needs. Madison argued in *Federalist #10* that people possess different interests because they have unequal abilities and thus varying success in accumulating property. People by nature also have "different opinions concerning religion, concerning government, and many other points." In a free society, they form factions on the basis of their conflicting ideologies and "the various and unequal distribution of property." He wrote:

> A landed interest, a manufacturing interest, a mercantile interest, a moneyed interest, with many lesser interests, grow up of necessity in civilized nations, and divide them into different classes, actuated by different sentiments and views. The regulation of these various and interfering interests forms the principal task of modern legislation, and involves the spirit of party and faction in the necessary and ordinary operations of the government.

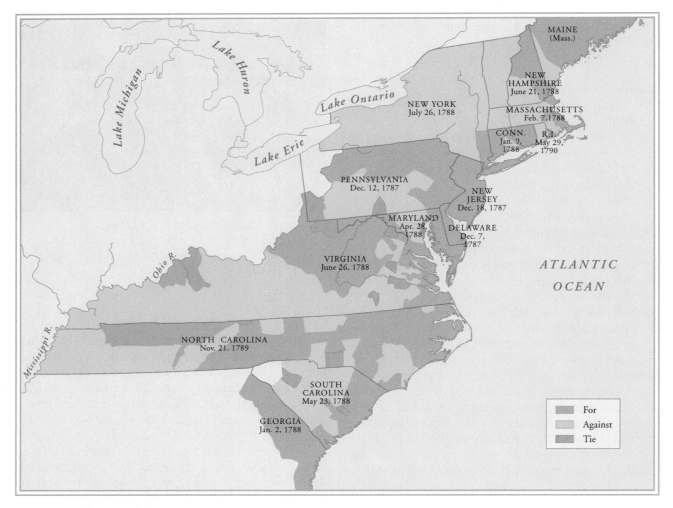

Map 6.4 *Ratification of the Constitution*
The pattern of support by relatively small states is visible in the votes of Delaware, New Jersey, Georgia, and Connecticut. In Pennsylvania, Massachusetts, and New York, the more populated urban areas supported ratification.

Madison claimed that the Constitution would be beneficial because a large republic contained more safeguards than a small one. In an extended polity, so many factions exist that the ability of a single interest to monopolize power is reduced. With the national government, "you take in a greater variety of parties and interests; you make it less probable that a majority of the whole will have a common motive to invade the rights of other citizens."

Antifederalists disagreed with this analysis, both because they favored small republics and because they feared the actions of men who would likely dominate the central government. Small farmers, many of them debtors who considered the mercantile elite their enemies, wanted nothing to do with this Constitution. At the core of their opposition was the belief

that power should remain in the states. The Antifederalists understood that, despite equal representation in the Senate, the new government was fundamentally different from the Articles. They argued that a republic must be geographically small with a homogeneous population in order to meet the needs of its people. They believed the new central government would be too large and too remote, that the interests of citizens of the thirteen states were too diverse. A congressman could never know the will of 30,000 constituents; with so few persons elected to Congress and such large electoral districts, affluent well-known candidates would have the advantage over ordinary men who ran for office. Thus, even the House of Representatives, the branch of government closest to the people, would become the domain of the rich. To the

Antifederalists, the Constitution lacked sufficient barriers against corruption and abuse of power. At the least, term limits on the president and senators were required to prevent these officials from keeping their offices for life. Annual elections (instead of every two years) would make the House of Representatives more responsive to the voters.

Antifederalists also pointed to the omission of a bill of rights as cause for rejecting the Constitution. They advocated freedom of speech, press, assembly, and religion; jury trials for civil cases; judicial safeguards such as the right to a speedy trial and to confront accusers and witnesses; and prohibitions against unwarranted searches and seizures. The Federalists answered that a bill of rights would be superfluous because state constitutions offered these protections (some did, but in no case was protection comprehensive), and because a bill of rights was needed against a powerful king, not when the people themselves were sovereign. This latter argument ignored the vulnerability of the individual to the will of the majority. The Federalists used poor judgment in failing to incorporate a bill of rights into the 1787 Constitution, for the Antifederalists gained momentum as a result. Omitting these rights, for which the patriots had fought, turned many Americans against the proposed frame of government.

Nevertheless, ratification proceeded rapidly at first as state legislatures called elections for the state ratifying conventions. Delaware was the first to ratify when its convention approved the Constitution unanimously on December 7, 1787. In Pennsylvania, where resistance was potentially heavy in the backcountry, Federalists moved quickly, securing approval by a two-to-one margin. New Jersey and Georgia then ratified unanimously. When Connecticut accepted the new government in January 1788 by a three-to-one vote, five states had joined the union. All of these states except Pennsylvania were relatively small and recognized the advantages of joining a union in which they had equal representation in the Senate.

Then the conventions became more acrimonious. North Carolina and Rhode Island rejected the document outright and New Hampshire put off its decision. Maryland and South Carolina ratified easily, but the vote in Massachusetts was close, as animosities from Shays's Rebellion colored the debate. Turnout for the Massachusetts convention was huge, as farmers in the central and western regions of the state believed the Constitution represented the interests of the eastern elite. The convention barely ratified the document by a vote of 187 to 168, recommending a series of amendments to protect individual rights and limit the powers of Congress. In June 1788, New Hampshire finally acted, becoming the ninth state to ratify, the number required to establish the new government. Nevertheless, two states remained crucial, Virginia and New York, whose size and economic importance made their approval necessary if the Constitution was to succeed. Virginia ratified in late June after a fierce debate, recommending to the first Congress a series of amendments, including a bill of rights. New York approved in late July, also with recommended changes, after New York City threatened to secede from the rest of the state if rural districts failed to accept the document.

CONCLUSION

The period from 1783 to 1788 was a crucial time for the United States, as it fixed the limits of revolutionary change and established a new government. Americans initially tried a political framework of thirteen small republics in which assemblies held the power to tax. All of the states (except New Jersey) restricted the vote—and political sovereignty—to propertied white men. "Republican motherhood" defined women's political role in the new nation. And despite a robust antislavery movement in the north, most African Americans remained enslaved.

The Congress, with little power under the Articles of Confederation, failed to solve its most pressing problems—the national debt, trade, and protection of U.S. borders against Spain and Great Britain. Even Congress's chief success, the legislation for governing and distributing land in the Northwest Territory, was marred by high land prices, delays in surveying, settlement by squatters, favoritism toward speculators, and conflict with Native Americans. When national government came to a halt and farmers rose in armed rebellion, nationalists demanded a constitution in which educated, propertied men like themselves would determine national economic policy and foreign affairs. These nationalists, who assumed the name Federalists, crafted the Constitution of 1787 to shift power from the states to a central government. The Antifederalists fought the new Constitution despite the "great compromise," which provided states equal representation in the Senate. The lack of a bill of rights intensified opposition. The Federalists prevailed, however, and with ratification by eleven states by July 1788, the United States began a new experiment in republican government.

Recommended Readings

Beeman, Richard, Botein, Stephen, and Carter, Edward C., eds. *Beyond Confederation: Origins of the Constitution and American National Identity* (1987). These essays provide an excellent introduction to the Confederation period and the making of the Constitution.

Berlin, Ira, and Hoffman, Ronald, eds. *Slavery and Freedom in the Age of the American Revolution* (1983). Important essays on change, or lack thereof, in the status of African Americans during the Revolutionary era.

Doerflinger, Thomas M. *A Vigorous Spirit of Enterprise: Merchants and Economic Development in Revolutionary Philadelphia* (1986). A very good study of Philadelphia merchants and their impact on economic growth in the emergent United States.

Greene, Jack P. *Peripheries and Center: Constitutional Development in the Extended Polities of the British Empire and the United States, 1607–1788* (1986). Links the constitutional structure of Britain and its colonies to the Constitution of 1787.

Hamilton, Alexander, Jay, John, and Madison, James. *The Federalist Papers* (1788). Defense of Constitution of 1787; seminal treatise of American political thought.

Hoffman, Ronald et al., eds. *Native Americans and the Early Republic* (1999). Essays focusing on the impact of the Revolution and founding of the new republic on white-Indian relations.

Kenyon, Cecilia M. "Men of Little Faith: The Anti-Federalists on the Nature of Representative Government," *William and Mary Quarterly*, 3d ser., 12 (1955): 3–43. Insightful essay on the men who opposed ratification of the Constitution of 1787.

Kerber, Linda K. *Women of the Republic: Intellect and Ideology in Revolutionary America* (1980). Evaluates the impact of the Revolution on attitudes toward women.

Rhoden, Nancy L., and Steele, Ian K., eds. *The Human Tradition in the American Revolution* (2000). Biographical essays of famous and more ordinary Americans during the Revolutionary era.

Richards, Leonard L. *Shays's Rebellion: The American Revolution's Final Battle* (2002). A recent study of the western Massachusetts revolt that challenges earlier interpretations.

American Journey Online and InfoTrac College Edition

Visit the source collections at http://ajaccess. wadsworth.com and infotrac.thomsonlearning.com and use the Search function with the following key terms to explore documents, images, audio and video clips, articles, and commentary related to the material in this chapter.

Shays's Rebellion	Constitutional Convention
James Madison	*The Federalist* essays
Northwest Ordinance	

Additional resources, exercises, and Internet links related to this chapter are available on the American Passages Web site: http://history.wadsworth.com/passages2e

7

THE FEDERALIST REPUBLIC
1789–1799

THE NEW GOVERNMENT

OPPOSING VISIONS OF AMERICA

EXPANSION AND CONFLICT IN THE WEST

FOREIGN ENTANGLEMENTS

THE ADAMS PRESIDENCY

Preparation for War to Defend Commerce *(1800), illustrating construction of the frigate* Philadelphia. *During the 1790s the United States tried to remain neutral in the European wars while prospering from international trade.*

After Ratification, the Federalists took leadership in creating the new government. Everyone expected George Washington to become president. The three authors of *The Federalist,* Alexander Hamilton, James Madison, and John Jay, who had been so important in achieving the Constitution, went on to play a central role in making it work. John Adams and Thomas Jefferson, who were serving as ministers to Great Britain and France during the convention, returned home to become, respectively, vice president and secretary of state.

Though many Federalists disagreed with specific parts of the Constitution, they accepted compromise and knew the weak Confederation had to be replaced. In the flush of victory over the Antifederalists, they set to the task of remedying the nation's ills. Differences soon became clear, however, between Hamilton on the one side, and Madison and Jefferson on the other, as the first administration tackled the national debt and foreign policy. As a result of their conflict over policy, varying interpretations of the Constitution, and competition for power, the nation's first political parties developed.

THE NEW GOVERNMENT

The first national elections went well, from the Federalist point of view, considering the whirlwind of Antifederalist opposition to the Constitution. The great majority of representatives and senators in the first Congress were Federalists. They fulfilled Madison's image of well-to-do men of national reputation and experience in politics. Many had served in the Constitutional Convention and signed the document. Most had military or political experience during the Revolution and Confederation period; just a few came from lower-class backgrounds. While the first congressmen were revolutionaries, they were also elites who believed that the country's interests coincided with their own. They wanted a stable government to foster economic growth.

George Washington Becomes President

The choice of George Washington as president was a foregone conclusion, though he would have preferred to stay at his Mount Vernon estate in northern Virginia. In February 1789, members of the electoral college met in their state capitals to cast unanimous votes for the former commander-in-chief. Washington's leadership during the war, his dignity and character, and his support for republican government made him the obvious choice. He might have tried to grasp power during the shaky Confederation, like a Napoleon or

CHRONOLOGY

1789 First Congress meets • Inauguration of George Washington as president • French Revolution begins • Judiciary Act of 1789

1790 Site on Potomac River chosen for permanent capital • Congress approves the funding and assumption plans • Samuel Slater builds first water-powered textile mill in the United States • First national census • Nootka Convention

1791 Bank of the United States is established • Native Americans of the Ohio Valley destroy Arthur St. Clair's army • Ratification of Bill of Rights

1793 France declares war on Great Britain and Spain • Washington begins second term • Proclamation of Neutrality • Genêt Affair • Britain seizes U.S. merchant fleet • Eli Whitney invents cotton gin

1794 Battle of Fallen Timbers • Whiskey Rebellion

1795 Senate approves the Jay Treaty • Treaty of Greenville • Treaty of San Lorenzo

1797 John Adams becomes second president

1798 XYZ Affair becomes public • Congress passes Alien and Sedition Acts • Kentucky and Virginia Resolutions

1798–1800 Quasi-War with France

1799 The Fries Rebellion • Napoleon takes power in France

Stalin, but he did not. The first president's commitment to the success of the Constitution ensured the nation's survival during the early years. John Adams, elected vice president, received fewer than half as many votes as Washington.

PICTURING THE PAST✦POLITICS & DIPLOMACY

GEORGE WASHINGTON IN NEW YORK CITY

The Granger Collection, New York

While ratification of the Constitution provided the political institutions to move forward as a republic, the nation lacked a unifying political culture. George Washington, hero of the Revolution, became a symbol of unity for all Americans, perhaps especially for those who could not vote or participate in government. He journeyed throughout the country, welcomed with triumphal arches and celebrations. An observer noted that if "every individual *personally* [were] consulted as to the man whom they would elect to fill the office of President of this rising empire, the only reply from New Hampshire to Georgia, would be *Washington.*"

As suggested in this illustration, thousands greeted George Washington upon his arrival in New York City for inauguration as president. The broad participation in such festivities—though not in actual suffrage and politics—is seen in the portrayal of Native Americans, African Americans, and women among the crowd. Other parades and pageants, most importantly the annual celebration of July 4th, helped to bond voters and nonvoters alike to the new nation.

The president-elect's trip from Mount Vernon to New York City, the temporary federal capital, became an eight-day triumphal march. In large and small towns along his way—Alexandria, Baltimore, Wilmington, Philadelphia—crowds of people, troops of infantry and cavalry, and local officials feted him with ceremonies, cannon fire, and banquets. Philadelphia citizens erected a Roman arch, crowning the revolutionary hero with a laurel wreath. In New Jersey, throngs saluted his military victories at Trenton and Princeton. On April 23, 1789, Washington crossed into Manhattan on a festooned barge, welcomed by thousands of cheering New Yorkers. He took the oath of office a week later.

The president and Congress, aware that they were setting precedent, initially placed a great deal of emphasis on titles and the comportment of officials. In this republic, in a world of monarchies, how should they be addressed? Should the president keep his door open or remain detached? While the ques-

tions may seem trivial, they indicate the novelty of this republican experiment. Adams, with diplomatic experience in Europe, urged Congress to adopt titles like those of other nations. A Senate committee suggested, for example, that Washington be called "His Highness the President of the United States of America, and Protector of their Liberties." After much debate, Congress dropped the notion of titles, preferring a more republican style. Washington and his successors have been addressed simply as "Mr. President."

For his part, the president wondered how to dignify his office and accomplish his work. He could easily have spent all of his time meeting with visitors, entertaining, and dining out. On the other hand, he did not want complete separation from the people. Washington's personality tended toward aloofness. He decided to hold a one-hour reception once a week, invite a few visitors to dinner, and sometimes attend the theater.

Washington also developed, by trial and error, the way in which the chief executive would deal with Congress. Early in his administration, in advance of negotiating a treaty with the Creek Indians, he attended the Senate to request their "advice and consent," as the Constitution seemed to direct. The senators were unprepared to discuss Washington's proposal, leading to embarrassment on both sides. The president resolved never to consult in formal session again. Instead, he set the precedent of private informal meetings with members of Congress. Heads of executive departments, such as the secretary of the treasury, would attend congressional hearings, not the president. And in the case of treaties, the executive would seek the Senate's consent *after* negotiations were complete, not advice—at least formally—beforehand.

Beyond titles and modes of operating, Congress and the president needed to establish executive departments and courts, and draw up a bill of rights, to fill gaps in the written Constitution. In creating executive departments, which included War, Treasury, State (foreign affairs), and the attorney general, the most crucial constitutional question concerned who would be able to remove the heads of departments from office. Some senators hoped to restrict the president's power by requiring Senate approval before officeholders could be fired, thus making them more accountable to the legislature. In rejecting this proposal, Congress clarified one aspect of the Constitution's balance of powers.

With the Judiciary Act of 1789, Congress put some flesh on the skeleton outlined in Article III of the Constitution, which stated that the "judicial power of the United States shall be vested in one Supreme Court, and in such inferior courts as the Congress may from time to time ordain and establish." Congress might have created a full-blown national court system, but supporters of states' rights opposed such enhancement of national power. Thus, the Judiciary Act, the result of compromise, established a Supreme Court of six justices and a system of federal inferior courts, which were few in number and restricted primarily to consideration of federal crimes. State courts retained original jurisdiction in most civil and criminal cases, with the U.S. Supreme Court taking appeals from the highest state courts. John Jay became the first chief justice.

The Bill of Rights

During its first months, Congress took up the question of amending the Constitution to satisfy criti-

cisms voiced during ratification, objections that by the summer of 1789 still kept North Carolina and Rhode Island out of the Union. More than the original document, the first ten amendments, called the Bill of Rights, represented the will of the American people.

The ratification campaign had elicited a mountain of proposals for amending the Constitution. Opponents offered two major grounds for altering the document or abandoning it altogether. Antifederalist leaders believed it took too much power from the states and from themselves as leaders of state and local governments, while popular opinion feared the loss of personal freedoms to a strong national government.

James Madison became the chief proponent of the Bill of Rights in Congress, despite his earlier advocacy of the Federalist position that the amendments were unnecessary. In order to get elected to the House of Representatives, he had promised his Virginia constituents to obtain the safeguards. Madison took his vow seriously, pushing his reluctant Federalist colleagues to the task. Antifederalist leaders, who wanted to scrap the Constitution entirely, now denied support to the Bill of Rights because they knew protection of individual freedoms would garner popular support.

After much negotiation between the Senate and the House, on September 25, 1789, Congress sent to the states for ratification a total of twelve amendments. By December 15, 1791, three-quarters of the states approved the ten amendments known as the Bill of Rights, thus putting them into effect. Of the two amendments not approved at the time, one was a rule concerning congressional salaries that was not ratified for two centuries, until 1992, and the other was a complicated formula for computing representation in Congress that was never adopted. Of the Bill of Rights, Articles 1 through 8 enumerated basic individual rights, while the intention of Article 9 was to protect any personal freedoms omitted from this list. Article 10 directed that "powers not delegated to the United States by the Constitution, nor prohibited by it to the States, are reserved to the States respectively, or to the people." It addressed concerns that the national government might assume powers that were not mentioned in the Constitution. Passage of the Bill of Rights by Congress attracted enough support to bring in the two remaining states; North Carolina ratified the Constitution in November 1789 and Rhode Island followed suit in May 1790.

The Bill of Rights, 1791

During the debates over ratification of the Constitution, many people argued for increased protection of individual rights, including freedom of religion, speech, the press, assembly, and petition, and judicial safeguards such as the right to a speedy trial and prohibition of cruel punishments. The Bill of Rights, or Amendments 1 through 10, added such provisions to the Constitution.

Amendment I

Congress shall make no law respecting an establishment of religion, or prohibiting the free exercise thereof; or abridging the freedom of speech, or of the press; or the right of the people peaceably to assemble, and to petition the government for a redress of grievances.

Amendment II

A well-regulated militia being necessary to the security of a free State, the right of the people to keep and bear arms shall not be infringed.

Amendment III

No soldier shall, in time of peace, be quartered in any house without the consent of the owner, nor in time of war, but in a manner to be prescribed by law.

Amendment IV

The right of the people to be secure in their persons, houses, papers, and effects, against unreasonable searches and seizures, shall not be violated, and no warrants shall issue but upon probable cause, supported by oath or affirmation, and particularly describing the place to be searched, and the persons or things to be seized.

Amendment V

No person shall be held to answer for a capital, or otherwise infamous crime, unless on a presentment or indictment of a grand jury, except in cases arising in the land or naval forces, or in the militia, when in actual service in time of war or public danger; nor shall any person be subject for the same offense to be twice put in jeopardy of life or limb; nor shall be compelled in any criminal case to be a witness against himself, nor be deprived of life, liberty, or property, without due process of law; nor shall

private property be taken for public use without just compensation.

Amendment VI

In all criminal prosecutions, the accused shall enjoy the right to a speedy and public trial, by an impartial jury of the State and district wherein the crime shall have been committed, which district shall have been previously ascertained by law, and to be informed of the nature and cause of the accusation; to be confronted with the witnesses against him; to have compulsory process for obtaining witnesses in his favor, and to have the assistance of counsel for his defense.

Amendment VII

In suits at common law, where the value in controversy shall exceed twenty dollars, the right of trial by jury shall be preserved, and no fact tried by a jury shall be otherwise reexamined in any court of the United States, than according to the rules of the common law.

Amendment VIII

Excessive bail shall not be required, nor excessive fines imposed, nor cruel and unusual punishments inflicted.

Amendment IX

The enumeration in the Constitution, of certain rights, shall not be construed to deny or disparage others retained by the people.

Amendment X

The powers not delegated to the United States by the Constitution, nor prohibited by it to the States, are reserved to the States respectively, or to the people.

The First Census

Congress also promptly ordered a census of the American population, which the Constitution required within three years of Congress's first meeting and every ten years subsequently. The census, the founders expected, would provide an accurate enumeration for apportioning delegates to the House of Representatives and electoral college. Congress set August 1790 as the date of the first census, appointing marshals to complete their work within nine months, which actually stretched to eighteen. The first census was less complicated than later ones, with just six questions: name of head of household, number of free white males aged sixteen years and over, number of free white males under sixteen, number of free white females, number of other free persons, and number of slaves. The separate listing of enslaved persons was required by the clause of the Constitution that counted three-fifths of slaves for representation and taxes. The distinction between free whites and blacks came from cultural values rather than some practical use. The census did not include Native Americans who lived outside areas settled by whites.

While sketchy and incomplete, the 1790 census served as a baseline for measuring the growth of a dynamic, expanding people. President Washington reported to Congress a total of 3.9 million people, of whom 60,000 were free blacks and almost 700,000 were slaves. The census covered the territory included in the thirteen original states and also Vermont, Kentucky, and Tennessee, which became states respectively in 1791, 1792, and 1796. It did not encompass the area north of the Ohio River where at least 4,000 white settlers had taken up land.

During the 1780s, the white population of the country had swelled by an extraordinary 44 percent, mostly through reproduction; in the 1790s, the increase remained high at 36 percent. After the Treaty of Paris, European immigrants once again began crossing the Atlantic Ocean, with the majority coming from Ireland. From 1783 to 1799, 156,000 Europeans entered the United States, of whom 69 percent were

Table 7.1	The U.S. Population, 1790	
United States	**Total 3,929,625**	**Slaves 697,624**
New England	**1,009,206**	**3,763**
Maine (part of Massachusetts)	96,643	0
New Hampshire	141,899	157
Vermont	85,341	0
Massachusetts	378,556	0
Rhode Island	69,112	958
Connecticut	237,655	2,648
Middle States	**1,017,087**	**45,210**
New York	340,241	21,193
New Jersey	184,139	11,423
Pennsylvania	433,611	3,707
Delaware	59,096	8,887
Southern States and Territories	**1,903,332**	**648,651**
Maryland	319,728	103,036
Virginia	747,610	292,627
North Carolina	395,005	100,783
South Carolina	249,073	107,094
Georgia	82,548	29,264
Kentucky	73,677	12,430
Tennessee	35,691	3,417

Irish, 14 percent were English, Scottish, and Welsh, and 6 percent were German. The African American population also grew quickly during the 1780s and 1790s, at a rate of 32 percent per decade.

Especially striking in the 1790 census are the small numbers of enslaved African Americans in New England and Pennsylvania compared with Maryland, Virginia, and the Carolinas, the result in part of northern abolition. This sectional difference would grow in the nineteenth century as the North focused more on commerce and developed a manufacturing sector, while the South cast its fate with agriculture, adopting cotton as its major crop.

OPPOSING VISIONS OF AMERICA

Almost immediately during Washington's first administration, political divisions arose between sides favoring commerce versus agriculture. Two divergent conceptions of the nation's future emerged among supporters of the Constitution. During the early 1790s, two political parties developed, though leaders avoided calling them that because public opinion considered parties "evil," or detrimental to unified republican government. As events unfolded in foreign and domestic affairs, the two parties contested one issue after another.

Alexander Hamilton, *1792, by John Trumbull. The first secretary of the treasury saw Great Britain, with its strong central government and expanding industrial economy, as a model for the new United States.*
© Bettmann/Corbis

Hamilton Versus Jefferson

Alexander Hamilton, appointed by Washington as secretary of the treasury, saw the future greatness of the United States in commerce and manufacturing. Born in the West Indies, Hamilton attended King's College in New York City, then served as Washington's aide-de-camp during the Revolution. Highly intelligent, full of energy and enthusiasm, he was a major proponent of the new Constitution. Appointment to the Treasury allowed Hamilton to promote his concept of a strong nation modeled on Great Britain, but his efforts to foster commerce and manufacturing aroused resistance among former allies, particularly Madison and Jefferson, leading to bitter partisan disputes.

Hamilton's party took the name Federalist though it was really nationalist. It favored commercial development, a national bank, high tariffs to spur manufacturing, and a strong central government based upon a "loose" interpretation of the Constitution, which allowed expansive powers to Congress and the president. The Federalists favored the British, abhorred the French Revolution after 1792, and were

generally suspicious of power wielded by ordinary folk. They were somewhat critical of slavery, however, and gained the allegiance of free blacks. Because their power base lay in New England and the Middle States, the Federalists had little enthusiasm for western expansion and sometimes supported the right of Native Americans to retain their lands.

The Republican party, in contrast, favored a "strict" interpretation of the Constitution, opposing a strong central government and federal privileges for manufacturing and commerce. It thought Hamilton's plans for funding the national debt, the bank, and protective tariffs infringed upon states' rights and helped the "few" at the expense of the "many." It disdained the British model and charged Hamilton with advocating a return to monarchy. With their power base in the south, west, and northern cities, the Republicans rejected efforts to abolish slavery and were ardent expansionists on the frontier. They had little sympathy for Indian rights.

Thomas Jefferson became the chief spokesman for the Republican party, though James Madison

U.S. Federal Census of 1790

This excerpt from the first U.S. Federal Census shows households on several streets in Philadelphia. The census provides much evidence about urban society in 1790, including the names, occupations, sex, and ethnicity of heads of household, but less information on other members of their households. Note that many more free blacks than slaves lived in this part of Philadelphia by 1790.

Name of Head of Family.	Free White Males of 16 Years and Upward Including Heads of Families.	Free White Males Under 16 years.	Free White Females Including Heads of Families.	All Other Free Persons.	Slaves.
PHILADELPHIA CITY—continued.					
North Fifth street from Market to Race street, East side.					
Wheelen, Israel (Grocer)	2	3	7		
Leacock, John (Coroner)	3	2	2		
Howell, Samuel (Brush Mak')	1		3		
Bell, Barbary (Widow)	1		2		
Shaw, John (Carpenter)	2	1	1		
Langdell, Margaret (Spinster)			3		
Snowden, George (Carpr)	3		4		
Shea, John (Shoe maker)	2	2	4		
Cruds, George (Breeches Makr)	1	3	2		
Paschall, Stephen (Gente)	1	3	5	1	
Detrick, Michael (Shoemaker)	3	1	1		
Shearer, Peter (Skinner)	2	3	2		
Church Burial Ground					
Gilmore, Daniel (Negroe)				2	
Davison, William (Gent.)	1	1	2	1	
Elton, Thomas (Joyner; S.)					
Gitz, John (plaisterer)	2	3	2		
Kroll, John (Barber)					
Wyman, Jacob (Taylor)	2	2	4		
Dutch Meeting Burial Ground					
North Fifth street from Market to Race street, West side.					
Cochran, Elizabeth (Widow)			1		
Yeager, Adam (Cedar Cooper)	2	2	4		
Boeush, Adam (Reed Makr)	1	5	5		
Facundus, Peter (Shoe Maker)	2		2		
Wolf, Lewis (Barber)	1	2	3		
Clark, Joseph (School Mast.)	1	1	1		
Enk, Jacob (Taylor)	3	1	5		
Wallace, Burton (Brick-layer & Mason)	1		3	1	
Randell, Thomas (Clerk)	1	1	3		
James, John (Mercht)	2	1	2		
Ogle, Cathe (Widow)	4		2		
Ritter, Henry (Baker)	1	1	7		
Steines, Frederick (Taylor)	1		3		
Field, Eleanor (Tayloress)			3		
Eckfelt, Jacob (Black Smith)	7	6	8		
Wilson, James (Coach Makr; S.)					
Clark, Samuel (Board Mercht)	2	1	4		
Alexander, Margaret (Spinster)			2		
Sadler, Matthew (Carpt; S.)					
Vandell, George (Negroe)				4	
Whig Quaker Meeting House					
Elwin, Hugh (Shoemaker)	1	1	2		
Weaver, William (Labr)	1	1	2		
Noah, Emanuel (Trader)	1	2	3		
Hartung, William (Scrivener)	1		3		
Robins, Isabella (Widow)	1	1	3		
Dawson, Elias (Merchant)	1	2	4		
Henbury, Thomas (Fish monger)	4		6		

Name of Head of Family.	Free White Males of 16 Years and Upward Including Heads of Families.	Free White Males Under 16 years.	Free White Females Including Heads of Families.	All Other Free Persons.	Slaves.
Newman, Frederick (Card maker)	1	1	3		
Kein, Christian (Bl. Smith; S.)	1		3		
Lawrence, Philip (Joyner)	2		2		
Rawlston, George (Custom hº Officer)	1		3		
Ross, Oliver (Comb Makr)	1	1	3		
Dougherty, Daniel (Shoe Maker)	2	1	3		
Wayne, John & Labʳˢ	3	3	5		
Miller, Jacob (Carter)	1		1		
Robinson, Ebenezar (Brush Makʳ)	1		2		
Dexter, James (Negroe)				7	
Roe, Thomas (Taylor)	3		3		
Howell, Reading (Surveyor)	4	2	4	1	
Evans, Cadwallader (Merchʳ)	1		3		
Taggart, Robert (Gent.)	1		3		
Evans, Robert (Ho. Carpʳ)	4	2	4		
Hudson, Samuel (Gentⁿ)	2		2		
Seyfreid, Jacob (Barber)	1	1	2		
Nail, Henry (Shoemaker)	1		3		
Dennis, John (Shoemaker)	2	1	3		
Meyer, Henry (Inn keeper)	4	3	2		
South Sixth street from Market to Chestnut street, East side.					
Clark, David	7	3	5	1	
Christie, Alexander (painter; S.)	1	2	4		
Gilmore, Samuel (Carpʳ)	1		5		
Hartong, Robert (Labʳ)	2		1		
South Sixth street from Market to Chestnut street, West side.					
Polk, Adam	1		1		
Ellcott, James (Innkeeper)	1	1	4		
Benge, Samuel (Umbrella M.)	2		1	1	
Street, Robert (Shoemaker)	1	1	1		
Welcher, Henry (Labʳ)	1		2		
Lace, William (Bl. Smith)	1	1	2		
Keen, Reynold. Esqʳ	4	2	8	2	2
Gray, Wᵐ & Joseph (Brewers)	1				
Matthar, Peter (Inn keeper)	1	1	4	2	1
North Sixth street from Market to Race street, East side.					
Donnalson, Joseph (Gent.)	1		4	2	
Redman, Joseph (Doctʳ P.)					
Simmons, William (Auditors Office)					
Erwin, Robert (Gentⁿ)	1	1	1		
Elmsley, Alexander (Carpʳ)	1	1	4		
Link, Frederick (Drayman)	3	3	7		
Albright, Michael (Cedʳ Cooper)	1	3	2		
Nusshag, Charles Willᵐ (Baker)	1	5	4		
Davis, Sampson (Lab.)	1	3	4		
Hudson, William	4	3	8		
Hawker, Godfrey (Baker)	2	2	4		
Elter, George (Coach Maker; S.)					
Fotter, Mattˢ (porter)	2		1		
Branger, William (Labʳ)	1	1	5		
Brinner, George (Taylor)	1		2		
Greer, Jacob (Butcher)	1	1	2		
Walker, Martha (Widow)		1	1		
Miney, Godfrey (Baker)	1	2	5		
Rust, Leonard (Meal Seller & Innkeeper; S.)	1		3		
Gray, Joseph (Brewer)	1	1	3		
Humphries, Amy (Spinstr)		1	3		
Harper, John (Bl. Smith; S.)					
Hallowell, Thomas (Joyner)	1	3	2		
Cunningham, Robert (Weaver)	1	1	4		
McConnell, John (Lab)	1		2		
Venables, Robert (Negroe)				4	
Sandiford, Rowland (Coach Makʳ)	1		3		
Dietz, Henry (Watchman)	2	1	3		
Guest, James (Taylor)	1	1	2		
Lambert, John (Chair Makʳ)	1		1		
Haseelback, Philip (Shoemaker)	2	2	2		
Hansell, Jacob (Bl. Smith)	1	3	1		

Thomas Jefferson, *1791, by Charles Willson Peale. The first secretary of state, who favored an agrarian republic, strict construction of the Constitution, and the French, quickly became Hamilton's chief opponent.*
Independence National Historical Park

collaborated in its growth. Jefferson, a wealthy planter and slaveholder, author of the Declaration of Independence, former minister to France, and now Washington's secretary of state, argued that Hamilton wanted too much national power. He believed the root of Britain's effort to destroy American liberty in the 1760s and 1770s had been commercial speculation and greed. Manufacturing in cities created poverty, dependency, and political corruption. Instead, the United States, with limitless land, should foster an agrarian society of small producers. A virtuous republic was one made up of small farmers whose goal was to produce enough to support their families. Commerce should exist primarily to allow them to sell their surplus in Europe and purchase manufactured goods in return. The farmers should be educated to participate wisely in republican government. Their self-sufficiency and education would make them virtuous, to act for the good of society rather than solely for their own gain.

Paradoxically, a large proportion of the Republicans were not small farmers. Many of the leaders were southern plantation gentry like Jefferson and Madi-

son, or old Antifederalist elites. The party drew together people who had opposed ratification of the Constitution as well as those who favored it but abhorred the government's direction under Washington and Hamilton. The Republicans received solid backing from farmers, especially in the south and west, and from urban craftsmen and small traders who watched wealthy speculators and merchants benefit from Hamiltonian policies.

Funding the National Debt

In becoming secretary of the treasury, Alexander Hamilton's primary challenge was the Revolutionary War debt. A strong nationalist, he viewed the debt more as an opportunity to enlarge national power than as a financial hurdle. The United States owed $10 million to foreigners, particularly to the French, and $40 million to Americans. The states also owed $25 million in domestic debts. To continue the War of Independence when funds were depleted, Congress and the states had issued certificates to merchants, artisans, and farmers for supplies and to soldiers for wages. After the war, many ordinary folks could not wait for the government to pay—or lost hope that the money was forthcoming—so they sold their certificates to wealthy speculators for a fraction of face value. Often the sellers received only 10 to 15 percent, rates that reflected the risk speculators were taking during the shaky Confederation period.

In his Report on Public Credit of January 1790, Hamilton formulated a plan by which the U.S. government would honor at face value all Revolutionary War debts, including those of the states. His "funding" proposal involved the exchange of new federal securities for the old debt certificates. He planned to pay off foreign creditors as soon as possible, but retain the domestic debt, paying only interest and a small amount of the principal each year. A customs duty on imports and an excise tax on whiskey would cover the interest; post office income would gradually reduce the principal. Hamilton's funding plan would tie wealthy Americans to the new government through their continuing investment. His "assumption" plan, by which the federal government assumed state war debts, expanded this strategy by reorienting the loyalty of investors from the states to the nation.

Congress eventually passed Hamilton's proposal, though with great opposition. Many people, including Madison, thought that repaying the domestic debt at face value was unfair, that speculators received a windfall at the expense of the poor. The split between Hamilton and Madison began over this issue.

Critics argued that funding allowed the "few" to benefit from the hardships of the "many," who had lost money when they sold their war bonds and who would pay again through import duties and the excise tax. Opponents feared the expansion of national power, and became convinced that the Treasury secretary was upsetting the balance between the central government and the states. Assumption raised additional questions because some states had more debt remaining than others. Massachusetts and South Carolina were keen on having the federal government assume their large debts, while Virginians opposed the plan, because they had satisfied most of the state's debt. Despite these divisions, the funding and assumption program passed Congress in July 1790, as part of a bargain struck by Hamilton, Jefferson, and Madison to situate the nation's permanent capital on the Potomac River, in Maryland and Virginia.

Planning Washington, D.C.

The choice of the Potomac for the nation's capital was controversial. While everyone agreed that a central location was necessary, regional interests surfaced as congressmen recognized its potential economic and political benefits. They also debated the question of the temporary capital. Should New York City or Philadelphia host the federal government until the permanent site was ready? The complicated negotiations over funding and assumption resulted in moving the temporary capital from New York to Philadelphia as well as locating the new city on the Potomac.

President Washington and his fellow Virginians supervised the development of the capital. The Residence Act of 1790 gave the president authority to select a ten-mile-square location somewhere along the Potomac; he chose the land on both sides of the river that included Alexandria, Virginia, and Georgetown, Maryland. The federal city would be built in neither of those towns, but on open land on the east bank of the river. Washington appointed a surveyor, three commissioners to manage the project, and Pierre Charles L'Enfant to design the layout of the capital and its major buildings. L'Enfant's grandiose street plan and Greek and Roman architecture expressed an exalted vision of the republic. The commissioners named the federal city "Washington" and the entire district "Columbia."

The president expected to finance construction by selling lots in the capital, thinking that land prices would skyrocket as citizens valued proximity to the seat of government. Instead, land sold poorly and lack of money undermined the project. At one of the failed auctions, even the participation of the president and a

Pierre Charles L'Enfant's intricate design for Washington, D.C., 1791, far outstripped the country's financial resources and interest in creating a national capital.
The Granger Collection, New York

parade of two brass bands and an artillery troop could not foster sales. When the commissioners suspended construction temporarily for insufficient funds, L'Enfant protested and was fired. His plan for grand boulevards, public squares, fountains, and imposing buildings was retained, but its execution would wait. For a decade the enterprise limped along, saved by grants from Maryland and Virginia. In 1800, when the government moved to Washington, the president's mansion was still unfinished and only one wing of the Capitol had been built.

The National Bank

The cornerstone of Hamilton's new commercial order was a national bank, to be patterned after the Bank of England. The Bank of the United States and its branches would hold the federal government's funds and regulate state banks. The chief purpose of the national bank was to expand the money supply, thereby encouraging commercial growth.

The Bank of the United States, which Congress chartered in 1791 for twenty years, would have assets of $10 million, including $2 million in government deposits. Private investors could purchase the remaining $8 million in stock. As the bank prospered, stockholders would receive dividends on their funds. Thus, Hamilton created a way for wealthy Americans, who had just profited from funding the Revolutionary War debt, to benefit further. Because the government was a major stockholder, it also received dividends that could be used to pay off the national debt. The bank made loans to merchants beyond the value of its stock of gold and silver (specie), thus increasing the supply of money, a critically important move for an economy short of specie. The bank notes circulated as currency; the federal government supported their value by accepting them for taxes. To Hamilton and his commercial backers, the Bank of the United States was essential for economic growth. The majority of the House of Representatives agreed, by a vote of thirty-nine to twenty, but the tally indicated important regional differences that fueled growth of political parties. Among northern congressmen, thirty-three voted for the bank and one against, while only six southern delegates supported and nineteen opposed Hamilton's bill.

The plan had many opponents, who variously considered the bank immoral, monopolistic, or unconstitutional. Some believed that all paper money should be based on gold and silver. "Every dollar of a bank bill that is issued beyond the quantity of gold and silver in the vaults," John Adams said, "represents nothing, and is therefore a cheat upon somebody." The wild frenzy to purchase the bank's stock—in which 25,000 shares sold in two hours and then the shares were bid up to 1,300 percent of their face value—reinforced fears that the national bank would undermine republican virtue. Jefferson called the bank's stock "federal filth." Others charged the bank with monopoly, complaining that

merchants could secure short-term loans to finance their commercial ventures, but farmers and artisans could not obtain mortgages for purchasing property or making improvements.

In Congress, Madison opposed the national bank on the constitutional grounds that the federal government lacked the power to create corporations, a strict interpretation of the Constitution. In particular, Madison said, the Tenth Amendment would deny the central government any power not expressly given. Hamilton and his supporters countered with a loose interpretation, that some powers of the federal government are implied. In the case of the bank, for example, the Constitution delegated to Congress and the president the power to lay and collect taxes, pay debts, regulate commerce, and coin and regulate money. It also provided the authority to "make all laws which shall be necessary and proper for carrying into execution the foregoing powers. . . ." Hamilton argued that the bank was a method by which the United States could fulfill its functions, and because some means was necessary, the power to establish the bank was implied. Though President Washington was initially unsure, he accepted Hamilton's reasoning and approved the bill.

Jefferson, like Madison, was convinced that the national bank was unconstitutional. By 1791, the secretary of state realized the political and economic consequences of the funding act—channeling more power to the federal government and more money to the rich—and thought the bank could only further these trends. He said he had been "duped" by Hamilton and "made a tool for forwarding his schemes" in accepting the assumption of state debts in return for the capital on the Potomac. He now believed that the Treasury secretary's program "flowed from principles adverse to liberty," as Jefferson told the president. It was "calculated to undermine and demolish the republic." Hamilton chafed at this criticism, stating "that Mr. Madison, cooperating with Mr. Jefferson, is at the head of a faction decidedly hostile to me and my administration; and actuated by views, in my judgment, subversive of the principles of good government and dangerous to the Union, peace, and happiness of the country."

Encouragement of Manufacturing

While the Treasury secretary won congressional support for the bank and funding the national debt, he was much less successful in his plan for industry. In 1791, the United States lacked a solid manufacturing base. Hamilton proposed high protective tariffs on certain goods to discourage Americans from buying

First Bank of the United States, Philadelphia. The imposing structure, designed by Samuel Blodget of New Hampshire, was intended to convey confidence in the bank's financial strength.

The Granger Collection, New York

imports and thus spur U.S. production. He also advocated bounties, or subsidies, on selected products to encourage entrepreneurs. Hamilton believed that a strong nation needed self-sufficiency in manufactures, especially for military defense, but failed to obtain congressional support for the subsidies. Madison contended that granting bounties would expand the power of Congress, while others argued that they were like monopolies and too expensive. A North Carolina congressman advised, "Establish the doctrine of bounties, [and] . . . all manner of persons—people of every trade and occupation—may enter at the breach, until they have eaten up the bread of our children."

In the 1790s, U.S. manufacturing remained on a small scale. Americans appreciated the quality of British imports; what they did not import, they produced themselves or purchased from neighboring artisans. Industry could not be stimulated overnight, for it required technology and the willingness of businessmen to invest time and capital for the long term. While some master craftsmen enlarged their shops and hired more workers, mechanized factories with mass production still lay in the future.

During the colonial and revolutionary periods, urban entrepreneurs had attempted large-scale textile manufacturing to provide employment for poor women and independence from British imports, but these efforts were short-lived and not mechanized. The "factories" had consisted of workhouses, in which large numbers of impoverished widows produced thread and yarn at traditional spinning wheels. Other businessmen used a "putting-out" system, whereby they distributed flax and wool for spinning at home.

In 1788, the Pennsylvania Society for the Encouragement of Manufactures and the Useful Arts introduced spinning jennies to their textile factory in Philadelphia. The jennies threatened to displace home spinners by producing cheaper yarn and thread. In 1790, however, the factory and its wooden jennies went up in flames, as did other early textile mills in the Delaware Valley. While the promoters believed that home spinners were sabotaging the factories, the fires may well have been accidental because the mills were highly flammable.

Samuel Slater, a twenty-two-year-old millworker and recent immigrant from Great Britain, in 1790 instituted a new phase in American cloth production by building a textile mill in Pawtucket, Rhode Island, using water power to run the spinning machines. From memory he constructed a spinning frame, a machine that produced stronger threads than the jenny produced. He had left Britain illegally; to keep its advan-

Until after 1815, households performed one or more steps in textile manufacturing. Here a family works together, with the wife spinning thread, which the husband then wove on his loom. Women also wove cloth, but men rarely—if ever—used a spinning wheel.
Rare Books Division, The New York Public Library Astor, Lenox and Tilden Foundations

tage in textile making, the government prohibited emigration of craftworkers or export of drawings of the machines. No satisfactory power loom yet existed, so Slater's mill performed only the first two steps of cloth production: carding, or preparing the cotton fibers for spinning, and spinning the thread. Slater then used the putting-out system of distributing the thread to families, who produced the cloth at home. Though Slater established additional mills in Rhode Island and Massachusetts, his workforce stayed fairly small, with about a hundred millworkers in 1800.

Alexander Hamilton tried an ambitious industrial program in Paterson, New Jersey, with the Society for Establishing Useful Manufactures. The society hoped to create an industrial town on the Passaic River where skilled craftsmen recruited from Britain would produce a variety of cloth and clothing, blankets, carpets, shoes, hats, pottery, metal wire, and paper. After obtaining a state charter from New Jersey, the society sold stock that sold quickly and appreciated in value. The project lost capital, however, when major stockholders sold their shares to make a fast profit. The managers failed to obtain reliable machinery and workers, closing shop in 1796.

While the results of Hamilton's plans were disappointing, the United States did make progress during the 1790s toward industrialization. In 1790, Congress passed patent legislation, giving inventors exclusive

*P*ICTURING THE PAST◆ECONOMICS & TECHNOLOGY

SAMUEL SLATER'S SPINNING FRAME

Smithsonian Institution

Samuel Slater pushed forward mechanization of the American textile industry by emigrating illegally from Great Britain. A young millworker, he built from memory the spinning frame that Richard Arkwright had invented in 1769, giving England its advantage in the early stages of the Industrial Revolution. The spinning frame was water-powered and produced stronger thread than the spinning jenny, which was already in use in the United States.

Slater built his first factory in Pawtucket, Rhode Island, initiating what was called the Rhode Island system: factory workers carded and spun thread, which was then distributed to skilled artisans in their homes to weave into cloth. In 1813, as discussed in Chapter 9, Francis Cabot Lowell originated the Waltham system, which mechanized weaving as well. Like Slater, Lowell appropriated English technology—in this case by recreating from memory the power loom.

rights to their work for seventeen years, and Slater initiated water-powered textile manufacture. Then, in 1793, while visiting a Georgia plantation, Eli Whitney, a New Englander, built the cotton engine, or gin. The device, which separated cotton fibers from husks and seeds, greatly increased the productivity of cotton cultivation, swelling the demand for African American slaves and fertile land in the Southwest, and spurring cloth production in the North. Because the gin could be duplicated easily, Whitney failed to make a fortune from the machine. In 1798, he further laid the basis for industrial growth by attempting to manufacture guns with interchangeable parts. After receiving a government contract for 10,000 weapons, he specified that each part be made identical to its counterparts so that it could be exchanged from one rifle to another, allowing less-skilled workers to build and repair the firearms. At this early date, however, such rigid stan-

dards were impossible to meet, and as a result, parts needed filing to fit together smoothly.

An inventor who would have benefited from Hamilton's proposed bounties was the Delaware-born artisan Oliver Evans, who apprenticed as a wagonmaker and became fascinated by machines. In 1772, at age seventeen, he heard that the Scottish inventor James Watt had improved the steam engine a few years earlier. Evans began building his own model but, for lack of money, thirty years passed before he actually installed a high pressure steam engine in his gypsum fertilizer factory in Philadelphia. This was the first such application of steam power to an industrial setting. In the meantime, in the 1780s, Evans also developed the idea of automating mills. He devised water-powered machinery for large grist mills that allowed one worker instead of three to supervise all the steps of producing flour. Evans obtained exclusive rights from the states of Pennsylvania and Maryland for his system of automated elevators, conveyors, and hoppers. With insufficient capital, however, he was unable to pursue many of his designs, including steam carriages and trucks, a machine gun, refrigeration, central heating, and gas lighting.

EXPANSION AND CONFLICT IN THE WEST

While Alexander Hamilton's financial policies aided commerce in the east, dynamic growth also occurred in the west. The expansion of settlers from east to west challenged the ability of the new government to keep their loyalty. In particular, Hamilton's excise tax on whiskey weighed heavily on westerners. The young nation also contended with Native Americans who were losing lands to the settlers; the British military, who kept forts in the northwest; and the Spanish, who contested U.S. territorial claims and rights to navigate the Mississippi.

Kentucky and Tennessee

During the 1780s, the region west of the Appalachians and south of the Ohio River developed quickly, as families left Virginia and North Carolina in search of fertile land and lower taxes. Even before the Revolution ended, settlers crossed the mountains in large numbers: Kentucky swelled from 150 settlers in 1775 to 61,000 whites and 12,500 enslaved blacks in 1790; Tennessee reported 32,000 whites and 3,500 slaves in the latter year.

White settlement of Kentucky and Tennessee proceeded quickly as state governments, speculators, and frontiersmen defeated the Cherokees, who claimed ancestral rights to the territory. Understanding that they were renting the land rather than selling it, in 1775 a group of Cherokee leaders, including Attakullaculla and Oconostota, traded 27,000 square miles to Richard Henderson and his associates for a cabin of consumer goods. Called Henderson's Purchase, the sale involved most of Kentucky and was illegal in Indian and English law. With the outbreak of the Revolution, most Cherokees joined the British, fighting for return of their lands. Receiving little help from Britain, the Cherokees were defeated in 1777 and forced to sign away even more territory.

Young militants led by Dragging Canoe, Bloody Fellow, and others, assisted by loyalist whites who intermarried and became members of the tribe, rejected these land cessions. In the 1780s and early 1790s, the militant Cherokees, called Chickamaugas, allied with Creeks and Shawnees against settlers along the frontier from Kentucky to Georgia. On both sides, fighting was vicious, with men, women, and children burned, scalped, and shot; and, as in so many cases, the whites failed to distinguish between enemy Indians and those who wanted peace.

The Washington administration attempted to end the hostilities with the Treaty of Holston in 1791, but gave responsibility for negotiating with the Cherokees to Governor William Blount of the Tennessee Territory, a land speculator the Indians called "dirt king" for his greed after land. Blount ignored Washington's promise to the Cherokees that if they ceded territory on which the whites had settled, the United States would guarantee their remaining lands. Instead, Blount required a cession of more than 4,000 square miles in return for an annual payment of $1,000 and no guarantee. When Blount surveyed the border without Cherokee witnesses, the treaty fell apart and war continued. In 1794, after Dragging Canoe died and the Spanish stopped supplying the Indians because of war in Europe, the Chickamaugas met defeat.

By the end of the war, parts of Kentucky and Tennessee had passed the initial stages of settlement. Early on, groups of settlers had gathered in frontier stations consisting of two-story log houses connected by a high wall to create a fort against Indian attack. As the population grew and the threat from Native Americans declined, families moved away from the stations. In the early years, all family members worked to provide food, clothing, shelter, and a few amenities such as soap and rough-hewn furniture. They needed to become familiar with their new environment. One Kentucky pioneer described how "the women the first spring we came out, wo'd follow their cows to see what they ate, that they might know what greens to get. My Wife and I had neither spoon, dish, knife, or any thing to do with when we began life. Only I had a butcher knife." The settlers grew corn, tobacco, hemp, cotton, vegetables, and fruits; raised cattle, sheep, horses, and pigs; hunted and fished. Soon they produced a surplus to trade for necessities they could not make themselves, such as nails, rifles, ammunition, needles, tools, and salt, as well as to pay taxes and fees. They sold furs, ginseng, agricultural produce, and livestock. As fertile lands such as Kentucky's Bluegrass region yielded bountiful crops, farmers sought markets by way of the Mississippi River and the port of New Orleans. Because transporting crops overland through the mountains was much more difficult and expensive than sending them downstream, southwestern farmers demanded that

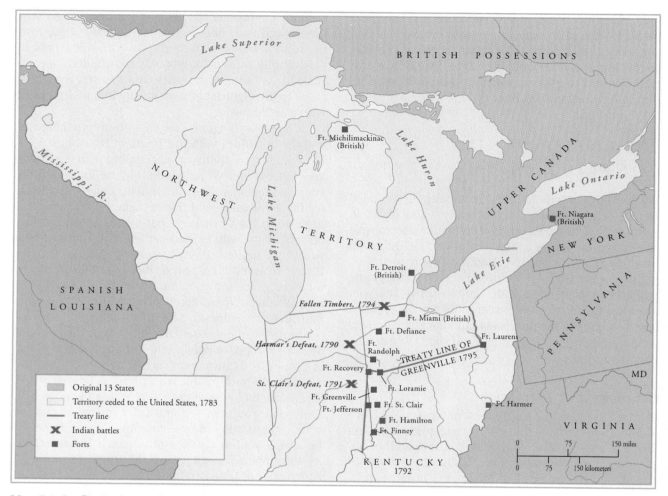

Map 7.1 *Conflict in the Northwest Territory, 1790–1796*
Native Americans continued to resist U.S. settlement in the Ohio region. They defeated U.S. forces in 1790 and 1791, but lost the Battle of Fallen Timbers in 1794. British forts in the Northwest Territory supported the Ohio Indians until that time.

the federal government convince Spain to end its restrictions on lower Mississippi shipping.

Though the population increased and a market economy developed in the 1790s, the trans-Appalachian region had few schools or church buildings. Most children, if taught at all, learned reading and arithmetic at home. In towns where schools existed, boys might attend for a few months but girls stayed at home. The exception were the children of wealthy families who entered academies with secondary school curricula. One man remembered the experience of most residents of Kentucky in the 1790s: "Our preachers and teachers were, in general, almost as destitute as the people at large, many of whom could neither read nor write, did not send their children to school, and of course, kept no books in the house."

Religion was the frontier's chief cultural institution. Throughout the region, Presbyterian, Baptist, and Methodist ministers held services in private homes. Baptist lay ministers farmed beside their neighbors through the week, then led services on Sunday. Methodist circuit riders traveled from one congregation to another, conducting worship services, baptisms, marriages, and prayer meetings. The churches expected members to avoid sin, including fighting, excessive drinking, adultery, and even celebrating the Fourth of July. If members committed offenses and failed to express regret, they were expelled, a serious consequence for people who had few social outlets. In addition to church, social activities included barn raisings, corn huskings, and log rollings. These events caused trouble when whiskey and frivolity led church members astray, as with one couple a Kentucky Methodist church expelled for "Disorderly Conduct." Another man was "Excluded from this Church for Fighting & Drinking to Excess."

The Ohio Country

White settlement moved more slowly north of the Ohio River, partly because the U.S. government kept tighter control in the Northwest Territory, but more because Native Americans resisted strongly. Delawares, Shawnees, Iroquois, and many others refused to cede lands that the federal government wanted to sell to land-hungry easterners. In the 1780s, the United States obtained a series of cessions, but from just some of the people who owned the land. Indians who were not party to the agreements rejected them. Forming a confederacy to withstand U.S. invasion, Ohio Indians attacked whites who risked settling in the region. This northern Indian confederacy allied with the Chickamaugas and Creeks in the south, establishing a pan-Indian defensive that gained help from the Spanish in the south and the British in the north. At one meeting in 1787, the Native Americans agreed to merge their forces "for a general defense against all Invaders of Indian rights."

In the early 1790s, President Washington challenged the northern confederacy by sending two expeditions, both of them unsuccessful. Arthur St. Clair, governor of the Northwest Territory, led the second invasion in 1791, in which 600 of his 1,400 men died. Washington believed that the disaster resulted from the use of militia, so instructed General Anthony Wayne to raise 5,000 regulars. Wayne trained the troops for two years, then on August 20, 1794, defeated the Native Americans decisively at the Battle of Fallen Timbers. Though the British had customarily given aid to the Ohio tribes, this time they closed the gates to Fort Miami, denying refuge to the retreating Indians. A year later, when it became clear to the Native Americans that their alliance with the British had ended, they signed the Treaty of Greenville ceding to the United States most of the land in present-day Ohio.

The Whiskey Rebellion

In 1794, the Washington administration also sent troops against western Pennsylvania farmers, who since 1791 had resisted the whiskey tax. Washington and Hamilton decided to take advantage of the unrest to demonstrate the power of the new central government. Farmers throughout the west resented the tax on spirits, for distilling whiskey from grain made their produce less bulky, thus less expensive to transport to

Signatures of Native Americans on the Treaty of Greenville, 1795. Indian leaders commonly used symbols such as diagrams of animals to sign deeds and treaties.
National Archives

eastern markets. They also used the whiskey instead of cash and consumed a good portion of it themselves. In much of the trans-Appalachian region, officials failed to collect the excise at all.

The administration found willing officials in western Pennsylvania, however, and there proceeded to enforce the law. The Pittsburgh area farmers held protest meetings and refused cooperation with the collectors. They tarred and feathered collaborators, burned barns, and destroyed stills of people who paid the tax. The farmers charged that the tax favored large distillers and was collected unevenly. Rebels left notes signed "Tom the Tinker" to warn distillers who registered for the tax that their stills would be "fixed" (that is, ruined) unless they joined the revolt. The insurgents understood their fight as a struggle for "the virtuous principles of republican liberty." But the whiskey tax was only one of the farmers' complaints, which included failure to open up the Ohio country and removal of Spanish trade restrictions on the Mississippi.

Indian Treaty of Greenville, *1795, by an unknown artist.*
Following General Anthony Wayne's victory at the Battle of
Fallen Timbers, the Miami leader Little Turtle and other
Indians signed the treaty, temporarily ending their military
resistance to white settlement in the Northwest Territory.
Chicago Historical Society, #P&S 1914.1

California Indians are lined up at the Spanish mission in
Carmel to greet French visitors.
Courtesy of the Bancroft Library, University of California, Berkeley

Events came to a climax in July 1794. When officials continued to collect the tax and arrest resisters, 500 men surrounded the excise inspector's home, exchanged gunfire killing several people, and burned the house. The official and his family escaped. In the days that followed, rebels set more buildings on fire, raised liberty poles, attacked collectors, and rumored secession. The uprising spread to central Pennsylvania, Virginia, Maryland, and Ohio. Washington sent commissioners to obtain oaths of submission, but when the insurrection continued, he called up 13,000 eastern militia, who marched west with the president briefly in command. By the time the soldiers reached western Pennsylvania, the revolt was over, as the show of force intimidated the rebels. The administration had demonstrated that armed resistance to federal policies would not be tolerated.

The Spanish Frontier

As settlers from the United States migrated across the Appalachians and traders extended their commercial networks, they came into contact with the Spanish. The 1790s marked the high point of Spain's control in North America, its provinces extending from East Florida across the Gulf Coast to Louisiana, Texas, New Mexico, and California. The Spanish govern-

ment continued to view these borderlands of their empire as a buffer against American and British designs on Mexican silver. Spanish officials recognized the phenomenal population growth of the United States. One warned that Americans were "advancing and multiplying . . . with a prodigious rapidity," while another took a dim view of the American frontier people, whom he considered "nomadic like Arabs and . . . distinguished from savages only in their color, language, and the superiority of their depraved cunning and untrustworthiness."

Nevertheless, the Spanish decided to open their territory to Americans, hoping to bolster the small settler populations. Spain offered free land in the Floridas and Louisiana, and even changed official policy to allow Protestants to keep their religion as long as they took an oath of allegiance to the Crown and had their children baptized Catholic. Because Spain could not provide desired consumer goods or adequate markets, it also relaxed mercantilist restraints, allowing plantation owners in the borderlands to sell their sugar, cotton, and indigo in the United States. These new immigration and economic policies facilitated later U.S. acquisition of the Floridas and Louisiana. Jefferson said prophetically, in 1791, that Spain had provided "the means of delivering to us peaceably, what may otherwise cost us a war."

Farther west, in New Mexico, the Spanish finally achieved peace with the Comanches and Apaches. Abandoning the attempt to make them subjects of the Crown, Spain signed a treaty recognizing their sovereignty. The Indians had forced the Spanish to set aside

Dances held by Native Americans for Alejandro Malaspina at Nootka Sound, 1791. Drawing probably by Tomás de Suria.
Courtesy, Museo Naval, Madrid and Robin Inglis

the goal of complete domination and to provide such gifts as guns, ammunition, clothing, mirrors, paint, tobacco, and sugar. Still, the Spanish sent prisoners of war to Cuba as forced laborers and settled other Apaches on reservations called *establecimientos de paz,* or peace establishments. Many Apaches refused to live on the reservations, however, steadfastly maintaining their independence. But the fighting stopped, making Texas, New Mexico, and Arizona safer for travel and economic development. Finally, settlers could journey directly between San Antonio, Santa Fe, and Tucson without fear of attack.

For several decades, fearing Russian and British incursions along the Pacific coast, Spain had expanded settlement in California. The government sent missionaries and soldiers north from Baja California in 1769 to set up missions and presidios along the coast from San Diego to San Francisco. José de Gálvez organized the effort, enlisting Junípero Serra, a zealous Franciscan priest, to establish the missions. Though fewer than 1,000 Hispanics lived in California by 1790, the missions controlled most of the arable land along the Pacific. With military force and by conversion, they put thousands of California Indians to work on mission lands. Before Spanish colonization, the re-

gion's native people possessed neither firearms nor horses; they lived in small villages with neither elaborate political structures nor much experience with war. In the earliest years after Spanish settlement, the natives lacked unity to avenge the crimes of Spanish soldiers or to refuse to serve as agricultural laborers. In 1775, however, one group burned the San Diego mission, followed by rebellions of other coastal Indians.

As elsewhere in North America, the California Indians declined sharply in population after contact with Europeans. People who went to work in the missions lived an average of ten to twelve years; their high death rate probably resulted from close quarters and exposure to disease. According to one missionary, "they live well free but as soon as we reduce them to a Christian and community life . . . they fatten, sicken, and die." The native population in the mission region along the Pacific coast declined from approximately 60,000 in 1769 to 35,000 at the end of the century.

The Spanish also looked to the Pacific Northwest, which they investigated in 1774, four years earlier than the British explorer Captain James Cook. After Cook publicized the trade for sea otter furs, however, British and American merchants sailed to Nootka Sound, at Vancouver Island, challenging the

Spanish claim to the area north of San Francisco. The traders made huge profits by purchasing the silky black otter pelts from the Tlingit, Haida, Nootka, and Chinook peoples, to sell in China for tea, porcelain, and silk. The Indians had formerly hunted the sea otter on a limited basis for fine clothing and food. When the Spanish seized two British ships, England threatened war. Spain signed the Nootka Convention (1790), yielding its sole claim to the Pacific Northwest and returning the confiscated vessels. Over the next several years, the two countries tried but failed to negotiate a northern boundary of California. Of more concern to Spain, Great Britain, and the United States during the 1790s was the outbreak of war in Europe and the Atlantic, in the wake of revolution in France.

FOREIGN ENTANGLEMENTS

In 1789, the United States rejoiced when the French abolished noble privileges and formed a constitutional monarchy. Americans believed that France had followed their example, for during the first phase of the French Revolution, its moderate leaders included friends of the United States, notably the Revolutionary War hero, the Marquis de Lafayette. In 1792, however, radicals took control and executed King Louis XVI the next year. The international situation became perilous when the French Republic declared war on Britain and Spain. The king's execution and thousands of deaths by guillotine during the second phase of the revolution cost the French support in the United States, particularly among Federalists, who feared the consequences of ordinary people, "the mob," taking power. Republicans, while not defending the excesses, remained sympathetic toward France because they hated monarchical Britain more.

Neutrality

The European war presented Americans with a tricky situation, for they had connections with both France and Britain that were potentially dangerous. The U.S.-France commercial and military alliance of 1778 remained in force. While it did not require the United States to enter the war, the French Republic expected favorable trade policies and informal military assistance. Though Secretary of State Jefferson favored France and despised Britain, he agreed that neutrality was essential. American commerce was closely tied with Britain, whose navy could sweep U.S. ships from the sea.

Hamilton was particularly concerned that British imports remain high because tariffs paid the lion's share of interest on the national debt. With all of this in mind, President Washington made the only reasonable decision, issuing his Proclamation of Neutrality in April 1793. The message warned citizens to avoid hostile acts against either side, including sale of weapons and privateering. Washington sought the belligerents' recognition of the U.S. right to trade in nonmilitary goods.

American neutrality quickly hit shoals with the activities of Edmond Genêt, the new minister from France. Citizen Genêt, as he was called in republican France, had arrived in Charleston several weeks before Washington proclaimed neutrality. He enlisted American mercenaries to man privateers and obtained ships to sail under the French flag against British shipping. The privateers, with largely American crews, seized British vessels, taking them to U.S. ports. There the French consuls sold the ships and their cargoes, paying the mercenaries with part of the proceeds. The French claimed this right under the 1778 alliance. The Washington administration, fearful of British reprisals and outraged by this violation of U.S. sovereignty, closed the ports to Genêt's privateers and requested his recall. The government prohibited foreign belligerents from arming vessels in U.S. ports and recruiting U.S. citizens in American territory; set the limit of U.S. territorial waters at three miles; and forbade foreign consuls from holding admiralty courts in U.S. cities to auction confiscated ships.

The Washington administration had greater success protecting the nation's sovereignty from French designs than from those of the British. The American republic's weakness became all too clear when the Royal Navy began impressing—recruiting by force—U.S. citizens from merchant ships. Then, in November 1793, the British ordered a total blockade of the French West Indies. Any ship intending to trade there would be confiscated. The blockade was timed to coincide with their invasion of St. Domingue, or Haiti, where enslaved blacks had risen up against their French masters in 1791. The British kept the blockade a secret until after U.S. ships headed for the Caribbean. Over the winter, their navy seized more than 250 American vessels, whether they were aimed for French, British, or neutral ports. The British impounded ships, cargoes, and even the sailors' possessions. Because international correspondence was so slow, Washington received no intelligence of the blockade and confiscations until March 1794.

The United States and Britain seemed headed for war. Exacerbating the crisis was the British refusal to vacate their forts and their aid to Native Americans in the Ohio country. Britain also helped Native Americans resist settlement in the west. In fact, in 1794 the governor of Canada, Lord Dorchester, told a group of Indians that they could expect war to break out between the United States and Britain within a year. With British victory, Dorchester promised, the Native Americans could reclaim the lands they had lost north of the Ohio River.

The Jay Treaty

The crisis abated when the British ended their total blockade of the French islands, now permitting Americans to trade foodstuffs and consumer goods but not war material. Rather than take retaliatory action, the president sent John Jay, chief justice of the Supreme Court, as special envoy to England. Jay's instructions were to convince the British to evacuate their forts in the west, pay for African American slaves who had left with their army after the Revolution, end impressment, open the British West Indies trade to American ships, and compensate recent shipping losses in the Caribbean.

Jay was unable to secure compensation for slaves, convince the British to stop impressment, or obtain recognition of all the neutral rights that Americans demanded. He did gain British withdrawal from the western forts by June 1, 1796, payment for confiscated ships in the Caribbean, and the opening of trade in the British West Indies to American vessels of 70 tons or less. He agreed, however, that American shippers would not export from the United States certain tropical products, including cotton, molasses, sugar, coffee, and cocoa, and that Americans would repay British creditors for prerevolutionary debts.

Washington received Jay's treaty in March 1795, keeping its contents secret until the Senate debate in June. Twenty Federalist senators voted to ratify while ten Republicans refused. The Federalists struck the provision forbidding U.S. merchants from exporting tropical crops. If they had agreed to this section, American trade would have faced a serious obstacle, particularly with the development of cotton. Thus, the Senate approved the treaty by exactly the two-thirds needed and sent it to the president, who signed the treaty as amended.

When the Jay Treaty became public, Republicans flew into a rage. Their opposition in large part was political: they abhorred *any* treaty with the British and privately bemoaned Jay's success on important issues. Publicly, they complained about his failures on impressment, neutral rights, and compensation for slaves. The Jay Treaty greatly hastened the growth of political parties, as Republicans gained support from

Dramatizing the intense party rivalries of the 1790s, this pro-Federalist cartoon shows President Washington leading troops against French radicals, as Thomas Jefferson and Citizen Genêt try to hold him back. The dog graphically shows its disapproval of a Republican newspaper.
Collection of The New York Historical Society

former Federalists, particularly in the south. While Hamilton defended the treaty, opponents roared that it surrendered American independence to the former imperial tyrant. John Jay was burned in effigy; mass meetings, petitions, and demonstrations protested the treaty throughout the country.

By spring 1796, however, the tumolt was over, in part because news arrived that Thomas Pinckney had concluded an agreement with Spain the previous October. The Treaty of San Lorenzo opened the Mississippi River to free navigation, allowed Americans to use the port of New Orleans without charge, and fixed the boundary between the United States and West Florida at the 31st parallel as specified in the Treaty of Paris.

Washington Retires

With the threat of war temporarily eased, the west open for settlement and trade, and a flourishing economy, the success of the republic seemed more certain. General Wayne's defeat of the Ohio Indians, the Jay Treaty, and Pinckney's diplomatic success gave westerners—and westward-looking Americans—resolution of their major problems: cession of lands in Ohio, removal of the British from the forts, free access to the Mississippi, and the right of deposit at New Orleans. Eastern merchants and farmers benefited from the lifting of trade restrictions in the British West Indies. Wartime demand for provisions in Europe and the Caribbean drove up farm prices and stimulated production. By the end of the century, American exports and shipping profits were almost five times their 1793 level. As a major neutral maritime nation, the United States assumed a greater place in world trade. With increased transportation profits, merchants invested more heavily in ships. The shipbuilding boom created demand for lumber, rope, and other supplies; wages for craftsmen and laborers rose, though so did the cost of living. Americans took advantage of their newfound prosperity to buy British imports, which in turn paid tariff income toward the national debt. Hamilton's funding plan was a success—the nation's credit was firm—despite resistance to the whiskey tax.

As the election of 1796 approached, George Washington announced his retirement, raising the question of his successor. The president had served two terms, his health had declined, and the battle over the Jay Treaty left him exhausted and angry. In his Farewell Address, Washington surveyed the accomplishments of his administration and gave the nation advice. The United States should avoid as much as possible becoming entwined in international affairs, he counseled. The European war demonstrated how perilous such involvement could be and how difficult it was to escape. "The great rule of conduct for us in regard to foreign nations is, in extending our commercial relations to have with them as little *political* connection as possible," Washington urged. His other major argument concerned factions. The outgoing president warned against parties based on sectional differences—North against South or East against West. And he cautioned against parties more generally, that the "disorders and miseries which result [from factionalism] gradually incline the minds of men to seek security and repose in the absolute power of an individual." In lamenting "the spirit of party," Washington blamed the Republicans for failing to support his administration. They had undercut his authority and the ideal of a consensual republic.

THE ADAMS PRESIDENCY

Though Washington's successors appreciated the wisdom of his "great rule" of foreign policy, they had less enthusiasm for his advice on factions. In 1796, the parties yet lacked full-scale national organization, and candidates did not campaign. But the contest was very much alive, as Federalists supported the policies of Hamilton and Washington, while Republicans opposed them.

Election of 1796

In the third presidential election under the Constitution, both parties had sufficient cohesion to offer national tickets: the Federalist candidates were John Adams for president and Thomas Pinckney for vice president; the Republicans put up Thomas Jefferson for president and Aaron Burr, a senator from New York, for the second spot. The results of the electoral college vote were close: Adams 71, Jefferson 68, Pinckney 59, Burr 30, and a number of other candidates totalling 48. As specified by the Constitution, Adams became president and Jefferson, vice president. Americans quickly realized the problem of this procedure for electing the executive, as the president represented one party and the vice president the other. In any event, the Federalists kept control of the presidency, though barely, and they increased their votes in Congress by a small margin, to 64 Federalists versus 53 Republicans.

For many Americans, John Adams possessed credentials from service in the Revolution and the new republic that made him a worthy heir to Washington. He had contributed to prerevolutionary agitation in Boston, served as a delegate to the Continental Congress, promoted the Continental navy, and assisted Jefferson in drafting the Declaration of Independence. He had helped negotiate the 1783 Treaty of Paris, and in 1785, became the first U.S. minister to Great Britain. While Adams was a skilled diplomat, an avid student of government, and entirely honest, he lacked Washington's charisma, military bearing, and understanding of executive leadership. As a lawyer, Adams's style was more intellectual and independent. He preferred to make decisions on his own, without consulting the cabinet or congressional leaders.

Like Washington, Adams denounced parties. He began his administration with the hope, soon abandoned, that he might bridge the gulf between Federalists and Republicans. Jefferson rebuffed the chief executive's peace overture and directed the Republican opposition from his post as vice president. After the first few days of the Adams administration, the president and vice president never consulted one another.

"Quasi-War" with France

The second president inherited an international situation that had worsened by the time he assumed office in March 1797. The French, now ruled by a dictatorial executive board called the Directory, declared that the Jay Treaty revoked the 1778 alliance. They confiscated American merchant ships and cut off diplomatic rela-

*P*ICTURING THE PAST ✦ POLITICS & DIPLOMACY

JOHN ADAMS

Independence National Historical Park

Elected the second president of the United States in 1796, Adams was the sole non-Virginian and the only president to serve a single term among the first five chief executives. He was also the only president whose son (John Quincy Adams) served in the nation's highest elected office until George W. Bush (son of George H. Bush) became president in 2001.

Both the presidential elections of 1796 and 1800 between John Adams and Thomas Jefferson were close. While each had contributed mightily to gaining independence from Great Britain and establishing the new nation, neither served as the symbol of national unity as had George Washington in 1789. Party spirit had grown during the 1790s, undermining even Washington's position. Differences between Adams and Jefferson became public in 1791, despite their earlier long-term collaboration. After both men had served as president, they renewed their correspondence and friendship. They died on the same day, July 4, 1826, the fiftieth anniversary of independence.

tions. Once again, the United States seemed destined for war.

Called by Adams into special session in May 1797, Congress authorized the mobilization of 80,000 militia, completion of three war vessels, and fortification of harbors. Adams also appointed a commission of three men to negotiate with France: John Marshall of Virginia, Elbridge Gerry of Massachusetts, and Charles Cotesworth Pinckney of South Carolina. Their assignment was to prevent war, stop the confiscation of American ships carrying nonmilitary cargoes, and obtain compensation for recent losses. In France, the commission corresponded with French Foreign Minister Talleyrand through three intermediaries, who later became known to the American public as X, Y, and Z. The French agents told the commissioners that, like other petitioners to the Directory, they must pay a bribe even to be heard. The amount specified in this case was $250,000. The Directory also required an

apology from Adams for criticizing France, a huge loan, and assumption by the U.S. government of any unpaid debts owed by France to American citizens. The commission refused these conditions and returned home. Their experience became known as the XYZ Affair.

In spring 1798, Adams received delayed correspondence that his envoys had been rebuffed. When he called for additional troops and warships, Congress responded by giving him more than he requested. Jefferson denounced the military buildup as "insane"; Republicans demanded to see evidence of France's treachery. When Adams made the commission's dispatches public, war fever engulfed the nation. The cry in the 1798 congressional elections became, "Millions for defense, but not a cent for tribute." Two patriotic songs "Adams for Liberty" and "Hail Columbia" were widely sung, the latter serving as the unofficial national anthem. Congress expanded the regular army

"Cinque-têtes," or the Paris Monster, an American cartoon showing the United States negotiators Elbridge Gerry, John Marshall, and Charles Cotesworth Pinckney refusing the demands for money of the French Directory (the five-headed monster).
This item is reproduced by permission of the Huntington Library, San Marine, California

The Constellation *Capturing the* Insurgente, *February 9, 1799. In the Quasi-War, the U.S. Navy, with British help, quickly outperformed the French.*
Courtesy, Peabody Essex Museum, Salem, MA

and war fleet, established the Department of the Navy, authorized naval vessels to protect American merchant ships, suspended commerce with France, and revoked the French alliance. George Washington assumed command of the army, with Alexander Hamilton in charge of field operations. To pay for all of this, Congress levied a direct tax of $2 million on dwelling houses, land, and slaves.

Without declaring war, the United States engaged France in hostilities from 1798 to 1800. In what was known as the Quasi-War, the U.S. Navy dominated the French, defeating their warships and sinking privateers. The British navy helped by protecting U.S. carriers. While some congressmen feared a French invasion and thereby justified further military preparations, French naval losses to Great Britain and the United States quickly removed that threat.

The Alien and Sedition Acts

The Federalists rode the crest of patriotism in 1798, using their majority in Congress to pass a series of acts that limited the rights of immigrants and critics of the administration. Congressional sponsors argued that the laws were necessary wartime measures. Their practical purpose, however, was to destroy the Republicans by undermining popular support and closing newspapers. The Federalists tried to take advantage of the Quasi-War to link their opponents with the enemy. This strategy worked in the short term, as the pro-French Republicans lost votes in the 1798 congressional election, but proved suicidal for Adams's party after the fear of invasion had passed.

The Federalist design resulted in four restrictive laws. The Naturalization Act of 1798 lengthened the period of residence needed for citizenship from five to fourteen years. The legislation was intended to stop the flow of Irish immigrants who, because they were anti-British and pro-French, swelled the number of Republican voters. The Alien Enemies Act established procedures in the event of declared war or invasion for jailing and deporting citizens of the enemy nation who were considered likely to spy or commit sabotage. The Alien Act, which had a term of two years, allowed the president to deport any non–U.S. citizens "he shall judge dangerous to the peace and safety of the United States, or shall have reasonable grounds to suspect are concerned in any treasonable or secret machinations against the government thereof." Like the Naturalization Act, this law potentially threatened Irish immigrants, but Adams refrained from using it.

The Federalists did enforce the fourth law, the Sedition Act, with serious results. Its term lasted until March 3, 1801, the day before the next president would be inaugurated. Thus the Federalists ensured that if the next chief executive were a Republican, he would not be able to retaliate without obtaining a new statute. In vague language, the Sedition Act made it illegal for "any persons [to] unlawfully combine or conspire together, with intent to oppose any measure or measures of the government of the United States" or to interfere with the execution of a law. Nor could a person "write, print, utter or publish . . . any false, scandalous and malicious writing or writings against the government of the United States, or either house of the Congress . . . or the President." In effect, this law permitted imprisonment and fines for criticizing the government. It was an obvious infringement upon freedom of speech and freedom of the press.

Nevertheless, the administration enforced the law. Adams believed that the Sedition Act was constitutional, that people who censured his policies threatened the future of the republic. The prime targets for prosecution were Republican newspapers, including the Philadelphia *Aurora*, edited by Benjamin Franklin's grandson, Benjamin Bache, who was one of Adams's most powerful critics. The official authorized to administer the act was Secretary of State Timothy Pickering, a staunch Federalist, who methodically reviewed the Republican papers for actionable offenses. He even ordered an inquiry into the private correspondence of a Republican congressman who reputedly called Adams a traitor; in this case, however, the investigation was dropped. Under the law, the Federalists indicted and tried at least seventeen people for sedition. They timed cases to reach court in the fall of 1799 or the following spring, with the goal of silencing the Republican press during the 1800 election. Some papers folded and others closed temporarily while their editors were imprisoned. All but one of the cases were prosecuted in New England and the Middle Atlantic states, where the Federalists controlled the courts and could pack juries.

The Republican Opposition Grows

Passage of the Alien and Sedition Acts and the jailing of Republican spokesmen shifted the political winds. In late 1798, the Kentucky and Virginia legislatures approved resolutions that protested the Alien and Sedition Acts on the grounds that they were unconstitutional. The Kentucky and Virginia Resolutions, drafted anonymously by Thomas Jefferson and James Madison, respectively, argued that these laws violated the First Amendment and granted powers to the national government not delegated by the Constitution. The Virginia assembly resolved that "in case of a deliberate, palpable, and dangerous exercise of other powers, not granted by the [Constitution], the states . . . have the right, and are in duty bound, to interpose, for arresting the progress of the evil." Virginia and Kentucky sent their resolutions to other legislatures, none of which agreed that states could declare a federal law unconstitutional. Rhode Island, for example, responded that the federal courts held the power to determine constitutionality; "that for any state legislature to assume that authority would be . . . Hazarding an interruption of the peace of the states by civil discord, in case of a diversity of opinions among the state legislatures." Nevertheless, the resolutions contributed toward a theory of "nullification," the idea that a state had the right to veto a federal law it considered unconstitutional. This theory was based upon the strict interpretation of the Constitution that denied, as in the controversy over the national bank, implied powers to the central government.

With the Alien and Sedition Acts, the Federalists made a strategic error. Where formerly the Republicans could be branded as a faction creating animosity and disunity, they now became legitimate defenders of revolutionary principles. The Republican party justified its opposition by warning that the Federalists were on the road to tyranny. The Sedition Act, the Virginia Resolutions argued, impeded free investigation of the actions of government officials and "free communication among the people thereon, which has ever been justly deemed the only effectual guardian of every other right."

The administration fanned the flames of indignation with its heavy-handed reaction to a tax rebellion among German Americans in eastern Pennsylvania, a group who had previously favored the Federalists or stayed out of politics entirely. The Republicans took advantage of the rural Pennsylvanians' aversion to the 1798 federal property tax to win their votes in the congressional election. They circulated petitions against the tax, the defense buildup, and the Alien and Sedition laws, petitions that Congress ignored. By early 1799, the people of Northampton and Bucks counties held public meetings and stopped tax assessors from doing their work. In March, after the U.S. marshal jailed eighteen suspected tax resisters in Bethlehem's Sun Tavern, John Fries, a fifty-year-old auctioneer of upper Bucks County, led a band of 140 armed men to release the prisoners.

The Fries Rebellion ended quickly, as the rebels considered the magnitude of their offense. Fries announced that he would pay the tax and would even welcome the assessor to his house for dinner. Nevertheless, the president decided to make an example of the episode. He dispatched troops that failed to march until almost four weeks after the resistance had ceased. The army descended upon the countryside, entering houses and arresting sixty men. One army officer wrote "that every hour's experience confirms me more and more that this expedition was not only unnecessary, but violently absurd." Contrary to the Judiciary Act of

1789, the prisoners were taken to Philadelphia for trial. Fries and two others were found guilty of treason by a Federalist court and sentenced to hang, but were subsequently pardoned by the president. The Republicans added the administration's unwarranted use of force to their arsenal of charges against the Federalists.

CONCLUSION

George Washington had warned in his Farewell Address that "the spirit of Party . . . agitates the Community with ill founded jealousies and false alarms, kindles the animosity of one part against another, foments occasionally riot and insurrection. It opens the door to foreign influence and corruption. . . ." He invoked the ideal of consensual community, challenging his fellow citizens to work together for the good of their country. The flaw of this conception was that Americans could not agree on which policies were best for everyone. The interests of farmers, merchants, and artisans, of residents of the north, south, and west, often diverged. The Federalist and Republican parties grew out of different visions of the nation's future. During the 1790s, the Federalists retained control of the central government, confident that their vision was correct. They denounced parties, identifying their government with the republic as a whole. When they tried to eliminate factions by silencing their adversaries with the Sedition Act, ironically they legitimized the party system in the eyes of many Americans.

Recommended Readings

Anderson, Margo J. *The American Census: A Social History* (1988). A very good source on the first federal census of 1790.

Cayton, Andrew R. L., and Teute, Fredrika J., eds. *Contact Points: American Frontiers from the Mohawk Valley to the Mississippi, 1750–1830* (1998). Essays about Indian-white relations in the backcountry from the prerevolutionary period through the early republic.

Cochran, Thomas C. *Frontiers of Change: Early Industrialism in America* (1981). A good introduction to industrialization in the early republic.

Elkins, Stanley, and McKitrick, Eric. *The Age of Federalism* (1993). Detailed narrative of the Washington and Adams administrations.

McCullough, David. *John Adams* (2001). An excellent biography of the second president.

McGaw, Judith A., ed. *Early American Technology: Making and Doing Things from the Colonial Era to 1850* (1994). Original essays on technology from agriculture to turnpikes.

North, Douglass C. *The Economic Growth of the United States 1790–1860* (1966). Includes a useful analysis of U.S. trade amid international conflict.

Onuf, Peter S., ed. *Jeffersonian Legacies* (1993). Wide ranging essays on Thomas Jefferson's character and politics.

Slaughter, Thomas P. *The Whiskey Rebellion: Frontier Epilogue to the American Revolution* (1986). An excellent book on the struggle between Alexander Hamilton and western Pennsylvania farmers over excise taxes.

White, Richard. *The Middle Ground: Indians, Empires, and Republics in the Great Lakes Region, 1650–1815* (1991). Influential study of Indian-white relations from New France through the War of 1812.

American Journey Online and InfoTrac College Edition

Visit the source collections at http://ajaccess.wadsworth.com and infotrac.thomsonlearning.com and use the Search function with the following key terms to explore documents, images, audio and video clips, articles, and commentary related to the material in this chapter.

George Washington	Alexander Hamilton
John Adams	Abigail Adams
Eli Whitney	Whiskey Rebellion
XYZ Affair	

Additional resources, exercises, and Internet links related to this chapter are available on the American Passages Web site: http://history.wadsworth.com/passages2e

8 THE NEW REPUBLIC FACES A NEW CENTURY 1800–1815

RELIGION IN AMERICAN SOCIETY

AFRICAN AMERICANS

JEFFERSON'S REPUBLIC

THE LOUISIANA PURCHASE

MORE FOREIGN ENTANGLEMENTS

MADISON AND THE WAR OF 1812

Methodist Camp Meeting, *engraving by E. Clay. During the Second Great Awakening, itinerant preachers held outdoor revivals that often lasted for several days.* Collection of the New York Historical Society

Americans confronted the nineteenth century with a variety of fears. For the Federalists, the growing Republican opposition warned that the evils of democracy and anarchy stood ready to take control. For the Republicans, the Alien and Sedition Acts and Federalist repression of the whiskey rebels and John Fries underscored the need for change. Both parties, still members of the revolutionary generation, thought in terms of the ideals for which they had fought against the British. They also measured events against what was transpiring elsewhere in the world. By 1800, the French Revolution and Napoleon Bonaparte's rise to power dismayed Americans. The never-ending European war threatened to involve the United States for twenty years, and finally did in 1812. The revolt by slaves in the French West Indies horrified southern slave owners.

Though Thomas Jefferson's presidency proved to be less revolutionary than many Federalists expected, the new century brought indelible changes to American politics and society. The Federalist party shriveled and died, the Louisiana Purchase expanded the nation's territory to the Rocky Mountains and beyond, slavery became more firmly embedded in the southern economy, and the republic fought once more against Great Britain. The Second Great Awakening, the series of religious revivals that began in the late 1790s and gained steam after the turn of the century, influenced the ways in which many people interpreted these events.

CHRONOLOGY

1800 Washington, D.C., becomes national capital • Gabriel's rebellion • Convention of 1800 with France • Jefferson's election as president • Rise of Handsome Lake as a Seneca prophet

1801 Adams's "midnight appointments" • John Marshall becomes chief justice • Tripolitan War • Cane Ridge, Kentucky, camp meeting

1802 Judiciary Act of 1801 repealed

1803 *Marbury v. Madison* case • Great Britain and France resume war • Louisiana Purchase

1804 Lewis and Clark expedition departs from St. Louis • Aaron Burr kills Alexander Hamilton • Twelfth Amendment ratified • Haiti founded • Reelection of Jefferson as president

1805 *Essex* decision in Britain

1806 Non-Importation Act

1807 Burr tried for treason • *Leopard-Chesapeake* affair • Embargo Act

1808 Federal ban on importation of slaves • Madison elected as president

1809–1811 Tecumseh organizes pan-Indian resistance to land cessions

1809 Giles's Enforcement Act • Embargo repealed; replaced with Non-Intercourse Act • Treaty of Fort Wayne

1810 Annexation of West Florida

1811 Charter of national bank expires • Battle of Tippecanoe

1812 U.S. declares war on Great Britain • Hull surrenders Detroit • Madison elected to second term

1813 Perry defeats British navy on Lake Erie • Battle of the Thames

1814 Battle of Horseshoe Bend • British burn public buildings in Washington, D.C. • Americans repel invasion on Lake Champlain • Hartford Convention • Treaty of Ghent

RELIGION IN AMERICAN SOCIETY

During the first decade of the nineteenth century, religion absorbed the energies of many different groups: frontier settlers and Native Americans caught up in revivals, organizations to provide welfare relief in towns and cities, new sects like the Shakers, and free African Americans who built separate churches as the cornerstone of their communities. Many people believed that renewed emphasis on religion would transform the nation through individual faith and communal action.

The Second Great Awakening

As the century began, people throughout the country sought spiritual renewal. Among New England Congregationalists, the revivals spread from one town to another between 1797 and 1801. The national Methodist conference of 1800 held in Baltimore witnessed an outpouring of religious fervor. These flames heralded a series of revivals—the Second Great Awakening—which lasted into the 1830s. In accepting the message of revival, large numbers of Americans embraced evangelicalism—the belief that they must take their message of salvation to others. They expected to create a more godly nation through conversion and good works.

In particular, eastern clergy worried that people on the frontier, with few churches, would let sin take control of their lives. As Americans streamed west across the Appalachians, by 1810, Ohio had 230,000 settlers, Kentucky and Tennessee had 668,000, and the Mississippi and Louisiana territories had 117,000. Evangelical ministers feared for the nation because so many westerners were unchurched. The clerics expressed their dread in terms of millennialism, the belief that the millennium—Christ's second coming—was at hand, as foretold in Revelation, the last book of the Bible. Pastors urged their congregations to prepare for the millennium by supporting missionary efforts in the West. They believed that Americans throughout the country must embrace Christianity and convert Native Americans and the people of other lands.

Circuit preachers and missionaries traveled throughout the frontier; the churches they started were often the first social organizations in new communities. The great western revivals of 1800–1815, which built upon this work, began when several Presbyterians summoned the first camp meeting, a religious gathering held outside over the course of several days. People came together, miles from their homes, to hear revivalist preachers. The most famous of the early camp meetings took place in August 1801, at Cane Ridge, Kentucky, where Presbyterian, Methodist, and Baptist clergy preached for about a week to a throng numbering about 20,000. From wagons and crude tents, the crowds listened to the spiritual message that Jesus Christ could save all people from their sins. People reacted emotionally and physically to this message, some jerking their heads or entire bodies, others falling to the ground in a faint.

Reminiscent of the Great Awakening in the South during the 1750s and 1760s, the camp meetings spread through Kentucky, Tennessee, and southern Ohio, gathering new congregations. The Methodist and Baptist churches, which placed less importance on the fine points of religious doctrine and a well-educated clergy than did the Presbyterians, benefited most from the revivals. The Methodists and Baptists saw extraordinary growth among ordinary people. As one minister wrote, "the illiterate Methodist preachers actually set the world on fire, (the American world at least) while [pastors of other denominations] were lighting their matches!"

Religion was important to black Americans, whether they remained enslaved or had achieved freedom. In the South, African Americans responded enthusiastically to revivalist preachers. The Methodists and Baptists welcomed free and enslaved blacks into their congregations as equals in spirit though not in governing the church. In hostile northern cities, free black communities depended upon separate churches for leadership and communal fellowship.

Growth of Sects

The period around 1800 witnessed the expansion of several dissenting sects: the Shakers, the Society of the Public Universal Friend, and the Universalists. They are called sects, rather than denominations, because they were new and fairly small. They held distinctive beliefs that set them apart from mainstream religions, yet had a significant influence on intellectual and social movements of their times.

The Shakers, whose official name was the United Society of Believers in Christ's Second Coming (the Millennial church), came to America in 1774, when Mother Ann Lee arrived from Britain with eight disciples. They left England to escape mob attacks and imprisonment. The group grew slowly at first, but expanded after Lee's death in 1784, as they reaped followers from revivals, especially Baptists. The sect offered an avenue for people who had been spiritually

The Shakers of New Lebanon—Religious Exercises in the Dining Room. *In religious worship, Shakers abandoned their strict, sex-segregated discipline.*
North Wind Picture Archives

reborn in the Awakening and sought a distinctive way to represent that rebirth in their lives.

From visions, Mother Lee believed that she embodied Christ's Second Coming, that the millennium had already arrived. As Christ had appeared as a man, and Lee (called Mother of the New Creation) came as a woman, God had both male and female elements. The Shakers believed in salvation by confession of sin, equality regardless of sex or race, opposition to slavery and war, and assistance to the poor. They abstained from sexual relations. In Shaker communities, which by 1809 existed from Maine to Kentucky, men and women ate, slept, and worked separately. They followed a strict discipline and aspired to economic self-sufficiency. Shakers sat on straight-backed chairs, cut their food into square pieces, and walked along paths laid out in right angles. But in religious worship, they abandoned this right-angle order. In a large open space without pulpit or pews, worshippers danced, shouted, and sang. The Shakers influenced other groups to organize communal, utopian experiments during the years after 1815.

A similar but smaller sect was the Society of the Public Universal Friend, founded by Jemima Wilkinson of Rhode Island. Disowned by Quakers in 1776 for joining the Baptists, Wilkinson became ill, believed that she died, and then returned to life as the Public Universal Friend. Her mission was to convince others to repent their sins and prepare for the millennium. Like Mother Lee, Wilkinson preached celibacy, peace, and opposition to slavery. She traveled sidesaddle on horseback, attracting a coterie of believers in New England and Pennsylvania. As one

convert said, Wilkinson was "the Messenger of Peace . . . Travelling far & wide to spread the glad tidings & news of Salvation to a lost and perishing & dying World who have all gone astray like Lost Sheep." In 1788, upon gathering over 200 Universal Friends, she organized a community called Jerusalem in western New York. The Universal Friends neither organized a communal economy like the Shakers nor continued to seek new members. Nevertheless, the community survived well past Wilkinson's death in 1819.

Another sect, the Universalists, rejected the Calvinist belief that only a minority of people, the elect, could attain salvation. They preached that "it is the purpose of God, through the grace revealed in our Lord Jesus Christ, to save every member of the human race from sin." The American Universalist Church, established in 1779 by an Englishman, John Murray, found a sympathetic audience among ordinary people caught up in the Second Great Awakening in New England and on the frontier. Its message of universal salvation had wide influence, though the Universalist Church itself remained small.

Revivalism among Native Americans

While the Second Great Awakening and dissenting sects claimed the imagination and souls of white and black Americans, a new wave of revivals drew together Native Americans. Among the Iroquois living on reservations in western New York and the Shawnees, Creeks, Cherokees, and other nations retaining lands in the trans-Appalachian region, prophets warned of imminent doom unless people changed their ways. Native Americans had continued to lose lands to whites throughout the area from the Appalachians to the Mississippi; by 1812, settlers in the region dwarfed the Indian population by seven to one. Decline in the numbers of fur-bearing animals caused economic hardship, while conflict over whether to cooperate with the United States created political factions within tribes.

Like the Delaware prophet Neolin in the 1760s, the new nativists blamed loss of land and power on the Indians' failure to maintain traditional rituals and on their adoption of wicked practices from the whites. Among many prophets, Handsome Lake of the Senecas (a nation of the Iroquois) and Tenskwatawa of the Shawnees wielded the greatest influence in the first decade of the nineteenth century.

Handsome Lake, a respected warrior and leader of the Allegany Senecas, fell ill in 1799, seemed to die, then came back to life saying that he

*P*ICTURING THE PAST✦SOCIAL & CULTURAL EVENTS

TENSKWATAWA, THE SHAWNEE PROPHET

National Art Gallery, 1985.66, 279, Smithsonian Institution

With his brother Tecumseh, Tenskwatawa organized pan-Indian resistance to white settlement in the Great Lakes region. He was one of a series of nativist prophets, including the Delaware Neolin and Seneca Handsome Lake, who challenged their followers to reject alcohol and Euro-American customs. The Shawnee Prophet and Tecumseh opposed accommodationist leaders who sold Indian land and, during the War of 1812, the brothers unsuccessfully allied with Great Britain against the United States.

George Catlin painted this portrait of Tenskwatawa in 1830, nineteen years after the Battle of Tippecanoe. It is one of many paintings produced by Catlin and other artists in the 1830s of individual Native American leaders and scenes demonstrating Indian customs, such as dances and the hunt. Unlike many Indians of the time, the prophet is wearing skins rather than a cloak. He has silver earrings, armbands, and a gorget at his throat, but not a peace medal indicating alliance with the U.S. or British government. In contrast, the drawing of Tecumseh later in this chapter shows the Shawnee leader wearing a military coat and British peace medal.

---

had a vision in which messengers told him to become a prophet. In a series of revelations over several years, Handsome Lake received a message of impending catastrophe and a means to salvation. He told his people to stop drinking alcohol and practicing witchcraft; instead they should perform their ancestral rituals. The prophet also advocated peace. He embraced the U.S. acculturation policy by which Quakers tried to convince the Iroquois to adopt white farming methods and gender roles, but he opposed further large-scale land cessions, the whiskey trade, social dancing in couples, and gambling with cards. Other Indians opposed acculturation, which required women to leave the fields and take up spinning, and men to farm rather than hunt. They

viewed the policy, accurately, as a way to justify further expropriation of hunting lands.

Handsome Lake served as a political leader of the Iroquois only briefly, from 1801 to 1803, but his spiritual message remained strong in the years that followed. Most influential was his drive against liquor. A former heavy drinker himself, the Seneca prophet advised, in the words of a white observer, that "the Whiskey is the great Engine which the bad Spirit uses to introduce Witchcraft and many other evils amongst Indians." Many Iroquois abstained from hard drink. One Quaker visitor "noted with satisfaction that in the course of our travels among all the Indians on the Allegheny River . . . we have not seen a Single individual the least intoxicated with

Liquor—which perhaps would be a Singular Circumstance to Observe in traveling among the same number of white Inhabitants."

Also influential was Tenskwatawa, called the Shawnee Prophet, who became prominent among the people of the Great Lakes and Ohio Valley. With his brother, Tecumseh, he inspired a nativist movement to resist the U.S. government's acculturation policy and land grabbing. To avoid fiery destruction, he warned, Indians must revitalize their traditional ceremonies, avoid liquor, and reject the new gender roles. One of the prophet's visions promised that the whites would be destroyed if his people obeyed these instructions.

AFRICAN AMERICANS

As slavery ended in the North, blacks faced discriminatory practices that kept the racial caste system in place, including segregation in churches and schools, and restriction from politics and many occupations. Despite this racism, northern blacks created new lives, institutions, and communities that offered a potent draw to African Americans in the South. Southern blacks also considered more violent means to end bondage, as in the case of Gabriel's revolt in Virginia.

Free Blacks in the North

By 1800, Pennsylvania, New York, and all of New England had passed gradual abolition acts or ended slavery outright. New Jersey in 1804 became the last northern state to pass a law for gradual emancipation, which, like those of other states, freed children henceforth born to slave mothers, but retained slaves born before that date in perpetual bondage. The black children who benefited from the law would be required to serve their mother's owner, much like indentured servants, until a certain age—in New Jersey, twenty-five for males and twenty-one for females.

Despite the gradual nature of these emancipation laws, slavery declined rapidly in the northern states. Responding to their slaves' requests for freedom and to the spirit of the abolition acts, owners freed people whom the laws left in bonds. Masters usually required some additional years of service for the promise of freedom. Frequently, blacks negotiated agreements for themselves or family members. In 1805, a New York slave, Margaret, obtained her owner's pledge of freedom in eight years if she behaved "as she always has done in an orderly manner as a servant ought to do." A New Jersey man promised to pay his owner $50 per year for four years in return for his release. When masters proved recalcitrant, blacks often forced the issue by running away.

The northern cities became magnets for escaped slaves. In addition, humanitarian concerns touched some southern masters, including George Washington, who freed his slaves in his will. Some owners in Delaware and the Chesapeake region, who held more slaves than they needed, emancipated their slaves, then sold them as indentured servants in the North. Between 1790 and 1810, the free black population of Philadelphia and New York City soared, while that of Boston also grew, though more slowly.

Philadelphia and New York City became centers of free African American culture, with churches fostering autonomous community growth. In Philadelphia, responding to hostility, freed men and women organized separate congregations in the 1780s and 1790s. Reverend Richard Allen, for example, led black worshippers from St. George's

Table 8.1	Number of Enslaved African Americans, 1800 and 1810	
	1800	**1810**
New England	1,339	418
New York	20,903	15,017
New Jersey	12,422	10,851
Pennsylvania	1,706	795
Delaware	6,153	4,177
Maryland & District of Columbia	107,707	115,056
Virginia	346,968	394,357
North Carolina	133,296	168,824
South Carolina	146,151	196,365
Georgia	59,406	105,218
Kentucky	40,343	80,561
Tennessee	13,584	44,535
Mississippi Territory	3,489	17,088

Table 8.2	Free Black Population in Northern Cities		
	1790	**1800**	**1810**
Philadelphia	1,849	6,028	8,942
New York City	1,036	3,333	7,470
Boston	766	1,174	1,484

Reverend Richard Allen, a former slave, was founder of the African Methodist Episcopal Church and a leader of the Philadelphia black community.
Moorland-Spingarn Research Center, Howard University

Methodist Episcopal Church when whites insisted on segregated seating. Allen described the scene as they were forced to move during prayer:

> We had not been long upon our knees before I heard considerable scuffling and loud talking. I raised my head up and saw one of the trustees, H_____ M_____, having hold of the Rev. Absalom Jones, pulling him off his knees, and saying, "You must get up, you must not kneel here." . . . we all went out of the church in a body, and they were no more plagued by us in the church.

Allen purchased a blacksmith's shop, converted it into a church, calling it Bethel. By 1803, the black Methodist church had 457 members, the result of revivals and Allen's fervent preaching. But while the evangelical message of Methodism appealed to African Americans, and "Mother" Bethel grew, the congregation found relations with the hierarchy of the white Methodist church difficult. In the early decades of the nineteenth century, black Methodists in Philadelphia, Baltimore, Wilmington, and New York struggled against white control, finally seceding to form separate denominations. In 1816, Philadelphia's Bethel became the first congregation of the African Methodist Episcopal church.

Urban black churches provided mutual aid, fellowship, and avenues for leadership. One benefit of belonging to a New York congregation became obvious to an eighty-year-old woman after a fire destroyed her home. When asked where she would find shelter, she answered, "O a sister in the church has promised to take me in." Shunned by white organizations, effectively barred from politics, and lacking equal opportunity for employment, African Americans created alternatives through the church.

Like white urban residents, freed men and women formed mutual benefit societies. The names African Americans chose for these organizations demonstrated pride in their African heritage. Philadelphians, for example, formed the Free African Society, Daughters of Ethiopia, Angola Society, Sons of Africa, and many others. The official purpose of these societies was to collect dues to provide relief to poor widows and children, but, just as important, the groups facilitated community involvement.

With little money or access to capital, few African Americans, perhaps one in ten, scraped together the funds to purchase a house, shop, or farm. In the first decades of the nineteenth century, many blacks were still completing terms of servitude, while others, though free, lived and worked in white households as domestic servants. Even if they established their own households, women generally washed clothes or performed domestic service for others. Most men were mariners or hired as common laborers. The African American community provided additional opportunity by employing its own. Residents supported black shoemakers, carpenters, food retailers, hucksters, barbers, hairdressers, seamstresses, tailors, cooks, bakers, schoolteachers, and ministers. In Philadelphia, a few African Americans achieved considerable wealth and fame. By 1807, James Forten employed thirty men—blacks and whites—to produce sails for the city's shipbuilders. Robert Bogle developed the idea of catering parties, weddings, and funerals, while Frank Johnson became the city's premier musician. He performed on trumpet and violin, composed dance music and songs, and organized a band that played at balls and public events.

Northern blacks faced daily challenges in their quest for economic success and equal status. But they revered their African roots. The word African in the name of most mutual aid societies and churches testified to their pride of origins, though many of the

*P*ICTURING THE PAST ✦ SOCIAL & CULTURAL EVENTS

THE AFRICAN EPISCOPAL CHURCH OF ST. THOMAS

The Historical Society of Pennsylvania (Bb 882 B756 44)

As the free African American population grew in Philadelphia, churches became central to the developing community. Black Philadelphians founded separate churches for several reasons, including the discrimination they experienced in white congregations and the desire for black leadership. Many of the African American community's key leaders were ministers, including the Rev. Richard Allen, founder of the Bethel African Methodist church, and Rev. Absolem Jones, leader of the African Church of Philadelphia, which affiliated with Episcopalians to become St. Thomas's.

The African Episcopal Church of St. Thomas, shown in this view by David Kennedy and William Lucas, was founded in 1794 and had 427 members the next year. Increasingly, black Philadelphians attended the separate churches. In explaining why former slaves sought their own institutions, Absolem Jones wrote, "to arise out of the dust and shake ourselves, and throw off that servile fear, that the habit of oppression and bondage trained us up in."

---

founders were two, three, even four generations removed from ancestral lands.

African Americans in northern cities also knew of recent struggles by slaves in St. Domingue and elsewhere; a large number of blacks in Philadelphia and New York City had come from the French island with their masters who fled the black revolt. During the 1790s, blacks on St. Domingue led by Toussaint L'Ouverture, a former slave, defeated local whites and the French, Spanish, and British armies. In 1802, Napoleon tried once again to take control of the island, but failed when disease decimated his forces. In 1804, the victorious rebels of St. Domingue established Haiti as an independent nation. Most white Americans dreaded the importation of black revolt. Thomas Jefferson opposed trade with the island, stating, "We may expect therefore

black crews, and supercargoes and missionaries thence into the southern states. . . . If this combustion can be introduced among us under any veil whatever, we have to fear it."

Slave Rebellion in the South

With more than 850,000 enslaved blacks in the American South in 1800, one-third of the population, whites had reason to be concerned about slave insurgency. After St. Domingue erupted, Georgia and the Carolinas declared black emigrés from the West Indies a threat, prohibiting their entry. South Carolina, in reopening its international slave trade in 1803, made every effort to avoid admitting rebels. The state excluded blacks from the West Indies and South America, and any who had ever lived in the French West Indies. Every man imported from another state needed a certificate indicating that he had not "been concerned in any insurrection or rebellion."

In August 1800, the worst fears of white southerners were nearly realized when an enslaved blacksmith named Gabriel organized an armed march against the capital of Virginia. With about 600 supporters from Richmond and surrounding counties, Gabriel planned a full-scale insurrection. His strategy included seizing guns from an arsenal, taking Governor James Monroe hostage, and forcing concessions from town officials. Gabriel expected poor whites to join him because they, like slaves, lacked political power. The attack failed when a torrential rainstorm washed out bridges, making travel impossible. Efforts to try again another day collapsed when two informers passed word of the conspiracy to authorities who rounded up suspects. Though Gabriel eluded capture for more than three weeks, he was arrested and hanged, as were twenty-six others implicated in the plot.

White Americans still held the revolutionary belief that all men and women desired freedom. Masters took seriously the threat of slave revolt. After Gabriel's rebellion, Governor Monroe observed about enslaved African Americans, "Unhappily while this class of people exists among us we can never count with certainty on its tranquil submission." In 1802, Virginians discovered additional conspiracies, with rumors of more violence heightening tensions. In 1805, after four whites had been poisoned in North Carolina, officials burned a slave woman alive, hanged three other slaves, and whipped and cut off the ears of another. Gabriel's plot, the St. Domingue uprising, and what appeared to be an upsurge of murders and arson by blacks convinced southern lawmakers to enact more stringent slave codes. South Carolina and Georgia tightened requirements for slave patrols and defined as treason any collaboration in slave rebellion. Hardening attitudes toward slavery snuffed out southern antislavery societies that were already faltering. On a more positive note, as the twenty-year constitutional restriction on prohibiting the slave trade expired, Congress officially banned the importation of slaves after January 1, 1808.

JEFFERSON'S REPUBLIC

In 1800, the federal government moved from the nation's cultural capital in Philadelphia to an unfinished village on the Potomac: Washington, D.C. The ruling party also changed, as voters voiced their dissatisfaction with the Federalists by electing Thomas Jefferson

and a Republican Congress. Jefferson's promise of reduced government and taxes appealed to a populace concerned about other things besides national politics—their finances, their souls, and local communities. Events prevented the young nation from wrapping itself in isolation, however, for its economic prosperity depended a great deal upon international commerce, a trade severely hampered by the ongoing European war.

The Election of 1800

Most recently, the United States had been involved in the Quasi-War with France, in which the French navy initially ravaged the American merchant fleet. Congress had expanded the army, authorized the

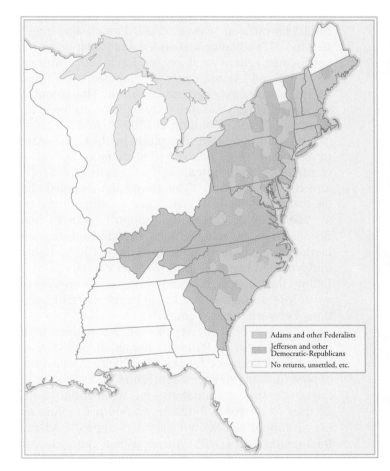

Map 8.1 *The Election of 1800*
The election Thomas Jefferson called "the revolution of 1800" was close, with Jefferson receiving 73 votes to John Adams's 65. The Federalist ticket, headed by Adams and Charles Cotesworth Pinckney, obtained considerable support from the Carolinas and mid-Atlantic as well as New England.

U.S. Navy to protect commercial ships, and revoked unilaterally the American-French treaty of 1778. The Federalists swept the congressional elections of 1798 on the crest of anti-French fervor; they tried to use war fever against the Republicans through the Alien and Sedition acts. Instead, the backlash of concern about civil liberties swelled the opposition.

As the 1800 election approached, many Federalists expected to take advantage of the unresolved difficulties with France in continuing to paint the Jeffersonian Republicans as pro-French, hence un-American. Nevertheless, President John Adams moved to end hostilities. He nominated a three-man commission, including William Vans Murray (minister to the Netherlands), Chief Justice Oliver Ellsworth, and Governor William R. Davie of North Carolina, to make peace with France. The commission received instructions that proved impossible to fulfill: its mission was to obtain French agreement that the 1778 alliance had ended and indemnities for confiscated American ships. In March 1800, Murray, Ellsworth, and Davie met with Napoleon, who had no intention of paying compensation. The commissioners reached an accord only by ignoring their instructions. The Convention of 1800, signed in France in October and ratified reluctantly by the U.S. Senate in February 1801, echoed provisions of the 1778 commercial treaty in calling for "a firm, inviolable, and universal peace." The Convention voided the defensive alliance of 1778, however, thus eliminating the French claim to U.S. support against Great Britain. The pact also included a vague confirmation by the French of neutral rights in international trade, but provided no restitution to American shippers, a failing that opponents said made the convention worthless. In fact, it had value in normalizing relations between the two countries.

The chief beneficiary of reduced tensions with France was Thomas Jefferson, named in May 1800 as Republican nominee for president, with Aaron Burr of New York for vice president. John Adams received the Federalist nomination for reelection, with Charles Cotesworth Pinckney of South Carolina as his running mate. Many Federalists opposed Adams for making peace with France. When the electoral votes were tallied, Jefferson and Burr each received 73 votes, Adams had 65, Pinckney 64, and John Jay 1. In lining up votes in the electoral college, the Republicans had failed to take account of the constitutional election procedures that lacked provision for party slates. The Constitution directed that each elector cast two votes, with the candidate receiving the highest number elected president and the

Aaron Burr, by Gilbert Stuart. Burr refused initially to follow the script and accept the vice presidency when he tied with Jefferson in the election of 1800.
From the Collections of The New Jersey Historical Society, Newark, New Jersey

runner-up vice president. The electors had no way of designating which candidate they supported for president and which for vice president. The Federalists avoided the difficulty by having one elector vote for John Jay, thus giving Pinckney one less vote than Adams.

If Burr had simply yielded to Jefferson in 1800, the problem would have been resolved without complication. The tie sent the election to the House of Representatives, which had a Federalist majority. Each state delegation received one vote. Some of the Federalists hatched a plan to support Burr, thinking that they might be able to control him as president. Hamilton opposed the plot vigorously, contending "Burr loves nothing but himself; thinks of nothing but his own aggrandizement, and will be content with nothing short of permanent power in his own hands." The former secretary of the treasury advised his party to make a deal with Jefferson to keep the system of public credit and the navy, retain Federalist appointees in office, and remain neutral in the war between Britain and France. The House of Representatives required thirty-six ballots over six days before the Federalist delegate from Delaware, James A. Bayard, shifted his position to break the tie.

Jefferson's "Revolution"

The third president assumed a conciliatory stance toward the Federalists as he took office. On March 4, 1801, Jefferson delivered his inaugural address to the new Congress, which the Republicans dominated in the House by 69 votes to 36, and in the Senate by an 18–13 majority. He gave the address almost in a whisper, for he was not a good public speaker. The speech reflected his Republican beliefs: emphasis on the power of state governments, freedom of religion and the press, majority rule but protection of minority rights, low government expenditures, and reduction of the federal debt. Jefferson upheld the Convention of 1800 with France implicitly by stating that he desired amity and trade with foreign nations and "entangling alliances with none." His most famous statement, "We are all republicans, we are all federalists," attempted to get beyond the partisan battles that had bedeviled his two predecessors. He later described his election as "the revolution of 1800" that "was as real a revolution in the principles of our government as that of 1776 was in its form; not effected indeed by the sword, as that, but by the rational and peaceable instrument of reform, the suffrage of the people." Despite bitter political enmity, American leaders had created a party system by which power could be contested in elections rather than through bloodshed. With the election of 1800, the Constitution passed a crucial test, with peaceful transfer of power from one party to its opponents.

The new president worked to put his principles into action, to create an agrarian republic in which the federal government kept its role to a minimum. The location in Washington, D.C., seemed the ideal setting for a weak government. In 1800, the town had fewer than 400 dwellings, which one government official described as mostly "small miserable huts." The Capitol was incomplete, with wings for the Senate and House but no center. What existed was poorly constructed: the acoustics were dreadful, the roof leaked, and the heating was "noxious." The president's house was not yet finished in 1814 when the British burned it. Construction materials littered the grounds during Jefferson's administration to the extent that, according to one guest, "in a dark night instead of finding your way to the house, you may, perchance, fall into a pit, or stumble over a heap of rubbish." Cows grazed on

The Capitol in Washington was incomplete at the time of Jefferson's election in 1800. With hogs running through the streets, the town seemed an appropriate seat for his agrarian republic.
The Granger Collection, New York

what later became the Mall; hogs ran through the city's streets.

Washington, D.C., remained a village in part because the federal government was small, and Jefferson had no interest in seeing it grow. In 1802, federal personnel throughout the country numbered under 10,000, of whom 6,500 served in military posts. Of the nonuniformed officials, fewer than 300 worked in the Capital. The president and Supreme Court each had one clerk, Congress employed thirteen, and the attorney general had none. The central government had relatively little to do, for state and local governments or voluntary associations took primary responsibility for keeping law and order, maintaining roads and bridges, supervising the militia, and providing welfare relief and schools.

Jefferson's lack of attention to building Washington, D.C., revealed his approach to the presidency. In contrast to Federalist efforts to reflect the grandeur of European courts and capitals, he adopted informality and frugality. Jefferson dealt with members of Congress and foreign diplomats personally, inviting small groups for dinner and conversation. He avoided making speeches, sending written messages to Congress. With only one clerk, he handled many documents himself.

The change of political power from the Federalists to the Republicans raised questions about

Thomas Jefferson's First Inaugural Address, March 4, 1801

Jefferson wrote this inaugural address, the first given by a president in Washington, D.C., in the two weeks following the confirmation of his election by the House of Representatives. In this speech, the third president sought to heal wounds from the contentious 1800 election and set forth his philosophy of government.

FRIENDS AND FELLOW-CITIZENS Called upon to undertake the duties of the first executive office of our country, I avail myself of the presence of that portion of my fellow citizens which is here assembled to express my grateful thanks for the favor with which they have been pleased to look toward me, . . .

During the contest of opinion through which we have passed the animation of discussions and of exertions has sometimes worn an aspect which might impose on strangers unused to think freely and to speak and to write what they think. But this being now decided by the voice of the nation, enounced according to the rules of the constitution, all will of course arrange themselves under the will of the law, and unite in common efforts for the common good. All too will bear in mind this sacred principle, that though the will of the majority is in all cases to prevail, that will, to be rightful, must be reasonable; that the minority possess their equal rights, which equal laws must protect, and to violate would be oppression. . . . We have called by different names brethren of the same principle. We are all republicans; we are all federalists. If there be any among us who wish to dissolve this Union or to change its republican form, let them stand undisturbed, as monuments of the safety with which error of opinion may be tolerated where reason is left free to combat it. . . .

About to enter, fellow citizens, on the exercise of duties which comprehend everything dear and valuable to you, it is proper you should understand what I deem the essential principles of this government, and consequently those which ought to shape its administration. I will compress them in the narrowest compass they will bear, stating the general principle, but not all its limitations. Equal and exact justice to all men, of whatever state or persuasion,

religious or political; peace, commerce, and honest friendship with all nations, entangling alliances with none; the support of the state governments in all their rights, as the most competent administrations for our domestic concerns and the surest bulwarks against anti-republican tendencies; the preservation of the general government in its whole constitutional vigor, as the sheet anchor of our peace at home and safety abroad; a jealous care of the right of election by the people, a mild and safe corrective of abuses which are lopped by the sword of revolution where peaceable remedies are unprovided; absolute acquiescence in the decisions of the majority, the vital principle of republics from which is no appeal but to force, the vital principle and immediate parent of despotism; a well disciplined militia, our best reliance in peace and for the first moments of war, till regulars may relieve them; the supremacy of the civil over the military authority; economy in the public expence, that labor may be lightly burthened; the honest payment of our debts and sacred preservation of the public faith; encouragement of agriculture, and of commerce as its handmaid; the diffusion of information and arraignment of all abuses at the bar of the public reason; freedom of religion; freedom of the press, and freedom of person under the protection of the habeas corpus, and trial by juries impartially selected. These principles form the bright constellation which has gone before us and guided our steps through an age of revolution and reformation. The wisdom of our sages and blood of our heroes have been devoted to their attainment. They should be the creed of our political faith, the text of civic instruction, the touchstone by which to try the services of those we trust; and should we wander from them in moments of error or of alarm, let us hasten to retrace our steps and to regain the road which alone leads to peace, liberty, and safety.

office holding and political spoils. At the highest level of executive appointments, the cabinet, Jefferson assumed his right to appoint trusted supporters. He named James Madison of Virginia, his closest ally, as secretary of state, and Albert Gallatin of Pennsylvania as secretary of the treasury. Other members of the cabinet included Levi Lincoln of Massachusetts as attorney general, Henry Dearborn of Massachusetts as secretary of war, and Robert Smith of Maryland as secretary of the navy.

The question of whether or not to retain bureaucrats was more difficult. Jefferson supported the idea of a civil service in which public officers held their positions on the basis of merit; during the election crisis he suggested that he would allow office-holders to keep their jobs. When he learned that Washington and Adams had appointed only six Republicans to about 600 positions, however, the new president replaced about one-half of the Federalists with Republicans. Most infuriating were the "midnight appointments," as Jefferson characterized them—the appointments Adams made as a lame duck after he knew that the election was lost. In February 1801, the Federalist Congress had passed a new Judiciary Act creating these additional judgeships and other offices, all of which Federalists received. Jefferson called upon the new Republican Congress to repeal the law.

Jefferson and Gallatin placed high priority in decreasing government expenditures, taxes, and the national debt. Gallatin opposed all spending by the federal government, including military. With support of the Republican Congress, the administration cut the defense budget in half. It repealed all excise taxes, including that on whiskey, relying primarily on import duties for income.

Jefferson's plan to reduce the navy and remain clear of international conflicts hit a snag when Yusuf Karamanli, the leader of Tripoli in North Africa, declared war on the United States. Karamanli demanded payments from the United States to "protect" American merchant carriers from pirates. To end this extortion, in 1801 Jefferson sent naval vessels to blockade Tripoli and protect shipping. The United States experienced a major loss when the ship *Philadelphia* ran aground while pursuing pirates, but when a small force of U.S. Marines and Arab mercenaries seized Derna, the Tripolitans agreed to peace. The war had propelled military expenditures upward, however, and convinced Jefferson of the navy's value, thus hindering somewhat the administration's plans for reduced government spending.

The Judiciary

Although the Republicans had captured the presidency and Congress in 1800, the judiciary remained firmly in the hands of the Federalists. Adams and the outgoing Congress had tried to solidify their party's power in the courts with the Judiciary Act of 1801, which amended the act of 1789. By appointing additional federal judges, the new law ended the onerous requirement for Supreme Court justices to ride from state to state holding circuit courts twice a year. The act also reduced the number of justices on the Court from six to five, thereby denying Jefferson the opportunity to make an appointment when a seat became vacant. The Republican Congress, in early 1802, repealed this law, reinstating the Judiciary Act of 1789, thus forcing some federal judges out of their jobs and the Supreme Court back to the circuit.

Jefferson's bitter relationship with the Supreme Court resulted in part from his antipathy toward Chief Justice John Marshall, his distant cousin, whom Adams had named to the bench in early 1801. Like Jefferson, Marshall was tall, informal in manner, and a native of Virginia. He had joined the patriot forces in 1775, serv-

Chief Justice John Marshall, *painted by Ferret de Saint Memin at the time of Marshall's appointment in 1801. During his tenure to 1835, the chief justice established federal judicial authority, in particular the Court's power to decide the constitutionality of laws.*
Courtesy of Duke University Archives

ing until 1781. He attributed his nationalism to that service, saying he became "confirmed in the habit of considering America as my country, and congress as my government." Marshall began a successful law practice after the war, served as a Virginia assemblyman, supported ratification of the Federal Constitution, then became the leading Federalist in his state. In the legal environment of the new republic, many colleagues appreciated his originality in building cases on logic and natural law rather than depending upon English precedent. On the Supreme Court, too, Marshall followed his own lights, creating the legal basis on which the power of the Court rests. During his long, illustrious career, which lasted until 1835, Marshall solidified the authority of the judicial branch of the federal government.

Marshall's most important decision, *Marbury v. Madison* (1803), commenced in a suit by William Marbury, nominated by Adams as a justice of the peace but not commissioned by the Jefferson administration. Marbury sued under the Judiciary Act of 1789, which granted the Supreme Court the power to require Secretary of State Madison to hand over Marbury's commission. Given the partisanship involved, most observers expected Marshall and his Federalist court to direct Madison to comply. Instead, the chief justice said that he could not remedy Marbury's situation, though he wished to do so, because the Congress had erred in giving the Court such authority. Marshall declared the provision of the 1789 Judiciary Act unconstitutional, thus establishing the Supreme Court's power of judicial review.

Jefferson decided that the federal judiciary, still dominated by Federalists and growing in power under Marshall, had to be controlled. Because federal judges constitutionally held their seats for life, "during good behavior," the president suggested to congressional Republicans that they start impeachment proceedings against objectionable Federalists. The Republicans impeached John Pickering, an official of the federal district court of New Hampshire, who was an alcoholic and insane, but who had not to anyone's knowledge committed any high crimes. The Senate found him guilty anyway and removed him from his position. Next, in January 1805, the House of Representatives impeached Samuel Chase of Maryland, an associate justice of the Supreme Court and extreme Federalist who castigated Jefferson's administration. But the prosecution failed to convince two-thirds of the Senate that Chase should be expelled from office for misconduct and other charges. Some moderate Republicans refused to adopt Jefferson's strategy to eject troublesome opponents. Thus ended Congress's attempt to remove Federalists from the bench by impeachment.

Domestic Politics

Jefferson and the Republicans gained in popularity as they steered a course more moderate than the "revolution" of 1800 had promised. The president had reduced taxes and attempted to limit the judiciary, but did not dismantle the Federalist edifice of national power, including the military and the national bank. He mixed republican theory, based upon a nation of small farmers, with practical politics aiding commerce. His policies, combined with booming exports, steadily increased Republican support, as many Federalist voters switched parties. In the election of 1802, the Republicans won 102 seats to the Federalists' 39 in the House of Representatives; the Republican margin in the Senate was 25 to 9.

Looking forward to the next presidential election, Congress acted promptly to avoid the deadlock that had occurred in 1800. The Republicans wanted a formal way to keep the Federalists from conspiring once again to elevate the Republican candidate for vice president to the presidency. The Twelfth Amendment to the Constitution, which required the electors to draw up distinct lists for president and vice president, was ratified by September 1804.

The election of 1804 demonstrated the demise of the Federalists as a national party. Jefferson defeated the Federalist presidential candidate, Charles Cotesworth Pinckney, by 162 electoral votes to 14.

Jefferson had replaced Aaron Burr as his running mate with George Clinton, also of New York, thus keeping the ticket balanced geographically. For his part, Burr ran for governor of New York against the Republican candidate, Morgan Lewis, but lost by a landslide. Alexander Hamilton played a decisive role in the defeat by publicly denouncing his longtime enemy. Burr challenged Hamilton to a duel. When the two faced each other at Weehawken, New Jersey, in July 1804, Burr shot Hamilton to death. In doing so, the vice president ended his own political career as well as the life of one of the architects of the American nation-state.

THE LOUISIANA PURCHASE

Jefferson had boosted his popularity prior to the 1804 election with the Louisiana Purchase, which marked the greatest success of his presidency. In pursuing the deal with France, he deviated from one of his beliefs—in limited power of the central government—to obtain land for his agrarian republic. Long interested in the

𝒫ICTURING THE PAST✦ECONOMICS & TECHNOLOGY

PLAN OF NEW ORLEANS, 1801

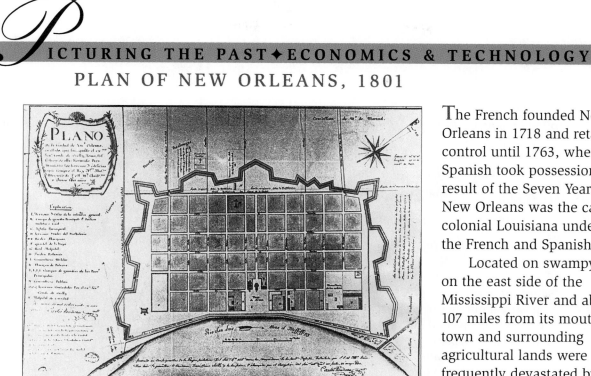

Courtesy, Archivo General de Indias, Seville, and the Spanish Colonial Research Center, University of New Mexico

The French founded New Orleans in 1718 and retained control until 1763, when the Spanish took possession as a result of the Seven Years' War. New Orleans was the capital of colonial Louisiana under both the French and Spanish.

Located on swampy land on the east side of the Mississippi River and about 107 miles from its mouth, the town and surrounding agricultural lands were frequently devastated by floods and hurricanes. In 1803, when the United States purchased Louisiana, New Orleans had a mixed population of free and enslaved blacks, Native Americans, French, Spanish, and U.S. citizens.

The key location of New Orleans near the mouth of the Mississippi emphasized its economic importance to Americans west of the Appalachians. When Spain closed the port once again in 1802, Americans feared a strategic loss. During the War of 1812, the British also recognized the significance of New Orleans to the expanding United States, when they unsuccessfully attacked the city in January 1815.

---

west, he scored a diplomatic coup that doubled the size of the United States and reduced Spain's dominance west of the Mississippi River.

The Bargain with Napoleon

The chain of events leading to the Louisiana Purchase began in 1800, when France signed a secret treaty with Spain for lands in western North America. France would get back the territory it had ceded to Spain in 1763. When Jefferson and Madison heard in 1801 of the impending transfer, they sent the new U.S. minister to France, Robert R. Livingston, with instructions to prevent the exchange or at least obtain West

Florida. The Americans wanted to prevent France from controlling the Mississippi Valley; the dilapidated Spanish empire caused trouble enough. In October 1802, the Spanish suspended once again the right of Americans to deposit goods for export at New Orleans. The Americans thought, incorrectly, that Napoleon was behind the ban. Many wanted to take New Orleans by force. Jefferson wrote to Livingston, "The day that France takes possession of N. Orleans . . . we must marry ourselves to the British fleet and nation." Jefferson pushed for negotiations, however, not war.

In response to Livingston's overtures, Napoleon decided to sell the entire Louisiana Territory to the United States. The French leader's zeal to construct

The Journals of Meriwether Lewis and William Clark 1805

*T*he following entries from the journals of the two explorers demonstrate the challenges the Corps of Discovery faced in mid-winter 1805. In early November 1804, in what is now North Dakota, they had built huts within a triangular palisade, naming it Fort Mandan, as Lewis wrote, "in honour of our Neighbours." Lewis and Clark used their diaries to record information about the Native Americans they met as well as the plants, animals, weather, and landscape along their route. On February 11, Lewis described the birth of a son to Sacagawea, the expedition's Shoshone interpreter and guide.

[Clark]   *14th January 1805 Monday.*

This morning early a number of indians men women children Dogs &c. &c. passed down on the ice to joine those that passed yesterday, we Sent Serg^t Pryor and five men with those indians to hunt (Several men with the Venereal cought from the Mandan women) one of our hunters Sent out Several days [ago] arived & informs that one Man (Whitehouse) is frost bit and Can't walk home.

[Clark]   *16th January Wednesday 1805.*

about thirty Mandans came to the fort to day, 6 chiefs. . . . the little Crow 2^d Chf of the lower Village Came & brought us Corn &c. 4 men of ours who had been hunting returned one frost'd

This War Chief gave us a Chart in his Way of the Missourie, . . .

[Lewis]   *3rd of February Sunday 1805.*

a fine day; the blacksmith again commences his opperations. we were visited by but few of the natives today. the situation of our boat and perogues is now allarming, they are firmly inclosed in the Ice and almost covered with snow—the ice which incloses them lyes in several stratas of unequal thicknesses which are seperated by streams of water.

[Lewis]   *8th February Friday 1805.*

This morning was fair wind S.E. the weather still warm and pleasent. visited by the *black-Cat* the principal chief of the Roop-tar-he, or upper mandane village. this man possesses more integrety, firmness, inteligence and perspicuety of mind than any indian I have met with in this quarter, and I think with a little management he may be made a usefull agent in furthering the views of our government. The black Cat presented me with a bow and apologized for not having completed the shield he had promised alledging that the weather had been too cold to permit his making it, I gave him some small shot 6 fishing-hooks and 2 yards of ribbon his squaw also presented me with 2 pair of mockersons for which in return I gave a small lookingglass and a couple of needles. the chief dined with me and left me in the evening. he informed me that his people suffered very much for the article of meat, and that he had not himself tasted any for several days.

[Lewis]   *11th February Monday 1805.*

. . . about five oclock this evening one of the wives of Charbono was delivered of a fine boy. it is worthy of remark that this was the first child which this woman had boarn, and as is common in such cases her labour was tedious and the pain violent; Mr Jessome informed me that he had freequently administered a small portion of the rattle of the rattle-snake, which he assured me had never failed to produce the desired effect, that of hastening the birth of the child; having the rattle of a snake by me I gave it to him and he administered two rings of it to the woman. . . . Whether this medicine was truly the cause or not I shall not undertake to determine, but I was informed that she had not taken it more than ten minutes before she brought forth. . . .

[Clark]   [13 February 1805.]

I returned last night from a hunting party [Feb. 4 to 12] much fatigued, haveing walked 30 miles on the ice and through Points of wood land in which the Snow was nearly Knee Deep. . . .

[9 Feb]—The Buffalow Seen last night provd to be Bulls. lean & unfit for to make use of as food, the Distance from Camp being nearly 60 miles and the packing of meat that distance attended with much dificuelty Deturmined me to return and hunt the points above, we Set out on our return and halted at an old Indian lodge 40 miles below Fort Mandan, Killed 3 Elk, & 2 Deer. . . .

I saw Several old Villages near the Chisscheter River on enquirey found they were Mandan Villages destroyed by the Sous & Small Pox. . . .

---

an American empire had cooled with the loss of his army in St. Domingue. In documents dated April 30, 1803, the United States agreed to pay France $15 million, to respect the rights of the French and Native Americans living in the territory, and to recognize the French residents as American citizens. Spain was furious because Napoleon had promised not to sell the region to the British or the Americans. Jefferson ignored the Spanish objections, but worried, as a strict constructionist, that the Louisiana Purchase was unconstitutional because the federal government had no specific power to acquire territory. He put aside these concerns, confident that it was right to avoid war and add vast lands for expansion of the American republic. "By enlarging the empire of liberty," the president argued, the nation could maintain its agrarian foundations, thus avoid descent into vice, luxury, and decay. A successful republic was dependent upon broad property holding, for virtuous, independent, middling farmers made ideal citizens. The Louisiana Purchase, Jefferson believed, would extend the life of the republic by providing space for generations of ordinary planters. While some Federalists disagreed, most Americans celebrated the end of friction over the Mississippi River and New Orleans. Western farmers could get their products to market; eastern merchants prospered from the trade.

Disputes with Spain

When U.S. officials gained formal possession of Louisiana in December 1803, the Spanish had only recently transferred control to the French. The ceremonies took place in New Orleans, a city of 8,000 that had been reconstructed in Spanish style since several great fires a decade earlier. With a cathedral, theater, impressive city hall, and mansions, New Orleans served as the cultural and economic center of the lower Mississippi Valley. In population, it was larger than other towns of the Spanish borderlands. The entire white population of the Louisiana Territory was approximately 50,000, including French, Spanish, Germans, English, and Americans.

Beyond Spain's objection to the U.S. purchase of Louisiana, the two nations also disputed the territory's boundaries, because the treaties transferring ownership were vague. Thomas Jefferson pushed for the most generous interpretation for the United States. He demanded West Florida, with an eastern boundary at the Perdido River, the present boundary between Alabama and the Florida panhandle. The president also thought his new acquisition extended in the southwest to the Rio Grande, incorporating all of Texas and part of New Mexico, and in the northwest to the Rocky Mountains. Spain, on the other hand, said the Louisiana Territory included only a constricted region along the west bank of the Mississippi from northern Missouri to the Gulf of Mexico.

In 1804, Jefferson sent troops to West Florida, hoping to convince Spain by threat of force to give up or sell the province. Americans already outnumbered Spanish residents in the territory, which later comprised parts of Mississippi, Alabama, and Louisiana. Jefferson also wanted East Florida. He decided not to attack, and instead attempted to purchase the Floridas over the next several years, but failed.

The Lewis and Clark Expedition

To strengthen U.S. claims to the West, Jefferson sponsored an exploratory mission to the Pacific Ocean. Several times since 1783, he had tried to organize expeditions for scientific knowledge and to promote American interests in the region. As president, he now had the authority and financial resources to support this major undertaking. By the early nineteenth century, however, others had surveyed parts of the territory. In 1792, an American sea captain Robert Gray explored the Columbia River, and George Vancouver, a British naval officer, sailed the northwest coast. A few

Page26.

Captains Lewis & Clark holding a Council with the Indians

Meeting of the Lewis and Clark expedition with Native Americans on the Missouri River, 1804. Illustration from the journal of Sergeant Patrick Gass, a member of the expedition.
Courtesy of Houghton Library, Harvard University

years later, fur traders working for the Spanish government ascended the Missouri River to present-day North Dakota, while British traders from Canada began moving west.

Even before buying Louisiana, the president had decided to send an expedition west; the purchase gave the project greater urgency. He appointed his private secretary, Meriwether Lewis, as captain of the enterprise. Lewis chose his friend William Clark to be his partner. Lewis and Clark had served in the army together in the old Northwest, so both were familiar with frontier conditions. Jefferson selected Lewis for his scientific interests as well as his wilderness experience. The president wanted "a person who to courage, prudence, habits & health adapted to the woods, & some familiarity with the Indian character, joins a perfect knoledge of botany, natural history, mineralogy & astronomy."

Jefferson had a long list of goals for his explorers. They were to travel to the source of the Missouri River to find the elusive Northwest Passage, fill in huge blanks in geographic knowledge of the West, and bring back descriptions of unknown species of plants and animals. He also hoped they would make peaceful contact with Native Americans to expand commercial networks for fur traders. Lewis and Clark more than fulfilled their assignment, keeping daily journals of their experiences, including descriptions of Indian societies and culture, systematic weather records, and observations of flora and

fauna, as well as a detailed map of their journey. Their relations with the people of the Northwest were for the most part amicable.

Lewis and Clark received commissions as army officers to lead the Corps of Discovery of about forty men who departed from St. Louis in May 1804. During that summer and fall they traveled up the Missouri River, using poles and tow ropes against the current. They battled the hot sun, diarrhea, and mosquitoes; several men deserted and one died, the only member of the Corps to perish during the entire trip. The adventurers met with the leaders of Indian nations along the way, telling them that the United States had taken possession of the territory from the Spanish. They arrived in the Mandan and Hidatsa villages of what is now North Dakota, where they spent the winter of 1804–1805.

In April 1805, the Lewis and Clark expedition set out with their guide Sacagawea, a Shoshone woman, and her French husband and infant son. They proceeded up the Missouri River, made an arduous crossing of the Rockies, and reached the mouth of the Columbia River before winter. On the way back, the corps divided in two, with Clark leading a party southeast along the Yellowstone River and Lewis taking a northern route through Montana. They joined forces once again in North Dakota, then returned to St. Louis by September 1806. They had been away so long that many assumed they had been killed by the Spanish or Native Americans.

Spies and Infiltrators

Spanish officials in fact had tried to intercept Lewis and Clark, whom they correctly suspected of making allies for the United States among the western Indians. General James Wilkinson, commander of U.S. troops in the west, governor of the Louisiana Territory, and a double agent known to the Spanish as "Agent 13," had tipped off New Spain about the expedition. The governor of New Mexico sent out search parties but failed to find Lewis and Clark. They did stop the mission of Thomas Freeman and Peter Custis, who in 1806 started from Louisiana to find the source of the Red River. Another Spanish party nearly intercepted Zebulon Pike, whom Wilkinson had dispatched to explore and spy in the region that is now Kansas, Colorado, and New Mexico. Pike became lost in the southern Rockies, was rescued by Spanish soldiers, arrested, then released.

Both the United States and Spain knew they were playing for high stakes. The United States could use exploration of the west and alliances with Native

Map 8.2 *Western Exploration, 1803–1807*
At about the same time Meriwether Lewis and William Clark led the Corps of Discovery along the northern route to treat with Native Americans, explore the natural resources, and locate a northwest passage, Zebulon Pike traveled north along the Mississippi River and west to the Rocky Mountains.

Americans to help confirm their claims to broad boundaries of the Louisiana Territory. The Spanish had by far superior documentation for Texas, New Mexico, Arizona, California, and western Colorado. But they also denied American rights to what is now western Louisiana. Jefferson sent General Wilkinson with troops to the undefined boundary between

Louisiana and Texas; the Spanish dispatched Lt. Col. Simón de Herrera to defend eastern Texas. The two officers avoided fighting by establishing a neutral zone until diplomats could negotiate the border.

Still concerned about protecting their silver mines in Mexico, the Spanish took steps to increase settlement in Texas. They welcomed Indian exiles—

Cherokees, Choctaws, and Alabamas—from lands overrun by American settlers east of the Mississippi, but the Hispanic population failed to grow significantly. New Spain officials specifically barred U.S. citizens from Texas, under threat of arrest and imprisonment. The Americans, one Spanish official feared, "are not and will not be anything but crows to pick out our eyes." Anglo-American traders continued to infiltrate Texas, however, to trap animals and bargain for horses with the Comanches and other Indians.

The Burr Conspiracy

While Lewis and Clark were reconnoitering the far Northwest, Aaron Burr conceived a plot to create a separate nation in the West. He contacted the double agent James Wilkinson, various unhappy politicians, and representatives of foreign governments. Burr suggested a variety of plans to those who would listen, including an invasion of New Spain, an attack on Washington, D.C., and secession of the West. Wilkinson cooperated with Burr at first, then turned informer when the conspiracy became public knowledge. Jefferson ordered Burr's arrest for treason, while applauding Wilkinson's "fidelity." Burr tried to escape to Europe, but was captured and taken to Richmond, Virginia, where he was tried in 1807.

The Burr conspiracy case, presided over by Chief Justice Marshall and involving three prosecutors and six defense lawyers, might have been called the trial of the century. An unbiased jury could not be found; one juror said before the case was heard that Burr should be hanged. The principal actors in the trial were Marshall, who ignored his responsibility as an impartial judge to favor the defense, and Jefferson, who directed the prosecution from afar. Because Marshall upheld a definition of treason that required actual gathering of troops, not just conspiracy, the case against Burr collapsed. Jefferson blamed Marshall and considered trying to impeach him, but found insufficient congressional support.

MORE FOREIGN ENTANGLEMENTS

The renewal of war in 1803 between Great Britain and France portended trouble for the United States. American merchants flourished, as they took advantage of neutrality and wartime demand for provisions in Europe and the West Indies. But their ships became vulnerable to the British navy and French privateers.

The British navy had practiced impressment, or forced recruitment, of American sailors since before the American Revolution. While claiming the men were British deserters, the navy often took native-born Americans, including free blacks.
The Granger Collection, New York

A Perilous Neutrality

Great Britain and France each wanted to prevent the United States from provisioning the other. In particular, the British intended to stop American traders from carrying foreign sugar, coffee, and other tropical products to Europe, even though the merchants conformed technically to British guidelines by taking the goods first to U.S. ports, then reexporting. In the *Essex* case of 1805, British courts stiffened their rules, stating that merely carrying Spanish and French goods to U.S. soil for reexport was insufficient, that only commodities originally meant for sale in the United States, then subsequently redirected to Europe, would be considered exempt from seizure. Few reexported cargoes met the new guidelines. With the *Essex* rule, the Royal Navy stepped up its confiscations of American ships. Then, in 1806 and 1807, the British and French established blockades of each other's harbors, in combination eliminating neutral trade with Europe and the British Isles. The British insisted that neutral ships sail to Britain first for inspection and licensing before trading in Europe. Napoleon's Berlin and Milan Decrees banned trade with Britain and threatened neutrals who obeyed the British rules with seizure.

After the British destroyed the French and Spanish navies in 1805 at Trafalgar, off the coast of Spain, the British restrictions and impressment of sailors were by far the most troublesome to Americans. Many Federalists and some Republicans cried for war. But Jefferson and the congressional majority looked for ways to avoid hostilities. With a trimmed federal budget and small military, the Republicans were unprepared for war. Congress passed a Non-Importation Act (1806) banning specified British goods, while the president opened negotiations with Great Britain to end impressment and recognize neutral trading rights. No agreement satisfactory to both sides could be reached. Then, in June 1807, the British ship *Leopard* fired upon the American frigate *Chesapeake* for refusing to submit to a search for British deserters. The *Chesapeake,* hit twenty-two times, managed to respond with only one shot. The *Leopard* boarded her, impressing four men.

The Embargo of 1807

As Americans briefly clamored for war, Jefferson closed U.S. ports and territorial waters to British vessels and recalled American ships from the Mediterranean, where they would have been trapped had war begun. The British refused to stop impressing American sailors. They challenged Jefferson's port closure by firing on coastal towns in Maine and sailing in Chesapeake Bay. The president resisted a declaration of war, but placed military posts and gunboats on alert. He chose economic warfare instead. Unfortunately, this policy destroyed the commercial boom that had meant high prices for farmers and employed thousands of sailors.

At the urging of President Jefferson and Secretary of State Madison, Congress passed the Embargo Act in December 1807. The law prohibited exportation to all other countries. The administration hoped in particular to defang the former parent country by withholding provisions to the British Isles and West Indies. A by-product of non-exportation would be a severe drop in imports of British manufactures. Jefferson and Madison argued that the boycott would hurt all warring parties, but Britain worst. During 1808, the administration faced difficulty enforcing the embargo because ships, especially from New England, left harbor pretending to sail to American coastal ports but headed for foreign destinations instead. The trade with the British West Indies continued illegally. Federal agents also had little success in preventing smuggling into Canada. In January 1809, the government resorted to an extreme measure,

Giles's Enforcement Act, which empowered the president to use the militia against smugglers. The act effectively ended trade.

The embargo had considerable impact on the U.S. economy. Agricultural prices declined, leading to farm foreclosures. According to official records, exports declined by 80 percent in 1808, though smuggling certainly lessened the effect. The U.S. Treasury suffered a loss in customs revenue, its chief source of income. The embargo stimulated further technological development of the textile industry, particularly in weaving cotton cloth with power looms.

With stern enforcement under Giles's Act, New Englanders became more strident in their demands for termination of the embargo. Jefferson became convinced that civil war was possible, but refused to support repeal. Republicans in Congress moved anyway, on March 1, 1809, replacing the embargo with a Non-Intercourse Act, which reopened trade with all countries except Great Britain and France. If either of the two belligerents changed its policy to favor neutral rights, the United States would resume commerce with that nation as well. While the new law banned trade with major markets, loopholes offered generous opportunities for smuggling.

Congress made this shift just days before the close of Jefferson's presidency. Jefferson thus ended his administration without solving the nation's international troubles, which Americans increasingly defined as an effort by Britain to subjugate its former colonies. As he returned to Monticello, however, the president could reflect favorably upon the goals he had achieved—lower taxes and national debt, smaller government, open doors to immigrants, and peace. He also took pride in an accomplishment he had not foreseen in 1801, the purchase of the Louisiana Territory. Jefferson's administration was remarkable for what it did—and for what it did not do, considering his opposition to Hamiltonian policies in the 1790s. Under Jefferson, the Republicans left intact the national bank, the federal administrative structure, and armed forces. Considering the war-torn world in which the young nation found its way, however, the Republican commitment to minimal government left the United States militarily unprepared.

MADISON AND THE WAR OF 1812

When Britain continued to impress American sailors and seize ships, Jefferson's successor had two choices: accept humiliation or declare war on Great

James Madison, *painted by Gilbert Stuart, a few years before he became the fourth U.S. president. Called the "Father of the Constitution," Madison also helped develop the two-party system through opposition to the Federalists in the 1790s.*
Colonial Williamsburg Foundation

Dolley Payne Madison, *by Gilbert Stuart. From a Quaker family, she met and married James Madison in 1794 while he was serving as congressman in Philadelphia. As first lady she brought elegance to the president's mansion.*
Copyrighted by the White House Historical Association

Britain. The British argued that they acted from necessity, as Napoleon conquered Europe. Americans upheld their rights as neutrals to sell provisions to both sides. They considered British impressment of 6,000 seamen as a violation of national sovereignty and human rights. Between 1809 and 1812, these conflicts developed into war.

The Election of 1808

Despite the embargo, Jefferson retained enough popularity to win a third term, had he chosen to run. When he withdrew, he designated James Madison, the secretary of state, as his successor. James Monroe, who had served as governor of Virginia and minister to Great Britain, challenged Jefferson's choice, but congressional Republicans endorsed Madison. Dissenting Republicans, called the Tertium Quids, gave Monroe some support, but his candidacy died quickly. George Clinton accepted renomination for vice president. The Federalists put up Charles C. Pinckney and Rufus King, hoping that the effects of the embargo might reverse their party's decline.

The Federalists improved upon their performance in 1804 and 1806, gaining twenty-four seats in Congress, but still had much less than a majority. The electoral vote for president was 122 for Madison and 47 for Pinckney. While Americans suffered from the embargo, most were unprepared to desert the Republicans. In electing the new president, citizens ratified Jefferson's political philosophy and policies, which Madison had helped formulate. The third and fourth presidents had jointly founded and nurtured the Republican party; together they had adjusted their ideals to meet the practical needs of the expanding nation. The country could expect a continuation of Jeffersonian policies, though the retiring president withdrew entirely from decision making.

In another way, however, the new administration presented a real departure. Madison brought his elegant wife Dolley Payne Madison with him to the executive mansion, which was still unfinished when they arrived. They made a remarkable couple, as one observer noted:

Mr Madison was a very small man in his person, with a very large head—his manners were peculiarly unassuming; and his conversation lively, often playful. . . . Mrs. Madison was tall, large and rather masculine in personal dimensions; her complexion was so fair and brilliant as to redeem this objection, in its perfectly feminine beauty. . . . There was a frankness and ease in her deportment, that won golden opinions from all, and she possessed an influence so decided with her little Man.

The first lady transformed the president's house into a proper executive mansion. She served as hostess to frequent teas and dinner parties, inviting Federalists and Republicans to socialize together.

Heading for War

After Madison's election, the European struggle continued to embroil the United States. While both Britain and France were hostile to free trade, the British dominated the seas, and as a consequence had substantial impact on U.S. commerce. Over the period to 1812, as Napoleon pushed across Europe, invaded Russia, and met defeat, he became inconsequential as a threat to the Americans. Indeed, his attempt to install his brother Joseph Bonaparte as king of Spain in 1808 undermined Spanish control in the New World. In West Florida, Anglo-Americans who had earlier pledged allegiance to Spain, in 1810 commandeered the Spanish fort at Baton Rouge, declared independence, and petitioned Madison for annexation by the United States. The president promptly claimed West Florida as part of the Louisiana Purchase and American troops occupied Baton Rouge. When Louisiana became a state in 1812, it included the western part of West Florida from Baton Rouge to the Pearl River.

In 1811, Madison appointed James Monroe, his former rival for the presidency, as secretary of state. Monroe took office hoping to reach an accord with the British, but soon decided that they wanted nothing less than to put the United States back into its colonial yoke. Great Britain adhered to its Order in Council that American exports go to England before shipment to Europe; the Royal Navy continued to impress American seamen. When Napoleon partially lifted his blockade in 1811, the United States resumed trade with France. Madison tried to convince the British to drop their restrictions as well, but instead they pounced on American ships headed for French ports.

Events in the West also intensified anger toward Britain, because Anglo-Americans believed

In 1811, Tecumseh attempted to unite northern and southern Indians to defend their remaining lands east of the Mississippi River. This portrait, which was based on sketches made c. 1811, is from Benjamin Lossing's Pictorial Field Book of the War of 1812 *(1869).*
Smithsonian Institution, Bureau of American Ethnology

that the British in Canada were stirring up Native American discontent. In fact, while some Indians traded with the British, many natives distrusted the whites of both Canada and the United States. An alliance between militant Indians and the British took time to evolve, as each group moved independently toward war with the Americans. The nativist message of Tenskwatawa, the Shawnee Prophet, and his brother Tecumseh found widespread support as a result of the Louisiana Purchase, expanding white settlement, and sales by accommodationist Indian leaders of a large proportion of native lands still remaining east of the Mississippi.

The nativists were spurred into action by the Treaty of Fort Wayne (1809), which turned over 2.5 million acres to the United States. Tecumseh met with William Henry Harrison, governor of the Indiana Territory, to request that the treaty be annulled. Failing that, the Indian leader went south to seek support from the Creeks, Cherokees, and Choctaws. He found allies

Map 8.3 *The War of 1812*

 Many of the battles occurred in the Great Lakes region, on the U.S.-Canadian border, shown in detail at bottom.

View an animated version of this map or related maps at http://history.wadsworth.com/passages2e

among militant factions of Creeks and Seminoles. These factions, called the Red Sticks, opposed the accommodationists among their own people who sold land to the United States and adopted Anglo-American ways of life. Tecumseh's effort to create a pan-Indian movement throughout the trans-Appalachian west ultimately failed, however, because by 1811, large white populations in Tennessee, Kentucky, and Ohio formed a barrier between north and south.

In November 1811, William Henry Harrison decided to cut short Tecumseh's efforts for unity. The governor did not believe the Indian leader's assurance that whites were "unnecessarily alarmed at his measures— that they really meant nothing but peace—the United States had set him the example by forming a strict union amongst all the fires that compose their confederacy." Harrison led a force against Prophetstown, the village Tenskwatawa had founded several years before on the Tippecanoe River. Before Harrison struck, the prophet attacked the encamped soldiers at night, but suffered casualties and withdrew. Harrison also lost men, but burned the town and claimed victory in what became known as the Battle of Tippecanoe. The nativists subsequently rebuilt their settlement; Harrison's action had little effect except to drive them closer to the British.

The War of 1812 Begins

When news of the battle reached Washington, many officials interpreted it as evidence that a British-Indian alliance already existed. The outcome, they mistakenly believed, showed that the British were weak, incapable of sustaining their allies. "War Hawks" in Congress, including the newly elected Speaker of the House Henry Clay of Kentucky and Representative John C. Calhoun of South Carolina, advocated preparations for war. They represented a new generation who had not participated in the Revolution and perceived Britain's actions as restoring colonial status. In Calhoun's words, his generation had to prove to "the World, that we have not only inherited that liberty which our Fathers gave us, but also the will and power to maintain it." By April 1812, President Madison agreed. The Federalists, only one-fourth of Congress and primarily from New England, opposed conflict with Great Britain in part to obstruct administration policy, in part for commercial interests. The Republicans were divided. Opponents claimed that Madison intended to wage war for territorial expansion in Canada and Florida.

The nation was ill-prepared when Madison issued his war message on June 1. Military funding would prove difficult because the charter of the national bank had been allowed to expire in 1811 due to politics and state banking interests, leaving state banks but no central agency as a source of loans. Lack of federal taxes beyond import duties, which fell sharply when the British blockaded the Atlantic coast, further limited the country's resources. The failure of New England leaders to provide their share of funds—indeed merchants' provisioning of the enemy and the desire of some New Englanders for a separate peace—severely hampered the war effort. The governors of Massachusetts and Connecticut refused to send their militia. Not everyone in New England opposed the war, however, for the majority of representatives from Vermont, New Hampshire, and Maine (still part of Massachusetts) voted in favor of the June 1812 declaration of war. Large numbers of the region's young men enlisted in the army.

Despite military deficiencies and lack of national unity, the Madison administration pushed forward into battle. Madison offered an armistice if the British stopped impressment, but they refused. Canada, with only 5,000 regular soldiers, seemed the logical target. The redcoats there had little hope for reinforcements as long as Napoleon marched through Europe.

U.S. military leaders planned three advances, one from Lake Champlain to Montreal, a second at the Niagara River, and the third from Fort Detroit east through Upper Canada. With American victories, they hoped, Canada would fall, forcing Britain to recognize U.S. rights. The Americans moved first in the west, where they expected more support from local militia than from New England. Both the Canadians and the United States needed control of the Great Lakes to retain access to lands farther west. General William Hull received orders to lead about 2,000 troops against Fort Malden, opposite Detroit, under command of British General Isaac Brock and reinforced by Tecumseh and his men. Hull dawdled long enough to allow more British soldiers to arrive. He failed to take Fort Malden and surrendered Detroit. The British and Native Americans then took control of much of the region by capturing Fort Michilimackinac, to the north, and Fort Dearborn, at the present site of Chicago. Another blow came for the United States in October, when the army lost the Battle of Queenston, opposite Fort Niagara, after the New York militia refused to leave American soil to assist the regular troops. William Henry Harrison, commissioned a general, reinforced Fort Wayne against Indian attack. The Americans held Fort Harrison (Terre Haute, Indiana) and other points along a line from Sandusky, Ohio, to St. Louis, and undermined Tecumseh's war effort by destroying Indian towns and cornfields in Ohio, Indiana, and Illinois.

Battle of Lake Erie, *painted by an unknown artist, c. 1820, commemorates the victory of Oliver Hazard Perry against the British at Put-in-Bay. The painting shows Perry moving to another vessel when his flagship became disabled.*
New York State Historical Association, Cooperstown

Fort Harrison in 1812, near present-day Terre Haute, Indiana.
From the Director of the Vigo County Historical Society Collection

"The Fall of Washington or Maddy in full flight," an
anonymous English cartoon, 1814. Two British sailors
ridicule President Madison and Secretary of State Monroe
as they escape the burning capital with state documents.
Anne S. K. Brown Military Collection, Brown University Library

During this frustrating campaign against
Canada, James Madison stood for reelection. Some
critics claimed that he had started the conflict to win
another term. His opponent was DeWitt Clinton, a
New York Republican. Clinton tried to gain support
from both political parties by advocating peace to the
Federalists while telling the Republicans that Madison
had failed to prosecute the war hard enough. The president won by an electoral tally of 128 to 89; he obtained substantial Republican majorities in the House
and Senate.

In contrast to the army's failures in 1812, the tiny
U.S. fleet had surprising success against the mighty
Royal Navy. The *Constitution* sank the British *Guer-
rière* in August; two months later the *United States*,
captained by Stephen Decatur, took the *Macedonian*;
in December the *Constitution* destroyed the *Java*. The
American defeats of an enemy considered master of
the seas greatly bolstered public opinion.

Victories and Losses, 1813–1814

On land, however, 1813 began with another disaster
for the Americans, as the British and Native Americans killed and captured nearly an entire force of 900
troops at Frenchtown, south of Detroit. The United
States managed to hold Fort Meigs and Fort Stephenson in northern Ohio. But to destroy British control
of Lake Erie and territory to the west, the army
needed naval support. The United States began

building ships at Presque Isle, Pennsylvania (now
Erie), and on September 10, 1813, Oliver Hazard
Perry defeated the British squadron at Put-in-Bay, establishing American dominance of the lake. This
naval victory cleared the way for General Harrison to
attack Fort Malden, from which the British and Indians hastily retreated toward Niagara. The Americans
caught up with them at Moraviantown on October 5,
winning a decisive victory known as the Battle of the
Thames. Tecumseh died on the battlefield; his
brother Tenskwatawa continued to fight alongside
the British during the rest of the war, but with little
success. To the east, the U.S. Army had burned York
(Toronto), the capital of Upper Canada. But the
Americans met defeat in an offensive against Montreal and lost Fort Niagara.

In the Mississippi Territory, the nativist Red
Sticks waged civil war against Creek leaders who accommodated Anglo-American demands for land.
The fratricidal conflict became a war against the
United States in July 1813 when 180 American militia struck a much smaller group of Red Sticks. A
month later, the nativists killed about 250 settlers
who had taken cover in a stockade called Fort Mims.
The Red Sticks, with 4,000 warriors but lacking adequate arms, faced overwhelming odds against the
combined forces of U.S. troops, accommodationist
Creeks, and Cherokee allies. Three armies entered
Red Stick territory, destroying homes and dispersing
families. The turning point came in March 1814,
when General Andrew Jackson, with 3,000 militia
and Indian allies, defeated 1,000 Red Sticks in the
Battle of Horseshoe Bend, killing 800. The surviving
militants escaped to Florida, where they joined nativist Seminoles and continued to fight. Despite the
fact that accommodationist Creeks assisted Jackson's troops in the battle, the United States forced
them to cede more than 20 million acres of land, including much of what was to become Alabama and
a fifth of present-day Georgia.

In the summer of 1814, the British turned
greater attention to the war in America, having defeated Napoleon in April. They sent 10,000 experienced redcoats to Canada, threatening New York until the American naval victory on Lake Champlain in
September cut short the British invasion. Britain also
sent forces to Chesapeake Bay, where in August they
attacked the nearly defenseless Washington, D.C.
Redcoats burned the Capitol and the president's
mansion, shortly after the Madison household fled
saving official documents and the Gilbert Stuart portrait of George Washington. The enemy promptly left
the capital, and the U.S. government returned.

The British then assaulted Baltimore. Despite heavy bombardment of Fort McHenry by the Royal Navy, the redcoats failed to take the city. James Monroe, who was by then secretary of war as well as secretary of state, took credit for Baltimore's stand. Francis Scott Key memorialized the scene of flaming rockets and exploding bombs in his poem "The Star Spangled Banner," which was later set to the tune of a popular English song and, in the early twentieth century, became the national anthem. The British sailed south to the Gulf Coast, intending to block off the Mississippi River. In late 1814, Andrew Jackson captured Pensacola, Florida, then organized the defense of New Orleans.

The Hartford Convention

Over the course of the war, sentiment had grown in New England for secession, as the British tightened their blockade of the region and occupied the Maine coast. The Massachusetts governor secretly contacted the British about a separate peace. In late 1814, a group of Federalists organized the Hartford Convention to find a more moderate course to remedy their loss of power within the Union. The convention issued a report supporting the right of states to declare federal laws unconstitutional (similar to the Virginia and Kentucky Resolutions of 1798) and arguing that states should be responsible for their own defense. The Hartford delegates called for significant amendments to the Constitution: removal of the three-fifths clause that counted slaves in apportioning delegates in the House of Representatives and electoral college; a two-thirds majority in Congress to declare war and admit new states; a one-term limit on the president and ban on residents from the same state succeeding one another in the office (obviously targeted at Virginia); and prohibition of naturalized citizens—who were largely Republican—from federal positions. These proposals, calculated to damage Republican power bases in the south and west and among new immigrants in the cities, fell on deaf ears when news of the peace treaty arrived from Europe.

The Treaty of Ghent

Peace came as both the British and the United States recognized that the end of the twenty-year struggle in Europe eliminated the rationale for war in America. The defeat of Napoleon removed Britain's need to regulate neutral trade and impress seamen. Both sides could also see that they had little hope of victory. Britain might continue its blockade and smother U.S. commerce, but to what purpose? Conquest of the former colonies, now expanded into the west, would require huge expenditures of manpower and funds. Victory at New Orleans would plug the Mississippi, but in late 1814 success was still uncertain. News arrived, as the British considered terms for peace, that the Americans had repelled the offensives at Lake Champlain and Baltimore. While some Britons desired revenge, more wanted to resume trade.

Madison authorized John Quincy Adams, Albert Gallatin, Henry Clay, and two others to meet the British peace delegation in August 1814 at Ghent, in what is now Belgium. After several months of stalemate, the negotiators agreed on Christmas Eve, 1814, to return to the status quo at the outbreak of war. The British dropped their demands for part of Maine and an independent Indian territory north of the Ohio River, while the Americans stopped insisting that the British renounce impressment, which had ceased.

Battle of New Orleans

Bad weather in the Atlantic delayed until February the ship bringing news of the Treaty of Ghent. In the meantime, British forces prepared to move against the Gulf Coast. A fleet of sixty ships and 14,000 men planned to attack Mobile, seize control of the coast and the rivers, then move against New Orleans.

For Americans unaware of the peace treaty, such a plan posed a serious threat. New Orleans, distant and disconnected from the cities of the east coast, lay vulnerable to invasion. Once the British established a foothold there, troops could move up the Mississippi River. Moreover, a British invasion threatened to bring free and enslaved African Americans, French and Spanish settlers, Native Americans, and even pirates into the conflict throughout the Gulf territories, igniting rebellions against white farmers and traders.

The commander in charge of the American forces, Andrew Jackson, was especially sensitive to the dangers settlers faced on the Gulf Coast. A Tennessee lawyer, planter, and militia leader, he had defeated the Red Sticks at Horseshoe Bend. He repelled the British at Mobile, then raced to New Orleans before the British troops could arrive. The Americans got there first, in December of 1814. When six hundred free blacks volunteered to help defend the city, Jackson gratefully accepted their offer.

A series of attacks by the British damaged the American forces but did not take New Orleans. The British general in charge, Sir Edward Pakenham, unleashed a frontal assault on January 8, 1815. Two Congreve rockets, launched by the British to signal the beginning of the assault and to frighten their opponents, screamed into the air. Jackson's troops, dug in behind earthworks, fired directly into the charging British troops; wave after wave of the onslaught fell as American troops took turns firing and reloading. In less than an hour it was over: Pakenham and two of his generals lay dead, along with over 2,000 of their troops. The Americans suffered only thirteen dead and a few dozen wounded or missing. Nearly a month later, word of Jackson's remarkable success reached the nation's Capital. "ALMOST INCREDIBLE VICTORY!!!," headlines trumpeted. Nine days later word of the Treaty of Ghent, ratified two weeks before the Battle of New Orleans, arrived in Washington.

CONCLUSION

With its simple provision to reinstate the *status quo ante bellum*, the Treaty of Ghent might appear to make the War of 1812 meaningless. The losses of lives and dollars, and disaffection of New England, all seem for nothing. Yet most Americans celebrated the peace, knowing they had withstood Britain's attempt to treat them as colonials. A second generation of Americans had proven they could survive a struggle with what was probably the world's most powerful nation. In addition, the United States had defeated Tecumseh's pan-Indian movement in the West, effectively ending Native American power east of the Mississippi.

Much had changed from 1800 to 1815. The Federalists transformed themselves from the architects of the national government in the 1790s to advocates of narrow sectional interests. Thomas Jefferson and James Madison, who had upheld states' rights, moved in the opposite direction during their administrations. Without denying their commitment to limited government, a skeleton military, low taxes, and republican principles, they expanded "the empire of liberty" by purchasing Louisiana and forcing Native Americans from their lands. Jefferson and Madison used every means short of armed conflict to protect commerce, then went to war when all else failed. In purchasing Louisiana, Jefferson relaxed his philosophy of strict interpretation of the Constitution in hope that the additional territory would extend the life of his agrarian republic. Madison facilitated the growth of nationalism by exacting respect from Great Britain. With the Atlantic world at peace once again, residents from Maine to Louisiana concentrated on making money and building their communities, all with a greater sense that they belonged to an American nation.

Recommended Readings

Andrews, Dee E. *The Methodists and Revolutionary America, 1760–1800: The Shaping of an Evangelical Culture* (2000). An excellent study, including important chapters on the role of women and African Americans.

Coles, Harry L. *The War of 1812* (1965). A readable, one-volume study.

Dowd, Gregory Evans. *A Spirited Resistance: The North American Indian Struggle for Unity, 1745–1815* (1992). Demonstrates the significance of religion in Native American resistance.

Ellis, Joseph J. *American Sphinx: The Character of Thomas Jefferson* (1996). A highly readable study of a complex president.

Freeman, Joanne B. *Affairs of Honor: National Politics in the Early Republic* (2001). A provocative study of the means of political conflict, including dueling.

McCoy, Drew R. *The Elusive Republic: Political Economy in Jeffersonian America* (1980). Insightful exploration of Jeffersonian politics and thought.

Moulton, Gary E., ed. *The Journals of the Lewis and Clark Expedition.* 7 vols. (1983–1991). Most comprehensive edition of manuscript maps and journals.

Nash, Gary B. *Forging Freedom: The Formation of Philadelphia's Black Community, 1720–1840* (1988). Insightful study of the challenges of freedom for one community of African Americans in the North.

Smelser, Marshall. *The Democratic Republic, 1801–1815* (1992). A useful, lively overview of the period.

Waldstreicher, David. *In the Midst of Perpetual Fetes: The Making of American Nationalism, 1776–1820* (1997). Study of popular political culture, including the ways in which African Americans and women participated in celebrations yet were excluded from voting.

American Journey Online and InfoTrac College Edition

Visit the source collections at http://ajaccess. wadsworth.com and infotrac.thomsonlearning.com and use the Search function with the following key terms to explore documents, images, audio and video clips, articles, and commentary related to the material in this chapter.

Thomas Jefferson	Louisiana Purchase
Lewis and Clark	*Marbury v. Madison*
Aaron Burr	Tecumseh
Tenskwatawa	Second Great Awakening

Additional resources, exercises, and Internet links related to this chapter are available on the American Passages Web site: http://history.wadsworth.com/passages2e

PASSAGES — 1815 TO 1855 —

THE UNITED STATES redefined itself during the forty years after 1815. The boundaries of the nation, the character of its population, the nature of its economy, and the religious beliefs of its people all took new shape. Some of the changes confirmed what the architects of the young nation had expected several decades before; other changes proved to be surprises and the bitterest of disappointments. The speed and scale of transformation astonished everyone.

In 1815, the young United States held only eighteen states, with Louisiana standing exposed at the western boundary, Florida in the hands of the Spanish, and an unsettled line between Canada and the United States. The western half of the continent remained only vaguely known to Anglo-Americans and seemed too far away to be of importance any time soon. Even within the country's sketchy borders, American Indians populated large and rich areas in both the north and the south.

Four decades later, the continental boundaries of the nation had expanded beyond recognition. Florida had come into the Union from Spain. War with Mexico had brought in vast territories from Texas to California. Negotiation with Great Britain had defined the northern boundary from Maine to Oregon. Military and economic pressure on the American Indian nations had driven them across the Mississippi River. A new state entered the Union about every two and a half years; by the end of the 1850s, thirty-three states—including two on the Pacific coast—claimed a place in the nation.

The population exploded. The number of Americans grew from 8.4 million in 1815 to 31.4 million by the end of the 1850s. Nearly 4 million of those people were held in slavery, while 3 million people had crossed the Atlantic from Europe in a mixture of hope and desperation. People spread out across the expanse of the burgeoning country, establishing farms and towns far from the older cities of the East. About half the population of an average town moved every ten years. By the end of the period the United States claimed 5 million more people than England, and the new country boasted eight cities of more than 150,000 inhabitants—more than any other country in the world.

Large changes altered the scale of life, tying people together as few could have imagined in 1815. Steamboats transformed water transportation in the 1810s, canals boomed in the 1820s, and railroads arrived in the 1830s. The United States claimed over 35,000 miles of railroad track by the end of the era. In the 1840s, the first telegraph wires carried information from one city to another in a clatter of keys; by the late 1850s, telegraph wires stretched across the Atlantic Ocean. Novels sold tens of thousands of copies in a few months. Newspapers, confined to just a few major cities in 1815, became staples of American life in the 1830s and 1840s, read and published in hundreds of communities of every size. Daguerreotypes and colorful lithographs decorated homes that had been empty of pictures a generation earlier.

The United States became integrated ever more tightly into the international economy. The capacity of ships arriving in American ports doubled in the 1830s, doubled again in the 1840s, and then again in the 1850s. American vessels plied the Atlantic with cargoes of cotton and wheat for England and Europe. Clipper ships sailed around South America and into the Pacific, carrying prospectors and immigrants along with tea. The United States, anxious about European intervention in Latin America and the Caribbean, claimed the hemisphere as a place under its jurisdiction and protection.

New York Public Library The Granger Collection, New York

Americans created lodges, clubs, and societies of every sort. Baptists, Methodists, and Presbyterians vied with one another for converts. Reform groups emerged to stamp out alcohol and war, to encourage education and humane treatment of the unfortunate, to improve diet and health, to bring the end of slavery. Women accounted for many members of these organizations, lending their energy and intelligence to activities beyond the home. Political parties mobilized nearly all adult white men, sweeping them up as Democrats, Whigs, Free Soilers, Know-Nothings, and Republicans. Men swore allegiance to their party, expressing their passions and beliefs in slogans, songs, and parades. On election days, as many as eight out of ten eligible voters went to the polls, publicly proclaiming their support for their candidates.

Foreign trade transformed cities in both the North and the South, as these paintings of New York and New Orleans in the 1850s reveal in striking detail.
The Granger Collection, New York

The expansion of the United States was the expansion of the largest and most powerful slave society in the modern world. Slavery grew stronger with each passing decade, embracing an ever larger part of the continent to the south and west, holding more people within its bonds, accounting for a larger share of the nation's exports. As the years passed, the discussions in the churches, the reform organizations, and the political parties increasingly turned to sectional conflict. Rivalry and distrust between the North and the South infected everything in the public life of the country.

The years between 1815 and 1855, then, did not witness a smooth passage through an "industrial revolution" or "growth of the common man" or "westward expansion." Rather, these years marked a passage filled with rapids and countercurrents and waterfalls. Panics and depressions, internal and external wars, massive migration and immigration, freedom and slavery—all came tumultuously.

	1815	1823	1831
Politics & Diplomacy	**1815:** Battle of New Orleans **1816:** Monroe elected president; "Era of Good Feelings" begins Clay calls for "American System" Indiana admitted to the Union **1817:** Mississippi admitted to the Union **1818:** Jackson invades Florida Illinois admitted to the Union **1819:** Transcontinental (or Adams-Onís) treaty with Spain Alabama admitted to the Union **1820:** Missouri Compromise Monroe elected president Maine admitted to the Union **1821:** Missouri admitted to the Union **1822:** Denmark Vesey Rebellion, Charleston	**1823:** Monroe Doctrine announced **1824:** Contested election of John Quincy Adams **1828:** Tariff of Abominations Calhoun's *Exposition* Election of Jackson **1829:** David Walker's *Appeal* Mexico tries to abolish slavery in Texas **1830:** Indian Removal Act Anti-Masonic party holds first national party convention **1831:** Nat Turner's rebellion Garrison's *The Liberator* Jackson reorganizes cabinet, Van Buren over Calhoun	**1832:** Bank War begins Nullification Crisis Virginia debates over slavery Jackson reelected **1833:** Force Bill against South Carolina Compromise Tariff Slavery abolished in British Empire **1834:** Whig party organized **1835:** Arkansas admitted to the Union Revolution breaks out in Texas Abolitionists' postal campaign War against Seminoles and runaway slaves in Florida **1836:** Congress imposes gag rule Battle of the Alamo; Texas Republic established **1838:** John Quincy Adams successfully defeats attempt to annex Texas
Social & Cultural Events	**1816:** American Colonization Society founded American Bible Society founded **1819:** Auburn penitentiary established	**1824:** Lafayette's visit American Sunday School Union founded **1825:** American Tract Society founded **1829:** David Walker's *Appeal* **1830:** *The Book of Mormon* Finney's revivals begin in Rochester	**1831:** Garrison's *The Liberator* Mormons migrate from New York to Ohio **1833:** Formation of American Anti-slavery Society **1837:** Grimké sisters lecture to mixed audiences Horace Mann becomes first secretary of Massachusetts State Board of Education Ralph Waldo Emerson, "The American Scholar" **1839:** Daguerreotypes introduced to the United States
Economics & Technology	**1815:** *Enterprise* first steamboat from New Orleans to Pittsburgh **1816:** Second Bank of the United States chartered **1817:** Mississippi admitted to the Union **1818:** Erie Canal begun National Road completed **1819:** *Dartmouth College v. Woodward* and *McCulloch v. Maryland* Financial panic and depression	**1824:** *Gibbons v. Ogden* **1825:** Completion of Erie Canal **1828:** Tariff of Abominations	**1831:** John Bull begins railroad operation **1832:** Bank War begins **1833:** Compromise Tariff **1834:** National Trades Union formed Cyrus McCormick patents reaper **1837:** Financial panic *Charles River Bridge v. Warren Bridge* decision **1839:** Depression worsens Daguerreotypes introduced to the United States

1840: Congress passes
Independent Treasury Act
Harrison elected president
Frederick Douglass escapes
from slavery
American Anti-slavery Society
splits
James G. Birney runs for
president as candidate for
Liberty party
1841: Harrison dies; John Tyler
becomes president
Amistad case heard before the
Supreme Court
1844: James K. Polk claims the
United States's claim to "all
Oregon"
1845: Texas and Florida admitted
to the Union

1846: Mexican War begins;
Stephen Kearny occupies Santa
Fe; Zachary Taylor takes
Monterey
Border between Canada and
United States established at
49th parallel
Wilmot Proviso ignites
sectional conflict
Bear Flag Republic in California
proclaimed by John C. Frémont
1847: Taylor defeats Santa Anna
at Buena Vista; Winfield Scott
captures Vera Cruz and Mexico
City
1848: Treaty of Guadalupe
Hidalgo
Attempts to buy Cuba from
Spain
Free-Soil party runs Van Buren
for president
Seneca Falls Convention
Zachary Taylor elected
president

1849: California seeks admission
to Union
1850: Nashville Convention
attempts to unify South
Fugitive Slave Law
Taylor dies; Millard Fillmore
becomes president
Compromise of 1850
1851: Maine adopts prohibition
Woman's rights convention in
Akron, Ohio
Indiana state constitution
excludes free blacks
1852: Franklin Pierce elected
president
1853: Gadsden Purchase
1854: Know-Nothings win
unexpected victories
Whig party collapses
Republican party founded
Kansas-Nebraska Act
Ostend Manifesto encourages
acquisition of Cuba

1840: Washingtonian temperance
movement emerges
1841: Brook Farm founded
P. T. Barnum opens the
American Museum
Amistad case heard before the
Supreme Court
1842: Edgar Allan Poe, "The
Murders in the Rue Morgue"
1844: Methodist Episcopal
church divides over slavery
Edgar Allan Poe, "The Raven"

1846: Hiram Powers completes
statue *The Greek Slave*
1847: Mormons reach Great Salt
Lake Valley
1848: Seneca Falls Convention
Oneida community
established
Mormons settle in Great Basin

1850: Nathaniel Hawthorne, *The
Scarlet Letter*
1851: Herman Melville, *Moby
Dick*
Maine adopts prohibition
Woman's rights convention in
Akron, Ohio
1852: Harriet Beecher Stowe,
Uncle Tom's Cabin
1854: Henry David Thoreau,
Walden

1840: Congress passes
Independent Treasury Act
1841: California sees arrival of
first wagon train
Oregon fever
1843: Oregon sees arrival of first
wagon trains
1844: Baltimore-Washington
telegraph line
Samuel F. B. Morse patents the
telegraph

1848: Gold discovered in
California
Regular steamship trips
between Liverpool and New
York City

1849: "Forty-niners" race to
California
Cotton prices invigorate South
1854: High-point of Immigration
Railroad reaches Mississippi
River

9 EXPLODED BOUNDARIES
1815–1828

NEW BORDERS

BUILDING A NATIONAL ECONOMY

REGIONAL GROWTH

CONSEQUENCES OF EXPANSION

THE REINVENTION OF POLITICS

The Erie Canal, connecting the Hudson River with Lake Erie, demanded a monumental engineering effort. It soon paid its way, however, as shippers and farmers rushed to use the new waterway.
The Granger Collection, New York

The sudden climax of the War of 1812 surprised everyone. The leaders of the United States had wondered whether a large and lightly governed republic could survive in the rough-and-tumble world of international conflict. When the new country held its own in the war against England, the most powerful military force on earth, Americans gained a new confidence. President James Madison, ending his term in 1816, announced that the Constitution had proven itself able to "bear the trials of adverse as well as prosperous circumstances."

James Monroe, another in a long line of Virginia Republicans, easily won the national election of 1816. He bore the reputation of being an honest and dependable man, less intellectually distinguished than Jefferson or Madison. Monroe and his wife set a new tone for the presidency, with greater emphasis on etiquette, style, and entertaining, on embodying and celebrating the new national stature of the United States. The Monroes had the executive mansion painted a brilliant white to cover the smoke stains from its burning during the war with England; the residence became known as the "White House." After his election, Monroe toured the Northeast, including New England. A Boston journalist, impressed, talked of a budding "Era of Good Feelings," an era without party rancor, a strong contrast to the bitter conflict of earlier decades. The term was an exaggeration but many people wanted to believe a new era of cooperation had begun. President Monroe relished the role of peacemaker and conciliator.

Newly secure, the United States entered upon a period of territorial expansion and economic growth no one could have foreseen just a few years earlier. Throughout the country, steamboats, canals, and turnpikes tied the countryside to the cities and the cities to one another. White settlers, freed from concern about the British and emboldened against the American Indians, pushed west in vast numbers, taking enslaved African Americans with them across the South. Such rapid growth led many Americans to worry that their society was changing too fast, that selfishness and ambition had come to rule.

NEW BORDERS

The borders of the United States had been fluid and in doubt throughout the nation's brief history. In every direction other nations and peoples contested American boundaries. To the north, English power loomed in Canada. To the west, American Indians resisted efforts by whites to buy or seize their ancestral lands. To the south, the Spanish held on in Florida. Moreover, many states had little economic dealing with one another, trad-

CHRONOLOGY

1815 Battle of New Orleans • *Enterprise* first steamboat from New Orleans to Pittsburgh

1816 Monroe elected president; "Era of Good Feelings" begins • Clay calls for "American System" • Second Bank of the United States chartered • Indiana admitted to the Union

1817 Mississippi admitted to the Union

1818 Jackson invades Florida • Erie Canal begun • Illinois admitted to the Union • National Road completed

1819 Transcontinental (or Adams-Onís) Treaty with Spain • *Dartmouth College v. Woodward* and *McCulloch v. Maryland* • Financial panic and depression • Alabama admitted to the Union • Auburn penitentiary established

1820 Missouri Compromise • Monroe elected president • Maine admitted to the Union

1821 Missouri admitted to the Union

1822 Denmark Vesey Rebellion, Charleston

1823 Monroe Doctrine announced

1824 Contested election of John Quincy Adams • Lafayette's visit • *Gibbons v. Ogden*

1825 Completion of Erie Canal

1826 Kidnapping of William Morgan

ing instead with England, Europe, and the Caribbean. As a result, states defended sharply conflicting policies, and their economies did not connect with one another very effectively. The peace after 1815 provided an opportunity for the United States to establish its borders more securely and to integrate itself more fully.

Native Peoples

President Monroe worked to establish clearer borders for the young nation. He succeeded in his dealing with Great Britain, when the two countries clarified the boundaries between the United States and Canada. The Rush-Bagot Treaty of 1817 calmed conflict on the Great Lakes and the Convention of 1818 fixed the border with Canada at the 49th parallel.

Relations with American Indians proved much more challenging. By the early nineteenth century, the American Indians had lived in contact with European culture for more than two hundred years. The native peoples had long combined their ancient practices with newer ones. Commercial hunting expeditions covered ever-expanding territory, tracking animals to trade with white trading partners. Trade networks stretched over thousands of miles.

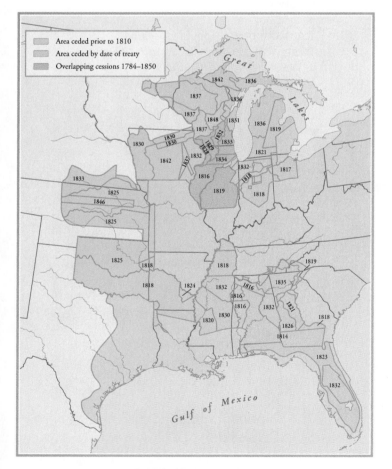

Map 9.1 *Lands Ceded by American Indians*
The United States negotiated one treaty after another with American Indians in the decades after 1815, acquiring land and pushing the natives of these areas to the west.

Indians' clothing reflected the combination of cultures, as they combined moccasins with woolen breeches, imported cloth turbans, and jewelry made of melted silver coins. The intermingling worked both ways, for considerable numbers of English and Scots traders lived among the Indians. Many men of European background adopted Indian dress and language and married into native families. African Americans, too, often took refuge with the Creeks and Seminoles, so that by 1815 mixed ancestry had become common.

The removal of the British troops after the War of 1812 dealt a strong blow to the hopes of the American Indians. Alliances with the British, both actual and threatened, had helped hold back the white Americans. Now that the alliance with England had been destroyed, the United States quickly sought to exert firm control over the eastern half of the continent. Andrew Jackson, triumphant general in the war, was placed in charge of negotiating with the Creek, Cherokee, Chickasaw, and Choctaw nations of Alabama, Florida, and Mississippi after the peace of 1815. Jackson used heavy-handed treaties to force Indians from their former lands. Many of the natives resisted the removal, objecting that the treaties extracted by Jackson had been signed by Indians who had no authority to make such concessions.

The various native peoples identified themselves by the location of their villages, their languages, and their traditional enemies, and often fought with one another, but whites insisted on lumping these diverse people into groups that could be more easily dealt with. Jackson and other officials relied on particular American Indians as allies in war but then deliberately punished all the tribes in the region regardless of earlier promises. Such policies weakened the power of Indian leaders and left their people little choice but to accept bribes and annual grants of money in return for their lands. As soon as Jackson managed to secure lands from the Creeks, Cherokees, and Chickasaws, white settlers rushed into the territories, hungry for the fertile land and the fortunes it could build. Such incursions occurred across millions of acres in North Carolina, Kentucky, and Tennessee as well as in Alabama, Mississippi, and Georgia; in each state, the Indians were pushed to the hilly and mountainous lands least desirable for farming. The U.S. government made it easy for white settlers to buy land and sold about a million acres a year throughout the next decade. Not surprisingly, tensions steadily mounted between the ancient residents of the land and those who now claimed it.

As in the South, white settlement in the Northwest was made possible by the subjugation of the na-

American Society for Improving Indian Tribes, 1824
The blessings of civilization

In this address to Congress, a prestigious religious group argues that the American Indians have suffered for generations at the hands of the United States. The only way to atone for these "national sins," the commissioners argue, is to educate the Indian people in the ways of white Americans. The document shows the good will that many white Americans held toward the Indians and the limitations of their understanding of the Indians' own desires.

. . . The history of our intercourse with Indians, from the first settlement of this country, contains many facts honorable to the character of our ancestors, and of our nation—many, also, too many, which are blots on this character; and which, in reflecting on them, cannot fail to fill us with regret, and with concern, lest the Lord of nations, who holds in his hand the scales of equal and everlasting justice, should in his wrath say to us, "As ye have done unto these Indians, so will I requite you." We here allude to the neglect with which these aboriginal tribes have been treated in regard to their civil, moral, and religious improvement—to the manner in which we have, in many, if not most instances, come into possession of their lands, and of their peltry: also, to the provocations we have given, in so many instances, to those cruel, desolating, and exterminating wars, which have been successively waged against them; and to the corrupting vices, and fatal diseases, which have been introduced among them, by wicked and unprincipled white people. These acts can be viewed in no other light, than as national sins, aggravated by our knowledge, and their ignorance; our strength and skill in war, and their weakness—by our treacherous

abuse of their unsuspicious simplicity, and, especially, by the light and privileges of Christianity, which we enjoy, and of which they are destitute. . . .

. . . It *is* desirable that our Indians should receive such an education as has been mentioned, we conceive, because the civilized is preferable to the savage state; because the Bible, and the religion therein revealed to us, with its ordinances, are blessings of infinite and everlasting value and which the Indians do not now enjoy. It is also desirable as an act of common humanity. The progress of the white population, in the territories which were lately the hunting grounds of the Indians, is rapid, and probably will continue and increase. Their game, on which they principally depend for subsistence, is diminishing, and is already gone from those tribes who remain among us. . . . There is no place on the earth to which they can migrate, and live in the savage and hunter state. The Indian tribes must, therefore, be *progressively civilized*, or *successively* perish.

Source: American Board of Commissioners for Foreign Missions, Memorial to the Senate and the House of Representatives, in *American Society for Improving Indian Tribes, First Annual Report*, 1824, pp. 66–68.

tive peoples. After northern Indians' disastrous losses in the War of 1812, they posed little threat to white settlers. The U.S. government quickly established a series of forts throughout the Northwest to intimidate any American Indians and to make sure that the British and Canadians did not regain a foothold. The growing

numbers of white farmers made it difficult for Native Americans to hunt for a living. President Monroe exulted in the "rapid and gigantic" spread of white settlers into the Northwest, an expansion the "rights of nature demand and nothing can prevent." The president argued that "the earth was given to mankind to support the greatest number of people of which it is capable, and no tribe or people have a right to withhold from the wants of others more than is necessary for their own support and comfort." Whites who moved to the Northwest confronted only scattered remnants of native peoples, trading with white merchants for food, sometimes begging from homesteaders.

The American Indians strove to adapt to white ways while maintaining their identity; the Cherokees, in particular, won praise for their "civilized" customs. One Cherokee, Sequoyah, devised an alphabet in his people's language in 1821. The wealthiest Cherokees purchased African American slaves and built substantial cotton plantations. No matter what accommodations they made, the American Indians suffered repeated conflicts with whites who relied on sheer numbers, trickery, violence, and the law to dispossess Native Americans of their land claims.

The Spanish in Florida

Like the American Indians, the Spanish who remained in Florida after 1815 had become vulnerable. Without the assistance of the British, they found it nearly impossible to resist American incursions into their territory. White Americans, for their part, felt they had a right, even an obligation, to drive the Spanish from the mainland, in part because Protestants had long distrusted the Catholic, monarchical Spanish. Many Americans thought it inevitable that Florida and Mexico would become part of the United States. To make relations even more volatile, sixty miles from the southern border of the United States stood the so-called Negro Fort, occupied by runaway slaves and their Indian allies.

In the spring of 1816 Jackson warned the Spanish commandant of Pensacola that the stronghold was "occupied by upwards of two hundred and fifty negros many of whom have been enticed away from the service of their master—citizens of the United States." The fugitives would "not be tolerated by our government," Jackson warned, "and if not put down by Spanish Authority will compel us in self Defence to destroy them." Spain was eager, in fact, to be rid of the fort as well, but did not have the military power to overthrow it. The Spanish feared, correctly, that Jackson would use the refuge as a pretext to invade Florida. Indeed, the Americans sent an expedition against the fort; a projectile hit a powder magazine, killing 270 of the men, women, and children inside.

In 1818, Jackson's forces also punished groups of Seminoles, who, with their Creek allies, had launched raids against white settlers in south Georgia and then fled into Florida. The American soldiers burned a Seminole town, only to see their foes retaliate by attacking a boat of soldiers, women, and children on the Apalachicola River, killing all but a few on board. Though his authorization from Washington was doubtful, Jackson invaded Spanish territory, executed a Creek prophet and two British men he accused of abetting the Indian cause, and overran the weak Spanish presence in the most important outposts. Some in Congress wanted to punish Jackson for what they considered his unauthorized attack. Jackson rushed to Washington to defend himself and his honor. Enraged by the appointment of a Senate committee to investigate his conduct during the war, Jackson threatened to slice off the committee chairman's ears. Unimpressed, the Pennsylvania Senator commented, "I have passed [Jackson's] lodging every day and still have my ears." Jackson also swore that he would kill Speaker of the House Henry Clay in a duel because of his speeches challenging Jackson's actions in Florida. In contrast, many white Americans thronged the cities where Jackson appeared along the way, celebrating him as a decisive hero rather than castigating him for being the military despot Henry Clay claimed. The congressional hearings on Jackson's behavior in the war had little effect except to make Jackson suspicious of the men in power in Washington.

Meanwhile, American and Spanish officials negotiated. The U.S. delegation was led by the brilliant and tenacious John Quincy Adams, son of the former president. With Jackson's military victories giving force to his words, Adams held out until the Spanish, in return for 5 million dollars in compensation of private claims, ceded to the United States all territories east of the Mississippi River. In this, the Adams-Onís Treaty of 1819, the Spanish kept the vast territory from Texas to present-day California, while the United States claimed a northern border that ran unbroken to Oregon and the Pacific Ocean. Adams called his handiwork the Transcontinental Treaty, for it stretched the borders of the United States from the Atlantic to the Pacific.

BUILDING A NATIONAL ECONOMY

The end of the Napoleonic Wars in 1815 unleashed the economies of Europe and the countries that dealt with Europe, including the United States. American prosperity grew as the population boomed, as people moved across the expanse of the continent, and as transportation advances knit once isolated settlers and small towns

PICTURING THE PAST◆POLITICS & DIPLOMACY

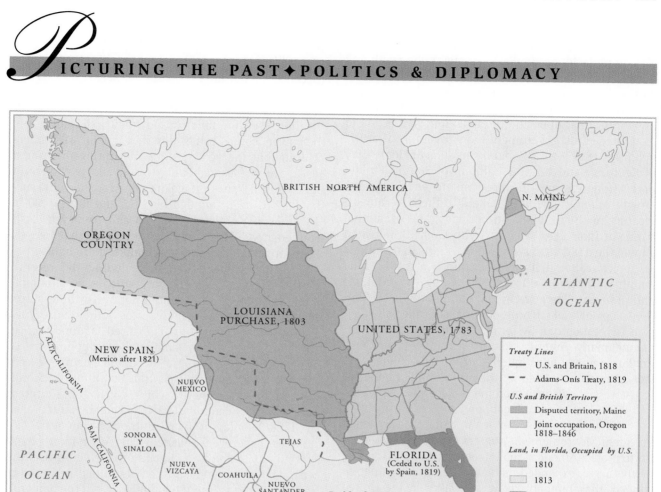

Map 9.2 *Redrawing the Nation's Boundaries*

View an animated version of this map or related maps at http://historywadsworth.com/passages2e

What now seem the "natural" boundaries of the continental United States were by no means obvious in 1815. As it stood, somewhat surprised in its lack of defeat by the powerful British in the War of 1812, the United States still had poorly defined and dangerous borders in almost every direction. The boundaries of Maine, the enormous area west of the Great Lakes, and Oregon remained contested with Great Britain in the north. Though we now think of the relationship between the United States and Canada as the very model of peaceful coexistence, at the time many people worried about this British territory looming over the United States. To the south, Spain (and runaway slaves and the Seminoles) controlled Florida and much of the Gulf Coast. The territory, so close to the booming areas of the South, posed a threat to slavery as well as to the territorial ambitions of the United States. To the west, the territory that would become Mexico remained contested, still in the process of defining its own nationhood. In the five years after the peace of 1815, the United States eagerly negotiated treaties with Great Britain and Spain to clarify and stabilize the young nation's borders. The settlement of the treaties helped create the conditions for rapid growth and economic development.

together. Slavery expanded along with free labor, farms along with factories, the East along with the South and the West. People made their livings in new ways and participated in an economy of ever-expanding scope.

Leading members of the Republican party, long known for their opposition to federal power, began to view the central government more favorably after the victory of 1815. Young Republicans such as Henry Clay of Kentucky and John C. Calhoun of South Carolina urged Congress and the president to encourage the growth of enterprise with the aid of the government, creating roads, canals, a strong navy, and a national bank. In their eyes, the war with Great Britain had shown the dangers of a sprawling American nation, its resources scattered, its defenses thin. The future of the country, Clay and Calhoun believed, lay in commerce and industry. The government should ally itself with the forces of trade. These nationalists called their vision the "American System." Despite the excitement among many Americans, representatives from New England joined with Virginia and North Carolina to reject projects supported by the mid-Atlantic and western states. They considered the projects too expensive and too threatening to local power.

Adopting some ideas of the "American System," President Monroe urged Congress to use protective tariffs to protect American manufacturing, to build roads to tie the newly expanded markets and farms together, to connect the abundant rivers and lakes in the United States with a system of canals to integrate "the whole coast from its southern tip to its northern extremity in one continued inland navigation." Monroe hoped his plan would be supported by a broad and nonpartisan consensus. He eagerly waited for agreement to develop.

The Second Bank of the United States announced its solidity and strength with its austere classical architecture.
The Granger Collection, New York

Banks, Corporations, and Law

No country needed credit more than the United States. Because far too little cash spread across its vast and growing territory, much business within the country rested on nothing more than trust and promises. Credit relations became tangled and fragile; the fall of one borrower could bring down a chain of lenders. Throughout the years before and during the War of 1812, states chartered banks to help alleviate the problems caused by a shortage of cash. More than 200 such banks had been founded by 1815 and nearly 400 by 1818, issuing notes that served as currency in cash-starved areas. Thomas Jefferson worried that "our citizens are clamoring for more banks, more banks."

Many influential men, including the recently elected President Monroe, supported a new national bank to stabilize the economy and distribute scarce money more uniformly. Advocates of the bank argued that the notes of state banks varied far too much in soundness and value, making the economic system dangerously unstable. The expanding country's economic system needed a central institution to coordinate the flow of money. Accordingly, in 1816 Congress chartered the Second Bank of the United States. Based in Philadelphia, it was authorized to establish branches wherever it wished. The new national bank was an amalgam of public and private enterprise: the federal government deposited its funds in the bank and appointed a fifth of the directors, but the bank ran as a private business. For the privilege of being the only such institution authorized to operate on a national basis, the bank handled, without fees, the funds of the federal treasury. The bank pumped large amounts of paper currency into the system in an attempt to feed the voracious hunger of the postwar economy, especially in the new states of the West.

The local, state, and federal courts of the United States also encouraged the growth of business in the years after the peace of 1815. Courts increasingly favored market forces over custom and stability in property relations, shifting the advantage from farmers and landowners to developers. Those who wanted to dam rivers for factories or build roads enjoyed increasing precedence over those threatened by floods, fires, or disruption caused by development. The courts assumed that the public good from the growth of business outweighed the stability favored by older notions of justice. Because many people bitterly protested this shift in emphasis, state legislatures sometimes sought to curb the power of business interests.

The Supreme Court under Chief Justice John Marshall issued a number of important decisions following the War of 1812 that also hastened economic development. Marshall was more concerned with establishing the power of the federal government than with furthering the economy, but by creating a more uniform legal environment that transcended the restrictions of particular states, the Court accelerated the growth of business. One decision of 1819 made bankruptcy laws more uniform across the country; another, *Dartmouth College v. Woodward,* sheltered corporations from legislative interference; yet another 1819 ruling, *McCulloch v. Maryland,* established the constitutionality of the Bank of the United States and protected it from state taxation. A fourth case in this period, *Gibbons v. Ogden* (1824), limited the rights of states to interfere in commerce with either special favors and monopolies or restrictive laws. "In all commercial regulations," Marshall pronounced, "we are one and the same people." In this new legal environment, increasingly emulated by state courts and legislators, business flourished in the years immediately following the end of war.

Roads and Canals

Americans threw themselves into a frenzy of road and turnpike building after 1815. New York alone chartered 300 companies that began construction of 5,000 miles of gravel roads. Investors, states, and even the federal government built thousands of miles of private roads—turnpikes—charging tolls to offset the roads' notoriously high maintenance costs. Some road builders laid logs side-by-side to provide a durable surface, though these so-called corduroy roads took a heavy toll on horse, wagon, and rider and wore out quickly besides. In 1818, the U.S. government opened the "National Road," connecting the Potomac River at Cumberland, Maryland, with Wheeling, [West] Virginia, on the Ohio River. The road was the best that technology could provide at the time, with excellent bridges and a relatively smooth stone surface. The road attracted so much business, however, that traffic jams slowed movement to a crawl and the road quickly fell into poor condition. Even on good roads, it often cost more to move bulky items such as corn or wheat than the price the products could bring at market.

Businesses and state governments began to plan dependable canals with controllable locks and a steady flow of water. Because Baltimore and Philadelphia enjoyed close connections with the West, benefiting from heavily used turnpikes, New York City merchants worried that their dominant position in the East would be lost if they did not establish fast and inexpensive connections as well. Fortunately for New York, a flat passage broke through the Appalachian

In the absence of a paper currency, notes such as this helped fuel the expansive growth of the American economy in these decades.
The Granger Collection, New York

Corduroy roads, while offering some relief from mud and stones, proved poor competition with newer kinds of transportation such as canals and steamboats.
The Granger Collection, New York

Mountains within the state's borders. New Yorkers believed that a canal through this area, connecting the Hudson River to Lake Erie, would far surpass any other kind of transportation. Such a canal would be ten times longer than any other canal then in existence: 364 miles through swamps and solid rock, through places where virtually no white settlers had bothered to migrate.

The mayor of New York City and future governor of the state, De Witt Clinton, became the foremost advocate of the canal, certain it would make his city "the great depot and warehouse of the western world." People scoffed at the money thrown away in

Ohio Board of Canal Commissioners, 1828
Annual Report

The commissioners of Ohio struggle here with a key question of an era when new kinds of transportation were rapidly growing: what role should state and federal government play in economic development? Should the government actively sponsor development, stay out of the way while private businesses competed among themselves, or try to regulate and coordinate private efforts? Here, the Ohio commissioners argue that it is more democratic for the government to take on the responsibility.

An important question may present itself for the consideration of the [Ohio] General Assembly, as connected with the proposed improvements; whether the contemplated canals should be made under the authority, and at the expense of the state, or charters should be granted to private companies for that purpose? The commissioners are of opinion, that the work should be undertaken by the state; chartered companies, possessing exclusive privileges, have always been popular in monarchical governments, because their powers and advantages were so much carved out of the sovereign power for the benefit of subjects—so much in fact gained from the monarchy. The judicial tribunals, influenced doubtless by the popular feeling upon this subject soon found means to secure them to the grantees—gave them a character of *immortality;* changed granted privileges, from the sovereign, into a contract between equals, and placed them beyond the reach of his power, under the protection of that ingenious fiction. Our jurisprudence which borrows its principles and reasonings from England, has very gravely adopted this doctrine of immortality in corporations; naturalized and established it as law in our free governments, and stretched over its dogmas, the aegis of the Constitution, so that in effect, whatever is granted to a private company by the legislature is holden to be intangible and irrevocable. A grant made under erroneous impressions, and which in its operation is found detrimental to, or even destructive of the public welfare, whether it involves the exercise of sovereign powers or not is, according to established principles of law, altogether irrevocable. The present generation may in this way not only bind themselves, but their posterity forever; and

government, instead of being at all times administered for the benefit of the people and in accordance with their will; may be parcelled out into monopolies, swallowing up their interests and counteracting their wishes. How long a free people will sanction such principles, or how consonant they are to the fundamental maxims of our social fabric, it is not our purpose to inquire; the existence of them, we remark, as evincing the risk and danger of granting to private companies any control over matters of public and general interest. Nothing can be more interesting to the whole community, than great navigable highways through the state, from the Lake [Erie] to the Ohio river, on the routes proposed; it does not consist with the dignity, the interest or the convenience of the state, that a private company of citizens or foreigners (as may happen), should have the management and control of them; the evils of such management cannot be fully foreseen, and therefore cannot be provided against; for experience is the only safe guide in legislation and of the operation of such grants we have no experience. Besides, such works should be constructed with a view to the greatest possible accommodation of our citizens; as a public concern, the public convenience is the paramount object; a private company will look only to the best means of increasing their profits, the public convenience will be regarded only as it is subservient to their emolument. We think therefore, that it would be extremely hazardous and unwise, to entrust private companies with making those canals, which can be made by the state.

Source: [Ohio] Board of Canal Commissioners, *Third Annual Report, Civil Engineer* (August 16, 1828), pp. 138–140.

STEAMBOAT

© Bettmann/Corbis

Steamboats began to ply the Mississippi River and other major waterways in the 1810s and 1820s, accelerating trade and fueling the growth of cities along the way. This boat is being loaded at Natchez, Mississippi, one of the earliest outposts of the new cotton economy in what would eventually be remembered as the "Old" South, even though it did not exist long enough to really deserve the name. The technology of the steamboat had been known before the War of 1812, but the end of the war opened the rivers of the United States to a rapidly increased trade. Though steamboat technology steadily improved so that steamboats become safer, larger, and more comfortable, they remained dangerous by their very nature. Built light and carrying large tanks under extreme pressure, streamboats were vulnerable to submerged obstacles and often exploded without warning and without obvious cause.

"Clinton's Big Ditch." But the largely untrained engineers learned as they went along. Aqueducts had to span rivers and gorges, aqueducts tight and strong enough to withstand the weight of the water and the boats they carried. Locks had to be constructed of heavy timbers and even heavier stone. The canal, 4 feet deep and 40 feet wide at the top, was dug by hands, backs, and shovels. Thousands of laborers, many of them foreign-born, moved with the canal, enlivening and sometimes frightening the more sedentary settlements on the route. Year after year, the canal edged toward Lake Erie, transforming the countryside along the way; by 1819, the canal stretched for seventy-five miles. As soon as workers completed a segment, boats crowded upon its waters, the tolls they paid financing the portions yet unfinished.

The completion of the Erie Canal in 1825 demonstrated that Americans could accomplish great things.

The constructors of the canal, bragged one speaker, "have built the longest canal, in the least time, with the least experience, for the least money and to the greatest public benefit." Soon after De Witt Clinton ceremoniously poured water from Lake Erie into the Atlantic, thousands of boats were traveling along the canal between Buffalo and New York City, pumping half a million dollars of tolls into the state coffers, sending a surge of prosperity along its route. By 1834, approximately nine boats passed through major locks on the canal each minute. Other states looked enviously upon the glorious and profitable Erie Canal and began their own plans and excavations.

Not everyone saw such transformations of the land in glowing terms. A contemporary satire mocked the pleasures of being dragged "along a muddy ditch, hour after hour, in constant dread of lifting your head above your knees for fear of having it knock'd off your shoulders by a bridge!" Although the canal had been envisioned as primarily a freight service, from the beginning more than 40,000 passengers traveled on the new waterway. Settlers, tourists, salesmen, and evangelical ministers took advantage of the convenience and low cost of the canal to reach new lands and wider audiences for their products.

Steamboats

Canals, though useful and exciting, reached only a limited part of the vast North American continent. Rivers offered faster and cheaper travel, especially along the Mississippi, Missouri, and Ohio. But their limitations were obvious as well. The rivers could be dangerously fast in some seasons and so slow as to be impassable in others. They often froze for months in the winter. Strong currents ran in only one direction. Those who wanted to transport goods northward had to push their boats against the current, sometimes with poles, sometimes by dragging the boats with ropes as the crews walked along the shore, sometimes merely by grabbing trees and bushes on the banks. It took three or four months to drag a boat upstream. Others simply sold their craft for scrap in New Orleans and walked back to Ohio or Illinois, a long and arduous trip.

Not surprisingly, people dreamed of using steam engines to drive riverboats. Robert Fulton's steamboats had traversed the quieter waters of the Northeast since 1807, but Fulton did not manage to build one for the rigors of the Mississippi until 1811. The War of 1812 slowed development of the steamboats, since engines could not be imported from England, but innovation resumed with the war's end. As soon as Jackson won New Orleans in 1815, the *Enterprise* churned its way upriver from Louisiana all the way to Louisville, Kentucky. Dozens of other craft soon joined, competing with one another. In 1817, the journey from New Orleans to Louisville took twenty-five days; in 1819, fourteen days. "If any one had said this was possible thirty years ago," a journalist marveled, "we should have been ready to send him to a mad-house." Though the shallow, high-powered, and top-heavy steamboats showed a dangerous propensity to explode, run aground, and slam into submerged obstacles, no one thought of going back to the old way of travel. Based on contemporary estimates, 40 percent of steamboats built prior to 1849 sank, burned, or exploded, frequently killing large numbers of passengers. To grasp the extent of the hazards of steamboat travel, a comparable rate of carnage today would involve six to nine serious accidents per motorist per year.

The increasing speed and frequency of the steamboats encouraged the growth of villages and towns along the rivers. Huge stacks of wood carted in from the countryside appeared wherever the steamboats regularly stopped for fuel; new stores sold the goods transported on the river; muddy villages dreamed of becoming major cities. Indeed, the populations of Louisville, Pittsburgh, and Cincinnati doubled or more than doubled between 1815 and 1825, developing into centers not only of trade but also of meatpacking and flour milling.

The small towns along the Ohio and Mississippi Rivers quickly grew into booming young cities like Cincinnati.
Cincinnati Historical Society

REGIONAL GROWTH

As the American economy grew, different parts of the country specialized economically. The more the regions integrated with one another, ironically, the more they differed. When roads, canals and steamboats lowered the cost of shipment, it made more sense for particular places to specialize in what they produced best. As a result, the South, Northeast, and Northwest, all pursuing growth and development, followed paths quite different from one another.

The different regions of the United States cannot be understood in isolation from one another. The South, for example, did not stand outside the political, cultural, and economic events that transformed the rest of the nation. Slavery played a critical role in the history of the entire country, producing the cotton that fueled the growth of the Northeast's textile factories and providing a large market for the farms of Ohio, Illinois, and Indiana. The South, moreover, changed as much as any part of the country in these years and often played a leading role in the nation's politics and foreign affairs. Unlike most texts, therefore, this one does set the South apart in a separate chapter but integrates its history into the story of the United States.

The Creation of the Cotton South

The demand for cotton in England took off after 1815, when cotton became, for the first time, the clothing of choice for large numbers of the world's

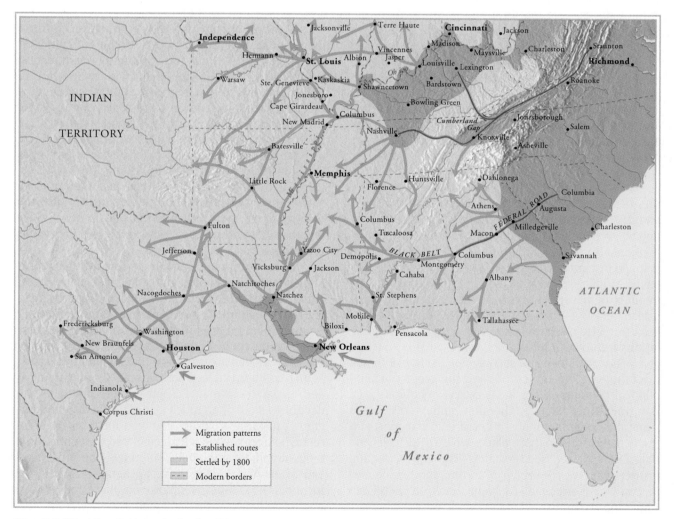

Map 9.3 *Migration Patterns in the Southeast*
White southerners followed rivers and valleys into the rich lands of the Southwest, with the wealthier among them relying on slaves to clear the lands for new plantations.

people. Cotton clothes were cheaper, easier to create, and more comfortable in warm weather than those made from wool or linen. No place in the world was as prepared to supply the burgeoning demand for cotton as the American South. Small farmers as well as planters from the older states of the southern seaboard saw opportunity in the new states of Alabama and Mississippi, especially now that Andrew Jackson had opened Mobile as a port for southern Alabama. Many white farmers also moved to western Tennessee and parts of Louisiana. The steamboat and the cotton gin gave southern planters powerful new tools, while slaves could clear and cultivate land for new plantations far more quickly than would have been otherwise possible. Slaveowners in the older states of the Atlantic seaboard, faced with what they considered a surplus of labor, eagerly sold slaves to planters moving to the "new" lands. One million slaves were sold from the states of the Upper South in the three generations after the ratification of the Constitution. This domestic trade, comprised of a complex network of traders, provisioners, and insurers, constituted as much as 13.5 percent of the total southern economy.

The expansion of the cotton kingdom broadened and deepened the slave trade. Many planters in the East took advantage of the opportunity to sell slaves "down south," especially as the price of slaves—stagnant or declining before 1815—began to rise. Hundreds of thousands of slaves endured forcible migration to the new states of the Southwest in the 1810s and 1820s; some moved in groups along with their owners to new plantations, but many were sold as individuals to slave traders in the East, who then shipped or marched them to slave markets in New Orleans, Mobile, and other cities in the Southwest. The families of many enslaved African Americans were broken apart, as slave traders eagerly bought those in their teens for the hard work of clearing land for plantations from virgin forest.

The movement west was not a simple march from the east, but rather followed the geographic and political contours of the areas recently acquired from the American Indians. The first settlements began along the rivers that made it possible to transport cotton to market and in those places where the Creeks and other Indians exercised no claims. The new plantation districts were disconnected from one another, centering on Montgomery in Alabama, Jackson in Mississippi, and Memphis in Tennessee, all areas taken from the natives of the region since 1814. Small farmers occupied the land farthest from the rivers, supporting themselves with hunting and foraging as well as with

growing small amounts of cotton. Young lawyers and editors headed out for the Southwest as well, eager to make their mark in the river towns and county seats growing up across Alabama and Mississippi.

"The Alabama Feaver rages here with great violence and has carried off vast numbers of our Citizens," wrote one North Carolina planter in 1817. "I am apprehensive, if it continues to spread as it has done, it will almost depopulate the country." The fever proved contagious, "for as soon as one neighbour visits another who has just returned from the Alabama he immediately discovers the same symptoms which are exhibited by the person who has seen the allureing Alabama." Even established men in the older states put their plantations up for sale; others saw the new states as a place for their grown children to get a fresh start. The combined population of Alabama, Mississippi, and Louisiana more than tripled between 1810 and 1820, growing from 117,000 people to 357,000.

The new plantations concentrated on cotton at the expense of everything else. Southerners who had just come into the vast and apparently inexhaustible lands of the Creeks and Seminoles worried little about conservation. The finest plantations clung to the rivers, for water offered the only way to get the ever-expanding cotton crop to market. Flatboats carried the bulky product to barges waiting at the docks of Natchez and Vicksburg on the Mississippi or to ships waiting in the bays of Mobile and New Orleans. Food and other provisions for the plantations came down the rivers from the new farms and cities to the north. A new national economy knitted together the enormous expanse of the young United States.

Some ambitious young men from northern states moved to the new cotton lands, the place in the United States, it seemed, where the greatest fortunes could be made in the shortest amount of time. Virgin land could produce a cotton crop in only one year; in two years, a plantation could be in full production. But most of the new residents came from older plantation states. Young southern men were especially eager to move and make their mark. Their wives, mothers, and daughters were often much less enthusiastic about migrating to Mississippi or Alabama, for it meant being removed from the kin who gave those women much of their happiness and social standing. The lure of the Southwest overrode concerns husbands may have felt for their wives' opinions, however, for the new states offered a chance at the independence they considered synonymous with manliness. They sought to build a world as much as possible like those of Virginia or Carolina, only more prosperous.

Slave trader, Sold to Tennessee,

Arise! Arise! and weep no more dry up your tears, we Shall part no more. Come rose we go to Tennessee, that happy Shore. to old virginia never — never — return. —

the Company going to Tennessee from Stainton, Augusta County, the law of Virginia Suffered them to go on. I was Astonished at this boldness, the carrier Stopped a moment, then Ordered the march, I Saw the plan it is Commonly in this State, with the negro's, in droves Sold,

The rapid spread of cotton plantations fueled the domestic slave trade. These enslaved people are being marched from Virginia into Tennessee.
Abby Aldrich Rockefeller Folk Art Center, Williamsburg, VA

Emergence of the Northwest

The area west of the Appalachians, north of the Ohio, and east of the Mississippi—the "Northwest"—was growing at an even faster pace than the Southwest. "Old America seems to be breaking up, and moving westward," one man wrote in 1817 as he watched people move down the Ohio River. The 280,000 white settlers of 1810 in Ohio, Indiana, and Illinois grew to 784,000 ten years later. In the first two decades of the new century, the trans-Appalachian population grew from about 300,000 inhabitants to more than two million. This immigration in the North bore considerable similarities to its southern counterpart. First of all, many of the settlers to the Northwest came from the states of the Upper South; large parts of southern Ohio, Indiana, and Illinois were settled by people from Virginia, Kentucky, Tennessee, and North Carolina. Some southern migrants to the North professed

Map 9.4 *Migration Patterns in the Northwest*
As in the South, migrants in the North wove their way into the West. New Englanders and New Yorkers followed a northerly path, while other people flowed in from the south, all of them following rivers, canals, and major roads.

themselves eager to move out of states with slavery, while others merely followed the easiest routes to good land. People from New England and New York filled the towns and farms of the northern parts of the new states of the Northwest. In 1824, Illinois voters defeated, by fewer than 2,000 votes, a proposition to hold a constitutional convention to authorize the continuance of slavery in the state.

As in the South, young people dominated migration to the Northwest. Migrants to both regions abandoned areas back east where land had become too expensive, crowded, or depleted. As in the Southwest, settlers to the Northwest did not move in a simple westward wave, but rather flowed up the rivers and spread from there, sometimes back towards the East. People often emigrated in groups, whether of families or of larger communities. "We are seldom out of sight, as we travel on this grand track towards the Ohio," one traveler noted, "of family groups behind, and before

us, some with a view to a particular spot, close to a brother perhaps, or a friend who has gone before, and reported well of the country." Family farms clustered closer together in the Northwest than in the Southwest because the absence of a large slave workforce meant that landholdings remained relatively small.

Most white settlers proved dissatisfied with the first land they claimed, for about two out of three migrants moved again within a few years. Rumors always circulated about richer land a bit farther west, about a new town certain to be a major city, about opportunity just over the horizon. Many people who had moved once found it easy to move again. Those who remained in a community became its "leading citizens," consolidating land into larger farms, setting up grist mills and sawmills, running for office, establishing the small towns that served as county seats and trading centers. In many cases, storekeepers were among the first to arrive and among those whose fortunes flourished best. Storekeepers became the bankers and wholesalers of their communities, often buying considerable amounts of land along the way, boosting the towns growing around the stores, churches, and schoolhouses. Courthouses were built early on to formalize land sales and taxation.

Farm and Factory in the Northeast

While the economies of the West and the South were being transformed by settlers and slaves, the economy of the East underwent its own fundamental change. Since the colonial years, people outside the major cities—more than nine out of ten Americans—had made in their own homes much of what they needed. This local production grew stronger when trade dried up during the war with England; in the war's wake, more than two-thirds of the clothes Americans wore were made in their own homes. The year of 1815, in fact, saw the peak of household manufacturing. Local blacksmiths, tailors, cobblers, and other artisans supplied what families could not produce for themselves, while local gristmills and sawmills processed crops and lumber.

Farms averaged a little over a hundred acres, about half improved and the other half occupied by wood lots for fuel and timber. Forests often dominated the farms of younger families, while mature families proudly claimed large areas of cultivation, the products of years of labor. Women and men, children and adults shared and divided the work among themselves. Farm families cleared their fields at spring thaw, manuring, plowing, and planting as soon as danger of frost passed. Livestock and poultry needed constant attention; sheep had to be washed and sheared and geese plucked in the spring. Farm families reaped flax in June, enjoyed a brief respite in August, and then pushed hard for the fall harvest. In winter, men and boys cut wood, while women and girls spun thread and wove cloth for clothes. The garden and dairy were the responsibility of women and girls, the cash crops the responsibility of men. Farmers, chronically short of cash, bartered among themselves and with merchants.

After 1815, the farms in many parts of New England, New York, and Pennsylvania would be tied ever more tightly into the economies of the towns and cities. Farm families produced more cash crops and bought more things with money rather than through barter. Women, especially widows and other single females, worked in their homes to produce palm hats, portions of shoes, or articles of clothing that merchants from nearby cities gathered and had assembled in workshops. These women added such work to their farm work, laboring in the evenings and throughout the winters. With so many young men leaving New England for the West, many communities found themselves with considerable numbers of young women who might never marry as well as older women who could not count on the support of sons. Piecework offered these women a chance to contribute to the economies of their households in a way the older farm economy had not, bringing in scarce cash. It was important to everyone in their families that those wage-earning women did not have to leave home to earn those wages.

The expanded cash economy thus overlapped with and conflicted with an older, more self-contained economy. Families sought opportunity in new jobs and new markets, even as they feared that the increasingly dense networks of trade would depress the value of their crops, make seasonal farm labor even more difficult to acquire, entice young people from the farm, and undermine local artisans. Rural folk both welcomed and worried over the changes. Although it would be generations before cities and factories dominated the economies of the Northeast, in the meantime, farms, towns, and small factories grew ever more interconnected.

The textile industry of New England stood as the most dramatic example of industrial growth. The cost of cotton clothing fell faster than the cost for any other product as machinery and cheaper cotton lowered the price. Francis Cabot Lowell of Boston designed a power loom in 1813, recreating from memory a machine he had seen on a recent trip to England. The same year, Lowell and a partner, Nathan Appleton, spent over $400,000 to open the first factory in the United States that could integrate all the steps of making cloth under a single roof: the Boston Manufacturing Company, in Waltham, Massachusetts, where a waterfall with a ten-foot drop offered free power. An expanded group of investors in the enterprise—the Boston Associates, they were called—pooled the resources of the city's most prominent merchant families.

Unlike earlier factories, that of the Boston Associates used unskilled labor and machines even for weaving, the most expensive part of the process. Lowell and Appleton, concerned that the introduction of factories into the United States might create the same alienated and despised working class they saw in England, recruited young New England farm women and girls as operatives. Young females had experience in producing yarn and cloth at home and they would work hard for low wages. Many were eager to earn money for themselves, to move out of crowded homes, and to send money back to their families. As Appleton

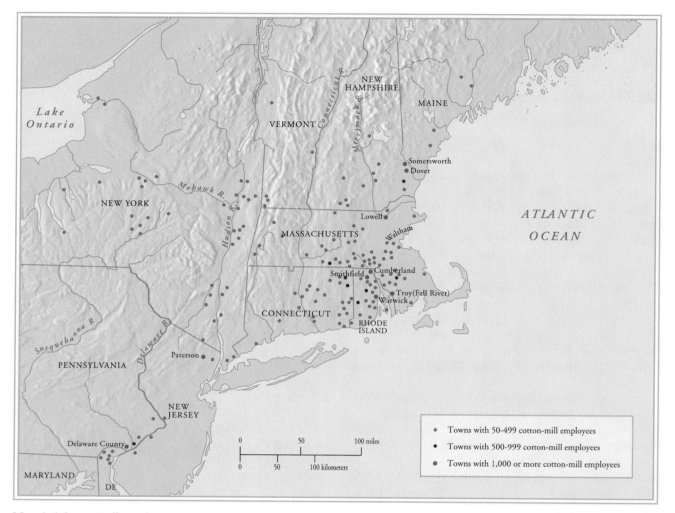

Map 9.5 *Cotton Mills in the Northeast*
The cheap cotton of the South combined with the cheap labor and abundant water power of the Northeast to create the United States's first industrial economy in small towns and cities located on streams.

put it, the young women supplied "a fund of labor, well educated and virtuous" for the factory.

The operatives, considering millwork a three- or four-year commitment before they married and began families of their own, worked fourteen hours a day, six days a week. When they signed a contract with the agents who received a dollar a head for each worker they could recruit, the young women agreed to stay with the mill for at least twelve months or to be put on a blacklist that would prevent them from getting a job elsewhere. The factory was unlike anything the young women had ever confronted: "You cannot think how odd everything seemed," one mill girl recalled; even those who had spun and woven for years could not be prepared for the "frightful" sight of "so many bands, and wheels, and springs in constant motion." Leaving

the factory in the evening, an operative could still hear the noise of the mill in her head, "as of crickets, frogs and jewsharps, all mingled together in strange discord."

The social and economic ground for industrialization had been broken in the Northeast. Mills, most of them small, grew up along the streams of Connecticut and the Delaware Valley of Pennsylvania and New Jersey, turning out not only textiles but also metal and wood products. These mills, like their bigger and more visible counterparts in Lowell, depended on low wages paid to workers without many other options. Many potential workers, competitors, and outside observers worried about the effects of the factories, even as investors and other supporters saw in the new buildings the hope for a richer and more productive American society.

*P*ICTURING THE PAST ✦ SOCIAL & CULTURAL EVENTS

THE EARLY TEXTILE MILLS

The Granger Collection, New York

The complex machinery, whirring spindles, and ceaseless web of threads to be pieced together when they broke took a toll on the health and safety of the young workforce of the early textile mills of New England. Women and girls were considered especially well-suited for this work because of their quick fingers and their familiarity with fabrics and thread. Most of the young women who came into the mills were adolescents and young women eager to get out on their own for a while before they married, and were able to contribute to the family income in a way not possible if they had stayed at home. New England at this time had a skewed sex ratio with a preponderance of females, as many of the younger men fled the hard farming of their native region to the easier lands of upstate New York and farther west.

CONSEQUENCES OF EXPANSION

The enlarged boundaries of the American nation, as exciting and promising as they seemed, brought troubles almost immediately. The newly integrated economy proved vulnerable to fluctuations in currency and to outside pressure. The rapid spread of slavery in the South threatened northerners who did not want to see the institution expand into new territories in the West. The resulting political fight over the future of slavery inspired slaves to launch a revolt in South Carolina. The leaders of the United States came to feel that their new status in the world called for an emboldened foreign policy, one that proclaimed an enlarged role for the United States in its hemisphere.

In all these ways, the explosive growth of the country in the fifteen years after 1815 brought consequences few could have imagined.

The Panic of 1819

In 1819, a series of events abroad and at home combined to bring a sudden halt to some of the growth in the economy of the United States. Prices for cotton lands in the Southeast, the most sought-after property in these years, skyrocketed as world demand for cotton cloth increased every year. Southern cotton rose to such an extent that in 1818 and 1819 British manufacturers turned to cotton from other sources, especially India. American cotton prices tumbled, along with the value of the land that produced it. And cotton was not the only crop whose value rapidly declined: tobacco plummeted from 40 cents a pound to 4 cents, wheat fell from $2.41 a bushel to 88 cents. State banks built on inflated, even fraudulent, credit wavered and then crashed. One year after authorizing the first military pensions for veterans of the Revolution, 16 percent of the federal budget was consumed by pensions just as financial crisis deepened. The Panic of 1819 had begun.

The panic proved a sudden and sobering reminder of just how complicated and interdependent the economy of the nation was becoming. The cities were hit the hardest. About half a million workers lost their jobs as business ground to a halt. Americans shuddered to see "children freezing in the winter's storm—and the fathers without coats and shoes." In the streets where new goods had been piled now wandered people without homes or food. Charitable groups opened soup kitchens. Wherever they could, families who had moved to towns and cities returned to the countryside to live with relatives. Things were not much safer in the country, however, where the failure of banks meant that apparently prosperous farmers saw household goods, farm animals, and the people they held as slaves sold in humiliating auctions.

Many people, including congressmen, began to call for the revocation of the charter of the Second Bank of the United States. States had chafed throughout the two years of the bank's life at what they considered its dictatorial power. Several states tried to limit that power by levying extremely high taxes on the branches of the Bank of the United States in their states, but it was at this point that the Supreme Court ruled in *McCulloch v. Maryland* that the laws of the federal government "form the supreme law of the land."

Despite the panic, James Monroe was reelected to the presidency in 1820 in one of the quietest and most lopsided elections in the nation's history. The Federalist party, fatally crippled by its opposition to the War of 1812 and its support of the Hartford Convention, offered no effective opposition. Neither did Monroe face an organized contest from others within his own Republican party, which was divided along sectional lines. He received every electoral vote but one. Most Americans seemed to blame someone other than President Monroe for the Panic of 1819 and the lingering hard times that followed it. The Era of Good Feelings somehow managed to survive in the White House—though, it turned out, not in the halls of Congress.

The Missouri Compromise

The recent admission of the new states of the Southwest and Northwest had left a precarious balance in the Senate between slave states and free, though northern states held a strong, and growing, preponderance in the House of Representatives. The Missouri territory posed a special challenge to the balance. Slavery had quickly spread in Missouri, stretching along the richest river lands. If Missouri were admitted with slavery—as its territorial legislature had decreed—then the slave states would hold a majority in the Sen-

ate. Slavery in Missouri, an area of the same latitude as much of Illinois, Indiana, and Ohio, seemed to violate the assumption long held by many people in the North that slavery, if it grew at all, would expand only to the south.

The three-fifths clause of the Constitution, northerners complained, gave the slave states twenty more members of Congress and twenty more electors for the presidency than they would have if only white population were counted. The South seemed to be getting extra representation unfairly.

The debates over slavery in Missouri in 1819 and 1820 were not debates between fervent abolitionists in the North and fervent proslavery advocates in the South. Neither of those positions had yet been defined. Instead, white northerners and southerners of all political persuasions agreed that as many blacks as possible should be shipped to Africa. White Americans who could agree on little else about slavery did agree that blacks and whites could not live together in the United States once slavery had ended. That was the message of the American Colonization Society, founded in 1816 and based in Washington, D.C. Many Americans shared the sentiments of a New Hampshire member who wrote, "This is not their country. . . . O let them breathe the air of the land of their fathers. . . . Send them home." The society bought land in Africa—naming the new country "Liberia"—and sent about 12,000 free African Americans there over the next fifty years. Disease took a terrible toll, however, and many died. Fewer African Americans migrated. In Philadelphia, they even staged protests against the notion of colonization.

In the meantime, slavery caused problems for the political system. A New York congressman, James Tallmadge, Jr., introduced an amendment to the bill that would admit Missouri as a state permitting entry only if it admitted no more slaves and if those slaves in the territory were freed when they became twenty-five years old. More than eighty of the North's congressmen supported the Tallmadge amendment and only ten opposed it. In the Senate, though, the slave states prevailed by two votes. A deadlocked Congress adjourned in March of 1819 to meet again in December.

During the months in between, politicians worked behind the scenes to prepare for the debates and decisions of December. The Union, so celebrated and expansive in the wake of the war with Britain, so peaceful for whites since the Creeks, Seminoles, and Cherokees had been quelled, now seemed in danger of breaking apart from within. Both northern and southern politicians talked openly of ending the Union if need be. Simmering northern resentment, held in

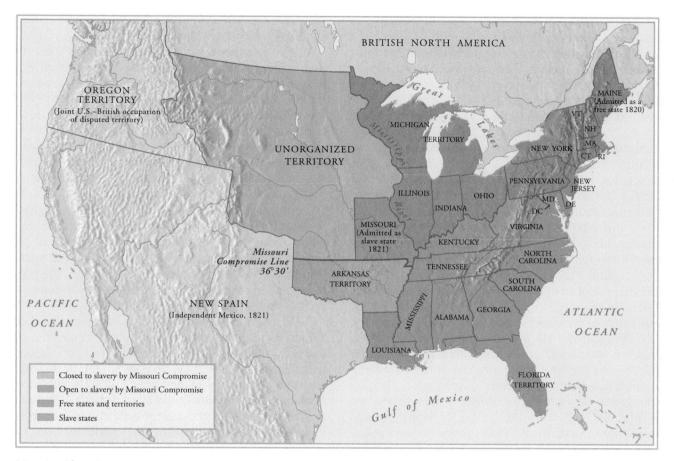

Map 9.6 *The Missouri Compromise*
The conflict over the fate of slavery in Missouri proved the first great sectional conflict over the issue. Under the provisions of the Missouri Compromise, Missouri entered the Union as a slave state while Maine entered as a free state. Slavery was prohibited in the remainder of the Louisiana Territory.

check for decades, was suddenly announced, even celebrated. Southerners felt betrayed. In their eyes, slavery was a thing they had inherited, something for which they bore no blame, an institution that would fade away naturally if it were left alone. White southerners thought northerners irresponsible and unrealistic to attack as the Tallmadge amendment did. The denial of Missouri statehood seemed to southerners nothing less than an assault on their character.

In northern states, where abolitionist societies had been relatively sedate, people suddenly announced the depth of their distaste for the institution. Furious meetings erupted in towns and cities across the North, turning out petitions and resolutions in large numbers. Slavery, these petitions thundered, was a blot on the nation, a violation of the spirit of Christianity, an abomination that must not spread into places it had not already ruined. The antislavery advocates of the 1820s expected colonization and aboli-

tion to occur simultaneously and gradually. But they were also determined to stop the spread of slavery toward the northern part of the continent.

After weeks of debate, a compromise emerged from the Senate: Missouri, with no restriction on slavery, should be admitted to the Union at the same time as Maine, thereby ensuring the balance between slave and free states. Slavery would be prohibited in all the lands acquired in the Louisiana Purchase north of the southern border of Missouri at 36° 309 latitude. Such a provision excluded the Arkansas territory, where slavery was already established, but closed to slavery the vast expanses of the Louisiana Territory—the future states of Iowa, Minnesota, Wisconsin, the Dakotas, Nebraska, and Kansas. Any slaves who escaped to the free states would be returned. Many of the northern men who voted for the measure found themselves burned in effigy back home and defeated when it came time for reelection. The South was no more satisfied than the North, furious to hear itself vilified in the national capital it had long dominated.

The debate broke out again when the Missouri constitutional convention not only authorized slavery but decreed that the state legislature could never emancipate slaves without the consent of their masters; the proposed constitution also pronounced that free blacks would never be permitted to enter the new state. The national House of Representatives refused to admit Missouri under this document, and the denunciation by both sides began again where it had paused. Finally, in early 1821, Henry Clay managed to fix a majority in the House in favor of a bill that would admit Missouri as long as the new state promised to pass no law barring the entry of a citizen from any other state. Exhausted, Congress ratified the law.

Northern and southern states had become wary and distrustful of one another as they had never been before. In a real sense, the debates over slavery in Missouri created "the North" and "the South," uniting the new states of the Northwest with the states of New England, New York, and Pennsylvania as they had not been united earlier, forging a tighter alliance between the new states of the Southwest and Virginia, the Carolinas, and Georgia. To the North, the South seemed greedy and corrupt; to the South, the North seemed greedy and hypocritical. The country became polarized as never before.

Vesey's Revolt

In Charleston, South Carolina, the heart of South Carolina's richest plantation district, a free black man named Denmark Vesey had closely followed in the papers the debates over the Missouri controversy. What he read there reinforced what he had seen in the Bible and the documents of the American Revolution: slavery was immoral. Vesey, a middle-aged mulatto of large stature who had bought his freedom twenty years earlier, stood as a commanding presence among the African American people of the low country. A skilled carpenter and preacher, Vesey traveled up and down the coast and into the interior, berating those blacks who accepted racial insult. Many African Americans were attracted to him; most were afraid to oppose him regardless.

Vesey drew not only upon his own strengths, but upon those of a powerful ally, a man known as Gullah Jack. This man, an Angolan, had arrived in South Carolina near the turn of the century, one of the 40,000 slaves brought into the state right before the end of the legal slave trade in 1807. Gullah Jack still looked very much the part of the conjurer he was, with huge whiskers, tiny arms, and unusual gestures setting him apart from American-born blacks.

The conspirators hoped to seize the city's poorly protected guardhouse, stores, and roads before the whites could gather themselves in opposition. House slaves would kill their white owners. Once Charleston was secure, the rebels, Vesey planned, would sail to Haiti, where Toussaint L'Ouverture had staged a black rebellion decades earlier and where slavery had been abolished. But a house servant broke under the pressure and alerted Charleston whites to the danger only two days before the revolt planned for June 16, 1822. The governor ordered out five military companies, and Vesey called off the attack. Over the next two months, white authorities hanged thirty-five alleged conspirators and banished thirty-seven more from the state. Few of the rebels would reveal the names of their allies, going to their deaths with the secrets of the revolt secure. Denmark Vesey was one of those killed.

Charleston Mayor James Hamilton bragged that "There can be no harm in the salutary inculcation of one lesson, among a certain portion of our population, that there is nothing they are bad enough to do, that we are not powerful enough to punish." Despite such boasts, white southerners blamed Vesey's Rebellion on the agitation against slavery by northern congressmen in the Missouri debate. "The events of 1822," a leading South Carolinian observed, "will long be remembered, as amongst the choicest fruits of the agitation of that question in Congress."

The Monroe Doctrine

The instability of the Spanish regime in Europe, exacerbated by the Napoleonic Wars, sent aftershocks into the colonies in the New World. Throughout the first and second decades of the nineteenth century, one struggle after another disrupted Latin America. Seeing Spain vulnerable in Europe and abroad, leaders in the colonies of the Western Hemisphere—Simón Bolívar in Venezuela, José de San Martín in Argentina, and Miguel Hidalgo in Mexico—pushed ahead with their long-simmering plans for national independence. By 1822, Chile, Mexico, Venezuela, and the Portuguese colony of Brazil had all gained their independence.

Neither the United States nor Great Britain wanted to see France fill the vacuum left by Spain in the New World. A French or Russian empire would pose a potentially dangerous economic and military threat much greater than any posed by the fading Spanish regime. Accordingly, in March of 1822 President Monroe urged Congress to recognize the new republics of Latin America. Throughout the next year, as the French army invaded Spain, the U.S. minister in England proposed that the United States and England jointly declare that neither country would annex any part of the tottering empire of Spain nor permit any other power to do so. Encouraged by former presidents Jefferson and Madison, Monroe wanted to make the joint declaration, but Secretary of State John Quincy Adams persuaded him that it would be more fitting and dignified for the United States to declare its policy independently instead of coming "in as a cockboat in the wake of the British man o'war." Adams's policy was directed more against outside intervention in Latin America than in favor of the new republics, which he considered weak and unlikely to endure an attack by a major power.

Accordingly, in December of 1823 the president used his annual message to Congress to announce what would eventually become known as the Monroe Doctrine: "The American continents, by the free and independent conditions which they have assumed and maintained, are henceforth not to be considered as subjects for future colonisation by any European power." The North American republic had exerted its first claim to recognition by the great powers of the world, making a show of acting independently even though Great Britain was the real power. The Russians and Spanish denounced the American policy as "blustering," "arrogant," "indecent," and "monstrous," meriting only "the most profound contempt." They tolerated the doctrine because the European powers, exhausted by wars among themselves, had little desire to expand their involvement on the other side of the world. The leaders of the Latin American revolts welcomed the warning to the European powers, but were less certain about the United States's own intentions toward Latin America. The Monroe Doctrine, after all, did not say that the United States would not interfere in the Western Hemisphere, only that it would not permit European countries to do so.

THE REINVENTION OF POLITICS

Two events of 1824 threw into sharp relief the accomplishments and dangers of the emerging nation. The first event was the thirteen-month tour of the United States by one of the heroes of the American Revolution: the Marquis de Lafayette. The second event was the presidential election of 1824. While Lafayette's visit tied the country together with bonds of memory and celebration, the election showed that Americans had become far more divided than had seemed possible only four years earlier.

Lafayette's Return

Lafayette sailed into New York and was met, fittingly enough, with a steamboat, symbol of the strides the United States had made since Lafayette's departure decades earlier. He spent tumultuous and tearful days in New York, where old comrades and young admirers poured out to see the living embodiment of the sacrifices and bravery of the Revolutionary War. Then Lafayette, along with his son, George Washington Lafayette, and his traveling companion, a radical young Scotswoman named Frances Wright, set out to see the rest of the United States. They went first to New England, visiting with John Adams, then down the coast to Philadelphia, Baltimore, Washington, Charleston, and then New Orleans. From there, they went up the Mississippi and on to Nashville, where he met Andrew Jackson.

Everywhere Lafayette traveled, the people tried to outdo what had been done before; the hero met with booming guns, torchlight parades, thousands of children dressed in the colors of France, beautiful young women, illuminated pictures, banquet after banquet, speech after speech. Some moments stood out: when the general cried, alone, at the grave of Washington at Mount Vernon, and when he traveled to Monticello to meet with Jefferson. Congress, knowing that the marquis was in serious financial difficulties, presented him with a gift of $200,000 (an enormous sum at the time) and a township of public land. Lafayette met with Cherokees in Georgia. Slaves, hearing of the patriot's opposition to slavery, lined the roads wherever he went to cheer him on.

A toast announced what Americans most admired in Lafayette, "the great apostle of liberty whom the persecutions of tyranny could not defeat, whom the love of riches could not influence, whom popular applause could never seduce." The Frenchman, in other words, was admired for his selflessness at the time of the American Revolution, for putting the cause of liberty before his own self-interest, for putting himself at risk in the pursuit of freedom. Such a posture of noble self-sacrifice was what Americans valued most in their public men and what they expected of those to whom power was given. In Lafayette, they could celebrate the best in themselves. While remembering their own Revolution and celebrating Lafayette, the 18th Congress defeated a resolution to express its sympathy with revolutionaries in Greece attempting to throw off Ottoman rule. Although backed by Henry Clay and

Daniel Webster, one of the resolution's opponents remarked that America would persuade others by "the moral influence of its example," not by actively supporting democratic movements abroad.

The Election of 1824

Many people felt that they saw the worst of the country in the presidential election going on while Lafayette toured the country. Few eligible voters had bothered to cast a ballot four years earlier when James Monroe had won the presidency without opposition, for his election seemed foreordained. But politicians and observers expected a more interesting contest in 1824. Many thought the next president would be William Crawford, secretary of the treasury, a Georgian and apparent heir to the Virginia dynasty. Others focused on John Quincy Adams, an experienced statesman, New Englander, and the secretary of state—the office from which many presidents had come. Others looked to John C. Calhoun of South Carolina, an impressive secretary of war and advocate of a strong national government. Yet others placed their bets on Henry Clay of Kentucky, Speaker of the House of Representatives for many years and one of the most visible members of Congress. Finally, Andrew Jackson of Tennessee hoped to parlay the widespread fame he won in the wars against the English and the Indians into the presidency.

Several of these men realized they did not command sufficient national support to win the election outright. They hoped, however, to prevail if the election went into the House of Representatives, where the top three candidates would vie if no candidate won in the electoral college. Cliques spread rumors, and alliances of convenience flourished. Openly partisan newspapers sang the praises of their man and published lacerating rumors about his opponents. The most novel was John Henry Eaton's successful press campaign to portray Jackson as a patriotic soldier, quietly tending his farm while Washington politicians schemed to block his election by ordinary voters because of his lack of polish and his incorruptible character.

While the Marquis de Lafayette serenely toured the United States, local and state politicians worked feverishly in taverns, caucuses, and newspaper offices. Many American voters seemed disenchanted with the crass politicking, though, and relatively few voted in 1824. Jackson's popular vote nearly equaled that of Adams and Crawford combined, but the election was thrown into the House of Representatives because no candidate received a plurality in the electoral college. The House could choose among the top three candidates: Jackson, Adams, and Crawford.

Since his fourth-place finish put him out of the running, Clay, the Speaker of the House, sought to strike the best deal he could with the other candidates, assuring himself of maximum power, visibility, and opportunities in subsequent elections. Clay, considering Jackson unworthy of the post and a potential military despot, discussed his future with Adams. When the vote came to the House of Representatives in early 1825, Adams won the presidency—taking the three states Clay had won in the electoral college. Two weeks later, Henry Clay received the appointment of secretary of state. "So you see," Andrew Jackson fumed, "the Judas of the West has closed the contract and will receive the thirty pieces of silver." Throughout the muddy little city of Washington, people speculated about the promises the upright John Quincy Adams had made to win the presidency. People often mentioned the cold sweat that broke out on his face when he received word of his election.

Adams wanted a stronger national government, internal improvements, and a tariff to protect American industry. But he could not mobilize support for his positions, either within Washington or among the voters. Adams refused to use patronage to persuade or coerce people to go along with his plans. His administration bogged down into factionalism and paralysis, always with the shadow of his supposed "corrupt bargain" with Clay darkening his reputation. Things seemed far removed, indeed, from the glorious days when Lafayette sacrificed for the American Revolution.

New York politicians sought to harness ambition into useful and organized forms in the 1820s, pioneering the development of the party system. Aaron Burr converted a simple patriotic club in New York City, the Society of Saint Tammany, into the beginnings of a major political machine. De Witt Clinton invented the "spoils system," in which it became the expectation that an incoming officeholder would remove those appointed by his predecessor and put his own supporters in their place. Martin Van Buren, a young lawyer and politician from New York, nicknamed the "Little Magician," combined the city machine and the spoils system into a powerful statewide organization. He used newspapers in Albany and New York City to spread the word of the party to the fifty small newspapers he controlled throughout the state, which also published vast numbers of handbills, posters, and ballots at election time. He built a large network of party men, many of them lawyers who traveled widely in the state and knew many of their counterparts. Van Buren's goal was to combine party unity with personal advancement for party members, creating a powerful and self-reinforcing cycle.

John Quincy Adams, a skilled and experienced statesman, had only limited success as president.
The Granger Collection, New York

Martin Van Buren opposed John Quincy Adams in the presidential contest of 1824 because Adams's nationally sponsored canals, roads, education, and other services would cut into the power of state government and state politics, elevating what Van Buren saw as dangerous federal power over power closer to home. Partly for this reason, Van Buren cast his lot in 1824 and the years thereafter with Andrew Jackson, who shared Van Buren's preference for localized power. As the next presidential election came closer, Van Buren, now a senator, worked ever more energetically for Jackson, hoping to spread the model of New York politics to the nation as a whole.

The Adams Twilight

The second half of John Quincy Adams's administration proved unhappy and unproductive. Neither Adams's talents nor his devotion to the Union had faded, but the public mood seemed little interested in either. The "corrupt bargain," in which Henry Clay allegedly conspired to hand the presidency to Adams, still hung over the White House in 1827. In the eyes of many, Adams had proven himself unfit for office, not only with his reputed bargain, but also, false rumor persisted, by procuring a young American girl for the Russian czar when Adams served as a fourteen-year-old member of the U.S. diplomatic corps in St. Petersburg. The president's elite education and even his purchase of a billiard table and chess set for the White House were disparaged by opponents as symbols of "aristocracy." Adams's many and diverse opponents organized against him and his policies almost from the beginning of his administration. It soon became clear that the president would be able to accomplish little of his ambitious agenda of internal improvements, a national university, and western exploration, ideals that might have won support in earlier years.

Supporters of Andrew Jackson of Tennessee, John C. Calhoun of South Carolina, and William Crawford of Georgia gradually joined forces in anticipation of the election of 1828, when they hoped to unseat Adams and his vision of an active and centralized government. The struggle, Calhoun wrote to Jackson, was between "power and liberty." The champion of power had had his turn, Adams's opponents believed; now it was time for the champions of liberty to step forward. After some jockeying, Andrew Jackson emerged as the man to challenge Adams.

Adams's supporters warned of the dangers of electing a raw and rough "military chieftain" such as Andrew Jackson to the presidency. Jackson's opponents distributed a handbill marked with eighteen coffins, each one representing a man Jackson had supposedly killed in a duel or ordered executed under his military command. The most incendiary charge, however, was that Jackson had married a woman married to another man, leading her to commit both bigamy and adultery in the process. The facts of the case were unclear—it appears that Rachel Jackson was a religious woman, trapped in a bad marriage, who thought she had received a divorce when she married Jackson—but the anti-Jackson forces made the most of any suspicions to the contrary.

Anti-Masons

Charges of conspiracy and corruption raged throughout American politics in the 1820s. Some of the suspicions seemed confirmed by events in New York. As the economy of that state prospered along with the Erie

Canal, so did fraternal organizations of every sort. The Ancient Order of Masons did especially well, claiming almost 350 lodges in the state. The Masons' exclusive society, surrounded by elaborate ritual and strict secrecy, many non-Masons felt, contradicted American ideals of democracy and openness, taking men away from their families and undermining organized religion. Since Masons were obliged to show business or political preference to a brother over "any other person in the same circumstances," some of those outside the order feared that Masons might win undue influence in their town, state, or country. As proof, they pointed out that every New York governor but one between 1804 and the late 1820s belonged to the Masons.

Suspicion of the Masons exploded when a brother named William Morgan turned against the order and decided to publish its secret rituals. Local Masonic leaders used their influence with county officials to harass and jail Morgan, who was later kidnapped in September 1826. He disappeared; many said he had been murdered. The investigation soon stalled, however, as Masonic law enforcement officers and others

Titillating depictions of the supposed Masonic rituals marked a flood of publications in the late 1820s and early 1830s such as this almanac from the Anti-Masons.
© Bettmann/Corbis

dragged their feet. Despite twenty trials and three special prosecutors, only a few convictions resulted and those convictions brought only minor jail terms. Congregations split and communities divided into warring factions over the Masons. Alleged Masonic skullduggery proved a convenient way to explain personal and political setbacks. A local Episcopal rector recorded his dismay: "I have lived here in the midst of fire, and . . . it has scorched my ears." Fury against the Masons soon spread from New York to the rest of the country, forcing one lodge after another to dissolve.

By 1827, nearly a hundred "Morgan committees" had met and formed in New York and began to spread across the entire northern half of the country, attracting men of reputation and prestige. Within two years, the "Anti-Masons" had established more than a hundred newspapers. They held public meetings and launched lobbying campaigns, bypassing local elites and inventing new means of pressuring legislatures directly. Unlike earlier reform organizations, such as those that supported Sunday schools and the distribution of Bibles, the Anti-Masons thrived on controversy. They devoted themselves to changing public opinion, to mobilizing people against a powerful entrenched force. They succeeded: Masonry lost more than half its members and created virtually no new lodges for the next fifteen years. So great was the Anti-Masons' success, in fact, that the movement's leaders dreamed of creating a new party to purify and energize American politics.

Birth of the Democrats

Even while the struggle over the Masons unfolded, Senator Martin Van Buren of New York was building a political coalition behind Andrew Jackson. Van Buren traveled throughout the United States, hammering out a new coalition of ambitious state politicians willing to back Jackson. The members of the coalition called themselves "Democratic Republicans," eventually to be shortened to "Democrats." Their candidates did extremely well in the off-year congressional elections of 1827, exploiting people's disapproval of the ineffectual Adams administration. The Democrats controlled both the House and the Senate.

Throughout 1827 and 1828, Van Buren and the other party leaders organized voters as they had never been organized before. Although Jackson himself was a prominent Mason, Van Buren adopted techniques not unlike those pioneered by the Anti-Masons in these same years. Using every strategy at their disposal—bonfires, speeches, barbecues, parades, professional writers, and the first campaign song—these Jacksonians claimed that they had found a true man of the people to strip the office from the aristocratic Adams. In towns across the country, "Old Hickory"—Jackson was supposedly as hardy as that toughest of trees—was celebrated with hickory poles, brooms, sticks, and trees. The National Republicans, as Adams's supporters became known, sniffed at what they considered the unseemly display that diverted attention from real issues, but they could not deny the power of the new methods to win voters' attention.

In the meantime, American politics became more democratic and inclusive. Most legislatures across the Union lowered property requirements for voting and made judicial offices elective rather than appointed. Voters seemed restless, hungry for someone to give direction and force to public life. Voting turnout in 1828 doubled that of the 1824 election. The dramatic confrontation of men and styles contributed to widespread voter interest, while politicians at every level and on both sides made sure voters went to the polls.

Jackson won easily over Adams, winning 178 of the 261 electoral votes, capturing the critical mid-Atlantic states and all the states of the South except Louisiana and Kentucky. The election proved bittersweet for Jackson, though, for his wife died soon afterward. Jackson blamed the slanderers of the other party for Rachel's death, for she had fallen ill after seeing an editorial denouncing her. The president-elect passed the weeks before his inauguration in sadness and bitterness.

CONCLUSION

The United States saw enormous economic change between 1815 and 1828. New states in both the Southwest and the Northwest joined the national and international economies. The nation's armies conquered and removed diverse peoples among the Native Americans. Cotton poured from Alabama and Mississippi in ever-growing amounts, while food flowed from Indiana and Illinois. Banks proliferated with the expanding population, and the Second Bank of the United States lent stability to the system. The major ports along the east coast grew as they had never grown before, connecting the expanding United States with the economies of England and Europe. New factory buildings went up along the streams and rivers of the Northeast, producing by water power what hands had made only a few years earlier. Turnpikes and roads covered the country in an increasingly dense network. Such changes seemed to mark the beginning of a new kind of security and prosperity for the United States.

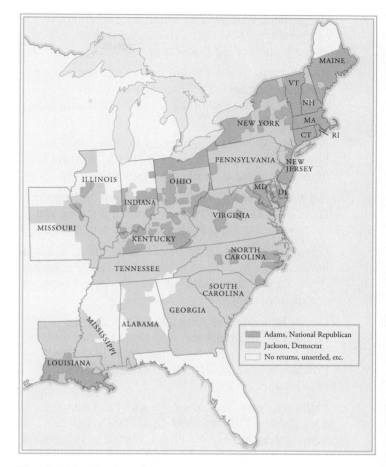

Map 9.7 *The Election of 1828*
Andrew Jackson overwhelmed John Quincy Adams almost everywhere except in Adams's native New England.

As the economy and territory grew, however, Americans had to reckon with the consequences of their expansion. The political system churned as people from different areas of the country and different economic factions jockeyed for power. Democracy turned out to be far messier than the Founding Fathers had imagined, creating new kinds of political figures, new kinds of political parties, and new kinds of political conflicts that threatened to pull the nation apart almost as soon as it came together.

Recommended Readings

Appleby, Joyce. *Inheriting the Revolution: The First Generation of Americans* (2000). Paints a wonderful picture of these years.

Cashin, Joan E. *A Family Venture: Men and Women on the Southern Frontier* (1991). Tells the story of the southwestern migration in a compelling way.

Dangerfield, George. *The Awakening of American Nationalism, 1815–1828* (1965). A classic interpretation of the postwar era.

Davis, David Brion. *The Problem of Slavery in the Age of Revolution, 1770–1823* (1975). Gives a magisterial overview of the international struggles with slavery.

Freehling, William W. *The Road to Disunion: The Secessionists at Bay, 1776–1854* (1990). Portrays the drama of sectional conflict throughout this era.

Horwitz, Morton J. *The Transformation of American Law, 1780–1860* (1977). Puts forward a strong and controversial argument about the law and commerce.

Larson, John Lauritz. *Internal Improvement: National Public Works and the Promise of Popular Government in the Early United States* (2001). The best treatment of this important subject.

Lewis, James E. *The American Union and the Problem of Neighborhood: The United States and the Collapse of the Spanish Empire, 1783–1829* (1998). Provides a fresh interpretation of this complicated relationship.

Mathews, Jean. *Toward a New Society: American Thought and Culture, 1800–1830* (1990). Offers a subtle interpretation of cultural history of this period.

Rohrbough, Malcolm J. *The Trans-Appalachian Frontier: People, Societies, and Institutions, 1775–1850* (1978). Tells this complex story well.

Saunt, Claudio. *A New Order of Things: Property, Power, and the Transformation of the Creek Indians, 1733–1816* (1999). Makes comprehensible the great complexities in the lives of American Indians in these crucial decades.

Sellers, Charles G. *The Market Revolution: Jacksonian America, 1815–1846* (1991). Gives a stirring portrayal of the period with economic change at the center.

Sheriff, Carol. *The Artificial River: The Erie Canal and the Paradox of Progress, 1817–1862* (1996). Offers a compelling account of the canal's origins, building, and effects.

American Journey Online and InfoTrac College Edition

Visit the source collections at http://ajaccess.wadsworth.com and infotrac.thomsonlearning.com and use the Search function with the following key terms to explore documents, images, audio and video clips, articles, and commentary related to the material in this chapter.

James Monroe   Monroe Doctrine
Henry Clay   Missouri Compromise
Erie Canal

Additional resources, exercises, and Internet links related to this chapter are available on the American Passages Web site: http://history.wadsworth.com/passages2e

10 THE YEARS OF ANDREW JACKSON 1829–1836

ANDREW JACKSON TAKES CHARGE

STRUGGLES OVER SLAVERY

POLITICAL TURMOIL AND THE ELECTION OF 1832

THE INDIAN PEOPLES AND THE MEXICAN NATION

REVIVAL

CHARACTER DEVELOPMENT

One of the most famous men in the United States due to his exploits in the War of 1812, Andrew Jackson of Tennessee seemed to many people an inspiring leader. Others, however, saw him as a "military chieftain" dangerous with the power of the presidency.

Tumultuous change came to the United States in the years Andrew Jackson served as president. Elections became sweeping public events that involved men of every class. Voters and leaders hotly debated and contested the role of government in American life. Religious revivals swept up entire communities in devotion and prayer. Working people created labor unions, and abolitionists launched a bold crusade against slavery.

Growing democracy was not the full story of these years, however. The people of the Creek, Choctaw, Cherokee, Seminole, Sac, and Fox nations were driven from their homes in the South and in the old Northwest. A crisis threatened to ignite a military struggle between South Carolina and the federal government. The revolt of Nat Turner and debates over slavery in Virginia unleashed a proslavery reaction throughout much of the South. The defeat of Mexico in Texas opened a vast new territory to slavery as well as to the settlement of free Americans. Few decades in American history witnessed more important and more fundamental changes.

Accompanying this rapid expansion of boundaries of every sort was considerable anxiety that American society threatened to spin out of control. The government held little power, and people worried that many Americans had moved beyond the influence of church, family, school, or employer. Some Americans began to suggest ways to contain the consequences of change. They offered political compromise, reform societies, and new ideals of the home as ways to counteract what they saw as threatening chaos.

ANDREW JACKSON TAKES CHARGE

Andrew Jackson, still dressed in black in mourning after the recent death of his beloved wife Rachel, traveled by steamboat from Nashville to Washington in the winter of 1829 to begin his presidency. The entire nation watched to see what sort of changes this new kind of leader might make, what sort of America he might help create.

The People's President

Once he arrived in Washington, Jackson began to assemble his cabinet, balancing North, South, and West. Martin Van Buren, leader of Jackson's successful campaign the year before, became secretary of state, a position traditionally reserved for the man next in line for

CHRONOLOGY

1828 Tariff of Abominations • Calhoun's *Exposition* • Election of Jackson

1829 David Walker's *Appeal* • Mexico tries to abolish slavery in Texas

1830 Indian Removal Act • *The Book of Mormon* • Finney's revivals begin in Rochester • Anti-Masonic party holds first national party convention

1831 Nat Turner's rebellion • Garrison's *The Liberator* • Jackson reorganizes cabinet, Van Buren over Calhoun • Mormons migrate from New York to Ohio

1832 Bank War begins • Nullification Crisis • Virginia debates over slavery • Jackson reelected

1833 Formation of American Anti-slavery Society • Force Bill against South Carolina • Compromise Tariff • Slavery abolished in British Empire

1834 Whig party organized • National Trades Union formed

1835 Arkansas admitted to the Union • Revolution breaks out in Texas • Abolitionists' postal campaign • War against Seminoles and runaway slaves in Florida

1836 Congress imposes gag rule • Battle of the Alamo; Texas Republic established • Treaty of New Echota • Election of Martin Van Buren

the presidency. Vice President John C. Calhoun, ambitious for the presidency himself, chafed at the appointment but could do little to change it; he and his wing of the party had to satisfy themselves with the appointment of one of their number as secretary of the treasury. The most controversial appointment, however, proved volatile for reasons that had little to do with political partisanship. Jackson wanted a close friend in the cabinet, someone in whom he could confide, and he chose an old Tennessee associate and influential editor, John Eaton, as his secretary of war.

Eaton, a widower in middle age, had married Peggy O'Neal Timberlake, an attractive and witty twenty-nine-year-old daughter of a well-known innkeeper in Washington. She was rumored to have driven her last husband to suicide, forcing him to defraud the government to pay debts she had run up. She was also rumored to have had sex with Eaton before their marriage—along with, one contemporary smirked, "eleven doz. others!" Eaton had asked Jackson's opinion of the marriage beforehand, receiving the old general's blessing; the president liked outspoken women and knew from bitter experience the power that unfounded rumors could hold. Jackson, in a gesture of friendship and support as the gossip flew, offered Eaton the cabinet position, apparently hoping he would decline. Unfortunately for Jackson, Eaton accepted. The decision electrified Washington.

Despite his rambunctious youth, Jackson disdained official Washington's fondness for strong drink, endless banquets, and overheated social life. He had witnessed that high life during his time as senator from Tennessee and he held it in contempt when he returned to the capital; he preferred instead to attend the city's churches. Jackson considered himself an outsider despite his power and popularity, an outsider determined to reform Washington, to make the city worthy of the nation it was supposed to serve.

As the inauguration day of March 4 neared, Washington's population doubled as men who considered themselves important in General Jackson's election arrived in the city to claim their fair share of glory, excitement, and jobs. They drank all the whiskey the city had to offer, slept five to a bed, and generally offended the more genteel residents of the capital. At the inauguration, 30,000 people crowded in to see the new president. After Jackson's brief address, members of the excited audience followed him back to the White House—as one observer put it, "country men, farmers, gentlemen mounted and dismounted, boys, women and children, black and white, carriages, waggons and carts all pursuing him." They surged into the White House, spilling barrels of orange punch, standing with muddy boots on expensive chairs to get a better look at the proceedings, smashing thousands of dollars worth of china. Servants attracted the mob outside by moving the liquor. Jackson, suffocated by admirers and disgusted

In a scene that soon grew legendary, celebrants at Jackson's inauguration overwhelmed the capacity of the White House to contain their numbers or their rambunctiousness.
The Granger Collection, New York

by the scene, climbed out a rear window and went for a steak at his boardinghouse.

Jackson and the "Spoils System"

Many people in Washington were as appalled at the events that followed the inauguration as they were with the inauguration itself. As the new administration got under way, Jackson and his advisors cleaned house in the federal government, removing those officials whose competence, honesty, or loyalty to Jackson and the Democrats were suspect. Although such a policy had become established practice in several major states, including Van Buren's New York, Jackson was the first president to make such sweeping changes on the federal level. He envisioned himself purging an arrogant bureaucracy of corruption, establishing the democratic practice of "rotation in office." As officeholders quaked and fretted, Jackson's lieutenants decided which custom houses and federal offices would be cleansed. Some of the incumbents clearly deserved to lose their jobs, having served jail terms, embezzled funds, or succumbed to drink, but others were guilty only of being active partisans for the other side in the recent election.

Jackson removed about 900 of 10,000 men from their offices and removed them in an especially brash spirit. One Jackson supporter unwisely announced to the Senate that the Jacksonians saw "nothing wrong in the rule that to the victors belong the spoils of the enemy." This proclamation gave an enduring notoriety to

Though Andrew Jackson saw his removal of federal officeholders as a reform, many critics saw it only as thinly disguised greed.
© Bettmann/Corbis

many more than his predecessors had, but Jackson also recognized the power of the postal system to aid partisan political aims. He elevated the postmaster general to a cabinet level position and worked to appoint friendly editors as local postmasters where they solicited subscriptions to Democratic publications and were frequently accused of misrouting or destroying rivals' pamphlets and newspapers.

The festering conflict within the administration over the so-called Eaton affair proved just how important matters of symbolism could be. The wives of the other cabinet members, Vice President Calhoun's wife, and even Emily Donelson—Jackson's daughter-in-law and hostess of the White House—refused to be in the same room with Peggy Eaton. But Jackson would not be swayed in his support for John and Peggy Eaton. The new cabinet found itself bitterly divided between pro-Eaton and anti-Eaton factions. Jackson labored to mend fences, calling an influential pastor to the White House and trying to find evidence to prove Mrs. Eaton's virtue. Nothing proved effective, though, and Jackson decided that the real villain of the story was Vice President Calhoun and his unbending wife Floride. By contrast, Martin Van Buren, a widower, cemented his friendship with the president by treating Mrs. Eaton with ostentatious respect. Jackson, embittered by the refusal of his other advisors to stand by Mrs. Eaton, largely abandoned his official cabinet and relied instead on an informal group of advisors, his so-called Kitchen Cabinet, and on Van Buren, the only winner in the Eaton episode.

STRUGGLES OVER SLAVERY

The years around 1830 saw several issues surrounding slavery come to a head. Southern states, worried about the rapidly growing population and power of the North, sought to define the limits of federal power. Feeling themselves neglected and abused by northern interests, South Carolina leaders tried to secure greater autonomy. At the same time, free blacks in both the North and South worked to replace the colonization movement with a campaign to end slavery and create freedom for African Americans in America. Even as these struggles unfolded, the largest slave revolt in the history of the United States erupted in Virginia. Combined, these events demonstrated that slavery and the issues on which it touched would bedevil the confident and boisterous young country far into the future.

what from then on would be called the "spoils system," a system that Jackson envisioned as reform, not cynical politics. A Washington woman observed, "Oh how dreadfully a parent must feel when he looks on his children gathered round him, and knows that one word spoken by a stranger, may reduce them to beggary. Such is the situation of hundreds . . . men too far advanced in life to be able to enter on new paths of industry."

Jackson further infuriated opponents by appointing partisan newspaper editors to important posts, leading to charges that Jackson was corrupting, rather than cleansing, American government. One key appointment, the collector of the Port of New York, did indeed prove disastrous, as the man eventually fled the United States with $1.2 million of the people's money. Over the course of Jackson's two terms he replaced only about 10 percent of all officeholders, not

The young wife of Secretary of War John Eaton became the center of a scandal that rocked Washington during Andrew Jackson's first term.
The Granger Collection, New York

The Tariff of Abominations, Nullification, and States' Rights

Before the election of 1828, Martin Van Buren and other Democrats had sought to broaden support for Jackson, whose strength lay in the South, by passing a tariff favorable to the economic interests of New Englanders and westerners. After elaborate deal making, the Democrats enacted a major tariff. But it came with a high cost: southerners were furious with what they called this "tariff of abominations," for it raised the price they would have to pay for manufactured items and threatened markets abroad for southern cotton. John C. Calhoun, like other South Carolina planters, feared not only that the tariff would bleed the state dry economically but that it would set a precedent for antislavery forces who might gain control of the federal government at some future date.

Accordingly, in the summer and early fall of 1828, a few months before he would take office as Jackson's vice president, Calhoun sought to find a principled way to reconcile his national ambitions and his local concerns. Rather than argue only against the tariff itself, Calhoun asserted the general rights of individual states within the Union. To do so, he returned to what he called "the primitive principles of our government," the foundations on which everything else rested. Calhoun insisted that interests had become so diverse in the United States that laws appropriate for one state or section might well harm another. Rather than merely letting the majority run roughshod over the minority, Calhoun believed, it made more sense to let a state "nullify" a national law within its own borders. Such nullification was constitutional, he said, because the federal system did not locate sovereignty in any one place, but rather divided it among the states and the nation. Should three-fourths of the states agree that a law must apply to all the country, then that clear majority could overrule the nullification. Calhoun thought he was finding a way to preserve order in an increasingly contentious Union. The document in which he laid out his ideas, the *South Carolina Exposition*, appeared in December of 1828; the pamphlet was published anonymously because it was too politically dangerous for the vice president of the United States to be publicly on record for nullification.

Calhoun's declaration of principles came at a celebration of Thomas Jefferson's birthday at the Indian Queen Hotel in Washington. Southern and western Democrats hoped that the gathering would reveal the strength of the alliance between the two sections, both of which wanted greater autonomy from the federal government. President Jackson, Vice President Calhoun, and Secretary of State Van Buren were all present. Van Buren urged the president to make clear his own position on nullification and states' rights. No one was really sure what Jackson thought on the issue, since he was identified as a southerner but had made his reputation fighting for the Union against the British. As the officeholders went around the table, one toast after another proclaiming the rights of the states, Jackson became ever more steely. When it was his turn, the president stood, lifted his glass, and—staring at Calhoun—pronounced words filled with a meaning obvious to those present: "Our Federal Union—it must be preserved." Van Buren climbed on a chair to see how Calhoun would respond to this rebuke. "The Union—next to our liberties the most dear," he retorted, his glass trembling, "may we all remember that it can only be preserved by respecting the rights of the states and distributing equally the benefits and burdens of the Union." There was no going back.

South Carolina planters persuaded themselves that they would have to do something soon. They watched with growing alarm as the newspapers told of the success of British abolitionists in ending slavery in the British West Indies—the place from which many elite white South Carolina families had come generations earlier. With the memory of Denmark Vesey's plan of 1822 and an 1829 revolt in the low country still fresh in their memory, white Carolinians felt they could display no weakness on the slavery issue. Unlike other southern states, where stark geographic differences between low country and hill country often divided voters and encouraged party differences, South Carolina witnessed broad agreement among its electorate on this crucial issue. Throughout the state, raucous crowds gathered to call for a fight against the federal government on the tariff. Those South Carolinians who favored a more conciliatory stance toward the federal government could not generate nearly as much support for their position.

When the toasts at the Indian Queen Hotel revealed that President Jackson had no sympathy for nullification, the leaders of the movement in South Carolina were surprised and disappointed. After all, Jackson, like them, was a planter and slaveholder and would suffer economically along with the South Carolinians. Jackson considered the tariff to be for the good of the nation as a whole. The tariff provided money for defense and prevented federal debt. The South Carolina challenge would limit the power of the U.S. government to make law for the country in matters that transcended state boundaries. Jackson did not believe the United States could afford to permit such divisiveness to impair its strength in the world of nations. Jackson, the old general, would tolerate no opposition on such matters.

Nullification, Jackson announced, would not stand. He could not have been any clearer: nullification was "incompatible with the existence of the Union, contradicted expressly by the letter of the Constitution, unauthorized by its spirit, inconsistent with every principle on which it was founded, and destructive of the great object for which it was formed." Disunion was treason, he warned, and would be treated as such; Congress passed a "Force Bill" to permit him to use military power to keep South Carolina in line. Recent opponents of Jackson such as Henry Clay and Daniel Webster were pleased—and surprised—at Jackson's nationalism; they had not expected such convictions from a Tennessee planter. Southerners in general were caught in a difficult position, disapproving of South Carolina's radicalism but distrustful of the centralizing precedent of the Force Bill.

Congress twisted and turned on the issue, not wanting South Carolina to get its way but unwilling to see Jackson use arms. After much debate, Congress, under the leadership of Henry Clay, offered compromise in early 1833: the tariff would be slowly but steadily lowered over the next decade, giving northern manufacturers time to adapt. South Carolina, secretly relieved, declared itself the victor and accepted the compromise tariff; in a final display of states' rights defiance, though, the Carolinians nullified the Force Bill. Jackson ignored them, recognizing the emptiness of the gesture.

Free Blacks and African American Abolitionism

Even as the white leaders of South Carolina struggled to define the extent of their powers within the Union, free blacks and slaves struggled to define their freedom. Communities of several thousand free blacks lived in every major northern city, establishing their own churches, newspapers, school, and lodges.

In many towns and cities along the coast of the Northeast, as many as 25 percent of all free black household heads worked as sailors. The dangers, poor pay, and family hardships opened seafaring posts for African Americans, though black men serving on whalers out of New England received equal shares in the profits with divisions made on the basis of skill rather than race.

More numerous were free African Americans in the Upper South slave states, especially Maryland and Virginia. Some had been emancipated during the decades after the Revolutionary War, when slavery seemed to be dying and when the ideals of the new nation and Christianity persuaded some masters to free their slaves. Although free blacks in the Upper South scattered throughout smaller towns and rural areas, they generally tended to gather in cities as they did in the North. The cities strung along the Atlantic and Gulf coasts—Norfolk, Savannah, Charleston, Mobile, and New Orleans—all contained several thousand free blacks. Outside of these cities, few free blacks lived in the deep South.

Free African Americans stayed in the South to be closer to family members held in slavery and because, ironically, southern cities held greater economic opportunity than the North. Because whites deemed many jobs in the South "nigger work," below the dignity of whites, black southerners dominated some fields of work. Black men constituted most of the barbers and teamsters, for example, while black women found work as laundresses and domestics. Free blacks in the South had to be careful, making sure that local officials kept records of their freedom, but they could acquire property and educate their children. They stayed in contact with African Americans in the North through newspapers, letters, and word passed by the many black sailors who plied the eastern seaboard.

Free blacks throughout the country debated the merits of leaving the United States altogether, as many whites encouraged them to do. The colonization movement struggled in the 1820s. Few black Americans were willing to be shipped to a place they had never seen; only about 1,400 black Americans went to Liberia in the 1820s. African Americans came to see in colonization an attack on their hard-won accomplishments in the United States, for their leaders insisted that people of color had earned a place in this country. Rather than spending moral energy and money on removing black people, they argued, Americans should work instead on making the United States a fairer place.

David Walker proved to be an important figure in this movement. Walker had lived in Charleston at the time of Denmark Vesey's conspiracy in 1822, becoming familiar with the long tradition of revolt and resistance in the Carolina low country. After the suppression of Vesey, Walker moved to Boston. There, he established a used-clothing store, one of the few businesses open to African Americans in the North. Walker did well in the business, bought a home, joined the African Methodist church, and became a black Mason, an organization that fought against slavery and the slave trade. He gave his support to *Freedom's Journal,* an anticolonization paper published by black people in Boston and New York City between 1827 and 1829.

In 1829, Walker released his *Appeal . . . to the Colored Citizens of the World.* Americans, whatever their skin color, had never read such a document. Walker denied that slaves felt or owed any bond to their masters. He called for black spiritual self-renewal, starting with African Americans' recognition of just how angry they were with their lot in the United States. They needed to channel that anger with God's love, Walker urged, making a group effort to end slavery immediately. He did not call for violence but for black Americans to be full Americans in both government and economy. Condemning Henry Clay's support for removing all free blacks to Africa, Walker accused Clay and those supporting colonization of concocting a "plan to get those of the colored people, who are said to be free, away from those of our brethren whom they unjustly hold in bondage, so that they may be enabled to keep them the more secure in ignorance and wretchedness. . . . For if the free are allowed to stay among the slaves, they will have intercourse together, and . . . the free will learn the slaves *bad habits,* by teaching them that they are MEN . . . and certainly *ought* and *must* be FREE."

Within weeks of its publication, Walker's *Appeal* appeared in Savannah, where it was seized, and then in Milledgeville, Georgia (the state capital), then in Virginia, North Carolina, South Carolina, and New Orleans. The *Appeal* created panic and repression wherever it appeared. Southern whites worried at this evidence of invisible networks of communication and resistance among the slaves, free blacks, and, perhaps, sympathetic whites in their midst. Events in Virginia bore out their worst suspicions.

The Crisis of Slavery in Virginia

Nat Turner was a field hand, born in 1800, who felt that God had called him for more than the lot of a slave. Well known even in his youth for his

David Walker, 1829
Appeal . . . to the Colored Citizens of the World, 1829

David Walker, a free black man, argues with Thomas Jefferson's assertion that slavery in the United States was more benign and beneficial than in ancient Greece and Rome, places to which educated Americans looked for the measure of true civilization. In Walker's eyes, the connection between the ancients and modern whites shows a strain of cruelty that runs throughout the history of western culture. He attacks the un-Christian behavior of slavetraders and slaveholders even as he looks to God for ultimate judgment.

I have been for years troubling the pages of historians to find out what our fathers have done to the *white Christians of America,* to merit such condign punishment as they have inflicted on them, and do continue to inflict on us their children. But I must aver, that my researches have hitherto been to no effect. I have therefore come to the immovable conclusion, that they (Americans) have, and do continue to punish us for nothing else, but for enriching them and their country. For I cannot conceive of any thing else. Nor will I ever believe otherwise until the Lord shall convince me. . . .

The whites have always been an unjust, jealous, unmerciful, avaricious and blood thirsty set of beings, always seeking after power and authority. — We view them all over the confederacy of Greece, where they were first known to be any thing, (in consequence of education) we see them there, cutting each other's throats — trying to subject each other to wretchedness and misery, to effect which they used all kinds of deceitful, unfair and unmerciful means. We view them next in Rome, where the spirit of tyranny and deceit raged still higher. — We view them in Gaul, Spain and in Britain — in fine, we view them all over Europe, together with what were scattered about in Asia and Africa, as heathens, and we see them acting more like devils than accountable men. But some may ask, did not the blacks of Africa, and the mulattoes of Asia, go on in the same ways as did the whites of Europe? I answer no — they never were half so avaricious, deceitful and unmerciful as the whites, according to their knowledge. . . .

Source: David Walker, *Appeal, in Four Articles; Together with a Preamble to the Colored Citizens of the World. . . .* (Boston: September 28, 1829. 3d ed. Boston: D. Walker).

---

intellectual abilities and his effectiveness as a preacher, on Sundays Turner traveled throughout the countryside around Southampton County, Virginia, coming to know most of the slaves and free black people who lived there. Praying and fasting, Turner saw visions: drops of blood that formed hieroglyphics on leaves, black shadows across the white moon. These things, he became certain, foretold a slave revolt, of the time "fast approaching when the first should be last and the last should be first." Turner, unlike Gabriel in Richmond in 1800 and Vesey in Charleston in 1822, chose to build his revolt around a small group of select lieutenants rather than to risk spreading the word broadly. Their plan was to begin the rebellion on their own and then attract compatriots along the way.

On August 22, 1831, Turner and his band began their revolt. They moved from one isolated farmhouse to the next, killing all the whites they found inside, including children. They gathered horses and weapons. Turner rode at the end of the group, praying for guidance on what plan they should follow. As

NAT TURNER

The Granger Collection, New York

In 1831, Americans hungered for news of Nat Turner. In the absence of photographs or of artists on the scene, people were left to imagine what Turner might have looked like— just as they imagined what his motives might have been. A white lawyer took down Turner's "confessions," which sold many copies throughout the nation. In those notes, Turner attributed his acts to directives from God and proclaimed his confidence that he acted properly.

Whites scoffed at such claims, assuming that Turner must have been simply insane. In this drawing, Turner is imagined as a sort of biblical character, inspiring a small band of lieutenants. This was in fact the way Turner worked, entrusting his plans to a small group of trusted men until the moment of the revolt, when they launched out on their journey from one white household to the next and gathered allies along the way. The swamp setting is a bit fanciful, however, portraying Virginia as a dark tropical region. Turner did apparently hope to escape into Virginia's Great Dismal Swamp, but most of his planning and raids took place on a considerably less exotic landscape.

---

the night went on, Turner's men had killed about seventy people, starting with the family of Turner's master. By morning, word had rushed to Richmond of the unimaginable events in Southampton. Whites huddled together in Jerusalem, the county seat, and troops arrived to put down the revolt. Blacks, many of whom had no connection with the rebellion, were killed by infuriated and frightened whites hundreds of miles away from Southampton. Turner's troops were all captured or killed, but he managed to escape and to hide in the woods of the county for two months. Once captured, Turner narrated a remarkable "confession" in which he told of his visions and prophecies. He had no regrets and no doubts that

God would stand in judgment of the people who held other people in slavery. At his hanging in November, he showed no signs of remorse.

White southerners saw in Nat Turner their worst nightmares. Here was a literate slave, allowed to travel on his own, allowed to spread his own interpretation of the Bible to dissatisfied slaves eager to listen to Turner's prophecies. The crackdown was not long in coming, as delegates to the state assembly gathered in Richmond a month after Turner's execution. In a series of remarkable debates, these white Virginians, some of them sons and grandsons of Thomas Jefferson, John Marshall, and Patrick Henry, openly admitted the debilitating effect of slavery on Virginia. They worried most about slavery's influence on whites, worried that slavery kept the economy from developing as it did in the North. Delegates from western Virginia, where relatively few slaves lived, expressed their misgivings most freely, but even large slaveholders from the East admitted slavery's negative effects. Petitions flowed into Richmond, particularly from the western counties where whites resented the domination of the state by the wealthy minority of tidewater slaveholders, urging the legislators to take a decisive step to rid Virginia of slavery. Defenders of slavery warned that the debates, published in the newspapers and discussed on the streets and in the shops and homes across the state, might result in more revolts. Enslaved Virginians were not an "ignorant herd of Africans," one delegate warned, but an "active, intelligent class, watching and weighing every movement of the Legislature, with perfect knowledge of its bearing and effect."

Some delegates urged that the state purchase all slaves born after a certain date—1840 was proposed—and colonize them in Africa or sell them to plantations farther south. Others argued that the state could not afford such a step, that the Virginia economy would collapse without slavery, that slaves born before the date of freedom would revolt, that property rights guaranteed in the Constitution made it ridiculous to talk about taking slaves from their owners. Others went much further, arguing that slavery was not wrong at all but rather God's plan for civilizing Africans otherwise lost to heathenism and barbarism. The disparate regions of Virginia found themselves in deep conflict; some discussed separating themselves from the rest of the state if one policy or another were followed. The lawmakers, starkly divided, ultimately decided that it was "inexpedient" to take any step at all against slavery at that time, that it would be left for subsequent legislatures to begin the process that would free Virginia from slavery. In the meantime, they passed harsher laws to limit the movement and gathering of free blacks and slaves.

POLITICAL TURMOIL AND THE ELECTION OF 1832

Andrew Jackson made fervent enemies as well as devoted followers throughout his presidency. No one could be neutral about him, for he seemed to touch everything in American life. The election of 1832 saw voters and leaders mobilize in opposition or support of Jackson, latching on to a wide range of issues. The president, furious at any resistance, lashed out, determined that his work not be wasted. The nation had never seen such political conflict, as citizens debated issues of the economy, states' rights, and morality.

Taking Sides

In September 1831, the first national political convention in U.S. history met in Baltimore. It was convened by the Anti-Masons. Despite their origins and their name, the Anti-Masons were concerned with the state of American politics in general, not merely with the threat posed by the Masons. They attracted an impressive list of ambitious and accomplished young men to their convention, including many who believed the Jackson White House was too pro-southern and too callous with the American Indians. The Anti-Masons found little appeal in John Quincy Adams's National Republicans, for that party seemed to be stuck in the past and hapless against the strong Jacksonian Democrats. The Anti-Masons promised to become a powerful third party, a wild card in an already tumultuous American politics.

The Jacksonians held their own convention the following spring. Jackson, fed up with the controversy over Peggy Eaton and alienated from Calhoun, early in 1831 asked all the members of his cabinet to resign. When the president reconstituted the cabinet, he replaced pro-Calhoun men with men more to his own liking. Van Buren, who had suggested the purge as a way of cleaning house before the election of 1832, was nominated by Jackson to be the new ambassador to Great Britain. Calhoun, in revenge, cast the Senate vote that rejected Van Buren's appointment. Van Buren and Jackson got the last laugh when the convention of 1832 filled the vice presidential slot with Van Buren and removed Calhoun from the ticket. Calhoun, it became clear, would never be Jackson's choice for president; Van Buren had supplanted him as heir apparent.

Other kinds of resentments also fueled the conflict of the early 1830s. As prices and rents rose more quickly than wages, urban working people found themselves falling behind. These working men and women felt their contributions slighted in the new economy, their labor no longer bringing the recognition and rewards it deserved. Workers formed unions to defend their rights. In the early 1830s trades' associations appeared in New York, Boston, Baltimore, Washington, and Louisville. They sponsored newspapers, lobbied legislatures, and supported one another

This poster sought to mobilize New York City's working people in favor of a new labor party.
From "The Union," 1835, courtesy of The New York Public Library

during strikes. By the mid-1830s, between 100,000 and 300,000 men and women belonged to unions.

A number of labor and political leaders, recognizing the power of such numbers, sought to mobilize the organized workers into politics. While union members generally liked Andrew Jackson's blows against monopoly, they thought he pulled up short in his attack on privilege. They sought to push the political system into doing more to protect working people. Some unions became deeply engaged in politics and put forward their own candidates.

The Bank War

Despite the tariffs intended to serve their interests, most people in the Northeast felt they had received little from Andrew Jackson's first term. They viewed him with distrust and growing anger, perceiving in Old Hickory an enemy to moral and commercial progress, a defender of the backward South and West against the East. The fate of the Second Bank of the United States stood as the key issue in this regard. Many merchants and others deemed it a stabilizing force in the American economy, holding an otherwise decentralized money system in place. It was the job of Nicholas Biddle, the president of the Bank of the United States, to make sure that state banks kept plenty of metal currency—specie—on

hand with which to pay the national bank when asked to do so. Such rules kept the state banks from putting out too many notes, from inflating the currency with paper money unsupported by gold or silver. When the economy fell into trouble, on the other hand, Biddle and the Bank of the United States would lessen their demands on the state banks, preventing panics and deflation.

While businessmen appreciated this role of the bank, many other Americans distrusted it. In their eyes, this largely private institution enjoyed far too much power for its own good or the good of the country. Why should privileged stockholders in the bank, they asked, profit from the business of the federal government? Why should the national notes be allowed to depress the value of state notes, with their origins closer to home?

For many voters, objections to the Bank of the United States were as much objections to banking and commerce in general as to any specific policies of the national bank. The whole business of banking seemed suspect, with its paper money, its profits seemingly without labor, its government-supported monopolies, its apparent speculation with public money. Andrew Jackson shared these feelings of mistrust. As a young man, he had lost a considerable amount of money to a speculator, and nothing he saw as president changed his mind about those who dealt in the mysteries of currency. He disliked monopoly, he disliked paper money, and he disliked the Bank of the United States.

The issue came to a head in 1832 as Henry Clay and other National Republicans, joined by South Carolina nullifiers such as Calhoun, sought to use the bank as a way to defeat Jackson for the presidency. A few months before the election in the fall, the bank's supporters steered its application for rechartering through Congress. Jackson heard of the news while he was ill in bed. "The bank," he told Martin Van Buren, "is trying to kill me, *but I will kill it!*" He vetoed the recharter, proclaiming that the bank was "unauthorized by the constitution, subversive of the rights of the States, and dangerous to the liberties of the people."

Jackson's opponents, in turn, saw the president, not the bank, as the usurper of American rights. How dare he single-handedly overturn what the people, in the form of Congress, had declared to be their will? Henry Clay and other opponents argued that his action posed a far greater threat to the American people than did the bank. If the president could force his way into the lawmaking process, the division of powers laid out in the Constitution would be violated and the Union

*P*ICTURING THE PAST ✦ ECONOMICS & TECHNOLOGY

THE BANK OF THE UNITED STATES AS A MONSTER

GENERAL JACKSON SLAYING THE MANY HEADED MONSTER.

The Granger Collection, New York

This elaborate cartoon conveyed a simple message but with many subtleties that informed people at the time could have decoded. Each of the heads of the "hydra" is labeled with the name of a state, representing the way the "monster" of the Bank of the United States had slithered its way into every corner of the nation. The largest head at the center of the hydra, that of Nicholas Biddle, is labeled "Penn" for Pennsylvania. The soldier on the right has dropped his axe, discovering that splitting one of the heads of the hydra only reveals another inside. President Jackson, elderly and yet still vigorous and determined, wields a sword labeled "veto," killing with a manly thrust a frightening opponent that seemed too formidable for anyone else to conquer. Vice President Martin Van Buren seems to be trying to help, albeit ineffectually. He contributes mainly by exclaiming "Well done general!"

---

would risk falling under the despotic rule of a president who would be king.

Before the bank could deploy its enormous financial resources to gather the two-thirds majority necessary to override his earlier veto, Jackson quickly moved all federal funds from the Bank of the United States to state banks. The newly appointed secretary of the treasury followed Jackson's plan and put the government deposits in seven state banks—promptly dubbed "pet banks" by opponents of the new strategy. Congressmen of both parties denounced Jackson's

move. Biddle and his bank's supporters fought on for two more years, but without the government's deposits they had little leverage. Jackson's lieutenants efficiently mobilized the votes they needed in Congress to prevent the renewal of the bank's charter. The Bank of the United States, deprived of government support, began a slow death.

The election of 1832 turned around these broad issues about the fate of the nation. Jackson portrayed himself as the champion of the common man fighting against a bloated aristocracy of privilege and monopoly. Clay, the candidate of the National Republicans, portrayed himself as the defender of the Union against an arrogant and power-hungry president, a man who had shown a disregard for morality and justice in his dealing with the American Indians and enacting the spoils system as well as with the bank. William Wirt, the candidate of the Anti-Masons, declared himself the opponent of conspiracies, corruptions, and subversions larger and more insidious than the bank, all the more dangerous for not being clearly defined.

Despite the challenges on the bank and by the Anti-Masons, Jackson won by a considerable margin, losing South Carolina to a nullifier, Vermont to the Anti-Masons, and the rest of New England and a few other states to Clay. Emboldened by his majority at the polls, the president went on the offensive.

Those opposed to Jackson began to call themselves "Whigs." Like their British namesakes, the American Whigs saw themselves as the counterbalance to otherwise unchecked monarchical power—in this case "King Andrew I," "the most absolute despot now at the head of any representative government on earth."

THE INDIAN PEOPLES AND THE MEXICAN NATION

Andrew Jackson's administration focused much of its energy on the native peoples of North America. The American Indians held immense areas of the South and the West when Jackson took office, land that many whites wanted and demanded. The southwestern border of the United States remained tantalizingly ambiguous as well. Mexico governed its Texas province loosely and many white Americans coveted that land. Both of these situations would undergo explosive change under Andrew Jackson.

Jackson and the American Indians

Andrew Jackson had announced, and acted upon, his attitudes toward the Indians years before he took office as president. The steady pressing of white population onto the rich lands of the Cherokee, Chickasaw, Creeks, Seminoles, and Choctaws, he thought, left the people of those nations with two choices. They could either become "industrious Citizens" who accepted the sovereignty of the states that claimed the lands on which they lived, or they could "remove to a Country

where they can retain their ancient customs, so dear to them, that they cannot give up in exchange for regular society." If they could adapt themselves to agriculture and law, they might remain where they were, protected by the laws they pledged to obey; if they could not adapt, they would have to leave. Their only other choice, Jackson thought, was extinction.

White people had mixed feelings about the Indians. Americans of European descent considered the Indians admirable in many ways, dignified and free, able to learn and prosper. Not a few "white" and "black" families were proud to claim some Indian ancestry. Andrew Jackson, for his part, adopted a Creek infant, Lyncoya, educated him, and brought him to live with him and his wife. In fact, the death of Lyncoya from tuberculosis in 1828, at age sixteen, hastened Rachel Jackson's heartbreak and decline. Many other white Americans, including some in Congress, had long contributed time and money to the Indians, helping to build and staff schools, sending seed and agricultural implements to ease the transition to farming.

By the late 1820s, the "civilized tribes" had adapted themselves to the dominant society. Many of the tribes were led by chiefs of mixed descent, leaders who lived in cabins, houses, and even mansions. Men such as John Ross negotiated land settlements and profited from such deals but also attempted to create systems of political representation and law. He joined the Methodist church and courted any political party he believed best advanced Cherokee interests. The wealthiest Indians, especially the Cherokee, bought African American slaves. The children of the Indian leaders and others went to schools established by white missionaries, who persuaded a considerable number of Indians to convert to Christianity. The Cherokees published a newspaper that included articles in both their own language and in English.

Despite these adaptations, the Indians of the Southeast showed no desire to leave the land on which they lived in the late 1820s. In their view, they had already given up more land than they should have—millions of acres over the preceding twenty years—and were determined to hold on to what remained. "We would not receive money for land in which our fathers and friends are buried," they declared. Most whites, especially those who lived nearby and coveted the rich cotton lands under the Indians' control, bristled at the continuing presence of the native inhabitants. Many white people longed to banish the American Indians to land on the other side of the Mississippi River, where, it seemed,

Memorial and Protest of the Cherokee Nation, 1836

The Cherokee nation, even while the federal and state governments prepared to force them from their homes in the South, desperately reminded Congress of the treaties struck between the two peoples. The Cherokee pleaded that they had done exactly what white Americans had urged them to do: assimilate, progress, and prosper. The arguments had little effect; the Trail of Tears soon commenced.

The undersigned representatives of the Cherokee nation, east of the river Mississippi, impelled by duty, would respectfully submit, for the consideration of your honorable body, the following statement of facts: It will be seen, from the numerous subsisting treaties between the Cherokee nation and the United States, that from the earliest existence of this government, the United States, in Congress assembled, received the Cherokees and their nation into favor and protection; and that the chiefs and warriors, for themselves and all parts of the Cherokee nation, acknowledged themselves and the said Cherokee nation to be under the protection of the United States of America, and of no other sovereign whatsoever: they also stipulated, that the said Cherokee nation will not hold any treaty with any foreign power, individual State, or with individuals of any State: that for, and in consideration of, valuable concessions made by the Cherokee nation, the United States solemnly guaranteed to said nation all their lands not ceded, and pledged the faith of the government, that "all white people who have intruded, or may hereafter intrude, on the lands reserved for the Cherokees, shall be removed by the United States, and proceeded against, according to the provisions of the act, passed 30th March, 1802," entitled "An act to regulate trade and intercourse with the Indian tribes, and to preserve peace on the frontiers." It would be useless to recapitulate the numerous provisions for the security and protection of the rights of the Cherokees, to be found in the various treaties between their nation and the United States. The Cherokees were happy and prosperous under a scrupulous observance of treaty stipulations by the government of the United States, and from the fostering hand extended over them, they made rapid advances in civilization, morals, and in the arts and sciences. Little did they anticipate, that when taught to think and feel as the American citizen, and to have with him a common interest, they were to be *despoiled by their guardian*, to become strangers and wanderers in the land of their fathers, forced to return to the savage life, and to seek a new home in the wilds of the far west, and that without their consent. An instrument purporting to be a treaty with the Cherokee people, has recently been made public by the President of the United States, that will have such an operation, if carried into effect. This instrument, the delegation aver before the civilized world, and in the presence of Almighty God, is fraudulent, false upon its face, made by unauthorized individuals, without the sanction, and against the wishes, of the great body of the Cherokee people. Upwards of fifteen thousand of those people have protested against it, solemnly declaring they will never acquiesce. . .

Source: Memorial and Protest of the Cherokee Nation, June 22, 1836, *Exec. Doc.* No. 286, 24th Cong., 1st sess., pp. 1-2.

whites would not want to live for a very long time, if ever.

In 1827, the Cherokees held a national convention and drew up a written constitution, patterned on that of the United States. They desired both to declare their sovereignty over their lands and to show whites just how devoted they were to American values. But the new constitution, U.S. courts ruled, violated the law of both the nation and the state of Georgia, which petitioned the federal government to remove

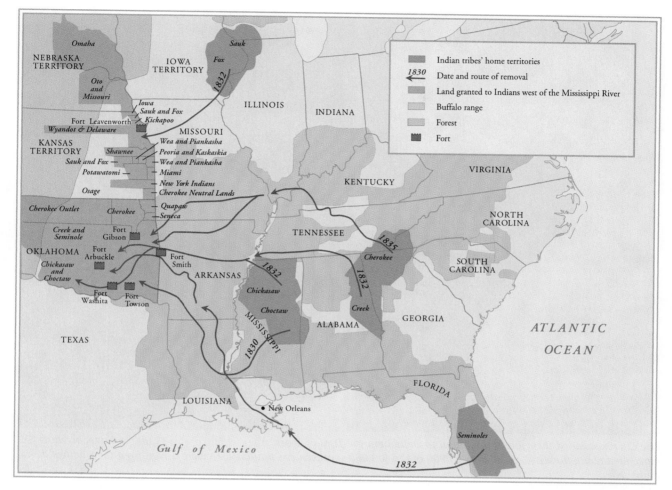

Map 10.1 *Removal of the American Indians*
In the early 1830s, the Indians of the North and South were "removed" to reservations in Oklahoma and Kansas.

the Cherokees. An already volatile situation worsened when gold was discovered on the Indian lands and white prospectors rushed in. The Georgia legislature declared the Cherokees' laws null and void, placing Georgia law into effect instead. The Cherokees suddenly found themselves even more vulnerable than before. White settlers invaded northern Georgia, taking Cherokee property.

Jackson told the Indians he was their friend, even their "father," but that he could do nothing to stop their mistreatment except to move them beyond the Mississippi River, where, he promised, they would be safe. The Indians and their supporters, mostly religious people in the North, responded bitterly to such claims, arguing that the rights of the Constitution should certainly extend to people who had lived in North America since time immemorial. Many northern men

and women who first organized to oppose Indian removal and participated in local and regional protests would later act together to oppose the expansion of slavery. But the Jacksonians quickly pushed through the Indian Removal Act of 1830. Two Supreme Court decisions in favor of the Cherokees, in 1830 and in 1832, proved to be without effect, since they depended on the federal government to implement them and Jackson had no intention of doing anything of the sort.

In the face of the impending removal, most of the Indian peoples split into pro-assimilation, "progressive," factions and anti-assimilation, "conservative," factions. They debated fiercely and sometimes violently among themselves. Missionaries and federal agents dealt primarily with the progressives, but many other Indians resisted, often by moving far into the backwoods. Many thousands of each nation remained

The Cherokee called their forced migration to Oklahoma the Trail of Tears. About 4,000 of the 15,000 Indians forced to move died along the way, as did over 25,000 of the 100,000 southeastern Indians who were driven from their homes in these years.
Woolaroc Museum, Bartlesville, Oklahoma

behind, either those who had passed into white or black society through marriage or those who lived outside areas of heavy settlement.

Agents, some of mixed blood, swindled the Indians as they prepared for the removal. The Choctaws, the first to move, underwent horrific experiences, suffering greatly and dying in large numbers as they traveled in the worst winter on record with completely inadequate supplies. The Creeks, too, confronted frauds and assaults. The Indians who moved sold whatever they could not take with them, usually at a great loss. Wagons and carts carried the old and the sick, while women and children drove livestock along the trail. Soldiers usually accompanied the Indians, along with an agent to hand out whatever support the government provided. Some of the migrants used steamboats to travel up or down the Mississippi River and then to Oklahoma along the Arkansas or Red River, while others proceeded over land. "To see the remnant of a once mighty people fettered and chained together forced to depart from the land of their fathers into a country unknown to them," an Alabama newspaper admitted, "is of itself sufficient to move the stoutest heart."

The Cherokee removal was the most prolonged. After years of negotiating, the government struck a bargain with a small and unrepresentative number of the Cherokee in the Treaty of New Echota in 1836. While groups of several hundred at a time left, including some of the wealthiest, 17,000 refused to leave by the deadline. General Winfield Scott then led 7,000 troops against them, driving people from their homes empty-handed, marching them to stockades and shipping them out by rail and water. About a quarter of all eastern Cherokees died in what they called the Trail of Tears. Some Cherokees remained in the mountains of North Carolina and Tennessee, but the power of the eastern Indians had been destroyed.

The Seminoles fought against removal as long as they could. Led by Osceola, the son of an English trader and the husband of an escaped slave, the Seminoles tried to break the will of the whites by killing soldiers and civilians and by burning their crops and homes. The Second Seminole War launched by the federal government to remove the 5,000 Indians began in 1836 and dragged on for six years. The conflict proved both unpopular and unsuccessful. About 36,000 U.S. soldiers fought and 1,500 died; many more suffered debilitating disease. The federal government spent $20 million in the fight, even though few white people wanted to settle on the Seminoles' land. The United States captured Osceola only by deception at a supposed peace conference. He died in captivity a few months later, after which some Seminoles finally migrated to Oklahoma. But most of the Seminole people, able to use the swampy landscape to hide, were never driven out of Florida.

Fighting also erupted in the Illinois Territory between white settlers and the Sac and Fox Indians. These people, under the leadership of Black Hawk, saw their lands along the Mississippi River taken over by whites while the Indians were on a hunting expedition in 1832. The whites burned the Indians' huts and plowed under their fields. In retaliation, the Sac and Fox destroyed white settlements. A large contingent of volunteers (including a young Abraham Lincoln), regular troops, and allied Indians set out after Black Hawk and his people, who also had allies from other Indian nations. Eventually, the whites outnumbered Black Hawk and overran his camp, killing nearly 500 as they tried to cross the Mississippi River. Taken prisoner, Black Hawk refused to repent, telling his captors that he "has done nothing for which an Indian ought to be ashamed. He has fought for his countrymen, the squaws and papooses, against white men who came, year after year, to cheat them and take away their land." Black Hawk's words and deeds, widely reported in the newspapers of the country, attracted considerable sympathy among whites in the East. Andrew Jackson met with Black Hawk and pardoned him; the chief's autobiography became a bestseller. The United States, using its defeat of the Sac as an example, found it much easier to induce the other Indians of the Old Northwest to cede 190 million acres for $70 million.

Conflict with Mexico

Speculators and settlers from the United States continually moved into Mexican Texas in the 1820s and 1830s. Sometimes the Mexican officials encouraged the newcomers; at other times, they sought to slow American settlement. Seeking the end of slavery in Mexico, they wanted settlers but they did not want the slaves white settlers often brought with them. The key leader in the American migration was Stephen F. Austin, a Virginia-born entrepreneur who first arrived in Mexico in 1821 on the heels of Mexican independence. Throughout the 1820s, Austin, negotiating with the changing Mexican governments, oversaw the arrival and settlement of hundreds of Americans. While the Mexican laws on slavery shifted repeatedly, most of the American settlers—the great majority of them southerners—argued that they had to have slaves if Texas were to develop as they and as Mexican leaders hoped. The Americans, with the tacit approval of local officials, improvised laws and took advantage of loopholes to keep slavery in fact if not in name.

American settlers and the Mexican government came into increasing conflict, as provincial officials attempted to collect tariffs and slow immigration into the district. Austin and the other Americans petitioned the Mexican government to let them become a separate Mexican state under its own administration, but they were rebuffed when Antonio López de Santa Anna took control of the government. In the 1830s, as Santa Anna consolidated his power in Mexico, his attempts to centralize control in Mexico City led to revolts in the Yucatan and Zacateces as well as in Texas. In Santa Anna's eyes, the Texans were clearly inviting an expansionist United States to take this province away from Mexico; he sent in troops to meet the threat.

In 1835, a convention of Texans voted to fight against Santa Anna, offering large amounts of land to all who would come help in the struggle. Volunteers and money flowed into Texas from throughout the United States, where people had been watching the events in that area with great interest. Southern states in particular sent hundreds of men. Nevertheless, they were greatly outnumbered by the Mexicans, who decimated the Americans at several battles. As the Mexican army sought to occupy San Antonio, 188 rebels—including Davy Crockett of Tennessee, famous for his frontier exploits and for his service in Congress—took refuge in the Mission of the Alamo. Most of the people inside were American, but they were joined by *tejanos,* Mexicans of the province who allied themselves with the revolt for independence. The defenders of the Alamo held out against 3,000 Mexican soldiers for nearly two weeks in 1836, until the Mexicans finally stormed the mission and killed all inside except three white women, two white children, and an African American slave. The Mexicans stripped the bodies of the insurrectionaries and burned them. After the Alamo, support for the rebellion grew rapidly in the United States, where it came to be seen as a moral struggle between the forces of freedom and the forces of autocracy. "Remember the Alamo" became the rallying cry.

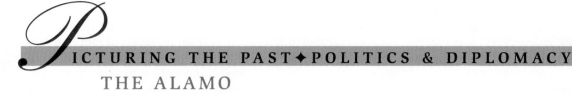

*P*ICTURING THE PAST✦POLITICS & DIPLOMACY

THE ALAMO

The Granger Collection, New York

A small force of Americans and *tejanos* were overwhelmed at the Almo mission in San Antonio. Although the Mexican army won the battle, its victory unleashed the support of the United States. Almost from the moment of the battle, the Alamo became the object of mythmaking. The press of the United States turned the men inside the mission into valiant heroes and imagined their deaths in ways that embodied the highet standards of masculine self-sacrifice. The newspapers back east talked little of the *tejanos* and instead celebrated the white soldiers in the Alamo as the vanguard of American civilization and decried the Mexicans as bloodthirsty and inhuman mercenaries defeating the men from the United States through sheer numbers.

Santa Anna seemed on the verge of victory until Sam Houston, the general of the American forces, surprised the larger Mexican force at San Jacinto in April of 1836. Rushing toward the Mexican camp, a force of 900 Texans and *tejano* cavalry commanded by Juan Seguín won a decisive battle in only eighteen minutes. Santa Anna himself was captured a day later. As a prisoner, he signed treaties removing Mexican troops from Texas, granting Texas its independence, and recognizing the Rio Grande as the boundary. The Mexican Congress, when they heard of this capitulation, announced that they would not be bound by its terms.

Texans and many Americans elsewhere urged the U.S. government to annex the new republic before it could be retaken by the Mexicans. That plea unleashed a heated and protracted debate between advocates of American expansion and those who thought such a step would be immoral and impolitic. Much of the debate raged between southerners, who saw Texas as a vast new empire, and northerners, especially abolitionists, who opposed annexation because it would lead to slavery's expansion. The fate of Texas was to be a key political issue for the next decade.

REVIVAL

The power and influence of Protestant churches surged to a new level in the Jacksonian era. Far more than in any previous generation, the Jacksonian years saw the churches take leading roles in every facet of life and in every part of the Union. Revivals pulled in scores of new members, firing them with the desire to remake their lives. Many of those who experienced the spiritual rebirth of the revivals sought ways to demonstrate their faith and their hope for America. A radical new movement against slavery gathered force with stunning speed. At the same time, other Americans sought purer forms of religion itself, listening to prophets who spoke of new churches and new possibilities. Everywhere in the late 1820s and early 1830s, religion seemed on people's lips.

Revivalism

Since the late eighteenth century, revivals led by the major Protestant denominations had periodically inflamed the United States. In those revivals, people who had never declared their faith in Jesus Christ or who had fallen away from the church made public expressions of their faith. Thousands of people gathered in the North, South, and West, in town and countryside, to pray and hear ministers tell them of God's love and forgiveness. Hearing of these gifts, and aware of their own sinfulness, men and women sometimes fell to the ground as if stricken. Others cried and screamed. The churches that devoted themselves to spreading the Gospel—known as "evangelical" churches because they sought to bring others to their faith in Scripture—periodically experienced revivals or "awakenings" when numbers of people expressed or renewed their faith. This revivalism burst out again in the mid-1820s.

Desires for personal relationship with God and a sense of community often linked new religious leaders with recent scientific advances to encourage beliefs in spiritualism, magnetic healing, phrenology, and mesmerism. Science and religion were not seen by those in the early nineteenth century as incompatible, as both the supernatural and scientific could explain the individual's role in creation. Samuel Gridley Howe, director of the New England Asylum for the Blind, chose to monitor a local deaf and blind girl to determine if morality and faith were inborn to humans. He chose Laura Bridgman, a local girl who had recently survived scarlet fever but lost her sight and hearing. She learned to read and became a celebrity, with as many as a thousand people turning out to see her as part of the asylum's efforts to raise money. She was also listed as a major attraction in contemporary tourist guides, so wealthy travelers from around the nation and Europe stopped in Boston to see her.

Many ministers and churches across the country were swept up in the religious awakening of the 1820s, but one man embodied its new and aggressive spirit: Charles Grandison Finney. Finney, a young attorney from Utica, New York, who had not regularly attended

SAVED IN THE LORD'S OWN TIME AND PLACE.

This engraving depicts Charles Grandison Finney's moment of conversion as he described the scene in his memoirs.
Oberlin College Archives, Oberlin

church until encouraged to do so by his fiancée, suddenly found himself struck with the power of God's love. "An overwhelming sense" of his wickedness brought Finney to his knees. "I wept aloud like a child [and] the Holy Spirit descended upon me in a manner that seemed to go through me body and soul," he recalled. "I could feel the impression like a wave of electricity, going through and through me." Finney spread the word of the Bible in the plain and straightforward language of everyday life. He told people that they had it within their power to take the first step toward God, that God would listen. Finney told people to seek out salvation, to throw themselves open to the mercy of Jesus.

Finney found in the new cities of western New York a receptive audience among young men, on their own in a rapidly changing America, and among women of every age. The churches, these people believed, had grown cold in the hands of the established ministry and needed a revival of spirit. They wanted a Christianity of activity, of prayer meetings, of spreading the word any way they could. Finney's influence grew in strength and numbers as women prayed with one another. The district of upstate New York that lay along the path of the Erie Canal became known as "The Burned-Over District," as one revival after another surged through its towns and farms.

The revivals took on a new scale and urgency in 1830 as they ignited Rochester. Like other rapidly growing towns and cities along the Erie Canal, Rochester was ripe for revival. Many people worried that the people of the young city barely knew one another, that husbands and wives, workers and employers, rich and poor were drifting apart. Politics appeared a morass of selfishness; alcohol seemed to drown hopes of social progress and family happiness; men seemed more concerned with their businesses, lodges, and politics than with their souls. When Finney came to town in 1830, accordingly, he was met by a populace hungry for something to stir them up, hungry for a new message.

Women's prayer groups met daily and traveled from home to home in efforts to bring the word of Jesus. Women pleaded with their husbands to listen to the Reverend Finney. Employers made it clear to the men who worked under them that it would be noticed whether or not they attended the revival. These efforts, combined with Finney's masterful sermons and hopeful message, transformed Rochester, bringing hundreds of people into the church who had not come before and reclaiming many who had strayed. All the Protestant denominations worked together, setting aside for a while their differences on baptism and other doctrines.

Such a powerful revival seemed evidence to many people that America could be changed by faith. As they watched saloons shut down, families brought together, and shops and stores closed while the revival was in progress, it appeared that the way was being prepared for God's kingdom on earth. If the United States could be adequately reformed, these people believed, the day of redemption could be hastened. The American Tract Society, eager to improve the nation's moral state, had delivered roughly 5 million gospel tracts by 1828, one for every three people in the United States and the equivalent to 90 million pamphlets today. It was up to Americans themselves to purge their country of sin, to make themselves better, and then to help others see the way as well. Such faith bred a demand for immediate reforms. When the means of change lay so close at hand, only a prayer away, delay seemed a rejection of God's love.

Joseph Smith was the founder of the Church of Jesus Christ of the Latter-Day Saints, also known as the Mormons.
© Bettmann/Corbis

The Birth of Mormonism

Like many American families of these years, that of Joseph Smith could not find a secure place. His father dreamed of bringing his family out of poverty, moving them from one community to another. Young Joseph, like hundreds of other people in upstate New York, looked for treasure rumored to have been buried long ago in the mountains; he watched with concern for his soul, too, as revivals came and went without his conversion. Smith reported that he felt the presence of an angel, however, who told him "that God had work for me to do, and that my name should be for good and evil among all nations, kindreds, and tongues. He said

there was a book deposited, written upon gold plates, giving an account of the former inhabitants of this continent, and the source from which they sprang. He also said that, the fullness of the everlasting Gospel was contained in it." Smith claimed that the angel directed him to the location of the sacred writings.

Smith began to transcribe what he had found; sitting in a tent divided by a partition, he read the plates to an assistant on the other side. *The Book of Mormon* took shape, telling of a struggle between the chosen ones and their persecutors, of a promised land reserved for the righteous. North America, the book said, had been visited by Jesus in the distant past but the people had lost their way and fallen into disputation. Those people had been cursed by God for their sins and marked with dark skins; their descendants were the American Indians, who had forgotten their lost paradise.

After 1830 Joseph Smith and several followers traveled throughout New York selling copies of what they called the "Gold Bible." They were met with hostility virtually everywhere they went, but they slowly gathered converts to their Church of Jesus Christ of the Latter-Day Saints. Many of the new members were poor, including some free blacks, but others had considerable resources. The most important converts were two brothers, Brigham and Joseph Young. As the movement gathered momentum, hundreds of people joined the church; entire congregations of churches of other faiths joined the Mormons and gladly contributed everything they owned to the church's common fund. The faithful moved first to Ohio and then to what Smith believed to be the original Eden: Missouri. But other settlers made no secret of their disapproval of the Mormons, firing shots, throwing stones through windows, and burning the crops of the Latter-Day Saints. One opponent depicted Mormonism as "the only form of religion in this country which refuses to conform either to the spirit of progress and improvement . . . which characterizes the age in which we live." The Mormons found no peace for the next decade. They were constantly harassed by non-Mormons who feared the growing number of converts and the local economic power that came from the church members' pooled resources and hard work.

CHARACTER DEVELOPMENT

For generations before the 1820s, Americans had relied on authority and reputation to keep their families and communities stable. Young men and women remained in their parents' households well into their twenties, subordinate to the demands and expectations of their fathers. Workingmen served for years as apprentices and journeymen to master artisans, slowly learning the craft and gradually working toward independence. Men and women carefully cultivated their reputations, projecting a polished image of themselves. Churches aided stability, encouraging deference to the authority of God and institution.

The early nineteenth century saw a new emphasis in American life, a new focus on what people called "character." In a society so mobile, so disconnected from traditional sources of stability and identity, people felt the need for new ways of ensuring appropriate behavior. Americans looked to new kinds of institutions suited for a new age, institutions that could better deal with strangers, new people, those cut off from older forms of social stability. Americans turned first to families, imparting to them primary responsibility for creating virtuous children and husbands.

Women at Home and Beyond

Women had long been recognized as the foundation of a good family. Women directly produced a large portion of the food farm families consumed, while town-dwelling families depended on women for running the household—especially hard work in the days before indoor plumbing and electricity. During the era of the Revolution and early republic, women had been encouraged to raise virtuous children befitting a nation of free people. Churches had long depended on women as the source of spiritual energy and admirable role models.

Women became central in yet another way. As Americans looked about them, they became concerned that little seemed to be holding their society together. People moved far beyond the reach of government and beyond the eyes of their parents. Men and women married at younger ages and left home far earlier than their parents had. The opening of land in the West undermined one of the principal forms of control exercised by fathers in earlier generations: the promise of passing on the family farm to sons who stayed at home. Now, sons could acquire land in the West with or without the support of their parents. Daughters might marry earlier and begin families of their own. The American population skyrocketed as so many young families established themselves.

The new economy, too, caused concern for many. Increasingly, men and women seemed pulled in different directions, away from a sole focus on the family farm or family artisan shop. Men found new opportunities in town, in businesses that kept offices or shops in a central area. Young men often worked for wages for a number of employers rather than serving for many years with one master. Middle-class women, too, saw their lives change, especially in towns and cities. Bakeries, butcher shops, clothiers, and candlemakers began to offer, more easily and cheaply, some of the things that women had long labored to produce at home. Schools and academies became more common, providing a place for children to receive education beyond the bounds of the home. Young women from poorer backgrounds came into cities looking for jobs as maids and laundresses, taking away some of the household burden for women well off enough to hire them. Families in towns and cities had fewer children

Depictions such as this portrait of Catherine Wheeler Hardy and her daughter celebrated the quiet domestic space enjoyed by children and presided over by the mother.
Jermiah Pearson Hardy, "Catherine Wheeler Hardy and her Daughter Anna Eliza Hardy" 1842. Museum of Fine Arts, Boston, M. and M. Kavolik collection

with each passing decade. Women's lives remained hard, as each birth threatened serious illness or death, but those lives began to change in important ways.

As ministers, journalists, and other opinion makers looked upon the changing nature of the households of the Northeast, they began to articulate an ideal of what has been called "domesticity." Families should seize the opportunities provided by the new situations, they said, and help lessen some of the costs created by the new order. Women could put their minds to higher purposes, focusing more on nurturing their children in spirit and mind as well as in body. Women would become the moral center of the household, the guardians of good thoughts, clean living, and a sense of safety for children and husbands. While the world beyond the household seemed increasingly threatening and disorienting, women could make the home a place of refuge and renewal.

Many middle-class women welcomed this message and this mission. It fit well with their own experiences and their own aspirations. In a time when public life made almost no provisions for female participation and when women found virtually no well-paying jobs open to them, the elevation of the home promised an elevation of women's role. Men believed what they said: they thought women naturally

better than themselves, more moral and feeling, more intuitive and spiritual. Men worried about the coarseness and callousness of the tumultuous marketplace even as they enjoyed the sense of freedom, excitement, and possibility it offered. Middle-class fathers wanted their children shielded from the hard world as long as possible, if only so they would be better able to handle the world when they emerged after their nurture at home.

Domesticity asked something of men as well. If the home were to be a haven, the center of society, men would have to make a greater investment in those homes than had their fathers. Men needed to acknowledge the feelings of their wives more, speaking in tones of respect and affection, respecting their wishes about sex and children. Fathers were expected to spend more time with their children, providing a firm male model to accompany the softer nurture of their wives. Drinking and cursing had no place at home.

Such models of domesticity did not emerge overnight, of course. The 1820s saw only the beginnings of a crusade to make all American homes fit this model. The effort began in towns and cities, making only gradual inroads into the raw and growing countryside. It was stronger in the Northeast than in the South and in the West. Working-class families could not afford this idealized model even if they wanted to follow its example. Women who had to work for others all day had little time to devote to their own families. Women who worked in their own homes mingled the market and the household in a way the creators of the domestic ideal deplored. Men who could not be certain of their next day's wages could not afford to keep children out of the workforce into their late teens. Slave families struggled to stay together in any way they could and could only imagine what it might be like to live in the homes held up as ideal in these years. Nevertheless, that ideal was celebrated and elaborated with each passing year, growing along with the booming towns and cities of the North.

An Eruption of Reform Movements

The same Americans who promoted the Christian, middle-class home as their ideal looked to other institutions and reforms in the 1820s to help remake American society. They sought to extend the ideals of character, self-control, and education to those who seemed to fall beyond the good effects of family and household. They worried about hungry children, desperate fathers, and distraught mothers. They noticed increasing numbers of women selling themselves on the city streets. They decried bulging jails and streets full of people without homes. They worried over the many young men and women who seemed adrift in this rootless new society. Reformers tapped the domestic impulses of improvement for the society as a whole.

Groups of reform-minded people mobilized themselves in the Northeast to counter these problems. Some of their efforts grew out of the churches, while others grew out of the ideals of the American Revolution and the marketplace. The American Bible Society intended to ensure the moral tone of American life and counteract what its founders feared was a dangerous trend towards irreligion and political licentiousness. The society launched an ambitious drive to put Bibles in every American home, pioneering steam presses and national systems of distribution, and ultimately issuing over 32 million Bibles. Individual denominations and publishers produced a range of Bibles to reach audiences of varying wealth and sophistication. The churches launched an ambitious drive to put Bibles in every American home, distributing a million Bibles each year.

The American Sunday School Union wrote and published materials for children to be used in Sunday schools across the country. Those schools, while based in churches, taught reading and writing as well as religion. They put the churches at the center of community life, giving children beyond the reach of traditional schooling a chance to learn some of the skills and attitudes necessary for spiritual and economic success. The American Tract Society produced millions of short inspirational pamphlets to reach those who might not set foot in a church or pick up a Bible. The new organizations prided themselves on being national in reach, extending to the Northwest and Southwest, knitting Americans together with a common faith. They preached nothing controversial, claiming only to spread the good news of the Protestant Christian faith. They depended on the hard work of women, who filled the membership rolls and helped raise funds.

Reformers created a new kind of institution—the "penitentiary"—in these years for those apparently most in need of reform: criminals. In a penitentiary, unlike a common jail, criminals would be locked in individual cells, free from the contamination of others, alone with their conscience and the Bible. There, reflecting on their crimes, they would become "penitent" and would emerge as better people. They would undergo some of the moral nurture they had obviously missed as children and would be ready to take their place in the economy of wages, self-discipline, and delayed gratification growing in the United States.

Penal reformers placed great faith in silence, order, and work, helping put the United States in the forefront of the growing penitentiary movement.
David A. Schorsch Co.

The most prominent penitentiaries were built in New York and Pennsylvania in the 1820s. Reformers argued over whether prisoners should be isolated at all times, the Philadelphia model, or whether they might be allowed to work together in silence, as they did at Auburn in New York. In either case, Americans were proud of their penitentiaries, among the first in the world, holding them up as examples of what the enlightened new nation could do. Almost every state in the nation, South as well as North, soon built its own penitentiary. Foreign observers such as Alexis de Tocqueville of France traveled to the United States to assess this innovation.

Alongside penitentiaries, asylums for the deaf and blind, for the insane, for orphans, and for the poor began to appear in the 1820s, replacing more informal kinds of care. Dorothea Dix became famous throughout the United States for her often lonely crusade on behalf of people otherwise forgotten. Dix lobbied ceaselessly for the construction of cleaner, healthier, and more hopeful kinds of institutions for those who could not care for themselves. Each institution placed its faith in strict order, in moral teaching, and in faith in the inherent good of human nature.

Abolitionism

While the great majority of white northerners thought Christians should seek holiness mainly in their own hearts, others were equally certain that society itself could and should be changed. To many, slavery seemed the place to start.

William Lloyd Garrison played a central role in the emergence of the new antislavery movement, bringing the attention of whites to what had been largely a crusade by African Americans. At the age of twenty-two, Garrison became the editor of the first newspaper dedicated to the prohibition of alcohol. Believing in the necessity of ending slavery as well as drunkenness, Garrison joined the colonization movement and soon became editor of its paper as well.

In the late 1820s Garrison attended the anticolonizationist meetings held by African Americans in eastern cities, including the group that published the first antislavery newspaper, *Freedom's Journal.* He experienced a mounting desire for a more aggressive antislavery crusade as he saw the limitations of the colonization movement and as he witnessed the passion of people such as David Walker. The balding and bespectacled young Garrison sought out other financial supporters and a partner to launch a paper of his own: *The Liberator.* It called for the immediate start toward emancipation, explicitly rejecting colonization. In 1831, the paper's first year, it had only six subscribers, but it acquired fifty-three by the following year, most of them African American. "I *will* be as harsh as truth," Garrison announced, "and as uncompromising as justice. On this subject, I do not wish to think, speak, or write, with moderation. . . . I am earnest—I will not equivocate—I will not excuse—I will not retreat a single inch—AND I WILL BE HEARD." He was.

Two hundred antislavery societies emerged in the early thirties. Ground that had been prepared by the evangelical crusades of the preceding few years proved fertile for the antislavery cause. Some northern church members argued that it was the duty of good Christians to cast out slaveholders and to work for immediate emancipation, to use the enormous power of the church as a force for freedom. These "immediatists" called for slaveholders to recognize the truth of what the abolitionists were saying, to free their slaves immediately, hire them as free workers, and help repay the former slaves for their years of unpaid toil. These early abolitionists hoped to convert the slaveholders by persuasion and prayer, by church and newspaper—not by law and force.

The American Anti-slavery Society formed in Philadelphia in 1833. Looking to the example of Great Britain, where the major denominations supported the antislavery movement that was at that moment triumphing over slavery in the British West Indies, the members of the society expected American church leaders to take the lead against American slavery. The North would have to be converted be-

William Lloyd Garrison played a key role in persuading many northern whites that slavery was morally wrong and should be brought to an immediate end.
The Granger Collection, New York

fore it could expect the South to follow. To convert the North, antislavery organizations held out the prospect of a free South, where 2 million freed slaves would constitute an "immense market" for the products of Northern "mechanics and manufacturers." These abolitionists expected the former slaves to remain in the South; they spoke little of the competition the freedpeople might provide to the workers of the North. Similarly, the antislavery people believed a free South would prosper, with planters and free whites flourishing as they had never flourished before; the South, they claimed, would "exhibit the flush of returning health, and feel a stronger pulse, and draw a freer breath."

The antislavery organizations proved volatile inside as well as out. Far more than any other organizations in the United States at this time, the antislavery cause brought together male and female, black and white, patrician and working class, Quaker and Unitarian, Baptist and Methodist, radical and moderate, political and anti-political people. Each of these groups had its own vision of how the abolitionists should spend their energies and influence. Black abolitionists, in particular, wanted the organizations to do more to help black communities in the North. Black women such as Maria W. Stewart published pamphlets that cried out that it "is of no use for us to wait any longer for a generation of well educated men to arise. We have slumbered and slept too long already; the day is far spent; the night of death approaches . . . Let every colored man throughout the United States, who possesses the spirit and principles of a man, sign a petition to Congress, to abolish slavery in the District of Columbia, and grant you the rights and privileges of common free citizens." Rejecting calls for removal of freedpeople to Africa, Stewart denied that "we can never rise to respectability in this country. They would drive us to a strange land. But before I go, the bayonet shall pierce me through."

The antislavery societies used pamphlets, leaflets, and other literature as their major weapons. Rapid innovations in printing lowered the cost of producing such materials, which flooded post offices and streets. The postal campaign reached its peak in 1834 and 1835, when a million pieces went out through the mail, much of it to the South, where the abolitionists hoped to appeal directly to ministers and others who might be willing to listen to their pleas. That literature, white southerners furiously protested, virtually invited slaves to follow Nat Turner's example. Georgia slaveholders offered a $12,000 reward for the capture of wealthy merchant Arthur Tappan, who, along with his brother Lewis, funded much of the postal campaign against slavery. Arthur received a slave's severed ear in the mail. Mobs in Charleston seized sacks of mail from northern cities and burned them in the streets.

The pamphlets infuriated people in much of the North as well. Mobs, led by some of the wealthiest merchants of northern towns but constituted in large part by white working people, rose up violently against the abolitionists. In 1835 mobs destroyed the home of African Americans, pelted antislavery speakers, and dragged William Lloyd Garrison himself through the streets of Boston at the end of a rope. The leaders of that mob announced that they had assaulted Garrison "to assure our brethren of the South that we cherish rational and correct notions on the subject of slavery." Many white Northerners believed the abolitionists to be hypocrites who cared nothing for America and everything for their own sanctimonious souls. Antislavery speakers risked a mob every time they spoke; one man counted over 150 attacks made on him. Abolitionists' churches were blown up and their school buildings dragged into swamps.

The persecution, ironically, strengthened the abolitionist cause. Denunciation and harassment only made the abolitionists more certain of the need for their efforts, of the moral decay caused by slav-

ery. The 200 antislavery societies of 1835 grew to over 500 in 1836. The reformers flooded Congress with petitions calling for the end of slavery in the District of Columbia, sending over 300 petitions signed by 40,000 people. The acceptance of these petitions by the House, southerners argued, besmirched slaveholders' honor and threatened to incite slaves to rebellion. The petitions should be rejected out of hand. Congress sought to avoid conflict by merely tabling the petitions, but the compromise pleased no one.

Over the next decade, Northerners of even a mild antislavery bent chafed at this "gag rule," which they saw as a clear violation of American freedom in the interests of slavery. Former President John Quincy Adams fought back in 1837 by attempting to present a petition from 22 slaves. Representatives from Georgia and Alabama demanded that Adams be expelled and the petition "taken from the House and burnt or the southern states would withdraw from the House." In their fury to squelch any petitions to Congress on the subject of slavery, southern representatives failed to notice that the petition from the slaves did not advocate abolition. Angered and embarrassed at Adam's trickery, one Mississippian decried this "outrage that has no parallel in parliamentary history" and condemned Adams as one who "rejoiced in the alarm and excitement he occasions like the midnight incendiary who fires the dwelling of his enemy, and listens with pleasure to the screams of his burning victims."

CONCLUSION

The years of Andrew Jackson changed America in profound ways. No longer would politics be a matter of remote personalities in Washington, for now a two-party system mobilized and articulated voters' desires. No longer would slavery be a matter beyond debate, for the nullification crisis, Walker's *Appeal,* Turner's revolt, and the emergence of an abolitionist movement made slavery a concrete and burning issue. After bitter debate and resistance, the power of the American Indians of the eastern United States had been broken and their people removed from homes they had occupied beyond memory. The aggressive young churches of the Second Great Awakening ensured that the Protestant faith became a matter of public action and testimony. The culture of the United States had become sharply divided over matters both public and private, as full of conflict as it was of possibility.

Recommended Readings

Bay, Mia. *The White Image in the Black Mind: African-American Ideas about White People, 1830–1925* (2000). Provides an extremely helpful perspective.

Feller, Daniel. *The Jacksonian Promise: America, 1815–1840* (1995). Offers an upbeat overview.

Freehling, Allison Goodyear. *Drift Toward Dissolution: The Virginia Slavery Debate of 1831–1832* (1982). Presents an interpretation of the crisis in Virginia.

Freehling, William. *Prelude to Civil War: The Nullification Crisis in South Carolina, 1816–1836* (1966). The standard account of the subject.

Johnson, Paul. *A Shopkeeper's Millennium: Society and Revivals in Rochester, New York, 1815–1837* (1978). Tells the story of revivals in an exciting way.

Hinks, Peter B. *To Awaken My Afflicted Brethren: David Walker and the Problem of Antebellum Slave Resistance* (1997). Reveals the crucial role black Americans played in the creation of the abolitionist movement.

Laurie, Bruce. *Artisans into Workers: Labor in Nineteenth-Century America* (1989). An excellent synthesis of this complicated history.

Mayer, Henry. *All on Fire: William Lloyd Garrison and the Abolition of Slavery* (1998). A comprehensive and fascinating biography.

Roberts, Randy, and Olson, James S. *A Line in the Sand: The Alamo in Blood and Memory* (2001). Relates a sophisticated understanding of this challenging topic.

Roediger, David R. *The Wages of Whiteness: Race and the Making of the American Working Class* (1991). Boldly interprets the uses the white working class made of the notion of "race."

Walters, Ronald. *American Reformers, 1815–1860* (1996). A fine analytical synthesis.

Watson, Harry L. *Liberty and Power: The Politics of Jacksonian America* (1990). A helpful and balanced interpretation of a subject that has been much debated by scholars.

Weber, David J. *The Mexican Frontier, 1821–1846: The American Southwest under Mexico* (1982). Tells the complex history of this region before war brought it into the United States.

American Journey Online and InfoTrac College Edition

Visit the source collections at http://ajaccess.wadsworth.com and infotrac.thomsonlearning.com and use the Search function with the following key terms to explore documents, images, audio and video clips, articles, and commentary related to the material in this chapter.

Andrew Jackson	*The Book of Mormon*
Free Blacks	Nat Turner
Abolitionism	Indian Removal Act
Texas Republic	Battle of the Alamo

Additional resources, exercises, and Internet links related to this chapter are available on the American Passages Web site: http://history.wadsworth.com/passages2e

11 PANIC AND BOOM
1837–1845

ECONOMIC CRISIS AND INNOVATION

LIFE IN THE NEW SLAVE SOUTH

REFORM TAKES ROOT

DEVELOPMENT OF AN AMERICAN CULTURE

THE TRANSFORMATION OF AMERICAN POLITICS

THE CHALLENGE OF THE WEST

The irony of a Fourth of July celebration during hard times fills this cartoon, in which symbols of poverty and decay pile on one another.
Museum of the City of New York

I n 1837 the largest financial panic and depression the nation had ever experienced descended on the United States. The hard times shaped reform, literature, politics, slavery, and foreign policy.

It was not surprising that economic troubles stimulated political conflict, but the reform spirit also flowered during these hard years. Men and women energetically championed public education, abstinence from alcohol, antislavery, and a host of other improvements to American life. The popular press burgeoned, along with art, photography, and literature. A few leading thinkers articulated a bold and distinctive American philosophy, one that bore the marks of its tumultuous time.

The hard times in the East drove westward expansion. These were the years in which the mass migration to the Pacific began, as pioneers began to push across the West to Oregon and California. Politics churned as the nation worried over the consequences of its rapid territorial growth.

ECONOMIC CRISIS AND INNOVATION

The late 1830s and early 1840s produced a surprising mixture of bad and good economic news. The economy fell into prolonged depression, but at the same time the creative energies of the American economy flourished. Courts and legislatures fostered an environment favorable to business, while inventors and investors plunged ahead despite the failures they saw all around them. In fact, the most important economic development of the entire century—the railroad—emerged from these years of turmoil.

Panic and Depression

Andrew Jackson sought to leave a comfortable legacy to his handpicked successor, Martin Van Buren, but even the inauguration ceremony in March 1837 accentuated the great disparities between the two men. Whereas Jackson's gaunt figure symbolized his sacrifices on the frontier and battlefield, Van Buren seemed the plump embodiment of a life spent in political office. Whereas Van Buren's inaugural speech inspired little enthusiasm in the crowd of 20,000, the mere sight of ex-President Jackson roused great cheers. Though Van Buren had been a principal architect of the so-called spoils system, he replaced few officeholders on the lower levels of government and made few changes in Jackson's cabinet. The new president seemed content to carry on Jackson's work.

CHRONOLOGY

1837 Financial panic • *Charles River Bridge v. Warren Bridge* decision • Grimké sisters lecture to mixed audiences • Elijah P. Lovejoy murdered in Alton, Illinois • Horace Mann becomes first secretary of Massachusetts State Board of Education • Ralph Waldo Emerson, "The American Scholar"

1838 John Quincy Adams successfully defeats attempt to annex Texas

1839 Depression worsens • Daguerreotypes introduced to the United States

1840 Congress passes Independent Treasury Act • Harrison elected president • Frederick Douglass escapes from slavery • American Anti-slavery Society splits • Washingtonian temperance movement emerges • James G. Birney runs for president as candidate for Liberty party

1841 Harrison dies; John Tyler becomes president • Brook Farm founded • California sees arrival of first wagon train • Oregon fever • P. T. Barnum opens the American Museum • *Amistad* case heard before the Supreme Court

1842 Edgar Allan Poe, "The Murders in the Rue Morgue"

1843 Oregon sees arrival of first wagon trains

1844 Methodist Episcopal church divides over slavery • James K. Polk claims the United States's claim to "all Oregon" • Baltimore-Washington telegraph line • Samuel F. B. Morse patents the telegraph • Edgar Allan Poe, "The Raven"

1845 Texas and Florida admitted to the Union • Baptist church divides over slavery

Alexis de Tocqueville,
Democracy in America, 1840

A young French nobleman, Tocqueville came to the United States to observe democracy in action. In the great book from which this selection is drawn, the sympathetic Tocqueville notes a central paradox of American life; all except slaves are free in virtually every facet of their lives and yet that freedom does not seem to bring happiness. Instead, it generates constant anxiety and a ceaseless yearning, as few seem able to grasp all that they can see.

. . . In America I saw the freest and most enlightened men, placed in the happiest circumstances which the world affords; it seemed to me as if a cloud habitually hung upon their brow, and I thought them serious and almost sad even in their pleasures.

. . . A native of the United States clings to this world's goods as if he were certain never to die; and he is so hasty in grasping at all within his reach, that one would suppose he was constantly afraid of not living long enough to enjoy them. He clutches everything, he holds nothing fast, but soon loosens his grasp to pursue fresh gratifications. In the United States a man builds a house to spend his latter years in it, and he sells it before the roof is on; he plants a garden, and lets [rents] it just as the trees are coming into bearing; he brings a field into tillage, and leaves other men to gather the crops; he embraces a profession, and gives it up; he settles in a place, which he soon afterward leaves, to carry his changeable longings elsewhere. If his private affairs leave him any leisure, he instantly plunges into the vortex of politics; and if at the end of a year of unremitting labor he finds he has a few days' vacation, his eager curiosity whirls him over the vast extent of the United States, and he will travel fifteen hundred miles in a few days, to shake off his happiness. Death at length overtakes him, but it is before he is weary of his bootless chase of that complete felicity which is for ever on the wing.

Among democratic nations men easily attain a certain equality of conditions; they can never attain the equality they desire. It perpetually retires from before them, yet without hiding itself from their sight, and in retiring draws them on. At every moment they think they are about to grasp it; it escapes at every moment from their hold. They are near enough to see its charms, but too far off to enjoy them; and before they have fully tasted its delights, they die. . . .

Source: Alexis de Tocqueville, *Democracy in America*, Vol. II (Boston: C. C. Little & J. Brown, 1841), Second Book, Ch. 13.

Within weeks of Van Buren's inauguration the American economy hit stormy waters. An unprecedented amount of silver poured into American banks in the mid-1830s, from abroad had fueling intense investment. Britain's economy expanded rapidly, increasing the demand for cotton, encouraging southern planters to buy land and slaves on credit, and boosting available credit for investment in American projects such as canals and turnpikes. British investors bought up state bonds and securities, while British exporters offered generous credit for purchase of a wide array of manufactured goods. American merchants, land speculators and state governments indulged in a feast of easy credit and seemingly endless profits.

Unfortunately, poor harvests in Britain disrupted the American economy when British firms demanded repayment of loans just at the time that prices for American cotton declined because of record production and reduced English demand. As a result, a major New Orleans cotton broker failed when it could not make its payments to British banks or pay debts in excess of a million dollars owed to J. & L., Joseph & Co., one of the nation's largest exchange brokers located in New York City. The collapse of Joseph's triggered panic. As a city official noted "everybody will fail—all Hell will fail." Desperate merchants and creditors tried to extract cash from debtors, credit evaporated, and thousands lost their jobs. Lots in Manhattan that had sold for $480 in September 1836 fell to $50 in seven months.

Despite the role of international trade in bringing on the crisis, many people blamed the problems on Jackson's banking policy, especially the practice of accepting only specie, not paper money, for the purchase of public lands. They looked to Van Buren to lead the repeal of this strategy, but Jackson made it clear to Van Buren that he did not want to see his work undone. Delegations of merchants came to the White House to plead with Van Buren, but to no avail. A "run" began on the banks; customers withdrew a million dollars in specie in only two days in early May. The panic of 1837 had begun. Soon it spread to every city and region of the country.

The panic quickly affected working people as well as the rich. Jobs dried up and many urban families had no idea of where they would get their next meal. In New York City, a poster warned that "Bread, Meat, Rent, Fuel—Their Prices Must Come Down. The Voice of the People Shall be Heard, and Will Prevail." Thousands of people gathered for a public meeting in the freezing weather. Told that a nearby warehouse held 50,000 barrels of flour, the protesters stormed the building; they took what they could and broke open hundreds of barrels. The riots continued for days until the police managed to regain order.

The panic of 1837 was followed by a better year in 1838, then by another panic in 1839. In the wake of that second panic, the stagnation of the economy spread more deeply and more widely, not ending until 1843. Labor unions weakened as workers grew afraid to risk their jobs. States' plans to finance canals, roads, and other public projects crashed. Nine states defaulted on the bonds with which they intended to finance those improvements, leading furious European investors to shun American investments. Governors and legislators found themselves under attack from voters angry that the states had permitted themselves to go so far into debt. Visions of a "glorious future" had vanished from the public imagination, a Chicago lawyer lamented.

Van Buren admitted that allowing state banks to hold federal funds had apparently fueled the speculation, but he would not even consider reinstating a national bank. Instead, he proposed what came to be known as the Sub-Treasury Plan or the Independent Treasury Plan. In that system, public funds would be disbursed by the secretary of the treasury as the economy seemed to dictate and banks would be kept out of the picture. It would be two more years before the plan passed, but by then it could do neither the country nor Martin Van Buren much good. The Whigs quickly won state-level offices and looked forward to harvesting more.

The Charles River Bridge Case

Even as the panic unfolded, some of the questions raised by the economic changes of the early 1830s worked their way through the American court system. American law still embodied many assumptions from the centuries before corporations and far-flung economic enterprises challenged local power.

The Charles River Bridge of Boston, for example, had been granted a franchise by the state legislature in 1785. The owners of the bridge charged a toll for everyone who crossed. As the population of Boston and Charlestown grew rapidly, so did the traffic and the tolls on the bridge. The bridge, which cost about $70,000 to build and improve, was bringing in $30,000 a year by the late 1820s. Another bridge also chartered by the state, the Warren Bridge, went up across the Charles, only 260 feet away. No sooner was the new bridge built than the traffic on the older bridge declined by more than half. The managers of the Charles River Bridge sued in court, claiming that their original charter implied a monopoly that the state had violated by building a competing bridge. Throughout the 1830s, the case proceeded to the U.S. Supreme Court and was heard in 1837.

The Chief Justice of the Supreme Court, Roger B. Taney, shared the Jacksonian animosity against monopolies. His decision in the *Charles River Bridge* case held that a state charter did not imply monopoly. Should old charters be permitted to hinder modern improvements, the country "would be obliged to stand still." The charters had perhaps been necessary in the past, he admitted, but by the 1830s such props no longer seemed necessary to attract capital investment. Taney's decision in the *Charles River Bridge* Case reflected a growing consensus among Democrats and Whigs that older forms of economic privilege had to make way for innovation and investment. It would take decades, and many political struggles, for the law to adapt to the new forms of American economic enterprise, but the process had begun.

This locomotive in New York State, like its other early counterparts, pulled passenger cars based on old-fashioned carriages. The technology evolved quickly in the 1840s, however, and the United States played an important role in that evolution.
Collection of the Albany Institute of History & Art. Photograph by Joseph Levy

Railroads

By the 1830s, Americans had devised several means for dealing with the vast spaces of their continent. Thousands of miles of canals cut across the East, while steamboats plied the waters of the North and South. Such means of transport, while cheap and dependable, remained relatively slow and limited in their reach. Inland cities longed for fast overland connections with the outside world, and they knew of experiments with railroads in England and the United States over the last decade. When New Jersey sponsored a bold rail and canal connection between New York and Philadelphia in 1831, it ordered a custom-built locomotive from an English company—the *John Bull*. The railroad became an immediate success, carrying over 100,000 passengers in 1834. That same year, Ralph Waldo Emerson noted in his journal the "uncomputed mechanical advantages" that "rides on the rail-road." He marveled that "men & trees & barns whiz by you as fast as the leaves of a dictionary."

American companies emulated and improved upon the English designs. By 1841, ten American railroad shops had sprung into existence. Those shops soon began changing the English designs, making the engines more powerful and the rails cheaper. Railroad companies quickly grew into some of the largest and most complex American businesses. Employing hundreds of people, they pioneered management and engineering innovations. In this era of panics and credit scarcity, how did rail companies finance the enormous expense of men, machinery, and maintenance?

Major manufacturers such as Matthew Baldwin expanded their locomotive works by attracting wealthy investors to join the firms as partners, whereas smaller, more specialized manufacturers plowed all profits back into new equipment. Governments—state, local and federal—also provided financial assistance. As an example, the state of Pennsylvania chartered 2,333 corporations by legislation between 1790 and 1860 and two-thirds of these entities were transportation companies.

Railroads almost immediately became the key form of transportation in the United States. Rail transport grew cheaper as the network expanded and trains could run when canals had frozen over. By 1840, American companies and states had spent $75 million dollars to build 3,300 miles of track, surpassing Great Britain; by 1850, the country claimed nearly 9,000 miles of railroad. New industries rose to serve the trains as iron, coal, and steel burgeoned with the railroads' demand. The railroads consumed prodigious amounts of wood for their ties, trestles, and boilers. Workers building and running the railroads operated in large gangs and frequently suffered from disease. Recruiters for companies in Illinois wrote of desertions when rumors of cholera appeared and the men would "scatter like frightened sheep." Accidents and misbehavior were common: "North bound freight ran into a drove of cattle, went down an embankment . . . nine cars with it," read one account. "Two engines delayed 24 hours, while engineers and firemen went off on a drunken spree."

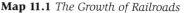

Map 11.1 *The Growth of Railroads*
A vastly expanded transportation network tied the United States together. The system exaggerated sectional differences by unifying the Northeast with the Northwest, creating the reality and perception of a "North" with interests different from those of a "South" stretching from the Atlantic to the Mississippi and beyond.

Despite such challenges, railroads gave farmers quick and certain access to markets, and towns prospered or died depending on their rail connection. Local artisans often found themselves undercut by cheaper finished goods from city merchants, while eastern farmers soon faced competition from the produce of rich Midwestern soils.

Railroads appeared in every region of the United States but not in a uniform network. Beginning from many different entrepreneurial efforts and adapting to widely varying terrain, railroads did not adapt a standard distance between the rails, or guage. As a result, trains could not travel from North to South; cargo had to be unloaded and reloaded. The South's trains focused on connecting coastal cities with inland planta-

tions and farms, while in the North and West railroads ran from city to city, knitting together a network of economic development that benefitted a wider area. In this way, railroads accelerated the growth of differences between the South and the rest of the country.

Telegraph poles marched alongside the railroads, preventing gruesome crashes on single-track lines and speeding the flow of information just as the railroads sped the flow of people and goods. Like the locomotive, the telegraph was the product of inventors in several different countries but received a major impetus from America. Samuel F. B. Morse patented his version of the electronic telegraph in 1840. Morse struggled with the invention for more than ten years, devising the code of dots and dashes that bears his name as well as devising ways to make the current travel farther. In 1842, he received half of a $60,000 research grant from Congress to run an experimental line from Washington to Baltimore. (The other portion of the grant provided $30,000 dollars to study animal magnetism or mesmerism, one of the great fads of the early decades of the century). Observers of the first public tests in 1844 were astonished by the telegraph: "Strange and wonderful discovery, which has made the 'swift-winged lighting' man's messenger, annihilated all space, and tied the two ends of a continent in a knot." Following its success, the telegraph spread across the country with great speed. In the four years after its initial test, more than 5,000 miles of wire had been strung with another 3,000 under construction.

LIFE IN THE NEW SLAVE SOUTH

The South, though increasingly dominated by slavery, remained an integral part of the United States. Southern cotton drove national economic growth and southern politicians controlled much of the nation's government. The South was a prosperous place for white people, whose average per capita incomes, while lower than those of northern whites, exceeded those of almost every other society in the world and were catching up to those in the North.

Thanks to the rapid expansion of newspapers and the telegraph, white southerners took part in all the national conversations about race, slavery, and politics. The growing connections between the regions, in fact, emphasized the differences between the North and the South. As people in each region read the hard words those across the Mason-Dixon line frequently said about them, their distrust of one another grew.

*P*ICTURING THE PAST ◆ ECONOMICS & TECHNOLOGY

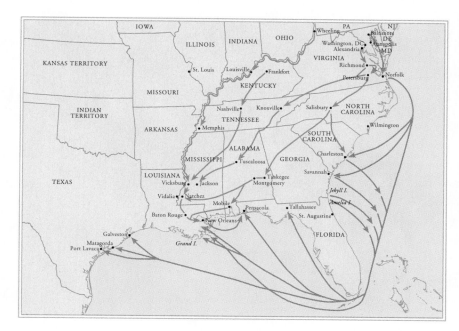

Map 11.2 *Paths of the Slave Trade*

The slave trade grew into a vast business in the years before the Civil War. Many people, including those who did not own slaves themselves, made their livings from supplying slavetraders with food, shelter, transportation, insurance, and banking. As this map shows, the trade ran strongly from the Upper South to the Lower South, from east to west. Although slavery remained firmly entrenched in states such as Virginia, Kentucky, and North Carolina, the demand for slave labor was so strong in the new plantation districts of Alabama, Mississippi, and Louisiana that slaveholders sold off "surplus" slaves to the traders who came through their counties each year. Traders gathered slaves in the cities of the Chesapeake, especially Alexandria, Virginia, to ship them around the Florida Keys to ports on the Gulf Coast, especially New Orleans. Meanwhile, other slaves were sold "down the river" from places close to the border with the North to the plantations surrounding Vicksburg, Natchez, and Baton Rouge. Other slaves were forced to walk or to take trains across the middle of the South. All along, even more slaves were bought and sold within states, being moved from one county to another in ways that do not appear on this disheartening map.

And as increasing numbers of people such as Frederick Douglass escaped to the North, northerners became ever more aware of their region's complicity in perpetuating slavery. The single profound difference between the North and South, slavery, became ever more significant as it grew ever stronger.

African Americans and the South

By the 1830s, slavery had spread over an enormous area stretching from Maryland to Texas. The decade had seen the domestic slave trade grow at a feverish rate, for the new planters of Mississippi, Alabama, and Louisiana eagerly imported slaves to clear land and plant cotton. By the time of the panic of 1837, Alabama, Mississippi, and Louisiana grew more than half the nation's cotton. American slavery became ever more diverse as it expanded. Enslaved people worked in hemp, wheat, rice, corn, sugar, and tobacco fields as well as cotton fields. They worked with livestock and racehorses, practiced trades such as carpentry and blacksmithing, and labored on the

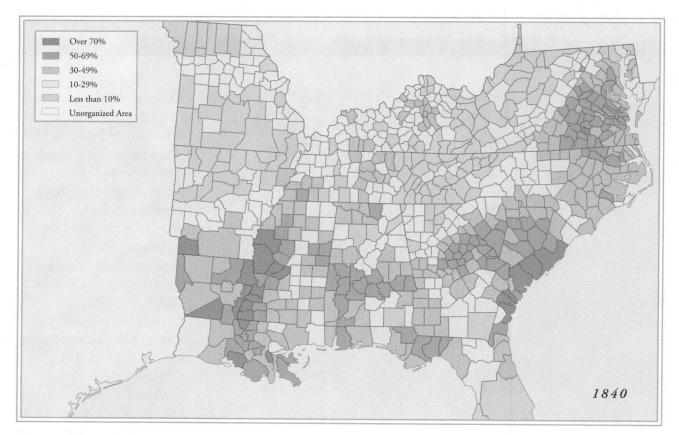

■	Over 70%
■	50-69%
■	30-49%
□	10-29%
□	Less than 10%
□	Unorganized Area

1840

Map 11.3 *The Spread of Slavery*
     Slavery moved to the lands taken from the American Indians in Georgia, Alabama, and Mississippi, even as the institution remained strong in the older plantation areas of the Atlantic coast.

docks of New Orleans, Mobile, and Memphis and in the shipyards of Baltimore. Some slaves lived where their families had dwelled for generations; others cleared new land along the Mississippi frontier. Some knew the white people among whom they lived quite well; others belonged to absolute strangers. Some worked in large groups of black people; others worked alone or beside whites.

     Southern culture mixed English, African, Scots-Irish, Caribbean, French, Indian, and Hispanic influences into a rich and complex blend. Language, food, music, and religion took on new shapes as black and white cultures interacted. In the meantime, African Americans prided themselves on the stories, songs, and dances they knew to be particularly their own, on the styles of the baskets, quilts, and clothes they sewed, or the way they carried themselves. Black culture remained distinct and vibrant, even as it influenced the larger American culture.

     African American families tended to rely on a broader range of kin than did white families. Grand-

parents, aunts, and uncles often played significant roles in child rearing in black families. When people of actual blood relation were unavailable, southern slaves created "fictive kin," friends and neighbors given honorary titles of "brother" or "aunt" and treated as such. These arrangements permitted slave families considerable resiliency and variety.

     Enslaved Americans generally lived in a relatively small community of others. About a quarter of all held in slavery lived on farms with fewer than nine slaves, whereas another quarter lived on the 3 percent of southern plantations that held more than fifty slaves. The remaining half lived on plantations with somewhere between ten and forty-nine bondspeople. African Americans often found wives or husbands on nearby farms, visiting one another on evenings and weekends.

Plantations and Farms

White slaveowners in the American South tended to live on the same plantation as their slaves, but wealth-

Pattern of Black Population

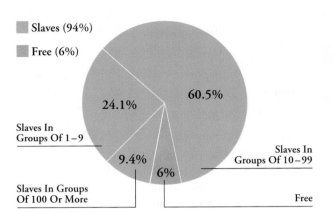

■ Slaves (94%)

■ Free (6%)

Slaves In
Groups Of 1–9 — 24.1%

Slaves In Groups
Of 100 Or More — 9.4%

60.5% — Slaves In
Groups Of 10–99

6% — Free

Chart 11.1 *Patterns of Black Population in the South*
Most black people lived on large plantations
with more than ten other enslaved people,
even while others were scattered on much
smaller farms and in towns and cities.

*Enslaved people of both genders and of all ages worked in
a variety of demanding tasks throughout the year as they
brought the South's valuable cotton crop from seed to bale.*
The Historic New Orleans Collection, Accension #1975.931 & 2

ier whites put day-to-day control of their plantations
in the hands of professional overseers. These overseers
were often ambitious young men of middling background who used the overseer position as a stepping
stone to their own plantation. Slaves could and did appeal to the owner if they thought the overseer unfair.
Since a master might indeed trust a well-known slave
more than a new overseer, the position involved tact
as well as brute force.

On larger plantations, where slaves often worked
in groups called gangs, trusted male slaves served as
"drivers." Such drivers tended to be especially strong
and skilled, commanding respect from whites as well
as blacks. Although whites held the ultimate threat of
force, they much preferred to keep the work moving
smoothly, with as little trouble as possible. The driver
could help both sides, protecting fellow slaves from
abuse and assuring that the work got done efficiently.
Drivers frequently found themselves caught between
the two competing sets of demands, however, and
slaves often resented or even hated drivers.

About three out of four enslaved people worked
mainly in the fields. Almost all of them went to the
fields during the peak times. Women, who worked in
the fields alongside men, also served in the house as
cooks and domestics. Slaves were well known for controlling the pace of work, reporting their tools broken
or "lost" when they were forced to work too fast or too
long. They traditionally had Sundays to garden for
themselves, do their domestic chores, or hunt.

Slaves' lives were by no means simple. Lines of
power often became complicated and tangled on plantations and farms, with masters, mistresses, sons,
overseers, and drivers claiming authority. Slaves
tended to work at several different jobs over the course
of the year. Some slaves were respected as purveyors
of healing or religious knowledge from Africa; some
slaves were admired for their musical ability; others
won recognition for their ability to read and preach the
Gospel. These abilities did not always correspond with
the opinions of whites, who frequently underesti-
mated the abilities and character of the people among
whom they lived.

Whites told themselves that they provided "their
people" a better life than they would have known in
Africa. Indeed, southern masters explained the justice
of slavery to themselves and to the North by stressing
their Christian stewardship for the slaves. As one clergyman wrote to his fellow slaveholders in the early
1840s, slaves "were placed under our control . . . not
exclusively for our benefit but theirs also."

Throughout the 1830s and 1840s, southern
slaveholders and ministers prided themselves on their
Christian mission to the slaves. Most masters would
not permit their slaves to learn to read, but they did
arrange to have Bible selections read to their slaves.
Although many slaves eagerly accepted the Gospel in
the white-dominated churches, others resented the obvious and shallow uses the masters made of the sermons, telling the slaves to accept their lot and to refrain from stealing food. Such slaves displayed their
deepest religious feelings only in their own worship, in
the secret meetings in brush arbors and cabins in the
slave quarters. There, they prayed to be free and to be
united in heaven with those they loved.

Largely oblivious to the lives their slaves led beyond their sight, masters pointed to the physical condition of the slaves as evidence of their concern for

Slaves Imported, 1500–1870

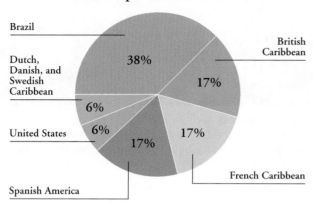

Proportion of Hemisphere's Slave Population, 1825

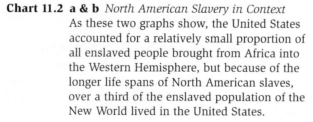

Chart 11.2 a & b *North American Slavery in Context* As these two graphs show, the United States accounted for a relatively small proportion of all enslaved people brought from Africa into the Western Hemisphere, but because of the longer life spans of North American slaves, over a third of the enslaved population of the New World lived in the United States.

"their people." Compared with slaves in other places in the hemisphere, it was true, those of the American South were relatively well-fed and healthier. They had limited and monotonous diets, but generally consumed enough nutrients. Slaves received ineffective or dangerous health care, their houses were small and drafty, and their clothing was limited to a few rough garments per year, but none of these conditions endangered slaves' physical survival. Slaves in the United States, working in relatively healthy settings and benefiting from a balanced ratio between men and women, generally lived longer than did their counterparts elsewhere in the hemisphere.

On the other hand, many slaveowners did not refrain from having their slaves whipped on small provocation, branded, shackled, or locked up in sweltering enclosures; slaves suffered sexual abuse. Partly because expectant mothers were often kept in the fields until the last minute, about a third of all black babies died before they reached their first birthday. American slavery, compared with slavery elsewhere, whatever ameliorating features it might have had, was a harsh institution.

The Politics of the White South

In the South as in the North, the Whigs portrayed themselves as the party of progress and prosperity. The lawyers, editors, and merchants who set up shop in the hamlets and towns of the South proved receptive to such views. The young men who followed such professions eagerly joined organizations such as the Masons, temperance groups, and political parties. They prided themselves on their broad views of national issues. In their eyes, only the Whigs reflected such enlightened perspectives. The large planters on the richest lands were also attracted to the Whigs. The Whigs drew, too, on the farmers in the mountains of the Upper South, men determined to develop connections to outside markets.

The Democrats, on the other hand, found their strongest supporters among the middling farmers and planters of the South. These men tended to resent and fear taxes on their lands and slaves. They admired the Democrats' aggressive approach to removing the American Indians and western expansion. Southerners distrustful of northerners and of commerce found the minimal-government pronouncements of the Democrats appealing.

In the South both the Whigs and the Democrats declared themselves the friends of southern slavery, but they differed in their emphases. The Democrats pledged that they would protect slavery by extending the power of the government as little as possible. The Whigs, on the other hand, argued that the best way to protect slavery was for the South to develop its region's economy and build strong economic and political bridges to the North.

REFORM TAKES ROOT

The wild swings of the economy of the 1830s seemed to drive Americans to improve their society. They could see dangers all around them but they could also

Horace Mann, 1846
Absolute Right to an Education, 1846

Horace Mann abandoned his successful law practice and position in the state legislature to become the first secretary of the Massachusetts Board of Education. Mann argued against those who resisted paying taxes to educate the children of others, insisting that every child had an "absolute right" to an education and that the state had an obligation to provide that education for the public good and at the public's expense.

. . . In the district-school-meeting, in the town-meeting, in legislative halls, everywhere, the advocates for a more generous education could carry their respective audiences with them in behalf of increased privileges for our children, were it not instinctively foreseen that increased privileges must be followed by increased taxation. Against this obstacle, argument falls dead. The rich man who has no children declares that the exaction of a contribution from him to educate the children of his neighbor is an invasion of his rights of property. The man who has reared and educated a family of children denounces it as a double tax when he is called upon to assist in educating the children of others also; or, if he has reared his own children without educating them, he thinks it peculiarly oppressive to be obliged to do for others what he refrained from doing even for himself. Another, having children, but disdaining to educate them with the common mass, withdraws them from the public school, puts them under what he calls "selecter influences," and then thinks it a grievance to be obliged to support a school which he [regards with contempt]. . . .

    It seems not irrelevant, therefore . . . to inquire into the nature of a man's right to the property he possesses; and to satisfy ourselves respecting the question, whether any man has such an indefeasible title to his estates, or such an absolute ownership of them, as renders it unjust in the government to assess upon him his share of the expenses of educating the children of the community up to such a point as the nature of the institutions under which he lives, and the well-being of society, require.

    I believe in the existence of a great, immortal, immutable principle of natural law, or natural ethics,—a principle antecedent to all human institutions, and incapable of being abrogated by any ordinance of man,—a principle of divine origin, which proves the *absolute right* to an education of every human being that comes into the world; and which, of course, proves the correlative duty of every government to see that the means of that education are provided for all.

    . . . To any one who looks beyond the mere surface of things, it is obvious that the primary and natural elements or ingredients of all property consist in the riches of the soil, in the treasures of the sea, in the light and warmth of the sun, in the fertilizing clouds and streams and dews, in the winds, and in the chemical and vegetative agencies of Nature. In the majority of cases, all that we call *property,* all that makes up the valuation or inventory of a nation's capital, was prepared at the creation, and was laid up of old in the capacious storehouses of Nature. For every unit that a man earns by his own toil or skill, he receives hundreds and thousands, without cost and without recompense, from the all-bountiful Giver. A proud mortal, standing in the midst of his luxuriant wheat-fields or cotton-plantations, may arrogantly call them his own; yet what barren wastes would they be, did not Heaven send down upon them its dews and its rains, its warmth and its light, and sustain, for their growth and ripening, the grateful vicissitude of the seasons!

continues

. . . The claim of a child, then, to a portion of pre-existent property, begins with the first breath he draws. The new-born infant must have sustenance and shelter and care. If the natural parents are removed, or parental ability fails; in a word, if parents either cannot or will not supply the infant's wants,—then society at large—the government having assumed to itself the ultimate control of all property—is bound to step in and fill the parent's place. To deny this to any child would be equivalent to a sentence of death, a capital execution of the innocent,—at which every soul shudders. It would be a more cruel form of infanticide than any which is practised in China or in Africa.

Source: Horace Mann, *Tenth Annual Report of the Secretary of the Board of Education* (1846), in *The Life and Works of Horace Mann* (Boston: Lee and Shepard, 1891), Vol. IV, pp. 114–17, 128–29, 131–34.

glimpse how things could be better. The new machinery of railroads, telegraphs, and printing presses held out exciting new possibilities for spreading the word, for pulling people together for common purposes.

Some Americans took practical routes to progress, focusing their efforts on schools and alcohol, whereas others explored philosophy and literature. Some used the new printing machinery of the age for entertainment, whereas others turned to the fight against social evils.

Public Schools

Many Americans had become dissatisfied with the way young people were schooled in the United States. No state had a statewide school system, and local districts ran their own affairs, often wretchedly. The rich attended private schools or employed tutors, whereas the parents of poorer children had to sign oaths declaring themselves "paupers" before their children could benefit from charity schools. Parents from the middle classes, charged a fee according to the number of children they had, sent their offspring to schools often taught by untrained teachers. Hundreds of districts, especially in the South, created no schools at all. Many American children never went to school in the 1820s and 1830s and those who did often attended for only a short time.

Reformers argued that unequal and inadequate education would not suffice in America, a country dependent upon informed democracy. These reformers wanted free schools. Taxes and other state support would make it possible for all children to go to public schools. The rich would be more likely to send their children to such schools, reformers reasoned, if their tax dollars were supporting them; the poor would be more likely to send their children if they were not stigmatized as paupers. Buildings and teachers could be improved with the increased support.

A Massachusetts lawyer and Whig politician, Horace Mann worked relentlessly to make rich citizens, especially manufacturers, see that a tax in support of schools was a wise investment. Think how much better workers would be, he argued, if they could read and calculate. Think to what good use women could be put as teachers, he argued, instilling future citizens with their virtues of cooperation and peacefulness. Mann gradually persuaded influential people in Massachusetts of the practicability of common schools. In 1837, he became the first secretary of the Massachusetts Board of Education.

When Mann took over, many schools were in session for only a couple of months a year. He transformed that system during his tenure. The minimum school year stretched to six months, buildings and teacher training improved significantly, and teachers' pay increased by more than half.

Women teachers became common in the Northeast. Oberlin College in Ohio admitted women in 1837, making it the first coeducational institution in the country. Females attended new "normal schools" that provided teacher training; they read educational journals, received professional supervision, and taught with uniform textbooks. These standards spread throughout the North and the West in the 1840s and 1850s, as did McGuffey's Readers. These books, which sold an astonishing 9 million copies between 1836 and 1850, blended Christian piety and the virtues of hard work. Though each book aimed at a specific grade, the underlying message was always the same: "God has given you minds which are capable of indefinite improvement."

The Washingtonians

Americans had long waged campaigns against intemperance, but the fight against drink took on a new urgency in the depression years of the late

These standardized textbooks offered millions of American schoolchildren moral as well as academic instruction.
Courtesy of Special Collections, University of Miami Libraries

1830s and early 1840s. Many people, religious and otherwise, saw alcohol as the scourge of American life. "You cannot go into hardly any man's house," an English visitor wrote, "without being asked to drink wine, or spirits, even in the morning." Men drank at work, farmers routinely turned their grain into whiskey, and rum was a major part of New England commerce. Americans aged fifteen or older consumed an average of 40 gallons of beer, spirits, and wine per capita.

The Washingtonian movement, named in honor of George Washington, gave great force and visibility to a crusade against alcohol. Whereas earlier temperance movements had mainly enlisted those who were already opposed to alcohol, the new movement marked an effort by drinkers to reform themselves. Earlier attempts at temperance had often pitted middle- and upper-class reformers against members of the working class, but the new movement grew among people in the lower ranks of American society. Older reform attempts had been largely the efforts of men, but now women became active.

The Washingtonians began in Baltimore in 1840, when six drinkers pledged to one another to quit drinking and to persuade other drinkers to do the same. Word of the new movement quickly spread up the eastern seaboard, and by 1843 the Washingtonians claimed millions of adherents. Unlike earlier temperance efforts led by upper class or religious leaders, Washingtonians prided themselves on an egalitarian ethos: "Exclusiveness was never intended to constitute . . . Washingtonianism. We write plain things for plain people." Partly as a result of the new organization, Americans' consumption of alcohol plummeted in the 1840s.

"Martha Washington" societies, for women only, grew rapidly, challenging the men's movement both in size and in fervor. These female temperance advocates were not well-to-do ladies stooping to help the fallen, but rather the wives of artisans and small businessmen. They helped families in distress to get back on their feet. They also provided a new edge to the temperance crusade, reminding men that drunkenness was more often than not a male failing and that it was the wives and children of drunkards who suffered most from their neglect, cruelty, and even violence.

Abolitionism Strengthened and Challenged

By the late 1830s the American Anti-slavery Society claimed over a quarter of a million members, primarily in the Northeast and Midwest. The first female abolitionist speakers—the Grimké sisters, Angelina and Sarah—were prize recruits into the antislavery ranks, for they were the daughters of a prominent South Carolina slave-owning planter. By telling New England audiences of their own experiences with slavery, the Grimkés held a credibility that white northern abolitionists could not match. In 1837, the Grimkés decided to exert their power in a new forum by lecturing to mixed audiences of men and women. Although some people strenuously objected to such an elevation of women in the public sphere, the Grimkés spoke to over 40,000 people in nine months in 1837 and 1838. *"All moral beings have essentially the same rights and the same duties,* whether they be male or female," Angelina Grimké admonished an audience. The female slaves of the South, who "now wear the rion yoke of slavery in this land of boasted liberty and law . . . are our countrywomen—*they are our sisters."*

PICTURING THE PAST ✦ SOCIAL & CULTURAL EVENTS

THE DANGERS OF DRINK

From the Collections of the Library of Congress

This print was a popular one in the United States early in its national history because many people considered alcohol the greatest threat to the country. In this one image, viewers could trace the devastating effects of drinking on a young man and his family. Everyone knew the excuses people told themselves about drinking. At first, in the lower left corner, the very young man shares a drink with a friend. He then proceeds to make weak excuses, such as drinking to "keep the cold out." From there, it is a short step to losing control, having "a drink too much," and becoming "riotous." At the "summit," the star of the story has become a "confirmed drunkard," wasting his life with equally drunken friends. His drinking leads quickly to poverty and then to desperate crime in order to support the habit. Finally, despairing, he turns to suicide as the only way out. Meanwhile, an abandoned wife and child, homeless, suffer on their way to the poor house. This was America's first war on drugs and it struck many of the same themes as those of later crusades.

As it grew stronger, the antislavery cause met with more determined opposition. When abolitionist Elijah P. Lovejoy offended readers of his religious paper in St. Louis—denouncing a local judge who prevented the trial of a mob who had burned a black man alive—citizens of Alton, Illinois, invited Lovejoy to move to their town. Alton prided itself on being a progressive place, but soon some prominent members of the community, angered at Lovejoy's paper for its dissemination of "the highly odious doctrines of modern Abolitionism," held a public meeting demanding that he quit printing such ideas. Lovejoy only intensified his attacks on slavery. Mobs destroyed two of Lovejoy's presses and vowed to tar and feather him, but he persisted. A mayoral candidate in Alton whipped a mob to a frenzy to destroy a replacement press as it was offloaded from the train in September. In November 1837, as his fifth press arrived, a battle erupted and Lovejoy was killed as he and his assistants fought the crowd. The mob shattered his press, and local law officers arrested the defenders of Lovejoy for inciting the violence.

The murder of Elijah P. Lovejoy, an abolitionist editor in Illinois, revealed the depth of opposition held by many northern whites to anyone who would speak forcefully against slavery.
North Wind Picture Archives

Abolitionists debated the proper response to such opposition. William Lloyd Garrison counseled his allies to offer no resistance to violence. He and his supporters renounced all allegiance to the established parties and churches, which had long since shown themselves tolerant of slavery. Other abolitionists, by contrast, used whatever means they could to bring slavery to an end, including political parties.

The differences among the abolitionists came to a head at the annual meeting of the American Anti-slavery Society in 1839. They differed most visibly in their attitudes toward the role of women. Women constituted perhaps half of all members of the antislavery organizations, but some male abolitionists sought to keep females in a subordinate role and prevent women members from voting, speaking publicly, or serving on committees with men. Unable to resolve their differences, the abolitionists split. The more conservative group, based in New York, created the Liberty party to run a candidate for president in the upcoming election of 1840. Garrison's organization maintained a more radical stance on the role of women and mocked those who sought "to sustain and propagate those eternal, immutable principles of liberty, justice, and equality" by denying "woman her right as a human being to speak and act with brethren on the anti-slavery platform."

Whatever their differences, abolitionists barraged Congress with petitions demanding that slavery be ended in the District of Columbia. Former President John Quincy Adams, now a congressman from Massachusetts, used all his parliamentary skill to fight the gag rule that prevented Congress from recognizing antislavery petitions; he finally succeeded in getting it overthrown in 1845. Adams also successfully defended Africans who had seized a slave ship bound for Cuba, the *Amistad,* and landed in Connecticut. Supported by a large network of abolitionists, Adams took the case before the U.S. Supreme Court and won not only the acquittal of the Africans for murdering the ship's captain but their freedom as well.

Black antislavery speakers greatly strengthened the antislavery cause. Speakers such as Henry Brown, Henry Bibb, Solomon Northup, Sojourner Truth, Harriet Tubman, and Ellen Craft electrified audiences. Slavery, they made clear, was nothing like the benign institution portrayed by its defenders. Public speakers such as Henry Highland Garnet urged listeners to "strike for your lives and liberties. Let every slave throughout the land do this, and the days of slavery are numbered. Rather die freemen than live to be slaves. Remember that you are FOUR MILLIONS! . . . Let your motto be resistance! resistance! RESISTANCE!"

Although white abolitionists valued the contributions of their black compatriots, they urged black speakers not to make too much of a fuss when confronted with the insults and indignities faced by black people in the North. African American abolitionists chafed under the restrictions they faced from fellow reformers and enemies alike; they demanded greater rights for northern as well as southern blacks. Their experiences showed the extent to which race was a national problem.

One of the most remarkable Americans of the nineteenth century burst into visibility in the early 1840s. Frederick Douglass had grown up in Maryland. Like other places in the Upper South, Maryland's economy was diversifying in the 1830s and 1840s as commerce intensified and railroads spread. Douglass learned to read from his mistress, though it was against the law for her to teach him. He carried with him a copy of *Webster's Spelling Book* and *The Columbian Orator,* a book of speeches, including a slave's persuasive argument with his master to set him free.

Sent to Baltimore by his owner, Douglass worked in the shipyards, continued to read widely, and plotted his escape to freedom. After several attempts, Douglass finally borrowed the papers of a free black sailor and rode a train to freedom. Douglass found himself in New York City, alone and without any notion of what he should do. A runaway slave

One of the most influential and famous Americans of the nineteenth century, Frederick Douglass fought tirelessly against slavery and in favor of a wide range of social reforms.
The Granger Collection, New York

might be hunted down by a slavecatcher for a reward. Fortunately for Douglass, he met a black man who introduced the young runaway to the New York Antislavery Society. After white abolitionists saw the skill with which he spoke, they sent Douglass to travel throughout the North with William Lloyd Garrison.

DEVELOPMENT OF AN AMERICAN CULTURE

European visitors had long scoffed at the failure of the United States to create anything they considered "culture." During the first desperate decades of the nation's experience, filled with war, economic panic, and political conflict, few Americans found opportunity to do philosophy, write novels, produce ambitious paintings, or carve sculpture. But in the 1830s and 1840s,

the new country experienced a sudden outburst of creativity in everything from the most elevated philosophy to the most popular amusements.

Transcendentalism

Leading thinkers saw the possibilities of improvement everywhere, not just in education or reform. Several of those thinkers came out of Unitarianism, a form of liberal Christianity especially strong in New England. Unitarianism encouraged people to emphasize feeling rather than dogma. Several young people raised within the Unitarian church took these ideas further than their elders intended, rejecting much Christian doctrine. A belief in the literal truth of the Bible, these youthful critics argued, trapped religion in the past. Better to appeal directly to the heart from the very beginning. These thinkers wanted religion to transcend churches and denominations.

Women played an active role in the effort to create an American philosophy, with Margaret Fuller becoming especially important. Fuller, raised in the Unitarian church in Cambridge, Massachusetts, received a fine education. But she felt herself adrift, full of "unemployed force," after her male classmates went on to college. She read widely and taught school with two other important figures in the revolt against Unitarianism: Elizabeth Peabody and Bronson Alcott. These three, like Horace Mann, believed that children were innately good and that education should be designed to let that goodness flourish. They argued that school, like church, should not be permitted to get in the way of people's natural connection with nature and with one another.

They soon took their lead from Ralph Waldo Emerson. Emerson had grown up around Concord, Massachusetts. Though descended from a distinguished ministerial family, he was raised by a widowed mother and forced to work his way through Harvard College. Uncomfortable as a minister and dissatisfied as a schoolteacher, Emerson set out for Europe. There he met exciting English intellectuals whose stirring ideas were to influence him deeply: Samuel Coleridge, Thomas Carlyle, and William Wordsworth. These writers, caught up in European romanticism with its rejection of the austere logic of the Enlightenment, provided Emerson with a perspective far removed from the cool Unitarianism on which he had been raised. Emerson perceived humankind as deeply tied to nature, filled with its rhythms and longings. He published such ideas in his first book, *Nature* (1836), a work that gained him considerable attention from the like-minded young people of New England.

Ralph Waldo Emerson was America's first popular intellectual, a combination of poet, lecturer, entertainer, and minister.
From the Collections of the Library of Congress

But it was Emerson's address before the Phi Beta Kappa initiates at Harvard in 1837 that announced his arrival to a larger audience. Emerson worried over the state of the nation after the panic of 1837. The panic directly touched one of Emerson's friends in Concord, Henry David Thoreau, who graduated from Harvard in the panic year and could find no decent job. Emerson, older than Thoreau, had finally achieved some economic security in the summer of 1837, thanks to an inheritance, but he was well aware of the difficulties facing even the Phi Beta Kappa graduates of Harvard during August of that hard year.

Emerson titled his speech "The American Scholar." He argued that the scholar should be a man of action, a man of nature, a man of risk and endeavor. Books and poetry held tremendous power, Emerson admitted, but it was in activity, in striving, that the American scholar became truly American. It was time to set the teachings of Europe aside long enough to find America's own voice, Emerson told the graduates.

Echoes of these ideas were also heard in the South. William Gilmore Simms, a leading essayist, novelist, and poet from South Carolina, traveled throughout the South delivering lectures to communities, universities, and learned societies on diverse topics such as "English Literature" and "The Philosophy of History." Like Emerson, Simms saw southern scholars as armed with "the sufficient spear of truth" who "shall compel the deference of sordid politicians."

Speakers developed these ideas throughout the late 1830s, enjoying growing fame and influence through public lectures. Railroads made it feasible for the first time for speakers to cover a large amount of territory. Public speaking generally paid much better than any kind of writing. The growth of newspapers and other printing facilitated advertising, getting word of the lectures out beforehand and spreading summaries of the lectures to those unable to attend. People flocked to the lectures. In the lecture hall, Emerson exulted, "everything is admissible, philosophy, ethics, divinity, criticism, poetry, humor, fun, mimicry, anecdotes, jokes, ventriloquism. . . ."

Emerson's home in Concord became the gathering place for a group who came to be called the transcendentalists, who sought to "transcend" the mundane into the mystical knowledge that every human possessed if he or she would listen to it. Margaret Fuller became the editor of the *Dial,* the transcendentalist magazine, while Elizabeth Peabody opened a bookstore catering to the interests of the group. Bronson Alcott and about eighty others founded Brook Farm, one of the many utopian communities that tried to get off the ground in the 1830s and 1840s. Brook Farm put people to work in the fields in the morning and on their books in the afternoon. The community produced both crops and an impressive weekly newspaper. Its schools stood as examples of enlightened education. The experiment failed economically after a few years, but for a while Brook Farm offered the possibility of combining intellectual excitement, physical work, and social responsibility in a way the transcendentalists craved.

Since the transcendentalists believed that people should establish a close connection to nature, Henry David Thoreau decided to conduct an "experiment in human ecology." He wanted to see—and show—how a modern man could live in harmony with nature. In 1845, he built an isolated house in the woods near Walden Pond, carefully calculating the cost of nails and other supplies and keeping a thoughtful journal. He strove to be self-sufficient and self-contained. The experiment proved important for the book Thoreau eventually published about his experience, *Walden: Life in the Woods* (1854).

Henry David Thoreau, a close friend of Emerson's, embarked on a characteristically American experiment when he went to live alone in the woods at Walden Pond.
The Granger Collection, New York

Emergence of a Popular Culture

The transcendentalists were not alone in their craving for intensity. American painters, sculptors, and writers found an increasing audience for their works in the 1830s. And so did entrepreneurs who sought out the largest audiences they could find with spectacle and controversy.

Thomas Cole was the key figure in the emergence of American painting. Though born in England, he came to the Ohio frontier as a small child. Cole taught himself to paint but went to England and Italy to perfect his art. He returned to the village of Catskill in New York to paint the Hudson River Valley in the late 1830s and early 1840s. Soon, other painters, such as Asher Durand and Frederick Church, joined Cole in their fascination with the stirring American landscape, creating what became known as the Hudson River School.

Cole also turned to richly symbolic allegorical painting. His journey to Europe had struck him by its contrasts, "both the ruined towers that tell of outrage, and the gorgeous temples that speak of ostentation." He believed America, by contrast, "to be the abode of virtue." He embodied his notions of the cycles of civi-

lization and personal life in two powerful allegorical series, *The Course of Empire* and *The Voyage of Life.* Engravings of these series became popular fixtures in American homes.

Other important artists followed their own paths through the American landscape. George Catlin spent much of the 1830s living among the American Indians of the Great Plains, making hundreds of drawings and paintings. As a young man he was moved by the sight of an Indian delegation visiting Philadelphia and vowed that "nothing short of the loss of my life shall prevent me from visiting their country and becoming their historian." In Catlin's paintings, easterners thought they might catch the last glimpse of a disappearing people.

Audiences could also view vanishing wildlife in the remarkable watercolors of John James Audubon. Audubon, born in Haiti and educated in France, settled on the Kentucky frontier as a merchant after he married. He loved the American wilderness too much to stay in his shop, though, and he launched out on daunting journeys to record the environment and appearance of the birds of the young nation. After ten years of work Audubon produced *The Birds of America, from Original Drawings, with 435 Plates Showing 1,065 Figures* in four immense volumes, completing the project in 1838.

The most famous artistic production of antebellum America was a statue: Hiram Powers's *The Greek Slave,* completed in 1846. Powers grew up in the raw country of Ohio but moved to Italy as he prospered. There, Powers sculpted his statue of a nude young woman bound in chains. The young woman represented, Powers said, a Greek girl captured by the Turks in the Greco-Turkish war. As such, she represented Christianity and whiteness, unbowed by the evil and darkness surrounding her. Powers sought, and received, the endorsement of a group of American clergymen, removing any qualms audiences might have. *The Greek Slave* served as the model for hundreds of miniature copies that appeared in the drawing rooms of the finest homes.

The same drawing rooms also contained a novelty of the age: daguerreotypes. This form of photography developed in France but arrived in the United States in 1838 soon after its creation. Within a few years, more than eighty young photographers practiced their craft in New York City alone and by 1850 as many as 10,000 daguerreotypists had set up shop. This early photography was cumbersome and required long periods of stillness before the camera, but the American people hurried to studios to have their portraits done.

Thomas Cole's painting View from Mount Holyoke, Northampton, Massachusetts, after a Thunderstorm (The Oxbow)
reflects a common theme in the work of American painters in these years: the power as well as the beauty of nature.
The Granger Collection, New York

Engravings based on paintings and photographs soon filled the publications coming off the presses. For the first time, illustrations could be produced cheaply. Etched metal plates replaced crude woodcuts for the mass production of lithographs of popular subjects such as Bible stories, sporting events, shipwrecks, and railroad disasters.

Seeing the opportunity afforded by this emergence of a popular audience for print, American writers worked hard to fill the hunger. One especially gifted author, Edgar Allan Poe, skillfully navigated between the market and his art. Poe wrote short stories, the kind of writing most in demand, but he brought to the form a kind of self-consciousness few had demonstrated before. Poe tapped into a widespread fascination with the occult, seances, and ghosts, filling his work with ruins, shadows, and legends. Works such as "The Murders in the Rue Morgue" marked the first appearance of the detective story. Throughout the 1840s, Poe published stories such as "The Masque of the Red Death," "The Pit and the Pendulum," and "The Tell-Tale Heart" and poetry such as "The Raven." Plagued by ill health, however, Poe did not survive the decade.

P. T. Barnum exploited the public fascination with the macbre and fanciful and opened his American Museum in New York in 1841. Barnum displayed oddities that strained the limits of belief but that could not be completely disproved. He displayed an aged black woman who he claimed was 161 years old and had been George Washington's nurse. Thousands turned out to gaze at her infirm body and hear her tales of "dear little George." Unlike earlier museums, Barnum's museum frankly offered entertainment, including magicians and midgets such as the famous Tom Thumb and the Feejee Mermaid, actually a monkey skeleton attached to the bones of a large fish. The fact that the "curiosities" were often attacked as fakes by scientists did not seem to deter visitors: Barnum's American Museum flourished for the next twenty years and his public tours with Swedish singer Jenny Lind enraptured millions and habituated Americans to a culture of celebrity and publicity stunts.

Hiram Powers's statue The Greek Slave became an American sensation, attracting large crowds and many imitators.
The New York Museum/Art Resource, NY

Edgar Allan Poe experimented with new literary forms, crafting remarkable stories and poems of terror and dread.
Courtesy of the Edgar Allan Poe Museum, Richmond, Virginia

P. T. Barnum's American Museum. *This painting captures the atmosphere of fascination and energy that surrounded everything the great American showman produced.*
The Granger Collection, New York

THE TRANSFORMATION OF AMERICAN POLITICS

Popular politics had been building in the United States since the 1820s, when Andrew Jackson electrified the electorate and when states lowered the obstacles of political participation. The two major parties, the Democrats and the Whigs, had experimented with ways to mobilize voters and to retain the power they won. The system grew throughout the 1830s, but no one was prepared for what happened in 1840.

The Election of 1840

The contest of 1840 should have offered an easy contest for the Whigs. Much of the nation remained mired in depression. Van Buren offered little effective leader-

ship during the economic crisis and many people held him to blame for the hard times. But the Whigs were not as strong as they might have been. Their party had been built piece by piece in the 1830s in reaction to Andrew Jackson. As a result, the party was a crazy quilt of interests and factions. In 1836, the party had even permitted three candidates to run against Van Buren because no one man could command the party's

Marching to the slogan of "Tippecanoe and Tyler, Too" in the campaign of 1840, the Whigs determined to keep their momentum strong. They rolled this ball, for example, all the way across Ohio.
Smithsonian Institution

full allegiance. Party leaders vowed that they would not make the same mistake in 1840.

The Whigs were determined to find the one man who stood for the common beliefs that unified Whigs beneath their surface differences. Those beliefs turned around faith in commerce, self-control, Protestantism, learning, and self-improvement. Most important, the Whigs wanted to make an active response to the depression plaguing the nation by putting money in circulation, building internal improvements, and strengthening banks. The trick was to find a candidate who embodied their beliefs without appearing to be "aristocratic" or hungry for power.

The Whig party found such a man in William Henry Harrison. Harrison had made his name as a general—most notably in his defeat of an Indian confederacy in the Battle of Tippecanoe in 1811—and later served in the House of Representatives and in the Senate. He had won fame without gathering many political liabilities and was identified with no particular position.

Seeking to balance their ticket, the Whigs chose Senator John Tyler of Virginia. Tyler shared few beliefs with his fellow Whigs, but his embrace of slavery helped mollify southerners. Moreover, his name made a nice pairing in the phrase that soon became famous: "Tippecanoe and Tyler, Too." One Whig warned that the combination of Harrison and Tyler had "rhyme, but no reason in it."

The Democrats were relieved that the Whigs had nominated Harrison. Democrats considered the old general a nonentity; one reporter commented sarcastically that if Harrison were merely given some hard cider and a small pension he would contentedly sit out the rest of his days in a log cabin. (He actually lived in a mansion and was a rich man.) The sarcasm backfired, though, for many Americans saw log cabins and home-brewed cider as evidence of American virtue and self-reliance. The Whigs, long frustrated at their reputation as snobs and elitists, seized on hard cider and log cabins as symbols of their party's loyalty to the common American.

All over the country, Whig speakers displayed paintings, signs, flags, and models of log cabins at huge outdoor rallies while freely dispensing cider to thirsty crowds. Harrison himself went out on the campaign trail, the first presidential candidate to do so. A new kind of American political style was being forged. For the first time, women became prominent at these rallies, encouraging their husbands, fathers, and suitors with smiles, waving kerchiefs, and riding in parades with pro-Harrison banners they had sewn. The Whigs embraced causes many women supported, such as temperance and allegiance to the church.

The Democrats had no idea of how to respond to the hard cider and log cabin campaign. Martin Van Buren proved an easy target for a Whig campaign that

PICTURING THE PAST ✦ POLITICS & DIPLOMACY

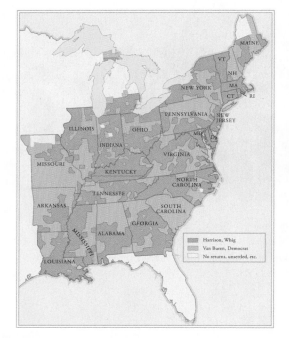

Map 11.4 *The Election of 1840*

The remarkable success of the two-party system in transforming the American political landscape was dramatized by the election of 1840. Slavery had torn at the nation ever since the Missouri Compromise, with the rapid spread of the institution all the way past the Mississippi River into Missouri, Arkansas, and Louisiana and the sudden rise of abolitionism in the North. Looking at this map, however, one would never know that these momentous things had happened. The great majority of states contained areas where either the Whigs or the Democrats dominated, the two areas balancing out almost evenly in most states so that both parties competed for every vote. The Whig party faced a difficult balancing act, for the map shows that the party won in Massachusetts and Connecticut, where antislavery was strong, and in the areas of Alabama and Georgia where plantation slavery dominated. National leaders had somehow to appeal to both constituencies if they were to remain in power.

---

emphasized homespun values. The president's portly figure and penchant for silk vests and doeskin gloves made the Democrats' long-standing claims of representing the common man look hypocritical. Andrew Jackson himself came out to campaign, firing the same charges against the Whigs that had worked so well in the past, charges of elitism, hostility to slavery, and softness on the bank issue. Even these charges failed. Harrison won nineteen of the twenty-six states, bringing about half a million new voters to the Whigs. Voter turnout surged to a level almost unimaginable just a decade earlier: Eight of every ten eligible voters went to the polls. After 1840, elections would demand the combination of active campaigning, the search for potent symbols, and boisterous public displays that had proven so successful in that year.

Tyler, Webster, and Diplomacy

The Whig celebration did not last long. Harrison, determined to prove his fitness despite his age, ex-

pounded the longest inaugural speech in American history in March 1841. Unfortunately, the weather was bitterly cold; Harrison contracted pneumonia and died exactly a month after taking office. John Tyler had become president even though he shared few of the prevailing ideals of the Whigs in Congress. Efforts on the part of Whig leaders to expand the power and reach of government with tariffs, banks, and internal improvements proved fruitless in the face of Tyler's opposition. Whig leaders in Congress responded by gathering in the Capitol gardens and excommunicating him from the party. Whig newspapers denounced him as "His Accidency" and the "Executive Ass." All but one of the members of the cabinet Tyler inherited from Harrison resigned in protest.

The only member to stay on, Daniel Webster, the secretary of state, did so because he feared his rival Henry Clay's ascendancy if he resigned and he did not think it proper to step down until important negotiations with England were complete. Conflicts between the two countries had broken out over the boundary between the United States and Canada. In 1837, armed men had fought along the border as Americans aided a rebel movement trying to overthrow British control of Canada; later, a Canadian militia burned an American steamboat carrying supplies for the insurgents, generating intense anger in the northern United States. Armed battle also erupted in the "Aroostock War" over the disputed boundary between Maine and New Brunswick.

Conflict had long been building between the British and the Americans, too, over the African slave trade. Great Britain insisted that its vessels be permitted to search American ships off the coast of Africa to prevent the transportation of slaves to British colonies. Americans resented the intrusion in its affairs and refused. The issue threatened to explode in 1841, when American slaves seized the slaving ship the *Creole*, which was taking them from Virginia to New Orleans. The slaves steered the vessel to the Bahamas and claimed their freedom under British law. Much to the anger of southern whites, the British gave sanctuary to the slaves.

Daniel Webster met with the British representative, Lord Ashburton, to settle these issues before they flamed up into a war that neither nation wanted. After extensive debate, the United States and Great Britain decided on a new boundary that gave each about half of what each had claimed in Maine and in the area to the west of Lake Superior. The Webster-Ashburton Treaty also established joint American-British patrols to intercept ships carrying slaves from Africa. Though the treaty stipulated that the United States must maintain a minimum presence totaling eighty guns along the African coast, Tyler's secretary of the navy undercut American effectiveness by sending only four ships mounting eighty guns instead of the approximately fifteen schooners better suited for the task. In 1850, while the U.S. Navy had captured only seven slavers since beginning the patrols, the British had captured over 500 ships and freed over 38,000 Africans.

THE CHALLENGE OF THE WEST

Americans of every sort kept their eyes to the west. Railroads, telegraphs, canals, and roads strained in that direction; population restlessly flowed there. But thoughtful people recognized that the lack of borders and limits posed threats as well as potential. When everything seemed possible, people placed few checks on their appetites. Every boundary was contested, every obstacle attacked.

The "Wests"

The hard times in the East made moving west seem an increasingly attractive option. Horace Greeley, the most influential newspaper editor of the day, warned people looking for a job in the midst of the depression not to come to the city but rather to "go to the Great West." To people in New England, migration to the West in the 1840s often meant migration to the lands of the northern plains and surrounding the Great Lakes. To people from Virginia and Kentucky, migration to the West might mean heading to the free states of Ohio, Indiana, or Illinois or, more often, to Mississippi, Louisiana, and Texas. For people from the cities of the East, the destination might be a booming new city such as Indianapolis, Chicago, or Detroit.

One "West" that captured the imagination of Americans in these years lay in Oregon and California, word of whose beauty and wealth had slowly filtered east throughout the preceding decade. Although many people considered it nothing less than suicide to attempt to cross the Rockies and what was considered "The Great American Desert," a growing stream of families decided to take the chance. Echoing earlier tall stories of the frontier, Peter H. Burnett, organizer of the the "Great Migration" of 1843, regaled listeners with tales of Oregon's wealth and fertility. "In Oregon, pigs are running about under great acorn trees, round and fat, and already cooked, with knives and forks sticking out of them so you can cut off a slice." Most of those who moved to the Pacific coast gathered in northern Missouri or southern Iowa. They set out in early May across undulating plains, with water and firewood easy to find, their wagons pulled by oxen. The settlers gradually ascended to Fort Laramie, at the edge of the Rockies. By July, they had reached the Continental Divide, the point at which rivers on one side flowed to the east and those on the other flowed to the west. On the trail for more than three months by this point, the settlers had covered two-thirds of the distance of their journey.

From the Divide, the settlers heading to California split off from those going to Oregon. Both faced enormous difficulties in the remainder of their trip. They raced the weather, for early mountain snowstorms could be deadly. Some of the mountainous areas were so steep that wagons had to be dragged up one side and let down the other with ropes, chains, and pulleys. Finally, by October, 2,000 miles and six months after they had left Missouri or Iowa, the settlers crossed one last ridge and looked down on the sparkling valleys of Sacramento or the Willamette River.

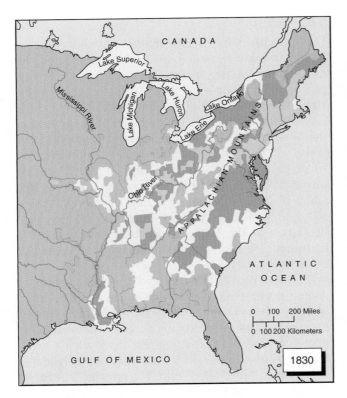

Migration to the Pacific began slowly, with only a few dozen families making the treacherous journey between 1840 and 1842. The numbers mounted between 1843 and 1845, when over 5,000 people passed through Utah on their way to Oregon and California. Throughout the 1840s, the great majority of migrants chose Oregon over California as their destination. Even so, distances still mattered: from the 1840s until the completion of the transcontinental railroad in 1869, Oregon grew from a few hundred white settlers to more than 100,000. By comparison, in the same period, Iowa's population jumped from a few thousand to 1.2 million. Oregon came to seem a respectable place for literate and upright Protestant families to settle, whereas California seemed a gamble, attractive mainly to single men willing to take their chances in a boom economy that could go bust.

Manifest Destiny

In 1842, the Great United States Exploring Expedition returned from a journey of 87,780 nautical miles. It had circumnavigated the globe, located Antarctica,

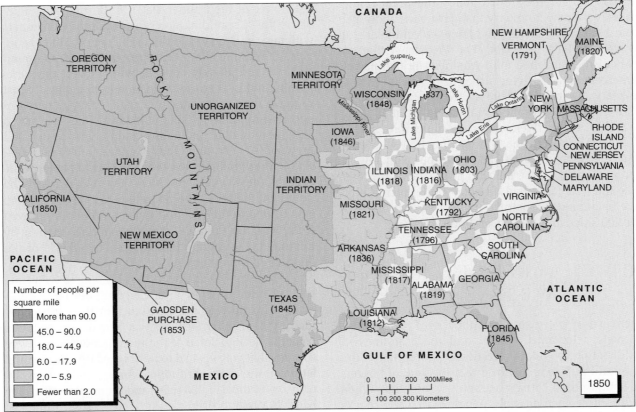

Map 11.5 a & b *Population Expansion, 1830–1850*
The population of the United States moved steadily westward at the same time that the Northeast became ever more densely settled. The population of the South remained thinner because plantations did not concentrate people as the family farms and towns of the North did.

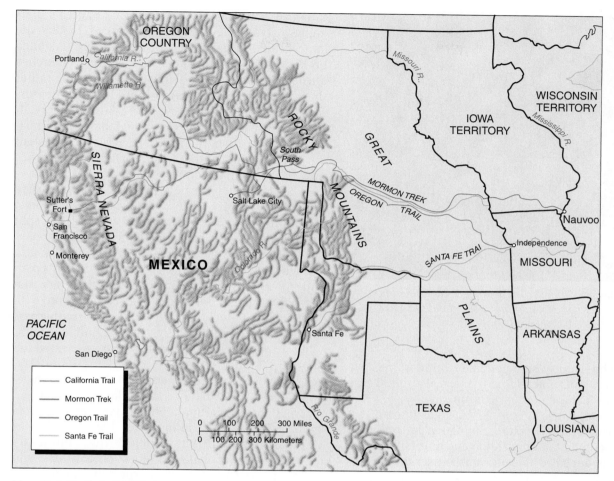

Map 11.6 *Trails to the West*
The trails to Oregon and California looked straightforward enough on a map but proved immensely challenging, even deadly, in practice.

and explored the Pacific coast. The captain of the expedition reported that Oregon was a treasure trove of "forests, furs, and fisheries." If the United States did not use its military to occupy the territory all the way to the 54°40′ boundary, it would be risking much more than the Oregon territory itself. California might throw off the light Mexican rule under which it rested and join with an independent Oregon to create a nation "that is destined to control the destinies of the Pacific." The Tyler administration sought to downplay this report, not wanting to disrupt negotiations still pending on the boundary of Maine and Wisconsin.

The forces of expansion proved too strong for the administration to contain, however. In 1845, newspaper editor John Louis O'Sullivan announced that it was the "manifest destiny"—the clear and unavoidable fate—of the United States "to overspread the con-

tinent allotted by Providence for the free development of our yearly multiplying millions." In other words, God intended white Americans to fill in every corner of the continent, pushing aside American Indians, Mexicans, English, or anyone else.

The Democrats in Congress and President Tyler supported this expansion, focusing first on Texas. If the United States did not quickly annex Texas, Democrats contended, it might fall under the sway of the British and become not only a barrier to further American migration but also a bastion of antislavery. If, by contrast, the United States acted quickly, Texas could attract not only slaveholders and their slaves but also emancipated slaves, keeping them away from the North and the other attractive lands such as California and Oregon. Midwestern Democrats, for their part, agreed that expansion was essential to the American

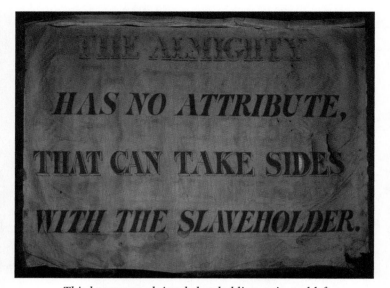

This banner proclaimed slaveholding a sin and left no room for excuse or explanation by slaveholders.
Courtesy of the Massachusetts Historical Society

future. The country simply could not afford to have major ports and potential markets sealed off. These Democrats had their eye on Oregon.

In 1844, James K. Polk, a former governor of Tennessee, got the Democratic nomination for president after an acrimonious convention and nine ballots. The Democrats appealed to both northerners and southerners with a program of aggressive expansion, attempting to counter fears of slavery's growth not by rejecting Texas but by embracing Oregon.

Politics in Turmoil

In 1844, the Whigs nominated Henry Clay for president on a program explicitly opposed to expansion. The apparently clear-cut choice between Clay and Polk soon became complicated, however. Clay announced that he would not oppose Texas annexation if it could be done peacefully and by consensus. Such a strategy backfired, attracting few advocates of expansion but alienating antislavery people in the North. Although Polk only won 49.6 percent of the vote, hardly a ringing endorsement of aggressive expansionism, his diaries indicate that he entered office with a clear vision of annexing large areas of Mexican territory, Texas, and Oregon.

Meanwhile, the early 1840s witnessed bloody battles over religion. A growing stream of immigrants from Ireland, the great majority of them Catholic, flowed into northern cities. In Protestant eyes, the Roman Catholic church posed a direct

threat to American institutions. That church's hierarchy was undemocratic, critics charged. In 1844 the largest anti-Catholic riot of antebellum America broke out in Philadelphia; several Catholic churches burned to the ground while local firemen, rather than fight the blaze, simply hosed down the surrounding buildings to prevent the fire from spreading. Because the Democrats proved far more sympathetic to the Irish than did the largely Protestant Whigs, the political differences between the parties now became inflamed with ethnic conflict.

Slavery, too, became an even more explosive issue in the early 1840s. In 1844 the Methodist church divided over slavery, and the Baptists split the following year. Southern church leaders were angry that many of their northern brethren refused to believe that American slavery was part of God's plan and bitterly resented their northern brethren's passage of a clause demanding no communion with slaveholders. Five hundred thousand southerners formed the Methodist Episcopal Church, South, while Baptists from nine southern states created the Southern Baptist Convention. Questions about slavery moved beyond laws and the Constitution into debates about sin, evil, and God's plan for the nation. As New York Governor William Marcy explained to John C. Calhoun, "I can fight your battles so long as you make the Constitution your fortress, but if you go to the Bible or make it a question of ethics, you must not expect me or any respectable member of the free states to be with you."

The conflicts over slavery exerted immediate political consequences. The abolitionist Liberty party won 62,000 votes in 1844. In New York, in fact, the Liberty party's strong showing took enough votes from Clay to give the state to Polk. And those electoral votes proved the difference in the national election, as Polk won the presidency by the narrowest of margins.

Even before Polk took office the Senate voted to annex Texas, an independent republic since 1836, as soon as Texas consented. Texas gave its approval in the fall of 1845 and won its vote in Washington at the end of that year. The Democrats sought to quiet concerns among northerners by also annexing Oregon. Though Americans, including some northern Democrats in Congress, clamored for all of Oregon to its northernmost boundary with Russian territory, chanting "Fifty-four Forty or Fight," Polk secretly negotiated with Britain to set the boundary at the 49th parallel, an extension of the northern U.S. boundary from the east. Northern Democrats who had supported Polk on Texas felt betrayed and cheated by this southern conspiracy to "strangle Oregon." Their resentment of Polk's handling of Oregon would smolder, ready to flare again.

CONCLUSION

The years between 1837 and 1845 bore the mark of the largest economic depression in the nation's history up to that time. Widespread dissatisfaction with the Democrats' handling of the economy laid the foundation for the remarkable Whig victory of 1840, when William Henry Harrison—and Tyler, too—campaigned under the banner of the log cabin and cider. The depression also drove settlers to the West and forced politicians to focus the energies and anxieties of the country on faraway opportunities and dangers.

Despite these economic problems, Americans remained profoundly optimistic about the long-term prospects of their nation. Painters, philosophers, and poets spoke in a confident new American vernacular. Reformers pushed hard for improvements in education, temperance, antislavery, and much else. Popular culture such as novels, magazines, and Barnum's museum entertained thousands of people. Many Americans focused so much on the future precisely because they had no desire to acknowledge the immediate problems surrounding them.

Map 11.7 *Oregon Boundary Dispute*
Although many Americans called for "54° 40' or Fight," the United States and England agreed on establishing the border at 49°, an extension of the boundary farther east.

Recommended Readings

Ballesein, Edward J. *Navigating Failure: Bankruptcy and Commercial Society in Antebellum America* (2001). Paints a compelling portrait of the financial turmoil of these years.

Fehrenbacher, Don E. *The Slaveholding Republic: An Account of the United States Government's Relations to Slavery* (2001). A magisterial overview of this important subject.

Genovese, Eugene. *Roll, Jordan, Roll: The World the Slaves Made* (1974). Stands as the most powerful portrayal of American slavery.

Hine, Robert V., and Faragher, John Mack. *The American West: A New Interpretive History* (2000). A fresh interpretation of a crucial American region.

Holt, Michael F. *The Rise and Fall of the American Whig Party: Jacksonian Politics and the Onset of the Civil War* (1999). A remarkable act of scholarship, describing important political change in every part of the nation.

Johnson, Walter. *Soul by Soul: Life Inside the Antebellum Slave Market* (1999). The best study of the vast domestic slave trade.

Kaestle, Carl F. *Pillars of the Republic: Common Schools and American Society, 1780–1860* (1983). The most thorough and balanced account of education reform.

Larson, John Lauritz. *Internal Improvement: National Public Works and the Promise of Popular Government in the Early United States* (2001). A valuable interpretation of one of the most important changes in these decades.

Licht, Walter. *Industrializing America: The Nineteenth Century* (1995). An extremely helpful overview.

Reiss, Benjamin. *The Showman and the Slave: Race, Death, and Memory in Barnum's America* (2001). Tells the fascinating story of the connection between popular culture, commerce, and race.

Stevenson, Brenda E. *Life in Black and White: Family and Community in the Slave South* (1996). Paints a subtle picture of both white and black southerners.

Von Frank, Albert J. *The Trials of Anthony Burns: Freedom and Slavery in Emerson's Boston* (1998). Tells a stirring story of what slaves and the abolitionists were up against.

American Journey Online and InfoTrac College Edition

Visit the source collections at http://ajaccess.wadsworth.com and infotrac.thomsonlearning.com and use the Search function with the following key terms to explore documents, images, audio and video clips, articles, and commentary related to the material in this chapter.

Frederick Douglass	*Amistad*
Harriet Tubman	Temperance movement
Manifest Destiny	transcendentalism
fugitive slave	Grimké
abolition	

> Additional resources, exercises, and Internet links related to this chapter are available on the American Passages Web site: http://history.wadsworth.com/passages2e

12 EXPANSION AND REACTION
1846–1854

WAR WITH MEXICO

AMERICANS ON THE MOVE

THE QUEST FOR PERFECTION

POPULAR CULTURE AND HIGH CULTURE

SLAVERY AND A NEW CRISIS IN POLITICS

POLITICS IN CHAOS

The 1840s and 1850s witnessed the peak of the American whaling industry. Ship after ship left New England to cover the oceans of the world in pursuit of the profitable prey. Whaling also served as the subject of the greatest novel of the era, though it went unappreciated at the time.
© Shelburne Museum, Shelburne, Vermont

The years of territorial expansion, population growth, and prosperity that accompanied a triumphant victory in a war with Mexico also proved to be years of unprecedented danger and foreboding for the United States. Heightened expectations of a transcontinental empire led to political conflict. Massive immigration from Europe fueled social conflict. Literature took on a more pessimistic tone. Female activists discovered that progress for women would come only as a result of prolonged effort. The attempt to open the West to settlement divided southerners and northerners. A stopgap compromise on slavery satisfied neither side.

WAR WITH MEXICO

Spanish territory to the south of the United States had been a major concern for generations. Throughout the 1820s American leaders had struggled with the promise and danger posed by Mexican independence and the annexation of Texas; throughout the 1830s and 1840s Americans had aided Texans in their fight against the Mexican army. The United States longed for the territories Mexico controlled in western North America, but Mexico pledged to keep those lands. No one could be sure that the United States could defeat Mexico in a large-scale war, but President Polk seemed determined to find out.

CHRONOLOGY

1846 Mexican War begins; Stephen Kearny occupies Santa Fe; Zachary Taylor takes Monterey • Border between Canada and United States established at 49th parallel • Wilmot Proviso ignites sectional conflict • Bear Flag Republic in California proclaimed • Hiram Powers completes statue *The Greek Slave*

1847 Taylor defeats Santa Anna at Buena Vista; Winfield Scott captured • Vera Cruz and Mexico City • Mormons reach Great Salt Lake Valley

1848 Gold discovered in California • Treaty of Guadalupe Hidalgo • Attempts to buy Cuba from Spain • Free-Soil party runs Van Buren for president • Zachary Taylor elected president • Seneca Falls Convention • Oneida community established • Regular steamship trips between Liverpool and New York City • Mormons settle in Great Basin

1849 California seeks admission to Union • "Forty-niners" race to California • Cotton prices invigorate South • Cholera epidemic returns

1850 Nashville Convention attempts to unify South • Fugitive Slave Law • Taylor dies; Millard Fillmore becomes president • Compromise of 1850 • Nathaniel Hawthorne, *The Scarlet Letter* • First land-grant railroad: Illinois Central • John C. Calhoun dies

1851 Herman Melville, *Moby-Dick* • Maine adopts prohibition • Woman's rights convention in Akron, Ohio • Indiana state constitution excludes free blacks

1852 Franklin Pierce elected president • Harriet Beecher Stowe, *Uncle Tom's Cabin* • Daniel Webster and Henry Clay die

1853 Gadsden Purchase • Nativism increases

1854 Know-Nothings win unexpected victories • Whig party collapses • Republican party founded • Kansas-Nebraska Act • Ostend Manifesto encourages acquisition of Cuba • Henry David Thoreau, *Walden* • High-point of immigration • Railroad reaches Mississippi River

The United States at War

The Mexican government had never recognized the independence of Texas, which Texans claimed as a result of their defeat of Santa Anna in 1836. President James K. Polk raised the stakes by insisting that the border between Texas and Mexico lay at the Rio Grande, not at the Nueces River farther north. Even before the formal annexation of Texas took effect in 1845, Polk ordered American troops under the command of General Zachary Taylor to cross the Nueces.

Polk had his eyes not only on the border with Texas but on larger prizes still: the sale of California and New Mexico. Polk ordered John C. Frémont, leading an army expedition to map rivers within U.S. borders, to California. Frémont, acting on instructions to seize California "in the event of any occurrence," supported the "Bear Flag Rebellion," an armed struggle by American settlers against the Mexican government. Disrupted, the Mexican provinces might be sacrificed more easily and more cheaply to the United States.

The president prepared for war in Texas, seizing on a skirmish between Mexican and American troops north of the Rio Grande as a convenient excuse. He declared that Mexico had started a war when it "invaded our territory and shed American blood on the American soil." Even though northern Whigs continually denounced the war and its motives, Whig congressmen believed they had to support appropriations for the soldiers in the field. The final vote for war was overwhelming, with only fourteen Whig congressmen and two senators opposing the president. While unpopular in New England, the war stirred widespread support in the South and West. Tasked to raise four regiments, enough volunteers to fill fourteen regiments swamped recruiters in Illinois. Thirty thousand men responded in Tennessee, earning the state the nickname the "Volunteer state."

Sixteen hundred American troops under the leadership of Colonel Stephen Kearney took Santa Fe in New Mexico with no casualties late in the summer of 1846. California proved to be a greater struggle, partly because Mexican settlers there put up more of a fight and partly because Frémont—now commanding a volunteer unit comprised of Indian mercenaries, Bear Flaggers, and sharpshooters—provoked fights and stimulated enraged Californios to drive the Americans from Los Angeles. In any case, the American forces won control of California a few months after they had taken New Mexico. The United States Army, under Zachary Taylor and Winfield Scott, achieved a series of victories in Mexico itself in 1846 and 1847, including an impressive amphibious landing at Vera Cruz by Scott's forces that ended in the conquest of Mexico City and "the halls of Montezuma."

Though the Mexicans outnumbered the Americans, the regular U.S. forces enjoyed impressive leadership from their officer corps. The Mexican War familiarized Americans with names like Ulysses S. Grant, Jefferson Davis, and Robert E. Lee. Nevertheless, Polk distrusted his two leading generals—Taylor and Scott—suspecting, correctly, that they might capitalize on their military success to seek the presidency. Soldiers were recruited throughout the nation, but in the 1840s as many as 40 percent of recruits were recent immigrants and 35 percent were illiterate. Conditions of service were harsh, with savage discipline, irregular pay, and poor supply. At any period during the Mexican War, one-third of the men on the muster rolls had deserted, the highest rate of desertion among American wars. Though it lost a high proportion of its men—about 14,000 of the 105,000 who fought—the United States Army proved remarkably effective.

The Consequences of War

Many northerners worried about the expansion of slavery that might accompany victory over Mexico. To put such concerns to rest, David Wilmot, a first-term Pennsylvania Democrat in favor of the war, made a bold move: when a bill to appropriate 2 million dollars to end the war and purchase California and Mexican territory north of the Rio Grande came before Congress in 1846, Wilmot offered a "proviso," or condition, that declared slavery could not be established in any territory the United States might win from Mexico as a result of the war. Still smarting over perceived mistreatment of their interests by Polk and aware of growing rejection of slavery's expansion among their section's voters, northern Democrats saw the proviso as "our *declaration of independence* from southern dictation, arrogance, and misrule." It passed the House by a vote of 83 to 64, with congressmen, with few exceptions, voting along sectional rather than party lines. The Wilmot Proviso eventually went down to defeat and the war proceeded, but from 1846 on, the opponents of slavery increasingly distrusted Polk and southern political leaders.

Henry David Thoreau protested the war with Mexico. As he wrote in his essay "On Civil Disobedience," Thoreau considered the Mexican War "the work of comparatively few individuals using the government as their tool." Thoreau decided to signal his disgust with the American government by refusing to pay his taxes. He spent only one night in jail before his friends paid his taxes for him, but Thoreau's essay proved influential later in American history when protesters looked for inspiration and justification.

~~P~~ICTURING THE PAST ✦ POLITICS & DIPLOMACY

Map 12.1 *War with Mexico, 1846–1847*

View an animated version of this map or related maps at
http://history.wadsworth.com/passages2e.

The war between the United States and Mexico ranged over an enormous territory, though the main battles occurred deep within Mexico. While the navy blockaded the Mexican coastlines, General Winfield Scott landed at Vera Cruz, marched more than 200 miles inland, and seized the capital, Mexico City, forcing a negotiated settlement to the war.

The small military of the United States coped with unprecedented challenges in equipping and supporting an army thousands of miles from supply bases. With the army short nearly 40 percent of authorized strength at the war's beginning, Congress more than doubled the size of the army and called upon the states to provide 50,000 volunteers. Overcoming the challenges of geography and distance, the junior officers and congressmen who managed and supplied U.S. troops in the Mexican War unknowingly conducted a dress rehearsal for similar difficulties during the Civil War.

The Mexican War was the first reported to Americans using telegraph and express riders to speed information of battles back to newspaper editors who competed fiercely to "scoop" their rivals with the latest news. The president reacted furiously to leaks of secret cabinet meetings and the *New York Herald's* publication of the still-secret Treaty of Guadalupe Hidalgo that ended the war. Attempting to frighten editors, Congress confined the *Herald's* reporter for leaking the treaty. His editor responded by releasing the names of congressmen who regularly slipped confidential stories to the press. The government backed down, and political reporting in Washington was changed permanently.

The war with Mexico limped to an end in late 1847 and the beginning of 1848. American troops controlled Mexico City, the Gulf Coast, and all the northern provinces claimed by the United States, but the Mexican government refused to settle on terms of peace. President Polk, General Winfield Scott, and peace commissioner Nicholas Trist bickered over the treaty. Northerners and southerners viewed one another with undisguised distrust and distaste. Some Americans urged Polk to lay claim to all of the conquered country, others insisted that the United States should seize no territory at all from the war, and many, such as John C. Calhoun, driven by racial fears, wanted to limit seized territories to the sparsely settled regions to prevent "the fatal error of placing these colored races on an equality with the white race." Trist, on his own in Mexico, finally signed a treaty in Guadalupe Hidalgo that brought the negotiations to an end in February 1848.

Mexico, for $15 million and the abandonment of American claims against the Mexican government and its people, agreed to sell California, New Mexico, and all of Texas above the Rio Grande. When the treaty finally appeared before Congress for ratification the following month, many doubted that it would pass. Declining popular support for the war derailed plans to send an additional 30,000 troops to occupy northern Mexico. The various cliques, however, swallowed their disagreements long enough to ratify the treaty in March. A prominent newspaper pronounced the treaty "a peace which every one will be glad of, but no one will be proud of." The Mexicans signed the treaty in May and the war finally closed, with Mexico surrendering nearly 600 million acres of territory to the United States.

War and Politics

James K. Polk did not seek reelection in 1848. The Democrats, scrambling to find someone to unite the northern and southern branches of the party, decided on Lewis Cass of Michigan. Cass, a rather colorless man except for his red wig, spoke for the majority of northern Democrats who sympathized with white southerners in their determination to keep black people enslaved. He called for "popular sovereignty," for people in the territories to make their own policies on slavery. Antislavery Democrats walked out of the Democratic convention and called their own convention in Buffalo, New York, where they nominated former president Martin Van Buren as the Free-Soil candidate for the presidency.

Abolitionists who had supported the Liberty party were intrigued to see a candidate who might win a substantial number of votes. Antislavery "Conscience Whigs" also threw their support behind Van Buren. These various groups forged a working alliance for the election of 1848, declaring their solidarity behind the name of the Free-Soil party and its stirring motto: "fight on and fight forever" for "Free soil, free speech, free labor, and free men."

The mainstream Whigs found themselves in an awkward spot, for they had fervently opposed the Mexican War but now sought to capitalize on the popularity of General Zachary Taylor. Taylor had several advantages as a candidate. He had no troubling political past. Though he was a slaveholding planter, he had opposed the war with Mexico before he had been sent there to lead American troops. Just what he thought about anything was quite unclear, but with his lack of connection to recent bitter party squabbles, Taylor appealed to voters in both sections who desired to "see the times of Washington, Monroe, and the younger Adams return, when the government was administered for the benefit of the country not of a faction."

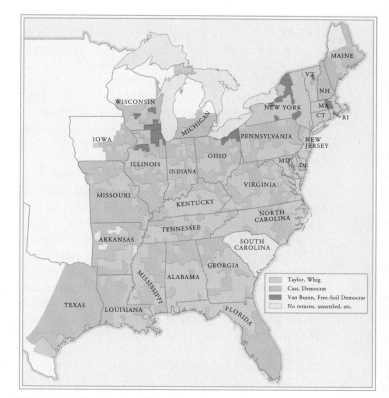

Map 12.2 *The Election of 1848*
The balanced strength of the two-party system across the entire country was demonstrated by this election, in which the candidates won northern and southern states in almost equal numbers.

Taylor won the election in the electoral college, but the popular vote revealed little consensus. Taylor, with 1,360,000 votes, won eight slave states and seven free ones, while Cass won eight free states and seven slave-holding ones, with 1,220,000 votes. Although the Free-Soilers' prospects as a third party appeared bleak, Van Buren came in second in several important states and his vote total was large enough to gain the respect of northern Democrats and send twelve men to Congress.

AMERICANS ON THE MOVE

Americans moved in massive numbers in the years around 1850. As the economy improved, transportation developed, boundaries became settled, and gold beckoned, people flooded to the states of the old Northwest and the old Southwest as well as to Texas, Oregon, and California. The suffering of Ireland and political conflict within Germany drove millions across the Atlantic, filling the cities and farms of the East.

Rails, Sails, and Steam

The late 1840s and early 1850s saw the emergence of the fastest-growing rail lines and the fastest ships in the world. Private investors poured tens of millions of dollars into rail expansion. The federal government aided railroads with free surveys and vast grants of land. The major cities of the eastern seaboard competed against one another to attract as many rail lines as possible. Owners of mines and factories subsidized new railroads, as did Wall Street speculators and investors from Great Britain.

Railroads proved more important for some parts of the country than for others. Railroads flourished in New England and New York, where the density of population and manufacturing permitted the new technology to work most efficiently. Midwestern states such as Ohio, Illinois, and Indiana also showed themselves well-suited to the railroads. Chicago had no railroads at all in 1850, but by 1860 twelve lines converged in the city. Three of those lines stretched from Chicago all the way to New York City; a trip that had taken ten days before the railroad now took only a day and a half. Daily, 120 trains moved in and out of Chicago, some hauling as many as forty cars loaded with freight.

Rural areas as well as cities immediately felt the effects of the railroad. Farmers now found it profitable to ship their produce to a city a hundred miles away. Previously, crops spoiled or were weather damaged in transit, or the cost and hazards of the journey eliminated the profit. Farmers specialized, becoming dairymen, veg-etable growers, and fruit producers. Corn, wheat, hogs, and cattle flowed out of Ohio, Illinois, Indiana, and Wisconsin. The older farms of New England, New York, and Pennsylvania turned to specialty products such as cheese, maple sugar, vegetables, and cranberries. These products rode the railroad tracks to market, tying countryside and city together. In 1843, Margaret Fuller noted that Chicago and Buffalo, linking the West and the Erie Canal system, were the "two correspondent valves that open and shut all the time, as the life-blood rushes from east to west, and back again from west to east."

In the South, still recovering from failed improvement schemes and loan repudiation after the economic crises of the late 1830s, railroad building trailed off in the 1840s. While spending levels did not match that of the North, states such as Virginia aggressively pursued rail construction beginning in 1847, and had spent over $15 million dollars by 1860 in loans to corporations and the building of two state-owned lines. North Carolina reversed decades of opposition to state supported improvements in 1849, building a major line and subsidizing plank roads, private rail lines, and navigational aids. With an uneven and fragmented system of railroads, most southern commerce and passengers relied instead on the steamboats that plied the Mississippi and other major rivers. The riverboats grew in size, number, and ornateness throughout the period. The 1850s marked the glory days of these riverboats, with cotton bales stacked on every square inch of deck.

Elsewhere, packet steamships carried mail, freight, and passengers up and down the eastern seaboard and over the Great Lakes. Over 57 million newspapers, pamphlets, and magazines and nearly 48 million letters crisscrossed the nation in 1847. Beginning in 1848, Americans could count on regular steam travel between New York and Liverpool, England. These innovations in transportation, exciting as they were, came at a steep cost. "I never open a newspaper that does not contain some account of disasters and loss of life. This world is going on too fast. Oh, for the good old days of heavy post-coaches," one diarist observed.

Clipper ships enjoyed a brief but stirring heyday in the late forties and early fifties. Clippers used narrow hulls and towering sails to attain speeds that had yet to be reached by any other sailing vessels of their size. They sailed from New York to San Francisco, all the way around South America, in less than a hundred days. Although they were to be displaced after 1855 by uglier and more efficient steamships, for a few exciting years the clipper ships thrived on the high prices, small cargoes, long voyages, and the desperate need for speed fueled by remarkable discoveries in California.

*P*ICTURING THE PAST✦ECONOMICS & TECHNOLOGY

CLIPPER SHIP

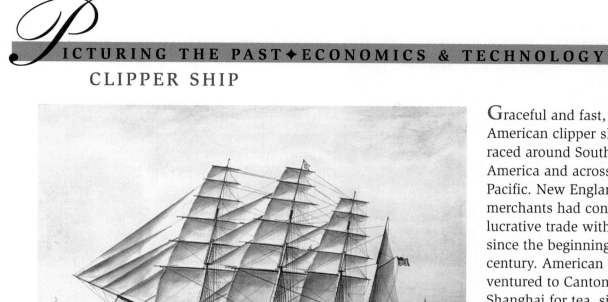

The Granger Collection, New York

Graceful and fast, American clipper ships raced around South America and across the Pacific. New England merchants had conducted lucrative trade with Asia since the beginning of the century. American ships ventured to Canton and Shanghai for tea, silks, furs, ginseng, and glassware. In 1852, reflecting the growth of Asian trade, over 150 various types of vessels rested at anchor in Honolulu. These wooden ships with towering expanses of canvas sails were the fastest craft of their day. Experiments with steam power and iron hulls would eclipse the great clipper ships by the 1860s, but their beauty and speed, preserved in memory and in thousands of contemporary prints and paintings, lingered even after they were replaced by more economical ships that carried larger cargoes.

The Gold Rush

The natives of California had long known of the gold hidden in the rocks and creeks of that vast territory. White American settlers, too, had found gold deposits in the early 1840s. But it was a discovery in January of 1848 that changed everything.

In 1839, John Sutter had emigrated from Switzerland to the area that became Sacramento, where he established a large fort, trading post, and wheat farm. Sutter hired a carpenter named James Marshall to build a mill on the American River. While working on the project, Marshall happened to notice "something shining in the bottom of the ditch." He realized that the nugget, about half the size of a pea, was gold. Sutter, Marshall, and the other men on the place tried to keep the find a secret, but word leaked to San Francisco. There, sailors abandoned their ships, soldiers deserted their barracks, and clerks left their shops to look for gold along the American River. Newspapers stopped publishing and

local governments shut down as Mexicans, Indians, and Americans in California rushed to the foothills. By the end of 1848, such men had gathered nuggets and dust worth about $6 million.

Back east, people remained calm, even skeptical, about the discovery until 230 ounces of almost pure gold went on display in the War Department in Washington and the president confirmed, in his State of the Union address in December 1848, that "the accounts of the abundance of gold in that territory are of such extraordinary character as would scarcely command belief." The gold rush began: "The coming of the Messiah, or the dawn of the Millennium could not have excited anything like the interest," one newspaper marveled. By the end of 1849, over 700 ships carrying over 45,000 easterners sailed to California. Some of the ships went around South America; others transported their passengers to the Isthmus of Panama, which they crossed by foot and canoe.

A diverse population of men rushed to the California goldfields in 1849. Recent immigrants from China worked alongside Indians, whites, and African Americans.
California History Section, California State Library

About 55,000 settlers followed the overland trails cut across the continent. Some traveled alongside the continuing stream of settlers to Oregon; others followed trails directly to the goldfields from destinations as far south as Mexico. Whether they went by sea or land, the participants in the gold rush were quite different from other immigrants to the West. The "forty-niners" tended to be either single men or groups of men from the same locality. Most of the men who flooded into California had little interest in settling there permanently. They intended to find their share of the gold and move on. Once in California, men of all classes, colors, and nations worked feverishly alongside one another in the streams and mountainsides. Disease and miserable living conditions hounded them, sending thousands to their deaths. Others, like Ramón Navarro of Argentina, kept diaries to record their wild swings of riotous wealth and desperate poverty punctuated by violence in the boomtowns of California. Like the vast majority of miners, after three years Navarro found wealth elusive and returned to South America no richer than when he arrived.

When some Chinese men returned home from California flush with American riches and stories of the "Golden Mountain," the fever spread in Asia. About 70 percent of the Chinese immigrants came from Guang-

dong Province, where many peasants and artisans had become impoverished and desperate enough to launch the dangerous journey. Young men, in particular, thought California might offer a way to attain the wealth they needed to acquire a farm and a wife back in China. Migrants could buy tickets from brokers on credit, with high interest. Upon their arrival in California, the Chinese immigrants discovered that they had to borrow yet more money from Chinese merchants in San Francisco to be transported to the goldfields. The miners worked continuously in hopes of paying off that debt, but the costs seemed worth the potential reward.

California held hope for African Americans, too. Most of the black migrants to California left from the coastal cities of New England. California beckoned with the promise of an American West where color really might not matter so much. Although abolitionists, black and white, warned that even California might not be safe for black migrants, several thousand African Americans decided to take the chance.

Whatever their race, few miners discovered a fortune. The average miner in 1848 found about an ounce of gold a day, worth around $20, or about twenty times what a laborer back east made with a daily wage. As the number of competing miners skyrocketed over the next few years, however, the average take declined until it reached about $6 a day in 1852. Mining became more mechanized, and soon the biggest profits went to companies that assaulted the riverbeds and ravines with battalions of workers, explosives, and crushing mills.

Although miners of every background went bust, California as a whole flourished. Towns appeared wherever people gathered to look for the gold. Men who tired of mining turned to farming instead, or teaching school or building houses. The largest fortunes were made supplying the miners. Men such as Levi Strauss, a dry goods salesman from New York, created tough denim jeans and Collis P. Huntington, later founder of the Central Pacific Railroad, met arriving ships and bought all the shovels on board for marked-up sale to miners. San Francisco was the big winner: by 1850, it had grown into a brash and booming city of 35,000 diverse residents.

The Mormon Migration

A different kind of westward movement was already in full force as the California gold rush got underway. These migrants were members of the Church of Jesus Christ of Latter-day Saints, or Mormons. In the face of relentless persecution, Joseph Smith, the founder of the church, had led his flock to Illinois. There they established the town of Nauvoo, which by the mid-1840s had become the largest city in Illinois with over 15,000 people. But conflict erupted when Smith decreed that

Ships filled the harbor of the small town of San Francisco as "forty-niners" descended on nearby goldfields.
The Granger Collection, New York

polygamy was God's will, that men within the church would marry several wives, and he created the Nauvoo Legion, an armed force to protect his followers. When Smith ordered the destruction of a Mormon press that printed a poster condemning polygamy, the paper's owners signed warrants for his arrest. In June 1844, a mob of non-Mormons broke into the jail where Smith was being held and killed both him and his brother.

After struggle among the elders, Brigham Young, a young loyalist of Joseph Smith, emerged as the new leader of the Mormons. Young decided to move to a place beyond the reach of the Mormons' many enemies. Young knew about the Great Salt Lake, a place cut off from the east by mountains and from the west and south by deserts. The Mormons abandoned Nauvoo in the spring of 1846 as anti-Mormons pounded the town with cannon, destroying the Great Temple. In a well-coordinated migration, 15,000 Mormons moved in stages to the Great Salt Lake. When they first arrived, in 1847, the valley presented a daunting picture of rock and sagebrush, but the settlers irrigated the land, turning it into a thriving community.

When frosts, insects, and drought ruined much of the crop in the spring of 1848, Young announced that the Mormons would pool their labor and their resources even more than before. They designed an ambitious city with wide streets surrounding a temple that would "surpass in grandeur of design and gorgeousness of decoration all edifices the world has yet seen." Young concentrated control of the city and its farms in his own hands and in those of his fellow church leaders.

As some non-Mormons settled at the Great Salt Lake, Young decided that a form of government other than the church must be established. He oversaw the creation of a state called "Deseret," a Mormon term meaning "honeybee." The Mormons began a successful campaign to attract new converts from Europe, Asia, and Latin America. In 1849, the residents of Deseret, with Brigham Young as territorial governor, petitioned Congress for admission into the Union as a new state—a status it was not to achieve for another half century.

Although polygamy was practiced by no more than 15 percent of Mormons, in 1852 the church decreed that plural marriage was a fundamental church doctrine. The pronouncement provoked outrage across the country and led President Buchanan to order the military to prepare for an attack on Salt Lake City.

Persecuted in Illinois in the 1840s, the Mormons launched a mass migration to the Great Salt Lake in the state they called "Deseret."
Mormon Panormana Eighteen/Crossing the Mississippi on the Ice, by C. C. A. Christensen © Courtesy Museum of Art, Brigham Young University, All rights reserved

The High Tide of Immigration

Even as Americans moved west, a vast immigration from Ireland surged into the eastern United States. Irish immigration was not new; about a million people had left Ireland for the United States between 1815 and 1844. But the situation in Ireland changed much for the worse beginning in 1845, when a blight struck healthy potato fields, turning the leaves black almost overnight and filling the air with "a sickly odor of decay." This, the Great Potato Famine, which would last for nearly a decade, destroyed the basic food for most of the Irish people. Over a million people died; another 1.8 million fled to North America. In all, about a fourth of the island's population departed, with more people leaving in the eleven years after 1845 than in the preceding 250 years combined.

The Irish emigrants tended to be young, single, poor, unskilled, and Catholic; they came over in the dead of winter, with virtually no money or property. Although some Irish immigrants spread throughout North America, most congregated in the cities of the North and Midwest. They lived from day to day on whatever money they could earn. Most men worked on docks, others in canal and railroad construction; women worked as domestics and as unskilled laborers in textile mills. Desperately poor and widely despised, the Irish figured prominently in arrest reports and on penitentiary rolls.

The high tide of Irish immigration occurred just before the peak of German immigration. Over a million Germans came to America between 1846 and 1854, many of them dislocated by a failed revolution in Germany in 1848. The Germans tended to be farmers who brought some money with them and established farms in the Midwest. The Germans, more than the Irish, were divided by wealth, generation, politics, regional background, and religion. Combined, the Irish and German immigrants accounted for almost 15 percent of the entire population of the United States.

Immigration to the United States, 1820–1860

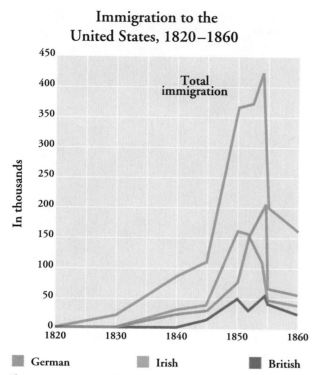

Chart 12.1 *Immigration from Europe*
The number of immigrants from Ireland grew markedly in the late 1840s and early 1850s as a result of the Great Potato Famine. German immigration reached its peak a few years later as political turmoil erupted there.

Hounded by poverty, Irish people gathered in their villages in search of transportation to America in the late 1840s and early 1850s.
The Granger Collection, New York

THE QUEST FOR PERFECTION

The late 1840s and early 1850s, though relatively peaceful and prosperous, led a number of people to resist the drift of American life. Some became so disenchanted that they established utopian communities where they could experiment with alternative ways of organizing labor, power, and sexuality. Others launched a crusade for woman's rights.

Perfect Communities

Most of the hundred or so utopian communities created in the United States between the Revolution and the Civil War were founded in the 1840s. Some communities were secular in origin and some religious. They all insisted that people truly dedicated to social improvement had to flee corruption and compromise. Though several prophets and leaders emigrated from Europe to the New World in hopes of establishing religious utopias, most of the idealistic communities grew directly from American origins.

The most notorious American communal experiment emerged in 1848. It was in that year that John Humphrey Noyes and his 250 followers created the Oneida Association in upstate New York. Noyes had become convinced that it was possible for humans to be "perfected," made free of sin. Most controversial, he argued that people in a state of perfection should not be bound by conventional monogamous marriages; all belonged to one another sexually in "complex marriage." He gathered a small group of disciples around him who put such beliefs into action, practicing birth control by having males withdraw during intercourse.

Oneida experimented not only with sex but also with economic cooperation. Everyone performed the full range of labor. The women of the group cut their hair, wore pantaloons rather than skirts, and played sports with their male compatriots. Unlike other utopian communities, Oneida focused its energies on manufacturing rather than farming. The community produced an improved and profitable steel animal trap. Later, Oneida transformed itself into a profitable business corporation specializing in silverware.

The utopian communities testified to the freedom the United States offered. People took advantage of the isolation offered by the enormous space of the young country to experiment with communities based on religious, sexual, or philosophical principles. The proliferation of such communities also testified, however, to

This antislavery meeting of 1850, like many others of this era, brought together men and women, blacks and whites, in a common cause.
The J. Paul Getty Museum, Los Angeles

John Humphrey Noyes founded the Oneida community in upstate New York, proclaiming sexual freedom in "complex marriage."
The Granger Collection, New York

how full of longing many Americans seemed for communal relations in a society changing from the influences of immigration, technological advances, and political conflict.

Woman's Rights

The seeds for the organized movement for woman's rights in the United States had been planted in 1840, when women attending the World's Anti-Slavery Convention in London, England, found themselves consigned to seats in a separate roped-off area. One of the delegates was Elizabeth Cady Stanton. Listening to the debates over the place of women in antislavery, Stanton felt "humiliated and chagrined, except as these feelings were outweighed by contempt for the shallow reasoning of the opponents and their comical pose and gestures." Stanton discovered an important ally at the London meeting: Lucretia Mott, a devout Quaker and feminist. The two women vowed that they would start a movement back in the States for woman's rights, but they did not soon find the opportunity they sought. Stanton devoted her time to raising her family in Boston. In 1847, she moved with her family to Seneca Falls, New York.

While living in Seneca Falls, Stanton grew frustrated with the narrowness of life in a small town and the limitations placed on women there. Meeting with Lucretia Mott again, Stanton told her friend how miserable she had become. The two women joined with three of Mott's Quaker friends to plan a convention in July in Seneca Falls, although only Mott had had any experience in organizing a reform meeting. Stanton recalled that they "felt as helpless as if they had been suddenly asked to construct a steam engine."

Casting about for a way to express their grievances most effectively, and rejecting the "reports of Peace, Temperance, and Anti-Slavery" as "too tame and pacific for the inauguration of a rebellion such as the world had never before seen," they decided to model their "Declaration of Rights and Sentiments" on the Declaration of Independence. It began with a ringing statement: "The history of mankind is a history of repeated injuries and usurpations on the part of man toward woman, having in direct object the establishment of an absolute tyranny over her." The Declaration demanded the right to vote and insisted on woman's full equality with men in every sphere of life, including property rights, education, employment, divorce, and in court. The organizers worried about how many people might attend the meeting—held in an obscure town during a busy season for farmers—but over a hundred people came, including a considerable number of men. Of those

Elizabeth Cady Stanton, one of the founders of the woman's rights movement, about the time of the Seneca Falls Convention of 1848.
Women's Rights National Historical Park, Courtesy of Seneca Falls Historical Society

Sojourner Truth, a former slave from New York, embodied for many people the pride and strength of black women, for she spoke out for both her gender and her race.
The Granger Collection, New York

men the most prominent was Frederick Douglass. Douglass's newspaper, the *North Star,* was one of the few papers to give the convention a positive notice.

The organizers of the Seneca Falls Convention succeeded in their major role: getting Americans to talk about woman's rights. Word of the Declaration spread among the many women's groups working in other reform organizations. Stanton, Mott, and their allies determined that they would hold a convention each year to keep the momentum going.

At the Akron meeting in 1851 a black woman spoke. She had escaped slavery in New York in 1827 and supported her family by working as a domestic. In 1843, she had a vision in which she was commanded to carry the word of God; she renamed herself "Sojourner Truth." In Akron, Truth celebrated women. "I have plowed and reaped and husked and chopped and mowed, and can any man do more than that?" she asked. The campaign for woman's rights developed a complex relationship to abolition and to

African Americans. The movement might have offered a rare opportunity for women such as Sojourner Truth to be heard, but white woman's rights advocates generally phrased their demands for equal rights in terms of education and refinement that neglected black women and their needs.

Not all activist women, moreover, dedicated themselves to woman's rights. More conservative women devoted their energies to acquiring public funds for orphanages, shelters for "fallen" women and the poor, using their connections to important men in state legislatures, on city boards, and in prosperous businesses to raise money and garner support. They asked for laws to criminalize seduction and to change property laws, to oppose Indian removal, restrict slavery, support colonization of free blacks in Africa, and stop the sale of liquor. They often proved successful

"Declaration of Sentiments" of the Woman Suffrage Movement, 1848

Sixty-eight women and thirty-two men signed this declaration, produced at Seneca Falls in 1848. Modeled on the Declaration of Independence, this document provided a touchstone for the woman's movement throughout the rest of the century and beyond.

The history of mankind is a history of repeated injuries and usurpations on the part of man toward woman, having in direct object the establishment of an absolute tyranny over her. To prove this, let facts be submitted to a candid world.

He has never permitted her to exercise her inalienable right to the elective franchise.

He has compelled her to submit to laws, in the formation of which she had no voice.

He has withheld from her rights which are given to the most ignorant and degraded men—both natives and foreigners.

Having deprived her of this first right of a citizen, the elective franchise, thereby leaving her without representation in the halls of legislation, he has oppressed her on all sides.

He has made her, if married, in the eye of the law, civilly dead.

He has taken from her all right in property, even to the wages she earns.

He has made her, morally, an irresponsible being, as she can commit many crimes with impunity, provided they be done in the presence of her husband. In the covenant of marriage, she is compelled to promise obedience to her husband, he becoming, to all intents and purposes, her master—the law giving him power to deprive her of her liberty, and to administer chastisement.

He has so framed the laws of divorce, as to what shall be the proper causes, and in case of separation, to whom the guardianship of the children shall be given, as to be wholly regardless of the happiness of women—the law, in all cases, going upon a false supposition of the supremacy of man, and giving all power into his hands.

After depriving her of all rights as a married woman, if single, and the owner of property, he has taxed her to support a government which recognizes her only when her property can be made profitable to it.

He has monopolized nearly all the profitable employments, and from those she is permitted to follow, she receives but a scanty remuneration. He closes against her all the avenues to wealth and distinction which he considers most honorable to himself. As a teacher of theology, medicine, or law, she is not known.

He has denied her the facilities for obtaining a thorough education, all colleges being closed against her.

He allows her in church, as well as state, but a subordinate position, claiming apostolic authority for her exclusion from the ministry, and, with some exceptions, from any public participation in the affairs of the church.

He has created a false public sentiment by giving to the world a different code of morals for men and women, by which moral delinquencies which exclude women from society, are not only tolerated, but deemed of little account in man.

He has usurped the prerogative of Jehovah himself, claiming it as his right to assign for her a sphere of action, when that belongs to her conscience and to her God.

He has endeavored, in every way that he could, to destroy her confidence in her own powers, to lessen her self-respect, and to make her willing to lead a dependent and abject life.

Now, in view of this entire disfranchisement of one-half the people of this country, their social and religious degradation—in view of the unjust laws above mentioned, and because women do feel themselves aggrieved, oppressed, and fraudulently deprived of their most sacred rights, we insist that they have immediate admission to all the rights and privileges which belong to them as citizens of the United States.

Source: Elizabeth Cady Stanton, et al., *History of Woman Suffrage*, Vol. 1 (Rochester, N.Y.: Fowler & Wells, 1889), 58–59.

and effective with these indirect means and saw little need for agitating for the vote for women.

POPULAR CULTURE AND HIGH CULTURE

The ever-growing acceleration of printing presses and railroads in the 1850s meant that Americans enjoyed more access to books, newspapers, plays, and lectures every year. People hungered for education and entertainment of all sorts. Performances of Shakespeare became widely popular, for example, as audiences flocked by the thousands to theaters in places as diverse as Philadelphia, Vicksburg, and San Francisco to see *Hamlet* and *King Lear*. But not all the products of popular culture proved as elevating.

Mass Appeal

Several authors, now forgotten, reached remarkably large audiences with their writing. Some achieved success by playing on the nativism and anti-Catholicism of these years with polemics such as *Maria Monk's Awful Disclosures,* supposedly by one Maria Monk of the Hotel Dieu Nunnery of Montreal. That titillating volume, imagining sordid behavior by priests and nuns, sold over 300,000 copies in the first twenty-five years after its publication in 1836. George Lippard composed a serialized melodrama entitled *The Quaker City; or the Monks of Monk Hall, A Romance of Philadelphia Life, Mystery, and Crime.* It sold 60,000 copies in 1844 and at least 10,000 copies annually for ten years. Lippard paraded the worst aspects of American life in order to stir his fellow citizens to reform them; instead, he merely entertained them.

Other authors used the new capacities of mass printing to produce an ever-growing flood of self-help books. Catherine Beecher reprinted an edition of her *Treatise on Domestic Economy* every year in the 1840s and into the 1850s. The book offered a comprehensive guide to women on how to live their lives in the new domestic world, providing tips on topics as diverse as etiquette and how to wash feathers (carefully). The book was more than a how-to compilation, however; it told women that their work stood at least equal in importance to the work their husbands did outside the home.

One of the most influential books of the era bore the intriguing title of *Ten Nights in a Bar-Room.* In that book, first published in 1854 and eventually selling more than 400,000 copies, Timothy Shay Arthur described how the weakness of drink dragged down not only the main characters who wasted their nights in a bar, but also their families, their neighborhoods, and even "a nation of drunkards."

In their popular reading, Americans showed themselves both excited and frightened by the large social changes through which they were living. Whether the books fed fear and suspicion or offered strategies for dealing with the new challenges—or both—Americans liked stories told in bold colors.

Hawthorne, Melville, and Whitman

While popular authors dealt with the changes around them in melodramatic and obvious ways, more enduring writers crafted literature of greater subtlety. Yet the books these more gifted writers produced were very much attuned to their time and place. Nathaniel Hawthorne's *The Scarlet Letter* and Herman Melville's *Moby-Dick* were ironic, dark, and complex allegories, but Walt Whitman's *Leaves of Grass* evoked a determinedly hopeful vision. All three captured a key part of the American mood in the 1850s. Their lives as well as their work bore the unmistakable marks of the times in which they lived.

Nathaniel Hawthorne's father died at sea and left his family to do the best it could with limited resources. Hawthorne went to Bowdoin College in Maine and

A writer deeply engaged with the history of his native New England, Nathaniel Hawthorne wove powerful allegorical stories of sin and regret such as The Scarlet Letter.
The Granger Collection, New York

Herman Melville became famous as a writer of sea stories but found little public interest in his 1852 masterpiece, Moby-Dick.
© Bettmann/Corbis

Walt Whitman, exuberant poet of New York and America, gloried in his connection to common people.
The Granger Collection, New York

then returned to his mother's home and set up as a writer. Quiet and ambitious, he did not marry until he was thirty-eight years old. He read almost indiscriminately, gulping down popular crime fiction as well as the latest literary products of Europe. Though he himself was not morose, Hawthorne was fascinated by the lingering consequences of sin. He turned to the history of New England as the setting for his best work, finding there an allegory for the struggles of his own age.

Hawthorne became an active supporter of the Democratic party. He wrote for the Democratic papers and won a job in the Salem customs house. Hawthorne's political experiences in the late 1840s embittered him, however, for his Whig opponents not only sought to remove Hawthorne from his post but also charged him with corruption. It was at this point that Hawthorne wrote *The Scarlet Letter,* a symbolic story about revenge and its costs. Though set in the colonial era, the novel opened with a biting portrayal of the Salem customs house and its petty (Whig) politicians. The novel propelled Hawthorne into literary fame.

After the arrival of Hawthorne's long-delayed prosperity, he and his family moved to Lenox, Massachusetts. There he met a younger writer, one who admired Hawthorne for his willingness to write complicated stories of guilt. The young author was Herman Melville. He had left school at the age of fifteen, tried his hand at writing, but, in need of work that paid better and more certainly, went to sea. His experiences gave him the subjects for most of his writing. His first two books, *Typee* and *Omoo,* adventure stories of the sea, did quite well. But Melville was not satisfied to write such books; he envisioned nothing less than an American epic.

Melville's masterpiece, about a ship captain's search for the great white whale "Moby-Dick," created a peculiarly American idiom: part Old Testament, part adventure story, part how-to book, part encyclopedia. Good and evil swirled together in *Moby-Dick.* Unlike *The Scarlet Letter, Moby-Dick,* published in 1852, did not do well on the market. Melville, disenchanted, made his work more cynical and biting. His novel *The Confidence-Man,* published six years after *Moby-Dick,* dwelt on the swindling, corruption, and self-deception that seemed at the heart of the United States in the 1850s. Few people at the time noticed Melville's bold experiments and he gradually fell silent.

Walt Whitman also labored on an epic work, *Leaves of Grass*, throughout the early 1850s. The collection of poems reflected America at mid-century in all its diversity, roughness, innocence, and exuberance. This poetry included everything and everyone, speaking in a language stripped of classical allusion and pretension. As Whitman wrote in the preface to this book, anyone who would be a poet in the mid-nineteenth century must "flood himself with the immediate age."

Whitman took the raucous city of New York as his subject. For him, cities were frontiers, full of democracy and possibility. Whitman participated fully in the life of the city, writing as a partisan Democratic journalist, running a shop, working as a building contractor, spending days in the public library, moving from one editing job to another, attending boisterous political meetings—all the while jotting notes for a new kind of epic poetry taking shape in his head.

As he invented a poetical style to match his kaleidoscopic vision of American life, Walt Whitman also invented an image of himself as the poet who would take in and express everything. Both his life and his poem would be "A Song of Myself." Whitman's book was literally self-made; in 1855 he set some of the type and hired friends—printers of legal work—to publish the book for him.

Leaves of Grass came out to no public recognition whatsoever. Whitman sent a few copies to people he admired, however, including Ralph Waldo Emerson. The reply could not have been more heartening: "I find it the most extraordinary piece of wit and wisdom that America has yet contributed." But most readers of the book, including several leading literary figures who read it on Emerson's recommendation, considered it vulgar, even obscene, shapeless, and crude. The hopeful words of *Leaves of Grass* soon became lost in years when a darker vision of the United States prevailed.

SLAVERY AND A NEW CRISIS IN POLITICS

The decade of the 1850s began with many signs of change and progress. The economy kicked into high gear. People flooded to the recently acquired territories of California and Oregon as well as to the upper and lower Mississippi region. Clipper ships, steamships, and railroads expanded their reach. Abolitionists, perfectionists, and feminists worked for the improvement of American society. Despite the generally positive turn of events, however, a persistent undercurrent of fear and anxiety wore at even the most privileged Americans.

The Crisis of 1850

Some of Americans' anxiety emanated from the new golden land of California, where lawlessness became rampant. The men who had left everything back east or in Europe to come to the goldfields showed little respect for the property rights—and even lives—of the Mexicans, Indians, or white men who were there before. In the eyes of many, anarchy threatened if California could not form a government quickly. As gold fever spread, the military governor urged the president to grant the territory a government as soon as possible. A territorial convention created such a government in 1849, helping to restore order, but one of the provisions of the new constitution created great disorder of another kind back in the United States. The new constitution declared that "neither slavery nor involuntary servitude . . . shall ever be tolerated in this state."

This straightforward statement exacerbated conflicts that had been brewing in Washington ever since the Wilmot Proviso three years earlier. White southerners of both parties considered the admission of a free California a grave threat to their own status in the Union, giving the Senate a free-labor majority. John C. Calhoun, the most vocal and extreme spokesman for the South, urged his fellow white southerners to band together. If they did not cooperate, Calhoun argued, they would be overwhelmed by the numbers and the energy of the free states of the North and the West. Southern congressmen talked of commercial boycotts, even of secession.

Southern Whigs had put Zachary Taylor forward for the presidency in 1848, assuming that, as a southerner himself, he would support the expansion of slavery. Wishing to avoid further rancorous debates over slavery in Congress, Taylor chose to send an agent secretly to California urging local leaders to design their government and submit their plan to Congress. To the disbelief and disgust of southerners, Taylor urged that California be admitted as it wished to be admitted, without slavery. But Taylor's support of the proposed California constitution unleashed a bitter debate in Congress. White southerners argued that to deny the South an equal representation in the Senate was to risk war between North and South. To give in on California was to lose the sectional balance on which their very safety rested. The most aggressive white southerners wanted to go on the offensive before northerners in Congress had time to act; in October 1849, they called a convention of the southern states to meet in Nashville in June of 1850.

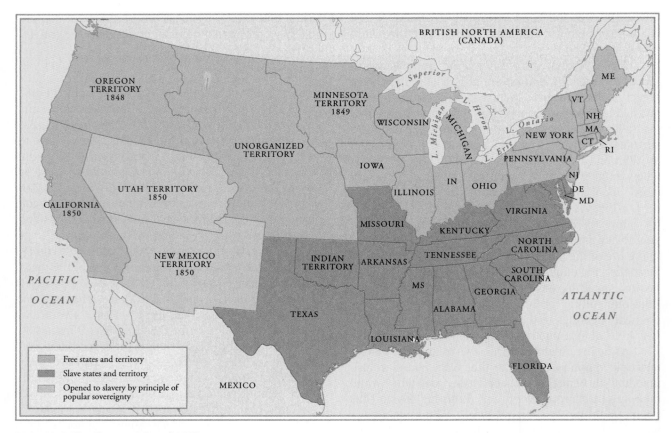

Map 12.3 *The Compromise of 1850*
This compromise, the result of elaborate and bitter negotiation, brought California into the Union as a free state, leaving the territories of Utah and Mexico open to the (slim) possibility of slavery.

A fabled session of Congress occurred as a result. In January 1850, the three most famous legislators of the first half of the nineteenth century—John C. Calhoun, Henry Clay, and Daniel Webster—assumed leading roles in the great national drama. Calhoun played the role of the southern protagonist, delivering fiery warnings and denunciations on behalf of the white South; Clay reprised the role of the Great Compromiser that had made him famous in the Missouri controversy thirty years earlier; Webster played the role of the conciliator, persuading the angry North to accept, in the name of the Union, the South's demand for respect. Clay and Webster rehearsed their lines in a private meeting before Clay presented his bill to Congress.

Clay's bold plan addressed in one inclusive "omnibus" bill all the issues tearing at the United States on the slavery issue. Balance the territory issue, he suggested, with other concerns that angered people about slavery. Leave slavery in the District of Columbia, but abolish the slave trade there. Provide a stronger law to capture fugitive slaves in the North, but announce that Congress had no power to regulate the slave trade among the states. Admit California as a free state, but leave undetermined the place of slavery in the other territories won from Mexico. Advocates on both sides hoped the compromise would buy time for passions to cool.

Clay made his plea with his characteristic eloquence and power. The eloquence appeared to have little effect, however, for the same bitter arguments went on for months after Clay's speech. In March, Calhoun, too ill to speak himself, wrote an address in which he conceded nothing; three days later, Webster claimed to speak "not as a Massachusetts man, nor as a northern man, but as an American." Webster found himself widely denounced in the North as a traitor, buckling under to the slave mongerers. Moreover, President Zachary Taylor—like Clay and Webster, a Whig—refused to support their compromise. William Seward of New York denounced the compromise as "radically wrong and essentially vicious."

The Nashville Convention of southern states, meanwhile, turned out to be ineffective, since six states sent no representatives, and the representatives who did come disagreed on the proper course of action. While a South Carolinian argued that "unite, and you shall form one of the most splendid empires in which the sun ever shone," most delegates still believed slavery was best preserved by remaining in the Union. In nine days of deliberations, the convention took no stand on the pending compromise; the representatives waited to see its provisions.

The omnibus bill appeared doomed. A series of unanticipated events, however, aided the compromise. Both Calhoun and Taylor died a few months apart. Millard Fillmore was now president, and Fillmore supported the omnibus bill. Webster resigned to serve as Fillmore's secretary of state, and Clay, after 70 addresses to the Senate defending the omnibus bill, left Washington to recover. Younger, less prominent, members of Congress steered the various components of the compromise through committees and votes. The compromisers were led by Stephen A. Douglas, a promising young Democrat of Illinois. The majority of northern and southern senators and representatives tenaciously voted against one another, but each part of the compromise passed because a small group of conciliatory congressmen from each side worked together. By September the various components of the compromise of 1850 had become law.

The problem of slavery, of course, would not go away merely because of a political compromise. The fugitive slave component of the Compromise of 1850 proved especially troubling. The Fugitive Slave Act directly implicated white northerners and insulted them with blatantly unjust provisions. The commissioners, who were appointed by a federal circuit judge and who decided the fate of black Americans accused of being runaway slaves, for example, received ten dollars if an accused fugitive were returned to his or her master but only five dollars if freed. Marshals and sheriffs could force bystanders to aid in the capture of an accused fugitive; if bystanders refused, they faced a substantial fine or even a jail term. The alleged runaway could not even testify in his or her own defense or call witnesses. Perhaps most horrifying of all was this provision: no matter how many years before slaves had escaped, no matter how settled or respectable they had become, they could be captured and sent back into bondage.

Most northern whites offered no opposition, and many, such as Daniel Webster, considered the law "essential to the peace of the country." Most of the two or three hundred alleged fugitives prosecuted under the law were ruled to be runaways and sent south. But abolitionists raged at the Fugitive Slave Law and they were not alone. Many northerners were furious. Armed opposition to the slavecatchers immediately

PRACTICAL ILLUSTRATION OF THE FUGITIVE SLAVE LAW.

This cartoon ridicules the Fugitive Slave Law that required northerners to help capture and return runaway slaves. It glorifies William Lloyd Garrison but assails Daniel Webster, who voted in favor of the law as part of the Compromise of 1850.
© Corbis

arose in cities across the North; mobs broke into jails to free ex-slaves; one slaveowner who came north to claim his property was shot. Ralph Waldo Emerson spoke for many when he asserted that "as long as men have bowels, they will disobey." The Fugitive Slave Law, far from calming the conflict between North and South, made it more bitter.

African Americans and the White North

The years surrounding the crisis of 1850, ironically, were also the years in which black minstrel shows reached their peak of popularity. The traveling troupes of minstrels offered the strange ritual of white men in blackface simultaneously ridiculing and paying homage to the creativity of African American culture. Although white people of all classes and backgrounds attended the minstrel shows, the quick-paced, humorous, and flashy skits and songs held special appeal for members of the white working class. Over the preceding decades, those workers had seen the value of their labor eroded by mechanization and immigration. In their eyes, the minstrel shows offered both a comforting dramatization of their own racial superiority and a way to associate imaginatively with carefree and fun-loving "black" people.

White northerners revealed their ambivalences about African Americans in other ways as well. Whites

Harriet Beecher Stowe, the author of Uncle Tom's Cabin, *wove Christianity and the domestic ideal into a powerful fable of slavery and its consequences.*
The Granger Collection, New York

Uncle Tom's Cabin *not only helped mobilize the white North's opinions on slavery, but it also proved an immediate and persistent best-seller.*
© Bettmann/Corbis

who argued that the new territory of the West must be free soil frequently insisted on the exclusion of free blacks. Ohio, Indiana, Illinois, and Oregon passed laws barring free blacks from entering or settling within their boundaries. Whites in cities associated black people with poverty and crime while unaware or unconcerned that recent immigrants had displaced blacks from jobs as stevedores, boatmen, and day laborers. A considerable majority of northern whites showed little interest in attending antislavery rallies.

Harriet Beecher Stowe's *Uncle Tom's Cabin or Life Among the Lowly* helped change white attitudes toward African Americans. Stowe had been writing throughout her life, but had not become prominent. In 1849, her infant son died of cholera in Cincinnati; the next year she moved back to New England. There, people talked angrily of the new Fugitive Slave Law. "You don't know how my heart burns within me at the blindness and obtuseness of good people on so very simple a point of morality as this," she wrote to her brother Henry Ward Beecher.

Stowe put her objections to the law and its effects into a story printed serially in a moderate anti-slavery newspaper beginning in June 1851. Stowe based her portrayals of black people on the African Americans she had known in Cincinnati, where they worked for her as domestic servants. They told Stowe of the terrors of being sold south to Louisiana, of their vulnerability to sexual exploitation. Stowe also drew on firsthand narratives of escape. She switched the usual roles of the freedom narratives, however, making a woman—Eliza—the active heroine and a man—Uncle Tom—the one left behind to endure slavery. The love of a mother for her children drove the story. The image of Eliza crossing the partially frozen Ohio River, baby in her arms, grew into one of the most powerful and familiar scenes of American culture.

The novel's 300,000 editions drove eight steam presses night and day to meet the demand in 1852 alone and eventually sold over 6.5 million copies in the United States and around the world, the best-selling novel of the nineteenth century. *Uncle Tom's Cabin* became the subject of the most popular play in American history. Readers and theatergoers were shocked at stories of cruelty, violence, and sexual

Harriet Beecher Stowe
Uncle Tom's Cabin, *1852*

Stowe's remarkable novel captured the moral energy of the antislavery movement. In this episode, the evil New England-born Simon Legree is confronted by the unbending Christian strength of Uncle Tom.

"And now," said Legree, "come here, you Tom. You see I telled ye I didn't buy ye jest for the common work; I mean to promote ye and make a driver of ye; and tonight ye may jest as well begin to get yer hand in. Now, ye jest take this yer gal and flog her; ye've seen enough on't to know how."

"I beg Mas'r's pardon," said Tom, "hopes Mas'r won't set me at that. It's what I an't used to—never did—and can't do, no way possible."

"Ye'll larn a pretty smart chance of things ye never did know before I've done with ye!" said Legree, taking up a cowhide and striking Tom a heavy blow across the cheek, and following up the infliction by a shower of blows.

"There!" he said, as he stopped to rest, "now will ye tell me ye can't do it?"

"Yes, Mas'r," said Tom, putting up his hand to wipe the blood that trickled down his face. "I'm willin' to work night and day, and work while there's life and breath in me, but this yer thing I can't feel it right to do; and, Mas'r, I *never* shall do it—*never!*"

Tom had a remarkably smooth, soft voice, and a habitually respectful manner that had given Legree an idea that he would be cowardly and easily subdued. When he spoke these last words, a thrill of amazement went through everyone; the poor woman clasped her hands and said, "O Lord!" and everyone involuntarily looked at each other and drew in their breath, as if to prepare for the storm that was about to burst.

Legree looked stupefied and confounded; but at last burst forth—

"What! ye blasted black beast! tell *me* ye don't think it *right* to do what I tell ye! What have any of you cussed cattle to do with thinking what's right? I'll put a stop to it! Why, what do ye think ye are? May be ye think ye're a gentleman, master Tom, to be a telling your master what's right and what an't! So you pretend it's wrong to flog the gal!"

"I think so, Mas'r," said Tom, "the poor crittur's sick and feeble; 't would be downright cruel, and it's what I never will do, not begin to. Mas'r, if you mean to kill me, kill me; but as to my raising my hand agin anyone here, I never shall—I'll die first!"

Tom spoke in a mild voice but with a decision that could not be mistaken. Legree shook with anger; his greenish eyes glared fiercely and his very whiskers seemed to curl with passion; but, like some ferocious beast that plays with its victim before he devours it, he kept back his strong impulse to proceed to immediate violence and broke out into bitter raillery.

"Well, here's a pious dog, at last, let down among us sinners!—a saint, a gentleman, and no less, to talk to us sinners about our sins! Powerful, holy crittur, he must be! Here, you rascal, you make believe to be so pious—didn't you never hear out of yer Bible, 'Servants, obey yer masters'? An't I yer master? Didn't I pay down $1,200 cash for all there is inside yer old cussed black shell? An't yer mine, now, body and soul?" he said, giving Tom a violent kick with his heavy boot. "Tell me!"

In the very depth of physical suffering, bowed by brutal oppression, this question shot a gleam of joy and triumph through Tom's soul. He suddenly stretched himself up, and, looking earnestly to heaven, while the tears and blood that flowed down his face mingled, he exclaimed—

"No! no! no! my soul an't yours, Mas'r! You haven't bought it—ye can't buy it! It's been bought and paid for by one that is able to keep it—no matter, no matter, you can't harm me!"

"I can't!" said Legree, with a sneer, "we'll see— we'll see! Here, Sambo, Quimbo, give this dog such a breakin' in as he won't get over this month!"

The two gigantic Negroes that now laid hold of Tom, with fiendish exultation in their faces, might have formed no unapt personification of the powers of darkness. The poor woman screamed with apprehension and all arose as by a general impulse while they dragged him unresisting from the place. . . .

Source: Harriet Beecher Stowe, *Uncle Tom's Cabin* (Boston: J. P. Jewett, 1852), pp. 419–423.

*P*ICTURING THE PAST ✦ SOCIAL & CULTURAL EVENTS

MINSTRELSY

© Bettmann/Corbis

White men in blackface mimicked southern slaves for white audiences in the era, acting out ambivalent feelings of contempt and envy. Minstrelsy centered on comedy, dance, skits, and song. On the eighteenth- and nineteenth-century stage, black characters normally were played by whites who painted their faces black and danced, mimed, and parodied exaggerated sexuality and foppishness to amuse white audiences, many of whom were recent immigrants. Crude racist humor combined with idealized plantation scenes of abundance and sloth to portray blacks as simultaneously foolish and sly, responding to their oppression with bemusement and a dance step. Ironically, black dance styles drawn from Africa would evolve into complex tap routines that became a staple of the American stage. These shows were wildly popular in all sections of the country and created stereotypes of black behavior and comic style that persisted well into the twentieth century in movies, radio, and television.

abuse. Stowe used techniques commonly found in domestic novels—the sanctity of the family, the power of religion, the triumph of endurance—to show that black people had the same feelings as white people.

That *Uncle Tom's Cabin* and minstrel shows reached their peak of popularity at the same time gives some idea of the confusion and ambivalence with which white northerners viewed African Americans in the early 1850s. Stowe's story was based on an antislavery message, but thousands of whites laughed at other whites in blackface. Only events could force northerners to decide what they really thought.

POLITICS IN CHAOS

The same years that saw struggle between the North and the South over race and slavery also saw profound conflicts over other issues. The high tide of immigration in the early 1850s unleashed a political backlash

as nativists organized themselves against the newcomers from Ireland and Germany. Meanwhile, the booming economy drove other Americans to lust for expanded territory beyond the bounds of the continental United States. And an effort by political leaders to quiet struggle between the North and the South by expanding in the West triggered the most violent conflict the nation had yet seen between the forces of slavery and antislavery.

The Know-Nothings

Franklin Pierce, the Democratic candidate for president in 1852, was a northerner friendly to the white South. Pierce's opponent—Winfield Scott—proved to be less impressive despite his fame as a general in the war with Mexico. The death of Henry Clay in 1850 and of Daniel Webster in 1852 left the Whigs adrift and directionless. Pierce crushed Scott in every state except four. "General opinion seems to be that the Whig party is dead and will soon be decomposed into its original elements," one diarist commented in the wake of the election.

Many influential Whigs took the 1852 election as a sign that the Democrats would always succeed by appealing to the lowest common denominator. The real, substantive issues that had originally shaped the two parties—banks, the tariff, and internal improvements—no longer distinguished them from one another. Neither did slavery and sectional issues sharply define the two parties, for each tried to appease voters in both the North and the South. Even the broader cultural orientation of the two parties had blurred in 1852, as the Whigs appealed to the burgeoning foreign-born vote and Protestant nativists grew disgusted with the Whigs.

In the eyes of many white Protestants, the new arrivals, especially from Ireland, appeared impossible to assimilate. "They increase our taxes, eat our bread, and encumber our street," commented one American diarist. The immigrants threatened to drive down wages because they were willing to work for so little. They also threatened to thwart enforced temperance. That movement gained momentum in 1851, when Maine became the first state to enact statewide prohibition of alcohol. The immigrants often received the right to vote in state and local elections soon after they landed, with Irish Catholics supporting the Democratic party and opposing prohibition, while English and German and Irish Protestants supported the Whigs and frequently voted in favor of prohibition.

In the face of such challenges to their values and power, "native Americans" organized against the immigrants. The most powerful manifestation of nativism appeared in New York City in 1849, when Charles Allen founded the Order of the Star Spangled Banner. Its membership was restricted to native-born white Protestants sworn to secrecy. When asked about the order by outsiders, members were instructed to say "I know nothing"—and thus they became popularly known as the "Know-Nothings." The order grew slowly at first, but it drew on deeply held and deepening prejudices.

The Know-Nothings moved into politics in 1854 in a way few expected. Mobilizing as many as 1.5 million adherents organized from local lodges to a national council, they did not announce their candidates beforehand, but rather wrote them in on the ballots, taking incumbents by complete surprise. The Know-Nothings won virtually all the seats in the legislature, the governor's chair, and the entire congressional delegation in Massachusetts with this strategy. By 1855, they dominated New England and displaced the Whigs as the major opponents to the Democrats through the Middle Atlantic states, in much of the South, and in California. Democrat and Whig leaders denounced "the 'Know Nothing' fever" that disrupted the campaigns and strategies of the parties.

THE PROPAGATION SOCIETY.___ MORE FREE THAN WELCOME.

The Know-Nothings played up a fear among Protestant Americans that the Roman Catholic church was invading the United States.
From the Collections of the Library of Congress

No one in the major parties had anticipated such a turn of events. The Whigs, after all, had long attracted the nativists, fervent Protestants, and temperance advocates to which the Know-Nothings now appealed. But these disgruntled voters proved extremely receptive to the Know-Nothing appeal. The Know-Nothings, unlike the Whigs, left control of the party close to the grassroots. They offered a revitalized political party, one more receptive than the Whigs to the anti-Catholic and anti-immigrant desires of its constituents and one that would attack problems rather than compromise on them. Many rural districts voted heavily for the Know-Nothings as a way to get back at the cities that had dominated the major parties for so long. Voters blamed standing politicians for corruption and sought a new organization free from the control of the "wire pullers" who ran campaigns from smoke-filled backrooms. "Thousands flocked into the order, not that they approved its principles," one observer noted, but as "the only chance for restoring the government, from a state of corruption, to comparative health and soundness." For such reasons, the Know-Nothings made strong showings in the South as well as the North.

The appearance of the Know-Nothings reflected a deep-seated change in the American political system. The party system began disintegrating at the local and state level, with the Whigs fading in some states as early as 1852 and in others not until three years later. Voters defected from the Whigs and Democrats to both the Know-Nothing and Free-Soil parties.

A Hunger for Expansion

The same forces of commerce and transportation that tied together the vastly expanded United States in the late 1840s and early 1850s pulled Americans into world affairs. American ships set out not only for England, but also for South America, Asia, Australia, New Zealand, and Tahiti. The ships carried lumber and hides, tea and silks, missionaries and scientists. American whaling ships patrolled the South Pacific, stopping for fuel and food at islands scattered over a vast territory. Some entrepreneurs, such as the American Guano Company, even rushed to mine 200 foot-high mountains of bird droppings piled up on remote Pacific islands. The droppings, called guano, offered a nitrogen-rich fertilizer much in demand on the farms and plantations of the eastern United States. American traders eager to break into the Asian market appeared in Japanese ports.

These exchanges in far-off ports often depended on the Hawaiian Islands as way stations. On a single day in 1852, for example, 131 whaling ships and eighteen merchant ships were tied up in Honolulu. Such trade came at a horrifying cost to the native population because of disease. Over the seventy-five years since the first contact with outsiders in the late eighteenth century, the Hawaiian population had declined from about 300,000 residents to only about 73,000. Around 2,000 foreigners lived in Hawaii by the early 1850s, a good many of them Americans. Though politicians and editors talked of annexing the islands for the United States, opposition on the islands and in Washington postponed any action.

Some well-placed Americans gazed at yet more Mexican territory with covetous eyes, urging the Pierce administration to acquire Baja California and other parts of northern Mexico. Mexico was not interested, though. Proponents of expansion had to settle for much less than they had wanted: after long wrangling, in 1853 the United States paid $15 million for a strip of Mexico to use as a route for a southern transcontinental railroad. This was the Gadsden Pur-

chase, named for the American diplomat who negotiated it. The purchase defined the final borders of the continental United States.

Cuba seemed the most obvious place for further expansion. Many Americans believed that Cuba should be part of the United States. Cuba was rich and growing, its slave trade flourishing even after the slave trade to the United States had ended. Abolitionists and others talked of freeing Cuba both from slavery and from the Spanish, whereas white southerners talked of adding this jewel to the slave empire.

The United States offered to buy Cuba from Spain in 1848, but met a rude rebuff. Franklin Pierce, pressured by the southerners in his party and in his cabinet, in the early 1850s renewed the effort to "detach" Cuba from Spain. American diplomats in Europe created a furor in October 1854 when they clumsily wrote the "Ostend Manifesto," a statement of the policy they wanted the administration to follow: gain Cuba peacefully or by force. When the "manifesto" was leaked to the press, the Pierce administration was widely vilified. London newspapers derided the manifesto as the "pursuit of dishonorable objects by clandestine means." Pierce publicly renounced any intention of taking over Cuba. The movement to expand the United States into the Caribbean came to a temporary halt.

Kansas-Nebraska Lets Loose the Storm

As the Cuban episode revealed, Franklin Pierce proved to be an ineffectual president. The best hope for the Democrats, Stephen A. Douglas determined, was to deflect attention to the West. Douglas called for two kinds of action: organizing the territories of the West, especially the Kansas and Nebraska area, and building a railroad across the continent to bind together the expanded United States with the route running through his home state of Illinois. The two actions were interrelated, for the railroad could not be built through unorganized territory. Partly to get southern votes for the territorial organization and

As this sketch by an American visitor shows, European and Polynesian cultures lived side by side in the capital of Hawaii. Protestant and Catholic churches stand beside consulates and native homes.
Sketch of Honolulu, Oahu, 1840, by James Dwight Dana, Courtesy of Mission Houses Museum Library, Collections of the Hawaiian Mission Children's Society

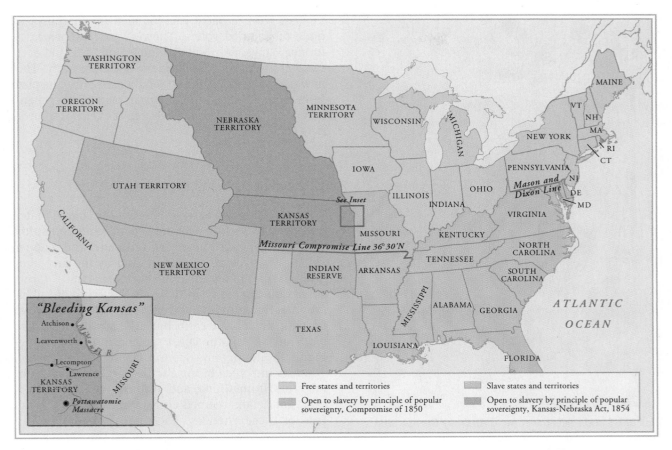

Map 12.4 *Kansas-Nebraska and Slavery*
The Kansas Territory, adjacent to slaveholding Missouri but well north of the Missouri Compromise line, stood as a place both slaveholders and Free-Soilers felt they could claim as their own.

partly because he believed that slavery would not survive in the northern territories, Douglas wrote a bill invalidating the Missouri Compromise line. He proposed that the people of the new territories decide for themselves whether or not their states would permit slaves and slaveholders. Adopting the phrase, "popular sovereignty," Douglas put it forward in the Kansas-Nebraska Bill.

Douglas's plan unleashed political and sectional resentments that had been bottled up by prior compromises. Six prominent Free-Soil senators, including Salmon P. Chase, Charles Sumner, and Joshua Giddings, denounced the plan as a plot by a "Slave Power" to make Nebraska a "dreary region of despotism, inhabited by masters and slaves." Northern ministers publicly protested the pending legislation, while newspapers throughout the North scornfully attacked the proposal. Despite the widespread opposition, however, the opponents of the Kansas-Nebraska Bill could not coordinate their efforts sufficiently to stop its passage.

The fight over Kansas-Nebraska inflamed northern resentment as never before. Many northerners determined that they could no longer trust southerners to keep a bargain and that northerners were no longer obligated to enforce the Fugitive Slave Act because the Kansas-Nebraska Act had nullified the Compromise of 1850. Attempts to arrest and extradite Anthony Burns, a fugitive slave in Boston, created such a turmoil that the mayor called out 1,500 militia to line the streets along the route between the courthouse and the ship that was to take Burns back to slavery in Virginia.

The Kansas-Nebraska Act sparked a chain reaction. It divided the Democratic party across the North; it upset the fragile balance of power between North and South in Congress; it provided a set of common concerns and language to unite disgruntled northern Whigs, Democrats, Free-Soilers, and abolitionists. Northern voters punished Democrats who had supported the Kansas-Nebraska Act as the party

This illustration tells the story of Anthony Burns's sale, escape, arrest, and return to slavery in Virginia. His highly publicized case further inflamed the conflict between the North and the South in the mid-1850s.
© Corbis

lost 66 of the 91 free-state House seats it had gained in 1852. As northern Democrats lost seats, southerners gained control of the party, fueling further resentment of southern dominance. The Know-Nothings took advantage of the widespread disillusionment with the two major parties to campaign against Catholics, immigrants, and corruption issues apparently unrelated to slavery.

Over the next two years the northern political system churned as voters looked for a party that would reflect their concerns and also have a chance of winning power. The Know-Nothings began to fade almost as quickly as they had emerged. They came to seem just another political party led by ambitious politicians who exploited patronage for personal gain. Violent gangs that terrorized immigrants under the Know-Nothing banner alienated many voters, and Know-Nothing legislators proved unable to control or punish Catholics as they had promised.

In 1854, a party was founded in Wisconsin to unite disgruntled voters. The new party appealed to former Whigs, Free-Soilers, Know-Nothings, and even Democrats fed up with their pro-southern party. This new party called itself the "Republican" party. Its platform announced that "no man can own another man" and it would not permit slavery in the territories or in new states.

CONCLUSION

The late 1840s and early 1850s saw the United States energized by victory over Mexico and the acquisition of vast new territories, by railroads and clipper ships, by westward migration, and by the arrival of millions of immigrants. As northern family farms spread during the good times, however, so did plantation agriculture and slavery. The gold of the West brought not only wealth but also lawlessness. The cities of the Atlantic coast seemed full to overflowing with immigrants from Ireland and Germany, whereas the cities of the Pacific burgeoned with immigrants from China and restless men from back east. Politicians seemed corrupt and helpless in the face of these changes. Each political compromise only seemed to make things worse. The parties that had held the country together for a quarter of a century began to buckle under the stress.

Recommended Readings

Anbinder, Tyler. *Nativism and Slavery: The Northern Know-Nothings and the Politics of the 1850s* (1992). Provides a full and balanced account.

Fehrenbacher, Don E. *The Slaveholding Republic: An Account of the United States Government's Relations to Slavery* (2001). Carefully analyzes this troubling issue.

Faragher, John Mack, and Hine, Robert V. *The American West: A New Interpretive History* (2000). A superb synthesis.

Fellman, Michael. *The Unbounded Frame: Freedom and Community in Nineteenth-Century American Utopianism* (1973). A helpful overview of perfectionist communities.

Foos, Paul. *A Short, Offhand, Killing Affair: Soldiers and Social Conflict During the Mexican-American War* (2002). A dark work on a neglected war.

Griffith, Elisabeth. *In Her Own Right: The Life of Elizabeth Cady Stanton* (1984). Tells the compelling story of this crucial leader of the woman suffrage movement.

Hedrick, Joan D. *Harriet Beecher Stowe: A Life* (1994). Gives a detailed portrait of the author of *Uncle Tom's Cabin.*

Lott, Eric. *Love and Theft: Blackface Minstrelsy and the American Working Class* (1993). Provides an original and challenging analysis.

Miller, Kerby A. *Emigrants and Exiles: Ireland and the Irish Exodus to North America* (1985). Contributes a full account of the origins and impact of this migration.

Morrison, Michael. *Slavery and the American West: The Eclipse of Manifest Destiny and the Coming of the Civil War* (1997). Details this complicated story.

Potter, David M. *The Impending Crisis: 1848–1861* (1976). Stands as the best overview of American politics from the wake of the Mexican War to the outbreak of the Civil War.

Reynolds, David S. *Beneath the American Renaissance: The Subversive Imagination in the Age of Emerson and Melville* (1988). A brilliant exploration of the "classic" era of American literature.

Rohrbough, Malcolm J. *Days of Gold: The California Gold Rush and the American Nation* (1997). Offers a fresh and exciting account of its subject.

American Journey Online and InfoTrac College Edition

Visit the source collections at http://ajaccess. wadsworth.com and infotrac.thomsonlearning.com and use the Search function with the following key terms to explore documents, images, audio and video clips, articles, and commentary related to the material in this chapter.

Elizabeth Cady Stanton	Sojourner Truth
Zachary Taylor	Nathaniel Hawthorne
William Lloyd Garrison	Walt Whitman
Uncle Tom's Cabin	Harriet Beecher Stowe
Mormons	Seneca Falls Convention
gold rush	Herman Melville
Fugitive Slave Law	Know-Nothings
Kansas-Nebraska Act	

Additional resources, exercises, and Internet links related to this chapter are available on the American Passages Web site: http://history.wadsworth.com/passages2e

PASSAGES

— 1855 TO 1877 —

Americans of the 1850s had no idea that the Civil War awaited them. They could not imagine that a vast war, larger than any Europe had known, could overwhelm the new republic. New farms and plantations, after all, spread rapidly in expectation of more boom years like the 1850s. Villages and workshops developed throughout the North, while cities, fed by millions of immigrants from Europe, grew at harbors and along railroads and rivers. In the South, cotton and slavery created a per capita income for white southerners higher than that of any country in Europe except England. Slavery, it was clear, would not collapse of its own contradictions any time soon; the institution had never been more profitable. Telegraphs, newspapers, steamboats, and railroads tied the North and South together more tightly every year.

The two sections viewed each other as aggressive and expansionist, intent on making the nation all one thing or another. The North claimed that the slaveholder South would destroy the best government on earth rather than accept the results of a fair election. The white South claimed that the arrogant and greedy North would destroy the nation rather than acknowledge what the Constitution had established. Both sides were filled with righteous rage, accepting violence to gain the upper hand, whether that involved capturing fugitive slaves or applauding John Brown's failed insurrection. Americans could not stop the momentum they had themselves created. Despite desperate efforts at compromise and delay, the war came.

Once the war could no longer be avoided, most people threw themselves into the conflict alongside their neighbors, regardless of whatever doubts they had held before. Confident that the war would be brief, young men on both sides enlisted to teach their enemies a lesson. Both the North and the South proved excellent at war. They innovated freely and successfully, fought relentlessly, discovered effective generals, and mobilized women as well as men. Indeed, the North's strengths and the South's strengths balanced so that the war went on for four years, killing 630,000 people, a proportion of the population equivalent to 5 million people in the United States today and a number larger than the country was ever to sacrifice in another war.

Throughout the conflict, from Lincoln's election to his death, the role of slavery remained both powerful and unclear. Lincoln announced that the war was for Union, not abolition. The Confederacy announced that the war was for independence, not merely slavery. Enslaved Americans in the South, however, forced slavery as an issue on both the Union and the Confederacy, risking their lives to flee to Union camps, undermining plantations and farms. Lincoln and much of the North came to see that ending slavery would end the Confederacy and help redeem the death and suffering. Two hundred thousand black men enlisted as soldiers and played a key role in bringing Union victory.

The North and the South struggled with themselves even as they fought one another. The North broke apart along lines of class, ethnicity, party, and locale. By 1864 a considerable portion of the northern population wanted the war to end, with compromise if necessary. The opponents of Lincoln expected to overwhelm him in the election that fall and even Lincoln shared that expectation. The white South broke apart along lines of class, locale, and gender. Poor soldiers deserted; upcountry communities shielded the deserters and resisted the Confederate government; impoverished white women rioted and resisted. Slaves rushed to the Union army at the first opportunity, every escape weakening the southern economy and Confederate morale.

Events on the battlefield, through 10,000 conflicts large and small, exerted their own logic and momentum. The Union army grew stronger as the Confederate army thinned and weakened. The victories of Grant and Sherman in 1864 destroyed the South's best hope of a negotiated peace. The relentless spread of the Union army throughout the South divided the Confederacy into smaller and smaller pieces, each helpless to aid the other. When Lee's army fell into defeat, the Confederate nation dissolved almost immediately.

Whatever Lincoln's plans for reuniting the nation, those plans ended at Ford's Theater in April of 1865. Lincoln's successor, Andrew Johnson, took the most cautious route possible, limiting the scope of black freedom in every way he could. The white South's resolve, indeed, seemed greater than any power the Union wielded in the South. African Americans struggled to make their freedom real: they mobilized politically, founded churches and schools, and reconstituted families. They demanded rights as Americans and did all they could to secure those rights. Black southerners found many white northern allies but many more white southern enemies who quickly turned to violence, as well as white northerners who supported or tolerated the violence. The years of 1866 and 1867 were full of a promise and a terror no one could have imagined ten years before. In many ways, the Civil War had not yet ended; its consequences had hardly begun.

For the next decade, Reconstruction in the South gradually receded. The process left blacks with greater political rights in law because of the Fourteenth and Fifteenth Amendments, but a more limited role in the day-to-day process of governing. The presidency of Ulysses S. Grant was a disappointment because the hero of the war proved unable to provide effective leadership, sectional reconciliation, or honest government. An economic collapse in 1873 helped the Democrats restore the national political balance and hasten the end of Reconstruction. The disputed election between Rutherford B. Hayes and Samual J. Tilden in 1876 saw the abandonment of black southerners to the rule of those who believed in white supremacy. The Civil War had preserved the Union and abolished slavery, but the unsettled problem of race cast a long shadow into the future.

Sunday Morning in Virginia. *This painting by Winslow Homer chronicled the great hunger of former slaves and their children for the blessings of literacy.*
Winslow Horner, "Sunday Morning in Virginia" 1877 Cincinnati Art Museum, John M. Emerey Funds Acc. 1924. 247

Politics & Diplomacy

1855: Proslavery and free-soil forces clash in Kansas
Massachusetts desegregates public schools
1856: John Brown's raid in Kansas
James Buchanan elected president
Congressman Preston Brooks canes Senator Charles Sumner
1857: *Dred Scott* decision
Lecompton Constitution
Hinton R. Helper, *The Impending Crisis of the South*
1858: Lincoln-Douglas debates
1859: John Brown's raid on Harpers Ferry
Vicksburg convention calls for reopening of African slave trade
Kansas ratifies free-soil constitution
1860: Democratic convention divides
Abraham Lincoln elected president
South Carolina secedes from the Union

1861: Mississippi, Florida, Alabama, Georgia, Louisiana, and Texas secede
Montgomery Convention creates Confederate States of America
Lincoln inaugurated
Firing on and surrender of Fort Sumter
Arkansas, Tennessee, Virginia, and North Carolina secede
Confederate victory at Bull Run (Manassas)
Jefferson Davis elected president of Confederacy with six-year term
Union navy seizes Confederate commissioners Mason and Slidell from British ship *Trent*
1862: Confederates surrender Fort Donelson to Grant
Virginia v. Monitor in Hampton Roads, Virginia
Grant wins dramatic victory at Shiloh
New Orleans surrenders to Admiral Farragut

1862: *(continued)* Jackson's Shenandoah Valley Campaign
Lee takes command of Army of Northern Virginia
Lee drives McClellan from Richmond in Seven Days' Battles
Confederate victory at Second Bull Run (Manassas)
Battle of Antietam (Sharpsburg)
First Emancipation Proclamation
Burnside replaces McClellan as commander of Army of the Potomac
Lee overwhelms Burnside at Fredericksburg
1863: Second Emancipation Proclamation
Culmination of Lee's victory over Hooker at Chancellorsville
Grant's successful campaign in Mississippi
Death of Stonewall Jackson
Union victory at Gettysburg
Vicksburg surrenders to Grant

Social & Cultural Events

1857: Mass revivals
1858: Frederick Law Olmsted begins design for Central Park in New York City

1863: Lincoln's Gettysburg Address
1865: First woman professor of astronomy appointed at Vassar College

1866: American Equal Rights Association founded to seek black and woman suffrage
1867: Horatio Alger begins publishing series of books for young boys

Economics & Technology

1857: Financial panic and depression
Baltimore–St. Louis rail service completed
1861: Suspension of specie payments
Mathew Brady begins photography of Civil War

1862: Legal Tender Act in North authorizes "greenbacks"
Homestead Act passed by Union Congress
Virginia v. Monitor in Hampton Roads, Virginia
1863: Confederate Congress passes Impressment Act
Union Congress passes National Bank Act

1863: Bread riot in Richmond
1864: Confederate Congress assumes new powers of taxation, impressment of slaves
George Pullman invents sleeping car
1866: National Labor Union organized

1863: *(continued)* Black troops fight at Fort Wagner, South Carolina Lincoln's Gettysburg Address Union victory at Chattanooga **1864:** Grant assumes command of all Union forces Battle of the Wilderness in Virginia Union victory at Cold Harbor Sherman captures Atlanta Lincoln reelected president Beginning of Sherman's march from Atlanta to the Atlantic **1865:** Congress passes Thirteenth Amendment, abolishing slavery Congress creates Bureau of Refugees, Freedmen, and Abandoned Lands (Freedmen's Bureau) Lincoln's second inauguration Fall of Richmond to Union Lee surrenders to Grant at Appomattox Court House Lincoln assassinated; Andrew Johnson becomes president	**1865:** *(continued)* Former Confederate states hold constitutional conventions through December; pass "black codes" Thirteenth Amendment to Constitution ratified, abolishing slavery **1866:** Congress passes Civil Rights Act and Freedmen's Bureau renewal over Johnson's veto Riots in New Orleans and Memphis Congress approves Fourteenth Amendment Ku Klux Klan formed **1867:** Congress passes Reconstruction Act and Tenure of Office Act Johnson dismisses Secretary of War Stanton, triggering impeachment proceedings First elections in South under Reconstruction Act Passage of Reconstruction Act Alaska purchase negotiations	**1868:** Andrew Johnson impeached and acquitted U.S. Grant elected president **1869:** Fifteenth Amendment passes Congress Woman suffrage starts in Wyoming Territory **1870:** Ku Klux Klan conducts terror raids in South **1871:** Tweed Ring exposed in New York City **1872:** Grant reelected **1873:** Salary Grab and Credit Mobilier Scandals **1874:** Democrats gain in congressional elections **1875:** Civil Rights Act passes Congress **1876:** Hayes and Tilden in disputed election **1877:** Hayes declared president after compromises settle election dispute
1868: Louisa May Alcott publishes *Little Women* **1869:** Licensing of women lawyers begins First intercollegiate football game played between Princeton and Rutgers	**1870:** First Greek letter sorority, Kappa Alpha Theta, founded **1871:** Cable car invented **1872:** American Public Health Association starts **1873:** Mark Twain and Charles Dudley Warner publish *The Gilded Age*	**1874:** Women's Christian Temperance Union founded **1875:** Smith and Wellesley College open to provide higher education for women **1876:** Centennial Exposition in Philadelphia
1867: Patrons of Husbandry (Grange) founded **1868:** First 8-hour day for federal workers **1869:** Gold Corner scheme of Jay Gould and Jim Fisk Transcontinental railroad completed	**1870:** Standard Oil Company of Ohio organized **1871:** Chicago fire burns center of city **1872:** Adding machine invented **1873:** Panic of 1873 starts depression	**1874:** Sale of typewriters begins Tomkins Square riot of unemployed in New York City **1875:** First dynamo for outdoor lighting constructed **1876:** Heinz tomato ketchup marketed **1877:** National railroad strike

13 BROKEN BONDS
1855–1861

NORTH AND SOUTH COLLIDE

AMERICAN SOCIETY IN CRISIS

THE NORTH AND SOUTH CALL EACH OTHER'S BLUFF

THE FIRST SECESSION

"Border Ruffians." The northern press depicted what it took to be the seedy character of the proslavery men who came over the border from Missouri into Kansas to support slavery.
The Granger Collection, New York

The United States had never seemed stronger than at the beginning of 1855. The economy was booming, settlers pushed into the West, railroads spread at a relentless rate, and immigrants streamed into American farms and factories. Churches, schools, asylums, and reform organizations grew faster than ever.

But the signs of danger were not hard to see. The conflict between the North and the South grew more bitter with each passing political crisis. Every year brought a clash more divisive than the one before. Disputes between North and South broke out in the Kansas Territory, in the village of Harpers Ferry, and finally in the contest for president. The party system, weakened by nativism and loss of faith by voters, seemed powerless to stop the disintegration.

NORTH AND SOUTH COLLIDE

Conflict between the North and the South had been a staple of American politics for decades before 1855. Territories proved a persistent problem, but northerners and southerners also argued over the tariff, nominees for high office, and religion. The arguments grew hot, but eventually calmed down until the next outbreak. Events of the late 1850s, however, broke the pattern. New crises came before the old ones could dissipate. The crises embroiled every political, economic, moral, and practical difference between the North and the South.

The White South Fortifies Itself

Slavery had never been stronger in the United States than it was in the 1850s. The three and a half million slaves of the South extended over a vast territory stretching from Delaware to Texas. Theorists devised ever more elaborate and aggressive defenses of slavery, no longer depicting it merely as a necessary evil or an unfortunate inheritance from the English. Rather, they claimed, slavery was an instrument of God's will, a means of civilizing and Christianizing Africans otherwise lost to barbarism and heathenism. Southern physicians went to great lengths to prove that Africans and their descendants were physically and intellectually inferior to whites.

Some defenders of slavery argued that slavery was *better* than free labor, more humane and Christian. If the hypocritical and self-righteous men of the North would admit it, white southerners argued,

CHRONOLOGY

1855 Proslavery and free-soil forces clash in Kansas • Massachusetts desegregates public schools

1856 John Brown's raid in Kansas • James Buchanan elected president • Congressman Preston Brooks canes Senator Charles Sumner

1857 Financial panic and depression • *Dred Scott* decision • Lecompton Constitution • Baltimore–St. Louis rail service completed • Hinton R. Helper, *The Impending Crisis of the South* • Mass revivals

1858 Lincoln-Douglas debates • Frederick Law Olmsted begins design for Central Park in New York City

1859 John Brown's raid on Harpers Ferry • Vicksburg convention calls for reopening of African slave trade • Kansas ratifies free-soil constitution

1860 Democratic convention divides • Abraham Lincoln elected president • South Carolina secedes from the Union

1861 Mississippi, Florida, Alabama, Georgia, Louisiana, and Texas secede • Montgomery Convention creates Confederate States of America • Lincoln inaugurated • Firing on and surrender of Fort Sumter

free labor exacted a great cost. Men, women, and children went hungry when unemployment, ill health, or old age struck. In the South, by contrast, slaveholders cared for their slaves even when those slaves had grown too old or feeble to work. The South's relative lack of schools, orphanages, asylums, and prisons, the defenders of the region insisted, testified not to backwardness but to a personalized society where individual responsibility replaced impersonal institutions.

Some white southerners in the late 1850s argued for the expansion of American territory in Cuba or Central America, places where slavery could flourish. William Walker, a young Tennesseean, dreamed of personal glory and a new territory for slavery. After several attempts at "filibustering," small-scale military efforts, in Mexico, Walker took advantage of a civil war to gain power in Nicaragua in 1855 and 1856. President Pierce granted diplomatic recognition of Walker's government, but Central American leaders united against him, cholera wiped out his dwindling, poorly supplied army, and Cornelius Vanderbilt, furious at Walker's revocation of Vanderbilt's Nicaraguan steamship charter, cut off his support from Washington. White southerners enthusiastically supported several attempts by Walker in the late 1850s to take Nicaragua, but he failed repeatedly, and finally was executed by a firing squad in Honduras in 1860.

Despite the agitation of a few editors and politicians for the reopening of the African slave trade, most white southerners wanted above all to keep and protect what they had, not jeopardize slavery by brashly ex-

panding it. Not only would a renewed slave trade with Africa ignite the opinion of the world against the South, but it would also drive down slave prices and create new problems of discipline and revolt. The white South prided itself on having created a stable and prosperous society during its two and a half centuries of slavery and did not want to endanger that society.

Moreover, the slave economy boomed in the late 1850s. Planters took advantage of improved cotton gins, river boats, railroads, and new kinds of seed to double, in the 1850s alone, their production of cotton. The claim of southern politicians that "Cotton is King" proved no empty boast. Even though northern factories and farms grew rapidly in the 1850s, cotton still accounted for fully half of all U.S. exports. Without cotton, many thousands of northern and British workers would have had no jobs.

The prosperity created by the cotton boom resonated throughout the southern economy. Southern cities grew quickly, attracting immigrants and businesses. Although the South could not keep up with the North, it actually did quite well by international stan-

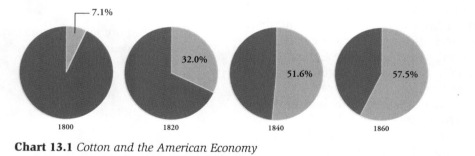

Chart 13.1 *Cotton and the American Economy*
Even as the economy of the entire nation boomed, cotton accounted for an ever-growing proportion of American exports to the rest of the world.

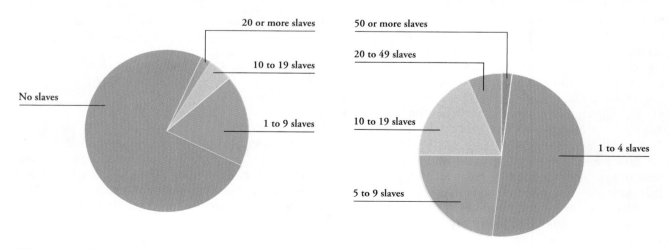

Chart 13.2 a & b *Slaveowning in the South*
About three-fourths of southern white families owned no slaves in 1860. More than half of those who did possess slaves claimed four or fewer.

*P*ICTURING THE PAST ✦ SOCIAL & CULTURAL EVENTS

A YEOMAN FARM

Painting of a block house in New Braunfels, by Carl G. von Iwonski. Courtesy of the Daughters of the Republic of Texas Library

Non-slaveholding whites in the antebellum South, living on farms such as this one in Texas, comprised approximately 75 percent of the white population. Most owned small plots of land they farmed themselves with the aid of their family and local networks of kin and community for access to market goods. They are frequently referred to as yeomen farmers, an ideal of the self-sufficient farm household as one of the cornerstones of American democracy.

Access to arable land and the prospects to purchase slaves became issues of increasing concern through the 1850s. Land exhausted by tobacco or cotton or that was tied up in large holdings of wealthier farmers raised the stakes of access to western lands. In many areas back east in Virginia and the Carolinas, poorer white families and younger sons found themselves unable to move from laborers and farm tenants to land ownership. While many southern yeomen families migrated to southern Illinois, Indiana, and Missouri to break ground in areas without slavery, many others considered the opportunity to own slaves part of their political birthright and supported slavery's expansion even if they owned no slaves themselves.

dards. Considered as a separate economy, the South stood second in the world in the number of miles of railroad, sixth in cotton textile factories, and eighth in iron production. Slaves proved to be adaptable both to factories and cities. The number of slaves in cities declined in the 1850s mainly because the demand for slaves in the countryside was so strong.

The southern economy, then, was not weak or weakening in the 1850s. On the other hand, the South was not urbanizing or industrializing nearly as quickly as the North. The South did not create a large class of entrepreneurs or skilled workers, nor did the region invest much money in machinery to make its farms and plantations more efficient. The southern plantation economy, in effect, was too profitable for its own good. The short-term gains of the 1850s, re-

flected in the escalating value of slaves, dissuaded wealthy southerners from investing in businesses that might have held greater potential for long-term development.

Northerners considered the southern economy the reverse image of the North: sick rather than healthy, backward rather than dynamic. Critics of the South argued that slavery victimized not only slaves but also "poor whites." In the antislavery portrayal, the Slave Power's domination began at home, where haughty self-proclaimed aristocrats lorded over ignorant whites, bullying them into supporting parties and policies that worked against their own interests. Antislavery advocates charged that slaves degraded white labor in the South and substituted a cheap sense of racial superiority for actual accomplishment.

The most effective criticism of the South in this vein came from a southerner: Hinton Rowan Helper, the son of a small slaveholding farmer in western North Carolina. In the late 1850s, a northern press, with aid from the Republican party, published Helper's book, *The Impending Crisis of the South*, which argued that the South's growth, prosperity, and cultural development were being held back by slavery. Helper deployed statistics from the census to prove his case, showing that land values, literacy levels, and manufacturing rates in the South were substantially lower than those in the North. He warned of the devastation caused by slavery, "It must be continually fed by new fields and forests, to be wasted and wilted under the poisonous tread of the slave." He proposed that slaveholders be taxed to colonize all free blacks in Africa or Latin America.

There is little indication that many southern whites agreed with Helper's assessment of them as ignorant, illiterate, and degraded. Most whites saw slavery as an avenue for their own advancement, not a hindrance. Many men and women bought a slave before they bought land. Slaveowners included women, shopkeepers, industrialists, lawyers, ministers, and even a few free blacks. No investment seemed to offer a more certain return than a slave, especially in the 1850s when slave prices rose rapidly. Although that rise in prices meant that a growing proportion of white people would be unable to afford a slave, most non-slaveholding whites apparently reconciled themselves to their situation or determined that they, too, would eventually join the slaveowning ranks. Many white southerners' livelihoods depended on servicing the slave trade, through insurance, medical care, and transport. The slave trade generated tens of millions of dollars in the antebellum South.

Politics reinforced the sense among southern white men that they lived in a fair and democratic society. Although many non-slaveholders in mountainous districts across the South voted against the large slaveholding districts, most southern white men voted in concert with the richest men in their immediate neighborhoods. In the eyes of the poorer men, their wealthy neighbors could act as spokesmen and brokers for the community in the state capital.

Southern whites identified themselves most of all as white people, tied to other whites by blood and heritage. Whites held black people in contempt, despite their knowledge that many African Americans were more intelligent, hardworking, and Christian than many whites. To be white was to be the inheritor of all the accomplishments of the ancients, of Christendom, and of the modern world. Such attitudes were reinforced at every level, from the daily rituals of life to the writings of leading thinkers from Europe. White southerners railed against the Republicans because that party threatened this bond of race between the white North and the white South. A senator from Mississippi outlined the rising threat to a large audience, "twenty years ago this [antisouthern] sentiment was confined to a few fanatics, now it pervades all classes, ages, and sexes of society."

Despite the solidarities of racial thinking, important political differences divided southerners. At one extreme were the so-called fire-eaters, virulent defenders of the South and slavery. These men were diverse. Some lived in cities, others on plantations. Some, such as J. D. B. DeBow, wanted to make the South more industrial and modern, whereas others rejected such development as a Yankee blight on the rural South. Whatever their differences, these men saw themselves as the voice of honesty. Men such as Robert Barnwell Rhett and Edmund Ruffin argued that the abolitionists and their Republican supporters intended to destroy the South. The only sane response, they believed, was to agitate the slavery issue constantly, to refuse to yield an inch in the territories or anywhere else.

At the other end of the political spectrum in the South were the former Whigs and Know-Nothings. They considered the Democrats, especially the fire-eaters, great threats to the future of the South and slavery. Former leaders of the Whigs and the nativist American party did their best to pull their allies into a new party opposed to the Democrats and attractive to a "thoughtful, sedate, constitution-abiding, conservative class of men." The many Unionists in the Upper South, in cities, and even in some of the richest plantation districts felt drawn to this position. The editors of the former Whig and American papers warned voters that the Democrats would sell out the South in Kansas, that the Democrats talked a tough game but always ended up caving in to the North.

Bleeding Kansas

The Kansas-Nebraska Act declared that settlers would decide for themselves, by "popular sovereignty," what kind of society they would create. But partisans from both the North and the South determined to fill the territory with settlers of their own political persuasion. "Come on, then, Gentlemen of the slave States," New York's Senator William H. Seward proclaimed soon after the Kansas-Nebraska Act passed, ". . . We will engage in competition for the virgin soil of Kansas, and God give the victory to the side which is stronger in numbers as it is in right."

The Massachusetts Emigrant Aid Company announced that it planned to raise $5 million to aid and encourage settlement in Kansas to ensure that the embattled territory became a free state. Advocates of slavery in Kansas believed that the forces of abolition would overwhelm the territory before slaveholders could move there. Fearing the exaggerated claims of the abolitionist press that 20,000 antislavery emigrants were moving to Kansas, advocates of slavery in Missouri depicted Kansas as "the unwilling receptacle of filth, scum, and offscouring of the East . . . to pollute our fair land."

Proslavery advocates in Missouri fought what they saw as Yankee invaders. On election day, they flooded across the border to vote in support of the proslavery candidates for the territorial legislature, casting roughly 3,400 more ballots than there were eligible voters. This action by the "border ruffians," as the northern press quickly labeled them, was not necessary, for southerners already accounted for six of every ten men settled in Kansas by 1855. In any case, the proslavery forces triumphed and took control of the territorial legislature in Lecompton. There, they passed a series of aggressive laws against free-soil advocates. Forbidding antislavery men to serve on juries or hold office, the legislature also decreed the death penalty for any person who assisted a fugitive slave.

Antislavery Kansans decided that their only recourse was to establish a rival government. They worked through the summer and fall of 1855 in Topeka to write a constitution of their own. Over the winter, the free-soil advocates "ratified" the constitution and elected their own legislature and governor. The free-soil delegates felt justified by the obvious injustice of their proslavery opponents.

Antislavery forces in New England and New York sent rifles to Kansas to arm what they saw as the side of righteousness. These arms became nicknamed "Beecher's Bibles" because Henry Ward Beecher's congregation, at his urging, funded part of their cost. Southerners, in turn, organized an expedition of 300 young men to reinforce their comrades. Not surprisingly, this volatile situation soon exploded into violence. On May 21, 1856, a group of slave-state supporters marched into the free-soil stronghold of Lawrence to execute warrants from the proslavery territory court against free-state leaders and two newspapers. They threw printing presses into the river, fired cannon at the Free State Hotel, and burned the hotel to the ground. Free-soilers labeled the episode the "sack of Lawrence."

The next day, in Washington, D.C., Representative Preston Brooks of South Carolina searched out

These settlers in Topeka, Kansas, armed themselves against their proslavery adversaries. The conflict quickly took on the trappings of a war.
The Kansas State Historical Society, Topeka, Kansas

SOUTHERN CHIVALRY — ARGUMENT versus CLUB'S.

Preston Brooks's attack on Charles Sumner in the United States Senate electrified the nation in the spring of 1856— even though this artist apparently did not have an image of Brooks from which to work.
The Granger Collection, New York

Senator Charles Sumner of Massachusetts. Sumner had delivered a series of bitter speeches against slavery. Sumner attacked Brooks's relative and fellow South Carolinian, the elderly Senator Andrew P. Butler, for taking "the harlot, slavery" as his "mistress." Brooks, defending the honor of his family and his state, demonstrated his contempt for Sumner by striking him repeatedly about the head with a heavy rubber cane as

Sumner wrote letters at his Senate desk. He did not return to his seat for two and a half years, the victim of shock. The empty seat became a symbol in the North of southern brutality; the incident became a symbol in the South of the only sort of response the arrogant North would respect. The *Richmond Enquirer* applauded Brooks's attack as necessary to keep in line "vulgar abolitionists in the Senate" who "dare to be impudent to gentlemen."

The next day, an event back in Kansas intensified the conflict. The episode swirled around one John Brown, a free-soil emigrant to Kansas. Brown had been a supporter of abolitionism since 1834 and followed five of his sons to Kansas in 1855. There, he became furious at the proslavery forces. He accompanied a group of free-staters to defend Lawrence, but they heard of the hotel's destruction before they arrived. Brown persuaded four of his sons and a son-in-law, along with two other men, to exact revenge for the defeat. The band set out for Pottawatomie Creek. There, acting in the name of the "Army of the North," they took five men from three houses and split open their skulls. The men had been associated in some way with the territorial district court, but no one was, or is, sure of Brown's precise motives. He was never punished for the killings.

In the wake of the "sack of Lawrence," the caning of Sumner, and the "Pottawatomie Massacre"— exploding in just a three-day period in May of 1856— the territory became known as "Bleeding Kansas." A new governor finally helped quiet the conflict in September, but the legitimacy of the territorial government remained an issue of heated contention. The South won a hollow victory when it seized the first election for the territorial government in Kansas. That government would soon pass, but the symbolic value of Bleeding Kansas would long endure.

The Republicans Challenge the South

The events in Kansas proved a disaster for the Democrats. In one state after another, Democratic representatives and senators lost office in the off-year elections of 1854. After a bitter two-month battle, a coalition of anti-Nebraska Democrats and nativists carried the Speakership of the House. To many Southerners, the Democrats seemed a mere tool of Stephen Douglas and his northern allies; to many Northerners, it seemed that Douglas's call for popular sovereignty was a cover for greedy slaveholders. President Franklin Pierce seemed incapable of leadership. The Democrats, needing someone who had not been tarnished by the events of the preceding two years,

President James Buchanan, a Pennsylvania Democrat, became the object of contempt among many northerners for his sympathy for the South in the political struggles of the late 1850s.
The Granger Collection, New York

turned to James Buchanan, the "Old Public Functionary," to run in 1856. As minister to England, Buchanan had conveniently been out of the country during the entire Kansas mess.

Although Know-Nothings were able to agree at the local and state level on issues of corruption and anti-Catholicism, slavery split them as they attempted to organize a presidential campaign and to develop consensus on sectional issues. In February 1856, Know-Nothing unity ended in a controversy over slavery when fifty northern delegates from eight states walked out of the National Council and called for a separate convention of northerners in June. Southerners who had voted with the Know-Nothings had nowhere to turn but to the Democrats, but northerners could devote their attention to the new Republican party. The Republicans bypassed their most outspoken

PICTURING THE PAST ✦ POLITICS & DIPLOMACY

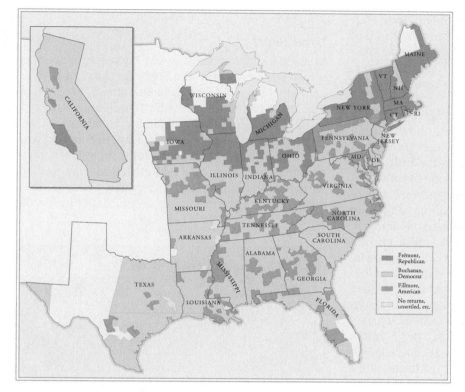

Map 13.1 *The Election of 1856*

Voters turned out in near record numbers for the presidential election in 1856. The Republicans, organized in only a few states in the North in the spring, rapidly consolidated their message and rallied voters in New England and the Upper North. A shift in a few thousand votes in key states such as Pennsylvania, and the Republicans might have won. Democrats celebrated victory, but their leaders recognized that the growing population of the North and Midwest would decide control of the House of Representatives. Southerners, now firmly in control of the Democratic party, escalated their demands for opening western territories to slavery and for federal protection of slave property. Northern Democrats faced defeat in home districts when they supported such policies, weakening the party's ability to resist the Republicans. The distribution of voter support for the various parties illustrates the inability of Democrats, Know-Nothings, or Republicans to appeal as a national party with a platform that appealed across the growing sectional divide. As the Know-Nothings faded as a serious competitor, the two remaining parties struggled to increase their appeal in the Lower North and Midwest, key areas that would determine the victor in the next election.

antislavery men for the 1856 nomination and turned to John C. Frémont, famed as an explorer of the West. He had taken almost no public positions and had accumulated almost no political experience. The Republicans thought they had found just the sort of vague candidate who would give few potential voters a reason to vote against him.

The new Republican party was antislavery but not pro-black; Republicans avoided talking about race. What they did talk about was the goodness of the North: the North, they argued, was everything the South was not, a place where hardworking white men could build a life for their families free from the threat of arrogant, powerful, and greedy slaveholders.

Abolitionists had succeeded in making slavery detested throughout the North and had created much of the anti-southern energy that flowed into the Republican party. But abolitionists distrusted that party. The Republicans seemed interested only in the welfare of the white North. They denied any intention of ending slavery in the South and even resurrected talk of colonization, the movement the abolitionists had abandoned twenty-five years earlier. The Republicans, although better than the pro-southern Democrats, still dissatisfied the abolitionists.

The Republicans talked of the "Slave Power," a political conspiracy of the most powerful slaveholders. Republicans saw everything from the three-fifths clause to the bloodshed in Kansas as the fruit of the Slave Power. How else to explain the long list of southern victories at a time when the North grew more populous and wealthy? Kansas and the caning of Sumner showed that the Slave Power, a Cincinnati paper raged, "cannot tolerate free speech anywhere, and would stifle it in Washington with the bludgeon and the bowie-knife, as they are now trying to stifle it in Kansas."

Republicans attacked Catholics as well, repeating the charges that nativists had made for decades. Ironically, rumors that Frémont was a Catholic quickly surfaced and refused to subside. Moreover, Frémont refused to give direction to the national campaign. To make matters worse, Millard Fillmore, the former president, ran under the banner of the American party, as the Know-Nothings called themselves. Fillmore hoped that the three-way election would split the electorate so that the final decision would rest with the House, where he would appear as a compromise candidate.

On election day in 1856, 83 percent of the eligible voting men went to the polls, one of the highest turnouts of the era. Although Buchanan won all of the South except Maryland, he received only 45 percent of the popular vote in the country as a whole. A difference of a few thousand votes in a few states would have denied Buchanan the election. The Democrats had won, but were filled with anxiety; the Republicans had lost, but were filled with confidence. It was clear to everyone that the American political system was in flux and transition.

Observers of all political persuasions believed that James Buchanan had it within his power to strengthen the Democrats in both the North and the South. His party, after all, still controlled the Senate. The Republicans, moreover, had drawn much of their power from the chaos in Kansas. Once Kansas had peacefully entered the Union as a free state under the banner of popular sovereignty, Democrats happily observed, no other territory awaited in which similar conflicts might be expected. Slavery, everyone seemed to agree, had no chance in Oregon, Nebraska, Minnesota, Washington, Utah, or New Mexico. The territorial issue that had torn at the country since 1820 might finally die down.

Dred Scott

In his inaugural address, James Buchanan mentioned a case pending before the Supreme Court, a case regarding a slave. Buchanan looked forward to the ruling, for he believed that the territorial issue was "a judicial question, which legitimately belongs to the Supreme Court . . . . To their decision, in common with all good citizens, I shall cheerfully submit, whatever they may be." That case had moved its way through various levels of courts for more than a decade. Dred Scott, born a slave in Virginia around 1800, had in the

The Dred Scott case attracted the attention of the entire country in 1856. This northern newspaper depicted Scott and his family sympathetically, emphasizing family ties and the women of the family.
The Granger Collection, New York

1830s been taken by his master, an army surgeon named John Emerson, to territories far in the upper Midwest. Scott had married Harriet Robinson, the slave of a federal Indian agent. Dr. Emerson bought Harriet and thus owned the two daughters she bore with Scott. When Emerson died in 1843, Scott and his family became the property of Emerson's widow, who moved to St. Louis. In 1846 the Scotts petitioned for their freedom, claiming that their residence in the free territory entitled them to free status.

A long series of postponements and delays dragged the case on into the early 1850s, when the legal environment had become much more divided by political controversy over slavery. Democratic judges and lawyers worked to deny the Scotts their freedom on the grounds that such a precedent would undermine the right of southerners to take slaves into the territories. A Republican lawyer agreed to carry the Scotts' case before the Supreme Court to counter the Democrats' aggressive claims. Unfortunately for the Republicans and the Scotts, five southern Democrats sat on the Court, along with two northern Democrats, one northern Whig, and one northern Republican. Presiding was Chief Justice Roger B. Taney (pronounced "tawney"), an eighty-year-old Marylander first appointed to the Court by Andrew Jackson in 1835.

The *Dred Scott* case came before the Supreme Court during the superheated months of 1856, when Kansas, the Brooks/Sumner affair, and the presidential election commanded the country's attention. Although the case could have been decided on relatively narrow grounds, the Democratic members of the Court wanted to issue a sweeping pronouncement that would settle once and for all the question of slavery in the territories. President-elect Buchanan pressured a fellow Pennsylvanian on the Court to side with the southerners. Two days after Buchanan took office in March of 1857, the Court announced its decision in the *Dred Scott* case. It took Chief Justice Taney two hours to read the opinion.

Taney spent half his time denying that Scott had the right to bring a case in the first place. Black people, Taney decreed, could not become citizens of the United States because "they were not included, and were not intended to be included, under the word 'citizens' in the Constitution." Taney declared that at the time the Constitution was written, throughout the "civilized and enlightened portions of the world," members of the "negro African race" were held to be "altogether unfit to associate with the white race . . . and so far inferior, that they had no rights which the white man was bound to respect." Therefore, Dred Scott had never been a citizen of Missouri and had no

right to sue his mistress. Taney also decreed that Congress had never held a constitutional right to restrict slavery in the territories and that therefore the Missouri Compromise of 1820 was invalid. Two justices dissented from the majority's opinion, but the decision stood as the law of the land.

Southerners and many northern Democrats exulted that they had been vindicated by the *Dred Scott* decision, that the Republicans' demand for territories free of slavery was simply unconstitutional. Democratic editors claimed that the decision "vindicates and sustains the Democratic Party in the patriotism and wisdom of its course" as "*sectionalism* has been rebuked, and abolitionism staggered." The Republicans, however, sneered at the decision, which they saw as one more corrupt act by the Slave Power Conspiracy designed to turn the nation in "one great slave pen." They reprinted the dissenting opinions in the *Dred Scott* case and denounced the decision in the state legislatures they controlled throughout the North. They argued that the Founding Fathers had never intended slavery to be a permanent part of the United States and merely tolerated bondage because they expected it to die of its own weight. If the *Dred Scott* decision were followed to its logical conclusion, they warned, the United States would reopen the slave trade with Africa and even extend slavery into northern states where it had been banned.

The Republicans thought the Court's audacious statement "the best thing that could have happened" to the Republican party. As an abolitionist newspaper put it, the "fiercer the insult, the bitterer the blow, the better." The Republicans expected the *Dred Scott* decision to make their party stronger. The Republicans needed to sweep the government in 1860, they argued, to clean out corruption and conspiracy from the executive, Congress, and now the courts.

AMERICAN SOCIETY IN CRISIS

The American economy boomed in the mid-1850s. Not only did cotton do well, but so did the farms, factories, railroads, and cities of the North and West. People cheered the laying of a telegraphic cable all the way across the Atlantic Ocean, an incredible feat that triggered celebrations in towns across the nation, including wild fireworks in New York City that set City Hall ablaze. Currier and Ives prints became the rage, brightening homes around the country with charming scenes of American life. The sale of newspapers,

Hinton Helper
The Impending Crisis of the South, *1857*

This book, a lacerating critique of slavery by a racist white southerner, proved even more incendiary in the South than had Harriet Beecher Stowe's *Uncle Tom's Cabin.* The Republican party seized on the book as a revelation from inside the slave power's empire, arguing that it revealed the secret resentments of the white majority. To the Republicans' surprise and dismay, however, the book bred anger against the North instead of Republican recruits in the South.

It is a fact well known to every intelligent Southerner, that we are compelled to go to the North for almost every article of utility and adornment, from matches, shoepegs and paintings, up to cotton-mills, steamships and statuary; that we have no foreign trade, no princely merchants, nor respectable artists; that, in comparison with the Free States, we contribute nothing to the literature, polite arts and inventions of the age; that, for want of profitable employment at home, large numbers of our native population find themselves necessitated to emigrate to the West, while the Free States retain not only the larger proportion of those born within their own limits, but induce, annually, hundreds of thousands of foreigners to settle and remain amongst them; that almost everything produced at the North meets with ready sale, while, at the same time, there is no demand, even among our own citizens, for the productions of Southern industry; that, owing to the absence of a proper system of business among us, the North becomes, in one way or another, the proprietor and dispenser of all our floating wealth, and that we are dependent on Northern capitalists for the means necessary to build our railroads, canals and other public improvements; that if we want to visit a foreign country, even though it may lie directly south of us, we find no convenient way of getting there except by taking passage through a Northern port; and that nearly all the profits arising from the exchange of commodities, from insurance and shipping offices, and from the thousand and one industrial pursuits of the country, accrue to the North, and are there invested in the erection of those magnificent cities and stupendous works of art which dazzle the eyes of the South, and attest the superiority of free institutions! . . . And now that we have come to the very heart and soul of our subject, we feel no disposition to mince matters, but mean to speak plainly and to the point, without any equivocation, mental reservation, or secret evasion whatever. The son of a venerated parent, who, while he lived, was a considerate and merciful slaveholder, a native of the South, born and bred in North Carolina, of a family whose home has been in the valley of the Yadkin for nearly a century and a half, a Southerner by instinct and by all the influences of thought, habits and kindred, and with the desire and fixed purpose to reside permanently within the limits of the South, and with the expectation of dying there also—we feel that we have the right to express our opinion, however humble or unimportant it may be, on any and every question that affects the public good. . . .

And now to the point. In our opinion, an opinion which has been formed from data obtained by assiduous researchers and comparisons, from laborious investigation, logical reasoning, and earnest reflection, the causes which have impeded the progress and prosperity of the South, which have dwindled our commerce and other similar pursuits, into the most contemptible insignificance; sunk a large majority of our people in galling poverty and ignorance, rendered a small minority conceited and tyrannical, and driven the rest away from their homes; entailed upon us a humiliating dependence on the Free States; disgraced us in the recesses of our own souls, and brought us under reproach in the eyes of all civilized and enlightened nations—may all be traced to one common source, and there find solution in the most hateful and horrible word, that was ever incorporated into the vocabulary of human economy—*Slavery*. . . .

In making up these [statistical] tables we have two objects in view; the first is to open the eyes of the non-slaveholders of the South to the system of deception that has been so long practiced upon them, and the second is to show slaveholders themselves—we have reference only to those who are not too perverse, or ignorant, to perceive naked truths—that free labor is far more respectable, profitable, and productive, than slave labor. In the South, unfortunately, no kind of labor is either free or respectable. Every white man who is under the necessity of earning his bread, by the sweat of his brow, or by manual labor, in any capacity, no matter how unassuming in deportment, or exemplary in morals, is treated as if he were a loathsome beast, and shunned with disdain. His soul may be the very seat of honor and integrity, yet without slaves— himself a slave—he is accounted as nobody, and would be deemed intolerably presumptuous, if he dared to open his lips, even so wide as to give faint utterance to a three-lettered monosyllable, like yea or nay, in the presence of an august knight of the whip and the lash. . . .

The lords of the lash are not only absolute masters of the blacks, who are bought and sold, and driven about like so many cattle, but they are also the oracles and arbiters of all the non-slaveholding whites, whose freedom is merely nominal, and whose unparalleled illiteracy and degradation is purposely and fiendishly perpetuated. How little the "poor white trash," the great majority of the Southern people, know of the real condition of the country, is, indeed, sadly astonishing. The truth is, they know nothing of public measures, and little of private affairs, except what their imperious masters, the slave-drivers, condescend to tell, and that is but precious little, and even that little, always garbled and one-sided, is never told except in public harangues; for the haughty cavaliers of shackles and handcuffs will not degrade themselves by holding private converse with those who have neither dimes nor hereditary rights in human flesh.

Whenever it pleases, and to the extent it pleases, a slaveholder to become communicative, poor whites may hear with fear and trembling, but not speak. They must be as mum as dumb brutes, and stand in awe of their august superiors, or be crushed with stern rebukes, cruel oppressions, or downright violence. If they dare to think for themselves, their thoughts must be forever concealed. The expression of any sentiment at all conflicting with the gospel of slavery, dooms them at once in the community in which they live, and then, whether willing or unwilling, they are obliged to become heroes, martyrs, or exiles. . . .

Non-slaveholders are not only kept in ignorance of what is transpiring at the North, but they are continually misinformed of what is going on even in the South. Never were the poorer classes of a people, and those classes so largely in the majority, and all inhabiting the same country, so basely duped, so adroitly swindled, or so unpardonably outraged.

Source: Hinton R. Helper, *The Impending Crisis of the South* (New York: A. B. Burdick, 1859), pp. 25–26, 28–29, 40, 42–43.

James D. B. DeBow
"The Interest in Slavery of the Southern Non-Slaveholder," 1860

DeBow used his statistical expertise as a former superintendent of the United States Census to argue that the South was actually more democratic in property holding than the North and that slavery actually helped the non-slaveholding white southerner in many ways.

[How does slavery benefit the non-slaveholding white man?]

1. The non-slaveholder of the South is assured that the remuneration afforded by his labor, over and above the expense of living, is larger than that which is afforded by the same labor in the free States.

2. The non-slaveholders, as a class, are not reduced by the necessity of our condition, as is the case in the free States, to find employment in crowded cities and come into competition in close and sickly workshops and factories, with remorseless and untiring machinery.

3. The non-slaveholder is not subjected to that competition with foreign pauper labor, which has degraded the free labor of the North and demoralized it to an extent which perhaps can never be estimated.

4. The non-slaveholder of the South preserves the status of the white man, and is not regarded as an inferior or a dependent.

5. The non-slaveholder knows that as soon as his savings will admit, he can become a slaveholder, and thus relieve his wife from the necessities of the kitchen and the laundry, and his children from the labors of the field.

6. The large slaveholders and proprietors of the South begin life in great part as non-slaveholders.

7. But should such fortune not be in reserve for the non-slaveholder, he will understand that by honesty and industry it may be realized to his children.

8. The sons of the non-slaveholder are and have always been among the leading and ruling spirits of the South; in industry as well as in politics.

9. Without the institution of slavery, the great staple products of the South would cease to be grown, and the immense annual results, which are distributed among every class of the community, and which give life to every branch of industry, would cease.

10. If emancipation be brought about as will undoubtedly be the case, unless the encroachments of the fanatical majorities of the North are resisted now, the slaveholders, in the main, will escape the degrading equality which must result, by emigration, for which they would have the means, by disposing of their personal chattels: whilst the non-slaveholders, without these resources, would be compelled to remain and endure the degradation.

Source: "The Non-Slaveholders of the South," in DeBow and others, *The Interest in Slavery of the Southern Non-Slaveholder. The Right of Peaceful Secession. Slavery in the Bible.* (Charleston: Evans & Cogswell, 1860), pp. 3–5, 7–12.

books, and magazines surged. Working people's organizations staged a comeback. Churches and schools spread with remarkable speed. The mileage of railroads tripled to more than 30,000 miles.

But underlying this prosperity ran a deep current of unease. Some people worried that Americans were growing soft and self-indulgent. Others felt guilt that as the economy boomed, slavery became stronger. Others despaired at the state of American politics, which seemed in disarray. The conflict between the North and the South embodied all these anxieties, giving them concrete shape.

Financial Panic and Spiritual Revival

Late in the summer of 1857, people warned that there had been too much speculation recently, that companies and individuals had borrowed too much money. The end of the Crimean War in Europe seemed ominous for the United States, for now the countries of the Old World could turn their energies toward growing their own food, undermining the heavy demand for American farm products that had buoyed the economy for several years. When a major insurance company went under in 1857, a panic spread among New York banks and railroad stocks plummeted along with western land values. Soon, banks and companies across the country began to fail.

Working people of all ranks lost their jobs. Not only unskilled laborers, domestics, and millworkers found themselves without work, but so did educated bookkeepers and clerks. Across the North, hundreds of thousands of people had no income and many were forced to rely on charity to feed and clothe themselves. Workers tried to organize, but employers shut down the mills and factories. As winter approached, many people wondered whether their families would survive through the cold months.

Southerners blamed northern financiers for bringing on the panic of 1857. Though the white and free black working people of southern cities suffered along with their counterparts in the North, white southerners bragged that their region quickly recovered from the panic. They also bragged that their slaves, unlike white workers, never starved or went without a roof over their heads: "The White Slave trade is more exacting and fraudulent than Black Slavery, . . . it is more cruel, in leaving the laborer to take care of himself and his family . . . which make his freedom an empty and delusive mockery."

Throughout the country, the panic and depression of 1857 caused people to pause and take stock of their situation. Some said that the political system had be-

trayed the country, that selfish politicians had allowed banking to become too loose or the tariff too strict—or vice versa, since no one could be certain. Others warned that Americans had grown too rich and lazy for their own good, becoming too wrapped up in their material welfare at the expense of everything and everyone else.

A wave of religious revivals emerged in response to the panic. They lasted for over a year, sweeping back and forth across the country. Unlike earlier revivals, the religious spirit emerged not in rural districts but in the largest cities of the Northeast. Unlike earlier revivals, too, those of 1857 attracted a conspicuously large number of men as well as women. In contrast to earlier revivals in rural areas, middle-class men in the commercial districts of larger cities met for daily prayer meetings, regularly covered in the press, that convened promptly at noon and with each member limited to a five-minute prayer to keep the group on schedule. The Young Men's Christian Association expanded rapidly during this time, providing young single clerks a venue for creating a "businesslike piety." The revivals also witnessed the first active participation of denominations such as the Episcopalians and Unitarians. It seemed to many people, in fact, that the revivals were the most heartening and significant in American history, showing that the people in the forefront of modern America were trying to change their ways. And as people read their newspapers they saw plenty that needed to be changed—especially in Kansas.

The Agony of Kansas

Most of the settlers who had arrived in Kansas in 1856 and 1857 were non-slaveholding migrants from the Upper South. They did not appear eager to establish slavery in Kansas. An open election, therefore, would likely install a constitutional convention in favor of free soil at the time Kansas became a state. The proslavery legislature elected in the earliest days of the territory, however, still controlled Kansas in 1857. Free-state advocates fought back, touring the North and raising money for the struggle against the Slave Power.

In November of 1857, the small band of proslavery delegates who still controlled the legislature proposed a new constitution. Kansas had to produce a constitution that the U.S. Congress would accept. The legislature provided that voters would choose between the constitution with slavery or without slavery. In either case, slaveowners already in Kansas would be permitted to keep their slaves. The Republicans portrayed the constitution as one more audacious act of the Slave Power, but in fact the "Lecompton Constitution" posed a serious problem for the Democrats.

*P*ICTURING THE PAST◆ECONOMICS & TECHNOLOGY

THE PANIC OF 1857

© Bettmann/Corbis

Nᴇw York City symbolized for many Americans the consequences of the high living and corrupt practices that brought on the panic of 1857. "With fifty-seven suspended banks . . . hundreds and thousands of bankrupt merchants, importers, traders, and stock jobbers . . . with her rotten bankruptcies permeating and injuring almost every solvent community in the nation," raged one New Orleans newspaper, New York stood as "the centre of reckless speculation, unflinching fraud and downright robbery." This cartoon dramatizes the moral corruption that many people believed lay at the heart of the panic.

The panic had more immediate and concrete causes. The end of the Crimean War in Europe triggered a decline in overseas demand for American agricultural products and reduction in specie flows into the nation from European investors. A wave of bankruptcies caused bank closures as cash became scarce and banks shut their doors on investors when cash supplies ran out. Small businessmen and managers, with no prospects of sales, laid off workers or offered them payment in kind instead of wages. Ironically, the southern cotton economy rebounded sooner, as European demand for cotton recovered by 1858, while northern and midwestern grain farmers faced low prices for the next two years.

Northern members of the party could not support it without appearing too sympathetic to the South; they could not oppose it without alienating the southern Democrats that made up the bulk of the party's strength. President Buchanan knew well that 112 of his 174 electoral votes had come from the South and that, of the 165 Democrats in both houses of Congress, 100 were southerners.

Stephen Douglas refused to endorse the Lecompton Constitution as a violation of popular sovereignty, but President Buchanan urged its adoption. When challenged by Douglas to support the rights of voters in Kansas, Buchanan warned Douglas, "no Democrat ever yet differed from an administration of his own [party] without being crushed." The president persuaded himself that the constitution was in fact a moderate compromise, letting Kansas enter the Union as a free state in the long run while protecting the slave-holders who were already there. Once Kansas was a state, he reasoned, its legislature could decide what to do with those slaves. Most northern voters saw the matter differently: though it was obvious that the great majority of Kansans wanted to enter the Union as a free state, those antislavery Kansans would be forced to accept slavery.

Republicans could hardly believe that Buchanan had handed them such an easy way to portray him as a tool of the South. And neither could Stephen Douglas, who recognized that Buchanan's actions would create enormous problems for the Democrats. The Democrats fought bitterly among themselves for months, Douglas denouncing the president for supporting "trickery and juggle" and seeking to use the Senate to block the Lecompton Constitution, Buchanan using the powers of the presidency to mobilize senators against Douglas.

Moderate southern and northern Democrats warned that the South was destroying its only hope for continued success: a strong Democratic party in the North. When Kansas voters overwhelmingly rejected the Lecompton Constitution in 1858, they rejected Buchanan and the South as well. The Democrats suffered widespread defeat in the state elections that spring and lost control of the House. Northern Democrats, still weak from the loss of seats after the 1854 elections, lost again as only 32 of 53 free-state Democrats survived the 1858 contest and 12 of those were opposed to the Lecompton Constitution. Douglas himself faced a tough election battle and Buchanan did everything he could to destroy this rival in his own party. Running against a promising Republican candidate, Abraham Lincoln, Douglas needed all the help he could get.

The Lincoln-Douglas Debates

Abraham Lincoln was very much the underdog in the Illinois senatorial race of 1858. As a Whig in a heavily Democratic state, Lincoln had not found it easy to win or hold office in the 1840s and 1850s. He had lost repeatedly, occupying national office for all of two years: elected to the House of Representatives in 1846, Lincoln lasted only one term and was sent back to his law office in Springfield. There, Lincoln made a good living as a lawyer, drawing on his own abilities and the connections that came with his marriage to Mary Todd, a member of a prominent family. Lincoln's modest beginnings on the Kentucky and Illinois frontier lay comfortably in the past. Still, he longed for a major public office.

Though the short, portly, experienced, pragmatic, and famous Stephen Douglas seemed the opposite of the tall, thin, inexperienced, principled, and obscure Abraham Lincoln, the two men in fact shared a great deal. Douglas, too, had grown up poor. Douglas, although the most prominent Democrat in the country, was actually four years younger than Lincoln. Both Lincoln and Douglas shared their constituents' moderate positions on most national issues.

Illinois's population was composed of many New England migrants in the northern half of the state, upcountry southern migrants in the bottom half, and German and Irish immigrants in Chicago. Both the factories and the farms of Illinois prospered in the 1850s, as did abolitionists, Know-Nothings, Whigs, and southern-leaning Democrats. The Illinois senatorial election of 1858 promised to throw all these groups into contention. At stake was this question: could the Democrats survive as a national party, with Douglas as their leader, or were they doomed to become a party of the South?

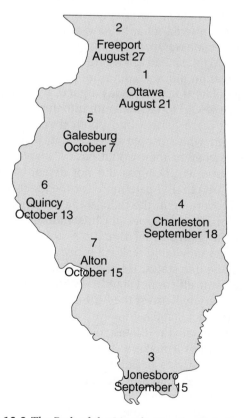

Map 13.2 *The Path of the Lincoln-Douglas Debates* The two candidates followed a long and circuitous route—nearly 1,300 miles long, on rail, river, buggy, and horseback—through Illinois in their efforts to win the voters over to their vision of the American future.

Douglas traveled by private railroad car from Chicago to Springfield, the state capital and Lincoln's base. All along the way, Douglas gave speeches to thousands of people, telling them that he was the voice of experience, principled compromise, and popular sovereignty. He also told them that Lincoln held "monstrous revolutionary doctrines" of abolitionism. To Douglas's great annoyance, Lincoln followed the senator to rebut his arguments and charges, sometimes appearing in the crowd, sometimes arriving the next day. Douglas, though reluctant to give the relatively unknown Lincoln a share of attention, finally agreed to hold seven joint debates in the late summer and early fall.

Lincoln was far from an abolitionist, refusing to join the antislavery Liberty and Free-Soil parties and staying with the Whigs longer than many of the men who became Republicans. He repeatedly brought up the *Dred Scott* decision from the previous year, however, arguing that it would permit slavery to spread into lands where Illinois men or their sons would otherwise migrate. The West must remain a region where "white men may find a home . . . where they can settle upon some new soil and better their condition in life." Douglas offered what he saw as practical, commonsense responses to such charges, arguing that slavery would not spread anywhere the majority of the white population did not want it to. A far greater and more immediate threat, Douglas argued, was that the Republicans would force the South into desperate acts by dragging moral issues into political contexts. Let the sovereign white people of each state decide for themselves whether they would have slavery or not, Douglas counseled. Douglas did not defend slavery, but he declared that "I care more for the great principle of self-government, the right of the people to rule, than I do for all the negroes in Christendom."

Lincoln charged that Douglas's strategy merely postponed an inevitable reckoning between the slave states and the free states. He argued that "a house divided against itself cannot stand. . . . Either the opponents of slavery will arrest the further spread of it, . . . or its advocates will push it forward till it shall become alike lawful in all the States, old as well as new." Notwithstanding Douglas's efforts to dismiss the morality of slavery as beside the point, that morality repeatedly surfaced in the debates. Lincoln argued that he, not Douglas, was the one defending true self-government. Douglas's policy permitted the forces of slavery to grow stronger and more aggressive, whereas Lincoln's would place slavery on the path toward "ultimate extinction." It would likely be several generations before that extinction occurred, Lincoln believed, but the process could begin in 1858.

Lincoln made a distinction between different kinds of rights. African Americans, he thought, had economic rights, but he did not believe in social equality between blacks and whites. He would not grant black men the right to intermarry with whites, serve on juries, or vote, but he did believe that black people had the right not to be slaves. Lincoln took the offensive, making Douglas appear more of a defender of slavery than at heart he was.

The election was close, but the state legislature, which elected U.S. senators in these decades, went to the Democrats and they returned Douglas to Washington. But Lincoln had become identified as the spokesman for a principled yet restrained antislavery. All across the North, in fact, the Republicans made impressive gains in 1858. In every state, many people wanted the nation to find some compromise. But the political environment did not have a chance to calm in 1859, for it was then that John Brown returned to the national scene.

John Brown and Harpers Ferry

John Brown had become famous in the three years since he had burst into prominence in Bleeding Kansas in 1855. Antislavery people back east, assured by journalists that Brown had not personally killed anyone at Pottawatomie, admired the hard man for his firsthand opposition to slaveholders. Thus, as he toured New England in search of funds to carry on the cause, he found willing listeners and open hands. Antislavery advocates were eager to contribute to the fight against slavery in Kansas, not realizing they were contributing to a fight against slavery much closer to home. Brown wrote letters to wealthy abolitionists requesting assistance for "an important measure, in which the world has a deep interest." Throughout 1857 and 1858, Brown planned for an attack on the federal arsenal at Harpers Ferry, Virginia. He had a thousand iron pikes forged to arm the slaves he believed would rise in rebellion once he and his men triggered the revolt. He tried to win the support of Frederick Douglass, who, while sympathetic, thought the plan doomed logistically. But Brown pressed on. One of his lieutenants moved to Harpers Ferry and even established a family there, preparing the way for the attack. In the meantime, Brown continued the fight against slavery in the West, freeing eleven slaves in Missouri, killing their master and leading them into Canada. Such exploits, though illegal, only heightened Brown's visibility and appeal in New England.

The assault on Harpers Ferry started in earnest in the summer of 1859, when Brown rented a farm seven

The campaign launched by John Brown and twenty-one black and white allies in 1859 failed in its immediate aims of unleashing a rebellion of the enslaved but succeeded in heightening the moral and political debate over slavery.
© Bettmann/Corbis

miles away and assembled his men and munitions. To his disappointment, he could recruit only twenty-one men, five of them African Americans.

The raid began easily enough on Sunday, October 16, as Brown's men quickly seized the arsenal and a rifle-manufacturing plant. Brown and his men remained in the small armory building, waiting for word to spread among the slaves of Virginia that their day of liberation had come. The word spread instead among local whites, who quickly surrounded Brown's men, killing or capturing eight of them. Militia from Virginia and Maryland arrived the next day, followed soon after by federal troops. The troops rushed the armory. Ten of the abolitionist forces were killed, five (including Brown) wounded, and seven escaped. Brown was tried within two weeks and found guilty. He was sentenced to be hanged exactly a month later, on December 2.

The entire episode, from the raid to Brown's execution, took only about six weeks to unfold. Yet those six weeks saw opinion in both the North and the South

change rapidly. Public opinion in the North and South, mixed at first, crystallized into sharply opposing viewpoints. Even those northerners who were appalled at the violence were also appalled at the speed with which Brown was tried and condemned. Even those southerners who read with reassurance early denunciations of Brown in the North were appalled when they realized that many northerners refused to condemn the raid. A senator from South Carolina denounced the raid as the result of "the miserable, intermeddling, nefarious spirit of many of the people of our associate States with [a] matter that concerns them not."

The rhetoric surrounding John Brown seemed almost cathartic, as both northerners and southerners said the worst they could imagine about the other. The many people of moderate sympathies on both sides watched, dismayed, as common ground eroded beneath their feet.

Brown had not set out to become a martyr. He fully expected to unleash a massive slave rebellion. Although his precise plans remain obscure, maps in his possession marked places where slaves outnumbered their masters and might overwhelm them with force. Brown wanted to play the role of Moses, leading the oppressed and chosen out of captivity. Once captured, however, Brown seemed to fit another role, that of Christ, selflessly dying for the salvation of others. In a letter to his wife he wrote, I "am sure I can recover all the lost capital occasioned by that disaster, by only hanging a few moments by the neck; & I feel quite determined to make the utmost possible out of a defeat." No longer the Old Testament figure of blood and vengeance, Brown now appeared to many in the North as a New Testament figure of suffering and dignified sacrifice. William Lloyd Garrison speculated that Brown planned "a desperate self-sacrifice for the purpose of giving an earthquake shock to the slave system and thus hastening the day of universal catastrophe." Many northerners came to believe that John Brown's body could be redeemed only with a return to the stern violence he had championed.

THE NORTH AND SOUTH CALL EACH OTHER'S BLUFF

Everyone knew the election of 1860 held enormous meaning for the United States, but no one could be sure what that meaning might be. Would this be the election that brought all to their senses? Would the border states be able to control the election? Would northern voters suddenly realize the South meant what it said? The actual events proved far more threatening than most Americans had believed possible.

The Election of 1860

White southerners automatically linked John Brown with the Republican party, though leading Republicans explicitly denied any connection. Southerners believed that "every village bell which tolled its solemn note at the execution of Brown proclaims to the South the approbation of that village of insurrection and servile war." The Republicans realized that they would be a purely northern party. Not only had any southern base of support disappeared, but Harpers Ferry and the public mourning and grief over Brown had made the Republicans far more attractive among northern voters than before.

The Democrats also felt the effects of Brown's raid. Meeting in Charleston in April 1860 to decide on their presidential nominee for the fall election, the northern Democrats nominated Stephen Douglas. The northern Democrats saw this as a compromise with the South. But southern Democrats demanded that the party explicitly support the rights of slaveholders to take their slaves into the territories. Northern Democrats could not afford to make that concession and still have a chance to win back home. The southerners proved heedless of this plea, however, and walked out of the convention. Several weeks later, the Democrats met in Baltimore and

As "Dred Scott" fiddles, the four candidates of 1860 dance to the tune of slavery. While Lincoln is accompanied by a black woman, Breckenridge, in the upper left, dances with the devil in the form of secessionist William L. Yancey.
From the Collections of the Library of Congress

nominated Douglas. Southerners, walking out once again, declaring themselves the "purified" Democratic party, nominated John C. Breckenridge of Kentucky.

Before the Democratic convention met again in June, Unionists in both the North and the South tried to avert catastrophe by nominating a compromise candidate. Calling themselves the Constitutional Union party, they settled on John Bell of Tennessee. Many of these Unionists were former conservative Whigs and Know-Nothings who no longer had a political home. They advocated an end to agitation over slavery, "the Union as it is, the Constitution unchanged," to safeguard the "priceless heritage of our fathers." They counted on the other candidates to create a deadlock that would have to be settled in the House of Representatives. There, the Unionists hoped, legislators would gratefully turn to their compromise candidate.

As the Democrats tore themselves apart, the Republicans met in Chicago. There, in efforts to put southern concerns at rest, the Republicans announced their belief in the right of each state to decide for itself whether it would have slavery. The Republicans cemented their appeal to voters unconcerned with the slavery issue by calling for protective tariffs, internal improvements, and free homesteads for anyone who would settle the West. The Republicans were much stronger than they had been only four years earlier. Party strategists calculated that they need only win Pennsylvania and one other state they had lost to the Democrats in 1856 to wrap up the election. The states they needed to take were Illinois, Indiana, or New Jersey—all of them on the border with the South and all of them far more moderate on the slavery question than states farther north. Thus, the Republicans turned to a moderate who was a favorite son of one of the crucial states: Abraham Lincoln of Illinois.

A certain air of unreality surrounded the election of 1860. People did not know that the way they voted would bring on a civil war, or even secession. Although Stephen Douglas constantly warned of such a danger, both Breckinridge and Lincoln downplayed any such dire consequence. Ironically, all the years of conflict had persuaded both the North and the South that the other talked tougher than it would act. The parties staged loud and raucous political events that proved long on emotion and short on clearly defined positions. Lincoln said nothing and stayed close to home while his party leaders displayed split fence rails and touted his honesty.

The election of 1860 was actually two separate elections, one in the North and one in the South. Lincoln made no attempt to explain himself to the South; Breckinridge made little attempt in the North. They never met face to face. Bell spoke mainly to the already converted.

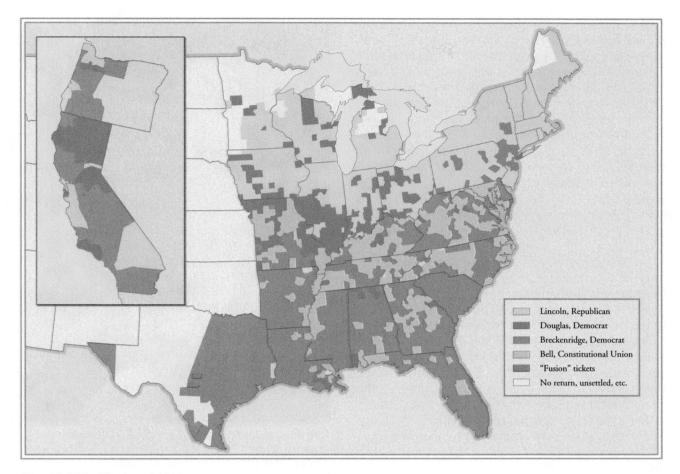

Map 13.3 *The Election of 1860*
This four-way election saw the North divided between Lincoln and Douglas, the South divided between Bell and Breckenridge.

Douglas, breaking with tradition, spoke from New England to Alabama, trying to warn people what could happen if they voted along sectional lines. While campaigning across the Deep South, he endured rotten fruit, insults, and injuries from a collapsed platform. Few men were willing to believe their opponents would have the nerve to act on their threats.

On election day, November 6, Lincoln won in every northern state except New Jersey, which divided between Douglas and Lincoln. Douglas won outright only in Missouri. Breckinridge won the entire South except the border states of Virginia, Tennessee, and Kentucky, which went with Bell. Even at this late stage of sectional division, voters did not fit into easy categories. It was hardly a contest between a rural South and an industrial urban North, for northern cities tended to vote for compromise candidates, not for Lincoln. Similarly, over half of southerners voted for Bell or Douglas, supporting the Union over the South.

Once the election returns were in, though, these complications seemed to evaporate. Even though Lincoln won only in the North, the election was not even close in the electoral college, where Lincoln won 180 electoral votes to Breckinridge's 72, Bell's 39, and Douglas's 12. In southern eyes, the North had arrogantly placed its own interests above those of the Union, insisting on electing a man who did not even appear on Southern ballots. In northern eyes, the South was to blame, walking out of nominating conventions and talking of disunion. The election of 1860 completed what John Brown's raid had started: the estrangement of North and South.

The South Debates Independence

The fire-eaters declared Abraham Lincoln's 1860 victory a sign that the North valued neither the Union nor the Constitution on which it was based. The South, they said, had every right, every incentive, to leave the Union. Although the Republicans claimed to work within the political system, Lincoln's supporters had violated an honored tradition of compromise.

Even though the Democrats still controlled the Senate and the Supreme Court, southerners believed that Lincoln would use the patronage of the federal government to install Republican officials throughout the South and possibly entice non-slaveholders with their free labor doctrines. Such officials could undermine slavery from within, eroding the authority of slaveowners. For years, Lincoln had talked of "a house" that had to be unified, of a nation that had to be all slave or all free. Would he not act to undermine slavery now that he was in power?

The nation's eyes turned to South Carolina. Influential men there, after all, had talked of secession since the nullification crisis nearly thirty years earlier. They believed that the same states that had created the Union could also dissolve that Union when it no longer served their purposes. The South Carolina legislature met on the day after Lincoln's election but did not secede immediately. Its members called for an election two months later to select delegates who would then decide the course the state should follow. In the meantime, they hoped, support for secession would grow. The next day, a local paper blustered, "the tea has been thrown overboard; the revolution of 1860 has been initiated."

States of the Deep South quickly lined up behind South Carolina. Carolina leaders, heartened by the response, seceded earlier than they had planned, on December 20. Southerners serving in Buchanan's cabinet began resigning and by the administration's annual New Year's Day reception, southerners in attendance all refused to shake Buchanan's hand or acknowledge the president. By February 1, Mississippi, Florida, Alabama, Georgia, Louisiana, and Texas had joined the secession movement. On February 4, delegates from these states met in Montgomery, Alabama, and created a provisional constitution, similar to that of the United States except in its explicit guarantee of slavery and states' rights. On February 18, the convention inaugurated a provisional president, Jefferson Davis of Mississippi, and a vice president, Alexander H. Stephens of Georgia. Davis was a strong states' rights advocate but not a fervent secessionist. With an eye towards opinion in the crucial states of Virginia, North Carolina, Kentucky, and Tennessee, these leaders of the new Confederacy portrayed themselves as a calm and conservative people, not wild-eyed revolutionaries.

The advocates of secession knew they had to strike before Lincoln took office. Two bad things could

Jefferson Davis, of Mississippi, a former U.S. senator and secretary of war, became the first—and only—president of the Confederate States of America in 1861.
© Bettmann/Corbis

happen if they waited to see what the new president did once in office. He might either attack the South by force or he might prove to be as moderate as he claimed to be. In the latter case, secessionists feared, white southerners would let the moment pass.

Many thousands of white southerners resisted secession. Some argued that secession was treason. Others warned that the South was committing suicide. Others argued that the southern states should wait until they could cooperate with one another more formally and fully. By presenting a united front to the North, these "cooperationists" insisted, the South would not need to secede at all. The North, recognizing that the South really was not bluffing, would grant concessions protecting slavery forever.

The arguments against immediate secession appealed to a large portion of southerners. Even in the southern states that rushed to secede in January of 1861, almost half of all votes went to delegates who had not supported immediate secession. The opposition to secession proved stronger still in the Upper

South. Upper South moderates warned that their states would bear the brunt of any conflict between the Lower South and the North. And voters listened: more than a month after the first seven states seceded, secession lost in Virginia by a two-to-one margin. The secessionists were stymied, too, in Tennessee, North Carolina, and Arkansas. The leaders of these border states believed they could bargain between the Gulf Confederacy and the North, winning the concessions the South wanted while maintaining the Union.

Recognizing the need to convince the border states to join the secession movement, five states from the Lower South dispatched agents to the Upper South to advocate and justify disunion. These commissioners wrote numerous letters to local politicians and spoke to legislatures, public meetings and private gatherings of community leaders in their efforts to cajole and persuade. These conversations among southerners clearly highlight the importance of race and slavery as the foundation of the states' rights argument. Delegates, such as Stephen Hale of Alabama, warned Kentucky's governor that Lincoln's election "was nothing less than an open declaration of war, for the triumph of this new theory of government destroys the property of the South, lays waste her fields, and inaugurates all the horrors of a San Domingo servile insurrection, consigning her citizens to assassinations and her wives and daughters to pollution and violation."

Northerners, too, remained quite divided at the beginning of 1861. Many recent immigrants viewed the conflict as none of their business. Northern Democrats called for conciliation with the South and many argued they were "for peace and not war . . . war is no remedy . . . and horribly wicked when waged without any cause, and by one portion of our people against another." Many black Northerners warned that a war for the Union alone did not deserve black support. A war to end bondage would be worth fighting, they argued, but in 1861 only the most aggressive white abolitionists spoke of such a cause.

People had plenty of opportunity to air their opinions, for events did not move quickly after Lincoln's election. After the first flush of secessionist victory at the beginning of 1861, people throughout the nation watched and waited to see what would happen when the new president officially assumed office on March 4. In the meantime, no one appeared to be in charge. James Buchanan, as lame-duck president, could not do much, and neither could the lame-duck Congress.

Most Republicans, including Lincoln, viewed the rhetoric and even the votes for southern secession as negotiating strategies rather than actual steps toward dissolving the Union. The Republicans

showed no inclination to bargain with the South over what remained the key question: federal support for slavery in the territories. Many recalled northern acceptance of defeat at the polls in 1856 and denounced southern rejection of the "lawfully elected administration." The tensions that had built up in the 1850s, Lincoln thought, could no longer be avoided. "The tug has to come," he argued, "and better now, than any time hereafter." If the North postponed action, Lincoln and other Republicans thought, the South would step up its efforts to gain new slave territories in the Caribbean and Central America, dragging the United States into war.

THE FIRST SECESSION

In the winter of 1861, the center of the conflict between the North and the South gradually shifted to two obscure forts in the harbor of Charleston, South Carolina. A Kentucky-born U.S. Army officer, Major Robert Anderson, worried that secessionists would attack his small federal force at Fort Moultrie in Charleston. Determined to avoid a war, on December 26 Anderson moved his small garrison from Fort Moultrie to Fort Sumter, a facility occupying a safer position in the center of the Charleston harbor. Tired of tension and stalemate, northern editors cheered Anderson's actions: "these are the times to develop manhood. God bless Major Anderson for setting us a good example." When South Carolina guns drove away a ship President Buchanan had sent with supplies for Anderson and his men, Buchanan chose not to force the issue. Meanwhile, South Carolina troops strengthened their position around the Charleston harbor.

Lincoln Becomes President

Men from both the North and the South worked frantically, but fruitlessly, to find a compromise during these weeks. Some urged the passage of a new constitutional amendment that would permit slavery forever; some urged the purchase of Cuba to permit slavery to expand; some urged that war be declared against another country to pull the United States together again. All the compromises were designed to placate the South. Abolitionists viewed such maneuvering with disgust and told their countrymen to let the South go. "If the Union can only be maintained by new concessions to the slaveholders," Frederick Douglass argued, "then . . . let the Union perish." Such views were not popular. Mobs attacked antislavery advocates throughout the North.

On February 11, Abraham Lincoln began a long and circuitous railway trip from Illinois to Washington, covering nearly 2,000 miles and using twenty separate rail lines, pausing frequently along the way to speak to well-wishers. At first, he played down the threat of secession—"Let it alone," he counseled, "and it will go down of itself." But as the train rolled on and the Confederate convention in Montgomery completed its provisional government, Lincoln became more wary. Warned of attempts on his life, Lincoln slipped into Washington under cover of darkness.

Lincoln assembled his government under the growing shadow of war. He sought to balance his cabinet with men of various backgrounds. The two most formidable cabinet members were Secretary of State William H. Seward, a moderate Republican, and Secretary of the Treasury Salmon P. Chase, a radical Republican inclined to take a harder line with the South. Fort Sumter stood as the most pressing issue facing the new administration. Any show of force to reclaim the fort from South Carolina, southern Unionists warned, and the secessionists would sweep border states such as Virginia into the Confederacy.

Lincoln, with Seward's advice, toned down the speech he delivered at his inauguration in March. He told the South that he had no intention of disturbing slavery where it was already established, that he would not invade the region, that he would not attempt to fill offices with men repugnant to local sensibilities. But he also warned that secession was illegal. It was his duty to maintain the integrity of the federal government, and to do so he had to "hold, occupy, and possess" federal property in the states of the Confederacy, including Fort Sumter. Lincoln pleaded with his countrymen to move slowly, to let passions cool.

People heard in Lincoln's inaugural what they chose to hear. Republicans and Unionists in the South thought it a potent mixture of firmness and generosity. Skeptics, on the other hand, focused on the threat of coercion at Fort Sumter. If Lincoln attempted to use force of any kind, they warned, war would be the inevitable result. Lincoln did not plan on war; he was trying to buy time, hoping that compromisers in Washington would come up with a workable strategy.

The Decision at Fort Sumter

But there was less time than Lincoln realized. On the very day after Lincoln's speech, Major Anderson reported to Washington that he would be out of food within four to six weeks. Initially unsure as to the wisdom of retaining the fort, Lincoln finally decided that he had to act: he would send provisions but not mili-

Abraham Lincoln took over the presidency at a time when the sectional conflict had reached a crisis; he had little time or room in which to maneuver as the federal soldiers in Fort Sumter ran out of food and had to be abandoned or supplied.
The Granger Collection, New York

tary supplies to Fort Sumter. By doing so, Lincoln would maintain the balance he promised in his inaugural speech, keeping the fort but not using coercion unless attacked first. He sent a note to South Carolina's governor of his intent to provision the fort, a note perceived by Confederate leaders not as a courtesy, but an ultimatum.

The president recognized that the Confederacy was determined to act. Jefferson Davis and his government had decided a week earlier that any attempt to reprovision the fort would be in and of itself an act of war. Davis believed that no foreign power would respect a country, especially one as new and tenuous as the Confederate States of America, if it allowed one of its major ports to be occupied by another country. The Union's resupply of the fort would mean the Union still controlled it.

The Confederate government decided that its commander in Charleston, P. G. T. Beauregard, should attack Fort Sumter before the relief expedition had a chance to arrive. The leaders understood the risks. The Confederate secretary of state warned Jefferson Davis that the attack would "lose us every friend at the North" and "wantonly strike a hornet's nest which extends from mountains to ocean, and legions, now quiet, will swarm out and sting us to death. It is unnecessary; it puts us in the wrong; it is fatal." Nevertheless, on April 12, at 4:30 in the morning, Beauregard opened fire on the Union garrison. The shelling continued for thirty-three hours. Anderson held out for as long as he could, but when fire tore through the barracks and his ammunition ran low he decided the time for surrender had come. Northerners agreed that the events in South Carolina could not go unanswered. Lincoln issued a call for 75,000 volunteers to defend the Union. Southerners agreed that they would have no choice but to come to that state's aid if the North raised a hand against their fellow southerners.

CONCLUSION

It was no accident that the slave states and free states experienced mounting animosity and distrust in the late 1850s. The rapid expansion of both the North and the South put the two regions on a collision course in the West.

Watching the events of those years unfold, however, it is clear that the conflict could certainly have taken other forms. Had Kansas been handled more adroitly by Buchanan and the Democrats, had Preston Brooks not caned Charles Sumner, had Chief Justice Taney not issued the *Dred Scott* decision, and had John Brown not given violence a martyr's sanction, the election of 1860 would not have become the watershed it did. This cascade of events washed the United States toward dissolution. Another cascade of events would soon push it into war.

Recommended Readings

Crofts, Daniel W. *Old Southampton: Politics and Society in a Virginia County, 1834–1869* (1992). Provides a detailed account of the way politics worked in communities of the Upper South.

Charles B. Dew. *Apostles of Disunion: Southern Secession Commissioners and the Causes of the Civil War* (2001). Offers excellent coverage of debates about secession among southerners.

South Carolina troops fire cannon at the federal forces under the command of Major Robert Anderson. Although no one was killed in the assault, the shots opened the Civil War.
The Granger Collection, New York

Fehrenbacher, Don E. *The Dred Scott Case: Its Significance in American Law and Politics* (1978). The classic account of this complicated episode.

Finkelman, Paul, ed. *His Soul Goes Marching On: Responses to John Brown and the Harpers Ferry Raid* (1995). Contains fascinating articles about this much-interpreted event.

Foner, Eric. *Free Soil, Free Labor, Free Men: The Ideology of the Republican Party Before the Civil War* (1970). Masterfully demonstrates the power of free labor ideology.

Holt, Michael F. *The Political Crisis of the 1850s* (1978). Stresses the dynamics of the two-party system in bringing on the Civil War.

Morrison, Michael A. *Slavery and the American West: The Eclipse of Manifest Destiny and the Coming of the Civil War* (1997). A subtle survey of this critical topic.

Stampp, Kenneth. *America in 1857: A Nation on the Brink* (1990). Shows the advantages of examining the simultaneous processes and events of this period.

Wyatt-Brown, Bertram. *Southern Honor: Ethics and Behavior in the Old South* (1982). Puts forward a powerful interpretation of white southern culture.

Zarefsky, David. *Lincoln, Douglas, and Slavery: In the Crucible of Public Debate* (1990). Recasts our understanding of these famous political debates.

American Journey Online and InfoTrac College Edition

Visit the source collections at http://ajaccess. wadsworth.com and infotrac.thomsonlearning.com and use the Search function with the following key terms to explore documents, images, audio and video clips, articles, and commentary related to the material in this chapter.

Dred Scott   Abraham Lincoln
Harpers Ferry   Fort Sumter
Lincoln-Douglas debates

> Additional resources, exercises, and Internet links related to this chapter are available on the American Passages Web site: http://history.wadsworth.com/passages2e

14 DESCENT INTO WAR
1861–1862

WAR BEGINS: APRIL 1861 TO JULY 1861

WAR TAKES COMMAND: AUGUST 1861 TO MARCH 1862

THE UNION ON THE OFFENSIVE: MARCH TO SEPTEMBER 1862

Thomas Nast. The Departure of the Seventh Regiment to the War, April 19, 1861. *The first days after secession saw great waves of enthusiasm fill both the North and the South as people mobilized for what they expected to be a short and glorious war.*
Seventh Regiment Fund

At the beginning of 1861, Americans could not imagine anything like the war that soon consumed their nation. Events piled on one another in ways that no one could have anticipated. The men who voted for Lincoln did not think the South would secede, the architects of secession did not think the North would resist, and neither side thought the other would or could fight for long. Events proved no more predictable once the war began. Last-minute reinforcements and retreats changed the outcome of battles; news from the battlefield shaped every political and diplomatic decision.

WAR BEGINS: APRIL 1861 TO JULY 1861

Neither the Union nor the Confederacy was ready for conflict in the spring of 1861. A number of states had yet to declare their loyalties and other states, communities, and families found themselves divided against themselves. In a matter of months, both the North and the South had to prepare for war.

Lincoln Calls for Troops

Two days after the Confederate flag went up over Fort Sumter on April 15, President Lincoln declared South Carolina in rebellion against the United States and called for 75,000 militiamen to help put the rebellion down. The president sought to appear restrained in his response. He demanded that forces gathering from the states of the Lower South "disperse and retire peacefully." He still hoped that Unionists in southern states besides South Carolina would rally to the nation's defense if he showed that he was no extremist. Lincoln also acted cautiously because he had not received the approval of Congress, which would not convene until July.

Lincoln's attempt to blend firmness and conciliation failed. Southern states saw the call to the militia as an act of aggression against South Carolina and state sovereignty. The Upper South states replied with defiance to Lincoln's requests for their troops on April 15, 1861. One Virginia representative responded to the president, "I have a Union constituency which elected me by a majority of one thousand, and I believe now that there are not ten Union men in that county today." Virginia seceded two days later. Although many people in Virginia still clung to hopes of avoiding war, two delegates to every one voted for secession on April 17. These Virginians, like white southerners of all inclinations and temperaments, refused to supply soldiers to

confront another slaveholding state. Recognizing the importance of moving President Jefferson Davis and his government closer to their armies, the Confederacy immediately voted to move its capital to Richmond in May of 1861.

In the North, even in areas like New York City, which had opposed Lincoln's election, 250,000 people filled the streets in a Unionist rally. Democrat Stephen Douglas addressed a tumultuous Chicago crowd. "There are only two sides to the question," he proclaimed. "Every man must be for the United States or against it. There can be no neutrals in this war, only patriots—or traitors." Ohio's governor informed Lincoln that "without seriously repressing the ardor of the people," he would raise twenty regiments to defend the nation rather than the requested thirteen. A Harvard professor, born during Washington's presidency, exclaimed, "I never knew what a popular excitement can be . . . The whole population, men, women, and children, seem to be in the streets with Union favors and flags."

The States Divide

Arkansas, Tennessee, and North Carolina quickly followed Virginia's example. North Carolinians, who over the winter rioted against secession and shot Confederate flags from their staffs, considered Lincoln's actions a call to arms for southern men that "as by a stroke of lighting, . . . made the South wholly South." The Oklahoma Territory, too, aligned itself with the Confederacy. There, leaders of the Five Civilized Tribes, slaveholders themselves, used the opportunity to fight against the U.S. government that had dispossessed them from their homes three decades earlier. The leaders of other Indian nations sided with the Union, however, and began to fight for control of the Indian Territory.

State leaders elsewhere frantically struggled with one another. In Maryland, rioters attacked Massachusetts troops as they marched through Baltimore two days after the secession of neighboring Virginia—spilling the first blood of the war when twelve civilians and four Union soldiers died in the gunfire. Maryland bitterly divided, the southern portion of the state sympathizing with the Confederacy, with Baltimore, where free blacks outnumbered slaves by eleven to one, and the western portion generally supporting the Union. Should the United States lose Maryland, the District of Columbia would be completely surrounded by Confederate territory. Accordingly, Lincoln acted quickly to keep Maryland in line, jailing secession advocates and suspending the writ of habeas corpus so they could not be released. He

CHRONOLOGY

1861

April	15	Lincoln calls for 75,000 militia
April	17–May 20	Arkansas, Tennessee, Virginia, and North Carolina secede
May	29	Richmond becomes capital of Confederacy
July	21	Confederate victory at Bull Run (Manassas)
	25	Frémont takes command in the West
	27	McClellan takes command of Union forces near Washington
August	30	Frémont declares martial law, and frees slaves, in Missouri
September	6	Kentucky remains in the Union
November	1	McClellan assumes command of all Union armies
	6	Jefferson Davis elected president of Confederacy with six-year term
	7	Union capture of Port Royal, South Carolina
	8	Union navy seizes Confederate commissioners Mason and Slidell from British ship *Trent*
	19	Halleck replaces Frémont as Union commander in West
December	26	Union government releases Mason and Slidell
	30	Suspension of specie payments

1862

February	6	Union captures Fort Henry on Tennessee River
	16	Confederates surrender Fort Donelson to Grant
	22	Inauguration of Jefferson Davis
	25	Legal Tender Act in North authorizes "greenbacks" Confederates evacuate Nashville
	27	Confederate Congress authorizes martial law and suspends habeas corpus
March	8–9	*Virginia v. Monitor* in Hampton Roads, Virginia

	17	McClellan begins move to James River Peninsula
April	5	McClellan begins siege of Yorktown
	6–7	Grant wins dramatic victory at Shiloh
	16	Confederacy passes Conscription Act
	25	New Orleans surrenders to Admiral Farragut
May	8–9	Jackson's Shenandoah Valley Campaign
	20	Homestead Act passed by Union Congress
	31	Lee takes command of Army of Northern Virginia
June	6	Confederates evacuate Memphis
	26	Lee drives McClellan from Richmond in Seven Days' Battles
July	11	Halleck appointed general-in-chief of Union armies
	12	Border states reject Lincoln plan for gradual emancipation
	17	Second Confiscation Act
	22	Cabinet hears Lincoln's draft of Emancipation Proclamation
August	3	Union decides to evacuate McClellan's troops from peninsula
	29–30	Confederate victory at Second Bull Run (Manassas)
September	4–6	Lee invades Maryland
	17	Battle of Antietam (Sharpsburg)
	22	First Emancipation Proclamation
October	3–4	Union victory at Corinth
November	7	Burnside replaces McClellan as commander of Army of the Potomac Republicans lose widely in mid-term elections in North
December	13	Lee overwhelms Burnside at Fredericksburg
	16–20	Crisis in Lincoln's cabinet
	27–29	Sherman defeated near Vicksburg

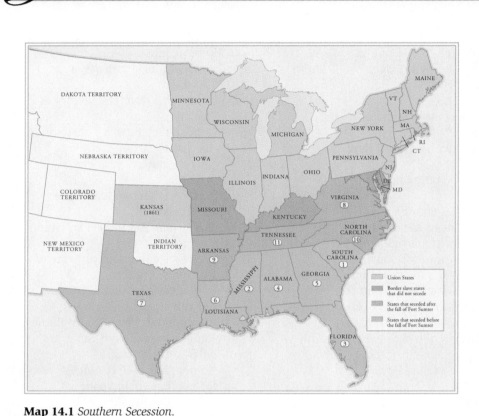

Map 14.1 *Southern Secession.*

View an animated version of this map or related maps at http://history.wadsworth.com/passages2e

The seven Gulf states seceded first, and on February 9th, delegates from these states met in Montgomery, Alabama, to create a provisional constitution, similar to that of the United States except in its explicit guarantee of slavery and states' rights. Advocates of secession traveled throughout the Upper South to convince voters and leaders to join the Confederacy. Regardless of the appeals to law and interpretations of the Constitution, the emotional heart of the debate white southerners conducted among themselves centered on three related issues: loathing of the prospect of racial equality, fear of servile insurrection and race war, and a surprisingly frank, if horrified, discussion of the inevitable miscegenation that would result if slavery were destroyed. While the language of states' rights appeared in these discussions, it focused on the states' rights to maintain slavery and preserve the standing racial order. Immediately after Lincoln called for troops to suppress the rebellion in South Carolina, Virginia, Arkansas, North Carolina, and Tennessee departed the Union. The other slave states—Kentucky, Maryland, Delaware, and Missouri—remained in the Union. Western Virginia would soon separate from the rest of the state and declare its loyalty to the Union.

admonished Baltimore leaders to send their "rowdies" home and if "they do attack us, we will return it, and that severely."

Kentucky, after months of determined attempts to remain neutral, decided for the Union in September after Confederate troops entered the state. Missouri officially remained in the Union but was ravaged from within for the next four years. Dissension took differ-

ent form in the mountains of western Virginia. In June, delegates from fifty counties met in Wheeling to renounce the Virginia secession convention, begin the gradual abolition of slavery, and declare their loyalty to the Union. Lincoln recognized these breakaway counties as the legal government of Virginia and their legislative delegations were seated in July 1861. After a complicated series of conventions and elections, the state of West Virginia came into being in 1862 and joined the Union the following year.

As it turned out, the Union and the Confederacy divided about as evenly as possible. Virginia, Tennessee, North Carolina, and Arkansas, all of which went into the Confederacy, might well have decided to remain with the Union; had they done so, the Confederacy would have had little hope of sustaining a successful war against the North. Those states accounted for half of all manufacturing and half of all food production in the Confederacy. Maryland, Kentucky, and Missouri, on the other hand, might well have joined the Confederacy; had they done so, the Union cause would have been weakened, perhaps fatally. Kentucky and Missouri occupied crucial positions along the major rivers that led into the South. Even the dissidents balanced: eight states along the border provided 235,000 white and 85,000 black troops to the Union and 425,000 to the Confederacy.

Although Abraham Lincoln was criticized from every angle in these months, he managed to bring into the Union fold the states he had to win. Had he lost these struggles, he might well have failed in all the other struggles that awaited him.

The Numbers

In retrospect, the cards seemed heavily stacked in the North's favor. The Union, after all, had vastly greater industrial capacity, railroads, canals, food, draft animals, ships, and entrepreneurial talent, all the things a mid-nineteenth-century war required. The Union could also claim four times as many white residents as the South. And although the 3.5 million enslaved people who lived in the Confederacy were extraordinarily valuable to the South, everyone recognized that the slaves could become equally valuable allies for the North.

Since the South acknowledged the North's advantages, many people then and since assumed that the Confederates must have been driven either by irrational rage or heedless bravery. Neither the Confederates nor the North, however, expected the secession crisis to turn into a full-fledged war, much less a four-year war. When Lincoln called for the 75,000 militia, he called them for only ninety days' service. When southern boys and men rushed to enlist for the Confederacy in the spring of 1861, they assumed they would be back home in time to harvest their crops in the autumn.

Southerners considered themselves natural soldiers, caricaturing their new enemies as clerks and factory workers. Though the Union did have more city men and immigrants than the South, most northerners, like southerners, were young men raised on farms. Since both sides believed that their opponents were weak and divided, northerners and southerners thought the conflict would likely come to a swift, and peaceful, resolution. Commanders on each side recognized their lack of experience. Lincoln calmed General Irvin McDowell: "You are green, it is true, but they are green also, you are all green alike." In such a struggle, sheer numbers did not seem nearly as important as they eventually became.

The Strategies

The military strategies of both sides sought to minimize actual fighting. The South saw itself as purely on the defensive; it would wait for northern armies to invade and then defeat them. The North, for its part, counted on General Winfield Scott's "Anaconda Plan," named after the snake of that name that slowly squeezes its prey to death. That plan depended on sending an overpowering force down the Mississippi River in the fall, dividing the South in two. At the same time, the Union navy would seal off the South from outside supplies. Ground troops and land battles would be kept to a minimum.

The Confederacy possessed considerable military advantages. It occupied an enormous area, larger than today's United Kingdom, France, Italy, and Spain combined. It possessed dozens of harbors and ports, connected by an excellent system of rivers and an adequate network of railroads. The Confederacy's long border with Mexico made it difficult to seal off outside supplies. The Confederacy could wage a defensive war, moving its troops internally from one point to another, whereas the Union had to move around the perimeter. The many country roads of the South, known only to locals, would provide routes for Confederate surprise attacks or strategic retreats.

For a model of how such a defensive plan might work, Southerners looked to the American Revolution. Like the American colonies eighty years earlier, the Confederates did not have to win every battle nor conquer northern territory. Southerners thought they had only to keep fighting long enough for the North's political, economic, regional, and ethnic divisions to overwhelm its temporary unity. Indeed, the Confederacy enjoyed advantages the American colonies had not enjoyed. The new southern nation covered twice as much territory as had the colonies, and the North possessed nowhere near the military power of the British at the time of the Revolutionary War.

Leadership

There was also the matter of leadership. In 1861, many observers would have given the advantage to the Confederates in this regard. Abraham Lincoln, after all, had held public office for only two years before he assumed the presidency, and his only military service had been a brief service in the militia. Jefferson Davis, by contrast, had distinguished himself in the war with Mexico. He had been secretary of war under Franklin Pierce and had served in the United States Senate. Davis, unlike Lincoln, directed his forces' military strategy with the confidence born of firsthand knowledge and experience.

At the beginning of the war, too, it appeared that the South had the better generals. The southern leaders certainly had more experience: the average age of the Union generals in 1861 was thirty-eight; of Confederate generals, forty-seven. Robert E. Lee of Virginia had served as an engineer, an officer in the Mexican War in the 1840s, and superintendent of West Point in the late 1850s. He resigned his U.S. military commission and accepted command of Virginia's forces. Lee made the same tortured decision so many southerners made when secession finally came: "With all my devotion to the Union and the feeling and loyalty of an American citizen, I have not been able to make up my mind to raise my hand against my relatives, my children, my home."

Neither the Union nor the Confederacy felt a need for a commanding general. Many lesser generals still had to be named quickly, however. Military experience and ability did not always prove to be the major considerations in these appointments. About a third of Union generals and half their Confederate counterparts had not been professional soldiers, though most had undergone some military training; overall, the North and the South placed roughly similar proportions of professional soldiers in command. The South did enjoy an advantage among junior officers, as seven of the nation's eight military colleges were in the South. In 1861, one-third of Virginia regiments' field grade officers had graduated from the Virginia Military Institute. Lincoln, forced to unify a people far more divided than the white population of the Confederacy, chose generals from the ranks of various constituencies he needed to appease: abolitionists, Democrats, Irish, and Germans. Jefferson Davis did the same to bind ambitious politicians from the various states to the new Confederacy.

Neither the Union nor the Confederacy enjoyed a clear advantage in civilian leadership. Both Lincoln and Davis assembled cabinets that balanced geography, political faction, personality, and expertise. The

Robert E. Lee rejected Lincoln's offer of command of the Union armies before he resigned his U.S. commission and swore allegiance to the Confederacy.
North Wind Picture Archives

Confederates had to create a government from scratch, including the design of flags, stamps, and money. Davis ran through several secretaries of war and secretaries of state before finding the two men on whom he felt he could rely, James A. Seddon and Judah P. Benjamin, respectively.

The Union enjoyed a head start in such matters, but the Republicans had many problems to iron out. Office seekers besieged Washington at the very time Lincoln was trying to keep the South in the Union; he felt like an innkeeper, he said, faced with customers demanding rooms in one wing while he tried to put out a fire in another. Lincoln's cabinet ended up containing men whom he barely knew and upon whom he was not always sure he could rely.

The First Conflicts

Battles began before anyone was ready. On the day following Lincoln's call for troops in April, federal officers in charge of the arsenal at Harpers Ferry and the naval yard in Norfolk, Virginia, sought to destroy the weapons under their command before secessionists could seize them. Despite their efforts, Virginia troops managed to recover valuable gun-making machinery, artillery, naval stores, and ships for the Confederate cause. A few weeks later, battles broke out along the B&O Railroad in what would become West Virginia, with Robert E. Lee, the new general for Virginia, leading an unsuccessful and embarrassing chase of troops under the command of George McClellan. Meanwhile, nearly 4,000 Confederates, most of them from Texas, pushed into New Mexico. They hoped to win the mineral riches of Colorado and perhaps even California for the Southern cause.

All these struggles showed both sides to be far from ready to fight a war in 1861. Not only were guns and uniforms scarce, but so were combat experience and even battlefield training. Even those men who had attended West Point had learned more about engineering than they had about tactical maneuvers. The United States Army contained only about 16,000 men, and nearly 12,000 of them were scattered across the vast territory west of the Mississippi River. The militiamen who first responded to the calls of the Union and Confederacy had scarcely been trained at all.

Mobilization

Both sides took immediate steps to create new armies, organized within local communities and led by local men. The Confederate Congress authorized 400,000 volunteers in May of 1861. In its special session beginning in July of 1861, the Union Congress authorized 500,000 troops, each signing on for three years; 700,000 eventually enlisted under this authorization. Much mobilization took place on the local level. Prominent citizens often supplied uniforms, guns, and even food for the troops from their localities. Units elected their own officers. States competed to enlist the largest numbers of men. A private mourned his state's slow mobilization, "New York and Pennsylvania and New Jersey are alive, while I am ashamed to speak of the apathy in Massachusetts." Local newspapers sought to make sure that state-level leaders dealt fairly with local troops and officers.

Some Northerners wondered whether the many divisions among classes, occupations, religions, and ethnic groups would hinder the Union war effort. Such doubters took heart at the response to the crisis of 1861. Both workingmen and wealthy men eagerly signed up. Members of ethnic groups took pride in forming their own units; the Irish and Germans supplied over 150,000 men each, with the total of foreign-born in service totaling nearly half a million. Northerners congratulated themselves that patriotism and self-sacrifice had not been killed, as many feared, by the spirit of commerce so strong in the land. Editor Horace Greeley sketched the transformation of Northerners from "a sordid, grasping money-loving people" to one in whom the "fires of patriotic devotion" still burned.

Southerners, too, found reason to be proud in 1861. The leaders of the South had secretly worried that when push came to shove the non-slaveholders would not fight for a cause that many identified with the defense of slavery. But Southern boys and men were activated by the same impulses that drove their Northern counterparts: dreams of glory, youthful self-confidence, and a burning desire to impress family, friends, and young women with their bravery. At this point in the war, white Southerners talked less about slavery than they had before or than they would later. In their eyes, they fought to defend their farms and homes from "foreign" invaders.

Editors, politicians, and citizens of both the North and the South demanded that the conflict be wrapped up immediately. "ON TO RICHMOND" ran the headline in northern papers while General Beauregard informed Jefferson Davis of his troops' readiness "to meet the enemies of our country under all circumstances." Confident of victory, they itched for the fight that would settle things once and for all. Only a few, such as William T. Sherman, dissented. This "is to be a long war,—very long,—much longer than any politician thinks."

The First Battle

Northerners soon grew impatient with the passive Anaconda Plan of cutting the South off from the outside. With so many men eagerly signing on to fight, Northerners thought they should get the war over early, before the South had time to consolidate its forces. The Union already had 35,000 men poised in northern Virginia, about twenty-five miles away from a Confederate force of 20,000 under the command of P. G. T. Beauregard. Beauregard's troops protected an important rail junction at Manassas, along Bull Run (a "run" is a stream). Confederate and Union troops also watched one another warily in the Shenandoah Valley, about fifty miles to the west.

These troop deployments reflected a primary goal of each side in the early stages of the war: capturing the capital of its enemy. Union leaders thought that if they could win Richmond—the industrial, commercial, and administrative center of the South— the rest of the Confederacy would soon follow. Confederate leaders thought that if they could conquer the capital of the United States, forcing Lincoln and

Despite his flamboyant appearance and cavalry tactics, J. E. B. Stuart, like a number of other Confederate generals, adhered to a strict religious discipline that prohibited drinking and swearing.
The Museum of the Confederacy, Richmond, Virginia. Copy Photography by Katherine Wetzel

The Battle of Bull Run (Manassas), the first major battle of the war, on July 21, 1861, suddenly turned into a rout of Union forces when confusion and Confederate reinforcements abruptly turned the tide.
Courtesy Sidney King

Early in the war, Thomas Jonathan "Stonewall" Jackson was the most beloved Confederate leader, admired for his military daring and his devout religious belief.
The Granger Collection, New York

his cabinet to flee, European powers would recognize the Confederacy's sovereignty and legitimacy.

The officers of both the Union and the Confederacy had learned their strategy at West Point although few had ever commanded units above the regimental level. These officers usually attempted to concentrate their force in hopes of overwhelming the enemy at the point of attack. The Union tried to take advantage of its greater numbers of men and resources; the Confederacy sought to use its interior lines, knowledge of the Virginia landscape, and aggressive maneuvers to gain an advantage. Educated with the same texts and serving together in peace and war, leaders on both sides knew what the others hoped and planned to do.

In the first major battle of the war, the South's advantages outweighed the North's. Both sides attempted to coordinate their troop movements near Washington and in the Shenandoah Valley. The valley had long served as a major corridor between the North and the South. If that corridor was left unprotected by the Union, Confederate forces could rush up the valley and capture Washington. But if too many troops protected the valley, the North would tie up men and resources that could be used more effectively elsewhere. The Confederacy employed cavalry, under the command of the flamboyant young colonel James E. B. (Jeb) Stuart, to move quickly up and down the valley, keeping the North off balance.

The Union, under the command of General Irvin McDowell, tried to concentrate most of its forces at Manassas by moving them from the valley. On July 21, the Northern troops were finally ready to attack. Congressmen and other spectators drove their carriages out from Washington to "see the Rebels get whipped." Union troops flooded over the battlefield, fording the creeks, flanking the strongest points in the Confederate lines. The Southern forces fell back to more defensible positions. When it looked as if the Confederates were to be routed, a Southern general pointed out Thomas J. Jackson to his men, "There is Jackson standing like a stone wall! Rally behind the Virginians!" "Stonewall Jackson," until recently an undistinguished mathematics professor at the Virginia Military Institute, had been christened.

The Confederate reinforcements that poured off the train at Manassas gave Beauregard a renewed spirit. The Union forces suffered confusion when the lack of a common uniform led some Northerners to mistake Confederates for their own troops. They began to pull back and then to run. Some civilian carriages got caught in the panicked flood of troops rushing back to Washington; the Confederates gleefully captured a New York congressman hiding in the woods and held him for the next six months in Richmond . . . as a prisoner.

The South had claimed its first victory. Each side had engaged about 18,000 soldiers, making Bull Run by a considerable margin the largest battle ever waged in the United States up to that time. Both the North and the South lost about 600 men. Nevertheless, the humiliating rout confirmed the Confederate belief that one Rebel could whip ten Yankees.

Key parts of Confederate lore emerged from Bull Run as well: the Rebel yell and the Confederate battle flag. The yell was not merely a scream or a roar, but a high wail, unnerving and strange. It served as the rallying cry for Southern troops for the rest of the war. The first flag of the Confederacy, the Stars and Bars, looked a great deal like that of the United States, leading to confusion in the heat of battle. After Bull Run, Beauregard designed a new flag—a square banner, red with a blue cross and white stars—to ensure that Southern troops did not fire on one another. It was that battle flag, never the official flag of the Confederacy, that later generations came to consider synonymous with the South.

For the next two years, the Battle of Bull Run emboldened Southern forces who fought in Virginia. The Confederacy, feeling itself invulnerable, fought aggressively, even recklessly, in the east. The Union fought cautiously, even tentatively, in Virginia. One Union

The battle flag (below) was adopted by the Confederates after Manassas because the official flag (top)—the so-called Stars and Bars—looked too much like the U.S. flag and led to deadly confusion in battle.
Courtesy of the National Park Service, Kennesau Mountain National Park. Photo, Harpers Peng Conservation Center (top)
Courtesy of the Carl Vinson Institute of Government—the University of Virginia. Photo by Ed Jackson (bottom)

soldier wrote home, "During the day one of the boys brought in a Virginia paper in which it stated that one 'Southerner could lick five Northern mudsills. It was not so comforting to feel we were to be killed off in blocks of five." Neither side forgot this conflict even though each side called it by different names. Northern forces generally named battles after physical features such as rivers and mountains; thus, they deemed this the Battle of Bull Run. Southerners usually named battles after nearby towns or villages; they called this one Manassas.

Louisa May Alcott
"Journal," April 1861

Thirty years old in 1862, Alcott, who had lived in her father's home her entire life, applied to become a nurse. She had no formal training, though she had cared for her dying sister. Her journal tells of her feelings at the beginning of her service, "full of hope and sorrow, courage and plans." She threw herself into the work, but grew ill with typhoid fever and endured mercury poisoning from the medication she received. She had to come home for the duration of the war. Alcott became a best-selling author with her enduring novel *Little Women*, published in 1868.

April. [1861]—War declared with the South, and our Concord company went to Washington. A busy time getting them ready, and a sad day seeing them off, for in a little town like this we all seem like one family in times like these. At the station the scene was very dramatic, as the brave boys went away perhaps never to come back again.

I've often longed to see a war, and now I have my wish. I long to be a man, but as I can't fight, I will content myself with working for those who can. . . .

September, October. [1862]— . . . War news bad. Anxious faces, beating hearts, and busy minds.

I like the stir in the air, and long for battle like a warhorse when he smells powder. The blood of the Mays is up! . . .

November.—Thirty years old. Decided to go to Washington as a nurse if I could find a place. Help needed, and I love nursing, and *must* let out my pentup energy in some new way. Winter is always a hard and a dull time, and if I am away there is one less to feed and warm and worry over.

I want new experiences, and am sure to get 'em if I go. So I've sent in my name, and bide my time writing tales, to leave all snug behind me, and mending up my old clothes,—for nurses don't need nice things, thank Heaven!

December.—On the 11th I received a note from Miss H. M. Stevenson telling me to start for Georgetown next day to fill a place in the Union Hotel Hospital. Mrs. Ropes of Boston was matron, and Miss Kendall of Plymouth was a nurse there, and though a hard place, help was needed. I was ready, and when my commander said "March!" I marched. Packed my trunk, and reported in B.[oston] that same evening.

We had all been full of courage till the last moment came, then we all broke down. I realized that I had taken my life in my hand, and might never see them all again. I said, "Shall I stay, Mother?" as I hugged her close. "No, go! and the Lord be with you!" answered the Spartan woman, and till I turned the corner she bravely smiled and waved her wet handkerchief on the doorstep. Shall I ever see that dear old face again?

So I set forth in the December twilight, with May and Julian Hawthorne as escort, feeling as if I was the son of the house going to war.

Friday, the 12th, was a very memorable day, spent in running all over Boston to get my pass, etc., calling for parcels, getting a tooth filled, and buying a veil,—my only purchase. A. C. gave me some old clothes, the dear Sewalls money for myself and boys, lots of love and help, and at 5 P.M., saying "goodby" to a group of tearful faces at the station, I started on my long journey, full of hope and sorrow, courage and plans.

A most interesting journey into a new world full of stirring sights and sounds, new adventures, and an evergrowing sense of the great task I had undertaken.

I said my prayers as I went rushing through the country white with tents, all alive with patriotism, and already red with blood.

A solemn time, but I'm glad to live in it, and am sure it will do me good whether I come out alive or dead.

All went well, and I got to Georgetown one evening very tired. Was kindly welcomed, slept in my narrow bed with two other room-mates, and on the morrow began my new life by seeing a poor man die at dawn, and sitting all day between a boy with pneumonia and a man shot through the lungs. A strange day, but I did my best, and when I put mother's little black shawl round the boy while he sat up panting for breath, he smiled and said, "You are real motherly, ma'am." I felt as if I was getting on. The man only lay and stared with his big black eyes, and made me very nervous. But all were well behaved, and I sat looking at the twenty strong faces as they looked back at me,—hoping that I looked "motherly" to them, for my thirty years made me feel old, and the suffering round me made me long to comfort every one. . . .

Source: Alcott's journals are located at Houghton Library, Harvard University, and have been published in Joel Myerson and Daniel Shealy, editors, *The Journals of Louisa May Alcott* (Boston, 1989).

 ## Women and War

Women had avidly studied the debates being waged in the newspapers. They had expressed their opinions in private conversation, in their letters, and in their diaries. Many had listened to the speeches on all sides. They had counseled their sons and husbands, sometimes urging their men on to join others of their community. They had worn cockades displaying their loyalties and had sung the latest songs. Once the speeches, songs, and toasts had come to an end and the fighting had begun, women became even more active. Within two weeks of the war's beginning, women on the two sides had formed 20,000 aid societies. These societies devoted themselves to supplying the armies' needs, especially clothing and medical supplies. One such organization in Alabama provided, in just one month, "422 shirts, 551 pairs of drawers, 80 pairs of socks, 3 pairs of gloves, 6 boxes and one bale of hospital supplies, 128 pounds of tapioca, and a donation of $18 for hospital use."

With the first battles, women claimed positions as nurses, even though men had served before as military nurses. Despite some initial grumbling by men, women converted themselves immediately into competent and devoted nurses. Dorothy Dix, long known as the champion of the mentally ill and other neglected people in the antebellum era, took matters in hand for the North. She became superintendent of nurses for the Union army, the highest executive appointment for a woman to date, organizing 3,000 women who volunteered to serve. Concerned both about the effectiveness and propriety of women min-

Women in both the North and South quickly stepped forward as nurses, sometimes against opposition, to save lives and relieve suffering.
© Corbis

istering to young male strangers, Dix decreed that she wanted only "plain" women, women over thirty, and women who would dress in brown and black. Unfortunately, by war's end, Dix's prudery, enthusiasm, and mismanagement had alienated military doctors, most of the Sanitary Commission, and many of her own nurses.

Women's efforts soon became legendary. They labored until they could no longer stand, until their long dresses trailed blood from amputations and wounds. Kate Cumming and Phoebe Pember played leading roles in the Confederacy, and Clara Barton took her aid to the front lines of the Union and later founded the American Red Cross. Most women stayed closer to home, working in factories, doing piecework in their households, or tilling fields. As Northern farmers departed for the military, observers in the Midwest saw "more women driving teams" and more "at work in fields than men."

WAR TAKES COMMAND: AUGUST 1861 TO MARCH 1862

The war spread across the continent in the fall, winter, and spring of 1861–1862. Armies consolidated command and launched campaigns thousands of miles from headquarters. Governments transformed their economies, invented or reinvented navies, conducted diplomacy, and cemented the loyalties of those at home. Families steeled themselves for a war longer than they had been willing to imagine.

McClellan Assumes Control

The North, while embarrassed by Bull Run, took from that defeat a determination to fight more effectively. Volunteers flooded into recruitment offices. Lincoln removed the leaders responsible for that battle and replaced them with George B. McClellan. Although short of stature and only thirty-four years old, McClellan exuded great authority. He was known as the "young Napoleon." McClellan had distinguished himself in the Mexican War and had studied military tactics in Europe. Moreover, he had already frustrated Confederate forces under Robert E. Lee in western Virginia. He now threw himself into reorganizing and reenergizing the Union troops under his command.

The press lavished praise on the young general. Already inclined toward grandiose visions of his abilities, McClellan developed an exalted sense of himself. The cocky commander considered Lincoln an "idiot" and his cabinet incompetent "geese." McClellan ignored, avoided, and insulted those men at every opportunity. McClellan wanted to make his army perfectly prepared before he risked it, and his reputation, in battle against Confederates whose numbers his spies consistently exaggerated. Meanwhile, months dragged by. Lincoln and newspaper editors became furiously impatient, but McClellan would not be moved.

Early in the war, Lincoln and the rest of the North placed great faith in the "young Napoleon," General George B. McClellan. Events would later lessen their admiration.
The Granger Collection, New York

The War in the West Begins

There was to be no waiting in the West. Four days after the battle at Bull Run, the Union installed a new commander in charge of the forces in Missouri: John C. Frémont, the "pathfinder of the West" and former Republican presidential candidate. Whereas the situation in Virginia unfolded slowly, the situation in Missouri burst into chaos in July and August of 1861. Guerrilla forces raged throughout the state. Confederate armies built up on the southern border, ready to attack in both the eastern and western parts of the state. Frémont decided that he had to protect the Mississippi River in the East and therefore left a weak force in the West. That force, outnumbered by the Confederates, staged a desperate attack, with terrible losses, at Wilson's Creek. As at Bull Run, the lack of a standard uniform color created deadly confusion. The Northern units fell into ragged retreat, exposing Missouri to Rebel incursions.

With the army so far from Washington, desperate for war materials and supplies, contractors took advantage of the situation, selling substandard goods to the Union army at inflated prices. With the populace of Missouri so divided in its loyalties, Frémont, who, a contemporary noted, had "all of the qualities of genius except ability," did not know whom to trust. Frantic, he declared the entire state under martial law, decreed the death penalty for captured guerrillas, and seized the slaves and other property of all Confederate sympathizers. Slaveholders in the border states of Kentucky and Maryland threatened to throw their allegiances to the South if Lincoln did not overrule Frémont.

The president, desperate to keep the border states within the Union, advised the general that the proclamation angered loyal slaveowners and threatened the loss of Kentucky and requested him to revoke his emancipation order. When Frémont resisted, demanding a public order overruling him, Lincoln felt that he had no choice but to remove Frémont from his post.

Events on the battlefield in the earliest stages of the war proved to be a poor guide to the long term. Although the North had been shaken by Bull Run and Missouri, it had lost neither Washington nor the border states. Although the South had apparently won at Bull Run, the Confederate forces, exhausted and bogged down in mud, had not taken advantage of the situation to attack the Union capital. Although slaveholders in the border states fumed at the Union government and military leaders, they remained in the Union. As a result, the South was deprived of a key strategic advantage: access to the Ohio River and a defensible border with the North. With the Union army able to move up and down the Ohio at will, the Confederates had to defend a vast, vague, and shifting border in Kentucky and Tennessee.

The war was not to be won by a decisive battle within a few months of the war's start. Instead, slower and less dramatic processes proved decisive. Armies and navies had to be built from scratch; economies had to be converted to wartime demands; households and families had to absorb growing sacrifices. These transformations began in earnest in the summer of 1861.

Paying for War

The Civil War, involving so many men over such an enormous territory, immediately became breathtakingly expensive. It was by no means clear how either side was going to pay. Although the Union and the Confederacy were, by any international standard, rich societies, neither had ever supported a large army or an active government. Taxes on imported goods and the sale of apparently endless public lands paid for what government there was. Ever since the Bank War of the 1830s, the federal and state governments did little to manipulate the currency. As a result, when the war came, the men responsible for paying for it had only a few options—loans, new taxes, or the creation of paper money.

Loans met the least resistance in both the North and the South, but this borrowing could provide only a third of the cost of the war. Taxes proved even less effective. The Confederacy quickly decided that it had no choice but to turn to paper money. As soon as it could find adequate engravers and printing presses, the South began producing millions of dollars in the new currency. Catastrophic inflation began to grow as early as the winter of 1861–1862. In Virginia, cash was scarce as women wrote husbands in the army for money and others turned away poorer friends, "I have no money by me at all" and "the wealthiest men in the county here have no money."

The situation was not quite as bad in the North, where taxes and bonds carried much more of the burden of financing the war, but the Union, too, was forced to issue paper money by the first winter of the war. People hoarded gold in anticipation of the deprivations a widened war would cause. New York banks felt they had no choice but to suspend specie payments in December of 1861. In February of 1862, the Union Congress reluctantly decided that it had no choice but to create paper money. The Legal Tender Act of that month permitted the treasury to release up to $10 million of the new currency, quickly dubbed "greenbacks." Over $450 million in paper notes circulated during the war, replacing the earlier system of state bank notes with a unified national currency.

The Confederate Homefront

Southerners watched helplessly as armies stripped their farms of food and livestock. They ministered to the bleeding young men dragged into their parlors and bedrooms. The residents of places where both Unionists and Confederates remained strong—such as Missouri and eastern Tennessee—became caught in internal civil wars that pitted roving gangs of thugs against one another. Governors received letters from women, their husbands and sons gone, who worried that they faced starvation if they did not get help soon.

Inflation ate away at the Confederacy like a cancer. The rapid rise in prices made currency worth less every day. The government issued war bonds that paid 8 percent interest per year at a time when inflation reached 12 percent per month in 1861. Speculators

Much of the Civil War turned around conflicts such as the one depicted in this painting, in which small groups of soldiers confronted one another and civilians far from the scenes of major battles.
©Bettmann/Corbis

could make money simply by buying up supplies and holding them while prices escalated. Farmers faced the temptation to grow cotton despite the needs of the armies. Cotton stored well and everyone knew that cotton would fetch a high price after the war, no matter who won. As a result, land and labor that could have grown food bent under the weight of cotton. A Georgia newspaper blamed speculators, for "a conscienceless set of vampires . . . are determined to make money even if one-half of the people starve."

Confederate leaders worried that the plantations could not produce the food the armies so desperately needed if white men did not force the slaves to work. African Americans wanted to hunt, fish, or work for themselves and their own families rather than to labor for the white people. Plantation mistresses often discovered that slaves would not work when the master—and the whips and guns he wielded—no longer hung over the slaves. Accordingly, the Confederate Congress passed laws exempting from the draft white men to supervise slaves on larger plantations. That a government in such need of every available soldier felt compelled to write such laws revealed how central slavery remained even in the midst of war.

To many poorer Southerners, the law was another in a growing list of grievances. Resentment against wealthy men and women—mediated during peacetime by family ties, common church membership, careful manners, and democratic politics—quickly came to the surface in the context of war. Common people were quick to notice when plantation slaves labored over cotton rather than corn, when the well-to-do hoarded gold or dodged taxes. Wealthy young men sometimes entered the Confederate army as privates, but others considered an officer's commission their just due as gentlemen. Scions of plantation fortunes often did little to disguise their disgust or amusement at the speech or clothing of the poorer men alongside whom they fought. The poorer soldiers noticed, as did their wives.

Navies

The navies of the North and South had to adapt most quickly. Just as many battles, starting with Bull Run, broke out at rail junctions, so did the leaders on both sides recognize the centrality of ports and rivers. The North's Anaconda Plan depended on control of the waterways, stopping the shipment of the South's immensely valuable cotton crop, cutting the region off from importations of weapons and other manufactured goods, and dividing the Confederacy along the Mississippi River.

The Union enjoyed a great initial advantage in its number of ships, but many of those ships were scattered around the globe. It took months to bring them home. Moreover, most of the Union's vessels were deep-sea ships. With remarkable speed, however, the Union naval department built new craft and deployed them against the South. In the first months of the war, the Navy Department armed merchant ships and sent them to blockade Southern ports. By the end of 1861, over 260 vessels patrolled the coasts and the skilled workers of the shipbuilding towns of the east coast had 100 more under construction, including the North's first ironclad ships.

The South had virtually no ships at the beginning of the war, but the Confederate navy seized, acquired, or built roughly 125 ships each year, including over 400 steam-powered ships. The Confederacy immediately contracted with large shipbuilding companies in England. Jefferson Davis authorized sailors to attack Northern ships on the high seas and turn them in for a share of the booty. For a few months, these "privateers" preyed on any unguarded ship they could find, but the Union navy quickly shut them down. The Confederates then used their naval officers to man ships that would attempt to sink rather than claim enemy ships. One intrepid officer, Raphael Semmes, escaped through the blockade in

CONFEDERATE SHIPS UNDER CONSTRUCTION IN ENGLAND

Williamson Art Gallery & Museum, Birkenhead, England

The Confederacy depended on English shipyards, such as this one in Liverpool, to construct vessels to run the Union blockade, attack Union ships on the seas, and defend its ports. English willingness to construct and equip Southern ships waned as battlefield defeats reduced the prospect of Confederate victory. The most effective arm of the Confederate navy consisted of commerce raiders, which destroyed roughly 255 Union ships and doubled the cost of marine insurance for Northern merchants. Two of the most successful, the *Alabama* and the *Shenandoah,* built at the Laird shipyards in Liverpool, were hybrid sail and steam-powered ships that disrupted Northern commerce and destroyed merchant ships in the Atlantic and Pacific Oceans. The *Shenandoah* fired the last official shot of the war across the bows of a whaler in the Bering Sea on June 28, 1865, as part of a month-long campaign that resulted in the capture of twenty-four whaling ships. Not until August 2nd did her captain James Waddell learn the war had ended. Fearing prosecution for piracy, Waddell sailed the *Shenandoah* warily back to England, arriving off the Irish coast on November 5, 1865.

1861 and seized eighteen Union ships before he was trapped at Gibraltar and forced to sell his ship and escape to England.

In the meantime, the North pushed its advantage. Larger ships began to blockade 189 harbors and ports from Virginia to Texas, patrolling 3,500 miles of coastline. Such enormous territory obviously proved difficult to control, especially because Northern ships periodically had to travel to ports hundreds of miles away for supplies and fuel. When Union craft left for such journeys, Southern blockade runners rushed into the unprotected ports. The Union navy decided to seize several Southern ports for use as supply stations.

The federal ships moved first in August, at Cape Hatteras in North Carolina, shelling the forts there and cutting off the supplies that dozens of blockade runners had brought into the Confederacy. The Northern navy also took a station near Biloxi, Mississippi, from which it could patrol the Gulf of Mexico. The most valuable seizure, however, was Port Royal, South Carolina. Not only did that place offer an excellent harbor, but it stood midway between the major Southern ports of Charleston and Savannah. The 77 ships and 16,000 sailors and soldiers dispatched to Port Royal were the largest combined force yet assembled in American warfare.

Diplomacy and the Trent Affair

On the day after the capture of Port Royal, a Union ship stopped a British mail packet, the *Trent,* as it traveled from Cuba to St. Thomas. The *Trent* carried James Mason and John Slidell, Confederate commissioners sailing to London and Paris to negotiate for the support of the British and French governments. The captain of the Union ship, Charles Wilkes, after firing two shots across the bow of the British vessel, boarded it and seized the Confederate emissaries. When Wilkes arrived in Boston to deposit Mason and Slidell in prison, he met with a hero's welcome. Congress ordered a medal struck in his honor.

The excitement began to wane, however, when people realized the possible repercussions of Wilkes's actions. Despite the growth of the Union navy, Great Britain still ruled the oceans. British newspapers and politicians called for war against the arrogant Americans: "We are pretty well accustomed to Yankee bluster and hot headedness, but we cannot think that they will be so utterly blind as to provoke a collision with a power which with little difficulty could blow to the four winds their dwarf fleet."

The *Trent* affair reflected the uneasy state of international relations created by the war. The Confederacy hoped that England or France, even both, would come to its aid. The importance of cotton in the international marketplace was such, Southerners argued, that the industrial powers of Europe could not long afford to allow the Northern navy to enforce its blockade.

The situation in the winter of 1861–1862 proved more complicated than people had expected, however. International law did not offer a clear ruling on whether Captain Wilkes had acted legally. And neither did self-interest offer a clear guide as to whether England should declare war on the United States or aid the Confederacy. The factories of Britain had stockpiled cotton in expectation of the war and did not clamor for intervention as Southerners had hoped. Anger over the *Trent* affair was balanced by resentment of Southern assumptions about British dependence on cotton. Confederates who "thought they could extort our cooperation by the agency of king cotton" would be disappointed, British leaders warned. They considered aid given in response to blackmail "ignominious beyond measure," completely unacceptable. France and England watched one another warily, neither country

Ulysses S. Grant distinguished himself in key battles in Tennessee and Mississippi in 1862. Many months and battles would pass, however, before Grant would assume command in the East.
The Granger Collection, New York

eager to upset the fragile balance of power between themselves by taking the first step in America.

Public opinion within England and France divided, for it was by no means clear to most Europeans which side had the better claim to their sympathies. Lincoln repeatedly declared that the war was not a war to end slavery. That declaration, Lincoln believed, was necessary to cement the support of the border states, but it undercut the support of English and European abolitionists for the Union cause. The Confederates claimed to be fighting for self-determination, a cause with considerable appeal in Europe, but potential supporters often viewed Southern slaveholding with disgust and distrust. One Confederate agent in London blamed Britain's failure to recognize the Confederate state on the South's "pernicious adherence to the institution of slavery." Both the English and the French waited for events on the battlefields of North America to clarify issues.

The *Trent* affair, however, had to be settled at once. Its settlement came through diplomatic evasion and maneuvering. The U.S. officials decided that

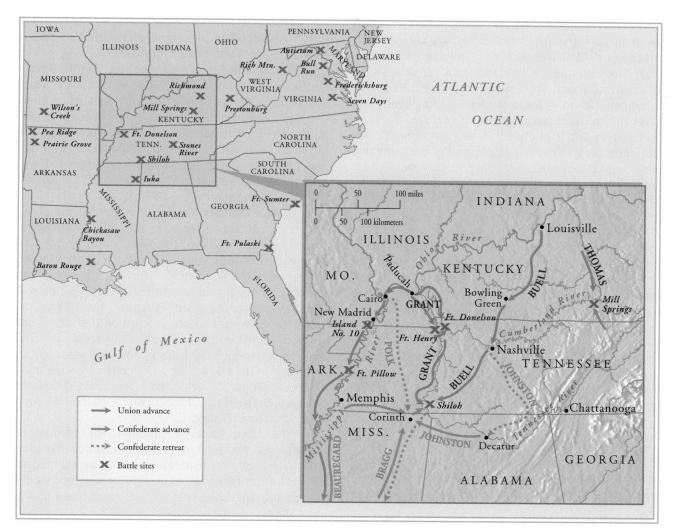

Map 14.2 *Campaigns in the West in 1862*
While Lee and McClellan remained immobilized in Virginia, U.S. Grant boldly pushed to the Mississippi border. View an animated version of this map or related maps at http://history.wadsworth.com/passages2e.

Wilkes had acted on his own, unauthorized by the government of the Union. Mason and Slidell were freed from prison and permitted to continue their journey. Although the Confederacy was jubilant at having "won," the underlying situation had not changed. Mason and Slidell found that though many powerful people elsewhere were sympathetic to the rebellious Southerners, they were unwilling to go to war against the United States.

The international situation remained tense and unsettled throughout the war. Leaders of both the North and the South could imagine situations in which England or France would intervene with weapons and supplies. Foreign intervention loomed as a fervent hope for the Confederacy and a great fear of the North.

The Rivers of the West

The Union felt starved for victories at the beginning of the hard winter of 1862. Northern troops remained bogged down in the eastern theater, but Union generals in the West moved aggressively. Deprived of control of the Ohio River when Kentucky sided with the Union, the Confederates under Albert Sidney Johnston desperately needed to stop the Union in the West. Troops under the command of Ulysses S. Grant, a relatively obscure general from Illinois, confronted a Confederate line of defense across southern Kentucky. Employing the Union's new river gunboats to great effect, Grant pushed down both the Tennessee and the Cumberland Rivers across the Kentucky border into Tennessee.

Important Confederate forts stood on both these rivers, but Grant hoped to overwhelm them by combined attacks on water and land. He assaulted Fort Henry on the Tennessee River in early February, easily overcoming the fort's defenses with the big guns on his river craft. The Union now commanded a river that flowed all the way through Tennessee into northern Alabama. Grant sent his boats steaming back up the Tennessee River to the Cumberland while he marched his men overland to Fort Donelson. There, the Confederates fought desperately, destroying several of the gunboats. Despite the Confederates' efforts, however, Grant pressed his advantage and overwhelmed Southern troops that attempted to break out of the fort and retreat to nearby Nashville.

When the Confederate general in charge of the 13,000 troops who remained in the fort attempted to negotiate with Grant (an old friend) for their surrender, Grant brusquely responded: "No terms except an unconditional and immediate surrender can be accepted. I propose to move immediately upon your works." Grant's phrase soon echoed through northern newspapers, jokes, and even mildly risqué love letters. Grant's first two initials, northern newspapers crowed, actually stood for Unconditional Surrender. Within days, Union troops pushed into nearby Nashville, the capital of Tennessee, making it the first great conquest of the war.

The Monitor and the Virginia

Even as Grant's troops seized their victories on the rivers of Tennessee, the Union navy continued its relentless attack on the eastern seaboard of the Confederacy. A well-planned amphibious assault allowed the Northern navy to consolidate its control of the North Carolina coast. The blockade steadily tightened.

Despite the Union's success, the Southern navy had reason for hope in early 1862. Confederate Secretary of the Navy Stephen Mallory had created an effective and innovative department. Mallory sought to take advantage of recent developments in shipbuilding and naval warfare such as steam power, the screw propeller, and armor. The Confederacy eagerly experimented, too, with mines in their harbors and developed the world's first combat submarine, the CSS *Hunley.*

Most important, the South examined the possibilities of iron-plated ships. In the years immediately preceding the Civil War, the French and British had been experimenting with such vessels, but the United States remained far behind. The Confederacy began building an ironclad almost from the very beginning of the war, converting a Union frigate, the USS *Merrimack,* captured in Norfolk in April of 1861. The confederacy added walls of two-feet-thick solid oak, covered with two-inch-thick iron plate, and installed an iron ram on the front to rip through the wooden hulls of enemy ships. It carried ten heavy guns. The Confederacy changed the ship's name from the USS *Merrimack* to the CSS *Virginia.*

The Union, for its part, hired a Swiss inventor to design a different kind of ironclad; his innovative plan called for a ship most of which would be submerged except for a rotating turret on top. Its inventor would refund the $275,000 cost to the government if the

The Union's use of riverboats provided a decided advantage when they quickly overran forts on the Tennessee River in February 1862. The boats played critical roles on other rivers as well, including the Mississippi.
Museum of the city of New York, The Harry T. Peters Collection. 57-300-51

In one of the most memorable episodes of the war, the two ironclad ships, the USS Monitor *and the CSS* Virginia, *bruised one another in the harbor of Hampton Roads, Virginia, in March 1862. Though neither ship won, the Union's* Monitor *proved the superior vessel.*
Collection of President Franklin P. Roosevelt U.S. Naval Historical Center Photograph

ship—condemned as a "cheesebox on a raft"—failed. It was by no means clear how such a craft might work in battle. No one was even sure it would stay afloat, much less fight effectively with its two guns. It was called the *Monitor*.

On March 8, 1862, the Confederates decided the time had come to unleash their new weapon. The *Virginia* attacked several Union ships occupying the harbor at Hampton Roads, Virginia. The ironclad sank two wooden ships and drove three others aground; their guns proved useless against the heavy iron sheathing.

In one of the more dramatic episodes of the young war, however, the Union happened to be sending its own ironclad to another Virginia port thirty miles away on the morning after the *Virginia* launched its attack. As soon as the sound of the guns in Hampton Roads reached the *Monitor*, it steamed down, arriving just in time. The two vessels pounded one another for hours. The imposing Southern ironclad had been neutralized and the blockade would continue. Although neither iron ship actually won the battle of March 9, the advantages of the Northern *Monitor* quickly became evident. Not only did that craft provide a much smaller target and a more maneuverable set of guns, but the *Monitor* required only half as much water in which to operate. The *Virginia* proved too big to retreat into rivers and too unwieldy for open seas. The Union began a crash campaign to build as many ironclads as possible, using the *Monitor* as its model. Britain, once the world's most formidable fleet, possessed only two ironclads. In the view of the *London Times*, "it would be madness" to engage "that little *Monitor*" with Britain's wooden fleet.

THE UNION ON THE OFFENSIVE: MARCH TO SEPTEMBER 1862

The Union strategy had long pivoted around the effort to take Richmond. With apparently unlimited resources, Northerners expected to make quick work of Virginia. Although the Confederacy had put up a surprisingly effective campaign, the Union believed it would win the war in the spring and summer of 1862. As with all things in this war, however, events followed directions no one could foresee.

The Peninsular Campaign Begins

On the very day that the CSS *Virginia* emerged at Hampton Roads, Abraham Lincoln gave his approval of General George McClellan's long-delayed plan to win the war in the East. Rather than fighting in northern Virginia, McClellan would attack on the peninsula between the James and York Rivers farther south, using the Chesapeake Bay as a supply route. By moving the war away from Washington, McClellan argued, he would lessen the threat to the nation's capital and find better roads from which to attack Richmond.

Four hundred watercraft of every description began transferring Union soldiers to the tip of the peninsula at Fort Monroe, about seventy miles from Richmond. The transfer of 100,000 men took weeks to unfold. McClellan required several more weeks to arrange them "just so" in preparation for what he expected to be his triumphant march into Richmond.

Shiloh

In the meantime, U.S. Grant and his fellow general William T. Sherman pushed their troops ever deeper into Tennessee. The Confederates, under Albert Sidney Johnston, had retreated to Corinth, Mississippi, where they regrouped and joined with other units arriving by train from throughout the Confederacy. They planned to attack Grant to regain momentum, if not the enormous territory and strategic rivers they had lost at Fort Henry and Fort Donelson. Grant established his own base of operations only twenty miles away, at Pittsburgh Landing, Tennessee. To the surprise of the Union, Johnston attacked the larger Union force at Shiloh Church on April 6.

The scattered woods and rough terrain around Shiloh turned the battle into a series of brutal fights among desperate groups of scattered men with little coordinated leadership. Johnston, killed leading an attack, was replaced by Beauregard, who succeeded in pushing the Union men back two miles. The Confederates' dominance proved short-lived, however, for 25,000 Northern reinforcements arrived overnight. The Southerners received no new men. The next day saw Grant and his army regain the ground they had lost, driving the Confederates back to Corinth. Though the Southern forces had been badly hurt, the Northern forces were themselves too exhausted and shaken to pursue.

The carnage at Shiloh exceeded anything anyone had ever seen. The bloodiest battle in the hemisphere up to that point, Shiloh exacted a horrible toll: about 1,700 killed and 8,000 wounded on each side. About 2,000 of the wounded men in both the Union and the Confederacy forces would soon die. Newspapers and generals debated the outcome of the battle for months, trying to decide the hero and the loser, but it eventually became clear that the Southern attempt to halt

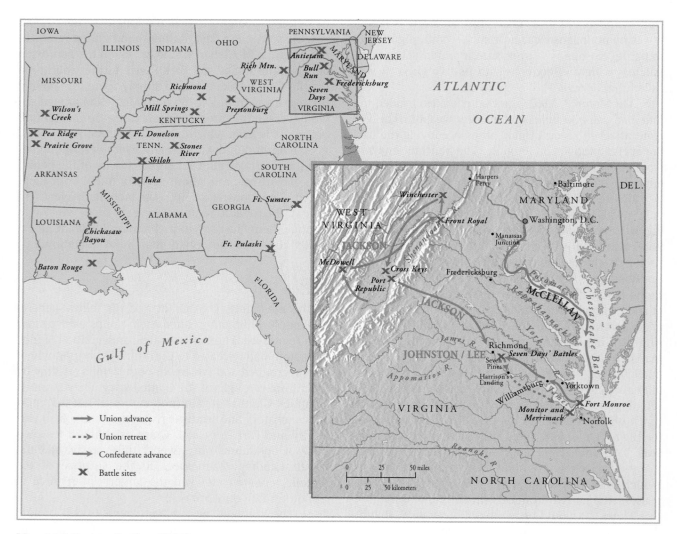

Map 14.3 *Eastern Battles of 1862*

 George McClellan's long-awaited campaign to take Richmond, Virginia, the capital of the Confederacy, began in March of 1862. The vast maneuver unfolded over many months and ended with the brutal stalemate of the Seven Days. Stonewall Jackson's Valley Campaign kept the Union forces divided. View an animated version of this map or related maps at http://history.wadsworth.com/passages2e.

Northern momentum in the Mississippi Valley had failed. Frustrated with McClellan's inertia, Lincoln turned aside criticism of Grant, "I can't spare this man, he fights."

New Orleans

Yet another drama played itself out in New Orleans. There, a Union naval force under David Farragut determined to do what Confederates considered impossible: overwhelm their largest city and largest port from the Gulf. Confederates recalled that the mighty British of 1815 had been unable to take New Orleans and fully expected the same fate to befall the Yankees. The city

lay under the protection of two forts claiming 115 guns as well as a river blocked with logs, barges, and thick cables. So safe did they consider New Orleans that Confederate troops abandoned the city to fight at Shiloh, leaving the port protected only by militiamen.

Farragut had his own weapons, however: 20 mortar boats, 17 ships with 523 guns, and 15,000 soldiers. The Union navy pounded the forts for days with the mortars, unsuccessfully. Frustrated, on April 24 Farragut audaciously led his ships, single file, past the forts and past Confederate ships that tried to ram the Union craft or set them on fire with flaming rafts. Once they had run this gauntlet, the Union ships had clear sailing right up to the docks of New Orleans. There,

In one of the bloodiest days of fighting in the war, the troops of Grant and William T. Sherman clashed with those of Albert Sidney Johnston and P. G. T. Beauregard at Shiloh. Johnston was killed and the Union forces seized a desperate, last-minute, and costly victory.

The Western Reserve Historical Society, Cleveland Ohio

they confronted no resistance as 4,000 Confederate troops withdrew from the city.

Troops under the command of Benjamin Butler occupied New Orleans while Farragut continued to drive up the Mississippi River. He took Baton Rouge and Natchez, but Vicksburg held Farragut off. Riverboats coming from the north soon took Memphis as well, giving the Union control of all the Mississippi River except the area near Vicksburg. Northern forces used the river as a major supply route. Rather than a highway uniting the Upper and Lower South, the Mississippi became a chasm separating one half of the Confederacy from the other.

The Confederate Draft

The end of April, then, seemed to promise the early end to the war that people had expected at its outbreak. Although many of the battles had been close that spring, they all seemed to turn out in favor of the

North. The first yearlong enlistments in the Confederate army were running out in April; many soldiers left for home. The Confederate Congress, fearful that its armies would be short of men as the Union stepped up its attacks, decided that it had no choice but to initiate a compulsory draft. All white men between the ages of eighteen and thirty-five were required to fight for three years. If men enlisted or reenlisted within the thirty days following passage of the law, they could choose the unit with which they fought.

Although the Confederacy eventually abolished substitution, a policy that allowed men with enough money to pay a substitute to fight in their place, it still permitted men from many occupations, such as teachers and apothecaries, to claim an exemption from military service. Governors appointed many men to positions in their state governments and militia so that they would be exempted from the draft. In Georgia and North Carolina, state and counties aided the families of poor soldiers by taxing slaves and large property owners.

Sarah Morgan
"Diary"

Sarah Morgan was a high-spirited teenager in Baton Rouge, Louisiana, when the Civil War broke out, the daughter of a respected judge. Though she and her father supported the Union during the secession crisis, both invested their loyalty in the Confederacy once the Civil War began. This part of her diary, begun in 1862, records the grief that struck the hundreds of thousands of American families who lost sons, brothers, and fathers in the war. Despite her sense of helplessness, Morgan went on to write for a leading newspaper in South Carolina after the war.

March

Dead! dead! Both dead! O my brothers! what have we lived for except you? We who would so gladly have laid down our lives for yours, are left desolate to mourn over all we loved and hoped for, weak and helpless; while you, so strong, noble, and brave, have gone before us without a murmur. God knows best. But it is hard—O so hard! to give them up without a murmur!

We cannot remember the day when our brothers were not all in all to us. What the boys would think; what the boys would say; what we would do when the boys came home, that has been our sole thought through life. A life time's hope wrecked in a moment—God help us! In our eyes, there is no one in the world quite so noble, quite so brave, quite so true as our brothers. And yet they are taken—and others useless to themselves and a curse to their families live on in safety, without fear of death. This is blasphemy. God knows best; I will not complain. But when I think of drunken, foolish, coarse Will Carter with horses and dogs his sole ambition, and drinking and gambling his idea of happiness, my heart swells within me. He lives, a torment to himself and a curse to others—he will live

to a green old age as idle, as ignorant, as dissipated as he is now. . . .

If we had had any warning or preparation, this would not have been so unspeakably awful. But to shut ones eyes to all dangers and risks, and drown every rising fear with "God will send them back; I will not doubt his mercy," and then suddenly to learn that your faith has been presumption—and God wills that you shall undergo bitter affliction—it is a fearful awakening! What glory have we ever rendered to God that we should expect him to be so merciful to us? Are not all things His, and is He not infinitely more tender and compassionate than we deserve? . . .

Sewed to the paper that contained the last words we should hear of our dear brother, was a lock of hair grown long during his imprisonment. I think it was a noble, tender heart that remembered that one little deed of kindness, and a gentle, pitying hand that cut it from his head as he lay cold and stark in death. Good heart that loved our brave brother, kind hand that soothed his pain, you will not be forgotten by us!

Source: From *The Civil War Diary of Sarah Morgan*, edited by Charles East. Copyright 1991 by the University of Georgia. Used by permission of University of Georgia Press.

The Confederacy also exempted one white man for every twenty slaves he supervised in the "twenty negro law." That law, like the draft in general, necessary though it was, divided Southerners more profoundly than anything else in the Civil War. A Mississippi private deserted to return home, refusing to "fight for the rich men while they were at home having a good time."

The Seven Days

"Every blow tells fearfully against the rebellion," a New York newspaper declared at the end of May. "It now requires no very far reaching prophet to predict the end of this struggle." From the viewpoint of the battlefields in Tennessee and Mississippi, the war did indeed seem to be nearing its end. And in Virginia George McClellan's troops, the pride of the Union and 100,000 strong, had pushed their way up the peninsula toward Richmond. By the end of May only five miles separated them from their destination.

Not that it would be easy for the Union troops to take Richmond. The river assaults that had worked so well two months earlier in Tennessee failed in Virginia. The Confederates were able to attack the river gunboats from the heights of Drewry's Bluff. Even the *Monitor* proved ineffectual when faced with an enemy one hundred feet above. Moreover, the Confederates had established imposing defenses around Richmond and concentrated many of their troops in the vicinity.

Defensive positioning proved more important in the American Civil War than in any prior conflict. Defenders gained their advantage from a new kind of weapon: the rifle. A rifle, unlike a musket, used a spiral groove in the barrel to put spin on a bullet, like a football pass, giving the bullet much greater stability and accuracy. A musket had been accurate at only about eighty yards, but a rifle could hit a target at four times that distance. Although the benefits of rifling had long been recognized, it was not until the 1850s that a French inventor, Charles Minie, devised a way to make it possible for a rifled gun to fire without requiring the grooves to be cleaned. Although the rifles still had to be loaded from the end of the barrel, preventing even the most skillful soldiers from firing more than three times a minute, rifles nevertheless made it much more difficult for attacking troops to overwhelm a defense.

Lincoln and McClellan believed that Washington faced a direct threat from Confederate troops in the Shenandoah Valley under the command of the increasingly impressive Stonewall Jackson. For three months in the spring of 1862, Jackson maneuvered his men up and down the valley, creating the impression that his forces were larger than they were and that they could attack anywhere, any time. As a result, the Union divided its forces, depriving McClellan's invasion of tens of thousands of soldiers that would have otherwise been available for the assault on Richmond.

The Union and the Rebel forces tested one another around Richmond in May and June, inflicting heavy casualties in battles that settled nothing. Robert E. Lee replaced Joseph Johnston, wounded in battle,

The fleet of David Farragut accomplished what the Confederates considered impossible, pushing past the elaborate defenses of New Orleans. Using the cover of darkness, much of the fleet managed to survive a thundering artillery assault.
Chicago Historical Society, P & S-1932.0027

as general of the Confederate forces in Virginia. Lee quickly proved himself aggressive and daring. He almost immediately planned an attack against the larger force under McClellan's command. Lee sent out J. E. B. Stuart, his cavalry leader, who rode all the way around McClellan's troops, reconnoitering their position and stealing their supplies. Stuart reported that part of McClellan's troops were vulnerable to attack. Lee brought Jackson and his men to join in an assault.

The resulting prolonged conflict around Richmond, which became known as the Seven Days' Battles, did not distinguish either side. Thirty thousand men had been killed and wounded. The Confederates' offensive did not work as planned and Jackson failed to carry out his part of the assault. For the North's part, McClellan, though possessing far more troops than his opponents' 90,000, believed himself outnumbered, wiring Lincoln that he faced 200,000 Confederates and "if this [army] is destroyed by overwhelming numbers . . . the responsibility cannot be thrown on my shoulders."

Slavery Under Attack

By the summer of 1862, the war seemed to have reached a stalemate. Both the Union and the Confederacy believed a decisive battle could still win the war.

MISSIONARIES AT PORT ROYAL

Corbis-Bettmann

In Union hands since 1861, the Sea Islands of South Carolina attracted slaves from the mainland who joined the 9,000 slaves who remained when their masters fled the federal army. These islands quickly became a testing ground for Northern ideals. Abolitionists quickly realized that these slaves, among the most isolated groups in the South, would prove a test for creating a community to disprove theories of black inability to adapt to a free labor society.

Societies formed in cities such as Boston, New York, and Philadelphia to organize financial and educational support for the newly liberated men and women on the islands. Missionaries and teachers of both genders came to the islands to instruct the newly freed residents in matters both secular and religious. The first group that sailed from New York in March 1862 also brought men to manage the production and sale of cotton, several of whom clashed with the antislavery activists when their interest in a profitable crop exceeded their concern for black welfare. Although eager to seize plots of land to support themselves and their families, many former slaves associated cotton with servitude and refused to plant it. Politicians, ministers, and newspapermen reported the conditions and progress made at Port Royal as a measure of what the end of slavery would mean for blacks and for the South.

The North took heart because Union ships controlled the coasts and rivers on the perimeter of the South even as Union troops pushed deep into Tennessee and Mississippi. The Confederacy took comfort because vast expanses of rich Southern farmland and millions of productive slaves remained beyond the reach of Union control.

President Lincoln, while detesting slavery personally, feared that a campaign against bondage would divide the North. As the war dragged into its second year, however, even Northerners who did not oppose slavery on moral grounds could see that slavery offered the South a major advantage: slaves in the fields meant more white Southerners on the battlefields.

More important, black Southerners themselves pressed slavery as a problem on the Union armies. Wherever those armies went, slaves fled to the federals as refugees. The Union called the black people who made their way to the Union ranks "contrabands," a word usually used to describe smuggled goods. The term revealed the confusion among white Northerners about the status of the black people in their midst. Although some Union officers returned the slaves to their owners, other officers seized the opportunity to strike against slavery and use former slaves to further their war aims. The slaves "bring much valuable information" and "are acquainted with all the roads, paths, fords," and "haunts of secession spies and traitors."

Northern leaders confronted such issues most directly near Port Royal, South Carolina. When the Union forces overran the Sea Islands along the coast in 1862, the relatively few whites who lived there fled, leaving behind 10,000 slaves. Almost immediately, various groups of Northerners began to vie for the opportunity to reshape Southern society. The Sea Islands claimed some of the largest and richest plantations in the South, growing rare and expensive long-staple cotton. Union leaders felt it crucial that freed slaves prove they would work willingly and effectively. Female abolitionist schoolteachers journeyed down from New England, while men came from New York City and the Northwest to demonstrate that plantations run on the principles of free labor could be both productive and humane.

The former slaves valued the opportunity to learn to read and write and wanted land of their own, but they did not always appreciate lessons from the newcomer whites about religion and agriculture. Black people knew how to farm and knew their God. Not only in South Carolina, but wherever the Union army penetrated, officers and civilians sought to control black labor and rich land. Sometimes, federal officials decreed that the freedpeople could sign contracts with whomever they chose—but they had to sign contracts with someone. In other times and places, Union leaders permitted black people to take responsibility for some of the land they had worked as slaves. Some white Northerners proposed seizing land from former slaveholders to give to the former slaves.

General David Hunter, a man of abolitionist sympathies, took advantage of his position in Port Royal in the late spring of 1862 to organize a number of black military units and to declare slavery abolished in South Carolina, Georgia, and Florida. Hunter stated that Union soldiers would not act "as a police force for the protection of property." Lincoln revoked Hunter's proclamation. Lincoln did not envision the immediate emancipation decreed by Hunter, with no compensation to slaveholders and with former slaves living alongside their former masters. Lincoln thought that slavery must end gradually, with payments to the slaveholders for their loss of property. Ideally, Lincoln argued, the former slaves would be colonized beyond the borders of the United States, perhaps in Haiti or Liberia.

Lincoln also resisted those members of his party and his cabinet who thought that black men should be enlisted into the Union army. Such Republicans, often called "Radicals" for their support of black rights, passed laws that forbade Northern commanders to return refugee slaves to their former masters, and they ended (albeit gradually and with compensation) slavery in the District of Columbia.

Many Northern Democrats firmly opposed such expansion of the war's purposes and means, warning that abolition would only embitter and embolden the Confederates. McClellan, a strong opponent of Radical Republicans, believed emancipation would "disintegrate our present armies." Democrats sympathetic to the South, called "Copperheads" by their opponents, marched under the motto "The Constitution as it is and the Union as it was." They wanted slavery to remain in place so that the South would come back into the nation.

Lincoln sought to steer a course between the Radicals and the Copperheads. But in the summer of 1862 he moved closer to an assault on slavery. The Union army had strengthened its position in Kentucky and Missouri, and it no longer appeared that the border states could effectively align themselves with the Confederates. Similarly, Lincoln came to see that the Southern Unionists could not or would not organize effective opposition to the Confederacy from within. Lincoln decided that to win the war he would have to hit slavery. Responding to a Southern Unionist, the president wrote, "This government cannot much longer play a game in which it stakes all, and its enemies stake nothing. Those enemies must understand that they cannot experiment for ten years trying to destroy the government, and if they fail still come back into the Union unhurt."

On July 22, 1862, Lincoln and his cabinet authorized federal military leaders to take whatever secessionist property they needed and to destroy any property that aided the Confederacy. That meant that Union officers could protect the black men and women who fled to Northern camps, using them to work behind the lines. Lincoln decided to wait for a victory on the battlefield before announcing the most dramatic part of his plan: that as of January 1, 1863, he would declare all slaves in areas controlled by the Confederates free. Although this proclamation would free no slaves under Union control in the border states, it ruled out compromise that would end the war and bring the South back into the Union with slavery. Knowing that this announcement would unleash harsh criticism in the North, Lincoln wanted to wait until the North was flush with confidence before he announced this preliminary Emancipation Proclamation. When and where that victory might occur, however, was by no means clear in July of 1862.

Second Manassas and Antietam

Confidence actually ran higher in the Confederacy than in the Union during the second summer of the war. The Union, after all, could draw little solace from

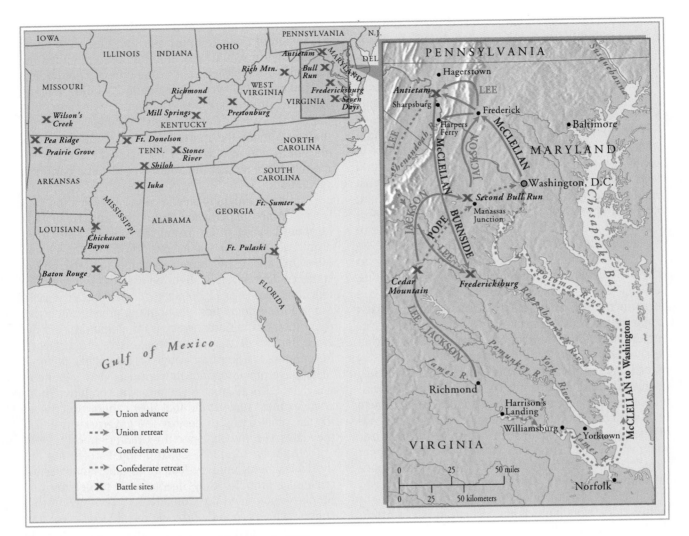

Map 14.4 *Campaigns in Virginia and Maryland, 1862*
As Union troops moved from the peninsula below Richmond to an area closer to Washington in August, Lee and Jackson used the opportunity to go on the offensive. Over the next several months, they clashed with Union forces at Manassas and Antietam in Maryland. View an animated version of this map or related maps at http://history.wadsworth.com/passages2e.

McClellan's sluggish performance in the ferocious Seven Days' Battles outside of Richmond in June. Lincoln placed Henry Halleck, who advocated a more aggressive stance toward southern civilians and their slaves, in charge of all Union troops. The president put John Pope, who had been fighting in the West, in charge of the new Army of Virginia. McClellan still commanded troops, but his role had been restricted. Pope issued a series of orders that signaled a new harder tone to the conflict. Troops would forage as needed, no longer guard Southern property, and hold local civilians responsible for damages caused by area guerillas.

The new Union leaders decided to remove McClellan's troops from the peninsula of Virginia and consolidate

them, under the joint command of Pope, with troops from the Shenandoah Valley. The forces began to move from the peninsula in August, creating a temporary opportunity for the Confederacy. Lee decided to attack Pope's troops while McClellan's were withdrawing. He hoped to occupy as much territory as possible, resting and resupplying his troops while complicating Union efforts to unify their forces.

Lee's plan worked better than he could have expected. Stonewall Jackson attacked Pope's men and pillaged a large federal supply depot at Manassas. Pope then fell under attack by James Longstreet's troops, who drove the new Yankee commander back into Washington. With McClellan no longer threaten-

The sunken road where Confederates battled Union soldiers on this Maryland battlefield became known as "Bloody Lane."
Bodies piled up six deep on the bloodiest single day of the Civil War.
From the Tharpe Collection of American Military Art

ing Richmond and Pope posing no danger to northern Virginia, Lee decided to push into Maryland. He believed that large numbers of Marylanders would rush to the Confederate cause. Lee had another audience in mind as well: England and France. In the wake of Union indecision and defeat in the summer of 1862, leaders in both countries were leaning toward recognition of the Confederacy. A major victory in Northern territory, Lee felt certain, would prove that the South deserved the support of the major powers.

Lee acted so confidently because he knew he would face George McClellan again. On September 17, the two old adversaries fell into battle once more, this time at Antietam Creek, near Sharpsburg, Maryland. The Confederates had 35,000 men to McClellan's 72,000, but the Southerners held the defensive ground. The terrible battle ended in confusion and stalemate. More men were killed, wounded, or declared missing on this day than on any other day in the Civil War: 13,000 for the Confederacy and 12,000 for the Union. Lee had lost nearly a third of his army; McClellan, despite his numerical advantage, had been unable to shatter the enemy.

Neither side could be satisfied with the battle's outcome, but the North made the best of the situation. Lincoln decided that Antietam represented enough of a victory to justify his announcement of the prelimi-

nary Emancipation Proclamation. The European powers decided that they would withhold their support for the Confederacy for the time being. The Confederacy decided that it would pull back into Virginia to fight another day.

Things could have turned out very differently at this juncture. Had McClellan destroyed Lee's army, the Confederacy might have given up its claims for independence before slavery had been ended. Had Lee merely held his ground in Virginia after driving McClellan away from Richmond and Pope back into Washington, England and France might have offered mediation—and the North might well have accepted, again without the end of slavery. As it was, however, both the North and the South would fight again and again.

Stalemate

While Northerners and Southerners slaughtered one another in Maryland with little clear advantage gained by either side, Southern forces under the command of Braxton Bragg pushed far into Kentucky, determined to regain ground lost early in the war. Confederates believed that Kentuckians would rush to the Southern flag if given a chance. But Kentuckians had little confidence that the Confederates could prevail in Kentucky and did not want to risk all they had in support of a losing

After the slaughter at Marye's Heights in December 1862, Confederates stripped the bodies of Union soldiers of their boots and uniforms. Here, Northern burial parties inter their dead.
© Stock Montage, Inc.

cause. Although the Confederates never suffered sharp defeat in Kentucky, they had too few men to occupy the state, and retreated after the battle of Perryville. Rather than risk losing his army, Bragg pulled his men into a more defensible position in Tennessee.

By the summer and fall of 1862, many men had died to little apparent purpose. Lincoln decided that generals in both the East and the West must be removed; George McClellan and Don Carlos Buell seemed too slow to react. Lincoln replaced Buell with William S. Rosecrans and replaced McClellan with Ambrose E. Burnside, an appealing man uncertain that he was qualified for the job. His doubts proved to be well founded.

In November, Burnside decided to establish a new base for yet another assault on Richmond. He moved his troops to Fredericksburg, Virginia, and launched an attack on a virtually impregnable Confederate position at Marye's Heights. With Southerners able to fire down on them at will from protected positions, over 12,000 Union soldiers were killed, wounded, or missing. Observing the suicidal Union charges, Robert E. Lee remarked to General Longstreet, "It is well that war is so terrible—we should grow too fond of it." At battle's end, both armies remained where they had been at the battle's beginning.

The North fell into mourning, humiliation, and anger at this sacrifice. Officers as well as enlisted men made no secret of their loss of faith in Burnside. Despondent, Lincoln responded to defeat at Fredericksburg, "If there is a worse place than Hell, I am in it." In

Tennessee, Rosecrans felt that he had to move against Bragg to demonstrate Union resolve and power. The two armies clashed on the last day of 1862 at Stones River near Murfreesboro. The two sides, losing about a third of their men each, fought to a virtual draw.

The winter of 1862–1863 saw the North and the South precariously balanced, both against one another and within their own societies. On the battlefield, the South had made impressive showings at Fredericksburg and at Second Manassas, but the Northern army had held Kentucky and Maryland. The Confederacy still possessed Vicksburg, but Grant and Sherman were planning ways to take the city. Slaves ran to Union armies at every chance. The preliminary Emancipation Proclamation gave the Union effort a new purpose and new credibility with liberals in Europe, but Lincoln faced mounting criticism within his own party and a growing threat from disgruntled Democrats. The North needed victories.

CONCLUSION

The bloody sacrifice without decisive victory of the Seven Days and Antietam fed disillusionment on both sides. The governments in both the North and the South found themselves the objects of bitter criticism. Military officers squabbled among themselves and with civilian leaders. The only thing people could agree on was that the war would not end soon.

The preceding year and a half had seen events and changes no one could have predicted. Eighteen months after Lincoln had begun his journey to Washington to become president, war had become a way of life. The boundaries between the Union and the Confederacy had been firmly drawn. The governments of both sides had begun to function effectively. The first volunteer units of both armies had been mobilized. Both the South and the North had claimed military victories. The Confederacy recalled the battle at Manassas with pride, whereas the Union took comfort in the steady success of its navy and the capture of New Orleans. The first international crisis, the *Trent* affair, had passed without dragging a major European power into the conflict. But in late 1862 both the North and the South felt that their cause must be clarified and given greater purpose.

Recommended Readings

Berlin, Ira, Fields, Barbarado, Miller, Steven F., Reidy, Joseph P., and Rowland, Leslie, eds. *Free at Last: A Documentary History of Slavery, Freedom, and the*

Civil War, (1997). A monumental collection of first-hand testimony about emancipation.

Boritt, Gabor. *Why the Civil War Came* (1996). A useful overview of thinking on this much-debated historical topic.

Crofts, Daniel W. *Reluctant Confederates: Upper South Unionists in the Secession Crisis* (1989). Analyzes the crucial border states with keen insight.

Crowley, Robert, ed. *With My Face to the Enemy: Perspectives on the Civil War* (2001). Offers interpretations from leading historians of the conflict.

Eicher, David J. *The Longest Night: A Military History of the Civil War* (2001). The best one-volume military history of the war.

Freehling, William W. *The South vs. the South: How Anti-Confederate Southerners Shaped the Course of the Civil War* (2001). Serves as a synthesis of various forms of Unionism by black and white Southerners.

Jones, Howard. *The Union in Peril: The Crisis over British Intervention in the Civil War* (1992). Provides a fresh interpretation of a critical episode.

McPherson, James M. *Battle Cry of Freedom: The Civil War Era* (1988). Stands as the best one-volume account of the Civil War.

Paludan, Phillip Shaw. *A People's Contest: The Union and the Civil War, 1861–1865* (1988). Paints a compelling portrait of the North during war.

Royster, Charles. *The Destructive War: William Tecumseh Sherman, Stonewall Jackson, and the Americans* (1991). Offers an original and disturbing meditation on war.

Thomas, Emory M. *The Confederate Nation, 1861–1865* (1979). The standard account.

American Journey Online and InfoTrac College Edition

Visit the source collections at http://ajaccess.wadsworth.com and infotrac.thomsonlearning.com and use the Search function with the following key terms to explore documents, images, audio and video clips, articles, and commentary related to the material in this chapter.

George B. McClellan
Civil War women
Antietam

Robert E. Lee
Stonewall Jackson
Vicksburg

Additional resources, exercises, and Internet links related to this chapter are available on the American Passages Web site: http://history.wadsworth.com/passages2e

15 BLOOD AND FREEDOM 1863–1867

PEOPLE AT WAR: SPRING 1863

THE BATTLEFIELDS OF SUMMER: 1863

THE WINTER OF DISCONTENT: 1863–1864

FROM WAR TO RECONSTRUCTION: 1865–1867

Ill and injured men filled the ground around the surgical and hospital tents where horrifying surgery often awaited them.

The Civil War enveloped the entire nation, homefront and battlefield alike. The outcome of a battle could win an election or trigger a riot, while events at home affected the leaders' decisions of when and where to fight. In the North, the strong political opposition to Abraham Lincoln and his policies exerted a constant pressure on his conduct of the war. In the South, slaves abandoned plantations and white families' hardships led soldiers to rethink their loyalties.

The outcome of the Civil War was not predetermined by the North's advantages of population and resources. Deep into the war, events could have taken radically different turns. Slavery might have survived the conflict had the Confederacy won at particular junctions or, more likely, had the United States lost the will to push the devastating war to the South's full surrender and the immediate abolition of slavery. Even with the war's end the future course of the nation remained in doubt as Americans confronted the greatest rupture in their history.

PEOPLE AT WAR: SPRING 1863

Both Northerners and Southerners expected the spring of 1863 to bring the climax of the Civil War. Much had been decided, organized, and mobilized over the preceding two years. Yet while generals and armies determined the result of battles, the women, slaves, workers, bureaucrats, draft dodgers, and politicians behind the lines would determine the outcome of the war.

Life in the Field

Soldiers eventually got used to the miseries of sleeping on the ground, poorly cooked food, driving rain, and endless mud. They learned to adapt to gambling, drinking, cursing, and prostitution, either by succumbing to the temptations or by steeling their resolve against them. They could toughen themselves to the intermittent mails and the arrival of bad news from home. Men recalled their initial mortification and humiliation of discovering the entire company infested with lice, a shame that turned to indifference when the sharper horror of wounds descended. Over time, veterans could even learn to absorb the deaths of men with whom they had shared so much.

But the most stalwart of soldiers could not adapt to the constant threat of diseases such as diarrhea, dysentery, typhoid, malaria, measles, diphtheria, and scarlet fever. As bloody as the battles were, disease killed twice as many men as died from the guns of the enemy. Soldiers feared disease and many shared a New England private's opinion, "I tell you there is no *honor* in a man's *sickness,* but there is about a *wound.*" Many doctors of the Civil War era used the same instruments of surgery on soldier after soldier, unwittingly spreading disease and infection. After every battle, screams filled the night as surgeons sawed off legs and arms, feet and hands, in often vain hopes of stopping gangrene.

Purposes

The North fought for ideals of union and democracy; the South fought for ideals of self-determination. Yet soldiers acted courageously not only because they believed in the official political purposes for which they were fighting, but also because they wanted to be admired by the people at home, because they wanted to do their part for their comrades, because they wanted to bring the war to a quicker end, and because they grew to hate the enemy.

Many men fought alongside their brothers, uncles, cousins. A steady stream of letters flowed back and forth between the units and the families and neighbors back home. Gossip, praise, and condemnation flourished. Any soldier who planned to return home knew that his deeds in the war would live with him the rest of his life. As a result, even fearful or half-hearted soldiers might throw themselves into battle to demonstrate their courage. A Southern mother, far from wanting her son home after three years of war, condemned his wrangling of a medical furlough. "You are bound by the duties of your position . . . Your time belongs to your Country." He was dead from wounds two months later.

Whereas about three-fifths of Civil War soldiers were over twenty-one at the age of enlistment, the largest single group of soldiers was eighteen. For those who passed the birthdays of their late teens or early twenties on the battlefields, the transition to manhood became inseparable from the war. A soldier from Illinois proudly wrote his family that "this war has made a man of your son." To be manly meant more than the simple ability to inflict violence on the enemy. It meant pride, responsibility, loyalty, and obedience. Every battle became a test of manhood, which had to be proven every time it was challenged under fire.

Courage developed, too, out of hatred. People on both sides spread the worst stories and rumors about one another. Newspapers printed exaggerated or fabricated atrocity reports about the enemy. While many were repelled by battlefield carnage, others took satisfaction. One Confederate artillery officer admired the

CHRONOLOGY

1863

January   Second Emancipation Proclamation

March   Union Congress passes Conscription Act • Confederate Congress passes Impressment Act

April   Bread riot in Richmond

May   Culmination of Lee's victory over Hooker at Chancellorsville

June   Lee's army crosses Potomac

July   Union victory at Gettysburg • Vicksburg surrenders to Grant • Port Hudson surrenders to Union • Lee retreats across Potomac into Virginia • New York City draft riots • Black troops fight at Fort Wagner, South Carolina

October   Grant assumes control of Union forces in West

November   Lincoln's Gettysburg Address • Union victory at Chattanooga

1864

March   Grant assumes command of all Union forces

May   Battle of the Wilderness in Virginia

July   Union failure at Battle of the Crater near Petersburg

September   Sherman captures Atlanta • Sheridan's victories in Shenandoah Valley

November   Lincoln reelected president • Beginning of Sherman's march from Atlanta to the Atlantic

1865

February   Columbia, South Carolina, burned; Confederates evacuate Charleston

March   Congress creates Bureau of Refugees, Freedmen, and Abandoned Lands (Freedmen's Bureau) • Lincoln's second inauguration • Confederate army authorizes recruitment of slaves into army

April   Fall of Richmond to Union • Lee surrenders to Grant at Appomattox Court House • Lincoln assassinated

May   Jefferson Davis captured • Former Confederate states hold constitutional conventions through December; pass "black codes" • African Americans hold conventions in South

December   Thirteenth Amendment to Constitution ratified, abolishing slavery

1866

February   Johnson vetoes Freedmen's Bureau bill

April   Congress passes Civil Rights Act and Freedmen's Bureau renewal over Johnson's veto

May   Riots in New Orleans and Memphis

June   Congress approves Fourteenth Amendment • Ku Klux Klan formed

1867

March   Congress passes Reconstruction Act and Tenure of Office Act Constitutional conventions in Southern states

August   Johnson dismisses Secretary of War Stanton, triggering impeachment proceedings • First elections in South under Reconstruction Act "severed limbs, decapitated bodies, and mutilated remains" at Fredericksburg and declared that it did "my soul good" to ride over the bodies of the federal dead. Union troops also hardened their attitudes. A Wisconsin soldier informed his fiancée that his unit wanted to fight until "we kill them all off and cleanse the country." The longer the war went on, the more people felt they had to hate one another to justify so much bloodshed.

The sermons men heard in the camps told them they were fighting on the side of the right. The Old Testament afforded rich imagery and compelling stories of violence inflicted for good causes. Many Americans believed that God enacted His will directly in human affairs. As the war ground on, the leaders, the soldiers, and the civilians of both sides came to feel that events were more than the product of human decision or even courage. Surely, they told themselves, so much suffering and sacrifice had to be for a larger purpose.

The Problems of the Confederate Government

Convinced that greedy merchants were holding supplies of flour until prices rose even higher, poor women in Richmond, in the spring of 1863, broke open the stores of merchants accused of hoarding the precious staple, taking what they needed. After President Davis climbed on a wagon and threw coins at the crowd, he ordered a militia unit to prepare to fire on them. The threat of violence and of arrest, as well as the promise of free supplies, broke up the riot, but similar events occurred in several other Southern cities such as Atlanta, Columbus, and Augusta. No one could tell when even larger riots might erupt again. Fearing the consequences for morale, military officers in Richmond ordered the press and telegraph office to suppress news of the riot, but word of the riot soon spread.

The rioters were not the only ones who took what they needed. Confederate officers in the field forced reluctant farmers to accept whatever prices the army offered, in an increasingly worthless currency. In the spring of 1863, the Confederate government attempted to curb the worst abuses of this practice in the Impressment Act. If a farmer did not think the prices he or she received were fair, the case could be appealed before local authorities. In practice, however, this cumbersome system failed. Farmers hid their produce from officers and resented it when they were forced to sell. North Carolina's governor denounced impressments to the War Department in Richmond: "If God Almighty had yet in store another plague . . . I am sure it must have been a regiment or so of half-disciplined Confederate cavalry."

The Southern government could not afford to lose civilian support. Although the absence of political parties originally appeared to be a sign of the South's consensus, that absence eventually undermined what original consensus the Confederacy had enjoyed. Jefferson Davis, without a party mechanism to discipline those who spoke out against him, could not remove enemies from office. Davis's own vice president, Alexander Stephens, became a persistent and outspoken critic of the Confederate president's "tyrannical" policies, actively undermining support for Davis and even allying with avowed enemies of Davis and his policies.

The Confederate government faced a fundamental dilemma. The whole point of secession had been to move political power closer to localities, protecting slavery in particular and self-determination in general. The government of the Confederacy, however, had to centralize power. If the armies were to be fed and clothed, if diplomats were to make a plausible case for the Confederacy's nationhood, if soldiers were to be mobilized, then the Confederate government had to exercise greater power than its creators had expected or intended. Jefferson Davis continually struggled with this tension. For every Southerner who considered Davis too weak, another considered the president dangerously powerful.

The Northern Homefront

In the North, the war heightened the strong differences between the Democrats and the Republicans. The Democrats won significant victories in congressional elections in the fall and winter of 1862, testifying to the depth and breadth of the opposition to Lincoln and his conduct of the war. Wealthy businessmen were eager to reestablish trade with their former Southern partners, whereas Irish immigrants wanted to end the risk of the draft and competition from freed slaves. Many citizens of Ohio, Indiana, and Illinois, whose families had come from the South, wanted to renew the Southern connections that had been broken by the war.

The Union passed its Conscription Act in March of 1863 because disease, wounds, and desertion had depleted the ranks of soldiers faster than they could be replaced. When drafted, a man could appear for duty, hire a substitute to fight in his place, or simply pay a fee of $300 directly to the government. Poorer communities resented the wealthy who could avoid service. Demonstrations broke out in Chicago, Pennsylvania mining towns, rural Vermont, and Boston. To avoid mob violence, state and federal governments often paid bounties—signing bonuses—to those who

Black men had called for their inclusion in the U.S. Army from the beginning of the war. In the spring of 1863, the U.S. Colored Troops were formed and over 180,000 African American men fought for the Union over the next two years.
© Bettmann/Corbis

volunteered. More than a few men took the bounties and then promptly deserted and moved to another locality to claim another bounty.

The opposition to the Lincoln government raised crucial issues. With the North claiming to fight for liberty, what limitations on freedom of speech and protest could it enforce? A Democratic congressman from Ohio, Clement Vallandigham, tested those limits in the spring of 1863. Hating both secessionists and abolitionists, Vallandigham refused to obey a general's orders to stop criticizing the Lincoln administration. He was arrested, tried before a military court, and sentenced to imprisonment for the rest of the war. Lincoln was dismayed by these events. He commuted Vallandigham's sentence, sending him to the Confederates in Tennessee, hoping to make Val-

landigham appear a Southern sympathizer rather than a martyr to the cause of free speech. Vallandigham quickly escaped to Canada, however, where he continued his criticisms. Ohio Democrats defiantly nominated Vallandigham for governor in the elections to be held in the fall of 1863. If things continued to go badly for the Union, who knew what kind of success a critic of Lincoln might find?

African American Soldiers

Though Northern civilian and military leaders remained deeply divided and ambivalent about black freedom, it became clear to everyone that black men could be of great value to the Union. In May 1863, the War Department created the Bureau of Colored Troops.

African American men from across the North rushed to enlist as soon as they heard of the new black regiments.

At first, black recruits found themselves restricted to noncombat roles and a lower rate of pay: ten dollars a month versus the thirteen dollars a month and three-fifty clothing allowance given to white soldiers. Black men, though eager to serve, protested that they could not support their families on such amounts. African Americans knew, and coveted, the rights and privileges of other Americans. They wrote petitions and appealed to higher authorities, often in the language of the Declaration of Independence and the Constitution.

Confederate officials who expected black soldiers to make reluctant or cowed fighters soon discovered otherwise. In May of 1863, two black regiments stormed, seven times, a heavily fortified Confederate installation at Port Hudson, Louisiana. Soon thereafter, black soldiers found themselves on the other side of the barricades. At Milliken's Bend, Louisiana, they fought Confederates hand-to-hand. Northern newspapers echoed the words of praise from generals in the field: "No troops could be more determined or more daring."

Encouraged and frequently supported financially by their communities, African American men in the North went to the recruiting tables in great numbers. Frederick Douglass, the leading spokesman for black Americans, celebrated the enlistments: "Once let the black man get upon his person the brass letters, *U.S.;* let him get an eagle on his button, and a musket on his shoulder, and bullets in his pocket, and there is no power on earth which can deny that he has earned the right to citizenship in the United States." From Rhode Island to Ohio, black troops prepared to head south.

THE BATTLEFIELDS OF SUMMER: 1863

Everything seemed in place for a climactic culmination of the war in the summer of 1863. The Union had almost severed the western half of the Confederacy from the eastern; the federal army had penetrated deep into Tennessee and stood on the threshold of Georgia. On the other hand, the Confederate army had toughened itself to its disadvantages and learned to make the most of the advantages it enjoyed.

Vicksburg and Chancellorsville

Union leaders needed all the help they could get in early 1863. Grant and Sherman remained frustrated in their goal of seizing Vicksburg; Rosecrans faced Bragg in Ten-

This magazine illustration detailed the many tasks and great deeds performed by the U.S. Colored Troops in one of their earliest challenges, at the Battle of Milliken's Bend in Louisiana.
© The Stock Montage

nessee; Lee's army had yet to be decisively defeated despite the men, resources, and determination thrown into battle against him. Lee would face General Joseph Hooker, whom Lincoln had chosen to replace Ambrose Burnside. Throughout the spring, "Fighting Joe" Hooker energized his men and repaired some of the damage to morale and readiness inflicted at Fredericksburg. But no one knew if he would be able to handle Lee.

The Northern public was especially impatient with Grant and Sherman. Grant knew the delays threatened his command. Vicksburg, heavily fortified by both geography and the Confederates, seemed most vulnerable to attack from the southeast, but to get there Grant would have to find a way to move his men across the Mississippi River without landing them in swamps. Throughout the long wet winter, Grant had tried one experiment after another, including digging canals. Nothing worked.

Grant finally decided on a bold move: he would run a flotilla of gunboats and barges past Vicksburg under the cover of night to ferry his men across the Mississippi south of the city, where the land was better. The guns of Vicksburg stood two hundred feet above the river, ready to fire down on any passing craft, but the Union men covered their ships' boilers with sacks of grain and bales of cotton to protect them from the shelling. Most of the boats made it through. Grant had Sherman create a diversion, confusing the Confederates, and then ferried his entire army across the Mississippi. Grant's army remained vulnerable, cut off from his allies

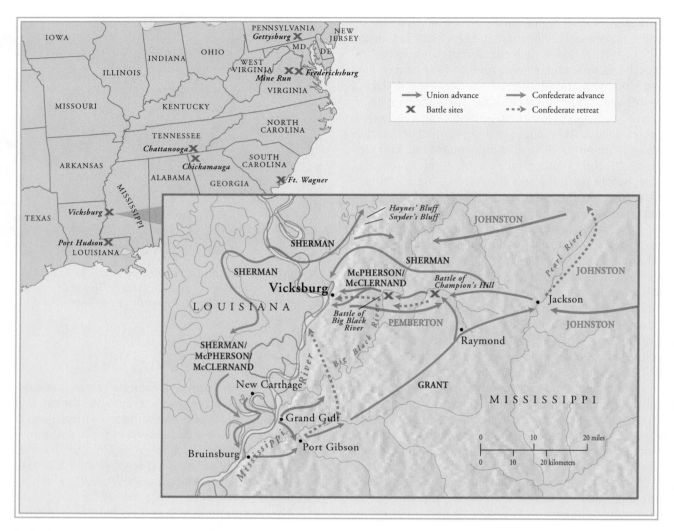

Map 15.1 *Vicksburg*

After months of frustration, Ulysses S. Grant and William T. Sherman found a way to attack Vicksburg from the south and east. Following great struggle, the Union generals were able to take the city on July 4, 1863.
View an animated version of this map or related maps at http://history.wadsworth.com/passages2e.

and his major supply base, but by mid-May, Grant had fought four battles, cost the South 8,000 dead and wounded, marched two hundred miles, and pinned 30,000 Confederates within Vicksburg's fortifications.

In the same week Grant made his landing near Vicksburg, Hooker began his attack on Lee, still based in Fredericksburg. Hooker commanded 130,000 men. Unlike Burnside, however, Hooker intended to outsmart Lee rather than try to overwhelm him with numbers. A large Union force would sweep around Lee and attack him from behind, even as another force attacked from the front. To keep from being bottled up in Fredericksburg, Lee would have to emerge from his well-entrenched defensive position. Lee met this bold move with an even bolder one. He would divide his forces and

send Stonewall Jackson to attack Hooker's men from the rear, outflanking Hooker's own flanking maneuver.

On May 2, Jackson assaulted Hooker's troops near Chancellorsville. The outnumbered Confederates defeated the surprised and indecisive Hooker, achieving a major victory. Southern jubilation, though, ended the very night of this triumph, for nervous Confederate soldiers accidentally shot Stonewall Jackson while he surveyed the scene near the front lines. The surgeons removed his arm that evening and hoped that he might live.

While Jackson lay in his tent, fading in and out of consciousness, Lee managed to contain another assault on Fredericksburg and to push the Union troops away from their positions. The losses had once again

Map 15.2 *Virginia, 1863*

The battle of Chancellorsville, not far from Fredericksburg, was a great victory for the Confederates. But it marked just the opening stage of a long summer of fighting that would culminate at Gettysburg two months later. In that battle, the Confederates sorely missed General Stonewall Jackson, accidentally killed by his own troops at Chancellorsville.

View an animated version of this map or related maps at http://history.wadsworth.com/passages2e.

been staggering—13,000 casualties, roughly 22 percent of the army—but Lee had overcome a larger opponent. After the last battles quieted, however, Jackson died. His death took with it Lee's most trusted general. Many on both sides shared the opinion of a New York paper: "Richmond papers scarcely exaggerate when they say the Confederacy could better have lost fifty thousand men!"

Gettysburg

Despite his victory at Chancellorsville, Lee recognized that the Confederacy was in trouble. Rosecrans still threatened to break through Tennessee into Georgia,

Grant clawed his way closer to Vicksburg, and the Union blockade drew an ever tighter net around the coast. Some of his generals urged Lee to rush with his troops to Tennessee to defend the center of the Confederacy and pull Grant away from Vicksburg. But Lee decided that his most effective move would be to invade the North again, taking the pressure off Virginia and disheartening the Union. A successful strike into the North might even yet persuade Britain and France to recognize the Confederacy and give heart to Peace Democrats in the North.

In early June, Lee began to move up through the Shenandoah Valley into southern Pennsylvania with 75,000 men. Hooker seemed confused. When, after a

The battle at Gettysburg, in an obscure town in southern Pennsylvania, provided some of the most memorable struggles of the entire war, especially the Confederate charge up an unprotected slope to Cemetery Ridge, where massed Union troops awaited.
The Granger Collection, New York

minor dispute, Hooker offered his resignation to Lincoln, the president quickly accepted and put General George Meade in charge. Meade had to decide how best to stop the greatest threat the Confederate army had yet posed to the North. Washington and Baltimore lay in danger, along with the cities, towns, and farms of Pennsylvania. There, the Confederate troops enjoyed taking food and livestock from the rich land. Free blacks and fugitive slaves were also seized and forced south into slavery.

Although Lee and his men moved unchecked across the Potomac and deep into Pennsylvania, they found themselves in a dangerous situation. Lee had permitted Jeb Stuart's cavalry, his "eyes," to range widely from the main army; as a result, the Confederates had little idea where the Union army was or what moves it was making. For their part, Meade and his fellow officers decided to pursue Lee, but not too aggressively, looking for a likely time and place to confront the enemy.

On June 30, units from the Confederacy and the Union stumbled over one another at a small town neither side knew or cared much about: Gettysburg. On July 1, they began to struggle for the best defensive position near the town, fighting over the highest and most protected land. It appeared at first that the Southerners had the better of the first day's battle, but as the smoke cleared both sides could see that late in the day the Union army had consolidated itself on the

most advantageous ground. Meade's men, after fierce fighting at the ends of their line, occupied a fishhook-shaped series of ridges and hills that permitted them to protect their flanks. The second day saw the Confederates slowly mobilize their forces for assaults on those positions and launch attacks late in the afternoon. The resulting battles in the peach orchard, the wheat field, Little Round Top, and the boulder-strewn area known as the Devil's Den proved horrific—with 35,000 men dead or wounded—but left the Union in control of the high ground.

Despite the Union's superior position, Lee decided on a frontal attack the next day. The Confederates hoped their artillery would soften the middle of the Union lines. The Confederates did not realize how little damage their guns had done until well-entrenched Union troops decimated waves of an attack led by George E. Pickett. Only a few Southern men made it to the stone wall that protected the Northerners, and even those Confederates quickly fell. It proved a disastrous three days for the Confederacy, which lost 23,000 men through death or wounds, about a third of its entire force. While the Union lost similar numbers of men, it had more to lose. The Northerners and their new general had fought a defensive battle; the Southern side, short on supplies and men, had gambled on an aggressive assault. Elation swept the North. "The glorious success of the Army of the Potomac has electrified all," a Northerner exulted. In the wake of Chancellorsville and Lee's apparently effortless invasion of Pennsylvania, he admitted, many Northerners "did not believe the enemy could be whipped."

The next morning, a thousand miles away, Vicksburg surrendered to Ulysses S. Grant. Unlike Gettysburg, where the battle had been fought in a place no one considered strategically important, Vicksburg held enormous tactical and psychological importance. It had been the symbol of Confederate doggedness and Union frustration. After six weeks of siege, after six weeks of near starvation behind the Confederate defenses, Vicksburg fell. The Mississippi River now divided the Confederacy while it tied the Union to the Gulf of Mexico.

Some Southerners, including Jefferson Davis, did not perceive Gettysburg as a defeat. In their eyes, Lee and his men had pushed deep into the Union, inflicted heavy losses, and damaged Northern morale without being trapped there. The losses at Gettysburg did embolden westerners to increase their complaints against the Confederate government's apparent fixation on the eastern theater. "Of what earthly use is this 'raid' of Lee's army into [the North], in violation of all the principles of war? Is it going to end the struggle, take Washington, or save the Mississippi Valley?"

Northerners at the time often agreed that Gettysburg had not been a decisive Union victory, pronouncing themselves more frustrated than satisfied with Meade, who had not destroyed Lee's army despite his greater numbers. During the Confederate retreat to Virginia, the Southerners found themselves caught between a swollen Potomac River and pursuing federal troops. Meade, his army exhausted and weakened, chose not to fight against the defenses Lee's men hurriedly put up against their pursuers. Meade could not know that the condition of the Southern troops was even worse than his own. Fortunately for the Confederates, the river soon calmed enough that they were able to escape back into Virginia.

The New York City Draft Riots

On the very day that Lee struggled across the Potomac to safety, riots broke out in New York City. Northern working people held complicated feelings about the war. Many of those who labored in the North's factories, mines, farms, and railroads had come to the United States in the last few years. These people, mostly Irish and Germans, volunteered in large numbers to fight for the Union cause. Between 20 to 25 percent of the Union Army consisted of immigrants, the great majority of them volunteers.

Despite their patriotism for their adopted country, many of the immigrants viewed black Americans with dread and contempt. Urban labor organizations divided over Lincoln's election and over the response to secession. Many Catholic Irishmen, almost all of them Democrats, proclaimed that they had no quarrel with white Southerners and that they resented the federal government's draft. The obvious effect of inflation on the wages of workers created strong resentments as well. Working people sneered at those men who had enough money to hire substitutes to fight in their place. Three hundred dollars, after all, constituted half a year's wage for a workingman.

Irish immigrants despaired at the losses among Irish-American units in the field. When their regiments were decimated at Fredericksburg, Gettysburg, and elsewhere, Irish people began to wonder if commanders valued their lives as highly as those of the native-born. When word came, just as the draft lottery was to take place in New York City on July 11, 1863, of the 23,000 men lost at Gettysburg, the fury of working people rose. On July 13, it exploded. Mobs began by assaulting draft officials, then turned their anger on any man who looked rich enough to have hired a substitute, then on pro-Lincoln news-

Riots in New York City were triggered by an impending draft lottery and by news from Gettysburg that told of heavy Union losses there. Black Americans suffered the most from the riots.
© The Stock Montage

papers and abolitionists' homes. They assaulted any African Americans they encountered on the streets, burning an orphanage, whipping men and women, and hanging victims from city lampposts. Lincoln was sickened by accounts of the riot and a city editor despaired, "Great God! What is this nation coming to?"

The police struggled for three days to control the riot. Eventually, troops (including all-Irish units) rushed from the battlefields of Pennsylvania to aid the police. The troops fired into the rioters; over a hundred people died and another 300 were injured. The working people got some of what they wanted: more welfare relief, exemptions from the draft for those whose families would have no other means of support, and an exodus of black people who feared for their lives.

Ironically, a few days after the New York draft riots, scores of black troops died during a bold nighttime assault on Fort Wagner near Charleston, South Carolina. Despite the bravery of the African Americans, the assault failed. The Confederates made a point of burying the African American soldiers in a mass grave along with their white officer, Robert Gould Shaw, intending to insult him and his memory. Instead, they elevated him to a Northern martyr. The *Atlantic Monthly* marked a change in Northern attitudes towards black soldiers: "Through the cannon smoke of that dark night, the manhood of the colored race shines before many eyes that would not see."

Chickamauga

After Gettysburg, Vicksburg, and the New York riots in July, events slowed until September, when Union General William Rosecrans left Chattanooga, near the Georgia border, and began moving toward Atlanta. His opponent, Braxton Bragg, hoped to entice Rosecrans into dividing his forces so that they could be cut off. The armies confronted one another at Chickamauga Creek—a Cherokee name meaning "river of death." The Confederates took advantage of Union mistakes on the heavily wooded battlefield, inflicting harrowing damage and driving Rosecrans back into Chattanooga. The Union troops were trapped there, the Confederates looming over them on Lookout Mountain and Missionary Ridge, with few routes of escape and limited supplies. The Northerners had gone from a position of apparent advantage to one of desperation.

Lincoln, judging Rosecrans "confused and stunned" by the battle at Chickamauga, used this opportunity to put Grant in charge of all Union armies between the Appalachian Mountains and the Mississippi River. In the fall of 1863, Grant traveled to Chattanooga, where Sherman joined him from Mississippi and Hooker came from Virginia.

The Gettysburg Address

The North's victories in the summer of 1863 aided Lincoln's popularity. The draft riots in New York City damaged the reputations of Democrats, whereas the bravery of black soldiers on the battlefields of Louisiana and South Carolina led white Northerners, particularly Union soldiers, to rethink some of their prejudices. In the fall of 1863, the Republicans won major victories in Pennsylvania and Ohio. Lincoln determined to make the most of these heartening events.

When Lincoln received an invitation to speak at the dedication of the cemetery at Gettysburg on November 19, he saw it as a chance to impart a sense of direction and purpose to the Union cause. The event had not been planned with him in mind and the president was not even the featured speaker. Edward Everett, a scholar and famed lecturer, had been asked weeks before to give the main address. But Lincoln recognized that a battlefield offered the most effective backdrop for the things he wanted to say.

Burial crews had been laboring for weeks on the Gettysburg battlefield. Thousands of horse carcasses had been burned; thousands of human bodies had been hastily covered with a thin layer of soil. Pennsylvania purchased seventeen acres and hired a specialist in rural cemetery design to lay out the burial plots so that no state would be offended by the location or amount of space devoted to its fallen men. Only about a third of the reburials had taken place when Lincoln arrived; caskets remained stacked at the station.

Lincoln, contrary to legend, did not dash off his speech on the back of an envelope. He had reworked and polished it for several days. The "remarks," as the program put it, lasted three minutes. Lincoln used those minutes to maximum effect. He said virtually nothing about the details of the scene surrounding the 20,000 people at the ceremony. Neither did he mention slavery directly. Instead, he spoke of equality as the fundamental purpose of the war. He called for a "new birth of freedom."

Lincoln was attempting to shift the purpose of the war from Union for Union's sake to Union for freedom's sake. He sought to salvage something from the deaths of the 50,000 men at Gettysburg. Democratic newspapers rebuked Lincoln for his claim, arguing that white soldiers had "too much self-respect to declare that negroes were their equals." But other Northerners accepted Lincoln's exhortation as the definition of their purpose. They might not believe that blacks deserved to be included as full participants in a government of, by, and for "the people," but they did believe that the Union fought for liberty broadly conceived. As battles and years went by, the words of the Gettysburg Address would gain force and resonance.

Just four days after Lincoln's speech, Grant gave the North new reason to believe its ideals might triumph. On November 23, Grant's men overwhelmed the Confederates on Lookout Mountain outside Chattanooga; two days later, Union soldiers accomplished the improbable task of fighting their way up Missionary Ridge because Confederate artillery could not reach opponents coming up directly from below. The Union, now in control of Kentucky and Tennessee, had a wide and direct route into Georgia. A clerk in the Confederate War Department reflected on the year's reverses: "calamity . . . utter ruin. Unless something is done . . . we are irretrievably gone."

England and France finally determined in late 1863 that they would not try to intervene in the American war. First Britain, then France detained or sold to foreign powers warships intended for the Confederacy. The Northern public, encouraged by events on the battlefield, supported Republican candidates in the congressional elections of 1863 more vigorously than had seemed possible just a few months before.

Abraham Lincoln
"The Gettysburg Address," 1863

Perhaps the most influential and memorable brief passage in American history, Lincoln's "remarks" at the opening of the Gettysburg battlefield in November of 1863 articulated the highest ideals with which the war could be associated: a government "of the people, by the people, for the people." The "new birth of freedom" Lincoln invoked proved, however, to take generations to come to pass.

Four score and seven years ago our fathers brought forth on this continent, a new nation, conceived in Liberty, and dedicated to the proposition that all men are created equal.

Now we are engaged in a great civil war, testing whether that nation, or any nation so conceived and so dedicated, can long endure. We are met on a great battle-field of that war. We have come to dedicate a portion of that field, as a final resting place for those who here gave lives that that nation might live. It is altogether fitting and proper that we should do this.

But, in a larger sense, we can not dedicate—we can not consecrate—we can not hallow—this ground. The brave men, living and dead, who struggled here, have consecrated it, far above our poor power to add or detract. The world will little note, nor long remember what we say here, but it can never forget what they did here. It is for us the living, rather, to be dedicated here to the unfinished work which they who fought here have thus far so nobly advanced. It is rather for us to be here dedicated to the great task remaining before us—that from these honored dead we take increased devotion to that cause for which they gave the last full measure of devotion—that we here highly resolve that these dead shall not have died in vain—that this nation, under God, shall have a new birth of freedom—and that government of the people, by the people, for the people, shall not perish from the earth.

Source: Abraham Lincoln, final text of the Gettysburg Address, from the *Collected Works of Abraham Lincoln*, Vol. VII, edited by Roy P. Basler (New Brunswick, N.J.: Rutgers University Press, 1953), p. 23.

THE WINTER OF DISCONTENT: 1863–1864

The battles of the summer had been horrific. Both sides held their victories close to their hearts and brooded over their losses. The resolve and fury of summertime faded into the bitterness and bickering of winter. As the cycle rolled around again, people steeled themselves for a final push.

Politics North and South

Lincoln hoped to end the war as soon as possible, using persuasion as well as fighting to entice white Southerners back into the national fold. In early December 1863, Lincoln issued his proclamation of amnesty and reconstruction. To those who would take an oath of loyalty to the Union, Lincoln promised a full pardon and the return of all property other than slaves. Though he excluded Confederate leaders and high officers from this offer, Lincoln tried to include as many white Southern men as possible. As soon as 10 percent of the number of voters in 1860 had sworn their loyalty to the Union, he decreed, the Southerners could begin forming new state governments. Education and apprenticeship programs would aid former slaves in the transition to full freedom. He did not provide for African American participation in the new governments of the South.

Two factors worked against acceptance of Lincoln's policy. First, Northern Republicans and much of the public overestimated the extent and depth of Southern Unionist sentiment after years of war and occupation. Second, even in areas under federal control such as Tennessee and Kentucky, guerilla bands and raiders terrorized the local population. Elections in parts of Tennessee were blocked by irregulars. "The people are warned . . . not to hold such an Election under pain of being Arrested and Carried South for trial," one observer reported. Civilians were often caught between threats. Those who failed to aid Union forces were perceived as "enemies of mankind" with "the rights due to pirates and robbers," whereas those who actively aided the federals were liable to find crops trampled, barns burned, and vigilante justice enacted by neighbors and guerillas.

Abolitionists and their allies attacked Lincoln's reconstruction plan as far too lenient to the Rebel masters and not helpful enough for the former slaves. In the Wade-Davis bill of February 1864, Republican congressmen attempted to inflict more stringent conditions on former Confederates and offer more help to former slaves. They wanted to use the power of the national government to enforce a standard set of laws across the South and to require 50 percent, rather than 10 percent, of the population to swear the loyalty oath, an oath of past as well as future loyalty. They feared that too weak a plan of reconstruction would permit former slaveowners and Confederates to negate much of what the war might win. Congressmen and Secretary of the Treasury Salmon P. Chase worked behind the scenes in opposition to Lincoln's plan. With an eye toward the upcoming election and the need to entice Arkansas and Louisiana to rejoin the Union, Lincoln refused to sign the Wade-Davis bill.

Although Jefferson Davis did not have to worry about his own reelection in late 1863—the Confederacy had established the presidential term at six years—he did have to worry about congressional elections. They did not go well: 41 of the new 106 representatives expressly opposed Davis and his policies, while he held only a slight majority in the Senate. Just as Northern Democrats called for compromise and peace, so did some Southerners. When Davis took a hands-off policy, he was criticized for doing too little. When he tried to assert more control, he found himself called "despotic" by his own vice president. Editors savaged Davis as responsible for the South's worsening fortunes: "Had the people dreamed that Mr. Davis would carry all his chronic antipathies, his bitter prejudices, his puerile partialities, and his doting favoritisms into the Presidential chair, they would never have allowed him to fill it." The Confederacy stumbled through the winter and into the spring of 1864, desperately watching for signs that the North might be losing heart.

Prisons

Early in the Civil War, both sides had exchanged prisoners of war rather than spending men and resources to maintain prisons. Such arrangements worked well enough into 1863, but then things began to break down. The Confederates decreed that any former slave captured would be executed or re-enslaved, not taken prisoner. The Union, as a matter of principle, refused to participate in any exchanges so long as this policy remained in effect. Prisoners began piling up on both sides, and stories of mistreatment became more frequent and more horrifying.

Northerners who heard of the Confederate camp at Andersonville, Georgia, became livid. The camp was built early in 1864 when the Confederates decided to move prisoners from Richmond. Not only would prisoners be less likely to be rescued by Northern troops moving south, but they could more easily be supplied by railroad away from the heavy fighting in Virginia. The camp, built for 10,000 men in an open, partly swampy field, soon became overcrowded; it held 33,000 by August. Gangs of Northern soldiers controlled daily life within the prison, routinely beating and robbing new arrivals. Of the 45,000 men eventually held at Andersonville, 13,000 died. The camp's commander, Colonel Henry Wirz, was the only Confederate official executed for war crimes after the war.

This Confederate prisoner of war camp in Andersonville, Georgia, witnessed great brutality and appalling death rates from disease and hunger.
The Granger Collection, New York

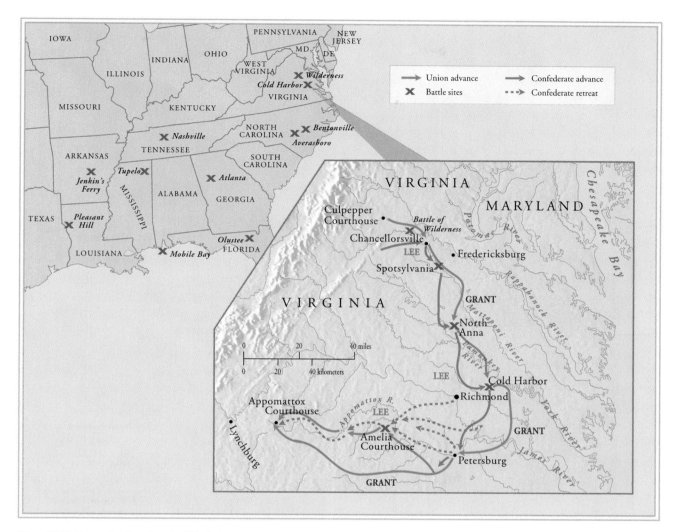

Map 15.3 *Grant Against Lee in Virginia*
 The two most important generals of the war confronted one another at one brutal battle after another between May 1864 and April 1865.
View an animated version of this map or related maps at http://history.wadsworth.com/passages2e.

Even higher proportions died at smaller camps in North Carolina. Although Confederates held in Northern prisons were better supplied, even there, death rates reached as high as 24 percent with rations often short and men reduced to eating rats. Overall, about 16 percent of Northern soldiers died in prison, 12 percent of Southerners. Many in the North criticized Lincoln for refusing to reinstitute exchanges, but Lincoln would not sacrifice the former slaves. Moreover, he knew that exchanges helped the soldier-starved Confederacy more than they did the North.

Union Resolve

In March 1864, Lincoln gave new direction and purpose to the Union effort by putting Ulysses S. Grant in charge of all Northern forces. Grant and Lincoln agreed that the Union had to use its superiority in materiel, manpower, and navy to attack the Confederacy on every front at once, forcing the South to decide what territory it would sacrifice. While Grant would fight in Virginia, Lincoln left William T. Sherman in charge in Chattanooga. Sherman would attack the young railroad center of Atlanta, cutting the Gulf South off from the Upper South. The loss of Atlanta would chop the Confederacy into pieces too small to resist the Northern army.

In retrospect, the events of 1864 may appear anticlimactic. The Confederates seemed to face overwhelming odds. Yet Southerners recognized that everything turned around holding the Northerners off until the presidential election in the North. If the

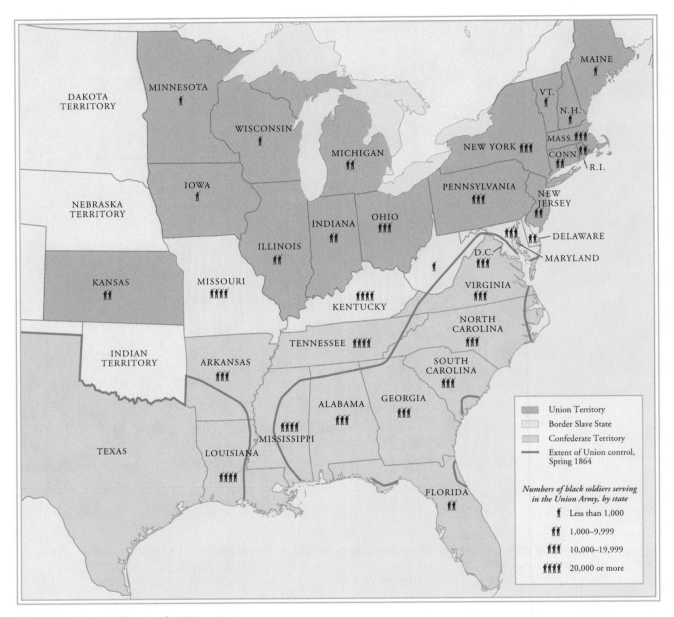

Map 15.4 *Black Soldiers in the Union Army*
African American men streamed into the U.S. army from all across the country, but they were especially prominent in the occupied South where they had been enslaved.

Southerners could inflict enough damage on the Union army, Northerners might elect someone willing to bring the war to an end through compromise. The Confederates knew, too, that the three-year terms of the most experienced veterans in the Union army expired in 1864. More than half of those veterans chose to leave the army, even though the war was not over. They would be replaced with younger, less seasoned soldiers. The Confederates also realized that Grant, new to his command, would be confronting Robert

E. Lee, who was fighting with an experienced army. All things considered, it was by no means clear in 1864 that the Union would win in Virginia or win the war.

African Americans played an increasingly large role in Union plans, for over 180,000 black soldiers enlisted just when the North needed them most. By the spring of 1864, the means of recruitment, training, and pay for these soldiers had become well established. The Confederates, however, refused to recognize the same rules of warfare for black soldiers that they acknowledged for whites. In April of 1864, at Fort Pillow in western Tennessee, Confederate cavalry under the command of Nathan Bedford Forrest shot down black Union soldiers and their white commander who attempted to surrender.

With the election clock running, Grant set out in May 1864 to destroy Lee's army. The Battle of the Wilderness near Chancellorsville saw brutal fighting and horrible losses. Fire in the tangled woods trapped wounded men, burning them alive. Grant lost more men than Hooker had in the battle of the previous year, but whereas Hooker treated such losses as a decisive defeat and retreated, Grant pushed on.

The two armies fought again and again over the next two months in the fields of Virginia. The Confederates turned the Union army back to the east of Richmond and rushed up the Shenandoah Valley to threaten Washington itself. While failing to take the capital, Confederate raiders "taxed" Maryland towns for thousands of dollars of greenbacks and burned the town of Chambersburg, Pennsylvania, when it refused to pay $500,000. The North repulsed the invasion and dispatched Philip Sheridan to the valley to make sure the Confederates did not regroup. With the Confederates pinned down in Petersburg, near Richmond, Pennsylvania coal miners volunteered to tunnel under the fortifications and plant explosives. Throughout July, they dug; finally, at the end of the month, they detonated a charge and blew an enormous crater in the Confederate lines. The attack that followed the explosion, however, failed. Union soldiers piled into the crater, where the rallying Confederates trapped them.

Fortunately for Lincoln, things were going better farther south. Throughout June and July, Sherman pushed relentlessly through north Georgia toward Atlanta. By the end of July, the Southern army had fallen back into Atlanta, preparing to defend it from siege. It seemed only a matter of time before the Union triumphed. But how much time? After rapidly advancing, federal troops slowed as they closed on Atlanta and many feared Sherman was "on the eve of disaster."

The Northern Election of 1864

The president had to fight off challenges even within his own party. Some Republicans considered Lincoln too radical; others considered him too cautious. Through adroit use of patronage, however, Lincoln managed to win renomination in June. The Republican party tried to broaden its appeal to Democrats by nominating Andrew Johnson, a former Democrat from Tennessee, to the vice presidency.

In the meantime, the Democrats confidently moved forward. They knew that in the eyes of his critics, Lincoln had caused the war, trampled on constitutional rights, consolidated too much power, and refused to end the war when he had a chance. The Democrats intended to take full advantage of such criticisms, especially by nominating George McClellan as their candidate. McClellan demonstrated that a person could oppose Lincoln's political purposes of the war without being a coward or traitor. McClellan and the Democrats portrayed themselves as the truly national party, for they were determined to restore the United States to its prewar unity and grandeur. McClellan said he would end the war if the South would reenter the Union—bringing slavery with it. It was a bargain that appealed to many in the North.

Just when it appeared that the Democrats would unseat Lincoln, however, news from the battlefield changed everything. Sherman swung around Atlanta and began destroying the railroads that made the small city an important junction. The Confederates, afraid they would be encircled and trapped within the city, set much of Atlanta on fire and abandoned it. Sherman and his army marched into the city on September 2. Two weeks later, Sheridan attacked the Confederates in the Shenandoah Valley, systematically destroying the valley's ability to support the Southern army again.

Even with these military victories, Lincoln won only 55 percent of the popular vote. Contrary to expectations, Lincoln carried the large majority of the armies' votes. In their letters, soldiers who identified themselves as Democrats rejected McClellan. A Vermont soldier who described himself as "a McClellan man clear to the bone" would not accept "peace by surrendering to the rebels"; instead "he would let his bones manure the soil of Virginia." Lincoln did much better in the electoral college, sweeping every state except three. The Republicans also elected heavy majorities to both houses of Congress and elected the governor and legislative majorities in all states except New Jersey, Delaware, and Kentucky. Lincoln believed the election validated the strength of republican government: "We can not have a free government without elections; and if the rebellion could force us to forego, or postpone a national election, it might fairly claim to have already conquered and ruined us."

The March to the Sea

Jefferson Davis traveled through the Lower South after the fall of Atlanta, exhorting citizens to remain defiant. A week after Lincoln's election, Sherman set out

ICTURING THE PAST◆POLITICS & DIPLOMACY

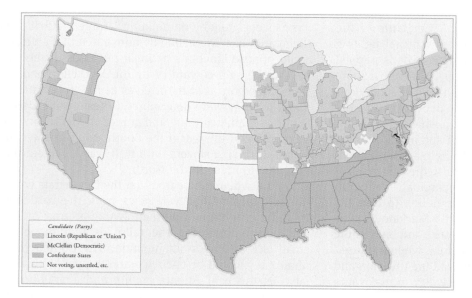

Map 15.5 *The Election of 1864*

To attract Democrats who supported the war, Lincoln and the Republican leadership renamed their party the National Union party and chose a Southern Unionist, Senator Andrew Johnson of Tennessee, as vice president. Though Lincoln won easily in the electoral college vote, he faced strong opposition throughout much of the North from George McClellan, who claimed 45 percent of the popular vote.

With the popular vote so close, in many states the outcome hinged on the votes of soldiers. In earlier wars, when soldiers departed home for service, they no longer voted, so no provision existed in law or practice for military personnel to vote away from their home polling site. By 1864, thirteen states permitted soldiers to vote in the field, while five continued to disenfranchise soldiers. Democrats had opposed absentee voting because they suspected soldiers would vote Republican, but hoped that General McClellan still enjoyed the favor of soldiers. Democrats lobbied senior generals while crying fraud. After three years of war, soldiers in the field, even those who considered themselves loyal to McClellan, would not support the Democratic peace platform. A Union colonel, a staunch Democrat, wrote his wife, "I have not come across an officer or a man that will vote for McClellan." This had always been considered a Democratic corps, but these formerly loyal Democrats voted for Lincoln by a factor of ten to one. Compare the distribution of votes for Lincoln in 1864 and 1860 (page 377) and note the areas where Lincoln gained and lost support.

---

across Georgia, provisioning his army along the way, taking the war to the Southern people themselves. Such a march would be as much a demonstration of Northern power as a military maneuver: "If we can march a well-appointed army right through [Confederate] territory," Sherman argued, "it is a demonstration to the world, foreign and domestic, that we have a power which Davis cannot resist." The triumphant

army of 60,000 made its way across the state throughout the fall of 1864. Large numbers of deserters from both sides, fugitive slaves, and outlaws took advantage of the situation to inflict widespread destruction and panic. Sherman arrived at Savannah on December 21. "I beg to present to you, as a Christmas gift, the city of Savannah," Sherman buoyantly telegraphed Lincoln. Contrasting with the devastation of the South,

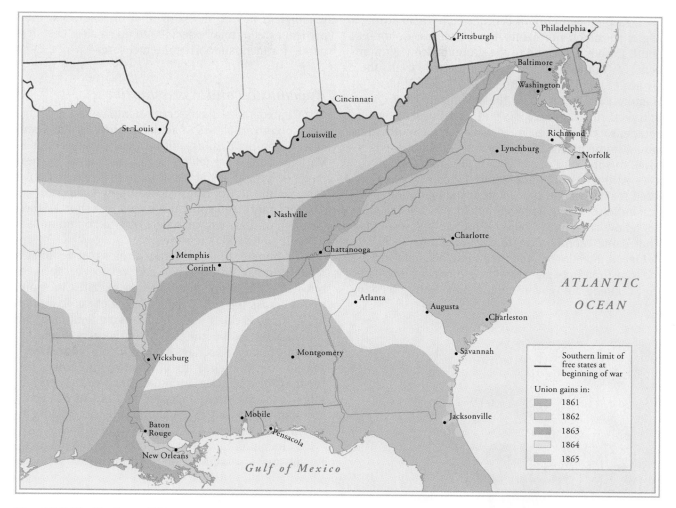

Map 15.6 *The Territory of War*

The Confederacy managed to protect large parts of its interior throughout the war, but the Union increasingly controlled the crucial rivers, rail lines, and ports.

View an animated version of this map or related maps at http://history.wadsworth.com/passages2e.

the president's annual message to Congress outlined a portrait of a North gaining strength with "more men now than we had when the war began . . . We are gaining strength, and may, if need be, maintain the contest indefinitely."

FROM WAR TO RECONSTRUCTION: 1865–1867

As the war ground to a halt in early 1865, Americans had to wonder if they remembered how to share a country with their former enemies. They had to wonder, too, how different the country would be with

African Americans no longer as slaves. Of all the changes the United States had ever seen, emancipation stood as the most profound.

War's Climax

Events moved quickly at the beginning of 1865. In January, Sherman issued Special Field Order 15, which reserved land in coastal South Carolina, Georgia, and Florida for former slaves. Those who settled on the land would receive forty-acre plots. Four days later, the Republicans in Congress passed the Thirteenth Amendment, abolishing slavery forever. Antislavery activists, black and white, packed the galleries and the House floor. Observers embraced, wept, and cheered. A Congressman wrote his wife that "we can now look other nations in the face without shame."

At the beginning of February, Sherman's troops began to march north into the Carolinas. Columbia, South Carolina, burned to the ground. Growing numbers of Confederate soldiers deserted from their armies. Lincoln met with Confederate officials at Hampton Roads on board the steamship *River Queen* to try to bring the war to an end, offering slaveowners compensation for their freed slaves if the Southerners would immediately cease the war. Jefferson Davis refused to submit to the "disgrace of surrender."

At the beginning of March, Lincoln was inaugurated for his second term. Rather than gloating at the impending victory on the battlefield, Lincoln called for his fellow citizens to "bind up the nation's wounds." That same month, Congress created the Bureau of Refugees, Freedmen, and Abandoned Lands to ease the transition from slavery to freedom. Nine days later, the Confederate government, after hotly debating whether to recruit slaves to fight as soldiers if their owners agreed, finally decided to do so after Lee, desperate for men, supported the measure.

Appomattox and Assassination

The Confederates' slave recruitment law did not have time to convert slaves to soldiers, however, for Grant soon began his final assault on Confederate troops in Virginia. Petersburg fell on April 2, Richmond the next day. Lee hoped to lead his army to the train station at Appomattox Court House to resupply them, but on April 9 Grant intercepted Lee's men just short of their destination. Lee, with nowhere else to go and no ally to come to his aid, surrendered.

A number of Confederate armies had yet to surrender, and Jefferson Davis had yet to be captured, but it was clear that the war had ended. Cities and towns across the North erupted in celebration and relief as crowds filled the streets to sing, embrace, fire salutes, and wave the flag. Southerners began to straggle home. Two days later, Lincoln addressed a Washington audience about what would come next for the freedmen. He admitted that Northerners differed "as to the mode, manner, and means of Reconstruction" and that the white South was "disorganized and discordant."

Lincoln did not live to take part in the planning, for he was assassinated on April 14 by John Wilkes

This picture of Lincoln, taken four days before his assassination, shows the toll four years of war had taken on the fifty-six-year-old president.
Corbis

Although John Wilkes Booth had been killed by Union troops twelve days after Lincoln's assassination in April of 1865, it was not until July that four of the eight convicted coconspirators—including a woman—were hanged.
The Granger Collection, New York

Booth, a failed actor and Southern sympathizer. Booth attacked Lincoln while the president sat with Mrs. Lincoln at Ford's Theater in Washington, shooting him in the back of the head and then leaping to the stage. Lincoln never recovered consciousness; he died early the next morning. After a long and frantic search, Booth was captured and killed in a burning barn.

The Costs and Consequences of the War

The North lost almost 365,000 men to death and disease in the Civil War, and the South lost 260,000. Another 277,000 Northerners were wounded, along with 195,000 Southerners. Black Americans lost 37,000 men in the Union army and another 10,000 men, women, and children in the contraband camps. Widows and orphans, black and white, Northern and Southern, faced decades of struggling without a male breadwinner. Many people found their emotional lives shattered by the war. Alcohol, drug abuse, crime, and violence became widespread problems. The war's legacy lingered in people's minds. Forty-eight years after the war, a former army surgeon on his deathbed fretted "that leg must come off—save a leg—lose a life."

The Southern economy fell to its knees. Major Southern cities had been reduced to ash. Railroads had been ripped from the ground, engines and cars burned. Fields had grown up weeds and brush. Farm values fell by half. Livestock, tools, barns, and fences had been stolen or destroyed by the armies of both sides. Recovery was slow. In Georgia, for example, as late as 1870 the state recorded 1 million fewer pigs, 200,000 fewer cattle, and 3 million fewer acres under cultivation than in 1860. Just as damaging in the long run, lines of credit had been severed. Before emancipation, planters had used slaves as collateral for loans. Now, without that basis, few people outside the South were willing to loan money to planters or other investors.

The Civil War did not mark a sudden turn in the Northern economy, but it did accelerate processes already well underway. The nationalization of markets, the accumulation of wealth, and the dominance of larger manufacturing firms all became more marked after 1865. Greenbacks, bonds, and a national banking system regularized the flow of capital and spurred the growth of business. The Republicans passed the Department of Agriculture Act, the Morrill College Land Grant Act, the Homestead Act, and the Union Pacific Railroad Act, all using the power of the federal government to encourage settlement of the West, strengthen public education, and spur economic de-

velopment. Despite the prosperity in the North, the hundreds of thousands of veterans faced many dislocations and readjustments as they returned to the farms, factories, and shops they had left months or years before.

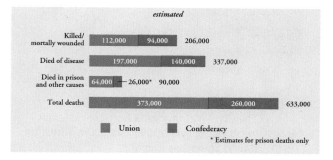

Chart 15.1 *The Causes and Numbers of Civil War Deaths* Disease killed even more men than did the bullets of the enemy.

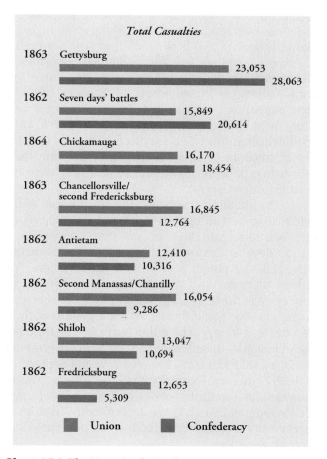

Chart 15.2 *The Most Costly Battles* Battles exacted horrible costs from early in the war until near its very end.

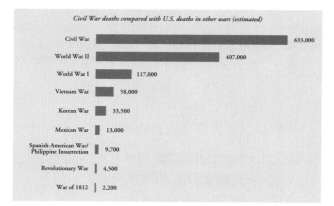

Chart 15.3 *Civil War Losses*
The Civil War exacted a horrible cost, far outstripping every other conflict in which the United States has fought.

Black Southerners took advantage of the presence of Union troops to leave the farms and plantations on which they had been held. Many set out to find family members.
North Wind Picture Archives

Emancipation and the South

As the battles ground to a halt, slaves became former slaves. Some, especially the young, greeted freedom confidently, whereas others, especially the elderly, could not help but be wary of anything so strange, no matter how long and how much they had prayed for it. Some seized their freedom at the first opportunity, taking their families to Union camps or joining the army. Others celebrated when the Yankees came to their plantations, only to find that their owners and white neighbors retaliated when the soldiers left. Others bided their time. Some refused to believe the stories of freedom at all until their master or mistress called them together to announce that they were indeed no longer slaves.

Upon hearing the news, the freedpeople gathered to discuss their options. For many, the highest priority was to reunite their families. Such people set off on journeys in desperate efforts to find a husband, wife, child, or parent sold away in earlier years. For others, sheer survival was the highest priority. Freedom came in the late spring, barely in time to get crops in the ground. Some former slaves argued that their best bet was to stay where they were for the time being. They had heard rumors that the government would award them land. Between July and September of 1865, however, those dreams died. Union officers promised land to former slaves in Virginia, Louisiana, Mississippi, and South Carolina, but then Washington revoked the promises. The land would be returned to its former owners.

Former slaveowners also responded in many different ways. Some fled to Latin America. Others tried to keep as much of slavery as they could by whipping

and chaining workers to keep them from leaving. Still others offered to let former slaves stay in their cabins and work for wages. The presence of black soldiers triggered resentment and fear among former slaveowners who marked the increased independence among blacks that was encouraged by "Negro troops." One slaveowner believed "the people of the South are in very great danger . . . I tell you most seriously that the whole south is resting upon a volcano."

African Americans had no choice but to compromise with white landowners. At first, in the spring of 1865, planters insisted that the former slaves work as they had worked before emancipation, in "gangs." In return for their work, they would receive a portion of the crop, shared among all the workers. Many black people chafed at this arrangement, preferring to work as individuals or families. In such places, landowners found that they had little choice but to permit black families to take primary responsibility for a portion of land. The former slaves provided the labor and received part of the crop as a result. Planters, though reluctant to give up any control over the day-to-day work on their land, realized they had few choices. They possessed little cash to pay wage workers and no alternative labor.

The Bureau of Refugees, Freedmen, and Abandoned Lands—the Freedmen's Bureau—oversaw the transition from a slave economy to a wage economy. Its agents dispensed medicine, food, and clothing from the vast stores of the federal government to displaced white and black Southerners. The Bureau created courts to adjudicate conflicts and to draw up labor contracts between landholders and laborers. It established schools and coordinated female volunteers who came from the North to teach in them.

PICTURING THE PAST ✦ ECONOMICS & TECHNOLOGY
DESOLATION OF THE SOUTH

© Bettmann/Corbis

After four years of war, little remained in many cities of the Confederacy. Atlanta, Columbia, and Richmond had been ravaged by fire; Vicksburg, Petersburg, and Fredericksburg had been pummeled by siege and battle. Union troops had destroyed railways, rivers were blocked by the refuse of war, and fields and farms had been stripped by the marauding troops of both sides or simply overrun by weeds. Roads, wagons, and riverboats were choked with civilian refugees, returning soldiers, and prisoners of war. In the countryside, even on farms and plantations untouched by combat, former slaves abandoned masters to seek family members and new opportunities.

Thousands of refugees from the countryside relied on federal aid and rations to survive. White women, particularly those from slaveholding families, found adjusting to defeat and emancipation trying. One woman from North Carolina bitterly lamented her transformation from "social queen" to "domestic drudge." African American women looked forward to working for the benefit of their own families.

Although many white Southerners resented and resisted the Freedmen's Bureau, it helped smooth the transition from slavery to freedom, from war to peace.

Black Mobilization

Black Southerners mourned the loss of Abraham Lincoln. Without his leadership, former slaves rightly worried, the forces of reaction might overwhelm their freedom. Southerners of both races watched to see what Andrew Johnson might do.

Throughout the South, former slaves and former free blacks gathered in mass meetings, Union Leagues, and conventions to announce their vision of the new order. They wanted, above all else, equality before the law and the opportunity to vote. They did not demand confiscation of land, nor did they speak extensively of economic concerns in general. Let us have our basic rights before the courts and at the ballot box, they said, and we will take care of ourselves. Such concerns and confidence reflected the perspective of the con-

ventions' leadership: former free blacks, skilled artisans, ministers, and teachers. The great mass of Southern blacks found their concerns neglected.

The Freedmen's Bureau, created in the spring of 1865, adjudicated conflicts between white landowners and black workers.
North Wind Picture Archives

PICTURING THE PAST ✦ SOCIAL & CULTURAL EVENTS

A BLACK SCHOOL

© Corbis

As growing numbers of African Americans gained literacy after emancipation, they increasingly taught in their own schools. To gain access to schools for their children and themselves, former slaves migrated to cities and towns and frequently demanded construction of a schoolhouse as a condition for signing a labor contract. Less than a month after the fall of Richmond, over 1,000 black children and adults attended schools begun by the city's black churches. Across the South, blacks organized and collected money to buy land, constructed schools with their own labor, and funded teacher salaries from self-imposed taxes and tuition. Teachers often advocated racial equality before the law and suffrage, as well as encouraging black political mobilization. Many Northern blacks, including a large number of women, helped found the first black colleges in the South, such as Fiske, Hampton, and Tougaloo. By 1869, black teachers outnumbered whites among the 3,000 teachers in the South.

Black Southerners agreed on the centrality of two institutions, however: the church and the school. At the very moment of freedom, they began to form their own churches. For generations, African Americans had been forced to worship alongside whites. For many ex-slaves, one of their first acts of freedom was to form their own churches. Before the war, 42,000 black Methodists in South Carolina attended biracial churches. By 1870, only 600 mostly elderly blacks remained. People who owned virtually nothing somehow built churches across the South. A black church in Charleston was the first building raised from the ruins of the city in 1865. Those churches often served as schools as well.

Andrew Johnson

In the meantime, events in Washington undermined the efforts of black Southerners to build a new world for themselves. Andrew Johnson wanted to attract moderates from both the North and the South to a political party that would change as little as possible. Johnson had been selected to run for the vice presidency because he was a Southerner who had remained true to the Union. As a result, both Northerners and Southerners distrusted Johnson. A longtime Democrat before the crisis of the Union, Johnson maintained a limited Jacksonian view of government. The new president's well-known disdain for the wealthy planters of the South appealed to equally disdainful Republicans in Washington. His public statements suggested a harsh peace for former slaveowners and Confederate leaders: "*Treason* is a crime, and *crime* must be punished." Unlike some Republicans, however, Johnson held little sympathy for black people or for expansion of the powers of the federal government. Johnson saw himself pursuing Lincoln's highest goal: reuniting the Union. He believed that re-

Andrew Johnson attempted to forge a new alliance between white Northerners and white Southerners, callously abandoning black Southerners in the process.
© Bettman/Corbis

lated, not merely as three-fifths of a people as before the war.

White Southerners could hardly believe their good fortune. The state conventions elected in 1865 flaunted their opinions of the North. Some refused to fly the American flag, some refused to ratify the Thirteenth Amendment, some even refused to admit that secession had been illegal. Former Confederates filled important posts in state governments. Georgia elected Alexander H. Stephens, the ex-vice president of the aborted nation, to Congress. Even Johnson recognized that far from inaugurating new regimes led by Unionist yeomen, "there seems, in many of the elections something like defiance."

The North erupted in outrage when the new state governments enacted the so-called "black codes," laws for the control of the former slaves. The Southern white legislatures granted only the barest minimum of rights to black people: the right to marry, to hold property, to sue and be sued. Most of the laws decreed what African Americans could not do: move from one job to another, own or rent land, testify in court, practice certain occupations. When the members of Congress convened in December of 1865, they reacted as many of their constituents did—with fury. To Northerners, even those inclined to deal leniently with the South, the former Confederates seemed to deny all the war had decided with this blatant attempt to retain racially based laws. And many Northerners blamed Johnson.

unification should start by winning the support of white Southerners.

Johnson could hardly have been placed in a more difficult position. Congress was not in session at the time of Lincoln's death and would not be for seven months, so Johnson used the opportunity to implement his vision of reunion. In what became known as "Presidential Reconstruction," Johnson offered amnesty to former Confederates who would take an oath of loyalty to the Union, restoring their political and civil rights and immunizing them against the seizure of their property or prosecution for treason. By 1866, Johnson granted over 7,000 pardons to wealthy Southerners and Confederate senior officers who applied individually for amnesty.

Johnson's plans for political reunion made no provisions at all for black voting. Indeed, his plan threatened to return the South to even greater national power than it had held before because the entire African American population would now be considered when the number of representatives was calcu-

Johnson and the Radicals

It was not that most Northerners, even most Republicans, wanted the kind of policies promoted by Radicals such as Thaddeus Stevens, who called for land to be seized from wealthy planters and given to the former slaves, or of Charles Sumner, who wanted immediate and universal suffrage for blacks. But neither did they want the sort of capitulation that Johnson had tolerated. A Chicago editor spoke for his readers: "As for Negro suffrage, the mass of Union men in the Northwest do not care a great deal. What scares them is the idea that the rebels are all to be let back . . . and made a power in the government again." Moderates tried to devise plans that would be acceptable to both sides.

The moderates sought to continue the Freedmen's Bureau. The Bureau was understaffed and underfunded—only about 900 agents covered the entire South—but it offered some measure of hope for former slaves. The Bureau saw itself as a mediator between blacks and whites. Its commissioner, General Oliver Howard, advocated education as the

"Letter to the Union Convention, 1865"
Black Citizens of Tennessee

In this petition by black Tennesseans to their white Unionist counterparts in the waning days of the Civil War, the themes of the Gettysburg Address receive eloquent endorsement. The fifty-nine men who signed the petition articulated the highest ideals of the American nation. There is no record of a response.

[*Nashville, Tenn., January 9, 1865*]

To the Union Convention of Tennessee Assembled in the Capitol at Nashville, January 9th, 1865: . . .

We claim to be men belonging to the great human family, descended from one great God, who is the common Father of all, and who bestowed on all races and tribes the priceless right of freedom. Of this right, for no offence of ours, we have long been cruelly deprived, and the common voice of the wise and good of all countries, has remonstrated against our enslavement, as one of the greatest crimes in all history.

We claim freedom, as our natural right, and ask that in harmony and cooperation with the nation at large, you should cut up by the roots the system of slavery, which is not only a wrong to us, but the source of all the evil which at present afflicts the State. For slavery, corrupt itself, corrupted nearly all, also, around it, so that it has influenced nearly all the slave States to rebel against the Federal Government, in order to set up a government of pirates under which slavery might be perpetrated. . . .

Devoted as we are to the principles of justice, of love to all men, and of equal rights on which our Government is based, and which make it the hope of the world. We know the burdens of citizenship, and are ready to bear them. We know the duties of the good citizen, and are ready to perform them cheerfully, and would ask to be put in a position in which we can discharge them more effectually. We do not ask for the privilege of citizenship, wishing to shun the obligations imposed by it.

Near 200,000 of our brethren are to-day performing military duty in the ranks of the Union army. Thousands of them have already died in battle, or perished by a cruel martyrdom for the sake of the Union, and we are ready and willing to sacrifice more. . . .

This is a democracy—a government of the people. It should aim to make every man, without regard to the color of his skin, the amount of his wealth, or the character of his religious faith, feel personally interested in its welfare. Every man who lives under the Government should feel that it is his property, his treasure, the bulwark and defense of himself and his family, his pearl of great price, which he must preserve, protect, and defend faithfully at all times, on all occasions, in every possible manner.

This is not a Democratic Government if a numerous, law-abiding, industrious, and useful class of citizens, born and bred on the soil, are to be treated as aliens and enemies, as an inferior degraded class, who must have no voice in the Government which they support, protect and defend, with all their heart, soul, mind, and body, both in peace and war. . . .

One other matter we would urge on your honorable body. At present we can have only partial protection from the courts. The testimony of twenty of the most intelligent, honorable, colored loyalists cannot convict a white traitor of a treasonable action. A white rebel might sell powder and lead to a rebel soldier in the presence of twenty colored soldiers, and yet their evidence would be worthless so far as the courts are concerned, and the rebel would escape. A colored man may have served for years faithfully in the army, and yet his testimony in court would be rejected, while that of a white man who had served in the rebel army would be received. . . .

There have been white traitors in multitudes in Tennessee, but where we ask, is the black traitor? Can you forget how the colored man has fought at Fort Morgan, at Milliken's Bend, at Fort Pillow, before Petersburg, and your own city of Nashville?

When has the colored citizen, in this rebellion been tried and found wanting? . . .

In this great and fearful struggle of the nation with a wicked rebellion, we are anxious to perform the full measure of our duty both as citizens and soldiers to the Union cause we consecrate ourselves, and our families with all that we have on earth. Our souls burn with love for the great government of freedom and equal rights. Our white brethren have no cause for distrust as regards our fidelity, for

neither death nor life, nor angels, nor principalities, nor powers, nor things present, nor things to come, nor height, nor depth, nor any other creature, shall be able to separate us from the love of the Union.

Praying that the great God, who is the common Father of us all, by whose help the land must be delivered from present evil, and before whom we must all stand at last to be judged by the rule of eternal justice, and not by passion and prejudice, may enlighten your minds and enable you to act with wisdom, justice, and magnanimity, we remain your faithful friends in all the perils and dangers which threaten our beloved country.

[*59 signatures*]

And many other colored citizens of Nashville

Source: *Free at Last: A Documentary History of Slavery, Freedom, and the Civil War.* Ira Berlin, et al., eds. (New York: New Press, 1992) pp. 497–505.

---

foundation for improving living conditions and prospects for blacks. By 1869, approximately 3,000 schools, serving over 150,000 students, reported to the Bureau, and these numbers do not include the many private and church-funded schools throughout the South.

The Bureau insisted on the innovation of formal contracts between laborer and landlord. Although these contracts infuriated Southern white men, the Bureau ended up supporting landowners as often as black laborers. The moderates also attempted to institute a Civil Rights bill to define American citizenship for all those born in the United States, thereby including blacks. Citizenship would bring with it equal protection under the laws, though the bill said nothing about black voting. The Bureau struggled against strongly held prejudice. Its Mississippi commissioner despaired of a public that failed to "conceive of the Negro having any rights at all."

Republicans supported the Freedmen's Bureau and Civil Rights bills as the starting place for rebuilding the nation. But Johnson vetoed both bills, claiming that they violated the rights of the states and of white Southerners who had been excluded from the decision making. Republicans closed ranks to override Johnson's veto, the first major legislation enacted over a presidential veto.

To prevent any future erosion of black rights, the Republicans proposed the Fourteenth Amend-

Thaddeus Stevens, a congressman from Pennsylvania, was among the leaders of the Radical Republicans.
North Wind Picture Archives

ment, which, as eventually ratified, guaranteed citizenship to all American-born people and equal protection under the law for those citizens. The

In this riot of July 1866, Southern whites killed thirty-four blacks and three white supporters after a Republican meeting in New Orleans.
Reproduced from the Collections of the Library of Congress

The Ku Klux Klan emerged in 1866, devoting itself to the maintenance of white supremacy in all its forms.
The Granger Collection, New York

amendment decreed that any state that abridged the voting rights of any male inhabitants who were twenty-one and citizens would suffer a proportionate reduction in its congressional representation. This clause offered white Southerners the choice of acceptance of black suffrage or reduced Congressional representation. It also was the first Constitutional amendment to use the word "male," angering feminist abolitionists who challenged the Republicans' denial of suffrage based on sex. Johnson urged

the Southern states to refuse to ratify the amendment, advice they promptly followed.

Throughout the second half of 1866 the North watched, appalled, as much that the Civil War had been fought for seemed to be brushed aside in the South. Not only did the Southern men who met in the state conventions refuse to accept the relatively mild Fourteenth Amendment, but they made clear their determination to fight back in every way they could against further attempts to remake the South. The spring of that year saw riots in Memphis and New Orleans in which policemen and other whites brutally assaulted and killed black people and burned their homes with little or no provocation.

It was in 1866, too, that the Ku Klux Klan appeared. Founded in Tennessee, the Ku Klux Klan dedicated itself to maintaining white supremacy. The Klan dressed in costumes designed to overawe the former slaves, hiding behind their anonymity to avoid retaliation. The Klan became in effect a military wing of the Democratic party, devoting much of its energy to warning and killing white and black men who dared associate with the Republicans.

Johnson toured the country in the fall of 1866 to denounce the Republicans and their policies. Even his supporters saw the tour as a "thoroughly reprehensible" disaster. The voters rejected both Johnson and the Democrats, as the governorship and legislature of every Northern state came under the control of the Republicans. In the next Congress, Republicans would outnumber Democrats sufficiently to override any presidential veto. The Republicans felt they held a mandate to push harder than they had before. They had only a few months, however, until their term ended in March, to decide what to do. They bitterly disagreed over the vote, land distribution, the courts, and education. Some wanted to put the South under military control for the indefinite future, whereas others sought to return things to civilian control as soon as possible. Finally, on March 2, 1867, as time was running out on the session, they passed the Reconstruction Act.

The Reconstruction Act

The Reconstruction Act placed the South under military rule. All the Southern states except Tennessee, which had been readmitted to the Union after it ratified the Fourteenth Amendment, were put in five military districts. Once order had been instituted, then the states would proceed to elect conventions to draw up new constitutions. The constitutions written by those conventions had to accept the Fourteenth Amendment and provide for universal manhood suffrage. Once a majority of the state's citizens and both houses of the national Congress had approved the new constitution, the state could be readmitted to the Union.

To ensure that Andrew Johnson did not undermine this plan—which soon became known as "Radical Reconstruction"—Congress sought to curb the president's power. With no threat of his veto after the 1866 elections, the Republicans could do much as they wanted. Congress decreed that it could call itself into special session. There, it limited the president's authority as commander-in-chief of the army and, in the Tenure of Office Act, prevented him from removing officials who had been confirmed by the Senate.

Johnson, characteristically, did not quietly accept such restrictions of his power. When he intentionally violated the Tenure of Office Act by removing Secretary of War Edwin Stanton in the summer of 1867, many in Congress decided that Johnson warranted impeachment. Matters stewed throughout the fall, while the first elections under the Reconstruction Act took place in the South.

African American men could vote in the South during Reconstruction, but often risked their livelihoods or their lives to do so.
The Granger Collection, New York

Reconstruction Begins

After word of the Reconstruction Act circulated in the spring and summer, both black and white men claimed leadership roles within the Republican party. Black Northerners came to the South, looking for appointive and elective office. Ambitious black Southerners, many of whom had been free and relatively prosperous before the Civil War, put themselves forward as the natural leaders of the race. Such men became the backbone of the Republican party in black-belt districts.

White Southerners sneered at white Northerners who supported the Republican cause. They called them "carpetbaggers." These men, according to the insulting name, were supposedly so devoid of connections and property in their Northern homes that they could throw everything they had into a carpetbag—a cheap suitcase—and head south as soon as they read of the opportunities created by Radical Reconstruction. The majority of white Northerners who became Republican leaders in the South, however, had in fact moved to the region months or years before Reconstruction began. Many had been well educated in the North before the war and many held property in the South. Like white Southerners, however, the Northern-born Republicans found the postwar South a difficult place in which to prosper. Black people were no more inclined to work for low wages for white

Northerners than for anyone else, and Southern whites often went out of their way to avoid doing business with the Yankees. As a result, when Reconstruction began, a considerable number of Northerners took up the Republican cause as a way to build a political career in the South.

White Southern Republicans, labeled "scalawags" by their enemies, risked being called traitors to their race and region. Few white Republicans emerged in the plantation districts, because they endured ostracism, resistance, and violence. "It costs nothing for a Northern man to be a Union man, but the rebuff and persecution received here . . . tells a horrible tale." In the upcountry districts, however, former Whigs and Unionists asserted themselves against the planters and Confederates. The Republican party became strong in the mountains of east Tennessee, western North Carolina, eastern Kentucky, north Alabama, and northern Georgia. Many whites in these districts, though unwilling to join with low-country African Americans or their white leaders, struck alliances of convenience with them. Black voters and white voters generally wanted and needed different things. Blacks, largely propertyless, called for an activist government to raise taxes to provide schools, orphanages, and hospitals. Most whites, on the other hand, owned land and called mainly for lower taxes.

Throughout the South, most whites watched, livid, as local black leaders, ministers, and Republicans mobilized black voters in enormous numbers in the fall of 1867. Membership in Union Leagues swept the region, with local leagues assisting with labor contracts and school construction as well as political activity. An Alabama league demanded recognition of black citizenship: "We claim exactly the same rights, privileges and immunities as are enjoyed by white men—we seek nothing more and will be content with nothing less." While many white Democrats boycotted the elections, the Republicans swept into the constitutional delegate positions. Although many black men voted, African American delegates made up only a relatively small part of the convention's delegates. They held the majority in South Carolina and Louisiana, but much smaller proportions elsewhere. About half of the 265 African Americans elected as delegates to the state conventions had been free before the war, and most were ministers, artisans, farmers, and teachers. Over the next two years, these delegates would meet to write new, much more democratic, constitutions for their states.

At the very moment of the success of the Southern Republicans, however, ominous signs came from the North. Republicans were dismayed at the election returns in the North in 1867, for the Democrats' power surged from coast to coast. Many white voters thought that the Radicals had gone too far in their concern with black rights and wanted officeholders to devote their energies to problems closer to home. Racism linked Democratic appeals against blacks in the Midwest with western diatribes against the Chinese and the specter of a nation menaced by a "Mongolian and Indian and African" alliance against ordinary white men. Integrated public schools and confiscation of plantation lands for former slaves were soundly defeated. The Republicans in Washington heard the message. They began scaling back their support for any further advances in Reconstruction.

CONCLUSION

The Civil War changed the United States more deeply than any other event in the nineteenth century. The conflict brought the deaths of over 625,000 soldiers. It saw bitter rioting in the streets and the first assassination of a president. It brought a major shift in the balance of power among the regions and an expansion of the federal government. Most important, the war brought what few Americans could have imagined at the end of 1860: the immediate emancipation of 4 million enslaved people.

Freedom emerged from the war through a circuitous route. The war began as a war for Union. As the deaths mounted and African Americans seized freedom at every opportunity, abolitionists and Republicans increasingly insisted that the war become a war to end slavery. Many white Northerners supported emancipation because it seemed the best way to end the war. Abraham Lincoln worked desperately to keep the support of both the advocates and foes of emancipation, knowing that moving too quickly would shatter the fragile support that kept him in office. The New York City draft riots and the close elections of 1863 demonstrated that many Northerners resisted the continuation of the war and its embrace of black freedom. Only Union success on the battlefield in late 1864 permitted Lincoln's reelection. His assassination made an already confused situation far more so, ending slavery and restoring the Union without a blueprint and without leadership.

The end of the fighting saw the conflict shift in the South, as people struggled to determine what freedom would mean. For black Southerners, the goal was autonomy and respect. For white Northerners, the goal was to reconstruct the South in an idealized image of the North. For white Southerners, the goal was the reassertion of the power they had held before the war, especially power over the black people in their midst. Such goals could not be reconciled. The era of Reconstruction would be devoted to the struggle among them.

Recommended Readings

Berlin, Ira, Fields, Barbara J., Miller, Steven F., Reidy, Joseph P., and Rowland, Leslie S., eds. *Freedom* (1985–). A rich and fascinating multivolume documentary collection.

Blight, David W. *Race and Reunion: The Civil War in American Memory* (2001). Documents the role of politics, myth, and race in shaping how the Civil War is remembered.

Donald, David. *Lincoln* (1995). Stands as the most elegant biography.

Faust, Drew Gilpin. *Mothers of Invention: Women of the Slaveholding South in the American Civil War* (1995). Offers a challenging and interesting interpretation.

Fellman, Michael. *Inside War: The Guerilla Conflict in Missouri During the American Civil War* (1989). Makes palpable the internal struggles in the border areas.

Foner, Eric. *Reconstruction: America's Unfinished Revolution, 1863–1877* (1988). A magisterial interpretation of the struggle over black freedom.

Gallagher, Gary W. *The Confederate War: How Popular Will, Nationalism, and Military Strategy Could Not Stave Off Defeat* (1997). Explores why the Confederacy could fight as long as it did.

Harris, William C. *With Charity for All: Lincoln and the Restoration of the Union* (1997). Offers a fresh assessment of Lincoln's attitudes toward the white South.

Hattaway, Herman, and Jones, Archer. *How the North Won: A Military History of the Civil War* (1983). Authoritatively describes strategy and tactics.

Litwack, Leon. *Been in the Storm So Long: The Aftermath of Slavery* (1979). Beautifully evokes the conflicting emotions and motives surrounding freedom.

Neely, Mark E., Jr. *The Union Divided: Party Conflict in the Civil War North* (2002). Examines the impact of political dissension in the North on war effort.

Roark, James L. *Masters Without Slaves: Southern Planters in the Civil War and Reconstruction* (1978). Describes the war from the perspective of those who lost the most in Southern defeat.

Rose, Willie Lee. *Rehearsal for Reconstruction: The Port Royal Experiment* (1964). A classic account of the first efforts to create Northern policy toward the freedpeople.

American Journey Online and InfoTrac College Edition

Visit the source collections at http://ajaccess. wadsworth.com and infotrac.thomsonlearning.com and use the Search function with the following key terms to explore documents, images, audio and video clips, articles, and commentary related to the material in this chapter.

Ulysses S. Grant	African American soldiers
Vicksburg	Gettysburg Address
Appomattox	Emancipation

Additional resources, exercises, and Internet links related to this chapter are available on the American Passages Web site: http://history.wadsworth.com/passages2e

16 RECONSTRUCTION ABANDONED 1867–1877

Reconstruction brought African American voters into southern politics for the first time. A drawing from Harper's Weekly *for November 16, 1867 depicts black workers, city dwellers, and soldiers casting their ballots.*
From the Collections of the Library of Congress

Republicans in 1867 believed that they had taken important steps toward a newer and more just society with their Reconstruction legislation. "We have cut loose from the whole dead past," said Timothy Howe of Wisconsin, "and have cast our anchor out a hundred years." But the struggle over black rights that had begun during the Civil War was far from over. The battle shifted from the halls of Congress back to the South. There, in the decade that followed, whites sought to recreate as many of the features of slavery as they could. Violence, brutality, election fraud, and raw economic intimidation ended the experiment in multiracial politics known as Reconstruction.

While racial prejudices were the main cause, other forces hastened the abandonment of Reconstruction. In the mid-1870s, a severe economic depression made African American rights seem a less urgent issue. White Americans feared that the national government was becoming too powerful; a renewed commitment to localism and states rights helped southern whites repress black aspirations. For many in the North, the hum of industry, the spread of railroads, and the rise of cities seemed more in tune with national progress than preserving the rights of former slaves. With a western frontier to open and Native Americans to subdue, the nation retreated from the principles for which the Civil War had been fought. By the disputed presidential election of 1876, it was evident that white Americans no longer wished to be involved with the fate of blacks in the South. After a decade of slow, painful withdrawal from a commitment to equality, an informal sectional compromise sealed the return of white rule to the South in 1877.

CHRONOLOGY

1867   Alaska purchase treaty signed

1868   Andrew Johnson impeached and then acquitted • Purchase of Alaska completed • Ulysses S. Grant wins presidency

1869   Ulysses S. Grant inaugurated as president • Transcontinental railroads link up • Licensing of women lawyers begins • Fifteenth Amendment passes Congress • "Gold Corner" scheme of Jay Gould and Jim Fisk • Woman suffrage enacted in Wyoming Territory

1870   Santo Domingo annexation treaty defeated • Ku Klux Klan terror raids in the South • First Greek letter sorority (Kappa Alpha Theta) founded

1871   Ku Klux Klan Act passes Congress • Tweed Ring exposed in New York City • Chicago fire burns three and a half miles of the city

1872   Liberal Republican movement challenges Grant • Grant wins reelection over Horace Greeley

1873   Panic of 1873 starts economic depression • Salary Grab and Credit Mobilier scandals • Mark Twain and Charles Dudley Warner publish *The Gilded Age*

1874   Woman's Christian Temperance Union founded • Democrats make substantial gains in the congressional elections • Sale of typewriters begins • Chautauqua movement for summer education starts

1875   Congress passes Civil Rights Act • Smith College and Wellesley College open to provide higher education for women

1876   Sioux defeat Custer at Little Big Horn • Centennial Exposition opens in Philadelphia • Tilden and Hayes are candidates in contested presidential election

1877   Hayes declared winner of presidency after series of compromises settles disputes • Reconstruction ends

A PRESIDENCY UNDER SIEGE: ANDREW JOHNSON IMPEACHED

The struggle between the executive and legislative branches over the fate of the South continued unabated into the second half of 1867. As President Andrew Johnson sought to impede the Radical Reconstruction program, Republicans in Congress argued that he should be impeached and removed from office. When the president tried to oust Secretary of War Edwin M. Stanton in August 1867, cries for impeachment mounted. For the moment the Republicans could do little until Congress reassembled in December. After lawmakers gathered, the sentiment for removing the president had receded and it appeared that the president would survive for the rest of his term. As he had done so often in the past, Johnson defied Congress and precipitated a confrontation. After the Senate in January 1868 refused to accept his dismissal of Stanton, Johnson replaced him anyway. Presidential stubbornness, Republicans said, was a clear violation of the Tenure of Office Act.

Emboldened by Johnson's defiance, the solidly Republican House voted for his impeachment and leveled eleven charges against him. None of the specifications in the articles of impeachment alleged violations of criminal laws; they dealt instead with Johnson's Reconstruction policies and his obstruction of Congress. The trial came in March. Two months later the Senate failed to achieve the necessary two-thirds vote to convict Johnson. The impeachment attempt lost because moderate Republicans feared that if Johnson were convicted on political grounds it would set a bad precedent. Moreover, Johnson himself eased up on his obstructive tactics. With the 1868 presidential election looming, it seemed less urgent to oust a man who would soon leave office. True to his nature, Johnson did not become more conciliatory. He encouraged southern whites to resist Reconstruction and contributed to the denial of rights to African Americans that marked the 1870s. Few presidents have done less with their historical opportunities than Andrew Johnson.

The Purchase of Alaska

During the months of Johnson's impeachment and trial, Congress concluded a major territorial acquisition that completed expansion on the North American continent. In March 1867, the Russian minister to the United States (Washington did not yet rate an ambassador from the European powers) hinted to Secretary of State William H. Seward that the government of the Tsar in St. Petersburg wanted to sell Alaska. The Russians knew that they could not defend their northern possession against the British in Canada. Seward worked out a treaty with the Russians that was signed on March 30, 1867. The United States paid $7,200,000 for Alaska; on April 9, 1867, the Senate, by a vote of thirty-seven to two, agreed to the deal.

Paying for the Alaska purchase required Congress to appropriate money. The House did not take action on the problem until July 1868 after Johnson had been impeached. Since the United States had already occupied the territory, the lawmakers went along and passed the bill on July 14. The Alaska purchase was a major strategic and geographic victory for the United States. For the moment, the impulse for expansion eased and the nation turned to its internal affairs.

The Election of 1868

Both parties looked ahead to the first postwar presidential contest but the issues of the Civil War defined the race. The Republicans nominated the great hero of the conflict, Ulysses S. Grant. As the architect of Union victory, his popularity transcended partisanship. Republicans believed that they had selected a candidate "so independent of party politics as to be a guarantee of peace and quiet." In his official letter of acceptance, Grant said "let us have peace" and that phrase became the theme of the Republican campaign. The Republicans were not campaigning on any promise to expand Reconstruction or black rights.

The Democrats turned to the former governor of New York, Horatio Seymour. Along with his running mate, Frank Blair of Missouri, Seymour relied on racial bigotry and white supremacy as the keynotes of his appeal. To win, the Democrats agreed, they had to arouse "the aversion with which the masses contemplate the equality of the negro." Seymour went out to campaign; Grant stayed home. The Republicans won, but not by a landslide. Grant garnered 53 percent of the vote; Seymour totaled 47 percent. Although Grant carried the electoral college by a margin of 214 to 80, the signs were not good for a continuation of Reconstruction. White voters were less willing to help African Americans, and the high point of post–Civil War racial reform was in the past.

The Fifteenth Amendment and Woman Suffrage

After the 1868 election, Republicans pushed for the adoption of the Fifteenth Amendment to the Constitution. Under its terms, the federal and state govern-

The Fifteenth Amendment 1870

The last of the three Reconstruction amendments, the Fifteenth Amendment said that race or color could not be a reason for denying a citizen the right to vote.

Sect. 1. The right of citizens of the United States to vote shall not be denied or abridged by the United States or by any State on account of race, color, or previous condition of servitude.

Sect. 2. The Congress shall have the power to enforce this article by appropriate legislation.

ments could not restrict the right to vote because of race, color, or previous condition of servitude. Congress approved the amendment in February 1869 over Democratic opposition. The purpose of the change was to limit the legal right of the southern states to exclude African Americans, and Democrats assailed it as a step toward black equality and a social revolution. In fact, the new amendment did not assure African Americans the right to hold office, and it left untouched the restrictions that northern states imposed on the right of males to vote. Literacy tests and property qualifications remained in place in some states outside of the South. State legislatures endorsed the amendment promptly and it was added to the Constitution in 1870.

The big losers in the adoption of the Fifteenth Amendment were women who had hoped that they might share in some of the expansion of political rights. In fact, several of the major advocates of woman suffrage, such as Susan B. Anthony, opposed the amendment because it left women out. In Anthony's mind, black and Asian men should be barred from voting if women did not have the right of suffrage too. Despite his earlier support for woman suffrage, Frederick Douglass, the major black leader, contended that "this hour belongs to the negro," by which he meant black males.

At a meeting of the Equal Rights Association in May 1869, the sharp differences about how to achieve woman suffrage produce an open break. Two distinct groups of suffragists emerged. The National Woman Suffrage Association (NWSA) reflected the position of Susan B. Anthony and Elizabeth Cady Stanton that the Fifteenth Amendment should be shunned until

Susan B. Anthony was a leading advocate of a woman's right to vote in the post–Civil War era. Her connection with that reform continued throughout the late nineteenth century.
The Granger Collection, New York

women were included. The American Woman Suffrage Association (AWSA), led by Lucy Stone and Alice Stone Blackwell, endorsed the amendment and focused its work in the states. Amid this dissension one small bright spot appeared. The new territory of Wyoming granted women the right of suffrage in 1869. The goal of the Wyoming legislature was to make Americans notice its underpopulated territory, not to expand women's rights. Nonetheless, a forward step had been taken. The discord between the major suffrage groups, however, lasted for two decades and slowed the progress toward reform.

THE GRANT ERA

Ulysses S. Grant came to the White House with almost no political experience. He believed that he should administer the government rather than promote new programs. "I shall on all subjects have a policy to recommend," he said in his inaugural address, "but none to enforce against the will of the people." He promised, unlike Andrew Johnson, to carry out the laws that Congress passed. Nineteenth century Americans did not expect a president to be an activist and neither did Grant himself. Those who hoped for a period of calm after the storms of Johnson's presidency were soon disappointed.

Grant's passive view of the presidency allowed Congress to play a dominant role in his administration. As a result, the executive office itself lost some of the authority Lincoln had given it during the Civil War. A generation passed before power shifted back toward the White House. Since Republicans were suspicious of strong presidents, that development aroused little protest from the governing party.

Hard choices confronted the new president. Southern Republicans begged for help from Washington to fight off resurgent Democrats. Yet, many party members in the North believed Reconstruction was no longer wise or practical. Support for black aspirations seemed a loser. As a result, the commitment to African Americans waned among Republicans. Within the party, differences also flared over the right of Republican leaders to hand out patronage. The government should follow a merit system of appointing officials said some Republicans; this idea became known as "civil service reform." Party regulars, who hated civil service reform, argued that Grant should side with them and defer to the wishes of congressional leaders when making appointments.

Grant tried to stay away from partisan battles. As a result, he followed a shifting policy in selecting his cabinet and making appointments. The president did not accept the advice of influential Republicans but depended instead on men who shared his cautious governing style. The president gave cabinet officers wide discretion to use merit rather than political connections in staffing their departments. Without the clear objective of a war before him, Grant seemed confused by the shifting demands of domestic politics.

When he took office, President Grant was seen as a constructive change from the turmoil of Andrew Johnson's administration. In office, he found that politics was more of a challenge to him than military success in the Civil War.
From the Collections of the Library of Congress

The most immediate problem for Grant in his first year was the South. The Democrats were trying to split the Republicans by making common cause with those party members unhappy about their existing leadership. Playing down their racism and dislike of blacks, the Democrats argued that former Confederates should now be allowed to participate in public life. The strategy produced mixed results in 1869. Republicans did well in Mississippi and won a close race for governor in Texas. Democrats triumphed in Virginia and Tennessee. Overall, the results suggested that Republican strength was eroding as the Democrats got back into politics. Southern white Republicans and their black allies found that Washington often left them on their own to confront the resurgent Democrats.

The Railroads Meet

While politics dominated Washington, an event in Utah captured public attention. The national economy needed secure and efficient transportation to the West Coast. Throughout the 1860s, two transcontinental railroads had been laying tracks across the country.

The completion of the transcontinental railroad at Promontory, Utah, in 1869, symbolized the joining together of the nation's two coasts. As the presence of photographers indicates, it also became an important media event.
The Granger Collection, New York

In the work of building the transcontinental railroad, the grueling labor of Chinese workers was indispensable. They worked for low pay in difficult conditions in a society that scorned them and often subjected them to harsh discrimination.
California History Section, California State Library

The Union Pacific had built westward and the Central Pacific eastward. The two lines faced imposing obstacles of money and geography. The Central Pacific had crossed the heights of the Sierra Nevada Mountains through rocky gorges and across treacherous rivers. Several thousand Chinese laborers did the most dangerous work. They tunneled into snowdrifts to reach their work sites and then toiled on sheer cliffs with picks and dynamite. Many died, all faced discrimination, and the railroad would not have existed without them. On the Union Pacific side, more than 10,000 construction men, many of them Irish immigrants, laid tracks across Nebraska and Wyoming.

On May 10, 1869, the two rail lines met at Promontory, Utah. Engine 119 of the Union Pacific placed its cowcatcher up against the cowcatcher of the Central Pacific's Engine No. 60. Railroad executives drove a golden spike into the ground with a silver sledgehammer after missing their target on the first few tries. The transcontinental lines were a reality. Loans and subsidies from the federal government to the railroads had enabled the lines to be built quickly. Following their completion, a period of railroad construction ensued. Soon the United States had one of the most developed transportation systems in the world.

With railroads in place, the entire West seemed open to settlement for white Americans eager to dominate the Great Plains. No longer did potential farmers think of this area as "The Great American Desert." The whole continent lay available. That meant, however, that hard decisions lay ahead regarding the Native Americans who had been pushed westward before the Civil War as well as the nomadic tribes of the Plains Indians already living in the area. These native residents of the West found their hunting grounds and traditional domains at risk as settlers appeared.

Grant's "Peace Policy"

Treatment of the Indians after the Civil War wavered between benevolence and cruelty. In the case of Grant, Native Americans found he treated them with more respect and insight than had many previous presidents. His administration pursued what became known as the "peace policy." While many western settlers advocated the extermination of the Indian tribes, most Americans applauded Grant's strategy of conciliation.

The approach took shape before Grant came to the White House. Advocates of the Indians contended that the hostile tribes should be resettled in Dakota Territory and in the Indian Territory (now Oklahoma). The government would stop treating the entire West as a giant Indian reservation. Instead, the government would allocate specific areas to the tribes. On these "reservations" Native Americans would learn the cultural values of white society, be taught to grow crops, and be paid a small income until they could support themselves. The plan was not yet in place when Grant became president.

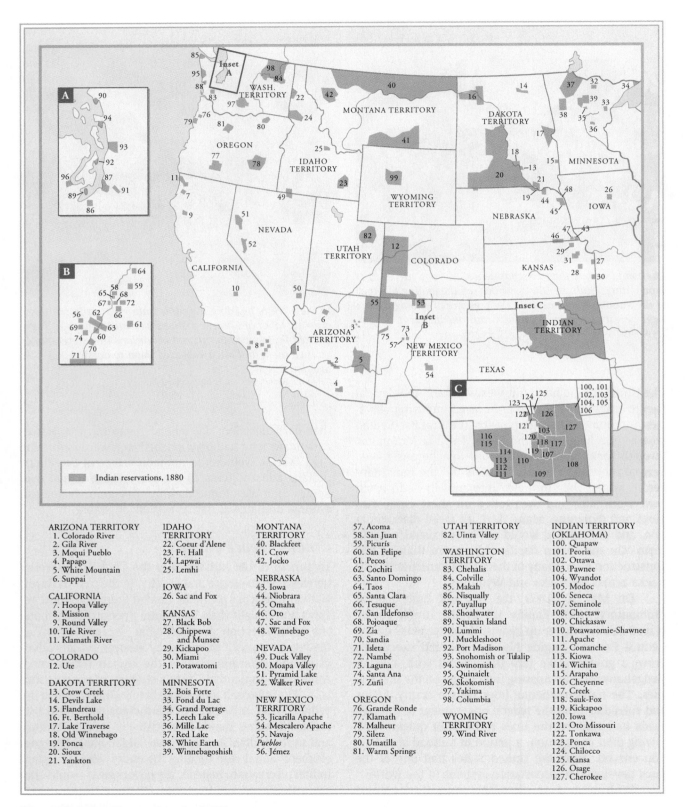

Map 16.1 *Indian Reservations in the West*
Following the end of the Civil War and with the adoption of the peace policy of President Ulysses S. Grant, a network of Indian reservations spread across the West. This map shows how extensive the reservation system was.

ARIZONA TERRITORY
1. Colorado River
2. Gila River
3. Moqui Pueblo
4. Papago
5. White Mountain
6. Suppai

CALIFORNIA
7. Hoopa Valley
8. Mission
9. Round Valley
10. Tule River
11. Klamath River

COLORADO
12. Ute

DAKOTA TERRITORY
13. Crow Creek
14. Devils Lake
15. Flandreau
16. Ft. Berthold
17. Lake Traverse
18. Old Winnebago
19. Ponca
20. Sioux
21. Yankton

IDAHO TERRITORY
22. Coeur d'Alene
23. Ft. Hall
24. Lapwai
25. Lemhi

IOWA
26. Sac and Fox

KANSAS
27. Black Bob
28. Chippewa and Munsee
29. Kickapoo
30. Miami
31. Potawatomi

MINNESOTA
32. Bois Forte
33. Fond du Lac
34. Grand Portage
35. Leech Lake
36. Mille Lac
37. Red Lake
38. White Earth
39. Winnebagoshish

MONTANA TERRITORY
40. Blackfeet
41. Crow
42. Jocko

NEBRASKA
43. Iowa
44. Niobrara
45. Omaha
46. Oto
47. Sac and Fox
48. Winnebago

NEVADA
49. Duck Valley
50. Moapa Valley
51. Pyramid Lake
52. Walker River

NEW MEXICO TERRITORY
53. Jicarilla Apache
54. Mescalero Apache
55. Navajo
Pueblos
56. Jémez

57. Acoma
58. San Juan
59. Picurís
60. San Felipe
61. Pecos
62. Cochiti
63. Santo Domingo
64. Taos
65. Santa Clara
66. Tesuque
67. San Ildefonso
68. Pojoaque
69. Zia
70. Sandia
71. Isleta
72. Nambé
73. Laguna
74. Santa Ana
75. Zuñi

OREGON
76. Grande Ronde
77. Klamath
78. Malheur
79. Siletz
80. Umatilla
81. Warm Springs

UTAH TERRITORY
82. Uinta Valley

WASHINGTON TERRITORY
83. Chehalis
84. Colville
85. Makah
86. Nisqually
87. Puyallup
88. Shoalwater
89. Squaxin Island
90. Lummi
91. Muckleshoot
92. Port Madison
93. Snohomish or Tulalip
94. Swinomish
95. Quinaielt
96. Skokomish
97. Yakima
98. Columbia

WYOMING TERRITORY
99. Wind River

INDIAN TERRITORY (OKLAHOMA)
100. Quapaw
101. Peoria
102. Ottawa
103. Pawnee
104. Wyandot
105. Modoc
106. Seneca
107. Seminole
108. Choctaw
109. Chickasaw
110. Potawatomie-Shawnee
111. Apache
112. Comanche
113. Kiowa
114. Wichita
115. Arapaho
116. Cheyenne
117. Creek
118. Sauk-Fox
119. Kickapoo
120. Iowa
121. Oto Missouri
122. Tonkawa
123. Ponca
124. Chilocco
125. Kansa
126. Osage
127. Cherokee

Chief Red Cloud of the Sioux sits in his regalia for a photographer. Fear and fascination were mingled in popular attitudes toward Native Americans after the Civil War.
The Granger Collection, New York

Jay Gould did not look like a financial pirate, but that was the way many in American society regarded his speculations, such as the "Gold Corner" in 1869, and later with numerous railroads.
From the Collections of the Library of Congress

The Peace Policy in Action

Grant's commissioner of Indian Affairs was Ely Parker, a Seneca. Congress appropriated $2 million for Indian affairs and set up a Board of Indian Commissioners to distribute the money. Indian agents were not to be political hacks; the Grant administration asked for nominations from Christian churches.

The peace policy blended kindness and force. If the Indians accepted the presence of Christian church officials on the reservations, the government would leave them alone. Resistance to the peace policy sparked the army to drive the Indians onto reservations. In its early months, the peace policy seemed a humane improvement over what had gone before. For the Indians, the new approach represented another attack on their way of life. They would not simply accept what whites offered to them without a final burst of armed resistance.

AN ERA OF SCANDALS

Periodic corruption has marked American government throughout its history, but the post–Civil War era seemed particularly prone to such behavior. Scandals plagued the Grant administration. In the summer of 1869, two speculators, Jay Gould and Jim Fisk, manipulated the gold market to achieve huge profits for themselves. The price of gold rose until on September 24, 1869, when financial turmoil erupted. Investors who had promised to sell gold at lower prices faced ruin. Then the government sold it own gold supplies, the price of gold broke, and the market returned to its normal level. In the resulting inquiries about what had happened, the public learned that some members of Grant's family had helped Gould and Fisk carry out their plan. Whispers had it that Julia Grant, the president's wife, might have been involved. The story was not true, but doubts spread about the ethical standards of Grant's presidency.

To the odor of corruption was soon added a sense of White House confusion and incompetence. The administration talked of forcing Spain to give up Cuba and then backed away from the idea. The president wanted to annex the Dominican Republic (Santo Domingo). An agent of the president worked out a treaty of annexation with Santo Domingo's rulers, and the pact was sent to the Senate. Grant pushed hard for approval of the treaty, but the Senate, fearful of the influence of speculators and lobbyists, was suspicious of the president's goals. As a result, the treaty was defeated and the president embarrassed.

Grant's administration had more success in the resolution of American claims for maritime losses against Great Britain over the *Alabama*, one of several Confederate raiders that had been constructed in British shipyards during the Civil War. The *Alabama* had sunk numerous Union vessels. Charles Sumner, chair of the Senate Foreign Relations Committee, wanted to use the claims as leverage in an effort to acquire Canada. In 1871, the State Department worked out an amicable settlement of the issue that left Canada alone.

Grant and Congress

Other issues troubled Grant's relations with Congress. Congressional Republicans were split on issues such as the protective tariff and the currency. The mainstream of the party believed that a tariff policy to "protect" American industries against foreign competition was in the best interest of business, workers, and the party itself. A minority of Republicans called the protective policy wrong economically and a potential source of corrupt influence from the affected industries. On the currency, eastern Republicans favored the gold standard and what was known as "hard money," where every dollar was backed by an equal amount of gold. Western Republicans advocated an expansion of the money supply through paper money, or "greenbacks," and, when necessary, even the issuance of dollars backed by silver as an alternative to gold.

The civil service issue also split the party. The reliance on political clout to get a government job came under fire as reformers argued that competence and nonpartisanship were better ways to staff these positions. Republicans who wanted to reduce the tariff, rely on the civil service, and treat the South with more leniency defected from the Grant administration. They formed "Liberal Republican" alliances with Democrats in such states as West Virginia and Missouri. In the 1870s, "liberal" meant someone who favored smaller government, lower tariffs, civil service, and most important, an end to Reconstruction.

Grant and His Party

With his presidency under attack, Grant turned to the Republican leaders in Congress for support. These Republicans disliked the Liberal Republican program and its leaders. Angry Liberals threatened to bolt the party. Grant knew that he could never satisfy the demands of the Liberals on Reconstruction or the civil service. The Democrats could always outbid him on those issues, and endeavoring to court his Republican opponents would only weaken the party further. The president understood that he had to please his base to win reelection in 1872. Grant was not a gifted politician, but he could read that lesson clearly.

Toward the 1870 Elections

Following that logic, Grant conciliated mainstream Republicans. He dismissed cabinet officers who disagreed with him and aligned himself with party members willing to defend Congress and the White House. Officeholders who supported Liberal Republican candidates or Democrats were fired. Despite these actions, the elections went for the opposition. Liberal Republicans won races in West Virginia and Missouri. The Democrats added forty-one seats to their total in the House and picked up another six seats in the Senate. The Republicans retained control of both houses, but their position was weakening. Grant's enemies even thought he might be defeated in 1872.

The Ku Klux Klan in the South

By the summer of 1870, reports reached Washington of violence against blacks and white Republicans across the South. Roving bands of whites calling themselves the Ku Klux Klan (see Chapter 15) made the attacks. Throughout the South, the Klan stamped out challenges to white dominance. One Republican in Louisiana pleaded that "murder and intimidation are the order of the day in this state."

The Klan and its offshoots, such as the Knights of the White Camelia, White Leagues, and the White Brotherhood, acted as the paramilitary arm of the Democratic party to stamp out Republicanism through any means. In Tennessee a black Republican was beaten after he won an election for justice of the peace. His assailants told him "that they didn't dispute I was a very good fellow . . . but they did not intend any nigger to hold office in the United States."

A CARTOONIST ATTACKS THE KU KLUX KLAN

The Granger Collection, New York

The use of political cartoons to convey ideas about contemporary issues became more sophisticated after the Civil War. One of the great popular artists of the day was Thomas Nast. In the 1870s, his images attacked the refusal of southerners to grant real freedom to African Americans and the increasing reliance in the South on such terror organizations as the Ku Klux Klan and the White Leagues. Nash dramatized for his audience that southern whites, in or out of a hood, had the same goal—"a white man's government." These striking pictures helped sustain the Republican party during the presidency of Ulysses S. Grant. Unfortunately for blacks in the South, neither Nast nor the white political leadership in the North persisted in their commitment to equal rights. By the end of the decade, other cartoons depicted blacks in a degrading manner that justified white dominance and paved the way in time for racial segregation.

The Klan stopped at nothing to eliminate its opponents. Leaders of the Republican party were hunted and killed. Four blacks died when the Klan attacked an election meeting in Alabama in October 1870. A "negro chase" in South Carolina left thirteen blacks dead. The Klansmen rode in white robes and hoods; their aim, they said, was to frighten their racial foes. The disguises also hid their identity from law enforcement. A wave of shootings and brutality undermined the chances of the Republican party to survive and grow below the Mason-Dixon line.

The Government and the Klan

Viewing the wreckage of their southern parties after the 1870 elections, Republicans recognized that the Klan's terror tactics had worked to intimidate voters and demoralize their leaders. But doing something posed problems. As 1871 began, the Republicans had less stomach for sending troops to the South to affect politics. As an Illinois newspaper observed, "the negro is now a voter and a citizen. Let him hereafter take his chances in the battle of life." Republican leaders asked themselves whether the cost of maintaining party organizations in the South justified the effort in the face of such resolute Democratic opposition.

The violence of the Klan presented a challenge that could not be ignored. Without firm action, the Republican party in the South might disappear. Congress adopted legislation to curb election fraud, bribery, and coercion in elections. When these measures proved inadequate, the lawmakers passed the Ku Klux Klan Act of 1871. This law outlawed conspiracies to deprive voters of their civil rights and banned efforts to bar any citizen from holding public office. The government also received broader powers to fight the Klan through the use of federal district attorneys to override state laws. As a last resort, military force could also be employed.

Reconstruction gave African Americans a real chance to serve in Congress. Robert Smalls was a Congressman from South Carolina for five terms in the 1870s and 1880s.
From the Collections of the Library of Congress

The Democrats labeled these laws an unconstitutional interference with the rights of the states. Their passage was "the crowning act of centralization and consolidation," said one critic. A Republican countered by saying: "Tell me nothing of a constitution which fails to shelter beneath its rightful power the people of a country."

Breaking the Power of the Klan

Republicans determined to end the lawbreaking and violence that the Klan embodied. The Justice Department, which had been established in 1870, argued that the threat the Klan posed to democratic government amounted to war. Officials in Washington mobilized federal district attorneys and United States marshals to institute prosecutions against the Klan. The legal offensive in 1871 brought results as in state after state Klan leaders were indicted. Federal troops assisted the work of the Justice Department in South Carolina. The Klan was discredited as

a public presence in southern politics; its violence became more covert and less visible. Even though the prosecutions of the Klan showed that effective federal action could compel southern states to comply with the rule of law, sentiment in the North for such stern measures was receding. Reconstruction did not seem to be a noble crusade for human rights but part of a troubling pattern of corruption and excessive government power.

The Tweed Ring in New York

The willingness to use national power to push Reconstruction receded in part when Americans became convinced that politics everywhere were corrupt. The most celebrated example of wrongdoing in this period was the Tweed Ring, which dominated New York City during the late 1860s.

William Magear Tweed, Jr. had risen through various city offices and by the early 1870s was a member of the New York state senate. He was closely identified with the Democratic party organization that met at a political clubhouse called Tammany Hall to plan strategy. The expanding cities of the post–Civil War years offered politicians chances to make money from providing lucrative contracts and official services. Tweed and his allies turned these new opportunities to their personal advantage. They padded the city's accounts and extracted kickbacks from contractors doing business with the city.

There was more to Tweed, however, than just corruption. His power rested on the votes of the city's heavily Democratic population. Long loyal to the Democrats who shared their suspicion of Republican efforts to regulate moral behavior, Irish Catholic immigrants supported the party that helped them and respected their lifestyle and religious values. Their votes were crucial to keep New York in the Democratic column in presidential contests. Tammany made sure that city services and jobs were available to those who supported their organization at the polls. Tweed and his "ring" thus reflected larger changes in American cities and urban politics that began in the 1860s.

In fact's Tweed's moment at the peak of New York politics was brief. The *New York Times* devoted endless columns to exposing the misdeeds of the Democratic party and its leaders. More significant from a national perspective, a cartoonist named Thomas Nast used his art to make Tweed an object of scorn. Nast's drawing depicted Tweed as the leader of a band of criminals, a money-grubbing scoundrel who was unfit for public office. The cartoon devastated

Few individuals were more notorious in the 1870s than William M. "Boss" Tweed of New York City. The Tweed Ring and the lavish expenditures of money that it made in New York City came to symbolize the corruption and boss rule that many Americans associated with the rise of the city.

The Granger Collection, New York

Tweed himself. As he told one editor: "I don't care a straw for your newspaper articles. My constituents don't know how to read, but they can't help seeing them damned pictures."

During mid-1871, an angry member of the Tweed Ring gave city account books to a reporter. The disclosure of how much had been spent on city projects stunned voters. A courthouse that had been projected to cost $250,000 came to $13 million. Within a year, Tweed had been indicted. He escaped conviction in his first trial but was later retried and found guilty on 204 counts. He fled the country and took refuge in Spain. Arrested there when an official recognized him from a Nast cartoon, he was returned to New York a broken man and died in 1878.

For many troubled Americans, Tweed's rise and fall symbolized the decline in ethical standards that had followed the Civil War. In the North, they thought that expanding the power of the government, as well as expanding the vote to all white males and many freed slaves, threatened the nation's political future. "We are in danger of going the way of all Republics," said one critic of the existing system. "First freedom, then glory; when that is past, wealth, vice, and corruption." That view was too gloomy, but it expressed the attitude of increasing numbers of middle-class citizens in the North.

Liberal Republicans Challenge Grant

Restoring ethical standards was the goal of the Liberal Republicans who wanted to field a candidate against President Grant in 1872. Only in that way could Reconstruction be ended and civil service reform achieved. Leading the campaign were Senator Carl Schurz, a Missouri Republican; Edwin L. Godkin, editor of *The Nation;* and Charles Francis Adams, the son of former president John Quincy Adams.

Liberals believed in smaller government and an end to the protective tariff. "The Government," wrote E. L. Godkin, "must get out of the 'protective' business and the 'subsidy' business and the 'improvement' business and 'development' business . . . It cannot touch them without breeding corruption." But Reconstruction was their main target. They saw what happened in the South as an unwise experiment in racial democracy. Jacob D. Cox, who had been secretary of the interior under Grant, maintained that "the South can only be governed through the part of the community that embodies the intelligence and the capital." In effect, black Americans in the South would have to look to whites in that region for protection of their rights and privileges.

The problem was that the Liberal Republicans did not have a good national candidate to run against Grant. Few party leaders were men with national stature. Schurz was a native of Germany and therefore ineligible to run under the Constitution. The race came down to Charles Francis Adams, Lyman Trumbull of Illinois, and Horace Greeley, editor of the New York *Tribune.* After six ballots, Greeley was the nominee. At sixty-one, Greeley was an odd choice. He favored the protective tariff, unlike most reformers, and he was indifferent about the civil service. His main passion was ending Reconstruction. Once a harsh critic of the South, he had now mellowed. His personal opinions, which included vegetarianism and the use of human manure in farming, made him an oddball to most

Americans. "That Grant is an Ass no man can deny," said one Liberal in private, "but better an Ass than a mischievous idiot."

The 1872 Election

Grant was renominated on a platform that stressed the need to preserve Reconstruction. Voters in the North must safeguard what they had won during the Civil War. The Democrats were in a box. If they rejected Greeley, they had no chance to win. Picking him, however, would alienate southern voters who remembered Greeley's passion against the Confederacy. In the end, the Democrats accepted Greeley as their only alternative. The Liberal Republican-Democratic nominee made a vigorous public campaign, while Grant observed the tradition that the incumbent did not take part in the race personally.

The Republicans made their appeal on the issues of the war. One speaker told his audience that they could either "Go vote to burn school houses, desecrate churches and violate women or vote for Horace Greeley, which means the same thing." The black leader, Frederick Douglass, said of the impending contest: "If the Republican party goes down, freedom goes down with it." When the voters went to the polls, the outcome was a decisive victory for Grant and his party. The president swamped Greeley in the popular vote and in the electoral tally. There were still enough Republicans in the South to enable Grant to carry all but five of the southern states in one of the last honest elections the region would see for many years. The Democrats had reached a low point behind Greeley. Worn out by the rigors of the campaign, he died in late November. The triumph was a mixed one for Grant. He remained in the White House, but scandals would soon plague his second term.

A Surge of Scandals

As the excitement of the 1872 election faded, allegations of corruption in Congress surfaced. The first controversy turned on the efforts of the Crédit Mobilier Company (named after a French company) to purchase influence with lawmakers during the 1860s. The directors of the Union Pacific had established Credit Mobilier to build the transcontinental line. By paying themselves to construct the railroad, the participants in the venture sold bonds that were marketed at a large profit to investors and insiders. The only problem was that much of the money in effect came from the federal government through loans and guarantees.

To avoid a congressional probe into the company, Credit Mobilier's managers offered leading Republicans a chance to buy shares in the company at prices well below their market value. When the lawmakers sold their shares, they pocketed the difference, the equivalent of a bribe. A newspaper broke the story in late 1872 and an investigation ensued. The probe produced a few scapegoats but cleared most of the individuals involved. Nevertheless, the episode damaged the credibility of public officials.

Another embarrassing episode occurred in February 1873. At the end of a congressional session, a last-minute deal gave senators and representatives a retroactive pay increase. The public denounced the action as the "Salary Grab." The *Chicago Tribune* said that it was "nothing more nor less than an act of robbery." When Congress reconvened in December 1873, repeal of the salary increase sailed through both houses as politicians backtracked. These two incidents produced widespread calls for reducing government expenditures and rooting out corruption. As the humorist Mark Twain said, "It could probably be shown by facts and figures that there is no distinctly native American criminal class except Congress."

Twain himself captured the spirit of the times in his novel *The Gilded Age*, published in 1873. The main character, Colonel Beriah Sellers, was an engaging confidence man who embodied the faith in progress and economic growth of the postwar years, along with a healthy amount of fraud and deceit that accompanied the rapid expansion of business. In time, the title of Twain's book came to be used for the entire era between the end of Reconstruction and the start of the twentieth century. Beneath its appealing surface, this period had significant problems. At the same time, the "Gilded Age" was a richer and more complex time than the stereotype of corrupt politicians and fraudulent businessmen that Twain portrayed.

THE PANIC OF 1873 AND ITS CONSEQUENCES

The sense of national crisis deepened in September 1873 when the banking house of Jay Cooke and Company failed. The bank could not pay its debts or return money to its depositors; it had to close. The disaster came because the bank could not market the bonds of the Northern Pacific Railroad in which it had invested heavily. As this important bank collapsed, others followed suit, businesses cut back on employment, and a downturn began. The problems

Table 16.1	Railroad Mileage, 1869–1876
1869:	46,844
1870:	52,922
1871:	60,301
1872:	66,171
1873:	70,268
1874:	72,385
1875:	74,096
1876:	76,808

The Panic of 1873 shook Americans's confidence in their economic system. This contemporary drawing of the New York Stock Exchange shows the names of the business failures being read.
From the Collections of the Library of Congress

rivaled similar panics that had occurred in 1819, 1837, and 1857; however, the Panic of 1873 was the worst of them all.

The immediate effects of the problem lasted until 1879. In fact, an extended period of economic hard times had begun that extended through the 1890s. A hallmark of the "Great Depression," as it was then called, was declining prices for agricultural products and manufactured goods. Americans faced an economy in which falling prices placed the heaviest burdens on people who were in debt or who earned their living by selling their labor. An abundance of cheap unskilled labor proved a boon for capitalists who wanted to keep costs down. For the poor, however, it meant that they had little job security and could easily be replaced if they protested against harsh working conditions. Industrialization went forward at a substantial human cost.

The panic occurred because of a speculative post–Civil War boom in railroad building. In 1869, railroad mileage stood at about 47,000 miles; four years later it had risen to 70,268 miles. The new railroad lines employed tens of thousands of workers and extended across a far larger geographical area than any previous manufacturing enterprise. When large railroads such as the Northern Pacific failed because of their overexpansion and inability to pay debts, the resulting impact rippled through society. Economic activities that were dependent on the rail lines, such as car making, steel rail production, and passenger services, also fell off. Layoffs of employees and bankruptcies for businesses followed. More than 10,000 companies failed in 1878, the worst year of the depression.

The Plight of the Unemployed

Americans who were thrown out of work during the 1870s had no system of unemployment insurance to cushion the shock of their plight. In some cities, up to

The hard times that arose from the Panic of 1873 produced labor unrest in many cities. Here an artist recreates the riot in Tompkins Square in New York in 1874.

a quarter of the workforce looked for jobs without success. Tramps roamed the countryside. The conventional wisdom held that natural forces had to restore prosperity; any form of political intervention would be useless and dangerous. When President Grant proposed that the national government generate jobs through public works, the secretary of the treasury responded: "It is not part of the business of government to find employment for people."

People out of a job during the mid-1870s could not afford such a philosophical attitude. Laborers in the Northeast mounted a campaign for "Work for Bread" that produced large demonstration in major cities. The marchers asked city and state governments to pay for projects to create parks and construct streets to provide work. In January 1874, a demonstration at Tompkins Square in New York City pitted a crowd of 7,000 unemployed laborers against police. Many marchers were arrested; others were injured in the melee.

Labor unrest crackled through the first half of the decade. Strikes marked 1874 and 1875. In Pennsylvania the railroads used their control of police and strikebreakers to put down the "Long Strike" of coal miners and their supporters. Twenty alleged members of a secret society called the Molly Maguires were hanged. Conservatives feared that the nation was on the verge of revolution.

Distress and Protest among the Farmers

Discontent also flared in the farm belt. The price of wheat stood at $1.16 a bushel in 1873; it skidded to ninety-five cents a bushel a year later. The price of corn stood at sixty-four cents a bushel in 1874 but went down to forty-two cents in 1875. These changes meant substantial drops in farm income. As a result, the debts that farmers had to pay for land and equipment posed an even greater burden. Faced with the economic power of the railroads and grain merchants, the farmer was, said one newspaper, "a mere bushwhacker, confronting organized and well-equipped enemies."

The Patrons of Husbandry, also known as the Grange, led the farm protests. Created in 1867, the nonpartisan Grange focused on complaints about the high mortgages that farmers owed, the prices they paid to middlemen such as the operators of grain elevators, and the discrimination they faced at the hands of the railroads in moving their goods to market.

Regulating the Railroads

Farmers argued that the answer to the power of the railroads was in using the authority of state governments to compel the rail lines to cease working against farm interests. In practice, that meant the creation of state railroad commissions with the power to establish fair rates and prevent unfair treatment of those who shipped agricultural products. In 1870, Illinois adopted a new state constitution that instructed the legislature to pass laws establishing maximum rates for the transportation of passengers and freight. The legislature responded with the creation of the Illinois Railroad Commission and gave the new agency wide powers. Neighboring states such as Iowa, Minnesota, and Wisconsin followed suit in the next several years. Railroad companies challenged some of these laws in court, and a case testing the constitutionality of the Illinois law worked its way toward the United States Supreme Court as *Munn v. Illinois.*

The pressure for regulatory legislation even affected Congress in 1873–1874. An Iowa Republican introduced legislation in the House to establish a national railroad commission. As an anonymous spokesman for western economic interests told a reporter, "Sir, you will never make me doubt that a government which could put down that mighty Rebellion can regulate the details of a few tariffs of some railroad corporation." The bill passed in the House, but the Senate never acted upon it. Federal legislation would not be enacted until 1887.

Inflationary Solutions

The decline in consumer prices and the growing burden of debt on farmers and businessmen in the South and West created pressure for laws to put more money into circulation. That would make debts easier to pay. The Treasury Department's decision to end the coinage of silver aroused particular anger among southern and western advocates of inflation; they called it the "Crime of 1873." Proponents of the move argued that an overabundance of silver in the marketplace required the move to a gold standard. By coining silver into money at a price above its market levels, the government was subsidizing American silver production and cheapening the currency. Opponents of the change responded that eastern bankers were setting financial policy to the detriment of farmers and debtors.

An effort to inject a modest amount of inflation into the economy came in 1875. A currency bill cleared both houses of Congress; it provided some $64 million in additional money for the financial system. President Grant decided, after getting conservative advice to do so, to veto the bill in April 1875. Congress sustained his action. The government would not intervene in the deepening economic crisis.

WOMEN IN THE 1870s

Amid the male-dominated political life that marked this period, occasional episodes reminded the nation that women were excluded from the government, elections, and most of public policy. Susan B.

Anthony sought the chance to address the Liberal Republican and Republican national conventions in 1872 but was turned away. On election day she and fifteen other women registered and voted at their polling place in Rochester, New York. Anthony and the voting officials were arrested. Her trial in federal court led to a $100 fine, which she refused to pay. Rather than giving Anthony a reason for appealing the case to a higher court, authorities did not collect the fine against her.

Another champion of women's rights was Victoria Claflin Woodhull. A faith healer and spiritualist from Ohio, she and her sister Tennessee Claflin came to New York, where, in 1870, Victoria announced her candidacy for president of the United States. She published a weekly newspaper that endorsed the right of women to practice free love outside of marriage. In 1872, she denounced one of the nation's leading ministers, Henry Ward Beecher, for having had an affair with a member of his congregation. The revelation led to one of the most sensational public trials of the nineteenth century. The proceedings ended in a hung jury and the Claflin sisters had to flee to England to escape public outrage. Woodhull's experience and social disgrace demonstrated the perils that faced women who defied the strict social conventions of the post–Civil War era.

The spread of industrialism brought new products into the home that were advertised as labor-saving devices for women. The reality was that the amount of work women did expanded as a result of the new machinery for domestic use.
From the Collections of the Library of Congress

Overcoming Barriers to Equality

For women from the middle and upper classes, the 1870s brought expanding educational opportunities. The number of women graduating from high school stood at nearly 9,000 in 1870, compared with 7,000 men. Aware of these trends, state universities and private colleges opened their doors to women students in growing numbers. By 1872, nearly one hundred institutions of higher learning admitted women. This process continued despite the fears of male academics. Edward Clarke, a retired Harvard medical professor, warned in 1873 that when women expended their "limited energy" on higher education, they put their "female apparatus" at risk.

Cornell University began accepting women applicants in 1875, and one of its first female graduates was M. Cary Thomas who received her B.A. in 1877. Five years later, she earned a Ph.D at a German university. By the 1890s, she had become the president of Bryn Mawr, a woman's college outside Philadelphia. Like other women in male-dominated institutions, she endured rudeness and indifference from her male colleagues. She later recalled that "it is a fiery ordeal to educate a lady by coeducation."

Obtaining a degree was not a guarantee of access to professions that males controlled. Myra Bradwell tried to become a lawyer in Illinois, but the state bar association rejected her application. She sued in federal court, and in 1873, the U.S. Supreme Court ruled that the law did not grant her the right to be admitted to the bar. One justice said that "the paramount destiny and mission of woman are to fulfill the noble and benign offices of wife and mother." That decision gave the Illinois legislature the authority to deny women the chance to practice law. In 1870, there were only five female lawyers in the nation.

The Supreme Court also rebuffed efforts to secure woman suffrage through the courts. Virginia Minor, president of the Woman Suffrage Association in Missouri, tried to vote during the 1872 election, but the registrar of voters turned her away. She sued on the grounds that the action denied her rights as a citizen. In the case of *Minor v. Happersett* (1875), the Supreme Court ruled unanimously that suffrage was not one of the rights of citizenship because "sex has never been made one of the elements of citizenship in the United States." To achieve the right to vote, women would have to amend the Constitution or obtain the right of suffrage from the states, a process that took another four decades to complete.

Minor v. Happersett
21 Wallace, 162 1875

This case involved the question of whether women were entitled to vote as citizens under the Fourteenth Amendment.

WAITE, C. J. The question is presented in this case, whether, since the adoption of the Fourteenth Amendment, a woman, who is a citizen of the United States and of the State of Missouri, is a voter in that State, notwithstanding the provision of the constitution and laws of the State, which confine the right of suffrage to men alone. . . . [Chief Justice Waite then discusses what constitutes citizenship in the Constitution.]

. . . Sex has never been made one of the elements of citizenship in the United States. In this respect men have never had an advantage over women. The same laws precisely apply to both. The Fourteenth Amendment did not affect the citizenship of women any more than it did of men. In this particular, therefore, the rights of Mrs. Minor do not depend upon the amendment. She has always been a citizen from her birth, and entitled to all the privileges and immunities of citizenship. . . .

If the right of suffrage is one of the necessary privileges of a citizen of the United States, then the constitution and laws of Missouri confining it to men are in violation of the Constitution of the United States, as amended, and consequently void. The direct question is, therefore, presented whether all citizens are necessarily voters.

The Constitution does not define the privileges and immunities of citizens. For that definition we must look elsewhere. In this case we need not determine what they are, but only whether suffrage is necessarily one of them.

It certainly is nowhere made so in express terms. The United States has no voters in the States of its own creation. The elective officers of the United States are all elected directly or indirectly by state voters. . . .

The [Fourteenth] Amendment did not add to the privileges and immunities of a citizen. It simply furnished an additional guaranty for the protection of such as he already had. No new voters were necessarily made by it. Indirectly it may have had that effect, because it may have increased the number of citizens entitled to suffrage under the constitution and laws of the States, but it operates for this purpose, if at all, through the States and the state laws, and not directly upon the citizen.

It is clear therefore, we think, that the Constitution has not added the right of suffrage to the privileges and immunities of citizenship as they existed at the time it was adopted. This makes it proper to inquire whether suffrage was co-extensive with the citizenship of the States at the time of its adoption. If it was then it may with force be argued that suffrage was one of the rights which belonged to citizenship, and in the enjoyment of which every citizen must be protected. But if it was not, the contrary may with propriety be assumed.

When the Federal Constitution was adopted, all the States, with the exception of Rhode Island and Connecticut, had constitutions of their own. . . . Upon an examination of these constitutions we find that in no State were all citizens permitted to vote. . . .

In this condition of the law in respect to suffrage in the several States it cannot for a moment be doubted that if it had been intended to make all citizens of the United States voters, the framers of the Constitution would not have left it to implication. . . .

It is true that the United States guarantees to every State a republican form of government. . . . The guaranty is of a republican form of government. No particular government is designated as republican, neither is the exact form to be guaranteed, in any manner especially designated. Here, as in other parts of the instrument, we are compelled to resort elsewhere to ascertain what was intended.

The guaranty necessarily implies a duty on the part of the States themselves to provide such a government. All the States had governments when the Constitution was adopted. In all the people participated to some extent, through their representatives elected in the manner specially provided. These governments the Constitution did not change. They were accepted precisely as they were, and it is, therefore, to be presumed that they were such as it was the duty of the States to provide. Thus we have unmistakable evidence of what was republican in form, within the meaning of that term as employed in the Constitution.

As we have seen, all the citizens of the States were not invested with the right of suffrage. In all, save perhaps New Jersey, this right was only bestowed upon men and not upon all of them. Under these circumstances it is certainly now too late to contend that a government is not republican, within the meaning of this guaranty in the Constitution, because women are not made voters. . . .

Certainly if the courts can consider any question settled, this is one. For nearly ninety years the people have acted upon the idea that the Constitution, when it conferred citizenship, did not necessarily confer the right of suffrage. . . .

Being unanimously of the opinion that the Constitution of the United States does not confer the right of suffrage upon any one, and that the constitutions and laws of the several States which commit that important trust to men alone are not necessarily void, we affirm the judgment.

The Rise of Voluntary Associations

Blocked off from politics, women carved out a public space of their own through voluntary associations. Black churchwomen established missionary societies to work both in the United States and abroad. Clubs and literary societies sprang up among white women as well. In New York City, women created Sorosis, a club for women only, after the New York Press Club barred women from membership. In 1873, delegates from local Sorosis clubs formed the Association for the Advancement of Women. The New England Woman's Club, located in Boston, had local laws changed during the early 1870s to allow women to serve on the School Committee. Later the club founded the Women's Education Association to expand opportunities for their sex in schools and colleges. During the two decades that followed, the women's club movement established strong roots in all parts of the nation.

Despite being turned away at the polls, women made their presence felt in an unexpected way in 1873. Protests against the sale and use of alcohol erupted among women in New York, Ohio, and Michigan. Women marched in the streets to demand that saloons and liquor dealers close down. They urged drunkards to reform. Middle-class women prayed in front of bars and smashed barrels of liquor to emphasize their determination. Men joined the temperance movement too, but it was the fervor of women that gave the antialcohol crusade new energy. "The women are in desperate earnest," said a Missourian who witnessed one of these campaigns.

The Woman's Christian Temperance Union

As their protest successes grew, women sought to make their antialcohol campaign more than transitory. In August 1874, a group of women in the temperance ranks met at Lake Chautauqua, New York, where they set a national meeting that developed into the Women's Christian Temperance Union (WCTU). Over the next five years, temperance leagues and local branches of the WCTU worked against intoxicating drink. By the end of the 1870s, a thousand unions had been formed, with an estimated 26,000 members. In 1879, Frances Willard became president of the WCTU, and she took the organization beyond its original goal of temperance and into broader areas of social reform such as woman suffrage and the treatment of children.

PICTURING THE PAST ✦ SOCIAL & CULTURAL EVENTS

THE WAR AGAINST DRINK

The Granger Collection, New York

The temperance crusades of the 1870s against alcohol and its evils brought women into politics in an era when they could not even vote in most of the nation. This cartoon links the campaign of the Women's Christian Temperance Union (WCTU) to the chivalry of the Middle Ages as the mounted women, armored in a righteous cause, destroy whisky, gin, brandy, and rum. The connection of reform with religion and patriotism gave the antialcohol crusade a powerful claim on middle-class sentiments. For those groups whose religious creed did not bar the use of liquor, the WCTU was an intrusive force seeking to interfere with personal rights. This cartoon thus reveals how long what are now called "social issues" have affected the nation's politics and how they grow out of cultural and economic divisions within American society. In fact, controlling the effects of alcohol has been one of the most persistent sources of social contention in the nation's history.

As industrialism took hold, women moved into the workplace. New inventions such as the typewriter gave women a larger place in offices and stores as secretaries and clerks.
The Granger Collection, New York

Women at Work

The 1870s also brought greater economic opportunities for women in sales and clerical jobs. The typewriter appeared in the early part of the decade. Young, college-educated women provided skilled labor to operate the new machines. E. Remington and Sons, which produced the typewriter, said in 1875 that "no invention has opened for women so broad and easy an avenue to profitable and suitable employment as the 'Type-Writer.'" By 1880, women accounted for 40 percent of the stenographers and typists in the country. These developments laid the foundation for growth in the numbers of female office workers during the rest of the nineteenth century.

The most typical experience of American women was toil. Black women in the South labored in the fields alongside their husbands who were tenant farmers or sharecroppers. They did "double duty, a man's share in the field and a woman's part at home." In the growing cities, women worked in textile factories or became domestic servants. Many urban women took in borders; their routine equaled that of a small hotel.

Middle-class women with domestic servants had some assistance, but they still did an impressive amount of work. Preparing food, washing laundry, keeping the house warm, and disposing of waste all demanded hand labor. Mary Mathews, a widowed teacher in the 1870s, "got up early every Monday morning and got my clothes all washed and boiled and in the rising water; and then commenced my school at nine." Other days of the week passed in the same fashion for her and other women.

To assist women in performing these tasks, manuals about housework became popular, along with private cooking schools and college courses in home economics. Catherine Beecher collaborated with her famous sister, Harriet Beecher Stowe, in writing *The American Woman's Home* (1869). In this work, they argued "that family labor and care tend, not only to good health, but to the *Highest culture of the mind*." Women, they continued, were "ministers of the family state." In the new coeducational colleges and universities, home economics programs offered instructions in operating kitchens and dining rooms efficiently. Cooking schools appeared in large cities with a separate class for "plain cooks" and a "Ladies Class" for affluent women who sought to link "the elegancies of artistic cookery with those economic interests which it is the duty of every woman to study."

The ease with which divorces could be obtained in many states produced a movement to tighten the conditions under which marriages could be dissolved. Laws to limit the sale of birth control devices and restrict abortions reflected the same trend. The New York Society for the Suppression of Vice was formed in 1872 under the leadership of Anthony Comstock. It lobbied successfully for a national law barring obscene information, including information about birth control and abortion, from the mails. Thus, while women had made some gains after the Civil War, they remained second-class citizens within the masculine political order of the Gilded Age.

POLITICS IN THE GILDED AGE

After the presidential election of 1872, the North's already weakened commitment to Reconstruction ebbed still more. The Panic of 1873 distracted attention from the rights of black Americans. The Grant administration backed away from southern politics, and the Justice Department prosecuted fewer individuals for violations of the Enforcement Act against the Klan and pardoned some of those who had earlier been convicted of terrorist activity.

Northern support for Reconstruction waned because of charges that the experiment in multiracial government was a failure. Liberal Republicans and northern Democrats spread racist propaganda to block the aspirations of southern blacks. The editor of *The Nation* said that black residents of South Carolina had an "average of intelligence but slightly above the level of animals." Northerners found it easier to believe that the South would be better off when whites were dominant. Black Americans should be left "to the kind feeling of the white race of the South."

A damaging setback to the economic hopes of African Americans came in 1874 with the failure of the Freedmen's Savings and Trust Company in Washington, D.C. Since its founding in 1865, the bank had managed the deposits of thousands of former slaves. It was supposed to provide lessons in thrift for its depositors. However, its manager sought larger returns by investing in speculative railroad projects. The Panic of 1873 caused huge losses, and the bank failed a year later. A few customers received a portion of their savings; most lost all their money.

The Stigma of Corruption

Corruption among southern Republican governments became a favorite theme of critics of Reconstruction. There were some genuine instances of wrongdoing, but these actions were far from widespread or typical. Moreover, the white governments that took over after Reconstruction also displayed lax political ethics and committed more serious misdeeds than their predecessors had. Nevertheless, the corruption issue gave the opponents of black political participation a perfect weapon, which they used to the full. Of course, it would not have mattered if Reconstruction governments had lacked any moral flaws. Any government that represented a biracial community was unacceptable to white southerners.

Although participation of African Americans in southern politics increased dramatically during Reconstruction, their role in the region's public life never approached that of whites. Sixteen blacks served in Congress during the period, most only briefly, and several were unseated by white opponents. Many more held offices in the state legislatures, but even there, their numbers were comparatively modest. In 1868, for example, the George legislature had 216 members, of whom only thirty-two were black. In only one state, South Carolina, did blacks ever hold a majority in the legislature, and they did so in only one

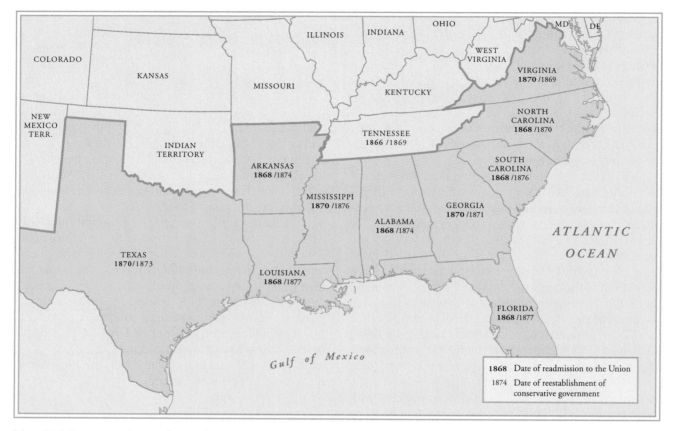

Map 16.2 *Reconstruction in the South*
This map shows the times at which the states of the former Confederacy reentered the Union and then saw the Democrats regain political control. Note how quickly this process occurred for most of the southern states. The relative brevity of Reconstruction is one of the keys to why more sweeping racial change did not take place.

house. One black man, P. B. S. Pinchback, served as governor of Louisiana for a little more than a month. Six African Americans held the office of lieutenant governor in the states of Louisiana, Mississippi, and South Carolina.

Two blacks served in the United States Senate. Hiram Revels became the first African American to enter the Senate. His term began in 1870 but lasted for only one year. From 1875 to 1881, Blanche K. Bruce represented Mississippi for a full term. Thus, by the 1870s, blacks had made their presence felt in politics, but the decline of Reconstruction made that trend a short-lived one.

The Resurgence of the Democrats

The return of the Democrats as a political force further weakened support for Reconstruction. Hard economic times arising from the Panic of 1873 worked against the Republicans. Discontented farmers wanted the government to inflate the currency and raise prices on

their crops. Factory workers clamored for more jobs to become available. In this setting, the fate of African Americans in the South became a secondary concern. Angry voters turned to the Democrats in the 1874 congressional races. The party used the issue of Republican corruption to regain control of the House of Representatives for the first time in sixteen years. The Democrats added seventy-seven seats in the House and also added ten seats in the Senate in what one happy party member called a "Tidal Wave."

In the South, the revitalized Democrats "redeemed," as they called it, several states from Republican dominance. They began with Texas in 1873, then won back Arkansas the next year, and elected most of the South's members in the U.S. House of Representatives. Louisiana saw the emergence of the White League, which was determined that "the niggers shall not rule over us." In September, open fighting erupted in New Orleans between armed Republicans and more than 3,000 White League partisans. President Grant sent in federal troops to restore calm. In Alabama, the

Democrats also relied on violence and murder to oust the Republicans. Some blacks who attempted to vote in that state's Barbour County election were shot; seven were killed and nearly seventy wounded. In view of the wide support for the Democratic party among southern whites, honest elections would probably have produced similar results for that party at the polls; but intimidation and violence were key elements in the victories that the Democrats secured in the South in 1874.

The Democrats intended to use their control of the House of Representatives to roll back Reconstruction and also prevent any further expansion of black rights. During the lame-duck congressional session of 1874–1875, Republicans, who were soon to lose power, enacted a pathbreaking civil rights law that gave black citizens the right to sue in federal courts when they confronted discrimination in public accommodations such as a hotel or restaurant. The law involved a further expansion of national power; it remained to be seen how federal courts would rule when black plaintiffs sued to enforce their rights under the new civil rights statute.

Early in 1875, the Grant administration used troops to prevent occupation of the Louisiana state capital and illegal seizure of the state government by the Democrats in the midst of an election dispute. The action drew widespread protests from many northern Democrats and a growing number of Republicans who said that the white South should handle its own affairs. Meanwhile, the Democrats used more violence to overturn Republican rule in Mississippi. The state's governor, Adelbert Ames, stated that he was "fighting for the Negro, and to the whole country a white man is better than a 'Nigger.'" Without a national consensus behind civil rights and Reconstruction, the fate of black Americans lay in the hands of white southerners who were determined to keep African Americans in economic, political, and cultural subjection.

Why Reconstruction Failed

Reconstruction failed to change American race relations because it challenged long-standing racist arrangements in both the North and South. The Civil War had called these traditions into question. In the years after the fighting ended, African Americans had acted to expand their political role and become more than passive recipients of white oppression or largesse. Then the Panic of 1873, the scandals of the Grant presidency, and waning interest in black rights led white Americans to back away from an expansion of racial justice.

To help the freed slaves overcome the effects of slavery and racial bias would have involved an expansion of national government power to an extent far beyond what Americans believed was justified during the nineteenth century. Better to keep government small, argued whites, than to improve the lot of the former slaves in the South. As a result, black Americans experienced segregation and deepening oppression. The political gains of the Reconstruction era, especially the Fourteenth and Fifteenth Amendments, remained unfulfilled promises.

THE END OF NATIVE AMERICAN RESISTANCE

While the United States was in the process of abandoning its Civil War commitments to African Americans, the long struggle of Native Americans to resist white encroachment also ended. Indian efforts to push back the wave of white settlers failed, and after 1876, Native Americans lacked the power to determine their own destiny.

During the 1870s, easterners and new immigrants surged westward to the prairies. The census reported over 2,660,000 farms in 1870 and just over 4 million ten years later. The newcomers competed with the Indians for space and resources. The amount of land devoted to wheat cultivation, for example, rose from nearly 21 million acres at the beginning of the decade to 62,545,000 in 1880.

The cattle industry exerted further pressure on the Indians in the late 1860s. Texans returning from the Civil War drove their herds north to markets in Kansas. These cattle and others in western territories such as Wyoming, the Dakotas, and Colorado occupied space on the prairies where Indians had traditionally pursued their nomadic hunting culture.

Annihilation of the Buffalo Herds

The systematic destruction of the buffalo herds dealt the most devastating blow to the Indians. In the societies of the Plains tribes, the meat of the bison supplied food, while the hides provided shelter and clothes. Removal of these resources was calamitous, but the cultural impact was even more ruinous. Buffalo represented the continuity of nature and the renewal of life cycles. Destruction of the buffalo ended the Indians' capacity to resist white incursions. As one Crow warrior observed after the herds had gone, "Nothing happened after that. We just lived. There were no more war parties, no capturing

PICTURING THE PAST ✦ ECONOMICS & TECHNOLOGY
SLAUGHTER OF THE BUFFALO

Kansas State Historical Society

The manner in which the opening of the West after the Civil War is depicted in textbooks has changed in dramatic ways during the last two decades. More attention is now given to the impact on the environment and on the nomadic lifestyle of the Native American residents of the Great Plains arising from the disappearance of the buffalo herds. The critical role that these animals played in sustaining the Indian way of life meant that the task of white settlers became much less dangerous when the buffalo were gone. Pictures such as this one of 40,000 hides pulled up outside Dodge City, Kansas, convey a dramatic sense of the extermination of these animals. Of course, no text can impart the odor of that many hides.

The individuals in the image are small compared to the mass of hides, but their presence reveals how the trade in buffalo had become a key aspect of the western economy. When the buffalo were gone, as happened within a few years, residents moved on to another boom and bust cycle, whether it was in cattle ranching or farming. The picture serves as an evocation of a vanished time and place, but also says something permanent about the nature of the West.

---

horses from the Piegan and the Sioux, no buffalo to hunt. There is nothing more to tell."

The decline of the buffalo herds began during the 1860s when drought, disease, and erosion shrank the animals' habitat. Then an expanding eastern market for buffalo robes and such products as pemmican (dried buffalo meat, berries, and fat) spurred the intensive hunting of buffalo. As railroads penetrated the West, hunters could transport their products to customers with relative ease. The result was virtual extermination of the buffalo. More than 5 million buffalo were slaughtered during the early 1870s. Along the Arkansas River, a British traveler reported, "there was a continual line of putrescent carcasses, so that the air was rendered pestilential and offensive to the last degree." By the end of the nineteenth century, only a few buffalo remained alive.

A Last Stand for Custer and the Indians

During the mid-1870s, Native American tribes mounted a last, futile effort to stem the tide that was overwhelming their way of life. The renewed strife in the West took place in spite of President Grant's peace policy. The original appointees of the president either resigned or left because of political attacks. Meanwhile, the church's influence over the operation of Indian policy receded as corruption and politics again shaped the treatment of Native Americans. The tribes that held on to their nomadic way of life confronted ever-increasing numbers of settlers and a hostile military.

Fighting broke out on the southern plains when Comanches and Kiowas attacked wagon trains. A conflict ensued between soldiers and Cheyenne, Kiowas, and Comanches that became known as the Red River War. The army did not prevail on the battlefield. Instead, Indian resistance collapsed because of a lack of food and supplies.

In the North, the discovery of gold in the Black Hills of Dakota increased pressure on the Sioux to give up the area for white development. The Indians refused, and the government sent soldiers to protect the miners. The Indian leaders, Crazy Horse and Sitting Bull, rallied their followers to stop the army. Near what the Indians called the Greasy Grass (known to whites as the Little Big Horn), Colonel George Armstrong Custer led a force of 600 men. With a third of his detachment, he attacked more than 2,000 Sioux warriors. The result was the annihilation of Custer and his force on June 25, 1876, in a battle that became legendary as "Custer's Last Stand." The Indian victory shocked the nation, but it was only a momentary success. The army pursued the Indians during the months that followed, and by the end of the Grant administration, the only Indians who were able to fight actively against the army were the Apaches in the Southwest. The bad treatment that the Apaches received from the government led to sporadic clashes during the 1880s, and the army prevailed by the end of the decade.

One more tragic encounter, the Battle of Wounded Knee, lay ahead for the Plains Indians in 1890. For the most part, however, the Grant presidency brought an end to the centuries of white-Indian warfare that had marked the history of the West in the United States.

THE ELECTION OF 1876

Several themes of late-nineteenth century life intersected as the 1876 presidential election neared. The centennial of the Declaration of Independence offered citizens an opportunity to reflect on the nation's progress and the social issues that remained unresolved. The race question confronted leaders and citizens even as the passions and commitments of Reconstruction faded. The contest for the White House seemed unusually important since it would shape the direction of the country for several decades.

The Continuing Shadow of Scandal

Toward the end of Grant's second term, political corruption continued to cast a shadow over the administration. Within the Treasury Department, the Whiskey Ring was exposed. Officials involved took kickbacks from liquor interests in return for not collecting federal excise taxes on whiskey. President Grant appointed a new secretary of the treasury, Benjamin H. Bristow,

The Centennial Exposition in 1876 summed a century of the nation's progress. The opening ceremonies were recorded in this painting.
From the Collections of the Library of Congress

and told him: "Let no guilty man escape if it can be avoided." The administration also faced queries concerning the secretary of war, W. W. Belknap. For some time, Belknap's wife had been receiving cash gifts from a man who sold supplies to the army. When these ties were revealed, Belknap faced impeachment by a congressional committee. He resigned abruptly and Grant accepted his hasty departure. Critics of the president argued that the trail of scandal had reached close to the White House. Few doubted Grant's personal honesty, but politicians recognized that he had not always exercised wise judgment in his cabinet selections.

Marking the Centennial

As the nation's one hundredth birthday neared, the Centennial International Exhibition to be held in Philadelphia attracted public fascination. In May of 1876, some 285 acres of fairgrounds held several hundred buildings crammed with exhibits, specimens, and artifacts from thirty-seven nations. The doors opened on May 10 for 200,000 spectators, including both houses of Congress, who heard a welcoming address by President Grant. The throng poured into the building to see what had been assembled as evidence of the advance of civilization in the United States. One of the stellar attractions was the huge Corliss steam engine. Standing forty feel tall, it weighed 700 tons. Equally alluring was the "harmonic telegraph" of Alexander Graham Bell, as the telephone was then called.

In the dramatic 1876 election, the Democrats put forward "Honest Sam Tilden," who lost to Rutherford B. Hayes in the disputed contest.
From the Collections of the Library of Congress

Amid the technological marvels, the complexity of American life in the 1870s slipped away. African Americans had almost no recognition. Native American cultures were depicted as "curiosities" consisting of totem poles, tepees, and trinkets. The Women's Pavilion stressed the joys of homemaking. That exhibit evoked a protest from Elizabeth Cady Stanton and Susan B. Anthony. On July 4, 1876, they read a "Women's Declaration of Independence" that contrasted their aspirations with the traditional attitudes toward women expressed at the fair.

Nearly 10 million Americans came to the fair during its run, which ended on November 10. They learned to eat bananas, and hot popcorn became a fad among city dwellers. The fair lost money, but at the same time contributed to a growing sense of national pride and confidence.

The Race for the White House

A key test of the nation's institutions occurred during the disputed election of 1876. The closest result in history produced a quarrel that threatened to renew hostilities between North and South. As the process commenced, the Democrats felt optimism about their chances to regain power for the first time since 1860. Most of the southern states would vote for the Democratic nominee; difficult economic times in the East and Middle West made voters sympathetic to the party out of power.

For its candidate, the party selected Samuel J. Tilden, the governor of New York. An opponent of the Tweed Ring, he was regarded as a reformer. A corporate lawyer, he believed in the gold standard, small government, and restraints on spending. The platform spoke of a "revival of Jeffersonian democracy" and called for "high standards of official morality." Since Tilden was not in good health, the custom that presidential candidates did not campaign during that era worked to his advantage.

Among Republicans, there was some talk of a third term for President Grant, but the scandals of his presidency made him a liability. The front-runner for the nomination was James G. Blaine, a former speaker of the House of Representatives. With the nomination seemingly in his grasp, Blaine came under fire for financial dealings with an Arkansas railroad while he was in the House. Despite his vigorous response to the charges, Republicans were wary of selecting him to run against Tilden.

At the national convention, Blaine took an early lead. As the balloting continued, his candidacy lost momentum. Instead, the Republicans selected Governor Rutherford B. Hayes of Ohio. Hayes had the virtues of a good military record in the Civil War and a spotless record in public office. In the campaign, the Democrats stressed Republican corruption and Tilden's honesty. In response, the Republicans relied on Reconstruction and war memories, as they had in 1868 and 1872. This rhetoric became known as "waving the bloody shirt," in memory of a Republican speaker who had held up a bloodstained Union tunic and urged voters to remember the sacrifices of the Men in Blue. As one Republican put it, "Soldiers, every scar you have on your heroic bodies was given to you by a Democrat." Hayes saw the wisdom of this strategy: "It leads people away from hard times, which is our deadliest foe."

When the election results rolled in, it seemed at first that Tilden had won. With most of the South in his column, the Democrat had carried New York, Connecticut, and New Jersey. The electoral vote totals in-

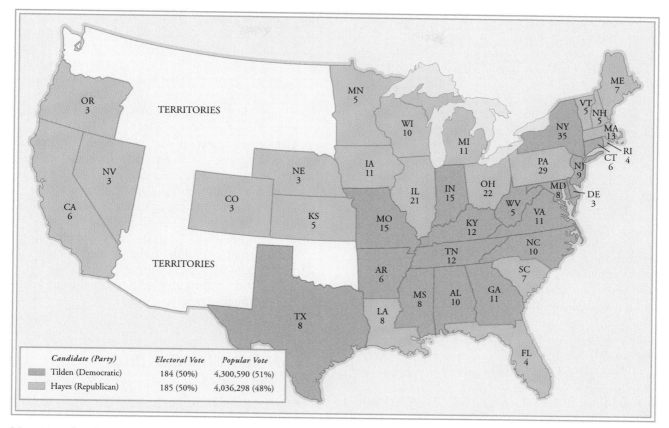

Candidate (Party)	Electoral Vote	Popular Vote
Tilden (Democratic)	184 (50%)	4,300,590 (51%)
Hayes (Republican)	185 (50%)	4,036,298 (48%)

Map 16.3 *The Election of 1876*

 The presidential election of 1876 between Samuel J. Tilden for the Democrats and Rutherford B. Hayes for the Republicans turned on the votes of Florida, Louisiana, and South Carolina to produce the narrow one-vote victory in the electoral college for Hayes.

View an animated version of this map or related maps at http://history.wadsworth.com/passages2e.

dicated that Tilden had won 184 votes, one short of the 185 he needed to become president. Hayes, on the other hand, had 165 electoral votes. Three southern states, Louisiana, Florida, and South Carolina, plus a disputed elector in Oregon, were still in doubt. If they all went for Hayes, he might be in the White House.

Republican operatives moved to contest the outcome in the three undecided states. Telegrams to party members asked for evidence that African American voters had been intimidated. Honest returns from these states, Republicans argued, would show that Hayes had carried each one. The Republicans believed, moreover, that they had the advantage. In the three states that they were contesting, the Republicans could rely on federal troops to safeguard state governments that were loyal to their cause. Otherwise, Democrats could simply occupy the state capitals and count the election returns their way.

The Constitution did not specify how a contested presidential election was to be resolved. With each of the states in question submitting two sets of election returns, the House of Representatives had the responsibility for electing a president if no one won a majority in the electoral college. At the same time, the Senate had the constitutional duty to tabulate the electoral vote. With Republicans in control of the Senate and with Democrats in control of the House, neither party could proceed without the support of the other.

To resolve the crisis, Congress created an electoral commission of fifteen members, ten from the Supreme Court. As originally conceived, the panel was to have seven Republicans, seven Democrats, and a politically independent Supreme Court justice named David Davis. Then Davis was elected to the U.S. Senate by the Illinois legislature with Democratic votes in a move to defeat a Republican incumbent. That tactic won a Senate place for the Democrat but injured Tilden's chances of prevailing in the election controversy. Davis resigned from the commission, and another member of the Supreme Court, this time a Republican, took his place. In a series of 8–7 votes along straight party lines, the electoral commission accepted the Republican returns from Louisiana, Florida, and South Carolina, and allocated the single disputed Oregon electoral vote to Hayes as well. The ruling declared that Hayes had received 185 electoral votes and Tilden 184.

Who had really been elected president in 1876? Tilden had a margin of 250,000 popular votes over Hayes and had carried sixteen states. Hayes had won eighteen states in addition to the three contested southern states. In Louisiana, Florida, and South Carolina, Tilden had received a majority of the white vote, but black Republican voters had been intimidated and terrorized to such an extent that an honest count was in doubt. Essentially the election had ended in a tie. Resolving the issue of which man would be president became an issue for the two political parties to decide.

Despite the decision of the electoral commission, the Democratic House still had to declare Hayes the winner. With the March 4, 1877, inauguration date approaching, the Democrats postponed tallying the electoral vote in an effort either to make Tilden president after March 4 or to extract concessions from the Republicans. To prevent a crisis, negotiations began among leaders from both sides to put Hayes in the White House in return for Republican agreement to end Reconstruction. The discussions were complex. They involved a variety of issues such as railroad subsidies for the South. The underlying issue was Reconstruction. If Hayes became president, the South wanted assurances that Republican rule would not be maintained through federal military intervention. After much discussion, an unwritten understanding along these lines led Congress to decide on March 2, 1877, that Rutherford B. Hayes had been elected as president of the United States.

CONCLUSION

The events that led to Hayes becoming president had great historical significance. Although the new president did not withdraw federal troops from the South, neither did he use them to keep Republican governments in power. Nor did Hayes attempt to enforce Reconstruction in the courts. Whites regained control of the South's political institutions, while black southerners remained second-class citizens with limited political and economic rights.

Several powerful historical forces produced that sad result. Pervasive racism in both the North and the South labeled African Americans as unfit for self-government. Pursuing Reconstruction into the 1880s

would have involved giving to the national government more power over the lives of individual Americans than would have been tolerated in that era. Weary of Reconstruction and its moral claims, the generation of white Americans who had fought the Civil War turned their attention to other national problems. In so doing, they condemned black citizens to continued segregation and oppression.

The era of the Civil War and Reconstruction did have a positive legacy. Slavery was abolished and the Union preserved. Black Americans had demonstrated that they could fight and die for their country, help make its laws, and function as full citizens when given an honest chance to do so. The Fourteenth and Fifteenth Amendments at least contained the promise of the further expansion of the rights of black Americans in the future. But for the moment the nation had missed a historical opportunity to created a more equitable, multiracial society.

Recommended Readings

Edwards, Laura F. *Gendered Strife and Confusion: The Political Culture of Reconstruction* (1997). Looks at the the role of women after the Civil War.

Foner, Eric. *Reconstruction: America's Unfinished Revolution, 1863–1877* (1988). An excellent treatment of the whole period, especially the decline of Reconstruction.

Perman, Michael. *Emancipation and Reconstruction, 1862–1879*, 2d ed. (2003). A good brief account of the issues and problems of Reconstruction.

Richardson, Heather Cox. *The Death of Reconstruction: Race, Labor, and Politics in the Post-Civil War North, 1865–1901* (2001). Considers how changing attitudes toward African Americans and labor undercut Reconstruction.

Simpson, Brooks D. *The Reconstruction Presidents* (1998). A treatment of Reconstruction from the perspective of the chief executives.

Smith, Jean Edward. *Grant* (2001). A full-scale, sympathetic biography of the general and president.

Summers, Mark Wahlgren. *The Era of Good Stealings* (1993). Uses the corruption issue of the 1870s to produce a political history of the decade.

Wang, Xi. *The Trial of Democracy: Black Suffrage and Northern Republicans, 1860–1910* (1997). Discusses how voting issues shaped the adoption and then the abandonment of Reconstruction.

American Journey
Online and InfoTrac
College Edition

Visit the source collections at http://ajaccess. wadsworth.com and infotrac.thomsonlearning.com and use the Search function with the following key terms to explore documents, images, audio and video clips, articles, and commentary related to the material in this chapter.

Andrew Johnson   Suffrage
Temperance   Reconstruction
Crazy Horse   Sitting Bull
George Armstrong Custer
Transcontinental railroad

Additional resources, exercises, and Internet links related to this chapter are available on the American Passages Web site: http://history.wadsworth.com/passages2e

PASSAGES
—1877
TO 1909—

To white Americans during the late 1870s, the sense that the Civil War and Reconstruction were receding into history represented a comforting illusion. African Americans knew best of all citizens how alive and painful the problem of race remained. Yet the popular belief that important forces now reshaped American life also described reality. The national journey was leaving behind an agricultural, rural, underdeveloped economy and culture, and gathering speed as an industrialized nation. The transformation took decades, but its consequences proved decisive in creating the modern United States.

Industry became the way in which more and more Americans made a living during the years from the presidency of Rutherford B. Hayes (1877–1881) through the end of Theodore Roosevelt's administration in March 1909. First came the railroads, but soon followed steel, oil, machinery, telephones, and, after 1900, the automobile. The relentless process of industrial growth drew families from the country to the city, changed the look and population of the cities themselves, and made society adapt to the pace of machinery and the factory. Business leaders emerged as national figures—Andrew Carnegie, John D. Rockefeller, and J. P. Morgan. Their fellow citizens wondered about the fate of the average person in the face of such concentrated economic power.

The result of industrialism was material abundance for some and great want for many others. The ability of factories to provide cheaper, standardized goods such as canned foods, sewing machines, tools, and clothes pleased those who could afford to buy them. For those left behind or shut out from society's bounty, the riches of the new system seemed a mockery. Industry knit the country together in a shared experience as consumers in a national market; it alienated others who saw their hard work bringing no fair reward for themselves.

The spread of technology during the late nineteenth century opened up new opportunities for women as this picture of female operators at a telephone exchange reveals.
Reproduced from the Collections of the Library of Congress #LC-US261-449

Immigration into the United States changed the shape of the nation's population and instilled an even richer diversity in the society. Older residents reacted with suspicion and hostility to the influx of newcomers from southern and eastern Europe, and ethnic tensions underlay voting decisions, residence patterns, and social conflict. The immigrants filled the nation's cities, tilled and settled the western plains, and did much of the work of the industrial sector. By the first decade of the twentieth century, pressures mounted for immigration restriction.

Politics struggled to keep pace with accelerating change in the business sector. An even balance between Republicans and Democrats from 1877 to 1894 kept the national government passive and slow to react. An expansion of governmental power took place on the state level despite claims that the era favored noninvolvement in social policy. An economic depression during the 1890s destroyed the national stalemate, wounded the Democrats, and gave the Republicans a majority of the electorate. A third party, the Populists, failed meanwhile to halt the erosion of the once powerful agricultural sector.

By the end of the 1890s, the United States stepped into the arena of international politics when it acquired an empire from Spain after a war over Cuba. The heyday of imperialism did not last; the consequences of overseas expansion endured. New responsibilities in the Atlantic and Pacific meant a growth in the power of the federal government to fulfill the world role. Currents of isolationism persisted to limit foreign adventures, but the movement toward world power continued.

The nation mixed confidence and doubt as the twentieth century opened. From the small nation of 1800 had emerged a continental giant, the world's largest internal free market, and a functioning experiment in political democracy. All that bred optimism by 1900. Social critics, however, pointed out the other side of the ledger. "We can feed ourselves, we are great and powerful," said a popular newspaperman in 1900, "but we have our

One of the driving forces of American economic growth between 1877 and 1909 was the flow of immigrants into the United States. Their travels from Europe were often harsh and uncomfortable. These immigrants had to sleep on deck as their ship made its way across the North Atlantic.
Courtesy American Antiquarian Society

The demand for labor swept up even young children. Here boys work in a shop in unsafe conditions with faces dulled by the toil they endured. Efforts to regulate child labor largely came to nothing before 1909.
The Library Company of Philadelphia

Urbanization, 1860–1910

Class and population size	1860	1870	1880
Urban territory	**392**	**663**	**939**
Places of 1,000,000 or more	– – –	– – –	1
Places of 500,000–999,999	2	2	3
Places of 250,000–499,999	1	5	4
Places of 100,000–249,999	6	7	12
Places of 50,000–99,999	7	11	15
Places of 25,000–49,999	19	27	42
Places of 10,000–24,999	58	116	146
Places of 5,000–9,999	136	186	249
Places of 2,500–4,999	163	309	467

Class and population size	1890	1900	1910
Urban territory	**1,348**	**1,737**	**2,262**
Places of 1,000,000 or more	3	3	3
Places of 500,000–999,999	1	3	5
Places of 250,000–499,999	7	9	11
Places of 100,000–249,999	17	23	31
Places of 50,000–99,999	30	40	59
Places of 25,000–49,999	66	82	119
Places of 10,000–24,999	230	280	369
Places of 5,000–9,999	340	465	605
Places of 2,500–4,999	654	832	1060
Places under 2,500	– – –	– – –	– – –
Rural territory	**6,490**	**8,931**	**11,830**
Places of 1,000–2,499	1,603	2,128	2,717
Places under 1,000	4,887	6,803	9,113

– – – Represents zero.

own galling Negro problem, our rotten machine politics, our legislative bribery, our municipal corruption, our giant monopolies, our aristocracy of mere riches, any one of which is a rock on which the ship of state, unless skillfully navigated, may go to its destruction."

The indictment had merit. Too many in the United States—African Americans, Hispanics, Indians, immigrants, and women—did not share in all that the country offered. In retrospect, the verdict would be that the late nineteenth century fell short of its historic duties. To Americans who lived through these times, who saw Hayes enter the White House and Roosevelt give way to William Howard Taft, it appeared that they had left the country better than they found it when they first addressed its problems during the 1870s. Their part in the American journey will be the underlying theme of the four chapters that follow.

This picture of the Wright Brothers starting their flight at Kitty Hawk, North Carolina in 1903 launched the age of aviation. Progress would be slow during the first decade of the new century, but the achievement of the Wright Brothers indicated how technology was transforming lives.
Courtesy American Antiquarian Society

	1877	1882	1888

Politics & Diplomacy

1877: Rutherford B. Hayes elected president after disputed election
Nationwide railroad strike
Supreme Court decides case of *Munn v. Illinois*
1878: Bland-Allison Act for silver passed over Hayes's veto
Congress passes Timber and Stone Act
1879: Exoduster movement of blacks to Kansas
1880: James A. Garfield defeats Winfield Scott Hancock in presidential election
1881: Garfield assassinated in July; dies in September
Chester A. Arthur becomes president

1882: Chinese Exclusion Act passed
1883: Supreme Court rules in *Civil Rights Cases* that Civil Rights Act of 1875 does not apply in southern states
Mongrel Tariff law enacted
Pendleton Civil Service Law passed
1884: Grover Cleveland defeats James G. Blaine in presidential election
1885: Ulysses S. Grant dies of cancer
1886: Haymarket Riot in Chicago
Great Southwestern Strike occurs
1887: President Cleveland calls for reform of tariff in annual message
1888: Benjamin Harrison defeats Cleveland in presidential election

1889: Opening of Oklahoma Territory to non-Native American settlement
Jane Addams starts Hull House settlement house program
1890: Passage of Sherman Silver Purchase Act, McKinley Tariff, and Sherman Antitrust Act
Battle of Wounded Knee
Candidates identified with the Farmers Alliance make electoral gains in South and West
Republicans suffer major losses in congressional elections
1891: Federal Elections Bill to regulate elections in South blocked in the Senate

Social & Cultural Events

1877: New York YMCA offers first typing course for women
1880: Metropolitan Museum of Art opens in New York City
1881: Helen Hunt Jackson publishes *A Century of Dishonor* about treatment of Native Americans
Boston Symphony Orchestra established

1882: American Association of University Women founded
1883: Lester Frank Ward publishes *Dynamic Sociology*
1884: Mark Twain's *The Adventures of Huckleberry Finn* is published
1885: William Dean Howell's book *The Rise of Silas Lapham* appears
1886: Death of poet Emily Dickinson
Coca-Cola goes on sale in Atlanta
Statue of Liberty dedicated
1887: William Randolph Hearst begins career as publisher of San Francisco *Examiner*
1888: Edward Bellamy's *Looking Backward* becomes best-seller

1889: Singer electric sewing machine introduced
Safety bicycle enjoys wide popularity
1890: Daughters of the American Revolution founded
Poems by Emily Dickinson published
1891: James Naismith invents basketball
University of Chicago opens

Economics & Technology

1877: Bell Telephone Company organized
Thomas Edison invents the phonograph
1878: General Assembly of Knights of Labor founded
1879: Thomas Edison invents incandescent lamp
Henry George publishes *Progress and Poverty*
1880: George Eastman patents first successful roll film camera
1881: American Federation of Labor (AFL) formed

1882: Standard Oil becomes first trust
Observance of Labor Day begins
1883: Railroads create national time zones
1884: Bureau of Labor established in federal government
1885: American Telephone and Telegraph Company organized
1886: Southern railroad tracks moved closer together to comply with national standards
1887: Interstate Commerce Act passed to regulate railroads
First electrical streetcar service in Richmond, Virginia

1888: George Eastman perfects Kodak hand camera
1889: Electric sewing machine developed
1891: Thomas Edison receives first radio patent in United States
1892: Homestead strike is broken in Carnegie Steel
1893: Panic of 1893 begins four-year depression
1894: Pullman Strike occurs in midst of economic hard times
1895: Supreme Court ruling in *U.S. v. E. C. Knight* case weakens Sherman Antitrust Act

1892: Cleveland defeats Harrison in 1892 presidential election
Democrats gain control of both houses of Congress
1893: Sherman Silver Purchase Act repealed
1894: Coxey's Army makes protest march to Washington
Republicans make large gains in congressional elections
1895: Venezuelan crisis with Great Britain
1896: McKinley defeats Bryan in presidential election
Supreme Court upholds segregation in *Plessy v. Ferguson*
1897: Dingley Tariff enacted

1898: Hawaiian Islands annexed
Spanish-American War begins; United States defeats Spain and acquires Philippine Islands
1899: Open Door policy in Far East announced by John Hay
1900: McKinley defeats Bryan again in presidential race
Theodore Roosevelt is McKinley's running mate
1901: McKinley assassinated
Theodore Roosevelt becomes president
1902: Northern Securities case filed by Justice Department
Anthracite coal strike settled
1903: Panama Canal Zone acquired; Canadian boundary dispute settled

1904: Theodore Roosevelt elected president over Alton B. Parker
1905: Roosevelt mediates Russo-Japanese War
1906: Hepburn Act passed to regulate railroads
Pure Food and Drugs Act and Meat Inspection Act passed
1907: Gentleman's Agreement with Japan over immigration policy
1908: William Howard Taft defeats Bryan for presidency
1909: Theodore Roosevelt leaves office; Taft inaugurated president

---

1892: *Ida Wells-Barnett* begins antilynching campaign
Ellis Island in New York opens to receive immigrants
Shredded Wheat created
1893: Mildred Hill publishes song that becomes "Happy Birthday to you"
Columbian Exposition offers "Great White City" in Chicago
1894: Radcliffe College for Women opens in Cambridge, Massachusetts
1895: Stephen Crane publishes *The Red Badge of Courage* about Civil War
Booker T. Washington proposes "Atlanta Compromise"
Anti-Saloon League established
1896: Trading stamps offered by stores in the United States
First commercial movie showing occurs
1897: Jell-O is introduced

1898: Condensed soups are offered to consumers
1899: Scott Joplin publishes "Maple Leaf Rag"
Edward Kennedy "Duke" Ellington born in Washington, D.C.
1900: Olds Motor Works begins mass-producing cars
1901: Dorothy Dix advice column begins in New York *Evening Journal*
Jazz trumpeter Louis Armstrong born in New Orleans
1902: Teddy Bear toy developed
Muckraking journalism begins in *McClure's Magazine*
1903: National Women's Trade Union League formed
Great Train Robbery, first western movie, premieres

1904: Ice cream cone marketed
1905: Edith Wharton publishes *The House of Mirth* about New York upper class
1906: Theodore Roosevelt attacks muckrakers
1907: Self-contained electric clothes washer developed
1908: Henry Ford introduces Model T automobile
First Mother's Day observed
Jack Johnson becomes heavyweight boxing champion
1909: National Association for the Advancement of Colored People founded

---

1896: Gold discovered in Klondike in Canada and helps ease deflation
1897: Depression of 1890s eases
1898: Burst of industrial consolidation as mergers accelerate
1899: Founding of National Consumers League
1900: Gold Standard Act passed
1901: United States Steel created as first billion dollar corporation
1902: Newlands Act passed to promote irrigation in the West
U.S. files suit against Northern Securities Company

1903: Department of Commerce and Labor created
Wright brothers make first airplane flight
1904: In *Northern Securities Co. v. U.S.,* Supreme Court upholds government position against railroad holding company and strengthens Sherman Antitrust Act
1905: In *Lochner v. New York,* Supreme Court rules that maximum hours law for bakers is not constitutional
1906: Bureau of Immigration established

1907: Panic of 1907 results in calls for banking reform
1908: In *Muller v. Oregon,* U.S. Supreme Court upholds law specifying maximum hours that women can work
1909: Payne-Aldrich Tariff enacted

17 AN ECONOMY TRANSFORMED: THE RISE OF BIG BUSINESS 1877–1887

RAILROADS AND A "LOCOMOTIVE PEOPLE"

BIG BUSINESS ARRIVES

THE CHANGING SOUTH AND WEST

LIFE AND CULTURE DURING THE 1880s

The pace of industrialization during the Gilded Age was symbolized by this image of a steam transport carrying railroad cars under a modern bridge. The rapid improvement in transportation helped to create a national market for industrial goods.
From the Collections of the Library of Congress

In the 1880s Americans talked of how complex and interdependent their nation was becoming. A surge of industrial growth moved the United States from the older agrarian ways to a new world of large industries, big cities, and pressing social problems. The issues of the Civil War and Reconstruction, though only a few years in the past, seemed stale. How would the country meet the new challenges it faced from big business and its consequences?

The agenda of social and political problems confronting the nation between 1877 and 1887 was formidable. The process of industrialization transformed how Americans lived and worked together. The ways in which the American people grappled with the effects of industrial growth defined the decades between the waning of Reconstruction and the end of the nineteenth century.

Table 17.1	Railroad Mileage, 1877–1887
1877	97,308
1878	103,649
1879	104,756
1880	115,647
1881	130,455
1882	140,878
1883	149,101
1884	156,414
1885	160,506
1886	167,952
1887	184,935

Source: *The Statistical History of the United States*, p. 427.

RAILROADS AND A "LOCOMOTIVE PEOPLE"

The belching, noisy, indispensable railroad stood as the most visible example of industrialization. One British writer noted that "The Americans are an eminently locomotive people." The completion of the transcontinental railroads underscored the energetic pace of rail development. During the 1880s, the amount of tracks rose steadily, reaching 167,000 miles in 1890. By that time, the United States had a more extensive railroad network than all the European countries combined, even with Russia included.

Creating the Railroad Network

This network of iron and steel drew the nation together as bridges and tunnels swept away the obstacles that rivers and mountains posed. Another step toward unification was the establishment of a standard gauge or width for all tracks. Some railroads used the standard gauge of 4 feet 8.5 inches; others relied on tracks as much as 6 feet apart. These inconsistencies translated into extra equipment, higher costs, and lost time. By 1880, the standard gauge dominated, with the South the principal holdout. Then, on a single day in 1886, all the southern lines moved their rails to the standard gauge. To put all railroads on the same set of working times, in 1883 the railroads agreed to set up four standard time zones across the country. Railroads could not operate with different times in different states, as had been the case before.

Consistency streamlined the operation of the railroads. Freight was moved with greater ease through bills of lading (a statement of what was being shipped), which all lines accepted. Standard freight classifications appeared and passenger schedules became more rational and predictable, especially after the establishment of standard time zones. After the enactment of the Interstate Commerce Act (1887) and the passage of other relevant legislation during the 1890s, all railroads adopted automatic couplers, air brakes, and other safety devices.

Railroad travel also became more comfortable for passengers and more accommodating to food and other perishables. The refrigerator car preserved food for transport to distant consumers. George Pullman pioneered the sleeping car. The railroads built huge terminals through which millions of passengers and countless tons of freight moved each day.

More than $4 billion was invested in the railroad system by 1877. The entire national debt was just over $2.1 billion. To finance this huge commitment of money, the railroads drew upon the funds of private investors both in the United States and Europe. An impressive amount, however, came from government. To aid in the construction of the western transcontinental railroads, for example, the federal government made direct loans of almost $65 million to the rail lines along with millions of acres of land grants. Total federal land grants to railroads exceeded 130 million acres, and state and local governments added another 49 million acres. Other examples of state aid included loans, tax reductions, and issuing of bonds. The total amount of all such assistance approached $500 million.

CHRONOLOGY

1877 After wages of railroad workers are reduced, national strike erupts • Desert Land Act passed

1878 Bland-Allison Act passed to buy silver • Timber and Stone Act passed

1879 Thomas Edison invents incandescent lamp • Cash register invented • Woman suffrage amendment introduced in Congress • Frances Willard becomes president of the Woman's Christian Temperance Union (WCTU) • Henry George publishes *Progress and Poverty*

1880 Metropolitan Museum of Art opens in New York City • James A. Garfield elected president

1881 Garfield assassinated; Chester Alan Arthur succeeds him • Boston Symphony Orchestra begins performances

1882 Chinese Exclusion Act • Standard Oil Company becomes first trust • American Association of University Women established

1883 Pendleton Civil Service Act passed • Railroads create national standard time zones • Lester Frank Ward publishes *Dynamic Sociology*

1884 Grover Cleveland defeats James G. Blaine for presidency • Mark Twain's *The Adventures of Huckleberry Finn* published

1885 Death of Ulysses S. Grant

1886 Haymarket Riot in Chicago (May 4) • Emily Dickinson dies in Amherst, Massachusetts • American Federation of Labor (AFL) formed

1887 Dawes Severalty Act passed • Interstate Commerce Act passed • Cleveland attacks tariff in annual message • First electrical streetcar service in Richmond, Virginia

By 1880 the railroad network had assumed a well-defined shape. East of the Mississippi River to the Atlantic seaboard ran four *trunk* (main line) railroads that carried goods and passengers from smaller towns connected by *feeder* (subsidiary) lines. The trunk lines were the Pennsylvania Railroad, the Erie Railroad, the New York Central Railroad, and the Baltimore and Ohio Railroad. The transcontinental lines included the Union Pacific/Central Pacific, Northern Pacific, and Southern Pacific. In the South the trunk lines emerged more slowly. During the 1880s and 1890s, southern railroads built five trunk lines, including the Southern Railway and the Louisville and Nashville Railroad.

Organizing the Railroad Business

Because they conducted their affairs on a grand scale, railroads became the first big business. Factories in a single location had fewer than a thousand workers; the railroads extended over thousands of miles and employed tens of thousands of workers.

The railroads required an immense amount of equipment and facilities; no single individual could supervise it all directly.

New management systems arose to address these problems. Executives set up clear lines of authority. Separate operating divisions purchased supplies, maintained track and equipment, handled freight, dealt with passengers, and transmitted information. Local superintendents took care of day-to-day matters; general superintendents resolved larger policy issues; and railroad executives made the overall decisions. By the 1870s, the organizational structure of the railroads included elaborate mechanisms for cost accounting.

Railroads stimulated the national economy. From the late 1860s through the early 1890s, the railroads consumed more than half the nation's output of steel. Railroads also used about 20 percent of coal production. Their repair shops created a market for industrial workers in Middle Western cities such as Chicago and Cleveland.

*P*ICTURING THE PAST ✦ ECONOMICS & TECHNOLOGY

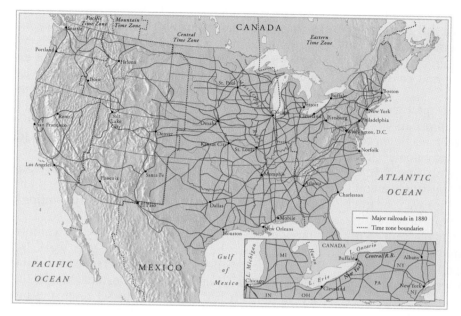

Map 17.1 *The Railroad Network*

A key economic development of the late nineteenth century was the spread of the railroad network and the national market that it helped to create for goods and services. This map shows the extent of progress by 1880 as well as the emergence of the system of time zones that facilitated the smooth operation of the railroad timetables. Note the more developed state of rail lines in the Northeast and Middle West where industrialism had taken hold.

The map also makes clear why the railroads were such a significant political issue in so many states and why those who used the rail lines often resented business practices that adversely affected their interests. Within a few years in 1887, Congress created the Interstate Commerce Commission to provide some degree of regulatory supervision for the railroads. Real control of the railroads did not come until the early twentieth century, and by then, the automobile and truck had challenged the railroad's dominance of transportation.

The United States was becoming a national economic market in which similar goods and services were available to people throughout the nation. The development of a national market also encouraged the growth of big business to meet consumer demand for canned goods, ready-made clothes, and industrial machinery. Thus, the expansion of the railroads was a key element in the dramatic changes that industrialization produced

The Railroad as a Political Issue

Because they shaped the economy in so many ways, railroads became a political issue. Land grants affected numerous communities, and railroad executives pro-

voked controversy. Cornelius Vanderbilt of the New York Central, Collis P. Huntington of the Southern Pacific, and Jay Gould of the Union Pacific, among others, were renowned for the ruthless methods they employed against their competitors. Their critics called them "robber barons."

Railroad leaders believed that too much competition caused their economic and political problems. Because a railroad ran constantly and had to maintain its equipment, facilities, and labor force on a continuing basis, its operating costs were inescapable or "fixed." To survive, a railroad needed a reliable and constant flow of freight and passengers and the revenue they supplied. One strategy was to build tracks and add lines in order to gain more business. Each new line required more business to pay off the cost of building it. Railroads therefore waged a constant economic struggle for the available traffic.

One obvious solution was to lure customers, either openly or secretly, with reduced prices. From 1865 to 1900, railroad rates were lowered. Some of the reduction in rates stemmed from the general deflation in prices that marked this period. Other price declines came about because the railroads and their workers found ways to move freight and passengers more efficiently.

To maintain their share of the total available business, railroads relied on secret procedures. The rebate was a discount on published rates given to a favored shipper in the form of cash payments. Other customers had to pay the listed rate or were charged more. When faced with potentially destructive competition, the railroads engaged in price wars or tried to acquire their rivals. Railroads (and other industries) also used the pool, a private agreement to divide the available business in an industry or locality. Working together, the railroads hoped to maintain rates at a level that ensured profits for all members of the pool.

Attractive as a means of restraining competition, pools were impossible to enforce because their secrecy violated state laws against economic conspiracies. Weaker railroads were willing to cheat on the pool if it would bring in more business. Railroad men wanted the federal government to legalize pooling through legislation, an approach that was politically unpopular because it meant price-fixing and monopolies. By the middle of the 1880s, therefore, the larger railroads moved toward consolidation as the answer to too many railroads and too much competition.

Regulating the Railroads

While rebates, pools, and consolidation made sense to the railroads, they angered those who traveled or shipped their goods by rail. Shippers who did not receive rebates regarded the tactic as unfair. Railroads often charged more for a short haul than for a longer one because fewer exchanges and stops made the long haul cheaper. Because of the advantage they gave to some shippers over others, railroad rates also served the interest of cities such as Chicago or Kansas City but hurt others in the Middle West. Railroads also posed dangers to the traveling public. In 1888 alone, some 5,200 Americans were killed while traveling or working on the railroad. Another 26,000 were injured.

Americans debated how society should respond to the railroads. Few advocated government ownership.

Using legislatures or courts to oversee the railroads was not popular either. Instead, Americans developed a middle way between those apparent extremes.

The Railroad Commission

The answer to the railroad problem during this period was the regulatory commission. Ideally, such a body, created by the state legislature, was composed of experts who decided issues of rates, finance, and service in a neutral, nonpartisan way. The first railroad commission had been created in New Hampshire in 1844; there were four in existence in 1861. After the war, the commission concept spread; there were twenty-eight such agencies by 1896.

Railroad commissions came in two kinds. One variety advised railroads of possible violations and publicized information about railroad operations. The most notable example of this form of commission was the one in Massachusetts. Critics claimed that the Massachusetts commission was weak because it lacked the power to set rates. The second kind of railroad commission was established in Illinois in 1871. It had the power to set rates and put them into effect in 1873. Because of this authority, which other Midwestern states adopted, the Illinois model became known as the strong form of the railroad commission.

During the 1870s railroads challenged the authority of these state commissions. The most important case involved Illinois, and it reached the U.S. Supreme Court in 1876. The decision of *Munn v. Illinois* (1877) declared that the state could establish a commission to regulate railroad rates. Railroads, the Court said, were "engaged in a public employment affecting the public interest." Because Congress had not yet acted to regulate interstate commerce in railroad matters, a state could make "such rules and regulations as may be necessary for the protection of the general welfare of the people within its own jurisdiction."

Despite such successes, reservations about the effectiveness of state commissions grew. Critics complained that the railroads had too much influence over the state commissions. There was some corruption, and the process of regulation was often cumbersome. Most important, however, the state commissions could not deal effectively with interstate railroads. In 1886, in the case of *Wabash, St. Louis, and Pacific Railway Company v. Illinois,* the Supreme Court ruled that enforcement of the Illinois law infringed on interstate commerce. Congress needed to establish a national policy for regulating the railroads.

The Interstate Commerce Act

Political and economic forces combined to stimulate the demand for railroad regulation in the mid-1880s. Western and southern farmers lobbied for such a policy. However, their influence was less significant than that of merchants and shippers on the East Coast, who wanted a government agency to ensure that they received fair treatment from the rail companies. Some railroads preferred federal regulation to the confusion of competing state commissions. Congress responded to these pressures by passing the Interstate Commerce Act in 1887. This law set up an Interstate Commerce Commission (ICC), composed of five members, that could investigate complaints of railroad misconduct or file suit against the companies. The law forbade rebates and pooling. The new regulatory agency was the first of its kind on the federal level. Despite a shaky start for the ICC in its first decade, commissions became a favored means of dealing with the problems of managing an industrial society.

BIG BUSINESS ARRIVES

While the growth of the railroads laid the basis for further industrial expansion, the overall success of big business came during difficult economic times. The depression of the 1870s ebbed by 1879, but the prosperity that followed was brief. From 1881 to 1885, there was another slowdown, with numerous business failures. Two years of good times preceded another recession during 1887 and 1888. In the late nineteenth century, businesses grew larger even though prosperity was elusive.

Deflation brought about by increased productivity, a tight money supply, and an abundant labor force set the tone for business. Companies with high fixed costs, such as railroads, oil, and steel, experienced intense, constant pressure to reduce competition and avoid its impact through arrangements such as pools. In a few industries it even seemed possible to escape competition and achieve monopoly.

John D. Rockefeller and Standard Oil

Oil was the most famous example of such an industry, and John D. Rockefeller of Standard Oil became the leading example of monopoly power and economic concentration. Rockefeller had been in the oil business since the mid-1860s. From his base in Ohio, he expanded rapidly while watching costs. He founded the Standard Oil Company in 1870. As Rockefeller's oil interests grew, he and his partner, Henry Flagler, used

A young looking John D. Rockefeller was on his way during this period to a dominance of the American oil industry
Courtesy of the Rockefeller Archive Center

Standard's size to secure rebates from the railroads. Able to assure the rail companies a dependable supply of oil to haul, they also obtained a share, or "drawback" of what their competitors paid. Despite these advantages, there were still too many producers in the industry. An oversupply of oil resulted.

The creation of Standard Oil was Rockefeller's effort to impose control on a chaotic business. Through rebates, drawbacks, and price-cutting against rivals whose companies he eventually acquired, he sought to dominate all the supplies of oil. By the end of the 1870s, he controlled about 90 percent of the nation's oil-refining capacity and had achieved a horizontal integration of the oil business.

The Emergence of the Trust

As a virtual monopoly in oil appeared, a political response followed. Under state law, Standard Oil of Ohio could not legally own stock in other oil companies or conduct its business in other states. Yet registering to do business in other states could reveal aspects of the company's business to competitors and expose it to legal challenges in the courts. In 1882, a lawyer for Rockefeller, S. T. C. Dodd, formulated a new use for an old legal device. Standard Oil became the first example of the *trust* in American business.

The forty-one stockholders of Standard Oil entered into an agreement that created a board of nine trustees. In return the board held the company's stock in trust and exercised "general supervision over the affairs of said Standard Oil Companies." The trustees could select the board of directors and set policy for all Standard Oil's subsidiaries in other states. In this way the trust escaped the restrictions of state laws everywhere. The term *trust* soon lost its legal connotation and became a general label for the rise of big business.

The trust device was used only for a brief period. In the late 1870s, several states passed laws that allowed corporations to own branches in other states, to hold the stock of other corporations, and to pursue a policy of consolidation to the extent that their industry and its conditions permitted. The "holding company" law, first enacted in New Jersey and later in Delaware, was more efficient than the trust approach. A large company simply held the stock of its subsidiaries. The spectacle of the trust swallowing up its rivals became ingrained in the popular imagination.

By the end of the 1880s, demands for state and congressional action arose to curb the growth of the trusts. In the 1888 presidential election, both major parties denounced trusts that aimed "to control arbitrarily the condition of trade among our citizens," as the Republicans put it. Fourteen states and territories passed laws to curb monopoly power. President Grover Cleveland said in 1887 that "competition is too often strangled by combinations quite prevalent at this time, and frequently called trusts." The political world seemed intent on taking at least symbolic action against large industrial combinations.

Andrew Carnegie and the Steel Industry

Almost as famous as Rockefeller was Andrew Carnegie. He was one of the few prominent businessmen of the era who rose "from rags to riches." An immigrant from Scotland, he worked first in a textile factory and then as a telegraph clerk. By 1853 he was the private secretary to Thomas A. Scott of the Pennsylvania Railroad. During the 1860s, he played the stock market through investments in railroading, oil, and telegraph company securities. By 1873, however, he focused on steel. He summed up his philosophy: "Put all your good eggs in one basket, and then watch that basket."

Andrew Carnegie integrated the American steel industry by making products more cheaply than his competitors.
From the Collections of the Library of Congress

In the 1870s, the technology of steelmaking relied on the Bessemer process of steel production in which molten pig iron was placed in a receptacle or converter and air was blown across it to remove impurities through oxidization. The result was a flow of steel in about fifteen or twenty minutes, much faster than the earlier process in which an individual "puddler" had worked the molten iron. Eventually the open-hearth method of steelmaking supplanted the Bessemer technique. In this method the iron ore was heated up and scrap metal was then added to the mixture. Subsequent modifications and refinements of the process allowed steelmakers to use American iron ores. The Bessemer process dominated the construction of steel rails; the open-hearth method proved better for heavy machinery, skyscraper beams, and other uses. By 1890, steel production had risen to 4,277,000 tons annually; it would climb still more, to 10,188,000 tons by 1900.

Carnegie became the dominant figure in steelmaking. A steel owner should "watch the costs and the profits will take care of themselves." Between 1873 and 1889, Carnegie cut the cost of steel rail from $58 a ton to $25 a ton. He poured money into new equipment and plowed profits back into the business. During the 1880s, steel production at Carnegie's works rose, costs went down, and his profits grew by over a million dollars annually. Carnegie sought to achieve the vertical integration of his steel interests; this meant controlling all the steps in the process of making steel. Carnegie acquired mines to ensure that he had raw materials, boats to move ore on rivers, railroads to carry it to his mills, and a sales force to market his many products.

Carnegie's innovations in steelmaking were felt throughout the economy. The lower cost of steel spurred the mechanization of industry. As machines became more complex and more productive, machine tools were needed to turn out these laborsaving and cost-cutting devices in sufficient amounts. In such industries as firearms, bicycles, and sewing machines, the use of machine tools spread technological innovations throughout the economy. Carnegie and Rockefeller's managers broke work down into specific, well-defined tasks for each employee. They made everyone in the workplace follow standardized procedures. Finally, they emphasized lower costs for every aspect of the business. Mass production and a continuous flow of resources into factories and of goods to the consumers were part of the larger process of industrialization that reshaped the American economy.

The Pace of Invention

Inventive Americans poured out a flood of new ideas with an average of 13,000 patents issued each year during the 1870s. In the next twenty years, the annual

Table 17.2	Steel Production, 1877–1887
1877	569,618
1878	731,977
1879	935,273
1880	1,247,335
1881	1,588,314
1882	1,736,692
1883	1,673,535
1884	1,550,879
1885	1,711,920
1886	2,562,503
1887	3,339,071

Source: *The Statistical History of the United States*, p. 416.

total climbed to about 21,000. Among the new devices were the phonograph (1877), the typewriter (1878), the cash register (1879), and the linotype in newspaper publishing (1886). The Kodak camera went on the market in 1888. The process of innovation led to such constructive changes as the twine binder, which made harvesting straw more efficient; time locks for bank vaults; and the fountain pen. As one writer put it, "Our greatest thinkers are not in the library, nor the capital, but in the machine shop."

Alexander Graham Bell and Thomas Alva Edison were the major inventors. A Scottish immigrant from Canada, Bell wanted to transmit the human voice by electrical means. In 1876, he and his assistant, Thomas A. Watson, created a practical device for doing so: the telephone. By 1877, it was possible to make telephone calls between New York and Boston; New Haven, Connecticut, established the first telephone exchange. Soon President Hayes had a telephone

This photograph shows Alexander Graham Bell, the inventor of the telephone, placing the first telephone call between New York and Chicago in 1892. The telephone was one of the inventions at the end of the nineteenth century that transformed how Americans communicated in business, politics, and private life.
The Granger Collection, New York

installed at the White House. Long-distance service between some cities arrived in 1884. After Bell overcame legal challenges to his patents, the Bell Telephone Company expanded into the American Telephone and Telegraph Company.

An even more famous inventor was Thomas Alva Edison, the "Wizard of Menlo Park." Born in 1847, Edison was a telegrapher during the Civil War with a knack for making machines and devices. By the end of the 1860s, he had already patented some of his nearly 1,100 inventions. In 1876, he established the first industrial research laboratory at Menlo Park, New Jersey. His goals, he said, were to produce "a minor invention every ten days and a big thing every six months or so." In 1877, he devised the first phonograph, although it would be another decade before he perfected it commercially. More immediately rewarding was the invention of the carbon filament incandescent lamp in 1879. Edison decided to use carbonized thread in the lamp, and it glowed for more than forty-five hours.

For the electric light to be profitable, it had to be installed in a system outside the laboratory. In 1882, Edison put his invention into operation in New York City. The area covered was about a square mile, and after a year in service there were 500 customers with more than 10,000 lamps. Electric power caught on rapidly. Edison's system, however, relied on direct electric current for power. As the distance traveled by the current increased, the amount of usable electric power decreased. One of Edison's business

Thomas A. Edison's many inventions enabled Americans to light their homes, listen to music, and in time to go to the movies.
From the Collections of the Library of Congress

rivals, George Westinghouse, discovered how to use a transformer to render electricity safe at the point where the consumer needed it. This device made possible alternating current, which could transmit higher amounts of electricity.

Electricity had an immediate impact on urban transportation. The electric streetcar was invented in Germany in 1879, and Edison and others adapted it for use in the United States. Granville T. Woods, a black inventor, devised the "third rail" to convey electric power to the cars. By 1882, there were more than 400 streetcar companies in the United States and they moved a total of 1.2 billion passengers annually.

Americans in the Workplace

Amid industrialization, individual Americans struggled to improve their lives within a society that resisted efforts to lessen the harmful effects of industrial growth. In 1877, there were 15 million nondomestic workers, more than half in agriculture and another 4 million in manufacturing. The economy was in the fourth year of a depression, stemming from the Panic of 1873, and almost 2 million people were unemployed.

The labor force grew by more than 29 percent during the 1870s. One-fifth of the increase came from immigrants. Four out of every ten of these working immigrants were unskilled; their sweat helped the new industries expand and the cities to rise. Most of the immigrants left from northern Europe as they had before the Civil War. Irish, Germans, British, and Scandinavians made up the bulk of the newcomers. The growth of the transatlantic steamship business and the aggressive work of emigration agents in Europe helped persuade many to come to the United States; hard times in Europe impelled others to make the trip. Western states and territories hoped that the new arrivals would become farmers, but the majority found work in the cities of the Northeast and Midwest. Soon distinctive ethnic communities grew up in New York, Boston, and Philadelphia.

Skilled Workers

Skilled labor faced dismaying changes in the new industrial setting. Technology replaced craft skills with machines, and market pressures led businesses to limit their dependence on trained artisans. A more hierarchical system of management stripped skilled workers of their autonomy and reduced their control over the workplace. The use of apprenticeship as a way of rising in industry receded, and the workforce was divided into unskilled and semiskilled employees.

Workers resisted these changes through mutual support in times of crisis. In 1882, the Amalgamated Association of Iron and Steel Workers struck for higher pay from the owners of steel rolling mills in Pennsylvania. For five months the union held together against unified management, but finally the workers were forced to go back on the job.

Women represented another new element in the labor force. They appeared in greater numbers as teachers and office workers, and as sales clerks in the expanding department stores. Eight thousand women worked in sales in 1880; a decade later the total was more than 58,000. Many stores preferred women, especially native-born white women. While many immigrant women toiled as domestic servants, they also found work in the sweatshops of the textile trades. For the most part, the jobs open to women were lower paid, required fewer skills, and offered less opportunity than those open to men.

Real wages for workers increased as the prices of farm products and manufactured goods fell during the deflation that lasted until the late 1890s. The hours that employees worked declined from more than sixty-five hours a week in 1860 to under sixty by 1900. Gradual though they were, these changes represented real gains.

The Dangers of Industrialism

Steelworkers put in twelve hours a day seven days a week amid the noise, heat, and hazards of the mills. In the coal mines, in the factories, and on the railroads, work was hazardous and fatal. From 1880 to 1900, some 35,000 of the 4 million workers in manufacturing died in accidents each year and another 500,000 were injured.

Workers had almost no protection against sickness, injury, or arbitrary dismissal. If an injury occurred, the courts had decided that the liability often belonged to another worker or "fellow servant" rather than to the company that owned the factory. For a worker who was fired during an economic downturn, there were no unemployment benefits, no government programs for retraining, and little private help. Old age pensions did not exist, and there were no private medical or retirement insurance plans. Child labor reached a peak during this period. Almost 182,000 children under the age of sixteen were at work in 1880 with no health and safety restrictions to protect them.

Workers had few ways to insulate themselves from the impact of harsh working conditions and often cruel employers. There were sporadic attempts at labor organization and strikes throughout the nineteenth century, but unions faced legal and political obstacles. The law said that a worker and his employer were equal players in the marketplace, one buying labor for the lowest price possible, the other selling labor for as much as could be obtained. Real equality in bargaining power rarely existed. The worker had to take what was offered; the boss set the conditions of employment.

The Rise of Unions

During the 1860s and 1870s, skilled workers in cigar making, shoemaking, and coal mining formed unions. The National Labor Union (NLU), a coalition of trade unions, was established in 1866. In 1868, its leader was William Sylvis, the head of the union of craftsmen in the steel industry known as iron-puddlers. Under his direction, the NLU pursued the eight-hour day and other improvements for labor. Sylvis's death in 1869 and the dominance of middle-class social reformers in the organization eroded the influence of the National Labor Union by the early 1870s. Still, the first national labor organization provided a model for others to imitate.

Because of the number of workers they employed, railroads were the first business to confront large-scale labor issues. The professional skills that engineers, firemen, brakemen, and others possessed made it more difficult for railroads to find replacements during a strike. Railroad workers joined unions based around these crafts such as the Brotherhood of Locomotive Firemen and the Brotherhood of Locomotive Engineers. "Unless labor combines," said one engineer, "it cannot be heard at all." The issue, according to one railroad executive, was, "who shall manage the road?" From this difference of opinion flowed the labor disputes that marked the decade from 1877 to 1887 and beyond.

The Railroad Strike of 1877

A bitter railroad strike erupted during the summer of 1877. On July 1, in the middle of an economic depression, the major eastern railroads announced a 10 percent wage cut. Facing their second pay reduction in a year, railroad employees launched an unplanned protest. Strikers disrupted train traffic across Pennsylvania, West Virginia, Maryland, and Ohio. In Baltimore and Pittsburgh, strikers battled state militia. A general strike spread to Chicago, St. Louis, and other large cities. Railroad unions played a relatively small part in these walkouts, however; during the depression their membership had declined as had their economic impact on the roads.

The Great Railroad Strike of 1877 left many railroads in ruins as vandals ripped up property along the tracks. The walkout became a symbol of the social disorder of the decade and its hard times.
The Granger Collection, New York

The leader of the Knights of Labor, Terence V. Powderly, pursued the vision of an all-embracing union that would unite the working classes against organized capital. It proved difficult for him to direct such a diverse coalition effectively, and by the mid-1880s, the Knights had fallen victim to a popular backlash against strikes in the Southwest and the Haymarket Riot in Chicago.
The Granger Collection, New York

The governors of the states with riots called out the militia. Some militia units refused to fire on their fellow citizens. As violence spread, the Hayes administration sent in the army. Deaths ran into the hundreds; many more were injured. Newspapers sympathetic to the strike said that "never before has the cause of justice been so thoroughly on the working-man's side." Faced with the overwhelming force of the government, the unrest died away. Nevertheless, the strike had touched most of the nation.

The Knights of Labor

The strike increased support for a new national labor organization: the Noble and Bold Order of the Knights of Labor. The Knights combined fraternal ritual, the language of Christianity, and belief in the social equality of all citizens. While advancing the cause of labor through unions and strikes where necessary, the Knights wanted government to play a larger role in protecting working people who produced goods and services for the economy. The order spoke about the "Commonwealth of Toil" and deplored "the recent alarming development of aggregated wealth." Instead it wanted "a system adopted which will secure to the laborer the fruits of his toil." By the mid-1870s, the Knights was es-

tablished among coal miners in Pennsylvania. After the railroad strike, the Knights saw membership grow to 9,000 in 1879 and 42,000 by 1882.

The leader of the Knights was known as the grand master workman. Terence V. Powderly was elected to that post in 1879, and became the first national labor figure. The Knights grew because it had few membership requirements, and its ideology reached out to the entire working population. Its ranks embraced workers from skilled craft unions, agricultural laborers in the South, and women who were new entrants into the workforce. The willingness of the Knights to include women and blacks set it apart from other unions. By 1885, the union claimed more than 100,000 members. Its message of working-class solidarity and mutual assistance among all producers appealed to many laborers.

The Knights in Decline

Success brought problems of internal strain and union discipline. In 1885, the Knights conducted a strike against a railroad owned by Jay Gould, one of the most hated of the rail executives. The Knights struck his Wabash, Missouri Pacific, and other lines, and achieved a form of official recognition that allowed the order to represent the company's employees in relations with management. Since it appeared that the Knights had beaten Gould, the order's popularity exploded among workers. By 1886, there were more than 700,000 members. A second walkout was called against Gould in February 1886, but this time the strike was broken through the use of police and violence against those who had walked out.

The Haymarket Affair

Other events put labor on the defensive. On May 4, 1886, workmen in Chicago gathered in Haymarket Square to protest police conduct during a strike at a factory of the McCormick Company that made farm reaping and harvesting machinery. As a heavy rain began to fall, the police endeavored to break up the meeting. Then a bomb exploded in the midst of the crowd. One police officer was killed; others fired into the throng. Seven policemen and two demonstrators were killed and seventy people were hurt.

Eight alleged participants in the bombing conspiracy were arrested and convicted, although none had taken part in the event itself. Their belief in anarchism made them likely targets for the police. Four were executed, one committed suicide, and three others went to prison. The Haymarket affair, with its undertones of radical unrest, shocked the nation. Public support for labor's demands for an eight-hour workday and other concessions dried up. In fact, widespread antiradical hysteria spread.

These events did most damage to the Knights of Labor. Even though Powderly had questioned the wisdom of strikes, business leaders and conservatives blamed the Knights for the violence and unrest. The union went into a permanent decline. To some workers, the failure of the Knights demonstrated the need for more violent action. To others, it indicated that Powderly's strategy of a broad, inclusive appeal and an avoidance of strikes had been wrong from the start.

The Knights of Labor had women as full members of its organization, and this picture shows eight delegates to the order's 1886 convention. The woman holding her two-month-old baby in the front is Elizabeth Rodgers. Although men dominated public life in this period, the role of women was expanding in ways that foreshadowed their greater participation after 1900.
Reproduced from the Collections of the Library of Congress

The American Federation of Labor

One vigorous critic of the Knights of Labor was Samuel Gompers. Because a philosophy of "pure and simple unionism" had worked for his own Cigar Makers International Union, he believed that only such an approach could help labor. The son of a British cigar maker, Gompers had come to the United States in 1863. During his years of employment in the cigar trade, he decided that labor should accept corporations as a fact of life, seek concrete and limited improvements in living and working conditions, and avoid political involvements.

Late in 1886, Gompers and others organized the American Federation of Labor (AFL) whose participating unions had 150,000 members. An alliance of craft unions and skilled workers, the AFL did not try to organize the masses of industrial workers. The union opposed immigrant labor, especially of the Chinese on the West Coast, and was cool toward the idea of black members. Nevertheless, the AFL's membership rose to more than 300,000 during its first ten years, and it achieved considerable benefits for its members through judicious use of strikes and negotiations with employers. Most of the men and women who worked as unskilled labor in the nation's factories and shops, however, derived little benefit from the AFL's policies.

Opposed to the inclusive policies of the Knights of Labor, Samuel Gompers, president of the American Federation of Labor (AFL) after 1886, wanted a labor movement that worked for well-defined objectives and better working conditions for its members. The craft unions that Gompers represented did not reach out to the large, unorganized mass of workers, and barred African Americans and Chinese from their ranks. Gompers believed that his strategy was more effective than what the Knights had tried to accomplish.
© Bettmann/Corbis

Social Darwinism

During these years, praise for industrialism crowded the popular press. Because clothes were now made so cheaply, said one observer, "the very beggars in our metropolitan cities, and the tramps sleeping in our fields or under the roof that shelters our cattle, wear a finer fabric than kings could boast a century ago." A more systematic justification for the existing social order was the philosophy known as Social Darwinism. Charles Darwin's famous work *On the Origin of Species,* published in 1859, offered an explanation for why some species survived and others became extinct. Darwin contended that a process of "natural selection" occurs in nature that enables the "fittest" animals and plants to evolve and develop. Darwin did not attach any moral virtue to the ability of one species to survive and reproduce as a result of the process of natural selection. He was simply analyzing the workings of the world. Advocates of Darwin's ideas, such as the English writer Herbert Spencer, applied them to human existence. If the doctrine of "survival of the fittest" operated in the natural world, Spencer argued, it governed human affairs as well. Since capitalists and the wealthy represented the "fittest" individuals, it was folly to interfere with the "natural" process that produced them. "The law of the survival of the fittest was not made by man and cannot be abrogated by man," said William Graham Sumner, a leading exponent of this doctrine. "We can only by interfering with it produce the survival of the unfittest." A professor at Yale University, Sumner won a wide audience for his ideas among middle- and upper-class Americans. On the other hand, few businessmen looked to Sumner or Spencer for advice about how to succeed in the marketplace when they sought government help through tariffs and subsidies.

The "rags to riches" novels of Horatio Alger, a popular writer of the day, spread these ideas. Alger argued that men of energy and determination (i.e., the "fittest") could triumph in the competitive system even against great odds. He wrote 106 books with such titles as *Brave and Bold* and *Paddle Your Own Canoe.* The central characters were impoverished young boys who used their natural talents to gain the support of wealthy benefactors and go on to achieve riches and success. The public consumed millions of copies of Alger's books despite repetitive plots. They taught the lessons of self-reliance and personal commitment, though few corporate leaders started at the bottom as Alger's characters did. Despite the popularity of Social Darwinism, the impact of these ideas was limited. While many Americans applauded Social Darwinism in theory, they also tolerated considerable government intervention in the economy and social relations.

Not everyone accepted the excesses and injustices of industrialism. One of the most famous social critics of the day was Henry George. A California newspaperman, George said that the cause of the gap between the wealthy and the poor was the monopoly of land by the rich and the rents that landowners charged. He expressed his ideas in a book titled *Progress and Poverty* (1879), which sold over 2 million copies in the United States and more abroad. Rent, he wrote, was "a toll levied upon labor constantly and continuously," and the solution for this social ill was

His book Progress and Poverty *(1879) made Henry George into one of the leading social reformers of the period. George diagnosed the problems of society in ways that captivated many who did not share his view that a single tax on land would provide the answers to the nation's ills.*
The Granger Collection, New York

a "single tax" on rising land values. With such a tax, all other forms of taxation would be unnecessary. George's writings enjoyed worldwide influence. Single-tax leagues flourished in the United States, and his ideas promoted social reform among clergymen in the 1890s and early 1900s. What gave *Progress and Poverty* its major impact was the moral intensity of George's analysis of the ills of capitalist society. The single-tax crusade was evidence that not all Americans favored an inactive and passive government.

Another challenge to Social Darwinism came in 1883 when a government geologist, Lester Frank Ward, published *Dynamic Sociology* in which he assailed Social Darwinism's view of evolution as applying to human society and not just to the natural world. The process of evolution did not work, he wrote, because of "the unconscious forces of nature, but also through the conscious and deliberate control by man." The idea that government should not interfere with the workings of society did not apply to its advocates: "Those who dismiss state interference are the ones who most frequently and successfully invoke it."

Ward's view of what Americans were doing was sound. All through this period, citizens asked government at all levels to take action on matters of health, safety, and finance.

THE CHANGING SOUTH AND WEST

The future of the West and South shaped the 1880s. In the South, race, industrial development, and agricultural growth combined in what was called the "New South." In the West, the vast spaces beyond the Mississippi Valley still were not fully part of the United States. Both of these regions also experienced changes stemming from the industrialization and urbanization of the North.

The Fate of Native Americans

The defeat of Custer at the Battle of the Little Big Horn in June 1876 was one of the final flurries of combat on the Great Plains. Some sporadic resistance continued. During 1877, the Nez Perce tribe in Oregon, led by Chief Joseph, resisted attempts to move them to a reservation. Through four months of running battles, Joseph led his band of 650 people toward Canada, but they were beaten before they could reach safety. "From where the sun now stands," said Joseph, "I will fight no more forever." The Nez Perces were sent to the Indian Territory in Oklahoma, where they fell victim to disease. As one white magazine said of Indian reservations, "If they [the Indians] cannot bear civilization, it will at least kill them decently."

Another famous example of Native American resistance was Geronimo, the Apache chief in New Mexico. With a small band of followers, he left the Arizona reservation where he had been living in 1881 and raided across the Southwest for two years. After brief periods of surrender he resumed his military forays. Finally, in September 1886, he was persuaded to surrender once again and was exiled to Florida.

As Native American resistance ebbed, the national government shaped policy for the western tribes. Many white westerners believed that the "Indian question" could be solved only when the tribes were gone. Easterners contended that Native Americans should be assimilated into white society. Organizations such as the Indian Rights Association lobbied for these policies, and a book by Helen Hunt Jackson, *A Century of Dishonor* (1881), publicized the plight of the Native Americans. Although the westerners had

The Apache leader Geronimo eluded capture in the Southwest until he surrendered to the army in 1886. Once in custody, he could be photographed with a rifle and menacing expression as a way of earning money from tourists.

The Granger Collection, New York

destructive motives toward the Indians while the eastern policies were more benevolent, their combined efforts devastated Indian culture.

The Dawes Act (1887)

Congress passed the Dawes Severalty Act in 1887. Named after Senator Henry L. Dawes of Massachusetts, the law authorized the president to survey Native American reservations and divide them into 160-acre farms. After receiving their allotment, Native Americans could not lease or sell the land for twenty-five years. Any Indian who adopted "habits of civilized life" became a U.S. citizen, but most Indians did not achieve citizenship. Any surplus land after this process was finished could be sold to white settlers. For the reformers, this law pushed Indians toward white civilization; for the western settlers it made Indian land available. During the next fifty years, the total land holdings of Native Americans declined from

138 million to 47 million acres. By dividing up tribal land holdings and putting Indians at the mercy of white speculators, the Dawes Act undermined the tribal structure and culture of the Native Americans.

The Mining Frontier

Mining "booms" drew settlers to seek riches in a series of bonanzas, first of gold, later of silver, and eventually of copper in territories and states such as Colorado, Montana, and the Dakotas. The mining camps became notorious for their violence and frenzied atmosphere. More than 90 percent of their inhabitants were men; most of the women were prostitutes. During the 1870s, the western mining industry came to resemble other businesses. Individual miners gradually gave way to corporations that used industrial techniques such as jets of water under high pressure to extract the metal from the ground. The ravaged land left farmers with fouled rivers and polluted fields.

In 1877, Leadville, Colorado, emerged as a major silver mining center, and Coeur d'Alene, Idaho, went through a similar process a few years later. In Butte, Montana, the development of the Anaconda Copper Mine would characterize the western mining business from the mid-1880s onward: an industrialized workforce, a company town, and bitter labor relations.

The Cattle Country

White settlement on the Great Plains during the 1880s started with the cattle ranchers, who dominated the open range in Wyoming, Colorado, and Montana. After the Civil War, ranchers in Texas found that their steers had multiplied during their absence. Enterprising cattlemen drove herds north to market at rail lines in Kansas and Nebraska. Up the Chisum and Goodnight-Loving Trails came Texas longhorns to the cattle towns of Ellsworth, Dodge City, and Abilene. Unlike the mining towns, these communities were not violent; respectable citizens quickly imposed law and order on their temporary guests. Dance halls and bordellos for the visiting cattlemen, though plentiful at first, soon were restricted.

During the late 1870s and early 1880s, cattle raising shifted from Texas to areas nearer the railroads and the Chicago stockyards. The growth of the railroad network gave ranchers access to eastern and foreign markets. Improved breeding and slaughtering practices produced beef for consumers both in the United States and in Europe, and the demand grew. With cattle easy to raise in the open spaces of the West and with an efficient transportation system, entrepreneurs in New York,

London, and Scotland wanted to buy cattle cheaply in the West and resell them to eastern buyers at a profit. Money poured into the West and increased the number of cattle on the ranges of Montana and Wyoming.

The Life of the Cowboy

Being a cowboy was not glamorous. Drudgery and routine marked ranch life. Cowboys worked fourteen-hour days with death near if the cattle stampeded. Much of what they did—riding the line, tending sick cattle, and mending fences—consisted of grinding physical labor in a harsh environment. One of every seven was African American. Former slaves from ranches in Texas or fugitives from the oppression in the South, these black cowboys gained a living but were not granted social equality. Other cowboys included Hispanics and Native Americans, and they also faced discrimination. From the Hispanic *vaqueros* and the Native Americans, other cowboys learned the techniques of breaking horses and the complex skills of managing cattle. Western development involved a subtle interaction of cultures that few whites understood.

The End of the Cattle Boom

The boom years did not last. As the ranges became overstocked in 1885 and 1886, prices for western cattle fell from thirty dollars to less than ten dollars. Then came the "hard winter" of 1886–1887. Thousands of cattle died in the blizzards. Before prices rose, investors from the East and Great Britain, including the young Theodore Roosevelt, lost all they had. Nine million cows in Wyoming Territory in 1886 had fallen to three million nine years later. The cattle industry became a more rational, routinized business.

Ranchers in the West faced other challenges. Sheep raisers moved onto the range and discovered that sheep could graze more economically than cattle. Range wars between cattle and sheep growers broke out in Arizona and Wyoming. In the long run, however, sheep raising proved to be a viable business, and by 1900, there were some 30 million sheep on western ranges.

Farming on the Great Plains

During the 1880s, hundreds of thousands of farmers swept onto the Great Plains. Advertising by the railroad companies drew them from Midwestern states and from northern Europe. Advertising said that land, water, and opportunity abounded. The Homestead Act of 1862 gave farmers public land, which they could use and eventually own. In practice, the 160-acre unit of the Homestead Act was too small for successful

The actual routine of work in the range cattle business was more deadening than glamorous. Here a group of cowboys makes camp after a long day of herding steers. Low pay and difficult conditions stimulated cowboy strikes on more than one occasion.
Reproduced from the Collections of the Library of Congress

farming; a serious settler had to purchase two or three times that acreage. The Homestead Act did not provide the money to go west, file a claim, and acquire the machinery required for profitable farming. Few laborers in the East became homesteaders and most of the settlers had some farming experience.

Congress complicated the land system. Cattle ranchers pushed for the Desert Land Act (1877), which allowed individuals to obtain provisional title to 640 acres in the West at twenty-five cents an acre. Before securing a title, they had to irrigate the land within three years and pay a dollar an acre more. Cowboys filed claims for their employer, threw a bucket of water onto the property, and swore that irrigation had occurred. A year later, lumber interests in the West obtained the Timber and Stone Act (1878). Directed at lands that were "unfit for cultivation" in Washington, Oregon, California, and Nevada, it permitted settlers to acquire up to 160 acres at $2.50 per acre. Lumber companies used false entries to gain title to valuable timber holdings.

Land and Debt

Most settlers obtained their land from the railroads or land companies. Congress had granted the railroads every other 160-acre section of land along their rights of way. Large tracts were closed to settlement until the railroads sold the land to farmers. From 1862 to 1900,

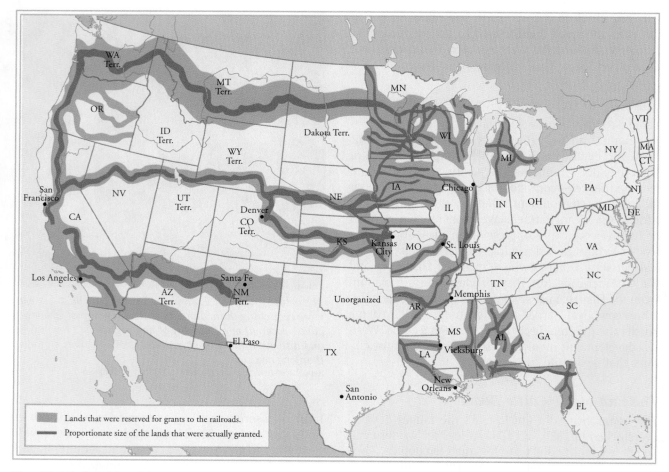

Map 17.2 *Railroad Land Grants*
To encourage the building of railroads across the West and to a lesser degree in the South, Congress and the states made sizable land grants in alternate sections to the rail lines. This map indicates how large these grants were and how they influenced patterns of settlement.

land companies acquired almost 100 million acres from railroads or the government. Other lands had been granted to eastern states to support their agricultural colleges under the Morrill Land-Grant Act of 1862. These western holdings went into the hands of speculators who purchased the lands, as did the land of Native Americans that had been sold off to white buyers.

Farmers had to purchase their land at prices that often ranged between five and ten dollars per acre. To buy the land, the farmers borrowed from loan companies in the East and Midwest. Interest rates on the resulting mortgages were as high as 25 percent annually. As long as land values rose and crop prices remained profitable, the farmers made the needed payments. When prices fell, however, they faced economic ruin.

Fences and Water

Industrial growth and technological advances made farming possible in the West. Joseph Glidden of Illinois devised the practical form of barbed wire in 1873. Soon Glidden's invention came to the attention of the Washburn and Moen Company of Massachusetts, which developed a machine to produce barbed wire. By 1880, some 80 million pounds had been produced and the price of fencing stood at ten dollars per pound. Improved plows, the cord binder for baling hay, and grain silos also aided western farming. During the 1880s, steam-powered threshers for wheat and corn-husking machines were developed.

Machines alone could not provide enough water for farming. West of the ninety-eighth meridian, which ran through the Dakotas, Nebraska, Kansas,

Howard Ruede
Sod-House Days, 1877

The settlement of the Great Plains often required the use of unfamiliar materials to create shelter. In this document, a settler in Kansas details for his relatives in Pennsylvania in 1877 how sod houses were constructed. The author, Howard Ruede, does not discuss how the sod house must have smelled to its inhabitants.

Perhaps you will be interested in the way a sod house is built. Sod is the most available material, in fact, the only material the homesteader has at hand, unless he happens to be one of the fortunates who secured a creek claim with timber suitable for house logs.

Occasionally a new comer has a "bee," and the neighbors for miles around gather at his claim and put up his house in a day. . . . The women come too, and while the men lay up the sod walls, they prepare dinner for the crowd, and have a very sociable hour at noon. A house put up in this way is very likely to settle and get out of shape, but it is seldom deserted for that reason. . . .

When the prairie is thoroughly soaked by rain or snow is the best time for breaking sod for building. The regulation thickness is 2 1/2 inches, buffalo sod preferred on account of its superior toughness. The furrow slices are laid flat and as straight as a steady-walking team can be driven. These furrow slices, 12 inches wide, are cut with a sharp spade into 18-inch lengths, and carefully handled as they are laid in the wall, one length reaching across the wall, which rises rapidly even when the builders are green hands. Care must be taken to break joints and bind the corners of the house. "Seven feet to the square" [top of the wall] is the rule, as the wall is likely to settle a good deal, especially if the sod is very wet when laid. The door and window frames are set in place first and the wall built around them. Building such a house is hard work.

At first these sod houses are unplastered, and this is thought perfectly all right, but such a house is somewhat cold in the winter, as the crevices between the sods admit some cold air; so some of the houses are plastered with a kind of "native lime," made of sand and a very sticky native clay. This plaster is very good unless it happens to get wet. In a few of the houses this plaster is whitewashed, and this helps the looks very much. Some sod houses are mighty comfortable places to go into in cold weather, and it don't take much fire to keep them warm. I will have to be contented with a very modest affair for a while, but perhaps I can improve it later. (P. 596)

Source *The American Heritage History of The Confident Years*, pp. 156–157, taken from Howard Ruede, *Sod-House Days* (Columbia University Press, 1937).

Oklahoma, and Texas, fewer than twenty inches of rain fell annually. Efforts to irrigate the land with the waters that ran from the Rocky Mountains worked in certain areas, but the region lacked adequate rivers. Ordinary wells did not reach the waters far below the surface. Windmills offered a possible solution but the high cost of drilling and installing a windmill made it too expensive. The most practical technique was "dry farming," cultivation using water that the land retained after rainfall.

Farm Life on the Plains

For the farm families, life on the western farms was a grind. With little wood available, shelter often consisted of a sod house made of bricks of dirt or dried sod. When it rained, the house became a mixture of mud and straw. To keep warm in the winter, the farmers burned buffalo chips (droppings) or dried sunflower plants. Grasshoppers ruined crops, animals trampled fields, and the weather was always uncertain.

$\mathcal{P}$ICTURING THE PAST ✦ SOCIAL & CULTURAL EVENTS

THE HARSHNESS OF FARM LIFE

Kansas State Historical Society

This picture of a farm woman and her daughter collecting Buffalo chips in Kansas conveys a striking image of the emptiness of the Great Plains at the end of the nineteenth century and the ways in which settlers had to adapt to a harsh, new environment. Given the photographic equipment of this time, the two figures were posed for maximum effect—the hardworking mother with her wheelbarrow full of buffalo and cattle chips, and the small daughter with her white doll. Behind them, the plains stretch endlessly away. Nonetheless, whatever its arranged qualities, the photo evokes a moment when traditional rural life met the immensity of a semiarid landscape. The crops that this woman and her husband produced then had to compete in a world market of falling prices. So the farm families who experienced these challenges would be the constituency for the farm protest movement called Populism that emerged in the late part of the 1880s.

The burdens of farmwork fell hardest on women. "I never knew Mama to be idle," the daughter of one farm woman recalled. The child of another farm woman remembered, "Bake day, mending day. A certain day for a certain thing. That is what I remember, those special days that my ma had." Amid the endless spaces, women labored on small plots of land, sustained by a network of friends and neighbors. Some women achieved a degree of independence in the male-dominated West. They operated farms, taught school, ran boardinghouses, and participated in politics and cultural life.

The Chinese in the West

Chinese immigrants came to California during the 1840s and 1850s to work the gold mines. They then constructed the transcontinental railroads in the 1860s. Energetic and thrifty, the Chinese soon engaged in manufacturing enterprises and farming. White Californians reacted. Laws barred the Chinese from professions in which they competed with whites. A movement to ban Chinese immigration grew. An 1868 treaty with China had guaranteed free access to Chinese immigrants to the United States. In 1880, the United States pressured China to change the treaty to grant it authority to regulate Chinese immigration. The Chinese Exclusion Act of 1882 barred Chinese entry into the United States for ten years.

From Territories to States

By the late 1880s, some of the western territories were ready for statehood. The territorial system had transferred eastern political ideas and values to the West and integrated settlers into the national political structure. In 1889 and 1890, Congress admitted the Dakotas, Montana, Washington, Idaho, and Wyoming into the Union.

Ranchers and settlers had overcome natural obstacles, political difficulties, and economic problems to build new societies on the Great Plains. Their efforts had created an elaborate economic and environmental system that linked the city and the country in mutually interdependent ways. By the end of the 1880s, however, the process of development stalled as farmers failed to achieve the anticipated prosperity. Crop prices fell, and the debts that settlers owed became an ever greater burden. Farm protest stirred in the West while similar anger marked the South in the same period.

The New South

The presidential election of 1876 ended what remained of Reconstruction. Democrats took over state governments in South Carolina, Louisiana, and Florida. In both the North and the South, the Democrats believed that white supremacy and limited government were the basic principles of political life. The bitter memories of Radical Reconstruction and the need to maintain the South as "a white man's country" made the Democrats dominant among white southerners. Not all southerners became Democrats, however. Blacks voted Republican, as did whites in the southern mountain regions. Independents and others cooperated with Republicans against the Democrats.

The men who took over the state governments in the South believed that they had "redeemed" the region from the mistaken Republican experiment in multiracial politics. Their policies, they claimed, lacked the corruption and waste of their Republican predecessors. In reality, the record of these politicians was worse as scandals and frauds marred the Redeemer administrations.

The Redeemers were a diverse lot. There were plantation owners, a generous assortment of one-time Confederate officers, and aspiring capitalists who sought a more urban and developed South. This coalition dominated the politics of many southern states throughout the 1880s, though they could agree on only the most general (and vague) principles. Slavery had vanished, never to return, but white supremacy remained entrenched.

Redeemers faced some opposition in the 1880s. In Virginia, the size of the public debt became a central issue, with William Mahone campaigning against using tax money to pay off out-of-state creditors. Mahone and his allies also advocated more money for public schools and other state services. These "Readjusters" even attracted some black voters. As a result, Democrats intimidated black voters from supporting Mahone's party. Soon the Readjuster movement had been defeated, in part by rigged elections and stuffed ballot boxes.

A key theme in the South during these years was embodied in the phrase "the New South" which argued that the region should welcome industrialization and economic expansion. An Atlanta newspaper editor named Henry Grady became the biggest backer of the idea. He thrilled northern audiences when he said, in 1886, that the South would soon have "a hundred farms for every plantation, fifty homes for every palace, and a diversified industry that meets the complex needs of this complex age." All over the region, steel mills, textile factories, and railroads arose.

The Industrial South

Manufacturing capacity expanded between 1870 and 1900. In the major cotton producing states of South Carolina, Georgia, Alabama, Mississippi, and Louisiana, capital invested in manufacturing increased about tenfold between 1869 and 1889. Southern railroads expanded during the postwar period; by 1880, there were 19,430 miles of track, double the total in 1860. Other key industries grew during this decade as well. Southern forests fell to satisfy the growing national demand for lumber. Almost 3 million board feet of yellow pine were produced in 1879 by crews working under dangerous conditions for less than a dollar per day. The region's ample deposits of iron ore stimulated the expansion of the iron and coal industries. Production of iron ore rose from 397,000 tons in 1880 to almost 2 million tons twenty years later. Birmingham, Alabama, became a center of the burgeoning southern iron industry. Large amounts of coal were mined in the southern Appalachian region of West Virginia and Virginia.

Before the Civil War, tobacco had been popular as something to chew, smoke in a pipe, or use as a cigar. During the war, northern soldiers tried the variety of bright leaf tobacco grown in North Carolina, and demand for Bull Durham and other products of the area increased. During the 1880s, James Buchanan Duke developed a practical cigarette-making machine. Production costs fell rapidly, and cigarette use skyrocketed. By the end of the 1880, Duke's company made more than 800 million cigarettes annually. Americans adopted smoking as an addictive habit.

The cotton textile industry also expanded. Employees of the cotton mills rose from about 16,000 in 1880 to more than 36,000 ten years later. Demand for southern products spurred the industry. Lower labor costs made southern mills competitive. Women and children labored in these clothing factories; often whole families worked to provide basic subsistence.

Industrialism led to greater prosperity for the South. New cities and towns sprang up as the South's economy expanded. Those who worked in the factories and mills bore the burden of progress. Wages were often low and conditions crude. Tobacco workers in North Carolina earned around a hundred dollars a year. In the cotton mills an average workweek might be more than sixty hours for wages that could be as low as fifteen cents a day. Influential southerners resisted arguments against child labor, even as others tried to end the practice.

Problems of Southern Agriculture

Southern agriculture faced serious problems after the Civil War. The success or failure of farming depended on cotton. Southern cotton farmers produced 3,111,000 bales of cotton in 1870; ten years later production had risen to 5,709,000 bales. Although newspaper editors and publicists urged farmers to grow other crops, few took this advice. Cotton rarely failed, caused less depletion of the soil, and brought a higher price per acre than any other crop.

World production of cotton was increasing, however, and prices fell between 1870 to 1885, rose somewhat at the end of the decade, and plunged again dur-

ing the 1890s. Unable to increase their productivity to make money despite lower prices, cotton farmers were debt ridden and dependent.

To make money, cotton farmers needed a reliable supply of cheap labor to pick the crop. With the end of slavery, the supply of field hands became uncertain. Whites held most of the land while blacks had less land and were forced to sell their labor. The result was a system that combined sharecropping, tenant farming, and the "furnish merchant" who provided the farmers with the "furnish" (whatever was needed) to get them through the year.

Sharecroppers received as their wage a designated proportion of the crops they produced. The landlord or owner controlled the crop until some of it was allocated to the sharecropper. Tenant farmers, on the other hand, owned the crop until it was sold. They then paid to the owner of the property either cash or a fixed amount of the crop. Both tenants and "croppers" depended on a local merchant for food, clothing, farm equipment, and crop supplies until their harvests were completed. To safeguard the merchant's investment, southern states passed crop lien laws that gave the merchant a claim on the crop if a farmer could not pay off his debt. Thus, the farmers in the South, both black and white, were in a cycle of debt first to the landlord and then to the "furnish" merchant. In bad years the farmers did not make enough to get out of debt. The interest that the merchants charged was often as much as 50 percent, and they exercised a degree of supervision over the croppers and tenants that recalled the era of slavery.

A Colonial Economy

The South had long lacked adequate capital, and losing the war made the situation worse. The National Banking Act of 1863 required banks to have up to $50,000 in capital and to be located in a small town to get a national bank charter. Few southern communities qualified, and so prospective borrowers competed for scarce local credit. Since national banks could not make mortgage loans, even those that opened in the South were of little help to the southern farm population. At the same time the national government followed monetary policies that promoted deflation. The South's lack of capital worsened during the 1880s.

Southern farmers believed that they faced an economic conspiracy. The furnish merchant represented the power of northern bankers, international cotton marketing companies, and industrialism. The cotton farmers tolerated these conditions because there appeared to be no other way to participate in the South's burgeoning economy. By the end of the decade, however, the problems of perpetual debt were becoming acute and political discontent mounted.

Segregation

Racial segregation evolved slowly but steadily across the South despite the national Civil Rights Act in 1875, which prohibited racial discrimination in public accommodations. In the *Civil Rights Cases* (1883), the Supreme Court ruled that under the Fourteenth Amendment Congress could prohibit only *state* actions that violated civil rights. For individual acts of racial discrimination in restaurants, hotels, and other public places, it was up to the states to ban discrimination. Southern states chose instead to allow and encourage racial segregation as a preferred policy.

During this period, segregation lacked the rigidity and legal power that it acquired later. In some southern states, black citizens used railroads and streetcars on a roughly equal basis with whites. Elsewhere in the region travel facilities were segregated. Under the regimes of the Redeemers, black men voted in some numbers before 1890, retained the right to hold office, could be members of a jury, and were permitted to own weapons.

Whatever opportunities were open to black citizens existed alongside an overall system of racial discrimination and bigotry. Black men often found their choices at the polls limited to approved white candidates, and if too many African Americans sought to cast ballots, white violence erupted. By the end of the 1880s, growing numbers of white politicians believed that blacks should be barred from the electoral process altogether.

Thus, for African Americans in the South, the fifteen years after the end of Reconstruction began with hopeful signs, but had a bleak outcome. Black families wanted to rent farms and work land for themselves rather than return to the plantation system. They believed that growing cotton in the delta of Mississippi gave them a chance to participate in that region's expanding economy. The area saw an influx of blacks at the end of the 1880s as African American men competed for new jobs and the opportunity to acquire land. Sharecropping and tenant farming were also present, but in this part of the South for a brief period there was a chance for black economic advancement.

African Americans created networks of black churches and endeavored to educate their children.

Booker T. Washington's leadership of the Tuskegee Institute in Alabama, which began in 1881, symbolized what education and training could do. Growing up with no direct experience of slavery, a new generation of southern blacks demanded their legal rights. When older blacks warned of the possible consequences of such behavior, the younger generation answered that "we are now qualified, and being the equal of whites, should be treated as such."

Some African Americans preferred to get out of the South if they could. At the end of the 1870s, rumors spread that Kansas offered a safer haven. During 1879, some 20,000 blacks, known as Exodusters because they were coming out of bondage as the children of Israel had in the Exodus, arrived in Kansas. More settled in the cities than actually farmed on the prairie. Hundreds of thousands of other blacks left the South in these years.

At the end of the 1880s, white spokesmen for the South boasted of the region's progress. The South produced more cotton than ever before; towns were growing throughout the region; industries had developed; and tens of thousands of black southerners had accumulated property. Yet there were danger signs. State legislatures wrote new laws to segregate first-class railroad passengers by race. Farmers who grew more cotton each year without getting ahead organized to oppose the power of merchants and railroads. Tenants and laborers of both races seemed restless and in constant motion. Racial violence reached unprecedented levels. Would the New South be any better than the Old?

LIFE AND CULTURE DURING THE 1880S

The daily rhythms of American life were those of the country and the small town. There were 50,155,783 people in the United States in that year. More than 70 percent of them lived in "rural territory." Another 3.5 million people lived in towns and villages with fewer than 5,000 inhabitants. Of the nearly 10 million households in the nation, the most common family consisted of a husband, a wife, and their three children. The father worked the family farm or at a job in an office or at the factory. The mother stayed at home and did the endless round of cleaning, cooking, sewing, and shopping. The children attended schools near their home or, in less prosperous families, labored to bring home income.

PICTURING THE PAST ✦ SOCIAL & CULTURAL EVENTS

A REFRESHING PAUSE

© Bettmann / Corbis

The continuities of American life are often best revealed in the routines of everyday existence. This advertisement for Coca-Cola attests to the enduring appeal of carbonated soft drinks to thirsty Americans and the devices advertisers have used to pitch their products. The well-dressed, respectable young woman quaffing the last drop of her coke in the 1880s, while watching the viewer outside the ad, would become one hundred and twenty years later a gyrating teenage heart throb hawking the same brand of sugar-laden refreshment. Only the price of the drink now seems historic. In their own bubbly way, soft drinks sparkled into one of the shared experiences of Americans in an industrialized, homogenized culture. Past advertisements from the pages of newspapers and magazines are thus one of the best windows into how Americans lived generations ago in ways that we still recognize.

Their Daily Bread

Americans ate large meals. For the middle class, breakfast often included fried eggs, biscuits, wheatcakes, potatoes, and steak. In 1878, John Harvey Kellogg invented a mixture of cornmeal, oatmeal, and wheat flour that, when baked into biscuits, became "granola." The afternoon and evening meals were also substantial. Among the upper classes a fancy dinner might provide ten or eleven courses of meats, fish, salads, and starchy foods. The poor found whatever they could scrape together.

Industrialism changed the way Americans ate. Millions of tin cans made vegetables and fruits available at the twist of a can opener. In large cities fresh meats became more accessible as the Armour meat company moved beef in iced railroad cars. The saltine cracker, shipped by the National Biscuit Company and other firms, provided a fresh and crisp product. Brand names told Americans that "Uneeda" biscuit and a portly Quaker figure appeared on containers of Quaker Oats. "Certified milk," freer from harmful bacteria than natural milk, became a staple; by the end of the 1880s, milk was being pasteurized. In 1886, an Atlanta druggist, John Pemberton, mixed syrup extracted from the cola nut with carbonated water and called it "Coca Cola." A year later he sold out to Asa Candler, who made Coca-Cola a household word.

Power for the Home

In the homes of city dwellers, gas and electricity provided new sources of power. No longer did people have to chop and gather wood, clean fireplaces, and maintain a multitude of candles and lamps. Running water replaced water drawn by hand. Refrigeration reduced the need for daily shopping; ready-made clothing relieved housewives of constant sewing chores. While machines reduced the burdens of the husband and children, the duties of the wife were still time-consuming. However fuel was supplied, she had to prepare the meals. Despite the availability of canned fruits and vegetables, many women canned and preserved. Sewing, cleaning, and household maintenance were done without the assistance of the male members of the family.

To a large extent, the wife and mother found herself alone in the house each day as the husband went to work and the children went to school.

The Middle-Class Family

Middle- and upper-class woman who could afford to hire domestics ended their child-rearing years earlier and gained more time for themselves. New magazines catered to this audience, including the *Ladies' Home Journal* in 1883 and *Good Housekeeping* in 1885. Women joined voluntary associations with other women of their class. Women's clubs spread during the 1870s and 1880s, and in time these groups sponsored middle-class social reform. The Young Women's Christian Association, founded in 1867, the Woman's Christian Temperance Union, established in 1874, and the Association of Collegiate Alumnae, formed in 1882, gave tangible expression to desires for association and service.

The children were educated in schools that were locally controlled and designed to instill patriotism and moral values. "We went to school to work," remembered one student; "our playing was done elsewhere." City children attended school for some 180 to 200 days a year. In rural areas, however, the demands of farmwork often limited school attendance to under one hundred days a year. Courses included arithmetic, the history of the United States, geography, reading, grammar, and spelling. Many students read the famous series of *McGuffey's Readers,* which stressed religion, obedience, and family. In the better school systems, students received instruction in Latin and at least one other foreign language; less attention was given to the sciences. For new immigrants, the school system taught the values of the dominant culture and prepared their children for citizenship.

Although only a small percentage of students attended high schools and even fewer pursued a college degree, the late nineteenth century brought rapid growth for institutions of higher learning. Wealthy businessmen created private universities such as Johns Hopkins in Baltimore (1876), the University of Chicago (1890), and Stanford in California (1891). State universities expanded in the Midwest and were created in the South. Modeled on the German educational system, these universities established academic departments and stressed research and graduate training. Higher education in the United States became increasingly professionalized. Teachers had to possess graduate degrees and prove themselves through research and publication.

Leisure in the 1880s

At Chautauqua meetings (named after the lake in western New York state where the program began) held in the summer, citizens gathered for ten-week sessions, read long lists of suggested and required books, and listened to lectures. Participants waved white handkerchiefs to show enthusiasm. Appealing to a wider audience were the circuses and Wild West shows. The first three-ring circus debuted in Manhattan in 1883, and P. T. Barnum, with his "greatest show on earth," became the entertainment equivalent to the giants of industry. During the same year, William "Buffalo Bill" Cody assembled a troupe of former Pony Express riders, stage coach robbers, and riding artists that toured the United States and Europe. Vaudeville, a form of entertainment consisting of a series of singers, comedians, and specialty acts, was a favorite of urban audiences.

Baseball was already popular. The National League, founded in 1876, entered an era of prosperity after 1880. Star players like Adrian "Cap" Anson of the Chicago White Stockings became household names. Anson's team won five pennants in ten years; its fastest player was Bill Sunday, later a popular religious evangelist. Baseball fans, known as "kranks," delighted in baiting the umpire. In the 1880s, many new rules were adopted, including the three strikes, four-balls format; overhand pitching; and substitutions of players. Attendance figures rose, with as many as 30,000 people turning out for games on Memorial Day. Sunday contests were banned, as was the sale of beer at ballparks. In 1888, Ernest L. Thayer wrote his famous poem "Casey at the Bat" and several generations of schoolchildren learned to recite how there was "no joy in Mudville" when "mighty" Casey struck out at the crucial moment. It was a golden age for baseball.

Literate citizens found an abundance of reading for varied tastes. The magazines of the day, some 3,300 in all, carried articles on every possible subject. Americans also read popular novels such as Lew Wallace's *Ben Hur* (1880), an engrossing blend of religion, ancient history, and a good story. The more serious novels of the decade included *The Rise of Silas Lapham* (1885), by William Dean Howells and *The Bostonians* (1885) by William James. Probably the most important literary work of the 1880s was *The Adventures of Huckleberry Finn,* written by Samuel L. Clemens ("Mark Twain") in 1884. In it, Clemens uses an adventure in which a boy helps a runaway slave to create a chronicle of the nation's experience with slavery, freedom, the wonders of childhood, and the ambiguities of adult life. The most popular writer of his era, Twain captured the

American art in the 1880s sought to portray the world in realistic terms. Thomas Eakins went into the operating theater of a medical school to show how an operation was conducted. Medicine was becoming scientific and professional, qualities that are shown in the attentive students, the authoritative surgeon, and the team of aids and a nurse in this painting titled The Agnew Clinic.
Courtesy of the University of Pennsylvania Art Collection, Philadelphia, Pennsylvania

images of a vanishing America of Mississippi riverboats, small towns, and the social tensions that lay beneath the tranquil surface.

Visual arts also fascinated Americans. Private acquisitions of paintings grew; about 150 such collections were in existence in 1880. Museums were founded in St. Louis, Detroit, and Cincinnati between 1879 and 1885, continuing a trend that had begun earlier in Boston, Philadelphia, and New York. Notable artists included Frederic Remington, who had gone west in 1880 to improve his health and arranged to accompany the army on campaigns against the Indians. His evocations of frontier life, published in *Harper's Weekly*, made him famous. Two of the most important figures of the decade were Thomas Eakins and John Singer Sargent. Eakins lived and worked in Philadelphia where he was forced to resign from the Pennsylvania Academy for using a naked male model in a class of female students. His most notable works included *The Swimming Hole* and *The Agnew Clinic.* Sargent became famous for portraits such as *The Daughters of Edward Boit* and *Mrs. Edward Burkhardt and Daughter Louise.*

During this era private institutions, universities, and the federal government encouraged the diffusion of scientific information. One scientist of the time,

Josiah Willard Gibbs, had became world famous for his work in theoretical physics and physical chemistry. The American Association for the Advancement of Science resumed operation after the war; other scientific societies expanded after 1877 as well. From the industrial laboratories of General Electric and other corporate giants to the facilities of research universities, the United States forged a partnership between science and technology that laid the basis for future innovations.

Two symbols were the Brooklyn Bridge in New York and the Statue of Liberty in New York City. Completed in 1883, the bridge allowed 11 million people to cross the East River from Brooklyn to Manhattan in its first year of operation. It took John A. Roebling and his son Washington Roebling twelve years to construct the longest suspension bridge in the world, but the resulting structure demonstrated what the new processes of industrialism could accomplish. The Statue of Liberty was dedicated three years later on October 28, 1886. The work of a French sculptor, Frédéric-Auguste Bartholdi, it was sponsored by a public fund-raising effort in the United States; the statue was placed on Bedloe's Island, now called Liberty Island, at the entrance to New York Harbor. Out of the campaign to raise money came the celebrated poem by Emma Lazarus that promised the "golden door" of opportunity to Europe's "huddled masses yearning to breathe free."

Politics and Public Policy, 1877–1887

In politics, both of the major parties sought to overcome an electoral stalemate. The Republicans won the presidency in 1876, 1880, and 1888; the Democrats triumphed in 1884 and 1892. Neither party controlled both houses of Congress on a regular basis. The Republicans had control twice, from 1881 to 1883 and 1889 to 1891; the Democrats only once, from 1893 to 1895. Outside the South, elections often were close and hard-fought.

Americans lavished time on their politics. Only men took part in elections, and most of them were whites. (A few black men voted in the South.) Those who did vote turned out at a record rate. About eight out of every ten eligible voters went to the polls. Women could vote only in Wyoming and Utah. When they were not voting, Americans listened to long speeches by candidates and read about politics in the extended stories that partisan newspapers printed.

Moral and religious values shaped the way that men voted and helped define which party won their support. The prohibition of alcohol, the role of religious and sectarian education in the public schools, and the observance of the Sabbath were hotly contested questions. Republicans favored government intervention to support Protestant values; Democrats thought the government should keep out of such subjects.

The most prominent national issues involved the kind of money Americans used, how the government raised revenue, and who served in the government itself. Some Americans believed that for every dollar in circulation an equal amount of gold should be stored in the Treasury or in banks. Others contended that the government should issue more money by coining silver into currency on an equal basis with gold. Debtors favored inflation, which made their loans easier to pay; creditors liked the deflation that raised the value of their dollars. The South and West wanted inflation; the Northeast and developed portions of the Midwest preferred the existing financial system.

Other major concerns were taxation and the protective tariff. There was no federal income tax; the government raised money from excise taxes on alcohol and tobacco, and customs duties (taxes) on imported goods. The protective tariff became a hot political issue. Those who favored it believed that high customs duties protected American industry, helped workers, and developed the economy. Republicans championed the protective system; Democrats countered that tariffs raised prices, hurt the consumer, and made government too expensive. The South liked the Democratic case, but Republicans found support from business and labor.

At bottom the argument was over the size and role of the national government. Should the government stimulate the economy, as the Republicans wanted, or allow natural forces to operate, as the Democrats advocated? Finally, there was the question of who should serve in government. Politicians preferred the "spoils" or patronage system. Allocating government jobs to partisan supporters enabled them to strengthen their party. Critics of the patronage system called it a corrupt and inefficient way to choose government officials. They favored a civil service, in which individuals, chosen through competitive examinations, would administer government without being subject to partisan pressure. Civil service reformers urged Congress to write laws to reduce the power of patronage during the 1870s, but incumbents of both parties liked the existing system.

From Hayes to Arthur

The Republicans began the period with Rutherford B. Hayes in the White House. He pushed for civil service reform and resisted pressure from Congress to base his appointments on candidates that Congress favored. He vetoed the inflationary Bland-Allison Act (1878), which called for monthly government purchases of silver, but Congress overrode his veto. Hayes had promised to serve only one term. To succeed him, the Republicans nominated James A. Garfield of Ohio, and Chester Alan Arthur of New York as his running mate. The Democratic candidate was a former Civil War general named Winfield Scott Hancock. After an intense campaign that focused on the tariff issue, Garfield won by a narrow plurality in the popular vote and a larger margin in the electoral college.

Garfield's presidency lasted only four months. On July 2, he went to the Washington railroad station to leave for a vacation. Presidents were not well guarded at this time, and a crazed assassin shot Garfield. He died on September 19, and Chester Alan Arthur became president. Much to everyone's surprise, Arthur, who was widely regarded as a mediocrity, proved a competent chief executive. During his single term, Congress passed the Pendleton Act (1883), which created a civil service system and limited the practice of assessing campaign contributions from federal employees. The act also established rules about where and how government officials could raise campaign funds. Arthur asked Congress to consider downward revision of the tariff. The lawmakers responded with the Mongrel Tariff of 1883 (so called because it pleased no one), which generally raised protective duties. The president vetoed a Chinese Exclusion Law, but after Congress revised it slightly, Arthur signed it.

Blaine Versus Cleveland, 1884

Arthur was a caretaker president. In 1884, the party selected its most popular figure, James G. Blaine of Maine, to run for the presidency. An excellent speaker and an advocate of the protective tariff, Blaine had been a potential presidential candidate in 1876 and 1880. Unfortunately for his chances in the general election, questions had been raised about his political honesty. His enemies said that Blaine had helped railroads while he was Speaker of the House in return for money (see Chapter 16). Despite these problems, the Republicans nominated him enthusiastically.

To run against Blaine, the Democrats selected the governor of New York, Grover Cleveland. Cleveland had risen from political obscurity. He was a lawyer in Buffalo, New York, when he was chosen to be its mayor in 1881. A year later he was the Democratic nominee for governor. Elected because of

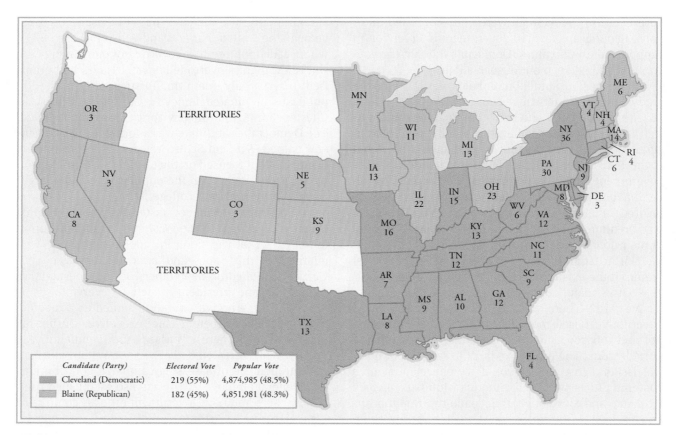

Candidate (Party)	Electoral Vote	Popular Vote
Cleveland (Democratic)	219 (55%)	4,874,985 (48.5%)
Blaine (Republican)	182 (45%)	4,851,981 (48.3%)

Map 17.3 *The Election of 1884*

This map illustrates the tight presidential race between Grover Cleveland for the Democrats and James G. Blaine for the Republicans in 1884. Amid talk of scandal and corruption, the two parties battled to a virtual dead heat. Cleveland carried New York and eked out a narrow victory.

View an animated version of this map or related maps at http://history.wadsworth.com/passages2e.

Republican disunity, Cleveland proved to be a popular state executive. The national Democrats wanted a fresh face, and the stocky Cleveland (relatives called him "Uncle Jumbo") was an attractive blend of honesty, conservatism, and independence. His campaign suffered a setback when it was revealed that some years earlier he had accepted responsibility for an illegitimate child in Buffalo. Cleveland acknowledged his part in the episode, however, and his candor defused the issue. Meanwhile, the issue of Blaine's public morality worked against the Republicans.

Cleveland was helped by the defection of upper-class Republicans in the Northeast. These voters, calling themselves "Mugwumps" (an Indian word meaning "Big Chief"), threw their support to the Democrats. The outcome of the election was very close, reflecting the even balance of the major parties. Cleveland carried the South, New York, New Jersey, Connecticut, and Indiana, receiving 219 electoral votes to Blaine's 182.

Cleveland in Office

Cleveland took office on March 4, 1885. During his first term, he established that his party could govern, and his political opponents gave him grudging respect. For the Democrats, however, Cleveland proved to be a mixed blessing. He was slow to turn Republican officeholders out of office, and he alienated many Democrats with his patronage policies. Still, Republicans made few gains in the congressional elections of 1886, and Cleveland seemed to have good prospects for a second term in 1888.

In December 1887, hoping to establish an issue for his reelection campaign, the president devoted his annual message to Congress (known as the State of the Union message) to tariff reform. With a surplus in the Treasury, Cleveland believed that the tariff could be reduced, leading to lower prices for consumers. The Republican reaction to Cleveland's move was one of delight. Now the 1888 election could be fought on the issue that united the Republicans and divided the Democrats.

With the stage set for the election, the stalemated politics of the 1880s slowly broke up. For the next twelve years, American politics would experience a turbulent and decisive period of change and partisan realignment.

CONCLUSION

The 1880s were lived out in the shadow of the recently concluded Civil War. As one veteran, Oliver Wendell Holmes, Jr., said in 1884, "Through our great good fortunes, in our youth our hearts were touched with fire." Having experienced so much as young people, between 1877 and 1887 they sought harmony, prosperity, and stability. They pursued industrialism and its benefits with intense energy. Their achievements—in terms of railroads and factories built, inventions developed, and society transformed—were striking.

Yet the transformation of the American economy came at a cost. In 1887, the United States was characterized by deep social divisions and economic inequality. Regional differences remained unresolved. Industrialism had produced serious changes in the environment that would imperil the natural resources available to future generations. The animosity between capitalists and workers smoldered behind a facade of calm. The nation had yet to work out the tensions that had accompanied industrial growth. That task would be addressed in the succeeding decade in a setting in which the rise of the American city would grow to be as important a force for change as industrialism had been in the years after 1877.

The first Democratic president since the start of the Civil War, Grover Cleveland, despite claims that he had fathered an illegitimate child as a younger man, won a close victory over James G. Blaine in 1884. He then demonstrated that his party could govern at a time of intense partisanship and even balance between the two major parties. This cartoon shows Cleveland reacting to the revelations about his personal difficulties.
From the Collections of the Library of Congress

Recommended Readings

Ayers, Edward. *The Promise of the New South* (1992). A fine modern treatment of the South in the years after Reconstruction ended.

Calhoun, Charles W. *The Gilded Age: Essays on the Origins of Modern America* (1996). A valuable assortment of excellent essays about this period.

Chandler, Alfred D. *The Visible Hand: The Managerial Revolution in American Business* (1977). A detailed examination of how industrial growth occurred.

Cherny, Robert. *American Politics in the Gilded Age, 1868–1900* (1997). A good, brief introduction to the public life of the period.

Edwards, Rebecca. *Angels in the Machinery: Gender in American Party Politics from the Civil War to the Progressive Era* (1997). Shows that women played a much larger part in political affairs than earlier historians had realized.

Porter, Glenn. *The Rise of Big Business, 1860–1920* (1992). An excellent short introduction to the economic trends of the Gilded Age.

Saum, Lewis O. *The Popular Mood of America, 1860–1890* (1990). Considers how the nation responded to social change.

Schlereth, Thomas J. *Victorian America: Transformations in Everyday Life, 1876–1915* (1991). A good survey of the impact of the changes brought by industrialism on the lives of Americans.

Summers, Mark Wahlgren. *The Gilded Age, or The Hazard of New Functions* (1997). A lively romp through the politics and leaders of the late nineteenth century.

American Journey Online and InfoTrac College Edition

Visit the source collections at http://ajaccess.wadsworth.com and infotrac.thomsonlearning.com and use the Search function with the following key terms to explore documents, images, audio and video clips, articles, and commentary related to the material in this chapter.

Rutherford B. Hayes
Andrew Carnegie
Thomas Edison
Geronimo

John D. Rockefeller
Alexander Graham Bell
Dawes Act

Additional resources, exercises, and Internet links related to this chapter are available on the American Passages Web site: http://history.wadsworth.com/passages2e

18 URBAN GROWTH AND FARM PROTEST 1887–1893

When the Oklahoma Territory was opened to white homesteaders in April 1889, a wild land rush ensued. This photograph conveys the frenzy with which prospective settlers hurried to establish their claims to the best holdings.

The Granger Collection, New York

Approaching its one hundredth birthday under the Constitution in 1889, the United States faced new problems in its growing cities. Huge gaps existed between the rich and poor. Rural values of the country clashed with the diversity and turbulence of the cities. The political system struggled to adjust to the new demands of the urban population.

The farm problems that had simmered throughout the 1880s also reached a crisis level. In the South and West, angry farmers formed a fresh political organization, the People's party, to make their grievances heard. For Indians and African Americans, the 1890s brought painful reminders of their vulnerability to bigotry and discrimination. By the end of the decade, both rural and urban residents saw the nation on the brink of becoming a world power.

THE NEW URBAN SOCIETY

During 1889, two events occurred in the center of the nation that reflected the persistence of rural ideas and the emergence of urban life. Shortly after Benjamin Harrison became president in March 1889, a climactic moment in the settlement of the West took place. Since the 1820s, the Five Civilized Tribes of Native Americans had lived in what is now Oklahoma. By the 1880s, however, pressure from white settlers to be given access to the territory proved irresistible in Congress. The Dawes Act of 1887 completed the process of stripping the Indians of their rights. President Harrison announced that unoccupied towns be settled beginning on April 22, 1889. One hundred thousand people rushed to acquire the newly available land. Within a few hours, the "Sooners," who entered the territory early, and the "Boomers" (a general name for eager new settlers) had created towns and staked out farms. Other "rushes" went on in the following four years until all the land that the Indians had once controlled was opened to white settlement.

A few months later, in August 1889, Jane Addams and Ellen Gates Starr founded Hull House, a settlement home in a Chicago neighborhood. The theory was simple. College educated young men and women "settled" in houses in the ethnic communities to school local residents in the ways of American life. Like the creators of similar houses that had started in New York a few years earlier, Addams and Starr hoped to develop solutions to the troubling problems of American city life. Hull House and Addams became famous as the settlement house idea grew in popularity among socially conscious, middle-class Americans. Her personal commitment to the experiment reflected

CHRONOLOGY

1888   Edward Bellamy publishes *Looking Backward* • Benjamin Harrison elected president over Grover Cleveland

1889   Oklahoma Territory becomes available for settlement by non-Native Americans • National Farmers Alliance and Industrial Union is organized • Jane Addams establishes Hull House in Chicago • Pan-American Congress held • First electric sewing machine marketed

1890   Congress enacts Sherman Silver Purchase Act, McKinley Tariff, and Sherman Antitrust Act • Mississippi constitutional convention establishes strict segregation laws • William Dean Howells publishes *A Hazard of New Fortunes,* a novel about the Haymarket Affair in 1886 • Republicans suffer large losses in congressional elections; Farmers Alliance makes strong showing • National American Woman Suffrage Association set up • Battle of Wounded Knee • Daughters of the American Revolution founded • Poems by Emily Dickinson published

1891   Queen Liliuokalani comes to power in Hawaii

1892   People's party founded • Homestead strike occurs • Ida Wells-Barnett begins campaigns against lynching • Grover Cleveland defeats Benjamin Harrison in presidential election • Ellis Island opens in New York to receive immigrants

1893   Hawaiian Revolution occurs • Grover Cleveland inaugurated for second term • Mildred Hill publishes song that becomes "Happy Birthday to You" • Columbian Exposition in Chicago

the views of many Americans that the rapid rise of large cities posed new challenges for the nation.

In 1860, Chicago had been the ninth-largest city, with a population of just under 109,000 people living in a seventeen-square-mile area. Thirty years later, Chicago was the second largest city, with 1,099,850 people within an area of 178 square miles. Through Chicago ran the major east-west railroads. To its stockyards came beef cattle from the West, to its elevators grain from the prairie, and to its lumberyards wood from the forests of Wisconsin and Minnesota. Chicago had survived the Great Fire of 1871, and from the ashes had risen the skyscrapers that gave it a distinctive skyline and the ethnic neighborhoods whose residents Hull House attempted to serve.

The Exploding Urban Population

Chicago's expansion typified the rocketing urban population growth. In 1869, only nine cities had more than 100,000 inhabitants; in 1890, there were twenty-eight with such populations. New York City had 1,515,301 residents in 1890; Chicago and Philadelphia had more than 1 million each, with Brooklyn, St. Louis, Boston, and Baltimore next in order.

Americans moved to the cities to escape the routine of "hard work and no holidays" that dominated rural life. Immigrants from Europe, many of them from cities in central and eastern Europe, remained in the large cities after they arrived. Newcomers came to Chicago and New York, worked there for months and years, and then either moved to other cities, returned to the rural areas, or, in the case of some immigrants, went back to their home country.

The Structure of the City

After 1880, American cities grew dramatically. Horse-drawn omnibuses and commuter railroads allowed the cities to spread outward. After the Civil War, the horsecar gave way to cable cars in San Francisco and other hilly cities. However, cable systems were clumsy, expensive, and inefficient; electric streetcars or the trolleys, which ran under overhead wires and moved at speeds of up to ten miles an hour, soon replaced them. Urban transit rapidly became electrified. To avoid traffic jams, some cities ran the streetcars on elevated tracks; others went underground to create subways. The older "walking city" soon disappeared.

As their populations moved from their core, the cities annexed their suburbs. In 1889, Chicago added 133 square miles of surrounding communities. Linked by the new streetcars, various parts of the city became distinguished by the race, income level, and ethnicity of their residents. Within the center of the city, race and ethnicity determined where people lived. The more

The clutter and congestion of the city was one of the hallmarks of the urbanizing of the United States. This scene of Dearborn Street in Chicago conveys some of the bustle and energy of the city as the 1890s began. Transportation by carriages and trolleys was common in the decade before the arrival of the automobile.
The Granger Collection, New York

affluent residents moved as far from the center as they could. Each class, racial, and ethnic group had fewer encounters with people in other sections of the city.

Central business districts emerged. Railroads built terminals; banks and insurance companies located their main offices downtown; and department stores anchored shopping districts. Streetcars brought customers from the suburbs to Macy's in New York, Marshall Field's in Chicago, and Filene's in Boston. In these "palaces of consumption," middle-class women spent their time in leisurely shopping for an array of attractive products. Museums, theaters, and opera houses added to the cultural resources of the industrial city.

Skyscrapers and Tenements

Architects created the *skyscraper* as a practical solution to the need to conduct economic activities in a compressed central business district. Louis Sullivan of Chicago developed techniques that made it possible for buildings to rise higher than the five to ten stories that had been the upper limits of tall structures in the past. Passenger elevators, lighter walls reinforced with iron piers, and a framework of structural steel led to buildings of twenty to forty stories or more. The principle, Sullivan wrote, was that "form follows function." Skyscrapers enabled the business district to accommodate thousands of office workers each day.

The Tenement and Its Residents

The people who crowded into Chicago, New York, Boston, and the other expanding cities between 1880 and 1900 strained the available living space. For the middle and upper classes, apartments were a practical answer. Apartment buildings, some of which were quite expensive, began to replace the single-family home in urban areas.

Poorer city residents lived in the *tenement houses,* six- or seven-story houses built on narrow lots. New York had 20,000 such structures, most of them twenty-five feet wide and one hundred feet deep, with windows only at the front and back. During the late 1870s after legislation mandated that at least some ventilation be provided, "dumbbell tenements" appeared; these had tiny, indented windows along the sides and often provided only crude sanitation facilities. In these buildings, dozens of people were crowded into small, dark rooms. Daily life often spilled out onto the surrounding streets. The buildings looked decent enough to a passerby, but as the novelist William Dean Howells noted, "To be in it, and not have the distance, is to

American artists incorporated the life of the city into their work in the 1890s. In W. Louis Sonntag, Jr.'s, The Bowery at Night, *the elevated railroads that moved people through the city become a striking visual image for the changes that were reshaping the nation's existence.*

W. Louis Sonntag, Jr., The Bowery at Night, 1895. Museum of the City of New York

inhale the stenches of the neglected street, and to catch the yet fouler and dreadfuller poverty-smell which breathes from the open doorways."

Inside the tenement or on the teeming sidewalks, urban residents strained the city's water and sanitation systems. The stench of manure, open sewers, and piled-up garbage filled their nostrils. Smoke from factories and grime from machinery were everywhere. One New York resident said that "the stink is enough to knock you down." Chicago's water systems were taxed to the limit during the 1880s, and residents of Philadelphia described their water as "not only distasteful and unwholesome for drinking, but offensive for bathing purposes."

The Need for Services

The cities expanded their facilities to provide better service. New York City created a system of reservoirs that brought water to the residents from surrounding rivers and lakes. Chicago faced immense difficulties in transporting water from Lake Michigan for drinking needs and providing adequate sanitation. By the end of the century, however, much progress had been made. Among other things, park building became a priority of urban political machines and reformers alike. Although most of the new parks appeared on the outskirts of the city, away from the poorer sections, the amount of parkland in the larger cities doubled during the years from 1888 to 1898.

The New Immigration

The cities grew because people flocked to them from the countryside and from other countries. For the twenty years after 1870, net immigration totaled more than 7.5 million people. Unlike the immigrants from northern and western Europe who had come during the first seventy-five years of the nineteenth century, these "New Immigrants" were mainly from southern and eastern Europe. These Italians, Poles, Hungarians, Russian Jews, and Czechs brought with them languages, lifestyles, and customs that often clashed with those of native-born Americans or earlier immigrants. Marrying within their own ethnic group, speaking their own language, and reading their own newspapers, they created distinctive, vibrant communities within the cities.

Many newcomers first saw the United States when they entered New York Harbor. They were processed at Castle Garden at the Battery in lower Manhattan. By the end of the 1880s, those immigration facilities had become inadequate; they were closed in 1890 and a new, more extensive immigrant station was opened in 1892 on Ellis Island in New York Harbor.

PICTURING THE PAST ✦ SOCIAL & CULTURAL EVENTS

TENEMENT LIFE IN THE GROWING CITIES

The Granger Collection, New York

Documentary photographs became a favored way of depicting social problems at the end of the nineteenth century, and Lewis Hine was one of the most famous practitioners of the technique. His camera went inside the tenements of the growing cities to show the crowded conditions that confronted urban families. In this nicely wallpapered room, a mother minds six small children, most of them under the age of ten. The photograph cannot convey the noise or the smells of the scene, nor the fate that awaits the children in a few years. The older girl on the right will soon have to earn a living to assist the harried mother with the family's upkeep. Yet this family is also a little better off than the more desperate urban poor who do not have metal beds, chairs to make cradles, or this much space for six children.

There the new arrivals were passed through a medical examination and questioned about their economic prospects. Sometimes even their names were changed. One often-told story was that of a German Jew confronted by an inspector who fired a volley of questions at him. When finally asked his name, the man responded in Yiddish: "Schoyn vergessen" (I forget). The inspector heard what the words sounded like and said that "Sean Ferguson" was eligible to enter the United States. Only about 1 percent of potential immigrants were excluded.

Immigrant Life in the United States

The new arrivals made their living any way they could. They provided the labor for city construction gangs that built New York City's subways, the steel mills of Pittsburgh, and the skyscrapers of Chicago. Some men sold fruits and vegetables from pushcarts, others worked as day laborers, and increasing numbers built their own small businesses. Italian immi-

grant women "finished" garments for the clothing industry or made artificial flowers.

Their cultural values and Old World experiences often dictated the jobs that men and women took. Italians preferred steady jobs with a dependable salary that left time for family life. Greeks joined railroad gangs where they could work in the open. Jews became shopkeepers, merchants, and peddlers, the trades that had been open to them in the anti-Semitic world of eastern Europe. Some nationalities, Bohemians and Slovaks for example, allowed women to work as domestic servants; others, such as Jews, Italians, and Greeks, barred women from domestic work outside the home.

The Rise of Ethnic Communities

Ethnic neighborhoods appeared. In New York City, immigrants from Naples lived on Mott Street while Sicilians resided on Prince Street. Churches and synagogues shaped community life. Newcomers formed self-help societies to ease the transition for those who came after them—the Polish National Alliance, the Bohemian-American National Council, and the Hebrew Immigrant Aid Society. They built theaters and concert halls, and created schools to educate their children. Some of the newcomers moved away from their ethnic roots as they prospered; other immigrants soon replaced them. In the Tenth Ward of New York, the Jewish immigrant population in 1900 had a density of 900 people per acre, one of the highest in the world.

The Nativist Reaction

As the communities of immigrants grew, older residents expressed fears about the impact of the newcomers on traditional values and customs. Prejudice and religious intolerance flared. Editors of urban newspapers called immigrants "the very scum and offal of the earth." During the 1880s, the anti-Catholic American Protective Association recruited those for whom the immigrants were a source of fear or economic competition. Its members resolved to limit the role of Catholics in politics. These sentiments that favored "native" Americans (hence "nativist") led to calls for legislation to restrict immigration through literacy tests for entrance into the United States or quotas based on national origin.

Anti-Semitism permeated American society during the Gilded Age. In addition to the long-standing religious roots of prejudice among Christians against Jews, the struggle over the currency revived notions that Jewish financiers dominated world banking and sought to perpetuate the gold standard. Among academics, social scientists, and historians, quasi-scientific arguments arose to justify exclusion of Jews from universities and businesses.

The Urban Political Machine

Politicians in the large cities grappled with this volatile mix of ethnicity, race, and economic class. Most cities had a mayor-council form of government in which the entire population elected the mayor, while council members represented individual districts or wards. Divided, ineffective government followed as council members traded favors and blocked legislation that hurt their districts. The urban "political machine" led by the "political boss" developed. The word *machine* masked a more complex reality. The organization that dominated city politics consisted of an interlocking system of operatives in each ward who delivered votes for their party at city and county conventions. The machine relied for its existence on the votes of the large inner-city population. They turned out faithfully on election day to support the candidates that the machine had designated.

The organization of the machine began in the ward. The leader of the ward got the vote by supplying his constituents with employment, helping in an economic crisis or brush with the law, and regularly attending the weddings, funerals, and wakes of the neighborhood. A ward leader like George Washington Plunkitt in New York or John F. "Honey Fitz" Fitzgerald in Boston was the man to see when disaster threatened an urban family. "I think that there's got to be in every ward somebody that any bloke can come to—no matter what he's done—and get help," said a Boston ward leader. *Help, you understand. None of your law and justice, but help.*

As the city grew, contracts were awarded to businesses to build the streets, install the sewers, lay the gas lines, and erect the trolley lines. There were abundant opportunities for politicians to decide how money was spent and who would benefit. With the power of its votes, the machine profited from the city services it allocated to the business community. Decisions about who built streets, parks, and sewer lines often depended on payoffs and graft to the boss and his associates. The flow of money, much of it based on corruption, enabled the machine to provide the social services that people wanted and a human sympathy for those in trouble.

In the public's mind, the political boss stood at the top of the machine. These men rarely held a public office and managed affairs from behind the scenes. "Honest John" Kelly and Richard Croker of Tammany Hall in New York City were among the most famous such leaders, but almost every major city had one. Their enemies depicted the bosses as unchallenged dictators of the city's destiny. In most cases, however, the bosses were shrewd politicians who balanced factions and interest groups in a constantly shifting political scene. They represented a response to the fragmentation of the city political system because of the coming of industrialism. In that sense they became an important and badly needed institutional innovation.

Reformers constantly challenged the power of the bosses. In their public comments, critics of the urban machine attacked its reliance on graft and corruption to sustain itself. The president of Cornell University said that cities in the United States were "the most corrupt in Christendom." Like-minded members of the middle and upper classes warred on the bosses and their machines throughout the late nineteenth century, seeking to replace them with more efficient, economical government. The machines often defeated the campaigns of the reformers because inner-city residents appreciated what the bosses did for them. Reformers came and went; the machine was always there. As George Washington Plunkitt said, reformers "were mornin' glories—looked lovely in the mornin' and withered up in a short time, while the regular machines went on flourishin' forever, like fine old oaks."

The rank-and-file residents also knew that the reformers wanted to shift power away from the lower classes. The reform programs often involved cutbacks in even the already minimal services that the poorer areas of the city received. On balance, the machines and bosses supplied reasonably good city government. Services were provided and economic opportunity expanded. City residents endorsed the results with their votes. Most cities had water, fire, and health services of a quality that compared with those found in the industrial nations of western Europe. In the city parks—Central Park in New York, the Boston park system, and the sprawling green spaces of St. Louis and Kansas City—the generation of the 1880s left a positive legacy to future urban residents.

A strong force for improving city life was the settlement houses that Jane Addams and others launched at the end of the 1880s. They held citizenship classes, provided training in cultural issues, and offered sports to local youth. Often settlement workers approached the ethnic neighborhood with arrogance and insensitivity. In time, some settlement workers gained a better understanding of the obstacles that the immigrants faced. Their experiences in the ghettos and streets of the cities prepared them for work in subsequent reform campaigns. At the same time, Addams and others also conveyed a strong sense of moralistic paternalism to the people they sought to serve. Their goal was to "build a bridge between European and American experiences" over which the immigrants could pass toward integration into the dominant culture. Despite this paternalistic attitude, the settlement house movement did soften the impact of the urban experience on the new immigrants. Still, the urbanizing process of the late nineteenth century had left the nation with accumulated social problems that would tax leaders and institutions for decades.

THE DIMINISHING RIGHTS OF MINORITY GROUPS

The United States was not a very tolerant nation at the end of the 1880s. For African Americans, Chinese immigrants, and Native Americans, these were years when their rights were at risk from repressive forces

The Battle of Wounded Knee provided this cartoonist with the opportunity to contrast how the United States denounced the imperialism of other nations with its own harsh treatment of Native Americans.
From the Collections of the Library of Congress

within white society. As a result, the period produced a narrowing of the possibilities for Americans in one of these distinct racial minorities.

Native Americans

For Indians, the end of large-scale armed resistance to white expansion left them with few viable ways to protest policies that destroyed their traditions and confined them to reservations or government schools. The Dawes Act was already taking away their lands. Bowed down by despair and hopelessness, the Plains Indians were receptive to any leaders who offered them a chance to regain their lost cultural values.

The appearance of a religious movement, called the Ghost Dance, promised Plains Indians the return of their buffalo herds and an end to white domination. If the Indians performed the rituals of the dance, said a Paiute messiah named Wovoka, the Indian dead would be reborn and the whites would vanish for all time. Apprehensive whites saw the Ghost Dance as a portent of another Indian uprising. When the army moved against the Sioux in December 1890, fighting occurred on Wounded Knee Creek on the Pine Ridge Reservation in South Dakota. Despite bitter hand-to-hand combat, the "battle" was no contest. The army's machine guns cut down the Indians; they suffered 146 dead and fifty-one wounded while army losses were twenty-five killed and thirty-nine wounded. The Battle of Wounded Knee was the last major chapter in the Indian wars.

"The Indian Situation," 1891

The Battle of Wounded Knee triggered much press comment about how the nation treated the Indians in general and in this tragic incident in particular. The following editorials from the *New York Herald,* January 4, 1891 and the *Detroit Tribune,* January 2, 1891 present contrasting perspectives on what had occurred and what the proper Indian policy should be.

N. Y. Herald, Jan. 4.—This Indian question is intensely interesting and pathetic. There is also an element of tragedy in it from which we recoil.

We have about a quarter of a million of red men on our territory. Their ancestors were originally the possessors of the rich lands which we now occupy. We have multiplied and they have decreased. Only a remnant remains, and we have apportioned to them large areas in different parts of the country—north of Texas, in Dakota, Arizona, Montana and Washington—and told them to stay there and behave themselves.

The continent is none too large for our purposes, and the red man has only a few more years to live. He hasn't kept up with the procession; by little and little he is dropping out and dying on the road side. He can't understand the situation, and once in a while puts on war paint, sharpens his tomahawk and fiercely resists the inevitable.

What a pity that when he meets the multitude in the happy hunting grounds he can't report that we have treated him fairly and kept our promises.

If he tells the truth he will say:—The white man made treaties and broke them. He has lied to me and starved me. When I rebelled he shot me, and here I am.

Our Indian record is wholly brutal and shameful.

Detroit Tribune, Jan. 2.—The present war was unavoidable. The Government and the military did all that was possible to prevent war, but all their efforts were futile. The hostile Indians must be conquered now once for all, and those of them who shall survive the war be forever deprived of all firearms and other war weapons.

Hereafter the only Indian policy that will be acceptable to the people of this country will be one that shall make impossible another Indian outbreak. Grant all that has been said about the wrongs the Indians of previous generations endured, the sentiment of the past cannot come into the situation of the present. For many years the Indians have been most humanely and generously dealt with by the Government and they have been growing more and more restless and treacherous. Doubtless they have sometimes been cheated and wronged by scoundrelly post traders and agents, but the Government has not countenanced such wrongs; it has sought to correct them. The present outbreak was entirely causeless, so far as any fault of the Government or the military is concerned; and the public good demands a speedy and permanent settlement of the war on the basis of everlasting peace.

Mexican Americans

In the Southwest, Mexican Americans were a majority in the territory of New Mexico, and their influence remained strong in southern California. A major political issue in New Mexico was land grants that the Spanish crown had made. Anglo lawyers acquired title to these properties in order to assemble large landhold- ings of their own. Hispanic residents grazed their cattle on communal lands that all ranchers shared. Anglo ranchers and settlers divided up the land with fences and sold it among themselves. Spanish Americans tried to resist this activity by forming a secret vigilante organization *Las Gorras Blancas* (The White Caps). In 1889, they removed the fences and burned Anglo property and businesses such as railroads and lumberyards. Thus ethnic and economic tensions led to social violence in the territory.

Chinese Immigrants

The prejudice that the 104,000 Chinese residing in the West faced became more institutionalized in the early 1890s. Congress moved to tighten the restrictions on immigration, embodied in the Chinese Exclusion Act of 1882. In 1889, the Supreme Court upheld the constitutionality of such laws and stated that such measures would help in "the preservation of our civilization there." In 1892, Congress extended the Chinese Exclusion Act for ten years, and by 1900 the number of Chinese living in the United States fell to 85,000. Most of the Chinese Americans resided in cities where they established laundries, restaurants, and other small businesses that served members of their own community. The Chinese Benevolent Association or "Six Companies" offered support for a Chinese culture that existed in a rich and complex setting of its own.

African Americans

The most elaborate and sustained policy of racial separation was aimed at African Americans in the South. As blacks tried to take part in politics and to seek wealth and happiness, white southerners created a caste structure to ensure their continued dominance. In the *Civil Rights Cases,* the Supreme Court had ruled that the Fourteenth Amendment did not give Congress the power to prohibit discrimination by individuals. That left southern states to write segregation laws against their black population.

An important national trend allowed the South to pursue these policies. White Americans in all parts of the nation believed that blacks were inferior to whites. Reconstruction was widely considered to have failed. White southerners, it was argued, should deal with their black population as they deemed best. Northern willingness to abandon the aims of the Civil War and Reconstruction was a key element in the rise of segregation.

With the tacit approval of the North, the white politicians of the South devised segregation laws that covered most spheres of human activity. Blacks were barred from white railroad cars and had to use the inferior and often shabby cars assigned to their race. Whites had their own hotels, parks, hospitals, and schools. Blacks had to either make do with lesser facilities or do without them entirely.

Informal restrictions also shaped the everyday life of blacks. African Americans were expected to step out of the way of whites, to be respectful and deferential, and never, by look or glance, to display resentment or anger. Courtesy titles for blacks disappeared. A young black man was a "boy" until he became old enough to be labeled "uncle." To call an African American person either "Mr." or "Mrs." would have implied a degree of individuality that the culture of segregation in the South could not tolerate.

Laws removed blacks from the political process. They could not serve on juries in judgment of whites. Punishments for their crimes were harsher than those for white offenders. Although some blacks had voted in elections during the 1880s, laws were passed to make it impossible for African Americans to vote. The South took its cue from Mississippi whose constitutional convention, held in 1890, required that voters demonstrate their literacy and pay a poll tax before they could cast a ballot. An illiterate man had to qualify to vote by demonstrating that he could "understand" a provision of the state constitution when it was read to him. A poll tax had to be paid in advance and a receipt presented at the polls. These laws worked against poor whites and most blacks who found it easier not to vote. In states like Mississippi and Louisiana, the number of registered black voters fell drastically during the early 1890s; the number of white voters declined as well.

If legal restrictions were not sufficient to maintain white supremacy, blacks faced the constant possibility of extralegal violence. In the 1890s, an average of 187 black Americans were lynched annually. Blacks convicted of crimes were imprisoned in brutal circumstances in overcrowded penitentiaries or made to work on gangs that the state leased out to private contractors. The convict-lease system produced inmate death rates as high as 25 percent in some states.

In Louisiana, blacks decided to test an 1890 law specifying that they must ride in separate railroad cars. On June 7, 1892, Homer A. Plessy, who was one-eighth black, boarded a train bound from New Orleans to Covington, Louisiana. He sat in the car reserved for whites, and the conductor instructed him to move to the car for blacks. He refused and was arrested. When his case came before Judge Thomas H. Ferguson, Plessy's claim that the law violated his constitutional rights was denied. His case was then appealed to the U.S. Supreme Court.

Black leaders resisted to the extent they could. The remaining African American members of southern legislatures argued against discriminatory legislation, but they were easily outvoted. A Richmond, Virginia Democrat boasted of the tactics used to exclude blacks from elections: "It was well understood that the blacks had to be beaten by hook or by crook—they knew what to expect and they knew who was putting the thing on them but they could not prevent it." By the mid-1890s, the South was as segregated as white leaders could make it. For most blacks the constitutional guarantees of the Fourteenth and Fifteenth Amendments existed only on paper. The fate of minorities had a low priority in a society where the values of Victorian life governed everyday existence.

A VICTORIAN SOCIETY

In the late nineteenth century, the social customs embodied in the term "Victorian" provided the context in which most white Americans lived. Like their counterparts in Great Britain, where Queen Victoria ruled between 1837 and 1901, these Americans professed a public code of personal behavior that demanded restraint, sexual modesty, temperate habits, and hard work.

The Rules of Life

The precepts of Victorian morality applied to every aspect of daily life. Relations between the sexes followed precise rules. Unmarried men and women were supposed to be chaperoned when they were together before marriage. A suitor asked a woman whether he might write to her before presuming to do so. A kiss resulted either in an engagement or social disgrace. Premarital sex was taboo. People married for life, mourned a dead spouse for at least a year, and showed fidelity by not remarrying. Some people did not follow these guidelines to their full extent, but many did and social conventions were strong.

Once married, a couple was expected to engage in sexual intercourse only for the purpose of having children. The wife was to tame the husband's baser instincts. She was considered to be naturally pure; he was thought to be dominated by animalistic drives. "The full force of sexual desire is seldom known to a virtuous woman," said one male writer, with the implication that women did not achieve the same pleasure in sex that men did.

In reality, women's desires did not conform to these masculine stereotypes. One mother of four in her thirties remarked that sexual relations "makes more normal people." A survey of forty-five married women, done by Professor Clelia Mosher in 1892, found that almost three-quarters of them experienced pleasure during lovemaking. Limits on the frequency of sex may have been to reduce unwanted pregnancies in a time before birth control devices became widespread.

The Moral Code

Men in Victorian society did the work of the world. They spent their days at the factory or office, and their children saw them in the evening and on Sundays. Males displayed the right virtues in what the age called their "character." In the middle and upper classes, men might sow their "wild oats" before marriage, but after that were expected to adhere to their wedding vows. The rising number of divorces (some 56,000 by 1900) indicated that many did not do so. People looked the other way when men patronized prostitutes or had discreet sexual adventures outside marriage. When it became known that a woman followed such a course, she was disgraced.

A strict moral code governed the raising of Victorian children. Parents instilled character in their children, who were required to show respect to their elders. Discussion of sex was rare. Many women knew nothing about it until they were married. Despite the constraints placed on children's behavior, youthful high spirits found an outlet in games and play. Entertainment was centered in the home, where families assembled to play board and card games, sing around a parlor organ or piano, and, for the wealthier Americans, play croquet or lawn tennis.

A Godly Society

Religion permeated the nation. In 1890, there were 145 different Christian denominations with nearly 22 million members. More than 8 million people were Roman Catholics; Presbyterians, Methodists, and Southern Baptists were the major Protestant denominations. Families reserved the Sabbath for churchgoing, rest, and quiet. Despite fears that religious convictions were waning in the face of growing secularism, thousands responded enthusiastically to the religious revivals conducted by Dwight L. Moody and other celebrated evangelists. Yet, by 1890, Victorian ideas were under attack as science and the teachings of Charles Darwin undermined traditional religious precepts.

Sports and Leisure

While thinkers debated the clash between religion and science, everyday Americans sought relaxation and recreation in the popular spectator sports. Among the upper and middle classes, football had emerged as second only to baseball in its appeal. The first intercollegiate football game occurred between Princeton and Rutgers in 1869; the modern game evolved as

By the end of the 1880s, college football was becoming a major spectator sport. Here a photographer records the crowd watching Cornell University and the University of Rochester in an 1889 game. The players performed without the equipment and padding of the modern game.
The Granger Collection, New York

African American fighters appeared in interracial bouts in some divisions, but before 1900 white heavyweight champions observed the "color line."

In 1891, James Naismith, an instructor at the Young Men's Christian Association Training School in Springfield, Massachusetts, developed a sport that could be played indoors during the winter. His early form of basketball soon spread across the nation.

Another popular diversion was bicycling, which became a craze after 1890. Before the development of the modern "safety" bicycle in the 1880s and the addition of pneumatic tires in 1889, cycling was a sport for those who could master the brakeless "ordinary" bikes with their large front wheels. But once technology put a convenient bicycle within the reach of the masses, the fad was on. Some 10 million bikes were in use by 1900. Cycling led women to adopt looser garments and, according to some enthusiasts, eased

rules for scoring became established. Walter Camp, the unofficial coach at Yale University and the founder of the "All-American" teams, devised the line of scrimmage and the requirement that a team gain five yards in three attempts in order to retain possession of the ball. Dividing the field into five-yard squares produced the "gridiron."

With regular rules came recruitment of talented athletes, charges of professionalism, and obsession with the sport among alumni. By 1890, the game held in New York City on Thanksgiving Day in which teams vied for the unofficial national championship drew crowds of 40,000 people. In fact, football appealed most to those who believed that young men should demonstrate commitment to a strenuous existence in a violent game that tested their masculine courage.

Beyond the Gridiron

Boxing had a wider appeal. Irish-American boxers dominated the sport, with John L. Sullivan the most famous champion. Some matches were held in secret and continued for as many as seventy-five bloody rounds. The contestants did not use gloves. Gloves and formal rules appeared during the 1880s. Sullivan lost his heavyweight crown in 1892 to James J. "Gentleman Jim" Corbett in the first gloved title fight.

Bicycling became a popular fad during the 1890s. Its low cost and convenience made it an attractive recreation for millions of Americans. It also brought men and women together in comfortable and socially approved surroundings.
© Collection of The New York Historical Society

childbirth. After the automobile appeared at the beginning of the twentieth century, the passion for bicycles receded and memories of the craze that had marked the early 1890s faded away.

VOICES OF PROTEST AND REFORM

Bicycles were not the only craze that swept the nation at the end of the 1880s. Edward Bellamy, a former reporter turned novelist, published a novel called *Looking Backward: 2000–1887* in 1888. Its main character, Julian West, had gone to sleep in 1887 and awoke in 2000. In the future he met Doctor Leete who told him how the world had changed during the 113 years he had been asleep. In the new industrial order of "Nationalism," efficiency and discipline had replaced the chaos of the late nineteenth century. Citizens had purpose in their lives. Members of an industrial army, they served the state that in turn provided them with material rewards. Bellamy's argument offered the promise of a nation organized for a common purpose in pursuit of abundance without the coercion of government.

Bellamy became an overnight celebrity. *Looking Backward* sold hundreds of thousands of copies. "Nationalist" clubs sprang up to spread his doctrine. The fad ebbed quickly, but Bellamy had struck a chord in a society that was dissatisfied with industrialism. His evocation of community and cooperative action was appealing in a competitive, capitalist society. Troubled individuals turned to their faith, to organization, and to political action to deal with their unease about the direction of the nation.

The Social Gospel

Religion offered one answer to the social ills of industrialism. Many clergymen had defended the inequalities of wealth and status in society. This harsh dogma offended younger members of the ministry who sought to improve society rather than to save individual souls. They rebelled against the tenets of Social Darwinism and what they regarded as its indifference to the ills of society. Walter Rauschenbush, a Baptist clergyman in Rochester, New York, had seen at firsthand the hardship and despair experienced by slum dwellers. He believed that it was necessary to "Christianize" the social order to bring it "into harmony with the ethical convictions which we identify with Christ." The church, he wrote, must "demand protection for the moral safety of the people."

Rauschenbush's ideas came to be known as the *Social Gospel.* He and other ministers went into the city to preach the Gospel to poor slum dwellers. Washington Gladden spoke out from the First Congregational Church in Columbus, Ohio, and wrote a book entitled *Applied Christianity,* which was published in 1886. "The Christian moralist," he wrote, had to tell "the Christian employer" that the wage system "when it rests on competition as its sole basis is anti-social and anti-Christian." Similar doctrines were promoted within Judaism and Catholicism. The Social Gospel contributed to the reform tendencies that extended through the 1890s.

Organized Women

Middle-class women spearheaded the reform efforts of the 1890s. The Woman's Christian Temperance Union (WCTU) expanded its role under Frances Willard, its president from 1879 to 1899. It pursued missions to the urban poor, prison reform, and protests against male-dominated politics. Alcohol reform became a means for many women to engage in other social concerns.

Women who had gained leisure time during the 1880s transformed their literary and discussion clubs into groups with more ambitious agendas. A leading feminist, Charlotte Perkins Gilman, saw clubs as "the first timid steps towards social organization of these so long unsocialized members of our race." In 1890, the General Federation of Women's Clubs (GFWC) was founded, with a core membership of 200 clubs and some 20,000 women on its rolls. It sponsored cultural and educational activities for workingwomen and homemakers. In Chicago, women's clubs supported the Legal Aid Society and other "child-saving" endeavors to help mothers raise their children in healthier settings.

The campaign to achieve woman suffrage had remained divided after the National Woman Suffrage Association and the American Woman Suffrage Association split over the Fifteenth Amendment and African American voting rights. The rift was healed through the efforts of Lucy Stone Blackwell, and in 1890 the National American Woman Suffrage Association (NAWSA) appeared. The president was Elizabeth Cady Stanton; Susan B. Anthony succeeded her in 1892. Progress toward suffrage was slow at first. Elections to secure suffrage usually failed, and by the middle of the 1890s only four states (Wyoming, Utah, Colorado, and Idaho) allowed women to vote. Nonetheless, NAWSA provided an important organizational foundation for future growth.

During the 1890s, social reformers continued their efforts to improve society. Frances Willard of the Woman's Christian Temperance Union sought to unite her organization with the work of the Populists and labor unions in an effort to build a broader coalition for change.
Courtesy Northwestern University Archives

Other reform goals attracted the support of committed women. Josephine Shaw Lowell animated the Charity Organization Society (COS), which sent "friendly visitors" into urban slums to instruct residents and "in great measure prevent the growth of pauperism." Homes were established for the impoverished mother and prostitute where she could obtain "Friends, Food, Shelter and a HELPING HAND by coming just as she is." Florence Kelley of Hull House carried the ideas of the settlement movement into the more ambitious Illinois Women's Alliance in 1892. The New York City Working Women's Society protested harsh working conditions in New York in 1890; its activities led to the formation of consumers' leagues in other cities. These diverse examples of social criticism and constructive action taught lessons about the effects of industrialism that would shape the experience of the coming generation.

LOOKING OUTWARD: FOREIGN POLICY IN THE EARLY 1890s

Interest in the outside world was also growing. After several decades of internal development, the United States sought a larger role in world affairs. The campaign for an expansionist foreign policy gained momentum slowly in the face of ingrained isolationism. Between 1887 and 1893, the United States took the first steps toward becoming a world power.

In 1889, the United States was a weak military and diplomatic force. The army was small, fewer than 25,000 men, who served in isolated posts in the West. The navy was equally insignificant. One congressman called the fleet "an alphabet of floating washtubs." Sails and wooden vessels were the rule until the end of the 1880s when four steel ships were built.

Overseas Markets and Foreign Policy

The Census Bureau announced the official closing of the frontier in 1890 with the disappearance of a clear line of unsettled territory. Further expansion would have to be international. Noting the size of the nation's industrial output, businesspeople and farmers worried about whether the home market could consume everything that factories and farms produced. Perhaps it would become necessary to secure overseas markets in order to relieve the pressure. The United States still imported more than it exported; in 1887 exports stood at $810 million, imports at $967 million. Exports fluctuated during the last quarter of the nineteenth century, but the overall trend was gradually upward. By the middle of the 1890s, the nation would export more than it imported.

Although there was much interest in overseas markets, the percentage of the gross national product devoted to exports remained low. Official economic policy toward foreign trade was protectionist, and proponents of the protective tariff resisted efforts to lower trade barriers in order to expand overseas commerce. Exporters lobbied for expanded foreign trade and reciprocal tariff legislation to lower foreign trade barriers, but their direct impact on policy and diplomatic decisions was less important than the general enthusiasm for a more aggressive policy that they generated.

The Roots of Imperialism

The example of other European powers engaged in a scramble for empire had the greatest impact. As Africa and Asia became colonies and protectorates of Great Britain, Germany, France, and other countries, Americans worried about being left behind. Applying the doctrines of Social Darwinism to foreign relations, advocates of empire said that a nation that did not expand would find itself unfit to survive.

A leader in the movement for expansion was Captain Alfred T. Mahan of the U.S. Navy. Mahan's research into naval history led to his most important work, *The Influence of Seapower on History, 1660–1783*, published in 1890. Mahan wanted his country to embark on the path to global greatness, and he believed that sea power was the way to achieve it. Only through naval bases, a powerful battleship fleet, and an aggressive foreign policy could the United States compete in a world of empires. He told policy makers that the United States should expand its foreign commerce, construct a strong navy, and acquire overseas bases. Of particular concern was a canal across Central America. Secretaries of the navy from 1889 onward listened to Mahan, as did such future leaders as Senator Henry Cabot Lodge of Massachusetts and Theodore Roosevelt.

The notion of Anglo-Saxon supremacy also fed the new interest in foreign affairs. The Protestant clergyman Josiah Strong contended in *Our Country: Its Possible Future and Its Present Crisis* (1885) that "God, with infinite wisdom and skill, is training the Anglo-Saxon race for an hour sure to come in the world's future." The popular author John Fiske gave lectures on "Manifest Destiny" that predicted that "every land on the earth's surface" that was not already civilized would become "English in its language, in its religion, in political habits and traditions, and to a predominant extent in the blood of its people." These statements helped expansionism gain popularity.

New Departures During the 1880s

During the brief administration of James A. Garfield, Secretary of State James G. Blaine tried to renegotiate the Clayton-Bulwer Treaty (1850) to give the United States control over any canal across Central America. Blaine hoped to create a Pan-American system that would promote stability and security in the Caribbean and South America. The end of the Garfield administration took Blaine out of office and postponed any further action on Pan-Americanism for almost a decade.

The gradual movement toward an expanded foreign policy continued under Presidents Chester Arthur and Grover Cleveland. Secretary of State Frederick T. Frelinghuysen pursued treaties for trade reciprocity with nations such as Mexico, Santo Domingo, and Colombia. Much as Blaine had done with South America, Frelinghuysen believed that these treaties would unite the interests of these countries with those of the United States. However, since the pacts involved concessions on the protective tariff policy, Congress declined to act on them.

Under Cleveland, the process slowed as the administration showed less enthusiasm for a canal in Nicaragua or an expanded role around the world. Still, the size and quality of the navy grew during the president's first term. When James G. Blaine returned to the State Department as Benjamin Harrison's secretary of state in 1889, the drive for an expansionist policy resumed.

The Pan-American Impulse

Blaine sent out invitations for a conference to Latin American countries in 1888. Delegates from nineteen nations gathered in Washington on October 2, 1889, for the first International American Conference. Blaine urged them to support the creation of a customs union and to work out procedures for settling their regional conflicts. Unwilling to accept what seemed to be the dominance of the United States, the conference declined to pursue these initiatives. Instead, it established the International Bureau of the American Republics, which became the Pan-American Union in 1910.

Blaine persuaded his Republican colleagues in Congress to include language allowing for reciprocity treaties in the McKinley Tariff Act of 1890. A number of products were placed on the free list, including sugar, molasses, coffee, and tea; the president could impose tariffs on such items if Latin American countries did not grant the United States similar concessions on its exports. Blaine used the reciprocity clause of the McKinley Tariff to negotiate treaties with South American countries such as Argentina. U.S. exports increased, disproving the claims of critics who warned that it would stifle trade with other nations.

The Harrison administration pursued a more aggressive foreign policy in two other key areas. Secretary of the Navy Benjamin F. Tracy urged Congress to appropriate money for a battle fleet that would not just protect the coastline of the United States but could engage enemies across the oceans. The lawmakers ultimately authorized four modern battleships, fewer than what Tracy wanted, but nonetheless an expansion of the nation's naval power. Tracy also carried out reforms that led to more efficient weapons and a better fighting force by the time he left office in 1893.

The Hawaiian Involvement

The United States had long sought to exercise greater influence in Asia. Religious leaders saw China and other Asian nations as sources of potential converts. Business leaders and farmers thought of potential markets for products and crops. In the quest to enter Asia, the Hawaiian Islands seemed a logical stepping-stone. Missionaries had been working in the islands since the 1820s, and their reports fed American fascination with Hawaii. Trade relations between the two countries had become stronger since the Treaty of Reciprocity, signed in 1875, which gave Hawaiian sugar and other products duty-free entry into the United States. In exchange, Hawaii agreed not to grant other countries any concessions that threatened the territorial or economic independence of the islands. The relationship was further strengthened in 1887 when the treaty was renewed and the United States received the exclusive right to use the superb strategic asset of Pearl Harbor.

Within Hawaii the white settlers and the native rulers clashed. The Hawaiian monarch, King Kalakua, had been inclined to accept the closer ties between the United States and his nation. He died in 1891, bringing to power his sister, Queen Liliuokalani. She resented the American presence in Hawaii and believed that the white minority should not have dominant power.

Hawaiian politics became more complex after the McKinley Tariff in 1890 which removed the duty-free status of Hawaiian sugar and granted bounties to American cane producers in Louisiana and beet sugar growers in the Rocky Mountain states. The Hawaiian sugar industry slumped and economic conditions on the islands worsened. Americans in Hawaii and in the Congress called for annexation of the islands.

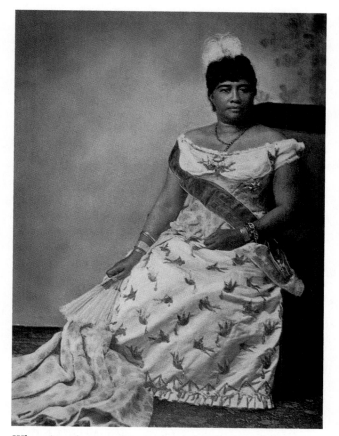

When Americans endeavored to bring the Hawaiian Islands under U.S. control, Queen Liliuokalani led the native Hawaiians in efforts to forestall the end of their independence. Her resistance led the Cleveland administration to block Hawaiian annexation for most of the 1890s.
The Granger Collection, New York

The Hawaiian Revolt

During 1892, the Hawaiian legislature and the queen had argued over the presence and role of foreigners in the country. As the new year began, the queen dismissed the legislature and established a constitution that stripped white settlers of many of the powers that they had enjoyed under the existing constitution. Proponents of annexation launched a revolt and called on the U.S. minister (the official representative of the United States in the islands) and the American navy for help. The coup was successful, helped by 150 U.S. Marines. The queen gave in, and a provisional government was created. The United States agreed to a treaty of annexation with the pro-American and predominantly white rebels on February 14, 1893. It looked as if Hawaii would become a possession of the United States. Then the incoming president, Grover

Cleveland, said that the treaty should not be ratified until the new administration took office. The fate of Hawaii remained in limbo.

Despite this temporary pause, the extent of American expansion during the Harrison administration was striking. The navy had been increased and its mission broadened. The nation's ties to Latin America had been extended, and the fate of Hawaii seemed to be linked to that of the United States. In the Pacific, the United States had become one of the three participants, with Great Britain and Germany, in a protectorate over the strategic islands of Samoa. Harrison and Blaine had launched the nation on a path of expansion that would be pursued throughout the 1890s. For the moment, however, internal ferment captured the nation's attention as social and political unrest flared in the heartland of the United States.

THE ANGRY FARMERS

Of all the groups who found themselves at odds with the direction of American society between 1887 and 1893, the unhappy farmers of the South and West had the greatest impact on the nation and its political system.

The Reaction to Republican Activism

The Republicans had regained national power in 1888 when Benjamin Harrison defeated Grover Cleveland for the presidency. Although Cleveland won the popular vote, Harrison triumphed in the electoral tally and the Republicans gained control of both houses of Congress from 1889 to 1890. Under the leadership of Speaker Thomas B. Reed, the Republicans enacted a wide-ranging program that included the McKinley Tariff, the Sherman Silver Purchase Act, and the Sherman Antitrust Act. Responding to the popular unhappiness with industrial consolidation, the antitrust law prohibited "combinations in restraint of trade." Not much enforced in the 1890s, the measure did not prove more than a symbolic gesture. Republicans believed that in raising tariffs through the McKinley law and in providing for limited government purchase of silver, they had crafted a winning program for the voters.

Instead, they confronted an aroused and cohesive Democratic party that took advantage of a host of grievances among voters in the Midwest. In states like Illinois, Wisconsin, and Iowa, Republicans had pushed an agenda of social change that reflected the party's activist religious sentiments. State legislatures passed laws to implement the prohibition of alcohol. Other measures required that schools chartered by a state teach subjects in English rather than in the languages of immigrant children. Still other laws restricted activities on the Sabbath. The Democrats realized that they could win the votes of the Catholic and German Lutheran voters who disliked these policies.

An appeal to the pocketbook strengthened the Democratic campaign. Party workers told homemakers that the McKinley tariff would raise the cost of living. The Democrats also tapped into racial fears in the southern and border states about a proposed Federal Elections bill to provide fair elections in the South. The results in November 1890 shocked Republicans. Their numbers in the House of Representatives dropped from 166 to 88, while the Democrats controlled 235 seats.

The Rise of the Populists

In addition to the shift in power between the two major parties, a new political force had appeared. Candidates identified with the Farmers Alliance, an agrarian protest group, made impressive gains in the South and West. Alliance candidates won nine seats in the House of Representatives; they also elected two members of the U.S. Senate. In the South, the governors of South Carolina, Georgia, and Tennessee were leaning toward the Alliance. Alliance men dominated a number of southern state legislatures, and they showed strength in Midwestern states such as Kansas, Nebraska, South Dakota, and Minnesota.

The crisis in southern and western agriculture had been building for decades. As productivity increased between 1865 and 1885, the prices of farm products declined. A bushel of wheat brought almost $1.20 in 1881 but fell to just under $.70 a bushel in 1889. Cotton was worth almost $.11 a pound in 1881; by 1890, that figure had fallen to $.085 per pound.

Two other grievances were the debts that farmers owed and the costs of moving their crops to market. During the 1880s, western farmers had borrowed from mortgage loan companies in the East to buy land and equipment. Rising land values and stable crop prices made this strategy appear sound. When farm prices declined, however, paying off debts became increasingly difficult. In the South, where sharecropping and farm tenancy tied many farmers to the credit that the "furnish merchants" provided, the slide in cotton prices meant that debts to the merchant increased each year. Another villain in the eyes of the farmers was the railroad that carried their crops to market. Growers in the Plains states complained about high rates and that the railroads discriminated against them in favor of manufacturers and middlemen. The railroads had this power, critics said, because they corrupted the political process.

The system of money and banking also attracted the scorn of western and southern farmers. Every dollar in circulation had to have an equal amount of gold bullion behind it to keep the nation's currency on "the gold standard." International production of gold was static and the amount of money in circulation did not keep pace with the growth of the population. The currency became deflated as the value of the dollar depreciated. Wheat farmers on the plains or cotton growers in the South had to work harder and harder to maintain the same level of income. Farmers sought to put more dollars into circulation. The prevailing perception among farmers in the South and West was that they were the victims of a rigged economic system. And so they looked eagerly at proposals that would relieve them of their debt burden.

Populist Party Platform,1892

When the Populist party wrote its platform in 1892, Ignatius Donnelly of Minnesota composed a stinging indictment of the existing political system. His words convey some of the passions that fueled the third party movement during the early 1890s. The reference to isolating voters at the polling places alludes to the use of the secret nonpartisan ballot rather than the party-oriented ballots of the earlier years of the Gilded Age.

Preamble

The conditions which surround us best justify our cooperation; we meet in the midst of a nation brought to the verge of moral, political, and material ruin. Corruption dominates the ballot-box, the Legislatures, the Congress, and touches even the ermine of the bench. The people are demoralized; most of the States have been compelled to isolate the voters at the polling places to prevent universal intimidation and bribery. The newspapers are largely subsidized or muzzled, public opinion silenced, business prostrated, homes covered with mortgages, labor impoverished, and the land concentrating in the hands of capitalists. The urban workmen are denied the right to organize for self-protection, imported pauperized labor beats down their wages, a hireling standing army, unrecognized by our laws, is established to shoot them down, and they are rapidly degenerating into European conditions. The fruits of the toil of millions are boldly stolen to build up colossal fortunes for a few, unprecedented in the history of mankind; and the possessors of these, in turn, despise the Republic and endanger liberty. From the same prolific womb of governmental injustice we breed the two great classes—tramps and millionaires. . .

Assembled on the anniversary of the birthday of the nation, and filled with the spirit of the grand general and chief who established our independence, we seek to restore the government of the Republic to the hands of the "plain people," with which class it originated. We assert our purposes to be identical with the purposes of the National Constitution; to form a more perfect union and establish justice, insure domestic tranquility, provide for the common defence, promote the general welfare, and secure the blessings of liberty for ourselves and our posterity. . .

The Farmers Alliance

The campaign to improve the lives of southern and western farmers had begun during the 1870s through the Patrons of Husbandry (the Grange). When farm conditions turned poor again in the mid-1880s, the Texas Farmers Alliance, formed to stop horse thieves in Lampasas County, Texas, attracted unhappy farmers. Elsewhere in the South, in Arkansas, Louisiana, and South Carolina, angry farmers organized into other alliances and associations that expressed their grievances.

Southern and western farmers first looked toward cooperative action. A self-taught doctor and lawyer, Charles W. Macune, became president of the Texas Alliance in 1886. He wanted to set up Alliance exchanges and cooperatives across the South. These institutions could provide farmers with supplies and equipment at a cost below what the "furnish merchants" charged. To spread the creed of the cooperatives, the Alliance relied on individual organizers or "lecturers." Alliance newspapers reprinted speeches and letters stating the complaints of agrarians and the merits of cooperation. Soon the Alliance claimed hundreds of thousands of members on its rolls.

$\mathscr{P}$ICTURING THE PAST ✦ POLITICS & DIPLOMACY

POPULISM AS RADICALISM

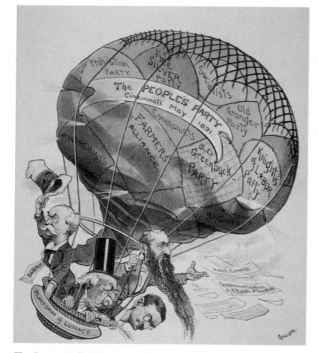

The Granger Collection, New York

Although historians treat the farm protest of the 1880s and 1890s with respect, during the Gilded Age the mainstream press viewed the unhappy agrarians with disdain. In this 1891 cartoon that followed an organizing meeting of the People's party in Cincinnati in May, the movement was depicted as a patchwork of old ideas from the 1870s first advanced by the Knights of Labor and the Greenback party. The participants are also caricatured as ineffectual cranks borne on the winds of discontent. Amused dismissal of Populism would, however, give way to fears for social stability when economic hard times arrived with the Panic of 1893. Such inflationary ideas as free silver, derided in the cartoon, would then be viewed as potentially destructive of the monetary system and the economy. Like so many American protest campaigns, the ideas scorned in this cartoon would in due course be incorporated into how the nation was governed.

Cooperatives proved easier to organize than to sustain. Marketing crops at a time other than harvest season required capital to store the crops until prices rose. The farmers lacked the resources to make such a scheme work. It also proved difficult to obtain the lower prices sought by the cooperatives. By 1889, it was clear that cooperatives were not the answer.

The Rising Tide of Farm Protest

While economic success eluded the Alliance between 1886 and 1890, its political power grew. The ideology of cooperative action appealed to farm families who often were isolated from one another. The Alliance meetings brought farmers together to hear speeches, enjoy entertainment, and share experiences. Alliance members told each other that they were part of a mass movement.

Some members of the Alliance saw African American farmers as potential allies. The Colored Farmers' National Alliance and Cooperative Union was formed in 1886 and had as many as 250,000 members by 1891. Cooperation between the black Alliance and its white counterpart was uneasy. Whites were usually landowners, even if impoverished ones; blacks tended to be either tenants or farm laborers. In 1891, the Colored Alliance in Arkansas tried to get higher wages for cotton picking. Their strike was met with violence. Fifteen of the strikers were lynched, and the Colored Alliance vanished.

As the farm depression worsened nationally, branches of the Alliance appeared in the Dakotas, Nebraska, and especially Kansas. Concerted national action was a logical next step. Representatives of the various state organizations met at St. Louis in December 1889 and created the National Farmers' Alliance and

Industrial Union. The delegates left out the word "white" from the organization's requirements, although state organizations in the South could exclude black members. Three key northern states, Kansas and the two Dakotas, joined the national organization.

The Subtreasury Plan

Charles Macune offered the most important policy proposal of the conference, the *subtreasury plan*. Cotton and wheat farmers usually sold their crops when prices were at their lowest point. A system of government warehouses or subtreasuries would start, a place where farmers could store their crops until prices rose. To bridge the months between storage and selling, the farmers would receive a certificate of deposit from the warehouse for 80 percent of the crop's existing market value with a 1 or 2 percent annual interest rate. Farmers would sell the crops for higher prices, repay their loans, and keep the resulting profits.

The subtreasury plan addressed the marketing and currency problems of staple crop farmers. However, if a majority of wheat or cotton farmers waited until prices rose and then sold their crops, the market glut would force prices down again. The certificates that the farmers would have received for storing their crops at the subtreasury warehouses would represent another form of paper money. The idea involved a large expansion of governmental power in an era suspicious of federal power. Nevertheless, to its agrarian advocates, the subtreasury seemed a plausible strategy.

The People's party used women to recruit new members and thus gave them a greater opportunity to be heard in political life. One of the most celebrated and controversial figures was Mary Elizabeth Lease of Kansas, here shown in a publicity photo for a lecturing career.
The Granger Collection, New York

The Alliance in the 1890 Election

During the 1890 election, the protest movement poured out its energy in speeches throughout Kansas and other friendly states. At a time when women took little direct part in politics, the Alliance allowed some female speakers to address audiences. One of them, Annie Diggs, was born in Canada, grew up in the Northeast, and came to Kansas during the 1870s. After some years in the East, she was working for a Topeka, Kansas, newspaper as the 1890 campaign got underway. Her speeches proved crowd-pleasers. Even more charismatic was Mary Elizabeth Lease. Her enemies changed her middle name to Ellen, which rhymed with "Yellin." She coined several phrases that became memorable parts of the agrarian cause. Kansas farmers, she reportedly said, should "raise less wheat and corn, and more hell."

The Alliance's success in electing congressmen and state legislators in the South and West led their leaders to consider a third party campaign during the next presidential election. They gathered in Ocala, Florida, in early December 1890 where they framed the Ocala Demands, including the subtreasury program, abolition of private banks, regulation of transportation facilities, and the free and unlimited coinage of silver into money at a fixed ratio to gold. Other planks asked for an income tax, restrictions on aliens owning land in the United States, and election of U.S. senators by the people rather than by state legislatures. The Alliance did not decide to become a third party. That issue was put off until February 1892 to allow the legislatures that had been elected with Alliance support to show what they could accomplish.

During the ensuing months, the economic situation of southern farmers worsened. Cotton prices fell sharply and the Alliance lost members. Facing increasing hostility from Democrats in the South, the Alliance men looked toward a third party at a national meeting scheduled for February 1892. There was already a name for the new party: the People's party, or Populists.

The People's Party

The delegates met in St. Louis and quickly decided to form a third party. The first national convention would be held in Omaha, Nebraska, on a symbolic date, July 4, 1892. The Omaha Convention nominated James B. Weaver, a longtime third party politician from Iowa, for president and named James G. Field of Virginia as his running mate.

The Populist platform proclaimed that "We meet in the midst of a nation brought to the verge of moral, political, and material ruin. Corruption dominates the ballot box, the legislatures, the Congress, and touches even the ermine of the bench." The specific planks echoed what had been said at Ocala. They endorsed the subtreasury, free coinage of silver, and other reform proposals.

The Shift to Free Silver

By 1892 the subtreasury plan was dead in Congress. Attention turned to another Populist proposal: free coinage of silver. To expand the currency, raise prices, and reduce the weight of debt on those who owed money, the best solution, Populists contended, would be to base the nation's currency on both gold and silver. If silver were coined into money at a ratio of sixteen to one with gold, there would soon be ample money in circulation.

The country needed controlled inflation. However, the market price of silver stood at more like twenty-five to one, relative to gold. A policy of free coinage would lift the price of the white metal in an artificial way. As a result, people would hoard gold, silver thus would continue to lose value, and inflation would accelerate. Meanwhile, if the nation went off the gold standard, its foreign trade would also suffer because international transactions were handled in gold. The Populists rejected these arguments. They maintained that the government could create money in any form the people desired. The idea of crop supports underlying the subtreasury plan and the manipulation of the money supply that could be achieved through free coinage of silver advocated would become common ideas during the twentieth century. But in 1892, they seemed radical to many Americans.

In 1892, the Republicans tried to use the tariff issue to obtain a second term in the White House for Benjamin Harrison, but he was defeated.
© David J. & Janice L. Frent Collection/Corbis

THE PRESIDENTIAL ELECTION OF 1892

The Republicans and Democrats watched the emergence of Populism with bewilderment and apprehension. The elections of 1890 had left the Republicans shocked at their losses and aware that President Harrison was not a strong candidate for reelection. His cold personality alienated fellow party members. The alternative to Harrison was Blaine who made a brief, doomed run at the nomination during the spring of 1892. Harrison was unenthusiastically renominated.

The Democrats felt more confident with Grover Cleveland, who had kept himself in the public eye since 1889. He easily won a third nomination from his party. Although he strongly favored the gold standard, he did not stress the point. Some party leaders in the South and West saw silver as the answer to the depression and the threat of populism. Cleveland muted his real beliefs to keep these Democrats willing to vote for him. In some western states the Democrats and the Populists struck deals and "fused" their two tickets, with Cleveland getting the electoral votes and the Populists electing state candidates.

The 1892 campaign was quiet on the surface. The political tradition at that time said that incumbent presidents should not make a formal reelection campaign.

PICTURING THE PAST ✦ POLITICS & DIPLOMACY

AN ELECTION WAGER

Chicago Historical Society, #CHI-03590

By the onset of the 1890s, the intense partisanship of the previous two decades was receding. Campaigns were more about education of the voters and less about marching men in columns like the Civil War. As this Joseph Klir painting shows, however, male voters still wagered on the outcome of election contests and paid off their bets in a most public way once the votes were counted. The banners and American flags attest to the patriotic aura of the proceedings. Election betting survives today in a more electronic format through casinos and on the Internet. In private transactions, the loser simply hands over the amount of the wager. The painting thus illustrates in its own artistic way the decline in interest in politics from these late nineteenth century rituals to the private, often individual, act of voting and celebrating the outcome that marks the twenty-first century.

Harrison did not make speeches, and Cleveland stayed home too. The two parties pitched their appeals more to educated voters who now read pamphlets and avoided rallies. Everyone talked of a quiet election.

The Homestead Strike

One significant event revealed the social tensions lying beneath the surface of politics. For workers at Andrew Carnegie's Homestead steel works outside Pittsburgh, Pennsylvania, the summer of 1892 brought misery and violence. The manager of the plant, Henry Clay Frick, cut wages and refused to negotiate with skilled workers who had unionized. A strike resulted and fighting broke out when Pinkerton detectives stormed through the town of Homestead as strikebreakers retook the mills. Detectives and workers died in the ensuing battle and state troops came in to restore order.

A few weeks later, an anarchist named Alexander Berkman shot and stabbed Frick. The industrialist sur-

vived his wounds, however, and the strike was broken. The walkout became a political issue that the Democrats exploited to their advantage. The Homestead strike seemed to embody the tensions between capital and labor that industrialism had fostered.

The Populist Campaign

The Populists tried to make the same argument about the struggle between agriculture and capital. Weaver drew big crowds, but the Democrats in the South subjected him to personal abuse and accused the third party of promoting black rule and a return to Reconstruction. Democrats in the South turned weapons of intimidation and violence against their Populist foes. Third-party candidates were counted out because the Democrats controlled the election machinery. Blacks who might have voted for the People's party candidate as the lesser of two bad choices were coerced to stay away from the polls. When the votes were counted, the Democrats had held the South solid for Grover Cleveland. Populists had

The Homestead Strike in Pittsburgh brought violence between the miners who had left their jobs and the troops sent in to break the walkout. This contemporary illustration depicts the violence that resulted.
© Bettmann/Corbis

A Populist leader, Thomas E. Watson of Georgia, argued that blacks and whites in the South should join to fight their common enemies in the early 1890s. Later in life he abandoned his racial tolerance and became an ardent exponent of segregation and racial violence.
Reproduced from the Collections of the Library of Congress

won some local offices in the region, but the Democrats were still dominant.

On the national level, Cleveland gained a second term by a decisive margin. His plurality over Harrison was almost 400,000 votes, and he won in the electoral college with 277 votes to 145 for the Republicans. The Democrats also controlled both houses of Congress for the first time since before the Civil War. Weaver carried four states and won electoral votes in three additional states for a total of twenty-two electoral votes. His popular vote total reached just over 1 million. The spirit that had driven the Populists was far from dead after the 1892 election, but in fact the movement had reached its high-water mark.

For the moment, it appeared as if the Democrats had emerged as the majority party from the long stalemate of 1874–1890. The Democrats had captured the mood of discontent that was sweeping the country during the early 1890s. They had resisted Republican activism and an expanded role for the federal government. It remained to be seen how Cleveland would carry out

the mandate to satisfy the many groups that had deserted the Republicans and appease the restless farmers who had supported Weaver and the Populists.

THE "GREAT WHITE CITY"

The American economy was in trouble at the beginning of 1893. Distracting the nation's attention from the gloomy forecasts was the prospect of a large popular spectacle that would sum up the state of civilization in the United States 400 years after Christopher Columbus had landed in the Americas. The World's Columbian Exposition in Chicago commemorated Columbus's arrival in what Americans of that time styled "The New World." Architect Daniel Burnham and his coworkers created a series of exhibition buildings that became known as the "Great White City" for their beauty and artistic harmony.

The American Historical Association held its annual meeting in Chicago in 1893 to commemorate the exposition. There a young historian from the University

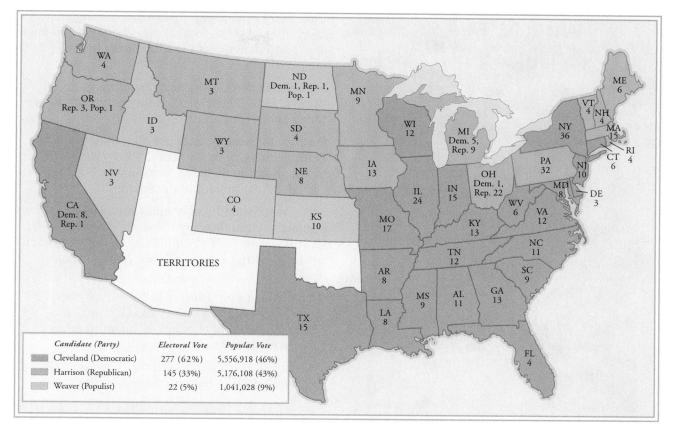

Map 18.1 *The Election of 1892*

In 1892, the new People's party reached the height of its electoral success in its first national race. James B. Weaver, the Populist candidate, did well in the Middle West and West, but he did not win enough electoral votes to disturb Grover Cleveland's progress toward a second term as a Democratic president.

View an animated version of this map or related maps at http://history.wadsworth.com/passages2e.

of Wisconsin, Frederick Jackson Turner, offered his interpretation of how the United States had changed and the challenges it faced in the immediate future. In his paper "The Significance of the Frontier in American History," he noted that the 1890 census had announced the end of the frontier as a clear dividing line between settled and undeveloped areas. He stressed that the availability of free land and the influence of the frontier had played a significant role in the development of democracy in the United States. He inquired about what would happen to the nation now that the possibility of free land and a new life in the West was vanishing. Turner's "frontier thesis" became a powerful and controversial explanation of the way the nation had developed.

CONCLUSION

As the 1890s approached their midpoint, Americans sensed that the country faced important new challenges.

The end of western settlement was one important element. So too was the rise of large cities and the attraction they exerted on the rural countryside. "The tendency is away from the farm and away from the rural districts," said James B. Weaver. "The trend is toward the city, where the needy congregate and where crime becomes organized and where the Republic is stabbed."

By 1893, however, such a simple choice between urban and rural life no longer existed. The country and the city had become interdependent in their need for products and services. There was no returning to the simpler republic for which so many longed. What remained to be decided were the terms on which the nation would go forward toward the twentieth century. The last seven years of the nineteenth century would be among the most divisive and controversial as any in the nation's history. An economic crash that occurred soon after Grover Cleveland took office in March 1893 provided the setting within which these issues of social change would be resolved.

The Columbian Exposition of 1892–1893 marked the 400th anniversary of the landing of Christopher Columbus. The "Great White City" in Chicago symbolized the progress of the nation and its technological accomplishments. The outbreak of the Panic of 1893 dulled the luster of the occasion for many Americans.
Chicago Historical Society

Recommended Readings

Ayers, Edward. *Southern Crossing: A History of the American South, 1877–1906* (1995). Very good on the changes in the South during the 1880s and 1890s.

Clanton, Gene. *Populism: The Humane Preference in America, 1890–1900* (1991). A sympathetic introduction to the unrest among southern and western farmers.

Crapol, Edward P. *James G. Blaine: Architect of Empire* (2000). An interpretive biography of one of the moving spirits behind American expansionism.

Cronon, William. *Nature's Metropolis: Chicago and the Great West* (1991). An interesting treatment of how Chicago grew and interacted with the region it dominated.

Duis, Perry R. *Challenging Chicago: Coping with Everyday Life, 1837–1920* (1998). An insightful book about how Americans lived their lives in the industrial cities.

McMath, Robert C. *American Populism: A Social History, 1877–1898* (1993). A thoughtful survey of forces behind Populism.

Perman, Michael. *Struggle for Mastery: Disfranchisement in the South, 1888–1908* (2001). A thorough synthesis of the ways in which blacks were excluded from politics in the South.

Schneirov, Richard. *Labor and Urban Politics: Class Conflict and the Origins of Modern Liberalism in Chicago, 1864–1894* (1998). Examines the impact of urban industrial growth on politics in a major American city.

Sklar, Kathryn Kish. *Florence Kelley and the Nation's Work: The Rise of Women's Political Culture, 1830–1900* (1995). An excellent biography of an urban reformer in Chicago in the 1890s.

Williams, R. Hal. *Years of Decision: American Politics in the 1890s* (1993). A fine introduction to the decade.

American Journey Online and InfoTrac College Edition

Visit the source collections at http://ajaccess. wadsworth.com and infotrac.thomsonlearning.com and use the Search function with the following key terms to explore documents, images, audio and video clips, articles, and commentary related to the material in this chapter.

Benjamin Harrison
National Farmers Alliance
Sherman Antitrust Act
Emily Dickinson
Ida Wells-Barnett
Grover Cleveland

Edward Bellamy
Jane Addams
Wounded Knee
Homestead strike
Ellis Island
Woman suffrage

> **Additional resources, exercises, and Internet links related to this chapter are available on the American Passages Web site: http://history.wadsworth.com/passages2e**

19 A Troubled Nation Expands Outward

1893–1901

THE PANIC OF 1893 AND ITS CONSEQUENCES

THE ECONOMIC AND SOCIAL IMPACT OF HARD TIMES

FOREIGN POLICY AND NATIONAL POLITICS

THE MCKINLEY PRESIDENCY: ACHIEVING WORLD POWER

THE UNITED STATES ON THE EVE OF THE TWENTIETH CENTURY

The belligerent figure of Uncle Sam preparing to fight Spain captures the passions that existed through the era of American Imperialism.
From the Collections of the Library of Congress

During the 1890s, social problems reached crisis proportions. An economic depression began in 1893 and Americans struggled with its effects for four years. With millions out of work and faith in national institutions eroding, the major political parties confronted unhappy voters. The Republicans emerged as the majority party, with the divided Democrats in disarray and the Populists unable to become a viable third party. The election of 1896 brought William McKinley to the White House, the architect of Republican success. He revitalized the presidency after its eclipse since the death of Abraham Lincoln.

As the condition of the economy improved at the end of the 1890s, Americans looked outward to an empire in the Caribbean and the Pacific. A war with Spain brought territorial gains and a debate about whether overseas possessions meant fundamental change. World power seemed alluring and troubling at the same time. American institutions and leaders faced the challenge of the new responsibilities.

THE PANIC OF 1893 AND ITS CONSEQUENCES

Grover Cleveland began his second term as president on March 4, 1893. In May 1893, the weakened economy collapsed in what became known as the Panic of 1893. Business had expanded during the late 1880s. In 1891 and 1892, investors turned cautious, worried about the soundness of the banking system and the stability of the currency. Banks failed as depositors withdrew their funds and hoarded cash. A decline in export trade further strained the economy. Business activity slowed, workers were laid off, and businesses cut back on production. Bad times spread across the country.

Effects of the Depression

By the end of 1893, some 600 banks had failed and 119 railroads were bankrupt and being run by court-appointed receivers. Another 15,000 businesses had closed. The stock market lost hundreds of millions of dollars. Most important, by early January 1894, 2.5 million people were unemployed. The economy was functioning at only three-quarters of its capacity.

The depression fell hardest on the average workers and their families. When their jobs vanished, there were no unemployment insurance payments, no government benefits, no temporary jobs programs to bridge the gap between a living wage and poverty.

States and cities provided some relief. In New York, daily newspapers distributed food, clothing, and fuel to the needy. Charity organization societies in Boston, New York, and Chicago coordinated volunteer efforts. Most well-off Americans believed the federal government should not intervene to alleviate a depression. As a result, people slept in the parks, camped out in railroad stations, and sought food at the soup kitchens that appeared in the big cities. Angry poor people called the soup kitchens "Cleveland Cafés."

To deal with the economic slump, Cleveland proposed a simple solution: repeal the Sherman Silver Purchase Act of 1890. That law had specified that the government buy a fixed amount of silver each month. Cleveland argued that the law produced inflation, undermined business confidence, and caused investors to take money out of the nation's gold reserve at the Treasury Department. If the amount of the reserve fell below $100 million, it would show that the credit of the United States was in danger. In fact, the amount was largely a psychological issue and did not measure the nation's economic condition.

In August 1893, Cleveland called a special session of Congress to repeal the Sherman Act. His own party was split over the issue of money. Northeastern party members believed in the gold standard with religious fervor. In the South and Far West, Democrats believed that the nation needed the free and unlimited coinage of silver into money at the fixed ratio to gold of sixteen to one. By asking his party to repeal the Sherman Act, Cleveland invited Democrats to wage war against each other.

The Special Session

Congress convened for its special session in August 1893. Over the protests of his party and with no tolerance of compromise, Cleveland insisted that Congress repeal the Sherman Act. With the aid of Republican votes, he won the battle. The bill repealing the Sherman Act was signed into law on November 1, 1893.

Having blamed the Sherman Act for the depression, Cleveland waited for a turnaround in the economy. Confidence in the dollar grew and the flow of gold out of the country eased somewhat. But prosperity did not return. As the new year approached, every indicator seemed headed downward. More railroads failed, more businesses closed, and more people were laid off to join the millions who were already unemployed.

The Tariff Disaster

The Democrats produced a bill to lower tariff rates in the House. With narrow control in their chamber, Senate Democrats had to write a tariff bill that in some instances raised customs rates on key products such as

CHRONOLOGY

1893 Grover Cleveland inaugurated as president • Panic of 1893 begins four years of depression • Sherman Silver Purchase Act repealed • National League of Colored Women established

1894 Coxey's army marches on Washington • Pullman strike occurs • Republicans make major gains in elections • Radcliffe College for women opens in Cambridge, Massachusetts

1895 Booker T. Washington proposes "Atlanta Compromise" • Venezuelan crisis brings threat of war with British • Utah adopts woman suffrage • Stephen Crane's *The Red Badge of Courage* published

1896 Republicans nominate William McKinley • William Jennings Bryan receives Democratic and Populist presidential nominations • Trading stamps are offered by stores in the United States • McKinley wins presidential election • *Plessy v. Ferguson* decision endorses racial segregation

1897 Dingley Tariff enacted • Jell-O is introduced

1898 Battleship *Maine* explodes in Havana Harbor • United States and Spain go to war • Treaty of Paris ends war and United States obtains Philippines and Puerto Rico

1899 Insurrection in Philippines begins • Open Door policy toward China announced

1900 McKinley and Bryan each renominated for presidency • Republicans win presidential election • International Ladies Garment Workers Union founded

---

sugar, coal, and iron. The law fell far short of the tariff reform that the Democrats had promised in 1892.

Congress finally passed the Wilson-Gorman Tariff Act in August 1894. It reduced rates on wool, copper and lumber, and raised duties on many other items. The measure repealed the reciprocal trade provisions of the McKinley Tariff, which had aimed at opening up markets and easing the political costs of protection. To make up for lost revenues, the Wilson-Gorman bill added a modest tax on personal incomes. Disgusted with the outcome, Cleveland let the bill become law without his signature.

The Industrial Armies

Outside of Washington, as the hard times lingered, some of the unemployed decided to present their grievances to Washington. In the Middle West, those out of work formed "Coxey's Army," uniting behind Jacob S. Coxey, a businessman from Massillon, Ohio. On Easter Sunday 1894, he left for Washington with 300 supporters to petition for a program of road building paid for by $500 million of paper money. Coxey and his son "Legal Tender Coxey" headed the proces-

sion, which included more than forty reporters. Slowly and painfully, the "Commonweal Army of Christ" approached Washington.

Across the nation other armies rode the rails, marched through cities, and demanded jobs from the government. The climax for Coxey and his followers came on May 1, 1894, when they reached Capitol Hill and tried to present their demands to Congress. Police intercepted Coxey, clubbed him and then arrested him for trespassing and "walking on the grass." The other armies were discouraged and dispersed but the protests undermined the political credibility of the Cleveland administration.

The Pullman Strike

Even more devastating was the major railroad strike that erupted shortly after the Coxey episode ended. George Pullman, the developer of the railroad sleeping car, had created a model town outside Chicago where his employees were to reside in apparent comfort and serenity. Employees who lived in Pullman and worked for the Pullman Palace Car Company found that their "model" town was expensive and

During the rioting that came with the Pullman strike in 1894 in Chicago, National Guard troops fired at the mob, as depicted in this contemporary drawing from Harper's Weekly.

Eugene V. Debs was the leader of the American Railway Union that struck in sympathy with the workers in the Pullman Palace Car Company. His experiences in this labor dispute helped persuade Debs to become a leader of the Socialist party.
© Bettmann/Corbis

oppressive. The prices that workers paid for services often ran 10 percent above what was charged in other communities.

When Pullman laid off employees and trimmed wages for others, he did not reduce the rents that his workers paid. As a result, in May 1894 the workers went out on strike. The strikers asked railroad workers across the nation not to handle Pullman's cars to help the walkout. The response from the American Railway Union (ARU) and its president, Eugene Victor Debs, was cautious at first. But by late June, the ARU started a sympathetic boycott and decided not to move trains with Pullman cars.

A National Railroad Strike

At its height the strike involved 125,000 men representing twenty railroads. The commerce of the nation stalled as freight shipments backed up in stations and train yards. The ARU did not interfere with the mails lest that action arouse the opposition of the federal government. Its economic power could not match that of the railroads' General Managers' Association, which had influence with Cleveland and his attorney general, Richard Olney, himself a former railroad corporation lawyer. On July 2, 1894, the president and the Justice Department obtained a court injunction to bar the strikers from blocking interstate commerce. Federal troops were ordered to Chicago.

Violence erupted as angry mobs destroyed railroad property and equipment. "We have been brought to the ragged edge of anarchy," Olney told the press. The strikers were not to blame for the episode; the rioters were local people. Police and National Guard troops put down the disturbance, but the public gave Cleveland and the federal government the credit. For the moment, the president regained his popularity among conservatives in both parties. His standing with ordinary voters remained low, however.

Debs went to jail for violating the court's injunction, and the U.S. Supreme Court confirmed his sentence in *In re Debs* (1895). By doing so the Court gave businesses a potent way to stifle labor unrest. If a strike began, management could seek an injunction from a friendly federal judge, jail the union leaders, and break the strike. Union power stagnated throughout the rest of the decade.

Politically, the strike divided the Democrats. Across the South and West, bitterness against the president became even more intense. Hate mail flooded into the White House, warning him of death if he crossed the Mississippi River. As one observer said, "If this keeps on long, fire and sword will devastate the country."

1894: A Realigning Election

Approaching the congressional elections of 1894, the Democrats were demoralized and divided. For the Populists, on the other hand, these elections seemed to offer an excellent chance to establish themselves as a credible challenger to the supremacy of the two major parties. The Republicans assailed the Democrats for failing to restore prosperity. Republican speakers urged a return to the policy of tariff protection that they had pursued under Benjamin Harrison. Party leaders, such as William McKinley, the governor of Ohio, crisscrossed the Midwest speaking to enthusiastic audiences. Former House Speaker Thomas B. Reed said, "The Democratic mortality will be so great next fall that their dead will be buried in trenches and marked unknown."

Reed's forecast was accurate. The Republicans prevailed in one of the most decisive congressional elections in the nation's history. The Democrats lost 113 seats in the largest transfer of power from one party to another in the annals of the two-party system. The Republicans regained control of the House of Representatives by a margin of 244 to 105. There were twenty-four states in which no Democrat won a federal office; six other states elected only one Democrat. In the Midwest 168 Republicans were elected to Congress, compared with nine Democrats.

The stalemated politics of the late nineteenth century had ended in an election that realigned the nation's politics. A Republican electoral majority would dominate American politics until 1929. The decision foreshadowed a Republican victory in the presidential contest in 1896.

The Populist Dilemma

The Populists were almost as disappointed as the Democrats with the outcome of the 1894 election. While the total vote for the Populists had increased over 1892, much of that rise occurred in the South where the Democrats then used their control of the electoral machinery to deny victory to Populist candidates. The

Table 19.1 Party Strength in Congress, 1886–1900

HOUSE OF REPRESENTATIVES

Congress and Year Elected	Republicans	Democrats	Other
Fiftieth (1886)	152	169	4
Fifty-first (1888)	166	159	– –
Fifty-second (1890)	88	235	9
Fifty-third (1892)	127	218	11
Fifty-fourth (1894)	244	105	7
Fifty-fifth (1896)	204	113	40
Fifty-sixth (1898)	185	163	9
Fifty-seventh (1900)	197	151	9

SENATE

Congress and Year Elected	Republicans	Democrats	Other
Fiftieth (1886)	39	37	– –
Fifty-first (1888)	39	37	– –
Fifty-second (1890)	47	39	– –
Fifty-third (1892)	44	38	3
Fifty-fourth (1894)	39	43	6
Fifty-fifth (1896)	47	34	7
Fifty-sixth (1898)	53	26	8
Fifty-seventh (1900)	55	31	4

Source: *The Statistical History of the United States* (Stamford, CT: Fairfield Publishers, 1965)

Populist delegation in Congress went from eleven members to seven. By 1894, the Populists were identified with the free coinage of silver, which appealed to the debt-burdened South and West. For industrial workers who had to survive on a fixed or declining income, higher prices arising from this inflationary policy seemed less attractive. The Populists told each other that they would do better in 1896, but they assumed that neither the Republicans nor the Democrats would adopt a free-silver position. In fact, the Populists' failure to mount a significant challenge to the major parties during the 1894 election signaled the end of their assault on the two-party system. The party remained a factor in the 1896 election, but its best days were past.

THE ECONOMIC AND SOCIAL IMPACT OF HARD TIMES

The economic impact of the depression of the 1890s was profound and far-reaching. By 1894, the economy operated at 80 percent of capacity. Total output of goods and services was down by some 13 percent. Unemployment ranged between 17 and 19 percent of the workforce. As the amount of money in circulation dropped, the nation experienced severe deflation. In the South, for example, cotton prices fell from 8.4 cents per pound in 1892 to 4.6 cents per pound in 1894. Since a figure of 10 cents per pound was necessary to break even, southern cotton farmers faced the prospect of disaster. For people with money, their dollars bought more goods. Among those out of work and without funds, however, lower prices were little comfort when they had no money to pay for the necessities of life.

In the South agricultural labor continued to be the lot of most African Americans. These four people had spent most of their lives in the cotton fields working for low wages and little economic future.
From the Collections of the Library of Congress

With their husbands, fathers, and sons laid off, women joined the workforce in greater numbers during the decade. During the 1890s, the total number of women with jobs rose from 3.7 million to just under 5 million. They gained employment in the expanding clerical fields, where they mastered typing and stenography. Traditional occupations such as teaching and nursing also attracted more women. In the factories, Irish-American, French-Canadian, and Italian-American women worked in textile and clothing establishments; or they did piecework for tobacco processors and shoemakers. In commercial food production and laundries the number of women employees also grew. The earnings of these women were necessary for the survival of their families. When the male wage earner brought home only $300 per year, and rents for a tenement dwelling were as much as $200 annually, the contributions of a daughter or wife were vital. However, the wages paid to women were as much as 40 percent below what men earned in industrial jobs.

The depression also brought young children back into the workforce. During the 1880s, the percentage of employed children between the ages of ten and fifteen had fallen from 17 percent to 12 percent. In the next decade, the percentage rose to 18 percent. By 1900, 1,750,000 children were employed. By the end of the century, thirty states had passed child labor laws, but these were often ineffective. Restricting the practice of child labor became an important social cause after 1900.

Reshaping the Economy

In the economy as a whole, the depression brought important changes. As a result of the downturn, the number of bankrupt businesses grew, revealing an obvious economic need for reorganization. In railroads, for example, major systems such as the Union Pacific were in receivership. The investment banker J. P. Morgan refinanced many of these rail lines and consolidated them to raise profits and increase efficiency. The thirty-two railroads capitalized at over $100 million controlled nearly 80 percent of the mileage of the nation. Shippers complained that these railroads gave larger customers unfair advantages in the form of rebates. By the end of the decade, there were increasing pleas from the South and Middle West to revive and strengthen the Interstate Commerce Commission whose power to oversee railroad rates had been reduced by court decisions.

In the 1890s, "finance capitalists" like J. P. Morgan challenged the dominance of the "industrial capi-

*P*ICTURING THE PAST✦SOCIAL & CULTURAL

CHILD LABOR IN THE 1890s

Brown Brothers, Sterling, PA

The spread of industrialism in the late nineteenth century expanded jobs and economic opportunity, but social problems arose as well. Young people found work in factories and small business, as this woman making shoes at her bench exemplifies. The conditions were often primitive and the workweek was very long and demanding. Few protections existed if she hurt herself on the job, and she might find herself discharged for small infractions of rules or the whim of her employer. Efforts to regulate child labor ran up against well-entrenched ideas that work built character in the young as well as the economic need in large families for extra income. Photographers educated the public about the existence of these conditions in the years 1890 to 1910, and images such as this one helped create the popular awareness behind the political and economic reforms of this period.

---

talists" of the 1870s and 1880s who had built large enterprises in steel, oil, and railroads. These financiers launched a wave of corporate mergers that began in 1895 and continued for a decade. An average of 300 companies a year were merged with larger firms. Twelve hundred mergers occurred in 1899. Some states such as New Jersey and Delaware made it easier for firms to locate holding companies there. In New York a market for industrial stocks enabled bankers to raise capital. In the case of *U.S. v. E. C. Knight* (1895), the Supreme Court ruled that the Sherman Antitrust Act applied only to monopolies of interstate commerce and not to those solely of manufacturing. This decision made it more difficult to enforce the antitrust laws and, as a result, the government took little action against any of the mergers that occurred during the 1890s.

When the economy began to recover in 1897, the public's attention turned to the growth of large businesses and trusts. Consumers believed that it was unfair for a few men or businesses to dominate a single industry or control the price of commodities.

The Revolt Against Bigness

The depression of the 1890s stretched on year after year. The accepted values of earlier generations came under scrutiny as people struggled to make sense of their situation. Writers questioned whether the government should simply promote economic expansion and then allow fate to decide who prospered and who did not. For the first time many argued that government should regulate the economy in the interest of social justice.

A growing number of social thinkers suggested that additional government action was necessary. In 1894, Henry Demarest Lloyd published a book entitled *Wealth Against Commonwealth* that detailed what he believed the Standard Oil Company had done to monopolize the oil industry and corrupt the nation. "Monopoly cannot be content with controlling its own business . . . . Its destiny is rule or ruin, and rule is but a slower ruin." Unimpressed with the idea of merely regulating the large corporations, Lloyd called for public ownership of many transportation and manufacturing firms.

The economic hard times strengthened the resolve of the Social Gospel movement. The church, said Walter Rauschenbusch in 1893, should be the "appointed instrument for the further realization of that new society in the world about it." Other young people of the day echoed similar themes. Ray Stannard Baker had reported on Coxey's army for his newspaper. He told his editor, "When such an ugly and grotesque fungus can grow so prominently on the body politic there must be something wrong. The national blood is out of order."

Women and Reform in the 1890s

In states such as Illinois and New York, bands of women joined together as consumers to push for better working conditions in factories and fair treatment of employees in department stores. Social workers and charity operatives decided that the plight of the poor was not simply the fault of those in need. Better government and more enlightened policies could uplift the downtrodden.

Women's participation in the process of change was significant. Julia Lathrop and Florence Kelley worked in Illinois improving state charitable institutions and inspecting factories. Ida Wells-Barnett rallied African American women against lynching. Mary Church Terrell led the National Association of Colored Women, founded in 1896, in making the women's clubs in the black community a more effective force for change. The suffrage movement and the women's clubs among white, middle-class women and their black counterparts slowly established the basis for additional reforms after 1900.

A leading voice for a new role for women was Charlotte Perkins Gilman, whose major work, *Women and Economics*, was published in 1898. Gilman advocated that women seek economic independence. The home, she argued, was a primitive institution that should be transformed through modern industrial practices lest it impede "the blessed currents of progress that lead and lift us all." Housework should be professionalized and homes transformed into domestic factories; women would then be free to pursue their own destinies, which could include social reform. Gilman's work influenced a generation of women reformers as well as future feminists.

Liquor Control and Reform

The renewed emphasis on reform during the 1890s also affected the long-standing campaign to control the sale and use of alcoholic beverages. In 1895, the

Charlotte Perkins Gilman's writings challenged the traditional roles that women occupied in the household. She became an important advocate for a new kind of thinking about how women should function in society.
From the Collections of the Library of Congress

Reverend H. H. Russell established the Anti-Saloon League in Oberlin, Ohio. Its organization relied on a network of local Protestant churches throughout the nation. They aimed to regulate saloons as tightly as possible. Unlike previous efforts to pass antiliquor laws, the League focused on a single issue, and it became a model for the kind of lobbying that would characterize reform campaigns during the first two decades of the twentieth century.

The prohibition campaigns in the South brought black and white women together in a brief alliance to cripple what they both regarded as an important social evil. In some parts of North Carolina, for example, white women organized chapters of the Woman's Christian Temperance Union (WCTU) among black women. When white volunteers did not appear, black women took over and set up their own organizations. Even as racial barriers rose in the

South, women continued to work together to curb drinking until at the end of the 1890s when it became politically impossible to do so.

To counter the drive for prohibition, brewers and liquor producers created lobbying groups to match the Anti-Saloon League and the persistent militance of the WCTU. Brewing associations appeared in battleground states such as Texas to coordinate strategies in local option elections and to get "wet" voters to the polls. Anti-prohibition sentiment flourished among Irish Americans and German Americans in the cities and towns of the Northeast and Midwest. The struggles over liquor often pitted the countryside dwellers against urban residents who wanted liquor to remain available.

Reform in the Cities and States

Reform appeared in the cities as the depression revealed social problems and political injustices. In Detroit, Hazen Pingree had been elected mayor in 1889. During the depression, he decided that city government ought to do more than just stand by while the poor suffered. He constructed his own political machine to pursue social justice through lower utility rates and expanded government services. That brought him into conflict with the streetcar companies and utilities that dominated Detroit politics. In Chicago, a British editor, William T. Stead, visited the city for the Columbian Exposition in 1893. What he saw in the slums led him to write *If Christ Came to Chicago* in 1894. Stead contended that the city needed a spiritual and political revival. He singled out the power of the street railway operator, Charles T. Yerkes, as particularly oppressive because of the high rates and poor service his companies provided. Stead's attack led to the formation of the Chicago Civic Federation, which sought to control gambling, clean up the slums, and limit the power of men like Yerkes. Similar reform groups sprang up in Wisconsin's cities to restrain corporations that provided vital municipal services at an exorbitant cost to taxpayers.

By the mid-1890s, these examples of urban reform sparked the creation of groups to address national urban problems. The National Municipal League came into existence in 1894; in the same year the First National Conference for Good City Government took place. Over the next several years reformers diagnosed the ills of American cities and recommended solutions. Out of these debates came the ideas that would flourish during the Progressive Era a decade later.

Reform in the States

As the depression worsened, citizens looked to their state governments for answers and instead found political and social problems that rivaled the plight of the cities. Critics complained of corruption, political machines, and a breakdown of democracy. In Wisconsin a Republican politician, Robert M. La Follette, built a political following by attacking the entrenched organization within his own party. He called for primary elections to choose candidates for office rather than leave the decision to the politicians and their rigged meetings. After his triumphs in the Spanish-American War, Theodore Roosevelt was elected governor of New York, where he displayed his vigorous leadership skills in publicizing the activities of large corporations and using state power to conserve natural resources.

The work of reform governors and their supporters in the states led to increased authority for these governments and greater reliance on experts and nonpartisan commissions in making decisions about public policy. Railroad commissions, public utility commissions, and investigative boards to oversee key industries were formed. By the end of the decade, however, observers believed that meaningful reform would come only when the federal government shaped national legislation to curb railroads and trusts engaged in interstate commerce.

Resistance from the Courts

Among the most powerful obstacles to reform were judges who upheld business interests. The doctrine of *substantive due process* gave state and federal judges a way to block legislative attempts to regulate economic behavior. According to this doctrine, the due process clause of the Fourteenth Amendment did not apply only to the issue of whether the procedure used to pass a law had been fair. Judges might consider how the substance of the law affected life, liberty, and property. They could then decide whether the law was so inherently unfair that it would be unjust even if the procedures for implementing the statute were unbiased. This approach gave the judiciary the right to decide whether a law regulating business enterprise was fair to the corporation being supervised.

Judges also interpreted federal laws in ways that limited efforts to curb corporate power. The same year (1895) that the Court issued the *E. C. Knight* decision, which constrained the scope of the Sherman Antitrust Act, it also ruled in *Pollock v. Farmers' Loan and Trust Co.* that the income tax provisions of the Wilson-Gorman Tariff were unconstitutional. In labor cases courts imposed injunctions to bar unions from boycotts and strikes.

A few jurists and lawyers, however, had doubts about this philosophy of favoring corporations. In Massachusetts, Oliver Wendell Holmes, Jr., had published a book on *The Common Law* in 1881. Holmes contended that "the life of the law has not been logic; it has been experience." By this he meant that judges should not base their rulings on abstract premises and theories but should consider the rational basis of a law in judging whether it was constitutional or not.

Conservative himself, Holmes was ready to defer to the popular will in legislative matters. If the Constitution did not prohibit a state from building a slaughterhouse or regulating an industry, his response was "God-dammit, let them build it." In Nebraska, Roscoe Pound was evolving a similar reality-based approach to legal thinking that became known as *sociological jurisprudence*. Louis D. Brandeis of Massachusetts was gaining a reputation as the "People's Lawyer" who believed that the legal system should serve small businesses and consumers as well as large corporations.

The Philosophy of Pragmatism

The philosopher William James of Harvard University evolved an explanation for what political and legal reformers were trying to do. He called it *pragmatism.* James wanted to show that truth is more than an abstract concept. He believed that truth must demonstrate its value in the real world. "What in short is the truth's cash value in experiential terms?" James asked. To James, pragmatism meant "looking away from first things, principles, 'categories,' supposed necessities; and of looking towards last things, fruits, consequences, facts." James divided the world into tough-minded people, who based their actions on facts and pragmatic truths, and tender-minded people, who were swayed by abstractions. His philosophy emphasized self-reliance and gritty reality. It appealed to a generation of reformers who sought practical solutions to the problems they saw in their communities and the nation as a whole.

Another spokesman for reform was a University of Chicago teacher and philosopher named John Dewey. In his major work, *The School and Society* (1899), Dewey contended that schools should undertake the task of preparing students to live in a complex, industrial world. The public school must do more than transmit academic knowledge for its own sake. As an institution, it should be a means of instilling democratic values and usable skills. Education,

The Harvard philosopher and psychologist William James advanced his theory of "pragmatism" as a way that individuals could deal with the realities of the world. His work was part of the intellectual ferment of the 1890s.
© Corbis

Dewey wrote, "is the fundamental method of social progress and reform."

Literary Naturalism and Realism

During the 1890s, writers and artists turned to the world around them. They preached the doctrine of realism, and they tried to capture the complexity of a natural world in which science, technology, and capitalism were challenging older values. William Dean Howells, a novelist, examined the impact of capitalism on workers and urban dwellers in New York City in *A Hazard of New Fortunes* (1890). During the depression Howell's novels and essays were sharply critical of the new industrial system. Stephen Crane depicted the ways in which the city exploited and destroyed a young woman in *Maggie: A Girl of the Streets* (1893).

Two noteworthy practitioners of literary naturalism were Frank Norris and Theodore Dreiser. Norris wrote about California railroads in *The Octopus* (1901) and about the wheat market in Chicago in *The Pit* (1903). In Norris's Darwinian world, humanity was trapped in the impersonal grip of soulless corporations.

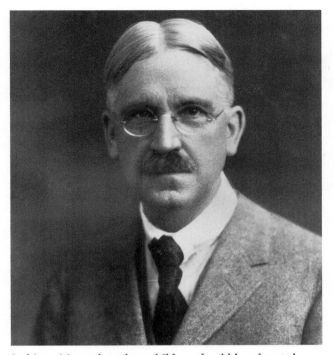

In his writings about how children should be educated, John Dewey influenced several generations of American teachers. He wanted schools to do more to prepare children to be productive members of society.
© UPI/Bettmann/Corbis

In *Sister Carrie* (1900), Dreiser described how a small-town girl went to work in Chicago and was consumed by its temptations. These novels reached a large audience, and their depiction of characters caught in an amoral universe intensified the sentiment for reform.

By the 1890s, then, the currents that would come together as the progressive movement of the 1900–1920 period were forming. Urban reformers, believers in the Social Gospel, politically active women, candidates angry with the established powers in their state's dominant party—all of these groups shared a pervasive discontent with the state of society. The volatile domestic and international events of the 1890s would prepare the ground for a generation of reform.

African Americans and Segregation

In addition to experiencing the same economic deprivations of the 1890s, African Americans confronted the ever-tightening grip of segregation in the South. Although blacks had made great strides in building viable communities and economic institutions since Reconstruction, white southerners disliked their advancement. Instead, whites endeavored to return African Americans to a subordinate position. The courts proved unreceptive to the pleas of blacks for equal treatment under the law.

A spokesman for blacks emerged in Booker T. Washington, who argued that African Americans should emphasize hard work and personal development rather than rebelling against their condition. Whites applauded Washington's philosophy, but bigotry continued in the form of race riots and lynchings. Washington believed that African Americans must demonstrate their worthiness for citizenship through their own achievements. In 1895, he reached a national audience when he spoke at the Cotton States and International Exposition in Atlanta. What he said made him the leading black figure in the United States for a generation.

"In all the things that are purely social, we can be separate as the fingers," Washington proclaimed, "yet one as the hand in all things essential to mutual progress." To his fellow blacks he said, "it is at the bottom of life we must begin" to create an economic base through hard work: "[C]ast down your bucket where you are" and be "patient, law-abiding and unresentful." Any "agitation of questions of social equality" would be "the extremest folly."

Washington's white audience gave him an enthusiastic response, and white philanthropists funded his school, the Tuskegee Institute generously. Behind the scenes, Washington dominated the political lives of blacks and even more secretly he funded court challenges to segregation. In public, however, he came to symbolize an accommodation with the existing racial system.

The Supreme Court put its stamp of approval on segregation as a legal doctrine a year later. Homer A. Plessy's appeal of the Louisiana court's decision upholding segregation of railroad cars had made its way to the Supreme Court. The court heard oral arguments in April 1896 and rendered its judgment five weeks later. By a vote of seven to one in the case of *Plessy v. Ferguson,* the justices upheld the Louisiana law and, by implication, the principle of segregation. Writing for the majority, Justice Henry Billings Brown said that the Fourteenth Amendment "could not have been intended to abolish distinctions based on color, or to enforce social, as distinguished from political equality, or a commingling of the two races upon terms unsatisfactory to either." He rejected the argument that "the enforced separation of the races stamps the colored race with a badge of inferiority." In a dissenting opinion, Justice John Marshall Harlan responded that "Our Constitution is color-blind, and neither knows nor tolerates classes among citizens." This ruling determined the legal situation of African Americans for more than half a century.

Petition from the citizens of New Jersey to the U. S. Congress praying for Congress to make the act of lynching a crime in the United States, 1900

At the end of the nineteenth century, lynchings directed against blacks became a frequent occurrence in the South. Some concerned citizens in the North protested against these crimes, as this petition from individuals in New Jersey shows, but the federal government took no action against this wave of extralegal violence.

We, the undersigned petitioners, citizens of New Jersey, beg most respectfully to represent to your honorable bodies, the Senate and House of Representatives, the alarming state of the country in respect to the appalling prevalence in the Southern States, of that species of lawlessness known as lynching whereby inhabitants of that section are deprived of life without due process of law by gangs of irresponsible and wickedly disposed persons; that the victims of these barbarous outbreaks and outrages are usually members of the Negro race, and that the crimes imputed to them by their self-constituted executioners, but never proved, and for which they suffer death, have ranged all the way from petty larceny to murder; that Negroes have been hanged and shot in the South by lynching mobs on mere suspicion, or because they have incurred the odium of being politically troublesome to the community in which they resided; that human life is frightfully cheap in the South, and that a Negro's life has absolutely no value whatever there when a Southern mob scents his blood; that the local police power offers him under such circumstances no adequate protection and often times are in actual or virtual connivance with his murderers:

WHEREFORE, your petitioners pray your honorable bodies to make the act of lynching a crime against the United States, to provide for its commission the sternest pains and penalties, and to empower the President of the United States and to make it his duty to intervene whenever and wherever necessary with the armed force of the nation to prevent the commission of this atrocious crime, and to rescue any person or persons from the hands of any mob in any state of the Union, and for the better prevention of lynching your petitioners further pray your honorable bodies for the creation of a Central Detective Bureau at Washington with branch offices in various parts of the section or sections subject to this kind of lawlessness, for the purpose of collecting and transmitting information promptly to the President relative to the intentions and movements of lynching bodies, and that such information may be used in subsequent prosecuting proceedings against such individuals in the Courts of the United States for violation of the law made and provided in that behalf.

Source: Petition presented to Congress, February 21, 1900, National Archives.

As the political rights of blacks diminished, white attacks on them increased. During the North Carolina elections of 1898, race was a key issue that led to a Democratic victory over the Populists, Republicans, and their African American allies. Once whites had won, they turned on the black-dominated local government in Wilmington, North Carolina. Several hundred whites attacked areas where blacks lived in December 1898, killing eleven people and driving residents from their homes. Lynchings in the South continued at a rate of more than one hundred per year.

Although black Americans faced daunting obstacles in the 1890s, they made substantial progress toward improved living conditions in ways that showed that they were more than simply the victims of white oppression. They founded colleges in the

_P_ICTURING THE PAST ✦ SOCIAL & CULTURAL
"CIVILIZING" NATIVE AMERICAN

© Smithsonian Institution

Few pictures better demonstrate how historical perceptions of images change over time than these photographs of Tom Torolino and friends at the Carlisle Indian School in 1886 and 1889. When the pictures were made, they could be used to show how three Native American boys gave up their tribal regalia and put on the clothing of white society as they moved toward "civilization." More than a century later, the photographs seem to trace a process whereby young men are stripped of their true identity and heritage to conform to the cultural dictates of white society. The images thus become a metaphor for the larger way in which American society has treated Indians. Those that were not killed outright in warfare were made to conform even at the cost of their real character as individuals and members of long-standing Native American ways of life.

South, created self-help institutions in black churches, and developed pockets of well-off citizens in cities such as Washington, Boston, Baltimore, and Philadelphia. In the South black women pursued social reform in states with impressive determination.

The National Association of Colored Women, founded in 1896, sought to become, in the words of its president, Mary Church Terrell, "partners in the great firm of progress and reform." African American resistance to segregation shaped the 1890s as much as did the white drive to subjugate blacks in the South and the North.

Native Americans

In the years after the Battle of Wounded Knee, efforts to assimilate the 250,000 Indians into the dominant culture went on. One favored method was to educate Native American children at schools either located on the reservation or many miles distant. The students were required to speak English, wear white people's clothes, and abandon their tribal ceremonies and religions. The most celebrated of these Indian schools was located in Carlisle, Pennsylvania, and was operated by Richard Henry Pratt between 1879 and 1904. "Transfer the savage-born infant to the surroundings of civilization," Pratt said, "and he will grow to possess a civilized language and habit." For many of the Indian children, however, these schools seemed more like a prison. They were malnourished, often treated cruelly, and stripped of their individuality. The goal of this policy seemed to be the extinction of Indian culture in the name of assimilation.

FOREIGN POLICY AND NATIONAL POLITICS

Amid the political turmoil of the second Cleveland administration, foreign affairs pressed for attention. The nation stood on the verge of becoming a world power, and national leaders debated how to respond to increasing competition with powerful international rivals and the upsurge of nationalism among colonial peoples.

Diplomatic Problems: Hawaii and Venezuela

The first issue was that of Hawaii. Grover Cleveland was not convinced that the revolution that had occurred in 1893 represented the will of the Hawaiian people. Holding the treaty of annexation, he dispatched a special commission to investigate conditions. Believing that the native population backed Queen Liliuokalani, he refused to send the treaty to the Senate and asked for restoration of the native government. The revolutionary government declined to yield power, however, and in 1894 the administration granted it diplomatic recognition.

Another foreign policy crisis occurred in 1894 when a dispute arose between Great Britain and Venezuela over the precise boundary line that sepa-

rated Venezuela and British Guiana. The Cleveland administration concluded that the controversy was also a test of the Monroe Doctrine. In 1895, the new secretary of state, Richard Olney, sent a diplomatic note to London that asserted that the United States was "practically sovereign on this continent, and its fiat is law upon the subjects to which it confines its interposition." The British responded slowly, and when their answer finally arrived it rejected the arguments of the Cleveland administration. Newspapers talked of a possible war. The president asked Congress for the power to name a commission to decide the boundary dispute and enforce its decision. The British found themselves in a difficult position. In South Africa they were encountering problems that would eventually lead to the Boer War (1899-1902), and they had few European friends when it came to foreign policy. Accordingly they decided to arbitrate their quarrel with Venezuela through a joint Anglo-American-Venezuelan commission to resolve the dispute, and the crisis passed.

The Cuban Rebellion

The most dangerous foreign policy issue that confronted Cleveland stemmed from the revolution that Cubans launched against Spanish rule in 1895. The Wilson-Gorman Tariff had increased import duties on Cuban sugar, damaging the island's economy, which depended on sugar. Rebels took to the battlefield in February 1895 seeking to oust the Spanish. Unable to defeat the rebels in direct combat, the Spanish drove the civilian population into cities and fortified areas. The "reconcentration" camps where these refugees were housed were disease-ridden and overcrowded. The architect of this harsh policy was General Valeriano Weyler, nicknamed "The Butcher" for his cruelty to the captive Cubans.

The American Stake in Cuba

The American public took a close interest in the Cuban situation. Investments in the island, totaling about $50 million, were threatened by the conflict. Religious denominations saw the brutality and famine of the rebellion as cause for concern and perhaps direct intervention. Sensational newspapers, known as "the yellow press," because one of them carried a popular comic strip about "The Yellow Kid," printed numerous stories about atrocities in Cuba. William Randolph Hearst, publisher of the *New York Journal,* and Joseph Pulitzer of the New York *World* were the most sensational practitioners of this kind of journalism. The Cubans also established an office in New York from which their "junta" dispensed propaganda to a receptive audience. Concern about Cuba was a significant element in the nation's foreign policy during the mid-1890s.

President Cleveland tried to enforce the neutrality laws that limited shipments of arms to Cuba. He did not recognize the Cubans as belligerents, and he informed the Spanish that they might count on the good offices of the United States in negotiating an end to the fighting. This position suited Spain, which followed a policy of procrastination to quell the revolt before the United States intervened. By the end of his administration, the president was pressing Spain to make concessions to the Cubans, but he never challenged Spain's right to exercise its sovereignty over the island.

The Election of 1896

The Cleveland administration did not recover politically from the disasters of 1894. Relations with the Democrats worsened. Preferring to work alone and wary of threats on his life, Cleveland increased the number of guards around the White House and rarely ventured out to meet his fellow citizens.

The reserves of gold were still shrinking, despite the repeal of the Sherman Silver Purchase Act in 1893. To bolster the reserves and bring in gold, the White House sold government bonds. The sale that took place in February 1895 was handled by New York banker J. P. Morgan, who made a nice profit from the transaction. Eventually there were four bond sales which supplied needed currency for the Treasury but also further alienated Democratic advocates of inflation and free silver.

The Political Lineup

As the 1896 election approached, the Republicans, after their sweep of the 1894 election, wanted to nominate a candidate who could cash in on their likely victory. The front-runner was William McKinley of Ohio, a veteran of the Civil War, former member of Congress, and governor of Ohio from 1892 to 1896. A popular speaker, he was identified with the protective tariff. With the aid of his close friend Marcus A. Hanna, an industrialist from Ohio, McKinley became the favorite for the Republican nomination. His campaign slogan proclaimed him as "The Advance Agent of Prosperity."

McKinley won on the first ballot at the Republican National Convention in St. Louis in June 1896. The only difficult issue was gold and silver. Eastern Republicans wanted the party to endorse the gold standard. The key plank contained that language, but it also conciliated

pro-silver Republicans with a promise to seek wider international use of silver. The Republicans expected to wage a tariff-centered campaign against a nominee saddled with the unpopularity of Cleveland.

The Rise of William Jennings Bryan

The Democratic convention, however, took an unexpected turn. After the elections of 1894, the free silver wing of the party dominated the South and West. By 1896, an articulate spokesman for the silver cause would appeal to many Democrats. Among the leading candidates for the nomination, however, none possessed the required excitement and devotion to silver. A young politician from Nebraska named William Jennings Bryan saw himself as the "logic of the situation." During 1895 and early 1896, he urged leaders to think of him as a possible second choice should the convention deadlock. By the time the Democratic National Convention opened in Chicago in July 1896, there was a good deal of latent support for Bryan among the delegates.

The Cross of Gold

Bryan's chance came during the debate over whether the party platform should endorse silver. He arranged to be the final speaker on behalf of free silver. Bryan had a clear, musical voice that could be heard across the convention hall. The speech he gave, entitled the "Cross of Gold," became a classic moment in American political oratory. He asked the delegates whether the party would stand "upon the side of the idle holders of capital, or upon the side of the struggling masses?" His answer was simple. To those who wanted a gold standard, the Democrats would say: "You shall not press down upon the brow of labor this crown of thorns, you shall not crucify mankind upon a cross of gold." His audience was enthralled.

The next day the convention nominated Bryan for president on a free silver platform. A wave of support for Bryan swept the country, and the Republicans found their careful plans for the campaign suddenly at risk. Since the Democrats could not raise much in the way of campaign funds, Bryan decided to take his message to the voters. He prepared for an extensive nationwide campaign tour to speak on behalf of the common man, a rural nation, and the older agrarian virtues.

The Populists and the Campaign

Bryan's nomination left the Populist party in disarray. The Populists had delayed their national convention until after the two major parties had named

At the age of thirty-six, William Jennings Bryan was a striking and handsome figure during his first race for the presidency in 1896. His musical voice and ardent advocacy of the silver issue gave him a powerful push in the summer until the effects of the Republican campaign turned the tide for William McKinley.
Reproduced from the Collections of the Library of Congress

The Republican magazines in the East attacked Bryan for his use of religious imagery in his famous "Cross of Gold" speech. In the cartoon, Bryan tramples on the Bible and his followers preach anarchy behind him.
The Granger Collection, New York

their candidates and now faced a dilemma. If they failed to select Bryan as their candidate, they would be accused of depriving silver of any chance of victory. Yet if they went along with Bryan's nomination, there would be no need for their party. With some reluctance, they ultimately decided to name Bryan as the presidential nominee.

Bryan Versus McKinley

Bryan pursued the presidency with youthful energy. He traveled 18,000 miles and gave more than 600 speeches; his audiences, estimated at a total of 3 million people, turned out to see "The Boy Orator of the Platte River." To counter Bryan, the Republicans raised between $3.5 million and $4 million from fearful corporations. The Democrats charged that the Republicans and their business allies were coercing workers to vote for McKinley. Most industrial workers voted Republican because they feared the inflationary effects of free silver. Mark Hanna, who managed McKinley's

The Republican candidate also came in for newspaper assault. A Democratic magazine ran a cartoon showing a dispirited Uncle Sam having to accept monopoly power in the nation's capital once McKinley was elected.
The Granger Collection, New York

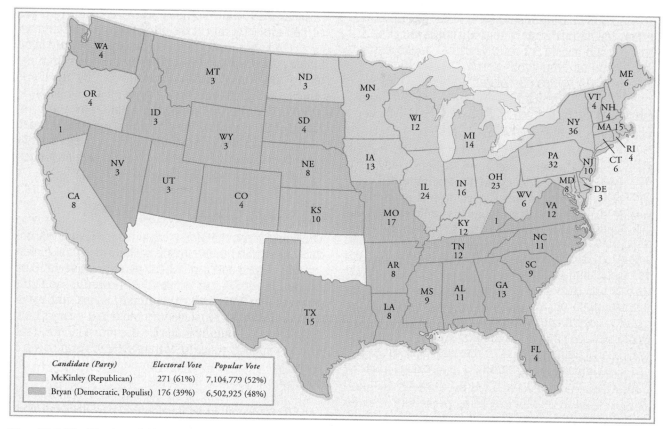

Candidate (Party)	Electoral Vote	Popular Vote
McKinley (Republican)	271 (61%)	7,104,779 (52%)
Bryan (Democratic, Populist)	176 (39%)	6,502,925 (48%)

Map 19.1 *The Election of 1896*

The election of 1896 was a climax to the upheavals of the mid-1890s. Note the sectional alignment that divided the nation between the agrarian South and West that supported William Jennings Bryan and the industrialized East and Middle West where William McKinley and the Republicans were strong.

View an animated version of this map or related maps at http://history.wadsworth.com/passages2e.

campaign, used the party's substantial war chest to distribute several hundred million pamphlets to the voters. Republican speakers took to the campaign trail; party newspapers poured out information about the merits of the tariff and the gold standard.

The key to the Republican campaign was McKinley. He stayed home in Canton, Ohio, and let the voters come to him. As the weeks passed, more than 750,000 people stood in McKinley's yard to hear his speeches about the dangers of free silver. These addresses appeared in newspapers across the country. By mid-September, the tide turned against Bryan, and there were signs that the Republicans would win in November.

A Decisive Election

The result was the most decisive outcome since the 1872 presidential contest. McKinley had a margin of 600,000 popular votes and won 271 electoral votes to 176 for Bryan. Bryan ran well in the South, the Plains states, and the Far West. McKinley dominated in the Northeast, the mid-Atlantic states, and the Midwest. Despite his appeals to the labor vote, Bryan ran poorly in the cities. Free silver might lead to inflation, an idea that had little appeal to workers on fixed incomes. McKinley's argument that the tariff would restore prosperity also took hold in the more industrialized areas of the country.

The 1896 results confirmed the outcome of the 1894 election. The Republicans had established themselves as the nation's majority party. The South remained solidly Democratic; the industrial North was Republican. The older issue of how much the government ought to promote economic expansion was giving way to the new problem of whether the government should regulate the economy so as to relieve injustices and imbalances in the way that society worked. Bryan and the Populists had suggested that government should play a larger regulatory role. The voters had chosen instead to accept the economic nationalism of the Republicans as embodied in the tariff and the gold standard.

THE MCKINLEY PRESIDENCY: ACHIEVING WORLD POWER

When Grover Cleveland departed in March 1897, he left a weakened presidency. McKinley improved relations with the press, which Cleveland had ignored; he traveled extensively to promote his policies; and he used experts and commissions to strengthen the operation of the national government. In domestic policy, McKinley persuaded Congress to enact the Dingley Tariff of 1897, which raised customs rates. He also sought, without success, to convince European nations to agree to wider use of silver through an international agreement. As a result, when the Republicans gained control of both houses of Congress after the 1898 election, the Gold Standard Act of 1900 established gold as the basis of the nation's currency. Gold discoveries in South Africa and Alaska inflated the currency by making more gold available. Returning prosperity relieved the agricultural tensions of the decade.

The Road to Empire

McKinley faced a growing crisis in Cuba. He wanted Spain to withdraw from Cuba if its forces could not suppress the rebellion quickly. Any solution must be acceptable to the Cuban rebels. Since they would accept nothing less than the end of Spanish rule, there was little basis for a negotiated settlement. During 1897, however, McKinley tried to persuade Spain to agree to a diplomatic solution. Yet, no Spanish government could stay in power if it agreed to leave Cuba without a fight.

At first it appeared that the president's policy might be working. In the fall of 1897 the Spanish government moved toward granting the Cubans some control over their internal affairs. Foreign policy, however, was to remain in Spanish hands. The practice of moving Cubans into reconcentration camps was abandoned. However, the situation worsened during the early months of 1898 as the rebellion persisted. On January 12, 1898, pro-Spanish elements in Cuba rioted against the autonomy program. To monitor the situation, the White House decided to send a warship to Havana. The battleship *Maine* arrived there on January 25. Spain was pleased at this sign of normal relations, but the diplomatic problem continued. On February 1, Spain insisted that its sovereignty over Cuba must be preserved even if it meant resisting foreign intervention.

On February 9, 1898, newspapers in the United States published a letter written by the Spanish minister to the United States, Enrique Dupuy de Lôme, which the Cuban rebels had intercepted. The letter described McKinley as "weak and a bidder for the admiration of the crowd." These insulting remarks led to de Lôme's recall and resignation. The minister's other statements revealed that Spain was playing for time in its negotiations with Washington.

The Sinking of the Maine

On February 15, the *Maine* exploded in Havana Harbor; 260 officers and men perished. The cause of the blast, according to modern research, was spontaneous combustion in a coal bunker. In 1898, however, the public believed that Spain had either caused an external explosion or had failed to prevent it. McKinley established a naval board of inquiry to probe the disaster. The deadline for its report was mid-March 1898. While he waited, McKinley made military preparations and explored unsuccessfully the idea of buying Cuba from Spain.

Time was running out for a peaceful solution. On March 17, a Republican senator who had visited the war, Redfield Proctor of Vermont, told the Senate that conditions in Cuba were horrible. The speech swayed the public toward intervention. Two days later, McKinley learned that the naval board had concluded, on the basis of the science of the time and the physical evidence, that an external explosion had caused the destruction of the Maine. When the report went to Congress, pressure on the president to intervene in Cuba mounted.

The Last Drive for Peace

McKinley pushed Spain either to agree to an armistice in the fighting that still raged in Cuba or to permit American mediation that would end in Cuban independence. However, the Spanish were opposed to independence for Cuba directly or through negotiations. Still, McKinley was able to hold off Congress until Spain had another chance to consider its options. When a negative answer arrived from Spain on March 31, 1898, McKinley prepared to put the issue before Congress.

There was one last flurry of diplomatic activity. On April 9, Spain agreed, at the urging of its European friends, to suspend hostilities in Cuba. It was not an armistice, which would have meant formal recognition of the Cuban cause. The Spanish military commander in Cuba would determine how long the cessation of the fighting would last. There was no agreement on Cuban independence from Madrid. Thus the Spanish had not yielded on the key demands of the United States.

McKinley sent his message to Congress on April 11. It requested presidential authority to end the fighting in Cuba through armed force if necessary. At the end of his message the president mentioned that Spain had proposed to suspend hostilities, but he gave the idea little significance. Later generations would argue that Spain's acceptance of a suspension of hostilities represented a surrender to the demands of the United States. In fact, the diplomatic impasse between the two countries was unbroken.

Over the following week Congress debated the president's request for authority to intervene. To show that the United States had no selfish motives, the lawmakers adopted an amendment offered by Senator Henry M. Teller, a Colorado Democrat. The Teller Amendment stated that the United States did not intend to control Cuba or annex it. Yet Congress also declined to extend official recognition to the Cuban rebels to preserve freedom of action for the United States. For McKinley, the important result was a resolution authorizing him to act; this was passed on April 19 and the president signed it the following day. Spain immediately broke diplomatic relations with the

United States; it declared war on April 24. Congress replied that a state of war had existed between the United States and Spain since April 21.

The War Begins

The war between the United States and Spain occurred because both sides believed that their cause was just. McKinley had pursued a diplomatic solution until it became clear that Spain would not agree to a negotiated settlement that would end its reign over Cuba. In the end, Spain preferred to lose Cuba on the battlefield rather than at the bargaining table.

The war began with a stunning naval victory. On May 1, 1898, Commodore George Dewey and the Asiatic naval squadron defeated the Spanish navy at Manila Bay in the Philippine Islands. The U.S. unit was in the waters of the Philippines because of war plans that had been developed in 1895 and updated as relations with Spain worsened. The goal was to hit the Spanish hard in the Philippines and thus pressure them to surrender Cuba. The triumph at Manila Bay made Dewey a national hero, but it confronted the president with new opportunities and problems in foreign policy.

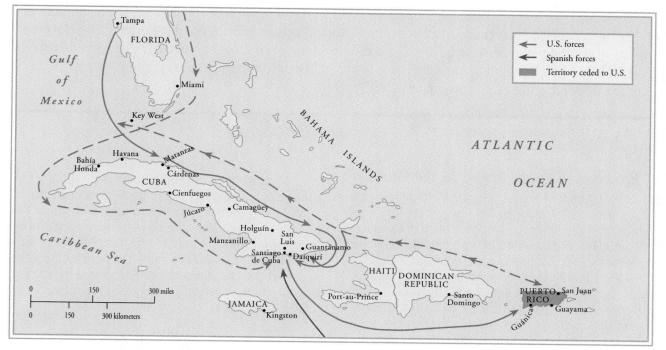

Map 19.2 *The Spanish-American War*

 The main focus of fighting in the war with Spain in 1898 was the island of Cuba and the Caribbean. This map shows the movement of American and Spanish naval forces toward the decisive battles in the vicinity of Santiago de Cuba as well as the capture of Puerto Rico.

View an animated version of this map or related maps at http://history.wadsworth.com/passages2e.

*P*ICTURING THE PAST ✦ SOCIAL & CULTURAL

"SMOKED YANKEES" AND THE WAR WITH SPAIN

The Granger Collection, New York

The Spanish-American War produced a surge of patriotic volunteers and enthusiasm, but the main brunt of the fighting fell to the small regular army that was ready for immediate action in Cuba. As a result, black troops played a significant, if now largely forgotten, role in the successful campaign to oust the Spanish from the Caribbean island. The picture records some of the black soldiers after a Cuban battle. American society credited white men such as Theodore Roosevelt and his Rough Riders with these victories, and African Americans were deleted from the historical record and their contributions to victory expunged. In the wake of imperialism, the nation became even more segregated. Placing a picture of black soldiers in a textbook is designed to emphasize that the American past is more complicated than the popular mind often recognizes.

A Broadening Commitment in the Pacific

To follow up on Dewey's success, the McKinley administration dispatched troops to the Philippines. The president wanted the option of acquiring the islands as a result of the war. He thought that a port in the Philippines might be enough, but he intended to maintain flexibility.

With the Philippines at stake, the Hawaiian islands gained in strategic value. A treaty of annexation had been worked out during 1897, but the pact stalled in Congress. After the war began, the president and congressional leaders turned to a strategy of annexation by means of a legislative resolution that needed only a simple majority from Congress. Through presidential persuasion, the required votes for the resolution were obtained in July 1898, and Hawaii was annexed.

Meanwhile, U.S. policy toward the Philippines became a source of tension with Filipino leaders, notably Emilio Aguinaldo, who wanted their islands to be independent. The administration instructed army and navy officers not to have any formal dealings with the Filipinos. The buildup of military strength continued, and the ambitions of the Filipinos were seen as an obstacle to American policy rather than as a legitimate expression of nationalism.

The "Smoked Yankees" in the War with Spain

The main combat of the war took place in Cuba. The U.S. Army numbered 25,000 men, so the nation turned to volunteers. In the first wave of national enthusiasm, there were 1 million volunteers, far more than the army could handle. Eventually about 280,000 men saw active duty. Soldiers complained about shortages of ammunition and supplies and the poor quality of the food rations. The army experimented with canned beef, creating an inedible meal and a postwar controversy over the product.

In the regular army, an important part of the force that fought the Spanish were the four regiments composed of African American soldiers, or the "Smoked Yankees," as the Spanish troops described them. Seasoned fighters against Indians, the black soldiers were ordered to move south and prepare to invade Cuba. On their way through the southern states they encountered scorn, segregation, and threats.

The African American soldiers did not endure such treatment quietly. When they boarded segregated railroad cars, they sat wherever they pleased. If they saw signs that barred their presence, they took down the signs. Violence broke out between white and black troops in Florida, and men were killed and wounded in the exchanges of gunfire. Seeing all this, one soldier asked poignantly: "Is America any better than Spain?" Once the black regiments reached Cuba, their military contribution was significant. They earned numerous decorations for bravery and five of them won the Congressional Medal of Honor.

Despite the bravery of the "Smoked Yankees," the Spanish-American War worsened the plight of African Americans. The ideology of imperialism that allowed whites to dominate Cubans and Filipinos also supported racial segregation in the South. McKinley's efforts to reconcile the whites of the North and South brought harmony at the expense of black Americans.

Victory in Cuba

In late June, the U.S. Navy found the Spanish fleet in the harbor of Santiago de Cuba, and army detachments went ashore to engage the Spanish forces holding the city. On July 1, the army, commanded by General William R. Shafter, defeated the Spanish defenders at the Battle of San Juan Hill. Theodore Roosevelt and his volunteer regiment of Rough Riders took part in the battle. Roosevelt became a national hero on his way to the presidency, but the Rough Riders might have been defeated had it not been for the timely support they received from their black comrades.

From War to Peace

On July 3, the navy destroyed the Spanish fleet when it tried to escape from Santiago Harbor. Negotiations for an armistice began. McKinley insisted that Spain

The war made Theodore Roosevelt a national hero. He poses with his Rough Riders atop San Juan Hill in Cuba shortly after his successful charge on July 1, 1898. African American soldiers, like those shown in the previous picture, helped Roosevelt and his men gain their objective, but Roosevelt gave them little credit later in his career for their timely assistance.
Theodore Roosevelt Collection, Harvard College Library

relinquish Cuba and Puerto Rico and that the fate of the Philippines be discussed at the peace conference. Spain did not like these terms, but it had no choice but to accept them, which it did on August 12, 1898.

John Hay, soon to be McKinley's secretary of state, called it "a splendid little war." Victory had been achieved at a low cost in terms of combat deaths, only 281 officers and men. However, malaria, yellow fever, and other diseases killed more than 2,500 others. A public outcry arose about the condition of the army, and McKinley named a commission to investigate the leadership of the War Department and the way the war had been conducted. The commission's report led to reforms such as general staff shakeups and improved organization that enhanced the future fighting ability of the army. The war also strengthened the power of the presidency because of McKinley's expansive use of his role as commander-in-chief of the armed forces.

The Peace Talks

The peace conference with Spain was held in Paris. McKinley appointed a commission that included several senators who would ultimately vote on any treaty that they negotiated. The president was aware that Germany and Japan had an interest in the Philippines, and he now intended that the United States should retain control of the islands. American officials did not believe that the Filipinos should determine their own destiny. Within the United States, opponents of such a policy, calling themselves anti-imperialists, aroused public sentiment against the administration.

To build support for his foreign policy, McKinley made effective use of the powers of his office. During October, he toured the Midwest. Ordinarily presidents did not take part in congressional election campaigns. However, though billed as a nonpartisan event, McKinley's tour helped Republican candidates in the 1898 congressional contest. It also gave the president an opportunity to state the case for a more expansive foreign policy. In a typical address he told an Iowa audience that "we do not want to shirk a single responsibility that has been put upon us by the results of the war."

The Philippines were the most divisive issue at the peace conference. On October 25, 1898, the president's commissioners asked him for instructions. On October 28, he responded that he could see "but one plain path of duty, the acceptance of the archipelago." The peace treaty was signed on December 10, 1898. The United States gained the Philippines, Guam, and Puerto Rico. Spain gave up its claims to Cuba and received a payment of $20 million for what it had lost. The United States obtained legal sovereignty over the Philippines but would soon face challenges from the island's inhabitants.

Approval of the Treaty

Opponents of imperialism tried to block acceptance of the treaty in the Senate. To win the necessary two-thirds vote, McKinley employed the power of the presidency in new and creative ways. In December, he went south to woo Democrats. He used patronage to persuade wavering senators and exerted pressure on the state legislatures, which elected senators. Believing that the Democrats would benefit if the issue was settled before the 1900 elections, William Jennings Bryan endorsed the treaty. That action divided the opposition at a key point. On February 6, 1899, the Treaty of Paris obtained Senate approval on February 6, 1899, by a vote of fifty-seven to twenty-seven, one more than the necessary two-thirds.

War in the Philippines

As the Senate voted, the nation knew that fighting had erupted in the Philippines between U.S. soldiers and the Filipino troops that Aguinaldo commanded. Relations between the two sides had worsened during December 1898 as it became clear that the United States did not intend to leave the islands. Although the president asserted that his nation had "no imperial designs" on the Philippines, anti-imperialists and the Filipinos were not convinced. For Aguinaldo and his supporters, it seemed that

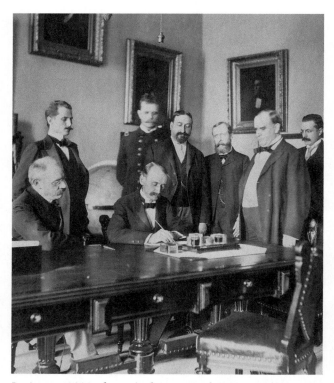

In August 1898, the United States and Spain reached an agreement on an armistice to end the fighting. This picture, which shows Secretary of State William Rufus Day signing the peace protocol with President McKinley (standing at right, in bow tie), was posed for photographers some days after the actual event.
Reproduced from the Collections of the Library of Congress

they had ousted the Spanish only to replace them with another imperial master, the United States.

During 1899, the U.S. Army defeated the Filipinos in conventional battles, and the administration sent out a commission to work out a civil government under U.S. sovereignty. However, the Filipinos turned to guerilla tactics. Their soldiers hit selected targets and then blended back into the population. Faced with this new threat, the U.S. Army responded by killing some Filipino prisoners and torturing others. The army's purpose was not genocidal, but many soldiers and their officers violated the rules of war and government policy in brutal and inhumane ways. With revelations of these misdeeds, enthusiasm for further imperialistic adventures ebbed.

The Battle over Imperialism

During the last two years of McKinley's first term, imperialism became a heated issue. An Anti-Imperialist League, created in November 1898, united the opposition against McKinley's foreign policy. Critics of expansionism charged that overseas possessions would damage the nation's democratic institutions. Some people used racist arguments to block the acquisition of lands where nonwhite populations lived. Others evoked moral concern about imperialism. A number of prominent Americans including Andrew Carnegie, Thomas B. Reed, and the longtime reformer Carl Schurz lent their voices to the anti-imperialist campaign.

Advocates of empire adapted the ideas of Social Darwinism and Anglo-Saxon supremacy to justify the acquisition of other countries. Theodore Roosevelt, Henry Cabot Lodge of Massachusetts, and their allies contended that the nation could not escape the world responsibilities that the war with Spain had brought. By 1900, the consensus was that the gains of empire should be retained and protected but not increased. The examination of the nation's goals and purposes contributed to the mood of reform and renewal that emerged at the turn of the century.

Other foreign policy issues emerged from the outcome of the war. The Teller Amendment blocked the annexation of Cuba, but the McKinley administration wanted to ensure that the island did not become a target of European intervention, most notably from Germany. A military government ran Cuba during 1899. As a civil government developed, the United States insisted on guarantees that Cuba would retain political and military ties with the country that had liberated it. The result of this process was the Platt Amendment of March 1901, which barred an independent Cuba from allying itself with another foreign power. The United States had the right to intervene to preserve stability and gained a naval base at Guantanamo in Cuba.

The Open Door in China and Beyond

The acquisition of the Philippines heightened interest about the fate of China, where European powers sought to establish economic and political spheres of influence. Worried about the nation's trade with China and concerned to preserve that country's territorial integrity, in September 1899 the administration, through Secretary of State John Hay, issued what became known as the Open Door Notes. The messages asked European countries active in China to preserve trading privileges and other economic rights that gave the United States a chance to compete for markets there. The replies of the powers were noncommittal, but Hay announced in March 1900 that the other nations had accepted the U.S. position in principle. The Open Door Notes became a significant assertion of U.S. interest in China.

When antiforeign sentiment in China led to the Boxer Rebellion during the summer of 1900, an important test of the Open Door principle occurred. Secret associations known as the "Righteous and Harmonious

The war in the Philippines of the United States against the native forces produced harsh fighting and in some instances atrocities on the part of American forces. This picture depicts the result of one such battle.
From the Collections of the Library of Congress

Fists" (hence Boxers) launched a series of attacks on westerners in China. Europeans who had taken refuge in Peking were rescued by an international force that included 2,500 U.S. soldiers. President McKinley justified sending the troops into a country with which the United States was at peace as a legitimate use of his war power under the Constitution. Secretary Hay reaffirmed the U.S. commitment to the Open Door policy in a diplomatic circular to the powers that he issued on July 3, 1900. McKinley withdrew the troops rapidly after their rescue mission had been completed.

Toward a Canal Across Central America

The Spanish-American War and the expansion of American commitments in the Pacific demonstrated the need for a waterway that would link the two oceans and enable the navy to conduct its growing worldwide responsibilities. The McKinley administration laid the groundwork for a canal across Central America when it renegotiated the Clayton-Bulwer Treaty of 1850 with Great Britain. That document prohibited both nations from exercising exclusive control over any future waterway. After extended negotiations with the British a treaty was worked out in the summer of 1901.

The 1900 Election

The signs seemed to point to McKinley's reelection. Prosperity had returned, and the conflict in the Philippines was being won. McKinley's vice president, Garret A.

Hobart, died in November 1899. Theodore Roosevelt, the popular young governor of New York, became McKinley's running mate. To oppose McKinley, the Democrats again turned to William Jennings Bryan. Bryan made another vigorous campaign. He attacked imperialism as a threat to the nation's institutions, and he accused the Republicans of being the tools of the trusts and the business community. The Democratic candidate also renewed his pleas for a free silver policy. The anti-imperialists did not trust Bryan, but they preferred him to McKinley.

Since in that era incumbent presidents did not make speeches, McKinley allowed Theodore Roosevelt to do most of the campaigning. Bryan made so many criticisms that his campaign lacked a clear theme. McKinley increased his margin in the popular vote over what he had achieved four years earlier. The result in the electoral college was 292 for McKinley and 155 for Bryan.

McKinley's Second Term

McKinley gained further victories in foreign policy. Congress set up a civilian government for the Philippines when the insurrection had ended, which occurred shortly after the capture of Emilio Aguinaldo in March 1901. On May 27, 1901, the Supreme Court ruled in the *Insular Cases* that the Philippines and Puerto Rico were properly possessions of the United States but that their inhabitants had not become citizens of the country. The decision upheld McKinley's colonial policy and provided legal justification for imperialism.

Meanwhile, the president was turning his attention to two major domestic issues: the growth of big business and the issue of high tariffs. By 1901, McKinley was persuaded that some action was necessary to enforce the Sherman Antitrust Act of 1890. He had also modified his earlier support for the protective tariff and now believed that reciprocal trade treaties should be adopted that would lower duties on products entering the United States. Treaties that had been negotiated with such foreign countries as France and Argentina had not yet received Senate action. McKinley intended to prod the Senate to take them up at the next session, which would convene in December 1901. As he had done to secure ratification of the treaty with Spain in 1898, he also planned to travel extensively during 1901 to raise the trade issue with the American people.

As the new century began, McKinley had revived the power of the presidency after the decades of congressional supremacy that followed the Civil War. He had expanded the size of the president's staff, begun to involve the press in the coverage of White House affairs, and personalized the office through his travels. In many respects, McKinley was the first modern president.

THE UNITED STATES ON THE EVE OF THE TWENTIETH CENTURY

The nation saw the arrival of the twentieth century on December 31, 1900, with a mixture of confidence about what the United States had accomplished and apprehension about what the future held. The depression of the 1890s remained a vivid memory for most citizens, even with the return of prosperity after 1897. The shift in attitudes toward government and its role that had occurred during the hard times led many people to advocate programs of social reform.

Calls for Change

With the end of the century in sight, and the experience of the war with Spain still vivid, there was a flurry of public debate about the direction of the nation. A National Social and Political Conference took place in Buffalo, New York, in 1899 that brought together Eugene V. Debs, Henry Demarest Lloyd, Samuel Gompers, and Hazen Pingree, among others. The delegates called for "equality of economic opportunity and political power." Their goals required a more activist government than had been common in the nineteenth century.

In 1900, other future advocates of change appeared. After a long political battle in Wisconsin, Robert M. La Follette finally won election as governor. His agenda looked toward changes in the way the state government functioned. A devastating hurricane in Galveston, Texas, in September 1900 caused significant damage to that Texas city. Political leaders there turned to a new form of government to deal with rebuilding. Commissioners of fire, water, police and other services replaced the older style of ward leaders. The idea of having officials tied to the workings of city departments rather than representing geographic areas would attract increasing attention after the turn of the new century.

In the academic world, a biting analysis of how Americans used the wealth that they had acquired during the process of industrialization was published. Thorstein Veblen was a professor at the University of Chicago when he wrote *The Theory of the Leisure Class* (1899). In this book he analyzed the ways in which citizens displayed their social status. Although his writings offered more diagnosis than solutions, Veblen was a provocative critic of capitalist institutions and practices at a time when his fellow citizens worried about their impact on national life.

At both ends of the economic spectrum, Americans looked to organizations to address social ills. In 1900, Italian and Jewish immigrants who worked in the

William McKinley: Reciprocal Trade Agreements, 1901

As he began his second term, President McKinley was urging his party and the nation to pursue a policy of trade expansion overseas. That theme dominated his last public address on September 5, 1901, where he called for reciprocity with our trading partners. The next day the president was assassinated.

By sensible trade arrangements which will not interrupt our home production, we shall extend the outlets for our increasing surplus. A system which provides a mutual exchange of commodities is manifestly essential to the continued and healthful growth of our export trade. We must not repose in fancied security that we can forever sell everything and buy little or nothing. If such a thing were possible, it would not be best for us or for those with whom we deal. We should take from our customers such of their products as we can use without harm to our industries and labor.

Reciprocity is the natural outgrowth of our wonderful industrial development under the domestic policy now firmly established. What we produce beyond our domestic consumption must have a vent abroad. The excess must be relieved through a foreign outlet, and we should sell everywhere we can and buy wherever the buying will enlarge our sales and productions, and thereby make a greater demand for home labor.

The period of exclusiveness is past. The expansion of our trade and commerce is the pressing problem. Commercial wars are unprofitable. A policy of goodwill and friendly trade relations will prevent reprisals. Reciprocity treaties are in harmony with the spirit of the times; measures of retaliation are not. If perchance some of our tariffs are no longer needed for revenue or to encourage and protect our industries at home, why should they not be employed to extend and promote our markets abroad?

---

clothing business in New York City united to form the International Ladies Garment Workers Union (ILGWU). The membership, predominantly female, used the ILGWU to spread the ideas of unionism to other immigrant workers and to discuss alternatives to the existing system. Also in 1900, the more well-to-do business leaders of the day created the National Civic Federation. Made up of representatives from organized labor, the business community, and the public, the NCF sought to promote harmony between labor and capital.

CONCLUSION

A balance sheet on the achievements of the late nineteenth century was a mixed one. Optimists cited the nation's burgeoning productive capacity, the totals of steel produced and railroad tracks laid, and the impressive per capita wealth of U.S. citizens. Most of the population could read, and there were more than 2,000 newspapers available covering a staggering variety of subjects. There was an equally dazzling array of magazines on the

As the twentieth century began, Americans were eating more mass-produced foods. In this advertisement for Postum, a substitute for coffee, two women discuss what the drink can do for their complexion and general health.
Culver Pictures, Inc.

newsstands with growing numbers of illustrations of national and world events. Advertisers spent $90 million in 1900 to tempt readers to try their products.

The United States was devoted to education. There were 1,700 libraries in the nation that held more than 5,000 volumes in their collections. Almost 240,000 students attended 977 colleges and universities at the turn of the century, or a little more than 1 percent of Americans between the ages of fifteen and twenty-five. Eighty percent of these institutions admitted women to their programs, although men received four times as many degrees as women did. Below the college level, 16 million children went to public schools. The educated, literate workforce that resulted was the envy of competing economies in western Europe.

On the negative side were the social problems that the nation confronted. An estimated 10 million Americans, or about 13 percent of the population, lived below the poverty line. A visitor to the United States said that half its population was "ill-housed, ill-fed, and ill-clothed." Although the often-anticipated social revolution of the 1890s had not occurred, influential leaders such as Theodore Roosevelt worried about the potential for violence and upheaval if moderate reforms did not take place. In addition, the nation faced the problems of race. Other issues were the fate of Native Americans and the place of immigrants in American society. Americans turned to these questions with an energy that made the twenty years between 1900 and 1920 famous as an age of political reform and government regulation.

Recommended Readings

Campbell, W. Joseph. *Yellow Journalism: Puncturing the Myths, Defining the Legacies* (2001). A skeptical look at the sensational journalism and the war with Spain.

Gilmore, Glenda. *Gender and Jim Crow: Women and the Politics of White Supremacy in North Carolina, 1896–1920* (1996). An excellent study of the ways in which black and white women interacted during the era of segregation.

Hoganson, Kristin L. *Fighting for American Manhood: How Gender Politics Provoked the Spanish-American and Philippine-American Wars* (1998). A provocative new study about the origins of the conflict with Spain.

Offner, John L. *An Unwanted War: The Diplomacy of the United States & Spain Over Cuba, 1895–1898* (1992). Valuable for the interplay of Cubans, Spaniards, and Americans as the war drew near.

Perez, Louis A. *The War of 1898: the United States and Cuba in History and Historiography* (1998). Offers an insightful, sympathetic look at the war from a perspective that takes Cuba into account.

Schlereth, Thomas J. *Victorian America: Transformations in Everyday Life, 1876–1915* (1991). Strong on the social and cultural changes that occurred during the 1890s.

Smith, Joseph. *The Spanish-American War: Conflict in the Caribbean and the Pacific, 1845–1902* (1994). A good one-volume account of the military history of the war.

Traxel, David. *1898: The Birth of the American Century* (1998). An interpretive survey of the war with Spain and its consequences for the nation.

Williams, R. Hal. *Years of Decision: American Politics in the 1890s* (1993). The best narrative account of this important decade.

Zimmerman, Warren. *First Great Triumph: How Five Americans Made Their Country a World Power* (2002). An interesting interpretation of the origins of American imperialism.

American Journey Online and InfoTrac College Edition

Visit the source collections at http://ajaccess. wadsworth.com and infotrac.thomsonlearning.com and use the Search function with the following key terms to explore documents, images, audio and video clips, articles, and commentary related to the material in this chapter.

Booker T. Washington	Atlanta Compromise
Grover Cleveland	Charlotte Perkins Gilman
Stephen Crane	Ida Wells-Barnett
William McKinley	*Plessy v. Ferguson*
Radcliffe College	William Randolph Hearst
Spanish-American War	Pullman strike

Additional resources, exercises, and Internet links related to this chapter are available on the American Passages Web site: http://history.wadsworth.com/passages2e

THEODORE ROOSEVELT AND PROGRESSIVE REFORM

1901–1909

THE AGE OF THEODORE ROOSEVELT

ROOSEVELT AND THE MODERN PRESIDENCY: THE FIRST TERM

PROGRESSIVE CAMPAIGNS TO REFORM THE NATION

ROOSEVELT AND THE MODERN PRESIDENCY: THE SECOND TERM

Theodore Roosevelt imparted his energy and enthusiasm to the first decade of the twentieth century. Here he sits astride a horse during one of his frequent trips around the United States. His intense smile became one of the trademarks of his public image.
The Granger Collection, New York

On September 6, 1901, President William McKinley was shot in Buffalo, New York. A week later he died and Vice President Theodore Roosevelt became president. The eight years that followed have come to be known as part of the Progressive Era. Responding to the social and economic impact of industrialism, Americans endeavored to reshape their nation to curb the power of large businesses, improve conditions for the consumer, and reform the political parties.

Americans confronted new issues. Citizens argued about whether government should regulate the economy and whether the power to do so should be local or national. The political party became a major source of controversy. Its critics contended that intense partisanship had corrupted government and weakened democracy. Power should be shifted toward the individual voter. Other advocates of change clamored for more voter participation in the electoral system by broadening the ability of citizens to propose laws, choose candidates, and overturn judicial decisions. Thus, during a time of prosperity at home and relative peace abroad, the United States experienced political ferment. The issues that Americans debated at the turn of the twentieth century would dominate the agenda of domestic policy for decades.

THE AGE OF THEODORE ROOSEVELT

At forty-two, Theodore Roosevelt was the youngest president. During the war with Spain his volunteer regiment of Rough Riders charged up Kettle Hill in Cuba against fortified Spanish positions. A national hero, he was elected governor of New York. When he criticized corporate abuses, Republican leaders exiled him to the vice presidency in 1900. McKinley's death thrust Roosevelt into the political spotlight.

The new president pledged to continue McKinley's policies. Yet the youthful and vigorous Roosevelt made news in ways that no previous president had done. He changed the official name of the president's residence to the White House and infused energy into its daily routine. His large family—he had six children—captivated

CHRONOLOGY

1901 United States Steel created • William McKinley inaugurated for second term • Theodore Roosevelt becomes president

1902 Antitrust suit filed against Northern Securities Company • Anthracite coal strike • Teddy Bear toy introduced • *McClure's Magazine* starts muckraking journalism

1903 Elkins Act outlaws railroad rebates • Alaska Boundary dispute settled • Panama Canal Zone acquired • Wright brothers make first successful powered flight • National Women's Trade Union League founded

1904 Roosevelt elected president; declines to run in 1908 • Roosevelt Corollary to Monroe Doctrine

1905 Niagara Movement to improve conditions for African Americans • Portsmouth Conference settles Russo-Japanese War

1906 Algeciras Conference in Morocco • President Roosevelt attacks muckrakers • Passage of Hepburn Act (railroads), Pure Food and Drugs Act, Meat Inspection Amendment

1907 Panic of 1907 • Self-contained electric clothes washer developed

1908 Henry Ford introduces Model T automobile • Election of William Howard Taft • Supreme Court upholds Oregon law limiting hours of work for women in *Muller v. Oregon*

1909 Taft inaugurated as president • National Association for the Advancement of Colored People (NAACP) founded • Roosevelt leaves for Africa

ICTURING THE PAST ✦ SOCIAL & CULTURAL EVENTS

Table 20.1	Immigration into the U.S., 1901–1909
1901	487,918
1902	687,743
1903	857,046
1904	812,870
1905	1,026,499
1906	1,100,735
1907	1,285,349
1908	782,870
1909	751,786

Source: *The Statistical History of the United States* (1965), p. 56.

Tables of historical numbers can seem dull and uninformative. In the case of these figures on immigration into the United States during the first decade of the twentieth century, the totals show a dramatic transformation in the population whose effects shaped politics, economics, and culture. The newcomers arrived primarily from southern and eastern Europe, as well as Asia, and soon put their stamp on cities as diverse as New York and San Francisco. Vibrant immigrant communities arose. The surge produced a backlash in efforts to restrict immigration that ultimately led to cutbacks by the 1920s. But the impact of these new Americans proved lasting in the way people lived and their expectations about the role of government. A more varied, turbulent, and interesting United States came out of the process that these numbers represent.

---

the nation. The president's oldest daughter, Alice Lee, made her debut in the White House, kept a pet snake, and drove around Washington in fast cars. "I can be President of the United States or I can control Alice," Roosevelt told friends who asked him to rein in his daughter. "I cannot possibly do both."

The Roosevelt Agenda

Roosevelt planned to be a strong and forceful president. In time, he decided that the president should be the "steward" of the general welfare. As long as the Constitution did not prohibit executive action, the president should stretch the limits of what was possible. Roosevelt built on McKinley's example but he went further, causing the public to see the president as the focus of national authority.

The nation watched him in fascination. Roosevelt reformed college football to make it less violent, pursued simplified spelling of English (*thru* instead of *through,* for example), and waged loud, frequent quarrels with political enemies. Like a preacher in church, he called the White House his "bully pulpit," using it to give sermons to the country about morality and duty.

The new president wanted to limit the power of big business to avoid pressure for more radical reforms from the Democrats or Socialists. He believed that the nation had to protect its natural resources. Before 1912, he saw the Republican party as the best means to implement his agenda. As a result, he did not challenge the party's leaders on the protective tariff. He cooperated with the conservative Republicans who dominated Congress during his first term. But after 1905 as he exerted presidential power more vigorously, his relations with Capitol Hill worsened.

Theodore Roosevelt was the first celebrity president. The spread of newspapers and the emergence of motion pictures made it possible for Americans to follow the nation's leader with greater attention than they had during the nineteenth century. Roosevelt dramatized what went on in Washington. By using the power of his office, he strengthened the presidency to meet future challenges.

The United States at the Outset of the Twentieth Century

In 1901, Americans balanced confidence about the future in a new century with worries about the direction in which their society was moving. The population stood at 76 million, up from 63 million ten years earlier. Immigrants accelerated the growth of the population.

New arrivals came in at a prodigious rate. There were 488,000 in 1900, 688,000 in 1902, and over 1.1 million in 1906. Like their late-nineteenth-century predecessors, the majority of these newcomers settled in the nation's growing cities.

Most Americans, however, still lived in rural areas or small towns with fewer than 2,500 residents. Not for another twenty years would the population become more urban than rural. As the cities expanded, tensions between rural and urban areas mounted.

A Longer Life Span

People lived longer in 1900, a trend that accelerated throughout the century. Life expectancy for white men rose from forty-seven years in 1901 to almost fifty-four in 1920. For white women, the increase was from around fifty-one years in 1901 to almost fifty-five in 1920. Life expectancy for members of minority groups rose from thirty-four years in 1901 to just over forty-five in 1920.

The population was young in 1900. The median age was twenty-three; it rose to just over twenty-five by 1920. The death rate for the entire population was seventeen per thousand in 1900. It fell to thirteen per thousand by 1920. For infants in the Progressive Era, the prospects were less encouraging. In 1915, the first year for which there are accurate numbers, almost sixty-one deaths were recorded for every 10,000 births. The situation worsened during the next several years, and the infant mortality rate reached more than sixty-eight deaths per 10,000 births in 1921. For nonwhite babies the picture was even worse: there were almost 106 deaths per 10,000 live births in 1915. Some positive changes occurred, however. More and more mothers gave birth in hospitals rather than at home. Improved medical techniques and the antiseptic setting of the hospitals helped reduce the incidence of infant mortality.

Children at Work

The problem of child labor persisted. In 1900 more than 1,750,000 children between the ages of ten and fifteen worked in the labor force. In the South, children worked in cotton mills. Conditions were so bad that reformers called the mills and their communities "the poorest place in the world for training citizens of a democracy." Abolishing child labor was a major goal of reform campaigns after 1900.

Changes in the Family

In families whose children did not have to work, child rearing became more organized and systematic. Kindergartens gained popularity as a way to prepare children for school. There were 5,000 in 1900 and nearly 9,000 twenty years later. The federal government held conferences on child rearing and issued booklets about infant care. Improved methods of contraception led to smaller families. In 1900, the average mother had 3.566 children compared with seven children in 1800. Attention shifted to rearing fewer children more successfully.

The status of women also changed after 1900. Divorce was easier and more common. About four marriages out of every thousand ended in divorce in 1900, but in the ensuing years the divorce rate increased three times faster than the rate of population growth. There were 56,000 divorces in 1900 and 100,000 in 1914. Some women delayed marriage to attend college. Yet opportunities for women to enter law, medicine, or higher education remained limited. In 1920, fewer than one and one half percent of all attorneys were women. In 1910, there were only 9,000 women doctors, about 6 percent of all physicians. Restrictive policies on admissions to medical schools and barriers to staff positions at hospitals posed obstacles to women who sought to become doctors. Nursing and social work were more accessible to women, but they still faced condescension from men.

Women at Work

Women in factories, mills, and garment sweatshops also saw little improvement in their condition as the new century began. Their workday was ten hours long, and six- and seven-day weeks were common. Men received more pay than women; labor unions regarded women as competitors for jobs held by men. Women set up their own unions, such as the Women's Trade Union League, established in 1903. They also formed the backbone of the International Ladies Garment Workers Union (ILGWU), which led strikes in New York City in 1910 and 1911.

Social trends slowly altered the status of women. Their clothes became less confining and cumbersome. The full skirt was still the fashion in 1900, but soon thereafter petticoats and corsets disappeared. Women began to show their ankles and arms in public. Some more daring young women, such as Alice Roosevelt, smoked in public; others used cosmetics openly. In dance halls and restaurants, young people danced the turkey trot and the bunny hug to the rhythms of ragtime.

The institution of marriage felt the effects of these changes. Marriage ceremonies used the word "obey" less frequently. Women asked more of their husbands, including companionship and sexual pleasure. Government programs were instituted to encourage family togetherness. In 1914, prodded by advocates of the traditional home (and the florist industry), Congress designated Mother's Day as a national holiday.

A Nation of Consumers

In 1900, 76 million people in the United States owned 21 million horses. Some forecasters said that the automobile would replace the horse, but in 1903 only a little more than 11,000 cars were sold. During the next decade, however, Henry Ford of Dearborn, Michigan, created the Model T. Ford's goal was to use mass production techniques to build an automobile that could be sold in large numbers. By 1908, the Model T was ready for distribution, priced at about $850. Sales increased as Ford reduced the car's price. In 1908, 5,986 Model T's were sold; by 1912, the total was 78,611. The mass-produced automobile was a key element in the evolution of the consumer society during the Progressive Era.

Standardized food products also gained popular acceptance. Asa Candler's Coca-Cola became available throughout the country when the parent company licensed bottling plants everywhere. There were 241 bottlers by 1905, 493 by 1910, and 1,095 a decade later. In 1912, Procter and Gamble introduced Crisco, a vegetable shortening, as a way of selling its cottonseed oil. The company used marketing campaigns in popular periodicals, held "Crisco teas" at which club women could try out their own recipes, and created cooking schools to spread awareness of the new product. By 1915, its advertising proclaimed that "Crisco is rapidly taking the place of butter and lard for cooking." Other famous brands, such as Kellogg's Corn Flakes, Uneeda Biscuit, and Kodak cameras, relied on mass advertising, billboards, and mail flyers to instill popular desire for these new and convenient consumer goods.

The Role of Advertising

Advertising became a central feature of American culture. Newspapers and magazines gave lower rates to advertisers who used entire pages. Billboards appealed to the new motoring public and outraged garden club members when they obscured scenic views. Advertising agencies shaped the content of product information. Men were urged to buy Gillette razors because "You Ought to Shave Every Morning." Toothbrush ads proclaimed that Americans should "keep their teeth and mouths clean." The Kodak camera was an essential part of the Christmas season as "your family historian."

To master these markets, advertisers surveyed potential purchasers. Agencies tracked customers through reports from salespeople, mail surveys, and questionnaires printed in magazines. Coca-Cola, for example, increased its advertising budget annually and in 1913 distributed 5 million metal Coca-Cola signs across the country.

The Example of Sears

Sears, Roebuck and Company was a leader in consumer marketing. Founded during the economic depression of 1893, the company was the brainchild of Richard Warren Sears, who believed in low prices as a selling technique. Beginning with mail-order watches, Sears expanded to general merchandise that was sold in a catalogue published annually. He cut prices for desirable products such as sewing machines and cream separators and soon produced record sales. Sears spent lavishly on advertising—over $1.5 million

The mail-order services of Sears, Roebuck and Company became a familiar part of countless American households as the new century began. In this Consumers Guide, Sears is instructing its customers about comparing the prices of local shopkeepers with the less expensive goods that can be obtained through the mail.

The Granger Collection, New York

in 1902—and promised low prices, guarantees of any products and parts, and the opportunity to order merchandise without prepaying. "Send No Money" was the Sears slogan. Volume sales at low prices built a market for Sears; the company sent out more than 1.5 million catalogues in 1902.

In many respects, the United States occupied an enviable position. A British visitor said that the standard of American life had reached a height "hitherto unrealized in a civilized society." National income stood at $17 billion; the average American's annual per capita income of $227 was the highest in the world. Innovations promised further abundance to a prosperous population.

Despite these positive trends, citizens worried about the nation's future. The growth of big business, the spread of labor organizations, the corruption in politics, the decline of the individual in a bureaucratic society—all these trends prompted fear that older values and attitudes were under assault. The early twentieth century saw a renewed debate about the purpose and accomplishments of the United States. For white Americans, however, the persistent issue of race and the treatment of minorities did not attract much attention during this period of reform.

Race Relations in the Roosevelt Era

On October 16, 1901, Booker T. Washington dined with Theodore Roosevelt and his family at the White House. The evening meal was social but the purpose of Washington's visit was political. Since he had emerged as a leading spokesman for African Americans during the 1890s, Washington had built a political machine among black Republicans in the South. He came to the White House to discuss the new president's nominations for patronage positions in the South. When southern newspapers learned that a black man had eaten with the president, they were furious. A Tennessee editor called the occasion "the most damnable outrage that has ever been perpetrated by any citizen of the United States."

Roosevelt saw himself as a friend of African Americans and the heir of Abraham Lincoln. He moved cautiously on race during his first term and conciliated white southerners during his second. Between 1901 and 1905, he defended black appointees to post offices and customs houses who were under attack in the South and he spoke out against lynching. After 1905, however, he criticized African Americans when blacks did not inform southern authorities where accused black criminals might be found. When black soldiers were falsely charged with at-

tempting to kill white residents of Brownsville, Texas, in August 1906, the president discharged their units without a hearing and blocked congressional efforts to reinstate the men.

Black Life in the Early Twentieth Century

For the majority of African Americans living in the era of Theodore Roosevelt, segregation was now an ever-present fact of life. "Don't monkey with white supremacy," warned a Mississippi newspaper, "it is loaded with determination, gun-powder, and dynamite." Between seventy and eighty black citizens of the United States were lynched during each year of Roosevelt's presidency.

Social and economic inequality were the lot of African Americans as well. Conditions had worsened since the passage of segregation laws in the South during the 1880s and 1890s. Nine million southern blacks lived in rural poverty. The field hands sang as they toiled: "Done worked all the summer/Done worked all the fall/And here comes Christmas/And I ain't got nothing at all." Black wage workers received much less per day and per hour than their white counterparts in the same trade. Other black men were industrial or agricultural peasants, virtual slaves who received only food and a place to sleep for their labor.

The system of segregation affected blacks in every aspect of their existence. "The white man is the boss," said one man. "You got to talk to him like he is the boss." Facilities for the races were supposed to be "separate but equal," but this was rarely the case in practice. In Florida, for example, the amount spent on educating white children was $5.92 per capita annually, as compared with $2.27 for black children.

Exclusion from Politics

Blacks no longer voted in significant numbers because of the barriers raised during the 1890s and early 1900s. The white primary barred black voters from elections that selected Democratic party candidates. In the one-party South, African Americans had no voice in the political contests that really mattered. They retained some role in the Republican party because their votes helped to choose the delegates to the national convention. A few black politicians in some states of the Upper South wielded influence. For the most part, however, the bitter comment of one African American politician summed up the situation: "The Negro's status in Southern politics is dark as Hell and smells like cheese."

W. E. B. Du Bois on What Blacks Felt During the Age of Roosevelt, 1903

The most notable advocate of the rights of African Americans at the beginning of the twentieth century was the scholar and publicist W. E. B. Du Bois. In his book *The Souls of Black Folk* (1903), he made a passionate case for the unique insights that the experience of African Americans in the United States had provided as well as stating with eloquence the obstacles that he and other blacks faced every day in a segregated nation.

After the Egyptian and Indian, the Greek and Roman, the Teuton and Mongolian, the Negro is a sort of seventh son, born with a veil, and gifted with second-sight in this American world—a world which yields him no true self-consciousness, but only lets him see himself through the revelation of the other world. It is a peculiar sensation, this double-consciousness, this sense of always looking at oneself through the eyes of others, of measuring one's soul by the tape of a world that looks on in amused contempt and pity. One ever feels his twoness—an American, a Negro; two souls, two thoughts, two unreconciled strivings; two warring ideals in one dark body, whose dogged strength alone keeps it from being torn asunder.

The history of the American Negro is the history of this strife, this longing to attain self-conscious manhood, to merge his double self into a better and truer self. In this merging he wishes neither of the older selves to be lost. He would not Africanize America, for America has too much to teach the world and Africa. He would not bleach his Negro soul in a flood of white Americanism, for he knows that Negro blood has a message for the world. He simply wishes to make it possible for a man to be both a Negro and an American, without being cursed and spit upon by his fellows, without having the doors of opportunity closed roughly in his face.

Source: W. E. B. Du Bois, *The Souls of Black Folk* (1903).

When he dined with Theodore Roosevelt, Booker T. Washington demonstrated to other African Americans that he could deliver the support of white politicians. To keep the president's friendship and to obtain money from wealthy whites, Washington had to accept the existence of segregation and the system it represented. Washington was doing what he had proposed in his speech in Atlanta in 1895. By the time Roosevelt became president, more militant blacks were saying that Washington's methods had failed.

The Stirrings of Militant Protest

Their leader was W. E. B. Du Bois, who had received a doctoral degree from Harvard and who taught sociology at Atlanta University, a black institution. After initially supporting Washington's policy, Du Bois decided that blacks had to confront segregation. "Separate schools for Whites and Blacks are not equal, can not be made equal, and . . . are not intended to be equal," he wrote. In *The Souls of Black Folk* (1903), Du Bois criticized Washington's methods as having "practically accepted the alleged inferiority of the Negro."

In June 1905, Du Bois led a delegation of twenty-nine blacks to Niagara Falls, New York, where they issued a call for political and social rights. The meeting denied that "the Negro-American assents to inferiority, is submissive under oppression and apologetic before insult." The Niagara Conference aroused Booker T. Washington's intense opposition, but it laid the basis for more lasting protests about the worsening situation of African Americans.

ICTURING THE PAST✦SOCIAL & CULTURAL EVENTS

W. E. B. DU BOIS AND THE STRUGGLE FOR AFRICAN AMERICAN RIGHTS

The Granger Collection, New York

The early twentieth century saw the worst era of racial segregation in the United States as the position of African Americans and other minorities steadily deteriorated North and South. A few voices were raised in protest. Of these, the black thinker who had the greatest impact was W. E. B. Du Bois. Pictured here in the conservative clothes and look of middle-class respectability that he favored in this phase of his life, Du Bois waged a vigorous assault on the public ideas of Booker T. Washington and the notion that blacks should accept their subordinate position. Du Bois led the intellectual efforts to repudiate the doctrine that African Americans were inferior to whites in brains and talent. His organizing efforts, especially the Niagara Conference of 1905, laid the basis for what would become the National Association for the Advancement of Colored People. His presence in the text attests to the rich history of African Americans that is too often omitted from popular accounts of the nation's development.

ROOSEVELT AND THE MODERN PRESIDENCY: THE FIRST TERM

On February 19, 1902, the Department of Justice announced that it was filing suit under the Sherman Antitrust Act (1890) against the Northern Securities Company. That firm, created in late 1901, merged major railroads in the Northwest, including the Great Northern, the Northern Pacific, and the Chicago, Burlington, and Quincy Company. The key leaders in assembling this large company were James J. Hill and E. H. Harriman; their financing came from J. P. Morgan. The merger sought to reduce destructive competition among warring railroads and make railroad rates more stable. Opposition to the merger came from states across which the company would operate, most notably in Minnesota. Farmers and business operators in the upper Midwest feared that a giant railroad would raise rates and limit their profits. They urged their governors to file suit against the new company in federal court. Many Americans believed that only the federal government could regulate such unbridled corporate power.

The creation of the Northern Securities Company was part of the trend toward larger economic units that had begun during the 1890s. A highly publicized case was the United States Steel Company, which had been formed earlier in 1901. The steel merger symbolized bigness in business in the same way that the railroad combine did. Indeed, the same forces that led to consolidation in railroads promoted a similar result in steel.

At the turn of the century, the Carnegie Steel Company dominated the industry, producing finished steel products at a lower unit cost than its rivals. For J. P. Morgan and the steel companies that he represented, Carnegie's power raised the possibility that competing firms might go bankrupt. The logical answer, Morgan concluded, was to buy out Carnegie and create a steel company that could control the entire industry. Morgan sent an aide to see Carnegie. "If Andy wants to sell, I'll buy," said Morgan. Go and find his price."

Morgan's agent, Charles M. Schwab, found Carnegie on the golf course. Carnegie sent his answer a day later. In a penciled note, he told Morgan that the price was $480 million. Morgan paused and responded: "I accept this price." The merger was made public on March 3, 1901, the day before William McKinley began his second term. Carnegie Steel joined other firms financed by Morgan such as Federal Steel and the National Tube Company. The half-billion dollars that Carnegie received for his holding was a staggering sum in an era when there was no federal income tax, no capital gains tax, and low inflation. In modern terms, Carnegie probably would have received more than $50 billion.

The Challenge of United States Steel

The new company, United States Steel, was capitalized at $1.4 billion. It had 168,000 employees and controlled 60 percent of the steel industry's productive capacity. Smaller steel companies would have to compete with the vertical integration Carnegie had achieved with the company that Morgan had acquired. Workers in steel now faced a powerful employer that could fix wage levels in any way it chose. The prospect worried outside observers. "We have billion dollar combines," said one editor, "maneuvered by a handful of men who have never been in a plant and think of a factory as just another chip in a gigantic financial poker game."

Theodore Roosevelt worried too. He saw the forces that led to business consolidation as the logical outcome of economic development, but he did not believe that the federal government should stand by. The large corporations, Roosevelt decided, should not be destroyed. Firms that were socially beneficial should be encouraged; those that misbehaved should be regulated. At first Roosevelt thought that publicizing the activities of corporations would be enough regulation. He soon concluded that he must establish the power of the federal government to intervene in the economy. The Northern Securities Company was unpopular, so the president acted.

Controlling the Trusts

After the Department of Justice announcement in February 1902, the stock market fell. J. P. Morgan hurried to Washington to ask the president if additional lawsuits were planned. No, said Roosevelt, "unless we find out . . . [that other companies] have done something wrong." Roosevelt argued that "trusts are creatures of the State, and the State not only has the right to control them, but it is in duty bound to control them wherever the need of such control is shown."

In 1904, the Supreme Court agreed with Roosevelt when the government won its case against the Northern Securities Company. By a 5–4 margin the justices ruled that the railroad company violated the Sherman Act. The case reestablished the power of the national government to use the Sherman Act, which had been called into question in the 1895 case of *U.S. v. E. C. Knight*. The American public saw Roosevelt as a "trustbuster" who was willing to curb the power of big business. Having established the principle that the government was supreme over any individual corporation, the president used trust-busting sparingly against "bad" trusts and sought to assist "good" trusts with policies that rewarded their positive behavior.

The Square Deal in the Coal Strike

The nation also applauded when Roosevelt intervened to end a strike in the coal industry during the autumn of 1902. The 140,000 members of the United Mine Workers walked off their jobs in the anthracite (hard coal) fields of Pennsylvania. The miners asked for a pay hike and for the railroads and coal operators to recognize their union. Having lost an earlier strike in 1900, management wanted to break the strike and the union. As the walkout stretched into autumn, fears

The Anthracite Coal Strike of 1902 required the intervention of Theodore Roosevelt to settle the dispute between organized labor and the mine owners by appointing the arbitration commission pictured here.
© UPI/Bettmann/Corbis

grew of winter coal shortages. If the voters were cold in November, the Republicans faced political losses in the 1902 congressional elections. Yet neither side in the walkout seemed prepared to yield.

As the crisis worsened, Roosevelt brought both sides to the White House in early October. Throughout a day of talks, Roosevelt urged the workers and owners to settle. The union's president, John Mitchell, agreed to arbitration, but the mine owners refused. Roosevelt responded that he might bring in the army to mine coal. Facing that threat, J. P. Morgan and Elihu Root worked out a deal in which a presidential commission was set up to look into the strike. The panel granted the miners a 10 percent pay increase, but the union was not recognized. Unlike Grover Cleveland during the Pullman strike, Roosevelt wielded presidential power to treat capital and labor on an equal basis. Roosevelt called his approach "the Square Deal."

Roosevelt's record limited Republican losses in the congressional elections. The results virtually assured the president's nomination as the Republican candidate in 1904. During the session of Congress that began in December 1902, Roosevelt endorsed the Elkins Act, which would outlaw the rebates railroads gave to favored customers. Roosevelt also called for a law to create a Department of Commerce. One of the agencies of this new department would be a Bureau of Corporations, which would publicize corporate records and indicate which businesses were behaving in the public interest. Roosevelt now had the weapons he sought to distinguish between businesses that he deemed socially good and those that behaved improperly. He attacked the unpopular meat-packing industry, known as the "Beef Trust," and then left business alone until he was safely reelected in 1904.

Roosevelt and Foreign Policy

Theodore Roosevelt wanted to complete the work left over from the Spanish-American War and make the United States a force in world affairs. Because the world was increasingly dangerous, military preparedness was a key goal. "There is a homely adage which runs," the president said, "Speak softly and carry a big stick; you will go far." By 1905, he had added ten battleships to the navy and improved its gunnery. Although Roosevelt loved to perform on the world stage without having to consult Congress, he always remembered the public's caution about overseas adventures. Except in the Philippines, where the guerilla war sputtered on, during his presidency Roosevelt sent no American forces into armed combat.

He did act vigorously in places where the power of the United States was dominant. In 1902, Germany and Great Britain used their navies to collect debts that Venezuela owed them; Roosevelt sent the U.S. Navy into the region to limit foreign involvement there. Similar problems with the Dominican Republic and its debts two years later led him to pronounce the "Roosevelt Corollary," which he believed was a natural extension of the Monroe Doctrine. In his annual message in 1904, he said that "chronic wrongdoing or impotence" of Latin American nations in paying their debts might lead the United States "to the exercise of an international police power." After 1905, the United States controlled customs revenues and tax services in the Dominican Republic.

Roosevelt also sought better relations with Great Britain. That policy would make it easier to secure a canal across Central America. A possible flashpoint between Washington and London was the boundary between Alaska and Canada. Discoveries of gold in the Yukon region attracted rival miners and speculators and raised the possibility of violence between Canadians and Americans. Roosevelt used an Anglo-American Commission to settle the dispute peacefully in favor of the United States.

The United States had wanted to see a waterway built across Central America for decades, but disease, mud, and the jungle defeated all construction efforts. The most ambitious project collapsed during the 1880s. The New Panama Canal Company, a French firm, left behind some construction work and large financial debts.

During the Spanish-American War, it took the battleship USS *Oregon* two months to go from San Francisco Bay around the tip of South America to join the navy near Cuba. In the Hay-Pauncefote Treaty (1901), Great Britain gave up its rights to participate in a canal project. Congress then decided in 1902 that the best route lay across Panama. Secretary of State John Hay opened talks with Colombia, of which Panama was then a part. In 1903, Hay and a Colombian diplomat concluded the Hay-Herran Convention. There would be a six-mile-wide canal zone, under American control, with a ninety-nine year lease. The Colombians would receive a $10 million payment and $250,000 per year in rent. The U.S. Senate ratified the pact.

Colombia was less cooperative. The Colombian Senate believed that the treaty infringed on their country's sovereignty, and the lawmakers wanted more money. Roosevelt was outraged. Within Panama, opponents of Colombian rule plotted revolution. Lawyers for the New Panama Canal Company lobbied for American intervention if a rebellion broke out. The uprising oc-

The Roosevelt Corollary to the Monroe Doctrine, 1904, 1905

In his annual message (State of the Union message) of 1904, President Theodore Roosevelt announced what became known as the Roosevelt Corollary to the Monroe Doctrine. His remarks emphasized the right and responsibility of the United States to intervene in the affairs of Latin American nations when they failed to fulfill their international responsibilities as Washington defined them. Roosevelt's comments represented a high point of American imperialistic attitude toward neighboring nations to the South.

. . . It is not true that the United States feels any land hunger or entertains any projects as regards the other nations of the Western Hemisphere save such as are for their welfare. All that this country desires is to see the neighboring countries stable, orderly, and prosperous. Any country whose people conduct themselves well can count upon our hearty friendship. If a nation shows that it knows how to act with reasonable efficiency and decency in social and political matters, if it keeps order and pays its obligations, it need fear no interference from the United States. Chronic wrongdoing, or an impotence which results in a general loosening of the ties of civilized society, may in America, as elsewhere, ultimately require intervention by some civilized nation, and in the Western Hemisphere the adherence of the United States to the Monroe Doctrine may force the United States, however reluctantly, in flagrant cases of such wrongdoing or impotence, to the exercise of an international police power. If every country washed by the Caribbean Sea would show the progress in stable and just civilization which with the aid of the Platt amendment Cuba has shown since our troops left the island, and which so many of the republics in both Americas are constantly and brilliantly showing, all question of interference by this Nation with their affairs would be at an end. Our interests and those of our southern neighbors are in reality identical. They have great natural riches, and if within their borders the reign of law and justice obtains, prosperity is sure to come to them. While they thus obey the primary laws of civilized society they may rest assured that they will be treated by us in a spirit of cordial and helpful sympathy. We would interfere with them only in the last resort, and then only if it became evident that their inability or unwillingness to do justice at home and abroad had violated the rights of the United States or had invited foreign aggression to the detriment of the entire body of American nations. It is a mere truism to say that every nation, whether in America or anywhere else, which desires to maintain its freedom, its independence, must ultimately realize that the right of such independence can not be separated from the responsibility of making good use of it.

curred in November 1903 amid strong signals that Washington supported the revolution. The presence of American naval vessels discouraged the Colombians from putting down the rebellion. The United States recognized the new Panamanian government, as did other European and Latin American nations.

In November 1903, discussions with the representative of Panama, a Frenchman named Philippe Bunau-Varilla, led to the Hay-Bunau-Varilla Treaty. The new pact created a ten-mile-wide zone across Panama in exchange for the $10 million payment and the $250,000 annual rent. Within the Canal Zone, the United States could act as a sovereign nation, a provision that subsequent Panamanian governments resented. Construction of the canal proceeded slowly until Roosevelt put the U.S. Army in charge in 1907. Roosevelt visited Panama himself in 1906, thus becoming the first president to leave the continental United States while in office.

*P*ICTURING THE PAST ✦ POLITICS & DIPLOMACY

THEODORE ROOSEVELT AND THE STRONG PRESIDENCY

From the Collections of the Library of Congress

One of the key features of politics and government during the twentieth century was the rise of the strong presidency. In the process, presidents became political celebrities. The youthful vigor of Theodore Roosevelt between 1901 and 1909, particularly his keen eye for the limelight, made him the darling of cartoonists in the nation's magazines and newspapers. In this image of the gigantic president striding the isthmus of Panama between the Atlantic and Pacific Oceans to build a canal, one gets a sense of how Roosevelt's larger-than-life qualities enhanced the power of his office and fixed public attention on the occupants of the White House. The dropping of the dirt from Roosevelt's shovel on the Colombian capital of Bogotá reflects as well how popular Roosevelt's disdainful treatment of the Colombians was as he made the Canal Zone a reality in 1903–1904.

It cost more than $350 million to build the Panama Canal, or the equivalent of several billion dollars in modern funds. Almost 6,000 workers died of disease and accidents during construction. The official opening took place on August 15, 1914. Theodore Roosevelt regarded the canal as the greatest achievement of his presidency.

The Election of 1904

Roosevelt's domestic and foreign policy triumphs made him the favorite in the 1904 election. The Democrats turned to Alton B. Parker, a very dull, conservative New York state judge. Despite last-minute Democratic charges that big business was behind the Roosevelt campaign, the American people voted for the incumbent. Roosevelt received more than 56 percent of the vote, compared with Parker's 38 percent. The number of Americans who voted, however, was more than 400,000 below the 1900 figure. Turnout also

slipped to under 65 percent of the voters in the North, compared with nearly 72 percent four years before.

On election night, Roosevelt said that the three years he had served represented his first term as president. He would not be a candidate for another term in 1908. By respecting the third-term tradition, he hoped to allay fears that he might remain president for life. Roosevelt thought he then could embark on a campaign of reform without being accused of personal ambition to stay in office.

In his 1904 annual message, Roosevelt asked Congress to strengthen the power of the Interstate Commerce Commission to regulate the railroads. Roosevelt contended that the power of the federal government should be used to make the whole society more just and equitable. He talked of carrying out the Square Deal. With his gift for understanding where public opinion was going, Roosevelt had caught the spirit of change that came to be called the

Progressive Movement. In his second term he put the power of the modern presidency behind the new agenda for reform.

PROGRESSIVE CAMPAIGNS TO REFORM THE NATION

Efforts to improve American life acquired national significance in the years just after 1904. Responding to the growth of cities, the problems of industrialism, and fears about the nation's future, the American people launched movements to clean up politics and society. The movement was called progressivism. It sought to expand the power of government and to make politics more just and democratic.

Consumers and Reformers

Progressivism occurred during a time of prosperity in which Americans saw themselves more as consumers than producers. A sense of well-being allowed middle-class citizens to address the social and economic problems that had emerged during the depression of the 1890s. After the deflation of the late nineteenth century, rising prices aroused popular concern about the high cost of living. Critics of the Republican protective tariff policies charged that customs duties added to inflation. Equally strong were fears of the effects of business consolidation on the smaller companies for which so many people worked. In 1909, 1 percent of firms accounted for 45 percent of manufactured goods.

When Americans focused on the products they bought and used, they listened when investigative reporters said that patent medicines were unsafe. The discovery that meat-packing plants and other food processors tolerated unsafe conditions led to federal regulation in 1906. Pure food and pure drugs were so necessary, reformers argued, that businesses would have to accept more governmental intrusion than ever.

The Currents of Reform

The movement for progressive reform drew upon forces that had been gathering strength for two decades. As the problems of industrialism and urban growth emerged, a coalition of groups proposed fresh answers. Despite their diversity of goals and approaches, shared assumptions united most people who called themselves progressives.

During the years before World War I in 1914, when Europe was at peace and society seemed to be improving, men and women believed that human na-

ture was basically good and could be made better. The human environment could be reshaped. Government at all levels could promote a better society, and the state had a duty to relieve the ills that were a result of industrial growth.

Differing Methods of Reform

Two approaches emerged within progressive reform. One answer for the problems of democracy was more democracy. Proposals for a *direct primary* to allow voters to choose the candidates of their political parties became popular. The selection of U.S. senators should be taken away from state legislatures and given to the people. The voters themselves should have the right to vote on public issues in *referenda,* to propose laws in *initiatives,* and to remove or *recall* officials or judges whose decisions offended majority sentiment in a city or state.

Another strand of progressivism focused on producing greater order and efficiency. Government had become corrupt, expensive, and clumsy. Accordingly, efforts were made to improve the structure of cities and states to make them work with more economy and less confusion. The commission form of city government did away with elected aldermen from local wards and replaced them with officials who were chosen in citywide elections and assigned to a specific department such as utilities, transit, or housing. Regulatory agencies like the Federal Trade Commission and the Interstate Commerce Commission, staffed with experts on the industries they supervised, would see that the marketplace operated in an orderly way without partisan influences. A strong distrust of political parties animated this style of reform.

The Ambiguities of Progressivism

Some reformers sought programs that emphasized social control of groups and individuals. Prohibition of the use of alcohol, restriction of immigration into the United States, and efforts to shift political power in cities away from the poor and unorganized reflected a desire to compel correct behavior or restrict democracy to native-born white Americans and the "respectable" classes. These coercive aspects of reform became less attractive to later generations.

Despite these failings, progressivism made constructive changes. The regulatory agencies, direct primaries, and other programs did not wipe out all the existing injustices, but they softened the impact of an industrial social order. The principle that government was responsible for the general welfare of the nation also became well established. Reform did not attack the preeminence of democratic capitalism, but the men and women who joined the crusades for change during the era of Theodore Roosevelt wanted to improve their country, not to revolutionize it.

The Muckrakers

Important figures in progressive reform were a group of journalists who exposed corruption and weaknesses in American society. They published their revelations in numerous monthly and weekly magazines. Selling for as little as ten cents a copy, these magazines gained large circulations and advertising revenues. New printing techniques made these periodicals economical and profitable. There were also more than 2,000 daily newspapers that gave reporters expanding opportunities to probe for scandals and scoops.

The Impact of McClure's Magazine

Samuel S. McClure, publisher of *McClure's Magazine*, helped launch the popular literature of exposure. By 1902, his monthly journal had attracted a wide middle-class audience for its appealing blend of fact and fiction. McClure wanted the magazine to address the major issues of the day. He decided that the rise of big business and trusts provided the "great theme" he sought. He sent one of his star reporters, Ida Tarbell, to look into the Standard Oil Company. With Tarbell's articles ready to run in the autumn of 1902, McClure decided to expand on an article that another reporter, Lincoln Steffens, had written about municipal corruption in St. Louis. That essay, "Tweed Days in St. Louis," led to a series on city government in the magazine that was published under the title *The Shame of the Cities* (1904). The January 1903 issue of *McClure's* carried articles by Tarbell and Steffens, along with an essay about the anthracite coal strike by Ray Stannard Baker.

Where McClure had led, other magazines soon followed. One writer called it "government by magazine." Samuel Hopkins Adams exposed fraud in patent medicines; his series contributed to the passage of the Pure Food and Drugs Act in 1906. Ray Stannard Baker wrote about unethical railroad practices; his revelations assisted President Roosevelt in his campaign for regulation. For almost five years, the popular press echoed with disclosures of this nature.

The End of Muckraking

In April 1906, Theodore Roosevelt, unhappy with press attacks on the Republican party and conservative senators, used the label "muckrakers" referring

The muckrakers became famous as investigative journalists. One of the most celebrated was Ida Tarbell, who explored how Standard Oil became such a powerful economic force.
The Granger Collection, New York

to investigative journalists. He was comparing them to a character in John Bunyan's *Pilgrim's Progress* who spent all his time raking the muck on the floor and therefore could not see heaven above him. The label stuck. Muckraking seemed to symbolize a style of reporting that emphasized only the negative. By 1907 popular interest in muckraking waned. While it lasted, however, muckraking gave progressivism much of its momentum. It supported the view of many reformers that once the facts of an evil situation were revealed, the political system would move to correct them.

Women and Progressive Reform

Women were the crucial foot soldiers of progressive reform who made these campaigns successful. Changes in the status of middle-class women gave them more time to devote to progressive causes. The settlement house movement continued to attract young women who were interested in social service. The number of such houses had risen steadily since the 1890s; and by 1905, there were over 200 of them. Jane Addams of the Hull House in Chicago remained in the forefront of the movement. Other women joined Addams to promote urban-oriented reforms. Florence Kelley guided the National Consumers League. Julia Lathrop supported child labor legislation and in 1912 became the first director of the federal Children's Bureau. In New York Lillian Wald used the Henry Street Settlement as a base for work to improve conditions for women and children. She also cooperated with the National Association for the Advancement of Colored People to pursue racial justice. Not all settlement house workers were women, but these institutions gave female reformers a supportive environment and a foundation on which to base their role in society.

Women also figured in the conservation movement. In garden clubs and women's improvement clubs, they criticized the spread of billboards, dirty streets, and neglected parks. They called their efforts "municipal housekeeping." Women joined the Audubon Society, the Women's National Rivers and Harbors Congress, and the Sierra Club. They saved species of birds from extinction, fought against dams and destructive logging in the West, and campaigned for more national parks.

The Continuing Fight for Woman Suffrage

The lack of the right to vote frustrated women, and the campaign for woman suffrage became a central concern. Giving women the ballot, said suffrage leaders, would be a "tool with which to build a better nation." Once they could participate in politics, women would promote progressive causes. Carrie Chapman Catt, president of the National American Woman Suffrage Association, said that "the enfranchisement of women will be the crowning glory of democratic government."

To reach that goal, however, the movement had to overcome substantial problems. In Congress, southern Democrats opposed suffrage because it might lead to votes for African Americans. Liquor interests feared that suffrage would help the prohibitionists. Within the suffrage campaign, fund-raising problems and organizational disarray limited the effectiveness of the drive for votes.

By 1910, it was evident that the strategy of pursuing a constitutional amendment at the federal level had stalled. Suffragists turned to the states where they devoted themselves to organizing campaigns that appealed to a majority of male voters. The result was a string of victories in western states such as Washington (1910), California (1911), Oregon (1912), Arizona (1912), Kansas (1912), Montana (1914), and Nevada (1914).

Reform in the Cities

Progressive reformers made their first important impact in the nation's cities. Two Ohio mayors, Samuel "Golden Rule" Jones of Toledo (1897–1903) and Tom L. Johnson of Cleveland (1901–1909), sought to produce changes in the way that their cities functioned. A wealthy businessman himself, Johnson lowered streetcar fares and introduced an electric lighting plan to show how rates could be kept low. Jones instituted municipal ownership of the trolley system, provided higher wages for city employees than private industry did, and founded free kindergartens for Toledo's children. Some cities, such as Milwaukee, Syracuse, and Minneapolis, elected Socialist mayors during the Progressive Era.

More typical of urban reform across the country were efforts to change the structure of city government itself. After Galveston, Texas, adopted the commission idea in 1900 and put each commissioner in charge of a separate city department, the "Galveston Idea" attracted national attention. Refined in Des Moines, Iowa, in 1908, commission government was in place in 160 cities by 1911. The shift away from ward representation also restricted the power of local interests in a nonpartisan way, according to its advocates. The new approach, however, sometimes reduced the voting impact of minority groups.

Soon, however, the commission form gave way to the "city manager" idea. Under this arrangement the city council named a nonpartisan executive who was trained to administer the city under policies that the council specified. The plan promised efficiency, cost-cutting, and reduced partisan influence. Smaller and medium-sized municipalities began instituting the city manager form around 1908.

Urban reform achieved positive results in many cities. Reduction of political influence and limits on the role of partisanship did produce better government. The consequences were not always constructive. Middle-class reformers who pursued these changes often did so at the expense of residents of poorer areas of the city who now found it harder to get a hearing from city hall. Stressing the interest of the city as a whole did not always translate into fair treatment for the less advantaged and less powerful.

Reform in the States

As urban reformers tried to improve their cities, they often confronted barriers within state government and opposition from state politicians. The constitutions of many states restricted the capacity of a city government to manage its own taxes, regulate its public utilities, or supervise the moral behavior of its citizens. By the beginning of the twentieth century, some cities had obtained "home rule," but frustrated reformers saw state governments as obstacles to change. When progressives looked at their problems on the state level, they detected patterns of corruption and business influence that resembled those they had fought locally. Reformers charged that the political party, tied to business interests, prevented meaningful improvements in state government.

At the state level, progressives favored the initiative and referendum because they limited the power of political parties to shape public policy. Allowing the people to propose laws or to vote on laws that had been enacted gave less authority to established political figures and institutions. The initiative and referendum first appeared in South Dakota in 1898; other western states adopted them before 1908. By 1915, twenty-one states had some form of these progressive procedures.

The direct primary spread across most of the nation by 1916; the recall was largely confined to a small number of western states. The primary was popular because it took the power to make nominations out of the hands of party leaders and gave it to the voters. The recall was more controversial. Angry conservatives charged that an election to remove a judge threatened the independence of the judiciary as a whole.

Progressivism drew much of its energy from reformers on the state level. Robert M. La Follette of Wisconsin was one of the most controversial. This cartoon shows what happened to Wisconsin as "Battle Bob" tamed the corporations and created a "model state." La Follette's thick hair made him a favorite of cartoonists.
The Granger Collection, New York

Increasing Regulatory Power

Greater emphasis on the regulatory power of state government accompanied these procedural reforms. Progressives strengthened the authority of existing state railroad commissions and created new commissions to oversee public utilities and insurance companies. These bodies, which would rely on experts in the field, seemed preferable to the whims of partisan lawmaking.

State government attracted popular and effective leaders during the twenty years after 1900. Theodore Roosevelt was a forceful executive for New York during his one term as governor. Also in New York, Charles Evans Hughes became famous for his probe of insurance companies, which gained him the governorship in 1906. Hughes increased the state's role in regulating utilities and railroads. Woodrow Wilson, elected governor of New Jersey in 1910, limited the power of corporations in that state.

La Follette of Wisconsin

The leading symbol of state reform was Robert M. La Follette of Wisconsin. When Republican party leaders opposed him after he was elected as governor in 1900, he launched a crusade against them. During his two

terms as governor, from 1901 to 1905, he established the direct primary, regulated Wisconsin's railroads, and levied higher taxes on corporations. He forged a close relationship between the state government and faculty members at the University of Wisconsin who advised him about policy. This reliance on academic experts was called "the Wisconsin Idea."

Progressivism as a National Force

By 1905, progressivism was moving on to the national stage. The issues that reformers faced in the states and cities now seemed to require action by the federal government. Corporations were interstate in character; only Washington could regulate them effectively. To solve the problems of political parties, the Constitution had to be changed. To create a more moral society, progressives contended, the national government had to grant women the vote, regulate the consumption of alcohol, and limit immigration into the United States.

With growth came problems. Where should the balance be struck between the goal of a more democratic society and that of greater efficiency? Efficiency required organization, expertise, and compulsion. Decision making should be left to the experts who knew how to regulate a railroad or a public utility. But that process enabled a well-organized interest group or lobbying campaign to exercise significant influence and sometimes corrupt the system. A major result of progressivism was more opportunities for organized groups to shape public policy.

The Problems of Reform

The changes that sought to make the political process more democratic sometimes had unexpected results. Conservative groups used the initiative and referendum for their own ends. Well-funded pressure groups could employ the ballot to pursue an issue such as lower taxes or to attack an unpopular idea or group. The initiative could also reduce the electorate to deciding such issues as how long the lunch hour of a fire department might last. The direct primary did not mean that good candidates replaced bad candidates. A wealthy but less qualified candidate could circumvent the party and achieve success in the primary.

The direct election of U.S. senators, mandated through the Seventeenth Amendment in 1913, took the power of choice away from the state legislatures and gave it to the voters in each state. It meant that candidates had to raise larger amounts of money for their campaigns and gave an advantage to wealthy men. Meanwhile, lobbying groups simply found new channels for improper influence. One unexpected consequence of these changes was the declining popular interest in voting that became evident in the 1904 presidential election and in later contests. Political parties, for all their weaknesses, had mobilized voters to come to the ballot box. The progressives never found a replacement for that function of the parties.

During the spring of 1905, however, reform was still fresh. Advocates of change believed that limited and gradual measures could improve society. With Roosevelt in the White House, they had a president who also believed that moderate reform was necessary to avoid radical transformations.

ROOSEVELT AND THE MODERN PRESIDENCY: THE SECOND TERM

In the four years after he was elected in his own right, Theodore Roosevelt traveled widely to promote his programs, built up the bureaucratic machinery of the national government, and pushed Congress to consider a wide range of social problems, from child labor to increased taxation of the wealthy. The president attracted bright young men to Washington to join him, and under Roosevelt the nation's capital became the focus of news and controversy.

Railroad Regulation and the Hepburn Act

Roosevelt began his reform campaign with the railroad regulation he had promised in his 1904 annual message. Customers of railroads in the South and West complained that rates were too high. Shippers and politicians maintained that the federal government, not the railroads themselves, should determine whether a rate was fair. To do that, the Interstate Commerce Commission (ICC) should have the power to review railroad rates to ensure that they were reasonable.

Roosevelt agreed. During 1905, he spoke for his program across the South and West. The Department of Justice launched well-publicized probes to find out whether railroads were still giving rebates in violation of the 1903 Elkins Act. Roosevelt dangled the threat of revising the tariff to sway Republican leaders in the House to favor his approach. He shared information about railroad misdeeds with sympathetic reporters. When the rail companies started their own public relations effort, it backfired because the public did not believe the railroad claims.

Still, getting a bill that the White House wanted through Congress was not easy. Matters went smoothly in the House. The Hepburn bill, named after William P. Hepburn of Iowa, initiated to give the ICC greater authority over railroads and their practices, was passed in February 1906 by a vote of 346 to seven. The Senate was the main obstacle. A long struggle ensued between Roosevelt and the conservative Republican leader, Nelson W. Aldrich of Rhode Island. The issue was whether the courts should have broad power to review the ICC's rulings. If courts had such authority, they could water down the law. The Senate won some victories on the issue, but the Hepburn Act was passed in late June 1906. The ICC now had the power to establish maximum rates and to review the accounts and records of the railroads. Most of all, the Hepburn Act showed what a strong president could do to achieve a major legislative goal when he summoned public opinion to support a popular cause.

The Expansion of Regulation

There was more to Roosevelt's regulatory program besides railroads. Muckrakers had revealed that patent medicines sold over the counter were usually ineffective and sometimes dangerous. Led by Dr.

A NAUSEATING JOB. BUT IT MUST BE DONE

The publication of Upton Sinclair's The Jungle *in 1906 angered the nation and led Roosevelt to support meat inspection legislation. A cartoonist depicts the president performing an unpleasant but necessary probe of the issue.*
The Granger Collection, New York

Roosevelt's diplomatic successes included his successful mediation of the war between Russia and Japan. He summoned delegates from both countries to Portsmouth, New Hampshire. This picture shows the Russians and the Japanese meeting with Roosevelt for what would later be called a "photo opportunity."
© Bettmann/Corbis

Harvey Wiley of the Department of Agriculture, the government conducted experiments on the purity of food that revealed that toxic chemicals made many food products unsafe. By early 1906, the clamor for reform had led to the introduction of a bill in Congress to restrict the sale of impure or adulterated food and drugs. The measure was passed by the Senate, but stalled in the House of Representatives.

During the winter of 1906, thousands of Americans read *The Jungle,* a novel about the meat-packing industry in Chicago. Written by a young socialist named Upton Sinclair, the book depicted shocking conditions in the plants. The public ignored Sinclair's political message; they were outraged that dirt and filth endangered their meat supply.

President Roosevelt was outraged as well. If the government did not take action, he feared that the socialism Sinclair favored might gain followers. The White House supported an amendment to the Agricultural Appropriation Act of 1906 that set up a federal program for meat inspection. The meat-packing industry tried to water down the bill, but the law represented a significant advance in regulatory power.

The controversy over meat inspection cleared the way for House action on the Pure Food and Drugs Act. As a result, that measure was passed on June 30, 1906. A happy president called the three regulatory laws passed during that year's congressional session "a noteworthy advance in the policy of securing Federal supervision and control over corporations."

To achieve that control, Roosevelt placed less emphasis on breaking up large corporations. Instead, he sought to use the Bureau of Corporations to supervise companies that the White House deemed socially responsible. Having decided which businesses and corporate leaders met his standards of morality in the marketplace, he made private agreements with International Harvester and United States Steel. In return for letting the government examine their financial records, these companies would not be subjected to antitrust prosecutions. Firms that Roosevelt disliked, including Standard Oil, would be disciplined by federal lawsuits. Presidential power, mixed with administrative discretion, would control corporate misdeeds.

Roosevelt and World Politics

Roosevelt matched his activism in domestic policy with equal energy in the conduct of foreign affairs. He carried on secret negotiations without Congress's knowledge, broadened the nation's activities in Asia and Europe, and tried to educate the American people to accept a new role as a world power.

Early in 1904, war broke out between Russia and Japan when the Japanese launched a surprise attack. Roosevelt sympathized with Japan because he regarded the Russians as a threat to the Open Door policy in China. As the Japanese won a series of decisive victories, however, the president concluded that a negotiated settlement would best serve the interests of the United States. He was ready to act as an intermediary when the two parties began negotiations.

Though victorious on the battlefield, Japan was financially exhausted. In April 1905, Tokyo invited Roosevelt to mediate. Roosevelt summoned the combatants to a peace conference to be held at Portsmouth, New Hampshire, in August. The two nations agreed to end the conflict; the Treaty of Portsmouth was signed in September 1905. Meanwhile the Roosevelt administration recognized the supremacy of Japan over its neighbor, Korea. In turn, Japan pledged that it had no aggressive designs on the Philippines. In 1906, Roosevelt received the Nobel Peace Prize for his diplomatic achievement.

Roosevelt's order that the American fleet should sail around the world proved to be a natural inspiration for advertising. The Prudential Insurance Company used the vessels to make an appeal to its customers.
Reproduced from the Collections of the Library of Congress

The Algeciras Conference

In Europe, Roosevelt sought to reduce the growing tension between Germany and the other major powers, France and Great Britain. Roosevelt sympathized with Britain and France, but he wanted to persuade Germany and its leader, Kaiser Wilhelm II, to be reasonable. During 1905, the Germans made a major issue of French dominance of Morocco. The Kaiser wanted a conference to determine Morocco's status. Roosevelt convinced Britain and France to accept a conference rather than go to war over the fate of the North African country. The president expanded the international role of the United States when he sent delegates to the Algeciras Conference.

The Gentlemen's Agreement

Later in 1906, the lingering problems in Japanese-American relations flared up again. Japan resented the nativist immigration policies of the United States that discriminated against Japanese newcomers. On the West Coast, the increasing number of Japanese workers and residents intensified nativist and racist sentiments. The San Francisco school board segregated children of Japanese ancestry, and Japan reacted angrily. Washington and Tokyo eventually worked out the "Gentlemen's Agreement" of 1907. The order of the school board was revoked, and Japan agreed to limit the number of immigrants who left that country for the United States.

The Great White Fleet

To increase funding for the navy, Roosevelt sent the American navy's "Great White Fleet" on a round-the-world tour from 1907 to 1909. When the vessels stopped in Japan in October 1908, the reception was enthusiastic and friendly. A month later, the two nations negotiated the Root-Takahira Agreement, which called for the Open Door in China, the independence of that country, and preservation of the status quo in the Pacific.

When he left office in March 1909, Roosevelt expressed pride that the United States was "at absolute peace" with the rest of the world. His policy in the Caribbean had reaffirmed the supremacy of the United States and made possible the construction of the Panama Canal. In Asia he had done his best with the limited power available to him. Roosevelt's involvement in Europe had been positive, but it had not addressed the interlocking alliance systems that would lead to war in 1914.

Labor and Socialists Challenge Roosevelt

As the congressional elections of 1906 approached, the Republican party was still dominant. Some voters were turning away from the Republicans, however, and the Democrats entered the contest with optimism. They had a new asset to help them against the Republicans: organized labor. The American Federation of Labor (AFL) had a membership of nearly 1.7

million by 1904. Its leaders hoped for legislation to limit the power of state and federal courts to block strikes through injunctions. When Republicans in Congress rejected such a program, the leader of the union, Samuel Gompers, called for the defeat of Republican candidates who were "hostile or indifferent to the just demands of labor."

In addition to the opposition of the AFL, Roosevelt worried about the growing power of the Socialist party and the most radical wing of the labor movement, the Industrial Workers of the World. Founded in 1905, the IWW, or as they were nicknamed, "Wobblies," criticized the AFL as timid and called for the overthrow of capitalism. The Socialist party, under the leadership of Eugene V. Debs, also gained strength at the polls. In 1904 Debs won some 400,000 votes. Roosevelt believed that his reforms were necessary to stave off more sweeping social change. During the 1906 election campaign, he sent out members of his cabinet to attack the IWW as violent and dangerous.

The 1906 Elections

The Republicans lost twenty-six seats in the elections, but the campaign of the AFL to unseat Republicans did not do as much damage as Gompers had promised. Nevertheless, the results revealed that the Republicans had significant problems. The protective tariff divided the party. Midwesterners wanted lower duties, whereas Republicans in the East would tolerate no tariff revision. Roosevelt's regulatory policies alienated party conservatives who became angry when Roosevelt regulated railroads, watched over the quality of food products, and attacked large corporations.

Problems with the Supreme Court

One barrier to reform was the Supreme Court where the justices often overturned progressive laws. In the case of *Lochner v. New York* (1905), for example, they struck down a New York law that limited the hours employees could work in a bakery. The Court ruled that the law infringed on the right of the bakers under the Fourteenth Amendment to get the best reward for their labor. Sometimes the justices made an exception. In the 1908 case of *Muller v. Oregon,* influenced by a brief submitted by Louis D. Brandeis, they upheld an Oregon statute that limited the hours women could work. In other decisions that same year, however, the Court invalidated the Employers Liabilities Act of 1906 and curbed the power of labor unions in the Danbury Hatters case *(Loewe v. Lawlor).*

In the South, women labored in the cotton mills of the region for long hours with low pay. Although the Supreme Court upheld the principle that a state could limit the hours that women worked in Muller v. Oregon, *the decision had little effect in North Carolina where these women worked in the spinning room of the White Oak Cotton Mill in Greensboro.*
The Granger Collection, New York

Roosevelt and Conservation

Roosevelt's campaign for the conservation of natural resources also reflected his presidential activism. Using the power of his office, he created refuges for wild birds, preserved the Grand Canyon against intrusion from development, and set aside national parks. During his first term he worked for passage of the Newlands Reclamation Act (1902), which established a system of irrigation reservoirs in the West financed through the sale of public lands. Over the long term, however, the Newlands Act helped large farming corporations more than it did small landowners.

Roosevelt worked closely with Gifford Pinchot of the United States Forestry Service to formulate conservation policy. Neither man thought that natural resources should be locked up and saved for some indefinite future use. Instead, the national parks, coal lands, oil reserves, water-power sites, and national forests in the West should be managed by trained experts from the federal government to achieve the maximum amount of effective use. For

Roosevelt and Pinchot conservation did not mean that large corporations should be excluded from developing such resources. In fact, corporations might be the best means of exploiting resources in the wisest possible way. Conservationists who were convinced that the wilderness should be preserved rather than developed opposed the Roosevelt-Pinchot policy.

Roosevelt had alerted the American people to a serious national problem. He raised important issues about the future of timber, water, wildlife, and mineral resources. He created national parks, including Mesa Verde and Crater Lake, and established four national game preserves, fifty-one bird reservations, and 150 national forests. He could be proud of the National Monuments Act (1906) and the Governors Conference on Conservation (1908).

Roosevelt's policies required a high degree of control by the federal government and the cooperation of large corporations. In the West, there was much resentment of programs that Washington had devised without much local support and implemented over the protests of the westerners themselves.

Deteriorating Race Relations

During his second term Roosevelt showed less sympathy for the plight of African Americans than he had as a candidate for the presidency. He made no public statement about a 1906 race riot in Atlanta, Georgia, in which four blacks were killed and many others injured. Later that year he discharged without a hearing or trial the African American soldiers who were falsely accused of shooting up Brownsville, Texas, in 1906, and he resisted all efforts to reopen the case of the men involved. Many blacks no longer believed that they had a friend in the White House.

The situation of African Americans worsened. In August 1908, whites rioted against blacks in Springfield, Illinois, Abraham Lincoln's hometown; two blacks were lynched. A tide of bigotry swept the nation. In 1909 in the face of presidential inaction, prominent white reformers such as Oswald Garrison Villard (grandson of the abolitionist William Lloyd Garrison), Mary White Ovington, and William E. Walling, met with W. E. B. Du Bois, Wells-Barnett, and other blacks to form the National Association for the Advancement of Colored People. They sought an end to segregation, voting rights for blacks, and equal education for all children. Du Bois became the editor of the NAACP's magazine, *Crisis*. The NAACP's use of the courts to attack segregation soon gave it a leading role in the struggle for racial justice.

"WILL YOU PLEASE HUSH?"
From the *Herald* (New York)

A cartoon attacks Roosevelt's antibusiness policies as a cause of the Panic of 1907.
Albert Shaw, *A Cartoon History of Roosevelt's Career* (1910)

Roosevelt's Last Years of Power

Roosevelt remained popular with the American people during the waning years of his administration. Among conservative Republicans, however, unhappiness with the president mounted. On Capitol Hill, party members in the House and Senate balked at Roosevelt's assertiveness. When problems in the banking industry led to the Panic of 1907, a momentary collapse of the financial system and a brief recession followed. Roosevelt's Republican opponents blamed the economic troubles on his regulatory policies. To stem the danger to banks, Roosevelt agreed to let United States Steel acquire the Tennessee Coal and Iron Company, a decision that came back to affect Roosevelt after his presidency.

The issue of Roosevelt's successor became a central problem for Republicans. Hoping to see his progressive policies carried on, the president decided to support his secretary of war, William Howard Taft. By early 1907, Roosevelt had become the real campaign manager of Taft's drive to win the Republican nomination.

During early 1908, Roosevelt endorsed more sweeping regulation of corporations, a tax on inheritances of great wealth, and compensation laws for workers. Congressional Republicans reacted coolly to these proposals, and relations between the White House and Capitol Hill worsened throughout 1908.

Meanwhile, Taft advanced toward the Republican nomination at the national convention in June where he won easily on the first ballot. In their platform the

In 1908, William Jennings Bryan made his third unsuccessful run for the White House. The "boy orator" of 1896 had less hair and more flesh, but he retained his capacity to enthrall Democratic voters.
By W. A. Rogers. From the Herald (New York)

WELL BEGUN AND WELL DONE
From the *Evening Mail* (New York)

The transition from Roosevelt to Taft was not as tranquil as this cartoon implies.
By Homer Davenport. From the Evening Mail (New York)

Republicans promised to revise the protective tariff at a special session of Congress shortly after the new president was inaugurated. The public assumed that any change in the tariff would lead to lower rates.

The 1908 Presidential Election

The Democrats nominated William Jennings Bryan for the third time and were optimistic about his chances. After all, Roosevelt was not a candidate and Taft had not been tested at the polls. In the early days of the campaign, Bryan ran well. Then Roosevelt threw his support behind Taft in a series of public statements. The Republicans won again: Taft garnered 321 electoral votes to Bryan's 162. The popular vote went solidly for Taft, although Bryan ran much better than Alton B. Parker had in 1904. The election was marked by ticket-splitting in which voters cast ballots for Taft for president and Democrats for other offices. The partisan allegiances and loyalties of the late nineteenth century were breaking down.

Roosevelt had picked Taft as his successor because he was convinced that Taft would carry on with his reform policies. Shortly after the election, however, tensions developed between Roosevelt and his political heir. Battles between Roosevelt and Congress flared as inauguration day approached. As Roosevelt prepared to leave office and embark on a hunting trip to Africa, the Republican party remained divided over its future.

CONCLUSION

Theodore Roosevelt had been an important president. In domestic policy, he had demonstrated how a chief executive could mobilize public opinion behind the policies of the national government. On the world stage, he had involved the nation in European and Asian affairs to preserve international stability.

Not all that Roosevelt did was positive. His handling of race relations was neither consistent nor principled, and he failed to exercise serious leadership on this troubled problem. Sometimes he flirted with excessive power in pursuit of his political enemies. He had also showed little respect for the constraints that the Constitution imposed on his office. Nevertheless, he offered an example of exciting leadership on which other presidents would build.

Theodore Roosevelt had neither caused the progressive movement to emerge nor encouraged all of its campaigns. He had given reform a visible national leader. As a result, progressives would point to numerous successes—railroad regulation, conservation, and pure food and drug legislation. The agenda of change was still incomplete, however. For the new president, the issue was whether to extend reform or to thwart it. Meanwhile, reformers in the states debated issues of cultural and economic policy—prohibition of alcohol, woman suffrage, immigration restriction, and procedural reforms. The Roosevelt years had been exciting, but the climax of progressivism would come during the presidency of William Howard Taft.

Recommended Reading

Cooper, John Milton, Jr. *The Pivotal Decades: The United States, 1900–1920* (1990). Offers a thoughtful and well-informed account of the first two decades of the new century.

Cordery, Stacy. *Theodore Roosevelt: In the Vanguard of the Modern* (2002). A new brief biography of Roosevelt that provides a good look at his historical impact.

Dalton, Kathleen. *Theodore Roosevelt: A Strenuous Life* (2002). A full biography that examines the psychological and family influences on Roosevelt's career.

Diner, Steven J. *A Very Different Age: Americans of the Progressive Era* (1998). An interpretive synthesis that emphasizes social and economic issues.

Gould, Lewis L. *Reform and Regulation: American Politics from Roosevelt to Wilson* (1996). Covers the politics of the era.

Gould, Lewis L. *The Presidency of Theodore Roosevelt* (1991). Reviews the president's achievements in office.

Graham, Sara Hunter. *Woman Suffrage and the New Democracy* (1996). A crisp, thoughtful examination of the evolution of woman suffrage as a progressive movement.

Milkis, Sidney M., and Mileur, Jerome M., eds. *Progressivism and the New Democracy* (1999). An interesting collection of essays on the impact of progressive reforms.

Naylor, Natalie, Brinkley, Douglas, and Gable, John, eds. *Theodore Roosevelt: Many-Sided American* (1992). A group of essays on the many aspects of Roosevelt's life.

Tilchin, William. *Theodore Roosevelt and the British Empire* (1997). A good brief introduction to Roosevelt as a world figure.

American Journey Online and InfoTrac College Edition

Visit the source collections at http://ajaccess.wadsworth.com and infotrac.thomsonlearning.com and use the Search function with the following key terms to explore documents, images, audio and video clips, articles, and commentary related to the material in this chapter.

Theodore Roosevelt	National Women's Trade
Muckraking	Union League
Niagara Movement	*Muller v. Oregon*
Model T	J. P. Morgan
Upton Sinclair	NAACP
Ida Tarbell	

Additional resources, exercises, and Internet links related to this chapter are available on the American Passages Web site: http://history.wadsworth.com/passages2e

PASSAGES
— 1909
TO 1933

Progress seemed everywhere in 1909. Aviators crossed the English Channel for the first time, wireless communication linked ships at sea with their destinations; at home Americans took to the open road in their new Ford automobiles. In such a heady climate of advancing technology and growing economic abundance, writers spoke of an end of war as nations talked out their disputes at the conference table rather than settling them on the battlefield. The path of history seemed well-lit and clear toward a bright future of hope and peace.

The two cars in the wheat field depicted here reveal the many ways in which Americans used the new freedom of the automobile to explore their vast country. With the open road and the motels, restaurants, and tourist attractions that arose in its wake, Americans became even more a traveling people.
From the Bostwick-Frohardt Collections, owned by KMTV and on permanent loan to Western Heritage Museum, Omaha, Nebraska

Twenty-four years later, in the winter of 1933, the United States lay in the grip of a severe economic depression. Banks had closed, unemployment had soared, and the homeless and destitute roamed the land. Newspapers and magazines ran articles that speculated on whether democracy had failed. To a minority of Americans, the opposing ideologies of communism and fascism seemed alluring. As the nation faced the prospect of a potential social revolution, its citizens looked back with nostalgia to the early years of the century and wondered what had happened to destroy that optimistic and confident world.

The outbreak of a world war in the summer of 1914 did the most to unhinge the sense of progress that then permeated the United States. If advanced nations could ravage each other on European battlefields, who could any longer believe in the perfectibility of humanity? Americans first tried to stay out of the conflict, but by 1917 they entered the war on the side of France and Great Britain.

In less than two years, the experience of World War I accelerated trends toward a more powerful federal government, a more bureaucratic society, and a nation in which large corporations exercised an even greater role. At the same time, the bitter national and ideological conflicts of Europe spilled over into American life. Racial, ethnic, and sectional tensions produced social unrest and group hatreds that raged between 1917 and 1933.

Net Production of Electric Energy by Central Stations, by Class of Ownership: 1907 to 1933	
Year	Total Utility and Industrial
1933	102,655
1932	99,359
1931	109,373
1930	114,637
1929	116,747
1928	108,069
1927	101,390
1926	94,222
1925	84,666
1924	75,892
1923	71,399
1922	61,204
1921	53,125
1920	56,559
1917	43,429
1912	24,752
1907	14,121

During the war, however, some aspects of prewar reform reached completion. Women gained the vote in 1920 after three generations of struggle. Their ballots did not transform national politics in the years that followed, but their presence in the process ended centuries of a male monopoly of the elective system. The war years also achieved the temperance dream of a national prohibition of alcohol. Despite this reform success, the nation remained divided over its attitude toward liquor, a condition that raised problems for enforcing the new constitutional amendment.

In the aftermath of World War I, Americans rushed forward to embrace the new world of consumer goods and economic affluence. Automobiles, appliances, and installment buying reshaped attitudes about frugality and the future. The spread of mass media and bigtime sports brought shared cultural experiences to many Americans. The decade seemed vibrant with the wailing of jazz, the roar of the metropolis, and the excitement of flaming youth.

Not all Americans shared in the prosperity or endorsed the headlong embrace of the modern world. Farmers never experienced the prosperity of the decade, and they encountered economic downturns sooner than did their city counterparts. Rural values remained strong even when transplanted to an urban setting. Some dislocated citizens sought the missing sense of community in an organization such as the Ku Klux Klan, which

The Stock Market Crash of October 1929 ended the ebullient optimism of the 1920s about the future of the American economy and the promise of wealth for millions. The entertainment newspaper Variety *caught the mood of disillusion that anticipated the Great Depression with its sarcastic headline the day after the averages had tumbled.*
The Granger Collection, New York

The rise of the Ku Klux Klan reflected the cultural tensions that accompanied the end of the First World War. The hooded order attained nationwide popularity before its own excesses discredited it and its leaders. This illustration shows the union of the cross and the American flag that made the Klan such a potent symbol of intolerance.
© Bettmann/UPI/Corbis

promised ritual, controversy, and social change in equal measure. Many Americans found that fundamentalist religious denominations spoke to their spiritual needs in ways that the modernist churches did not. Strains between the city and country showed themselves in politics in the 1928 presidential election when the urban, Catholic background of Democrat Al Smith turned many in his party toward the Republican nominee, Herbert Hoover.

Throughout the 1920s, the confidence that the economy would move ever upward sustained people even when they lacked wealth themselves. By the end of the decade, however, the prosperity that consumers had built and that corporations relished began to totter. Poor distribution of income, corporate excesses, weaknesses in the banking structure, and mounting problems with international finance led to a stock market crash in 1929 and a Depression that grew steadily worse during the early 1930s.

A generation raised on the prospect of burgeoning prosperity found itself confronted with want, destitution, and despair. Organized charity seemed inadequate for the task of relief, and government at all levels also failed to address the economic problems in effective ways. By the winter of 1932, the nation experienced a tightening spiral of gloom and fear. The sunny days of progressivism and reform were only a grotesque echo of an age that had disappeared. In the American passage, the early 1930s seemed as close as any citizen wished to get to the valley of the shadow.

The dramatic flight of Charles Lindbergh across the Atlantic alone in 1927 symbolized the promise of technology for the 1920s. "The Lone Eagle" became a popular celebrity, and thousands flocked to see him and his plane, "The Spirit of St. Louis," when he traveled around the country after his epic adventure.
From the Collections of the Library of Congress

Herbert Hoover campaigned as "The Great Engineer" in 1928. Here he poses on his campaign train with railroad workmen. The American people chose Hoover over Al Smith during a time of prosperity. The onset of the Depression in the 1930s eroded Hoover's popularity and left him a discredited leader by 1932 when he lost in a landslide.
Reproduced from the Collections of the Library of Congress

	1909	1913	1917
Politics & Diplomacy	**1909:** Ballinger-Pinchot controversy over conservation begins **1910:** Roosevelt proclaims his New Nationalism Democrats regain control of House of Representatives in elections **1911:** Taft pursues Canadian Reciprocity on tariff but fails **1912:** Republican party splits between Roosevelt and Taft Roosevelt forms Progressive party Democrats nominate Wilson for president and he is elected	**1913:** Wilson addresses Congress in person, breaking longtime precedent Underwood Tariff passed Sixteenth Amendment adopted allowing income tax **1914:** Clayton Antitrust law passed Vera Cruz incident leads to intervention in Mexico World War begins in Europe **1915:** *Lusitania* sunk Leo Frank lynched in Georgia **1916:** Germany makes *Sussex* Pledge about submarines Americans intervene in Mexico to attempt capture of Pancho Villa Wilson defeats Hughes in presidential election	**1917:** Zimmerman Telegram released United States declares war on Germany **1918:** Wilson announces Fourteen Points Armistice ends World War I Democrats are defeated and Wilson repudiated in congressional elections **1919:** Wilson attends Peace Conference, but League of Nations is defeated in Senate Prohibition adopted **1920:** Woman suffrage adopted Harding defeats Cox and is elected president **1921:** Harding inaugurated United States signs separate peace with Germany
Social & Cultural Events	**1909:** Massachusetts forms first public commission on aging Motion Picture Trust formed out of early movie companies **1910:** Mann White Slave Traffic Act passed to discourage transportation of women across state lines for "immoral purposes" Jack Johnson defeats James Jeffries ("the Great White Hope") in heavyweight title fight Boy Scouts of America founded **1911:** Harriet Quimby becomes first licensed woman pilot **1912:** S S *Titanic* hits iceberg and sinks in North Atlantic Children's Bureau established Girl Scouts of America begins	**1913:** Armory Show provides introduction to modern art Massive suffrage march occurs in Washington, D.C., on March 3 Brillo pads introduced **1914:** President Wilson proclaims first national Mother's Day Margaret Sanger introduces term "birth control" *New Republic* magazine begins publication **1915:** *The Birth of a Nation* becomes hit movie Support for woman suffrage grows Charlie Chaplin becomes movie star Great Migration of African Americans to the North continues **1916:** First birth control clinic opens in Brooklyn, New York National Woman's party founded	**1917:** Frozen food processing developed Woman suffrage advocates jailed for picketing White House **1918:** Influenza epidemic sweeps the globe and kills 20 million people First granulated soap ("Rinso") introduced **1919:** Dial telephones introduced Red Scare about Bolsheviks occurs **1920:** Edith Wharton wins Pulitzer Prize for her novel *The Age of Innocence* Miss America beauty pageant begins Marcus Garvey's United Negro Improvement Association claims more than 2 million members **1921:** Immigration laws set quotas for eastern Europeans Shepard-Towner Maternity and Infancy Protection Act passed
Economics & Technology	**1909:** Payne-Aldrich Tariff enacted International Ladies Garment Workers Union begins prolonged strike in New York City **1910:** Mann-Elkins Act to strengthen railroad regulation passed **1911:** Triangle Fire in New York City produces regulation of sweatshop conditions **1912:** Strike occurs in woolen mills in Lawrence, Massachusetts **1913:** Federal Reserve Act passed and system of twelve regional banks created	**1914:** Ludlow, Colorado, strike leads to deaths of nineteen people by state militia Henry Ford introduces $5 day for auto workers **1915:** Preparedness movement and war orders revive American economy **1916:** Federal Farm Loan Act passed Adamson Act creates eight-hour day for railroad workers **1917:** Production and use of food is regulated through food administration War Industries Board created	**1918:** Webb-Pomerene Act passed to promote foreign trade National War Labor Board established **1919:** Economy reverts to peacetime status with little government supervision Strikes and labor disputes occur nationwide Inflation becomes problem **1920:** Esch-Cummins Act passed to return railroads to private control and broaden powers of Interstate Commerce Commission Woman's Bureau created in Department of Labor

1922: Washington Naval Conference
Democrats make gains in congressional elections
1923: Teapot Dome scandal breaks
Harding dies of heart attack
Calvin Coolidge becomes president
1924: Miriam Amanda Ferguson and Nellie Tayloe Ross elected as first woman governors
Democratic convention takes 103 ballots to nominate John W. Davis
Coolidge defeats Davis and third party candidate Robert M. La Follette

1925: Scopes trial on evolution in Dayton, Tennessee
1926: United States membership in World Court fails
Democrats make gains in congressional elections
1927: President Coolidge says he will not run in 1928
Sacco and Vanzetti executed
1928: Hoover defeats Smith in presidential election
1929: Hoover becomes president
1930: London Naval Conference on disarmament
Democrats erase most of Republican House majority in elections

1931: Depression deepens
Hoover declares moratorium on war debts
1932: Bonus Marchers dispersed in Washington
Roosevelt defeats Hoover in election
1933: Roosevelt inaugurated president as Depression intensifies

---

1922: Sinclair Lewis's, *Babbitt* is published
Radio gains in popularity as stations spread
Reader's Digest begins publication
1923: *Time* magazine is launched
Blues singers such as Alberta Hunter and Bessie Smith become popular
1924: Kleenex is introduced
1925: Red Grange becomes national football hero and signs professional contract
Publication of F. Scott Fitzgerald's *The Great Gatsby*
Harlem Renaissance at height in New York City
New Yorker magazine starts
1926: Publication of Ernest Hemingway's *The Sun Also Rises*
Gertrude Ederle becomes first woman to swim English Channel

1927: Babe Ruth hits sixty home runs
Charles Lindbergh flies across the Atlantic alone
Al Jolson makes talking pictures popular in *The Jazz Singer*
1928: Walt Disney releases his first cartoon, "Plane Crazy"
Eugene O'Neill's play *Strange Interlude* wins Pulitzer Prize
1929: Sales of processed baby food begin
Museum of Modern Art founded in New York City
The first Blue Cross health insurance group starts in Dallas
Amos 'n' Andy radio show becomes nationally popular
1930: Sliced bread introduced commercially
First supermarket opens

1931: Southern Commission on the Study of Lynching formed
Empire State Building, world's tallest, opens in New York City
Al Capone, leading mobster, sentenced to jail for tax evasion
1932: Charles Lindbergh's son kidnapped and found dead
Amelia Earhart makes first solo transatlantic flight by a woman
Radio City Music Hall opens in New York City
1933: Prohibition ends

1921: Nation experiences business recession as intense deflation occurs
1922: Fordney-McCumber Tariff Act passed
1923: Supreme Court in *Adkins v. Children's Hospital* invalidates law providing for minimum wage for women in Washington, D.C.
1924: McNary-Haugen Bill to help farmers is introduced
1925: Florida land boom flourishes

1926: Revenue Act produces substantial tax reduction
Florida land boom collapses
1927: Henry Ford introduces Model A car
1928: Federal Reserve raises interest rates to curb speculation
1929: Stock Market crash occurs in September and October
1930: Great Depression begins
Smoot-Hawley Tariff enacted

1931: Hoover administration relief measures address condition of unemployed but do not bring upturn in economy
1932: Reconstruction Finance Corporation created to deal with bank and corporate failures in Depression
Revenue Act cuts government spending
1933: Depression intensifies as Franklin D. Roosevelt takes office

21 PROGRESSIVISM AT HIGH TIDE 1909–1914

TAFT'S PRESIDENCY

PROGRESSIVE VICTORIES

LABOR PROTEST IN A CHANGING WORKPLACE

REPUBLICAN DISCORD AND DEMOCRATIC OPPORTUNITY

WILSON'S PRESIDENCY

SOCIAL AND CULTURAL CHANGE DURING THE WILSON YEARS

NEW FREEDOM DIPLOMACY

WORLD WAR I

The Triangle Fire in New York City in 1911, which took dozens of lives, represented the problems that American society faced in the Progressive Era. How far should the nation go to regulate business in the interests of health and safety?
From the Collections of the Library of Congress

When Theodore Roosevelt left office in March 1909, progressivism entered a phase of partisan upheaval. Under William Howard Taft the Republicans split as conservatives and reformers struggled for control. The Democrats moved toward a more active role for the national government and away from state rights. The Socialists mounted a vigorous challenge from the left. For five years it seemed as though the party system might fragment.

Political ferment also revealed the tensions among reformers. Campaigns for woman suffrage, the prohibition of alcohol, restriction of immigration, and social justice created new coalitions that sometimes followed party lines and at other times disrupted them. In the process, progressivism provoked a conservative reaction that limited the possibilities for reform.

The social and economic forces that were producing a consumer society also gathered strength. Henry Ford's low-priced automobile gained greater popularity while other products of industrialism attracted more customers. Women found more opportunities for employment. For minorities, however, these years saw continuing tension and racial strife.

International strains in Europe and revolutions in Latin America and Asia made foreign policy more of a national concern than it had been since the war with Spain. Still, the outbreak of fighting in Europe during the summer of 1914 came as a shock to the United States. World War I did not resolve the crisis in which progressivism found itself. Instead, it added new complexity to an already turbulent period.

TAFT'S PRESIDENCY

Soon after William Howard Taft took office on March 4, 1909, Theodore Roosevelt left for his hunting safari in Africa. The hope on Wall Street, ran a joke of the day, was that a lion would do its duty. A celebrity as an ex-president, Roosevelt found that his activities were news, even across the ocean. The issues of regulation, social justice, and corporate power with which he had struggled were also on the agenda for his successor.

Taft came to the White House facing complex problems. Republican conservatives expected him to slow the movement toward reform. Party progressives, on the other hand, wanted the new president to expand Roosevelt's legacy. The Republicans had promised in their 1908 platform to revise the tariff but had not specified whether rates would go up or down. The president planned to call a special session of Congress to address the issue. Republicans waited to see what Taft would do.

CHRONOLOGY

1909 William Howard Taft inaugurated as president • Enactment of Payne-Aldrich Tariff

1910 Ballinger-Pinchot controversy over conservation worsens • Roosevelt returns from Africa, announces New Nationalism
• Camp Fire Girls founded • Democrats regain control of House of Representatives

1911 Triangle Fire in New York City kills 146 people • Harriet Quimby becomes first licensed woman pilot

1912 Taft defeats Roosevelt for Republican nomination • Bitter strike in Lawrence, Massachusetts, woolen mills • S S *Titanic* hits iceberg and sinks in North Atlantic • Roosevelt forms Progressive party • Woodrow Wilson defeats Taft and Roosevelt in presidential race

1913 Suffragettes stage large march on the day before Woodrow Wilson is inaugurated • Federal income tax adopted • Armory Show of Modern Art held in New York City • Federal Reserve System established

1914 Henry Ford announces Five-Dollar Day program • Fighting occurs at Vera Cruz in Mexico • Outbreak of First World War

A native of Cincinnati, Ohio, Taft was fifty-one. He had been a lawyer and a federal judge before heading the Philippine Commission in 1900. He proved to be an adept colonial administrator, but Roosevelt summoned him back to the United States in 1904 to serve as secretary of war.

During Roosevelt's presidency, Taft acted as troubleshooter for the administration. When Roosevelt went on vacation, he told reporters that he felt confident because the portly Taft was in Washington "sitting on the lid." Roosevelt looked forward to a continuation of his policies under his successor.

A Conservative President

Taft was a conservative man who had taken on some of Roosevelt's reform spirit. He did not agree with the expansive view of presidential power that Roosevelt had advanced. Taft believed that the president should act within the strict letter of the law and the constitutional boundaries of his office. Such a philosophy was bound to disappoint Roosevelt and the progressive Republicans.

Taft lacked Roosevelt's sure sense of public relations. He played golf at fashionable country clubs and vacationed with wealthy men at a time when riches were associated with political corruption. He quarreled with the press and often delayed writing speeches until the last minute. The success he had enjoyed as a speaker during the 1908 campaign was soon forgotten as he failed to sway audiences or committed political gaffes. Taft also depended on the advice of his wife, Helen Herron Taft, in political matters, but during the spring of 1909, she had a serious illness that deprived him of her emotional support.

The Dilemma of the Tariff

In revising the tariff, Taft confronted the consequences of Roosevelt's postponement of the issue. Progressive Republicans favored reductions in customs duties and a move away from protectionism. Conservatives regarded the tariff as the cornerstone of Republicanism and felt that high rates were justified.

To maintain Republican unity in Congress, Taft supported the reelection of conservative Joseph G. Cannon as Speaker of the House. If Taft challenged the Speaker, who enjoyed the support of a majority of House Republicans, Cannon could easily stall action on the tariff program.

Once Congress assembled in March 1909, Taft sent it a message asking for a new tariff law. In April, the House passed a tariff bill that lowered rates on sugar, iron, and lumber and placed coal and cattle hides on the free list. The measure was named the Payne bill after its author, Sereno E. Payne, chairman of the Ways and Means Committee.

After it passed the House, the bill then went to the Senate where the Republicans had sixty-one members, the Democrats thirty-one. The Republican leader, Nelson Aldrich of Rhode Island, was regarded as a virtual dictator of the Senate.

In fact, Aldrich's position was much more vulnerable than it seemed. Among the Senate Republicans, there were seven to ten midwesterners, such as Robert La Follette of Wisconsin, Albert J. Beveridge of Indiana, and Jonathan P. Dolliver of Iowa, who wanted to see lower tariffs and limits on Aldrich's power. On the other side of the debate, senators from the East and Far West insisted that goods from their states must be protected against foreign competition. Aldrich did not have a majority of votes for the Payne bill.

Aldrich had the Senate Finance Committee write a bill with 800 amendments, half of which raised rates back toward those of the Dingley Tariff. During the summer of 1909, Dolliver, La Follette, and Beveridge attacked Aldrich's bill. They said that the public expected lower tariffs and they denounced attempts to protect it. The Aldrich version finally cleared the Senate in early July by a vote of forty-five to thirty-four. Ten Republicans voted against Aldrich.

The Political Consequences

As a House-Senate conference committee hammered out the final version of the bill, both sides looked to Taft. The president used his leverage to obtain some concessions, such as lower duties on gloves, lumber, and cattle hides, but he failed to obtain reductions on wool, cotton, and industrial products. Convinced that he had gained all he could, Taft signed the Payne-Aldrich Tariff in early August 1909. The battle had split the Republicans.

Taft endorsed the new tariff during a tour of the Midwest in September. Speaking at Winona, Minnesota, he called the law "the best tariff bill that the Republican party ever passed." Conservatives applauded his remarks while progressives fumed. The president then refused to appoint individuals whom the progressives recommended for federal offices in their states. Republican harmony thus took a beating throughout the autumn of 1909.

The Battle over Conservation

Taft also found himself engaged in a battle that threatened to disrupt his friendship with Theodore Roosevelt. Federal government control of natural resources had been one of Roosevelt's favorite policies. His principal aide had been Chief Forester Gifford Pinchot. Taft disliked Pinchot and doubted whether the policies Roosevelt had pursued were legal. The president and his secretary of the interior, Richard A. Ballinger, pursued conservation policies that conformed to existing laws and allowed less room for presidential initiative. When Ballinger opened lands for development that Pinchot had closed off to settlers and businesses, Pinchot struck back. He accused Ballinger of acting as an agent for J. P. Morgan and a syndicate trying to sell valuable coal lands in Alaska. After looking into the charges, Taft sided with Ballinger.

Pinchot then leaked information about the episode to the press. In early 1910, he went even further, writing a letter of protest that a senator released to the public. Taft thereupon fired Pinchot for insubordination. In the ensuing controversy, a congressional probe revealed that Taft and Ballinger had not done what Pinchot had charged.

Taft seemed to be attacking a key Roosevelt policy. Roosevelt in Africa received letters from friends saying that Taft was betraying him. The former president responded that perhaps he had made a mistake in picking Taft. Washington buzzed with talk that Roosevelt might run in 1912.

The congressional session in the spring of 1910 compounded Taft's problems. Progressive Republicans joined with Democrats to restrict the power of Speaker Cannon to hold up legislation. Because Taft had supported the Speaker, this move was seen as a rebuke to the White House. Some constructive measures emerged from the session. Railroad legislation broadened the power of the Interstate Commerce Commission over the railroads. The navy was given more

Table 21.1 Party Strength in Congress, 1894–1918

SENATE

Congress	Year Elected	Republicans	Democrats	Other
Fifty-fourth	(1894)	43	39	6
Fifty-fifth	(1896)	47	34	7
Fifty-sixth	(1898)	53	26	8
Fifty-seventh	(1900)	55	31	4
Fifty-eighth	(1902)	57	33	– –
Fifty-ninth	(1904)	57	33	– –
Sixtieth	(1906)	61	31	– –
Sixty-first	(1908)	61	31	– –
Sixty-second	(1910)	51	41	– –
Sixty-third	(1912)	44	51	1
Sixty-fourth	(1914)	40	56	– –
Sixty-fifth	(1916)	42	53	– –
Sixty-sixth	(1918)	49	47	– –

HOUSE

Congress	Year Elected	Republicans	Democrats	Other
Fifty-fourth	(1894)	244	105	7
Fifty-fifth	(1896)	204	113	40
Fifty-sixth	(1898)	185	163	9
Fifty-seventh	(1900)	197	151	9
Fifty-eighth	(1902)	208	178	– –
Fifty-ninth	(1904)	250	136	– –
Sixtieth	(1906)	222	164	– –
Sixty-first	(1908)	219	172	– –
Sixty-second	(1910)	161	228	– –
Sixty-third	(1912)	127	291	17
Sixty-fourth	(1914)	196	230	9
Sixty-fifth	(1916)	210	216	6
Sixty-sixth	(1918)	240	190	

Source: The information in this table is derived from *The Statistical History of the United States* (Stamford, CT: Fairfield Publishers, 1965).

By the end of Taft's first year as president, his political troubles multiplied and many republicans looked to Roosevelt again in 1912.

Courtesy of the Theodore Roosevelt Coll., Widener Library, Harvard University

money, and progressives enacted a law to encourage private citizens to use federal banks located in post offices. Taft got little credit for these improvements. Progressives charged that he did more to frustrate reform than to push it.

Roosevelt's Return

Meanwhile, Theodore Roosevelt had returned to the United States, his ears filled with Taft's alleged misdeeds. Roosevelt decided that it was up to him to get the Republican party back on the right course. He received a tumultuous welcome when his ship entered New York Harbor. Guns boomed and fireboats shot water into the air. A crowd of 100,000 people cheered him as he rode up the streets. His popularity seemed as strong as ever.

At first, Roosevelt refrained from public quarrels with the president. Meanwhile, the Republicans' internal warfare intensified. Taft used his appointment power against the Middle Western progressives in his party; their candidates were not nominated for positions in the federal government. Taft went even further, trying to organize loyal Republicans against reform leaders such as Dolliver, La Follette, and Beveridge. These moves failed, and the president's inability to rally support within his own party emphasized his weakness. Taft knew that his troubles with Roosevelt were growing.

Roosevelt and the New Nationalism

Roosevelt sharpened his quarrel with Taft in a series of speeches during the summer of 1910. He called his program "The New Nationalism." In a speech at Osawatomie, Kansas, in August, he said that "The New Nationalism regards the executive power as the stew-

ard of the public welfare." The Square Deal of his presidency should be expanded. The "rules of the game" should be "changed so as to work for a more substantial equality of opportunity and reward for equally good service." There should be an income tax, inheritance taxes on large fortunes, workmen's compensation laws, and legislation to protect child labor. Roosevelt was advocating the modern regulatory state and wanted to achieve it as president.

In the congressional elections of 1910, the Democrats gained control of the House of Representatives when the Republicans lost fifty-eight seats. In the Senate, the Republicans dropped ten seats. They still had a ten-seat majority, but the progressive Republicans often voted with the Democrats. Republicans suffered their biggest losses in the industrial East where twenty-six Republican House members were defeated. Stressing inflation and the high cost of living, Democrats won governorships in New York, New Jersey, Ohio, and Indiana. After years of being the opposition party, they looked forward to the presidential election of 1912.

PROGRESSIVE VICTORIES

Between 1910 and 1913 progressivism peaked, as the movement for social change gathered momentum. The reformers seemed to have public opinion behind them, and conservatives in both parties were on the defensive. In the short term the forces of reform pushed forward.

Woman Suffrage

In April 1910, the National American Woman Suffrage Association (NAWSA) presented Congress with a petition that more than 400,000 people had signed. The document sought a constitutional amendment allowing women to vote. Although Congress refused to act, one suffrage worker, surprised by the size of the petition, said that her cause "is actually fashionable now."

Under the leadership of Anna Howard Shaw, NAWSA's membership had grown. In states like Washington (1910), California (1911), and Arizona, Kansas, and Oregon (1912), woman suffrage triumphed. However, referenda to give women the vote failed in Ohio, Wisconsin, and Michigan. Within the movement, younger women, eager for results, urged the older leaders to concentrate on obtaining a constitutional amendment.

Alice Paul led the radical wing of the suffrage movement. She had fought for the vote in England and now wanted to apply tactics of picketing and civil disobedience to the United States. Other women joined her, including Lucy Burns and Harriot Stanton Blatch, daughter of Elizabeth Cady Stanton. For a few years, Paul and her allies worked on NAWSA's congressional

The militant spirit of the woman suffrage movement was embodied in the young and dynamic leader Alice Paul, who broke away from the National American Woman Suffrage Association to pursue a more aggressive course.
© Bettmann/UPI/Corbis

The Anti-Saloon League was one of the primary forces behind the drive for national Prohibition. Its use of cartoons and leaflets made it a precursor of modern issue-oriented campaigning for social causes.
Reproduced from the Collections of the Library of Congress

committee. On March 3, 1913, before Woodrow Wilson became president, they staged a well-publicized suffrage parade in Washington. Frustrated at the cautious tactics of NAWSA, Paul and Burns left the organization in early 1914 to form the Congressional Union.

Significant obstacles to suffrage remained. The liquor industry feared that women who voted would support Prohibition. White southerners worried that woman suffrage might lead to votes for African Americans. Men saw their dominance threatened if women took part in politics. To counter these arguments, NAWSA stressed that female voting meant purer and more honest politics. They also played down the argument that women should have equal political rights. Instead, they contended that woman suffrage would offset the votes of immigrants and racial minorities in large cities. Thus, suffragists would be protecting traditional values against "alien" assaults.

Prohibition

Efforts to restrict the use and sale of alcohol also prospered. The Anti-Saloon League had held a dominant position among prohibitionist organizations since its founding during the 1890s . Older groups, such as the Woman's Christian Temperance Union, played an important role in the crusade, but the Anti-Saloon League used interest group politics. The league sought to limit the power of the liquor industry to sell its product. At first the league sought elections to give voters in a county or state the "local option" to ban the sale of alcohol. By 1906, impatient with the slowness of the local option, the league turned to statewide elections.

Oklahoma adopted Prohibition in 1907. By 1914, eight other states had banned the sale of alcohol. Militant prohibitionists (they were called "drys"; anti-prohibitionists were "wets") found the state-by-state process discouraging. In 1913, prohibitionists in Congress passed the Webb-Kenyon Act, which outlawed the shipment of alcohol into dry states. President Taft vetoed the bill, but Congress overrode him. The Anti-Saloon League's next goal was a constitutional amendment to ban the sale of alcohol in the United States.

*P*ICTURING THE PAST ✦ SOCIAL & CULTURAL EVENTS

CHINESE IMMIGRATION ON THE WEST COAST

The Granger Collection, New York

Immigration into the United States between 1900 and 1914 was not solely a European experience. Despite such obstacles as the Chinese Exclusion Act of 1882, Chinese-Americans found ways to bring young men from their native country to the United States. This picture shows a group of such Chinese newcomers as they went through immigration. They had to demonstrate that they were being brought in as the sons or relatives of American citizens of Chinese origin. Small numbers of Japanese immigrants also entered the country during these years. Both Asian immigrant groups built prosperous lives in the face of the resentment of white Americans at their economic success. Racial tensions persisted and led to friction between the Japanese and American governments during the presidency of Theodore Roosevelt. Sentiment on the West Coast to restrict Asian immigration remained strong into the 1920s and beyond.

Restriction of Immigration

The effort to restrict immigration into the United States also accelerated. The flow of newcomers from southern and eastern Europe persisted. There were more than 1 million immigrants in 1910, nearly 2 million in 1913, and over a million more in 1914, before the outbreak of World War I. In addition, revolutionary upheavals in Mexico drove thousands of Hispanic immigrants into the Southwest.

Protestants wanted to keep out Catholic and Jewish newcomers. Labor unions feared that immigrants would become strikebreakers; rural residents saw urban populations growing at their expense. Prejudice against the Chinese and Japanese fed nativist sentiments on the West Coast. Diplomatic friction with Japan followed. By 1913, a bill to impose a literacy test on immigrants passed both houses of Congress. President Taft vetoed the measure and Congress was unable to override.

Progressivism and the Immigrant

Progressive reform offered some support to the nativist and racist feelings. Since businesses favored a loose immigration policy, opposition to immigration was portrayed as a way to help workers already in the United States. A feeling that cultures from southern and eastern Europe threatened traditional values led some progressives to endorse restriction.

An incident in Atlanta, Georgia, in 1913, underlined the tensions surrounding immigration restriction. When a young factory worker, Mary Phagan, was murdered, suspicion fell on her superintendent, Leo Frank. A Jew whose parents had come from Russia, Frank was innocent, but he fell victim to anti-Semitism and fear of outsiders. As a "victim worthy to pay for the crime," he was convicted and sentenced to death. After the governor of Georgia commuted his sentence, a mob abducted and lynched him in August 1915. The episode helped to promote the rise of the Ku Klux Klan, a further testament to the xenophobia and bigotry in the age of reform.

Saving the Children

Americans worried about the future of their children in a changing world. Three organizations sprang up to address these concerns. In 1910–1911, the Boy Scouts of America, modeled on the British precedent created by Robert Baden-Powell, began training young men in loyalty and service. Boys twelve through eighteen enrolled to receive instruction in "the military virtues such as honor, loyalty, obedience, and patriotism."

For young women, there were the Girl Scouts, founded by Juliette Low in 1912, and the Campfire Girls, founded two years earlier. These two groups prepared American girls for future domestic responsibilities. "The homemaker of tomorrow," said one Girl Scout leader, "must be made efficient in her task and happy in it." With the constructive activities that the Girl Scouts, Campfire Girls, and Boy Scouts supplied, delinquency and crime among the young would be reduced, or so their advocates maintained.

The struggle against child labor overshadowed all the other drives to improve the condition of children. In 1910, some 200,000 youngsters below the age of twelve labored in mills and factories. Attempts to limit child labor in textile firms in the South brought meager results. In 1912, the reformers succeeded in establishing a Children's Bureau within the federal government, but Congress failed to pass any legislation that directly addressed the child labor problem. Proponents of child labor laws hoped to make it an issue for the parties in the 1912 presidential contest.

Despite the many obstacles that progressive reformers faced, there was a sense that the nation was making genuine gains. William Allen White, a Kansas newspaper editor and a friend of many of the leading progressives, recalled that "All over the land in a score of states and more, young men in both parties were taking leadership by attacking things as they were in that day." Women, too, experienced feeling a sense of possibility that infused middle-class reform during the years before World War I.

LABOR PROTEST IN A CHANGING WORKPLACE

Conflict marked the relations between labor and capital. Bitter struggles between workers and employers occurred in the garment unions of New York, among the textile workers of Massachusetts, and in the coal mines of Colorado. American laborers measured their progress in violent and bloody confrontations against harsh conditions in the workplace.

Changes in the Corporation

As industrialization spread, factories and businesses grew. In Chicago, Marshall Field had 5,000 salespeople in its many store departments. The meat-packing firm of Swift and Company employed 23,000 people in its seven plants by 1903. The Amoskeag Company textile mills in Manchester, New Hampshire, dominated the lives of its 17,000 employees with welfare programs and company organizations.

The nature of large corporations was changed. Important companies applied scientific research techniques and social science procedures in ways that altered the working experience of Americans. The need to develop new products at a regular rate led such corporations as DuPont and General Electric to emulate the example of German firms. General Electric set up links to universities that allowed scientists and engineers on their faculties to address the needs of the corporations in their research. The ties between business and education helped propel economic growth for the rest of the century.

New Rules for the Workplace

Within the large factories, relationships between employers and workers became more structured and routinized. The informal dominance that the foreman had exercised during the nineteenth century gave way to bureaucratic practices. To control costs and ensure steady production, companies set up procedures for regular reporting on expenditures, centralization of purchasing and maintenance, and measurement of worker productivity.

Out of these innovations came a new way to run the factory and workplace. *Scientific management* was developed by Frederick Winslow Taylor. As a mechanical engineer in the steel industry, Taylor believed that careful study of how each individual task was conducted would lead to efficiency. Once the maximum amount of time to do a specific job was established, workers could be instructed on how to complete the task without any wasted motion. Stopwatches measured the speed of work down to the split second.

As a concept, Taylorism enjoyed great popularity among businesspeople. Although most employers did not adopt all of Taylor's ideas, the principle of managing factories and shops systematically took hold. Since the core of scientific management meant reducing all jobs to a set of simple steps that required little skill, workers resented practices that made them perform repetitive, routine movements all day long. Henry Ford claimed that "no man wants to be burdened with the care and responsibility of deciding things." Thus, he believed that workers welcomed freedom from mental strain. In fact, however, employees objected to being "reduced to a scientific formula," said one machinist.

The Limits of Paternalism

While scientific management viewed workers in a detached and bloodless way, some corporations revived paternalism through welfare and incentive programs for their employees. Lunchrooms and toilet areas were cleaned up, recreational facilities established, and plans set up for pensions and profit sharing. National Cash Register of Dayton, Ohio, was a leader in the field, along with H. J. Heinz Company, the Amoskeag Mills, and Remington Typewriter.

Yet the situation for most American workers showed only marginal improvement. Businesses used a variety of techniques to block unions and prevent workers from improving their condition. The National Association of Manufacturers (NAM) pushed for laws to outlaw the union shop (mandating membership in a union to work in the plant) in favor of what was called the "open shop" in which unions were not allowed. Blacklists of pro-union employees were circulated, and new workers often had to sign contracts that barred workers from joining a union. When strikes occurred, employers used nonunion labor (strikers called them "scabs") to end the walkouts. Court injunctions limited the ability of strikers to picket and organize. Violent clashes between workers and police accompanied many strikes.

Unorganized Workers

The working classes in the cities faced the ravages of inflation during these years. While wages rose, prices accelerated at a faster rate. Many consumer products remained out of reach of the average laborer. These workers faced dangerous conditions in their factories and sweatshops. Many laborers turned to strikes and unions as their best weapons. In New York City and Philadelphia from 1909 to 1911, the International Ladies Garment Workers Union organized workers within the shirtwaist manufacturing business. Twenty thousand women strikers took their grievances into the streets to demonstrate their solidarity. They managed to wrest some concessions from their employees in the form of union shops and improved working conditions.

Many manufacturers forced their employees to work in deplorable conditions with poor ventilation, dirt and filth, and danger to the lives of those who labored. In March 1911, a fire erupted at the Triangle Shirtwaist Company on New York City's Lower East Side. As the workers fled the flames, they found locked doors and no fire escape routes. The conflagration claimed 146 lives. Many women were killed when they jumped to the pavement below. The Triangle Fire spurred reform efforts among politicians in the New York legislature.

Varieties of Labor Protest

Labor unions grew between 1900 and 1914. The American Federation of Labor, led by Samuel Gompers, had several million members. The politics of the AFL had not changed since the end of the nineteenth century. Its craft unions discouraged organization among industrial workers. Women employees received little support from Gompers and his allies.

The Industrial Workers of the World (IWW) appealed to the unskilled masses. Its ultimate goal was still a social revolution that would sweep away industrial capitalism. To the IWW's leadership, including William D. "Big Bill" Haywood and Elizabeth Gurley Flynn, violent strikes seemed the best way to promote industrial warfare.

Strikes in Lawrence and Ludlow

The IWW gained national attention when a strike erupted in the textile mills of Lawrence, Massachusetts, in mid-January 1912. After the textile companies announced substantial wage reductions, the workers walked out. Haywood came to Lawrence to support the strike. The children of strikers were sent to live in other cities, a tactic that publicized the walkout and swayed public opinion to the workers' cause. On March 1, the companies granted them a pay hike. Women strikers were key participants in the victory. As one of their songs put it, they sought "bread and roses" by which they meant a living wage and a life with hope. Despite this local success, the IWW did not build a strong following in the East.

Another controversial strike occurred in Colorado. The United Mine Workers struck against the Colorado Fuel and Iron Company in September 1913. The workers complained about low wages and company camps with brutal guards. "The miners get very poor food," said one man, "and some of the children are dressed in gunny-sacks and their fathers are working every day." John D. Rockefeller, who controlled the coal company, asked the governor to call in the National Guard to maintain order. Confrontations between soldiers and miners ended in the "Ludlow Massacre" of April 1914, in which troops fired on miners in a tent city at Ludlow. Five strikers and one soldier were shot, and two women and eleven children died in the flames that broke out in the tents. Federal inquiries followed, and the workers obtained some concessions. Yet later in 1914 they were forced to end the strike without gaining union recognition.

Changes in the workplace during the progressive period had benefited the employers far more than they had improved the lot of the people who labored

The New York *Tribune* Reports the Triangle Fire, March 26, 1911

The Triangle Fire of March 1911 was a tragic event that dramatized the desperate working conditions that often confronted the poor in an industrial society. The deaths that the fire caused spurred the New York legislature to consider remedial legislation for workers in the garment district. The news story from the New York *Tribune* conveys some of the drama and tragedy of the episode.

Scores of Girls Leap to Death In Streets Ten Stories Below Them,
Had No Chance For Life
Unable to Reach Elevators or Stairways, Employees Rush to Windows,
Croker Blames Escapes
None on Outside of Building, Says Fire Chief, Saying That is Reason For Fearful Loss of Lives in Disaster, Elevators Save Hundreds
Frightful Panic as Trapped Workers Fight Like Furies in Cars, Almost The Only Means of Escape, As Flames Sweep Through Workrooms.

Nearly one hundred and fifty lives were lost in a fire that swept through the three upper stories of a ten story factory loft building at the Northwest corner of Washington Place and Green Street at 5 o'clock yesterday afternoon, occupied by the Triangle Waist Company and a clothing house. At midnight 142 bodies had been taken to the morgue.

Fire Chief [Edward] Croker said:
"This calamity is just what I have been predicting. There were no outside fire escapes on this building. I have been advocating and agitating that fire escapes be put on building such as this. This large loss of life is due to this neglect."

Thirteen of the victims were men; 129 were women and girls.

The cause of the fire is unknown. No one has tried to do more than guess at it.

Scenes of almost indescribable horror attended the catastrophe. Scores of girls leaped from windows eight, nine, and ten stories above the street to their death. In one place so many bodies fell that the glass and iron deadlights in the pavement were broken.

A fire escape in a light shaft proved a veritable death trap. More than fifty girls were found dead at the bottom of the shaft.

---

in factories and shops. Some social legislation had been enacted to protect the worker from the effects of industrial accidents. The length of the working day had been reduced somewhat. Unlike Great Britain or Germany, however, the United States still did not provide social insurance when a worker became unemployed, pension benefits for old age, or equal bargaining power on the job.

Dollar Diplomacy

In foreign affairs, William Howard Taft and his secretary of state, Philander C. Knox, adopted the policy of "dollar diplomacy" toward Latin America and Asia.

When U.S. corporations traded and invested in underdeveloped areas of the world, peace and stability increased. Instead of military force, the ties of finance and capital would instruct countries in the wise conduct of their affairs. "The borrower is the servant of the lender," said Knox. Military intervention should be a last resort to restore order.

Latin America offered an ideal location for applying the principles of dollar diplomacy. No European countries challenged the supremacy of the United States in that region. In 1909, Taft and Knox induced bankers to loan money to Honduras to prevent British investors from achieving undue influence. In 1911, they compelled the government of Nicaragua to accept

This cartoon, which appeared on the day of Woodrow Wilson's inauguration, March 4, 1913, illustrates the condescending attitude of the American media toward Mexico and its problems.
From the Collections of the Library of Congress

another loan from U.S. investors. Unfortunately, some Nicaraguans regarded the scheme as an intrusion in their affairs, and they rebelled against the government that had made the deal. The Taft administration sent Marines to Nicaragua; the resulting U.S. military presence continued for several decades. A lasting feeling of bitterness marked relations with Latin America.

Taft and Knox also applied dollar diplomacy to China. The government wanted American capitalists to support a railroad in China, first to develop the country and then to offset Japan. Roosevelt had recognized Japanese dominance in the region; Knox challenged it economically. A syndicate of nations would lend China money to purchase existing railroads in Manchuria. The plan collapsed when the British, Russians, and Japanese rejected the idea in early 1910. Instead of promoting stability in China, Knox drove the Japanese and Russians to join forces against American interests. The Knox initiative sparked resentment in Japan, and relations between that country and the United States remained tense. Dollar diplomacy proved to be an ineffective way to achieve world influence.

A foreign policy problem closer to home emerged in 1911. Porfirio Diaz had ruled Mexico for almost forty years. American investment came because he had maintained apparent calm and stability. In fact, however, his dictatorial rule eventually erupted in a revolution. Francisco I. Madero, the leader of the rebels, came to power hoping to transform the nation. But he

aroused the opposition of conservative forces, including the military, large landowners, and the Roman Catholic church. Shortly before Taft's term ended in 1913, Madero was overthrown and murdered. Mexico remained in revolutionary ferment.

REPUBLICAN DISCORD AND DEMOCRATIC OPPORTUNITY

Following Republican losses in 1910, Taft and Roosevelt agreed not to attack each other during the first half of 1911. Republican progressives still looked for an alternative to Taft in 1912. To placate the progressives, Taft eased Ballinger out of the cabinet and named two supporters of Roosevelt as secretary of the interior and secretary of war.

Taft's Embattled Presidency

Taft's troubles with Congress persisted. He negotiated a trade agreement with Canada based on reciprocal concessions on tariffs. Neither the Democrats nor the progressive Republicans liked Canadian Reciprocity because it lowered import duties on products that affected their districts. Taft pushed the agreement through Congress, but then Canadian voters rejected the government that had supported it.

Then the president's fragile friendship with Roosevelt collapsed. Unlike Roosevelt, Taft really believed in "busting" the trusts, and his Justice Department attacked large corporations. In October 1911, the Department of Justice filed an antitrust suit against United States Steel. One of the practices that violated the law, according to the indictment, was the company's acquisition of the Tennessee Coal and Iron Company during the Panic of 1907.

Since Roosevelt had approved the merger, the indictment held him up to ridicule. Roosevelt was furious. By the early part of 1912, he decided to challenge Taft for the Republican nomination. "My hat is in the ring, the fight is on, and I am stripped to the buff," he said in February 1912.

The Struggle Between Roosevelt and Taft

Throughout the spring of 1912, a bitter battle for the Republican nomination raged. For the first time, a few states held primary elections to choose delegates to the Republican convention. That change gave an obvious advantage to Roosevelt, who attracted a majority of these

This cartoon depicts the tensions of the 1912 presidential race among Theodore Roosevelt, William Howard Taft, and Woodrow Wilson; by election day, however, a Wilson victory was almost a certainty.

Courtesy, Clifford K. Berryman Collection, U.S. Senate, Center for Legislation Archives

voters. Taft ran strongly among party regulars, who controlled the nominating conventions. As the Republican National Convention opened in Chicago, neither man had a clear majority. Several hundred delegates were contested but the Republican National Committee awarded most of them to Taft. When the national convention upheld what the national committee had done, Roosevelt believed that Taft had stolen from him a prize that was rightfully his. Summoning his followers to leave the convention, Roosevelt denounced Taft and promised to fight on. "We stand at Armageddon and we battle for the Lord," he said. For the next two months, Roosevelt prepared to run as a third-party candidate.

The Democratic Opportunity

To exploit the disarray of their opponents, the Democrats needed a credible presidential candidate. One attractive newcomer was the governor of New Jersey, Woodrow Wilson, who had carried that staunchly Republican state by a sizable majority in 1910. Woodrow Wilson was fifty-six years old in 1912. Born in Virginia, he grew up in the South and shared its racial views. He

attended Princeton University in New Jersey, studied law for a time, and then earned a doctorate in history and political science at Johns Hopkins University. He joined the Princeton faculty in 1890, was quickly recognized as an outstanding instructor, and became president of the university in 1902. After initial successes, he ran into resistance from more conservative alumni and faculty when he attacked the eating clubs that dominated Princeton's social life. He resigned from the Princeton presidency in 1910. New Jersey Democrats urged Wilson to run for state office and he won the New Jersey governorship in his first try at elective office.

The Wilson Candidacy

Wilson had been a conservative Democrat for much of his life; political opportunity led him to reform. Some Democrats preferred the safer and less inspiring leadership of the Speaker of the House, James Beauchamp "Champ" Clark of Missouri. Wilson, Clark, and several other Democratic hopefuls fought for the nomination in primaries and state conventions.

When the national convention met in Baltimore in late June, no candidate was in sight of the two-thirds majority needed for the nomination. After forty-six ballots, Wilson was nominated and the hopes for victory looked bright in November.

The Socialist Challenge

Once again the Socialist party selected Eugene V. Debs as its candidate. Debs had run in every election since 1900, and his total vote had increased each time. The party also made gains at the state and local levels. Seven hundred thousand voters supported Socialist candidates in 1910, and the following year Socialist mayors or city officials were chosen in seventy-four cities. Labor unrest seemed to be growing, especially in the Lawrence, Massachusetts, textile strike that broke out in January of 1912. "Comrades," Debs cried, "this is our year."

Socialism gained followers because the party spoke to the grievances of the agricultural and working poor. Disputes within their ranks over whether to pursue reform at the ballot box or through more violent means prevented the party from offering a united front. Moreover, since he had little chance of winning, Debs did not have to frame programs with a view to carrying them out in office.

The Creation of the Progressive Party

President Taft decided not to campaign for reelection since he expected to lose and the Republicans were short of money. Many conservative Republicans supported

Theodore Roosevelt's new Progressive party tried to raise campaign funds from small contributors. Those who gave received these certificates for their participation in the third party effort.

Wilson in order to retain control of their party and keep Roosevelt out of the presidency.

Roosevelt campaigned with his usual energy and excitement, and he attracted many reformers to his cause. The Progressive party held its national convention in Chicago during August. The atmosphere mixed the fervor of a revival meeting with the backroom bargaining of a traditional political conclave. Delegates sang "Onward Christian Soldiers" as the theme of the convention.

To woo the white South, the delegates excluded African Americans from the convention. Roosevelt defended the protective tariff and attacked reciprocity with Canada. The main financial support for the new party came from wealthy newspaper publishers and corporate executives, who liked Roosevelt's attitude toward big business.

At its core, however, the Progressive party's endorsement of expanded social justice legislation made it more forward-looking than either the Republicans' or the Democrats.' Jane Addams and other social justice reformers joined Roosevelt's crusade for that reason. The party supported woman suffrage, limits on child labor, and a system of "social insurance." The centerpiece of Roosevelt's New Nationalism was the proposal for an "administrative commission" that would "maintain permanent, active supervision over industrial corporations engaged in interstate commerce." Roosevelt continued his policy of distinguishing between "good trusts" that served the public interest and "bad trusts" that harmed

society. As a joke of the time went, the difference between a good trust and a bad trust was that when you tickled a bad trust it said "Tee Hee," and when you tickled a good trust it said "TR."

Enacting Roosevelt's program involved a broadening of national authority and an expansion of the bureaucratic machinery of the federal government. The role of the president would also expand to ensure that the public's rights were protected. Roosevelt's position in 1912 looked forward to the regulatory and welfare state that emerged later in the twentieth century. Critics at the time warned that in the wrong hands this increased national power could also threaten individual liberty.

Woodrow Wilson and the New Freedom

At first Woodrow Wilson did not plan to campaign much. As Roosevelt laid out his program, however, the Democratic nominee soon decided that he would have to confront his major rival. Wilson told the voters that only a Democratic president could govern effectively with the Democratic Congress that was certain to be elected. He then offered a program of his own to counter Roosevelt's New Nationalism. He called it the New Freedom.

As Roosevelt began his campaign, Wilson consulted with Louis D. Brandeis, a prominent lawyer in Boston and reformist thinker. Brandeis believed that big business was inefficient economically and dangerous to democracy. He told Wilson that the issue Roosevelt was raising could be met with a simple question: shall we have regulated competition or regulated monopoly? Wilson should emphasize the need for greater competition to control monopoly and call for stricter enforcement of the antitrust laws. Rather than relying on trusts and large corporations to act in a socially responsible manner, as Roosevelt contended, the government should create conditions in which competition could flourish.

As for social justice, Wilson said that he supported the goals of eliminating child labor, improving wages for women, and expanding benefits for employees, but he questioned whether the federal government should supply these benefits. In that way he appealed to progressives but also prevented southern Democrats from opposing him as an enemy of state rights (and segregation). The New Freedom was, like most campaign slogans, broad and vague. It gave Wilson a mandate for action without tying his hands.

Wilson Victorious

The 1912 election was turbulent down to election day. From the outset of the campaign it was clear that the Democrats had the electoral advantage over the divided Republicans and Progressives. Wilson received 435 electoral votes to eighty-eight for Roosevelt and eight for Taft. The Democrats swept Congress. They had fifty-one seats in the Senate to forty-four for the Republicans and their margin in the House was 291 to 127. Nevertheless, Wilson was a minority president. He received about 42 percent of the popular vote. Eugene Debs won just over 900,000 popular votes, or 6 percent of the total, and Roosevelt and Taft divided the rest. Voter turnout for the election was lower than it had been in 1908. It was now up to Woodrow Wilson to prove that the Democratic party could govern the nation.

WILSON'S PRESIDENCY

In the White House, Woodrow Wilson was a brilliant speaker whose moral rhetoric spoke of lofty ideals. He strengthened the power of the presidency, increased the regulatory role of the national government, and led the nation to play a greater part in international affairs. Even more than Roosevelt, he had the capacity to articulate national values in effective and moving language.

With these strong qualities came important limitations. Before he became president, Wilson had suffered a series of small strokes that increased his natu-

The Democrats selected Woodrow Wilson to oppose Roosevelt and Taft in 1912. Seated in the chair, Wilson talks to supporters at a rally.
The Granger Collection, New York

ral stubbornness and made him reluctant to accept unwelcome advice. Although he often called for open government and sought what he called "common counsel," he kept his decisions to himself and consulted only a few friends about his policies. His righteousness and sense of personal virtue caused his political enemies to develop an intense dislike of his methods and tactics. However, when the tide of events ran with Wilson, as they did during his first term, he was a powerful leader.

Launching the New Freedom Program

Wilson lost no time in demonstrating his intention to be a strong president. In his inaugural address on March 4, 1913, he spoke eloquently of the negative aspects of industrialism. To implement his program, Wilson first asked Congress to take up the issue of the tariff. He called the lawmakers into a special session in April 1913. To dramatize the problem, he decided to deliver his message to Congress in person. No president had done so since Jefferson had abandoned the practice in 1801, but presidential appearances before Congress became more common once Wilson resumed the technique. The move proved to be an important step in expanding presidential influence both on Capitol Hill and in the nation at large.

In the speech itself, Wilson urged the House and Senate to reduce import duties. The Democratic House responded with a measure to lower tariffs, named after Oscar W. Underwood, the chairman of the Ways

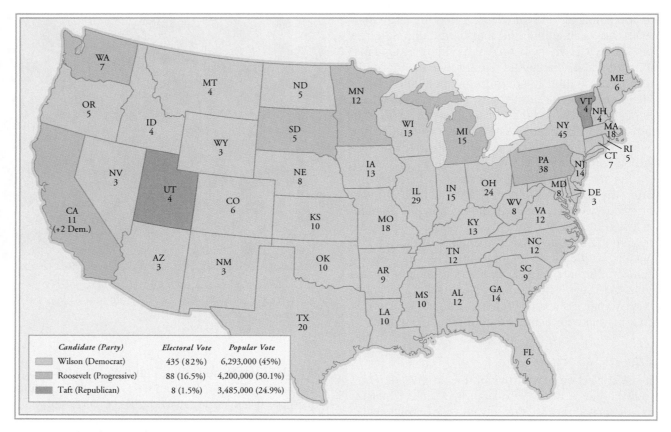

Map 21.1 *The Election of 1912*

Because Democrat Woodrow Wilson faced a divided opposition in the presidential election of 1912, the result was a landslide victory in the electoral vote. Theodore Roosevelt's Progressive party ran second, and William Howard Taft's Republicans were a distant third.

and Means Committee. The Underwood bill cut duties on raw wool, sugar, cotton goods, and silks. To compensate for the revenue that would be lost, the new tariff imposed a small tax on annual incomes over $4,000 with rates increasing for those who made more than $20,000 a year. Progressives had secured ratification of the Sixteenth Amendment in February 1913, which made the income tax constitutional.

Democrats worried about what would happen when the Underwood bill reached the Senate. They remembered the experience of 1894 and the Wilson-Gorman Tariff, and the Payne-Aldrich Law of 1909, when the Senate changed the House bill in a protectionist way. In fact, the Democrats were relatively unified in 1913, and pressure from large corporations for higher rates had eased. Only smaller businesses, fearing foreign competition, pushed hard for tariff protection. President Wilson added his voice on May 26, when he publicly denounced the "industrious" and "insidious" lobby that was trying to weaken the drive for tariff reform. He said

that he would be the people's lobbyist. It was a dramatic gesture, but it was not really necessary. The Democrats stuck together, lowered the duties that the House had set, and passed the bill in August by a vote of forty-four to thirty-seven. The conference committee's version of the bill passed both houses in October. Wilson signed the Underwood Tariff into law on October 3, 1913. The president and his party had demonstrated that they could provide positive leadership.

The Federal Reserve System

Building on his momentum with the tariff, during June 1913 Wilson turned to another important subject. Since the Panic of 1907, there had been a clear need for reform of the nation's banking system. A modern economy could not function efficiently without a central bank with the capacity to control the currency, meet the monetary needs of different sections of the country, and ensure that the money supply was adequate to the

The Social Cost of Industrialism
An Excerpt from Woodrow Wilson's First Inaugural Address, March 4, 1913

Woodrow Wilson's first inaugural address on March 4, 1913, offered an eloquent statement of how a major national progressive saw the nation's task in dealing with the social cost of industrialism and rapid change. Wilson's reference to "the groans and agony of it all" may be compared with the earlier document in this chapter on the Triangle Fire.

. . . We see that in many things that life is very great. It is incomparably great in its material aspects, in its body of wealth, in the diversity and sweep of its energy, in the industries which have been conceived and built up by the genius of individual men and the limitless enterprise of groups of men.

It is great, also very great, in its moral force. Nowhere else in the world have noble men and women exhibited in more striking forms the beauty and the energy of sympathy and helpfulness and counsel in their efforts to rectify wrong, alleviate suffering, and set the weak in the way of strength and hope. We have built up, moreover, a great system of government which has stood through a long age as in many respects a model for those who seek to set liberty upon foundations that will endure against fortuitous change, against storm and accident. Our life contains every great thing, and contains it in rich abundance.

But the evil has come with the good, and much fine gold has been corroded. With riches has come inexcusable waste. We have squandered a great part of what we might have used, and have not stopped to conserve the exceeding bounty of nature, without which our genius for enterprise would have been worthless and impotent, scorning to be careful, shamefully prodigal as well as admirably efficient. We have been proud of our industrial achievements, but we have not hitherto stopped thoughtfully enough to count the human cost, the cost of lives snuffed out, of energies overtaxed and broken, the fearful physical and spiritual cost to the men and women and children upon whom the dead weight and burden of it has fallen pitilessly the years through. The groans and agony of it all had not reached our ears, the solemn, moving undertone of our life, coming up out of the mines and factories, and out of every home where the struggle had its intimate and familiar seat. With the great Government went many deep secret things which we too long delayed to look into and scrutinize with candid, fearless eyes. The great Government we loved has too often been made use of for private and selfish purposes, and those who had used it had forgotten the people. . . .

demands of the growing economy. The issue became whether private banking interests or the national government should be in charge of the central bank.

Before Wilson was elected, the National Monetary Commission, headed by Nelson Aldrich, had offered the idea of a system of reserve banks that private bankers would supervise. Wilson initially favored this approach until Secretary of State William Jennings Bryan and his allies in Congress insisted that the federal government must be supreme over the reserve banks and the currency they would issue. At the urging of Louis Brandeis, Wilson accepted Bryan's ideas.

It took six months to get a banking bill through Congress. Wilson had to appease southern and western

*P*ICTURING THE PAST✦POLITICS & DIPLOMACY
WOODROW WILSON ADDRESSES CONGRESS IN PERSON

Reproduced from the Collections of the Library of Congress

The spectacle of presidents addressing Congress on national television for State of the Union messages and other important occasions has become a traditional feature of American public life. Yet the modern practice of presidents going to Congress in person to deliver their ideas is less than a century old. Woodrow Wilson in April 1913 resumed a practice that Thomas Jefferson had abandoned in 1801. This photograph records the innovation that Wilson was making. While the change provided more visibility to the president and more information to the American people, what Wilson did accelerated the process whereby presidents became celebrities. Over time, as motion pictures and then television covered these events, the presidential address took on more and more of the trappings of show business and became moments staged for the greatest political impact outside the halls of Congress.

Democrats, who wanted two changes in the proposed law. These members sought to expand the credit available to farmers, and they wanted to outlaw the practice known as interlocking directorates, in which banking officials served as directors of banks with which they competed. For reformers, such arrangements symbolized the power of finance capital. The president withstood criticism from the banking community itself, and used patronage and persuasion to win over potential opponents among Democrats in the Senate.

Congress completed its action in mid-December, and Wilson signed the Federal Reserve Act on December 27. This act was one of the most important pieces of economic legislation of the first half of the twentieth century. It established the Federal Reserve Board, whose members the president appointed, and created a structure consisting of twelve reserve banks located in different parts of the country. The Federal Reserve had the power to determine the amount of money in circulation, to expand or contract credit as needed, and to respond to some degree to changes in the business cycle.

Wilson and the Trusts

Wilson had now gone a good distance toward fulfilling his campaign pledges to reduce the tariff, reform the banking system, and deal with the problem of trusts. Early in 1914, the president asked Congress to consider trusts in a constructive spirit. Some of the legislation passed in that year followed the principles that Wilson had outlined in his campaign. The Clayton Antitrust Act (1914) endeavored to spell out precisely the business practices that restricted competition and then prohibit them.

As time passed, however, the president's thinking shifted. He came to favor the creation of a trade commission that would respond to business practices as they evolved, an idea that resembled what Theodore Roosevelt had proposed in 1912. The Federal Trade Commission was established during the fall of 1914. A delighted Wilson said that he had almost completed the program he had promised in his 1912 presidential campaign.

Wilson and the Progressive Agenda

The president's statements left many progressives disappointed. They wanted the Democratic administration to push for social justice legislation. Wilson did not yet believe that Washington should support the demands of progressive interest groups. He also worried about the precedent that might be set by a government that used power to address specific social issues. Such a policy might lead to attacks on racial segregation in the South that Wilson supported. In fact, the Wilson administration expanded racial segregation in the federal government. The color line, Wilson told a black delegation that came to protest such policies, "may not be intended against anybody, but for the benefit of both."

When supporters of woman suffrage sought Wilson's backing in 1913 and 1914, he turned them down. He also opposed federal aid for rural credits, restrictions on child labor through congressional action, and Prohibition. Court decisions had subjected organized labor to the workings of the antitrust laws, and the unions wanted that policy changed through legislation. Again, Wilson declined to act. Worsening economic conditions during the spring and summer of 1914 reinforced Wilson's belief that his administration should remain conservative on social issues. He tried to reassure businesses that the administration was friendly toward them. These gestures did not appease the Republicans or their business supporters, however. There were indications that the Democrats would have a difficult time at the polls in the 1914 congressional elections.

SOCIAL AND CULTURAL CHANGE DURING THE WILSON YEARS

While politicians worked out Wilson's New Freedom programs during 1913 and 1914, social and cultural transformations accelerated. The Victorian era, with its cultural restraints, seemed to be fading. Americans

Henry Ford's cheap and efficient car became very popular during the first decade of the new century. This photograph gives a good sense of the simplicity and durability of the Model T.
From the Collections of Henry Ford Museum & Greenfield Village

with a literary or artistic bent turned to the ideas of European thinkers, who emphasized greater freedom for the individual in an uncertain world. Some of these principles came to be defined as *modernism*. In the days just before World War I, a sense of optimism and possibility filled the air. "Looking back upon it now," wrote Mabel Dodge Luhan, a sponsor of artists and their work, "it seems as though everywhere, in that year of 1913, barriers went down and people reached each other who had never been in touch before."

Automobiles for a Mass Market

When Wilson went to his inauguration on March 4, 1913, he drove in an automobile. It was the first time a president-elect had traveled to his swearing-in by car. This action symbolized the vast changes that were making the people of the United States more mobile in their daily lives and more eager for the consumer products of an industrial society. In particular, the innovations in both production and marketing of Henry

ICTURING THE PAST✦ECONOMICS & TECHNOLOGY

| Table 21.2 Manufacturing and Marketing of Model T Fords, 1908–1916 |

Calendar Year	Retail Price (Touring Car)	Total Model T Production	Total Model T Sales
1908	$850	n.a.	5,986
1909	950	13,840	12,292
1910	780	20,727	19,293
1911	690	53,488	40,402
1912	600	82,388	78,611
1913	550	189,088	182,809
1914	490	230,788	260,720
1915	440	394,788	355,276
1916	360	585,388	577,036

Source: Table is taken from David A Hounshell, *From the American System to Mass Production, 1880–1932* (Baltimore: Johns Hopkins University Press, 1984), p. 224.

The table about Henry Ford's Model T is a revealing look at the impact of the automobile on American society in the years preceding entry into World War I. As Ford introduced assembly line methods into his production facility at Highland Park, Michigan, the output of cars rose steadily. The economies of scale that Ford's engineers achieved allowed them at the same time to bring down the cost to the consumer by more than half in an eight-year period ($850–360). Sales rose as well, enabling Ford to finance his $5 per day program for workers and to put more capital into his productive capacity.

A careful scrutiny of the table thus discloses some key points about the emergence of a mass economy in the early twentieth century. Ford understood that lower costs for each unit produced greater and more dependable profits for his company. At the same time consumers needed a secure income to afford to buy cars and other products. The information in the table thus offers a snapshot of an economy and society moving away from the industrial system of Andrew Carnegie and John D. Rockefeller, and toward the mass production, consumer-oriented system of the modern United States.

Ford were bringing cars within the reach of the average middle-class American.

If Ford wanted to fulfill his dream of building "a motor car for the great multitude," he had to devise a means of producing cars continually and in even greater quantities. He borrowed the concept of the assembly line from the meat-packing industry and his engineers adapted it to carmaking. The Ford plant covered more than sixty-five acres in Highland Park, Michigan. It featured a large belt, fed by smaller belts, that brought the chassis of the car and its windshields,

tanks, batteries, and other parts together in a smoothly functioning operation. At first, it took the work force ninety-three minutes to turn out a single Model T. By 1920, the cars were coming off the line at the rate of one per minute. In 1914 the Model T cost under $500 and Ford produced more than 260,000 cars.

On January 5, 1914, Ford proclaimed that he would pay his workers $5 for an eight-hour day. The announcement was headline news across the country, and Ford became a national hero. He was not a serious economic thinker, but he understood that people needed to earn enough money in wages to be able to afford the cars he was making. He realized that he could make more money by selling large numbers of low-priced vehicles than he could by selling a few expensive cars. Ford thus could be described as an apostle of the emerging mass society.

The Five-Dollar Day program was also designed to head off potential unrest among Ford workers. Absenteeism and high turnover among employees hampered production schedules. In addition, unhappiness among workers might lead to the organization of unions. To offset these trends, the new program aimed at sharing profits in a way that would keep workers at their jobs. In addition, Ford developed a "Sociological Department" to instill in employees the values required for efficient mass production. Workers who were productive and cooperative received higher wages. Those who were not were discharged.

The Growing Use of Electricity

The Five-Dollar Day was an apparent sign of progress. Another was the spreading reliance on electricity. Average annual use of electricity doubled during the twenty years after 1912. New products offered homemakers the chance to ease the dull routines of domestic work. General Electric introduced the Radiant Toaster in 1912, which promised "Crisp, Delicious, Golden-Brown Toast on the Breakfast Table." The Hoover Suction Sweeper would "Sweep With Electricity for 3¢ a Week." Newer stoves and washing machines also came into use. Women could also buy ready-made clothes and spend less time on the sewing that had occupied much of their time a generation earlier.

Other technological developments were still in their early stages. The Wright Brothers had made the first power flight in 1903, but aviation began in earnest five years later. Harriet Quimby of the United States was the first woman to fly a plane across the English Channel. Meanwhile, the use of wireless telegraphy in marine navigation expanded. The disaster of the *Titanic,* which hit an iceberg in April 1912 and sank with the loss of hundreds of passengers, underlined the need for reliable radio communications for all vessels. Congress enacted a bill mandating the navy to promote radio usage. Within a few years tentative steps would be taken toward broadcasting voices over the airwaves.

Artistic and Social Ferment

Artistic and cultural ferment accompanied the peak years of progressivism. In 1913, the International Exhibit of Modern Art took place at the 69th Regiment

Greater freedom for women in the Progressive Era brought them into places previously reserved for men. These four women are drinking in the bar of a New York hotel.
© Bettmann/UPI/Corbis

Armory in New York City. Quickly dubbed "the Armory Show," it displayed the works of such European painters as Pablo Picasso and Henri Matisse. The modernist paintings offended many critics, who attacked them in vicious terms. Yet the public flocked to see the paintings, and American artists were stimulated and challenged to adopt the new forms of expression. As one critic predicted, "American art will never be the same again."

The period also produced innovative literary figures who would become even more famous during the 1920s. Reporters and novelists clustered in New York's Greenwich Village. Among them were Max Eastman, publisher of *The Masses,* a magazine that assailed conventional values and the established political system; Eugene O'Neill, a playwright; and John Reed, a radical journalist. Outside of New York, Theodore Dreiser was continuing a literary career that included *The Financier* (1912), a novel depicting a ruthless tycoon; Sherwood Anderson was a short story author who criticized middle-class life in the nation's heartland.

Among the influential writers of the day was Walter Lippmann, a Harvard-educated commentator and social critic, who published *A Preface to Politics* (1913) and *Drift and Mastery* (1914). Lippmann sympathized with the New Nationalism of Theodore Roosevelt, and was one of the cofounders, with Herbert Croly, of *The New Republic,* soon a leading journal of political opinion and cultural commentary. Another

The American painter George Bellows records the teeming life of New York City in 1913 in his painting that reflects the newer currents of art at the time of the Armory Show and the onset of World War I.
George Bellows, "The Cliff Dwellers" 1913. Los Angeles County Museum of Art, Los Angeles

important critical voice was H. L. Mencken, editor of *Smart Set,* a New York magazine; he assailed the cultural provincialism of much of American culture.

Women, too, sought to gain greater rights and to share the freedoms that men enjoyed. In 1912, women in Greenwich Village founded a club called Heterodoxy whose only demand was that its members should "not be orthodox" in their views. In their discussions and in the public meetings they sponsored, they called their doctrine "feminism," which they defined as an attempt on the part of women to be "our whole big human selves."

Heterodoxy represented only a small proportion of American women, but cultural changes occurred even for those who did not call themselves feminists. Women's skirts had become several inches shorter since the beginning of the century. Bobbed hair became fashionable, and more women smoked openly in public. When movie stars like Mary Pickford became famous, the use of cosmetics spread as women emulated the images of feminine beauty that appeared on screen. The "flapper," an image associated with the 1920s, actually made her appearance at about this

time. The years between 1910 and 1920 saw greater opportunities for women in employment and cultural affairs than would occur in the 1920s.

Americans at Play

The ways in which Americans used their leisure time reflected a trend toward mass entertainment. Boxing was still a major sport. When Arthur John "Jack" Johnson became the first African American heavyweight champion in 1908, the public clamored for a "white hope" to reclaim the title. Jackson defeated each of his white challengers in the ring, but fled the country when the government accused him of transporting women across state lines for immoral purposes. In 1915, an aging Johnson lost the heavyweight title.

Baseball attained new heights of popularity. The two professional leagues had emerged, and the World Series had become an annual fall ritual to decide the "world's champion." The public avidly absorbed the ample news coverage that baseball received.

Motion Pictures and the Vaudeville Stage

Motion pictures and vaudeville competed for entertainment dollars. In elaborate vaudeville houses, audiences saw such stars as Fanny Brice, Al Jolson, and Sophie Tucker in well-developed routines aimed at the whole family. A circuit of theaters gave performers a reliable market in which to perfect their craft and maintain their popularity. By the time Wilson became president, however, motion pictures challenged the dominance of vaudeville. Movies were evolving from short features into real stories of an hour or more. The places where patrons saw films were upgraded, while the price of admission remained reasonable. An average family of five could see a movie for less than a half a dollar. Within a decade, the movies emerged as the mass entertainment of the nation. They were lively and up-to-date and conveyed a sense of modern life and spontaneity that made nineteenth-century ideas appear even more dated and obsolete.

NEW FREEDOM DIPLOMACY

Throughout the Progressive Era, domestic political and economic concerns dominated. Newspapers covered international news, and readers could follow the unfolding of European diplomacy if they wished. Isolated from the tensions of world affairs by two vast oceans, Americans allowed their elected leaders to conduct foreign policy as long as the general policies of isolation and noninvolvement with Europe were observed.

Woodrow Wilson and the World

Woodrow Wilson came to the presidency without any experience in foreign policy. In fact, early in 1913 he remarked to a friend that "[it] would be the irony of fate if my administration had to deal chiefly with foreign affairs." Nevertheless, Wilson had definite ideas about how the nation should behave in world affairs. During his first eighteen months in the White House, Wilson applied his precepts to diplomatic problems in Asia and Latin America, situations that trained him for the greater trials he would face in World War I.

The president handled most of the business of foreign affairs himself. He appointed William Jennings Bryan as secretary of state, but he never allowed Bryan to have a significant role in shaping policy. Bryan spent some of his time making speeches about public issues and promoting international treaties of conciliation that he thought would end the threat of war. Many countries signed these treaties before the war broke out in 1914; they provided for a "cooling-off" period before countries could begin fighting.

Wilsonian Ideas in Practice

In foreign affairs, Woodrow Wilson believed that the United States should set an example for the world because of the nation's commitment to democracy and capitalism. "Morality and not expediency is the thing that must guide us," he said in 1913.

In Asia, the Wilson administration stepped back from Taft's commitments, instructing American bankers to withdraw from the Chinese railroad consortium that Taft and Knox had sponsored. The United States also recognized the Republic of China which had come into power following the 1911 revolution that ousted the Manchu dynasty. Wilson and the Democrats put the Philippine Islands on the road toward independence, but their efforts to counter the rise of Japanese influence in Asia proved less successful.

Wilson wanted his policy toward Latin America to be less intrusive and less dominant than Roosevelt's had been. To that end, he worked out a treaty with Colombia that apologized for Roosevelt's actions in 1903–1904. The pact outraged the former president, and the Senate did not approve the treaty while Wilson was in office. Better relations with Latin America did not, in the president's mind, mean accepting governments that offended his moral values. "I am going to teach the South American Republics to elect good

One of the more controversial episodes of Wilson's early foreign policy was the intervention in Mexico in 1914. Marines march through the streets of Vera Cruz to carry out the president's pressure on the Mexicans.
Reproduced from the Collections of the Library of Congress

men," he said. That principle led him into the kinds of intervention that he would have preferred to avoid. He kept troops in Nicaragua and extracted further concessions from that country. Other military detachments went to Cuba, Haiti, and the Dominican Republic.

The Mexican Involvement

In Mexico, Wilson confronted a revolution. The Madero government, which had taken over from Porfirio Díaz in 1911, was ousted just before Wilson was inaugurated in March 1913. The man who toppled Francisco Madero was General Victoriano Huerta. Although most European nations quickly recognized Huerta's government, the United States did not. To win recognition from the United States, the Mexicans would have to install a government that relied on law rather than "arbitrary and irregular force."

Wilson instead threw the weight of the United States behind Venustiano Carranza, a rebel against the Huerta government, but his offers of cooperation were not accepted. If Carranza agreed to Wilson's insistence on some U.S. economic and political presence in Mexico, he would have been regarded as pro-American, a fatal weakness to the sensitive Mexican populace.

To block the flow of munitions into Mexico, Wilson had sent the navy to patrol the Gulf of Mexico. Sailors from the USS *Dolphin* went ashore at Tampico on April 9 without the necessary permission, and Mexican authorities arrested them. Released quickly and without further incident, they returned to their ship. The admiral on the scene nonetheless demanded that the Mexican authorities apologize and make a twenty-one gun salute to the American flag. Huerta's government replied that the Mexican flag should be saluted.

The president asked Congress for authority to use force at a time when a German vessel was unloading arms on the Mexican shore. Wilson ordered troops to occupy the port of Vera Cruz. Heavy fighting erupted in which more than one hundred Mexicans and nineteen Americans died. All the warring parties in Mexico denounced the United States. The two countries seemed on the edge of outright war.

Wilson drew back and accepted mediation. The negotiations led to the evacuation of Vera Cruz on November 14. Dependent on outside funds to pay his army, Huerta left office when his money ran out in July 1914. Carranza took power, and Wilson promptly recognized his government. A rebellion against Carranza by one of his generals would lead to further confrontations with the United States during the rest of Wilson's first term.

Hispanics in the Southwest

Revolutionary upheavals in Mexico produced an increase in immigrants from that country into the United States after 1910. A mix of social, political, and economic forces had already produced a rising number of Mexican immigrants after 1900. Although many of those immigrants returned to Mexico after working in the United States for several months, some 35,000 to 75,000 Hispanic immigrants stayed on each year. The dictatorial regime of Porfirio Díaz impelled political dissidents and impoverished peasants to travel north. Once the revolution began in 1911, it drove more Mexicans toward the border. Throughout these years the spread of irrigation agriculture, railroads, and mining in the Southwest increased the demand for inexpensive labor. The closing off of Japanese immigration after 1907 made Mexican laborers an attractive option for Anglo businesses.

The newcomers from south of the border found work in the sugar beet fields of Colorado; the agricultural valleys of south Texas and southern California, where they picked the lettuce and citrus fruits that grew in irrigated fields; and the towns of Arizona and New Mexico. Other Hispanics labored for daily wages in Los Angeles, El Paso, and San Antonio. They paved streets, built houses, and processed food for the Anglo community. Their wages were low, sometimes under $1.25 per day.

Major centers of Hispanic life emerged in the southwestern cities. Ethnic communities sponsored mutual aid societies and established Spanish language newspapers to ease the immigrants' adjustment to a new culture. Religious prejudice remained strong, however. When Mexican immigrants settled in San Bernadino, California, one longtime resident warned that he "might use a shotgun on these aliens if necessary." In Texas and California, segregation and poverty limited the opportunities open to Mexican Americans.

The international tension between Mexico and the Wilson administration led to periodic "brown scares" along the border. Anglo residents feared vague conspiracies to reclaim land lost by Mexico during the nineteenth century. Cross-border incursions from Mexico further heightened tensions. By 1915, a violent cultural conflict that claimed hundreds of lives was in progress in south Texas. As a result of these struggles, the Mexican Americans lost much of the land they held in the area. Nevertheless, Hispanics had achieved the basis for a greater presence in the United States during the twentieth century.

WORLD WAR I

By 1914, the major European nations were on edge. If one country found itself at war with another, all the other powers could be drawn into the struggle. On one side stood Germany, in the center of Europe. Its powerful industries and efficient army worried its neighbors, France and Russia. The Germans sought the international respect they believed to be their rightful due. They had built up a large navy that had fueled tensions with Great Britain. Their leader, Kaiser Wilhelm II, had erratic dreams of world influence that his generals and admirals adapted for their own expansionist purposes. The Germans had treaty links to the sprawling and turbulent nations of Austria-Hungary and the even more ramshackle regime of the Ottoman Turks. Italy had been part of the so-called Triple Alliance with Germany and Austria-Hungary, but these ties were frayed by 1914.

Against the Germans stood the French (who coveted territory they had lost in the Franco-Prussian War of 1871), the Russians, and, if the Germans attacked France, the British. The Russian Empire was in decay, with revolutionary sentiments just below the surface. The French feared another defeat at the hands of Germany, and the British worried about German naval strength and Berlin's plans for dominance of Western Europe. All the powers had elaborate plans for mobilization in a general crisis. Once these timetables went into effect, the relentless pressure of military events would frustrate efforts at a diplomatic resolution.

Map 21.2 *Europe on the Eve of World War I*
In the summer of 1914, when the First World War erupted, Germany and Austria-Hungary dominated the center of the European land mass. France, Great Britain, and Russia counterbalanced the Central Powers. Once the fighting began, the system of alliances drew most of Europe into the conflict.

The Road to World War

World War I began in the Balkans. On June 28, 1914, the Austrian archduke, Franz Ferdinand, and his wife were murdered in the town of Sarajevo in Bosnia, a province of the Austro-Hungarian Empire. The Austrians soon learned that the killer was paid by the Serbians. The Austrians made harsh demands on Serbia that would have left that nation defenseless. The Germans supported their Austrian allies, with the result that the Russians came to the defense of the Serbs. Soon all the European countries were drawn into the conflict.

By early August of 1914, the general war that Europeans had long feared and anticipated was under way. Germany, Austria-Hungary, and Turkey, known as the Central Powers, were fighting against Great Britain, France, and Russia, now called the Allies. Italy remained neutral. Soon the guns of August began a conflagration that lasted four years and consumed the flesh and blood of a generation.

America and the European War

The sudden outbreak of fighting in Europe surprised Americans, even those who were well-informed about world events. Although the arms race among the great powers had seemed potentially dangerous, it had been a century since a major war had involved all the major European countries. Surely, the conventional wisdom of the day said, the self-restraint and wisdom of the great nations made a destructive war unlikely. Faith in progress and the betterment of humanity, so much a part of the Progressive Era's creed, made war unthinkable. When the armies marched, Americans were shocked. The world war came at a time of emotional distress for Wilson. His wife, Ellen, died on August 6, 1914. This personal loss devastated the president, who occupied himself in dealing with the war. On the domestic political scene, the Democrats expected serious losses in the congressional elections. The Republicans had won back some of the Progressive voters who had followed Roosevelt in 1912. Until war broke out, it seemed as if politics might be returning to something resembling its normal patterns.

CONCLUSION

The war, however, produced a lasting change in the course of American history. The nation's isolation from world events ended. Americans had to confront the challenges of a world role. During the seven years that followed, Woodrow Wilson would pursue neutrality, enter the war in 1917, and see his dreams of world peace collapse in 1921. Social and political reform continued for a time and then gave way to conservatism. With all these developments, the impact of progressivism on the direction of American politics remained significant. The issues that had been identified in domestic affairs between 1901 and 1914, particularly the question of the government's role in the economy, endured.

Recommended Readings

Batchelor, Robert. *The 1900s (American Popular Culture Through History)* (2002). A brisk look at the way Americans lived and entertained themselves at the start of the twentieth century.

Chambers, John Whiteclay II. *The Tyranny of Change: America in the Progressive Era, 1890–1920* (1992). Considers the Taft and Wilson years in the context of reform.

Clements, Kendrick. *The Presidency of Woodrow Wilson* (1992). Provides a crisp, informed look at Wilson in office.

Gilmore, Glenda E., ed. *Who Were The Progressives?* (2002). A thoughtful collection of essays about how historians have viewed early twentieth century reformers.

Margulies, Herbert F. *Reconciliation and Revival: James R. Mann and the House Republicans in the Wilson Era* (1996). Supplies a good guide to the politics of the Taft-Wilson years.

Miller, Char. *Gifford Pinchot and the Making of Modern Environmentalism* (2001). Places one of the leaders of the progressive conservation movement in a broader context.

Rodgers, Daniel T. *Atlantic Crossings: Social Politics in a Progressive Age* (1998). Looks at the international aspects of reform.

Sanders, Elizabeth. *Roots of Reform: Farmers, Workers, and the American State, 1877–1917* (1999). Provides insights into how reform legislation fared in Congress.

Stansell, Christine. *American Moderns: Bohemian New York and the Creation of a New Century* (2000). Discusses how New York City and Greenwich Village affected cultural change.

Unger, Nancy. *Fighting Bob La Follette: The Righteous Reformer* (2000). A biography of the Wisconsin senator who challenged Roosevelt for progressive leadership.

American Journey Online and InfoTrac College Edition

Visit the source collections at http://ajaccess. wadsworth.com and infotrac.thomsonlearning.com and use the Search function with the following key terms to explore documents, images, audio and video clips, articles, and commentary related to the material in this chapter.

William Howard Taft
Alice Paul
Woodrow Wilson
Henry Ford

Triangle Shirtwaist
Woman suffrage
Prohibition
Vaudeville

Additional resources, exercises, and Internet links related to this chapter are available on the American Passages Web site: http://history.wadsworth.com/passages2e

22 OVER THERE AND OVER HERE: THE IMPACT OF WORLD WAR I 1914–1921

STAYING NEUTRAL IN A WORLD CONFLICT

SOCIAL CHANGE DURING THE PERIOD OF NEUTRALITY

THE PERSISTENCE OF REFORM

A NATION AT WAR

THE ROAD TO VICTORY

FROM WAR TO PEACE

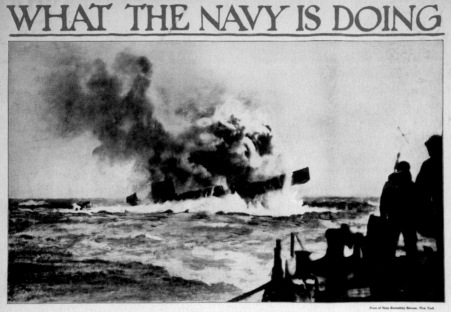

The submarine was the most controversial weapon of World War I. Its use helped bring the United States into the war. Once the war had broadened to include the United States in April 1917, the Navy tuned to dealing with the submarine menace as this recruiting advertisement shows.

From the Collections of the Library of Congress

Americans wanted to keep out of the European war. Yet events in the conflict influenced domestic politics, altered the Progressive movement, and changed the fortunes of women, African Americans, and socialists. The nation's traditional values came under repeated attack as the war went on. U.S. entry into the war in April 1917 transformed the country in an even more striking fashion.

The era of progressive reform ended. World War I brought several campaigns for social change, most notably Prohibition and woman suffrage, to national success. Yet by the time these results occurred, the movement for reform had lost momentum. The nation rejected an activist government, expensive programs, and efforts to improve society. When Woodrow Wilson left the White House on March 4, 1921, he gave way to Warren G. Harding, who promised a return to older values and a respite from moral uplift.

STAYING NEUTRAL IN A WORLD CONFLICT

President Wilson in August 1914 asked his fellow citizens to "be neutral in fact as well as in name" and "impartial in thought as well as in action." Wilson himself had more sympathy for the Allies than he had for Germany and its wartime partners. He also believed that some kind of "association of nations" must prevent future world wars. In conducting foreign policy, however, he was as evenhanded toward the two sides as any president could have been.

The War and National Politics

The initial results of Wilson's neutrality decisions came in national politics. Going into the congressional elections of 1914, the Republicans anticipated gains in the House and Senate, but the war issue changed things. In the 1914 elections, the Democratic slogan was "War in the East! Peace in the West! Thank God for Wilson!" The Republicans picked up sixty-three seats in the House, but the Democrats retained control. In the Senate, the president's party actually added five seats.

The issue of peace and war held potential benefits for the president in 1916. The Democrats did well in the Midwest, where support for progressive reforms remained strong. As Wilson looked toward reelection, he decided to form a coalition of southern and western voters united on a platform of peace and reform.

To do so, the president had to pay attention to the interest groups—union workers, farmers, and woman suffrage advocates—that he had rebuffed between 1913 and 1915. If the war stimulated the economy, the combination of peace, prosperity, and reform might give the president a chance at reelection.

The Dilemma of Neutrality

Economic links with Great Britain were strong, and they intensified as the war progressed. Exports to Britain and France totaled $754 million in 1914; in 1916, they stood at $2.75 billion. Meanwhile, trade with Germany, which had totaled $190 million in 1914, virtually ceased because of the British blockade. The United States could have embargoed all trade with belligerent powers, as many American supporters of Germany recommended, but that strategy would have devastated the U.S. economy.

The Germans had strong support in the United States. The more than 5 million German Americans, most numerous in the Middle West, represented a sizable bloc of votes that usually favored Republicans. The 3 million-plus Irish Americans hated England and cheered for its enemies. Germany conducted an expensive propaganda campaign consisting of pamphlets and newspaper advertisements. Money directed through the German-dominated brewing industry paid for the campaign. Undercutting their public relations image, however, the Germans also used espionage and sabotage to cripple the British war effort and to hamper American assistance to the Allies.

The British matched German expenditures on propaganda describing the alleged atrocities of their foe. They also relied on their cultural ties with the upper classes and opinion makers in the Northeast to set forth the British case in magazines and newspapers.

The Course of the War and American Public Opinion

The way the Germans waged the war did the greatest damage to their cause with Americans. In the opening days of the fighting, the German army violated Belgium's neutrality, crossing that nation's borders to invade France. Confronted with a British naval blockade designed to strangle its economy and capacity to wage war, Germany turned to a new weapon, the submarine, early in 1915. In contrast to surface ships, the submarine relied on surprise attacks based on its ability to submerge. Passengers on torpedoed ships were left to drown. Submarines could not provide warnings without risk to themselves, and the Germans resisted pleas that they should do so.

CHRONOLOGY

1914 Wilson declares American neutrality in World War I • President also proclaims first National Mother's Day

1915 *Lusitania* torpedoed with loss of 128 Americans • Wilson announces preparedness campaign • *The Birth of a Nation* promotes revival of Ku Klux Klan • Great Migration of African Americans continues

1916 Army pursues Pancho Villa into Mexico • Wilson wins second term over Charles Evans Hughes

1917 Wilson makes "Peace Without Victory" speech • Woman suffrage advocates arrested and jailed for picketing the White House • Germans resume unrestricted submarine campaign • United States enters world war • Military draft enacted to raise army

1918 Wilson announces "Fourteen Points" for peace settlement • American troops join in Allied drive toward Germany • First granulated soap ("Rinso") introduced • Influenza epidemic sweeps the globe and kills 20 million people • Armistice ends First World War

1919 Wilson negotiates Treaty of Versailles • Dial telephones introduced • Prohibition amendment adopted • Wilson stricken with stroke

1920 Senate defeats League of Nations for second time • Woman suffrage amendment ratified • Warren G. Harding wins presidency • Edith Wharton wins Pulitzer Prize for her novel *The Age of Innocence*

1921 Harding becomes President

Germany declared that enemy vessels would be sunk on sight, a policy many Americans regarded as a violation of the civilized rules of war. Despite this aggressive strategy, Germany had only twenty-one submarines when the fighting began. These new vessels could not win the war by themselves but use of the submarine put Germany in direct conflict with the United States, the leading neutral country.

The Lusitania Crisis

On May 7, 1915, a German submarine fired a torpedo into the British liner *Lusitania* off the Irish coast. The huge vessel sank quickly. Among the nearly 1,200 passengers who died were 128 Americans. To most people this event was an audacious atrocity, not an inescapable by-product of modern warfare. Wilson had said that Germany would be held to "strict accountability" for submarine attacks on Americans. He decided, however, that the *Lusitania* was not worth a war.

The president was applauded when he said, three days after the *Lusitania* incident, that "there is such as thing as a man being too proud to fight. There is such a thing as a nation being so right that it does not need to

convince others by force that it is right." Allied sympathizers denounced Wilson's words, but the president's readiness to negotiate was generally approved.

Wilson and the Submarine Crisis

Wilson sought an apology and a pledge to limit submarine warfare. His diplomatic protest was strong enough, however, that Secretary of State William Jennings Bryan resigned in protest in June 1915. He was replaced by Robert Lansing, a pro-Allied diplomat. During the remainder of the summer, the Germans kept the negotiating process going without apologizing or yielding on any point.

Then, in August, the Germans torpedoed a British liner, the *Arabic,* wounding two Americans. Wilson told the Germans privately that the United States would break diplomatic relations with them if submarine warfare continued. Still unsure whether the submarine alone could win the war, Berlin offered a conditional pledge not to make unannounced attacks on passenger liners; this defused the situation briefly. In the following year, the Germans sank thirty-seven unarmed liners.

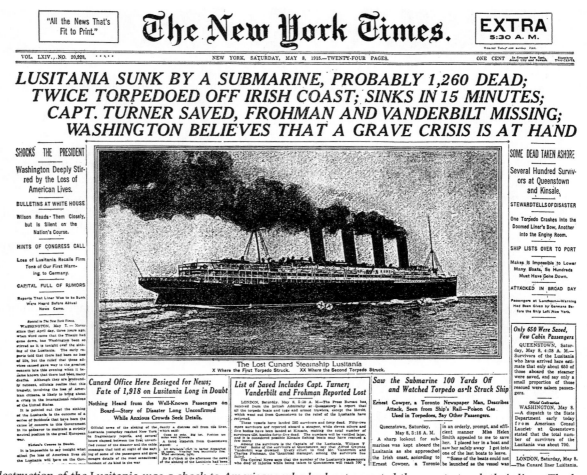

The Lost Cunard Steamship Lusitania
X Where the First Torpedo Struck.   XX Where the Second Torpedo Struck.

The destruction of the Lusitania *was a shock to Americans who had not expected the war to touch their lives. The banner headlines in the* New York Times *convey something of the sense of amazement and surprise that accompanied the sinking of the passenger liner.*
The Granger Collection, New York

The United States and Its World Role

The neutrality issue forced Americans to consider the nation's future role in a warring world. Many groups wanted the United States to maintain its traditional posture of noninvolvement. German Americans and Irish Americans saw no need to help the British. Progressive reformers regarded war and foreign commitments as the death of reform. In the Midwest and on the Pacific Coast, peace sentiments were widespread.

Theodore Roosevelt, Elihu Root, and other northeastern Republicans supported the allies and called for military "preparedness" in the event of ultimate American entry into the war. Army and navy officials knew that they would have to expand their

forces greatly if they were to play any significant role on the Allied side. In late 1914, Wilson had blocked programs to strengthen the military defense. By the summer of 1915, however, he changed his position and sought a larger army and navy. He promised a navy "second to none" and more troops for the regular army. Many Democrats in the South and West opposed Wilson on the issue of preparedness and the increased spending that it entailed. In early 1916, the president made a speaking tour to arouse popular support for his policy.

As the debate over preparedness intensified, some opinion leaders argued that a world organization should be formed to keep the peace once the fighting stopped. The League to Enforce Peace was created in June 1915, with William Howard Taft as its leader. As 1915 ended, Wilson had not yet thrown his influence behind the idea of a world organization.

SOCIAL CHANGE DURING THE PERIOD OF NEUTRALITY

During 1915, Americans flocked to theaters to see a new motion picture that vividly depicted sensational events in the nation's past. David Wark Griffith's *The*

Birth of a Nation, based on an antiblack novel by Thomas Dixon entitled *The Clansman,* portrayed the Reconstruction period in the South as a time when ignorant African Americans terrorized whites and made a travesty of government. An artistic triumph because it used new techniques such as flashbacks and close-ups, the movie twisted history to glamorize the Ku Klux Klan and the white South. Audiences were enthusiastic, box office records were broken, and President Wilson reportedly said: "It is like writing history with lightning." Efforts by African Americans to have the film banned were largely unsuccessful.

Inspired by the film's portrayal of the Klan, a group of white men burned a cross at Stone Mountain, Georgia. At first the revived Klan's membership remained under 5,000 nationally, but the social tensions of the postwar era proved a fertile ground for organizing in the South and Midwest.

The political prospects for improved rights for blacks remained as bleak as they had been since the 1890s. The Wilson administration and the Democratic party proved unsympathetic to any efforts to reduce racism. After protests from blacks and a few progressives, the White House retreated from efforts to enforce segregation in the federal government, but that was a minor victory. The Supreme Court did, however, rule in the case of *Guinn v. United States* (1915) that

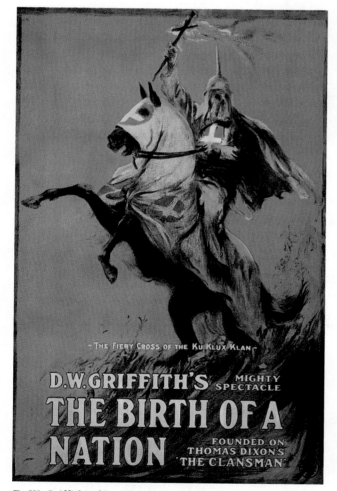

D. W. Griffith's film The Birth of a Nation *was an artistic triumph with a racist theme. This photograph advertising the film depicts the Ku Klux Klan as akin to medieval knights in the garb of chivalry. White audiences ignored the Klan's violent reality for African Americans.*
The Granger Collection, New York

This lynching in Waco, Texas in 1915 became known as the "Waco Horror" for the cruel way the mob killed the victim. Lynching remained an accepted part of race relations in the South.
Photographs and Prints Division, Schomburg Center for Research in Black Culture, New York Public Library, Astor, Lenox and Tilden Foundations

PICTURING THE PAST ✦ SOCIAL & CULTURAL EVENTS

THE GREAT MIGRATION OF AFRICAN AMERICANS TO THE NORTH

Photographs and Prints Division, Schomburg Center for Research in Black Culture, New York Public Library, Astor, Lenox and Tilden Foundations

The Great Migration of African Americans from the South to northern cities during the second decade of the twentieth century reshaped the nation's cities and, in time, its political, social, and cultural life. This photograph of a black family arriving in Chicago in 1916 reveals in their faces the determination and pain that the journey out of the segregated South demanded. The expressions underscore the rigors of the process, the way in which a few belongings and their best clothes prepared them for the trip, and their apprehension about the uncertain future that they faced in the North.

This photograph comes from the rich collection of images of black life in the Schomburg Center for Research in Black Culture at the New York Public Library. The photographic documentation of African American life in such twentieth century records enables history texts to do better justice to the everyday life of all Americans and the individual families of which they were a part. Thus a simple scene of a family in search of a better life for themselves and their children becomes a symbol of a larger national quest for these values.

the grandfather clause that Oklahoma used to exempt whites from a literacy test for voting was unconstitutional. Oklahoma found other ways to register whites and restrict blacks, but the decision foreshadowed future racial progress toward greater protection of minority rights.

The Great Migration

For African Americans in the South, life was still painful and burdensome. Southern agriculture experienced crippling problems during the first fifteen years

Table 22.1	Migration of African Americans to Five Northern Cities, 1910–1920		
	1910	**1920**	**Percent Rise**
New York	91,709	152,467	66.3
Chicago	44,103	109,458	148.2
Philadelphia	84,459	134,229	58.9
Baltimore	84,749	108,322	27.8
Detroit	5,741	40,838	611.3

Source: Robert B. Grant, *The Black Man Comes to the City* (Chicago, 1972).

of the century. Natural disasters hit the region in the form of floods and droughts. The boll weevil, an insect that destroys cotton, undermined the farm economy. Blacks began leaving the South for cities in the North. The "Great Migration" started slowly around 1910 and then accelerated between 1914 and 1920 when more than 600,000 African Americans left the South.

The outbreak of the war played a key role in this process. Immigration from Europe ended. The result was an expanding labor market for unskilled workers in the North. Those who came to the North found a better life, but not a paradise. They secured work in the coal mines of West Virginia, the stockyards of Chicago, and the steel mills of Pittsburgh. In Chicago, some 60,000 blacks moved to the city between 1916 and 1920, a 148 percent increase in its African American population. Similar percentage increases occurred in Pittsburgh, Cincinnati, and Detroit.

As their population in the North grew, blacks encountered discrimination in housing and public services. Long-standing residents of African American communities in northern cities looked down on the new arrivals. But the southern blacks continued to move north in an historic population shift that reshaped the politics and culture of the nation's largest cities.

The Rise of the Movies

In 1914, a young British comedian began appearing in films for the Keystone company, a filmmaking venture in Los Angeles. Although most of his thirty-five pictures were very short, one film, *Tillie's Punctured Romance,* ran for thirty minutes. Audiences began asking about the funny actor in the derby hat and little tramp costume. By 1915, the whole nation was talking about Charlie Chaplin and a craze called "Chaplinitis" swept the land. In January 1915, Chaplin signed with Essanay Pictures for the then-huge sum of $1,250 a week. (An industrial worker made around $600 per *year.*) Within twelve months Chaplin moved on to the Mutual Film Corporation at $10,000 a week. Stardom had come quickly for the twenty-six-year-old actor.

After a shaky start at the beginning of the century, motion pictures had arrived as mass entertainment. There were more than 10,000 nickelodeon theaters by 1912, and up to 20 million Americans went to the movies on a regular basis. Soon movies became longer, and exhibitors began constructing motion picture theaters that could seat up to 5,000 customers.

Although Chaplin was the most famous male performer of his time, he was not the only "star" that the studios created during the era of the silent movie. Executives found that audiences wanted to know

By 1915, Charlie Chaplin had become one of the most recognizable people in the world. This advertising montage gives a good sense of his varied characters and the popular appeal that he enjoyed.
Washington Evening Star, November, 1915

about the private lives of the people they saw on the flickering screens. Mary Pickford became "America's Sweetheart" in a series of roles that depicted a demure damsel in acute distress. Douglas Fairbanks used his athletic ability as the swashbuckling hero of such films as *American Aristocracy* (1916) and *Wild and Woolly* (1917). Theda Bara became the "vamp" in *A Fool There Was* (1915). Advertisements described her as having "the most wickedly beautiful face in the world."

The business of making movies became concentrated in a few large studios that controlled the process of production and distribution. Because of its mild climate, Hollywood, California, emerged as the center of the picture industry. Studios like Vitagraph and Paramount dominated the making and marketing of films.

Most moviegoers lived in cities where the large theaters were located. Immigrants found that they could learn about American life at the movies. Parents worried when their children saw such films as *Women and Wine* or *Man and His Mate.* Reformers clamored for censorship boards to screen films for scenes that showed lustful images or suggested that criminals profited from their crimes.

Shifting Attitudes Toward Sex

Continued challenges to the nation's family and sexual values arose. In 1916, one of every nine marriages ended in the divorce courts. Meanwhile, family size was decreasing. By 1920, two or three children were born to the average mother; in 1860, the average had been five or six.

The most daring women of the decade were the "flappers." They cut their hair short in the fashionable "bob" and wore shorter skirts. The flapper, wrote social commentator H. L. Mencken in 1915, "has forgotten how to simper; she seldom blushes; it is impossible to shock her." Norms of sexual behavior slowly moved away from the restrictions of the Victorian era. For women born around 1900, the rate of sexual intercourse before marriage was twice as high as it had been for women born a decade earlier. Nevertheless, the overall incidence of premarital sexual behavior remained very low in comparison with the present.

Birth Control

Despite the changes in actual sexual practices, the official attitudes of the nation remained restrictive. Homosexual relationships were outlawed, even though some college-educated women maintained "partnerships" or "Boston marriages." Laws governing the dissemination of information about birth control discouraged the use of contraception. In many states and cities it was a crime to sell condoms or to distribute information about how to avoid pregnancy. A federal statute, the Comstock Law of 1873, barred the making, selling, distribution, or importation of contraceptives, as well as any transmission of birth control information through the mails. The only ground on which abortions were permitted was to save the life of the mother.

Margaret Sanger, a thirty-two-year-old radical living in Greenwich Village, New York City, saw women suffering from disease and poverty because of the large number of children they bore. Often women had many babies because they lacked knowledge about ways to limit births. In 1914, Sanger coined the term *birth control* and began publishing a periodical called *Woman Rebel.* Women, she wrote, "cannot be on an equal footing with men until they have full and complete control over their reproductive function." Indicted for sending such information through the mails, she went to Europe, consulted with experts on family planning, and returned to the United States determined to arouse support for birth control.

A year later she founded a clinic in a poor neighborhood of Brooklyn that distributed information about contraception to the female residents. The police soon closed the clinic down, and Sanger went to jail. When the case was appealed, a higher court affirmed the right of doctors to prescribe birth control devices. Sanger then organized the Birth Control League to promote her cause. Some feminists regarded birth control as a liberating idea; others saw the availability of contraceptive devices as likely to encourage promiscuity and thus promote male dominance.

THE PERSISTENCE OF REFORM

Progressive reform campaigns pressed ahead despite the distractions of the European war. Prohibition capitalized on anti-German sentiment to reduce the political power of the brewing industry. The end of the flow of immigrants from Europe enabled advocates of immigration restriction to gain support for tighter laws. Supporters of woman suffrage also used the war as a way of mobilizing women behind their cause.

Renewed Momentum for Woman Suffrage

Woman suffrage gained strength after 1914 despite serious divisions among the movement's leaders. Alice Paul and the militant Congressional Union pressed for a constitutional amendment to obtain votes for women. Their tactics included demonstrations and a direct challenge to the Democrats as the party in power. In contrast, the National American Woman Suffrage Association (NAWSA), led by Carrie Chapman Catt after 1915, emphasized nonpartisanship and state-by-state organization. Paul and her allies formed the National Woman's party to defeat Wilson and the Democrats. NAWSA, on the other hand, continued its efforts to win the right to vote in individual states, but it now sought a constitutional amendment as well. As the election approached, the momentum for suffrage seemed to be building. Even President Wilson, who had previously opposed the idea, now said that individual states could adopt woman suffrage if they wished.

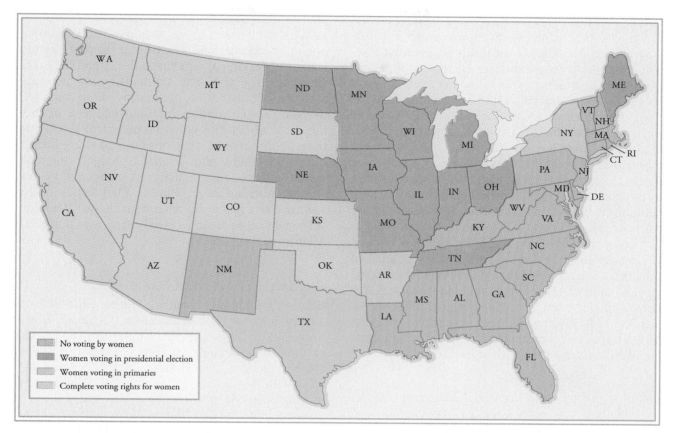

Map 22.1 *The March of Woman Suffrage*
This map tracing the progress of woman suffrage gives an excellent sense of the sectional split over the issue with the West and Middle West in favor and the South and East in opposition.

The Drys on the Offensive

The drive for Prohibition, the second major cultural reform campaign, also intensified. In 1914, the Anti-Saloon League decided to press for a constitutional amendment to ban the sale of alcohol. At the same time, the efforts to make the states liquor-free went forward, with notable success. In 1913–1914, more than a dozen states adopted Prohibition legislation or held referenda in which the voters adopted Prohibition. Nine more states adopted Prohibition in 1915. Gradually, prohibitionist candidates within the major parties won seats in Congress.

Closing the Golden Door

The war in Europe shut off immigration to the United States from the eastern European countries. The reduced flow of newcomers did not stop the campaign to cut down on immigration. Proponents of immigration restriction contended that the eventual peace would open the door to an even greater influx of outsiders. The eth-nic tensions that the neutrality debate produced heightened sensitivity about what came to be called "hyphenated Americans." Congress again passed an immigration restriction law with a literacy test in 1915 which President Wilson again vetoed. In the 1916 election, neither major party wanted to alienate ethnic voters.

The Enactment of Reform

After 1914, progressive reformers looked to the federal government for help with the agenda of social change. In light of the results of the 1914 congressional elections, Wilson understood that he must move left to win four more years in office. Putting aside his earlier reservations about the use of national power to achieve such reforms as child labor legislation or agricultural credits for farmers, he shifted toward the progressive side. He also became more willing to use the authority of his office to push for reform.

One notable step that Wilson took was to nominate Louis D. Brandeis to the U.S. Supreme Court in

January 1916. Brandeis had advised Wilson on the New Freedom, and had won renown as the "People's Lawyer" and a foe of consolidated business enterprise. Since Brandeis was a longtime champion of reform causes and a prominent Jew, his appointment aroused intense, often anti-Semitic, feelings among conservatives. In the end he was confirmed, and Wilson's strong endorsement of him convinced progressives that the president was on their side.

During the months before the election campaign began, Wilson came out for laws to restrict child labor, to promote federal loans to farmers (known as agricultural credits), to provide federal aid for highway construction, and cover federal employees with workers' compensation laws. When a national railroad strike threatened in August 1916, Wilson compelled Congress to pass the Adamson Act, which mandated an eight-hour working day for railroad employees. Labor responded with strong support for Wilson's reelection bid. Meanwhile, the improving economy, driven by orders from the Allies for American products and foodstuffs, helped the Democrats.

Foreign Policy and the 1916 Election

Wilson's reelection chances hinged on the uneasy neutrality he had maintained toward the Germans and the British throughout 1916. The Republicans seemed divided between those who wished to do more for the Allies and those who either disliked overseas involvement or wished to help Germany. Wilson would benefit if he could find a middle position that combined defense of American rights with preservation of neutrality.

The president had to deal with several related wartime issues during the first half of 1916. The main problem remained the submarine. By the end of 1915, Wilson had succeeded in obtaining a German apology and indemnity for the Americans who had died on the *Lusitania.* After the sinking of the *Arabic,* the Germans had also pledged not to attack passenger liners without warning. Then the United States suggested an arrangement in which the Germans would limit submarine warfare and the Allies would not arm merchant ships. When this proposal (or *modus vivendi*) collapsed because of British and German opposition, Germany resumed submarine attacks on *armed* shipping, whether it was belligerent or neutral, in February 1916.

The Sussex Pledge

On March 24, 1916, a German submarine attacked an unarmed steamer, the *Sussex,* in the English Channel. American passengers on board were injured, and another diplomatic crisis ensued. Wilson sent an ultimatum to Berlin that continued attacks on unarmed merchant vessels without warning would lead to a breaking of diplomatic ties, a prelude to U.S entry into the war. The Germans again faced the question of whether the submarine alone could win the war. At the time, only about eighteen of their fifty-two submarines could be on patrol at any one time. With hopes of a victory on land still glimmering before them, the Germans pledged that they would not conduct attacks on merchant vessels without warning them. The so-called *Sussex* Pledge seemed like a major diplomatic success for Woodrow Wilson because it had staved off a war that most Americans dreaded.

Seeking a Negotiated Peace

During these same months, Wilson also tried to arrange for a negotiated settlement of the war. In December 1915, he sent his close friend, Colonel Edward M. House, to discuss peace terms with the British, French, and Germans. House's talks led to an agreement with the British foreign minister, Edward Grey, for Anglo-American mediation of the war; if the Germans rebuffed the idea, the United States would enter the war on the side of the Allies. The House-Grey Memorandum, as the agreement was called, never took effect because Wilson watered it down and the British ignored it.

During the first half of 1916, Wilson emerged as a forceful national leader. His speaking tour calling for preparedness swung public opinion behind his program to provide more weapons and personnel for the army and navy. When Congress sought to assert itself through resolutions warning Americans not to travel on the ships of the warring powers, the president pressured Congress to have the resolutions defeated on the grounds that they interfered with his power to conduct foreign policy. In May 1916, the president argued, in a speech to the League to Enforce Peace, that the major nations of the world should find a way to band together to preserve peace.

The Mexican Problem

During the spring of 1916, the issue of Mexico once again grabbed the nation's headlines. The Mexican civil war had continued after the American intervention at Veracruz in 1914. Although Wilson did not like the regime of Venustiano Carranza, he extended diplomatic recognition to it when it became clear that Carranza had emerged as the nation's effective leader.

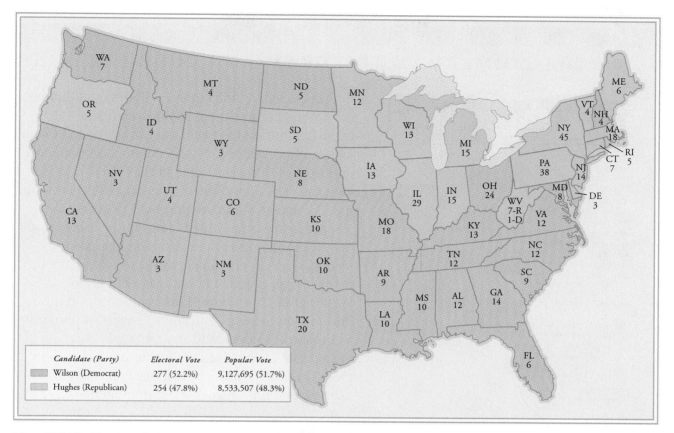

Map 22.2 *The Election of 1916*

The election of 1916, fought under the shadow of World War I in Europe, saw Woodrow Wilson campaign on a platform of peace, prosperity, and progressive reform. That was enough to enable the Democratic incumbent to run well in the West and compile a tight victory over Charles Evans Hughes and the Republicans.

Then a rebel named Pancho Villa raided towns in New Mexico and Texas in 1916, killing and wounding numerous Americans. The U.S. Army under General John J. Pershing pursued him across the Rio Grande. Heedless of Mexican feelings about this intrusion on their sovereignty, the United States seemed to be headed for a war. Wilson negotiated a diplomatic settlement. Nevertheless, American troops remained in Mexico for two years, placing a continued strain on relations between the two nations.

The 1916 Elections

The Democrats approached the election of 1916 with confidence. The president's program of progressive domestic legislation was moving through Congress; the international situation appeared to have vindicated Wilson's leadership; and the economy was prosperous because of the war orders that the British and French had placed for munitions, food, and industrial products. The Republicans first had to win back the

Progressives, some of whom found Wilson's reform program attractive. Eastern Republicans wanted the United States to intervene on the side of the Allies. In the Midwest, progressive Republicans and German Americans opposed a pro-Allied policy.

The Republicans Select Hughes

Theodore Roosevelt hoped to be the Republican nominee, but his pro-Allied policy made him too controversial. The Republicans turned to Supreme Court Justice Charles Evans Hughes. He had been a progressive governor of New York, was not scarred with the wounds of 1912, and had said little about foreign policy. A remnant of the Progressive party nominated Roosevelt, but he declined and the party soon disappeared. The Republicans offered assurances that they favored some domestic reforms and carefully straddled the more controversial questions of preparedness, neutrality, and loyalty of ethnic groups such as the German Americans.

*P*ICTURING THE PAST ✦ POLITICS & DIPLOMACY
THE ZIMMERMAN TELEGRAM AND CODE BREAKING

The Granger Collection, New York

The use of codes and ciphers, although traditional in warfare, became more sophisticated and important during the twentieth century as radio and telegraphy developed. One of the most sensational examples of this trend came in the First World War with the revelation of the Zimmerman Telegram. In that document, Germany proposed to Mexico an alliance against the United States in the event of war in 1917. British code-breakers, who had been reading German diplomatic traffic, easily intercepted the message, decoded it, and passed it on to Washington. The White House, in turn, used the information to sway reluctant members of Congress to support President Wilson as war with Germany neared. Secret intelligence thus became a publicity tool as well as a military weapon. Published in the newspapers in its encoded and unbroken form, the telegram as pictured here provided a brief but elusive glimpse into a secret world that grew in importance even after the First World War ended.

"He Kept Us Out of War"

For the Democrats, Wilson's nomination was never in question. The excitement occurred over the party's platform and the campaign slogan that arose from it. In his keynote address to the Democratic delegates, a former governor of New York, Martin Glynn, noted that Wilson had maintained neutrality. Each time he referred to this fact the audience exclaimed: "What did we do? What did we do?" and he shouted back: "We didn't go to war! We didn't go to war!"

In the campaign that followed, Wilson employed the themes of peace, progressivism, and prosperity in his speeches. Meanwhile, Hughes had difficulty finding a way to appeal to Republicans who shared Roosevelt's position and to the German-American voters who wanted the nation to stay out of the conflict. Hughes also proved to be a less effective campaigner than the Republicans had hoped, but he had the benefit of a party that still attracted a majority of voters outside the South. To win, the Democrats assembled a coalition of voters in the South

and West, the peace vote, women (who could vote in western states), and Midwestern farmers who were happy with wartime prosperity. Wilson won one of the closest elections in the nation's history. He gained 277 electoral votes from thirty states, while Hughes won 254 electoral votes from eighteen states. The president amassed a little more than 49 percent of the vote, polling 600,000 more popular votes than Hughes did.

Wilson's Attempts to Mediate

The war and its problems had not disappeared during the campaign. Wilson now believed that the time had come to press for a negotiated settlement. Relations with the British had soured during 1916 because of the way the Royal Navy and the British Foreign Office interfered with American shipping in enforcing their blockade against Germany. Meanwhile, the British were becoming more dependent on American loans and credits to pay for the supplies that they had been buying since 1914. Under the circumstances, the president believed, London might be receptive to an American mediation effort. The president also knew that pressure was rising within the German military for unrestricted use of submarines.

On December 18, 1916, Wilson asked the warring countries to state their terms for a negotiated peace. Both the British and the Germans rejected the president's offer; the solution would have to come on the battlefield. In response, Wilson addressed the U.S. Senate on January 22, 1917, in a speech that called for a "Peace Without Victory." He argued that "only a peace among equals can last," and set out a program that included plans to create a league of nations. The attitude of the warring powers was skeptical. The idea of a league of nations also aroused opposition in the Senate. Wilson' failure to consult with his political enemies on this matter was an error that would later plague him.

American Intervention in the War

The German military decided on January 9, 1917, that the submarine could win the war before the United States could move troops to Europe. Unrestricted submarine attacks would be resumed on February 1. Wilson learned of the German decision on January 31 and realized that Berlin had not been negotiating in good faith. He broke diplomatic relations on February 4. The submarine campaign began as scheduled, and American lives were lost. On February 26, the president asked Congress for authority to arm U.S. merchant ships. With peace sentiment still strong on Capitol Hill, the administration faced a tough fight to get the bill passed.

An unexpected revelation about German war aims then happened. British intelligence had intercepted and decoded a secret German diplomatic telegram to its ambassador in Mexico. The "Zimmerman Telegram," named after the German foreign minister Arthur Zimmerman, dangled the return to Mexico of Arizona, New Mexico, and Texas as bait to entice the Mexicans to enter the war on the German side. Wilson released this diplomatic bombshell to the public on March 1, and the House promptly passed the bill to arm merchant ships. Eleven senators, led by Robert M. La Follette of Wisconsin, filibustered against the bill until Congress adjourned on March 4. In fact, Wilson could arm the ships on his own authority, which he did on March 9.

The Outbreak of Hostilities

The submarine campaign was hurting the Allies badly, and defeat seemed possible. One stumbling block to American support for the Allied cause had always been the presence of Russia on the side of the British and French. Alliance with that autocratic monarchy seemed to mock the notion that the Allies were fighting for democratic values. However, the outbreak of revolution in Russia toppled the regime of Czar Nicholas II and seemed to offer some hope for reform. Meanwhile, the Germans sank three American ships on March 18 with large losses. Wilson decided to call Congress into special session on April 2. On a soft spring evening, the president asked for a declaration of war against Germany. "The world must be made safe for democracy," he told them. "It is a fearful thing to lead this great peaceful people into war, into the most terrible and disastrous of all wars, civilization itself seeming to be in the balance. But the right is more precious than peace." Evoking the language of the sixteenth-century German religious reformer, Martin Luther, Wilson said of his nation, "God helping her, she can do no other."

Congress declared war on Germany on April 6, 1917. Although the votes were overwhelming (82 to 7 in the Senate; 373 to 50 in the House), the nation was divided. In large parts of the South and West, peace sentiment was strong because the public felt no need to become involved in European quarrels or to benefit eastern business interests that might profit from the fighting. Opposition to the war remained high among German Americans and Irish Americans. Dedicated reformers and Socialists saw the war as a betrayal of reform ideals.

For Wilson himself, involvement in the war seemed to be the price the nation had to pay to influence the peace settlement. His lofty rhetoric encouraged Americans to believe that a better world could be obtained through the use of military force. In that sense the president paved the way for the later disillusion among Americans that frustrated his ambitious plans for world leadership.

A NATION AT WAR

World War I produced significant changes in the way the United States functioned. The power of the federal government increased dramatically in response to the need to mobilize the nation for war. Average citizens found that they had to respond to government programs and directives in strange and unfamiliar ways, such as accepting bureaucratic rules for their businesses, listening to government propaganda, and changing their eating habits.

Wilson's War Message to Congress, April 2, 1917

In his message to Congress on April 2, 1917, Woodrow Wilson put the decision to go to war with Germany in a strongly moral context that helped make the American involvement in the conflict a war to make the world safe for democracy. The president's language in these concluding paragraphs of his message elevated a foreign policy decision to a national crusade.

. . . It will be all the easier for us to conduct ourselves as belligerents in a high spirit of right and fairness because we act without animus, not in enmity towards a people or with the desire to bring any injury or disadvantage upon them, but only in armed opposition to an irresponsible government which has thrown aside all considerations of humanity and of right and is running amuck. We are, let me say again, the sincere friends of the German people, and shall desire nothing so much as the early reëstablishment of intimate relations of mutual advantage between us,—however hard it may be for them, for the time being, to believe that this is spoken from our hearts. We have borne with their present Government through all these bitter months because of that friendship,—exercising a patience and forbearance which would otherwise have been impossible. We shall, happily, still have an opportunity to prove that friendship in our daily attitude and actions towards the millions of men and women of German birth and native sympathy who live amongst us and share our life, and we shall be proud to prove it towards all who are in fact loyal to their neighbors and to the Government in the hour of test. They are, most of them, as true and loyal Americans as if they had never known any other fealty or allegiance. They will be prompt to stand with us in rebuking and restraining the few who may be of a different mind and purpose. If there should be disloyalty, it will be dealt with with a firm hand of stern repression; but, if it lifts its head at all, it will lift it only here and there and without countenance except from a lawless and malignant few.

It is a distressing and oppressive duty, Gentlemen of the Congress, which I have performed in thus addressing you. There are, it may be, many months of fiery trial and sacrifice ahead of us. It is a fearful thing to lead this great peaceful people into war, into the most terrible and disastrous of all wars, civilization itself seeming to be in the balance. But the right is more precious than peace, and we shall fight for the things which we have always carried nearest our hearts,—for democracy, for the right of those who submit to authority to have a voice in their own Governments, for the rights and liberties of small nations, for a universal dominion of right by such a concert of free peoples as shall bring peace and safety to all nations and make the world itself at last free. To such a task we can dedicate our lives and our fortunes, everything that we are and everything that we have, with the pride of those who know that the day has come when America is privileged to spend her blood and her might for the principles that gave her birth and happiness and the peace which she has treasured. God helping her, she can do no other.

The State of the Conflict in 1917

The government assumed that the American contribution to the war would consist of furnishing money and supplies to the Allied cause. It soon became apparent that American soldiers would have to go across the Atlantic and join in the fighting to achieve an Allied victory. Otherwise, a German military success seemed probable.

As of April 1917, the German army still occupied large portions of France that it had seized in 1914. On the "western front" the two sides fought in elaborate trenches from which soldiers fired at each other or mounted attacks against well-fortified positions. Dug-in artillery and machine guns gave the advantage to the defense. The French suffered more than 1,430,000 casualties on the western front in 1915. The Germans tried to break the will of the French at Verdun in 1916; both sides lost more than 300,000 men in the ensuing struggle. The British attacked in northern France in 1916; 60,000 men were killed or wounded in a single day's fighting. Similar carnage occurred when the British renewed their offensive on the Somme River in 1917. After the French went on the attack in 1917 with heavy casualties, their broken armies mutinied against further slaughter.

U.S. Armed Forces

The Wilson administration did not want to raise an army through volunteer methods. Experience in Europe had shown that a volunteer system was undependable and did not keep trained individuals at their jobs in key war industries. In May 1917, Congress adopted the Selective Service Act. Men between the ages of twenty-one and thirty had to register for the draft; local boards were set up to administer the program. By the end of the war some 24 million young men had been registered, and about 3 million had been called into the armed forces. Another 340,000 men tried to evade the draft and became "slackers." There were also 65,000 men who claimed exemptions for religious reasons.

To command the American Expeditionary Force (AEF), Wilson selected General John J. Pershing, who had pursued Pancho Villa into Mexico. The nation was ill-prepared for war. The army had no plans for a war with Germany in western Europe, and it did not have the rifles and machine guns necessary for a modern conflict. Its staff structure was loaded with old officers who lacked initiative and experience in commanding large numbers of men.

Training the Army

Training the troops for warfare in Europe was not a simple process, and the indoctrination that the men received often reflected progressive ideals. The government endeavored to maintain the purity of troops with extensive programs to limit excessive drinking and venereal disease. The army also provided an optional opportunity to acquire inexpensive life insurance, which increased popular interest in such programs after the war.

Enlisted men also received intelligence tests that had little impact on their fighting ability but did enhance psychology's reputation as a social science. Men who could read were asked to identify the unit of electromotive force from a list consisting of *ohm, ampere,* and *watt.* Soldiers who could not read were asked to specify the missing item in pictures of a tennis court without a net, or a camel without a hump. When the tests showed

no significant difference in intelligence between black soldiers and white soldiers, the army recalculated the results to conform with its prejudices.

While the army was being raised, the navy faced a more immediate challenge. During April 1917, German submarines sank almost 900,000 tons of Allied shipping. At that rate, half the oceangoing shipping available to the British would disappear by the end of 1917. The British had only enough food for six weeks in reserve.

The American naval commander in Europe, Admiral William S. Sims, turned to convoys to escort vulnerable merchant ships across the Atlantic. American destroyers on escort duty became a key part of the strategy that eventually ended the submarine threat. Troops began to move toward Europe. The Germans did not regard troopships as significant targets because of their belief that American soldiers lacked fighting ability. Two million men were shipped to France before the Armistice was signed and they provided the margin for an Allied victory.

Financing the War

The government raised a third of the money for the war, some $9 billion, through increased taxes. The remainder came from citizens who purchased "Liberty Bonds" from the government. These interest-bearing securities brought in more than $15 billion. Children were taught to save their pennies and nickels for thrift stamps. They learned a rhyme to urge them on:

> Hush little thrift stamp,
> Don't you cry;
> You'll be a war bond
> By and by.

Those who were unwilling to contribute were told that failure to buy bonds was unpatriotic and helped the Germans. In some cases, violence was used to coerce the reluctant contributors.

The total cost of the war exceeded $35 billion because the United States loaned more than $11.2 billion to the Allies. In June 1917, one British official told his government that "If loan stops, war stops." President Wilson counted on the Allies' financial dependence on the United States as a weapon to use in achieving the goals of his postwar diplomacy.

Herbert Hoover and Food for the Allies

The Allies also desperately needed food. The British depended on supplies from their empire, which took a long time to reach Europe by ship and were

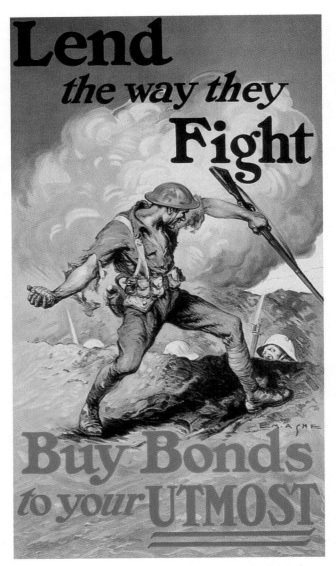

The government also employed advertising to sell bonds. This poster showing an American soldier at the front was one of the ways that Washington sought to awaken public opinion to the need for bond sales.
Gift of Henry Colgate, Picker Art Gallery, Colgate University

vulnerable to submarine attack. Without American food, sent via convoys under the protection of the U.S. Navy, serious shortages would have impaired Allied ability to wage war. To mobilize the agricultural resources of the United States, Congress passed the Lever Act, which established a Food Administration. Wilson selected Herbert Hoover to head this new agency. A mining engineer from California, Hoover had gained international fame through his work to feed the starving people of Belgium. He threw his abundant energy into persuading Americans to save their food for shipment overseas.

Hoover asked Americans to observe "wheatless days" and "meatless days" because "wheatless days in America make sleepless nights in Germany." Women and children planted "war gardens" to raise more fruits and vegetables. Higher prices induced farmers to expand their production. The wheat crop was 637 million bushels in 1917; a year later it stood at 921 million bushels.

Prohibition and the War Effort

The campaign to conserve food boosted the effort to restrict the sale and use of alcoholic beverages. Scarce grain supplies had to be reserved for soldiers in the field and Allied populations overseas. As a wartime slogan put it, "Shall the many have food or the few have drink?" Prohibitionists argued that drink impaired the fighting ability of the armed forces and those working in defense plants. The connection of the brewing industry with the German Americans also worked in favor of the prohibitionist cause.

Congress passed legislation to restrict the production of liquor, and in December 1917 the lawmakers approved the Eighteenth Amendment, which banned the production and sale of alcoholic beverages. All that remained was to ensure ratification of the amendment by the required number of states, a task that the Anti-Saloon League was well equipped to handle.

Managing the Wartime Economy

Coordination of the economy was not limited to the agricultural sector. The president used his power to wage the war to establish the expanded bureaucracy required to manage production of war supplies and oversee their shipment to the Allies. Wilson did not seek to have government take over business. He hoped that a business-government partnership would develop naturally. However, much government encouragement and direction were needed before the business community fully joined the war effort.

The eventual record of mobilization was a mixed one. The United States tried to build ships and planes under the direction of government agencies. Those efforts produced at least one British-designed plane that used American-built engines, and large numbers of merchant ships were constructed in American shipyards. On the other hand, Pershing's men used British and French artillery and equipment. The government had more success with expanding the production of coal through the Fuel Administration. Coal prices were raised in order to stimulate production, and "daylight savings time" was established in order to reduce the use of fuel for nonmilitary purposes.

Wartime Economic Problems

The nation's railroads became so confused during the first year of the war that immense and costly transportation snarls resulted. The armed forces insisted on immediate passage for railcars with war supplies; tieups of rail traffic all over the East Coast resulted. Finally the government took over the railroads in January 1918, placing the secretary of the treasury, William G. McAdoo, in charge of operations. McAdoo raised the wages of railroad workers, dropped inefficient routes, and allowed the lines to raise their rates. The tieups soon disappeared.

Even before U.S. entry into the war, the government had made plans for coordinating industrial production. Staffed with "dollar-a-year men" whose salaries were paid by their former companies, the War Industries Board (WIB) was supposed to make sure that the purchasing and allocation of supplies for the armed forces followed rational programs. The WIB fell well short of this standard during 1917. In March 1918, under pressure from Congress and Republican critics such as Theodore Roosevelt, Wilson placed Bernard Baruch, a Wall Street speculator and contributor to the Democratic party, at the head of the War Industries Board.

Bernard Baruch and the War Board

Baruch and his aides attacked needless waste in production. They standardized products, established priorities for the shipment of important goods, and set prices to encourage factories to turn out goods quickly. Simply by altering bicycle designs, the WIB saved 2,000 tons of steel for war goods.

Not all industries cooperated willingly. Baruch had to compromise with both the automobile and the steel industries to induce them to abandon peacetime production in favor of handling wartime orders. In the process, the industries made significant profits from their government contracts. As one steel executive put it, "We are all making more money out of this war than the average human being ought to."

Labor and the War

The American Federation of Labor and its president, Samuel Gompers, threw their support behind the war effort. In return for the government's agreement to allow unions to participate in economic policy making, Gompers and the AFL promised not to strike or to press for union shops in factories. Between 1917 and 1920, the AFL gained more than 2 million members.

Nonunion workers also benefitted from the government's wartime policies. The National War Labor Board, headed by former President William Howard Taft, set standards for wages and hours that were far more generous and enlightened than those private industry had provided. A minimum wage was mandated, as were maximum hours and improved working conditions. The government also created housing for war workers and began a system of medical care and life insurance for federal employees.

Black Americans in the War

While some blacks wanted no part of the European conflict, most African American leaders agreed with W. E. B. Du Bois that they should "forget about special grievances and close our ranks shoulder to shoulder with our own fellow white citizens." Some 367,000 black soldiers served during the war; 42,000 of them saw combat in France. Most of the African American servicemen, however, were assigned to labor battalions and supply duties. The War Department moved very slowly to commission black officers; at the end of the war there were only 1,200. Several African American units fought bravely. Others were given inadequate training and equipment, but when they performed poorly in combat the blame was placed on their supposed inferiority. Blacks had little motivation to fight in the first place. Moreover, for some blacks in France, the experience of being in a country without a long tradition of racism made them long for greater freedom at home.

African American troops stationed in the United States faced familiar dangers. In August 1917, in Houston, Texas, black soldiers reacted to segregation and abuse by the police with attacks on the police and on white citizens that left sixteen whites and four soldiers dead. The army indicted 118 soldiers, of whom 110 were convicted by courts-martial. Nineteen black soldiers were hanged.

Growing Racial Tension

Racial tensions intensified elsewhere in the nation. During the summer of 1917, race riots in East St. Louis, Illinois, resulted in the deaths of forty blacks and nine whites. Forty-eight lynchings occurred in 1917 and sixty-three in 1918. Facing discrimination and violence, blacks responded with a heightened sense of outrage. Marches were held to protest the race riots. Banners called upon President Wilson to "Bring Democracy to America Before You Carry It to Europe."

During the war the black migration to northern cities accelerated. As the African American communities in Chicago, New York, Philadelphia, and other northern cities grew, black newspapers began publishing articles about "The New Negro" who did not "fear the face of day. The time for cringing is over." The repressive actions of the Wilson administration fed the new currents of militance among black Americans.

Women in Wartime

The great achievement of American women during World War I was winning the right of suffrage. The leaders of the National American Woman Suffrage Association decided that identification with the war offered the surest and fastest road to achieving their goal. Carrie Chapman Catt argued that giving women the vote would enable them to offset disloyal elements at home. "Every slacker has a vote," said Catt, a vote that newly enfranchised women could counter. Members of NAWSA appeared at rallies and proclaimed that suffrage should be a "war measure" that would repay women for their contributions to the war. The National Woman's party, on the other hand, picketed the White House to embarrass Wilson for failing to support woman suffrage. The combined impact of these tactics led to the passage of the woman suffrage amendment in the House of Representatives in January 1918. Wilson came out in favor of the amendment just before the congressional elections of that year. The Senate still had to act, but the war had made possible the eventual victory of the campaign to give women the vote.

Beyond the success of woman suffrage, however, the war did not go on long enough to produce lasting changes in the condition of American women. Only about 400,000 more women joined the labor force; some 8 million found better-paying jobs as a result of the conflict. More than 20,000 women served in the military. The navy and the marines enlisted 13,000 of them, largely in office jobs. The army employed more than 5,000 as nurses. In industry, women were hired as drivers, farm workers, and secretaries. As soon as the war ended, they were expected to relinquish these jobs to returning servicemen. As a Chicago woman complained, "During the war they called us heroines, but they throw us on the scrapheap now."

Civil Liberties in Wartime

The Wilson administration believed that winning the war required mobilization of public opinion to offset potential opposition to the conflict. As a result, the White House mounted a campaign of laws, agencies, and popular spirit to arouse support for the war and to quell dissent. In doing so, however, Woodrow Wilson

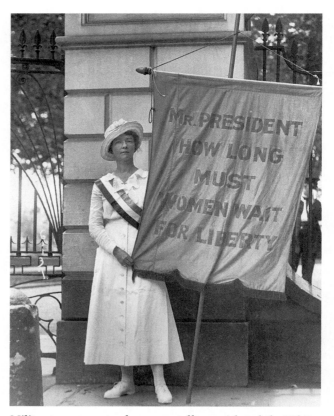

Militant proponents of woman suffrage picketed the White House in 1917–1918 to move President Wilson to support their cause. Their presence embarrassed the president and several of the picketers went to jail for their beliefs.
© Bettmann/UPI/Corbis

and the men around him abused and restricted the civil liberties of many Americans.

To awaken national enthusiasm, the government created the Committee on Public Information (CPI) on April 13, 1917, and President Wilson named George Creel, a former newspaperman, as its head. Creel called his task "the world's greatest adventure in advertising"; he saw his role as one of fusing Americans into "one white-hot mass . . . with fraternity, devotion, courage, and deathless determination." To spread its message, the CPI used pamphlets, billboards, and motion pictures such as *The American Indian Gets into the War Game*. Seventy-five thousand speakers known as "Four-Minute Men" (because of the length of their talks) spoke to audiences throughout the nation.

The themes of the CPI's appeal were simple, patriotic, and strident. Four-Minute Men asked listeners: "Do you want to take the slightest chance of meeting Prussianism here in America?" The great national goal was unity; the Germans were depraved animals; and the nation was engaged in a crusade to "make the world safe for democracy." Wilson's wartime speeches described the United States as "an instrument in the hands of God to see that liberty is made secure for mankind."

The Limits of Dissent

To guard against opposition to the war, the Wilson administration and Congress placed legislative limits on the ability of Americans to criticize the government or the war effort. The Espionage Act of 1917 curbed espionage and sabotage, but made its definitions so sweeping that they embraced even public criticism of the war and its conduct. A person who violated the law could be sentenced to twenty years in prison. The Trading with the Enemy Act, passed in October 1917, authorized the postmaster general to suspend the mailing privileges of foreign-language periodicals and newspapers that he deemed offensive to the government. Postmaster General Albert S. Burleson used that law and the Espionage Act to bar from the mails publications that he considered treasonous or seditious. In 1918, Congress passed the Alien Act, which gave the government broad powers to deport any noncitizen who advocated revolution or anarchism. Most sweeping was the Sedition Act of 1918, which prohibited "uttering, printing, writing, or publishing any disloyal, profane, scurrilous, or abusive language" about either the government or the armed forces.

These laws were vigorously enforced. Burleson pursued critics of the administration relentlessly. The Socialist magazine *The Masses* was barred from the mails for carrying articles claiming that "this is Woodrow Wilson's and Wall Street's War." The Justice Department was equally vigilant. People were sent to prison for saying that "Wilson is a wooden-headed son of a bitch" or remarking that this was "a rich man's war." Eugene V. Debs, the perennial Socialist candidate for president, received a ten-year prison sentence for opposing the draft and the war. The American Protective League, a volunteer organization designed to locate draft evaders, became a vigilante branch of the Justice Department that used wiretapping, illegal searches, and other lawless techniques to find "slackers" and other opponents of the war.

Wartime Hysteria

The zeal of the government to stamp out dissent was matched by private hysteria toward Germans. Sauerkraut became "liberty cabbage," hamburgers reemerged as "Salisbury steak," and some cities gave up pretzels. Speaking the German language in public was banned in

half of the states by 1918, and German literary works vanished from libraries. Musicians with German names, such as the violinist Fritz Kreisler, found their careers crippled.

Some German Americans suffered more serious injuries. When they refused to buy war bonds, mobs beat them until they promised to contribute. Editorials warned: "YOUR NEIGHBOR, YOUR MAID, YOUR LAWYER, YOUR WAITER MAY BE A GERMAN SPY." Radicals, too, were the victims of mob violence. Frank Little, an organizer for the Industrial Workers of the World, was hanged from a railroad trestle in Montana for denouncing the war at a labor rally.

The Political Legacy of Repression

The government had a legitimate reason to be concerned about German espionage, but the repression of civil liberties during the war was excessive. President Wilson did not order cabinet officials to engage in such conduct, but he failed to keep them in check when he learned about what they were doing. The government's campaign against radicals and progressives undermined support for the president in domestic politics. In his eagerness to win the war, Wilson had allowed his government to destroy part of his own political base. He and the Democrats paid for that policy in the 1918 and 1920 election campaigns.

THE ROAD TO VICTORY

During the late winter of 1918, as American troops arrived in France, the Allies faced a dangerous military crisis. In November 1917, the Communist revolution in Russia had taken that nation out of the Allied coalition and enabled the Germans to move troops to the western front. Berlin hoped to achieve victory before the Americans could reinforce the Allies. The German attack came on March 21, 1918, and made impressive gains until the Allies held. When further attacks were made against the French in April and May, American reinforcements helped stop the assault. At battles near Chateau-Thierry and in Belleau Wood in early June, the men of the AEF endured frightful losses but halted the Germans.

The Germans made one more offensive thrust in mid-July, and the British, French, and Americans repelled it as well. Counterattacks moved the Germans backward, a retreat that continued until the end of the war. In September 1918, the American army went on the offensive at the town of Saint-Mihiel near the southern end of the trenches. At the end of the month,

Map 22.3 *American Participation on the Western Front*
This map indicates how the American Expeditionary Force helped to repel German offensives in 1918 and then pushed the enemy back toward the German border.
View an animated version of this map or related maps at http://history.wadsworth.com/passages2e.

Americans launched another thrust toward the Meuse River and the Argonne Forest. Their casualties were heavy, but the AEF pierced the German defenses to threaten key supply routes of the enemy.

Wilson's Peace Program

Wilson had set out his views on peace in a major address to Congress on January 8, 1918. Using the archives of the Czarist government, the Russian Communists had released secret treaties that the Allies had made before 1917 dividing up Europe and the Middle East once victory was achieved. These documents cast doubt on Allied claims that they were fighting for unselfish reasons. Wilson endeavored to shape the Allied answer and regain the diplomatic initiative.

To present the American cause in a better light, Wilson offered a peace program with fourteen specific elements that became known as the Fourteen Points. Among the key provisions were freedom of the seas, free trade, and more open diplomacy. Freedom of the seas would prevent a repetition of the submarine threat the United States had faced before entering the war. Wilson believed that secret treaties and balance of power diplomacy had helped bring about the war itself. The president advocated national self-determination for all nations. He meant that the borders of countries should reflect the national origins of the people who lived in a particular area. He also advocated an "association of nations" to keep the peace.

The End of the Fighting

The Fourteen Points would not be easy to achieve. After four years of slaughter, Britain and France wanted to punish Germany and cripple its ability to wage war. They disliked Wilson's criticism of their war aims and his interference with European policies. For the desperate Germans, the Fourteen Points seemed much more appealing than negotiations with London and Paris. In early October a civilian government in Germany asked Wilson to arrange an armistice based on the Fourteen Points. Working through Colonel House, the president negotiated an agreement for an end to the fighting. He also used the threat of a separate settlement with the Germans to induce the British and French to accept the Fourteen Points and attend the peace conference. The fighting ended on November 11, 1918, at 11:00 in the morning.

Woodrow Wilson had achieved a diplomatic triumph with the conclusion of the armistice, but his success proved to be temporary. Even as he prepared to lead the American delegation to Paris, his domestic political base was eroding. During the war, he had proclaimed, "politics is adjourned." In fact, however, partisan battles continued with both Wilson and his enemies using the war for their own political purposes.

The 1918 Elections

Throughout the conflict President Wilson kept the Republicans at arm's length and treated the conflict as a war for Democrats only. He did not bring Republicans into his government at the highest levels, and he attacked Republicans who opposed his policies. Meanwhile, his enemies capitalized on the unhappiness of farmers and workers over the administration's domestic programs. Midwestern farmers, for example, disliked the price controls that had been imposed on wheat. They complained that southerners in Congress had prevented similar price controls from being put on cotton. As a result, wheat farmers saw their profits held down while cotton producers did well. Progressives who had supported Wilson in 1916 recoiled from the administration's repressive tactics toward dissenters. In late October 1918, Wilson tried to stave off the defeat with an appeal to the American people to elect a Democratic Congress. The statement allowed Wilson's enemies to claim that he had been decisively repudiated when the

The American Expeditionary Force saw major combat during the closing stages of the war. An artillery detachment supports an advance of soldiers in France.
U.S. Signal Corps. Photo No. 111-SC-26063 in the National Archives

results showed that both the House and the Senate would have Republican majorities. For a president who needed bipartisan support in the Senate for any treaty he might write at the up-coming Peace Conference in Paris, it was a major blunder.

The Paris Peace Conference

In a break with the tradition that presidents did not travel outside the country, Wilson had already decided to attend the Peace Conference. Despite Republican criticism, he believed that he needed to direct the negotiations himself. Moreover, his selection of delegates to accompany him showed his continuing insensitivity to bipartisanship. The five men he chose were his close allies, with only one nominal Republican among them.

Wilson did not send any senators to Paris. Had he done so, he would have had to include Senator Henry Cabot Lodge of Massachusetts, the next chairman of the Foreign Relations Committee. Wilson and Lodge hated each other. If Wilson could not take Lodge, he could not invite any other senators. Unwilling to accept advice or share the credit, Wilson also declined to select other prominent Republicans such as William Howard Taft or Elihu Root.

The President in Europe

Europeans greeted Wilson with rapturous applause. When he arrived in Paris, 2 million people cheered him as he rode up the Champs-Elysees. They called him

President Wilson's Appeal to the Voters to Return a Democratic Congress October 24, 1918

Faced with worsening Democratic prospects in the 1918 elections, President Wilson issued an appeal to the voters to elect candidates of his party to strengthen his hand in making peace. His tone, however, alienated Republican voters without rousing Democrats to get out and vote. The appeal was a political disaster for the president and his party.

My Fellow Countrymen:

. . . This is no time either for divided counsels or for divided leadership. Unity of command is as necessary now in civil action as it is upon the field of battle. If the control of the House and the Senate should be taken away from the party now in power an opposing majority could assume control of legislation and oblige all action to be taken amid contest and obstruction.

The return of a Republican majority to either house of the Congress would, moreover, be interpreted on the other side of the water as a repudiation of my leadership. Spokesmen of the Republican party are urging you to elect a Republican Congress in order to back up and support the President, but, even if they should in this impose upon some credulous voters on this side of the water, they would impose on no one on the other side. It is well understood there as well as here that Republican leaders desire not so much to support the President as to control him.

The peoples of the allied countries with whom we are associated against Germany are quite familiar with the significance of elections. They would find it very difficult to believe that the voters of the United States had chosen to support their President by electing to the Congress a majority controlled by those who are not in fact in sympathy with the attitude and action of the Administration.

I need not tell you, my fellow countrymen, that I am asking your support not for my own sake or for the sake of a political party, but for the sake of the nation itself in order that its inward duty of purpose may be evident to all the world. In ordinary times I would not feel at liberty to make such an appeal to you. In ordinary times divided counsels can be endured without permanent hurt to the country. But these are not ordinary times.

If in these critical days it is your wish to sustain me with undivided minds, I beg that you will say so in a way which it will not be possible to misunderstand, either here at home or among our associates on the other side of the sea. I submit my difficulties and my hopes to you.

WOODROW WILSON

"Wilson *le Juste* [the Just]" and expected him to fulfill their desires for a peaceful world and for revenge against the Germans. Wilson came to believe that he could appeal to the peoples of the world over the heads of their leaders to support his program of international peace.

The other major figures at the conference were David Lloyd George, the prime minister of Great Britain, and Georges Clemenceau, the premier of France. Both men were hard-headed realists who did not share Wilson's idealism. "God gave us the Ten Commandments, and we broke them," said Clemenceau. "Wilson gives us the Fourteen Points. We shall see." Along with the prime minister of Italy, Vittorio Orlando, Wilson, Clemenceau, and Lloyd George made up the "Big Four" who directed the Peace Conference toward a settlement of the issues that the war had raised.

The Shadow of Bolshevism

Four years of war had left the world in disorder, and nations large and small came to Paris to have their fate decided. A striking absentee was the new Soviet

Union, the Communist nation that the Russian Bolsheviks had established after their successful revolution. Civil war raged in Russia between the "Reds" of Communism and the "Whites," who wanted to block Bolshevik control of the nation. Meanwhile, the Bolsheviks' authoritarian leader, Vladimir Ilyich Lenin and his colleagues wished to extend Communist rule beyond Russia's borders.

In 1919, national leaders worried that the infection of Communism might spread into western Europe, and they had not recognized the government in Moscow. The French and British had tried to strangle the new regime by providing financial support for its enemies and intervening militarily in some areas of Russia. Helping its allies and trying to undermine Bolshevism, the United States had dispatched small detachments of troops to Siberia and Vladivostok in 1918 and 1919. The American presence in Russia became a long-standing grievance for the Soviet regime that emerged from the Bolshevik victory.

The Terms of Peace

The negotiations about the terms of peace with Germany produced both victories and defeats for Wilson. He had to accept the inclusion in the treaty of a clause that assigned Germany "guilt" for starting the war in 1914. That language proved to be a source of discontent for a resurgent Germany in the 1920s and 1930s. The Germans were also assessed severe financial penalties in the form of reparations that eventually amounted to $33 billion, a provision that further fueled their resentment in the 1930s.

Wilson also achieved partial success in his efforts to establish self-determination in the peace settlement. He accepted Italian desire for control of the city of Fiume on the Adriatic Coast, could not block Japan from territorial gains in China, and was unable to prevent several groups of ethnic and national minorities in eastern Europe from being left under the dominance of other ruling groups, as in the case of Germans in the new nation of Czechoslovakia.

The League of Nations

Wilson's main goal was establishment of the League of Nations. The league consisted of a General Assembly of all member nations, a Council made up of Great Britain, France, Italy, Japan, and the United States, with four other countries that the Assembly selected; and an international court of justice. For Wilson, the "heart of the covenant" of the League of Nations was Article X, which required member nations to preserve

When Wilson arrived in Europe, he received a hero's welcome. As he embarked in Great Britain and walked in with Lloyd George and King George V, schoolgirls threw flowers in his path.
U.S. Signal Corps. Photo No. 111-SC-62979 in the National Archives

each other's independence and take concerted action when any member of the league was attacked.

In February 1919, Wilson returned to the United States for the end of the congressional session. Senator Lodge then circulated a document that thirty-seven senators signed. It stated that the treaty must be amended or they would not vote for it. This "round-robin" had drawn enough votes to defeat the treaty unless Wilson made changes in the document. The president attacked his critics publicly, further intensifying partisan animosity.

Wilson and the Treaty of Versailles

To secure changes in the treaty for the Senate, Wilson had to make concessions to the other nations at the Peace Conference when he returned to Europe. These included the imposition of reparations on Germany, the war guilt clause, and limits on German's ability to re-arm. In return, Wilson obtained provisions that protected the Monroe Doctrine from league action, removed domestic issues from the league's proceedings, and allowed any nation to leave the world organization with two years' notice. The final version of the Treaty of Versailles was signed on June 28, 1919, in the Hall of Mirrors at the Palace of Versailles outside Paris. For all of its problems and weaknesses, the treaty was the closest thing to a reasonable settlement that Wilson could have obtained.

Map 22.4 *Europe after the Peace Conference, 1920*
The Treaty of Versailles attempted to contain Germany against future aggressive behavior. Note the number of new states created out of the old Russian and Austro-Hungarian empires. Nonetheless, Germany remained a major force in Central Europe.

The most dedicated political opponent of Woodrow Wilson was Senator Henry Cabot Lodge of Massachusetts. He said that he had never expected to hate anyone in politics with the intense dislike that he felt toward Wilson. The feeling was mutual.
© Bettmann/Corbis

The Senate and the League

The Republicans now controlled the Senate forty-nine to forty-seven, so the president could not win the necessary two-thirds majority without the votes of some of his political opponents. Some Republicans were opposed to the treaty as an infringement upon American sovereignty, no matter what it said. These were the fourteen "irreconcilables"; two Democrats were also part of this group. Wilson had to seek help from the twelve "mild reservationists," who wanted only changes in the wording, and the twenty-three "strong reservationists," who sought to limit the league's power over American actions. The president could count on about thirty-five of the forty-seven Democrats in the Senate. Assuming that some of the mild reservationists would support the treaty, the Democrats had to find twenty Republican votes to gain the necessary sixty-four votes to approve the treaty.

In the political battle that ensued, Senator Lodge focused on Article X and the issue of whether Congress should be able to approve an American participation in the league's attempts to prevent international aggression. Lodge also played for time, hoping that public opinion would turn against the treaty. He had the lengthy treaty read aloud to the Senate. Meanwhile, Wilson insisted that the treaty be approved without changes or "reservations."

Wilson's Tour and Collapse

By September 1919, with the treaty in trouble, Wilson decided to take his case to the American people. Despite audience approval of his speeches, Wilson's

ICTURING THE PAST◆SOCIAL & CULTURAL EVENTS

THE INFLUENZA EPIDEMIC OF 1918

National Archives #165-WW-269.c-7

The impact of disease on American history is still understood only in an incomplete way. The influenza epidemic of 1918–1919 was such an event: it shaped the behavior of Americans during the last months of the First World War and into the early period of peacetime. The flu virus, which spread around the world so rapidly, swamped the existing medical facilities and public health apparatus of major cities. Believing that the malady might be spread by mouth, citizens took precautions like the one used by the policeman shown in this photograph directing traffic and selling Liberty Bonds.

Nothing that was done to halt the pandemic really did much good. In the end, the sickness simply ran its course, leaving millions of people dead worldwide. Some earlier books about the World War I period barely mentioned it, but in recent years historians have become more sensitive to how sickness and infection operate to influence the course of history. This picture and its appearance in your text is a testament to that change in how historians think about the past. Other examples of similar episodes of illnesses in American history appear elsewhere in the text.

---

health broke under the strain. The circulatory problems that had bothered him for years erupted. He was rushed back to Washington, where he suffered a massive stroke on October 2, 1919. His left side was paralyzed, seriously impairing his ability to govern.

The president's wife and his doctors did not reveal how sick Wilson was. The first lady screened his few visitors and decided what documents her husband would see. Wilson was only a shell of a president and the government drifted.

The Defeat of the League

The Senate voted on the treaty on November 19, 1919, with reservations that Lodge had included in the document. Lodge would have required Congress to approve any sanctions imposed by the league on an aggressor. When the Democratic leader in the Senate asked Wilson about possible compromises, he replied

that changing Article X "cuts the very heart out of the Treaty." The Senate rejected the treaty with reservations by a vote of thirty-nine to fifty-five. Then the lawmakers voted on the treaty without reservations. It lost, thirty-eight in favor and fifty-three against. In the end, the decision about a possible compromise with Lodge was Wilson's to make. He told Senate Democrats: "Let Lodge compromise."

FROM WAR TO PEACE

Meanwhile the nation experienced domestic upheaval. Citizens grappled with labor unrest, a Red Scare (fear of Communist or "Red" subversion), a surge in prices following the end of the war, and an influenza epidemic. The postwar period was one of the most difficult that Americans had ever experienced.

The influenza epidemic began with dramatic suddenness at the end of 1918 and spread rapidly through the population. No vaccines existed to combat it; no antibiotics were available to fight the secondary infections that resulted from it. More than 650,000 Americans died of the disease in 1918 and 1919. The number of dead bodies overwhelmed the funeral facilities of many major cities; coffins filled a circus tent in Boston. Children skipping rope made the epidemic part of their song:

> I had a little bird,
> And his name was Enza;
> I opened the window,
> And in flew Enza!

The influenza pandemic receded in 1920, leaving a worldwide total of 20 million people dead.

The Waning Spirit of Progressivism

By 1919, the campaigns for Prohibition and woman suffrage were nearing their goals. Enough states had ratified the Prohibition amendment by January 1919 to make it part of the Constitution. In October 1919, Congress passed the Volstead Act to enforce Prohibition. Wilson vetoed the measure, but Congress passed it over his objection. The United States became "dry" on January 15, 1920. Prohibitionists expected widespread compliance and easy enforcement.

After the House passed the woman suffrage amendment in 1918, it took the Senate another year to approve it. Suffrage advocates then lobbied the states to ratify the amendment. When the Tennessee legislature voted for ratification in August 1920, three-quarters of the states had approved woman suffrage. Women would now "take their appropriate place in political work," said Carrie Chapman Catt.

The Struggles of Labor

After the Armistice, the nation shifted from a wartime economy to peacetime pursuits with dizzying speed. The government declined to manage the changeover from a wartime to a peacetime economy. High inflation developed as prices were freed from wartime controls, and unemployment rose as returning soldiers sought jobs. The government's index of the cost of living rose nearly 80 percent above prewar levels in 1919 and it went up to 105 percent a year later. Unemployment reached nearly 12 percent by 1921.

Unions struck for higher wages. Seattle shipyard workers walked off their jobs, and the Industrial Workers of the World called for a general strike to support them. When 60,000 laborers took part in the protest, the mayor of Seattle, Ole Hanson, responded with mobilization of police and soldiers that made him "the Saviour of Seattle." Newspapers depicted the strike as a prelude to communist revolution.

The Reaction Against Strikes

The largest industrial strike of the year occurred in the steel industry. The American Federation of Labor tried to organize all steelworkers to end the seven-day week and the twelve-hour day. In September, 350,000 steel workers left the mills. The steel manufacturers refused to recognize the union. Strikebreakers were hired from among the ranks of unemployed blacks, Hispanics, and immigrants. The steel companies kept their factories running while they waited for the strike to be broken through police harassment and internal divisions within the unions. Conservatives attacked the radical background of one of the strike organizers, William Z. Foster. Although the strikers remained united for several months, they could not withstand the accumulated financial and political pressure from management. This first effort at a strike by an entire workforce failed in early 1920.

Other strikes of the year included a walkout by coal miners and a strike by police in Boston. Inflation had hit the Boston police hard, and they struck late in 1919. When looting and other criminal acts occurred because of the absence of police, public opinion turned against the striking officers. The governor of Massachusetts, Calvin Coolidge, became a national celebrity when he said: "There is no right to strike against the public safety, by anybody, anywhere, any time." To many middle-class Americans, the social order seemed to be unraveling.

An Upsurge of Racial Violence

Racial tensions also flared up. There were frequent lynchings in the South. In the North, the tide of African American migration produced confrontations with angry whites. Rioting against blacks occurred in Washington, D.C., in June 1919. During the same summer a young black man was stoned and killed when whites found him on a Chicago beach from which African Americans had been excluded. Angry blacks attacked the police who had stood by while the killing occurred. Five days of violence followed in which thirty-eight people, most of them black, were killed and another 500 were injured. Two dozen other cities saw violent episodes during what one black leader called "the red summer."

The Communist "Menace"

Searching for a cause of the social unrest that pervaded the nation, Americans looked to radicalism and communism. The emotions aroused by the government's wartime propaganda fueled the "Red Scare" of 1919–1920. About 70,000 people belonged to one of the two branches of the Communist party. However, the radicals' reliance on violence and terrorism inflamed popular fears. When several mail bombs exploded on May 1, 1919, and dozens of others were found in the mail, press and public called for government action.

Attorney General A. Mitchell Palmer established a division in the Justice Department to hunt for radicals; the division was headed by J. Edgar Hoover, who later became director of the Federal Bureau of Investigation. In November 1919, Palmer launched raids against suspected radicals, and a month later he deported 300 aliens to the Soviet Union. In the process, the legal rights of these suspects were violated, and they were kept in custody, away from their families and attorneys.

Throughout the country civil liberties came under assault. State legislatures investigated alleged subversives. Communist parties were outlawed, antiradical legislation was adopted, and Socialists were expelled from the New York legislature. Suspected members of the IWW and other groups were subjected to vigilante violence and official repression.

The U.S. Supreme Court upheld the constitutionality of most of the laws that restricted civil liberties during the war and the Red Scare. Justice Oliver Wendell Holmes, Jr., devised a means of testing whether the First Amendment had been violated. In *Schenck v. United States* (1919), he asked whether words or utterances posed "a clear and present danger" of interference with the government, the war effort, or civil order. The answer was that they had. The Court also sustained the conviction of Eugene V. Debs for speaking out against the war.

By 1920, however, the Red Scare lost momentum. Palmer forecast a violent uprising on May 1, 1920, and when it did not occur, his credibility suffered. Some government officials, especially in the Department of Labor, opposed Palmer's deportation policies. Other public figures, such as Charles Evans Hughes, denounced New York's efforts against socialist lawmakers. During this period, however, police in Massachusetts arrested two anarchists and Italian aliens, Nicola Sacco and Bartolomeo Vanzetti, for their alleged complicity in a robbery and murder at a shoe company in South Braintree, Massachusetts.

Gradually, the frenzy of Red-hunting abated. During the Wilson administration a dangerous precedent had been set for government interference with individ-

In the 1920 election, Warren G. Harding promised "normalcy." To evoke the spirit of bygone days, he began his campaign from his front porch. Later he took to the campaign trail in a more modern manner. Harding won an overwhelming victory.
Brown Brothers

ual rights. The bureaucratic machinery was in place for future attempts to compel loyalty and punish dissent.

Harding and "Normalcy"

In early 1920, with Wilson ill and the government leaderless, the Senate took up the Treaty of Versailles with reservations once again in March. On March 19, the treaty received forty-nine votes in favor and thirty-five against, seven short of the number needed to ratify it. Wilson had said that he would not approve the pact with reservations, but the vote showed that a compromise could have been reached. Wilson hoped that the election would be a "solemn referendum" on the treaty, but that did not happen.

The Republicans had expected that Theodore Roosevelt would be their nominee in 1920, but he died on January 6, 1919, of circulatory ailments and heart problems. The Republicans turned to Senator Warren G. Harding of Ohio. To run with him, the convention named Governor Calvin Coolidge of Massachusetts. Harding emphasized a return to older values, which he labeled "normalcy." He called for "not heroics, but healing."

For the Democrats the nominee was Governor James M. Cox of Ohio, a moderate progressive from the party's anti-prohibitionist wing, and his running mate was Franklin D. Roosevelt of New York. The Democratic candidates supported the League of Nations; the Republicans generally dodged the subject until the end of the campaign when Harding advocated rejection of the treaty. The issue did not have much effect. Voters wanted to turn the Democrats out of office. They did so in a landslide. Harding received 16 million votes to 9 million for Cox.

CONCLUSION

With the election of the conservative Harding, the era of progressivism ended. The voters associated reform and uplift with big government, high taxes, and intrusion into their private lives. For a time they wanted no more of such programs. Disillusioned by the outcome of the war and the upheaval of 1917–1919, Americans longed for quiet and conservatism.

The legacy of progressivism was a stronger presidency, a larger national government, and a weakened party system. The regulatory machinery to oversee business was still in place if a future president wished to use it. Progressives had addressed many serious issues—child labor, working conditions for men and women laborers, the plight of the unemployed. They had improved the quality of politics and opened up the system to middle-class citizens. Woman suffrage had been achieved, and the experiment of Prohibition was underway. However, reformers had done less for African Americans, Hispanics, immigrants, and Native Americans. Despite the excesses of the war, the United States was a more humane and just nation in 1920 than it had been in 1901.

Recommended Readings

Auchincloss, Louis. *Woodrow Wilson* (2000). A brief, readable life of this important president.

Chambers, John Whiteclay. *The Tyranny of Change: America in the Progressive Era, 1890–1920* (2000). A helpful synthesis of this whole period.

Clements, Kendrick. *The Presidency of Woodrow Wilson* (1992). Offers a thorough guide to the accomplishments of Wilson in office.

Cooper, John Milton. *Breaking the Heart of the World* (2002). An excellent examination of the fight over the League of Nations.

Davis, Donald E., and Trani, Eugene P. *The First Cold War: The Legacy of Woodrow Wilson in U.S.-Soviet Relations* (2002). Considers the impact of Wilson's policies on these two nations.

Graham, Sally Hunter. *Woman Suffrage and the New Democracy* (1996). Describes how women obtained the vote during World War I and afterward.

Levin, Phyllis Lee. *Edith and Woodrow: The Wilson White House* (2001). Looks at the effect of Wilson's illness on his presidency.

Saunders, Ronald M. *In Search of Woodrow Wilson: Beliefs and Behavior* (1998). A very critical account of the president and his record.

Schaffer, Ronald. *America in the Great War: The Rise of the War Welfare State* (1991). An informative text about woman suffrage and race.

Trotter, Joe William, ed. *The Great Migration in Historical Perspective* (1991). An excellent collection of essays about the movement of African Americans to northern cities.

American Journey Online and InfoTrac College Edition

Visit the source collections at http://ajaccess. wadsworth.com and infotrac.thomsonlearning.com and use the Search function with the following key terms to explore documents, images, audio and video clips, articles, and commentary related to the material in this chapter.

Lusitania	Great Migration
Woodrow Wilson	Fourteen Points
Margaret Sanger	Carrie Chapman Catt
W. E. B. Du Bois	New negro

> 🌐 **Additional resources, exercises, and Internet links related to this chapter are available on the American Passages Web site: http://history.wadsworth.com/passages2e**

23 THE AGE OF JAZZ AND MASS CULTURE 1921–1927

THE SHAME OF AMERICA

Do you know that the <u>United States</u> is the <u>Only Land on Earth</u> where human beings are <u>BURNED AT THE STAKE?</u>

In Four Years, 1918-1921, Twenty-Eight People Were Publicly BURNED BY AMERICAN MOBS

3436 People Lynched 1889 to 1922

This poster that the National Association for the Advancement of Colored People issued in 1922 to support the antilynching bill recounts that 3,436 people had been killed in this way since 1889.

THE AFTERMATH OF WAR

During the 1920s the United States became modern as the automobile and other technological developments reshaped the economy and society. While the country became more urban, cosmopolitan, and uniform, the shared experiences of Americans made the nation more cohesive. Social attitudes toward sex and family life moved away from Victorian restraints. Movies, radio, and big-time sports shaped everyday existence. Young people emerged as a distinct group. Advertising made public relations a significant characteristic of the period.

After a postwar depression, the economy rebounded from 1922 to 1927. The Republican administrations of Warren G. Harding and Calvin Coolidge lowered income taxes and encouraged private enterprise. Issues of culture and morality shaped politics more than did questions of economic reform. Prohibition and the Ku Klux Klan split the Democrats.

In foreign affairs, the decade was officially a time of isolation after the rejection of the League of Nations in 1919–1920. Although involvement in world affairs increased more slowly, the United States maintained a significant stake in the postwar European and Asian economies.

A More Urban Nation

The census of 1920 gave one important indicator of the country's new course. For the first time, the government reported that more Americans lived in towns and cities with 2,500 or more residents than in the countryside. The small-town and rural experience still dominated the lives of most citizens, but the trend toward urban residence was transforming the nation.

More than 10 million Americans lived in cities with a million people or more in 1920; that figure rose to more than 15 million by 1930. Such places as New York, Detroit, and Los Angeles saw large increases in their populations during these years. Some 19 million people left the country for the city over these ten years. The migration of African Americans from the South to the North continued unabated during this period. The percentage of blacks listed as urban residents rose by nearly 10 percent between 1920 and 1930, compared with a rise of about 5 percent for whites.

For the young people who flocked to Chicago, New York, and Los Angeles, the city offered a degree of excitement and energy that the sedate farm could not match. Within the concrete canyons and electric

avenues, visitors found theaters, dance halls, and vaudeville artists that they could never hope to see in a small town. Many Americans resented the temptations of the city and associated them with foreign influences and assaults on traditional values.

CHRONOLOGY

1921 Warren G. Harding becomes president • Immigration laws set quotas for eastern and southern Europeans • Sheppard-Towner Maternity and Infancy Protection Act passed

1922 Fordney-McCumber Tariff enacted • Sinclair Lewis's *Babbitt* published • Supreme Court rules minimum wage for women is unconstitutional in *Adkins v. Children's Hospital*

1923 Teapot Dome scandal • *Time* magazine starts publishing • Equal Rights amendment drafted by Alice Paul • Death of Warren G. Harding • Calvin Coolidge becomes president

1924 Coolidge wins presidential election • Nellie Tayloe Ross (Wyoming) and Miriam Amanda Ferguson (Texas) became first elected women governors

1925 Scopes trial in Tennessee over teaching of evolution • Publication of F. Scott Fitzgerald's *The Great Gatsby*

1926 Publication of Ernest Hemingway's *The Sun Also Rises* • Gertrude Ederle beomes first women to swim English Channel

1927 Charles Lindbergh flies the Atlantic alone • Sacco and Vanzetti executed • Babe Ruth hits sixty home runs • Henry Ford introduces Model A car • Calvin Coolidge announces "I do not choose to run" for president in 1928

Immigration Restricted

After the war immigration returned to its former pattern. Over 430,000 people sought entry to the United States in 1920, and another 805,000 came in 1921. In response, advocates of immigration restriction renewed their campaign to shut off the flow of entrants from southern and eastern europe.

Proponents of restriction argued that the immigrants lacked the qualities needed to be successful American citizens. Madison Grant, one of the leading advocates of immigration restriction, said that "these immigrants adopt the language of the [native-born] American, they wear his clothes, they steal his name, and they are beginning to take his women, but they seldom adopt his religion or understand his ideals."

The widespread tension about immigration played a significant part in the fate of Nicola Sacco and Bartolomeo Vanzetti who in June 1921 were on trial for a murder and robbery committed in South Braintree, Massachusetts, a year earlier. There were allegations that authorities framed two Italians who believed in anarchism. In July, both men were found guilty. Numerous appeals for a new trial were made, and the case soon became a focus for liberals and intellectuals convinced that Sacco and Vanzetti had not received a fair trial because of their foreign origin.

Immigration Quotas

The pressure on Congress grew to block immigration. The American Federation of Labor, which feared the use of aliens as strikebreakers, added its weight to the campaign for immigration restrictions. In 1921, Congress enacted an emergency quota law that limited immigration from Europe to 600,000 people annually. Such countries as Great Britain and Germany were given the highest quotas. Three years later, the lawmakers passed the National Origins Quota Act, which reduced annual legal immigration from Europe to about 150,000 people, gave preference to entrants from northern European countries, and blocked Asian immigrants entirely. The quota of immigrants from each country was determined by the number of residents from these countries counted in the 1890 census.

New Patterns of Immigration

Despite their racist premises, the new laws did not end immigration during the 1920s. After 1924, the recorded number of immigrants totaled about 300,000 annually until the beginning of the Great Depression. However, the impact on people who wished to emigrate from southern and eastern Europe was dramatic. Some 95,000 immigrants had come into the United States from Poland in 1921; the annual total from that country was about 28,000 over the next three years.

Since the immigration law did not affect Mexicans, some half-million newcomers from that country crossed the border during the 1920s and swelled the ranks of Americans of Hispanic ancestry. Mexicans were concentrated in California and Texas.

The Ku Klux Klan

The pressures of immigration from abroad and the movement of Americans from the country to the city produced intense social strains. The most sensational and violent of these developments was the Ku Klux Klan. Revitalized after 1915 in the South, the Klan gained followers slowly until the end of World War I. By 1920, the Klan had become a marketing device for clever promoters who used the Klan's brew of racism, anti-Catholicism, and anti-immigrant views to acquire converts. The Klan claimed that it had 3 million members in the early 1920s. The masks and sheets that members of the order wore provided an anonymity that attracted recruits in the southern countryside and in the cities of the Midwest where formerly rural residents had moved.

A secret ritual added to the mystique of the hooded movement. Members contributed a ten-dollar entrance fee, called a "klecktoken." They read the Kloran and dedicated themselves to "Karacter, Honor, Duty." In time they might rise to become a King Kleagle or a Grand Goblin of the Domain. Members asked each other "Ayak," for "Are you a Klansman?" The proper reply was "Akia," meaning "A Klansman I am."

The Klan's program embraced opposition to Catholics, Jews, blacks, Asians, violators of the Prohibition laws, and anyone else who displeased local Klansmen. In their rallies, marching members carried signs that read "COHABITATION BETWEEN WHITES AND BLACKS MUST STOP." Even more than the Klan of the Reconstruction era, the Klan of the 1920s based its appeal on the desire of many white Americans for a more tranquil and less confusing social order. The Klan's efforts to create such an order initially made it attractive to many citizens who never wore a hood. But the Klan also contained an ugly strain of violence and vigilantism. In many states its members lynched people they disagreed with; tortured blacks, Catholics, and Jews; and made a mockery of law enforcement.

Soon the Klan went into politics. In 1922, its members elected a senator in Texas and became a powerful presence in the legislatures of that state and others in the Southwest. In Indiana, members of the order dominated the police of the state's major cities. The Klan also wielded significant influence in the Rocky Mountain states and the Pacific Northwest.

For the Democrats, the Klan posed a difficult problem. The party was already divided over cultural issues. Southern members favored Prohibition and disliked large cities. In the North, Democrats were ethnically diverse, opposed to Prohibition, and rooted in the new urban lifestyles. The Klan intensified these tensions. Some "dry" Democrats saw the Klan as a legitimate form of political protest. The "wets" in northern cities regarded the Klan as an expression of cultural and regional intolerance.

The Rise of Black Militance

The resurgence of the Klan came when African Americans were asserting their identity and independence. Black sacrifices during World War I had made blacks impatient and resentful of the indignities of segregation. The recurrence of white on black violence, such as the brutal attack on the African American area of Tulsa, Oklahoma, in 1921, underlined the predicament of blacks. A growing spirit of assertiveness and militancy appeared in the art and literature of black intellectuals. A poet named Claude McKay issued his rallying cry in 1922: "If we must die, let it not be like hogs / Hunted and penned in an inglorious spot." Instead, he concluded, "Like men we'll face the murderous, cowardly pack, / Pressed to the wall, dying, but—fighting back."

For the African Americans who crowded into the large northern cities during the Great Migration, the promise of America seemed to be an illusion. They lived in substandard housing, paid higher rents for their apartments than whites did, and could obtain only menial jobs. The Harlem neighborhood of New York City might be "the greatest Negro city in the world," as author James Weldon Johnson called it, but it was also a place where every day blacks saw how white society discriminated against them.

Marcus Garvey and Black Nationalism

In 1916, a Jamaican named Marcus Garvey immigrated to the United States. Garvey preached a doctrine of Pan-Africanism and promised to "organize the 400,000,000 Negroes of the World into a vast organization to plant the banner of freedom in the great continent of Africa." He worked through the Universal Negro Improvement Association (UNIA) to establish societies that were not controlled by imperialist nations. He founded his campaign on international shipping lines and newspapers that would enable blacks to travel to Africa and com-

municate among themselves. Rallies and conventions in New York and other cities drew up to 25,000 people and raised funds for the UNIA.

Garvey's business ventures failed. The shipping lines collapsed and the investors, mostly African Americans, lost their money. Blacks were divided in their views of the charismatic Garvey. The National Association for the Advancement of Colored People bristled when Garvey attacked its political agenda and met with a Klan leader. His criticisms of labor unions alienated key African American leaders such as A. Phillip Randolph of the Brotherhood of Sleeping Car Porters. Black opponents sent damaging information about Garvey's finances to the Department of Justice and the government indicted him for mail fraud. He was convicted and went to prison in 1925. The important legacy of Garvey and the UNIA was the idea that urban blacks could band together to wield economic and political power.

Dry America: The First Phase

The initial impact of Prohibition on the lives of Americans achieved much of what its proponents had predicted. The national consumption of alcohol declined from about two gallons per capita annually to around three-fourths of a gallon in 1921 and 1922. Alcoholism as a medical problem became less prevalent. Many hospitals closed their alcoholism wards because of a lack of patients. Contrary to later legend, Prohibition did change drinking habits in the United States.

Yet the extent of compliance with Prohibition was spotty. Some people made their own liquor; instructions for doing so were easily obtained. In cities like San Francisco and Boston, centers of "wet" sentiment, the law was never enforced. Several states did not even ratify the Eighteenth Amendment. Others failed to pass state laws to support the federal legislation. Believing that compliance ought to be voluntary, Congress appropriated inadequate funds to the Treasury Department's Prohibition Bureau. There were never enough federal men to cover the nation adequately. Even when agents acted decisively, the rising number of arrests led to huge backlogs in the federal court system.

The upper classes expected the working poor to obey the Prohibition law, but they resisted any change in their own drinking practices. With a ready market for illegal liquor in the major cities, enterprising individuals moved alcohol across the border into the United States. These "rum runners" and "bootleggers" brought in shipments of alcohol from Canada and the Caribbean. Their wares were sold at illegal saloons or "speakeasies" where city dwellers congregated in the evenings.

Claude McKay,
If We Must Die! 1922

The First World War led many African Americans to resent their second-class status in the United States. Black artists and poets like Claude McKay expressed their feelings in verse. McKay's passionate affirmation of his sense of self captured the spirit that also expressed itself in the Harlem Renaissance and the campaign of Marcus Garvey.

If we must die, let it not be like hogs
   Hunted and penned in an inglorious spot,
While round us bark the mad and hungry dogs,
   Making their mock at our accursed lot.
If we must die, let it not be like hogs
   So that our precious blood may not be shed
In vain; then even the monster we defy
   Shall be constrained to honor us, though dead!

Oh kinsman! We must meet the common foe;
   Though far outnumbered, let us still be brave,
And for their thousand blows deal one deathblow!
   What though before us lies the open grave?
Like men we'll face the murderous, cowardly pack,
   Pressed to the wall, dying, but—fighting back!

Prohibition did not, however, create organized crime. Nor were the 1920s a decade of rising crime rates. The nation became more aware of crime as a social problem, because of the well-publicized activities of gangsters like Alphonse "Al" Capone and Johnny Torrio in Chicago. Prohibition offered individuals already involved in crime another incentive to tap the immense profits to be had from easing the thirst of upper-class Americans. Capone in particular devoted himself to gaining control of gambling, prostitution, and bootlegging in the Chicago area. In New York, other mobsters built up networks of criminal enterprises to provide the same services. These sensational cases undermined faith in the positive effects of Prohibition. The Klan, immigration restriction, and Prohibition reflected the power of older cultural values.

HARDING AS PRESIDENT

Because of the scandals associated with his administration, Warren G. Harding is often depicted as the worst president in American history. During his brief term, however, he was very popular. Harding surrounded himself with what he called the "Best Minds," as his selection of Charles Evans Hughes as his secretary of state, banker Andrew Mellon as secre-

The campaign to enforce Prohibition produced some results. Here police pour beer down a sewer.
From the Collections of the Library of Congress

tary of the treasury, and Herbert Hoover as secretary of commerce attested. After years in which the presidency had seemed separated from the people, Harding

ICTURING THE PAST ✦ SOCIAL & CULTURAL EVENTS

Table 23.1	Estimated Alcohol Consumption in the United States, 1920–1930 (Gallons Per Capita)
Year	**Estimated Consumption**
1920	n/a
1921	.54
1922	.91
1923	1.07
1924	1.05
1925	1.10
1926	1.18
1927	1.12
1928	1.18
1929	1.20
1930	1.06

Source: Derived from table in Joseph R. Gusfield, "Prohibition: The Impact of Political Utopianism," in John Braeman, Robert H. Bremner, and David Brody, eds., *Change and Continuity in Twentieth-Century America: The 1920s* (Columbus, Ohio: Ohio State University Press, 1968), p. 275.

This table on estimated alcohol consumption between 1920 and 1930 is more than just a representation of how much people drank in that period. It is part of the evidence in the debate about the effectiveness of Prohibition as a way of changing individual behavior toward alcohol. One school of thought has it that liquor control was an utter failure and that Americans drank as much as they ever did in the 1920s.

These estimates, compiled from tax information, hospital records, and police statistics, indicate that Prohibition did achieve substantial reductions in alcohol consumption during the first four years of the decade. Then, as enforcement loosened and evasion of the law grew, consumption crept up again. But it is not enough to deride Prohibition as a failed experiment that was doomed from the start. The issue was more complex than that. This table reveals that historical clichés about social movements should always be tested against the best available evidence and not simply accepted at face value.

and his wife Florence opened up the White House and greeted visitors with evident pleasure. Throughout the country Harding was a well-regarded president whose speeches appealed to a desire for a calmer, less activist chief executive.

The new administration pressed for a legislative program that combined some constructive reforms with a return to older Republican trade policies. The 1921 Budget and Accounting Act gave the government a more precise sense of how the nation's funds were being spent. It established an executive budget for the president, a General Accounting Office for Congress, and a Bureau of the Budget in the executive branch. The Republicans rebuilt tariff protection in an emergency law of 1921 and then wrote the Fordney-McCumber Tariff Law a year later. Reflecting the party's suspicion of a powerful national government, Treasury Secretary Mellon pushed for lower income tax rates, particularly for individuals with higher incomes.

Harding and the World

The Harding administration stayed aloof from the League of Nations, and a separate peace with Germany came in 1921. Throughout the 1920s, Washington withheld recognition from the new Soviet Union. American interests turned back toward Latin America. To reduce the nation's military role in the region, the administration withdrew marines from Haiti, the Dominican Republic, and Nicaragua. Trade and investment expanded south of the border.

The Far East claimed a large amount of attention as Japan expanded its power in China. The United States wanted to preserve the Open Door policy and restrain Japanese influence. The White House relied on diplomacy and economic pressure as its main weapons. Both nations were, however, increasing the size of their navies at this time. Congress and the administration concluded that a conference in which representatives of Great Britain, Japan, and the United

States would meet to discuss naval issues and peace in the Far East was a logical move. The United States and Great Britain arranged for such a meeting in Washington in November 1921.

The Washington Conference and Beyond

The Washington Naval Conference began with a dramatic proposal by Secretary of State Hughes to scrap outright sixty battleships of all nations. Limits should also be placed on the number of battleships and aircraft carriers that Japan, the United States, and Britain could build. Out of the conference came the Five Power Treaty, which provided a fixed ratio for warship construction. For every five ships the United States built, the British could also build five, and the Japanese could build three. The Japanese were not happy with the 5-5-3 arrangement, but in return they secured an American pledge not to construct defenses in such U.S. possessions as Guam and the Philippines. For the time, the naval arms race in the Pacific slowed.

The Washington Conference also resulted in two other pacts—the Four Power Treaty and the Nine Power Treaty. The Four Power Treaty ended a long-standing alliance (since 1902) between Great Britain and France, and committed the United States, France, Great Britain, and Japan to respect each country's territorial possessions. In the Nine Power Treaty, the various nations agreed to avoid interference with China's internal affairs. The Washington Conference achieved much without the United States having to make commitments that entailed the risk of force or greater international involvement.

THE NEW ECONOMY

The continuing postwar recession dogged the first two years of the Harding administration. Hard times contributed to substantial Republican losses in the 1922 congressional elections. The Democrats gained seventy-four seats in the House and six in the Senate. Yet the long-range news proved beneficial for Republicans. The economy slowly picked up in 1922 and 1923, productive output returned to its 1918 levels, and employment rose. As wages climbed, discontent ebbed and the Republicans looked forward to the 1924 presidential election with greater optimism.

Prosperity and Its Benefits

The improvement in the economy's performance during 1922 began a period of unprecedented prosperity. The gross national product soared almost 40 percent,

increasing from nearly $76 billion in 1922 to $97.3 billion in 1927. The per capita income of Americans went up about 30 percent during the same period. Real earnings for wage workers rose over 20 percent, whereas hours worked declined slightly. The unemployment rate fell from 12 percent of the labor force in 1922 to 4 percent in 1927.

The Car Culture

The number of cars registered in 1920 totaled 8.25 million, while the number of trucks was 1.1 million. By 1927, there were more than 20 million cars on the roads along with more than 3 million trucks and buses. Automobiles needed oil and gasoline to operate, steel for their frames, rubber for their tires, glass for windshields, and service businesses for dealers and drivers. For the traveler on the road, motels offered accommodations, billboards advertised attractions, and roadside restaurants provided food and diversion. The Federal Highways Act of 1921 left road construction to the states, but set national standards for concrete road surfaces and access to roads. The size of the road network grew from 7,000 miles at the end of the war to 50,000 miles in 1927. Gasoline taxes brought in revenues for the states, enabling them to build more roads, which, in turn, fostered the development of suburbs distant from the old city centers.

No longer did young women and men have to carry on courtship within sight of parents and chaperones. When fathers urged their daughters not to go out driving with boys, the young women replied: "What on earth do you want me to do? Just sit around all evening?" Cars consumed a large chunk of the working family's income as Americans readily took to the practice of buying their cars on the installment plan.

Table 23.2	Automobile Registrations, 1921–1929
1921	9,212,158
1922	10,704,076
1923	13,253,019
1924	15,436,102
1925	17,481,001
1926	19,267,967
1927	20,193,333
1928	21,362,240
1929	23,120,897

Source: *The Statistical History of the United States*, New York: Fairfield Press, 1965, p. 462.

For many African Americans in the South, owning a car gave them at least some mobility and escape from a segregated life. The enclosed car, initially a prestigious model, soon became standard on the road; by 1927, 83 percent of cars were of this type.

Henry Ford Gives Way to General Motors

As the decade began, Henry Ford was still the most famous carmaker in the nation. His showplace was the huge factory on the Rouge River near Detroit. Sprawling across 2,000 acres, the Rouge plant employed 75,000 workers to turn out the reliable, familiar Model T car. In 1921, Ford made more than half of the automobiles produced in the United States, turning out a new vehicle every ten seconds. A car cost under $300.

The Model T was a popular car but not a very attractive one. The joke was that you could get a Model T in any color, so long as it was black. Ford's failure to develop different car models opened a competitive opportunity to General Motors (GM). Although GM had been in severe financial difficulty in 1920, the DuPont family acquired the firm. They brought in Alfred P. Sloan, Jr., as chief assistant to the president. In 1923, he became president. Sloan set up a system of independent operating divisions that produced models of Chevrolets, Buicks, and other vehicles annually. GM introduced self-starters, fuel gauges, reliable headlights, and other features that consumers liked. The constant flow of new models induced customers to want a fresh vehicle every few years. The General Motors Acceptance Corporation made it easy to acquire a car on the installment plan.

By the middle of the 1920s, Ford's sales fell as those of General Motors rose. Ford dealers switched to General Motors while the used-car market undercut

Automobile Manufacturers competed for car buyers with advertising that stressed the mobility and freedom that these vehicles provided to Americans in the 1920s.
From the Collections of the Library of Congress

Ford at the other end of the price scale. Henry Ford had revolutionized American transportation before 1920. Now he was losing out because of his resistance to marketing and manufacturing innovation.

Electrical America

By 1928, electricity drove 70 percent of factory equipment. Two-thirds of the families in towns and cities had electricity in their homes as well, stimulating demand for the electrical appliances that industry was turning out in abundance. Homemakers bought some 15 million electric irons and another 7 million vacuum cleaners. Advertisers appealed to women with descriptions of the all-electric kitchen "Where Work is Easy!" Sales of consumer appliances were one of the major economic stimulants of the decade. The electric power industry expanded rapidly, as did the firms that made equipment for the power plants.

The diffusion of electricity facilitated the growth of radio. The first station, KDKA in Pittsburgh, went on the air in 1920. There were only four in 1922; a year later, 566 were in operation. In 1923, a New York station, WBAY, began selling time to anyone who would pay for it. Commercial radio caught on quickly. Soon announcers and performers became popular attractions. Listeners wrote to them for advice about love affairs and to praise the human contact that radios provided. In 1923, there were radios in 400,000 households.

Three years later, the Radio Corporation of America (RCA), led by its president David Sarnoff, established the first national network of stations, the National Broadcasting Company (NBC). Telephone wires carried the broadcast signals to stations scattered across the country. NBC consisted of two networks, the "red" and the "blue." Programming was diverse, and commercial sponsors oversaw the content of such programs as *The Maxwell House Hour* and the *Ipana Troubadours*.

Movies in the Silent Era

Each week, 100 million people went to see movies at one of the 20,000 theaters that showed silent pictures. Some movie houses were plain and functional. Others featured expensive lobbies and plush furniture. Ticket prices were relatively low and stable, usually about fifty cents. As one college student recalled, "You learn plenty about love from the movies." Pictures shaped how young people kissed on dates, what they wore, and what they said. "I cling to my dream world woven about the movies I have seen," said another student.

From their uncertain beginnings at the turn of the century, motion picture studios had developed into large enterprises employing hundreds of people. Studio

The spread of mass entertainment through radio made the 1920s the first decade when Americans could experience simultaneously the same programs and stars. Radios became elaborate products as this expensive model, complete with "radiotrons" for $495, reveals.

Exotic themes and portraying a sexy hero such as the hero in The Son of the Sheik made Rudolph Valentino a box office superstar before his untimely death.
The Granger Collection, New York

heads like Adolph Zukor of Paramount Pictures and Louis B. Mayer of Metro-Goldwyn-Mayer (MGM) controlled chains of theaters, to which they allocated the pictures they made on a rigidly controlled basis. To get a popular feature film, theater owners would have to accept the entire yearly production of a major studio.

Motion picture stars were the bedrock of the business. Charlie Chaplin's popularity rose to even greater heights during the early 1920s in such films as *The Gold Rush* (1925). Other box-office attractions included Rudolph Valentino, whose sudden death in 1926 brought thousands of weeping fans, in a line stretching for eight city blocks, to his New York funeral.

To maintain its hold on the popular mind, Hollywood reacted quickly when sexual scandals tarnished the industry's image early in the 1920s. The studios recruited Will H. Hays, a prominent Republi-

can, to serve as president of the Motion Pictures Producers and Distributors Association in 1922. Hays tried to persuade moviemakers to inject more moral content into films. Skillful directors such as Cecil B. deMille circumvented these mild warnings. He argued that the sexual scenes in *The Ten Commandments* were based on biblical descriptions.

Advertising America

Advertisers developed new and effective ways to persuade Americans to acquire the products coming out of the nation's factories and workshops. The advertising business boomed. Before World War I, the total amount spent on advertising stood at about $400 million annually. It soared to $2.6 billion by 1929. Radios brought advertising into the home; billboards attracted the attention of millions of motorists. Advertising, said one of its practitioners, "literally creates demand for the things of life that raise the standard of living, elevate the taste, changing luxuries into necessities."

Among the products that advertising promoted was Listerine, which was said to eliminate halitosis, the medical term for bad breath. Other consumers were urged to ingest yeast at least twice a day to fight constipation and skin problems. The ingenious advertising executive Albert Lasker succeeded in inducing Americans to drink orange juice daily at breakfast, breaking the taboo against advertising the sanitary napkin Kotex, and describing Kleenex as "the handkerchief you can throw away." He also claimed Pepsodent toothpaste would remove "film" from the fortunate user's teeth.

The most celebrated advertising man of the decade was Bruce Barton, who wrote a biography of Jesus Christ in order to demonstrate that advertising went back to biblical times. In *The Man Nobody Knows* (1925), Barton retold the New Testament in terms that Americans of the 1920s could easily grasp. Jesus, wrote Barton, "recognized the basic principle that all good advertising is news." The twelve disciples were a model of an efficient business organization, and Jesus himself was a master salesman. "He was never trite or commonplace; he had no routine." Barton's book became a national best-seller. As long as the economy expanded, advertising prospered and fed the demand of consumers for products they had never known they needed.

Those Left Behind

Not all segments of society shared equally in the return of good times. The postwar depression hit the farm sector with devastating force. Farmers had never benefitted from the upturn that marked the cities. For labor also, this was a time of retreat.

Despite the shift toward city living, the United States still relied on farming as a key element in the economy. The 7 million families who lived on farms in 1920 did not generally enjoy the modern conveniences and appliances that had appeared in the cities. In some areas farm life resembled that of the pioneers more than it did the city dwellers. Overproduction of crops drove down prices and led to massive harvests that could not be marketed. In the South, for example, the price of cotton was forty cents a pound in 1920 but slid to ten cents a pound in 1921. Wheat stood at $1.82 per bushel in 1920, sagged to $0.926 in 1924, and then recovered to $1.437 in 1925. The postwar recovery of agriculture in Europe meant that overseas markets

were smaller as well. The per capita income of most farmers did not rise substantially after 1919, and there was a widening gap between what farmers earned and what city dwellers made.

To improve their lot, farmers sought higher tariff duties on imported products. They also revived the idea of farm cooperatives to market more effectively. Federal legislation to regulate the trading of grain futures and extend more credit to farmers was marginally helpful, but the underlying problem of overproduction continued.

In 1921, a plow manufacturer named George Peek proposed that American farmers ship surplus products overseas and dump them on the world market at whatever price they could obtain. The government would buy farm products at the market price and then sell them abroad. Taxes on the processing of crops would cover the cost to the government and the taxpayer. The chairs of the House and Senate Agriculture Committees introduced a bill to enact such a program in January 1924. Known as the McNary-Haugen Plan, it gained much support in the Midwest and soon commanded national attention. Critics called it price-fixing at government expense.

Labor in Retreat

After World War I, the Red Scare of 1919–1920 stalled labor's drive to organize coal mining, steel, and other industries that employed thousands of unskilled workers. The number of unionized laborers dropped from nearly 5 million in 1921 to fewer than 3.5 million eight years later. The American Federation of Labor (AFL), under its president William Green, presented only weak challenges to employers. It accepted what management called "business unionism," or the nonunion "open shop," which was labeled the "American Plan." Efforts to organize unskilled workers were abandoned.

Government and business threw up numerous obstacles to labor's interests. The U.S. Supreme Court struck down minimum wages for women in Washington, D.C. In the case of *Adkins v. Children's Hospital* (1923), the Court ruled that the law infringed on the right of workers to sell their labor for whatever they could obtain. This "liberty-of-contract" doctrine accordingly barred Congress from passing such a law. In addition to an unsympathetic Supreme Court, unions faced opposition from the White House. When strikes occurred in railroading during 1922, the Harding administration obtained harsh court orders that effectively ended the walkouts.

Businesses used less repressive tactics as well. Some of the bigger and more enlightened firms provided

*P*ICTURING THE PAST ✦ ECONOMICS & TECHNOLOGY

THE CHANGING FACE OF AGRICULTURE

American farmers in the 1920s struggled with the problems of abundance. The introduction of mechanized tractors and tillers, like the one depicted here from North Dakota, made it possible for farmers to increase their production far beyond what had been done with horse-drawn equipment. The family watching the new machine from their horse and buggy indicate the transition that farmers were experiencing. As farmers brought their cash crops in through the use of this kind of machinery, they found that success in growing wheat and other staple crops only intensified their economic dilemmas. The price of wheat, for example, plunged during the first half of the decade as a result of national and international overproduction. Small farmers learned that they could not survive in a market that favored larger enterprises with the capital to purchase modern equipment like this plow and keep costs low.

what became known as welfare capitalism. General Electric, International Harvester, and Bethlehem Steel represented companies that sought to appease workers with recreational facilities, benefit plans, and sometimes even profit-sharing opportunities. Estimates indicated that as many as 4 million workers received such rewards. After the middle of the decade, however, these programs stalled as the lack of labor militancy removed the incentive to make concessions to workers. Most workers remained dependent on the goodwill of their employer for whatever job security they possessed.

The Harding Scandals

By early 1923, Harding's presidency was mired in rumors of scandal. Attorney General Harry Daugherty was a political ally of the president, but his loose direction of the Justice Department allowed corruption to flourish. Scandals also festered in the Veterans Bureau and the Office of the Alien Property Custodian.

The most serious wrongdoing involved the secretary of the interior, Albert B. Fall. Federal oil reserves at Elk Hills, California, and Teapot Dome, Wyoming (where the rocks vaguely resembled a teapot), were leased to private oil companies. Fall received $400,000 in loans from friends in the industry in what many interpreted as payoffs for his leasing decisions. The Teapot Dome scandal emerged after Harding died, but it established his administration's reputation as one of the most corrupt in American history.

A weak president and a poor judge of people, Harding allowed cronies and crooks to infest his administration. By 1923, he knew about the ethical problems in the Veterans Bureau, and he suspected that scandals lurked in the Department of the Interior and the Justice Department. During a tour of the Pacific

Northwest in July 1923, the president fell ill. He died in San Francisco on August 2 of heart disease.

Keep Cool with Coolidge

Harding's successor was Calvin Coolidge, the former governor of Massachusetts. Coolidge came to be viewed in Washington as a stereotypical New Englander, a man of few words. In fact, Coolidge was quite talkative in the regular press conferences that he held twice a week. Although he slept twelve hours a day, Coolidge worked hard greeting visitors and addressing the needs of those who told him their problems with the federal government. His wife Grace brought glamour and a sense of fun to the White House, offsetting her husband's dour personality.

Coolidge was much more committed to the conservative principles of the Republicans than Harding had been. He proclaimed that "the business of America is business," and he endorsed policies designed to promote corporate enterprise. He extended the tax-cutting policies of Treasury Secretary Mellon. The president also appointed pro-business individuals to head the regulatory agencies and departments that the progressives had established a generation earlier. Meanwhile, he removed the Harding holdovers, such as Harry Daugherty, who might prove politically embarrassing when Coolidge ran for the presidency in 1924.

Coolidge cultivated a dour New England demeanor to set himself apart from the excesses of the Harding years. His grim expression hides the playful spirit that liked to inflict practical jokes on his White House staff.
© Bettmann/Corbis

Coolidge lost little time in gaining control of the Republican party. The president used modern public relations techniques to bolster his image as an embodiment of old-time virtues of morality and frugality. Movie stars came to the White House to endorse the president and, under the leadership of the stylish Grace Coolidge, sing the campaign theme song: "Keep Cool with Coolidge."

The Discordant Democrats

The Democrats hoped that the Teapot Dome scandal and other revelations of wrongdoing in the Harding years would be their ticket back to the White House. When the Teapot Dome scandal could not be linked to anyone in the White House, the issue faded away. Prohibition had split the Democrats between the dry faithful of the South and West, who wanted strict enforcement of the Volstead Act, and the wet residents of the large cities of the North and Midwest, who saw Prohibition as a foolish experiment. The two leading candidates for the Democratic party nomination reflected this regional tension. William G. McAdoo represented the progressive, prohibitionist wing. Governor Alfred E. Smith of New York was a Roman Catholic who opposed Prohibition. The Democratic National Convention left the party with almost no chance of defeating President Coolidge. McAdoo and Smith deadlocked through dozens of ballots. Finally, after 103 ballots, the exhausted delegates compromised and chose a former member of Congress and Wall Street lawyer named John W. Davis.

Senator Robert M. La Follette of Wisconsin, who had been seeking the presidency for many years, became the champion of what remained of the progressive spirit and the anger of the Midwestern farmers. Although he was nominated for president at a convention of the Progressive party, he did not attend the meeting or identify himself with the party. The American Federation of Labor and the railroad unions backed La Follette but with little money or enthusiasm.

The 1924 Election in Perspective

The Republicans ignored Davis and concentrated on the alleged radicalism of La Follette and his supporters. The choice, they said, was "Coolidge or Chaos." Coolidge polled more than 15,718,000 votes, more than the combined total of his two rivals. The Republicans retained firm control of both houses of Congress. Yet beneath the surface, electoral trends were moving toward the Democrats. In the northern cities the party's share of the vote grew during the 1920s. If a candidate appeared who could unite the traditionally

Democratic South with the ethnic voters of the Northeast, Republican supremacy might be in jeopardy.

A BLOSSOMING IN ART AND LITERATURE

While politics followed a conservative path during the 1920s, the nation's cultural life experienced a productivity and artistic success that would be unrivaled during the rest of the twentieth century. In music, drama, and literature, the decade brought forth a rare assembly of first-rate talents.

The Harlem Renaissance

In the wake of the Great Migration, African American intellectual life centered in New York City. There authors and poets lived in the black section known as Harlem. The "Harlem Renaissance" owed much to W. E. B. Du Bois's encouragement of African American writing in *The Crisis,* the journal of the National Association for the Advancement of Colored People (NAACP). In the New York of the early 1920s, the ferment associated with Marcus Garvey, the exciting night life, the relative absence of racial bigotry, and the interest of wealthy white patrons enabled a few black writers to pursue literary careers. Their moment of celebrity proved brief, but their impact was significant.

The Harlem Renaissance reached its peak in 1925, when a national magazine ran an article on "Harlem: Mecca of the New Negro." In the same year, Alain Locke's book *The New Negro* was published. Locke argued that African Americans' "more immediate hope" depended on the ability of blacks and whites to evaluate "the Negro in terms of his artistic endowments and cultural contributions, past and prospective." Other major figures in the Renaissance were the poets Langston Hughes ("The Weary Blues"), Countee Cullen ("Do I Marvel"), Zora Neale Hurston (the play *Color Struck*), Claude McKay (*Harlem Shadows*), as well as the memoirist and songwriter James Weldon Johnson (*God's Trombones*). Although these writers' artistic merit was undeniable, the Harlem Renaissance did little to alter the segregationist laws and customs that restricted the lives of most African Americans.

The Sound of Jazz

After World War I, the improvised music that came to be called jazz brought together black musicians and a few white players in Kansas City, Chicago, and New York. At the rent parties where Harlem residents raised

The Harlem Renaissance gave an opportunity for numerous black writers and poets to gain a larger audience than would have been possible even ten years earlier. One of them was the story writer and novelist Zora Neale Hurston, who wrote about the African American masses.
The Granger Collection, New York

money to pay their landlords, in the nightclubs that organized crime controlled, and in the after-hours jam sessions, jazz became a unique American art form.

The major innovators of jazz included trumpeter Louis Armstrong and tenor sax player Coleman Hawkins, who took the new music beyond its roots in New Orleans toward a more sophisticated style. Blues artists such as Bessie Smith and Ma Rainey sold "race records" to black and white audiences. Edward Kennedy "Duke" Ellington and Fletcher Henderson led larger orchestras that showed what jazz could accomplish in a more structured setting. The rhythms and sounds of jazz gave the 1920s its enduring title: the Jazz Age.

Writers looked at the postwar world in a critical spirit that grew out of the European ideas and a skepticism about older values. The most popular novelist of the early 1920s was Sinclair Lewis, whose books *Main Street* (1920) and *Babbitt* (1922) examined with unsparing honesty small-town life in the Midwest. His novels *Arrowsmith* (1925) and *Elmer Gantry* (1927) enhanced his reputation, but his artistic powers failed in the 1930s.

The Cotton Club in Harlem was the nightly center of the social scene of the Harlem Renaissance. The Cotton Club orchestra in 1925 entertained the white patrons who came up from Manhattan to sample the excitement of black music and culture.
© Frank Driggs/Corbis

Young people devoured the work of the acidic essayist and social critic Henry L. Mencken, who wrote for the *American Mercury.* Mencken was a Baltimore newspaperman who had little time for the sacred cows of middle-class culture or, as he called them, the "booboisie." He characterized democracy as "the worship of jackals by jackasses" and said that puritanism was "the haunting fear that somebody, somewhere may be happy." Aimed more at the middle-class audience was *Time,* started in March 1923 by Briton Hadden and Henry Luce. *Time* sought to present the week's news in readable and sprightly prose.

The most influential fiction author of the decade was Ernest Hemingway, whose terse, understated prose spoke of the pain and disillusion that men had suffered during the fighting in World War I. In *The Sun Also Rises* (1925) and *A Farewell to Arms* (1929), Hemingway expressed the anguish of young Americans who had lost faith in the moral customs of their parents.

Another serious novelist of the day was F. Scott Fitzgerald. Like Hemingway, he, along with his wife Zelda, captured attention as the embodiment of the free spirit of the Jazz Age. At the same time, Fitzgerald was a dedicated artist who sought to write a great novel that would ensure his fame. In *The Great Gatsby* (1925), he came as close to that goal as any author of the time. The book chronicled how the young man Jay Gatsby sought to recapture a lost love among the aris-

tocracy of the Long Island shore. In Gatsby's failure to win his dream, Fitzgerald saw the inability of Americans to escape the burdens of their own pasts.

An Age of Artistic Achievement

The list of important authors during the 1920s was long and distinguished. It included such artistic innovators as T. S. Eliot, who lived in Great Britain and whose poems such as "The Waste Land" (1922) influenced a generation of poets on both sides of the Atlantic. Novelists such as John Dos Passos, Sherwood Anderson, Edith Wharton, Willa Cather, and William Faulkner produced a body of work that delved into the lives of aristocratic women (Wharton), prairie pioneers (Cather), the working poor and middle class (Dos Passos), the residents of small towns (Anderson), and the Deep South (Faulkner).

The theater witnessed the emergence of the Broadway musical in the work of Richard Rodgers and Lorenz Hart (*Garrick Gaieties*), George and Ira Gershwin (*Lady, Be Good*), Jerome Kern and Oscar Hammerstein II (*Showboat*) and Cole Porter (*Paris*). The great age of the American popular song, inspired by the musicals, began in the 1920s and lasted for three decades. Serious drama drew upon the talents of the brooding and pessimistic Eugene O'Neill as well as Elmer Rice and Maxwell Anderson.

PICTURING THE PAST ✦ SOCIAL & CULTURAL EVENTS

F. SCOTT FITZGERALD AND THE JAZZ AGE

© Bettmann/UPI/Corbis

This picture of F. Scott Fitzgerald, his wife Zelda, and their daughter in a smart roadster in the 1920s provides an image of domestic harmony that was at odds with the author's real, troubled life. Anxious for the artistic success and acclaim that came with such novels as *The Great Gatsby*, Fitzgerald worked hard at his writing but also drank and partied with equal intensity. He and his wife became celebrities whose lives were the subject of the popular press. Even this picture, posed for the news cameras, was designed to feed the public appetite for personal details of the famous.

The facade soon crumbled. Zelda Fitzgerald succumbed to mental illness, in part because of tensions with her husband over her desire to write fiction too. With the end of the 1920s and the Jazz Age, Scott Fitzgerald's own career hit rough spots and he died in 1940, his fame almost forgotten. In the decades since, his reputation as a keen interpreter of the 1920s has rebounded to the point that his fame is more widespread than when this picture was taken.

In architecture, although the innovative work of Frank Lloyd Wright had given him a reputation for artistic daring before 1920, commercial success eluded him. American architects designed planned, suburban communities modeled on historical models from England or the Southwest. Skyscrapers and city centers such as Rockefeller Center in New York City embodied a building style that emphasized light and air. Amid the prosperity and optimism of the 1920s, it seemed that the possibilities for a lively and vibrant culture were limitless.

FUNDAMENTALISM AND TRADITIONAL VALUES

For most Americans, the literary and artistic ferment of the 1920s was part of a broader set of challenges to the older lifestyles with which they had grown up.

Residents of small towns and newcomers to the growing cities sought to find reassurance in the older ways that they fondly remembered. The currents of religious and social conservatism remained dominant.

The Klan in Decline

The Klan's influence peaked around 1923. As the Klan sought greater political power, the two major parties, especially the Democrats, absorbed some of the Klan's appeal and weakened its hold on the public. In a key state such as Indiana, parts of the Klan's program, including reading the Bible daily in schools and restrictions on parochial schools, aroused fears that religious freedom might be at risk. Scandals also sapped the Klan's moral fervor. In Indiana the Klan leader, David Stephenson, went to prison for the death of a woman he had assaulted. Faced with jail, he revealed the bribes he had offered to state officials. The tawdry mess broke the Klan's hold on Indiana and hastened its decline elsewhere in the nation.

The Continuing Controversy over Sacco and Vanzetti

Meanwhile, the ordeal of Sacco and Vanzetti in the Massachusetts legal system continued as their attorneys filed a series of appeals to overturn their 1921 conviction. The lawyers challenged the conduct of the jury, attacked the quality of the evidence against the two men, and questioned the identifications of the defendants that various witnesses had made. Intellectuals became more convinced that the prosecution had either framed Sacco and Vanzetti or railroaded them into prison.

None of this changed the mind of the presiding judge, and by October 1924, all motions for another trial had been denied. The two defendants had hired a new attorney, and a campaign for a new trial and their eventual release gained greater national attention during 1925 and 1926. Within Massachusetts, where animosity against immigrants still ran strong, the state government did not waver in its belief that Sacco and Vanzetti were guilty.

The Fundamentalist Movement

Amid the social ferment that accompanied the rise of the Ku Klux Klan, the tensions over nativism, and the reaction against modern ideas, American Protestantism engaged in a passionate debate over the proper position of Christians toward science, the doctrine of evolution, and liberal ideas. Conservative church leaders in northern Baptist and Presbyterian pulpits spoke of the dangers to faith from a society that had moved away from the Bible and its teachings. In 1920, a minister called the movement "Fundamentalism" because it sought to reaffirm precepts of the Christian creed such as the literal truth of the Bible and the central place of Jesus Christ in saving humanity.

Fundamentalism had a political and social agenda as well as a religious message. On the local and state levels, believers sought to eradicate traces of modern ideas that contradicted biblical teachings. The doctrine of evolution became a special target of fundamentalist wrath. William Jennings Bryan emerged as a leading champion of the crusade. "It is better to trust the Rock of Ages," he said, "than to know the age of rocks." In a dozen state legislatures, lawmakers introduced bills to ban the teaching of evolution in public schools. The Anti-Evolution League hoped to amend the Constitution to bar the teaching of evolution anywhere in the nation. In 1924, Tennessee passed a law that prohibited the spending of public money "to teach any theory that denies the story of the Divine Creation of man as taught in the Bible."

The Scopes Trial

In 1925, a schoolteacher named John T. Scopes taught evolution in Dayton, Tennessee. The local authorities indicted Scopes, and his case came to trial. William Jennings Bryan agreed to help prosecute Scopes, and the American Civil Liberties Union brought in the noted trial lawyer Clarence Darrow for the defense. The proceedings attracted national attention and the trial became a media circus. The judge refused to let Darrow call in scientists to defend evolution.

Darrow summoned Bryan as an expert witness on the Bible. The two men sparred for several days. Bryan defended the literal interpretation of the Bible, but to the reporters covering the trial he seemed to wither under Darrow's cross-examination. Sophisticated Americans regarded Bryan as a joke, but in rural America he remained a hero. The jury found Scopes guilty and assessed him a small fine. Bryan died shortly after the trial. To many Americans, the Scopes trial seemed to signal the end of fundamentalism, and the political side of the movement did lose momentum during the late 1920s. But during the same period fundamentalism returned to its roots. It concentrated on creating a network of churches, schools, and colleges where its doctrines could be taught to future generations. The forces underlying fundamentalism during the 1920s would remain a potent element in American culture.

Prohibition in Retreat

By the middle of the 1920s, the Prohibition experiment was faltering. Enforcement and compliance waned. The spread of bootlegging and its ties with organized crime meant that state and federal authorities faced an ever-growing challenge in attempting to stop movement of illegal liquor across the Canadian border or from ships that gathered near major U.S. ports. The brewing and liquor interests called for a campaign to repeal the Eighteenth Amendment, and the Association Against the Prohibition Amendment became a strong lobbying force.

Consumption of alcohol rose to over one gallon annually per capita by 1923 and reached almost one and one-quarter gallons three years later. With the national law on the books, the Anti-Saloon League lost some of its intensity during the 1920s. When the problems associated with drinking declined, its urgency as a social issue receded. The consensus that had brought Prohibition into existence during World War I was crumbling as the 1928 presidential election approached. As yet, however, a majority of Americans opposed outright repeal of Prohibition.

Flaming Youth

During the 1920s, changes in the family gave youth more importance. Women stopped having children at a younger age, and they thus had more time to devote to their own interests. Divorce gained favor as a way of ending unhappy marriages; in 1924, one marriage in seven ended in divorce. The emphasis shifted to making marriages more fulfilling for both partners. Marriage counseling gained in popularity, as did manuals telling men and women how to achieve greater sexual gratification.

As the nature of marriage changed, the role of children in the household was also transformed. Parents were no longer regarded as the unquestioned rulers of the home. One major influence on how American children were raised was the work of the behavioral psychologist John B. Watson. He taught that by manipulating the stimuli that a child experienced, the parents could create the kind of adult they wanted. Children, he said, "are made, not born." He instructed parents to follow a system of reward and punishment to shape the character of their offspring.

The ability of parents to decide what their children should read and think came under attack from the growing pervasiveness of the consumer culture. Young people were bombarded with alluring images of automobiles, makeup, motion pictures, and other attractions. Since children no longer were so important to the wage-earning power of the family, they were given greater freedom to spend their leisure time as they deemed best. A teenager might have four to six evenings a week to spend away from home. Adolescence came to be seen as a distinct phase in the development of young Americans in which they lived within their own subculture and responded to its demands for fun, excitement, and novelty. Dating became a ritualized form of courting behavior carried on at movies, dances, and athletic events, as well as in automobiles.

More young Americans attended high school during the 1920s than ever before, and the percentage of those who went to college increased. The college experience became the model for middle-class white youth across the nation. Freed from parental supervision, college women could smoke in public, go out on dates, and engage in the latest trends in sexual activ-

The Scopes trial over the teaching of evolution resulted in a notorious legal confrontation between Clarence Darrow (left) and William Jennings Bryan. Many observers saw their duel as a symbol of the urban-rural tensions roiling the nation during the 1920s.
The Granger Collection, New York

ity, "necking and petting." Male students with enough income joined fraternities, drank heavily, and devoted endless amounts of time to athletic contests and dates.

The college experience for students from lower-class families, different religious backgrounds, or minority groups was less comfortable. Informal quotas limited the numbers of Jewish students admitted to Yale, Columbia, or Harvard. In the South, African Americans of college age were forced to attend predominantly black institutions that struggled with fewer resources and less distinguished faculties. Poorer students at state universities and private colleges worked their way through, often performing the menial tasks that made life pleasant for their affluent colleagues.

Big-Time Sports

During the 1920s, college football grew into a national obsession as money was poured into the construction of stadiums, the coaching staffs, and in many instances, the players themselves. Large stadiums sprang up on the West Coast and in the Midwest. The most famous football player of the era was Harold "Red" Grange of the University of Illinois. When he scored four touchdowns in twelve minutes against the University of Michigan in 1924, his picture appeared on the cover of the new *Time* magazine. After he left college, Grange joined the newly formed National Professional Football League and received some $12,000 per game at the start.

Boxing attracted millions of followers. The first popular champion was William Harrison "Jack" Dempsey, who received $1 million for his fight against the Frenchman Georges Carpentier in 1921. To avoid confronting the leading African American contender Henry Willis, Dempsey and his manager agreed to fight James Joseph "Gene" Tunney. Tunney defeated an overconfident Dempsey in 1927.

Baseball: The National Sport

Of all the American sports, however, baseball symbolized the excitement and passion of the 1920s. The game experienced a wounding scandal in 1919 when it was revealed that members of the Chicago White Sox had conspired to fix the World Series. Although the players were ultimately acquitted of any crime, the "Black Sox" scandal cast a shadow over the game. The owners hired a new commissioner, Kenesaw Mountain Landis, a former federal judge, and gave him sweeping authority over the operations of baseball. Landis barred the "Black Sox" players from the game for life

In the heyday of big-time sports, no one was more popular or well known than George Herman "Babe" Ruth of the New York Yankees. His prodigious home runs and gargantuan appetites made him a larger-than-life hero. This picture shows his powerful swing.
Chicago Historical Society

for having cheated and exercised his power vigorously to keep baseball pure.

Baseball underwent even more dramatic changes on the field because of the emergence of a new kind of player in the person of George Herman "Babe" Ruth. Ruth was a pitcher for the Boston Red Sox when they sold him to the New York Yankees for $400,000 in 1918. Ruth believed that he could hit home runs; he belted out fifty-four during the 1920 season. Fans flocked to see him perform. The Yankees decided to construct Yankee Stadium ("the House that Ruth built") to accommodate the customers who wanted to be there when Ruth connected. The Yankees won American League pennants from 1921 to 1923, and in 1923 they won the World Series. Batting averages rose in both leagues, as did attendance records. Professional baseball remained a white man's game, however; talented black players such as Josh Gibson labored in obscurity in the Negro leagues.

NEW ROLES FOR WOMEN

After the achievement of woman suffrage, most people expected the newly enfranchised voters to produce a genuine change in politics. It soon became apparent that women cast their votes much as men did. The possibility of a cohesive bloc of female voters evaporated. Yet while women did not change politics, they found that their place in society underwent significant transformations.

Women in Politics

After 1923, the more militant wing of the suffragists, identified with Alice Paul and the National Woman's party, advocated the Equal Rights Amendment (ERA). The amendment stated that "men and women shall have equal rights throughout the United States and every place subject to its jurisdiction." Other female reformers, such as Florence Kelley and Carrie Chapman Catt, regarded the ERA as a threat to the hard-won legislation that protected women in the workplace. These women favored an approach such as the Sheppard-Towner Act of 1921, which supplied federal matching funds to states that created programs in which mothers would be instructed on caring for their babies and safeguarding their own health.

Two states, Wyoming and Texas, elected female governors. Nellie Tayloe Ross of Wyoming was chosen to fill out the unexpired term of her husband after he

Elsie Hill on Why Women Should Have Full Legal Equality, 1922

In the wake of woman suffrage, the National Woman's party pressed forward with a feminist agenda that is well expressed in this statement of the movement's goals by Elsie Hill.

The removal of all forms of the subjection of women is the purpose to which the National Woman's Party is dedicated. Its present campaign to remove the discriminations against women in the laws of the United States is but the beginning of its determined effort to secure the freedom of women, an integral part of the struggle for human liberty for which women are first of all responsible. Its interest lies in the final release of woman from the class of a dependent, subservient being to which early civilization committed her.

The laws of various States at present hold her in that class. They deny her a control of her children equal to the father's; they deny her, if married, the right to her own earnings; they punish her for offences for which men go unpunished; they exclude her from public office and from public institutions to the support of which her taxes contribute. These laws are not the creation of this age, but the fact that they are still tolerated on our statute books and that in some States their removal is vigorously resisted shows the hold of old traditions upon us. Since the passage of the Suffrage Amendment the incongruity of these laws, dating back many centuries, has become more than ever marked. . . .

The National Woman's Party believes that it is a vital social need to do away with these discriminations against women and is devoting its energies to that end. The removal of the discriminations and not the method by which they are removed is the thing upon which the Woman's Party insists. It has under consideration an amendment to the Federal Constitution which, if adopted, would remove them at one stroke, but it is at present endeavoring to secure their removal in the individual States by a blanket bill, which is the most direct State method. For eighty-two years the piecemeal method has been tried, beginning with the married women's property act of 1839 in Mississippi, and no State, excepting Wisconsin, where the Woman's Party blanket bill was passed in June, 1921, has yet finished. . . .

The present program of the National Woman's Party is to introduce its Woman's Equal Rights Bill, or bills attaining the same purpose, in all State legislatures as they convene. It is building up in Washington a great headquarters from which this campaign can be conducted, and it is acting in the faith that the removal of these discriminations from our laws will benefit every group of women in the country, and through them all society.

---

died in office. Miriam Amanda Ferguson of Texas won election in 1924 because her husband, a former governor, had been impeached and barred from holding office in the state. She became his surrogate. Eleven women were elected to the House of Representatives, many of them as political heirs of their husbands. Many more won seats in state legislatures or held local offices. Eleanor Roosevelt, the wife of a rising Democratic politician in New York, built up a network of support among women in her party.

Social causes enlisted women who had started their careers in public life years earlier. Margaret Sanger continued to be a staunch advocate of birth control. She founded the American Birth Control League, which became Planned Parenthood in 1942. Sanger capitalized on a popular interest in "eugenics," a quasi-scientific movement to limit births among "unfit" elements of the population. The racist implications of the theory stirred only modest controversy before the rise of Nazi Germany in the 1930s. Sanger found increased support for birth control among doctors as the 1920s progressed. The greatest effect of the campaign was seen in middle-class women. The poor and minorities turned to older, less reliable methods of avoiding pregnancy and often resorted to abortions when pregnant.

The Flapper and the New Woman

Social feminism confronted a sense that young women were more interested in fun and diversion than in political movements. The "flapper," with her bobbed hair and short skirts, captivated the popular press. Older female reformers noted sadly that their younger counterparts were likely "to be bored" when the subject of feminism came up. In their relations with men, young women of the 1920s practiced a new sexual freedom. Among women born after 1900, the rate of premarital intercourse, while still low by modern standards, was twice as high as it had been among women born a decade earlier.

Women on the Job

Women joined the workforce in growing numbers. At the beginning of the decade, 8.3 million women, or about 24 percent of the national workforce, were employed outside the home. Ten years later, the number stood at 10.6 million, or 27 percent. A few occupations accounted for 85 percent of female jobs. One-third of these women worked in clerical positions, 20 percent labored as domestic servants, and another third were employed in factory jobs. Many women with factory jobs worked a full week and continued to spend many hours on household chores as well. The median wage for women usually stood at about 55 percent of what men earned for comparable jobs. At the same time women entered new professions and became celebrities. Amelia Earhart, for example, was the first woman pilot to cross the Atlantic, and emerged as the most famous woman flier of the era.

For the majority of women, however, the barriers to advancement and opportunity remained high. Poor white women in the South often worked at dead-end jobs in textile mills or agricultural processing plants. Black women found it difficult to secure nondomestic jobs either in the North or the South. When African Americans were employed to move supplies or equipment in factories, they did the heavy, menial laborer that white workers shunned. In the Southwest, Hispanic women picked crops, shelled pecans, or worked as domestic servants. Labor unions rarely addressed the situation of female workers. When strikes did occur, as in New Jersey and Massachusetts during the middle of the decade, employers sometimes granted concessions—and then moved their factories to the South where labor was cheaper and unions were weaker.

The Plight of the Career Woman

Career women faced formidable obstacles. When a woman schoolteacher married, many school districts compelled her to resign. College faculties, the medical profession, and the law had more women members but they made it difficult for women to advance in these careers. In government, men received favorable treatment. Although many women worked outside the home out of economic necessity, they were expected to juggle their careers and domestic responsibilities. Women who were "creative" or who had "administrative gifts or business ability," said the feminist Crystal Eastman, and who also had "the normal desire to be mothers, must make up their minds to be sort of supermen."

COOLIDGE IN THE WHITE HOUSE

The inauguration of President Coolidge on March 4, 1925, was the first to be broadcast over the radio. The administration's policy goals were modest. In 1926, Coolidge asked Congress for a cut in taxes. The lawmakers responded with a measure that lowered the surtax on those people who made more than $100,000 annually, reduced the estate tax to 20 percent, and eliminated the gift tax. Few married couples earned more than the $3,500 exemption and only about 4 million Americans filed tax returns during this period. The changes in the law affected only the most affluent in the society.

The president also supported laws to oversee the expansion of the new airline industry and regulate the growing radio business. On the other hand, Coolidge vetoed a bill to develop the electric power potential of the Tennessee River at Muscle Shoals, Alabama, for public purposes. When Congress twice passed the McNary-Haugen Plan to assist agriculture, Coolidge vetoed it on the grounds that trying to raise crop prices through government intervention was both expensive and wrong.

Coolidge's Foreign Policy

Although the United States remained out of the League of Nations, it was not an isolationist country during the 1920s. The Coolidge administration participated in foreign relations in ways that would have seemed impossible a decade earlier. Its effort to have the United States join the World Court (a part of the League whose official title was the Permanent Court of International Justice) in 1925 and 1926 collapsed when the Senate insisted on major conditions for American membership, including limits on the court's ability to issue advisory opinions on disputed issues. The government encouraged the expansion of American business around the world, and Washington used corporate executives as ambassadors and in framing monetary policy. Americans applauded U.S. policy in Latin America, Asia, and Europe because it did not involve the use of force or the commitment of soldiers. Sentiment for peace remained strong.

In Latin America, troubled relations with Mexico, especially over control of oil reserves, persisted. The administration sent an emissary, Dwight Morrow, who mediated an agreement to protect American oil companies from further expropriation. Marines were withdrawn from Nicaragua in 1925 but were sent back a year later when civil war erupted again. American efforts to instruct the Nicaraguans in what Washington said were democratic procedures did not produce the desired results by the time the Coolidge presidency ended.

Diplomacy and Finance in the 1920s

After the decision not to join the League of Nations, the U.S. interest in Europe became chiefly financial. American bankers and investors played a large part in providing the reparation payments required of Germany in the Treaty of Versailles. Because of the size of the sums they had to pay, the Germans were unable to meet their obligations without American help. In 1924, the Coolidge administration endorsed a plan that scaled back German reparations and loaned that country money to meet its debts. During the next four years, Germany borrowed almost $1.5 million from the United States. European nations in turn used the money paid to them by the Germans to buy American farm and factory products.

The Coolidge administration continued the policy of nonrecognition of the Soviet Union, but it did not object when business interests, including Henry Ford, made substantial investments there. Americans also sent large amounts of aid and food when the Soviets faced famine during the early 1920s. In China, the U.S. government watched apprehensively as revolution and civil war wracked that nation. Washington extended de facto recognition to the government of the Nationalist leader, Chiang Kai-shek. That stance reflected the general policy of encouraging positive developments overseas without assuming any direct obligations. A symbol of that sentiment came in American support for the idea of outlawing war altogether. When the French foreign minister, Aristide Briand, proposed a mutual security agreement between his country and the United States, the State Department, under Frank B. Kellogg, proposed instead a multilateral agreement to have signatory nations renounce war. Peace groups supported the idea and the Kellogg-Briand Pact was signed in 1928 and ratified a year later.

1 9 2 7 : THE YEAR OF THE DECADE

The crosscurrents of the 1920s merged during 1927. One significant event after another grabbed the headlines. The most striking individual achievement came in May, when Charles A. Lindbergh flew alone across the Atlantic Ocean from New York to Paris. Lindbergh did not make the first nonstop flight across the ocean. Two English aviators accomplished that feat eight years earlier, flying from Ireland to Newfoundland in 1919. By 1926, however, a $25,000 prize was offered for the first nonstop flight between New York and Paris, a distance of 3,600 miles. Charles Lindbergh had been an army flier and was working as an airmail pilot for the government when he heard about the contest. He raised money from civic leaders in St. Louis and other cities. He called his monoplane the *Spirit of St. Louis.* On May 10, a tired Lindbergh (he had not slept the night before) took off from Roosevelt Field in New York on his way to Paris. When he landed in the French capital thirty-six hours later, he was a worldwide celebrity. He received a ticker tape parade in New York City, medals from foreign nations, and a lifetime in the public eye. To the generation of the 1920s, Lindbergh's feat symbolized the ability of a single person to bend technology to his will and overcome nature.

It was a period of enthusiasm for science and technology both in and out of government. The achievements of Henry Ford and Frederick Winslow

Charles Lindbergh's solo flight across the Atlantic Ocean in 1927 made him an international hero. Here the youthful Lindbergh stands stiffly in front of his plane, the Spirit of St. Louis.
The Granger Collection, New York

Taylor in industry captured worldwide attention. Sigmund Freud's psychological theories attracted popular notice. Terms from his writings, such as "id" and "libido," became part of the everyday language. Universities and corporations supported scientific research, especially in physics; chemistry and astronomy also benefitted. In this climate, a hero like Lindbergh found a ready audience.

A Heyday for Sports and a Big Change for Films

On athletic fields, stunning accomplishments marked 1927. The New York Yankees became known as "Murderers Row" because of their many hitters, of whom Babe Ruth was the most famous. Ruth hit sixty home runs, a record that stood for thirty-four years. In boxing, Gene Tunney and Jack Dempsey had a rematch of their heavyweight championship fight. Dempsey knocked Tunney down in the seventh round but failed to go to a neutral corner quickly. The result was a "long count" that enabled Tunney to come off the canvas and win.

**WARNER BROS.
Supreme Triumph**

AL JOLSON
in
The JAZZ SINGER

Al Jolson in "the Jazz Singer" brought sound to the movies in 1927 and opened a whole new phase of popularity for the cinema. Soon silent pictures had became obsolete as audiences flocked to the new talking movies.
From the Collections of the Library of Congress

Motion pictures enjoyed strong popularity at the beginning of the year but there was growing evidence that silent films were boring audiences. Filmmakers believed that talking movies were the logical next step. Fearful that they might lose their hold on the public, the major studios agreed that none of them would make talking pictures unless they all did. One of the smaller studios, Warner Brothers, was working on a sound picture called *The Jazz Singer.* Its star was Al Jolson, who specialized in blackface renditions of popular tunes. When he ad-libbed his catch phrase, "You Ain't Heard Nothing Yet,"and sang several songs, the audience response was enthusiastic. Within two years, silent pictures gave way to sound.

Ford Introduces the Model A

By the end of the 1920s, the simple Model T was no longer the car of choice for Americans. General Motors was offering Chevrolets that were only a little more expensive than Model Ts but offered features and options that Ford did not. In addition, the annual models that Alfred P. Sloan had introduced promised consumers novelty and excitement as well as a better product. By 1926, the Model T had become an economic liability and Ford's sales had slumped.

During the spring of 1927, Henry Ford ended production of the Model T and turned to the development of a new car. Within months the Model A was ready for consumers. Interest in the product was high; orders for hundreds of thousands were taken before the new model was introduced. Although it would be months before Ford could fill the consumer demand for the automobile, on December 1, 1927, the company unveiled the Model A. Like General Motors, Ford marketed the Model A through a huge advertising campaign. It also created a credit corporation, again modeled on what General Motors had done, to enable buyers to obtain their cars on credit.

The Execution of Sacco and Vanzetti

The fate of Sacco and Vanzetti continued to attract international attention. By the spring of 1927, the appeals process had almost run its course. Despite strong evidence that the two men had not received a fair trial, and substantial indications that they were not guilty, the legal machinery moved them toward the electric chair. The date of their execution was set for July 1927. The campaign to save the two defendants had become worldwide. The governor of Massachusetts appointed a special commission to review the case. After flawed and biased proceedings, the panel decided to affirm the convictions. Finally, the two men were electrocuted on August 23, 1927. The case convinced many radicals that more drastic measures would be necessary to reform American society.

"I Do Not Choose to Run"

Calvin Coolidge could easily have sought another term in 1928. The president, however, may have sensed the weaknesses in the economy that would become evident two years later. While vacationing in the Black Hills of South Dakota during the summer of 1927, the president gave reporters a simple statement: "I do not choose to run for President in 1928." This surprise announcement opened up the race for the Republican presidential nomination to other potential contenders such as the secretary of commerce, Herbert Hoover.

As 1927 ended there were some signs that the economy was not as robust as it had been. A slight recession occurred in which wholesale prices fell nearly 4.5 percent. Production slowed, and consumer spending also dropped. Despite these warning signs, the banking system continued to expand credit, and stock market speculation persisted. For the average American there was little concrete evidence that the boom years might be coming to a close.

The longest running legal case of the 1920s was the controversial murder conviction of Nicola Sacco (right) and Bartolomeo Vanzetti (left). Their appeals of the verdict became a cause that many intellectuals in and out of the United States supported before the two men were executed in 1927.
© Bettmann/UPI/Corbis

CONCLUSION

The years between World War I and the start of the Great Depression have never lost their reputation for excitement and novelty. Bathtub gin, flappers, syncopation, and gangsters remain part of the national image of that time. Prohibition did encounter serious opposition from the upper classes, and evasion of the law was widespread. On the other hand, liquor control did change drinking habits, so the experiment was not a complete failure.

For women the sense that the 1920s represented a new age of sexual and social liberation was actually rather superficial. Sexual practices did become more flexible, but marriage and family continued to be viewed as the goals toward which most women should aspire. The number of women in the workplace rose, but the percentage of women in the labor force did not change very much. Politics saw an infusion of women into both major parties, but genuine equality remained elusive. The 1920s did not produce anything like the gains in political or social status that had been achieved by women during the previous decade.

In its culture, the United States went through an artistic renaissance. Literature, art, and music explored new channels and brought forth important figures whose influence remained strong through the 1930s and beyond. The works of Hemingway, Fitzgerald, and Mencken, the jazz of Ellington and Armstrong, and the achievements of numerous other artists made the 1920s a high point of American artistic expression.

The 1920s brought important economic changes for many Americans. A consumer culture based on mass appeal tied middle-class society together through common experiences of driving automobiles, listening to radios, and attending films each week. The cultural response was more complex. The Ku Klux Klan, the movement for immigration restriction, and the rise of fundamentalism challenged the newer ways and revealed that the United States was still divided between the values of town and country.

While the potential for social conflict persisted, the economic good times of the decade left few avenues for effective protest and unrest. For a brief period it seemed possible that discord might vanish in a rising tide of economic growth. However, the prosperity of the 1920s did not alter the inequities between rich and poor. If the national belief in a prosperous future were to disappear, the latent strains within American life might resurface.

Recommended Readings

Brophy, Alfred I., and Kennedy, Randall. *Reconstructing the Dreamland: The Tulsa Race Riot of 1921* (2002). Looks at a case study of racial violence in the decade.

Coben, Stanley. *Rebellion Against Victorianism: The Impetus for Cultural Change in 1920s America* (1991). Discusses how Americans in the 1920s reacted against the ideas and values of an earlier time.

Douglas, Ann. *Terrible Honesty: Mongrel Manhattan in the 1920s* (1995). A cultural history of the decade from the perspective of events in New York City.

Dumenil, Lynn. *The Modern Temper: American Culture and Society in the 1920s* (1995). An excellent analysis of the major trends of the period.

Ferrell, Robert H. *The Strange Deaths of President Harding* (1996). Explodes many of the sensational myths about Harding's career.

Ferrell, Robert H. *The Presidency of Calvin Coolidge* (1998). Provides a good survey of what Coolidge did as president.

Goldberg, David J. *Discontented America: The United States in the 1920s* (1999). Provides a thoughtful narrative about the main currents of this period.

Larson, Edward J. *Summer for the Gods: The Scopes Trial and America's Continuing Debate over Science and Religion* (1997). A prize-winning look at the celebrated trial about evolution.

Leinwand, Gerald. *1927, High Tide of the Twenties* (2001). Considers the year that defined the spirit of the decade.

Parrish, Michael E. *Anxious Decades: America in Prosperity and Depression* (1992). A fascinating treatment of the interwar years.

American Journey Online and InfoTrac College Edition

Visit the source collections at http://ajaccess.wadsworth.com and infotrac.thomsonlearning.com and use the Search function with the following key terms to explore documents, images, audio and video clips, articles, and commentary related to the material in this chapter.

Warren G. Harding	Sinclair Lewis
Calvin Coolidge	Marcus Garvey
Charles Lindbergh	Zora Neale Hurston
Babe Ruth	Flapper
Alain Locke	New Negro Renaissance
Marcus Garvey	National Woman's party
Woman suffrage	Sacco and Vanzetti

Additional resources, exercises, and Internet links related to this chapter are available on the American Passages Web site: http://history.wadsworth.com/passages2e

24 THE GREAT DEPRESSION
1927–1933

THE ELECTION OF 1928

THE STOCK MARKET CRASH OF 1929

THE GREAT DEPRESSION

HOOVER'S PROGRAMS TO FIGHT THE DEPRESSION

A DARKENING WORLD

A POLITICAL OPPORTUNITY FOR THE DEMOCRATS

Herbert Hoover was an effective candidate against Al Smith in 1928 even though his main reliance was on a few speeches that were broadcast nationally.
From the Collections of the Library of Congress

As the end of the 1920s approached, some well-off Americans viewed the future with confidence. Accepting the Republican presidential nomination in 1928, Herbert Hoover proclaimed: "We in America today are nearer to the final triumph over poverty than ever before in the history of any land." Farmers would not have shared Hoover's optimism, nor would African Americans and the poor. Among those who had benefitted from the boom of the 1920s, however, the prosperity and abundance enjoyed by the fortunate seemed destined to extend into the immediate future.

Then came the shocks, first of the crash of the stock market in October 1929, then a severe economic depression that worsened during the early 1930s. The good times of the 1920s were replaced with bread lines, soup kitchens, and the wandering homeless. The administration of President Herbert Hoover took unprecedented actions to relieve the crisis, but nothing seemed to work. Resentment against the president, the economic system, and the wealthy grew. The specter of social revolution arose. Pressures for political change led to the election of Franklin D. Roosevelt in 1932.

By 1933, the Great Depression, as it came to be called, affected almost everyone in American society. It worsened the already difficult situation of the nation's farmers. For African Americans, Hispanics, and the poor, it meant even more misery and suffering than they usually faced. A generation of Americans looked to the federal government for answers to the social and economic problems they confronted.

THE ELECTION OF 1928

After the withdrawal of President Coolidge in 1927, Herbert Hoover, the secretary of commerce, moved to the front of the Republican field for 1928. He presented an attractive blend of scientific expertise as an engineer and traditional values based on his rural upbringing.

Herbert Hoover: The Engineer as Candidate

Hoover had been reared as an orphan in a modest Quaker home in Iowa. He built a career as a mining engineer after graduation from Stanford University. He first gained world attention during World War I, when he managed the campaign to bring food relief to the starving people of Belgium. He ran the Food Administration and then sent relief and food to war-torn Russia. During his years in the Commerce Department, Hoover skillfully used the new technology of radio and

---

CHRONOLOGY

1928 Republicans nominate Herbert Hoover as their presidential candidate • Democrats select Alfred E. Smith • Hoover elected president of the United States

1929 Stock market crash, September–October 1929

1930 Smoot-Hawley Tariff bill passed to raise tariff rates • Birds Eye frozen foods and Wonder sliced bread introduced • Democratic gains in congressional elections

1931 President Hoover declares moratorium on payment of war debts • Association of Southern Women Against Lynching starts • Japanese invade Manchuria

1932 Bonus March in Washington • Amelia Earhart makes first transatlantic solo flight by a woman • Democrats nominate Franklin D. Roosevelt who promises New Deal • Roosevelt wins landslide election victory

1933 Banks fail during first two months • Depression worsens • Roosevelt inaugurated March 4, 1933

---

motion pictures to spread his name and face to all corners of the United States.

The leaders of the Republican party were less enthusiastic about Hoover. They recognized that "Sir Herbert," as they called him in private, had few direct connections with the traditional methods of partisan politics. Since Hoover had worked for the Wilson administration and had internationalist sympathies, he was not popular among Republicans who wanted to limit foreign involvement. Nevertheless, Hoover was the most attractive Republican hopeful in the race and he was easily nominated at the party's convention.

In his acceptance speech for the nomination, Hoover promised abundant jobs and spoke out strongly against religious intolerance. Hoover was never an exciting speaker. He read this address in a monotone, with little effort to arouse the enthusiasm of the audience. In 1928, however, sober and calm rhetoric impressed many voters as precisely what the times demanded.

From the Sidewalks of New York: Al Smith

The Democrats still felt the wounds of their disastrous convention in 1924 and wished to avoid the mistakes of that year. The nomination of Alfred E. Smith, the governor of New York and the clear front-runner, was almost a certainty. Because he had been denied the prize in 1924, a second rejection would split the Democrats irrevocably. Yet to nominate Smith was likely to release the passions and prejudices that had dogged the Democrats for twenty years.

Al Smith had grown up in New York City, working in the Fulton Fish Market. He had a natural talent for politics and soon made his mark in the New York legislature. He was elected governor in 1918, defeated in 1920, returned to office in 1922, and then reelected twice more. As governor, Smith championed moderate social welfare policies, administrative efficiency, and public works. He enlisted former progressives, women reformers, and social scientists in his administration in ways that foreshadowed the New Deal of the 1930s.

Smith's Political Weaknesses

For all his political skills, however, Smith had liabilities that alienated intolerant voters in 1928. A devout Roman Catholic, he confronted the currents of prejudice that limited presidential candidates to Protestant men. In his daily life, the governor attended Mass, pledged religious obedience to the Catholic clergy, and displayed the visible symbols of his faith. As a public official, he defended separation of church and state, challenging the position of his church when he supported divorce legislation in New York.

The governor also disliked Prohibition and its impact on national politics. He favored the right of an individual state to allow liquor to be sold within its borders, and indicated that he had served liquor at his official residence. At the Democratic convention, he came out for "fundamental changes in the present provisions of national prohibition," a move that outraged southerners in his party. Despite reservations among his southern and western opponents, Smith's strength won him the nomination at the Democratic National Convention in Houston.

Cartoonists had a fine time depicting the Smith-Hoover contest. Smith was known as the "Happy Warrior" because Franklin Roosevelt had given him that title in 1924.
The Granger Collection, New York

Hoover Versus Smith: The 1928 Campaign

Most of the electoral advantages rested with Herbert Hoover. Many parts of the nation were prosperous, and those who suffered from economic difficulties thought that they still had a chance to improve their lives. Will Rogers, the cowboy humorist, summed up the public mood: "Prosperity—millions never had it under Coolidge, never had it under anybody, but expect it under Hoover."

Hoover campaigned in a highly structured manner. He gave his acceptance address and six other major speeches during the autumn of 1928. The Republicans took as their campaign slogan "a chicken in every pot and two cars in every garage." Well financed and cohesive, the Republicans easily outmaneuvered the divided Democrats.

The Smith Response to Hoover

Smith did not campaign as a liberal alternative to Hoover. He said little about economic distress, played down differences over the tariff and tax policy, and stressed his allegiance to a government that interfered "as little as possible with business." On the radio, Smith came across to Americans outside the Northeast as an alien, strange voice who once asked reporters which states were located west of the Mississippi River.

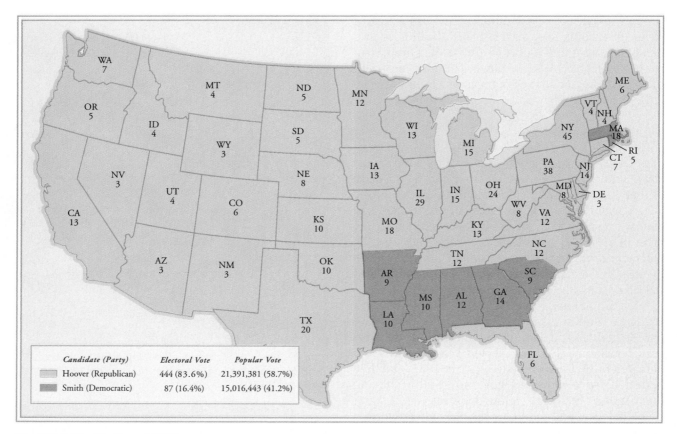

Candidate (Party)	Electoral Vote	Popular Vote
Hoover (Republican)	444 (83.6%)	21,391,381 (58.7%)
Smith (Democratic)	87 (16.4%)	15,016,443 (41.2%)

Map 24.1 *The Election of 1928*

In the election of 1928, Herbert Hoover achieved an electoral landslide and cracked the "Solid South" for the first time since Republican successes in Reconstruction. Alfred E. Smith did carry Massachusetts and Rhode Island, whose heavily Roman Catholic populations supported him. Those victories anticipated Democratic gains in the 1930s. View an animated version of this map or related maps at http://history.wadsworth.com/passages2e.

The religious issue made the 1928 campaign infamous in American political history. Some devout Protestants saw in Smith's candidacy the specter of Catholic domination of the government. Even though Smith had announced his belief "in the absolute separation of Church and State," the forces of religious intolerance rallied against him. A Baptist minister in New York City called the Democratic candidate "the nominee of the worst forces of hell." When Smith campaigned in the South, he faced burning crosses and angry voters.

A Landslide for Hoover

Hoover received 21.4 million ballots to 15 million for Smith. In the electoral college, Hoover won the 444 electoral votes of forty states. Hoover carried five southern states, including Texas, and thus broke the "Solid South" that had provided the Democrats with an electoral foundation for so long.

Beneath the electoral wreckage, however, lay some modestly encouraging signs for the Democratic party. Smith carried the nation's largest cities and ran strongly in areas with substantial immigrant and Catholic populations. At the same time, however, the Democratic candidate did less well in his party's traditional areas of strength, the South and West.

Hoover Takes Office

Herbert Hoover worked long hours in the White House. "All days were alike to him," recalled a servant. He was the first president to have a telephone installed in the Oval Office and the last to dress formally for dinner with his wife each evening.

A problem left over from previous administrations was Prohibition. By 1929, enforcement of the policy took different forms across the nation. In regions where "dry" sentiment remained strong, penalties for violators could be harsh. Elsewhere, in states with "wet" majorities, legislatures voted for repeal of the Eighteenth Amendment. Many Americans believed that Prohibition was becoming either a joke or a failure. Hoover had endorsed the amendment as "noble in motive and far-reaching in purpose," and he still hoped that it could succeed.

To address the problems, in May 1929, Hoover named a Commission on Law Enforcement to examine the nation's justice system and particularly "the enforcement of the Eighteenth Amendment." The panel studied the impact of Prohibition for nearly two years as the difficulties of stopping the alcohol traffic worsened. In January 1931, the Commission issued its report, which said that enforcement was not working; a majority of the members favored revising the Eighteenth Amendment but did not call for repeal.

For the time being, President Hoover remained a strong backer of Prohibition. Lobbying efforts by organizations such as the Association Against the Prohibition Amendment were beginning to take hold, however, and popular support for Prohibition was eroding. In the 1932 election campaign, the Democrats and their presidential candidate came out strongly for repeal of the Eighteenth Amendment.

Despite his early successes in the White House, Hoover had certain political weaknesses that would impair the effectiveness of his presidency when the economy worsened. He had very poor relations with the White House press corps. Reporters resented his insistence on saying little at news conferences, playing favorites, and becoming upset with unfavorable press coverage. Hoover also stayed aloof from Congress and made little effort to persuade lawmakers to support his favorite programs. Above all, Hoover lacked the capacity to inspire public confidence in a crisis. His success depended on the national faith that he could carry on the prosperity of the Harding-Coolidge era. When that spirit evaporated, so did Hoover's presidency.

THE STOCK MARKET CRASH OF 1929

During the first six months of Hoover's administration, the president pushed for reforms in the treatment of Native Americans and addressed a number of conservation issues such as increasing forest reserves and expanding waterpower facilities. Hoover also was an activist in foreign policy. He reduced American military commitments in Latin America and explored ways of achieving savings in military expenditures.

To the average American, the economic signs during the summer of 1929 also seemed to be encouraging. The prices of stocks traded on the New York Stock Exchange were reaching ever-higher levels. At the beginning of 1928, for example, the industrial index of the *New York Times* was recorded at 245. Within twelve months, it had risen to 331. It soared to 452 by September 1929. Radio Corporation of America stock shot up from $85 a share to $420 a share during 1928. DuPont's stock price went from $310 to $525. A poem appeared in a popular magazine:

> Oh, hush thee, my babe, granny's bought some more shares,
> Daddy's gone out to play with the bulls and bears,
> Mother's buying on tips, and she simply can't lose,
> And baby shall have some expensive new shoes!

The Crash Occurs

These rosy statistics and forecasts made the stock market crash of October 1929 even more of a shock. The problem began in September as stock prices neared their record levels. Stock prices declined early in the month, regained some strength, and then drifted downward. Yet no abrupt collapse had occurred, and to many on Wall Street these events seemed to be another one of the temporary "corrections" that usually preceded upward surges. A few people warned of impending problems, but they were dismissed as chronic naysayers who had been wrong before. Even President Hoover told his financial broker to sell off some of his holdings because "possible hard times are coming." But most owners of stock simply waited for the rise in prices to begin again.

Then on October 24, 1929, which became known as "Black Thursday," traders began selling stocks and quickly realized that there were few buyers. Prices collapsed and the total number of shares traded reached 13 million, an all-time record. Stockholders were estimated to have absorbed a $9 billion loss. During the afternoon a banking syndicate led by J. P. Morgan, Jr., and Co. urged investors to be calm. As the syndicate bought stocks, the market quieted.

On October 29, however, the selling of stocks resumed at an even more intense rate. More than 16 million shares changed hands in a single day. Prestigious industrial stocks such as American Telephone and Telegraph and General Electric recorded twenty-eight-point declines. Fistfights occurred on the trading floor and rumors of suicides swept through the Exchange.

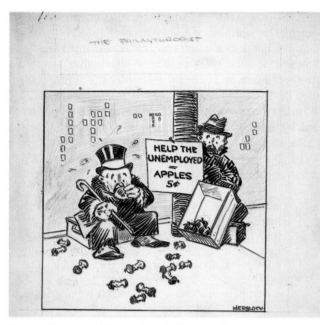

During the Great Depression, selling apples became one of the ways that poor people eked out an income. This satiric cartoon by Herbert Block (Herblock) from the early 1930s shows a rich man helping out a poor apple seller by buying and eating all the fruit that he can.
From the Collections of the Library of Congress

Causes of the Stock Market Crash

What forces produced the stock market crash of 1929? The 1920s had been characterized by an investment fever that led people into risky ventures. In Florida, for example, there had been a land boom that saw prices for some lots rise to $15,000 or $20,000 a foot for coveted waterfront acreage. When the hysteria ended in 1926, after a devastating hurricane, land prices headed downward again. Willing investors then looked for other speculative opportunities that promised a quick and profitable return.

By 1927, the stock market seemed to be just the place to make easy money. The issuance of Liberty Bonds during World War I had shown Americans the potential value of stocks. Corporations increasingly turned to the public through stock offerings to finance their business expansion. Stockbrokers sold their products with aggressive advertising techniques developed for other consumer goods. Finally, during the Harding and Coolidge years government tax policies enabled the wealthy to retain money to invest in securities. The richest Americans sometimes paid no income taxes at all. Five hundred families had incomes of more than $1 million in 1929.

Many of these surplus funds fueled the rise in the stock market.

Playing the Market: Margin Buying and Investment Trusts

One tempting device for less well-off investors was to buy stocks in "margin" trading. An investor could purchase a stock on credit, putting up only 10 or 15 percent of the actual price. Since Wall Street sentiment believed that stock prices were going up, a person could sell the stock at a higher level, pay off the broker, and still pocket a substantial profit. Just as someone might acquire a house or a car on credit, so brokers urged their customers to invest a hundred dollars with the prospect of controlling $1,000 or more worth of stock. People borrowed money to buy on margin. In this way, a tiny investment might represent a commitment to buy several thousand dollars worth of stock. Of course, the investor could be required to provide the full price of the stock at any time. But with the market headed ever upward, that risk seemed a small one.

Abuses of this practice soon followed. Investors with inside knowledge manipulated a stock's price up and down in order to fleece the unwary public. A firm called Kolster Radio had no earnings in 1929, but insiders drove the value up to ninety-five dollars before the value collapsed back to three dollars a share. New companies often consisted of nothing more than schemes to issue stock based on the assumption that the market would rise. These firms produced no goods; they were paper empires with no real value, such as Ivar Kreuger's International Match Company. Government regulation of stock issues on both the state and federal levels was very lax, and the stock exchanges themselves had few requirements for revealing the true financial status of these companies. Some of the investment trusts, as they were called, were frauds; those who put money into them lost their entire investment.

The Impact of the Crash

The number of Americans who participated in the stock market in 1929 stood at between 1.5 million and 2 million. Most of the corporate dividends in that year went to about 600,000 stockholders whose annual incomes were above $5,000. These individuals were betting on the nation's economic future and sought to benefit from a prosperity that appeared to be permanent. The crash of 1929 wiped out many of these investors. Others cut back on their stock holdings and trimmed their personal expenditures.

The stock market collapse revealed serious underlying weaknesses in the economy. The well-to-do citizens who played the market were confident that other investors would buy their stocks at the higher price levels of the precrash period. Because of the way income was distributed in the United States, with the rich getting a far higher share than that of other segments of the population, there were not enough people in the upper brackets for that assumption to be realistic. Once the wealthy investors began to sell their stocks, there were no other potential buyers to keep security prices high. A fall in the market became unavoidable.

The consequences of the stock market's decline were striking. The prices of individual stocks underwent a sustained downward slide. Within a few months such a high-flying issue as General Electric had dropped from $403 a share to $168. Standard Oil shares fell from eighty-three dollars to forty-eight. One index of stock prices had gone to 469.5 in September and was at 220.1 by November. During the next twelve months, the gross national product went down from nearly $88 billion to $76 billion.

THE GREAT DEPRESSION

Although the stock market crash represented a serious setback for the nation's economic health, the Great Depression of the 1930s arose from causes more deeply rooted than just the decline in stock values that occurred in October 1929. Despite the apparent prosperity of the 1920s, the United States had not dealt with a number of serious structural problems that combined to cause the prolonged economic downturn.

The most pervasive dilemma that the United States economy faced had to do with the distribution of income during the 1920s. By 1929, the 5 percent of Americans at the top income level were receiving one-third of the total annual personal income. Those who made up the lowest 40 percent of the population received about one-eighth of the available income. For an economy that depended on the purchase of consumer goods for its expansion, there were not enough people with money to buy the products that industry was turning out. The amount of spendable income that the top 1 percent of the population received rose from 12 percent in 1920 to 19 percent nine years later. That gain for the wealthy meant that there was less money for the mass of consumers to spend on the products of American factories and businesses than might otherwise have been possible.

Wealth was also concentrated in the hands of those with the highest incomes. More than 21 million families, or 80 percent of the national population, did not have any savings at all. About 2.3 percent of families with incomes above $10,000 a year, on the other hand, possessed two-thirds of the available savings. A consumer society had emerged, but the bulk of the consumers were unable to participate fully in the economic process. While wealth had been more concentrated earlier in the century, the disparities of the late 1920s had more impact in contributing to the onset of the Depression.

Instead of using the profits that their businesses gained from selling goods during the mid-1920s to invest in new factories or a better-paid workforce, industry leaders had put their gains into the stock market or speculative ventures. Loans to New York stockbrokers, for example, went from $3.5 billion in July 1927 to $8.5 billion in September 1929. By 1927, the market for new cars and new houses began to weaken, indicating that demand for consumer goods was decreasing.

Other Economic Problems

Another chronic weakness of the economy was in agriculture, a sector that never shared in the general prosperity of the 1920s. The problem of overproduction of farm goods had not been addressed successfully, and as prices fell at the beginning of the Depression, the farmers felt the effects most acutely. At the beginning of 1931, cotton stood at nine to ten cents per pound; when farmers brought in their crop in the fall, the price had skidded to under six cents a pound. Since farmers could not pay off their mortgages, rural banks soon failed. The ripple of banking failures strained a banking system that was already weakened by the effects of the stock market crash. In the countryside, crops rotted because they could not be sold, and farmers talked of strikes and other protests.

The International Situation

The world economy was also fragile as the 1920s came to an end. The settlement of World War I had imposed heavy reparation payments on the defeated Germans. Since the Germans could not pay these sums, they borrowed from investors and banks in the United States. In that way Americans financed the German debt payments to the victorious British and French. Those countries, in turn, could use the funds to pay off their war debts to the United States.

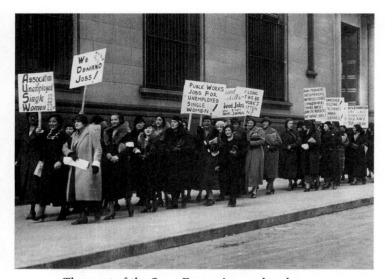

The onset of the Great Depression produced mass unemployment that the nation had not seen for four decades. The downturn hit women as much as men, and these women protested the lack of jobs and asked for public works employment.
© Bettmann / UPI / Corbis

Table 24.1	Bank Suspensions, 1927–1933
1927	669
1928	499
1929	659
1930	1352
1931	2284
1932	1458
1933	4004

Source: *Historical Statistics of the United States,* 1985, p. 536.

In 1924, the United States had reduced the burden of German war debts, and in 1929, another plan was offered that further cut back on the amount that Germany owed while establishing a payment schedule that extended the length of time for retiring the debt. These concessions alleviated the situation to some degree, but the basic problem persisted. This intricate and interlocking process hinged on the strength of the American economy. The United States, however, created tariff barriers that discouraged European imports and steered American capital toward internal economic development. When the European economies experienced difficulties themselves after 1929, the weakened structure of debts and loans soon collapsed, further damaging the economy of the United States. In fact, President Hoover would later argue that the entire Depression arose from causes beyond the borders of the United States. The debts were important in the overall situation of the world economy, but they were a contributing cause to the Depression in the United States rather than the main element in the crisis.

A Worsening Economic Situation

In 1929–1930, the United States lacked many of the government programs that could have lessened the cumulative effects of a depression. There was no government insurance of bank deposits. Individual banks were vulnerable to sudden demands by depositors to withdraw their money. Many banks had invested in the stock market and thereby placed their assets at risk. Other prominent bankers had embezzled some of the funds under their control to finance their investing. Among banks in general, there was little cooperation when a crisis occurred. To save themselves, the stronger banks called in loans made to smaller banks, thus worsening the condition of weaker banks.

For an individual employee thrown out of work, there was no unemployment insurance to cushion the effect of a layoff. Old age pensions were also rare. Conventional economic thinking taught that the government should play a minimal role during hard times. Many people believed that the natural forces of the economy must work themselves out without the government intruding into the process. Secretary of the Treasury Andrew Mellon told President Hoover that "a panic was not altogether a bad thing" because "it will purge the rottenness out of the system." Americans who did not have Mellon's wealth and secure income were less persuaded of the therapeutic effects of hard times.

The President, Congress, and the Depression

The stock market crash did not cause the Depression, and for some months after the disaster on Wall Street it seemed as though the economy might rebound without much assistance from Washington. President Hoover endeavored to strike an encouraging note when he said in late 1929: "the fundamental business of the country is sound." He conferred with leading business figures about measures to maintain public confidence, especially programs to bolster prices and wages. He asked the Federal Reserve System to facilitate business borrowing. For the moment, events seemed to be going Hoover's way. During the first several months of 1930, stock market prices recovered from their 1929 lows.

In 1930, Congress enacted the Smoot-Hawley Tariff, which raised customs duties to high levels. Republicans believed that tariff protection would enable American agriculture and industry to rebound. The bill passed the Senate by a narrow margin, and despite some reservations Hoover signed the measure on June 17, 1930. The Smoot-Hawley law has been blamed for the severity of the worldwide Depression because it made it more difficult for European business to sell goods in the United States. The negative impact of the Smoot-Hawley Tariff has probably been overstated, relative to the other, more severe causes of the Depression. In any case, by the middle of 1930, the effects of the downturn began to be felt in many areas of government activity.

Foreign Policy in the Depression

President Hoover had come to the White House with well-formulated ideas about the national role in foreign affairs. Since future wars were unlikely, he believed, it was time to pursue disarmament and let the force of world opinion maintain peace. Secretary of State Henry L. Stimson did not share the president's optimism. The two men agreed, however, on the basic goals of diplomacy during the first phase of the new administration.

In Latin America, the president announced the "good neighbor" policy. He promised not to repeat previous U.S. interventions in the region and he withdrew marines from Nicaragua and Haiti. In 1930, the State Department renounced the Roosevelt Corollary of 1904. Despite outbreaks of revolutions in South America during his term, Hoover kept his word and left Latin American nations alone.

Drawing upon his Quaker roots, Hoover thought that wars were senseless and sought disarmament as a key goal. A naval conference in Geneva in 1927 had brought Great Britain, Japan, and the United States back to the diplomatic table. Disagreements about the size of vessels covered by the proposed pact caused that meeting to break up in failure. Hoover now reassembled the major naval powers in London for a conference on disarmament. They deliberated for three months before reaching an apparent understanding. The London Treaty of 1930 made only a modest contribution to peace, however. To reduce military spending, the provisions of the Washington Conference were extended for five years. The United States won parity with Britain in all naval vessels, and the Japanese gained the same result for submarines. The outcome did not alter the military balance. Japan remained the dominant power in the Pacific, but there was little that the Hoover administration could do to change that reality. The London Treaty also contained language that allowed the signers to resume building ships if they were threatened with aggression.

The Effects of the Economic Crisis

As the United States economy deteriorated, however, the effects spread to Europe. Fewer American investors could lend money to European governments, especially in Germany. The Smoot-Hawley Tariff made it more difficult for Europeans and other importers to sell their products in the United States. International trade stagnated; production in all industrial countries declined. In 1931, Germany and Austria endeavored to set up a customs union to deal with their common problems, but the French objected to the plan and cut off payments to banks in the two countries. In the resulting turmoil, the Creditanstaldt, Austria's central bank, collapsed. The entire structure of international banking stood on the brink of disaster.

Hoover decided that the only answer was a moratorium on the payment of war debts to give the European countries time to regain their financial stability. He declared on June 21, 1931, that the United States would observe an eighteen-month moratorium on the collection of its foreign debts. The French held back for two weeks, putting further strain on German banks. In the end, all the countries involved agreed to Hoover's initiative.

The moratorium was the only possible answer, but it came too late to stop the erosion of the international financial system. A few months later, Great Britain devalued the pound when it could no longer maintain the gold standard. This step reduced the price of British products and made them more competitive in world markets. Other nations soon followed this course.

Domestic Issues for Hoover

At home, President Hoover experienced problems in his dealings with Congress. After naming Charles Evans Hughes as chief justice of the U.S. Supreme Court to replace William Howard Taft early in 1930, he had another Court vacancy to fill soon thereafter. He selected John J. Parker of North Carolina for the post. Organized labor opposed Parker's nomination because of Parker's issuance of antiunion injunctions in labor disputes. The National Association for the Advancement of Colored People assailed his racial views. The Senate rejected Parker's selection.

During the 1930s and afterward, many Americans would blame the Great Depression on President Hoover and his policies. Yet more than any previous chief executive, Hoover endeavored to use the power of his office to address the economic crisis. He favored reduction of taxes, easing of bank credits, and a modest program of public works to provide jobs. Some members of Congress opposed these ideas as too activist; others said that Hoover proposed too little. Meanwhile, the White House issued a series of confident statements to bolster public faith that the economic downturn would be brief. When the stock market turned upward briefly in 1930, for example, the president told the nation: "I am convinced we have passed the worst and with continued effort shall rapidly recover."

The Deepening Depression

But as 1930 continued, it was clear that the Depression was not going away. Bank failures soared from 659 in 1929 to 1,350 a year later. Businesses were closing, investment was declining, and corporate profits were falling off. Industrial production was 26 percent lower at the end of 1930 than it had been twelve months earlier. By October 1930, 4 million people were without jobs (almost 9 percent of the labor force), and the trend worsened as each month passed. Within a year, nearly 16 percent of the labor force was out of work.

To encourage confidence, Hoover exhorted businesses to keep prices up and employees at work. Conferences with industry leaders at the White House were covered extensively in the press. These sessions were designed to show the American people that the Depression was being addressed. The president lacked the power to make corporations retain workers or to prevent price-cutting. Despite any public pledges they might offer to Hoover, corporate executives trimmed payrolls and reduced costs when it seemed necessary. These actions further undercut Hoover's credibility.

HOOVER'S PROGRAMS TO FIGHT THE DEPRESSION

The president sought to apply his principles of voluntary action to keep the banking system afloat. In October 1931, he persuaded bankers to set up the National Credit Corporation, a private agency that would underwrite banks that had failed and safeguard their depositors. Unfortunately, the banks proved reluctant to acquire the assets of their failed competitors. The experiment was a disaster.

Despite his broadened use of the powers of his office, Herbert Hoover did not view government action as an appropriate way of responding to the Depression. Instead, he believed that the traditional self-reliance and volunteer spirit of the American people provided the most dependable means of ending the economic slump. His policies promoting economic recovery and providing relief for the unemployed stemmed from that fundamental conviction. He asked Americans who had jobs to invest more in their neighbors, to spend something extra to ensure that everyone could work. He set up presidential committees to coordinate volunteer relief efforts for the unemployed. One of those committees was the President's Organization of Unemployment Relief (or POUR).

The Persistence of Unemployment

These programs were inadequate for the size of the unemployment situation. By 1931, 8 million people were on the jobless rolls. They overwhelmed the resources of existing charitable agencies that normally provided help to the blind, the deaf, and the physically impaired. Nor were the cities and states capable of providing relief at a time when the Depression reduced their tax revenues and increased the demand for services.

In this situation, the president's informal committees for dealing with unemployment proved ineffective. The POUR program coordinated relief agencies and urged people to help their neighbors. The First Lady, Lou Hoover, long a leader of the Girl Scouts, mobilized its members for the same purpose. These efforts, commendable as they were, did little to deal with the mass unemployment that gripped the country. But when politicians clamored for action by the national government, Hoover remained resolutely opposed.

A symbolic event underscored the president's political ineptitude in dealing with the Depression and its effects. When a drought struck the Midwest in 1930 and 1931, Congress proposed to appropriate $60 million to help the victims of the disaster buy fuel and food. Hoover accepted the idea of allocating money to feed animals, but he rejected the idea of feeding farmers and their families. One member of Congress said that the administration would give food to "jackasses . . . but not starving babies." The president accepted a compromise that spent the money without saying that some of it would be used for food.

Everyday Life During the Depression

For most Americans, there was no single decisive moment when they knew that the economy was in trou-

ℱICTURING THE PAST✦ECONOMICS & TECHNOLOGY

Table 24.2	Unemployment, 1927–1933	
Year	**Unemployed**	**% of Labor Force**
1927	1,890,000	4.1
1928	2,080,000	4.4
1929	1,550,000	3.2
1930	4,340,000	8.7
1931	8,020,000	15.9
1932	12,060,000	23.6
1933	12,830,000	24.9

Source: *Historical Statistics of the United States*, 1985, p. 73.

The dimensions of the Great Depression of the 1930s are sometimes hard to grasp in human terms. This table about the rise of unemployment during the late 1920s and into the early 1930s provides the raw totals of people out of work. As the numbers show, the modest unemployment of 1929 rose dramatically by 1930 and then nearly doubled a year later. The increase in the number of people out of work strained the resources of relief agencies, which were then largely private. Mass unemployment had not been seen for four decades since the hard times of the 1890s. By 1932, the percentage of those unemployed had risen to almost 24 percent, and many other workers saw pay cuts and reductions in the hours that they spent on the job. With no unemployment insurance or organized system of government relief to tide workers over, poverty was the inescapable result. The impact of these stark numbers lingered for more than a decade on the people who found themselves the unexpected victims of this massive and prolonged economic downturn.

ble. A husband might find his pay reduced or his hours of work cut back. Soon families were making changes in their lifestyle, postponing purchases and sending children out to find jobs. When a person lost a job, savings helped tide the family over until another job could be found. As time passed and no jobs appeared, savings ran out and the family home went on the market or the mortgage was foreclosed. The family slipped into the ranks of the unemployed or the poor. In a trend that became a lasting image of the Depression, men selling apples appeared on the street corners in major cities. Beggars and panhandlers became a common sight as well.

For those who were at the bottom of the economy even during boom times, the Depression presented still greater challenges. Blacks had not shared in the relative prosperity of the 1920s. "The Negro was born in depression," said one African American. "It only became official when it hit the white man." In the South, whites seeking work took over the low-paying service jobs that African Americans had traditionally filled. Some black workers in the South encountered violence when whites compelled them to leave their

jobs. Elsewhere, white laborers went on strike, insisting that African American workers be dismissed.

Women were told that they too should relinquish their jobs to men to end the unemployment crisis. Some corporations fired all their married women employees, and school districts in the South dismissed women teachers who married. Because women did the domestic and clerical tasks that men did not care to do even in hard times, the number of women employed did not decline as fast as the number of men. Nevertheless, the Depression retarded the economic progress of women.

For Native Americans, the hard times perpetuated a legacy of neglect that had endured for decades. The Bureau of Indian Affairs (BIA) did not address the many social problems that the people under its jurisdiction confronted. Nearly half the Indians on reservations had no land; the other half subsisted on poor quality land. Poverty pervaded Indian society along with a rate of infant mortality that far exceeded the rate for the white population. Criticism of the BIA mounted, but, despite a commitment to reform, the Hoover administration accomplished little to improve Native American life.

℘ICTURING THE PAST ✦ ECONOMICS & TECHNOLOGY

DISTRESS ON THE FARM IN THE GREAT DEPRESSION

© Bettmann / UPI / Corbis

This picture of a farm being sold at auction during the Great Depression shows the culmination of the agricultural problems depicted in an earlier photograph (page 647). Even with the prosperity of the 1920s, farmers remained trapped in a cycle of overproduction and falling commodity prices. As the bottom dropped out of the economy in the early 1930s and deflation hit all sectors, many farmers found it impossible to pay their debts and make a living. One by one, smaller, less efficient farms went under. As farm bankruptcies spread, scenes like the one in this photograph became commonplace in rural America. The potential for violence from the resentful neighbors became so strong that armed state troopers and National Guardsmen were needed to keep order as the sales went forward. The sense of imminent anger and protest that pervades this picture was a common thread throughout American life during the hard times of the 1930s.

Crisis on the Farms

On the nation's farms, abundant crops could not find a market, so they rotted in the fields. Mortgages were foreclosed, and many former landowners fell into the status of tenant farmers as the Depression went on. In 1929, President Hoover had persuaded Congress to pass an Agricultural Marketing Act that created a Federal Farm Board whose purpose was to stabilize farm prices. When farm surpluses around the world swamped grain markets in 1930, it proved impossible to prevent commodity prices from falling. Talk of strikes and protests was common among farmers during 1931 and 1932. During the summer of 1932, Milo Reno, an Iowa farmer, created the Farmers' Holiday Association that urged growers to hold their crops off the market until prices rose. The association put its program into verse:

> Let's call a farmers' holiday
> A holiday let's hold;
> We'll eat our ham and wheat and eggs
> And let them eat their gold.

In the Southwest, the Hoover administration, faced with growing unemployment in that region, endeavored to reduce the number of people looking for jobs with a program to send Hispanic workers and their families back to Mexico and other Latin American countries. Some 82,000 Mexicans were deported and another half million immigrants crossed the border out of fear that they would be sent back under duress. For Hispanic Americans who stayed in the United States, relief from the government was often hard to find because of a belief that it should be limited to "Americans."

The Plight of the Homeless

As the Depression deepened, the homeless and unemployed took to the roads and rails, looking for work or better times. Migratory workers moved through the agricultural sections of California, picking figs and grapes for whatever they could earn. Others went from city to city, finding inadequate meals at relief stations, shuffling through a breadline in some cities, stealing or begging for food in others. The homeless lived in shantytowns outside of cities that were dubbed "Hoovervilles." Soon derogatory references to the president spread throughout the nation. A pocket turned outward as a sign of distress was "a Hoover flag." In the Southwest, people killed armadillos and renamed the meat "Depression Pork."

By 1931, a sense of despair and hopelessness pervaded many segments of society. People who had been out of work for a year or two had lost the energy and inner resources to rebound even if a job was available. Others began to question the nation's values and beliefs. Bread riots occurred in several cities; the Communist party forecast that the system was toppling; and the nation's political leaders seemed out of touch with the downward trend of economic events.

The Depression did not touch every American in the same way. Despite the economic disruptions, daily life in much of the nation went on as it always had. Families stayed together with the father holding a job, the mother running the home, and their children growing up and attending school. There might be less money to spend, but there was not extensive poverty. Breadlines and people selling apples happened somewhere else. Nevertheless, the economic uncertainty that gripped so many people contributed to a general sense of unease and doubt that permeated the early 1930s.

Mass Culture During the Depression

Amid the hardships of the Depression, Americans found diversions and amusements in the mass media and popular entertainment that had emerged during the 1920s. Radio's popularity grew despite the hard times. Sales of radio sets in the United States reached $300 million annually by 1933. Radio broadcasters and stores were less successful financially between 1929 and 1932, but the habit of listening for a favorite

The shantytowns where the homeless and unemployed lived became known as "Hoovervilles." Their presence on the outskirts of the large cities became a common site as the Depression deepened.
© Bettmann / Corbis

The radio was a form of inexpensive entertainment that Americans depended on during the Depression. In this photograph a family clusters around its set to listen to programs such as Amos 'n' Andy or Fibber McGee and Molly.
© Bettmann / Corbis

program was an integral part of the daily lives of many families.

Radio was becoming more commercial every year. Programming appealed to popular tastes and sought the

PICTURING THE PAST ♦ ECONOMICS & TECHNOLOGY

A BANK FAILS

© Bettmann / Corbis

One of the most unsettling aspects of the Great Depression was the increasing numbers of bank failures. Since there was no national system to insure bank deposits, those who had money in a financial institution were vulnerable when a bank failed or a "run" occurred as depositors sought to get out whatever money they could. With no federal authority to help banks in trouble, the collapse of one major bank could trigger a ripple effect of failures that could paralyze commerce in an entire region or state. This picture shows an anxious crowd milling about outside a bank in New York City that until this crisis had paid 4 percent interest on "thrift accounts." The sense of fear that is evident in the body language of passersby peering into the bank conveys the worry that more and more Americans felt about their financial security as the Depression continued its downward course in the early 1930s.

---

largest available audience. Listeners preferred daytime dramas such as *One Man's Family* and *Mary Noble, Backstage Wife,* quickly dubbed "soap operas" after the detergent companies that sponsored them.

The most popular radio program of the Depression years was *Amos 'n' Andy,* which portrayed the lives of two African American men in Harlem as interpreted by two white entertainers, Freeman Gosden and Charles Correll. Performed in heavy dialect, the show captured a huge audience at 7 o'clock each evening. The tales of black life appealed to white stereotypes about African Americans, but they also gained an audience among blacks because the characters' experiences were comparable to those of minority listeners.

Off to the Movies

With ticket prices very low and audiences hungry for diversion from the trials of daily life, Hollywood presented a wide choice of films between 1929 and 1932. Sound movies had replaced the silent pictures of the 1920s, and escapist entertainment dominated the movie screens across the country. Audiences laughed at the Marx Brothers in *Cocoanuts* (1929) and *Monkey Business* (1931). Musicals found a ready audience, and there was a vogue for gangster films such as *Little Caesar* (1931) with Edward G. Robinson and *The Public Enemy* (1931) with James Cagney. During the early 1930s, Hollywood pressed the limits of tolerance for sexual innuendoes and bawdy themes with stars such as Mae West.

Despite the hardships of the economic downturn, the cultural flowering that had begun during the preceding decade continued. In Kansas City and other midwestern cities, African American musicians were developing a new jazz style that would become known as "swing" when white musicians smoothed its hard edges to make it appealing to their audiences. The hardships of the era evoked artistic creativity and a vibrant popular culture that would dominate the entertainment scene for half a century.

A DARKENING WORLD

With the economies of the democratic nations weakened and the structure of international relations tottering, authoritarian forces around the world asserted themselves against the existing order. The first test came in the Far East.

In September 1931, Japanese troops detonated a weak explosive charge under a Japanese-owned railroad in Manchuria and blamed the episode on the Manchurians. The Japanese military had fabricated the incident as an excuse for attacking Chinese positions in Manchuria. During the weeks that followed, the Japanese army invaded Manchuria and advanced deep into the countryside. The Japanese bombed Chinese cities to deter any opposition to their effort to occupy all of Manchuria.

Frustrated by the power of the Western countries and desperate for raw materials, Japan and its military wanted to establish their nation as the dominant force in Asia and expel the foreign countries that had achieved a political and economic presence in China and the Far East. Anger at the discriminatory racial policies of the United States, Great Britain, and other European powers fed this frustration. Japan was also fearful that a resurgent China might pose a threat to Japanese ambitions and access to crucial materials for Tokyo's economy. Desire for political and economic supremacy in the Pacific completed the Japanese agenda.

A Challenge to the League of Nations

Japan's attack into Manchuria posed a threat to the League of Nations. It confronted the United States with the problem of what to do about a clear violation of policies and treaties to which Washington was a party, such as the Open Door policy and the Nine-Power Treaty. Yet the American army was no match for Japan's, and the administration had not maintained naval strength at the levels allowed in the various treaties that had been signed during the preceding

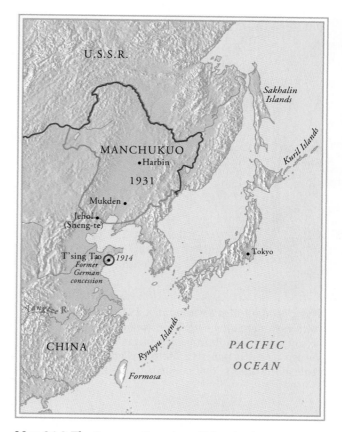

Map 24.2 *The Japanese Invasion of Manchuria*
The Japanese invasion of Manchuria extended Japan's power up from Korea to the border of the Soviet Union and also presented them with a base for their ultimate attack on China later in the 1930s. The failure of the western nations to take effective action against these Japanese actions began a process that would lead in time to the end of the European colonial presence in Asia.

decade. In addition, Congress would not have been sympathetic to U.S. intervention in a remote foreign quarrel. For the same reason, Washington could not look to European countries. Nor could it endorse an economic boycott against Japan under the sponsorship of the League of Nations. Secretary of State Stimson issued statements to China and Japan that proclaimed the unwillingness of the United States to recognize territorial changes in China produced by aggressive actions. This policy of nonrecognition became known as the Stimson Doctrine. The Japanese pressed ahead with their campaign to occupy Manchuria and intimidate China despite the secretary's comments.

The League of Nations criticized the Japanese policy, and Japan responded by withdrawing from the organization early in 1933. The United States and

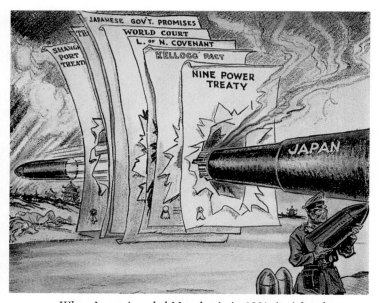

When Japan invaded Manchuria in 1931, it violated a number of international agreements that it had signed. This cartoon provides an American commentary on these actions. The depiction of Japanese militarism would be a running theme in the United States throughout the 1930s and 1940s.
The Granger Collection, New York

Adolf Hitler's rise to power in Nazi Germany was a sobering backdrop to the course of events in the United States. Hitler is the third from the right at a Nazi rally in Nuremberg, Germany. Hermann Goering is on Hitler's left, Ernst Roehm is on Hitler's right, and Heinrich Himmler is to Roehm's right.
Reproduced from the Collections of the Library of Congress #USZ62 045911
903241

Japan were now embarked on a course that would lead to ever more bitter encounters and ultimately to all-out war.

Germany Moves Toward the Nazis

In Germany, where resentment about the Treaty of Versailles had grown during the Depression, the National Socialist party of Adolf Hitler was gaining support. Hitler's message of national revenge and hatred of the Jews proved intoxicating to the German people, and during 1932, he stood on the brink of obtaining power. Some Americans, insensitive to Hitler's ideology of racial hatred, even admired the policies of Hitler and the Italian dictator Benito Mussolini because they apparently offered decisive action to deal with the economic crisis. The situation of democratic governments, on the other hand, was perilous as the United States entered the third year of the Depression.

A POLITICAL OPPORTUNITY FOR THE DEMOCRATS

At the beginning of 1932, the Hoover presidency was in dire political trouble. Even his advisors were critical. One official remarked that the president "has a childlike faith in statements," while a political commentator concluded that "there seems to be no class or section where Hoover is strong."

By 1932, the limits of the president's voluntary approach had become evident even to him. During the winter he supported a congressional initiative to establish the Reconstruction Finance Corporation (RFC). Congress authorized this agency to loan up to $2 billion in tax money to save banks, insurance companies, and railroads from financial collapse. The law that set up the RFC repudiated the principle of voluntary action that Hoover had been following since the Depression began. It put the federal government behind the effort to achieve economic recovery and signaled that Washington could no longer take a passive or hands-off role when the economy turned downward.

Republican problems meant opportunity for the Democrats if they could seize the initiative. In their congressional programs, however, the Democrats were not much more creative than their opponents. A deep split persisted within the party over the proper role of government in dealing with the Depression. Many of the conservatives who had supported Al Smith would

Franklin D. Roosevelt: Commonwealth Club Address

In the campaign of 1932, Franklin D. Roosevelt offered a vision of somewhat greater governmental action to meet the Depression. He did not, however, offer a radical program, as this excerpt from his speech to the Commonwealth Club of San Francisco on September 23, 1932, indicates.

. . . This implication is, briefly, that the responsible heads of finance and industry, instead of acting each for himself, must work together to achieve the common end. They must, where necessary, sacrifice this or that private advantage; and in reciprocal self-denial must seek a general advantage. It is here that formal government—political government, if you choose—comes in.

Whenever in the pursuit of this objective the lone wolf, the unethical competitor, the reckless promoter, the Ishmael or Insull whose hand is against every man's, declines to join in achieving an end recognized as being for the public welfare and threatens to drag the industry back to a state of anarchy, the government may properly be asked to apply restraint. Likewise, should the group ever use its collective power contrary to the public welfare, the government must be swift to enter and protect the public interest.

The government should assume the function of economic regulation only as a last resort, to be tried only when private initiative, inspired by high responsibility, with such assistance and balance as government can give, has finally failed. As yet there has been no final failure, because there has been no attempt; and I decline to assume that this nation is unable to meet the situation.

The final term of the high contract was for liberty and the pursuit of happiness. We have learned a great deal of both in the past century. We know that individual liberty and individual happiness mean nothing unless both are ordered in the sense that one man's meat is not another man's poison. We know that the old "rights of personal competency," the right to read, to think, to speak, to choose, and live a mode of life must be respected at all hazards. We know that liberty to do anything which deprives others of those elemental rights is outside the protection of any compact; and that

government in this regard is the maintenance of a balance, within which every individual may have a place if he will take it; in which every individual may find safety if he wishes it; in which every individual may attain such power as his ability permits, consistent with his assuming the accompanying responsibility.

All this is a long, slow task. Nothing is more striking than the simple innocence of the men who insist, whenever an objective is present, on the prompt production of a patent scheme guaranteed to produce a result. Human endeavor is not so simple as that. Government includes the art of formulating a policy and using the political technique to attain so much of that policy as will receive general support; persuading, leading, sacrificing, teaching always, because the greatest duty of a statesman is to educate. But in the matters of which I have spoken, we are learning rapidly, in a severe school. The lessons so learned must not be forgotten, even in the mental lethargy of a speculative upturn. We must build toward the time when a major depression cannot occur again; and if this means sacrificing the easy profits of inflationist booms, then let them go; and good riddance.

Faith in America, faith in our tradition of personal responsibility, faith in our institutions, faith in ourselves demand that we recognize the new terms of the old social contract. We shall fulfill them, as we fulfilled the obligation of the apparent utopia which Jefferson imagined for us in 1776, and which Jefferson, Roosevelt, and Wilson sought to bring to realization. We must do so, lest a rising tide of misery, engendered by our common failure, engulf us all. But failure is not an American habit; and in the strength of great hope we must all shoulder our common load. . . .

Source: *New York Times*, September 24, 1932.

not look kindly on a candidate who wished to expand government's part in dealing with the Depression.

The Democrats in Congress

In the 1930 elections, the Democrats picked up eight seats in the Senate. The Republicans retained control of the upper house by only a single vote. In the House, the Democratic gain was forty-nine seats, not enough to give the Democrats a majority, although their total of 216 members put them close.

When Congress reassembled late in 1931, the Democrats had gained several other seats because of the death or retirement of four Republicans. As a result, John Nance "Cactus Jack" Garner of Texas became the new Speaker of the House. His answer to the growing budget deficit that the Depression produced was to offer a national sales tax. Such a proposal would have hurt lower income Americans and, by taking money out of the economy, would also have been deflationary at a time when the economy needed stimulation. Before the bill could pass the House, angry rebels in both parties killed the sales tax idea.

The Rise of Franklin D. Roosevelt

The front-runner for the Democratic nomination in 1932 was Franklin D. Roosevelt. He came from a wealthy branch of his family that lived on the Hudson River in Hyde Park, New York. After attending the aristocratic Groton School and Harvard University, he had studied law in New York City. In 1910, he won a seat in the New York state senate, and three years later he became assistant secretary of the navy in the Wilson administration. Seven years in Washington had given him a thorough introduction to the politics of that city.

Although Franklin D. Roosevelt was only a distant cousin of Theodore, his wife, Eleanor, was the former president's niece. His connection to a famous name helped Roosevelt secure the Democratic vice presidential nomination in 1920. Although the Democrats lost, the race gave Roosevelt valuable national exposure.

Roosevelt's Illness and Political Comeback

In 1921, Roosevelt was stricken with polio and lost the use of his legs. For the rest of his life he could not walk without crutches and usually used a wheelchair. Counted out of politics because of his illness, Roosevelt worked his way back into Democratic affairs during the mid-1920s and in 1928 was elected governor of New York by a narrow margin despite the Hoover landslide. Two years later, he won reelection by a huge majority.

In public, the fifty-year old Roosevelt, his wife, and their five children were the picture of a robust American family. But behind this facade lay personal difficulty.

During 1918–1919, the marriage had almost collapsed because of Franklin's affair with another woman. The Roosevelts stayed together, but theirs became a political partnership of convenience. During the 1920s, Eleanor Roosevelt played a greater role in politics herself and gained prominence as an advocate of social reform.

As for his political views, Roosevelt shared many of the ideas of the mainstream of the Democratic party. He believed in balanced budgets, the gold standard, and capitalism. Yet he also had an instinctive rapport with people in all segments of society, and he relished the exercise of power. His progressive views on the role of government separated him from conservatives in his party, who longed for a return to the pre-Wilsonian traditions. Roosevelt trusted no one completely and never confided his deepest thoughts about his political destiny. Many observers judged him to be superficial and shallow.

The Roosevelt Appeal

Roosevelt was one of the most gifted politicians in the nation's history. He recognized earlier than most public leaders of his time the power of radio to reach the American electorate. His jaunty manner and courage in the face of his disability conveyed a message of hope and optimism that was contagious during the Depression.

Roosevelt's campaign got off to a strong start. His manager, James A. Farley, had been wooing potential delegates since 1930, and he had mapped out a strategy to attract both big-city leaders, whose support for the Democrats had been growing, and the Solid South. As a source of ideas for his campaign, Roosevelt turned to the academic community in the Northeast. He recruited several professors from Columbia University in New York to write speeches and formulate concepts for his programs. These scholars were promptly named "the brain trust." In his speeches, Roosevelt talked of "the forgotten man at the bottom of the economic pyramid" who was suffering from the effects of the Depression. The answer, Roosevelt said, was "bold, persistent experimentation."

The Struggle for the Nomination

As Roosevelt's campaign gathered strength and it became clear that Hoover was going to lose, other Democrats challenged the front-runner. Still angry over his 1928 defeat and no longer friendly with Roosevelt, Al Smith wanted another chance at the White House. He became a more active candidate as the weeks passed, and his strength in the Northeast made him a serious rival to Roosevelt. Roosevelt was clearly the choice of a majority of the Democrats, but party rules mandated that a nominee receive two-thirds of the votes of the convention delegates. If Garner and Smith teamed up against him and their delegates stood firm, Roosevelt could not win.

The Democratic National Convention opened in Chicago on June 20, 1932. The Roosevelt forces faced many difficulties during the days that followed, but when it came to the balloting, his opponents could not rally around anyone else. In the end, Speaker Garner decided to release his delegates to Roosevelt; his reward would be the vice presidential nomination, which he said was "not worth a pitcher of warm piss." At the same time, the California delegation swung its support to Roosevelt on the fourth ballot.

A New Deal

In a dramatic break with the political tradition that barred candidates from appearing at a convention to accept a nomination, Roosevelt boarded a plane and flew to Chicago through stormy weather. There he delivered his speech in which he used a phrase that would become the trademark of his presidency: "I pledge you, I pledge myself to a new deal for the American people." The candidate seemed poised and self-assured, and he radiated optimism. The convention band played the new Democratic theme: "Happy Days Are Here Again." Meanwhile, the gloomy Republicans nominated Hoover and braced for defeat.

The Economy in Distress

To deal with the growing budget deficit, Congress imposed new taxes in the Revenue Act of 1932. The sales tax idea had been dropped, but other levies on corporations, estates, and incomes made this the greatest peacetime increase in taxes in the nation's history. At a time when the economy needed fiscal stimulus, the tax measure drew funds out of the hands of consumers. Raising taxes in an election year added to Hoover's growing unpopularity.

The weakening of the Hoover administration and the increasing power of the Democrats led to an important change in labor policy during 1932. For many years employers had used friendly federal judges and the power of injunctions to cripple the ability of labor unions to win strikes. The Norris-LaGuardia Act of 1932, by contrast, extended to workers "full freedom of association" and labor representation, restricted the use of injunctions, and barred reliance on "yellow-dog" contracts, which prevented workers from joining unions.

As the Depression worsened during its third year, the plight of unemployed Americans deteriorated well beyond the ability of cities and states to provide aid. Congress became restive as the Reconstruction Finance Corporation extended loans to large corporations and the White House resisted legislation to help the needy and distressed. Bills were introduced to provide direct assistance to the unemployed, but a coalition of Republicans and southern Democrats blocked their passage. As news spread about how much money businesses had received from the RFC, pressure intensified for Congress to do something. The result was the Emergency Relief and Construction Act of 1932, which required states to attest that they could not raise any money themselves before federal funds were allocated to them. The law limited the kinds of construction projects that could be funded, but it represented at least a symbolic step toward a greater federal role in meeting the needs of desperate Americans in the midst of an economic crisis.

The Bonus March

During the summer of 1932, other desperate citizens sought immediate relief from the government in the form of cash. After World War I, Congress had promised war veterans cash bonuses in the form of paid-up life insurance to be disbursed in 1945. During the Hoover presidency, the needs of veterans as a group had been generously funded, and on the whole they had suffered less from the Depression than had some other groups. As the Depression worsened, however, the veterans clamored for early access to their "bonus" money. Hoover vetoed a proposal to allow veterans to borrow against the value of their bonuses in 1931. During the spring of 1932, Congress decided not to authorize early payment of the bonuses.

To make their presence felt, thousands of veterans organized the Bonus Expeditionary Force, or the Bonus Army, which came to Washington during the summer of 1932 to listen to Congress debate the bonus proposal. They camped out in tar paper dwellings and tents on the banks of the Anacostia River; some slept in government buildings. The authorities in Washington generally cooperated with the veterans and did what they could to provide them with food and shelter during their stay. Hoover ignored them. When it became clear that Congress was not going to help the Bonus Marchers and would adjourn in mid-July 1932, the Hoover administration urged the Bonus Army to leave Washington and even allocated $100,000 to pay for the cost of sending the men home. Some of the marchers took advantage of this offer and left Washington. Others stayed on, hoping for a change in government policy.

A Violent Climax to the Bonus March

Some officials in the Hoover administration wanted a confrontation with the marchers in order to bolster the president's reputation as a champion of law and order.

On July 28, the secretary of war ordered the police to remove marchers from government buildings. When the police moved in, the veterans resisted and fighting occurred. A police pistol went off; other officers began shooting; and soon two Bonus Marchers lay dead. The president ordered the federal troops in Washington, commanded by General Douglas MacArthur, to restore order. The general took his men, armed with tanks and machine guns, across the Anacostia River into the main camp of the Bonus Army. The veterans fled in terror as the soldiers approached. Tear gas canisters were hurled, tents were burned, and the crowd dispersed in a panic. Motion picture cameras caught MacArthur in full military regalia directing the attack, and moviegoers across the nation saw newsreels of American soldiers ousting the Bonus Army from its camp.

The Hoover administration laid the blame for the incident on the influence of Communists inside the veterans' camp. There were a few Communists among the veterans, but they had little influence on the protest. Law enforcement agencies found no evidence of an organized conspiracy among the marchers, and public opinion favored the veterans. "If the Army must be called out to make war on unarmed citizens," said a newspaper editor, "this is no longer America."

The 1932 Election

The economic devastation produced by the Great Depression offered groups outside the two-party system a promising chance to win votes for more radical solutions to the nation's problems. The Communists, for example, organized Unemployed Councils to stage protests against high rents and evictions of tenants. Socialists and other left-wing groups cooperated with the Communists in protest marches and petitions for relief. Efforts to organize sharecroppers and tenant farmers in the South also went forward under the sponsorship of the Communists during these years. The Communists wooed African American support when they defended the "Scottsboro boys," a group of young black men who had been unjustly accused of raping two white women in Alabama in 1931. In 1932, some prominent intellectuals endorsed the Communist presidential campaign or supported the Socialist candidate, Norman Thomas.

For the majority of Americans, however, the only real choice lay between Roosevelt and Hoover. Many of Roosevelt's advisors told him that he did not have to campaign to win the race. Roosevelt saw the matter

The Hoover administration sent in troops to disperse the Bonus Marchers after Congress refused to pay the veterans their bonuses early. The use of armed force against protesting citizens, especially the deployment of tear gas, made the episode a public relations disaster for the White House.

© Bettmann / UPI / Corbis

The case of the African American men accused in the Scottsboro trial became another controversial episode in racial injustice in the early 1930s. Guarded by state troopers, the defendants in the case consult with their attorney.

The Granger Collection, New York

differently. If he ran a passive, traditional campaign, he would not persuade the voters who were looking for a change. A front-porch campaign would also have fed rumors that he could not withstand the physical rigors of the presidency. So Roosevelt crisscrossed the country, making speeches that assailed the Republican leadership and attacked Hoover's record.

Roosevelt's Campaign

Roosevelt wanted to occupy the political middle ground, and as a result his campaign speeches took a variety of contradictory positions. At times he seemed to be calling for a more activist federal government that would adapt "existing economic organizations to the service of the people." On other occasions he attacked Hoover's budget deficits and wasteful government spending. Most of Roosevelt's appeal came down to hope, confidence, and the promise of political change.

The incumbent president knew he was going to lose, but he campaigned doggedly. Hoover told the voters that the nation faced a choice between "two philosophies of government." Abandoned by many of his fellow Republicans and unpopular with the voters, Hoover staggered through his lifeless campaign.

Hoover Defeated

On election day, the Democratic candidate won overwhelmingly in the popular vote and scored a 472-to-59 triumph in the electoral college. His party secured almost 57 percent of the popular vote and made significant gains in Congress: ninety seats in the House and thirteen in the Senate. The election proved a major disappointment to both the Socialists and the Communists. Norman Thomas, running on the Socialist ticket, received fewer than a million votes. William Z. Foster, the Communist candidate, gained just over 100,000 ballots.

Roosevelt and Hoover

By 1932, politicians realized that the four-month period between the time that a president was elected and the inauguration was too long for a modern industrialized

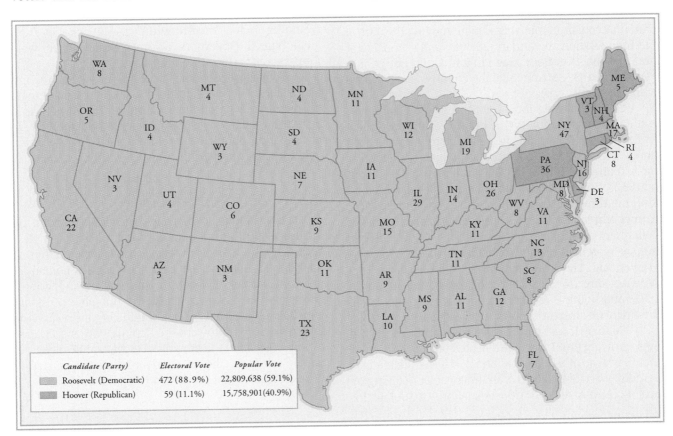

Candidate (Party)	Electoral Vote	Popular Vote
Roosevelt (Democratic)	472 (88.9%)	22,809,638 (59.1%)
Hoover (Republican)	59 (11.1%)	15,758,901 (40.9%)

Map 24.3 *The Election of 1932*
As the Depression hit bottom in 1932, the voters rejected Herbert Hoover and the Republicans in favor of Franklin D. Roosevelt and the Democrats. The incumbent and his party did well only in the traditional Republican bastions of New England and two states in the Middle Atlantic region.
View an animated version of this map or related maps at http://history.wadsworth.com/passages2e.

By the end of the 1932 campaign, President Hoover knew he had lost. He made a final radio address the day before the election when his hopes had vanished.
© Bettmann / UPI / Corbis

nation. A constitutional amendment moving the date of the inauguration to January 20 was under consideration, but the Twentieth Amendment would not go into effect until 1937. Meanwhile, the country faced a worsening economic crisis.

During these four months, the Depression reached its lowest point. One-quarter of the workforce could not find jobs and the relief system had broken down. The gross national product, which had stood at more than $103 billion in 1929, had slid to $58 billion by 1932. Wheat sold for thirty cents a bushel compared with the three dollars a bushel it had brought in 1920. Farmers threatened more action to stop foreclosures of delinquent mortgages in their states. In December, hunger marchers came to Washington to ask for government aid. The growing numbers of failing banks presented a dire threat: 1,453 banks shut their doors in 1932, and political leaders feared that the nation's entire financial structure could be threatened.

Neither Hoover nor Roosevelt was able to deal with these growing problems. The defeated president believed that the cause of the Depression lay beyond the nation's borders. Wary of making commitments before taking office, Roosevelt dodged Hoover's efforts to obtain his backing. Hoover became convinced that Roosevelt cared little for the welfare of the country, whereas Roosevelt saw his defeated rival as a sore loser who was trying to win through subterfuge what he had lost at the polls.

Roosevelt devoted most of his energy to forming a cabinet and getting ready to take over the presidency.

The president-elect also survived an assassination attempt two weeks before the inauguration. At a speaking engagement in Miami during a break from a fishing trip, Roosevelt was talking with the mayor of Chicago, Anton Cermak, when a would-be assassin fired five shots at Roosevelt. None hit him, but one wounded Cermak, who died shortly afterward.

The Banking System Nears Collapse

A crisis of confidence in banks gripped the country. Alarm about the banking system had been spreading since October 1932. During that month the governor of Nevada proclaimed a twelve-day bank "holiday" to end depositor runs on banks. The news spurred depositors in other states to remove funds from their local banks. In Michigan, two banks in Detroit seemed about to fail by mid-February. Hoover tried to persuade business leaders, including Henry Ford, to place deposits in the troubled banks. Ford was willing, but others were not. The governor of Michigan intervened and declared a bank holiday on February 14. Depositors in other states, fearing that their deposits would be frozen, tried to withdraw their money from local banks. Governors in nine other states were forced to announce bank holidays.

Hoover pressed the incoming president for immediate joint action. Roosevelt was still reluctant to tie his own hands before he took office. The days passed as February ended with no agreement on either side to do anything about the banking crisis. The two men held one last awkward business meeting on March 3.

A Spreading Sense of Crisis

As the transition of power neared, general apprehension increased. By the morning of March 4, banks in New York City, the nation's financial capital, were shutting their doors. A weary Hoover concluded in a moment of personal despair: "We are at the end of our string." Shortly before eleven o'clock, the outgoing president joined Franklin Roosevelt in a waiting limousine and the two men drove off toward the Capitol. Roosevelt waved to well-wishers in the crowd as Hoover sat in silence. A nation mired in the worst depression in its history waited to hear what the new president would say.

CONCLUSION

The economic slump of the early 1930s was one of the most significant events in American history. It called into question faith in the brighter future that the nation promised to all. The Depression also changed the way Americans viewed the federal government. While they retained their suspicion of intrusive national power, they expected that Washington would prevent future depressions and relieve the effects of the one that was occurring. Radical solutions that involved dismantling capitalism or redistributing income on a large scale gained relatively few adherents.

The Depression discredited the Republican party for two decades in presidential elections. The memory of President Hoover and his failed policies was so strong that Democratic candidates ran against him for a generation. Although Hoover lived thirty years after he left the White House, his reputation never recovered.

The popular esteem for large corporations also fell dramatically during the 1930s when the public learned how their executives had profited from inside information and tax advantages. A congressional probe in early 1933 disclosed that Wall Street executives had benefitted from inside information about stock market transactions. Other similar revelations followed once Roosevelt took office.

The major political and economic institutions that had governed the nation for half a century—the Republican party and corporate power—were challenged by the force and size of the Great Depression. Industrialism had become embedded in American life, but there remained serious questions about how society ought to respond to the inequities and injustices that often accompanied industrial growth. Would the United States turn to radical solutions as European countries had done? Could democratic institutions respond to the demands of economic hardship? Franklin D. Roosevelt had now promised a "new deal" for the American people. Noon approached in Washington, and Roosevelt walked on crutches the thirty-seven painful and difficult steps from his seat to the place in front of the Capitol where he would take the oath of office.

Recommended Readings

Clements, Kendrick. *Hoover. Conservation and Consumerism: Engineering the Good Life* (2000). Offers a probing study of the president's attitude toward nature and society.

Cook, Blanche Wiesen. *Eleanor Roosevelt, 1884–1933* (1992). The first volume of a biography of the important first lady.

Doherty, Thomas. *Pre-Code Hollywood: Sex, Immorality, and Insurrection in American Cinema, 1930–1934* (1994). Considers the role of popular entertainment during the Depression.

Finan, Christopher M. *Alfred E. Smith: The Happy Warrior* (2002). An engaging biography of the Democratic candidate in 1928.

Houck, Davis W. *Rhetoric as Currency: Hoover, Roosevelt, and the Great Depression* (2001). Examines how Hoover's speaking style affected his presidency.

Kennedy, David M. *Freedom from Fear: The American People in Depression and War, 1929–1945* (1999). Provides a prize-winning discussion of the Depression and its impact.

Liebovich, Louis. *Bylines in Despair: Herbert Hoover, the Great Depression, and the U.S. News Media* (1994). Looks at the troubled relations between Hoover and the press.

McElvaine, Robert S. *The Depression and the New Deal: A History in Documents* (2000). A well-chosen collection of revealing documents about the economic crisis.

Parrish, Michael E. *Anxious Decades: America in Prosperity and Depression, 1920–1941* (1992). An excellent synthesis of the interwar period.

Watkins, T. H. *The Great Depression: America in the 1930s* (1993). Offers a popular account of the events of the Depression decade.

American Journey Online and InfoTrac College Edition

Visit the source collections at http://ajaccess. wadsworth.com and infotrac.thomsonlearning.com and use the Search function with the following key terms to explore documents, images, audio and video clips, articles, and commentary related to the material in this chapter.

Stock market crash of 1929	Herbert Hoover
Amelia Earhart	Alfred E. Smith
Hoovervilles	Marx brothers
Scottsboro	

Additional resources, exercises, and Internet links related to this chapter are available on the American Passages Web site: http://history.wadsworth.com/passages2e

PASSAGES
—1933 TO 1960—

Americans who grew up in the Depression, served their country during World War II, and ushered in the enormous prosperity of the 1950s and beyond have been celebrated in recent books and movies as "the greatest generation." There are good reasons for such praise. In no other period except the Civil War and Reconstruction was America as severely tested, its direction as radically changed. The 1930s saw the worst economic catastrophe in modern history. Banks collapsed, farms failed, factories closed, breadlines formed in the cities. Yet what truly defined the nation in this decade was its passionate response to misfortune—the way Americans mixed protest, innovation, and reform. Dramatic changes occurred. The Great Depression not only increased the social responsibilities of government, it also opened the political process to millions of "forgotten Americans," who exercised power by joining labor unions, switching political parties, and migrating to places where they could vote and be represented. In contrast to the violent ideological struggles that gripped much of Europe in the 1930s, the United States witnessed a remarkable expansion of the democratic principles it held so dear.

Although the Great Depression would linger until World War II, the federal government provided Americans with food and employment, optimism and hope. Furthermore, the vast public works projects of that era—the roads, dams, bridges, tunnels, schools, hospitals, post offices, airports, parks, and playgrounds—created a physical infrastructure that tied the nation together while it spurred its future success. World War II brought on new challenges and opportunities. Battling on two fronts, the nation resolutely mobilized a superb U.S. fighting force and a masterful homefront effort in which almost everyone took part. The war provided better employment for minorities and for women, although

The New Deal forged a legacy of magnificent public works structures, including the Grand Coulee Dam, the 100-mile causeway linking Florida to Key West, the Triborough Bridge in New York City, and the Golden Gate Bridge in San Francisco.
© Bettmann / UPI / Corbis

The landing craft—or LST—became a symbol of American fighting power during World War II. Thousands were produced to carry troops, vehicles, and equipment ashore in the Pacific, North Africa, Anzio, and Normandy.
U.S. Coast Guard photo no. 26-WA-6J-14 in the National Archives

discrimination in wages and skilled jobs remained. So, too, did segregation in the armed forces—a hypocrisy that did not end till 1948. Nevertheless, Americans stood shoulder-to-shoulder against the villainy of fascism, Pearl Harbor, and Nazi genocide.

The enormous prosperity following World War II quickly pushed fears of economic depression aside. What remained in place, however, were the structural reforms that made banks safer, capitalism stronger, and people more secure. Postwar Americans strongly supported an active government role in domestic and foreign affairs. There was little opposition to expanding the Social Security system, increasing the defense budget, or providing hefty benefits to veterans of the war. Soldiers came home and picked up their lives. The marriage rate soared, a baby boom followed, and young families rushed to the suburbs. Peacetime consumption replaced wartime production as the key to national prosperity, with the sale of new homes, automobiles, and appliances reaching record heights.

The prosperity and good feelings generated by World War II, however, were not equally shared. Employment opportunities for women fell dramatically after the veterans returned. Racial prejudice remained a national disgrace. The South still required segregation by law, while other regions discriminated more subtly in housing, education, and jobs. Furthermore, growing fears about Soviet expansion and domestic communism dissolved the political unity, or bipartisanship, that had marked American foreign policy throughout the war. The resulting Red Scare, fueled by opportunistic politicians like Senator Joseph R. McCarthy, challenged America's most cherished ideals.

Still, the nation prospered and grew. The 1950s saw the spread of a powerful civil rights movement and the demise of Senator McCarthy. Breakthroughs in medicine and technology ended the nightmare of polio, fueled the space race, and brought the miracle of television into almost every American home. The economic boom continued, raising living standards and national confidence to even greater heights. As 1960 approached, the nation appeared content and comfortable—thanks in large part to "the greatest generation," now approaching middle age.

The housewife holding a baby while watching the Army-McCarthy hearings illustrates the combined influence of domesticity, anti-communism, and television in post–World War II American society.
© Bettmann / UPI /Corbis

Following the former Soviet Union's spectacular launch of Sputnik I, *the United States created the National Aeronautics and Space Administration (NASA) in 1958 to manage civilian space operations. Among its first tasks was the selection and training of astronauts (pictured) for Project Mercury, the human spaceflight program.*
© Bettmann / UPI / Corbis

	1932	1940	1946
Politics & Diplomacy	**1932:** Franklin Roosevelt elected president **1933:** Adolph Hitler becomes chancellor of Germany U.S. recognizes the Soviet Union **1935:** Congress passes Social Security **1936:** Spanish civil war **1937:** Court-packing plan defeated **1939:** Nazi forces invade Poland	**1940:** Roosevelt wins unprecedented third term **1941:** Japanese bomb Pearl Harbor **1942:** Incarceration of Japanese Americans **1943:** German army crushed at Stalingrad **1944:** Normandy Invasion **1945:** Germany surrenders Atomic bombs dropped on Hiroshima and Nagasaki Japan surrenders	**1946:** Cold War emerges **1947:** Truman Doctrine and Marshall Plan implemented **1948:** Alger Hiss indicted for perjury **1949:** Communists triumph in China
Social & Cultural Events	**1932:** Bonus Army march **1933:** Prohibition ends **1935:** Congress of Industrial Organizations formed **1936:** Jesse Owens dominates the Berlin Olympics **1939:** John Steinbeck publishes *The Grapes of Wrath* Marian Anderson sings at Lincoln Memorial	**1941:** A. Philip Randolph threatens March on Washington **1943:** Race riot in Detroit **1944:** GI Bill passed **1945:** 12.5 million Americans in uniform	**1946:** Dr. Spock publishes *Common Sense Book of Baby and Child Care* **1947:** Jackie Robinson breaks baseball's color line **1948:** *Kinsey Report* **1949:** Sears, Roebuck catalogue advertises television set
Economics & Technology	**1932:** Unemployment reaches 25 percent Thousands of banks close **1933:** Tennessee Valley Authority created **1937:** Severe recession	**1942:** Manhattan Project begins **1945:** United States produces more than half the world's manufactured goods	**1946:** Reconversion **1949:** Soviet Union tests atomic bomb

1950: Senator Joseph McCarthy raises Communist issue
Korean War begins
1952: Dwight Eisenhower elected president
1953: Cease-fire in Korea
Stalin dies
1954: U.S. Senate censures Joseph McCarthy
Brown v. Board of Education

1956: Hungarian Revolution
Suez crisis
1957: Federal troops sent to Little Rock

1959: Cuban Revolution
1960: John F. Keenedy elected president

1951: Alan Freed hosts rock 'n' roll radio show
1955: Montgomery bus boycott

1956: Elvis Presley appears on *Ed Sullivan Show*
1957: Jack Kerouac publishes *On the Road*

1959: TV quiz show scandals

1954: IBM markets business computer
1955: Salk polio vaccine

1956: Federal Highway Act
1957: *Sputnik* launched

1958: U.S. manned space program begins

25 THE NEW DEAL
1933–1939

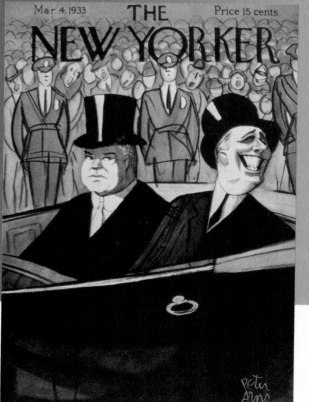

This New Yorker *cartoon, sketched well before the inauguration, accurately predicted feelings of both men—the glum Hoover and the exuberant Roosevelt— as they rode down Pennsylvania Avenue together on March 4, 1933.*

Franklin D. Roosevelt Library / The New Yorker

ON MARCH 4, 1933, Franklin Roosevelt took the presidential oath of office in a steady, chilling rain. "Only a foolish optimist can deny the dark realities of the moment," he told the huge crowd and the millions who listened on radio. Roosevelt's voice radiated confidence and concern. "This nation asks for action, and action now," he declared. Comparing the Depression to an all-out war of survival, he vowed to ask Congress for the "broad executive power . . . that would be given to me if we were in fact invaded by a foreign foe."

Roosevelt offered few specifics in his inaugural address. His objective was to convince a dispirited people to have faith in him and in themselves. Standing erect in his cumbersome leg braces, Roosevelt stressed four major themes: sacrifice, discipline, compassion, and hope. "The only thing we have to fear," he assured the nation, "is fear itself."

 ## ROCK BOTTOM

This fear was understandable. The winter of 1932–1933—the political interregnum between Hoover's defeat and Roosevelt's inauguration—was a time of intense suffering and despair. Unemployment reached a staggering 25 percent. Banks were failing everywhere. Food prices had collapsed, forcing farmers from their land. Roosevelt understood how deeply the Depression had shaken the country and sapped its confidence. "I have [seen] the faces of thousands of Americans," he confided to a friend. "They have the frightened look of children. . . . They are saying, 'We are caught in something we don't understand; perhaps this fellow can help us out.' "

Taking Charge

Roosevelt's words reflected both his compassion for common people and his detachment from their lives. He would become a father figure to them in perilous times—bold and caring, yet distant and elusive. He would be their protector, their steward, but not their social peer.

No peacetime president ever faced a tougher challenge, or a greater opportunity. Respected commentators were predicting the end of capitalism if the Depression hung on much longer. At the very least, Americans were desperate for change. And that meant almost any initiative designed to revive the economy, feed the hungry, and put people back to work.

CHRONOLOGY

1933 Franklin D. Roosevelt inaugurated as president • Eighteenth Amendment is repealed, ending Prohibition • "First hundred days" of New Deal includes passage of Agricultural Adjustment Act and National Industrial Recovery Act • Adolf Hitler becomes chancellor of Germany • United States extends diplomatic recognition to the Soviet Union

1934 Senator Huey Long establishes "Share Our Wealth Society" • Labor violence erupts in major American cities • Democrats add to huge congressional majorities in midterm elections

1935 Huey Long assassinated • "Second New Deal" emerges with passage of Wagner Act and Social Security Act • Congress passes first Neutrality Act, reflecting the nation's isolationist mood

1936 FDR reelected to second term • John L. Lewis and other labor leaders break with AFL to form the CIO • Civil war erupts in Spain

1937 Roosevelt unveils "Court-packing plan" • Autoworkers stage "sit-down strike" at GM plant in Flint, Michigan • Severe economic recession begins

1938 Passage of Fair Labor Standards Act • Anti–New Deal forces make gains in midterm elections • Hitler wins major concessions from French and British leaders at Munich Conference

1939 Marian Anderson gives concert at Lincoln Memorial • German forces attack Poland after Hitler and Stalin sign a "non-aggression" pact

♱ICTURING THE PAST ✦ POLITICS & DIPLOMACY

FDR AND POLIO

© Bettmann / UPI / Corbis

Franklin Roosevelt contracted infantile paralysis, later known as polio, in 1921, at the age of thirty-nine. The disease permanently paralyzed him from the waist down. Though Americans, of course, were aware of his disability, it did not seem a part of the Roosevelt they knew. As president, FDR had an unspoken agreement with the press not to be photographed in a wheelchair or in a helpless position. The Secret Service prepared for his appearances by constructing wooden ramps and putting handgrips on the podium. When Roosevelt fell—as at the 1936 Democratic National Convention—the press did not report it. The photograph here typifies what Americans saw: FDR on his feet, leaning on a cane while grasping the arm of an aide. As biographer Hugh Gallagher, himself a polio victim, has written: "Among the thousands of political cartoons and caricatures of FDR, not one shows the man physically impaired. In fact, many of them have him as a man of action—running, jumping, doing things." Some have criticized Roosevelt for hiding his disability and not doing enough to alter the popular image of the handicapped. But the president believed that concerns about his health and stamina would detract from his ability to lead the nation in perilous times.

Roosevelt possessed neither a comprehensive plan to end the Depression, nor a rigid set of economic beliefs. What he did have was the willingness to experiment, to act decisively, and to use the government as a powerful weapon in the struggle for economic recovery. "Take a method and try it," he liked to say. "If it fails admit it frankly and try another."

Roosevelt surrounded himself with men and women of talent, accomplishment, and wide-ranging progressive views. His closest advisors included Republicans and Democrats, agricultural theorists and urban planners, college professors and political pros. In addition, the New Deal attracted thousands of young people to Washington, drawn by the opportunity to do something meaningful—and perhaps historic—with their lives.

The Bank Crisis

More than 5,000 banks had failed in the United States between 1930 and 1932, wiping out countless savings accounts and stalling the nation's credit. Panicked depositors, unable to tell a good bank from a bad one, lost faith in them all. An avalanche of withdrawals resulted. By the time Roosevelt took office, nineteen states had declared "bank holidays" (or closings) to head off a full-scale collapse.

On March 6, 1933, the president called Congress back into special session and proclaimed a national "bank holiday." Three days later, his emergency banking proposal was enacted in a matter of hours. The new law provided for the federal inspection of all banks. Those with liquid assets would be allowed to reopen with a license from the Treasury Department; the others would be reorganized, if possible, or closed for good.

On March 12, Roosevelt addressed the nation in the first of his "fireside chats." About half of America's homes had radios in 1933, and the president's audience that Sunday evening was estimated at 60 million people. "I want to talk for a few minutes about banking," he began, assuring everyone that the system was now safe. The listeners believed him. In the following days, as the stronger banks reopened, deposits greatly exceeded withdrawals. By the end of March, almost $1 billion had been returned from mattresses to bank vaults. The crisis was over.

Roosevelt's handling of the bank emergency revealed his essential pragmatism. In the midst of such turmoil, he could easily have taken a more radical approach—by nationalizing the banks, for example, or by instituting much tighter controls. Instead, he demonstrated that his primary mission would be to preserve capitalism, not to replace it. And that meant *reforming* its institutions with substantial federal aid.

The president also showed himself to be a master of communication. His ability to reach people in the radio age, to win their confidence, was perhaps his greatest gift. He would use it often in the coming years, as the nation faced the twin crises of economic hardship and global war.

Extending Relief

The special session of Congress lasted from March 9 to June 16, 1933, a period known as "the first hundred days." In that time, more than a dozen major bills proposed by the White House were enacted. With both the House and the Senate now under firm Democratic control, Roosevelt had little trouble getting his legislation passed. As the banking crisis ended, he moved quickly to help those too desperate to help themselves.

The problem was daunting. By conservative estimates, more than 30 million Americans were now living in family units with no income at all.

The Hoover administration had refused to consider federal payments to the jobless. As a result, state and local governments had been forced to ration what little relief they could muster. In 1932, the average weekly payment to an "out-of-work" family in New York City was $2.39. In Detroit, the figure dropped to fifteen cents a day before the money ran out. Some cities were forced to limit relief to families with three or more children; others offered free food and fuel.

Roosevelt believed that relief efforts should be a local responsibility. He, too, worried about the cost of funding such efforts, and about the consequences of giving people money that they hadn't actually earned. Yet there seemed to be no alternative. It was essential,

As banks failed and unemployment soared, breadlines became an ominous symbol of human misery during the Great Depression.
© Bettmann / Corbis

said one of Roosevelt's advisors, to pursue "long-run" economic growth. The problem, he added, is that "people don't eat in the long run—they eat every day."

On March 21, the White House sent two major relief proposals to Capitol Hill. The first one created the Civilian Conservation Corps (CCC). Based on a program that Roosevelt had implemented as governor of New York, the CCC combined the president's enthusiasm for nature with his belief in national service for the young. It provided government conservation jobs to "city boys," age seventeen to twenty-four, in isolated camps run by the U.S. Army. The pay was $30 a month, with $22 going directly to the worker's family.

The CCC was both popular and successful. It eased unemployment a bit, lowered crime rates in the cities, and kept countless families off relief. It also helped to protect and restore the nation's environment, while teaching young men about the discipline of hard work. More than half a million recruits cleaned beaches, built wildlife shelters, fought forest fires, and stocked rivers and streams.

Roosevelt's second relief measure was the Federal Emergency Relief Administration (FERA), which had a budget of $500 million to assist individual states in their efforts to help the unemployed. Hoping to spend the money as quickly and humanely as possible, Roosevelt chose Harry Hopkins, a former social worker who had directed New York's relief effort, to run the FERA. With boundless energy and an ego to match,

One of the New Deal's most popular programs was the Civilian Conservation Corps, which took unemployed young men from the cities and put them to work on conservation projects in the country.
© Bettmann / Corbis

Hopkins personified the New Deal's activist, free-wheeling style. He became Roosevelt's closest advisor.

Most of the funding went to the jobless in the form of free food or a simple "dole." This troubled Hopkins, who understood both the need for such relief and the damage it could do. Real work "preserves a man's morale," he insisted. Knowing that Roosevelt felt the same way, he convinced the president to approve a federal work relief program for the unemployed.

With Hopkins in charge, the Civil Works Administration (CWA) hired more than 4 million people in a matter of months. Its aim was to create jobs and restore self-respect by handing out pay envelopes instead of relief checks. In reality, CWA workers sometimes performed worthless tasks, known as "boondoggles," such as raking leaves in huge circles or lugging shovelsful of dirt to faraway piles.

But this was only part of the story. The CWA spent much of its $1 billion budget on projects of lasting value. Its workers built over 400 airports and 200,000 miles of roads. They ran nursery schools and taught more than a million adults to read and write. They immunized children, served hot school lunches, and took garbage off the streets. Yet Roosevelt ended the CWA experiment after only four months, citing its spiraling costs. He expected federal job programs to be short-term experiments, nothing more. Otherwise, he warned, they will "become a habit with the country."

Conservation, Regional Planning, and Public Power

In the spring of 1933, FDR appeared to be governing the nation by himself. His proposals were so sweeping, and so easily enacted, that Congress seemed to have no independent function of its own. Never before had the White House taken such initiative on domestic legislation; never before had it been so successful.

At Roosevelt's behest, Congress created the Securities and Exchange Commission (SEC) to oversee the stock and bond markets. It established the Federal Deposit Insurance Corporation (FDIC) to insure bank deposits up to $5,000. It provided funds to refinance one-fifth of the nation's home and farm mortgages. And it effectively ended Prohibition by permitting the sale of beer and wine with an alcoholic content of 3.2 percent. (The Eighteenth Amendment would be repealed on December 5, 1933.)

Some of Roosevelt's early proposals had very personal roots. The Civilian Conservation Corps was one example; the Tennessee Valley Authority (TVA), created in May 1933, was another. Like many progressives, Roosevelt had a deep interest in the related issues of conservation, regional planning, and public power. Believing that poverty could be eradicated through the careful development of natural resources, he turned the Tennessee Valley into a laboratory for his most cherished ideas.

Covering seven states and 40,000 square miles, the Tennessee Valley was America's poorest region. Most of its 4 million people—mainly small farmers and sharecroppers—lived in isolated communities, without electricity, medical care, proper schooling, or paved roads. The TVA transformed this region in fundamental ways. Within a decade, sixteen huge dams and hydroelectric plants were in operation along the Tennessee River, providing flood control, cheap, abundant power, and thousands of jobs. Per capita income rose dramatically. Electric power gave local residents what millions of other Americans already took for granted: radios and refrigerators, plumbing, lights in houses and barns.

TVA was widely viewed as one of the New Deal's greatest achievements. Yet its critics included many residents of the Tennessee Valley, whose complaints reflected the changing face of reform. To their thinking, TVA displaced thousands of people, attracted low-wage factory jobs, and caused serious environmental damage. At best, they argued, it brought a measure of comfort and prosperity to a badly depressed region. At worst, it allowed distant bureaucrats to decide how local people should live.

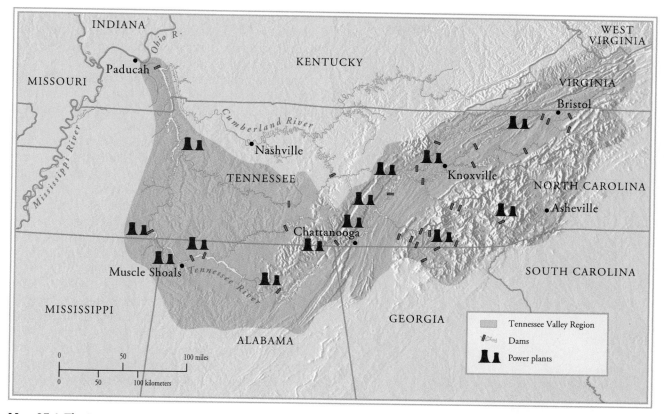

Map 25.1 *The Tennessee Valley*
  The Tennessee Valley Authority, acclaimed as the most visionary model of government planning in the New Deal era, brought electric power, flood control, and employment to one of the nation's most impoverished regions.

ECONOMIC RECOVERY

With the bank crisis over and federal relief flowing to those most desperately in need, the Roosevelt administration turned to the long-term issue of providing a structure for the nation's economic recovery. In agriculture, which accounted for one-quarter of all American jobs, the problems were severe. Most farmers had been slumping badly since the 1920s. The introduction of tractors and high-grade fertilizer had made them more productive than ever. Yet their share of the world market had declined because of high tariff walls and tough foreign competition.

If overproduction plagued American agriculture in this era, the problem facing American industry was quite the reverse. So many factories had closed their doors during the Depression that too little was being produced. The resulting unemployment caused a drop in purchasing power, which forced even more factories to shut down. Something had to be done to break this vicious cycle.

Trouble on the Land

The Roosevelt administration turned first to the agricultural problems. Farmers in 1932 were earning less than one-third of their meager 1929 incomes. As food prices collapsed, there was talk of open rebellion in the heartland. Farmers blocked roads, clashed with police, and threatened to lynch any official who foreclosed a family farm. Roosevelt was sympathetic. He believed that low farm income was a leading cause of the Depression, and he needed the support of rural legislators to get his New Deal programs adopted. The proposal he sent Congress, therefore, incorporated the ideas of the nation's major farm interest groups. Passed in May 1933, the Agricultural Adjustment Act confronted the problems of overproduction and mounting surpluses that had conspired to erode farm income over the years. The act also created the Agricultural Adjustment Administration (AAA) to oversee this process.

The AAA had one clear goal in mind: to raise farm prices by encouraging farmers to produce less. The idea was no longer to win back world markets,

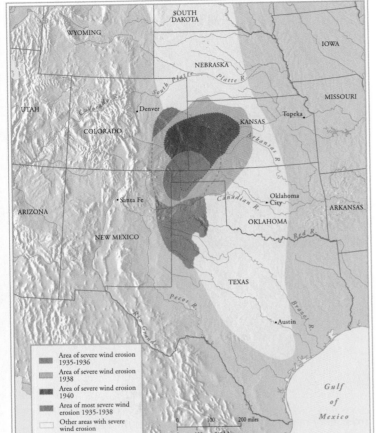

Map 25.2 *The Dust Bowl*
The immense dust storms that blew through the high plains in the 1930s covered nearly 100 millions acres in the hardest hit states of Texas, Oklahoma, Kansas, Colorado, and New Mexico. Though some historians blame local farmers for causing this environmental catastrophe by wearing out the land in search of quick profits, others see them as the unfortunate victims of a prolonged drought. Either way, the dust storms caused terrible economic hardship and a mass migration from the high plains, with tens of thousands of displaced farmers heading west to California.

but rather to limit domestic output in order to achieve "parity," or fair price levels, within the United States. The act compensated farmers who voluntarily removed acreage from production. And it funded these payments through a tax upon farm processors—such as flour millers, meatpackers, and cotton gin operators.

Problems quickly arose. Because spring planting was already underway, the AAA encouraged farmers to plow under a large portion of their crops. Producing

less food while millions were going hungry was difficult for people to understand. But destroying food seemed particularly senseless and cruel. Secretary of Agriculture Henry A. Wallace described the process as "a shocking commentary on our civilization." Yet there seemed to be no other way to fix an economic system awash in idle workers and empty factories, hungry people and abundant food.

Within a year, more than 3 million farmers had signed individual contracts with the AAA. The early results were encouraging. Cotton, wheat, and corn production fell significantly as farmers cultivated fewer acres and cashed their government checks. Farm income shot up almost 60 percent between 1932 and 1935—the result of rising food prices, generous mortgage assistance, and federal loans to those who stored their surpluses in government warehouses.

Nature played a role as well. During the 1930s, the American farm belt experienced record highs in temperature and record lows in rainfall. The Great Plains were hardest hit. Terrifying dust storms swept through Kansas, Nebraska, Colorado, Oklahoma, Texas, and the Dakotas like a black blizzard, packing gale force winds and stripping nutrients from the soil. Cornfields were turned into sand dunes and livestock were buried in their tracks. "This is the ultimate darkness," a Kansas woman wrote in her diary. "So must come the end of the world."

The "Dust Bowl" disaster triggered one of the largest internal migrations in the nation's history. More than 3 million people abandoned their Dust Bowl farms in the 1930s, with Oklahoma, Kansas, and South Dakota losing huge chunks of population. By one account, "The people did not stop to shut the door—they just walked out, leaving behind them the wreckage of their labors: an ugly little shack with broken windows covered by cardboard, a sagging ridgepole, a barren, dusty yard, the windmill creaking in the wind."

Many set out for California, where the "fortunate" among them found work picking fruit, boxing vegetables, and baling hay. Living in hellish squatter camps, enduring disease and discrimination ("Negroes and Okies Upstairs," read a local theater sign), they moved from field to orchard in the San Joaquin and Imperial Valleys, earning pitiful wages and "going on relief."

Tenants and Landowners

The AAA helped countless farm families and ignored countless others. The large farmers got the biggest subsidies. Yet the system barely touched those at the bottom of the pile: the tenants and sharecroppers who comprised almost one-half of the nation's white farm families and three-quarters of the black farm families. Most of them lived in desperate poverty, working the cotton fields of the rural South. Under AAA regulations, these tenants were supposed to get a fair share of the acreage reduction payments. But this rarely occurred. Few landlords obeyed the rules, and some evicted their tenants in order to take even more land out of production.

In response, tenants and sharecroppers formed their own organization, the Southern Tenant Farmers' Union (STFU), to fight for their rights. "The landlord is always betwixt us, beatin' us and starvin' us," complained a black sharecropper from Arkansas. "There ain't but one way for us to get him where he can't help himself and that's for us to get together and stay together."

This would not be easy. Despite the strong support of Norman Thomas and his Socialist party, the STFU could not match the power and resources of its opponents. Tenants who joined the union were evicted from their shacks, blacklisted by employers, and denied credit at banks and stores. Union organizers were beaten and jailed.

President Roosevelt did not intervene. He understood the racial implications of this struggle—most tenants were black; the landlords were white. He did not want to jeopardize the AAA by offending powerful southern interests in Congress. "I know the South . . . ," he told Thomas, "and we've got to be patient." In the meantime, Roosevelt created the Resettlement Administration, with modest funding, to assist evicted tenants and migrant farm workers. Headed by Rexford Tugwell, an outspoken civil rights advocate, the RA became a kind of "mini-AAA" for the rural poor—the New Deal's most class-conscious agency.

Conditions were no better in the Southwest and Far West, where destitute Mexican farm workers struggled to survive. Many had been brought north by American ranchers and growers seeking cheap labor in better times. Now, as the demand for workers decreased, and job competition with poor whites (including the Dust Bowl refugees) intensified, their desperation grew. Since most of these farm workers were not U.S. citizens, local governments often denied them relief. Between 1930 and 1935, moreover, the federal government deported at least 200,000 Mexicans, some of whom were longtime residents of Texas, Arizona, and California, while a larger number returned to Mexico on their own. Those who stayed behind toiled for starvation wages in the fields. Like the Tenant Farmer's Union in Arkansas, their attempts to union-

Texas Dust Bowl refugees on the long road to California.
© Bettmann / Corbis

ize were crushed by local vigilantes and police. In 1936, John Steinbeck reported on a strike of Mexican lettuce workers near his home in Salinas, California. "The attitude of the employer," he wrote, "is one of hatred and suspicion, his method is the threat of the deputies' guns. The workers are herded about like animals. Every possible method is used to make them feel inferior and insecure."

The AAA revolutionized American agriculture. Never before had the federal government been as deeply involved in the affairs of the American farmer; never before had it encouraged its citizens to produce fewer goods, not more. Though key elements of the AAA would be struck down by the Supreme Court in *United States v. Butler* (1936), the concept of federal farm subsidies continues to dominate America's agricultural policy to the present day.

Centralized Economic Planning

The Roosevelt administration had an equally ambitious plan to revive the economy, reopen idle factories, and put people back to work. On June 13, 1933, Congress passed the National Industrial Recovery Act (NIRA) amidst a flood of optimistic projections. Modeled upon both the voluntary trade associations of the 1920s and the industrial mobilization during World War I, the NIRA was designed as a vehicle for centralized economic planning. Roosevelt himself viewed it as the primary weapon in his crusade against the Depression. The act, he boasted, "is the most important and far reaching legislation ever enacted by the American Congress."

The NIRA created two more federal agencies: the Public Works Administration (PWA) and the National Recovery Administration (NRA). The former, with a budget of $3.3 billion, was supposed to "prime the economic pump" by providing jobs for the unemployed and new orders for the factories that produced steel, glass, rubber, cement, and heavy equipment. What made the PWA so appealing was its emphasis on private employment. Workers were to be hired and paid by individual contractors, not by the federal government.

Roosevelt selected Secretary of the Interior Harold Ickes, a veteran progressive, to run the PWA. It proved to be a controversial choice. Known for his prickly, tightfisted ways, Ickes scrutinized almost every construction contract himself, sometimes line by line. He wanted PWA projects to be free of graft, and he insisted that each one add something useful to a community's well-being. In the end, the PWA would spend only $2.8 billion of its budget.

Still, Ickes's legacy was immense. Under his leadership, the PWA constructed schools, hospitals, post offices, and sewage systems. It built the Golden Gate Bridge in San Francisco and the Triborough Bridge in New York City, the Grand Coulee Dam in Washington state and the Boulder Dam in Colorado. No one brought more honest efficiency to government than Harold Ickes, and no one got more value for the dollar.

The key to Roosevelt's recovery program, however, was the NRA. Under the flamboyant leadership of General Hugh S. Johnson, the NRA encouraged representatives of business and labor to create codes of "fair practice" designed to stabilize the economy through planning and cooperation. Johnson's agency promised something to everyone, though not in equal amounts. Business leaders, who dominated the code-writing process, got the biggest gift of all: the suspension of antitrust laws which had dogged them for years.

In return for such generosity, these leaders agreed to significant labor reforms. Each NRA code featured a maximum hour and minimum wage provision (usually forty hours and twelve dollars per week). Child labor was forbidden, and yellow-dog contracts were banned. Most important, Section 7A of the NIRA guaranteed labor unions the right to organize and bargain collectively.

General Johnson barnstormed the country by airplane, giving speeches and lining up support. His tactics were the same ones he had used to mobilize Americans in the bond drives and mass rallies of World War I. With a patriotic symbol (the blue eagle) and a catchy slogan ("We Do Our Part"), Johnson organized the biggest public spectacles of the Depression era. In the summer of 1933, more than 250,000 New Yorkers paraded down Fifth Avenue singing:

> Join the good old N.R.A., Boys,
> and we will end this awful strife.
> Join it with the spirit
> that will give the Eagle life.
> Join in folks, then push and pull,
> many millions strong.
> While we go marching to Prosperity.

Johnson signed up the big industries—coal, steel, oil, autos, shipbuilding, chemicals, and clothing—before going after the others. By the end of 1933, the NRA had 746 different agreements in place. There was a code for the mop handle makers, another for the dog food industry, and even one for the burlesque houses that determined the number of strippers in each show.

Before long, however, the NRA was in trouble. Small businessmen complained that the codes encouraged monopolies and drowned them in paperwork. Labor leaders charged that employers ignored the wage and hour provisions, while cracking down on union activity. And consumers blamed the NRA for raising prices at a time when their purchasing power was extremely low.

All of this was true. Because the codes were voluntary, they carried no legal weight. (Johnson naively assumed that the power of public opinion would keep potential violators in line.) The large companies obeyed them when it was in their interest to do so, and ignored them when it wasn't. As a result, the codes became a device for fixing prices, stifling competition, and limiting production. This may have guaranteed a profit for some companies, but it was the wrong remedy for solving an economic crisis in which the revival of consumer spending was a key to recovery.

In 1934, General Johnson suffered a nervous breakdown, leading Roosevelt to replace him with a five-member executive board. The president seemed relieved when the Supreme Court, in *Schechter Poultry Company v. United States* (1935), struck down the NRA on the grounds that Congress had delegated too much legislative authority to the executive branch. "It has been an awful headache," Roosevelt confided to an aide. "I think perhaps NRA has done all it can do."

NEW DEAL DIPLOMACY

Foreign affairs were not high on President Roosevelt's agenda. His riveting inaugural address had devoted one sentence to the entire subject. "In the field of

PICTURING THE PAST✦ECONOMICS & TECHNOLOGY

CHILD LABOR IN THE 1930s

© Bettmann / Corbis

Few employment issues have proved as contentious and enduring as child labor. From colonial times forward, children worked on farms and in family businesses, often alongside parents and siblings. With the coming of industrialization, children labored in coal mines, canneries, sweatshops, and factories (like the spindle boys pictured here in a Georgia cotton mill), working long hours for pitifully low wages. By 1900, the abolition of child labor had become a powerful force in American politics, supported by progressive reformers, but opposed by many business groups. In 1918, the U.S. Supreme Court, in *Hammer v. Daggenhart*, struck down the first national child labor law. In the 1920s, a proposed constitutional amendment to end this shameful practice also fell short. But the movement gained fresh support during the Great Depression, as adult unemployment rose dramatically and new technologies decreased the need for unskilled factory labor. In 1938, with FDR's blessing, Congress passed the Fair Labor Standards Act, which largely ended child labor in the United States. Three years later, a more liberal Supreme Court unanimously upheld this law. Today, child labor is again on the rise, especially among illegal aliens and school dropouts. The issue is far from resolved.

---

world policy," he declared, "I would dedicate this nation to the policy of the good neighbor"—a theme already sounded by outgoing President Herbert Hoover. The United States was in turmoil, struggling through the worst economic crisis in its history. "I favored as a practical policy," said Roosevelt, "the putting of first things first."

The Soviet Question

FDR was no isolationist. He believed deeply in the concepts of international cooperation and global security, as Americans would shortly discover. One of his first diplomatic moves, in November 1933, was to extend formal recognition to the Soviet Union. The move was criticized by groups as varied as the American Legion and the American Federation of Labor, which viewed the Soviet Union as a godless, totalitarian society bent on exporting "communist revolution" throughout the world. But Roosevelt believed that the United States could no longer afford to ignore the world's largest nation.

The move did not pay quick dividends to either side. Trade with the Soviet Union remained low, partly because Soviet dictator Joseph Stalin was determined to make his nation self-sufficient. The

Russians also ignored their promise not to spread "communist propaganda" in the United States, and then refused to pay their $150 million war debt to Washington. Yet for all of these problems, a major hurdle was cleared. Relations between the United States and the Soviet Union would slowly improve in the 1930s and early 1940s, as ominous world events drew them closer together. For FDR, recognition of Stalin's regime seemed less a threat than an opportunity.

The Good Neighbor

The Roosevelt administration showed a growing interest in Latin America, where U.S. companies had billions of dollars invested in the production of foodstuffs like coffee and sugar, and raw materials such as copper and oil. Along with efforts to increase trade in this region, the United States extended the Good Neighbor Policy by affirming at the 1933 Pan-American Conference in Uruguay that no nation "has the right to intervene in the internal or external affairs of another." Shortly thereafter, the Roosevelt administration recalled several hundred U.S. Marines stationed in Haiti and signed a treaty with Panama recognizing the responsibility of both nations to operate and defend the Panama Canal.

There were exceptions, however. In Cuba, a nation of vital economic and strategic importance to the United States, intervention was a way of life. In 1934, the State Department used its considerable leverage to help bring an "acceptable" government to power in Havana, more sympathetic to North American business interests. With a friendly new regime in place, led by Sergeant Fulgencio Batista, the United States agreed to renounce direct intervention under the Platt Amendment in return for permission to keep its huge naval base at Guantánamo Bay.

The Good Neighbor Policy faced its sternest test even closer to home. In 1934, President Lázaro Cárdenas of Mexico began a national recovery program much like FDR's New Deal. Pledging "Mexico for the Mexicans," Cárdenas attempted to nationalize the agricultural and mining properties of all foreign corporations, as required by the Mexican Constitution of 1917. Though Cárdenas promised "fair compensation" for these holdings, American and British companies demanded more than the Mexicans were willing to pay. (American oil interests wanted $262 million; the Cárdenas government offered $10 million.) Over the objections of many businessmen, the Roosevelt administration convinced Mexico to pay $40 million in compensation for foreign-owned lands it had seized, and another $29 million for the oil fields.

Roosevelt's caution was understandable. The president realized that better relations with Latin America required a new approach. "Give them a share," he urged in private. "They think they are just as good as we are, and many of them are." Roosevelt's policy was also tied to larger world events. With fascism rising in Europe and in Asia, the need for inter-American cooperation was essential.

CRITICS: RIGHT AND LEFT

By 1934, the Depression seemed to be easing. Though enormous problems remained, there was less talk about the dangers of starvation, violent upheaval, or complete economic collapse. The New Deal had injected a dose of hope and confidence into the body politic. Yet as things got better, people inevitably wanted more. The spirit of unity, the shared sense of hardship and struggle, began to dissolve.

The American Liberty League and the 1934 Election

The first rumblings came from the political right. In the summer of 1934, a group of conservative business leaders formed the American Liberty League to combat the alleged "radicalism" of the New Deal. They believed that Roosevelt was leading the country down "a foreign path" by attacking free enterprise, favoring workers over employers, and increasing the power of the federal government. "There can be only one capital," said a Liberty League spokesman, "Washington or Moscow."

The league generously supported Roosevelt's political opponents in the 1934 congressional elections. But the results served only to reinforce the president's enormous popularity, or so it appeared. Instead of losing ground—the normal pattern for the majority party in midterm elections—the Democrats picked up nine seats in the Senate and nine in the House. Few pundits could recall a more lopsided election, and some questioned the future of the Republican party. As publisher William Allen White put it, Roosevelt had been "all but crowned by the people."

In reality, the election results were a mixed blessing for the Democrats. Most Americans approved of the New Deal. Their main criticism was that it had not gone far—or fast—enough to end the Depression. In Minnesota, for example, Governor Floyd Olsen was reelected on an independent "Farmer-Labor" ticket that advocated the state ownership of utilities and railroads.

In neighboring Wisconsin, the sons of "Fighting Bob" LaFollette formed a new Progressive party that endorsed the idea of a welfare state. And in California, Upton Sinclair, author of *The Jungle,* ran for governor on a program called EPIC (End Poverty in California), which promised to hand over idle factories and farmland to the poor and unemployed. Sinclair received almost 900,000 votes in a bitter, losing effort—a sign of things to come.

"Every Man a King"

The most serious challenge to Roosevelt's leadership was offered by Louisiana's Huey P. Long. Known as the "Kingfish," after a strutting, smooth-talking character on the popular radio program *Amos 'n' Andy,* Long combined a gift for showmanship with ruthless ambition. On the campaign trail, he wore a white linen suit, orchid shirt, pink necktie, straw hat, and two-toned shoes. A superb orator and a master storyteller, he understood the value of the spoken word in a state where few people owned radios, read newspapers, or traveled far from home.

As governor of Louisiana, Long pushed his unique brand of southern populism. By revising the tax codes to make corporations and wealthy citizens pay more, he was able to construct new hospitals, bring paved roads and bridges to rural areas, and give free textbooks to the poor. At the same time, he built a political machine of almost totalitarian proportions. When Long vacated the governor's chair to enter the U.S. Senate in 1932, he controlled the legislature, the courts, and the civil service system of Louisiana.

"I came to the United States Senate," Long wrote, "to spread the wealth of the land among all of the people." As a Democrat, he campaigned hard for Roosevelt in 1932 and supported much of the early New Deal. But as time passed, he grew restless with the slow pace of reform. In 1934, Long proposed his own agenda for economic recovery. Once in place, he promised, it would "make every man a king."

Under Long's plan, no one would be allowed to earn more than $1.8 million per year or to keep a personal fortune in excess of $5 million. After confiscating this surplus, the government would provide each family with a house, a car, a radio, and an annual income of at least $2,500. Veterans would get their bonus, the elderly would receive pensions, and deserving students could attend college free of charge.

Most economists were appalled. They knew that there weren't nearly enough millionaires around to finance Long's proposal. According to one study, the government would have had to confiscate all yearly incomes above $3,000—not $1.8 million—to provide

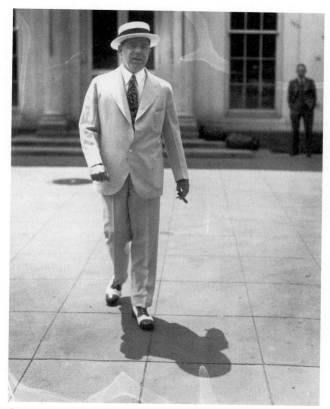

Senator Huey P. Long combined showmanship with ruthless ambition to become Franklin Roosevelt's most influential critic and political rival. Claiming the New Deal did not do enough to help poor people, Long proposed a radical program to redistribute wealth that attracted millions of followers.
© Bettmann / UPI / Corbis

each family with $2,500. Long didn't much care about the arithmetic. "You don't have to understand it," he told his followers. "Just shut your damned eyes and believe it. That's all."

By 1935, Long's "Share Our Wealth Society" claimed 8 million members nationwide. It lured in people by promising them what the New Deal could not possibly deliver. At local meetings across the nation, his followers sang:

Every man a king, every man a king
For you can be a millionaire
But there's something belongs to others
There's enough for all to share.

The Radio Priest and the Pension Doctor

Long did not lack for competitors. In Royal Oak, Michigan, a working-class suburb of Detroit, Father Charles Edward Coughlin was busy leading a protest movement of his own. As the pastor of a small Catholic church called the Shrine of the Little Flower, Coughlin became a towering figure in the 1930s by mixing prayer with politics in a way that touched millions—and frightened millions more.

Coughlin could be heard every Sunday on seventeen CBS radio outlets nationwide. An early Roosevelt supporter, he compared the New Deal to "Christ's Deal," assuring listeners that "Gabriel is over the White House, not Lucifer." Like Senator Long, Coughlin deplored the fact that too much wealth was concentrated in too few hands. Unlike Long, however, he blamed this evil on a tight money supply, manipulated by international bankers in London and New York.

Coughlin believed that "free silver"—the old Populist nostrum—would solve this problem and bring prosperity to all. His attacks on British bankers won him strong support in the Irish-Catholic community, and his call for monetary reform appealed to debt-ridden farmers and merchants in America's small towns. Before long, Coughlin's radio show, *Golden Hour of the Little Flower*, had more listeners (an estimated 40 million) than *Amos 'n' Andy* and *Gracie Allen*. He needed 150 clerks and four personal secretaries to handle the thousands of letters and donations that poured into his office. Some of this money was used to construct a new church of granite and marble, seven stories high, bathed in floodlights, with a huge Christ figure on top.

By 1934, the "Radio Priest" was souring on the New Deal. Angered by Roosevelt's disinterest in his "silver solution," he formed the National Union for Social Justice to challenge the president's leadership. "I glory in the fact that I am a simple Catholic priest," Coughlin declared, "endeavoring to inject Christianity into the fabric of an economic system woven upon the loom of the greedy."

A third protest movement, led by Francis E. Townsend, a retired physician living in California, offered yet another solution to the ills of the 1930s. Townsend had no desire to punish the rich, alter the money supply, or challenge the capitalist order. What disturbed him was the sight of elderly men and women sifting through garbage cans for food. In 1934, Townsend proposed a measure to revive the economy by meeting the specific needs of older Americans. It guaranteed a pension of $200 per month to those over sixty who promised to stay out of the job market and to spend the $200 by month's end. The pensions would be funded by a 2 percent sales tax on all "business transactions."

According to Townsend, his plan would create jobs for the young, increase the country's purchasing power, and provide security for the elderly. What he didn't say was that his plan, known as Old Age Revolving Pensions Limited, was impossibly expensive. By most estimates, Townsend needed a sales tax approaching 70 percent in order to properly fund his proposal. When asked about this at a congressional hearing, the doctor replied: "I'm not in the least interested in the cost of the plan."

Neither were his followers. By 1935, more than 10 million Americans had signed petitions supporting Townsend's idea, and public opinion polls showed strong support for a government-sponsored pension plan. Townsend had unleashed a powerful new interest group, the elderly, and American politics would never be the same.

THE SECOND NEW DEAL

The American Liberty League, the victories of Floyd Olsen and the La Follette brothers, the rumblings of Long, Coughlin, and Townsend—all raised nagging problems for Franklin Roosevelt and the New Deal. Though national income in 1935 was a full 25 percent above the 1933 level, millions were still living on handouts, without much hope of a permanent job. Inside the White House, Roosevelt's key advisors were nudging him further to the left. "Boys—this is our hour," said the opportunistic Harry Hopkins. "We've got to get everything we want—a works program, social security, wages and hours, everything—now or never."

Jobs, Jobs, Jobs

In the spring of 1935, Roosevelt presented Congress with a "must" list of reforms, the so-called "second New Deal." He requested—and received—$4.8 billion in work relief for the unemployed, the largest single appropriation in the nation's history. After allocating generous shares to his favorite projects, such as the CCC, Roosevelt established yet another agency, the Works Progress Administration (WPA), with Hopkins in charge, to create "jobs, jobs, jobs!"

In that task, it was very successful. At its height in 1936, the WPA employed 25 percent of the nation's entire workforce. Many of these jobs, however, were low-paying and temporary so as to avoid competition with private enterprise. Concentrating on small construction projects, the WPA built schools and playgrounds, repaired countless bridges and landing fields, and improved 650,000 miles of roads. Its National Youth Administration, inspired by Eleanor Roosevelt, provided part-time work to several million high school and college students.

Huey P. Long Condemns FDR and the New Deal

During his first term in office, President Roosevelt was criticized by the political right for expanding the role of government to help end the Great Depression, and by the political left for not expanding that role even further. Among FDR's most vocal critics was Senator Huey P. Long of Louisiana, a self-styled "populist" with presidential aspirations. Shortly before his assassination, the flamboyant Long accused Roosevelt of reneging on earlier promises to help the poor, the hungry, the unemployed.

I was the first man to say publicly—but Mr. Roosevelt followed in my tracks a few months later and said the same thing. We said that all of our trouble and woe was due to the fact that too few of our people owned too much of our wealth. We said that in our land, with too much to eat, and too much to wear, and too many houses to live in, too many automobiles to be sold, that the only trouble was that the people suffered in the land of abundance because too few controlled the money and the wealth and too many did not have money with which to buy the things they needed for life and comfort.

So I said to the people of the United States . . . that the only way by which we could restore our people to reasonable life and comfort was to limit the size of the big man's fortune and guarantee some minimum to the fortune and comfort of the little man's family. . . .

. . .So we convinced Mr. Franklin Delano Roosevelt that it was necessary that he announce and promise to the American people that in the event he were elected President of the United States he would pull down the size of the big man's fortune and guarantee something to every family—enough to do away with all poverty and to give employment to those who were able to work and education to the children born into the world.

Mr. Roosevelt made those promises; he made them before he was nominated in the Chicago convention. He made them again before he was elected in November, and he went so far as to remake those promises after he was inaugurated President of the United States. And I thought for a day or two after he took the oath as President, that maybe he was going through with his promises. No heart was ever so saddened; no person's ambition was ever so blighted, as was mine when I came to the realization that the President of the United States was not going to undertake what he had said he would do, and what I knew to be necessary if the people of America were ever [to be] saved from calamity and misery.

Source: *New York Times*, January 26, 1936.

Social Security

The president's "must" list included a social welfare plan that challenged the cherished concepts of voluntarism and individual responsibility. At the urging of Labor Secretary Frances Perkins, the nation's first woman cabinet member, Roosevelt proposed legislation (passed as the Social Security Act of 1935) to create a national pension fund, an unemployment insurance system, and public assistance programs for dependent mothers and children, the physically disabled, and those in chronic need. The pension was financed by a payroll tax to begin in 1937. Benefits were purposely modest—about twenty to thirty dollars per month—because Roosevelt did not intend "Social Security" to be the *main* source of personal retirement income, as it has become for many people today.

The act had numerous defects. It excluded millions of vulnerable wage earners from the pension fund, such as domestics, farm workers, and the self-employed.

*P*ICTURING THE PAST ✦ SOCIAL & CULTURAL EVENTS

THE NEW DEAL AND THE ARTS

WPA Mural; Coit Tower, San Francisco

Among the most controversial parts of FDR's New Deal was "Federal One," an experiment to provide government funding for the arts. Established under the huge Works Progress Administration, Federal One aimed to employ out-of-work professionals to help bring "culture" to the masses. Its Federal Theater Project performed everything from Shakespeare to puppet shows for audiences that rarely, if ever, had seen a live production. Its Federal Arts Project produced museum exhibits, murals for public buildings (like the one pictured here in San Francisco's Coit Tower), and painting classes for the poor. Playwright Arthur Miller worked for Federal One, as did Actor Burt Lancaster, artist Jackson Pollock, and writers Saul Bellow and Richard Wright. Though some criticized these projects as wasteful and politically slanted to the New Deal (note the clean, well-fed, contented workers in the mural), they remained popular with the American public. Asked about the artwork, FDR said: "Some of it is good, some of it not so good, but all of it is native, human, eager and alive—all of it painted by their own kind in their own country."

It taxed all participants at a fixed rate, forcing those with the lowest incomes to pay a far greater share of their wages into the system. Over time, the Social Security fund emerged as the country's most important and expensive domestic program.

"Class Warfare"

Roosevelt had never been a strong supporter of organized labor. He wanted to help workers through his own social programs, rather than having them organize unions to help themselves. He felt uneasy about the tactics of labor leaders such as John L. Lewis, head of the United Mine Workers, who had tripled his membership (from 150,000 to almost 500,000) with an ag-

gressive organizing campaign that declared, "The president wants you to join a union!" Roosevelt worried that labor's militant new spirit would accelerate the violent confrontations of 1934, when pitched battles erupted between striking workers and police on the streets of Minneapolis, San Francisco, and Detroit.

In the wake of these disturbances, Senator Robert Wagner of New York authored a bill to protect the rights of workers to organize and bargain collectively. His legislation filled a dramatic void, because the Supreme Court had just declared parts of the NIRA—including Section 7A—to be unconstitutional. Passed in 1935, the National Labor Relations (Wagner) Act prohibited employers from engaging in a wide range of "unfair labor practices," such as spying on

Unemployment 1925–1945

Chart 25.1 *Unemployment 1925–1945*
This chart shows the two great peaks of unemployment—the first in 1933, as FDR took office; the second (and smaller one) during the recession of 1938, when federal spending was reduced. The chart also shows the enormous impact of World War II in bringing unemployment—and the Great Depression itself—to an end.

Secretary of Labor Frances Perkins, the first woman to hold a cabinet position, was instrumental in the formulation and passage of the Social Security Act.
© Bettmann / UPI / Corbis

their workers. The law also created the National Labor Relations Board (NLRB) to supervise union elections and determine the appropriate bargaining agents.

The Wagner Act revealed deep divisions within the union movement. At the American Federation of Labor's annual convention in 1935, John L. Lewis pleaded with fellow leaders to begin serious membership drives in the steel mills, automobile plants, and rubber factories. Lewis wanted these mass production workers to be organized by industry rather than by craft. Only then, he argued, could the power of big business be successfully confronted.

Most AFL leaders were unmoved. As representatives of skilled craftsworkers, such as masons and carpenters, they had little interest in organizing industrial unions composed largely of African Americans and ethnic groups from eastern and southern Europe. Indeed, after Lewis finished his emotional plea to the AFL convention, Carpenters' President "Big Bill" Hutcheson called him a "bastard." Lewis floored Hutcheson with a solid right to the jaw and stormed out of the convention.

In November 1935, Lewis formed the Committee for Industrial Organization (CIO) to charter new unions in the mass production industries. He was joined by a handful of AFL leaders from the needle trades, including Sidney Hillman of the Amalgamated Clothing Workers and David Dubinsky of the International Ladies' Garment Workers. Although the AFL suspended these men and their unions for

Police in Minneapolis battle striking truck drivers in 1934. Labor violence was common in this era, as workers demanded and employers often resisted the right to organize unions and to press for better wages and working conditions.
Franklin D. Roosevelt Library

"fomenting insurrection," Lewis never looked back. His attention had turned to the CIO's organizing drives in the auto and steel industries. Labor's "civil war" had begun.

THE FASCIST CHALLENGE

As the 1936 presidential election approached, Americans watched events in Europe with growing apprehension. From the Soviet Union came stories about a regime that was brutalizing its people in an attempt to "collectivize" the society and stamp out internal dissent. In Germany and Italy, powerful dictators emerged, preaching race hatred and vowing to expand their nation's borders. For millions of Americans, the scene was frighteningly familiar—a replay of events that had led Europe, and eventually the United States, into the bloodiest war of all time.

Hitler and Mussolini

Adolf Hitler became the German chancellor in January 1933, a few months before FDR was sworn in as president. Born in Austria in 1889, Hitler had moved to Bavaria as a young man and fought in the German army during World War I. Wounded and jobless, he helped form the National Socialist (Nazi) party, one of the many extremist groups that thrived in the economic chaos of war-battered Germany. In 1923, Hitler was arrested in Munich for staging an unsuccessful coup against the Weimar government. From his prison cell, he wrote *Mein Kampf* ("My Struggle"), a rambling account of his racial theories, plans for Germany, and hatred of Jews.

As the Weimar government collapsed in the Depression, the Nazis gained strength. Millions welcomed their promise to create jobs, restore German glory, and avenge the "humiliation" of Versailles. Nazi representation in the *Reichstag* (parliament) rose from twelve in 1928 to 230 by 1932. A year later, Hitler became chancellor of Germany. The results were alarming. Constitutional rights were suspended and competing political parties were banned. Nazi supporters held mass book-burning rallies, drove Jews from universities, boycotted their businesses, and attacked them in the streets. "Hitler is a madman," President Roosevelt told a French diplomat.

Under the Nazis, the state increased its control over industry, while leaving it in private hands. This allowed Hitler to begin a massive rearmament program, which produced badly needed jobs. By 1934, German factories were producing tanks and military aircraft. A year later, Hitler proposed a 500,000-man army and instituted the draft. In 1936, Nazi forces marched into the Rhineland—a clear violation of the Versailles treaty—and reoccupied it without firing a shot. "Today Germany," the Nazis chanted, "tomorrow the world."

Hitler had modeled himself, to some degree, after Italian dictator Benito Mussolini, the father of fascism in modern Europe. Born in 1883, Mussolini had served in the Italian army during World War I. Playing upon the social unrest and economic turmoil of the postwar era, he seized national power in 1922 and proclaimed *Fascismo*. As the supreme leader, or *Duce*, he preached national unity and state management (though not ownership) of Italy's industrial base. Like Hitler, he destroyed labor unions, censored the press, abolished all political parties but his own, and relied on a secret police force to maintain order and silence his critics.

In 1935, Italian forces invaded Ethiopia from their neighboring colonies of Eritrea and Somaliland. For Mussolini, the attack was a way of restoring Italy's ancient glory. The fighting in Ethiopia was brutal and one-sided, pitting Italian tanks and machine guns against local defenders armed with little more than spears and bows and arrows. At the League of Nations, Ethiopian Emperor Haile Selassie pleaded for support. The league responded by branding Italy the aggressor, but sending no military help. After annexing Ethiopia in 1936, Mussolini signed a pact of friendship with Hitler, known as the Rome-Berlin Axis.

The Neutrality Acts

Americans did not want to become involved in European squabbles, as they had in the past. They were determined that history must not repeat itself—that American blood must not be shed again on foreign soil. There was only one way to avoid another war, most people believed, and that was to remain truly neutral in world affairs.

Although this sentiment had deep historical roots, running all the way back to George Washington, the key to understanding America's anxiety in the early 1930s was the legacy of World War I—the belief that U.S. participation had been a mistake, that America had been lured into the conflict, against its vital interests, by a conspiracy of evil men. In 1934, the U.S. Senate set up a committee, chaired by isolationist Gerald P. Nye of North Dakota, to investigate the reasons for America's involvement in World War I. The Nye committee highlighted a series of well-known facts: large banks and corporations had made huge profits during World War I by giving loans and selling arms to the various combatants. It followed, therefore, that the United States had been led into this conflict by greedy bankers and businessmen determined to protect their investments. The press dubbed them "merchants of death."

This was a simplistic explanation, to be sure. It ignored the rather tangled reality of American intervention—from submarine warfare to the Zimmermann Telegram, from President Wilson's rigid morality to the defense of neutral rights. Yet the Nye committee findings enjoyed wide popular support in a nation determined to avoid another war.

The isolationist impulse was particularly strong in the Great Plains and Upper Midwest, where populist suspicions of Wall Street and international bankers went back a long way. It attracted many Americans of German descent, who remembered their brutal treatment during World War I; of Irish descent, who opposed aid to Great Britain in any form; and of Italian descent, who viewed Mussolini as a hero in these years. Isolationism—in some cases combined with pacifism—also appealed to ministers, peace groups, and college students.

Congress responded to this public mood with legislation designed to avoid the "entanglements" that had led to American participation in World War I. The first Neutrality Act, passed after the Ethiopian invasion of 1935, empowered the president to determine when a state of war existed anywhere in the world. In that event, the president would declare an embargo on all combatants. American arm shipments would cease, and American citizens would be warned against traveling on the vessels of belligerents. In February 1936, Congress passed a second Neutrality Act, prohibiting American banks from extending loans or credits to any nation at war.

President Roosevelt did not like these bills. He believed that absolute neutrality favored powerful aggressor nations by forcing the United States to treat all sides equally. Yet FDR signed them into law for political reasons. The Neutrality Acts had wide popular support. He knew that a veto would give strong ammunition to the Republicans in the coming presidential campaign.

MANDATE FROM THE PEOPLE

As the 1936 election approached, FDR had reason for concern. Although personal income and industrial production had risen dramatically since he took office in 1933, neither had reached the pre-Depression levels of 1929. Millions of Americans were still unemployed, labor violence was spreading, and the federal deficit continued to climb. In addition, more than 80 percent of the nation's newspapers and most of the business community remained loyal to the Republican party,

meaning that Roosevelt's major presidential opponent could count on strong editorial and financial support.

The 1936 Election

In June, the Republicans gathered in Cleveland to nominate their presidential ticket. Herbert Hoover, anxious for another crack at Roosevelt, received a thunderous ovation. But the convention delegates, seeking a winner, not a martyr, chose Kansas Governor Alfred M. Landon to head the Republican ticket, and Frank Knox, a Chicago publisher, to be the vice presidential nominee.

Landon, a political moderate, promised "fewer radio talks, fewer experiments, and a lot more common sense." His problem was that he radiated little of the compassion and confidence that made Roosevelt so popular with the masses. Worse, Landon's bland pronouncements were overshadowed by the broadsides of more conservative Republican leaders, who denounced the New Deal as a radical plot to subvert free enterprise and individual rights.

Roosevelt also faced presidential challenges from the left. Both the Communists and the Socialists ran spirited campaigns in 1936, demanding more federal aid for the poor. But Roosevelt's most serious concern—a political merger involving Coughlin, Townsend, and Long—was effectively eliminated in September 1935, when an assassin's bullet killed the Louisiana senator in Baton Rouge. To replace the charismatic Long, these dissident forces nominated William "Liberty Bill" Lemke, an obscure North Dakota congressman, to be their presidential candidate on the new Union party ticket.

Roosevelt's political strategy differed markedly from 1932. In that campaign, he had stressed the common hopes and needs that bound people together; in 1936, he emphasized the class differences that separated those who supported the New Deal from those who opposed it. Time and again, Roosevelt portrayed the election as a contest between common people and privileged people, between compassion and greed. In his final campaign speech at New York's Madison Square Garden, he declared that the "forces of selfishness" had "met their match" in the Roosevelt administration. "They are unanimous in their hatred of me," the president thundered, *"and I welcome their hatred."*

On November 3, FDR crushed Landon and Lemke in the most one-sided election since 1820. The final totals showed Roosevelt with 27,752,869 popular votes, Landon with 16,674,665, and Lemke with 882,479. (The Socialist and Communist party candidates polled fewer than 300,000 votes between them.) Roosevelt won every state except Maine and Vermont, while the Democratic party added to its huge majorities in both houses of Congress. A few days after the election, Father Coughlin announced his retirement from the radio.

African Americans and the New Deal

Roosevelt's landslide victory signaled a dramatic shift in American politics. A new majority coalition had emerged. In the farm belt, Roosevelt won over long-time Republicans with federal subsidies and price supports. In the cities, he attracted workers grateful for welfare benefits and WPA jobs. And he appealed to ethnic minorities by filling so many White House positions, cabinet posts, and federal judgeships with Catholics and Jews.

Adding to the president's strength was the support he received from the CIO. Describing Roosevelt as "the worker's best friend," the CIO campaigned tirelessly for him in key industrial states, and the effort paid off. FDR captured the working-class vote in 1936 by a margin of four to one.

The most striking political change, however, occurred within the nation's African American community. The steady migration of blacks to northern cities, where they could vote, increased their political power. Historically, most blacks supported the Republican party, an allegiance that dated back to Abraham Lincoln and the Civil War. In 1932, Herbert Hoover won an overwhelming share of their votes.

With the New Deal, a massive switch took place. In large part, African Americans became Democrats because the Roosevelt administration provided jobs and welfare benefits to all Americans, regardless of race. This federal assistance was especially welcome in black communities, where poverty and discrimination had long been facts of life. "The Negro was born in depression," a black leader recalled. "It only became official when it hit the white man."

By 1933, black unemployment had reached a staggering 50 percent. Fortunately, the two New Deal administrators most responsible for creating jobs were sympathetic to minority needs. At the PWA, Harold Ickes insisted that blacks receive equal pay and minimum quotas on all construction projects. Though local officials often ignored these rules, the PWA provided thousands of jobs for African Americans, while building black schools and hospitals throughout the segregated South. At the WPA, Harry Hopkins set the same standards with somewhat better results. Blacks received a generous share of WPA work in northern cities—a testimony to both their joblessness and political clout. "Let Jesus Lead You and Roosevelt Feed

Although few blacks voted in the South during the 1930s, their growing numbers in northern cities like Chicago and New York increased their political influence within the New Deal coalition.
© Bettmann / UPI / Corbis

You," became a rallying cry in African American churches during the election of 1936.

Many blacks viewed the New Deal as a progressive social force. They welcomed an administration that showed some interest in their struggle. And they particularly admired the efforts of First Lady Eleanor Roosevelt, who served as the White House conscience on matters pertaining to minority rights.

Eleanor Roosevelt had a passion for public service and a deep commitment to the poor. Her interest in civil rights had been fueled, in large measure, by her friendship with prominent African Americans such as Mary McLeod Bethune, founder of Bethune-Cookman College in Florida. Born in a sharecropper's shack, the fifteenth child of former slaves, Bethune had acquainted the first lady with the special problems facing African Americans—from the scandal of lynching to the crisis in public education. In 1936, Eleanor Roosevelt recommended Bethune to head the National Youth Administration's Office of Negro Affairs.

As the New Deal's highest-ranking black appointee, Bethune presided over the administration's "black cabinet," which advised the White House on minority issues. Working together with Eleanor Roosevelt and other civil rights advocates, she helped to encourage—and monitor—the New Deal's racial progress. Much of it was symbolic. In an age of rigid segregation, Eleanor Roosevelt visited black colleges, spoke at black conferences, and socialized with black women. (She raised eyebrows by inviting Bethune to tea at the White House.) When the Daughters of the American Revolution refused to allow Marian Anderson, a gifted black contralto, to perform at Washington's Constitution Hall, Eleanor Roosevelt resigned from the organization. A few months later, Harold Ickes arranged for Anderson to sing at the Lincoln Memorial on Easter Sunday, 1939. An integrated audience of 75,000 gathered to hear her.

Yet the good work of Eleanor Roosevelt and others could not mask larger New Deal failures in the field of civil rights. Throughout his presidency, for example, Franklin Roosevelt never attempted to challenge southern racial customs. He made no effort to break down segregation barriers or to enable blacks to vote. And he remained on the sidelines as federal anti-lynching bills were narrowly defeated in Congress. Without his leadership, not a single piece of civil rights legislation was enacted in the New Deal years.

Roosevelt argued that he could not support civil rights legislation without alienating southern Democrats who controlled the most important committees in Congress. "They will block every bill I [need] to keep America from collapsing," Roosevelt said. "I just can't take that risk."

The president's position did not prevent blacks from supporting him in 1936. Roosevelt received 76 percent of their votes—the same total that Herbert Hoover had won four years before. On balance, African Americans viewed the New Deal as a clear improvement over the Republican past. "My friends, go turn Lincoln's picture to the wall," a black editor wrote in 1935. "That debt has been paid in full."

POPULAR CULTURE IN THE DEPRESSION

The economic struggles of the 1930s shaped not only the politics of American life, but the culture as well. Hard times encouraged federal participation in the arts and triggered a leftward tilt among many intellectuals and writers. A flurry of "proletarian literature"

Marian Anderson entertained a crowd of 75,000 at the Lincoln Memorial on Easter Sunday, 1939, after the Daughters of the American Revolution refused to allow her to perform at Washington's Constitution Hall.
© Bettmann / UPI / Corbis

emerged in the early Depression years, emphasizing the "class struggle" through stories about heroic workers resisting the exploitation of evil employers. Several important black writers—including Ralph Ellison, Richard Wright, and Langston Hughes—identified with the Communist party because it appeared to actively support civil rights. For most intellectuals, however, the fascination with communism was fleeting. As free thinkers, they could not adjust to the party's rigid conformity or its blind support of the Soviet dictator Joseph Stalin.

The Depression era also witnessed the spread of a popular culture born in the preceding decades. Photojournalism came of age in the 1930s with the publication of magazines such as *Life* and *Look,* and the vivid imagery of government-sponsored photographers like Walker Evans and Dorothea Lange. In the comics trade, "Superman" (1938) demonstrated that Americans were anxious to get beyond the tame characters from the newspaper strips. He was quickly followed by comic books featuring "Batman" and "Captain Marvel." In popular music, the "swing era" brought the jazz of African American artists to a much broader public. In radio and in movies, the changes were most dramatic and profound.

The Big Screen

By the 1930s, the motion picture was the leading form of popular culture in the United States. Most Americans attended at least one movie a week; many followed the lives of their favorite stars in gossip columns and fan magazines. Theater owners attracted customers by offering inducements such as the "double feature," which dramatically increased the number of films produced during this decade. In the larger cities, movie theaters were transformed into fantasy palaces, with thick carpets, winding staircases, ushers in tuxedoes, and the twinkling lights of chandeliers. For millions, the theater became a temporary escape from the bleak realities of the Depression.

Hollywood mirrored the changing attitudes of the 1930s. It was no accident that the most popular movie of 1932, the year America hit rock bottom, was Mervyn LeRoy's *I Am a Fugitive From a Chain Gang,* the story of a decent man, unjustly convicted of a crime, who escapes from a brutal southern penal farm. In the final scene, the hero meets his former girlfriend, who asks him how he survives. From the shadows of a dark alley—representing the Depression itself—he whispers: "I steal."

Other early films from this decade, such as *Little Caesar* (1930) and *Public Enemy* (1931) focused on big city mobsters who ruthlessly shot their way to the top. Although these "bad guys" were either killed or brought to justice on screen, the public's fascination with criminal activity reached a peak in these years with the romanticizing of bank robbers (and cold-blooded murderers) like John Dillinger, Bonnie Parker and Clyde Barrow, Baby Face Nelson, and Ma Barker. All died in shoot-outs with local police or the FBI.

The evolving optimism of the 1930s—the promise of better times—was apparent in Hollywood films. The 1930s saw Fred Astaire whirling Ginger Rogers across the nightclub dance floor; Mickey Rooney courting Judy Garland in the blissfully innocent "Andy Hardy" movies; and Walt Disney raising the animated cartoon to an art form in his feature film *Snow White and the Seven Dwarfs* (1937). Wildly popular in this decade (and beyond) were the Marx brothers—Groucho, Harpo, and Chico—whose classic comedies demolished upper-class snobbery, foolish tradition, and much of the English language.

More significant were the moral dramas of director Frank Capra, including *Mr. Deeds Goes to Town* (1936), starring Gary Cooper, and *Mr. Smith Goes to Washington* (1939), with Jimmy Stewart. Both the movies and the leading men represented the inherent virtues of heartland America, with its strong sense of decency and cooperation. Common people could be fooled by greedy bankers and selfish politicians, but not for long. Life got better when "good folks" followed their instincts.

The most memorable films of this era, *Gone with the Wind* and *The Grapes of Wrath,* showcased Holly-wood's ability to transform best-selling fiction into successful movies, seen by millions who had read the novels of Margaret Mitchell, John Steinbeck, and others—and millions more who had not. Both films related the epic struggle of families in crisis, trying desperately to survive. *The Grapes of Wrath,* set in the Depression, depicts the awful conditions faced by the Dust Bowl farmers who migrated to California. True to the 1930s, it is a story of marginal people confronting economic injustice—people who stick together and refuse to give up. The hero, Tom Joad, promises his Ma that "wherever they's a fight so hungry people can eat, I'll be there. Wherever they's a cop beatin' up a guy, I'll be there." Ma Joad is a source of strength and common sense. "They ain't gonna wipe us out," she insists. "Why, we're the people—we go on."

The Radio Age

Like the movie boom, the rapid growth of radio in the Depression encouraged the spread of popular culture. Politicians and public figures such as President Roosevelt and Father Coughlin used radio to great effect. So, too, did companies seeking to mass market their products. Organized along commercial lines in the 1920s, radio continued firmly down that path in the 1930s, with two giant firms—the National Broadcasting Company (NBC) and the Columbia Broadcasting System (CBS)—dominating the nation's airwaves.

In an odd way, the economic turmoil of the 1930s aided radio by weakening other forms of entertainment. As vaudeville failed and the infant recording industry struggled, popular performers, including Al Jolson and Jack Benny, continued their careers on the radio. For morning and afternoon fare, the networks relied on domestic dramas such as *Ma Perkins* and *Helen Trent,* which appealed to women working in the home. Often sponsored by soap and beauty companies, these programs, known as "soap operas," doled out the story line in daily fifteen-minute installments. In the evenings, as entire families gathered around the radio, the entertainment broadened to include quiz shows, talent contests, and adventure programs like *Inner Sanctum* and *The Green Hornet.* Surveys showed that the average American in the 1930s listened to more than four hours of radio each day.

Radio carried sporting events, political conventions, and the news. Millions followed the 1936 Berlin Olympics, where Jesse Owens, the African American track star, embarrassed Adolf Hitler by winning four gold medals. Two years later, the heavyweight title fight from Yankee Stadium between Joe Louis, the black champion, and Max Schmeling, the German challenger, was broadcast throughout the world. When Louis knocked out Schmeling in the first round, Americans celebrated in the streets.

Perhaps nothing better demonstrated the power of radio than the infamous "War of the Worlds" episode. On Halloween evening, 1938, actor Orson Welles, star of CBS's *Mercury Theater,* did a powerful reading of the H. G. Wells novel, presenting it as a simulated newscast in which violent aliens from Mars land in the New Jersey town of Grovers Mills. "I can see the thing's body," sobbed a "roving reporter" at the scene. "It's large as a bear and it glistens like wet leather. That face . . . the black eyes and saliva dripping from its rimless lips." Although Welles repeatedly interrupted the program to explain what he was doing, a national panic ensued. Thousands fled their homes, believing that the Martians had wiped out the New Jersey State Police and were advancing toward New York City. Traffic came to a halt in parts of the Northeast; bus and train stations were jammed; churches overflowed with weeping families. A few commentators blamed the hysteria on world events; the rising tide of fascism in Europe made people uneasy. Everybody else blamed Welles for misusing—or at least misjudging—the power of radio. Newspaper headlines screamed: "Radio War Terrorizes U.S." and "Panic Grips Nation As Radio Announces 'Mars Attacks World.'" When the furor died down, President Roosevelt invited Welles to the White House. "You know, Orson," he joked, "you and I are the two best actors in America."

Orson Welles, arms upraised, caused a national panic during his radio dramatization of "War of the Worlds" in 1938.
© Bettmann / UPI / Corbis

THE SECOND TERM

In his second inaugural address, FDR emphasized the New Deal's unfinished business. "I see one-third of a nation ill-housed, ill-clad, ill-nourished," he declared. The president was optimistic. The election had provided him with a stunning popular mandate and with huge Democratic majorities on Capitol Hill. To Roosevelt's thinking, only one roadblock lay in his path: the Supreme Court.

A confrontation seemed inevitable. The Supreme Court was dominated by elderly, conservative justices, appointed in the Harding-Coolidge years, who despised the New Deal and worked zealously to subvert its legislation. In Roosevelt's first term, the Court had struck down the NRA, the AAA, and a series of social welfare laws. In the coming months, it would be reviewing—and likely overturning—the National Labor Relations Act and the Social Security Act, two of the New Deal's most precious accomplishments.

Roosevelt struck first. In February 1937, without consulting Congress, he unveiled sweeping legislation to reorganize the federal court system. Under his plan, fifty new judgeships would be created by adding one judge for each sitting justice over the age of seventy who refused to retire. The Supreme Court would get a maximum of six new members, raising its total to fifteen.

The plan was legal. The Constitution sets no limits on the size of the Supreme Court; indeed, the number of justices, determined by Congress, had fluctuated between six and ten in the previous century. Roosevelt assumed that his overwhelming reelection in 1936 had given him the green light to crush all opposition to the New Deal, regardless of the source.

He was badly mistaken. His plan met quick and furious opposition. Many Americans, including Louis D. Brandeis, the Supreme Court's oldest and most liberal justice, were offended by Roosevelt's jab at the elderly. Others worried that his "Court-packing" plan would undermine judicial independence and threaten the balance of power among the three branches of government. As the opposition grew stronger, aides urged Roosevelt to withdraw the bill.

In the spring of 1937, the Supreme Court changed course. By votes of five to four, with one moderate justice switching sides, it upheld both the Wagner Act and the Social Security Act. Then, one by one, the old conservatives decided to retire. This allowed Roosevelt—

the only president in American history to make no Supreme Court appointments during his first four-year term—to fill five vacancies in the next three years. The justices he chose—including Hugo Black, Felix Frankfurter, and William O. Douglas—would steer a more liberal course for decades to come.

Nevertheless, the Court battle wounded Roosevelt in significant ways. By refusing to withdraw his legislation, he subjected fellow Democrats to a bitter Senate debate—and to eventual defeat. The Court-packing incident also emboldened Roosevelt's opponents by proving that the president could be beaten. "The New Deal," wrote one observer, "would never be the same."

Union Struggles

Away from Washington, new battles raged in the automobile plants of Michigan, the textile mills of North Carolina, and the coal fields of Kentucky as industrial workers demanded union recognition under the banner of the CIO. In perhaps the most spectacular episode, autoworkers at a General Motors plant in Flint, Michigan, went on strike *inside* the factory, refusing to leave. Their spontaneous technique, known as the "sit-down," spread quickly to other sites. Though Roosevelt privately criticized these strikers for violating property rights, he declined to send in troops. In February 1937, GM recognized the CIO's United Automobile Workers (UAW) as the bargaining agent for its employees. Chrysler came to terms a few months later.

Autoworkers celebrate the end of their "sit-down" strike at a General Motors plant in Flint, Michigan, in 1937.
© Bettmann / UPI / Corbis

The victory at GM forced other employers into line. Firestone signed a contract with the CIO's Rubber Workers, General Electric and RCA with the Electrical Workers. Even U.S. Steel, an old enemy of organized labor, agreed to generous terms with the Steelworkers—union recognition, a 40-hour week, and a 10-percent wage increase.

There were some holdouts, however. Henry Ford hired an army of thugs to rough up union organizers and disrupt strikers on the picket lines. Republic Steel of Chicago stockpiled more weapons than did the city police department. "I won't have a contract with an irresponsible, racketeering, violent communistic body like the CIO," fumed Republic President Tom C. Girdler.

The worst violence occurred outside Republic's South Chicago mill on Memorial Day 1937. There heavily armed police battled rock-throwing strikers on the picket line. Before it ended, ten workers had been killed by gunfire, and dozens more had been injured. In the following months, Ford and Republic Steel came to terms. Under pressure from the National Labor Relations Board, they gradually accepted industrial unionism as a legitimate force in American life. With a membership approaching 3 million, the CIO had come a long way since its break with the conservative, craft-oriented American Federation of Labor a few years before.

LOSING GROUND

The Court battle and the sit-down strikes slowed down the political momentum that followed FDR's reelection landslide in 1936. Further problems loomed in Europe, where fascism continued to gain strength, and in the United States, where a serious recession in 1937 eroded public confidence in the New Deal. For President Roosevelt, the road ahead appeared even more menacing than before.

Fascist Advances

Late in 1936, civil war broke out in Spain. A group of military officers, led by General Francisco Franco, attempted to overthrow the recently elected government. Because Franco represented the *Falangist*, or fascist elements in Spain, he received military aid from Hitler and Mussolini. On the other side, Joseph Stalin aided the government (or "loyalist") forces, which contained a large socialist and communist contingent. The war itself was brutal, with extreme cruelty on both sides. Before it ended, more than 600,000 people were killed.

The Spanish civil war triggered strong emotions in the United States. Some Americans praised Franco as a bastion against communism and a strong supporter of the Catholic church. Others condemned him as a fascist thug, determined to overthrow a popularly elected government by force. Several thousand Americans went to Spain as part of the Abraham Lincoln Brigade, organized by the Communist party, to fight on the Loyalist side. As Ernest Hemingway said of Franco, "There is only one way to quell a bully and that is to thrash him."

Most Americans disagreed. In 1937, Congress passed a third neutrality bill that extended the arms embargo to include *civil wars* like the one raging in Spain. The bill also prohibited Americans from traveling on belligerent vessels, even at their own risk. However, it did permit nations at war to purchase "nonmilitary" goods if they paid cash (no loans) and carried them away on their own ships. President Roosevelt quickly signed the bill into law.

The Rising Nazi Menace

In central Europe, meanwhile, Hitler marched boldly toward war. Vowing to unite all German-speaking people, he moved on Austria in 1938, adding 6 million "Germans" to the Third Reich. Then he demanded the Sudentenland, a region in western Czechoslovakia where 3 million ethnic Germans lived. The Czechs possessed both a well-trained army and a defense treaty with France. As central Europe's only remaining democracy, Czechoslovakia looked to the French and British for support against the Nazi threat.

That support never came. Neither France nor England wanted a showdown with Germany. France had lost half of its male population between the ages of twenty and thirty-two during World War I. In Britain, Oxford students adopted a resolution in the 1930s declaring that they would not take up arms for their country under any circumstances. Antiwar feeling was so strong that a kind of diplomatic paralysis set in. The result was the Munich debacle of 1938.

At Munich, Prime Minister Neville Chamberlain of England and Premier Edouard Daladier of France agreed to Hitler's demand for the Sudetenland. In return the German leader promised not to take any more territory. Daladier then pressured the Czechs to accept this dismal bargain, while Chamberlain congratulated everyone—Hitler included—for bringing "peace in our time."

The news from inside Germany was even worse. Early in 1938, the Nazis torched Munich's Great Synagogue and began the initial deportation of Jews to the infamous concentration camp at Buchenwald. On the

Hitler Youth in Germany rounding up books to be burned, including the works of Thomas Mann and Albert Einstein. As Joseph Goebbels, the Nazi propaganda minister, declared: "These flames not only illuminate the final end of an old era; they also light up the new."
© Bettmann / UPI / Corbis

At the fateful Munich Conference in 1938, British Prime Minister Neville Chamberlain appeased Adolf Hitler's demands for territorial expansion, claiming the agreement would bring "peace in our time."
AP / Wide World Photos

In 1939, more than a thousand Jews fleeing from Germany aboard the ocean liner St. Louis *were refused entry into the United States at the port of Miami and forced to return to Europe—and certain death.*
© Bettmann / UPI / Corbis

Table 25.1	Key New Deal Programs and Legislation
1933	Emergency Banking Act
	Civilian Conservation Corps
	Agricultural Adjustment Act
	Tennessee Valley Authority
	Glass-Steagall Banking Act (creates Federal Deposit Insurance Corporation)
	Federal Emergency Relief Act
	National Industrial Recovery Act
	Civil Works Administration
1934	Securities and Exchange Act
1935	National Labor Relations Act
	Social Security Act
	Emergency Relief Appropriation Act (creates Works Progress Administration)
	Revenue Act ("Wealth Tax")
	Rural Electrification Administration
	National Youth Administration
1936	Soil Conservation Act
1937	National Housing Act
1938	Fair Labor Standards Act

evening of November 9—known as *Kristallnacht,* the "night of broken glass"—Nazi mobs burned synagogues, looted stores, and attacked Jews in cities throughout Germany. Dozens were murdered, hundreds were beaten and raped. In addition, the Nazis passed new laws to confiscate Jewish property, bar Jews from meaningful employment, and deprive them of ordinary liberties such as attending school and driving a car.

When word of these events reached the United States, President Roosevelt was furious. "I myself could scarcely believe that such things could occur in a twentieth century civilization," he told reporters. Roosevelt immediately called a conference of thirty-two nations to discuss plans for accepting desperate Jewish refugees from Germany, Austria, and Czechoslovakia. But no country, with the exception of small and densely populated Holland, showed a willingness to help. In the United States, a combination of anti-Semitism, isolationist sentiment, and hard times kept the "golden door" tightly shut. Most Americans did not want "foreigners" competing with them for jobs and resources in the midst of the Depression.

The result was disastrous. At a time when many Jews had the ability to flee Hitler, there was almost no place for them to go. Between 1935 and 1941, the United States took in an average of 8,500 Jews per year—a number far below the annual German quota of 30,000 set by the National Origins Act of 1924.

(Among those allowed to enter were "high profile" Jewish refugees such as Albert Einstein and composer Kurt Weill.) Furthermore, President Roosevelt refused to take additional steps against Hitler because he feared a political backlash. Thus, he did not make a strong diplomatic protest or attempt to lessen trade with the Nazi regime.

AN END TO REFORM

Until 1937, the American economy had been making steady, if uneven, progress. National income and production finally reached 1929 levels, stock prices were climbing, profits were up. Roosevelt now hoped to slow down government spending as the business picture improved. He wanted to balance the federal budget and cut the mounting national debt.

The president knew that national recovery had been fueled by the New Deal's farm subsidies, relief programs, and public works. He was familiar with the writings of British economist John Maynard Keynes, who advocated a policy of deficit spending in hard times to spur economic growth. Yet Roosevelt had never been fully comfortable with government's expanding role. He feared that the growing national debt would generate inflation, and he worried about the effect of federal welfare programs upon the recipients' initiative and self-respect.

In 1937, Roosevelt slashed funding for both the PWA and WPA, cutting almost 2 million jobs. At the same time, the new Social Security payroll tax took effect, removing billions of dollars of purchasing power from the economy. The result was recession—the most serious economic plunge of the Roosevelt years. As unemployment rose and production plummeted, the nation slipped back toward the nightmare of 1933, with breadlines and soup kitchens dotting the landscape.

In October, Roosevelt called Congress into special session. Within weeks, a $5 billion expenditure was approved for federal relief and public works. The economy responded, showing the impact of government spending once again. But the recession further weakened Roosevelt's image as a forceful leader in perilous times.

By 1938, the New Deal had clearly lost momentum. Harry Hopkins blamed it on six grinding years of Depression and reform, claiming the public was "bored with the poor, the unemployed, the insecure." Facing a more combative Congress—Republicans and conservative Democrats made significant gains in the 1938 elections—Roosevelt decided to "tread water" for a while. Among his few legislative achievements that year was passage of the Fair Labor Standards Act, which abolished child labor in most industries, while providing a minimum hourly wage (forty cents) and a maximum workweek (forty hours) to be phased in over time. Like Social Security, the act did not cover those who needed it most, such as farm workers and domestics. Yet almost a million Americans had their wages raised immediately by this law, and countless millions had their work hours shortened as well.

CONCLUSION

The New Deal altered politics and society in fundamental ways. It forever changed the role of the federal government in American life, making it bigger, costlier, and more attentive to previously forgotten groups. For the first time in our history, the government provided massive assistance to the poor and the unemployed. It stabilized the banking system, protected farmers with price supports, guaranteed the rights of organized labor, encouraged collective bargaining between workers and employers, and created a national pension plan. The New Deal also produced a more class-oriented Democratic party, appealing to industrial workers, hard-pressed farmers, and urban minorities. Under Franklin Roosevelt's leadership, a kind of broker state emerged in which diverse groups pushed their competing demands upon the federal government and received tangible rewards. Avoiding the political extremes that plagued other nations in the Depression era, Roosevelt steered a middle course between laissez faire and socialism—a course that combined free enterprise and democracy with national planning and social reform.

What the New Deal could not do, however, was to restore prosperity at home. Fearful of mounting budget deficits and ever-growing relief rolls, President Roosevelt never committed himself to the level of consistent federal spending urged by economists like John Maynard Keynes. When the New Deal ended in 1939, more than 8 million Americans were still unemployed. It would take a world war, and the full mobilization that followed, to put them permanently back to work.

Recommended Readings

Brinkley, Alan. *Voices of Protest: Huey Long, Father Coughlin, and the Great Depression* (1982). A revealing account of Depression era dissidents.

Cohen, Lizabeth. *Making a New Deal: Industrial Workers in Chicago* (1990). Examines working-class protest and culture during the Depression.

Cooke, Blanche Wiesen. *Eleanor Roosevelt* (1992). Follows the life of the nation's most active first lady.

Fraser, Steve, and Gerstle, Gary, eds. *The Rise of the New Deal Order* (1989). Contains a series of original essays about the New Deal's impact on American life.

Goodman, James. *Stories of Scottsboro* (1994). Vividly recreates the most important civil rights trial of the 1930s.

Leuchtenburg, William. *The Supreme Court Reborn: The Constitutional Revolution in the Age of Roosevelt* (1995). Studies the conflicts and changes that altered the Supreme Court in the 1930s and beyond.

McElvaine, Robert S. *The Great Depression* (1984). An excellent survey of American life and politics during the New Deal era.

Terkel, Studs. *Hard Times* (1970). Views the Depression through the oral histories of those who lived through it.

Ware, Susan. *Holding Their Own: American Women in the 1930s* (1982). Explores the role of women in America's worst economic crisis.

Worster, Donald. *Dust Bowl: The Southern Plains in the 1930s* (1979). Examines the causes and the impact of this ecological disaster.

American Journey Online and InfoTrac College Edition

Visit the source collections at http://ajaccess. wadsworth.com and infotrac.thomsonlearning.com and use the Search function with the following key terms to explore documents, images, audio and video clips, articles, and commentary related to the material in this chapter.

Franklin D. Roosevelt
Civilian Conservation Corps
Tennessee Valley Authority
Huey P. Long
Mary McLeod Bethune

New Deal
Dust Bowl
The Grapes of Wrath
Marian Anderson

 Additional resources, exercises, and Internet links related to this chapter are available on the American Passages Web site: http://history.wadsworth.com/passages2e

26 THE SECOND WORLD WAR
1940–1945

The collapse of France in 1940 raised fears that Hitler would soon control all of Europe.
© Bettmann/Corbis

Prime Minister Neville Chamberlain's "peace in our time" lasted fewer than six months. In March 1939, the Germans marched into central Czechoslovakia. To the south, Franco's forces won a final victory in the Spanish civil war, while Mussolini's army annexed neighboring Albania. Throughout the summer months, Nazi threats multiplied. "So long as Germans in Poland suffer grievously, so long as they are imprisoned away from the Fatherland," warned Hitler, "Europe can have no peace."

President Roosevelt declared neutrality, reflecting the clear sentiment of the American people. At the same time, he worked to mobilize the nation's defense effort and to shape public opinion steadily against the Axis powers. If possible, Roosevelt hoped to aid Great Britain and the Allies through "all measures short of war." If need be, however, he vowed to use military force to prevent a Nazi victory in Europe.

WAR IN EUROPE

In August 1939, Hitler and Stalin stunned the world by signing a "non-aggression" pact. Both dictators were buying time for an inevitable showdown between their armed forces. And both had designs upon Polish territory, which they secretly divided in their agreement. On September 1, German ground troops and armored divisions stormed into Poland from the west, backed by their powerful air force *(Luftwaffe)*. Two weeks later, Soviet troops attacked from the east, reclaiming the territory that Russia had lost to Poland after World War I. In the following months, Stalin moved against the Baltic states, subduing Estonia, Latvia, and Lithuania.

Blitzkrieg

Hitler's *Blitzkrieg* (lightning strike) into Poland shattered the lingering illusions of Munich. Having pledged themselves to guarantee Poland's borders, England and France reluctantly declared war on Germany. The British sent a small, ill-equipped army to defend western Europe against further Nazi aggression. The French reinforced their "impregnable" Maginot Line facing Germany, while the Nazis fortified their Siegfried Line in the Rhineland facing France. An eerie calm settled over Europe, as all sides prepared for battle.

CHRONOLOGY

1940 Germany conquers the Low Countries and France • British Air Force beats back Luftwaffe in skies over England, preventing Nazi invasion • Selective Service Act brings first peacetime draft • Franklin Roosevelt elected to an unprecedented third term in the White House

1941 Lend-Lease Act passed by Congress • Nazi armies invade the Soviet Union • Atlantic Charter is issued • Japan attacks Pearl Harbor, bringing United States into war

1942 Japanese forces capture the Philippines • Internment of Japanese Americans begins FDR authorizes top secret Manhattan Project to build an atomic weapon • U.S. forces land in Africa to begin Operation Torch • U.S. Navy halts Japanese advance at the Battle of Midway

1943 Soviets win pivotal victory over Nazis at Stalingrad • Race riot in Detroit, "zoot-suit" riots in Los Angeles • U.S. forces invade Italy • U.S. Marines capture Guadalcanal

1944 Allies launch Normandy Invasion • U.S. forces, led by General MacArthur, recapture Philippines • Roosevelt elected to fourth term

1945 Allied leaders discuss postwar issues at Yalta • FDR dies; Harry Truman becomes president • Hitler commits suicide days before Germany surrenders • United States captures Iwo Jima and Okinawa • Atomic bomb is successfully tested in New Mexico desert • United States drops atomic bombs on Hiroshima and Nagasaki • Japan surrenders, ending World War II

That six-month calm, known as the "phony war," ended in April 1940 when the Nazis overran Denmark and Norway. In May, they invaded Belgium, Holland, Luxembourg—and France itself. From the skies, the Luftwaffe strafed fleeing civilians and flattened cities such as Rotterdam. On the ground, German troops and armor swept through the Ardennes Forest, skirting the Maginot Line. The huge French army collapsed in disarray. Within weeks, German units had reached the French coastline, trapping the British army at Dunkirk, with its back to the sea. In early June, a flotilla of small ships from England—tugs, pleasure craft, and naval vessels—ferried 330,000 soldiers to safety. It was both a defeat and a deliverance for the British forces, who had been badly mauled but rescued from disaster.

In mid-June, as Paris fell to the advancing Nazi army, Mussolini attacked France from the south. Following the French surrender on June 22, the German Luftwaffe attacked England in force. Hitler's plan was to gain control of the skies in preparation for a full-scale invasion of the British Isles. Day and night, German planes dropped their bombs on London, Coventry, and other cities in a murderous attempt to break civilian morale. Day and night, the British Royal Air Force rose up to meet the Luftwaffe, with devastating effect. By early fall, Nazi air losses forced Hitler to abandon his invasion plans. "Never in the field of human conflict," said England's new Prime Minister Winston Churchill of the brave pilots who fought the Battle of Britain, "was so much owed by so many to so few."

A Third Term for FDR

Events in Europe shattered America's isolationist façade. Unlike Woodrow Wilson in 1914, President Roosevelt did not ask the people to be "neutral in thought as well as in action." If England fell to the Nazis, he believed, the United States would become an isolated fortress, vulnerable to attack from the air and the sea. Most Americans felt the same way. A national poll found 83 percent hoping for a British victory, 16 percent neutral, and only 1 percent supporting the Nazis.

The German Blitzkrieg increased American concerns about defense. In August 1940, as the Battle of Britain raged in the skies over England, President Roosevelt and Congress worked to fashion the first peacetime draft in American history, the Selective Service Act, as well as a $10.5 billion appropriation for defense. With factories now open round-the-clock to build tanks, war planes, and naval vessels, unemployment virtually disappeared. The Great Depression was over.

Building a strong defense was one thing, aiding the Allies quite another. As Michigan Senator Arthur Vandenberg, a leading isolationist, put it: "I do not believe that we can become an arsenal for one belligerent without becoming a target for another." Vandenberg used World War I as his example, charging that America's support for the allied war effort had led to its participation in the war itself. With a presidential election on the horizon, FDR would have to answer this charge.

Until the last moment, however, there was no assurance that Roosevelt would even run. The loss of New Deal momentum and the Court-packing disaster pointed to his political retirement. Furthermore, no American president had ever served a third term—a taboo that reflected the public's deep suspicion of entrenched federal power.

By 1940, the picture had changed. The idea of tested presidential leadership took on added appeal. Roosevelt expected to run again. Hoping to defuse the third-term issue, he allowed himself to be "drafted" by the Democratic National Convention in Chicago, thus appearing reluctant but dutiful in the public's mind. "The salvation of the nation rests in one man, because of his experience and great humanitarian thinking," declared Mayor Edward J. Kelly of the host city. Roosevelt selected the enigmatic Henry Wallace to be his vice presidential running mate.

The Republicans, meeting in Philadelphia, nominated Wendell Willkie of Indiana for president and Senator Charles McNary of Oregon for vice president. As a Wall Street lawyer and the head of a large utilities corporation, Willkie held two positions almost guaranteed to make the voters suspicious. He had never run for public office or held an appointive government position. His political ascent was due, in large part, to the public relations skills of his advisors.

The 1940 campaign was dominated by foreign affairs. Though Willkie shared Roosevelt's views about the dangers of Nazi aggression, he attacked the president for moving too quickly on the European stage. Among Willkie's complaints was a controversial decision by FDR to supply England with "overage" destroyers. In the summer of 1940, Churchill had begged the United States for naval support to protect British sea lanes from Nazi submarine attacks. In September, without consulting Congress, the president sent fifty old but serviceable warships to England in return for long-term leases to British military bases in Newfoundland, Bermuda, and other parts of the Western Hemisphere. The agreement outraged isolationists, who viewed it as a clear violation of American neutrality. Willkie charged that FDR's foreign policy meant

***P*ICTURING THE PAST ✦ POLITICS & DIPLOMACY**

BREAKING TRADITION: A PRESIDENTIAL THIRD TERM

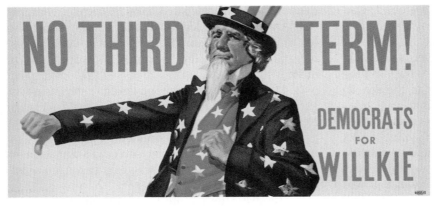

Franklin D. Roosevelt Library

Franklin Roosevelt's decision to seek a third term in 1940 broke a long-standing precedent. Note the political poster here, which uses the authoritative, nonpartisan image of Uncle Sam to make this point. At that time, the Constitution set no limits on the number of terms a president could serve. In the nation's formative years, Presidents George Washington, Thomas Jefferson, and James Madison had all retired after two full terms in office, setting an informal standard for the future. Though former President Ulysses S. Grant had unsuccessfully sought the Republican nomination for a third term in 1880, and former President Theodore Roosevelt was defeated in his quest for a third term on the Progressive party ticket in 1912, no *sitting* president had campaigned for a third term until FDR. Given the state of world affairs in 1940, the third term issue generated little interest; Americans were far more focused on the coming of war. When Roosevelt ran for a fourth term in 1944, Republicans raised the issue obliquely, describing the president and his advisors as "tired old men." In 1947, however, a Republican-led Congress passed an amendment that limited presidents to two terms. The Twenty-Second Amendment was ratified, with little public rancor or discussion, in 1951.

"more wooden crosses for sons and brothers and sweethearts," forcing the president to make a promise that he would not be able to keep. "I have said this before, but I shall say it again and again and again," Roosevelt told a cheering crowd in Boston. "Your boys are not going to be sent into any foreign wars."

Roosevelt defeated Willkie with ease—27 million votes to 22 million, 449 electoral votes to eighty-two. He carried all of America's major cities, piling up impressive totals among blacks, Jews, ethnic minorities, and union members. New York Mayor Fiorello La-Guardia put it well: "Americans prefer Roosevelt with his known faults to Willkie with his unknown virtues." Still, the margin of FDR's popular victory made this the closest presidential election since 1916.

THE END OF NEUTRALITY

Shortly after the election, Roosevelt learned that England could no longer afford the supplies it needed to fight the Nazi war machine. He responded by asking Congress for the authority to sell or lease "defense material" to any nation he judged "vital to the defense of the United States." Roosevelt compared his "Lend-Lease" proposal to the simple act of lending a garden hose to a neighbor whose house was on fire. In Europe, he said, the British desperately needed tanks, guns, and planes to extinguish the raging inferno of Nazism. Only one nation had the ability to supply them. "We must be the great arsenal of democracy," Roosevelt declared.

Lend-Lease

Lend-Lease set off a furious national debate. In 1940, FDR's opponents organized the America First Committee to keep the nation "neutral" by defeating Lend-Lease. Supported by Henry Ford, Charles Lindbergh, and Robert E. Wood, chairman of Sears, Roebuck, it appealed to the isolationist notion that America should be prepared to defend its own territory, leaving Europe's wars to the Europeans. At times, however, the committee's message became muddled and conspiratorial, as when Lindbergh described American Jews as the "principal war agitators" behind Lend-Lease.

By 1941, Roosevelt gained the upper hand. Public opinion moved sharply against isolationism as Hitler became a more ominous threat. Polls showed a clear majority of Americans willing to risk war with Germany in order to help the British survive. In March, a $7 billion Lend-Lease bill sailed through Congress, assisted by powerful lobbying groups such as the Committee to Defend America by Aiding the Allies.

In June 1941, Hitler shattered the recent Nazi-Soviet Pact by invading Russia with more than 2 million troops. Roosevelt responded by offering Stalin immediate Lend-Lease support. The idea of aiding a Communist dictator was hard for Americans to accept. But Roosevelt stood firm, believing that wars made strange bedfellows and that Hitler must be stopped at all costs. At his insistence, the Soviets received $12 billion in aid over the next four years.

With Lend-Lease in place, Roosevelt abandoned all pretense of neutrality. To ensure that American goods reached England, he instructed the navy to protect merchant shipping in the North Atlantic sea lanes. In August 1941, Roosevelt and Churchill met aboard the USS *Augusta,* off the Newfoundland coast, to discuss their mutual aims and principles. The result was a communiqué known as the Atlantic Charter, which called for freedom of the seas, freedom from want and fear, and self-determination for all people in the post-war world.

At this meeting, Roosevelt secretly promised Churchill that the United States would try "to force an 'incident' that could lead to war" with Germany. In the fall of 1941, as Nazi submarines sank one Britain-bound freighter after another, the president armed America's merchant fleet and authorized U.S. destroyers to hunt these U-boats under a policy known as "active defense." In October, a German submarine sank a U.S. destroyer off Iceland, with the loss of one hundred American lives. In his ballad to the men who died, Woody Guthrie asked:

Millions of Americans, including Charles Lindbergh, opposed President Roosevelt's attempt to aid the Allies against the onslaught of Nazism, claiming it would lead the United States into the European war.
© Bettmann/UPI/Corbis

> What were their names, tell me,
> what were their names?
> Did you have a friend
> on the good *Reuben James?*

War would come shortly, but not where Roosevelt expected.

The Road to Pearl Harbor

As Hitler swept relentlessly though Europe, another power was stirring halfway around the globe. Like Germany and Italy, Japan had become a militarist state controlled by leaders with expansionist ideas. In the 1930s, the Japanese had invaded China, routing its army, terror-bombing cities, and brutalizing civilians in the infamous "rape of Nanking." The United States barely protested. With his focus on the Nazis, Roosevelt sought to avoid a crisis with Japan, even after its planes bombed an American gunboat, the *Panay,* on the Yangtze River in 1937, killing three sailors and injuring forty-three more.

In 1938, the Japanese unveiled their plan for empire, known as the "Greater East Asia Co-Prosperity Sphere." Viewing themselves as superior to their neighbors, they aimed to rule their region by annexing European colonies in Southeast Asia and the Western Pacific. Control of French Indochina, the Dutch East Indies, and British Malaya would provide the food and

The Japanese attack on Pearl Harbor—December 7, 1941—destroyed eighteen warships, killed 2,400 Americans, and plunged the nation into World War II.
© Bettmann/UPI/Corbis

raw materials to make Japan self-sufficient and secure. Only one obstacle stood in the way—the United States.

Japan purchased the bulk of its steel, oil, heavy equipment, and machine parts from U.S. suppliers. To help prevent further Japanese expansion, the Roosevelt administration placed an embargo on certain strategic goods to Japan and moved the Pacific Fleet from San Diego to Pearl Harbor. The Japanese responded by negotiating a defense treaty (the so-called Tripartite Pact) with Germany and Italy. Relations steadily declined. Hitler's Blitzkrieg left defeated France and Holland unable to defend their Asian colonies. When Japan moved against Indochina in April 1941, Roosevelt retaliated by freezing all Japanese assets in the United States and blocking shipments of scrap iron and aviation fuel to Japan. In September, Japanese leaders requested a meeting with Roosevelt to end the deepening crisis. The president agreed—but with certain conditions. Before sitting down together, he said, the Japanese must withdraw from both China and Indochina.

The Japanese refused. Though talks were held at a lower level, both sides prepared for war. Military analysts expected Japan to move southwest, toward the Dutch East Indies and British Malaya, in search of needed rubber and oil. Instead, on November 26, 1941, a huge Japanese naval fleet, led by Admiral Chuichi Nagumo, left the Kurile Islands, just north of mainland Japan, and headed due east into rough Pa-

cific waters. The armada included six aircraft carriers with 400 warplanes, two battleships, two cruisers, nine destroyers, and dozens of support vessels. Traveling at thirteen knots, under complete radio silence, the fleet was destined for Pearl Harbor, Hawaii, 5,000 miles away.

On Sunday morning, December 7, 1941, Admiral Nagumo's fleet reached its takeoff point, 220 miles north of Pearl Harbor. At 7:40 A.M., the first wave of Japanese warplanes appeared. The wing commander radioed back the words, "Tora (tiger), Tora, Tora," meaning that surprise had been complete. The battleship *Arizona* suffered a direct hit and went up in flames. More than 1,200 of her crew were killed. The *Oklahoma* capsized after taking three torpedoes, trapping 400 men below deck. A second Japanese assault at nine o'clock completed the carnage. All told, eighteen warships had been sunk or were badly damaged, 300 planes had been lost, and 2,400 Americans had died.

It could have been worse. The aircraft carriers *Lexington* and *Enterprise* were away from Pearl Harbor on maneuvers. And Japanese commanders made a strategic error by not launching a third air attack against the oil depots, machine shops, and repair facilities. As a result, most of the damaged warships were back in action within two years.

Why was Pearl Harbor so woefully unprepared? By the fall of 1941, the United States had broken the Japanese diplomatic code, known as MAGIC. American planners knew that war was coming. On November 27, Army Chief of Staff George C. Marshall sent a warning to all American military outposts in the Pacific. "Negotiations with Japan appear to be terminated to all practical purposes," it said. "Japanese future action unpredictable, but hostile action possible at any moment."

Yet Pearl Harbor was not viewed as the likely point of attack. It was thousands of miles from Japan, and supposedly well defended. The very idea of a Japanese fleet sailing so far without detection seemed utterly fantastic. At Pearl Harbor, the commanders most feared sabotage from the large Japanese population living in Hawaii. Though some Americans believed that Roosevelt secretly encouraged the Japanese attack in order to bring the United States into World War II, the truth is more mundane. The debacle at Pearl Harbor was caused by negligence and errors in judgment, not by a backroom conspiracy at the White House.

On December 8, Congress declared war against Japan. Only Montana's Representative Jeanette Rankin dissented. (A longtime peace activist, she also had voted against President Wilson's war message in 1917.) On December 11, Germany and Italy honored

An American Soldier Remembers The Bataan Death March

In April 1942, more than 10,000 American soldiers surrendered to the Japanese on Bataan Peninsula in the Philippines. Badly weakened by starvation and disease, the soldiers were marched under brutal conditions to an internment camp sixty-five miles away. Hundreds died on the march, and thousands more died in captivity.

Capt. LLOYD MILLS, Company C, 57th Infantry,

Philippine Scouts:

The nights were the worst times for me. We walked all day, from early morning until dusk. Then we were put into barbed-wire enclosures in which the conditions were nearly indescribable. Filth and defecation all over the place. The smell was terrible. These same enclosures had been used every night, and when my group got to them, they were covered by the filth of five or six nights.

I had dysentery pretty bad, but I didn't worry about it because there wasn't anything you could do about it. You didn't stop on "the March" because you were dead if you did. They didn't mess around with you. You didn't have time to pull out and go over and squat. You would just release wherever you were. Generally right on yourself, or somebody else if they happened to be in your way. There was nothing else to do. Without food it was water more than anything. It just went through me . . . bang.

I was in a daze. One thing I knew was that I had to keep going. I was young, so I had that advantage over some of the older men. I helped along the way. If someone near you started stumbling and looked like he was going to fall, you would try to literally pick him up and keep him going. You always talked to them. Tried to make them understand that if they fell they were gone. 'Course, there was nothing you could do about the people who fell in the back.

Source: Capt. Lloyd Mills, in Donald Knox, *Death March*, 1981, p. 133.

---

the Tripartite Pact by declaring war on the United States. Almost instantly, Americans closed ranks. The foreign policy battles were over. As Roosevelt's former enemy Senator Burton Wheeler put it, "The only thing to do now is lick the hell out of them."

Early Defeats

The attack on Pearl Harbor began one of the bleakest years in American military history. In the North Atlantic, allied shipping losses reached almost a million tons per month. On the Eastern front, Nazi forces approached the outskirts of Moscow, where Soviet resistance was fierce. In Egypt, German General Erwin Rommel's elite Afrika Korps threatened the Suez Canal.

The news from Asia was grimmer still. Following Pearl Harbor, Japan moved quickly against American possessions in the Pacific, overrunning Guam, Wake Island, and eventually the Philippines. On December 10, 1941, the Japanese attacked the British fleet off Malaya, sinking the battleship *Prince of Wales* and the cruiser *Repulse*. In the following weeks, Burma, Hong Kong, Singapore, Malaya, and the Dutch East Indies fell like dominoes to Japanese invaders. Japan now had the resources—the oil, tin, rubber, and foodstuffs—to match its appetite for empire.

For Americans, the most galling defeat occurred in the Philippines, where 100,000 U.S. and Filipino troops surrendered to the Japanese after a bloody six-month struggle. The military campaign had actually been lost on December 8, 1941, when the Japanese successfully bombed Clark Field, destroying one hundred planes based there to defend the islands. (The failure to prepare for such an attack one day after Pearl Harbor was scandalous.) Lacking air cover, the defenders retreated to the jungles of the Bataan Peninsula, just north

The Bataan Death March, following the surrender of U.S. troops in the Philippines, further fueled America's boiling hatred of Japan.
© Bettmann/UPI/Corbis

of Manila. As food ran out, they ate snakes, monkeys, cavalry horses, plants, and grass. Their songs were of hopelessness and despair.

> We're the battling bastards of Bataan;
> No Mama, no papa, no Uncle Sam.
> No aunts, no uncles, no cousins, no nieces;
> No pills, no planes, no artillery pieces.
> . . . And Nobody gives a damn!

In March 1942, President Roosevelt ordered commanding General Douglas MacArthur to slip out of the Philippines, leaving his troops behind. The trapped defenders made their stand at Corregidor, a fortresslike island in Manila Bay. After two months of constant bombardment, General Jonathan Wainwright surrendered to the Japanese. His diseased and starving men were brutalized by their captors on the infamous Bataan Death March—an event that further fueled America's boiling hatred of Japan.

Despite these disasters, the nation remained united and confident of victory. The road ahead would be long, the challenges immense. As *Time* magazine reminded its readers,

> At the end of six months of war, the U.S. has:
> Not yet taken a single inch of enemy territory,
> Not yet beaten the enemy in a single major
> battle . . .
> Not yet opened an offensive campaign.
> The war, in short, has still to be fought.

THE HOMEFRONT

The United States had begun to mobilize for World War II before the attack on Pearl Harbor. The draft was already in place, and defense plants were hiring new workers in the mad scramble to keep England, then the Soviet Union, and now America, fully supplied. Furthermore, the positive feelings about this conflict—a "good fight" against Nazi and Japanese aggression—eased many of the problems associated with a democratic nation going to war. Few men refused to register for military service, unlike World War I, and millions rushed to enlist. On the homefront, Americans vowed to outproduce their enemies and to sacrifice for the "boys" at the front. "Our great strength," said a defense worker from San Diego, "is that we're all in this together."

War Production

FDR named Donald Nelson of Sears, Roebuck to run the newly created War Production Board (WPB). Nelson's main job was to oversee the transformation of American factories—to get companies such as Ford and General Motors to make tanks and warplanes instead of automobiles. To accomplish this, the federal government offered generous incentives. Antitrust laws were suspended so military orders could be filled quickly without competitive bidding. Companies were given low interest loans to retool, and "cost-plus" contracts which guaranteed them a profit. Not surprisingly, the industrial giants made out best. As the war progressed, America's top one hundred companies increased their percentage of the nation's total production from 30 to 70 percent. Ford, for example, began construction of a huge new factory in 1941, named Willow Run, to build B-24 Liberator bombers. In the next four years, it turned out 8,685 airplanes—one every sixty-three minutes. When questioned about these enormous profits and market shares, Secretary of War Henry Stimson replied that "in a capitalist country, you have to let business make money out of the process or business won't work."

Between 1940 and 1945, the nation's gross national product doubled, while the federal budget reached $95 billion, a tenfold increase. In the first half of 1942, the government placed over $100 billion in war orders, requesting more goods than American factories had ever produced in a single year. The list included 60,000 planes, 45,000 tanks, 20,000 antiaircraft guns, and 8 million tons of merchant shipping. The orders for 1943 were even larger. By war's end, military spending exceeded $300 billion.

Roosevelt hoped to finance this effort without dramatically raising the national debt. That meant taxation over borrowing, a policy Congress strongly opposed. The result was a compromise that combined both of these elements. The Revenue Act of 1942 added millions of new taxpayers to the federal rolls and dramatically raised the rates paid by Americans in higher income brackets. Along with increases in corporate and inheritance rates, taxation provided about 45 percent of war's total cost—less than Roosevelt wanted, but far more than the comparable figures for World War I or the Civil War.

Borrowing accounted for the rest. The national debt reached $260 billion in 1945, six times higher than that in 1941. The government relied on banks and brokerage houses for loans, but common people did their share. "There are millions who ask, 'What can we do to help?' " said Treasury Secretary Henry Morgenthau in 1942. "Right now, other than going into the Army and Navy or working in a munitions plant, there isn't anything to do. . . . The reason I want a [war bond campaign] is to give people an opportunity to do something."

Morgenthau sold bonds in inventive ways. Hollywood stars organized "victory tours" through 300 communities. Hedy Lamarr promised to kiss anyone who bought a $25,000 bond. Carol Lombard died in a plane crash on her way home from a bond rally. Factory workers participated in payroll savings plans by putting a percentage of their earnings into government bonds. The Girl and Boy Scouts raised $8 billion in bond pledges.

By 1942, the problem was no longer finding enough work for the people, it was finding enough people for the work to be done. Factories stayed open around the clock, providing new opportunities to underemployed groups such as women, blacks, and the elderly. Seventeen million new jobs were created during World War II. Wages and salaries more than doubled, due in large part to the overtime that people put in. Per capita income rose from $373 in 1940 to just over $1,000 by 1945. As a result, the United States experienced a rare but significant redistribution of wealth, with the bottom half of the nation's wage earners gaining a larger share of the pie.

Making Do

Though Americans took home larger paychecks than ever before, they found less and less to spend them on. In 1942, Congress created the Office of Price Administration (OPA) to ration vital goods, preach self-sacrifice to the public, and control the inflation caused

American fighter planes roll off the assembly line during World War II.
© Bettmann/UPI/Corbis

by too much money chasing too few goods. Gas, tires, sugar, coffee, meat, butter, alcohol—all became scarce. Most car owners were issued coupon books limiting them to three gallons of gasoline per week. Pleasure driving virtually ended, causing thousands of restaurants and drive-in businesses to close. As manufacturers cut back on cloth and wool, women's skirts got shorter, two-piece swimsuits (midriff exposed) became the rage, and men's suits no longer had cuffs. Metal buttons, rubber girdles, and leather shoes simply disappeared.

Changes on the homefront could be seen through the prism of baseball, the national game. Many wanted major league baseball suspended during the war, but Roosevelt disagreed, claiming that it united Americans and built up their morale. The 1941 season had been one of the best ever, with Ted Williams batting over 400, and Joe DiMaggio's fifty-six-game hitting streak. The next year was very different, indeed. Night games were banned because of air-raid "blackouts." Spring training took place in the northern cities, rather than in Florida, to cut back on travel and save fuel. Ballparks held blood drives and bond drives, and soldiers in uniform were admitted free of charge. In 1942, Detroit Tigers slugger Hank Greenberg became the first major leaguer to be drafted into the armed forces. By 1943, most of the stars were gone, replaced by men who were too old or physically unfit for duty, such as Pete Gray, a one-armed outfielder for the St. Louis Browns. In response to public concerns, FBI Director J. Edgar Hoover declared that his agents had investigated the new major leaguers and found no draft-dodgers among them. But recruiting ball players became so difficult that the St. Louis Cardinals placed an advertisement in the *Sporting News:* "We have positions open on our AA, B, and D minor league clubs," it said. "If you believe you can qualify for one of these good baseball jobs, tell us about yourself."

OPPORTUNITY AND DISCRIMINATION

In many respects, World War II produced a social revolution in the United States. The severe labor shortage caused an enormous migration of people from rural areas to cities, from South to North, and especially to the West Coast, where so many war industries were located. With defense factories booming and 15 million people in the armed forces, Americans were forced to reexamine long-held stereotypes about women and minorities in the workplace and on the battlefield. The war provided enormous possibilities for advancement and for change. It also unleashed prejudices that led to the mass detention of American citizens, and others, on largely racial grounds.

The labor shortages of World War II created new employment opportunities for women, most of whom were married and over thirty-five. More than 6 million women worked in defense industries across the country, including shipyards, munitions plants, and aircraft factories.
Reproduced from the Collections of the Library of Congress

Women and the War Effort

The war brought new responsibilities and opportunities for American women. During the Depression, for example, women were expected to step aside in the job market to make way for unemployed men. A national poll in 1936 showed an overwhelming percentage of both sexes agreeing that wives with employed husbands should not work. Furthermore, the majority of employed women held poorly paid jobs as clerks and "salesgirls," or as low-end industrial workers in textile and clothing factories.

The war brought instant changes. More than 6 million women took defense jobs, half of whom had not been previously employed. They worked as welders and electricians, on assembly lines and in munitions plants. More than three-quarters of these women were married, and most were over thirty-five—a truly remarkable change. Some had husbands in the armed forces. (The standard monthly allotment for a serviceman's family was $50.) Young mothers were not expected to work, although a sizable number did. Since the government and private industry provided little childcare assistance, absenteeism and job turnover among younger women were extremely high.

The symbol of America's new working woman was "Rosie the Riveter," memorialized by Norman Rockwell in *The Saturday Evening Post* with her overalls, her work tools, and her foot planted on a copy of *Mein Kampf,* helping to grind fascism to dust.

> All the day long whether rain or shine—
> She's a part of the assembly line—
> She's making history working for victory—
> Rosie the Riveter.

Rosie was trim and beautiful, signifying that a woman could do a man's job—temporarily—without losing her feminine charm. Advertisers played heavily on this theme. A hand-cream company praised the "flower-like skin of today's American Girl, energetically at work six days a week in a big war plant." A cosmetics ad went even further: "Our lipstick can't win the war, but it symbolizes one of the reasons why we are fighting . . . the precious right of women to be feminine and lovely."

Although this work paid very well, wage discrimination was rampant in the defense industries, where women earned far less than did men in the same jobs. Employers and labor unions rationalized such inequities by noting that men had seniority, put in more overtime, and did the really "skilled" work. In 1945, female factory workers averaged thirty-two dollars per week, compared with fifty-five dollars for men.

Women also were told that their work would end with the war's completion, when defense spending dropped and the veterans came home to reclaim their old jobs. Many women welcomed a return to domesticity after four years of struggle, sacrifice, and separation from a husband overseas. But a survey of female defense workers in 1944 showed that most of them—particularly married, middle-aged women—hoped to continue in their present jobs.

This was not to be. Though more women than ever remained in the labor force following World War II, the bulk of them were pushed back into lower-paying "feminized" work. Still, a foundation had been laid. As a riveter from Los Angeles recalled, "Yeah, going to work during the war made me grow up and realize I could do things. . . . It was quite a change."

The "Double V" Campaign

For millions of American blacks, the war against racist Germany and Japan could not be separated from the ongoing struggle to achieve equal rights. The *Pittsburgh Courier*, an influential African American newspaper, demanded a "Double V" campaign from the Negro community—"victory over our enemies at home and victory over our enemies on the battlefields abroad." To the cynical suggestion that minorities secretly wished for an American defeat, black heavyweight champion Joe Louis responded: "America's got lots of problems, but Hitler won't fix them."

One obvious problem was the small number of blacks employed in high-paying factory jobs. "The Negro will be considered only as janitors," stated North American Aviation, one of the nation's leading military contractors. "Regardless of their training as aircraft workers, we will not employ them." In 1941, A. Philip Randolph, president of the Brotherhood of Sleeping Car Porters, an all-Negro labor union, proposed a "March on Washington" to protest job discrimination in the defense industries and segregation of the armed forces. "We loyal Americans," he said, "demand the right to work and fight for our country." Fearing the negative publicity, President Roosevelt convinced the organizers to call off their march in return for an Executive Order (8802) declaring that "there shall be no discrimination in the employment of workers because of race, creed, or national origin." To facilitate the order, Roosevelt appointed a Fair Employment Practices Committee (FEPC) to "investigate complaints" and "redress grievances." With a tiny budget and no enforcement powers, the FEPC held public hearings, preached equality in the workplace—and was largely ignored.

Still, the desperate need for labor provided new opportunities for minorities. More than a million blacks migrated to the North and West during World War II, taking factory jobs in New York and California, Michigan and Illinois. Most were attracted by the higher wages and the chance to escape stifling oppression; many came from the Deep South, where the invention of the mechanical cotton-picker forced them from the land. The percentage of African Americans in the war industries reached 7.5 percent by 1944—less than their share of the population, but a vast improvement over 1941. The work itself was often menial, such as cleaning factory bathrooms and sweeping the floors. Black workers had little access to the skilled, high-paying jobs, because powerful craft unions, like the Machinists and the Carpenters remained lily-white. But thousands of African Americans took semiskilled positions on the assembly line, which meant higher wages than ever before.

For black working women, the changes were more dramatic. On the eve of World War II, about 70 percent of them labored as servants in private homes. By war's end, that figure had fallen below 50 percent, as 400,000 black females left domestic work for the defense plants. "The war made me live better, it really did," recalled an aircraft worker who moved from rural Texas to Los Angeles. "My sister always said that Hitler was the one that got us out of the white folks' kitchen."

Where racial barriers were crossed, however, violence often followed. In Mobile, Alabama, the promotion of eleven black welders led white shipyard workers to go on a rampage through the African American community, severely beating dozens of residents. In Philadelphia, white transit workers walked off their jobs to protest the elevation of eight blacks to the rank of motorman. Their stoppage brought the city to a halt, effectively closing the vital Philadelphia Navy Yard. Moving quickly, federal officials sent 8,000 fully armed soldiers to run the buses and streetcars, while threatening to fire the strikers and draft them into the armed forces. The walkout collapsed two days later.

The worst racial violence flared in Detroit, the nation's leading war production center. With good jobs available on the assembly lines of Chrysler, General Motors and Ford, Detroit's areawide labor force grew from 400,000 in 1940 to almost 900,000 by 1943. With the war effort receiving the government's full attention, little thought was given to building new homes, schools, and hospitals. Indeed, state spending for health and education actually declined in Michigan during World War II. Those who arrived in Detroit, mainly poor, rural people of both races, found themselves competing for living space and social services

PICTURING THE PAST ✦ SOCIAL & CULTURAL EVENTS

AFRICAN AMERICAN NURSES IN WORLD WAR II

© Bettmann/UPI/Corbis

Thousands of African American women enlisted in the armed forces during World War II. Some joined the newly created Women's Army Corps, taking noncombatant positions as clerks, cooks, and drivers. Others (pictured here) served in the Army and Navy Nurse Corps, helping to evacuate casualties and staffing hospitals throughout the United States, Europe, and the Pacific theater. As with African American men, African American women were forced to serve in racially segregated units. Indeed, despite a shortage of nurses, the Surgeon General issued a directive limiting the service of black nurses to "hospitals or wards devoted exclusively to the treatment of Negro soldiers." As one African American newspaper complained: "There are hundreds of young colored nurses. They are eager to serve in the Army, the Navy, the Marine Corps . . . and [possess] skills acquired through long apprenticeship in recognized hospitals. Given equal opportunity for training, the Negro nurse has no superior in any national or racial group in the world." By 1945, as the demands of war increased, African American nurses often treated wounded soldiers regardless of race.

---

with Detroit's established blue-collar labor force—and with each other. One half of Detroit's wartime black population lived in miserable, substandard housing, often one family to a room, with no indoor toilets or running water. Bulging public schools went to half-day sessions. Infant mortality rates skyrocketed, and tuberculosis reached epidemic proportions.

In 1942, an angry mob in Detroit kept several black families from moving into a public housing project in a white neighborhood. The following year, a fight between whites and blacks at a municipal park sparked a race riot involving huge mobs with guns, knives, and clubs. Detroit's poorly trained police force, weakened by the departure of its best men to the armed forces, did little to stop the carnage. By the time federal troops established calm in the city, thirty-five people were dead, and more than 700 were wounded.

The police shot seventeen "looters" during the riot, all of whom were black.

Mob violence on the West Coast involved other victims. In California, a hate campaign led by local politicians and the press blamed Mexican Americans for an alleged rise in drugs, crime, and gang warfare. In June 1943, white sailors from surrounding naval bases roamed the Mexican districts of Los Angeles, Long Beach, Pasadena, and other cities looking for "zooters"—young Mexican Americans in ducktail haircuts wearing long jackets with wide pleated pants, pegged at the cuff. Cheered on by white crowds, the sailors became a vigilante mob—stripping the young men of their "zoot suits," cutting their hair, and beating them senseless. "Throughout the night the Mexican communities were in the wildest possible turmoil," wrote a Los

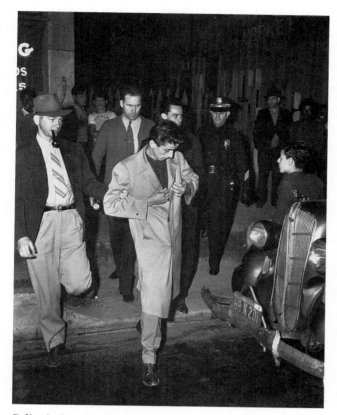

Police in Los Angeles take a young man to jail during the 1943 "zoot-suit" riots in which hundreds were injured and arrested.
© Bettmann/UPI/Corbis

Angeles reporter. "Scores of mothers were trying to locate their youngsters and several hundred Mexicans milled around the police substations and the Central jail trying to get word of the missing members of their families."

The zoot-suit violence had other roots as well. Unlike the Depression era, when jobs were scarce and Mexicans were deported in large numbers, the United States now needed all the labor it could get. In 1942, the American and Mexican governments agreed to a so-called "bracero" (contract labor) program in which several hundred thousand Mexicans were brought to the United States to plant and harvest crops. In addition, the shortage of factory labor during World War II led to an influx of Hispanic workers in the shipyards and defense plants of Southern California. In cities like Los Angeles, where African American and Hispanic workers arrived at a rate of 10,000 per month, crowding and competition bred resentment and fear.

To many residents of Southern California, the "zooters" came to represent the Hispanic commu-

nity as a whole. Rumors flew that Mexican Americans were hindering the war effort by evading the draft. In fact, the reverse was true. Mexican Americans served in numbers far greater than their percentage of the general population—350,000 out of 1.4 million—and seventeen were awarded the Congressional Medal of Honor.

Mexican Americans were integrated in the armed forces during World War II; African Americans were not. All branches except the tiny Coast Guard practiced race discrimination as a matter of course. The marines did not take blacks until 1943, when 20,000 were recruited to unload supplies and munitions during the amphibious Pacific landings—an extremely hazardous duty that subjected them to withering artillery and sniper fire from dug-in Japanese defenders. The navy segregated blacks by occupation, with most working as food handlers, stevedores, and "messboys." In July 1944, a huge explosion at an ammunition depot in Port Chicago, California, killed 250 black sailors from a segregated work unit. When fifty survivors refused an order to return to work, claiming they had been singled out for these dangerous jobs on account of race, they were court-martialed, convicted of mutiny, and sentenced to prison. Following an intense publicity campaign in the Negro press, the black sailors were returned to duty.

More than 500,000 African Americans served in the army, which placed them in segregated divisions, commanded by white officers. Since most training facilities were located in the Deep South, where the weather was mild and construction costs were low, black recruits faced hostile surroundings. Racial clashes at military posts were regularly reported in the Negro press, as were the murders of black soldiers by white mobs in Arkansas, Georgia, Mississippi, and Texas.

Only one black army division saw significant combat—the 92nd Infantry in Italy. When questioned about this, Secretary of War Henry Stimson claimed that "Negroes have been unable to master efficiently the techniques of modern weapons." The truth, however, was that racial prejudice dominated the military chain of command. When given the opportunity, black units performed superbly. The 99th Air Force Fighter squadron, known as the Tuskegee Airmen, earned two Distinguished Unit Citations and shot down a dozen Nazi planes during the Anzio invasion of 1943. Escorting American bombers over Germany in 1944 and 1945, pilots of the 99th compiled a perfect record. Not a single bomber under their protection was lost to enemy fire.

Such treatment fueled anger, protest, and pride. The Negro press became more assertive in the drive for

African Americans were rigidly segregated in the armed forces during World War II. One of the most celebrated black units was the 99th Air Force Fighter squadron, known as the Tuskeegee Airmen.
© Bettmann/UPI/Corbis

equal rights. America's leading black organization, the National Association for the Advancement of Colored People (NAACP), increased its wartime membership from 70,000 to 500,000. In 1942, young activists, black and white, formed the Congress of Racial Equality to challenge segregated restaurants in Washington and Baltimore, chanting, "We die together. Let's eat together." A powerful civil rights movement was slowly taking shape.

Internment of Japanese Americans

President Roosevelt was determined to avoid a recurrence of the federal repression and vigilante activity that had marred the homefront during World War I. Yet the years between 1942 and 1945 witnessed the most glaring denial of civil liberties in American history. The victims included people of Japanese ancestry—citizen and noncitizen alike—living mainly on the West Coast of the United States.

On December 8, 1941, Roosevelt issued a standard executive order requiring enemy aliens to register with local police. Before long, however, the president lifted the enemy alien designation for Italians and Germans in the United States, but not for the Japanese. The attack on Pearl Harbor, the Bataan Death March, the fall of Hong Kong and Singapore, Wake Island and the Philippines—all sent shock waves across the United States. Though J. Edgar Hoover saw no evidence of a Japanese "threat" to American security, the public thought otherwise. *Time* magazine published an article after Pearl Harbor entitled "How to Tell Your Friends from the Japs," which included such tips as "Japanese—except for wrestlers—are seldom fat," and "Japanese are likely to be stockier and broader-hipped than Chinese." More ominous were the words of Henry McLemore, a columnist for the *San Francisco Examiner.* "I am for the immediate removal of every Japanese on the West Coast to a point in the interior," he wrote. "Herd 'em up, pack 'em off, and give 'em the inside room in the badlands. . . . Personally, I hate the Japanese. And that goes for all of them."

More than 90 percent of the 125,000 Japanese Americans lived in California, Oregon, and Washington. (Two-thirds were citizens, or Nisei, born in the United States; the rest were noncitizens, or Issei, born in Japan and ineligible for naturalization under the Immigration Laws of 1882 and 1924.) Few in number, politically powerless, and less well assimilated than European ethnic groups, the Japanese in America made perfect targets. Military leaders raised the dangers of allowing them to live so close to aircraft plants and naval bases. Patriotic groups linked them to the atrocities committed by the Japanese armed forces 8,000 miles away. Local farmers and fishermen resented the economic success of these hardworking people. All wanted their removal from the West Coast.

President Roosevelt capitulated. In February 1942, he issued Executive Order 9066, giving Secretary of War Stimson the authority to designate military zones inside the United States "from which any or all persons may be excluded." A few days later, the army interpreted that order to include the entire West Coast and all people of Japanese extraction. "A Jap's a Jap," said General John DeWitt, head of the West Coast Defense Command. "It makes no difference whether he is an American citizen or not."

Roosevelt preferred a "voluntary" removal and resettlement to rural parts of the West. The problem, however, was that the Japanese Americans were unlikely to leave their homes and businesses voluntarily, and the western states were unwilling to take them. As the governor of Idaho said, "If you send them here, they'll be hanging from every tree in the state. Why not send them back to Japan? They live like rats, breed like rats, and act like rats."

Japanese Relocation Order February 19, 1942
(Federal Register, Vol. VII, No. 38) Issued by Franklin D. Roosevelt

On February 19, 1942, President Roosevelt issued Executive Order 9066, authorizing the evacuation of more than 100,000 people of Japanese ancestry—most of whom were American citizens—from the West Coast. Although Roosevelt framed the order as a measure to protect national security, other factors, including war hysteria and racism, played a major role.

Executive Order

Authorizing the Secretary of War to Prescribe Military Areas

Whereas the successful prosecution of the war requires every possible protection against espionage and against sabotage to national-defense materials, national-defense premises, and national-defense utilities. . . .

Now, therefore, by virtue of the authority vested in me as President of the United States, and Commander in Chief of the Army and Navy, I hereby authorize and direct the Secretary of War, and the Military Commanders whom he may from time to time designate, whenever he or any designated Commander deems such action necessary or desirable, to prescribe military areas in such places and of such extent as he or the appropriate Military Commander may determine, from which any or all persons may be excluded, and with respect to which, the right of any person to enter, remain in, or leave shall be subject to whatever restrictions the Secretary of War or the appropriate Military Commander may impose in his discretion. The Secretary of War is hereby authorized to provide for residents of any such area who are excluded therefrom, such transportation, food, shelter, and other accommodations as may be necessary, in the judgment of the Secretary of War or the said Military Commander, and until other arrangements are made, to accomplish the purpose of this order. . . .

I hereby further authorize and direct the Secretary of War and the said Military Commanders to take such other steps as he or the appropriate Military Commander may deem advisable to enforce compliance with the restrictions applicable to each Military area hereinabove authorized to be designated, including the use of Federal troops and other Federal Agencies, with authority to accept assistance of state and local agencies. . . .

In March, the president issued Executive Order 9102, establishing the War Relocation Authority. Milton Eisenhower—brother of General Dwight D. Eisenhower—became its director. Internment camps were set up in the deserts of California and Arizona, the mountains of Wyoming, and the scrublands of Utah and Colorado. Japanese Americans on the West Coast were given a few weeks to sell their belongings, get their affairs in order, and report to "processing centers" at converted racetracks, ballparks, and fairgrounds. By June, 120,000 men, women, and children—most of them American citizens—reached the internment camps.

Conditions there were harsh, but not brutal. Families lived together in Spartan army barracks with little privacy and poor sanitation. Most worked as farm laborers. "All of Manzanar was a stockade, actually—a prison," wrote a young Japanese American woman of her California camp. "We were in jail. There was barbed wire all around, there were great big watch towers in the corners, and there were spotlights turned on during the night."

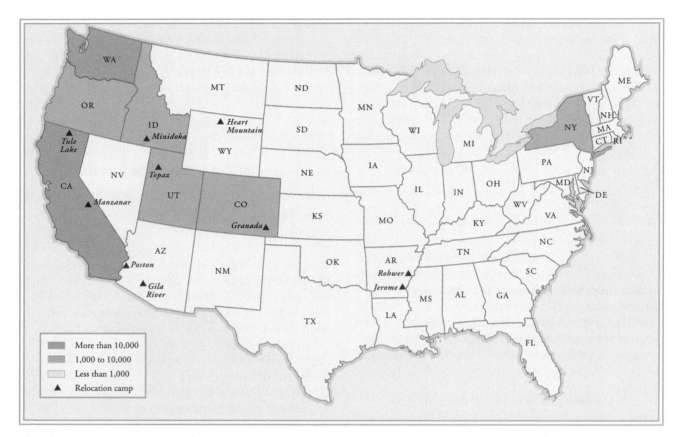

Map 26.1 *Japanese American Relocation*
The 120,000 Japanese Americans removed from the West Coast during World War II were sent to internment camps in six states, run by the newly established War Relocation Authority. The relocation order did not affect the small number of Japanese Americans living elsewhere in the United States or the large Japanese population living in Hawaii.

Executive Order 9066 provided for the removal of 120,000 people of Japanese ancestry from the West Coast of the United States to isolated internment camps like this one in Manzanar, California.
© Bettmann/UPI/Corbis

The Supreme Court did not intervene. In *Hirabayashi v. United States* (1943) it upheld a curfew ordinance against Japanese Americans in Seattle on the grounds that wartime conditions sometimes justified measures that "place citizens of one ancestry in a different category from others." The Court also ruled (*Korematsu v. United States*, 1944) that the evacuation of Japanese Americans was appropriate, but added (*Endo v. United States*, 1944) that the War Relocation Authority should attempt to separate "loyal" internees from "disloyal" ones, and set the loyal free.

It took almost forty years for a measure of justice to prevail. In 1981, a congressional panel concluded that the internment program had resulted from a combination of race prejudice, war hysteria, and the failure of political leadership. It had nothing to do with "military necessity," as its supporters had claimed. In 1988, Congress awarded each survivor of the internment camps $20,000 in "reparations" for the terrible wrong that had been done.

THE GRAND ALLIANCE

Most Americans saw Japan as the primary villain of World War II. Opinion polls showed the public overwhelmingly in favor of concentrating the war effort in the Pacific against a "barbaric" and "treacherous" foe. Yet President Roosevelt and his military advisors felt otherwise. To their thinking, American power should be directed against the stronger enemy—Germany. Roosevelt viewed the Nazis as the real threat to world peace, and Europe as the key battleground.

North Africa, Stalingrad, and the Second Front

America's two major allies had conflicting strategies, interests, and concerns. The British did not believe in confronting Hitler with immediate, massive force. They remembered their staggering losses to the Germans during World War I, and they had felt the power of the Nazis at Dunkirk and in the London air raids. The British, moreover, had a far-flung empire to defend. Their strategy was to strike at "the soft underbelly" of the Axis in North Africa and the Mediterranean, rather than to confront Hitler directly in France.

The Russians strongly disagreed. Already facing a huge Nazi force deep inside their territory, they wanted the United States and Britain to open a "second front" in western Europe so as to relieve German pressure on them in the east. That meant a major allied invasion of France. As one American diplomat said of Soviet Foreign Minister V. M. Molotov, "He knows only four words of English—'yes,' 'no' and 'second front.' "

Though America's top military advisors leaned toward the Russian strategy, President Roosevelt favored the British approach. At present, he realized, the United States was unprepared for a full-scale invasion of Europe. But a smaller operation against Nazi forces in North Africa, as the British proposed, had the benefit of getting the United States into the war quickly on the proper scale.

To make this possible, the United States had to gain control of the ocean. In the first three months of 1942, German submarines sank almost 1 million tons of allied shipping. The so-called "wolf-packs" were so close to American shores that bathers on the New Jersey and Virginia coasts watched in horror as merchant ships were torpedoed. By 1943, however, technological advances in antisubmarine warfare turned the tide. The use of sonar and powerful depth charges made German U-boats more vulnerable underwater, while the development of long-range attack planes and so-phisticated radar allowed American aircraft to spot and destroy them as they surfaced to recharge their batteries. The toll was enormous. More than 900 of the 1,162 German submarines commissioned during World War II were sunk or captured.

In November 1942, American troops under the command of General Dwight D. Eisenhower invaded the French North African colonies of Morocco and Algeria in an operation code-named TORCH. At virtually the same moment, British forces badly mauled General Rommel's army at El Alamein in Egypt, ending Nazi hopes of taking the Suez Canal. Though Hitler rushed reinforcements to North Africa, the Allies prevailed, capturing 250,000 German and Italian troops and taking enemy-held territory for the first time in the war.

In North Africa, the Allies fought and defeated twelve Nazi divisions. In the Soviet Union, the Russians were fighting 200 German divisions along an enormous 2,000-mile front. The pivotal battle occurred at Stalingrad, a vital transportation hub on the Volga River, in the bitter winter of 1942–1943. As the Germans advanced, Stalin ordered his namesake city held at all costs. The fighting was block-to-block, house-to-house, and finally hand-to-hand. Hitler would not let his forces retreat, even after they ran out of fuel and food. Surrounded by Russian forces, overwhelmed by starvation, exposure, and suicide, the German commander surrendered on February 2, 1943.

Stalingrad marked the turning point of the European war. The myth of German invincibility was over. The Russians were advancing steadily in the east, aided by a stream of tanks, planes, food, and clothing from the United States under Lend-Lease. Now Stalin expected an allied thrust from the west—the long-promised second front.

Churchill had other ideas. At a meeting with Roosevelt in Casablanca, he convinced the president to put off a cross-channel invasion in favor of an assault on Axis troops across the Mediterranean in Italy. Roosevelt attempted to pacify Stalin by promising to open a second front the following year and to accept nothing less than Germany's unconditional surrender. But the Soviets, having sacrificed more troops at Stalingrad than the United States would lose in the entire war, were suspicious and displeased.

The Italian campaign began in the summer of 1943. Sicily fell in a month, and Mussolini along with it. Overthrown by antifascist Italians, the Duce fled to Nazi lines in the north. The new Italian government then declared war on Germany and was recognized as a "co-belligerent" by England and the United States. The battle for Italy was intense. A young American soldier, badly injured in the campaign, wrote to his wife:

So many buddies gone and so many wounded! . . . We walked straight into death, not one man flinched or tried to save himself. I am proud to say, darling, that I was one of those brave lost children. We were only children after all. The dead boys were cuddled up, the wounded cried for dead friends. All children, after all.

The Italian campaign dragged on for almost two years, draining troops and resources for the planned invasion of France. (In April 1945, antifascists captured Mussolini, killed him, and strung him up by his heels.) Suspicions between Stalin and his wartime allies deepened as Roosevelt and Churchill set the terms of Italy's surrender without consulting the Soviet leader. In addition, postponement of the second front gave Stalin the opportunity to gobble up much of central Europe as his troops pushed toward Germany from the east.

The three allied leaders met together for the first time in November 1943 at the Tehran Conference in Iran. Roosevelt and Churchill promised to launch their cross-channel invasion the following spring. The future of Poland, the partition of Germany, and need for a United Nations were also discussed. In public, at least, allied unity was restored. "We are going to get along fine with Stalin and the Russian people," Roosevelt declared.

On June 6, 1944, allied troops stormed the beaches of Normandy in the massive D-Day invasion. By nightfall, more than 150,000 troops were ashore, and others quickly followed, beginning the long-awaited "second front" that sealed Hitler's fate.
© Bettmann/Corbis

The Normandy Invasion

By 1944, the Allies were in complete control of the skies over western Europe, and in command of the seas. Their amphibious landings in North Africa and Italy had provided valuable experience for the job that lay ahead. In April and May, General Eisenhower assembled his huge invasion force in England—3 million men, 2.5 million tons of supplies, thousands of planes, landing craft, and escort vessels. Meanwhile, allied aircraft pounded the Atlantic Wall, a line of German fortifications stretching hundreds of miles along the coast of France and the Low Countries.

Despite meticulous preparation, Eisenhower faced enormous risks. The Nazis had fifty-five divisions in France. To keep them dispersed and guessing, allied intelligence spread false information about the planned invasion sites. The deceptions worked. Hitler and his generals put their strongest defense at Pas de Calais, the English Channel's narrowest point.

The massive D-Day invasion—Operation OVERLORD—began on the morning of June 6, 1944. Eisenhower's biggest worry was the weather. A channel storm had postponed one attempt, and another storm was predicted. Before the men left, he told them: "You are about to embark upon the Great Crusade, toward which we have striven these many months. The eyes of the world are upon you."

The invasion succeeded. With overwhelming air cover, allied forces assaulted Normandy and dropped paratroopers behind enemy lines. The heaviest fighting took place at Omaha Beach, where U.S. Rangers scaled sheer cliffs under withering fire to silence Nazi gunners. By nightfall, 150,000 men were ashore.

Others quickly followed. Within two months, more than a million allied troops were in France—liberating Paris in August, reaching the German border by September. With the Soviets pressing from the east, a Nazi surrender seemed only weeks away. But the Germans counterattacked in December 1944, taking British and American forces by surprise. The Battle of the Bulge was Hitler's last gasp—a failed attempt to crack allied morale. U.S. troops took heavy casualties, but stood firm. Germany lost 100,000 men and the will to fight on. Hitler committed suicide in his Berlin bunker on April 30, 1945, with Russian soldiers a few miles away. Germany surrendered a week later. The Thousand-Year Reich had lasted a dozen murderous years.

Facing the Holocaust

In the spring of 1945, allied troops liberated the Nazi concentration camps in Poland and Germany. Ghastly

Map 26.2 *The War in Europe*
The U.S. military effort against German and Italian forces in World War II began in North Africa, moved to Italy, and culminated in the D-Day invasion of France in 1944. With the aid of England and other nations, the Allied forces reached Germany from the West in 1945. Meanwhile, following a tenacious defense of their homeland, Russian troops pushed deep into Germany from the East, destroying the bulk of Nazi fighting forces and playing a key role in the German surrender.

ICTURING THE PAST ✦ POLITICS & DIPLOMACY

THE WAR IN THE PACIFIC

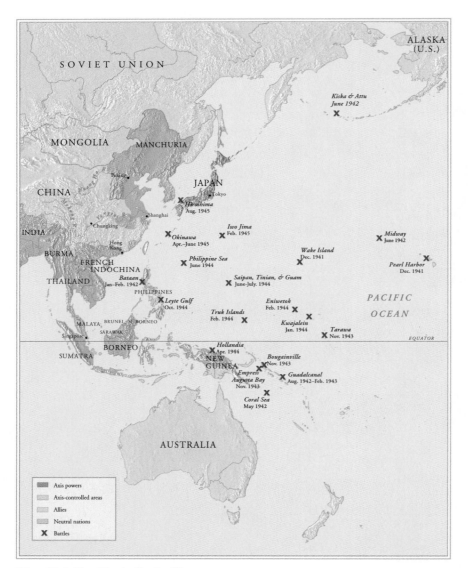

Map 26.3 *The War in the Pacific*

America's war against Japan was fought differently than the war against Germany. In the Pacific, the United States did the great bulk of the allied fighting; in Europe, that burden was shared by others, including Great Britain, and most important, the Soviet Union. As shown on the map, the war against Japan was waged largely at sea and from the air; though American marines met fierce resistance in clearing Guadalcanal, Saipan, Iwo Jima, Okinawa, and other Japanese-held strongholds, there were no massed land battles to match the Soviet defeat of German forces at Stalingrad or the allied counterattack at the Bulge. In Europe, armor and artillery were essential to the allied victory; in the Pacific, it was aircraft carriers and submarines. By war's end, the United States had lost 128 combatant vessels to Japanese warships and aircraft, but only 29 to German fire. The Japanese surrender in 1945 ended the largest naval war in history.

---

pictures of starving survivors and rotting corpses flashed around the world, recording the almost inconceivable horror in which 6 million European Jews and 4 million others (including Poles, Gypsies, homosexuals, political dissidents) were exterminated during World War II.

To American leaders, these photos of the Holocaust produced shock, but hardly surprise. Evidence of the death camps had reached the United States in 1942, yet the government paid scant attention to the consequences. The State Department, well known for its anti-Semitism in that era, made it virtually impossible for refugees fleeing the Nazis to enter the United States. An applicant for a wartime visa had to provide the names of two American sponsors before submitting six copies of a form that measured four feet in length. As a result, only 10 percent of America's immigration quotas were met during World War II, leaving almost 200,000 slots unfilled.

President Roosevelt did not seriously intervene. Consumed by the responsibilities of leading his nation in a global war, he insisted that the best way to aid the victims of Nazism was to defeat Hitler's armies as quickly as possible. His only acknowledgement of the impending disaster came in 1944, when he created the War Refugee Board, which helped finance the activities of Raoul Wallenberg, the courageous Swedish diplomat who prevented thousands of Hungarian Jews from being deported to the death camps. Had it been formed earlier, and supported more firmly by the White House, the War Refugee Board might have played a major role in the saving of innocent lives.

The United States had other options as well. Its bombers could have attacked the rail lines leading to the death camps, as well as the gas chambers and crematoria that lay inside. The War Department avoided these targets, claiming they were too dangerous and too far away. This clearly was not true. In 1944, allied bombers flew hundreds of missions within a 35-mile radius of Auschwitz.

When liberation came to the concentration camps, the vast majority of prisoners were dead. One survivor at Dachau recalled the very moment the American troops arrived. "We were free. We broke into weeping, kissed the tank. A Negro soldier gave us a tin of meat, bread, and chocolate. We sat down on the ground and ate up all the food together. The Negro watched us, tears in his eyes."

THE PACIFIC WAR

Shortly after the attack on Pearl Harbor, Admiral Isoroku Yamamoto, Japan's leading naval strategist, issued a stern private warning. "In the first six months to a year of war against the U.S. and England," he said, "I will run wild and I will show you an uninterrupted succession of victories: I must tell you that, should the war be prolonged for two or three years, I have no confidence in our ultimate victory." Yamamoto understood America's overwhelming advantage in population and productivity. What he doubted was the will of its people to fight—and win—a long, bloody struggle.

Turning the Tide

The Japanese hoped to create an impregnable defense line in the Pacific. Their strategy included new conquests, such as Australia, and a naval thrust against the U.S. carrier fleet. Yet two key engagements in the spring of 1942 shattered Yamamoto's illusion about American will power and naval strength. On May 7, a task force led by two American carriers—the *Lexington* and *Yorktown*—held its own against a larger Japanese force at the Battle of the Coral Sea, just north of Australia. Though the "Lady Lex" was sunk, heavy Japanese losses saved Australia from invasion or certain blockade.

A month later, the two sides clashed again. Admiral Yamamoto brought a huge fleet to Midway Island, 1,000 miles west of Hawaii, to flush out and destroy the American carrier fleet. But the U.S. Navy, having broken the Japanese military code, was well aware of his intentions. In a three-day battle, brilliantly commanded by Rear Admiral Raymond A. Spruance, the Americans sank four Japanese carriers (losing the *Yorktown*) and shot down 320 planes. Japan would never fully recover from this beating.

Closing in on Japan

After Midway, the United States followed a two-pronged plan of attack. Admiral Chester Nimitz was to move west from Hawaii toward Formosa, while General Douglas MacArthur was to come north from Australia toward the Philippines, with their forces combining for an eventual assault on Japan. The Pacific theater would see no massed land battles like Stalingrad or the Bulge. The fighting would be sporadic but brutal, involving air attacks, naval duels, and amphibious landings by U.S. Marines on selected Japanese-held islands. It would be "a war without mercy," with bitter racial hatreds on both sides.

The first American offensive occurred at Guadalcanal, a small tropical island in the Solomons, off New Guinea, in August 1942. Guadalcanal had strategic importance as both a supply depot and a base from which to assault the Japanese air and naval complex at Rabaul. For six months, American marines waged a desperate campaign in swamps and jungles, battling intense heat, malaria, dysentery, infection, and leeches, as well as the Japanese. When the island was finally secured in February 1943, General MacArthur began a "leapfrog" campaign across New Guinea to the Philippines, attacking some islands while bypassing others. By 1944, Manila was in his sights.

In the central Pacific, Admiral Nimitz was moving west, ever closer to Japan. In November 1943, the marines assaulted Tarawa, a tiny strip of beach in the Gilbert Islands, taking 3,000 casualties in a successsful three-day assault. Next came the Marshall Islands; the Marianas—Guam, Tinian, and Saipan—followed. Control of the Marianas, only 1,200 miles from Tokyo, placed major Japanese cities within range of America's new B-29 bombers. The battle for Saipan raged through June and July of 1944. The Japanese defenders fought, quite literally, to the last man. Worse, thousands of Japanese civilians on the island committed suicide—a preview, some believed, of what lay ahead in Japan.

The end seemed near. In October 1944, MacArthur returned to the Philippines in triumph, while an American naval force destroyed four Japanese carriers at the Battle of Leyte Gulf, outside Manila. To the north, American troops took the island of Iwo Jima in brutal combat, and then attacked Okinawa, less than 400 miles from Japan. Admiral Nimitz assembled a huge force for the invasion—180,000 troops, most of his carriers, and eighteen battleships. The Japanese had an army of 110,000 on Okinawa, the final barrier to the homeland itself.

The battle took three months, from April through June of 1945. Waves of Japanese kamikaze (suicide) planes attacked the allied fleet, inflicting terrible damage. American troops suffered a casualty rate of 35 percent, the highest of the war. Seven thousand were killed on land, 5,000 at sea, and 40,000 were wounded. The Japanese lost 1,500 kamikazes and virtually all of their soldiers. These appalling losses would be a factor in America's decision to use atomic weapons against Japan.

Table 26.1	Second World War Casualties	
Country	**Battle Deaths**	**Wounded**
Canada	32,714	53,145
France	201,568	400,000
Germany	3,250,000	7,250,000
Italy	149,496	66,716
U.S.S.R.	6,115,000	14,012,000
Australia	26,976	180,864
Japan	1,270,000	140,000
New Zealand	11,625	17,000
United Kingdom	357,116	369,267
United States	291,557	670,846

Source: *Information Please Almanac* (Boston: Houghton Mifflin Co., 1988).

A CHANGE IN LEADERSHIP

In November 1944, the American people reelected Franklin Roosevelt to an unprecedented fourth presidential term. Roosevelt defeated Republican Thomas Dewey, the moderate forty-two-year-old governor of New York. The president's handling of the war was not an issue in the campaign. Dewey hammered away at problems on the homefront, such as food shortages, gas rationing, squalid housing for war workers, and government "red tape." Roosevelt campaigned as the war leader, urging voters "not to change horses in midstream." To bolster his chances, Democratic party leaders removed the increasingly unpopular Vice President Henry Wallace from the ticket and replaced him with Senator Harry S. Truman of Missouri.

The Yalta Accords

When Truman visited the White House to plan campaign strategy with Roosevelt, he was appalled by the president's feeble condition. In February 1945, with Germany near collapse, an exhausted FDR met with Churchill and Stalin at Yalta, in southern Russia, to lay the groundwork for peace and order in the postwar world. On several issues, agreement came easily. The Russians promised to enter the Pacific war after Germany's defeat in return for territorial concessions in the Far East. The three leaders also blessed the formation of a new international body, known as the United Nations.

But agreement on the larger issues proved elusive. The Soviet Union had suffered staggering losses at German hands. At least 20 million Russians were dead or wounded; thousands of towns, factories, and collective farms had been destroyed. From Stalin's perspective, the Soviets deserved more than simple gratitude for their role in defeating the great bulk of Hitler's army. They needed the means to rebuild their nation and to protect it from further attacks.

Stalin hoped to ensure Soviet security through the permanent partition of Germany. And he demanded huge reparations from the Germans—at least $20 billion—with Russia getting half. Furthermore, Stalin had no intention of removing Soviet troops from the lands they now controlled in eastern Europe. In both world wars, Germany had marched directly through Poland to devastate the Russian heartland. Stalin would not let this happen again.

Roosevelt and Churchill had other ideas. Both men viewed a healthy, "de-Nazified" Germany as essential to the reconstruction of postwar Europe, and both feared the expansion of Soviet power into the vacuum created by Hitler's defeat. The British also claimed a moral stake in Poland, having declared war on Germany in 1939 to help defend the Poles from the Nazi assault. To desert them now—to permit a victorious Stalin to replace a defeated Hitler—smacked of the very appeasement that had doomed allied policy a decade before. Few believed that the Polish people would pick Stalin or communism if given a free choice.

The Yalta Accords created a legacy of mistrust. The parties agreed to split Germany into four "zones of occupation"—American, Russian, British, and French. Berlin, deep inside the Soviet zone, also was divided among the Allies. Yet the vital issue of reparations was postponed, as were plans for Germany's eventual reunification. At Roosevelt's urging, Stalin accepted a "Declaration for a Liberated Europe" that promised "free and unfettered elections" in Poland and elsewhere at some unspecified date. But these words did not mean the same thing in Moscow as in the West. An American advisor accurately described the agreement as "so elastic that [Stalin] can stretch it all the way from Yalta to Washington without ever technically breaking it."

In the weeks following Yalta, Roosevelt's optimism about Soviet-American relations seemed to fade. Pledges of free elections in Europe were ignored. The Yalta Accords did not prevent Stalin from ordering the murder of political dissidents in Romania and Bulgaria and the arrest of anti-communist leaders in Poland. His ruthlessness seemed to highlight the unpleasant truth that America had little or no influence in the nations now occupied by Soviet troops. "We can't do business with Stalin," FDR complained privately. "He has broken every one of the promises he made at Yalta."

Truman in Charge

On April 12, 1945—less than two months into his fourth term—FDR died of a massive stroke at his vacation retreat in Warm Springs, Georgia. The nation was shocked. Roosevelt had been president for twelve years, leading the people through the Great Depression and World War II. "He was the one American who knew, or seemed to know, where the world was going," wrote *Life* magazine. "The plans were all in his head."

The new president was largely unknown. Born on a Missouri farm in 1884, Harry Truman had served as an artillery officer in World War I before jumping into local politics in Kansas City. Elected to public office in the 1920s with the aid of Tom Pendergast, a crooked Democratic boss, Truman walked a fine line between efficient service to his constituents and partisan loyalty to a corrupt political machine. Fair and honest himself,

Truman went about the business of building better roads and improving public services while ignoring the squalor of those who put him in office.

Working for the Pendergast machine sensitized Truman to the needs of different people, fueled his belief in a welfare state, and got him elected to the U.S. Senate in 1934. On the other hand, the label of "machine politician" would plague him for years. It was hard to earn respect as a legislator when the newspapers kept referring to him as "the senator from Pendergast."

Truman did not inspire immediate confidence in his ability to fill Roosevelt's giant shoes. Small in stature, with thick glasses and a high-pitched midwestern twang, he seemed thoroughly ordinary to all but those who knew him best. As vice president, he was largely excluded from the major discussions relating to foreign policy and the war. After taking the presidential oath of office, Truman turned to reporters and said, "Boys, if you ever pray, pray for me now."

As expected, Truman received conflicting advice. A number of FDR's confidantes, including Henry Wallace and Eleanor Roosevelt, urged him to keep the wartime alliance alive by accommodating Russia's economic needs and security demands. But others like Averell Harriman, U.S. ambassador to the Soviet Union, prodded Truman to demand Russia's strict compliance with the Yalta Accords. The new president did not want a confrontation with Stalin. He still hoped for Soviet help in ending the Pacific war and building a lasting peace. Yet the more Truman learned about events in Poland and eastern Europe, the angrier he became. Ten days after taking office, he confronted Soviet Foreign Minister V. M. Molotov at the White House, claiming that Russia had ignored the Yalta Accords, and warning him that economic aid to Russia would never get through Congress so long as this attitude persisted. When Truman finished, Molotov told him that "I've never been talked to like that in my life." "Carry out your agreements," Truman shot back, "and you won't get talked to like that."

In July 1945, Truman left the United States aboard the USS *Augusta* for his first face-to-face meeting with Stalin and Churchill at Potsdam, near Berlin. The three leaders agreed on a number of important issues, including the terms of peace for defeated Germany and public trials for Nazi war criminals. "I can deal with Stalin," Truman wrote in his diary. "He is honest—but smart as hell."

His optimism didn't last long. The conference was halted for several days by the stunning defeat of Winston Churchill's Conservative party in the British parliamentary elections. Churchill returned to England, replaced by the new Labour prime minister, Clement

Winston Churchill, Harry Truman, and Joseph Stalin clasp hands at the Potsdam Conference in July 1945. The good feeling did not last long, as Churchill's ruling party was defeated at the polls in England, while relations between the United States and the Soviet Union moved swiftly downhill.
AP/Wide World Photos

Attlee. When the talks resumed, Stalin brushed aside Truman's concerns about Poland and eastern Europe, while Truman rebuffed Stalin's attempt to claim reparations from the western zones of occupation in Germany. The conference ended on a chilly note. There seemed little doubt that Russia would remain in the lands it now controlled, and that Germany would remain divided for some time to come.

The Atomic Bomb

One of Truman's first decisions concerned the use of atomic weapons. As the United States took control of the island chains east of Japan in 1944, a ferocious bombing campaign of the Japanese home islands took place. In March 1945, 300 American B-29s led by Major General Curtis LeMay firebombed Tokyo, killing 100,000 people, leaving 1 million homeless, and destroying much of the city. These raids were particularly devastating because Japan had few planes left to defend its densely populated areas. In the following months, conventional (nonatomic) bombings pounded half of Japan's sixty-six major cities.

Shortly after taking office, President Truman was told about the atomic bomb by Secretary of War Stimson, who called it "the most terrible weapon ever known in human history." The decision to build this bomb had been made by President Roosevelt in response to reports from refugee scientists, such as Italy's Enrico Fermi and Germany's Albert Einstein, that the Nazis were already at work on one. The American effort, known as the Manhattan Project, included top-secret facilities in Hanford, Washington; Oak Ridge, Tennessee; and Los Alamos, New Mexico, to design and construct this bomb, and produce the fissionable material for an atomic explosion.

At President Truman's direction, an Interim Committee was formed to advise him about the bomb. Chaired by Henry Stimson, the committee recommended the use of atomic weapons against Japan, without warning, as soon as they became available. Another group, the Target Committee, chose four major cities—Hiroshima, Kokura, Niigata, and Nagasaki—based on their strategic importance, and the fact that each of them, unlike Tokyo, was untouched by war. On July 16, 1945, the atomic bomb was successfully tested near Alamogordo, New Mexico. The explosion, equivalent to 15,000 tons of dynamite, was visible 200 miles away. Truman learned of the test while attending the allied Summit meeting in Potsdam. He immediately issued a public ultimatum to the Japanese, calling on them to surrender unconditionally or face "prompt and utter destruction."

A number of top scientists on the Manhattan Project objected. Having urged one president to build the atomic bomb to counter Germany, they now found themselves begging another president not to use it against Japan. These scientists were joined by several ranking civilian and military officials, who argued that Japan was close to surrender, that the naval blockade was going well, and that use of the bomb would trigger a dangerous arms race with the Russians.

But Truman held firm, believing that the bomb would save American and Japanese lives by ending the war quickly. On the morning of August 6, 1945, a B-29 named *Enola Gay* dropped an atomic bomb over Hiroshima, incinerating the industrial city and killing at least 100,000 people. (Thousands more would die of radiation effects, a problem poorly understood by scientists at that time.) Three days later, a B-29 named *Bock's Car* dropped a second atomic bomb on Nagasaki, with much the same effect. On August 14, the Japanese asked for peace.

Though Americans overwhelmingly supported these bombings, the decision remains controversial to this day. Some believe that Truman dropped the bomb to scare the Russians in Europe and to keep them out of the Asian war. Others think the decision was based on racism and revenge. Still others argue that the

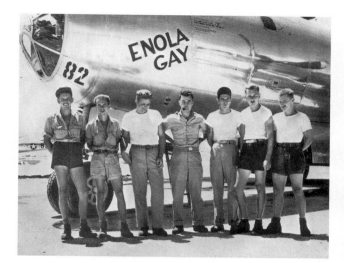

On August 6, 1945, a B-29 named after the mother of Colonel Paul W. Tibbets, and piloted by him (center), dropped an atomic bomb on the Japanese city of Hiroshima, killing at least 100,000 people. Since that time, a debate has raged over the atomic bombings of Hiroshima and Nagasaki—in particular, their role in ending the war.
© Baldwin H. Ward/Corbis

Japanese representatives signed the formal declaration of surrender aboard the battleship Missouri on September 2, 1945.
© Bettmann/UPI/Corbis

United States should have provided a "demonstration" of the bomb's power for the Japanese or made it clear to them that the terms of "unconditional surrender" did not mean that the emperor would have to be removed. For all the controversy, however, one inescapable fact remains: Japanese leaders could not bring themselves to surrender until two atomic bombs had been dropped.

World War II formally ended on September 2, 1945, when the Japanese signed the document of surrender aboard the battleship *Missouri* in Tokyo Bay. More than 25 million soldiers and civilians died in the struggle. Speaking from the deck of the *Missouri* that day, General MacArthur issued a warning for the new atomic age. "We have had our last chance," he said. "If we do not devise some greater and more equitable system, Armageddon will be at our door."

CONCLUSION

World War II shattered the illusion that Americans could remain separate from the world's problems. By leading the Grand Alliance against Nazi and Japanese aggression, the United States took on the full responsibilities of a global power—morally, economically, militarily. In doing so, it served notice that America's commitment to, and influence upon, world affairs

would be substantial in the postwar era, whether in containing the spread of communism, constructing a nuclear arsenal, spending billions in foreign aid, or rebuilding the battered economies of Western Europe and Japan.

World War II had an equal impact on domestic affairs. It ended the Great Depression, created full employment, and increased mean family income an astonishing 25 percent. It demonstrated the ability of an ethnically diverse nation to unite in a just cause, although basic civil liberties, in the case of Japanese Americans, were tragically denied. And it opened new opportunities for women and minorities, although economic and political equality in the United States remained a dream unfulfilled. In 1945, Americans looked to the future with cautious optimism—proud of their accomplishments and yearning for better times.

Recommended Readings

Birdwell, Michael. *Celluloid Soldiers* (1999). Carefully examines Hollywood's war effort against the Nazis.

Dower, John. *War Without Mercy: Race and Power in the Pacific War* (1986). Explores the racial attitudes of the United States and Japan in the brutal Asian conflict.

Hartmann, Susan. *The Homefront and Beyond: American Women in the 1940s* (1982). Documents the extraordinary impact of World War II on women at home and in the workplace.

Jeffries, John. *Wartime America* (1996). Concentrates on the homefront during World War II.

Kennett, Lee. *G.I.: The American Soldier in World War II* (1997). Describes the day-to-day order of life of the average American soldier in the training camps, in combat, and in victory.

O'Neill, William. *A Democracy at War: America's Fight at Home and Abroad in World War II* (1993). Examines both the military front and the homefront in lively detail.

Robinson, Gregg. *By Order of the President: FDR and the Internment of Japanese Americans* (2001). Offers a sobering account of Roosevelt's personal role in the internment process.

Tuttle, William. *Daddy's Gone to War* (1993). Recreates these years in generational terms through the eyes of America's wartime children.

Walker, J. Samuel. *Prompt and Utter Destruction: Truman and the Use of Atomic Bombs Against Japan* (1997). Offers a balanced account of the factors leading to the president's fateful decision.

Wyman, David S. *The Abandonment of the Jews* (1984). Examines the failure of American policy makers, the press, and the larger public to provide a sanctuary for victims of the Holocaust.

American Journey Online and InfoTrac College Edition

Visit the source collections at http://ajaccess. wadsworth.com and infotrac.thomsonlearning.com and use the Search function with the following key terms to explore documents, images, audio and video clips, articles, and commentary related to the material in this chapter.

Franklin D. Roosevelt	Lend-Lease
Pearl Harbor	Executive Order 9066
Enola Gay	Harry S. Truman

Additional resources, exercises, and Internet links related to this chapter are available on the American Passages Web site: http://history.wadsworth.com/passages2e

27 POSTWAR AMERICA
1946–1952

American soldiers return home at the end of World War II.
© Bettmann/UPI/Corbis

enry R. Luce was a man of grand visions and powerful views. One rival dubbed him "Lord of the Press" because his publishing empire included *Time, Life,* and *Fortune,* among other mass circulation magazines. In February 1941, Luce composed an editorial prodding the American people to accept their new role as citizens of "the strongest and most vital nation in the world." The time had come, he insisted, to exert "the full measure of our influence, for such purposes as we see fit" in the dawning "American Century."

The belief in America's destiny was as old as the country itself. Yet the challenges of World War II had turned this rhetoric into reality by placing the United States at the very center of the international stage. Old empires lay in ruins; an atomic era had begun. Only the United States seemed to possess the combination of military strength, economic resources, and political stability to rebuild a world battered by war. What worried Luce and others was the failure of American resolve. As columnist Dorothy Thompson put it, the United States "must lead now or take a back seat in history."

RECONVERSION

The United States faced two major problems following World War II. The first one concerned relations with the Soviet Union. Would the two nations be able to maintain the Grand Alliance, or would their obvious differences about the shape and direction of postwar Europe degenerate into conflict, and possibly war? The second problem related to the domestic economy. Many Americans feared that the Great Depression might return after World War II, as defense spending dropped and factory jobs disappeared. In the months following Japan's surrender, the federal government cancelled more than $30 billion in military contracts, forcing 800,000 layoffs in the aircraft industry alone. Could the United States handle the difficult reconversion from a wartime to a peacetime economy? Or would it slip back into the dark days of joblessness, poverty, and despair?

The Veterans Return

President Truman's first job was to bring the soldiers home. Twelve million Americans were still in uniform in 1945, most of them young men, age eighteen to thirty-four, who had experienced the dual hardships of economic depression and war. Their dream was to return home quickly and get on with their lives. Throughout Europe and the Pacific, GIs grumbled about the

	CHRONOLOGY
1946	Dr. Spock publishes *Common Sense Book of Baby and Child Care* • Republicans capture both houses of Congress
1947	Truman Doctrine is unveiled • Marshall Plan is implemented • Jackie Robinson breaks baseball's color line
1948	Harry Truman upsets Thomas Dewey in tight presidential race • Whittaker Chambers confronts Alger Hiss
1949	Soviet Union successfully tests an atomic bomb • China falls to the Communists
1950	Senator Joe McCarthy charges that Communists have penetrated the State Department • Korean War begins
1951	General Douglas MacArthur is relieved of his command in Korea
1952	Richard Nixon delivers dramatic Checkers speech • Dwight Eisenhower is elected president

slow pace of demobilization, while their loved ones barraged Congress and the White House with angry mail. One soldier put his feelings in a poem:

Please Mr. Truman, won't you send us home?
We have captured Napoli and liberated Rome.
We have licked the master race.
Now there's lots of shipping space.
So, won't you send us home.

This pressure brought results. Within a year, the number of men and women in the armed forces had dropped to 3 million, despite the growing Soviet threat.

For many GIs, however, these were anxious, difficult times. The divorce rate shot up dramatically in 1945, reflecting the tensions of readjustment to civilian life. A major housing shortage, brought on by the virtual absence of home-building during World War II, made things even worse. Washington, D.C., reported 25,000 homeless veterans, Chicago more than 100,000. North Dakota veterans took to living in converted grain bins. One serviceman complained: "You fight a damn war and you finally come home and everybody slaps you on the back and tells you what a wonderful job you did . . . but when it comes to really doing something, then nobody's home."

In fact, however, assistance for returning veterans had received careful attention from the wartime Congress, which passed the popular Servicemen's Readjustment Act in 1944. Known as the GI Bill, it provided almost $20 billion for various programs in the decade following World War II. The social and economic effects of this legislation were enormous. The GI Bill fueled a nationwide construction boom by providing long-term, low-interest mortgages to veterans, plus a $2,000 bonus toward the purchase of a new home. Furthermore, it allowed former soldiers to fulfill the dream of a college degree, thereby expanding the system of higher education as never before. In 1947, for example, more than half of the 30,000 students at the University of Minnesota were veterans of World War II. Older, more serious, and determined to make up for lost time, they formed the nucleus of America's expanding white-collar workforce in the prosperous years ahead.

Lurching Toward Prosperity

The fear of another economic depression in the United States did not last long. The increase in federal spending for veterans helped to offset the decrease in defense spending. And a surge of consumer demand held out the promise of prosperity based on peace. For the past five years, Americans had worked overtime in offices and factories, banking their paychecks, buying savings bonds, and dreaming of the day when cars, appliances, prime beef, and nylon stockings would reappear in the nation's stores and showrooms. Between Pearl Harbor and the Japanese surrender, the public had accumulated an astonishing $140 billion in savings and liquid securities, while the average weekly wage had almost doubled, from $24.20 to $44.30. "I'm tired of ration books and empty shelves," said one factory worker. "I'm ready to spend."

But factories could not change from fighter planes to automobiles overnight. Reconversion took time. With the demand for consumer goods far outracing the supply, President Truman hoped to keep inflation in line by extending wartime price controls. His plan met strong opposition from the business commu-

Veterans register for college. The GI Bill of 1944 expanded and democratized higher education as never before.
© Bettmann/UPI/Corbis

nity, which lobbied hard to "strike the shackles from American free enterprise." In June 1946, controls were lifted and prices shot up. The cost of meat doubled in two weeks, leading the *New York Daily News* to quip:

PRICES SOAR, BUYERS SORE
STEERS JUMP OVER THE MOON

Not surprisingly, the labor movement took a militant stance. Since higher prices meant a drop in real wages, the United Automobile Workers (UAW) demanded an average pay hike of 33 cents an hour from General Motors in 1946, from $1.12 to $1.45. When the corporation offered a ten-cent hourly raise, the union struck for 113 days, eventually settling for eighteen cents. Shortly thereafter, the UAW and the auto companies agreed to a cost-of-living adjustment (COLA) clause in future contracts.

The country was soon plagued by a wave of strikes. In 1946 alone, 5 million workers were involved in 4,630 work stoppages totaling 120 million days of lost labor. When two railroad brotherhoods threatened a national strike designed to shut down the country's rail service, President Truman signed an executive order seizing the railroads. "If you think I'm going to sit here and let you tie up this whole country," he told union leaders, "you're crazy as hell." A few weeks later, the United Mine Workers (UMW) went on strike, forcing power stations and factories to close for lack of fuel.

An advertisement for the "dream kitchen." A surge of consumer spending after World War II quickly erased fears that America would slip back into economic depression.
Peter Newark's American Pictures

In response, President Truman went on radio to demand that the miners return to work at once. They did, coaxed along by a federal court injunction that led to $3.5 million in damages against the UMW. For Truman, these victories came at a heavy cost. Not only did he offend large parts of the labor movement, he also appeared incapable of governing a nation wracked by consumer shortages, labor strife, soaring inflation, and an approaching cold war.

In November 1946, the Democratic party suffered a crushing defeat at the polls. Campaigning against the ills of reconversion ("Had Enough?") and the president's alleged incompetence ("To Err Is Truman"), the Republicans gained control of the Senate and the House for the first time since 1928. When the Truman family returned to Washington from a campaign trip on election eve, no one showed up to greet them. The train station was deserted. "Don't worry about me," the president told his daughter, Margaret. "I know how things will turn out and they'll be all right."

AFFLUENCE AND ANXIETY

The pain and sacrifice of the Great Depression and World War II led most Americans to yearn for both emotional security and material success. As expected, the family grew in importance, providing a sense of comfort and stability to people after years of separation and loss. Along with the focus on families came a changing middle-class culture, based on suburban living, a baby boom, an emphasis on more traditional sex roles, and an explosion of consumer goods. In the coming years, the nation's unprecedented prosperity would be measured by the increased size and abundant possessions of its thriving middle class.

The Postwar American Family

One of the songs among returning American veterans was titled "I've Got to Make Up for Lost Time." Beginning in 1946, the United States experienced a surge in marriage and birthrates, following record lows in the Depression decade. The young adults of this era (eighteen to thirty) became the most "marrying" generation in American history, with 97 percent of the women and 94 percent of the men taking marriage vows. By 1950, the age of marriage for American women had dropped below twenty, another record, while the percentage of divorces, initially high among returning veterans, reached an all-time low.

The baby boom was equally dramatic. The number of children per family in the United States jumped from 2.6 in 1940 to 3.2 by decade's end. Birthrates doubled for a third child, and tripled for a fourth, as the American population grew by 20 million in the 1940s. At a time when access to birth control information was rapidly increasing, U.S. population growth rivaled not England's, but rather India's.

These spiraling marriage and birthrates went hand in hand with a shift back to more traditional sex roles following World War II. Actress Ann Sothern exemplified the reordering of domestic priorities when she advised women, shortly before Japan's surrender, to begin "planning our house—our perfect house" and to think about the nursery. "I know a lot of men are dreaming of coming back not only to those girls who waved goodbye to them," she added. "They are dreaming of coming back to the mothers of their children and the least we can do as women is to try to live up to some of these ex-

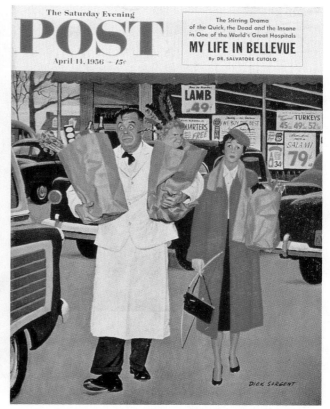

Marriage and birthrates rose dramatically in the postwar years, following record lows in the Depression era.
J. R. Eyerman/Life Magazine © 1953 Time, Inc.

A trip to the suburban supermarket in postwar America.
© Curtis Publishing Company

pectations." Indeed, one of the most popular wartime advertisements showed a mother in overalls about to leave for the factory. She is at the door when her little daughter asks: "Mother, when will you stay home again?" And she responds: "Some jubilant day, mother will stay home again doing the job she likes—making a home for you and daddy when he gets back."

Quite naturally, this emphasis on family life strengthened long-held prejudices against married women holding full-time jobs outside the home. As a result, the gains made in female employment during World War II largely disappeared. Returning veterans reclaimed millions of factory jobs held by women and minorities. The female labor force dropped from a wartime high of 19 million in 1945 to less than 17 million by 1947. On the Ford and General Motors assembly lines, the percentage of women plummeted from 25 to 6 percent. Though many women gladly returned to their former domestic lives, the vast majority, according to postwar surveys, hoped to keep their jobs. "I'd stay if they wanted me to," said a female aircraft worker, "but without taking a man's place from him."

The social pressures on women were enormous. A host of "experts," including psychiatrists, psychologists, and pediatricians, asserted that women belonged in the home for their own good as well as the good of society—that women *needed* to be housewives and mothers in order to be fulfilled. In their 1947 best-seller, *Modern Women: The Lost Sex*, Marynia Farnham and Ferdinand Lundberg noted that "all mature childless women are emotionally disturbed," and that "the pursuit of a career is essentially masculine." Furthermore, these experts claimed that returning veterans needed special love and attention after so many years away from home.

The concept of "mothering" as central to the postwar family was further popularized by Dr. Benjamin Spock, whose *Common Sense Book of Baby and Child Care* (1946) became the standard reference for parents of the "baby boom" generation. While most reviewers noted Spock's relaxed, more permissive attitude toward child rearing, another message came through as well. Women must be the primary caregivers, Spock insisted. It was their role to shape the infant into a normal, happy

*P*ICTURING THE PAST ✦ SOCIAL & CULTURAL EVENTS

DR. KINSEY AND THE SEXUAL REVOLUTION

Corbis/Bettman

In 1948, Dr. Alfred Kinsey, a professor at Indiana University, became a national celebrity with the publication of his 804-page study, *Sexual Behavior in the Human Male.* The photo of Kinsey here, with his crew cut and bow tie, conveys the conservative, old-fashioned image he liked to portray. In truth, his personal habits were anything but conventional. Kinsey had experienced many different sexual relationships throughout his life. His scientific research, based on thousands of detailed interviews, showed that American men were more sexually active—and less bound by traditional codes of morality—than had previously been imagined. His book became a best-seller, followed in 1953 by a sequel, *Sexual Behavior in the Human Female,* which drew similar conclusions about American women. Kinsey hoped that his work would lead to greater tolerance for a wide range of sexual behavior, including homosexuality. He was mistaken. Though opinion polls showed most Americans in agreement with his findings, angry critics, led by church leaders and politicians, condemned Kinsey for undermining the nation's moral standards. In response, his main benefactor, the Rockefeller Foundation, withdrew its financial support, undermining future projects. Kinsey died shortly thereafter, in 1956, at the age of sixty-two.

---

adult. For Spock and countless others, a man's success was measured by his performance in the outside world, a woman's success by her skills in raising well-adjusted children. As feminist author Betty Friedan recalled, "Oh, how Dr. Spock could make me feel guilty!"

The emphasis on traditional sex roles also affected female education. World War II had opened up new opportunities for women in science, engineering, and medicine. For the first time in history, women constituted a majority of the nation's college graduates. But the return of male veterans, combined with the educational benefits provided them by the GI Bill, reversed these temporary gains. Although the number of

college women increased after World War II, the percentage of females in the college population declined dramatically. At Cornell University, for example, women comprised 50 percent of the wartime classes, but only 20 percent of the postwar classes. More significantly, the percentage of college women who actually graduated fell from 40 percent during World War II to 25 percent by 1950.

The steepest declines occurred in professional education. Engineering colleges, which doubled their enrollments to more than 200,000 by 1946, accepted fewer than 1,300 women, with more than half of these schools accepting no women at all. Female enrollments biles, 20 million refrigerators, 5.5 million electric stoves, and more than 2 million dishwashers. This consumer explosion resulted from a combination of factors: the baby boom, the huge savings accumulated during World War II, the availability of credit, and the effectiveness of mass advertising in creating consumer demand. The average American now had access to department store charge accounts and easy payment plans with almost no money down. "Buy Now, Pay Later," urged General Motors, and most people obliged. In 1950, as consumer debt surpassed $100 billion, the Diner's Club introduced America's first credit card. The Depression age virtues of thrift and savings seemed as remote as the Depression itself.

Ironically, this new consumer society led millions of women back into the labor force. By 1950, more women were working outside the home than ever before. The difference, however, was that postwar American women returned to low-paying, often part-time employment in "feminine" jobs such as clerks, salespeople, secretaries, waitresses, telephone operators, and domestics. Working to supplement the family income, to help finance the automobile, the kitchen appliances, the summer vacation, the children's college tuition, American women earned but 53 percent of the wages of American men in 1950—a drop of 10 percent since the heady years of "Rosie the Riveter" during World War II.

Suburbia

No possession was more prized by the postwar American family than the suburban home. In 1944, fewer than 120,000 new houses were built in the United States, a figure that rose to 900,000 by 1946, and 1.7 million by 1950. More than 80 percent of these new houses were built in suburban areas surrounding established cities. While prosperity and population growth produced the need for more housing, the rush to suburbia was accelerated by a flood of federal mortgage money and a revolution in the building of affordable, single-family homes.

The GI Bill provided the cash to bolster demand. With mortgage money now available, the housing shortage quickly disappeared. Leading the way were builders like William Levitt, who purchased several thousand acres of farmland in Hempstead, New York, twenty-five miles east of Manhattan, for the mass production of private homes. Levitt modeled his operation after Henry Ford's automobile assembly plants. His building materials were produced and precut in Levitt factories, delivered by Levitt trucks, and assembled by Levitt work crews, each performing a single

The vast majority of working women in the postwar era were employed in low-paying, often part-time, jobs as clerks, secretaries, waitresses, domestics, and telephone operators.
AP/Wide World Photos

in medical schools dropped from a high of 15 percent during World War II to 5 percent by 1950. A study of medical students in this era showed deep prejudice among the men and self-limiting attitudes among the women. The majority of men, believing they made better doctors, thought that women should face tougher admission standards. The majority of women, insisting that marriage was more important than a career, claimed they would cut back their hours, or even stop working, to meet their family obligations. On campuses across the nation, educators struggled to find the proper curriculum for female students. The ideal, said one college president, was to enable women "to foster the intellectual and emotional life of her family and community"—to fill the American home with proper moral values, a love of culture, and an appreciation of good wine and gourmet cooking.

Before long, the postwar American woman became the nation's primary consumer. Between 1946 and 1950, Americans purchased 21 million automo-

The routine of suburban life often included a wife delivering her husband to the train station.
© Curtis Publishing Company

The GI Bill helped fuel the boom in suburban housing after World War II.
© Bettmann/UPI/Corbis

task such as framing, pouring concrete, or painting window shutters. In good weather, Levitt workers put up 180 houses a week. The typical dwelling—a solid, two-bedroom Cape Cod, with a kitchen–dining room, living room with fireplace, single bath, and expansion attic—sold for $7,900. When completed, Levittown, Long Island, contained 17,000 houses, plus dozens of parks, ballfields, swimming pools, churches, and shopping areas for the 82,000 residents. Levitt followed his Long Island venture with similar towns in Pennsylvania and New Jersey.

City dwellers were attracted by Levittown's good schools, safe streets, and open space. The idea of owning one's home, moreover, was a central part of the American dream. And these suburban neighborhoods, filled with young families, provided a sense of shared experience and community that large cities sometimes lacked.

What stood out to others, however, was the "sameness" of Levittown—a place where people lived

in similar houses, accumulated similar possessions, and conformed to similar rules. Levitt salesmen restricted their communities to white applicants, who then signed pledges saying they would not resell their homes to blacks. As late as the 1960s, the percentage of African Americans living in the three Levittown developments was well below 1 percent, a figure that represented most suburban areas nationwide. Furthermore, Levittown appeared to reinforce the traditional family roles of postwar America, with mothers caring for their children while fathers commuted long distances to work.

THE SOVIET THREAT

Relations between the United States and the Soviet Union were moving swiftly downhill. The failure to find common ground on a host of vital issues—from "free elections" in Poland to the German payment of reparations—raised anger and suspicion on both sides. Soviet leaders now viewed the United States as largely indifferent to the security needs of the Russian people, while American leaders increasingly portrayed the Soviet Union as a belligerent force in the world, bent more on expanding its empire than on defending its territory. The Grand Alliance was over; the Cold War had begun.

Containment

Within hours of Germany's surrender, President Truman had signed an executive order ending Lend-Lease aid to the Allies. Though Truman reversed himself under a storm of criticism, Congress abolished Lend-Lease following Japan's surrender in August 1945. A few months later, the United States gave England a low-interest $3.75 billion loan, while ignoring a similar request from the Russians.

Stalin angrily viewed these moves as a sign of American indifference to the suffering of his people. In February 1946, the Soviet leader delivered a major address predicting the collapse of capitalism and the dawn of a communist world. The following month, with Truman at his side, former Prime Minister Churchill told an audience at Westminster College in Missouri that Russia had drawn an "iron curtain" across Europe. The West must unite against Soviet expansion, Churchill said, adding that "God had willed" the atomic bomb to Britain and America so as to ensure their ultimate triumph over this totalitarian foe.

A more compelling rebuttal to Stalin's speech came from a forty-two-year-old foreign service officer stationed at the U.S. Embassy in Moscow. In an 8,000-word telegram, George F. Kennan laid out the doctrine of "containment" that would influence American foreign policy for the next twenty years. According to Kennan, Russia was an implacable foe, determined to expand its empire and to undermine Western democratic values. America must be patient, Kennan believed. It must define its vital interests and then be prepared to defend them through "the adroit and vigilant application of counterforce at a series of constantly shifting geographical and political points."

Kennan's "long telegram" arrived in Washington at the perfect time. Poland and Eastern Europe were now lost causes; there seemed little that the United States could do to change their dismal fate. The present objective, Truman believed, was to block communist expansion into new areas vulnerable to Soviet influence and control. "Unless Russia is faced with an iron fist and strong language another war is in the making," he predicted. "I am tired of babying the Soviets."

The Truman Doctrine and the Marshall Plan

The new trouble spot appeared to be the Mediterranean, where Russia was demanding territorial concessions from Iran and Turkey, and where communist-led guerillas were battling the Greek government in a bloody civil war. Early in 1947, Great Britain, the traditional power in that area, informed the United States that it could no longer provide military and economic assistance to Greece and Turkey. Exhausted by World War II, England urged the United States to maintain that aid in order to prevent further Soviet expansion.

At a White House meeting six days later, General George C. Marshall, the new secretary of state, presented the case for American aid to congressional leaders from both parties. When Marshall's soft-spoken approach failed to rally the meeting, his assistant Dean Acheson took over. In sweeping terms, Acheson portrayed the future of Greece and Turkey as a test case of American resolve against Soviet aggression. If Greece fell to the communists, Acheson warned, other nations would follow "like apples in a barrel infected by one rotten one." When he finished, Republican Senator Arthur Vandenberg of Michigan summed up the feeling in the room. "Mr. President," he said, turning to Harry Truman, "if you will say that to Congress and the country, I will support you and I believe most members will do the same."

On March 12, 1947, the president offered his Truman Doctrine before a joint session of Congress and a national radio audience. In the present crisis, he be-gan, "every nation must choose between alternative ways of life." One way guaranteed "individual liberty" and "political freedom," the other promoted "terror" and "oppression." In a world of good and evil, Truman declared, it "must be the policy of the United States to support free peoples who are resisting attempted subjugation by armed minorities or by outside pressures."

Some critics noted that the regimes in Greece and Turkey were a far cry from the democratic ideals that the president lauded in his speech. Others worried that the Truman Doctrine would lead the United States into an expensive, open-ended crusade against left-wing forces around the globe. Yet most Americans supported Truman's position, and Congress allocated $400 million in military aid for Greece and Turkey.

On June 5, 1947, at the Harvard University commencement, Secretary of State Marshall unveiled a far more ambitious proposal known as the European Recovery Plan (ERP), or the Marshall Plan. The danger seemed clear: without massive economic aid, European governments might collapse, leaving chaos in their wake. "Our policy is not directed against any country or doctrine," Marshall said, "but against hunger, poverty, desperation, and fear."

Several weeks later, seventeen European nations, including the Soviet Union, met in Paris to assess their common needs. But the Russians walked out after a few sessions, forcing nations like Poland and Hungary to leave as well. The Soviets balked at the idea of divulging critical information about their economy to outsiders. And they surely feared that massive American aid would tie them and the nations they now controlled to a capitalist orbit that might undermine the communist system.

Truman was not sorry to see them leave. He had been forced to invite all European nations to participate in order to avoid the appearance of worsening the Cold War. Yet he realized that Congress would not look favorably upon the prospect of spending billions of dollars to reconstruct a nation that seemed so brutal to its neighbors and so threatening to the United States. With the Russians and their satellites out of the picture, the remaining European nations prepared an agenda for economic recovery that came to $27 billion, a staggering sum. After six months of bitter debate, Congress reduced that figure by about one-half. The largest expenditures went to England, Germany, and France.

The Marshall Plan proved a tremendous success on both sides of the Atlantic. By creating jobs and raising living standards, it restored economic confidence throughout Western Europe while curbing the influence of local Communist parties in Italy and France.

The Truman Doctrine, March 12, 1947

While recommending military aid for the anti-Communist governments of Greece and Turkey, President Harry Truman warned the American people about a grave new threat to world peace and democratic ideals. His graphic warnings about Soviet expansion, and the need to combat it, set a militant tone in foreign policy for decades to come.

At the present moment in world history nearly every nation must choose between alternative ways of life. The choice is too often not a free one.

One way of life is based upon the will of the majority, and is distinguished by free institutions, representative government, free elections, guarantees of individual liberty, freedom of speech and religion, and freedom from political oppression.

The second way of life is based upon the will of the minority forcibly imposed upon the majority. It relies upon terror and oppression, a controlled press and radio, fixed elections, and the suppression of personal freedoms.

I believe that it must be the policy of the United States to support free peoples who are resisting attempted subjugation by armed minorities or by outside pressures.

I believe that we must assist free peoples to work out their own destinies in their own way. . . .

Should we fail to aid Greece and Turkey in this fateful hour, the effect will be far reaching to the west as well as to the east. We must take immediate and resolute action.

I therefore ask the Congress to provide authority for assistance to Greece and Turkey in the amount of $400,000,000 for the period ending June 30, 1948. . . .

The seeds of totalitarian regimes are nurtured by misery and want. They spread and grow in the evil soil of poverty and strife. They reach their full growth when the hope of a people for a better life has died. We must keep that hope alive. The free peoples of the world look to us for support in maintaining their freedoms.

If we falter in our leadership, we may endanger the peace of the world—and we shall surely endanger the welfare of this nation.

Great responsibilities have been placed upon us by the swift movement of events. I am confident that the Congress will face these responsibilities squarely.

Source: *Congressional Record,* March 12, 1947.

Furthermore, the Marshall Plan increased American trade and investment in Europe, opening vast new markets for U.S. goods. As President Truman noted, "peace, freedom, and world trade are indivisible."

The rising prosperity in Western Europe was matched by growing repression in the East. Stalin moved first on Hungary, staging a rigged election backed by Russian troops. Opponents of the new Communist regime were silenced and imprisoned. Next came Czechoslovakia, where the Soviets toppled a coalition government led by Jan Masaryk, a statesman with many admirers in the West. A few days later, Masaryk either jumped or was pushed to his death from an office window in Prague. Against this ominous background, President Truman proposed legislation to streamline the nation's military and diplomatic services. Passed as the National Security Act of 1947, it unified the armed forces under a single Department of Defense, created the National Security Council (NSC) to provide foreign policy information to the president, and established the Central Intelligence Agency (CIA) to coordinate intelligence gathering abroad. By 1948, the Cold War was in full swing.

LIBERALISM IN RETREAT

In foreign affairs, President Truman could count on strong bipartisan support. Republican legislators had joined with Democrats to endorse early Cold War initiatives like the Truman Doctrine and the Marshall Plan. But the president had no such luck on domestic issues. For one thing, the widening rift with Russia produced a growing concern about the influence of communists and their "sympathizers" inside the federal government. For another, the president's attempt to extend the liberal agenda through ambitious social and economic legislation—known as the "Fair Deal"—met with stiff resistance in Congress after 1946. As one Republican leader put it: "We have to break with the corrupting idea that we can legislate prosperity, legislate equality, legislate opportunity."

The Cold War at Home

The Iron Curtain that descended on Europe had a tremendous psychological impact on the United States. Americans were fearful of communism and frustrated by the turn of global events. The defeat of fascism had not made the world a safer place. One form of totalitarianism had been replaced by another. The result was an erosion of public tolerance for left-wing activity, spurred on by prominent government officials like Attorney General Tom Clark, who warned that communists were "everywhere" in the United States—"in factories, offices, butcher shops, on street corners, in private businesses, and each carries with him the germs of death for society."

In fact, the American Communist party was far weaker in 1947 than it had been a decade before, and its numbers were dwindling by the day. Yet that did not stop President Truman from establishing a Federal Loyalty–Security Program for the first time in American history. Truman acted, in large part, to keep congressional conservatives from fashioning an even tougher loyalty program. The one he put in place called for extensive background checks of all civilian workers in the federal bureaucracy. The criteria for disloyalty included everything from espionage to "sympathetic association" with groups deemed "subversive" by the attorney general. The Loyalty–Security Program provided minimal safeguards for the accused. Even worse, it frightened the country by conceding the possibility that a serious problem existed.

The congressional assault on domestic subversion was led by the House Un-American Activities Committee (HUAC). Formed in the 1930s to investigate Nazi propaganda in the United States, HUAC had

The Marshall Plan at work in West Berlin. Billions of dollars in American aid helped rebuild much of war-ravaged Europe.
© Bettmann/UPI/Corbis

been revived after World War II as a watchdog against communist propaganda. Among its more visible members was a young congressman from southern California named Richard M. Nixon. In 1947, HUAC launched a spectacular investigation of the motion picture industry, alleging that "flagrant communist propaganda films" had been produced during World War II on the specific orders of President Roosevelt. The committee subpoenaed a number of pro-communist writers and directors, who angrily refused to answer questions about their political beliefs and associations. Known as the "Hollywood Ten," these individuals were cited for contempt, sent to jail, and "blacklisted" from working in the entertainment industry, a practice that became increasingly common in the late 1940s and 1950s. HUAC also heard from a host of "friendly" Hollywood witnesses, including movie stars Gary Cooper, Ronald Reagan, and the dapper Adolphe Menjou, who declared: "I am a witch-hunter if the witches are communists. I am a Red-baiter. I would like to see them all back in Russia."

The following year brought HUAC even more publicity. A witness named Whittaker Chambers, then a senior editor for *Time* magazine, claimed to have once

Alger Hiss is sworn in at a hearing of the House Un-American Activities Committee in 1948. Accused by Whittaker Chambers of being part of a Soviet espionage ring, Hiss went to federal prison in 1950 after a jury convicted him of perjury.
© Bettmann/UPI/Corbis

been part of a "communist cell" in Washington that included Alger Hiss, a former government official who had advised President Roosevelt in foreign affairs. Hiss denied Chambers's allegations in testimony before HUAC a few days later. When Chambers repeated the charge on a national radio broadcast, Hiss sued him for libel.

Chambers struck back hard, producing dozens of classified State Department documents from the 1930s that, he claimed, had been stolen by Hiss and passed on to the Russians. Suddenly the ground had shifted to espionage, a more serious charge. The evidence—known as the "Pumpkin Papers" because Chambers had briefly hidden it in a pumpkin patch on his Maryland farm—included five rolls of microfilm and summaries of confidential reports written by Hiss in longhand or typed on a Woodstock typewriter he once owned. In December 1948, a federal grand jury indicted Hiss for perjuring himself before HUAC. (The ten-year statute of limitations on espionage had just run out.) The first trial ended in a hung jury; the second one sent Hiss to jail.

The guilty verdict sent shock waves through the nation. Not only did it bolster Republican charges

about the threat of communists in government, it also served to undermine the liberal-internationalist philosophy that had guided the Democratic party since 1933. If Alger Hiss was a traitor, some wondered, how many just like him were still loose in the Truman administration, working secretly to help the Soviet Union win the Cold War? This question would come to dominate American politics over the next several years.

The Domestic Agenda

The Republican landslide of 1946 appeared to signal the decline of American liberalism. In the following months, the Republican Congress brushed aside President Truman's proposals for national health insurance and federal aid to education, while passing major legislation, known as the Taft-Hartley Act, to curb the power of organized labor. Taft-Hartley generated strong public support, given the crippling strikes of the previous year. Republican leaders viewed the union movement as both an ally of the Democratic party and a threat to the employer's authority in the workplace. In 1947, organized labor was at the height of its influence, with 15 million members nationwide. More than 35 percent of all nonagricultural workers belonged to a union, the highest total ever reached in the United States.

To counter the threats of powerful unions like the United Mine Workers, Taft-Hartley gave the president authority to impose an eighty-day "cooling-off" period to prevent strikes that threatened the national interest. More important, the bill outlawed the closed shop, a device that forced workers to join a union at the time they were hired, and it encouraged the states to pass "right to work" laws which made union organizing more difficult. Though Truman strongly opposed Taft-Hartley, the Republican Congress easily overrode his veto.

Truman also confronted the issue of racial discrimination, long ignored in the White House and on Capitol Hill, by forming a special task force on civil rights. Its final report included a series of bold recommendations, such as the desegregation of the armed forces and the creation of a special division within the Justice Department devoted solely to civil rights. Truman endorsed these recommendations, although his personal feelings about them were mixed. As a political leader, he had to balance the interests of two distinct Democratic party voting blocs: southern whites and northern blacks. As an individual, he believed that all citizens deserved political rights and equal opportunity, yet he felt uncomfortable with the notion of *social* equality for African Americans, as did most white people of that era. Addressing the NAACP's national convention in 1947—the first

American president to do so—Truman spoke out strongly against prejudice and hate. "The only limit to a [person's] achievement," he declared, "should be his ability, his industry, and his character."

Breaking the Color Line

Truman's statement seemed particularly appropriate in 1947. On April 15, Major League baseball broke its long-standing "color line" in an opening day game at Brooklyn's Ebbets Field. "History was made here Tuesday afternoon," reported the *Pittsburgh Courier,* an African American newspaper, "when smiling Jackie Robinson trotted out on the green-swept diamond with the rest of his Dodger teammates."

Baseball had been all-white for generations. Blacks played in the so-called Negro Leagues. Poorly paid, they often barnstormed from town to town, taking on local teams in exhibitions that combined great baseball with crowd-pleasing entertainment. The top players—pitcher Leroy "Satchel" Paige, catcher Josh Gibson, infielder George "Cool Papa" Bell—were as good, if not better, than the top Major League stars. Hall of Fame pitcher Walter Johnson claimed that Gibson "can do everything. He hits the ball a mile. He catches so easy he might as well be in a rocking chair. Throws like a rifle. Too bad this Gibson is a colored fellow."

The vast majority of Major League owners opposed integration. Branch Rickey of the Brooklyn Dodgers was an exception. Mixing deep religious values with shrewd business sense, Rickey insisted that integration was good for America, for baseball, and for the Dodgers. "The Negroes will make us winners for years to come," he said, "and for that I will happily bear being called a bleeding heart and a do-gooder and all that humanitarian rot."

To break the color line, Rickey selected Jack Roosevelt Robinson, twenty-seven, a man of tremendous talent and pride. The son of sharecroppers and the grandson of slaves, Robinson moved from rural Georgia to Pasadena, California, where his athletic skills earned him a scholarship to UCLA. A letterman in four different sports—baseball, football, basketball, and track—he also won tournaments in tennis and golf. Drafted into the army during World War II, Robinson fought bigotry at every turn. As a second lieutenant in a segregated tank unit, he was court-martialed for insubordination, and acquitted, after refusing to move to the rear of an army bus. Honorably discharged in 1944, he joined the Kansas City Monarchs, a Negro League team, as a shortstop at $400 a month. On a road trip to Oklahoma, teammate Buck O'Neill recalled, Robinson personally broke the color line at a

Jackie Robinson, who broke Major League baseball's color line in 1947, led the Brooklyn Dodgers to six pennants and a World Series victory in his brilliant career.
AP/Wide World Photos

local filling station by demanding to use the rest room. When the attendant refused, Robinson told him: "Take the hose out of the tank. If we can't go to the rest room, we won't get gas here." Startled, the attendant replied: "Well, you boys can go to the rest room, but don't stay long."

Rickey met secretly with Robinson in the fall of 1945. Talent was not an issue. Robinson was hitting .385 for the Monarchs and stealing bases by the bunch. What most concerned Rickey was Robinson's temper. How would he react to racial slurs, to pitches thrown at his head, to runners sliding into him spikes first? For three hours, Rickey grilled Robinson about the need for absolute self-control. "Do you want a ballplayer who's afraid to fight back?" Robinson asked. "I want a ballplayer with enough guts *not* to fight back," Rickey answered. "You will symbolize a crucial cause. One incident, just one incident, can set it back twenty years." "Mr. Rickey," Robinson replied, "if you want to take this gamble, I will promise you there will be no incident."

Robinson kept his word, enduring segregated hotels, racial insults, even death threats against his family. His pioneering effort caught the public's fancy, and huge crowds followed him everywhere. Chicago, Cincinnati, Philadelphia, Pittsburgh, St. Louis—all set attendance records when Robinson appeared, with black fans leading the way. As one writer put it, "Jackie's nimble/ Jackie's quick. Jackie's making the turnstiles click." By season's end, Robinson had led the Dodgers to the National League pennant and won "Rookie of the Year."

The struggle was far from over. It would be another decade before all Major League teams accepted integration. Yet the efforts begun by Branch Rickey and Jackie Robinson helped change the face of America by democratizing its "National Game." Looking back on the events of 1947, sportswriter Jimmy Cannon recalled a side of Robinson that captured both his courage and his pain. He was, said Cannon, "the loneliest man I have ever seen in sports."

Man of the People

As the 1948 presidential election approached, Harry Truman seemed a beaten man. His relations with Congress were stormy and unproductive, especially in domestic affairs. The press, remembering the elegant and fatherly FDR, portrayed Truman as too small for the job. Likely supporters deserted him in droves. In December 1947, a band of left-wing Democrats formed the Progressive Citizens of America, with an eye toward the coming election. Their leader was Henry Wallace, the former vice president and secretary of commerce, who had been fired by Truman for criticizing the administration's firm stance toward the Soviet Union. Wallace opposed both the Truman Doctrine and the Marshall Plan. Though he had no hope of winning the presidential election in 1948, his Progressive party seemed likely to split the Democratic vote.

Some urged Truman not to run. A number of Democratic leaders suggested other presidential candidates, including General Dwight D. Eisenhower. *The New Republic,* a favorite of liberals, ran the front cover headline: "HARRY TRUMAN SHOULD QUIT." The Democrats convened in Philadelphia, where the heat was oppressive and tempers grew short. When word reached the convention that Eisenhower was unavailable, "Boss" Frank Hague of Jersey City threw down his cigar. "Truman," he mumbled. "Harry Truman, oh my God!"

Left with no alternative, the delegates nominated Truman for president and Alben Barkley, the popular but aging Senate majority leader from Kentucky, for vice president. Barkley had strong ties to the South. Yet even he could not prevent the convention from dividing along sectional lines when northern liberals, led by Mayor Hubert Humphrey of Minneapolis, demanded the endorsement of Truman's civil rights initiatives. "The time has arrived," said Humphrey, "for the Democratic party to get out of the shadow of states' rights, and walk forthrightly into the bright sunshine of human rights."

The passage of a strong civil rights plank led many southern Democrats to walk out of the convention. Two days later, waving Confederate flags and denouncing Harry Truman, they formed the States' Rights (Dixiecrat) party at a gathering in Birmingham, Alabama. The Dixiecrats chose governors Strom Thurmond of South Carolina and Fielding Wright of Mississippi to be their presidential and vice presidential candidates. Their platform demanded "complete segregation of the races."

Divided into three camps, the Democratic party appeared hopelessly overmatched. Not only did President Truman face Henry Wallace on his left and Strom Thurmond on his right, but the national Republican ticket of New York Governor Thomas E. Dewey for president and California Governor Earl Warren for vice president was the strongest in years. Truman's campaign strategy was to portray himself as a common people's president, protecting the voters and their hard-earned New Deal benefits from a heartless Republican assault. To highlight these differences, he called a special session of Congress to demand passage of an eight-point program that included civil rights, public housing, federal aid to education, a higher minimum wage, and storage facilities for farmers. When the Republican Congress refused to act, calling Truman's move a "publicity stunt," the president lambasted the Republicans as selfish politicians, interested only in the rich.

Truman also used his presidential power in significant ways. He showed support for the new state of Israel by offering it political recognition and economic assistance. He issued his promised executive order desegregating the armed forces. And he forcefully confronted Stalin in a showdown over Germany and Berlin.

In June 1948, Russian troops blockaded West Berlin to protest the merging of the French, British, and American occupation zones into the unified nation of West Germany. The city lay deep inside Soviet-controlled territory. With all roads and rail lines through East Germany now closed to allied traffic, its future seemed bleak. Truman ruled out force to break the blockade because American troops were greatly outnumbered. Instead, he and his advisors decided to supply West Berlin from the air. In the coming months, Western pilots made close to 300,000 flights into the city, delivering food, fuel, and medical supplies. By the time the Russians called off their blockade, Berlin, the former Nazi capital, had become the symbol of resistance to communist oppression.

Truman could see his fortunes rising as the 1948 campaign progressed. Crisscrossing the nation by train, he drew huge, friendly crowds at each whistle stop. To shouts of "Give 'em hell, Harry!" he ripped into the "do-nothing" Republican Congress and their "plans" to dismantle Franklin Roosevelt's work. "The Republican politicians don't like the New Deal. They want to get rid of it," Truman repeated. "This is a crusade of the people against the special interests, and if you back me up we're going to win."

The experts didn't think so. Opinion polls showed Dewey with a substantial lead. On election eve, the staunchly Republican Chicago *Tribune* carried the now-famous mistaken headline: "Dewey Defeats Truman."

In fact, Truman won the closest presidential contest since 1916, collecting 24.1 million votes to Dewey's 22 million, and 303 electoral votes to Dewey's 189. Strom Thurmond captured 1.1 million votes and four southern states under the Dixiecrat banner, while Henry Wallace won no states and barely a million votes. Ironically, the three-way Democratic split appeared to help Truman by allowing him to speak out forcefully against Soviet expansion and to aggressively court African American voters in the pivotal northern

After Soviet troops blockaded the roads and rail lines leading into West Berlin in 1948, American and British pilots led a massive effort to keep the isolated city supplied from the air.
© Bettmann/UPI/Corbis

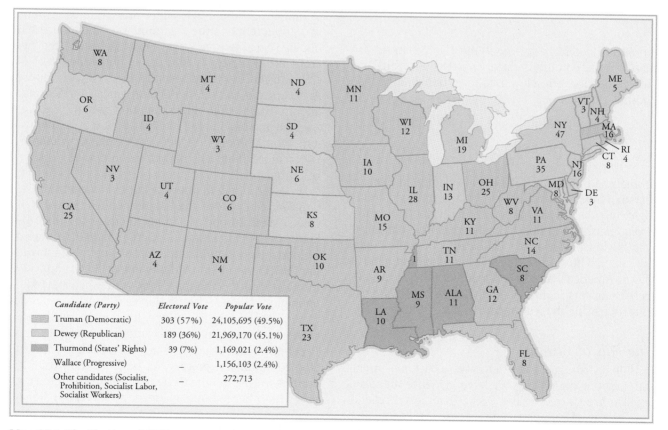

Candidate (Party)	Electoral Vote	Popular Vote
Truman (Democratic)	303 (57%)	24,105,695 (49.5%)
Dewey (Republican)	189 (36%)	21,969,170 (45.1%)
Thurmond (States' Rights)	39 (7%)	1,169,021 (2.4%)
Wallace (Progressive)	—	1,156,103 (2.4%)
Other candidates (Socialist, Prohibition, Socialist Labor, Socialist Workers)	—	272,713

Map 27.1 *The Election of 1948*

The presidential election of 1948 is considered one of the greatest upsets in American political history. Because there were four significant candidates, two running on third-party tickets, the victor, President Truman, captured a majority of the electoral votes without actually winning a majority of the popular vote.

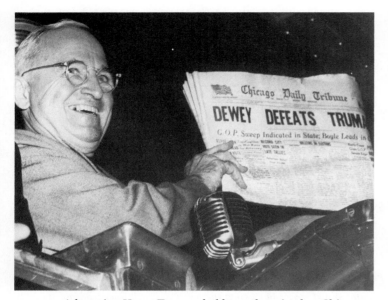

A beaming Harry Truman holds up the mistaken Chicago Daily Tribune *headline following his upset victory over Republican candidate Thomas Dewey in the 1948 presidential election.*
AP/Wide World Photos

industrial states. In the end, the people chose Truman's frank, common appeal over Dewey's stiff, evasive demeanor. The New Deal coalition had held for another election.

TROUBLE IN ASIA

Truman had little time to savor his victory. In the summer of 1949, an American spy plane returned from a flight over the Soviet Union with photographs revealing strong traces of radioactive material. The conclusion was obvious: Russia had exploded an atomic device. Combined with alarming new developments in Asia, the loss of America's atomic monopoly served to heighten global tensions in the coming months while dramatically increasing the fear of communism at home.

The Fall of China

President Truman broke the news in a one-sentence statement to the press: "We have evidence an atomic explosion occurred in the USSR." Domestic reaction was severe. Ever since Hiroshima, Americans had been taught to depend on nuclear superiority in the Cold War and to believe that Russia, a supposedly backward nation, could not possibly develop an atomic bomb before the mid-1950s, if ever. That could

mean only one thing: espionage. The Soviets, it appeared, had stolen the biggest secret of all.

The news from China was equally grim. Following World War II, Chiang Kai-shek and his Nationalist (Kuomintang) forces had renewed their offensive against the communist forces of Mao Tse-tung. Chiang counted heavily on American support. He believed that his fight against communism, his powerful friends in Congress, and his image as China's savior would force the Truman administration to back him at all costs.

Chiang was mistaken. The president and his advisors were far less interested in Asia than they were in Western Europe. They were not about to be trapped into an open-ended commitment in the Far East. From 1946 to 1949, the United States gave Chiang's government about $2 billion in military aid—enough, it was hoped, to satisfy Chiang's American friends without seriously affecting the more important buildup in Europe.

As civil war raged in China, Chiang's forces met defeat after defeat. Much of the American weaponry was discarded by fleeing Nationalist troops; it would end up in communist hands. In August 1949, the State Department issued a 1,054-page "White Paper on China," conceding that the world's largest country was about to fall to the communists. "The unfortunate but inescapable fact," said Dean Acheson, the new secretary of state, "is that the ominous result of the civil war in China was beyond [our] control." Though Acheson was correct, his White Paper sounded more like an excuse than an explanation. Americans were angered and bewildered by Chiang's demise. How well did "containment" really work, many wondered, when more than 600 million people were "lost" to communism?

Determined to prevent further communist expansion elsewhere, the United States joined with eleven West European nations to create the North Atlantic Treaty Organization (NATO) in 1949. The treaty was extremely significant; in promising to support fellow NATO members in the event of Soviet attack, it formally ended America's long tradition of avoiding entangling alliances abroad. A year later, Secretary of State Acheson and Paul Nitze, his deputy, produced a secret document known as National Security Council Paper 68, which advocated the use of military force to stop communist aggression throughout the world. According to NSC 68, the United States should act in concert with other nations wherever possible, but alone if need be. The document called for an unprecedented peacetime increase in military spending—from $13 billion to $50 billion per year—and for the construction of a huge new "thermonuclear device," the hydrogen bomb. Though Truman never showed this document to Congress, it became, in Acheson's words, "the fundamental paper" governing America's defense policy in the coming years.

War in Korea

On June 25, 1950, troops from Communist North Korea invaded anti-Communist South Korea with infantry, armor, and artillery in a massive land assault. Korea had been arbitrarily divided by Russian and American troops at the end of World War II. In 1948, an election to unify Korea had been cancelled when the Soviets refused to allow U.N. observers north of the dividing line at the 38th parallel. A stalemate thus developed, with Kim Il Sung, the pro-Communist dictator of North Korea, and Syngman Rhee, the anti-Communist dictator of South Korea, making daily threats to "liberate" each other's land.

The North Korean attack put great pressure on President Truman. His administration had treated the Rhee government with indifference, removing American combat troops from Korea in 1949 and implying that Korea itself was not vital to the free world's security. Yet here was a classic case of aggression, Truman believed. To ignore it was to encourage it elsewhere— and to turn away from NSC 68.

There were political considerations, too. If the president did nothing, he would only reinforce the Republican charge that his administration was "soft" on communism. Thus, Truman moved quickly, proposing a U.N. resolution that offered "such assistance to South Korea as may be necessary to repel armed attack." (The Russians, boycotting the Security Council to protest the U.N.'s refusal to seat Communist China, were unable to cast a paralyzing veto.) A week later, without consulting Congress, Truman dispatched ground troops to South Korea.

Public opinion seemed favorable. Letters and telegrams of support poured into the White House, and the news from the front kept improving. After two months of backward movement, U.N. troops under the command of General Douglas MacArthur took the offensive. In September 1950, MacArthur outflanked the enemy with a brilliant amphibious landing at Inchon, on South Korea's west coast. By October, U.N. troops had crossed the 38th parallel in pursuit of the routed North Korean army. As the public listened in amazement, MacArthur spoke of having his men "home before Christmas."

There were ominous signs, however. First, by sending troops into North Korea, President Truman and the United Nations had gone beyond their original mandate to defend South Korea from outside aggres-

Map 27.2 *The Korean War*

This map shows the main offensive thrusts: the North Korean attack into South Korea in June 1950; the Inchon Landing of September 15, 1950; the U.N. offensive in the fall of 1950; and the Communist Chinese counter-offensive beginning in November of 1950. The war ended in stalemate, with the final truce line almost identical to the previous division of Korea into North and South at the 38th parallel.

sion. Second, General MacArthur appeared oblivious to the possibility that Communist China might enter the war. As U.N. forces drove north, they captured scores of Chinese Communist troops near the Yalu River that divided North Korea and Manchuria. On November 5, the Chinese attacked—300,000 strong— pushing MacArthur's startled army back toward the

38th parallel. In the following weeks, American army and marine units fought their way through mountain blizzards and a wall of Chinese infantry to form a defense line just south of the 38th parallel. Although disaster had been averted, the nation was shocked by what *Time* magazine described as "the worst military setback the United States has ever suffered."

By March 1951, the Communist offensive had stalled. U.N. forces pushed ahead to the 38th parallel, where the two sides faced each other in a bloody standoff. Not surprisingly, General MacArthur called for an escalation of the war. Killing Chinese soldiers was not enough, he argued, for replacements could always be found. MacArthur recommended a naval blockade of China's coast, massive bombing of its factories and power plants, and an invasion of the Chinese mainland by the forces of Chiang Kai-shek.

This plea for an expanded war was understandable. MacArthur, like most Americans, believed in the concept of total victory. His message, quite simply, was that the lands surrendered to the Communists by weak-kneed civilians like Truman and Acheson could be recaptured through the full exercise of American military power.

The president saw things differently. Any attempt to widen the war, he realized, would alarm other U.N. participants and perhaps bring Russia into the conflict. The Soviets might send troops to the Asian front or put pressure on Western Europe. Furthermore, Russia's involvement raised the threat of nuclear attack. As General Omar Bradley noted, MacArthur's strategy was the very opposite of the one proposed by President Truman and the Joint Chiefs of Staff. "So long as we regard the Soviet Union as the main antagonist and Western Europe as the main prize," he said, "it would involve us in the wrong war, at the wrong place, at the wrong time, and with the wrong enemy."

Despite repeated warnings from the president, MacArthur refused to keep his views to himself. The final blowup came in April 1951, when Republicans in Congress released a letter that MacArthur had sent them from the battlefield that criticized Truman's refusal to meet force "with maximum counterforce," and ended with the oft-quoted phrase: "There is no substitute for victory." Furious at such insubordination, the president relieved MacArthur of his command.

MacArthur returned to the United States a genuine folk hero, a man who symbolized old military values in a world complicated by the horrors of nuclear war. Cities across the nation burned President Truman in effigy. Letters to the White House ran twenty to one against MacArthur's firing. On Capitol Hill, angry representatives placed some of the telegrams they received into the *Congressional Record*: "Impeach the Imbecile" and "We Wish to Protest the Latest Outrage by the Pig in the White House." Harry Truman's old standard—"If you can't stand the heat, stay out of the kitchen"—had never been more strenuously tested.

General Douglas MacArthur and President Harry Truman meet to discuss Korean War strategy at Wake Island shortly before Communist China entered the conflict.
© Bettmann/UPI/Corbis

MCCARTHYISM AND THE ELECTION OF 1952

On a bleak February evening in 1950, a little-known politician delivered a speech about "communist subversion" in the federal government to a Republican women's club in Wheeling, West Virginia. The topic was a common one, and large portions of the speech had been lifted word for word from a recent address by Congressman Richard Nixon. Only one explosive sentence had been added. "I have here in my hand," Senator Joseph R. McCarthy of Wisconsin told his audience, "a list of 205 Communists that were made known to the secretary of state and who are still working and shaping the policy of the State Department." The message was clear: America, the strongest nation on earth, was losing the Cold War to the evil forces of communism because the U.S. government was filled with "dupes" and "traitors" like Alger Hiss who *wanted* the communists to win.

*P*ICTURING THE PAST ✦ POLITICS & DIPLOMACY

THE BLACKLIST

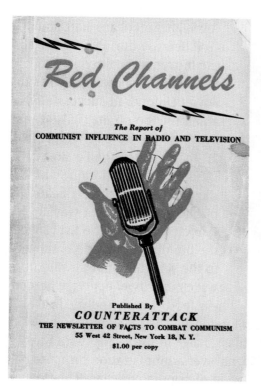

Red Channels

The Report of
COMMUNIST INFLUENCE IN RADIO AND TELEVISION

Published By
COUNTERATTACK
THE NEWSLETTER OF FACTS TO COMBAT COMMUNISM
55 West 42 Street, New York 18, N. Y.
$1.00 per copy

As the Cold War heated up in the late 1940s, a number of powerful sources in and out of government charged that Communists and their sympathizers were polluting the nation's entertainment industry—radio, television, and movies—with subversive propaganda. Fearful of an angry public reaction, industry leaders agreed to check the political backgrounds of their employees. This, in turn, led to the blacklisting of dozens of entertainers, who were denied work for allegedly supporting the Communist cause. The most influential blacklist of this era, *Red Channels* (pictured), demonstrates the "guilt by association" technique often used by Red-hunters of this era, who made accusations against people based on their connection, however fleeting, with groups deemed "communist" or "un-American." Compiled by three former FBI agents, *Red Channels* included the names of conductor Leonard Bernstein, composer Aaron Copeland, actress Lena Horne, and more than one hundred others. Much of the information was erroneous. In the late 1950s, a Texas broadcaster named John Henry Faulk exposed the sordid nature of *Red Channels* by successfully suing its publisher for libel. The final blow came in 1960, when a major Hollywood studio hired the blacklisted writer Dalton Trumbo to do the screenplay for the hit movie *Spartacus* under his own name. "The blacklist was a time of evil," Trumbo observed. "None of us—right, left, center—emerged from that long nightmare without sin."

The Rise of Joe McCarthy

Wisconsin's junior senator was an erratic politician, known for his reckless ambition and raucous behavior. He held no list in his hand that night in Wheeling. He knew nothing about communists in government or anywhere else. But the newspapers printed his charges, and the public was aroused. McCarthy had struck a nerve in the country, rubbed raw by Soviet aggression in Europe, the Communist victory in China, the Alger Hiss case, and the news of the Russian atomic bomb. As Americans searched for explanations, McCarthy provided the simplest answer of all. The real enemy was not in Moscow, he thundered, but rather in Washington, D.C.

McCarthy's charges of treason in high places made him an instant celebrity. His face adorned the covers of *Newsweek* and *Time*. The *Washington Post* cartoonist Herblock coined a new word to describe his reckless behavior: "McCarthyism." But prominent Republicans, sensing the political benefits of the "communist issue," rallied to his side. Senator Robert Taft of Ohio, known as "Mr. Republican," privately dismissed McCarthy's charges as "nonsense." Yet he told McCarthy to keep punching—"if one case doesn't work, try another."

President Truman viewed McCarthy as a shameless publicity hound who would say anything to make headlines. He was right about the senator, yet helpless

*P*ICTURING THE PAST ✦ SOCIAL & CULTURAL EVENTS

CIVIL DEFENSE IN THE ATOMIC WORLD

© Bettmann/UPI/Corbis

Though Americans had practiced civil defense during World War II, the movement gained new momentum following reports that the Soviet Union had successfully tested an atomic bomb. In 1951, at the height of the Korean War, President Truman created the Federal Civil Defense Administration, which used most of its budget to educate the public about the best ways to survive a nuclear attack. The list ranged from the building of private bomb shelters to the scheduling of air raid drills in which city dwellers were herded into designated areas—mainly basements and subway tunnels—where food, water, and medical supplies were stockpiled. The photograph here shows one of the civil defense drills, with students ducking under their desks and shielding their eyes from an atomic blast. Later in the 1950s, with the development of the more powerful hydrogen bomb, the Eisenhower administration promoted a different version of civil defense relying on the mass evacuation of populated areas. The policy, said one critic, had changed from "Duck and Cover" to "Run Like Hell." Never popular with most Americans, who viewed such measures as a futile response to the threat of nuclear annihilation, civil defense all but disappeared with the signing of the Limited Nuclear Test Ban Treaty in 1963.

to stop him. The fear of communism kept growing, aided by the outbreak of war in Korea. Air raid drills, including simulated bombings of American cities, became the order of the day. In school practice drills, students were taught to dive under their desks and shield their eyes against atomic blasts. In New York City, school officials distributed metal "dog tags." "If a bomb gets me in the street," a first-grader explained, "people will know what my name is." In Washington, a typical real estate ad read: "Small farm—out beyond the atomic blasts." Mayor Mike DiSalle of Toledo, Ohio, tried to calm worried residents by joking that he would build large neon signs directing communist pilots to Cleveland and Detroit.

McCarthy's attacks grew bolder. As the 1952 presidential campaign approached, he called George C. Marshall a traitor, mocked Dean Acheson as the "Red Dean of fashion," and described President Truman as a drunkard, adding, "the son-of-a-bitch ought to be impeached." Yet party colleagues continued to encourage McCarthy, viewing him as the man who could turn public anxiety and distrust into Republican votes.

"I Like Ike"

By 1952, Harry Truman's public approval rating had dropped to 23 percent—the lowest ever recorded by an American president. *The New Republic* called Truman "a spent force politically" and urged him to withdraw from the coming presidential campaign. In March, Truman did just that. "I shall not be a candidate for re-election," he declared.

Truman did not sulk on the sidelines, however. As the leader of his party, he wanted the Democratic nominee to defend the New Deal–Fair Deal philosophy with the same energy and enthusiasm that he himself had shown in 1948. The most impressive candidate, Governor Adlai Stevenson of Illinois, had earned a reputation as a liberal reformer. Eloquent and witty, he appealed both to party regulars and to the liberal intelligentsia, much like FDR had. Stevenson had his handicaps, including a recent divorce and a past friendship with Alger Hiss. The Democrats nominated him for president on the third convention ballot. Senator John Sparkman of Alabama, a Fair Dealer and a segregationist, was given the vice presidential nod.

The battle for the Republican presidential nomination was in many ways a battle for control of the Republican party. The moderate wing, represented by Governor Thomas Dewey of New York and Senator Henry Cabot Lodge, Jr., of Massachusetts, was committed to internationalism and to many New Deal reforms. The conservative wing, led by Senator Robert Taft of Ohio, was suspicious of the New Deal and wary of America's expanding global commitments, especially the defense and reconstruction of Europe. Beyond these views was a yearning for the past, for the pre-Depression days when government was smaller, cheaper, and less intrusive.

Senator Taft, the son of former President and Chief Justice William Howard Taft, had earned the respect of his colleagues and the plaudits of Washington reporters, who voted him "best senator" in 1949. On many domestic issues, such as public housing, Taft was more flexible than his conservative supporters. Yet he, too, feared that a powerful commitment to Western Europe could lead the United States into another world war.

Only one man stood between Taft and the Republican nomination. But he was a very powerful opponent. In 1948, the leaders of both major political parties had begged him, unsuccessfully, to enter their presidential primaries. "I don't believe a man should try to pass his historical peak," said General Dwight D. Eisenhower. "I think I pretty well hit mine when I accepted the German surrender in 1945." Yet his moderate Republican supporters, believing that Eisenhower alone could defeat Taft for the presidential nomination, convinced the general that people wanted him, the country needed him, duty called once again.

Eisenhower, sixty-one, was raised in Abilene, Kansas, a prairie town west of Topeka. He attended schools with no lights or plumbing and earned his diploma while working the night shift in a dairy. In 1911, the young man—nicknamed Ike—won an appointment to the U.S. Military Academy at West Point.

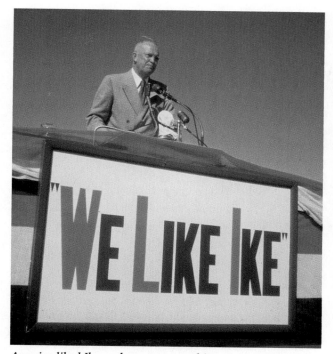

America liked Ike—who won a smashing victory at the polls in 1952, ending twenty years of Democratic party rule.
© Bettmann/Corbis

After graduating near the middle of his class, Eisenhower married Mamie Dowd, the daughter of a Denver businessman, and began his swift climb through the ranks. In the 1930s, he served as chief aide to General Douglas MacArthur, recalling: "Oh, yes, I studied dramatics under him for seven years." In 1941, he moved to the War Department and helped plan the D-Day invasion of France. His work was so outstanding that President Roosevelt named him Commanding General, European Theater of Operations—a promotion that jumped him over hundreds of officers with greater seniority.

It turned out to be one of the best decisions of World War II. Eisenhower commanded history's most successful coalition force—American, British, French, Polish, and Canadian troops—with courage, diplomacy, and skill. He was brilliant at handling people and reconciling the most diverse points of view. In the following years, Eisenhower served as Army Chief of Staff, president of Columbia University, and commander of NATO forces.

The Republican convention nominated Eisenhower on the first ballot. Most delegates did not believe he would make a better president than Taft, simply a better candidate. Eisenhower defused the bitter feelings of conservatives by selecting Richard Nixon to

Following charges that he kept a secret political slush fund, Republican vice presidential candidate Richard Nixon saved his political career in 1952 with a televised explanation that included his pet cocker spaniel Checkers.
© Bettmann/UPI/Corbis

be his running mate and by accepting a party platform that accused the Democrats of lining their pockets, shielding traitors in high places, and bungling the Korean War. As the campaign began, Republican leaders summed up their strategy with a simple formula: K1, C2—Korea, Communism, and Corruption.

On the campaign trail, General Eisenhower talked about leadership and morality, while Senator Nixon attacked from below. Traveling by train on the "Look Ahead Neighbor Special," Eisenhower visited more than 200 cities and towns. At every stop, he introduced Mamie, praised America, bemoaned the "mess in Washington," and promised to clean it up. Then the whistle sounded and the train pulled away to the chants of "I Like Ike."

On September 28, 1952, the *New York Post,* a pro-Democratic newspaper, broke the biggest story of the campaign: "Secret Rich Men's Fund Keeps Nixon in Style Far Beyond His Salary." The Nixon fund (about $18,000) had never been a secret; it had been used for routine political expenses; and it was similar to those of other politicians. Nixon responded by blaming the "Reds" for his troubles. "The communists, the left-wingers, have been fighting me with every smear," he declared. "They did it yesterday. They tried to say I had taken the money."

The campaign ground to a halt. Aboard the Eisenhower train, anxious advisors suggested that

Nixon resign from the ticket. How could the general campaign against Democratic party corruption, they wondered, when his own running mate stood accused of taking secret gifts? On September 23, Nixon went on national television to explain his side of the story. To an audience estimated at 55 million, he spoke about his boyhood, his family, his war record, his finances, and his admiration for General Eisenhower. He explained how the fund worked, asked the American people to support him, and then described the one gift he would never return. It was, said Nixon, "a little cocker spaniel dog and our little girl named it Checkers. And you know the kids love that dog and I just want to say that we're going to keep it."

The reaction was volcanic. More than 2 million phone calls and telegrams poured into Republican offices across the country. They were followed by millions of letters, running three hundred to one in Nixon's favor. Eisenhower had no choice but to keep his running mate on the ticket. The "Checkers Speech" saved Nixon's career.

It also demonstrated the emerging power of television in national affairs. In the campaign's final weeks, the Republican party ran dozens of 20-second TV spots for Eisenhower, who used the ads to soothe voter anxiety about his views on popular New Deal welfare programs. "Social security, housing, workmen's compensation, unemployment insurance—these are things that must be kept above politics and campaigns," he said. "They are rights, not issues." The general also vowed that if elected, he would visit Korea "to help serve the American people in the cause of peace."

Stevenson tried to ridicule the announcement. "If elected," he replied, "I shall go to the White House." But few Americans were amused. On November 4, Eisenhower overwhelmed Stevenson—33.9 million votes to 27.3 million, and 442 electoral votes to 89. Eisenhower became the first Republican in decades to crack the Solid South, winning four states and coming close in several others. He did well in cities, where ethnic voters, concerned about the rise of communism in Europe, deserted the Democrats in droves. Nearly 25 percent of Eisenhower's total came from men and women who had supported Harry Truman in 1948.

Some observers spoke of a new Republican era, but this was not the case. Almost everywhere, Eisenhower ran well ahead of his ticket. Although the Republicans managed to gain a slim majority in Congress, they did so by riding the general's coattails to victory.

CONCLUSION

The Roosevelt-Truman years had come to a close, yet the New Deal legacy remained largely undisturbed. The American people had voted for a new president, not a return to the days of Harding and Coolidge. Dwight Eisenhower accepted the idea that government must provide a safety net for its citizens in time of personal need and economic distress. And like Harry Truman, he intended to contain communist expansion around the globe.

After two decades marked by the Great Depression and World War II, most Americans were finally enjoying the benefits of economic security, material comfort, and stable family lives. They wanted a leader who would steer a moderate course in domestic and foreign affairs; a leader who would heal old wounds and moderate angry passions without turning back the clock; a leader who would end the present conflict in Korea without widening it or compromising the nation's honor. In 1952, Dwight D. Eisenhower seemed to be the one.

Recommended Readings

Ackerman, Marsha. *Cool Comfort* (2002). Well describes how air-conditioning changed the way middle-class Americans lived and worked in this new age of affluence.

Bennett, Michael. *When Dreams Came True* (1996). Studies the impact of the GI Bill on the making of modern America.

Boyer, Paul. *By the Bomb's Early Light* (1985). Considers the impact of atomic weaponry on American society in the early Cold War years.

Grossman, Andrew. *Neither Dead Nor Red* (2001). Focuses on the often bizarre plans of American officials to fight and survive a nuclear war.

Hamby, Alonso. *Man of the People* (1995). Examines the personal life and political career of President Harry Truman.

Jackson, Kenneth. *Crabgrass Frontier* (1985). Analyzes the suburbanization of America, especially after World War II.

Jones, James. *Alfred Kinsey: A Public/Private Life* (1997). The biography of the nation's leading sex researcher and his impact on American culture.

Spock, Dr. Benjamin. *Common Sense Book of Baby and Child Care* (1946). Had a lasting impact on child rearing and gender roles in the United States.

Tanenhaus, Sam. *Whittaker Chambers* (1997). Tells the absorbing story of the man who helped ignite the nation's anti-Communist crusade in the late 1940s.

Tygiel, Jules. *Baseball's Great Experiment* (1983). A fine account of Jackie Robinson and the integration of Major League baseball.

American Journey Online and InfoTrac College Edition

Visit the source collections at http://ajaccess.wadsworth.com and infotrac.thomsonlearning.com and use the Search function with the following key terms to explore documents, images, audio and video clips, articles, and commentary related to the material in this chapter.

Harry S. Truman	Thomas Dewey
Marshall Plan	Truman Doctrine
Jackie Robinson	Alger Hiss
Joseph McCarthy	Baby boom
HUAC	General Douglas MacArthur

Additional resources, exercises, and Internet links related to this chapter are available on the American Passages Web site: http://history.wadsworth.com/passages2e

28 THE EISENHOWER YEARS
1953–1960

A NEW DIRECTION

THE COLD WAR AT HOME AND ABROAD

THE CIVIL RIGHTS MOVEMENT

THE AGE OF TELEVISION

YOUTH CULTURE

CRISES AND CELEBRATION

A SECOND TERM

An American street scene at mid-twentieth century, with a mother and children in the new suburbia.
AP/Wide World Photos

The United States at the middle of the twentieth century was far different from the nation we live in today. The Cold War was at its height, U.S. soldiers were dying in Korea, and communism seemed a formidable foe. The American population of 153 million contained a small and declining number of foreign born, the result of strict immigration quotas installed in the 1920s. Most blacks still lived in the South, where racial segregation was the law. Blue-collar workers outnumbered white-collar workers, and labor unions, led by charismatic figures like John L. Lewis and Walter Reuther, were at the height of their power. Major League baseball had only sixteen teams, none west of St. Louis. There were no supermarkets or shopping malls, no motel chains or ballpoint pens. Television was just beginning, rock music still a few years away. More than half of the nation's farm dwellings had no electricity. It cost three cents to mail a letter and a nickel to buy a coke.

Marriage rates were at an all-time high, while divorce rates kept declining. In 1954, *McCall's* magazine used the term "togetherness" to describe American family life, with shared activities such as Little League, car rides, and backyard barbecues. Though more women worked outside the home in 1950 than in 1944, the height of World War II, they did so mainly to supplement the family income, not to seek full-time careers. In the growing cult of motherhood, fulfillment meant meeting the needs of others. Feminism was described in psychology books as a "deep illness," entirely out of place.

America at mid-twentieth century saw an acceleration of postwar trends. As 40 million people moved to the suburbs, the large cities declined in population, political power, and quality of life. Racial lines remained rigid, with census data showing the suburbs to be more affluent than the cities they surrounded—and 98 percent white. Automobile sales skyrocketed, creating whole new industries to service the American traveler. Inventions poured forth, from the computer to the prevention of polio. And a new president was elected to guide the country through these anxious, demanding times.

A NEW DIRECTION

Dwight Eisenhower entered the White House in 1953 on a wave of good feeling. His lack of political experience appeared to be an asset after the turmoil of the Truman years. Americans trusted Eisenhower's judgment and admired his character. They believed that his enormous skills as a military leader would serve him equally well as president of the United States.

Modern Republicanism

Yet few Americans knew where Eisenhower stood on important domestic or international issues. His presidential campaign in 1952 had been intentionally vague. On the political spectrum, he stood somewhere between the Fair Deal Democrats of Harry Truman and the conservative Republicans of Robert Taft. The new president described himself as a moderate, using the term "modern Republicanism" to define his political approach.

Eisenhower filled his cabinet with prominent business leaders. For secretary of defense, he chose Charles E. ("Engine Charlie") Wilson, former president of General Motors, who proclaimed at his confirmation hearing that "what was good for our country was good for General Motors, and vice versa." For secretary of the treasury, Eisenhower selected George Humphrey, a fiscal conservative. "We have to cut one-third out of the budget and you can't do that just by eliminating waste," Humphrey declared. "This means, whenever necessary, using a meat axe."

Eisenhower avoided such rhetoric. He had no intention of dismantling popular New Deal programs such as Social Security or unemployment insurance,

**Urban, Suburban, and Rural Americans
1940–1960**

■ Central-city dwellers

■ Suburban dwellers

■ Rural and small-town dwellers

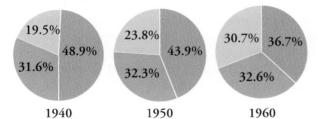

1940   1950   1960

Chart 28.1 *Urban, Suburban, and Rural Americans 1940–1960*
These charts point to a number of important changes. First is the steady loss of population in small-town America. Second is the stagnation of the inner cities, reflecting both a loss of population in the older northern and midwestern cities and a growth in the sunbelt cities of the South and West. Third is the surge of population in the suburbs, which continues to this day.

CHRONOLOGY

1953 Truce ends fighting in Korea • Soviet dictator Joseph Stalin dies

1954 Supreme Court issues school desegregation ruling in *Brown v. Board of Education* • U.S. Senate censures Joseph McCarthy

1955 Bus boycott begins in Montgomery, Alabama • Elvis Presley signs with RCA Records • Brooklyn Dodgers finally win World Series

1956 Federal Highway Act passed, forging massive interstate highway system • Hungarian Revolution and Suez crisis strain U.S.–Soviet relations • Eisenhower easily reelected

1957 Russians launch *Sputnik* • Federal troops sent to enforce school integration order in Little Rock

1958 U.S. manned space program begins

1959 Fidel Castro leads successful revolution in Cuba • Soviet Premier Nikita Khrushchev visits United States

1960 American U-2 spy plane shot down over Soviet Union • John F. Kennedy elected president

and he supported a significant hike in the minimum hourly wage, from seventy-five cents to a dollar. Yet wherever possible, he worked to balance the budget, trim government expenditures, and stimulate private enterprise. "I'm conservative when it comes to money," Eisenhower claimed, but "liberal when it comes to human beings."

In his first year as president, federal spending and federal income taxes were both cut by 10 percent. Eisenhower also opposed expansion of such popular but expensive federal programs as price supports for farmers and cheap public power from government dams and electric plants. In perhaps his most controversial early move, the president strongly supported passage of the Tidelands Oil Act, which transferred coastal oil land worth at least $40 billion from the federal government to the states. Critics, fearing the exploitation of these vital reserves by a few giant corporations, described "Tidelands" as the "most unjustified giveaway program" of the modern era.

A Truce in Korea

One member of Eisenhower's cabinet, Secretary of State John Foster Dulles, stood above the rest. The son of a minister and grandson of a former secretary of state, Dulles trained from his earliest days to serve God and country. Most observers found him arrogant, stubborn, and sour. Yet Eisenhower respected his secretary as a tough, knowledgeable advisor who willingly took the heat for actions the president himself had formulated. "I know what they say about Foster—dull, duller, Dulles—and all that," Eisenhower told a friend. "But the [critics] love to hit him rather than me."

The president's first priority in foreign affairs was to end the Korean conflict. Though willing to accept the same terms that Truman had proposed—two Koreas, North and South, divided at the 38th parallel—Eisenhower demanded a prompt resolution. To speed this process, Dulles apparently warned the Communist Chinese (through diplomatic channels in India) that the United States would not rule out the use of atomic weapons if the Korean stalemate dragged on.

The impact of this "nuclear threat" is difficult to gauge. The Chinese Communists probably viewed Eisenhower, a military leader, as a more dangerous foe than Harry Truman. Yet huge Communist battlefield losses, coupled with the sudden death of Joseph Stalin, helped spur the peace process. In July 1953, a truce was signed that stopped the fighting without formally ending the war. More than 50,000 Americans were killed and 103,000 were wounded in Korea. The Pentagon estimated that 2.4 million civilians died or were seriously injured in the three years of terrible fighting, along with 850,000 troops from South Korea, 520,000 from North Korea, and 950,000 from Communist China.

THE COLD WAR AT HOME AND ABROAD

When Republicans took control of Congress and the White House in 1953, the "communist issue" gained center stage. On Capitol Hill, 185 of the 221 House Republicans applied for duty on the House Un-American

*P*ICTURING THE PAST ✦ POLITICS & DIPLOMACY

SEARCHING FOR "REDS" IN GOVERNMENT

Culver Pictures

The search for communists in government became one of the key political issues of the early Cold War era. This cartoon gives the impression that communists were rampant in the federal bureaucracy in the 1950s and that Uncle Sam was adept at the tough but vital job of weeding them out. Was this perception correct? Recent evidence—gleaned from newly opened Soviet security archives and a supersecret American code-breaking project known as Venona—suggests that communist espionage in government was, indeed, a serious problem during the late 1930s and World War II and that among those Americans who spied for the Soviet Union was Alger Hiss (pages 751–752). The new evidence, however, does not support the sensational charges of Senator Joseph R. McCarthy and others that hundreds of communists were still at work in the federal government in the 1950s. Indeed, it appears that such penetration declined dramatically after World War II, due, in large part, to the defections of key communist espionage agents in the United States. In 1953—the time of this cartoon—the Eisenhower administration announced that 1,456 federal employees had been fired under the Federal Loyalty Program. It turned out, however, that the vast majority were released for offenses such as alcoholism, malingering, and "sexual misconduct." Almost none was dismissed for reasons pertaining to disloyalty.

Activities Committee, where Chairman Harold Velde of Illinois vowed to hunt down communists like "rats." At the White House, President Eisenhower promised both a crackdown on "subversives" in government and a "New Look" in military affairs, designed to streamline American forces for the continuing struggle against "worldwide communist aggression."

The Hunt for "Subversives"

Shortly after taking office, President Eisenhower issued an executive order that extended the scope of the Federal Loyalty Security Program. A few months later,

he announced that 1,456 federal workers had been fired as "security risks," including "alcoholics," "homosexuals," and "political subversives." The most controversial security case involved J. Robert Oppenheimer, the distinguished physicist who directed the Manhattan Project during World War II. Oppenheimer's prewar association with left-wing radicals was widely known. He had been checked and rechecked by the FBI, cleared and recleared by the Atomic Energy Commission until 1953, when the Eisenhower administration suspended his top security clearance. Many believed that Oppenheimer's troubles resulted from his public opposition to the building of

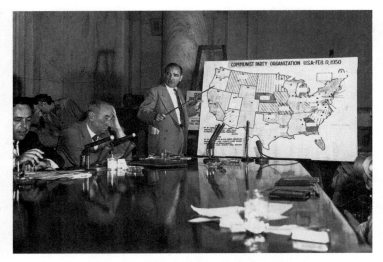

Senator Joe McCarthy, America's premier Red-hunter, lectured army counsel Joseph Welch (hand on head) about the Communist party during the celebrated Army-McCarthy hearings in 1954.
© Bettmann/UPI/Corbis

the hydrogen bomb—a charge the administration vigorously denied.

In Congress, the Red-hunting fervor was even more intense. The Senate assault was led by Joseph McCarthy, newly appointed chairman of the Committee on Government Operations and its powerful Subcommittee on Investigations. Filling key staff positions with ex-FBI agents and former prosecutors like Roy M. Cohn, an abrasive young attorney from New York, McCarthy looked for "communist influence" in the State Department and other government agencies. His hearings didn't uncover any communists. They did, however, ruin numerous careers, undermine worker morale, and make the United States look fearful in the eyes of the world. Not surprisingly, Republican criticism of McCarthy began to build. After all, he was now attacking a federal bureaucracy controlled by his own party.

Many expected Eisenhower to put the senator in his place. But the new president was slow to respond, believing that a brawl with McCarthy would divide Republicans into warring camps and seriously demean the presidential office. Time and again, he told his aides: "I just will not—I *refuse* to get into the gutter with that guy."

Eisenhower changed his mind after McCarthy's subcommittee, spearheaded by Roy Cohn, began to investigate charges that a "communist spy ring" was operating at Fort Monmouth, New Jersey, home of the Army Signal Corps. Army officials responded that Cohn was harassing the service in order to win prefer-

ential treatment for a close friend and part-time McCarthy staffer named G. David Schine, who had recently been drafted into the army. Early in 1954, the Senate agreed to investigate these conflicting allegations. Furious at the attacks upon his beloved army, Eisenhower convinced Republican Senate leaders to televise the hearings. The president wanted the American people to see McCarthy in action, and it proved to be a very shrewd move. For thirty-six days, the nation watched the senator's frightening outbursts and crude personal attacks. The highlight of the hearings came on June 9, 1954, when army counsel Joseph Welch sternly rebuked McCarthy for his menacing behavior, asking: "Have you no sense of decency, sir? Have you left *no sense of decency?*" The spectators burst into applause.

A few months later, the Senate censured McCarthy for bringing that body "into dishonor and disrepute." The vote was sixty-seven to twenty-two, with only conservative Republicans opposed. Many believed that McCarthy's censure was linked to the easing of Cold War tensions at home. The Korean War was over, Stalin was dead, and the radical right was in disarray. For McCarthy, things came apart at a wicked rate of speed. Reporters and colleagues ignored him, and his influence disappeared. Unable to get his message across, McCarthy spent his final days drinking in private and railing against those who had deserted his cause. He died of acute alcoholism in 1957, virtually alone, at the age of forty-eight.

Brinksmanship and Covert Action

Like Truman before him, President Eisenhower supported the containment of communism through military, economic, and diplomatic means. What most worried him were the spiraling costs. "If we let defense spending run wild," he said, "we get inflation . . . then controls . . . then a garrison state . . . and *then* we've lost the very values we were trying to defend." Eisenhower called his solution the "New Look." It was fruitless to match the communists "man for man, gun for gun," he reasoned. The Korean stalemate showed the folly of that approach. In place of conventional forces, the United States must emphasize "the deterrent of massive retaliatory power." This meant using America's edge in nuclear weapons and long-range bombers to best advantage.

The "New Look" allowed Eisenhower to cut defense spending by 20 percent between 1953 and 1955. The number of men and women in uniform went down each year, while the production of atomic warheads dramatically increased. Secretary of State Dulles viewed the "New Look" as a way to intimidate potential enemies with the implied threat of atomic attack. He called this "brinksmanship," claiming that "the ability to get to the verge without getting into the war is the necessary art."

Critics, however, saw brinksmanship as a dangerous game. Intimidation meant little, they warned, if the United States did not intend to back up its words. Was Eisenhower willing to consider atomic weapons as a viable option in every international crisis? If not, he undermined America's credibility; if so, he risked nuclear destruction. To increase his flexibility in foreign affairs, the president needed other options as well.

In 1953, Eisenhower appointed Allen Dulles, younger brother of the secretary of state, to head the Central Intelligence Agency (CIA). Dulles emphasized "covert action" over intelligence gathering—a change the president fully endorsed. Most of the CIA's new work was cloaked in secrecy, and much of it was illegal. Covert action became one of Eisenhower's favorite foreign policy tools.

Iran was a case in point. In 1953, the new government of Mohammed Mossadegh nationalized the British-controlled oil fields and deposed the pro-Western Shah of Iran. The United States, believing Mossadegh's government to be pro-communist, feared for its oil supplies in the Middle East. President Eisenhower thus approved a CIA operation that toppled Mossadegh and returned the young Shah to power. A few months later, Iran agreed to split its oil production among three Western nations, with American companies getting 40 percent, British companies 40 percent, and Dutch companies 20 percent. The grateful Shah told the CIA: "I owe my throne to God, my people, my army, and to you."

In 1954, the CIA struck again, forcing the overthrow of Guatemala's democratically elected president, Jacobo Arbenz. Guatemala was one of the world's poorest nations. Its largest employer and landholder, the American-owned United Fruit Company, controlled much of the Guatemalan economy. After taking office, Arbenz supported a strike of banana workers on United Fruit plantations, who were seeking wages of $1.50 a day. Far more provocative, however, was a new law, known as Decree 900, which expropriated millions of acres of private property for the use of landless peasant families. Under this law, the Arbenz government offered United Fruit $1.2 million for 234,000 acres of its land—a figure based on the absurdly low tax assessments given United Fruit in the past.

The company had powerful allies in the United States. Numerous government officials, including both Dulles brothers, were linked to United Fruit through their previous corporate positions. Defending the company's interests came naturally to them, while the idea of expropriating American property smacked of "communist thinking." If Arbenz succeeded, the notion could spread across Latin America like wildfire.

Eisenhower moved quickly, authorizing the overthrow of Arbenz by Guatemalan exiles trained at CIA bases in Honduras and Nicaragua. The small invasion force, backed by CIA pilots, tore through Arbenz's poorly equipped army. The American press, meanwhile, accepted the Eisenhower–Dulles account that Guatemalan liberators had ousted a dangerous, pro-communist regime with minimal American help. In the following months, the new government of General Carlos Castillo Armas established a military dictatorship, executed hundreds of Arbenz supporters, and returned the expropriated lands to United Fruit.

Events in Indochina (or Vietnam) did not turn out as well. Following World War II, nationalist forces in that French colony, led by Ho Chi Minh, a popular Marxist leader, began an armed struggle for independence. The United States, viewing Ho (incorrectly) as a puppet of Moscow, supported French attempts to crush the Vietnamese resistance, known as the Vietminh. By 1953, American military aid to France in the Indochina conflict totaled nearly $3 billion.

It failed to turn the tide. The Vietminh grew stronger. In 1954, Ho's forces surrounded 12,000 elite French troops at an isolated garrison called Dien Bien Phu. Facing sure defeat, the French appealed to the United States for help. When Secretary of State Dulles, Vice President Nixon, and several U.S. military officials suggested tactical nuclear weapons, Eisenhower was appalled. "You boys must be crazy," he said. "We can't use those awful things against Asians for the second time in ten years. My God!"

Eisenhower also refused to send American ground troops to Indochina. And he rejected the use of conventional air strikes to save Dien Bien Phu unless the British took part—but Churchill sternly said no. On May 7, 1954, the battered garrison surrendered, effectively ending French rule in Vietnam.

At peace talks in Geneva, Switzerland, the two sides agreed to a cease-fire and a temporary partition of Vietnam at the 17th parallel, with French troops moving south of that line and Vietminh forces moving north. Free elections were scheduled for 1956, at which time the French were to fully withdraw. The United States refused to recognize the Geneva Accords. Eisenhower and Dulles were not about to acquiesce in a unified Vietnam under the leadership of Ho Chi Minh, the certain winner in the proposed election of 1956. The U.S. plan, therefore, was to prevent that election, while creating a permanent anti-communist government in South Vietnam supported by American economic and military aid.

To Eisenhower, the survival of South Vietnam became the key to containing communism in Asia. He described the so-called "domino theory" at a press conference about Indochina in 1954. "You have a row of dominoes set up," he began. "You knock over the first one, and what will happen to the last one is a certainty that it will go over quickly. So the possible consequences of the loss [of Vietnam] are just incalculable to the free world."

THE CIVIL RIGHTS MOVEMENT

The 1950s witnessed enormous gains in the struggle for minority rights. In federal courts and in cities throughout the South, African Americans struggled to eradicate the system of racial segregation that denied them dignity, opportunity, and equal protection under the law. Though the Eisenhower administration proved far less sympathetic to the cause of civil rights than the Truman administration had been, the movement for racial justice took on a power and a spirit that would transform the nation in the coming years.

Attorneys representing the NAACP's Legal Defense Fund, led by Thurgood Marshall (center) celebrate Brown v. Board of Education *on the steps of the Supreme Court, May 17, 1954.*
© Bettmann/UPI/Corbis

Brown v. Board of Education

In September 1953, Chief Justice Fred Vinson died of a heart attack, requiring President Eisenhower to make his first appointment to the U.S. Supreme Court. Eisenhower offered the position to California Governor Earl Warren, who won prompt Senate approval. Warren had been the Republican party's vice presidential nominee in 1948. Far more liberal than Eisenhower on social issues, he would sometimes anger the president in the coming years, but rarely lose his respect.

The major issue facing the Supreme Court in 1953 was civil rights. For more than a decade, a group of talented African American attorneys had been filing legal challenges to segregated public facilities in the South, hoping to erode the "separate but equal" doctrine of *Plessy v. Ferguson.* Led by Thurgood Marshall and William Hastie of the NAACP's Legal Defense Fund, these attorneys targeted specific areas, such as professional education (law, medicine, teaching), to establish precedents for the larger fight.

This strategy worked well. In 1950, the Supreme Court stretched the *Plessy* doctrine to its limits in two lawsuits brought by the NAACP. In *Sweatt v. Painter,* the Court ruled that Texas authorities must admit a black applicant to the all-white state law school in Austin because they had failed to provide African Americans with a comparable facility, thereby violating the equal protection clause of the Fourteenth Amendment. And in *McLaurin v. Oklahoma,* the Court struck down a scheme that segregated a black student *within* that state's graduate school of education, forcing him to sit alone in the library and the lecture halls in a section marked "Reserved for Coloreds." "State-imposed restrictions which produce such inequalities," the Court noted, "cannot be sustained."

With these victories, the NAACP took on the larger challenge of racial segregation in the nation's public schools. Unlike *Sweatt* and *McLaurin,* which involved a small number of adult students, the new cases touched millions of children, white and black, in twenty-one states and the District of Columbia. By 1953, five separate lawsuits had reached the Supreme Court, including *Brown v. Board of Education of Topeka.*

The case involved a Kansas law that permitted cities to segregate their public schools. With NAACP support, the Reverend Oliver Brown sued the Topeka

Chief Justice Earl Warren
Opinion of the Court in Brown v. Board of Education *May 17, 1954*

Ruling that racial segregation of the nation's public schools violated the due process clause of the Fourteenth Amendment, a unanimous Supreme Court, led by Chief Justice Earl Warren, overturned the "separate but equal" doctrine set down fifty-eight years earlier in *Plessy v. Ferguson.*

These cases come to us from the States of Kansas, South Carolina, Virginia, and Delaware. . . .

In each of the cases, minors of the Negro race, through their legal representatives, seek the aid of the courts in obtaining admission to the public schools of their community on a nonsegregated basis. In each instance, they had been denied admission to schools attended by white children under laws requiring or permitting segregation according to race. . . .

Today, education is perhaps the most important function of state and local governments. Compulsory school attendance laws and the great expenditures for education both demonstrate our recognition of the importance of education to our democratic society. It is required in the performance of our most basic public responsibilities, even service in the armed forces. It is the very foundation of good citizenship. Today it is a principal instrument in awakening the child to cultural values, in preparing him for later professional training, and in helping him to adjust normally to his environment. In these days, it is doubtful that any child may reasonably be expected to succeed in life if he is denied the opportunity of an education. Such an opportunity, where the state has undertaken to provide it, is a right which must be made available to all on equal terms.

We come then to the question presented: Does segregation of children in public schools solely on the basis of race, even though the physical facilities and other "tangible" factors may be equal, deprive the children of the minority group of equal educational opportunities? We believe that it does. . . .

To separate them from others of similar age and qualifications solely because of their race generates a feeling of inferiority as to their status in the community that may affect their hearts and minds in a way unlikely ever to be undone. . . . Whatever may have been the extent of psychological knowledge at the time of *Plessy v. Ferguson,* this finding is amply supported by modern authority. Any language in *Plessy v. Ferguson* contrary to this finding is rejected.

We conclude that in the field of public education the doctrine of "separate but equal" has no place. Separate educational facilities are inherently unequal. Therefore, we hold that the plaintiffs and others similarly situated for whom the actions have been brought are, by reason of the segregation complained of, deprived of the equal protection of the laws guaranteed by the Fourteenth Amendment. This disposition makes unnecessary any discussion whether such segregation also violates the Due Process Clause of the Fourteenth Amendment. . . .

Source: *Brown v. Board of Education,* 349 U.S. 294, 1954.

school board, arguing that his eight-year-old daughter should not be forced to attend a Negro school a mile from her home when there was a white public school only three blocks away. The Supreme Court was badly divided. Several justices supported the *Plessy* doctrine, while others argued that it fostered racial inequality. Believing racial segregation to be both unconstitutional and morally wrong, Chief Jus-

tice Warren insisted that the Supreme Court speak in a powerful, united voice against this evil. Anything less, he reasoned, would encourage massive resistance in the South.

On May 17, 1954, the Supreme Court overturned *Plessy v. Ferguson* in a stunning 9–0 decision, written by Warren himself. Relying on the studies of social scientists such as Kenneth Clark, the chief justice claimed that racial segregation had a "detrimental effect" on black children by making them feel inferior to whites. "In the field of public education the doctrine of 'separate but equal' has no place," he stated. "Separate educational facilities are inherently unequal."

The Supreme Court put off its implementation guidelines (known as *Brown II*) for a full year, hoping to let passions cool in the South. *Brown II* required local school boards to draw up desegregation plans with the approval of a federal district judge. But there were no timetables, and the wording was intentionally vague. Integration should proceed, it said, "with all deliberate speed."

White southern reaction was intense. "You are not required to obey any court which passes out such a ruling," Senator James O. Eastland of Mississippi told his constituents. "In fact, you are obligated to defy it." Violence flared across the South. "In one school district after another," wrote an observer, "segregationists staged the same drama: forcing young blacks to enter a school by passing rock-throwing white mobs and white pickets shouting 'Nigger,' 'Nigger,' 'Nigger.' " The Ku Klux Klan came alive in the 1950s, and new groups like the White Citizens' Council were formed to defend segregation and the "Southern way of life." In the summer of 1955, a black Chicago teenager named Emmett Till, visiting relatives in Mississippi, was murdered for allegedly flirting with a white woman at a country store. Two suspects—the woman's husband and his half-brother—were acquitted by an all-white jury in just over an hour. "If we hadn't stopped to drink pop," a juror noted, "it wouldn't have taken so long."

Many Americans looked to the White House for guidance about civil rights. But Eisenhower had little to say about the issue, partly because he personally opposed the "forced integration" of the races. When asked at a press conference if he had any advice for the South on how to handle the *Brown* decision, Eisenhower replied: "Not in the slightest. The Supreme Court has spoken and I am sworn to uphold the constitutional processes in this country; and I will obey."

The Montgomery Bus Boycott

The battle over public school integration was but one of many such struggles in the South during this era. Some were fought by attorneys in federal courtrooms; others involved ordinary men and women determined to challenge the indignities of racial segregation and second-class treatment in their daily lives. "Nothing is quite as humiliating, so murderously angering," said one African American, "as to know that because you

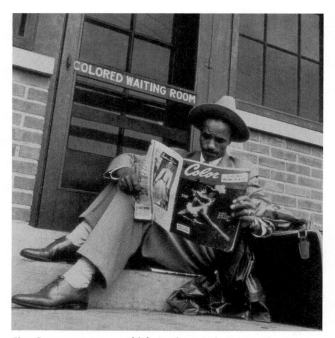

Jim Crow was a way of life in the South, where theaters, restaurants, trains, buses, blood banks, hospitals, drinking fountains, waiting rooms, and cemeteries were all segregated by law.
© Bern Keating/Black Star

are black you may have to walk a half mile farther than whites to urinate; that because you are black you have to receive your food through a window in the back of a restaurant or sit in a garbage-littered yard."

The black people of Montgomery, Alabama, had experienced such treatment for years. Known as "the cradle of the Confederacy," Montgomery enforced segregation and racial etiquette in meticulous detail. Blacks always tipped their hats to whites, always stood in the presence of whites unless told to sit, and always addressed whites with a title of respect. ("Boss," "Sir," and "Ma'am" were most common.) Restrooms, drinking fountains, blood banks, movie theaters, cemeteries—all were separated by race. It was illegal for whites and blacks to play checkers together on public property or to share a taxi cab. On the local buses, blacks paid their fares in the front, got off the vehicle, and entered the "colored section" through the rear door. They also had to relinquish their seats to white passengers when the front section filled up.

On December 1, 1955, a simple yet revolutionary act of resistance occurred on a crowded Montgomery bus. Rosa Parks, a forty-two-year-old black seamstress, and member of the local NAACP, refused to give up her seat to a white. The bus driver called the police. "They got on the bus," Parks recalled, "and one of them asked me why I didn't stand up. I asked him, 'Why do you push us around?' He said, '. . . I don't know, but the law is the law and you're under arrest.' "

News of Parks's defiance electrified the black community. Within days a boycott of Montgomery's bus system was begun, organized by local clergymen and the Women's Political Council, the black alternative to the all-white League of Women Voters. Calling themselves the Montgomery Improvement Association (MIA), they chose a young minister named Martin Luther King, Jr., to lead the struggle for open seating in public transportation, a small but highly symbolic step.

King, twenty-six, was a newcomer to Montgomery. He was selected, in part, because his youth and vocation made him less vulnerable to economic and political pressure from whites. The son of a well-known Atlanta pastor, King earned his college degree at Morehouse and his doctorate at Boston University's School of Theology before heading south with his new wife, Coretta Scott King, to serve as pastor of Montgomery's Dexter Avenue Baptist Church in 1954. Dr. King was familiar with the works of Gandhi and Thoreau. He viewed mass action and nonviolent resistance as essential weapons in the war against racial injustice.

King rallied the black community with the eloquent passion of his words. "There comes a time when people get tired," he told a packed rally after Rosa Parks's arrest. "We are here this evening to say to those who have mistreated us so long that we are tired—tired of being segregated and humiliated, tired of being kicked about by the brutal feet of oppression. We have no alternative but to protest."

King's reputation soared. He kept the movement together, despite police harassment and the firebombing of his home. Blacks in Montgomery formed car pools to get people to their destinations. The churches raised money for fuel, while black-owned garages did repair work free of charge. Many people rode bicycles or simply walked for miles. The boycott nearly bankrupted the city bus system and badly hurt the white merchants downtown. Mother Pollard, bent with age, inspired the movement with her simple remark: "My feets is tired, but my soul is rested."

In November 1956, the federal courts struck down the Alabama law requiring racial segregation in public transportation. A month later, blacks sat in the front of the Montgomery buses without incident. The boycott, lasting 381 days, demonstrated both the power of collective action and the possibility of social change. In 1957, Dr. King joined with other black ministers to form the Southern Christian Leadership Con-

Rosa Parks rides a nearly empty but integrated Montgomery bus following the successful boycott she triggered in 1955.
© Bettmann/UPI/Corbis

ference (SCLC), an organization devoted to racial justice through peaceful means. "Noncooperation with evil," King declared, "is as much a moral obligation as is cooperation with good."

THE AGE OF TELEVISION

In the 1950s, social commentators analyzed a host of new issues in American life. Some worried about the struggle between individuals and organizations, the apparent quest for security over adventure, the monotony of modern work. A few focused on the supposed emptiness of suburban living, the growing cult of domesticity among women, the changing standards of success. Yet what struck virtually all critics and commentators in the 1950s was the impact of television upon American life—an impact that altered politics, news gathering, consumer tastes, and popular culture in truly revolutionary ways.

The Magic Box

When World War II ended, there were 17,000 TV sets in the United States. The late 1940s saw major changes in television technology, such as the use of coaxial cable and the introduction of color. In 1949,

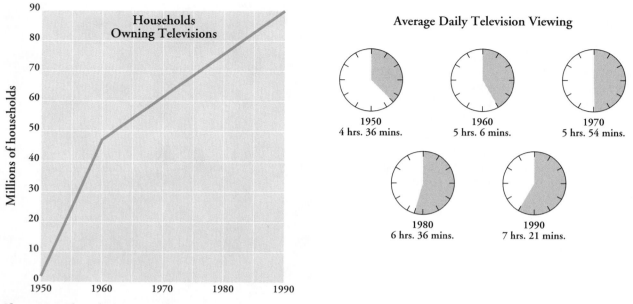

Chart 28.2 *The Television Revolution 1950–1990*

As television became commonplace in the 1950s, TV viewing altered the nature of American politics and culture. Average daily television viewing has increased in each decade, with Americans now spending almost half their waking hours with their sets turned on.

Source: Statistical Abstracts of the United States.

a TV set appeared for the first time in the Sears, Roebuck catalogue—$149.95 "with indoor antenna." A year later, Americans were buying 20,000 television sets a day. The two most popular shows of that era were Milton Berle's *Texaco Star Theater* and Ed Sullivan's *Toast of the Town*. Berle, a physical comedian, seemed perfect for a visual medium like TV. His fast-paced humor relied on sight gags instead of verbal banter. The press called him "Mr. Television."

Sullivan, a former gossip columnist, was awkward and unsmiling on camera. What made him unique was his ability to provide fresh entertainment to Americans of all tastes and ages. Sullivan's Sunday night variety show, mixing opera with acrobats, ran for twenty-three years on CBS. His guests included Elvis Presley, Dean Martin and Jerry Lewis, pianist Van Cliburn, dancer Rudolf Nureyev, singer Lena Horne, and the Beatles. "Ed Sullivan will last," said pianist Oscar Levant, "as long as other people have talent."

Television's potential was impossible to ignore. In 1951, an obscure Tennessee politician named Estes Kefauver became a national figure by holding televised hearings into organized crime. Senator Kefauver grilled prominent mobsters like New York's Frank Costello as 25 million viewers watched in amazement. The TV cameras perfectly captured Costello's discomfort by focusing for several minutes on his jittery, sweat-soaked hands.

Nixon's "Checkers speech" and the Army-McCarthy hearings further highlighted the impact of television in the political arena. Above all, however, TV possessed the power to sell. In 1950, local stations, desperate for programming, aired a series of old "Hopalong Cassidy" movies starring an obscure cowboy-actor named William Boyd. Within months, "Hopalong Cassidy" clothing and six-guns were in frantic demand, grossing $30 million before the craze died out. Walt Disney struck gold with his three-part series on Davy Crockett, which aired nationally in 1954. Millions of children wore coonskin caps to school. There were Davy Crockett shirts and blankets, toothbrushes and lunch boxes. One department store chain sold 20,000 surplus pup tents in less than a week by printing "Davy Crockett" on the flap.

By 1954, three national networks were firmly in place. As the major radio powers, ABC, CBS, and NBC held a decided advantage over potential competitors in technology and talent. Indeed, these networks filled their early airtime by moving popular radio programs like *Jack Benny, Burns & Allen,* and *Amos 'n' Andy* over to TV. The faster television grew, the more its schedule expanded. Important advertisers signed on, sponsoring entire programs such as *Kraft Television Theater* and *Motorola Playhouse.* This, in turn, provided work for hundreds of performers at a time when the motion picture industry was losing ground to television. New York City, the early center of TV production, became a magnet for young actors and writers like Paul Newman, Sidney Poitier, Joanne Woodward, Rod Serling, Neil Simon, and Mel Brooks.

Some critics called this era the "golden age" of television. They pointed to the high quality of plays and dramas, the original comedy of Sid Caesar and Jackie Gleason, and the powerful documentaries of Edward R. Murrow on *See It Now.* Yet by 1955, this "golden age" was largely over. The networks abandoned most live broadcasts in favor of filmed episodes, with Hollywood quickly replacing Manhattan as television's capital. Popular new shows like *Dragnet* and *I Love Lucy* showed the advantages of film over live TV. Production was less demanding. Errors could be corrected, scenes could be shot at different locations, and episodes could be shown more than once, creating additional revenues.

Many television shows of the 1950s reflected both the yearnings and stereotypes of American society. Popular comedies such as *Father Knows Best, Ozzie and Harriet,* and *Leave It to Beaver* portrayed the charmed lives (and minor problems) of middle-class white families in the suburbs. Mother was a housewife. Dad held a pressure-free white-collar job. The kids were well-adjusted and witty. Money was never a problem. No one stayed angry for long. "You know, Mom," said Beaver Cleaver, "when we're in a mess, you kind of make things seem not so messy." "Well," June Cleaver replied, "isn't that sort of what mothers are for?"

Married women in TV "sit-coms" did not work outside the home. Their husbands would not permit it. This rule even applied to childless couples like Ralph and Alice Kramden of *The Honeymooners,* one of television's rare programs about urban, working-class people. Furthermore, single women in sit-coms rarely took their jobs seriously. Like Eve Arden in *Our Miss Brooks* and Ann Sothern in *Private Secretary,* they spent most of their time hunting for a husband.

Though racial minorities almost never appeared in these sit-coms, they did play major—if stereotypical—roles in two or three popular shows of the 1950s. There was "Beulah," the big-hearted domestic in a white suburban household, and "Rochester," the wisecracking butler on the *Jack Benny Show.* Above all, there was *Amos 'n' Andy,* an adaptation of the popular radio show created by two white men, Freeman Gosden and Charles Correll, that featured an all-black cast. The NAACP angrily denounced *Amos 'n' Andy* for portraying blacks as "clowns" and "crooks," but others praised the performers for transforming racist stereotypes into "authentic black humor."

The Quiz Show Scandals

No event raised more concerns about the control and direction of commercial television in the 1950s than the quiz show scandals. Quiz shows were a throwback to the radio era; they appeared early on television but did not generate much interest until Revlon cosmetics produced a "big money" version called *The $64,000 Question,* which aired on CBS in June 1955.

The rules were simple. After choosing a topic such as science or baseball, the contestant fielded questions that began at $64 and doubled with each correct answer. At the $16,000 plateau, the contestant entered a glass "isolation booth." The tension was enormous, since a wrong answer wiped out all previous winnings. The show drew the highest ratings in TV history—a whopping 85 percent audience share—when contestants went for the $64,000 question.

Contestants Charles Van Doren and Vivian Nearing battle it out on the rigged quiz show Twenty-One.
© Bettmann/UPI/Corbis

Revlon products literally flew off the shelves. Annual sales rose from $34 million to $86 million, while Revlon stock jumped from twelve to twenty.

Before long, the airwaves were flooded with imitations. In 1956, *The $64,000 Question* lost its top rating to NBC's *Twenty-One*, which pitted two competitors in a trivia contest structured like the blackjack card game. The stakes grew ever larger. Charles Van Doren, a handsome English instructor at Columbia University, won $129,000 on *Twenty-One* and became an instant national hero.

His good fortune did not last long. A grand jury investigation revealed that numerous quiz show contestants had been given the questions in advance. It turned out that both *The $64,000 Question* and *Twenty-One* were rigged, with players coached about every detail of their performance. The contestants blamed the producers, who then implicated the sponsors. Van Doren admitted the painful truth after first protesting his innocence. "I was involved, deeply involved, in a deception," he said, adding, "I would give almost anything to reverse the course of my life."

The public was outraged. President Eisenhower condemned the "selfishness" and "greed" of the perpetrators. Yet there was nothing illegal about these shows. Indeed, some sponsors defended them as a form of *entertainment*, akin to professional wrestling or a "ghostwritten" book. As public anger mounted, however, Congress passed legislation to prevent the rigging of TV quiz shows, and the networks promised to regulate themselves. *The $64,000 Question, Twenty-One*, and other big money game shows quickly left the air.

The quality of television did not appear to improve. New programs became clones of each other—bland sit-coms or violent westerns and crime dramas. Advertising now consumed 20 percent of television airtime, with more money spent making commercials than producing the shows themselves. "The feeling of high purpose that lit the industry when it was young," wrote the *New York Times*, "is long gone." Yet television's power kept expanding. One study in the 1950s estimated that an American youngster spent 11,000 hours in the classroom through high school and 15,000 hours in front of the TV. Another concluded that adults spent more time watching television than working for pay. There were complaints that television tended to isolate people and to shorten their attention spans. Nobody needed to concentrate for more than a half hour—and not very hard at that.

As television expanded, other media outlets declined. Mass circulation magazines such as *Look* and *Collier's* folded in the 1950s, and newspaper readership went way down. Movie attendance dropped and radio lost listeners, forcing both industries to experiment in order to survive. Hollywood tried Cinemascope, Technicolor, 3D glasses, drive-in movies, and big budget spectacles like *The Ten Commandments* and *Ben Hur*. Radio moved from soap operas and big band music to "hip" disc jockeys spinning rock 'n' roll. Nevertheless, television was now king. People watched the same programs in Boston and San Diego, in rural hamlets and in cities, in rich areas and in poor. America's popular culture, consumer needs, and general information—all came increasingly from TV.

YOUTH CULTURE

In the 1950s, a distinctive "teenage culture" emerged, rooted in the enormous prosperity and population growth that followed World War II. America's young people were far removed from the grim events of the previous two decades. Raised in relative affluence, surrounded by messages that undermined traditional values of thrift and self-denial, these new teenagers were perceived as a special group with a unique subculture. They rarely worked, yet their pockets were full. By 1956, the nation's "teenage market" topped $9 billion a year. The typical adolescent spent as much on entertainment as had the average family in 1941.

A New Kind of Music

Nothing defined these 13 million teenagers more clearly than the music they shared. In the 1940s, popular music was dominated by the "big bands" of Glenn Miller and Tommy Dorsey, the Broadway show tunes of Rodgers and Hammerstein, and the mellow voices of Bing Crosby, Frank Sinatra, and the Andrews Sisters. These artists appealed to a broad white audience of all ages. Other forms of popular music—blue-grass, country, rhythm-and-blues—were limited by region and race.

But not for long. The huge migration of rural blacks and whites to industrial centers during World War II profoundly altered popular culture. The sounds of "race" music, "hillbilly" music, and gospel became readily available to mainstream America for the first time. Record sales tripled during the 1950s, aided by technological advances like the transistor radio and the 45 rpm vinyl disc (or "single"). The main consumers were young people who acquired new tastes by flipping the radio dial.

In 1951, a Cleveland, Ohio, record dealer noticed that white teenagers at his store were "going crazy" over the songs of black rhythm-and-blues artists like Ivory Joe Hunter and Lloyd Price. He told a local disc jockey named Alan Freed, who decided to play these records on the air. Freed's new program, *The Moondog Party,* took Cleveland by storm. Soon Freed was hosting live shows at the local arena to overflow crowds. Pounding his fists to the rhythm, chanting "go man, go," Freed became the self-proclaimed father of rock 'n' roll.

"I'll never forget the first time I heard his show," a writer recalled. "I couldn't believe sounds like that were coming out of the radio." Freed understood the defiant, sensual nature of rock 'n' roll, the way it separated the young from everyone else. It was their music, played by their heroes, set to their special beat. Indeed, rock's first national hit, "Rock Around the Clock," by Bill Haley and the Comets, became the theme song for *Blackboard Jungle,* a movie about rebellious high school students set to the throbbing rhythms of rock 'n' roll.

The Rise of Elvis

Haley's success was fleeting. He didn't generate the intense excitement or sexual spark that teenagers craved. As Haley faded, a twenty-one-year-old truck driver from Memphis exploded onto the popular music scene. His name was Elvis Presley; the year was 1955.

Born in rural Mississippi, Presley was surrounded by the sounds of country music, gospel, and blues. As a teenager in Memphis, he listened to WDIA—"the Mother Station of Negroes"—and frequented the legendary blues clubs along Beale Street. The music moved him deeply, providing both spiritual force and physical release.

Memphis was also home to Sun Records, a label with strong southern roots. Owned by Sam Phillips, Sun recorded white country singers like Johnny Cash and black bluesmen such as B. B. King. What Phillips most wanted, however, was an artist who combined these two sounds instinctively, without appearing artificial or forced. "If I could find a white man who had the Negro sound and the Negro feel," Phillips said, "I could make a million dollars."

Presley was that man. Signing with Sun Records in 1954, he took the region by storm. The press described his unique style as "a cross between be-bop and country," and "a new hillbilly blues beat." It wasn't just the sound. Tall and handsome, with long sideburns and slicked-back hair, Presley was a riveting performer, combining little boy shyness with enormous sexual drive. A fellow artist described young Presley on tour:

Combining the sounds of black and white music with enormous sexual drive, Elvis Presley became the most successful recording star in history.
© Bettmann/UPI/Corbis

This cat came out in red pants and a green coat and a pink shirt and socks, and he had this sneer on his face. And he stood behind the mike for five minutes, I'll bet, before he made a move. Then he hit his guitar a lick, and he broke two strings. I'd been playing ten years, and I hadn't broken a *total* of two strings. So there he was, these two strings dangling, and he hadn't done anything yet, and these high school girls were screaming and fainting and running up to the stage, and then he started to move his hips real slow like he had a thing for his guitar.

When Presley became too big to handle, Sun Records sold his contract to RCA for $35,000, a sizable amount at that time. Before long, he was a national sensation. His early hits topped the charts in popular music, country, and rhythm-and-blues—the first time that had ever occurred. In less than a year, Elvis recorded eight number-one songs and six of RCA's all-time top twenty-five records. When he appeared on *Ed Sullivan,* the cameras carefully shot him from the waist up. The ratings were extraordinary. "I want to say to Elvis and the country," Sullivan told his audience, "that this is a real decent, fine boy."

Young Elvis was modest and polite. He didn't smoke or drink or use drugs. He was so devoted to his parents that friends laughingly described him as a mama's boy. Yet his exaggerated sexuality on stage made him the target of those who believed that rock 'n' roll was a vulgar and dangerous assault upon

America's youth. "Popular music," wrote one television critic, "has reached its lowest depths in the grunt and groin antics of Mr. Presley."

Such criticism served only to enhance Presley's stature in the teenage world. And his success led the major record companies to experiment more aggressively with black rhythm-and-blues. At that time, white "cover artists" still were used to record toned-down versions of "race" music for white teenage audiences. In 1954, Big Joe Turner's legendary "Shake, Rattle, and Roll" did not make the popular charts, while Bill Haley's cover version became a number-one hit. Turner began:

> Well you wear low dresses
> The sun comes shinin' through [*couplet repeated*]
> I can't believe my eyes
> That all of this belongs to you.

Haley sang:

> You wear those dresses
> Your hair done up so nice [*couplet repeated*]
> You look so warm
> But your heart is cold as ice.

In 1956, rock music reached a milestone when Little Richard's sensual recordings of "Long Tall Sally" and "Rip It Up" outsold the "sanitized" versions of Pat Boone, America's leading white cover artist.

There was more to rock 'n' roll, of course, than Elvis Presley and rhythm-and-blues. Teenagers adored the sweet sounds of the Everly Brothers, the lush harmony of the Platters, and the clean-cut innocence of Ricky Nelson. Furthermore, jazz and folksinging retained a healthy following, as did popular artists like Sinatra, Perry Como, and Nat "King" Cole. Nevertheless, the music that defined this era for most Americans, but for teenagers in particular, was hard-edged rock 'n' roll. It was the car radio blasting Presley's "Hound Dog," Chuck Berry's "Maybellene," and Little Richard's "Tutti Frutti" on a carefree Saturday night. *A wop bop a lu bop a lop bam boom!*

The Beat Generation

Whatever else might be said about Elvis Presley and other rock heroes, they loved the system that made them millionaires. Elvis spent lavishly. His first royalties were used to purchase three new homes and matching Cadillacs for his parents, though his mother didn't drive. Material rewards were the standard by which Presley, and countless others, measured their success.

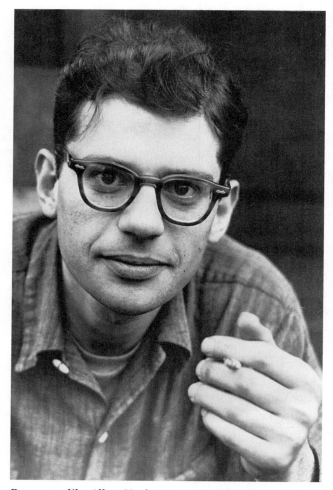

Beat poets like Allen Ginsberg assaulted the politics and culture of middle-class America in the 1950s with anthems of despair.
© Bettmann/UPI/Corbis

The Beat movement was different. Composed of young writers and poets based mainly in San Francisco and New York, it blossomed in the mid-1950s as a reaction against mainstream standards and beliefs. The word "beat" described a feeling of emotional and physical exhaustion. The Beats despised politics, consumerism, and technology. They viewed American culture as meaningless, conformist, banal. Their leading poet, Allen Ginsberg, provided a bitter portrait of generational despair in *Howl* (1955).

The Beats linked happiness and creativity with absolute freedom. Their model was Dean Moriarty, the hero of Jack Kerouac's *On the Road,* an autobiographical novel about the cross-country adventures of Kerouac and his friends finding adventure and renewal (not to mention sex and drugs) beyond the confines of middle-class life. *On the Road* became both a national best-seller and a cult book on America's college campuses. In a sense, Kerouac and Presley had something important in common: both appealed to young people who seemed dissatisfied with the apparent blandness of American culture.

CRISES AND CELEBRATION

In September 1955, President Eisenhower suffered a heart attack while vacationing in Colorado. The news raised obvious questions about his present and future course. At sixty-five, Eisenhower was one of the oldest presidents in American history. How quickly would he recover, if at all? Who would guide the nation in his absence?

Eisenhower spent the next four months recovering in the hospital and at his Gettysburg farm. Fortunately, the fall of 1955 was a time of political tranquility, with Congress out of session, no bills to sign or veto, and no crises looming on the international scene. The president stayed in close contact with his advisors as he slowly regained his health. Returning to the White House early in 1956, he announced his plan to seek reelection. The public was vastly relieved. As columnist James Reston noted, Eisenhower was more than a president; he was "a national phenomenon, like baseball."

Conquering Polio

The president's full recovery was not the only positive "health news" of 1955. On a far larger front, a medical research team led by Dr. Jonas Salk, a virologist at the University of Pittsburgh, announced the successful testing of a vaccine to combat poliomyelitis, the most frightening public health problem of the postwar era. More than 50,000 polio cases were reported in 1954, mostly of children who took sick during the summer months. The disease produced flulike symptoms in most cases, but a more virulent form, which entered the central nervous system, led to paralysis and sometimes death. The cause of polio was uncertain; the virus seemed to be excreted in fecal matter and then passed through hand-to-hand contact. Not surprisingly, the epidemic produced a national panic. Cities closed swimming pools and beaches; families cancelled vacations, boiled their dishes, and avoided indoor crowds. Children were warned against jumping in puddles, drinking from water fountains, and making new friends.

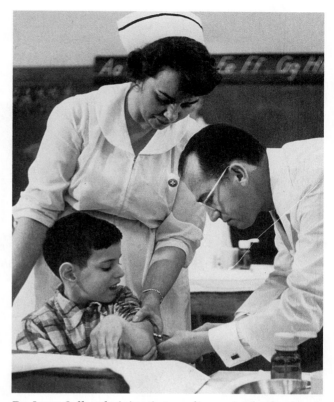

Dr. Jonas Salk, administering a polio vaccine he developed in 1954, helped eradicate a disease that terrorized Americans in the postwar era.
AP/Wide World Photos

The March of Dimes became America's favorite charity, raising millions to find a cure for polio and to finance the care of patients through therapy, leg braces, and iron lungs. Determined to provide immediate protection against the disease, Dr. Salk began testing a "dead" polio virus vaccine on schoolchildren in 1954. (His critics, led by Dr. Alfred Sabin, insisted that only a "live" polio vaccine would trigger the immunities needed to provide a lasting solution.) Aided by the March of Dimes and an army of volunteers, Salk tested the vaccine—and a placebo—on several million youngsters nationwide. "It was the largest peacetime mobilization of its kind," wrote one observer, "one in which the mothers of America rose up to save, in many cases, their own children."

The testing proved extremely successful. The federal government approved the polio vaccine in 1955, touching off emotional public celebrations. "People observed moments of silence, rang bells, honked horns, blew factory whistles, drank toasts, hugged children, attended church." Although the government did not provide the funds to vaccinate all school-age children immediately—in part because the American Medical

PICTURING THE PAST✦ECONOMICS & TECHNOLOGY

AMERICA'S DREAM CAR

Happy Resolution for a Happy New Year!

Cadillac

CADILLAC MOTOR CAR DIVISION • GENERAL MOTORS CORPORATION

The decade following World War II marked the height of America's love affair with the automobile. Each year's sales proved better than the last; in 1955 alone, more than 7 million cars rolled off the nation's assembly lines. This dramatic growth was not shared equally, however. As the 1950s progressed, the "Big Three" automakers—General Motors, Ford, and Chrysler—took over the market as the poorly funded "independents" disappeared: Kaiser and Willys in 1955, Nash and Hudson in 1957, Packard in 1958. As this advertisement demonstrates, the American automobile of the postwar era became ever more powerful and luxurious, representing not just a means of transportation, but a status symbol as well. Indeed, General Motors produced five different cars with five distinct images: Chevrolet for "hoi polloi," Pontiac for "the poor but proud," Oldsmobile for "the comfortable but discreet," Buick for "the striving," and Cadillac (pictured here) for "the rich." Yet even the cheaper models came with a V-8 engine, automatic transmission, air-conditioning, tail fins, miles of chrome, and white wall tires. Around 1957, a series of small, economical European imports, led by the Volkswagen "beetle," arrived to compete with America's overdesigned, gas-guzzling behemoths. The battle was on.

Association objected to this "socialist" proposal—public opinion soon forced a more compassionate approach. In 1960, fewer than a thousand new polio cases were reported in the United States.

Interstate Highways

The nation's confidence soared even higher with passage of the Federal Highway Act of 1956, which authorized $25 billion in new taxes on cars, trucks, and

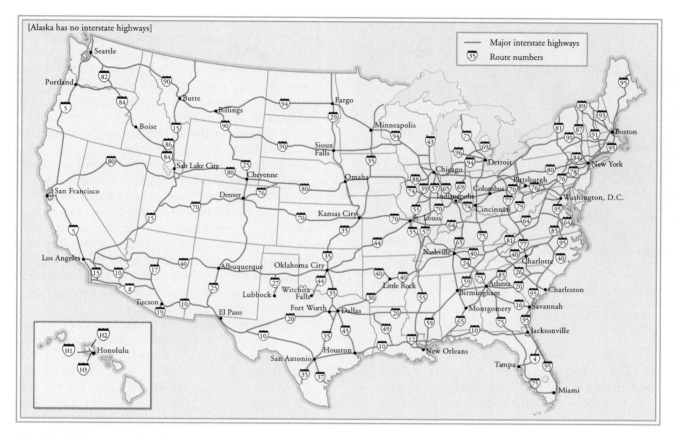

Map 28.1 *The National Highway System*
The ability to drive almost anywhere in the continental United States on a super highway transformed the nation's economy as well as its culture. Private transportation overwhelmed public transportation. Workers commuted longer distances between their homes and their jobs, spending more time on the road. Whole new industries arose to service the business traveler and vacationer, who no longer had to drive through the center of small towns or large cities to reach their destination.

gasoline for the construction of 40,000 miles of interstate roads over the next ten years. The huge highway network, linking all cities with more than 50,000 people, allowed a driver to travel the continent uninterrupted, save stops for food and gas. Eisenhower viewed this project as both a convenience to motorists and a boost to the economy. The president also linked good highways to Cold War events, warning that cities must be evacuated quickly in the event of nuclear war.

The Highway Act spurred enormous economic growth. Improved roads meant higher oil revenues, soaring car sales, more business for truckers, and greater mobility for travelers. The so-called "highway trade" took off. Ray Krock opened his first McDonald's in 1955 in Des Plaines, Illinois, a suburb of Chicago. In Memphis, meanwhile, Kemmons Wilson unveiled the first Holiday Inn, featuring a restaurant, a swimming pool, and clean, air-conditioned rooms with free TV. Before long McDonald's golden arches and Holi-

day Inn's green neon lettering were among the most recognizable logos in America.

Opposing the Highway Act of 1956 was akin to opposing prosperity, progress, and national defense. A few social critics like Lewis Mumford expressed concern about the deterioration of urban centers, the stink of auto pollution, and the future of interstate rail service, but they were drowned out by the optimistic majority. As the prestigious *Architectural Forum* noted, America's new highway system was "the greatest man-made physical enterprise of all time with the exception of war."

Hungary and Suez

In the fall of 1956, at the height of the presidential campaign, foreign affairs took center stage. From central Europe came a dangerous challenge to the Eisenhower-Dulles rhetoric about liberating nations

Protesters in Budapest stand on a captured Soviet tank during the Hungarian uprising of 1956.
AP/Wide World Photos

from communist oppression. From the Middle East came a crisis that pitted the United States against its most loyal allies—Israel, England, and France.

Following Stalin's death in 1953, Russian leaders called for "peaceful coexistence" between the Communist bloc and "differing political and social systems." In 1956, Soviet Premier Nikita Khrushchev stunned the Twentieth Communist Party Congress in Moscow by denouncing Stalin's brutality and hinting at a relaxation of the Soviet grip on central and eastern Europe.

The reaction was predictable. Protests flared throughout the Soviet bloc, demanding an end to Russian rule. In Warsaw, angry crowds sacked the Communist party headquarters, while in Budapest street battles escalated into full-scale civil war.

The Hungarian revolt put Eisenhower on the spot. In 1952, his campaign rhetoric had blasted the Democrats for being "soft" on communism. From 1953 forward, his administration had vowed to "roll back" the communist wave, not simply to contain it. Now the time had come to put words into action by supporting the anti-communist freedom fighters in Hungary. Yet Eisenhower refused to send American troops, or even to airlift supplies to the resisters, for fear of starting an all-out war with the Soviet Union. In October 1956, Russian tanks and troops stormed into Budapest to crush the revolt.

At the very moment of the Hungarian revolt, another crisis erupted in the Middle East, a region of growing interest and concern to the United States.

Though American policy supported the new State of Israel, it also recognized the strategic importance and economic power of Israel's Arab neighbors. In 1952, a young Egyptian military officer named Gamal Abdel Nasser had dramatically altered Middle Eastern politics by overthrowing the corrupt regime of King Farouk. As an Arab nationalist, Nasser steered a middle course between the Cold War powers, hoping to play off one side against the other. To the Egyptian people, he promised both the destruction of Israel and an end to British control of the Suez Canal.

The United States tried to woo Nasser with economic aid. It even agreed to finance his pet project, the Aswan Dam, a huge hydroelectric plant on the Nile River. But trouble arose in 1956, when Secretary Dulles withdrew the Aswan offer to protest Egypt's recognition of Communist China. Unable to punish the United States directly, Nasser did the next best thing by seizing the Suez Canal.

The move could not be ignored. In 1955, Nasser had blockaded the Gulf of Aqaba, Israel's sole outlet to the Red Sea. Now he controlled the waterway that linked western Europe to its oil supply in the Middle East. On October 29, 1956, Israeli armor poured into the Sinai, routing Egyptian forces. Two days later, French and British paratroopers landed near Alexandria and easily retook the Suez Canal.

Eisenhower immediately condemned this invasion. At the very least, he believed, the attack undermined Western interests in the Middle East by forcing Egypt and other Arab states closer to the Soviet bloc. Fearing the worst, Eisenhower placed U.S. armed forces on full alert. If the Russians "start something," he warned, "we may have to hit 'em—and, if necessary, with *everything* in the bucket."

It never came to that. Privately, the White House pressured England, France, and Israel to withdraw. Publicly, the United States supported a U.N. resolution that denounced the invasion and called for negotiations regarding the canal. On November 6, a cease-fire was signed, ending the crisis but not the ill will.

Events in Hungary and Suez came in the midst of Eisenhower's 1956 reelection campaign. Expecting an easy victory, the president worried most about picking the proper running mate, a critical choice given his advanced age and questionable health. Eisenhower did not believe that Vice President Nixon was the best person to lead the nation in a crisis. "I've watched Dick a long time and he just hasn't grown," Ike told an aide. "So I just haven't honestly been able to believe that he is presidential timber."

In a private meeting, Eisenhower urged Nixon to trade in his vice presidential hat for a cabinet post.

Yet when Nixon resisted, the president backed down, fearing a backlash within Republican ranks. In November 1956, Eisenhower and Nixon trounced the Democratic slate of Adlai Stevenson and Senator Estes Kefauver by almost 10 million votes, a margin of victory even wider than in 1952. Nevertheless, the Democrats easily retained their majorities in both houses of Congress, demonstrating that Eisenhower, who accepted New Deal reforms as a permanent part of American life, remained far more popular than the political party he led.

A SECOND TERM

Eisenhower returned to office on an optimistic note. Events in Hungary and the Middle East faded momentarily from view. *Time* magazine even praised the president for his moderation "in time of crisis and threat of World War III." The economy was strong, unemployment was low. The nation seemed confident, prosperous, and secure.

Confrontation at Little Rock

These good feelings did not last long. Throughout the South, opposition to the *Brown* decision was spreading, with some white southerners interpreting Eisenhower's virtual silence on the issue as a sign that he supported their resistance to integrated schools. In 1956, more than a hundred congressmen from the former Confederate states issued a "Southern Manifesto" that vowed to resist court-ordered integration "by all lawful means." A year later, in Little Rock, Arkansas, Governor Orval Faubus triggered the inevitable confrontation between national authority and "states' rights" by defying a federal court order to integrate the all-white Central High School. First the Arkansas National Guard, and then a crowd of angry whites, turned away the nine black students.

As televised scenes of mob violence in Little Rock flashed around the world, President Eisenhower finally, but firmly, took command. Vowing to use "the full power of the United States . . . to carry out the orders of the federal court," he nationalized the Arkansas Guard and dispatched a thousand fully equipped army paratroopers to surround the high school and escort the black students to their classes. The soldiers remained for months, though peace was quickly restored. Ironically, Dwight Eisenhower became the first president since Reconstruction to protect the civil rights of African Americans through the use of military force.

President Eisenhower nationalized the Arkansas Guard and dispatched army paratroopers to escort black students to Little Rock's Central High School in the fall of 1957. Although reluctant to act, Eisenhower became the first president since Reconstruction to use military force to protect the constitutional rights of African Americans.
© Bettmann/UPI/Corbis

Sputnik and Its Aftermath

On October 4, 1957, the Soviet Union launched *Sputnik I* (or "traveling companion"), the first artificial satellite, weighing less than 200 pounds. The admiral in charge of America's satellite program dismissed *Sputnik I* as "a hunk of iron almost anybody could launch." But one month later, the Russians orbited *Sputnik II,* a 1,100-pound capsule with a small dog inside.

The news provoked anger and dismay. Americans had always taken for granted their technological superiority. Even the Soviet atomic bomb was seen as an aberration, most likely built from stolen U.S. blueprints. But *Sputnik* was different; it shook the nation's confidence and wounded its pride. The feeling grew that America had become complacent in its affluence, and that danger lay ahead. "The time has clearly come," said an alarmed senator, "to be less concerned with the depth of the pile of the new broadloom or the height of the tail fin of the new car and to be more prepared to shed blood, sweat, and tears."

The nation's educational system came under withering fire. Critics emerged from every corner, bemoaning the sorry state of America's schools. In an issue devoted to the "Crisis in Education," *Life* magazine followed a sixteen-year-old Russian student and his American counterpart through a typical high

The launching of Sputnik *in October 1957 raised serious doubts about America's military and technological superiority in the Cold War era.*
Sovfoto/TASS

school day. Alexi took difficult courses in science and math. He spoke fluent English, played chess and the piano, exercised vigorously, and studied four hours after class. Stephen, meanwhile, spent his day lounging through basic geometry and learning how to type. The students around him read magazines like *Modern Romance* in their English class. No one seemed to study. The end result, warned the *Life* editors, was a generation of young Americans ill-equipped "to cope with the technicalities of the Space Age."

The embarrassments continued. In December 1957, millions watched on television as the U.S. Navy's much-publicized Vanguard rocket caught fire on takeoff and crashed to the ground. (The newspapers dubbed it *"Flopnik"* and *"Kaputnik."*) A month later, the army launched a ten-pound satellite named *Explorer I* aboard its new Jupiter rocket. Determined to calm public fears, President Eisenhower insisted that the United States was well ahead of the Soviet Union in nuclear research and delivery systems. But the people thought otherwise, especially after the Russians orbited a third satellite weighing almost 3,000 pounds.

In fact, however, Eisenhower was correct. His own information, not available to the public, made two vital points. First, the Russians *needed* more powerful missiles because the warheads they carried were heavier and cruder, owing to inferior technology. Second, the Soviets did not have enough intercontinental ballistic missiles (ICBMs) to counter America's huge lead in manned nuclear bombers.

Put simply, the United States was in no real danger of being outgunned.

Eisenhower got this information from the CIA's U-2 spy planes, which crossed the Soviet Union at 70,000 feet. The U-2 flights were both secret and illegal, a clear violation of Russian air space. But the cameras on board, capable of picking up license plate numbers in the Kremlin's parking lot, provided American intelligence with a detailed picture of the Soviet war machine. Of course, the president could not speak candidly about Russian military power without also admitting the existence of these U-2 flights.

This was an awful dilemma. Critics now demanded expensive crash programs for weapons research, missile construction, and community "fallout" shelters to protect against nuclear attack. Eisenhower vigorously opposed these programs, claiming that they undermined economic prosperity and threatened the "very values we are trying to defend." Using his exalted stature as general and war hero, he battled hard—and successfully—to keep military budgets stable during these years. Defense spending increased from $38 billion in 1957 to $41 billion in 1960, a tiny jump after inflation.

Still, the impact of *Sputnik* did not quickly disappear. For the first time, Americans started to view their educational system in terms of national security. This meant greater emphasis on science, mathematics, and foreign language study. In 1958, Congress passed the National Defense Education Act, which funded high school programs in these fields and college scholarships for deserving students. That same year, Eisenhower reluctantly endorsed the creation of the National Aeronautical and Space Agency (NASA), in response to overwhelming public pressure.

End of an Era

In November 1958, the Democrats won a smashing victory in the off-year elections, increasing their majorities in the House (282–153) and the Senate (62–34) to the largest level since 1936. *Sputnik* was partly responsible for this landslide, but so, too, was an economic recession in 1957 that lingered for the next two years. Determined to avoid the inflationary risks of increased federal spending, Eisenhower did little to counter a steady rise in unemployment and a sharp (if temporary) decline in the annual rate of economic growth.

There were optimistic signs, however. In the summer of 1959, Vice President Nixon visited Moscow at Khrushchev's invitation to open a trade show featuring consumer products from Russia and

THE KITCHEN DEBATE

© Elliot Erwitt/Magnum Photos, Inc.

This famous photograph of Soviet Premier Nikita Khrushchev and Vice President Richard Nixon squaring off in their impromptu "Kitchen Debate" in Moscow in 1959 demonstrates that the Cold War had a cultural component that went beyond military confrontation. Standing nose-to-nose in a "model" American kitchen, the two leaders argued about the merits of western consumer culture. Khrushchev saw America's love affair with "gadgetry" as a sure sign of capitalist laziness and decay. Looking grumpily at the array of gleaming appliances, he asked: "Don't you have a machine that puts food in your mouth and pushes it down?" But Nixon, known as a militant anti-communist, won praise for responding to Khrushchev that it was "better to compete in the relative merits of washing machines than in the strength of rockets." The Cold War would continue for years, but for the moment, the battlefield seemed a far different place.

---

the United States. Several weeks later, Khrushchev accepted President Eisenhower's invitation to visit the United States. Khrushchev toured an Iowa farm and an IBM plant near San Francisco. At a Hollywood studio, he watched the filming of *Can-Can* and then, offended by the skimpy costumes, launched into a diatribe against capitalist "pornography." When his trip to Disneyland was canceled for security reasons, Khrushchev was furious. "What's wrong?" he yelled. "Do you have rocket launching pads there? Or have gangsters taken hold of the place?"

The trip ended on a hopeful note with a visit to the presidential retreat at Camp David, where Khrushchev and Eisenhower spent two days in leisurely conversation. They announced that Eisenhower would visit the Soviet Union in 1960 following a summit meeting of world leaders in Paris. The main issues, they agreed, were nuclear disarmament and the future of Berlin.

The summit meeting was a disaster. As he left for Paris in May 1960, Eisenhower learned that a U-2 spy plane was missing. A few days later, Khrushchev revealed that an American aircraft had been shot down deep inside the Soviet Union. Assuming that the pilot was dead, Eisenhower falsely described the U-2 as a weather research plane that had veered off course during a routine flight over Turkey. But Khrushchev then produced the pilot, Francis Gary Powers, frightened but very much alive.

At the summit, Eisenhower took full responsibility for the incident, but refused to apologize. Indeed, he justified the U-2 flights by insisting that Soviet espionage inside the United States was rampant and that U-2 photographs were essential to America's defense, given the closed nature of Russian society. In response, Khrushchev turned the summit into a tirade against Western "banditry," adding that Eisenhower was no longer welcome on Soviet soil.

The failure at Paris deeply wounded the president. In his "farewell address" to the people, he warned that years of Cold War tensions were sapping America's strength and concentrating too much power in the hands of "a military-industrial complex." Speaking boldly, at times sadly, he urged the people to be on guard against militarism and greed, and to reject a "live for today" mentality. At risk, the president concluded, was "the loss of our political and spiritual heritage."

The Election of 1960

Who would lead the United States into the next decade? Unlike the predictable Eisenhower landslides of 1952 and 1956, the election of 1960 generated drama from the start. Both major candidates were tough, hard-driving campaigners. Both were born in the twentieth century—a political first—and both entered Congress in 1946 after serving as junior naval officers during World War II. But the similarities ended there.

Richard Nixon, the forty-seven-year-old vice president, grew up in modest circumstances. His Quaker parents ran a small grocery store in Whittier, California, near Los Angeles, where Nixon worked as a boy. Neighbors and classmates recalled him as serious and socially ill at ease. After graduating from Whittier College and Duke Law School, he married Patricia Ryan in 1940 and obtained his naval commission the following year.

Nixon's political rise was dramatic. As a new Republican congressman, he played a major role in the Alger Hiss case and then won a U.S. Senate seat in 1950 after accusing his Democratic opponent of being "soft on communism." As vice president from 1953 to 1960, Nixon emerged as the Republican party's most aggressive defender.

John Kennedy took a different path to power. Born to wealth and privilege, he grew up in Boston, attended the finest private schools, and graduated from Harvard. His self-made millionaire father, Joseph P. Kennedy, served as ambassador to England under Franklin Roosevelt. Preaching competition and excellence, Joseph Kennedy expected his oldest son, Joe, Jr., to become the first Catholic president of the United States. When Joe, Jr., died in combat during World War II, the torch was passed to John Kennedy, the next oldest son. In 1943, John barely escaped death himself after his PT boat was rammed by a Japanese warship in the South Pacific. Elected to Congress in 1946, and to the Senate in 1952, Kennedy did not excel as a legislator. In constant pain from his war wounds, he un-

derwent delicate spinal surgery and then was diagnosed with Addison's disease, an adrenal malfunction that required daily doses of cortisone. While recuperating, Kennedy won the Pulitzer Prize for *Profiles in Courage,* an intriguing book, written almost entirely by his staff, about politicians who took brave but unpopular positions on the great issues of their time.

In 1956, Kennedy ran a close second to Estes Kefauver for the Democratic party's vice presidential nomination. "You know, if we work like hell the next four years," Kennedy told an aide, "we will pick up all the marbles." Healthy once again, he traveled the country with his glamorous wife, Jacqueline, to line up presidential support. The crowds they drew were so large and adoring that reporters used the Greek word *charisma* to describe the growing Kennedy mystique.

The Republican convention nominated Richard Nixon on the first ballot. As expected, Nixon chose a moderate easterner, Henry Cabot Lodge, Jr., of Massachusetts, to be his vice presidential running mate. The Democratic convention was more dramatic. While also winning a first ballot victory, Kennedy surprised almost everyone by selecting Senator Lyndon Johnson, a longtime rival, for the vice presidential slot. As a Texan with liberal instincts, Johnson was expected to help Kennedy in the South without hurting him in the North. "The world is changing," Kennedy proclaimed in his acceptance speech. "We stand today on the edge of a New Frontier."

The two candidates were evenly matched. Nixon campaigned on the eight-year Eisenhower record, reminding Americans that their nation was prosperous and at peace. Kennedy attacked that record without criticizing the popular Eisenhower by name. Portraying the United States as stagnant in a changing world, he promised new leadership "to get the country moving once again."

Kennedy had two main hurdles to overcome: religion and inexperience. No Roman Catholic had ever been elected president, a fact underscored by the crushing defeat of Al Smith in 1928. Religion became an open issue in the 1960 campaign after a group of Protestant ministers issued a statement questioning Kennedy's fitness to govern on the grounds that Roman Catholicism was "both a church and a temporal state." Kennedy confronted this issue in a powerful speech to a Baptist audience in Texas. Vowing to uphold the constitutional separation of church and state, he added: "If this election is decided on the basis that 40,000,000 Americans lost their chance of being president on the day they were baptized, then it is the whole nation that will be the loser in the eyes of history."

President Eisenhower's Farewell Address, Jan. 17, 1961

In the most quoted and best remembered speech of his eight-year presidency, Dwight Eisenhower spoke about the future obstacles to individual liberty and world peace. While urging Americans to remain vigilant in the struggle against communist expansion, he also raised concerns about the rise of "a military-industrial complex" and the erosion of national values based on sharing and trust.

We now stand ten years past the midpoint of a century that has witnessed four major wars among great nations. Three of them involved our own country. Despite these holocausts America is today the strongest, the most influential and most productive nation in the world. . . .

A vital element in keeping the peace is our military establishment. Our arms must be mighty, ready for instant action, so that no potential aggressor may be tempted to risk his own destruction.

Our military organization today bears little relation to that known by any of my predecessors in peacetime, or indeed by the fighting men of World War II or Korea.

Until the latest of our world conflicts, the United States had no armaments industry. American makers of plowshares could, with time and as required, make swords as well. But now we can no longer risk emergency improvisation of national defense; we have been compelled to create a permanent armaments industry of vast proportions. Added to this, three and a half million men and women are directly engaged in the defense establishment. We annually spend on military security more than the net income of all United States corporations.

This conjunction of an immense military establishment and a large arms industry is new in the American experience. The total influence—economic, political, even spiritual—is felt in every city, every statehouse, every office of the federal government. We recognize the imperative need for this development. Yet we must not fail to comprehend its grave implications. Our toil, resources, and livelihood are all involved; so is the very structure of our society.

In the councils of government, we must guard against the acquisition of unwarranted influence, whether sought or unsought, by the military-industrial complex. The potential for the disastrous rise of misplaced power exists and will persist.

We must never let the weight of this combination endanger our liberties or democratic processes. We should take nothing for granted. Only an alert and knowledgeable citizenry can compel the proper meshing of the huge industrial and military machinery of defense with our peaceful methods and goals, so that security and liberty may prosper together. . . .

Another factor in maintaining balance involves the element of time. As we peer into society's future, we—you and I, and our government—must avoid the impulse to live only for today, plundering, for our own ease and convenience, the precious resources of tomorrow. We cannot mortgage the material assets of our grandchildren without risking the loss also of their political and spiritual heritage. We want democracy to survive for all generations to come, not to become the insolvent phantom of tomorrow. . . .

Source: *Public Papers of the President, Dwight D. Eisenhower, 1960–1961,* no. 421.

Kennedy's other hurdle—inexperience—was removed in a series of televised debates with Nixon that marked the beginning of modern presidential campaigns. The first debate had the greatest impact, as more than 80 million Americans watched on television or listened on radio. Though both candidates spoke well, the difference lay in cosmetics and style. The handsome, well-groomed Kennedy radiated confidence and charm. Nixon, by contrast, seemed awkward and pale. The hot TV lights made him sweat

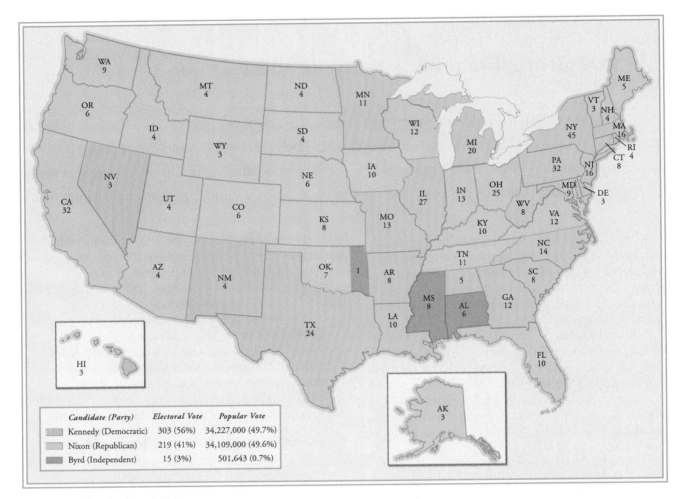

Candidate (Party)	Electoral Vote	Popular Vote
Kennedy (Democratic)	303 (56%)	34,227,000 (49.7%)
Nixon (Republican)	219 (41%)	34,109,000 (49.6%)
Byrd (Independent)	15 (3%)	501,643 (0.7%)

Map 28.2 *The Election of 1960*
In winning one of the closest presidential contests in American history, John F. Kennedy barely kept the Democratic New Deal coalition together. Several key factors were at work in this election, including the impact of the first televised presidential debates, the Catholic issue, and the suspicion of voter fraud in the key states of Texas and Illinois.
View an animated version of this map or related maps at http://history.wadsworth.com/passages2e

profusely, smudging his makeup. Those who heard the debate on radio scored it a draw. Those who saw it on television thought Kennedy the clear victor.

Kennedy won the election with 303 electoral votes to Nixon's 219. Yet the popular vote was the closest since 1888, with Kennedy getting 34,227,000 (49.7 percent) and Nixon 34,109,000 (49.6 percent). A swing of several thousand votes in Texas and Illinois, where suspicions of ballot fraud were rampant, would have given the election to Nixon. Kennedy did well among traditional Democrats (minorities, urban dwellers, the working class), and swept the Catholic vote, yet polls showed his religion costing him dearly in rural Protestant areas. Kennedy suspected that television won him the White House, and he may have been correct. The four debates, and a flood of prime-time advertisements, appeared to influence voters as never before.

CONCLUSION

The 1950s were far more tranquil than the war-torn 1940s or the Depression-scarred 1930s. For most Americans, the fifties were years of economic security and personal fulfillment, yet nagging questions remained. Would prosperity and racial justice ever reach into the far corners of the land? Would the civil rights movement retain its momentum and nonviolent stance? Would the nation's expanding Cold War military commitments drain its economic strength—and moral authority? Would the lure of materialism and

Nixon and Kennedy revolutionized political campaigning with the first televised presidential debates in American history.
AP/Wide World Photos

consumerism undermine precious national values? These questions would dominate the American agenda in the tumultuous years ahead.

Recommended Readings

Biskind, Peter. *Seeing Is Believing: How Hollywood Taught Us to Stop Worrying and Love the Fifties* (1983). Examines the way moviemaking shaped popular culture.

Dudziak, Mary. *Cold War, Civil Rights* (2000). Examines the impact of America's civil rights movement on the international scene.

Guralnick, Peter. *Last Train to Memphis: The Rise of Elvis Presley* (1994). Traces the early years of rock 'n' roll's most popular artist and the reasons for his extraordinary success.

Gilbert, James. *A Cycle of Outrage* (1986). Looks at the nation's reaction to juvenile delinquency in the 1950s.

Halberstam, David. *The Fifties* (1993). Offers an encyclopedic account of this decade, from McCarthyism to McDonalds.

Kahn, Roger. *The Boys of Summer* (1971). Recalls the glory days of Major League baseball in a simpler time.

Lewis, Tom. *Divided Highways* (1997). Shows how the building of the interstate highway system transformed American life.

Marling. Karal Ann. *As Seen on TV* (1994). Looks at the rise of visual culture in a new age of leisure.

May, Elaine. *Homeward Bound: American Families in the Cold War Era* (1988). Ties the anxieties associated with anti-communism and the atomic bomb to the national quest for security and stability in the American home.

Oshinsky, David M. *A Conspiracy So Immense: The World of Joe McCarthy* (1983). Explores the life of America's great Red-hunter and the era that bears his name.

American Journey Online and InfoTrac College Edition

Visit the source collections at http://ajaccess. wadsworth.com and infotrac.thomsonlearning.com and use the Search function with the following key terms to explore documents, images, audio and video clips, articles, and commentary related to the material in this chapter.

Dwight D. Eisenhower
Sputnik
Rosa Parks

Brown v. Board of Education
Montgomery Bus Boycott

Additional resources, exercises, and Internet links related to this chapter are available on the American Passages Web site: http://history.wadsworth.com/passages2e

PASSAGES

—1960 TO 2003—

Who could have predicted the turmoil and tragedy of the 1960s? The previous decade, after all, gave scant warning that trouble lay ahead. Filled with powerful milestones, such as the National Highway Act and *Brown v. Board of Education*, the 1950s seemed to reflect the optimism and stability of a confident nation—a place of widely shared values and little public complaint. All was well in prosperous postwar America, or so it appeared.

The tumult of the 1960s came suddenly, without letup or relief. It began with the jailings and beatings of civil rights workers in the South, which turned many activists against the philosophy of nonviolence. The civil rights movement, in turn, spawned a women's movement, and then a student movement, which further challenged the status quo. Meanwhile, the escalating Vietnam War eroded the credibility of American officials and divided the nation in dangerous ways. Against the backdrop of increasing bloodshed in Southeast Asia, the United States endured a horrifying cycle of home-grown violence in the 1960s, including inner city riots, militant campus upheavals, and the assassination of prominent public figures like President John F. Kennedy, his brother Robert, and the Reverend Martin Luther King, Jr.

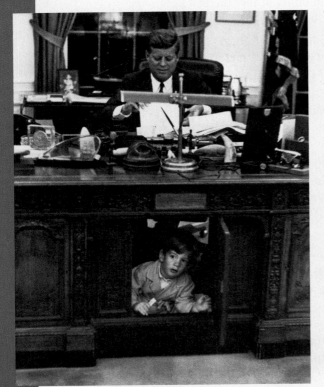

In the Oval Office in 1963, a vigorous young president, with son John, Jr., represented the hopes of a new generation.
© Bettmann; Stanley Tretick, 1963/Corbis

The 1970s brought little relief. An American president resigned from office for the first time in the nation's history. The North Vietnamese Communists took over South Vietnam. Americans faced gas shortages, high unemployment, and staggering inflation. They watched with anger and embarrassment as their embassy in Iran was attacked and 52 Americans were held hostage for more than a year.

Republican Ronald Reagan won the 1980 presidential election by promising to reverse the nation's apparent decline. Mixing personal charm and optimism with the darker politics of resentment, he attracted mainstream voters by vowing to strengthen family values, reward hard work, and increase respect for America around the world. At the same time, he reinforced the notion among white working-class voters (known as "Reagan Democrats") that the party of Franklin Roosevelt had deserted their interests—that the real enemies of working people were no longer big business and the very rich, but rather big government and the very poor. During the 1980s, the Reagan administration's policies regarding taxes, wages, unions, banking, and antitrust produced one of the most dramatic redistributions of wealth in American history, with the top 1 percent seeing its yearly income rise by 75 percent, while the rest of the nation experienced almost no gain at all. Nevertheless, Reagan remained a popular president, a politician who articulated the fears and dreams of Americans with extraordinary skill.

Through all the tumult of these decades, one certainty remained—the specter of international communism, centered in Moscow. Although the fear of domestic subversion stirred up by Senator Joseph McCarthy had largely subsided by 1960, the anxieties generated by Soviet power and influence remained solidly in place. During the 1960s, the United States and Russia tangled over Berlin and Cuba, where the placement of offensive missiles, ninety miles from the Florida coast, led to the most dangerous confrontation of the entire Cold War. In Vietnam, meanwhile, American officials defended the growing involvement as a test of will against Soviet-inspired aggression. The larger goals, they insisted, were to halt the spread of world communism and to maintain American credibility around the globe.

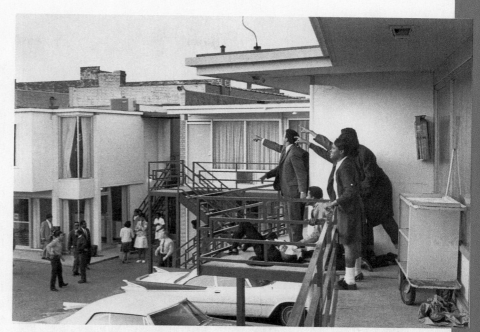

Rushing to the fallen body of Dr. Martin Luther King, Jr., aides and friends point in the direction from which the fatal shot was fired. The assassination of Dr. King in Memphis on April 4, 1968, stunned and saddened a nation now deeply divided by political, cultural, and racial unrest.
© Joseph Louw/Life Magazine

The 1970s brought an apparent thaw in U.S.-Soviet relations. The two sides signed a momentous agreement limiting nuclear weapons known as SALT 1. President Nixon also visited the Soviet Union as well as Communist China, raising hopes for serious dialogue, or détente. It didn't happen. As Nixon freely admitted, his visit to China was intended, in large part, to drive a wedge between the Russians and the Chinese, the world's two leading Communist powers. Furthermore, the very idea of negotiating with the Soviet Union over issues such as human rights and arms control offended hard-line anti-communists who believed that American military power must largely determine the outcome of the Cold War. In the 1980 presidential campaign, Ronald Reagan promised a much tougher stand against communism in the future.

The Reagan administration dramatically increased the nation's defense budget. It also funded military campaigns against leftist rebels and Marxist governments in Africa, Asia, and Latin America. In one instance, it funneled money from a secret arms deal with Iran to illegally finance a right-wing guerilla army in Nicaragua. President Reagan made no apologies for this activity. The Soviets had created an "Evil Empire," he declared, and it had to be destroyed.

President George W. Bush addresses Congress about the war on terrorism and the challenges that the conflict posed on the United States.
© Getty Images

In fact, that empire was already in trouble. Assuming power in 1985, Soviet Premier Mikhail Gorbachev well understood the problems his nation faced. Believing that communism must become more democratic and market-oriented in order to survive, he encouraged the policies known as *glasnost* (openness) and *perestroika* (restructure). In trying to save communism, however, Gorbachev set in motion the very forces that would bring it down. A wave of protest swept through Eastern Europe, demanding more freedom and closer contacts with the West. Unlike Hungary in 1956 and Czechoslovakia in 1968, the Soviet Union did not rush in troops to restore order. On a trip to West Berlin in 1987, President Reagan encouraged the protesters by demanding: "Mr. Gorbachev, tear down this wall." In 1989, the Communist governments in Eastern Europe fell like dominoes—Hungary, Poland, Czechoslovakia, East Germany, Romania. It was one of those rare instances, noted *Time* magazine, "when the tectonic plates of history shift beneath men's feet, and nothing after is quite the same."

In 1991, the Soviet Union collapsed and the Cold War officially ended. For the United States a new set of challenges emerged. President Bill Clinton saw the economy achieve unprecedented levels of prosperity and the problem of budget deficits ease for a time. Yet the good times at home did not mean political calm, The Republicans regained control of the House of Representatives in 1994 for the first time in four decades. Nonetheless, Clinton was reelected in 1996 and then impeached over a sex scandal in 1998–1999. Even with his acquittal, his presidency ended under a cloud. His successor was Republican George W. Bush who won the disputed election in 2000. In September 2001, a terrorist attack transformed the global landscape and confronted the United States, the only remaining super power, with new challenges. Humanity faced the prospect of environmental disaster in global warming, spiraling population growth, and political turbulence worldwide. With the start of the twenty-first century, American leadership as the only superpower remained crucial and also under assault in a rapidly changing world.

The seven Columbian astronauts perished when their spacecraft burned up during reentry into the atmosphere in 2003.
Courtesy of NASA

	1960	1972	1983

Politics & Diplomacy

1960: John Kennedy elected president
1961: Berlin Wall erected
1962: Cuban missile crisis
1963: President Kennedy assassinated
1964: President Johnson elected by record margin
Landmark Civil Rights Act passed
1965: U.S. troop levels exceed 100,000 in Vietnam
Malcolm X assassinated
1967: Antiwar protests multiply
1968: Tet offensive
Martin Luther King, Jr., assassinated in Memphis
Robert Kennedy assassinated in Los Angeles
Richard Nixon elected president
1970: U.S. troops invade Cambodia

1972: President Nixon visits mainland China
Watergate burglary
1973: Vice President Agnew resigns
1974: President Nixon resigns
1975: South Vietnam falls
1976: Jimmy Carter elected president
1977: Panama Canal treaties
1978: Camp David Accords
1979: Hostage crisis in Iran
1980: Ronald Reagan elected President
1981: Reagan survives assassination attempt
Sandra Day O'Connor becomes first woman appointed to Supreme Court
1982: Democrats gain seats in congressional elections

1983: Strategic Defense Initiative (SDI) proposed
Invasion of Grenada
1984: Geraldine Ferraro becomes first woman to be nominated for vice president by major party
Reagan wins sweeping reelection
1985: Mikhail Gorbachev becomes leader of Soviet Union
1986: Democrats regain control of Senate
Iran-Contra scandal begins
1987: Nomination of Robert Bork to Supreme Court defeated
1989: George H. W. Bush wins presidential election over Michael Dukakis on "no new taxes" pledge
Berlin Wall torn down
1990: Iraq invades Kuwait
Bush abandons "no new taxes" pledge

Social & Cultural Events

1961: Freedom Rides
1962: Students for a Democratic Society formed
1963: Betty Friedan publishes *The Feminine Mystique*
1964: Beatles tour the United States
1965: Race riot in Watts
1966: National Organization for Women formed
1967: Haight-Ashbury "summer of love"
1968: Cesar Chavez leads California grape strike
Antiwar protests disrupt Democratic National Convention

1969: Woodstock music festival
1970: College protesters killed at Kent State and Jackson State
1973: Abortion legalized
1974: Antibusing protests in Boston
1981: AIDS epidemic begins in United States
1982: Vietnam War Memorial dedicated in Washington
David Letterman show premiers on NBC late night

1983: Sally Ride first American woman in space
1984: Summer Olympics in Los Angeles
1985: Rock Hudson dies of AIDS
1986: *Challenger* space shuttle explodes
1987: Scandals engulf televangelist ministry of Jim and Tammy Faye Bakker
1988: Antidepressant drug Prozac introduced
1989: Actresses Bette Davis and Lucille Ball die
Oil tanker *Exxon Valdez* goes aground in Alaska causing environmental damage

Economics & Technology

1960: Oral contraceptive marketed
1962: John Glenn orbits the earth aboard *Friendship 7*
1969: Apollo moon landing
1973: Arab oil embargo triggers energy crisis
1979: Nuclear accident at Three Mile Island
1981: Reagan tax cut package adopted
Air traffic controllers strike

1982: Recession ends
Budget deficit exceeds $100 billion for first time
1983: Social security reforms adopted
1984: Macintosh computer introduced
1985: President Reagan signs Gramm-Rudman-Hollings Act to reduce government spending
1986: Tax Reform Act passed

1987: Stock market closes about 2,000 on Dow Jones, but loses 508 points on the index in October in a single day
1988: U.S., Canada arrive at free trade agreement
President George H. W. Bush approves $300 billion plan to bail out savings and loan industry
1990: American dependence on foreign oil reaches historic high

1991	1996	2000

1991: Persian Gulf War brings Iraq's ouster from Kuwait
Clarence Thomas-Anita Hill controversy erupts
1992: Bill Clinton defeats George H. W. Bush and Ross Perot in presidential race
1993: Branch Davidians besieged in Waco, Texas, which results in fiery confrontation
Clinton's deficit-reduction plan passes Congress by a single Democratic vote in Senate
1994: Republicans regain control of House of Representatives for first time in forty years
1995: Bombing in Oklahoma City kills more than 160 people; fears about militias aroused
Republicans force government shutdown
Settlement of Bosnian conflict reached at Dayton, Ohio

1996: Clinton and Bob Dole wage presidential contest
Clinton reelected to second term
1997: Balanced budget agreement reached
1998: Clinton sex scandals break
President Clinton impeached by House of Representatives in December
1999: Clinton acquitted by Senate
NATO launches air war against Serbia over treatment of Albanians in Kosovo
School massacre in Littleton, Colorado, sets off debate about violence and gun control
Air war against Serbia ends successfully

2000: Disputed election results in Florida end in Supreme Court ruling that George W. Bush is president
Hillary Rodham Clinton elected to the U.S. Senate
2001: Terrorist attack occurs on September 11
War in Afghanistan
2002: Republicans regain control of Senate and dominate all branches of government
2003: United States at war against Iraq

1990: Hubble Space telescope launched
1991: Basketball star Magic Johnson reveals that he is HIV positive (AIDS virus)
1992: Vice President Dan Quayle attacks single mother premise of sit-com *Murphy Brown*
1993: Author Toni Morrison wins Nobel Prize for literature
1994: O. J. Simpson murder trial grips nation
Death of Jacqueline Kennedy Onassis
1995: Simpson's acquittal sparks national furor

1996: Jazz singer Ella Fitzgerald dies
Virginia Military Institute admits women
1997: Movie *Titanic* sets all-time box office record for receipts
Princess Diana killed
Spice Girls group has top pop album *Spice*
1998: Singer Frank Sinatra dies
Slugger Mark McGwire hits 70 home runs for all-time record

1999: Death of baseball star Joe DiMaggio
Michael Jordan (basketball) and Wayne Gretzky (hockey) retire from professional sports
Star Wars, Episode I, The Phantom Menace opens to long lines and critical panning
2001: Michael Jordan returns to basketball.
2002: Former President Jimmy Carter receives Nobel Peace Prize
2003: Columbia space shuttle explodes, killing all seven astronauts
Fred Rogers dies

1991: Economy enters recession that will last until late 1992
1992: Unemployment reaches 7.8 percent, the highest since 1983
1993: United States and Europe agree on new terms for General Agreement on Tariffs and Trade (GATT)
Clinton administration proposes national health care plan
North American Free Trade Agreement (NAFTA) approved in Congress

1994: Clinton health care plan dies in Congress
1995: Budget battle in Congress produces closing of federal government in December
1996: Congress passes sweeping welfare reform bill
2001 Congress passes Bush's tax cut

1997: Unemployment rate in May falls to 4.8 percent, the lowest since 1973
Budget surplus reported and future surpluses are projected
1998: Dow Jones average closes above 9,000 in April
1999: Dow Jones hovers around 11,000 in May
United States has strongest economy in world as twentieth century draws to a close, but stability of world financial system is still a concern

29 THE TURBULENT YEARS 1960–1968

President Kennedy delivered a stirring inaugural address on a cloudless, bitter-cold afternoon in January 1961.
© 1998 JP Owen/Black Star

The 1960s opened on an ambivalent note. The gross national product reached $500 billion for the first time, yet talk of economic recession was in the air. The darkest days of McCarthyism were over, yet the fear of communism remained. The development of new products and technologies bred optimism, yet the spread of new weapons caused alarm.

Hints of protest and trouble had begun to appear. In Greensboro, North Carolina, four black college students sat down at a Woolworth lunch counter and were denied service, but refused to leave. Word of their defiance triggered "sit-in" protests across the South, with demonstrators bravely confronting Jim Crow. Half a world away, supporters of North Vietnam's Communist ruler Ho Chi Minh announced the formation of a National Liberation Front to overthrow the anti-Communist government of President Ngo Dinh Diem in South Vietnam. President Diem did not seem concerned. With U.S. support, he boasted, his forces would quickly subdue these "Viet Cong" (or Vietnamese Communists) and bring peace to his land.

EARLY TESTS

The 1960 election was a landmark event in American political history. At age forty-three, John Kennedy became the first Catholic president, the youngest candidate to win a presidential election, and the first president to be born in the twentieth century. His inauguration on January 20, 1961, seemed to herald a new era of idealism, commitment, and change. Kennedy declared that the "torch has been passed to a new generation of Americans," adding: "Ask not what your country can do for you; ask what you can do for your country."

Idealism and Caution

The new administration appeared to mirror these words. Young people converged on Washington with a fervor reminiscent of the early New Deal years. Public service became a badge of honor. Kennedy's White House staff included fifteen Rhodes scholars and numerous Ivy League professors. The new secretary of state, Dean Rusk, came from the Rockefeller

CHRONOLOGY

1961 Bay of Pigs invasion fails • East Germany erects Berlin Wall • Peace Corps established

1962 Cuban missile crisis sparks nuclear confrontation • War on Poverty is formulated • Students for a Democratic Society (SDS) is organized

1963 Martin Luther King, Jr., delivers "I Have a Dream" speech at Lincoln Memorial • United States and Soviet Union sign treaty banning above-ground nuclear tests • President Kennedy is assassinated; Lyndon B. Johnson becomes president

1964 Congress passes Gulf of Tonkin Resolution • Freedom Summer voting rights campaign begins in Mississippi • Congress passes landmark Civil Rights Act • President Johnson elected by record margin

1965 American ground troops sent to Vietnam, escalating commitment • Race riot erupts in Watts, Los Angeles • Congress passes Voting Rights Act • Malcolm X assassinated

1966 Black Panthers organized in California • U.S. combat deaths in Vietnam increase tenfold to 6,664 • Antiwar protests spread to major state universities

1967 Race riots erupt in Detroit, Newark, and other cities • Thousands gather in Haight-Ashbury, San Francisco, for "summer of love"

1968 Communists launch Tet offensive in South Vietnam • President Johnson announces he will not seek reelection • Martin Luther King, Jr., is assassinated in Memphis • Robert Kennedy is assassinated in Los Angeles • Richard Nixon is elected president

Foundation, while the new defense secretary, Robert McNamara, left the presidency of the Ford Motor Company to help "streamline" the nation's armed forces. Kennedy chose his younger brother Robert to become attorney general. Under Jacqueline Kennedy's direction, the White House became a center for the arts. Cellist Pablo Casals performed at the Executive Mansion, as did the American Shakespeare Festival Theatre.

Despite the lofty rhetoric and the fanfare, Kennedy took a measured approach to his early presidential duties, particularly in domestic affairs. For one thing, he lacked the huge popular mandate given to previous first-term presidents such as Franklin Roosevelt in 1932 and Dwight Eisenhower in 1952. For another, he worried about his relations with a Congress in which conservative Republicans and southern Democrats held the balance of power.

Several of Kennedy's early initiatives were in the New Deal tradition. He worked successfully to increase social security benefits and to raise the minimum wage from $1 to $1.25. Yet the Congress easily blocked his efforts to provide health insurance for the aged and to create a cabinet-level Department of Urban Affairs. Worse still was the defeat of Kennedy's $2.3 billion education bill for school construction and higher teachers' salaries, which raised nagging questions about the federal role in education. Would funds be given to racially segregated public schools or to private religious schools? At first, Kennedy opposed parochial school assistance, fearing a political backlash. Amid the confusion, the education bill died in committee.

In other areas, the new administration achieved success. By executive order, Kennedy launched the Peace Corps in March 1961, an idea modeled partly on Franklin Roosevelt's Civilian Conservation Corps. Directed by the president's brother-in-law R. Sargent Shriver, the Peace Corps sent thousands of American volunteers to underdeveloped nations to provide educational and technical assistance. With a tiny budget, it became one of Kennedy's great triumphs, showcasing American idealism and know-how throughout the world. Within three years, almost 10,000 volunteers were at work in forty-six countries, teaching school, staffing hospitals, and planting new crops.

Even more popular, though far more expensive, was the space program. Unlike Eisenhower, who opposed a costly "race to the moon with Russia," the new president viewed an American victory in this contest as essential to national prestige. Setting the goal of a manned moon landing "before this decade is out," Kennedy convinced a skeptical Congress to allocate billions of dollars for space research and rocketry, an astronauts training program, and a mission control center in Houston.

The "space race" captivated the world. In April 1961, Soviet Cosmonaut Yuri Gagarin orbited the globe in less than two hours. A month later, Commander Alan Shepard rocketed 300 miles from Cape Canaveral in a suborbital flight, and in February 1962, Lieutenant Colonel John Glenn orbited the earth three times aboard *Friendship 7* before touching down in the Caribbean. Glenn became a national hero, with ticker tape parades and a televised address before a joint session of Congress.

The Bay of Pigs

Kennedy inherited his first crisis from the previous administration. As president-elect, he was told of a secret plan, personally approved by Eisenhower, to overthrow the new Marxist government of Fidel Castro in Cuba. The plan called for several hundred anti-Castro exiles, trained and equipped by the CIA, to invade Cuba and trigger an anti-communist revolution.

Kennedy endorsed the plan for several reasons. He believed that Castro set a dangerous example by aligning Cuba with the Soviet Union and by expropriating the property of American corporations. Kennedy had promised to "get tough" with Castro during the 1960 campaign. He could not easily back down now.

On April, 17, 1961, a brigade of 1,500 waded ashore at the Bay of Pigs, on Cuba's southern coast. Nothing went as planned. The landing site had sharp coral reefs and swampy terrain, making it hard to unload supplies and move out from the beaches. Local workers quickly spotted the invaders, and news of their arrival sparked no popular uprising against Castro.

Kennedy refused to lend vital air and naval support to the brigade in a futile attempt to hide America's role in this disaster. More than a hundred invaders were killed, and 1,200 were captured. After reviewing the events with his advisors, Kennedy took a walk on the White House lawn. It was "the first time in my life," a friend recalled, "that I ever saw tears come to his eyes."

The Bay of Pigs fiasco left a troubled legacy. On the one hand, it angered other Latin American governments and drove Castro even closer to the Russian embrace. On the other, it fueled Kennedy's interest in covert operations and his desire to control them more directly. After removing longtime CIA Director Allen Dulles, the president approved a top-secret program, code-named Operation Mongoose, to topple the Cuban government and assassinate its leaders. Its plans included the destruction of Cuba's vital sugar crop, and a box of exploding cigars for Castro.

Most important was the public reaction. Rather than hurting Kennedy, the incident marked him as a man of action, willing to take chances in the war against communism. Opinion polls gave him higher ratings after the Bay of Pigs than at any other point in his presidency. "It's just like Eisenhower," he quipped. "The worse I do the more popular I get."

The Berlin Wall

In June 1961, Kennedy met with Soviet leader Nikita Khrushchev in Vienna. Khrushchev tried to bully the new president, threatening to give East Germany full control over road and rail access to West Berlin, in violation of previous guarantees. Berlin was both a danger and an embarrassment to Khrushchev. The prosperous Western sector stood as a model of democratic capitalism behind the Iron Curtain. Each day, more than a thousand refugees from the communist side poured into West Berlin. At this rate, East Germany would lose most of its skilled workers to the West.

Kennedy was not intimidated. Calling West Berlin "the great testing place of courage and will," he declared that NATO forces would defend the city at all costs. To emphasize this point, the president tripled draft calls, mobilized reserve units, and requested $3 billion in additional defense appropriations, which Congress quickly granted. The crisis ended in August 1961. As the world watched in amazement, workers in East Berlin constructed a wall of barbed wire and concrete around the western edge of their city, sealing off East Berlin, and eventually all of East Germany, from the noncommunist world. In a tactical sense, Khrushchev achieved his objective of stopping the East German exodus to the West. In a larger sense, however, the wall became an admission of failure—a monument to oppression and to freedom denied.

The Freedom Riders

Kennedy's first domestic crisis occurred in the field of civil rights. An integrationist at heart, the president wanted change to come slowly, without the mass protests and violent incidents that had made headlines around the world. He worried, too, that White House support for *immediate* desegregation would cost him the good will of powerful southerners in Congress.

Yet, as Kennedy discovered, the real momentum for civil rights came from below. In 1961, the Congress of Racial Equality (CORE) announced plans to test a recent Supreme Court decision, *Boynton v. Virginia*, which prohibited racial segregation in bus terminals, train stations, and airports engaged in interstate transportation. CORE's objective, said its national director, was "to provoke the southern authorities into arresting us and thereby prod the Justice Department into enforcing the law of the land."

| **Table 29.1** | **Persons Below Poverty Level: 1959–1969** |

	NUMBER BELOW POVERTY LEVEL (IN MILLIONS)			*PERCENT BELOW POVERTY LEVEL*		
Year	Total	White	Black and Other Races	Total	White	Black and Other Races
1969	24.3	16.7	7.6	12%	10%	31%
1968	25.4	17.4	8.0	13	10	33
1967	27.8	19.0	8.8	14	11	37
1966	28.5	19.3	9.2	15	11	40
1965	33.2	22.5	10.7	17	13	47
1964	36.1	25.0	11.1	19	15	50
1963	36.4	25.2	11.2	19	15	51
1962	38.6	26.7	12.0	21	16	56
1961	39.6	27.9	11.7	22	17	56
1960	39.9	28.3	11.5	22	18	56
1959	39.5	28.5	11.0	22	18	56

Note: The poverty threshold for a nonfarm family of four was $3,743 in 1969 and $2,973 in 1959.
Source: Congressional Quarterly, *Civil Rights: A Progress Report*, 1971, p. 46.

PICTURING THE PAST✦ECONOMICS & TECHNOLOGY

POVERTY IN AMERICA

© Joffre Clarke/Black Star

In an era of increased abundance and consumerism, it was easy to forget that our country's great wealth and prosperity were not shared by all. This painful truth became the subject of a pathbreaking book, *The Other America,* by socialist author Michael Harrington, in 1962. Harrington estimated that more than 40 million people—almost one-quarter of the nation's population—lived in an "economic underworld" of joblessness, marginal wages, hunger, and despair. He emphasized that poverty could be found in every corner of the nation—among whites and blacks, natives and immigrants, rural folk and city dwellers. The picture here is from Appalachia, one of the region's highlighted in Harrington's book. It demonstrates the author's point that poverty is "a culture, an institution, a way of life" passed from one generation to the next. The powerful response to Harrington's book led to a vast array of social programs popularly known, in the words of President Lyndon Johnson, as the War on Poverty.

In May 1961, thirteen "freedom riders"—seven blacks and six whites—left Washington on a Greyhound bus bound for New Orleans. Most were veterans of the sit-ins. At each stop, they ignored the "white" and "colored" signs that hung by the toilets, lunch counters, and waiting rooms in defiance of federal law. Trouble erupted in Anniston, Alabama, when their bus was firebombed by a white mob. As the passengers struggled outside, they were beaten with fists and clubs. One rider suffered permanent brain damage from repeated blows to the head.

When the violence continued in Montgomery and Birmingham, Alabama, Attorney General Robert Kennedy urged CORE to end the freedom rides, claiming that they embarrassed President Kennedy on the eve of his summit with Premier Khrushchev. "Doesn't the attorney general know," a black Alabaman responded, "that we've been embarrassed all our lives?"

As new freedom riders arrived to replace the wounded, the Kennedy administration sent in federal marshals to protect them. It had no choice, given the violent scenes that flashed around the world. In September 1961, the federal government banned interstate carriers from using any terminal that segregated the races. After months of bloody struggle, the freedom riders prevailed.

The New Economics

Despite his increasing focus on civil rights, President Kennedy considered the economy to be his number-one domestic concern. Economic growth in the Eisenhower years had been steady, but increasingly slow. Though real wages for an average family rose a remarkable 20 percent in the 1950s, a series of recessions toward the end of Eisenhower's second term prompted both a drop in factory production and a rise in unemployment. By the time Kennedy took office, more Americans were out of work than at any time since the end of World War II.

In 1962, Kennedy unveiled an economic program that differed sharply from the spending model of the New Deal and Fair Deal. Instead, he proposed a major tax cut for consumers and businesses, designed to stimulate purchasing power and encourage new investment. For Kennedy, the goal of full employment required sizable budget deficits in the short run as tax revenues declined. What worried him was the specter of inflation as the economy heated up.

To prevent this, Kennedy lobbied business and labor leaders to respect the wage-price guidelines his administration recommended to keep inflation in check. The Teamsters, Auto Workers, and Steel Workers all agreed to modest wage hikes in 1962 with the understanding that their employers would not raise prices. Two weeks later, U.S. Steel, the nation's third largest corporation, announced a whopping price increase of six dollars a ton, leading other steel companies to do the same.

Calling the move an "irresponsible defiance of the public interest," Kennedy used his influence to roll back the price increase. Within days, the Justice Department threatened to investigate antitrust violations in the steel industry, while the Defense Department announced that it might not purchase steel from the "price-gouging" offenders.

Under enormous pressure, the steel companies gave in. The president had won a major victory in his battle against inflation, although his rough tactics aroused deep anger in the business community. Nevertheless, the economy prospered in the early 1960s, achieving low unemployment, stable prices, and steady growth.

SOCIAL AND POLITICAL CHALLENGES

Before long, President Kennedy's political caution began to ease. A year of trial and error led him to take more confident stands in certain areas, such as U.S.–Soviet relations and the push for civil rights. As events unfolded in 1962, the president faced challenges in familiar places—the Deep South and the waters off Cuba. This time, the stakes were much higher.

The Battle for Ole Miss

In the fall of 1962, a federal court ordered the admission of James Meredith, a black air force veteran, to the all-white University of Mississippi, known as Ole Miss. Governor Ross Barnett led the opposition. A virulent racist, who claimed that "God made the Negro different to punish him," Barnett had kept a previous black applicant from entering Ole Miss by having him committed to a mental hospital. Now Barnett invoked the doctrine of interposition—a throwback to antebellum times—by warning that Mississippi would ignore all federal rulings in order to keep segregation in place.

Kennedy responded to Barnett's challenge by dispatching several hundred federal marshals to Ole Miss. They were met by a well-armed mob, more than 2,000 strong. In the riot that followed, two people were killed and hundreds were injured, including twenty-eight marshals hit by gunfire. Like Eisenhower during the Little Rock crisis, Kennedy rushed in troops and federalized the State Guard. With 23,000 soldiers on campus—five times the student population—Meredith registered for classes under army bayonets. The battle at Ole Miss was over; the larger struggle for Mississippi lay ahead.

The Missiles of October

In October 1962, the world faced the most dangerous confrontation of the entire Cold War. It began with rumors, confirmed by U-2 spy plane photos, that the Russians were deploying Intermediate-Range Ballistic Missiles (IRBMs) in Cuba. Speed was essential, for the missiles would become operational in less than a month. Kennedy convened an executive committee (known as ex-Comm) to provide a suitable response.

Castro's need for security was understandable. In addition to Operation Mongoose, the Kennedy administration had imposed an economic embargo on Cuba and engineered its expulsion from the Organization of American States. At Castro's urging, the Soviet Union sent thousands of military advisors to Cuba, as well as defensive missiles to shoot down invading planes. Yet the deployment of *offensive* weapons, capable of reaching Chicago or Washington with nuclear warheads, was an alarming escalation designed to tip the balance of terror in Moscow's favor.

MEDIUM RANGE BALLISTIC MISSILE BASE IN CUBA
SAN CRISTOBAL
LAUNCH POSITION
MISSILE-READY TENTS
MISSILE ERECTORS
LATE OCTOBER

U-2 photos, such as this one, of missile bases being constructed in Cuba led to the most dangerous confrontation of the Cold War.
© Bettmann/UPI/Corbis

Some ex-Comm members recommended immediate air strikes to take out the missile bases. Others, including Robert Kennedy, proposed a naval blockade of Cuba. The president carefully studied both options before choosing the latter. A blockade shifted the burden of responsibility to Khrushchev while allowing both sides to seek a solution short of war.

On October 22, 1962, Kennedy revealed the existence of the missiles in a nationally televised address. After describing the naval blockade, he demanded that Russia remove the IRBMs already in place. Any missile fired from Cuba, he warned, would be regarded "as an attack by the Soviet Union on the United States," requiring a "full retaliatory response." American forces went on full alert. A U-2 plane over Cuba was shot down, and its pilot killed. The entire world watched anxiously as Russian vessels in the Caribbean inched closer to American warships enforcing the blockade.

On October 26, Kennedy received an emotional note from Khrushchev suggesting a settlement: Russia would remove its missiles if the United States pledged never to invade Cuba. Before the president could respond, however, a second note arrived demanding that the United States also remove its Jupiter missiles along the Soviet border in Turkey. This new demand did not pose a security problem, since the Jupiter mis-

siles were obsolete and about to be scrapped. Yet the president could not remove them without appearing to buckle under Soviet pressure.

Robert Kennedy provided the solution. Respond to the first note, he said, and ignore the second one. On October 27, the president vowed not to invade Cuba if the IRBMs were dismantled. In private, meanwhile, Robert Kennedy assured Soviet Ambassador Anatoly Dobrynin that the Jupiter missiles would be removed from Turkey in the near future. Kennedy also gave Dobrynin a deadline. If the Cuban missiles were not dismantled within forty-eight hours, the United States would destroy them.

On October 28, Khrushchev accepted the deal. The Soviet premier had badly miscalculated the stern American reaction to the placement of offensive missiles in Cuba, though his restraint in the crisis helped to assure a peaceful solution. Khrushchev soon left office in disgrace, while Kennedy's reputation soared. For two weeks in October, the world seemed headed for nuclear war.

That fact alone seemed to sober both sides. In July 1963, a direct telephone link, known as the "hotline," was established between the White House and the Kremlin. In August, the United States and Russia joined with ninety other nations to sign the "Treaty Banning Nuclear Weapons Tests in the Atmosphere, in Outer Space, and Under Water." The treaty did not prevent underground testing or provide for on-site inspection, and several emerging atomic powers, such as France and China, refused to take part. Yet a first step had been taken to cleanse the environment of radioactivity—a symbolic step on the road to a safer world.

Trouble in Vietnam

President Kennedy came away from the missile crisis with greater confidence in his ability to manage foreign problems. His primary goal, in military terms, was to replace the Eisenhower-Dulles doctrine of "massive retaliation" with a "flexible response" policy that would maximize his options in any foreign crisis. The plan called for a buildup in nuclear missiles, conventional ground troops, and Special Forces such as the "Green Berets." Not surprisingly, the defense budget rose rapidly in the Kennedy years, with Congress approving virtually all of the president's military spending requests. Under JFK, the armed forces added ten Polaris submarines, 200,000 ground troops, and 400 Minutemen missiles, giving the United States a sizable advantage over Russia in nuclear weapons.

When Kennedy entered the White House, American aid to South Vietnam topped $1 billion, and several hundred American military advisors were in the field. Like Eisenhower, Kennedy hoped to formalize Vietnam's temporary partition at the 17th parallel by turning the South Vietnamese regime of Ngo Dingh Diem into a military and economic power capable of defending itself against attacks from Ho Chi Minh's Communist government in the North.

Kennedy welcomed the challenge. Under the doctrine of "flexible response," U.S. Special Forces were dispatched to train South Vietnam's army, along with CIA personnel to direct covert operations and economic experts to supervise the aid programs intended to stabilize Diem's regime. Among the worst problems, it turned out, was Diem himself. Educated in the United States, a Catholic in a largely Buddhist land, Diem had little in common with the people he ruled. The South Vietnam he envisioned did not include the vital measures, such as land reform and religious toleration, that were needed to keep him in power.

In 1963, protests erupted in Saigon and other South Vietnamese cities over Diem's autocratic rule. The Buddhists held mass demonstrations against religious oppression, with several monks setting fire to themselves. As the protests escalated, army units attacked Buddhist temples and arrested their priests, sparking even greater protests from the Buddhist majority. Isolated in his presidential palace, Diem seemed oblivious to the crisis.

That fall, Diem was overthrown in a military coup engineered by South Vietnam's top generals. American officials knew about the coup, but did nothing to stop it. To their surprise, however, the generals murdered Diem and his brother, Ngo Dinh Nhu, after taking them prisoner on the palace grounds.

By that time, 16,000 American "advisors" were stationed in South Vietnam. For Kennedy and his advisors, the struggle had become a test of will against "communist aggression." Yet the president also worried that the use of American troops created a dangerous momentum of its own. "It's like taking a drink," he said. "The effect wears off and you have to take another."

THE RIGHTS REVOLUTION: EARLY STEPS

In the early 1960s, the fires of social and political protest slowly came alive, fanned by the civil rights movement and the New Frontier's vision of idealism and change. In 1962, as James Meredith challenged the once impene-

Quang Duc, a Buddhist monk in Saigon, burned himself to death in June 1963 to protest the crackdown on Buddhists by South Vietnamese President Ngo Dinh Diem. The Buddhist protests helped bring down the Diem government later that year.
AP/Wide World Photos/Malcolm Browne

trable wall of segregation at Ole Miss, a thirty-five-year-old Mexican American named Cesar Chavez moved to Delano, California, with his wife and eight children. A naval veteran of World War II, Chavez toiled in the plum orchards and strawberry fields of central California before turning to community organizing. With unshakable conviction, he aimed to better the lives of impoverished migrant farm laborers by uniting them under a single banner—the black Aztec eagle of the infant United Farm Workers of America.

The year 1962 also witnessed the publication of two pathbreaking books about the underside of modern society: Michael Harrington's *The Other America* and Rachel Carson's *Silent Spring.* Carson, a marine biologist, exposed the contamination of wildlife, water supplies, and farmland by pesticides such as DDT. Her book helped revive America's naturalist movement. In 1963, two more seminal works appeared: Betty Friedan's *The Feminine Mystique,* which spurred the struggle for women's rights, and James Baldwin's *The Fire Next Time,* which warned of the growing racial divide. "To be a Negro in this country and to be relatively conscious," wrote Baldwin, "is to be in a rage all the time."

From Birmingham to Washington

By 1963, racial injustice in America was a central issue. Birmingham, Alabama, became the new battleground, as a coalition of civil rights groups, led by Martin Luther King's Southern Christian Leadership

Led by Eugene ("Bull") Connor, Birmingham police used attack dogs and high-pressure fire hoses to disperse civil rights demonstrators.
AP/Wide World Photos

Conference, attempted to break down the walls of discrimination in a city where African Americans had few economic opportunities or political rights. Birmingham was so rigidly segregated that a book featuring black rabbits and white rabbits eating together was removed from city libraries, and a campaign was underway to banish "Negro music" from "white" radio stations.

Dr. King hoped to integrate Birmingham with a series of nonviolent protests code-named "Project C," for confrontation. Using the local black churches as meeting houses, he recruited hundreds of followers with his revivalist appeals.

The demonstrations challenged segregation on many fronts. There were sit-ins at lunch counters, kneel-ins at white churches, and voter registration marches to city hall. Boycotts were organized to protest the all-white hiring practices of downtown department stores. Birmingham authorities cracked down hard. Led by Commissioner Eugene ("Bull") Connor, city police dispersed the protesters—many of them schoolchildren—with attack dogs and high-pressure fire hoses.

Dr. King was among the hundreds arrested for violating local court orders against marching and picketing. From his jail cell, he defended the morality of civil disobedience, noting that "segregation statutes are unjust because segregation distorts the soul." President Kennedy offered firm support. After dispatching

federal troops to Birmingham, he assisted in an agreement that integrated the city's lunch counters and department stores. At that very moment, however, Governor George C. Wallace—proclaiming "Segregation Now! Segregation Tomorrow! Segregation Forever"—vowed to block the admission of two black students to the University of Alabama by "standing in the schoolhouse door." When federal marshals arrived, Wallace dramatically stepped aside.

The president's decisive action in Alabama signaled a major change. Viewing civil rights for the first time as a *moral* issue, Kennedy delivered a moving appeal for justice on national television. "One hundred years have passed since President Lincoln freed the slaves," he said, "yet their heirs, their grandsons, are not fully free. . . . And this nation, for all its hope and all its boasts, will not be fully free until all its citizens are free." Later that evening, civil rights activist Medgar Evers was assassinated outside his Jackson, Mississippi, home by a member of the Ku Klux Klan.

In June 1963, Kennedy sent Congress one of the most sweeping civil rights bills of the twentieth century. The bill, which prohibited discrimination in employment, federally assisted programs, and public accommodations such as restaurants and hotels, caused a furor on Capitol Hill. Southern legislators accused the president of "race-mixing," while others, including Senator Barry Goldwater of Arizona, criticized him for abusing the "property rights" of business owners. As the bill's momentum stalled, a number of civil rights groups led by A. Philip Randolph, longtime president of the Brotherhood of Sleeping Car Porters, announced a "March on Washington for Jobs and Freedom."

On August 28, 1963, more than 200,000 people gathered at the Lincoln Memorial in the largest civil rights demonstration ever held on American soil. They listened to the spirituals of Mahalia Jackson, locked arms in solidarity as Joan Baez sang "We Shall Overcome," the anthem of the civil rights struggle, and rose in thunderous applause to the final words of Martin Luther King's now legendary address, "I Have a Dream."

Feminist Stirrings

The civil rights movement always possessed a strong female strain. From Rosa Parks in Montgomery to Fannie Lou Hamer of the Mississippi Freedom Democratic party, women played a prominent role in the struggle for black equality. By 1963, the spirit of these protests created a sense of determination that sparked other movements, such as women's rights.

The revival of feminism in the 1960s seemed long overdue. More than four decades after winning the vote,

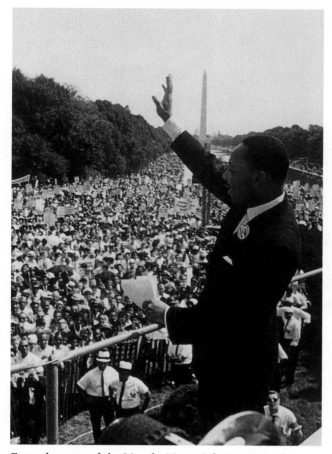

From the steps of the Lincoln Memorial, Martin Luther King, Jr., delivered his eloquent address "I Have a Dream" to a gathering of 200,000 people who had come to Washington to push for passage of a landmark civil rights bill in August 1963.
© Bettmann/UPI/Corbis

1962) and Esther Peterson, an assistant secretary of labor, the commission detailed a wide range of problems, including job discrimination, unequal wages, lack of child care, and legal restrictions that prevented women, in some states, from sitting on juries or making wills. In direct response, President Kennedy issued an executive order banning sex discrimination in federal employment. A few months later, Congress passed the Equal Pay Act of 1963, requiring employers to provide equal wages to men and women who did the same work.

Even more important in terms of the emerging women's movement was the publication of *The Feminine Mystique.* In the opening chapters, Betty Friedan described "the problem that has no name," the emptiness felt by middle-class women who sacrificed their dreams and careers to become the "happy homemakers" of suburban America. Blaming educators, advertisers, social scientists and government officials for creating a climate in which femininity and domesticity went hand in hand, Friedan concluded that "we can no longer ignore that voice in women that says: 'I want something more than my husband and my children and my home.' "

The Feminine Mystique became an instant bestseller because it voiced the unspoken feelings of so many women. Their unhappiness was not caused by individual neuroses, Friedan argued, but rather by a set of cultural values that oppressed women while pretending to improve their lives. The message, she added, was that women must grasp their common problems in order to solve them.

American women played a minor role in government affairs. In 1963, there were no women governors, cabinet officers, or Supreme Court justices. The U.S. Senate contained one female member, Margaret Chase Smith of Maine. Women comprised 51 percent of the population, but only 3 percent of state legislators nationwide.

Discrimination also pervaded the workplace. Though more women were working outside the home in the early 1960s than ever before, they were increasingly concentrated in low-paying service and clerical jobs, despite their rising level of education. Fewer than 4 percent of the nation's lawyers, and 1 percent of the top business executives, were female. As a result, full-time working women earned about 60 percent of the income of men.

These inequities were highlighted in 1963 by the final report of the Presidential Commission on the Status of Women. Led by Eleanor Roosevelt (who died in

TRAGEDY AND TRANSITION

By the fall of 1963, the fast pace and rapid changes of the new decade were leaving their mark. A growing economy, an emerging rights revolution, an expanding war in Southeast Asia, a frantic race to the moon—each would serve to reshape the fabric of American life in the years ahead. First, however, tragedy intervened.

Dallas

In late November 1963, John and Jacqueline Kennedy traveled to Texas on a political fence-mending tour. The 1964 presidential race was approaching, and Texas, which had narrowly supported the Kennedy–Johnson ticket three years before, could not be taken for granted. After greeting friendly crowds in Fort

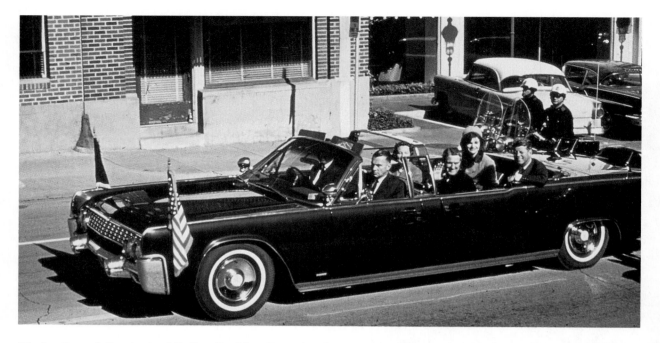

Moving through the streets of Dallas, President Kennedy's limousine headed toward Dealy Plaza—and tragedy—on November 22, 1963.
© Bettmann/UPI/Corbis

Worth, the Kennedys took a motorcade through Dallas, with the bubble-top of their limousine removed on a warm and cloudless day. Along the route, people waved from office buildings and cheered from the sidewalks. As the procession reached Dealy Plaza, shots rang out from the window of a nearby book depository. President Kennedy grabbed his throat and slumped to the seat. Texas Governor John Connally was wounded in the back, wrist, and leg. The motorcade raced to Parkland Hospital, where the president was pronounced dead.

Within hours, the Dallas police arrested a twenty-four-year-old suspect named Lee Harvey Oswald. Two days later, Oswald was shot and killed in the basement of Dallas police headquarters by Jack Ruby, a local nightclub owner with a shady past. These shocking events led many Americans to conclude that Oswald was innocent or that he did not act alone. Dozens of theories surfaced about the Kennedy assassination, blaming leftists and rightists, Fidel Castro and the Mafia, the Ku Klux Klan and the CIA. The most logical theory, that a deranged man had committed a senseless act of violence, did not seem compelling enough to explain the death of a president so young and full of life.

Few events in the nation's history produced so much bewilderment and grief. Charming and handsome, a war hero with a glamorous wife, Kennedy seemed the ideal president for the electronic political age. The media likened his administration to Camelot, a magical place that symbolized courage, chivalry, and hope. His tragic death added the further dimension of promise unfulfilled.

The reality was rather different, of course. Kennedy's 1,037 days in office were marked by failures as well as successes, and his leadership was more decisive in foreign policy than it was in domestic affairs. Since his death, moreover, evidence of his extramarital affairs and other personal shortcomings have raised legitimate questions about his character and morality. Still, the president's final months were his most productive by far. The Test Ban Treaty offered hope for a safer world, and a new civil rights bill had been sent to Capitol Hill. There is also the suggestion—disputed by some—that Kennedy was rethinking his position on Vietnam. "If I tried to pull out completely now," he told Senator Mike Mansfield, "we would have another Joe McCarthy red scare on our hands, but I can do it after I'm reelected."

The trip to Dallas shattered those hopes and plans.

LBJ

Within hours of the assassination, Lyndon Johnson took the presidential oath of office aboard *Air Force One,* with his wife, Lady Bird, and Jacqueline Kennedy

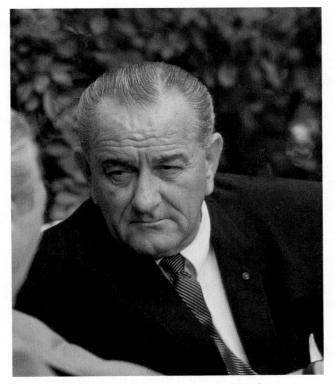

Lyndon Johnson provided a smooth transition by promising to continue the programs and policies of President Kennedy. Yet retaining Kennedy's key advisors served to limit Johnson's options, particularly in foreign affairs.
© Dennis Brack/Black Star

standing at his side. As the nation mourned its fallen leader, President Johnson vowed to continue the programs and policies of the Kennedy administration. "All I have," he told a special session of Congress, "I would gladly have given not to be standing here today."

Lyndon Baines Johnson—known as LBJ—bore little resemblance to the president he replaced. Born in the Texas hill country in 1908, Johnson came from a different region, a lower social class, and an older political generation. After graduating from a public college, he worked in the Washington office of a Texas congressman before returning home to become state director of the National Youth Administration, a New Deal agency that provided work-study funds for needy students. Under Johnson's leadership, the Texas NYA became a model for the nation, providing employment for blacks and whites in the construction of neighborhood playgrounds and roadside parks. The experience turned him into an avid New Dealer, with confidence in the government's ability to help people in need. Johnson described Franklin Roosevelt, his mentor and role model, as "like a daddy to me."

In the following years, Johnson won a seat in Congress, served as a naval officer during World War II, and became a U.S. senator in 1949. (His margin of victory, a mere eighty-seven votes, earned him the nickname "Landslide Lyndon.") Elected Senate majority leader by his Democratic colleagues in the 1950s, Johnson worked efficiently with the Eisenhower White House to craft important legislation on defense spending, highway construction, and civil rights.

LBJ lacked the good looks and regal charm of John Kennedy. He seemed crude and plodding by comparison, with his heavy drawl, cowboy boots, and earthy language. Yet few people in Washington knew more about the political process—how things really got done. Johnson recognized the true pockets of power. He knew when to flatter, when to bully, and when to bargain. Incredibly ambitious and hardworking—he survived a near-fatal heart attack in 1955—Johnson entered the White House with three decades of political experience under his belt.

Tax Cuts and Civil Rights

The new president moved quickly to restore public confidence through a smooth transition of power. To calm mounting suspicion of conspiracy, he appointed a seven-member commission, headed by Chief Justice Earl Warren, to investigate the Kennedy assassination and issue a report. To provide stability in the executive branch, he convinced Secretary of State Dean Rusk, Secretary of Defense Robert McNamara, chief economic advisor Walter Heller, and other key officials to remain at their jobs. Where Kennedy had proclaimed "Let us begin," Johnson added "Let us *continue!*"

One of his first acts as president was to work for the tax cut that Heller and Kennedy had supported. To please fiscal conservatives in Congress, Johnson agreed to slash the federal budget. He believed that lower taxes would spur economic growth and lower unemployment, thereby increasing federal revenues down the road. In February 1964, Johnson signed a measure that cut taxes by $10 billion over the next two years.

The economy responded. With more money available for investment and consumption, the gross national product shot up 7 percent in 1964 and 8 percent the following year, while unemployment fell below 5 percent for the first time since World War II. Furthermore, the economic boom generated even greater federal revenues—just as Johnson had predicted.

Within weeks after taking office, the president met with Martin Luther King, Jr., and other black leaders to assure them of his commitment to civil rights. This was essential, for Johnson's public record was mixed. As a young senator, he had opposed virtually all of President Truman's civil rights initiatives. Yet as majority leader, he had helped pass legislation giving the Justice Department more authority to enforce school integration and protect black voting rights. In his heart, Johnson considered segregation to be an immoral system that retarded an entire region's advancement. "He felt about the race question much as I did," a Texas friend recalled, "namely that it obsessed the South and diverted it from attending to its economic and educational problems."

The civil rights bill had strong public backing outside the South. In February, the House of Representatives easily approved it by a vote of 290 to 130, but the bill hit a wall in the Senate, where southern opponents used the filibuster to prevent its passage. The bill's success depended on a vote for cloture, ending debate, which required the agreement of two-thirds of the Senate. Working together, Senators Hubert Humphrey (D-Minnesota) and Everett Dirksen (R-Illinois) gathered bipartisan support. The Senate voted for cloture on June 10, 1964 (ending a seventy-five-day filibuster), and passed the bill the following afternoon. Described by the *New York Times* as "the most far-reaching civil rights [legislation] since Reconstruction days," it withheld federal funds from segregated public programs, created an Equal Employment Opportunity Commission, and outlawed discrimination in public accommodations, such as theaters, restaurants, and hotels. Furthermore, a last-minute lobbying effort by Senator Margaret Chase Smith and other women's rights supporters added another category—"sex"—to the clause in Title Vll that prohibited employment discrimination based on race, creed, or national origin. What seemed like a minor addition became a powerful asset to working women in the future.

President Johnson signed the bill into law on July 2, 1964. Though compliance came slowly, the Civil Rights Act marked a vital turning point in the struggle for equal rights. Citing Victor Hugo, Senator Dirksen declared that "no army can withstand the strength of an idea whose time has come."

Landslide in 1964

LBJ entered the 1964 presidential campaign on a tidal wave of popularity and good will. His early months in office were blunder-free. The nation prospered, Vietnam appeared as a distant blip on the screen, and the only war on Johnson's public agenda was the one against poverty, which he promised to wage—and win—after his expected victory at the polls.

The summer of 1964, however, offered signs of the trouble to come. In Mississippi, an attempt to register black voters by local activists and northern college students met violent resistance from white mobs. On June 21, three volunteers—James Chaney, Andrew Goodman, and Michael Schwerner—disappeared after inspecting the ruins of a firebombed black church. Because Goodman and Schwerner were northern whites, the incident made the front pages of newspapers across the country. Five weeks later, FBI agents found three bodies buried in an earthen dam. The civil rights workers had been murdered by local Klansmen and police, seven of whom were eventually convicted and sent to jail.

Racial tensions that summer were not confined to the South. In July, a confrontation between residents and police officers in Harlem led to several nights of arson and looting. The trouble was followed by disturbances in the black neighborhoods of Philadelphia, Pennsylvania; Paterson, New Jersey; and Rochester, New York. At the Democratic National Convention in Atlantic City, moreover, the race issue took center stage. While the nomination of President Johnson and Senator Humphrey, his running mate, went smoothly, a floor fight erupted over the seating of two rival Mississippi delegations—one composed of state party segregationists, the other representing the biracial Mississippi Freedom Democratic party (MFDP).

Led by Fannie Lou Hamer, the twentieth child of illiterate sharecroppers, the MFDP spoke for the disenfranchised black majority in Mississippi. "I was beaten till I was exhausted," Hamer told the national convention. "All of this on account we wanted to register, to become first class citizens. If the Freedom Democratic party is not seated now, I question America."

Johnson hoped to compromise. Acting through Senator Humphrey, he offered the Freedom party two voting delegates and the promise of a fully integrated Misssissippi delegation at future national conventions. The compromise pleased no one. Mrs. Hamer rejected it as a "token" gesture, while several white Mississippi delegates left Atlantic City in a huff.

At the Republican National Convention in San Francisco, the simmering feud between moderates and conservatives boiled over, with delegates shouting down opponents with catcalls and boos. After bitter debate, the convention chose Senator Barry Goldwater of Arizona for the presidential nomination, and Representative William Miller of New York for the vice presidential spot. In a defiant acceptance speech, Goldwater promised a "spiritual awakening" for America, adding: "Extremism in the defense of liberty is no vice. Moderation in the pursuit of justice is no virtue."

*P*ICTURING THE PAST ✦ POLITICS & DIPLOMACY

A NEW ERA IN POLITICAL ADVERTISING

"Ten, nine, eight, seven . . .   six, five, four, three . . .   two, one . . .

These are the stakes. To make a world in which all of God's children can live . . .   or to go into the dark. We must either love each other or we must die . . .   The stakes are too high for you to stay home."

VOTE FOR PRESIDENT JOHNSON ON NOVEMBER 3.

By 1964, the use of television for political advertising was on the rise. But negative TV spots, so common in election campaigns today, were still relatively rare. All that changed, however, with an ad (shown here) produced for the Democrats by Doyle Dane Bernbach, one of America's largest advertising firms, which portrayed Republican presidential candidate Barry Goldwater as a dangerous extremist who could easily plunge the world into nuclear war. By following the individual frames, one can see a little girl innocently pulling the petals from a daisy. As she reaches the number nine, an adult voice begins a reverse countdown for the launching of an atomic device. At zero, the girl's face is engulfed by a huge mushroom cloud. The ominous voice-over appears under the final three frames. Ironically, the notorious "Daisy Ad" aired only once on television; the Democrats pulled it after the Republicans filed a formal complaint with the Fair Campaign Practices Committee. But news programs showed the ad over and over again, sending the message into millions of American homes.

Goldwater opposed "big government" in domestic affairs, but supported large military budgets to deter "Communist aggression." His Senate record included votes against social security increases, the Nuclear Test Ban Treaty of 1963, and the Civil Rights Act of 1964. In contrast to Goldwater, President Johnson came across as the candidate of all Americans, with promises galore. "We're in favor of a lot of things and we're against mighty few," he said.

Even in foreign affairs, his least favorite subject, Johnson appeared confident and controlled. In August 1964, two U.S. Navy destroyers, the *Maddox* and *C. Turner Joy,* engaged several North Vietnamese torpedo boats in the Gulf of Tonkin. The truth about this incident—Did a battle really occur? Who fired first? What were American warships doing in these waters?—was overshadowed by Johnson's dramatic re-

sponse. First he ordered U.S. planes to bomb military targets deep inside North Vietnam. Then he requested—and received—a congressional resolution authorizing the president to "take all necessary measures" to repel "further aggression."

The Gulf of Tonkin Resolution gave Johnson the authority he would need to escalate the Vietnam War. During the 1964 campaign, however, he assured voters that nothing could be further from his mind. "We don't want American boys to do the fighting for Asian boys," he declared. "We don't want to get tied down in a land war in Asia."

The election was never in doubt. Johnson projected optimism and energy, while Goldwater appeared defensive and out-of-touch. The president won 61 percent of the popular vote (43 million to 27 million) and forty-four of the fifty states (486 electoral votes to

Goldwater's 52). In addition, his lopsided margin of victory allowed the Democrats to increase their substantial majorities in both houses of Congress.

For Republicans, however, the news was not all bad. The election returns showed that a new coalition was forming in their ranks, with the party gaining strength among middle-class white voters in the South and Southwest. Furthermore, Goldwater attracted thousands of young recruits who were determined to reshape the Republican party along more conservative lines. For these legions, 1964 was a beginning rather than an end.

THE GREAT SOCIETY

President Johnson viewed his landslide victory as a mandate for change. Anxious to leave his mark on history, he spoke of creating "a great society" for Americans in which the "quality of our goals" exceeded the "quantity of our goods," a society in which poverty, ignorance, and discrimination no longer existed, and the spirit of "true community" prevailed.

Declaring War on Poverty

The centerpiece of Johnson's expansive vision was his "War on Poverty," a concept that President Kennedy and his aides had explored shortly before his death. To maintain continuity, Johnson named R. Sargent Shriver, Kennedy's brother-in-law, to coordinate the numerous programs created by the Economic Opportunity Act of 1964, including the Job Corps, the Neighborhood Youth Corps, and Volunteers in Service to America (VISTA), a domestic service program modeled on the Peace Corps. Though Congress allocated $3 billion for these programs in 1965 and 1966, this figure would decline as the Vietnam War expanded.

The most controversial aspect of the "War on Poverty" was its emphasis on "community action," which encouraged neighborhood groups to play an active role in federally funded projects. Some initiatives, such as food stamps and Head Start, a preschool enrichment program, proved very successful. Others were cited for waste and fraud. Of greatest lasting impact, it appeared, was the increase of minority participation in local affairs.

Poverty did decline dramatically in this era—the result of an expanding economy as well as federal programs aimed directly at the poor. In 1960, more than 40 million Americans (20 percent of the population) lived beneath the poverty line; by 1970, that figure had dropped to 24 million (12 percent). For all of its prob-

lems, the much maligned and seriously underfunded War on Poverty achieved a fair measure of success.

Health Care and Immigration Reform

The Great Society included a mixture of original programs and borrowed ideas. A kind of infectious optimism gripped Washington, much like the early days of the New Deal. Nothing seemed politically impossible with Lyndon Johnson in charge.

Health care was a good example. When Johnson took office in 1963, a majority of older Americans were without health insurance, one-fifth of the nation's poor had never visited a doctor, and the infant mortality rate showed no signs of declining, despite the introduction of lifesaving vaccines. Johnson believed that medical care for the poor and the elderly was an essential part of the Great Society. Yet the idea of federal involvement raised fundamental questions about the role of government in a free enterprise system. The American Medical Association (AMA) and private insurers strongly opposed such intervention, calling it "socialized medicine."

After months of intense lobbying, Congress passed the landmark legislation, known as Medicare and Medicaid, that Johnson requested. Medicare provided federal assistance to the elderly for hospital expenses and doctors' fees, while Medicaid extended medical coverage to welfare recipients through matching grants to the states. Both programs grew rapidly, reaching 40 million Americans by 1970. Though supporters pointed with pride to statistics showing both an increase in life expectancy and a drop in infant mortality, critics noted the exploding federal costs, the gaps in coverage, and the inferior quality of health care to the poor. Few government programs proved more controversial and expensive to maintain than Medicare and Medicaid, and none would prove more difficult to reform.

The Great Society also included a new immigration law, passed in 1965. Though vitally important to the nation's future, it went largely unnoticed at the time. In one bold sweep, the Immigration Act removed the "national origins" quotas, as well as the ban on Asians, which dated back to 1924. While setting a ceiling of about 300,000 immigrants per year, the law permitted the family members of American citizens (both naturalized and native-born) to enter the United States without limit.

The impact was dramatic. Prior to 1965, Europe accounted for 90 percent of the new arrivals to the United States; after 1965, only 10 percent. By the mid-1970s, a majority of legal immigrants came from seven

Asian and Latin American countries: Korea, Taiwan, India, the Philippines, Cuba, the Dominican Republic, and Mexico.

THE EXPANDING WAR

Lyndon Johnson inherited a rich agenda from the Kennedy White House, including the War on Poverty and the push for civil rights. But nothing proved as important, or damaging, to his presidency as the conflict in Vietnam. When Johnson assumed office, there were fewer than 20,000 American "advisors" in that divided country, training the soldiers and bureaucrats of anti-Communist South Vietnam. Within three years, that number had risen to almost 500,000, with no end in sight. Vietnam quickly became Johnson's war, and, ultimately, his nightmare.

Point of No Return

Vietnam was part of a larger "containment" effort that had guided American foreign affairs since the end of World War II. Like Presidents Truman, Eisenhower, and Kennedy, LBJ based his commitment to Vietnam on a series of powerful assumptions, such as saving "democracy" in Asia, halting the spread of communism, and maintaining America's credibility around the globe. It hardly mattered that South Vietnam was neither a democracy nor the victim of an international communist plot. What did matter was the need for strength and staying power in a world crisis—the belief that a defeat for the United States anywhere would undermine its standing everywhere.

Johnson understood the political stakes. "I am not going to lose Vietnam," he said. "I am not going to be the president who saw [it] go the way China went." His plan was to pressure the communist enemy in a measured fashion that would neither alarm the American public nor divert resources from his cherished domestic programs. The Gulf of Tonkin Resolution gave him the authority to move forward. The Viet Cong attack at Pleiku provided the motive.

Pleiku, a market town in the central highlands of South Vietnam, was home to a military air strip guarded by American Special Forces. In February 1965, a Viet Cong mortar barrage killed eight Americans and wounded more than a hundred. Several days later, U.S. warplanes began the massive bombing of North Vietnam. Known first as Operation Rolling Thunder, the air strikes hit targets checked personally by President Johnson, who boasted that "they can't even bomb an outhouse without my approval." The problem, however,

was that air power had little impact on North Vietnam's ability to wage war. The bombings killed thousands, flattened factories and power plants, and ravaged the economy; yet the flow of communist troops and supplies into South Vietnam never stopped.

In March 1965, two marine batallions arrived at the huge new U.S. Air Force base in Da Nang, raising the American troop total in South Vietnam above 100,000. By December, troop levels reached 184,000 and rose each month thereafter. Draft calls zoomed from 100,000 in 1964 to 340,000 by 1966, leading millions of young men to seek student deferments or to join the National Guard in the hope of avoiding combat in Vietnam.

By 1965, at least half of South Vietnam was controlled by Viet Cong or North Vietnamese troops. The new South Vietnamese government of General Nguyen Van Thieu appeared more stable than previous ones, but its army was no match for the well-disciplined communist soldiers. As Johnson saw it, American forces would defend South Vietnam until its people were ready to defend themselves. "We will not be defeated," the president vowed. "We will not withdraw."

American strategy in Vietnam had both a military and political objective: to wear down the enemy with superior firepower, and to "win the hearts and minds" of the South Vietnamese people. Neither proved successful. North Vietnam, a nation of 19 million, continued to field a large army despite enormous casualties, while the Viet Cong provided able support. Fighting on native soil, these soldiers waged relentless, often brutal war against a "foreign aggressor" and its "puppets" inside South Vietnam. Between 1965 and 1966, U.S. combat deaths rose tenfold, from 636 to 6,664.

Americans fought bravely, and morale at this point remained high. Yet the very nature of the war alienated these soldiers from the people they had come to defend. It would have been trying, under the best of circumstances, to distinguish between innocent civilians and Viet Cong. Unfamiliar with the language and culture of Vietnam, Americans increasingly viewed everyone as the enemy. Each village appeared as "a dark room full of deadly spiders," a soldier recalled.

American planners tried numerous strategies to isolate the Viet Cong and deprive them of their sanctuaries. Most included the movement of peasant populations from their ancestral lands to "strategic hamlets" or to cities unprepared for the arrival of thousands of homeless refugees. Between 1960 and 1970, the percentage of South Vietnamese living in urban areas jumped from 20 to 43 percent. In these bulging cities, jobs were scarce, prostitution flourished, and families split apart.

Those who remained in the countryside faced terror from all sides. There were North Vietnamese mortar attacks, Viet Cong assassination squads, and American assaults from the ground and the air. U.S. planes and helicopters defoliated the fields and forests with chemical sprays, and pounded suspected enemy strongholds with bombs and napalm (jellied gasoline). In one of the most telling remarks of the war, an American officer explained his mission bluntly: "We had to destroy this town in order to save it."

Early Protests

Even as President Johnson escalated the war in 1965, he expected the Great Society to move freely ahead. A "rich nation can afford to make progress at home while meeting its obligations abroad," he declared. The United States could have both guns and butter; there was no need to choose.

For a time, his domestic agenda remained impressive. Fueled by the immense economic prosperity of 1965 and 1966, the Great Society added an Education Act that extended federal aid to public and private schools, and a Model Cities Act that provided funds to upgrade housing, health services, crime prevention, and parks. In addition, LBJ reaffirmed his commitment to civil rights by appointing the first African American Supreme Court justice, Thurgood Marshall, and the first African American cabinet member, Robert Weaver, to head the new Department of Housing and Urban Development (HUD).

The momentum didn't last. The decision to escalate in Vietnam divided the nation and sapped the president's strength. The first rumblings of antiwar protest came from the college campuses, where a new group, calling itself Students for a Democratic Society (SDS), was gaining ground. Formed in Port Huron, Michigan, in 1962, SDS issued a "Declaration of Principles" that denounced "racism" and "militarism," among other evils, and promised a new politics based on socialist ideals. Limited at first to "elite" colleges and major state universities, such as Harvard, Berkeley, and Wisconsin, the organization expanded in direct proportion to the war itself.

The early student leaders called their movement the "New Left." Some of them, known as "Red-diaper babies," were the children of "Old Left" radicals from the 1930s and 1940s. Others came from the burgeoning civil rights movement. Impatient and idealistic, they identified with the "revolutionary" movements of the emerging Third World. To their eyes, Fidel Castro and Ho Chi Minh were positive forces in history, representing a fundamental shift in power from the privileged elites to the struggling masses. Not surprisingly, Vietnam be-

came the New Left's defining issue—a symbol of popular resistance to America's "imperialist" designs.

Early in 1965, antiwar students and faculty at the University of Michigan held the nation's first "teach-in" to discuss the consequences of escalation in Vietnam. The idea spread rapidly from campus to campus—with the University of Maine's teach-in attracting 300 people, and Berkeley's drawing more than 12,000. On Easter Sunday, a crowd of 30,000 attended the first major antiwar rally in Washington, sponsored by SDS. The speakers, including radical journalist I. F. Stone and folk singer Joan Baez, linked the Vietnam demonstrations to other issues that were percolating within the larger society, such as civil rights, women's rights, and the role of universities in fostering protest and dissent.

THE RIGHTS REVOLUTION: CENTER STAGE

The national mood of unity and reconciliation that followed President Kennedy's assassination in November 1963 did not last much beyond the landslide election of 1964. The war in Vietnam created divisions that grew wider by the year. Americans became more skeptical of their leaders and less likely to believe official explanations of events. Even a master consensus-builder like Lyndon Johnson faced an overwhelming task.

Voting Rights

Following passage of the landmark Civil Rights Act of 1964, the struggle for racial justice moved to the next battleground: voting rights in the Deep South. The campaign was already underway in places like Selma, Alabama, where local activists, facing intense white resistance, asked Martin Luther King, Jr., and his Southern Christian Leadership Conference for support.

The Selma demonstrations began early in 1965. Local blacks marched daily to the courthouse, where Sheriff Jim Clark—wearing a huge button with the single word NEVER—used force to turn them away. Thousands were arrested, beaten with clubs, and shocked with cattle prods for attempting to register with the local election board. In March, Dr. King decided to lead a protest march from Selma to Montgomery, the state capital, fifty miles away. "We are not asking, we are demanding the ballot," he declared.

On March 9—known as Bloody Sunday—a contingent of Sheriff Clark's deputies and Alabama state police attacked the marchers, sending seventeen to the

*P*ICTURING THE PAST ✦ POLITICS & DIPLOMACY

BLACK VOTER REGISTRATION

Table 29.2 Black Voter Registration

State	1960	1966	Percent Increase
Alabama	66,000	250,000	278.8
Arkansas	73,000	115,000	57.5
Florida	183,000	303,000	65.6
Georgia	180,000	300,000	66.7
Louisiana	159,000	243,000	52.8
Mississippi	22,000	175,000	695.4
North Carolina	210,000	282,000	34.3
South Carolina	58,000	191,000	229.3
Tennessee	185,000	225,000	21.6
Texas	227,000	400,000	76.2
Virginia	100,000	205,000	105.0

Source: U.S. Bureau of the Census, *Statistical Abstract of the United States: 1982–83* (103d edition) Washington, D.C., 1982.

Black voter registration in the South was one of the great accomplishments of the civil rights movement. Spurred by the Selma demonstrations, President Johnson signed the Voting Rights Act on August 6, 1965, which abolished discriminatory practices such as the literacy test, and authorized federal examiners to register voters, instead of relying on the individual states. As this table demonstrates, the act profoundly altered the political landscape of the South. Within months of its passage, more than 2 million black Southerners were registered to vote. Most supported the Democratic party of Presidents John F. Kennedy and Lyndon Johnson, which had endorsed the cause of civil rights. At the same time, however, white southerners deserted the Democrats and moved overwhelmingly into the Republican party. In the 1968 presidential election (see map, page 826), Democratic candidate Hubert Humphrey would win only one southern state, beginning a trend of Republican dominance in the South that has lasted, with few notable exceptions, to the present time.

---

hospital. Hundreds of civil rights leaders, entertainers, politicians, and clergy rushed to Selma to lend their support, but the violence continued. James Reeb, a Unitarian minister from Boston, was beaten to death by a gang of whites, and Viola Luizzo, a civil rights activist from Michigan, was shot and killed by the Klan.

On March 15, President Johnson made a special trip to Capitol Hill to urge passage of a new voting rights bill. In the most eloquent speech of his career, Johnson said:

> What happened in Selma is part of a larger movement which reaches into every section and state of America. It is the effort of Negroes to secure for themselves the full blessing of American life.
>
> Their cause must be our cause, too. Because it is not just Negroes, but really it is all of us who must overcome the crippling legacy of bigotry and injustice.
>
> And we shall overcome.

The Watts Explosion

Five days later, on August 11, a riot erupted in Watts, a black section of Los Angeles, triggering the worst urban violence since World War II. The disturbance began with the arrest of a black motorist by a white highway patrolman. A crowd gathered, police reinforcements arrived, and several arrests were made. As word of the incident spread, several thousand people—mostly young men—rampaged down Crenshaw Boulevard, looting stores, burning buildings, and overturning cars. The violence flared each evening for a week. It took 14,000 National Guardsmen to restore order. At least thirty-four people were killed, 1,000 injured, and 4,000 arrested, with property damage estimated at $200 million.

News of the riot shocked President Johnson. "We simply hadn't seen the warnings," recalled Attorney General Ramsey Clark. "We had looked at [civil rights] as basically a southern problem, but . . . in fact

The Watts riot of 1965 began a cycle of urban destruction that engulfed dozens of cities in the coming years.
© Bettmann/UPI/Corbis

the problems of the urban ghettos exceeded any that we were dealing with in the South."

Times had changed. By 1965, almost half of America's black population lived outside the South, mostly in large cities, and Watts epitomized the conditions of day-to-day urban life. Good housing was scarce. As black neighborhoods became overcrowded, residents wishing to move elsewhere were trapped by racial discrimination. Inferior schools hampered upward mobility. Two out of three adults in Watts lacked a high school education, and one in eight was illiterate. Watts had the highest unemployment rate, and lowest income level, of any Los Angeles neighborhood except Skid Row. Two hundred of 205 policemen assigned to Watts were white. Crime was rampant, public services poor. "The sewers stank in the summer, there was not enough water to flush toilets, not enough pressure to fight fires," said one Watts resident. "The social fabric just couldn't stand the strain."

Some rioters targeted white businesses in Watts for arson and looting. The Los Angeles police, suspecting a radical plot, stormed the Black Muslim Temple and arrested fifty-nine people. Local residents knew better. The riot was a spontaneous event, not a planned act of destruction. In the next three years, hundreds of northern black neighborhoods would explode. The worst riots, in Newark and Detroit, would begin, as Watts did, with an incident between local blacks and white police.

Most African Americans deplored the riots and took no part. Yet a competing vision, far different from the one preached by Dr. King, was gathering strength in the black community. As he walked the streets of Watts after the riot, King met a group of youths shouting, "We won!" He asked how anyone could claim victory in the face of such violence and destruction. "We won," a young man answered, "because we made them pay attention to us."

Black Power

By the mid-1960s, Dr. King's leadership in the civil rights movement was increasingly under attack. Younger African Americans, in particular, seemed reluctant to follow his course. At a 1966 rally in Mississippi, a recent Howard University graduate named Stokely Carmichael brought this issue to a head. Just released from jail for leading a peaceful civil rights protest, Carmichael vented his anger as a clearly uncomfortable Dr. King sat behind him on the stage. "This is the twenty-seventh time I've been arrested," Carmichael shouted, "and I ain't going to jail no more. The only way we gonna stop them white men from whuppin' us is to take over. What we gonna start saying now is 'Black Power.' " The crowd took up the chant: "Black Power! Black Power! Black Power!"

Black Power became a symbol of African American unity in the mid-1960s, stressing group strength, independent action, and racial pride. In local communities, black activists lobbied school boards to add African American history and culture to the curriculum. On college campuses, black students pressed administrators to speed up minority recruitment, establish Black Studies programs, and provide separate living quarters—a demand that alarmed integrationists, black and white. In the political arena, Carl Stokes of Cleveland and Richard Hatcher of Gary, Indiana, became the first African American mayors of northern cities by combining hard work with racial solidarity. Across the nation, black men and women donned African clothing, took on African names, and wore their hair unstraightened in an "Afro" style. "Black is Beautiful" became a powerful slogan in this era, as did "Say it loud, I'm black and I'm proud" by soul singer James Brown.

To militants like Stokely Carmichael, Black Power meant a political separation of the races. His position reflected a generational split between "old" civil rights groups such as the NAACP, which viewed racial integration as the key to black advancement, and "new" movement groups like Carmichael's Student Nonviolent Coordinating Committee (SNCC), which began to exclude whites. "Black people," said Carmichael, "must be seen in positions of power doing and articulating for themselves."

The separatist impulse had deep roots in the African American community. Its renewed strength in the 1960s was due, in large part, to a black nationalist movement that appealed to young people in the bleakest neighborhoods of urban America, far removed from civil rights and the Great Society. "There is a different type of Negro emerging from the the 18- to 25-year-old bracket," said a black leader in Watts. "They identify with Malcolm X's philosophy."

Malcolm X was the most popular and controversial Black Muslim leader of the 1960s. Born Malcolm Little, he joined the Nation of Islam while serving a prison term for robbery and adopted the "X" to replace "the white slave-master name which had been imposed upon my paternal forebears by some blue-eyed devil." The Nation of Islam was a black nationalist group, organized in Detroit in 1931, which preached a doctrine of self-help, moral discipline, and complete separation of the races. Its code of behavior, based on the rejection of racist stereotypes, stressed neatness, abstinence, and a firm division of male and female roles. Black Muslims were forbidden to smoke, drink alcohol, eat pork or cornbread, or have sex outside of marriage. "Wake up, clean up, and stand up," their motto declared.

Created by Elijah Poole, who renamed himself Elijah Muhammad, the Black Muslims were strongest in the urban ghettos, where their membership reached upwards of 100,000, with a far larger mass of sympathizers. Assigned by Elijah Muhammad to a temple in Harlem, Malcolm X became a charismatic figure to young black men, in particular, with his bold statements about the impact of white injustice on black behavior and self-esteem. "The worst crime the white man has committed," he said, "is to teach us to hate ourselves."

Malcolm also preached self-defense, saying that blacks must protect themselves "by any means necessary" and that "killing is a two-way street." Such rhetoric made it easy to label the entire Black Muslim movement as extremist, and to construe its message as one of violence and hate.

Malcolm created a public furor by describing the assassination of President Kennedy as an instance of "the chickens come home to roost." Expelled from the

Malcolm X, the charismatic Black Muslim minister, preached a doctrine of black nationalism, self-help, and racial separation that held wide appeal for thousands of African Americans. He was assassinated by a rival Muslim group in 1965.
© Bettmann/UPI/Corbis

Nation of Islam by Elijah Muhammad, he traveled to Mecca on a spiritual pilgrimage and discovered, to his surprise, the insignificance of color in Islamic thought. This led him to form a rival Muslim group, the Organization of Afro-American Unity, which emphasized black nationalism in a manner that did not demonize whites. Assassinated in 1965 by followers of Elijah Muhammad, Malcolm became a martyr to millions of African Americans, some praising his militant call for self-defense, others stressing his message of self-discipline and self-respect.

Occasionally Black Power became a vehicle of rage and racial revenge. SNCC Chairman H. Rap Brown, for example, urged a crowd in Cambridge, Maryland, to "burn this town down," adding: "Don't love the white man to death, shoot him to death." And some went beyond rhetoric by forming terrorist groups like the Black Panthers to take their grievances to the streets.

Betty Friedan attends the second NOW convention in 1967. At her side is Dr. Kathryn Clarenbach, who chaired the convention.
© Bettmann/UPI/Corbis

Founded in 1966 by an Oakland, California, ex-convict named Huey Newton, the Panthers provided a violent alternative to other black movements of this era. Portraying themselves as defenders of "oppressed" people against a "racist-capitalist police state," the Panthers demanded the release of all blacks from prison and the payment of "slave reparations" by whites.

Adept at self-promotion, the Panthers won modest support in black neighborhoods through their community work. With perhaps 5,000 members nationwide, most in the San Francisco Bay area, they ran food banks, health clinics, and preschool programs in run-down city neighborhoods. At the same time, however, Newton and his aides routinely engaged in extortion, drug dealing, and other criminal acts. Heavily armed, wearing black clothing and dark sunglasses, the Panthers became a feared enemy—and primary target—of law enforcement, including the FBI. At least twenty-eight members and eleven policemen were killed in shoot-outs and ambushes between these forces.

"Sisterhood Is Powerful"

The rights revolution of the 1960s included demands for sexual, as well as racial, equality. Both the Equal Pay Act of 1963 and the Civil Rights Act of 1964 were important steps in the battle against gender discrimination, yet progress had been slow. In the fall of 1966, a band of activists formed the National Organization for Women to speed the pace of change.

At NOW's first convention, the 300 delegates elected Betty Friedan president and issued a statement endorsing "the world wide revolution for human rights taking place within and beyond our national borders." Never radical, NOW pursued its major goals—passage of an equal rights amendment and sexual equality in the workplace—through political means. Its leaders took pains to portray NOW as an organization *for* women, not of women, which welcomed male support.

NOW grew slowly. Its membership in 1970 totaled 15,000—mostly white, middle-aged, and middle-class. Yet NOW's impact upon the emerging women's movement was enormous, both in what it represented and what it seemed to lack. For many younger women, raised in the affluence of suburban America, the resurgence of feminism went beyond the fight for political and economic equality. What attracted them was the call for female solidarity—the power of sisterhood—in the larger struggle for sexual liberation.

Some of these women were veterans of the civil rights movement. Others worked for SDS and were active in the antiwar protests on college campuses. Although deeply committed to these causes, they discovered that sexism—the assumption of male superiority—also existed in organizations devoted to justice and equal rights. Thus, women found themselves thankful for the skills and self-confidence they had developed, yet resentful of their expected roles as cooks, secretaries, and sexual objects. When asked what positions women filled in his organization, Stokely Carmichael brought roars of male laughter by noting: "The position of women in SNCC is prone."

Committed to equal rights, adept at organizing, and determined to confront sexism on all fronts, these "new feminists" developed strategies and communities of their own. As women's liberation emerged in the mid-1960s, feminist study groups appeared, along with feminist newspapers, health clinics, and bookstores. The more radical elements, viewing men as the enemy, opposed heterosexual relationships, denounced marriage as "legal whoredom," and regarded the nuclear family as a form of female slavery. While rejecting such notions, liberal feminists also struggled with the dilemma of how to achieve greater power and fulfillment in a male-dominated culture.

The new feminism met immediate resistance—and not only from men. Surveys of American women in the 1960s showed both a growing sensitivity to issues of sex discrimination and a strong distaste for "women's lib." Most housewives expressed pride in their values and experiences and resented the "elitism" of the feminist movement—the implication that outside employment was more fulfilling than house-work or that women degraded themselves by trying to appear attractive to men. As the country artist Tammy Wynette sang: "Don't Liberate Me, Love Me." A long and difficult struggle lay ahead.

The Counterculture

The emerging radicalism of America's youth in the 1960s had both a cultural and political base. Bound together with civil rights, women's rights, and the antiwar protests was a diffuse new movement, known as the counterculture, which challenged traditional values. To many young people, the counterculture symbolized personal liberation and generational strength—a break with the humdrum, hollow world of adults.

In 1965, a San Francisco journalist used the term "hippie" to describe a new breed of rebel—passionate, spontaneous, and free. Like the Bohemians of the early 1900s and the Beats of the 1950s, the hippies defined themselves as opponents of the dominant culture, with its emphasis on competition, consumerism, and conformity. By rejecting such "empty values," they tapped into a seam of youthful alienation so brilliantly portrayed in Mike Nichols's *The Graduate* and Paul Simon and Art Garfunkel's "Sounds of Silence." Unlike the "uptight" nine-to-five crowd, the hippies wore their hair long, dressed in jeans and sandals, and sought a "higher consciousness" through experimentation and uninhibited living.

The counterculture offered numerous attractions. Many young people embraced the chance to try out new arrangements and ideas. A few joined communes, explored ancient religions, studied astrology, or turned to the occult. Far more pervasive was the sexual freedom, the vital new music, and the illegal drug use that marked these turbulent times.

The counterculture did not begin the sexual revolution of the 1960s. That process was already underway, fueled by the introduction of oral contraceptives in 1960, the emergence of a women's rights movement, and a series of Supreme Court decisions that widened public access to "sexually explicit" material. The counterculture played a different but equally important role by challenging conventional morality at every turn.

The results were dramatic. When the Beatles took America by storm in 1964, their chart-busting songs included "I Want to Hold Your Hand," "She Loves You," and "Please, Please Me." Marijuana use, a federal crime since 1937, was rare in middle-class society, and lysergic acid diethylamide (LSD) was largely unknown. By 1967, however, the Beatles were

Thousands of young people migrated to the Haight-Ashbury section of San Francisco in 1967 for a "summer of love." Having no means of support, many turned to drug dealing, panhandling, and prostitution.
© 2003 Gene Anthony/Black Star

imagining "Lucy in the Sky with Diamonds" (LSD) and wailing, "Why Don't We Do It in the Road!"

The counterculture spread inward through America from the east and west coasts. In Cambridge, Massachusetts, a Harvard researcher named Timothy Leary became the nation's first psychedelic guru by promoting LSD as the pathway to heightened consciousness and sexual pleasure. In San Francisco, author Ken Kesey (*One Flew over the Cuckoo's Nest*) and his Merry Pranksters staged a series of public LSD parties, known as Acid Tests, that drew thousands of participants in 1966. Wearing wild costumes, with painted faces, the revelers danced to the sounds of Jerry Garcia and his Grateful Dead.

To much of the public, San Francisco became synonymous with the counterculture. Acid rock flourished in local clubs like the Fillmore West, where Jimi Hendrix ("Purple Haze"), Steppenwolf ("Magic Carpet Ride"), and the Jefferson Airplane ("White Rabbit") celebrated drug tripping in their songs. In 1967, more than 75,000 young people migrated to San Francisco's Haight-Ashbury district to partake in a much publicized "summer of love." The majority of arrivals, studies showed, were runaways and school dropouts with no means of support. By summer's end, Haight-Ashbury was awash in drug overdoses, venereal disease, panhandling, and prostitution.

At first the national media embraced the counterculture as a "hip" challenge to the blandness of middle-class suburban life. Magazines as diverse as

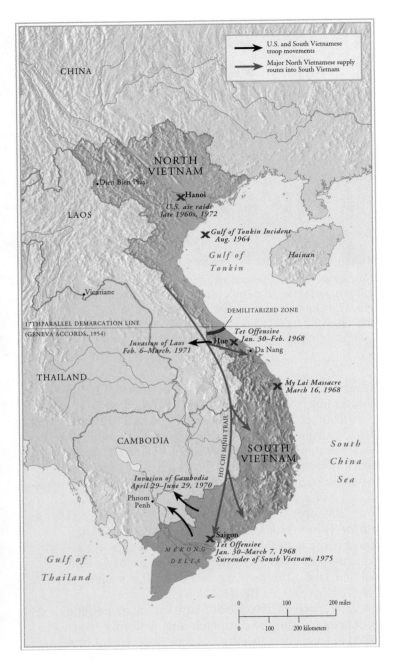

Map 29.1 *The Vietnam War*
The map charts the evolution of American military involvement from the Gulf of Tonkin incident in August 1964 to the surrender of South Vietnam in April 1975. In 1970 and 1971, U.S. and South Vietnamese troops briefly expanded the land war into Cambodia and Laos, stirring further antiwar sentiment inside the United States.

Time and *Playboy* doted on every aspect of the hippie existence, while the Levi-Strauss corporation used acid rockers to promote its new line of jeans. Hollywood celebrated the counterculture with films such as

Easy Rider, about two footloose drug dealers on a motorcycle tour of self-discovery, and *I Love You, Alice B. Toklas,* in which a dull lawyer becomes a fun-loving hippie after accidentally taking hashish. The smash hit of the 1968 Broadway season was the rock musical *Hair,* depicting a draft evader's journey through the pleasure-filled Age of Aquarius.

Yet most young people of the 1960s experienced neither the nightmare of Haight-Ashbury nor the dream world of *Hair.* Millions of them remained on the margins of the counterculture, admiring its styles and sounds while rejecting its revolutionary mantra. And millions more entered adulthood without the slightest sign of protest or alienation. Indeed, some commentators spoke of a serious *intra*generational split in this era, pitting young people who accepted, or aspired to, America's middle-class promise against more radical young people who did not.

A DIVIDED NATION

As 1968 began, General William Westmoreland, commander of U.S. forces in Southeast Asia, offered an optimistic assessment of the Vietnam War. In his view, American and South Vietnamese (ARVN) troops were gaining strength and confidence as the fighting progressed. Their new vitality, he insisted, stood in direct contrast to the enemy's sagging morale.

The Tet Offensive

Four days later, 70,000 Communist troops assaulted American and ARVN positions throughout South Vietnam. Their lightning offensive, begun on the lunar New Year holiday of Tet, took Westmoreland by surprise. In Saigon, Viet Cong units reached the American Embassy before being driven back. After capturing Hue, one of South Vietnam's oldest cities, Communist soldiers murdered thousands of civilians and dumped their bodies into a mass grave.

As a military operation, the Tet offensive clearly failed. Using their overwhelming firepower, American and ARVN forces inflicted frightful casualties upon the enemy. In the three-week battle to recapture Hue, more than 5,000 Communist soldiers were killed, along with 400 ARVN troops and 150 American marines. Viet Cong losses were so severe that the brunt of the ground fighting after Tet would have to be shouldered by North Vietnamese troops.

In psychological terms, however, the Tet offensive marked a turning point in the war. The sheer size of the Communist attacks, their ability to strike so many targets in force, made a mockery of Westmoreland's optimistic claims. Reporting from Saigon after the Tet offensive, Walter Cronkite, America's most popular television journalist, claimed that a military victory was nowhere in sight. At best, Cronkite predicted, "the bloody experience of Vietnam is to end in a stalemate."

A stalemate was exactly what Americans feared most. The Tet offensive accelerated Johnson's political decline. His approval rating dropped from 48 to 36 percent, with most Americans expressing skepticism about official claims of military progress in Vietnam. Columnist Art Buchwald compared LBJ to General Custer at the Little Big Horn, while the prestigious *Wall Street Journal* warned that "the whole war effort is likely doomed."

The President Steps Aside

As Lyndon Johnson pondered his political future, the memory of Harry S. Truman was fresh in his mind. In 1952, Truman decided not to seek reelection after losing the New Hampshire Democratic presidential primary to Senator Estes Kefauver of Tennessee. The main issue then was the stalemate in Korea. In 1968, LBJ faced a spirited challenge in New Hampshire from Senator Eugene McCarthy of Minnesota. The main issue now was the stalemate in Vietnam.

McCarthy's presidential campaign reflected the deep divisions within Democratic party ranks. The "peace faction," led by younger activists like Allard Lowenstein hoped to "dump Johnson" by mobilizing antiwar sentiment against him in key primary states. Hundreds of college students arrived in New Hampshire to work for the McCarthy campaign. Long hair and beards were taboo, as well-scrubbed volunteers in sports coats and dresses ("be clean for Gene") ran phone banks, stuffed envelopes, and canvassed house to house. "These college kids are fabulous," one Democratic leader remarked. "They knock at the door and come in politely, and actually want to talk to grown-ups, and people are delighted."

The New Hampshire results sent shock waves through the political system. McCarthy came within a whisker of defeating President Johnson, who received less than 50 percent of the Democratic primary vote. Polls showed McCarthy winning the support of "hawks" who demanded victory in Vietnam, as well as "doves" who wanted to pull out at once. For Johnson, the results amounted to a vote of "no confidence" on his handling of the war.

Four days later, Robert Kennedy entered the presidential race. As the former attorney general and a cur-

Although U.S. troops inflicted heavy casualties on the Viet Cong and the North Vietnamese during the Tet offensive of 1968, the intensity of the fighting shocked the American public and increased public criticism of the war.
© Robert Ellison/Black Star

rent U.S. senator from New York, he was both a critic of the Vietnam War and a champion of minority causes, especially in the field of civil rights. Millions saw "Bobby" as the keeper of Camelot, the heir to his fallen brother's legacy.

On March 31, President Johnson announced his political retirement in a stunning televised address: "I shall not seek, and I will not accept, the nomination of my party for another term as your President." A few weeks later, Vice President Hubert Humphrey entered the presidential race as the "regular" Democratic candidate, endorsed by Johnson himself. Humphrey's strategy was to line up delegates for the presidential nomination without contesting Kennedy or McCarthy in the volatile state primaries, where his chances of winning were slim.

A Violent Spring

Early in April, Martin Luther King, Jr., traveled to Memphis to support a strike of city garbage workers for better wages and conditions. His social vision was ever expanding, as he challenged Americans to confront the "interrelated" evils of racism, militarism, and poverty. In 1968, Dr. King's projects included a "Poor People's March on Washington" and a "moral crusade" to end the war in Vietnam.

On the evening of April 3, King delivered a passionate sermon at a Memphis church. Demanding justice for the poor and the powerless, he

An Open Letter to the Grape Industry

For years, Cesar Chavez had been struggling to earn better wages and livable working conditions for the men, women, and children who toiled in the fields and orchards of central California. In 1969, with the United Farm Workers on strike and a national boycott of table grapes gaining momentum, Chavez described the tactics and goals of his union in an open letter to E. L. Barr, Jr., president of the California Grape & Tree Fruit League.

YOU MUST understand, I must make you understand, that our membership—and the hopes and aspirations of hundreds of thousands of the poor and dispossessed that have been raised on our account—are, above all, human beings, no better no worse than any other cross section of human society; we are not saints because we are poor but by the same measure neither are we immoral. We are men and women who have suffered and endured much and not only because of our abject poverty but because we have been kept poor. The color of our skins, the languages of our cultural and native origins, the lack of formal education, the exclusion from the democratic process, the numbers of our slain in recent wars—all these burdens generation after generation have sought to demoralize us, to break our human spirit. But God knows we are not beasts of burden, we are not agricultural implements or rented slaves, we are men. And mark this well, Mr. Barr, we are men locked in a death struggle against man's inhumanity to man in the industry that you represent. And this struggle itself gives meaning to our life and ennobles our dying.

As your industry has experienced, our strikers here in Delano and those who represent us throughout the world are well trained for this struggle. They have been under the gun, they have been kicked and beaten and herded by dogs, they have been cursed and ridiculed, they have been stripped and chained and jailed, they have been sprayed with the poisons used in the vineyards. They have been taught not to lie down and die or to flee in shame, but to resist with every ounce of human endurance and spirit. To resist not with retaliation in kind but to overcome with love and compassion, . . .

This is not to pretend that we have everywhere been successful enough or that we have not made mistakes. And while we do not belittle or underestimate our adversaries, for they are the rich and powerful and possess the land, we are not afraid nor do we cringe from the confrontation. We welcome it! We have planned for it. We know that our cause is just, that history is a story of social revolution, and that the poor shall inherit the land.

Once again, I appeal to you as the representative of your industry and as a man. I ask you to recognize and bargain with our union before the economic pressure of the boycott and strike take an irrevocable toll; but if not, I ask you to at least sit down with us to discuss the safeguards necessary to keep our historical struggle free of violence. I make this appeal because as one of the leaders of our nonviolent movement, I know and accept my responsibility for preventing, if possible, the destruction of human life and property.

For these reasons and knowing of Gandhi's admonition that fasting is the last resort in place of the sword, during a most critical time in our movement last February, 1968, I undertook a 25-day fast. I repeat to you the principle enunciated to the membership at the start of the fast: if to build our union required the deliberate taking of life, either the life of a grower or his child, or the life of a farmworker or his child, then I choose not to see the union built.

MR. BARR, let me be painfully honest with you. You must understand these things. We advocate militant nonviolence as our means for social revolution and to achieve justice for our people, but we are not blind or deaf to the desperate and moody winds of human frustration, impatience, and rage that blow among us. Gandhi himself admitted that if his only choices were cowardice or violence, he would choose violence. Men are not angels and the time and tides wait for no man. Precisely because of these powerful human emotions, we have tried to involve masses of people in their own struggle. Participation and self-determination remain the best experience of freedom; and free men instinctively prefer democratic change and even protect the rights guaranteed to seek it. Only the enslaved in despair have need of violent overthrow.

This letter does not express all that is in my heart, Mr. Barr. But if it says nothing else, it says that we do not hate you or rejoice to see your industry destroyed; we hate the agribusiness system that seeks to keep us enslaved and we shall overcome and change it not by retaliation or bloodshed but by a determined nonviolent struggle carried on by those masses of farmworkers who intend to be free and human.

Sincerely yours, CESAR E. CHAVEZ
1969

Source: Susan Ferriss and Ricardo Sandoval, *The Fight in the Fields: Cesar Chavez and the Farmworkers Movement,* 1997, pp. 150–51.

---

seemed to sense the danger he was in. "I've been to the mountaintop," he cried. "I may not get there with you, but I want you to know that we as a people will get to the promised land." The following night, King was shot by James Earl Ray, a white racist, as he stood on the balcony of the Lorraine Motel. He died instantly, at the age of thirty-nine.

News of Dr. King's death touched off riots in African American communities from Boston to San Francisco. At the White House, President Johnson proclaimed a day of national mourning for Dr. King against a backdrop of wailing police sirens and billowing smoke. Forty-five people died in these national riots, including twenty-four in Washington, D.C.

Among the presidential candidates, Robert Kennedy seemed closest to the message of Dr. King. Centering his campaign on the connection between domestic unrest and the Vietnam War, Kennedy visited migrant labor camps, Indian reservations, and inner-city neighborhoods to highlight the problems of disadvantaged Americans and the work to be done. He also supported the labor strike of Cesar Chavez and his National Farm Workers against the grape growers in central California.

The two had met when Kennedy chaired a Senate investigation into the squalid living and working conditions of migratory labor. Both men were close to forty, both were devout Catholics, and both admired the nonviolence of King and Gandhi in the struggle for justice and social change. As Kennedy campaigned in California, the grape strike was entering its third year. To protest the stalemate, and the growing violence on both sides, Chavez began a fast that continued for twenty-one days. He ended it, in poor health, by breaking bread with

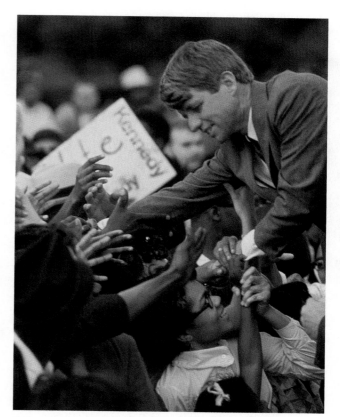

Robert Kennedy's presidential campaign in 1968 both energized and split the Democratic party, leading, in part, to Lyndon Johnson's decision to announce his political retirement. Kennedy was assassinated after winning the vital California primary in June 1968.
© Steve Schapiro/Black Star

Senator Kennedy at a Mass of thanksgiving. Despite enormous media coverage, and a national boycott of table grapes, the strike dragged on.

United Farm Workers leader Cesar Chavez led a series of strikes and boycotts to win better wages and working conditions for union members. Behind him is the symbol of the organization, the black Aztec eagle.
© Bettmann/UPI/Corbis

Chicago police wade into a crowd of protesters during the Democratic National Convention in 1968.
© Bettmann/UPI/Corbis

In June 1968, Kennedy took a major step toward the Democratic presidential nomination by defeating Eugene McCarthy in the delegate-rich California primary. That night, after greeting supporters at a Los Angeles hotel, Kennedy was shot and killed by a deranged Arab nationalist named Sirhan Sirhan. The nation went numb. Who could have imagined the horror of four national leaders—John F. Kennedy, Malcolm X, Martin Luther King, Jr., and Robert F. Kennedy—all dead at the hands of assassins? "My dreams were smashed," a young man recalled. "I shared with a lot of other people these feelings of loss and despair and grim, grim days ahead."

The Chicago Convention

Throughout the spring of 1968, a coalition of antiwar groups prepared for a massive peace demonstration at the Democratic National Convention in Chicago. Originally expecting 500,000 people, the organizers dramatically lowered their estimates following the withdrawal of President Johnson in March and the murder of Senator Kennedy in June. Furthermore, Mayor Richard Daley made it clear that protesters were not welcome in his city, no matter how well they behaved. Fearing serious bloodshed at the Democratic convention, Senator McCarthy urged young demonstrators to stay away.

There was reason for concern. The continued military buildup in Vietnam had created a violent cycle of protest and response at home. That spring, thousands of young men burned their draft cards in public; some were beaten by angry crowds. Demonstrators tried to block troop trains and army induction centers, leading to bloody clashes with police. At Columbia University, students from SDS took over several buildings and trashed them to protest "war-related" research on campus. Hundreds were arrested, a general strike followed, and the university closed down for the semester.

Chicago resembled a war zone in August 1968, with 6,000 army troops, 5,000 National Guardsmen, and hundreds of Chicago riot police patrolling the streets. Denied permits to rally in public places, the protesters—perhaps 4,000 strong—gathered in a park opposite the Hilton Hotel, where many Democratic party leaders were staying. Conflict was inevitable. Radical speakers from SDS and the Black Panthers harangued the crowd with calls for "guerilla warfare," while Abbie Hoffman and Jerry Rubin, founders of the Youth International ("Yippie") party, held workshops on LSD production and then chose a pig as their candidate with the slogan: "They nominated a president and he eats the people. We nominate a president and the people eat him."

On the evening of August 28, the demonstrators tried to march to the convention arena. As millions watched on television, the police moved in with clubs and mace, while National Guardsmen fired tear gas at the crowd. Hundreds were badly beaten, including reporters and bystanders, in what investigators later described as a "police riot." Even so, the blame did not rest entirely with one side. "We were not just innocent people who were victimized," Abbie Hoffman admitted. "We came to plan a confrontation."

News of the street violence shocked the Democratic convention. From the podium, Senator Abraham Ribicoff of Connecticut condemned "the

Gestapo tactics on the streets of Chicago." His remark set off booing, cursing, and wild applause. Television cameras caught a furious Mayor Daley hurling ethnic insults at Ribicoff and telling the "lousy mother_____" to "go home."

The shaken delegates chose Hubert Humphrey and Senator Edmund Muskie of Maine to be their presidential and vice presidential nominees. A staunch liberal, with strong ties to organized labor and the civil rights movement, Humphrey exemplified the New Deal Democratic tradition of Roosevelt, Truman, Kennedy, and LBJ. His great weakness in 1968 was his loyal (if reluctant) support for Johnson's handling of the war. To many Americans, Humphrey endorsed the very policies that had divided the nation and left the Democratic party in disarray.

Nixon's the One

Meeting in Miami, the Republicans faced a much simpler task. The Goldwater defeat of 1964 opened the door for candidates with broader political appeal, such as Richard Nixon. Having lost a bruising election for president in 1960 and another for governor of California in 1962, Nixon kept his fortunes alive by marketing himself as both a devoted Republican and an experienced public figure. After choosing him on the first ballot in 1968, the delegates selected Governor Spiro T. Agnew of Maryland to be his vice presidential running mate.

Nixon campaigned as the spokesman for America's "silent majority"—the people who worked hard, paid their taxes, went to church, obeyed the law, and respected the flag. In a nation grown weary of urban riots and campus demonstrations, he vowed to make "law and order" his number one domestic priority, while bringing "peace with honor" to Vietnam.

For the first time since 1948, the presidential campaign attracted a serious third-party candidate, Governor George Wallace of Alabama. An ardent segregationist, Wallace showed surprising strength in white working-class areas of the North and West, where issues such as rising crime rates, draft deferments for college students, and the court-ordered busing of schoolchildren to achieve racial integration were vital concerns. In blunt, sometimes explosive language, Wallace lashed out at "liberal judges," "welfare cheats," and "pot-smoking freaks in their beards and sandals."

Early opinion polls showed Nixon far ahead of Humphrey, with Wallace running a strong third. Yet the gap closed considerably in the campaign's final

Richard Nixon and family celebrate his long-awaited presidential victory in November 1968.
© Bettmann/UPI/Corbis

weeks when President Johnson ordered a temporary bombing halt in North Vietnam, and millions of Democratic voters, fearful of a Nixon presidency, returned to the party fold. On election day, Nixon won 43.4 percent of the votes and 301 electoral votes, to 42.7 percent and 191 for Humphrey, and 13.5 percent and 46 for Wallace.

CONCLUSION

Few decades in American history provided more drama and tragedy than the 1960s. What began with such hope and promise, with a popular young president and a firm belief in the possibilities of eradicating racism, poverty, and other national problems gave way to deep suspicion and despair by 1968, as Americans reeled from one crisis to another. Race riots, social protests, and generational conflict served to divide the country dangerously, while political assassinations and the escalating war in Vietnam combined to erode the public's trust and confidence in government itself.

To a large degree, Richard Nixon rode the political whirlwind that swept America in 1968. His margin of victory against Hubert Humphrey was nearly as narrow as his margin of defeat against John Kennedy

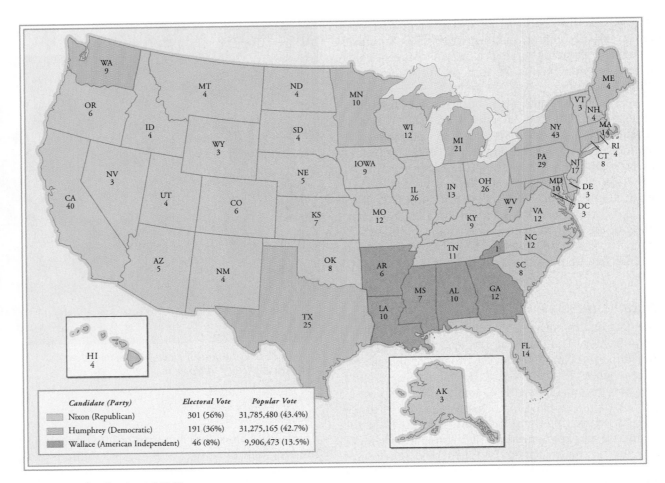

Candidate (Party)	Electoral Vote	Popular Vote
Nixon (Republican)	301 (56%)	31,785,480 (43.4%)
Humphrey (Democratic)	191 (36%)	31,275,165 (42.7%)
Wallace (American Independent)	46 (8%)	9,906,473 (13.5%)

Map 29.2 *The Election of 1968*

 In a bitterly fought three-way contest for the presidency, held against the backdrop of a nation badly split by the Vietnam War, Richard Nixon won with a razor-thin victory with only 43 percent of the popular vote. View an animated version of this map or related maps at http://history.wadsworth.com/passages2e.

in 1960. Yet the combined total for Nixon and Wallace in 1968—almost 57 percent—signaled a major swing to the right. The radical protests of the 1960s had fueled an inevitable backlash against the liberal party in power. The Great Society lay in ruins. The Nixon years had begun.

Recommended Readings

Baughman, James. *The Republic of Mass Culture* (1992). Assesses the media's enormous impact on modern American culture.

Brennan, Mary. *Turning Right in the Sixties* (1995). Analyzes the impact of Goldwater conservatism on a changing Republican party.

Farber, David. *Age of Great Dreams* (1994). Provides an excellent synthesis of the political and cultural changes of the 1960s.

Friedan, Betty. *The Feminine Mystique* (1963). A pathbreaking account of the domestic restrictions placed on women following World War II by those who shape American culture.

Harrington, Michael. *The Other America* (1962). Riveted national attention on the issue of poverty, leading to major government programs and reforms.

Horne, Gerald. *Fire This Time* (1995). Offers an interesting analysis of the Watts riot and the rise of black nationalism.

Karnow, Stanley. *Vietnam* (1983). Remains the best one-volume survey of American involvement in our nation's longest war.

Munoz, Carlos, Jr. *Youth, Identity, Power* (rev. ed. 2000). Carefully examines the origins of the Chicano movement.

McDouglall, Walter. "*. . . The Heavens and the Earth": A Political History of the Space Age* (1985). Captures both the policy making and the drama behind the race to the moon.

Miller, James. *Democracy in the Streets: From Port Huron to the Siege of Chicago* (1987). A thorough history of the student movement that revolutionized American culture and politics in the 1960s.

American Journey Online and InfoTrac College Edition

Visit the source collections at http://ajaccess. wadsworth.com and infotrac.thomsonlearning.com and use the Search function with the following key terms

to explore documents, images, audio and video clips, articles, and commentary related to the material in this chapter.

John F. Kennedy
Bay of Pigs
U-2
The Feminine Mystique
Tonkin Resolution
Black Power
Tet offensive
Richard Nixon

Students for a
  Democratic Society
Martin Luther King, Jr.
Fannie Lou Hamer
Lyndon B. Johnson
Watts riots
Malcolm X
Cesar Chavez

Additional resources, exercises, and Internet links related to this chapter are available on the American Passages Web site: http://history.wadsworth.com/passages2e

30 CRISIS OF CONFIDENCE 1969–1980

AMERICA UNITED AND DIVIDED

ACTIVISM, RIGHTS, AND REFORM

NEW DIRECTIONS AT HOME AND ABROAD

FOUR MORE YEARS?

GERALD FORD IN THE WHITE HOUSE

THE CARTER YEARS

"One giant leap for mankind." Neil Armstrong sets foot on the moon's surface, July 20, 1969.
© Bettmann/UPI/Corbis

Richard Nixon had been in politics for most of his adult life. As a congressman, a senator, and a vice president, he thrived on controversy and kept moving ahead. Bitter defeats in the presidential election of 1960 and the California gubernatorial race of 1962 did not diminish his ambition or ruin his dreams. On the morning after his presidential victory in 1968, Nixon addressed a nation battered by racial turmoil, urban violence, generational conflict, political assassinations, and continuing war. Vowing to unite the country and to restore confidence in its institutions, he recalled a campaign stop he had made in the little town of Deshler, Ohio. Near the back of the crowd a teenager held up a sign reading "Bring Us Together." That message, he assured his listeners, "will be the great objective of this administration . . . to bring the American people together." The tragic presidency of Richard Nixon was underway.

AMERICA UNITED AND DIVIDED

The new era began with optimistic signals and improbable events. For a time, the dark days of 1968 were pushed aside by the miracles of 1969. In January, the New York Jets, led by "Broadway" Joe Namath, the nation's most celebrated bachelor, won the football Super Bowl by crushing the heavily favored Baltimore Colts. In October, the New York Mets, once regarded as the worst team in Major League baseball history, defeated the Baltimore Orioles in a World Series that left millions of Americans screaming, "Ya gotta believe!" Sandwiched between these events were two enormous spectacles, each affecting the nation in a very different way.

CHRONOLOGY

1969 Neil Armstrong sets foot on the moon • Woodstock rock festival attracts 400,000 people • First antiwar "moratorium" attracts huge crowds nationwide

1970 U.S. troops invade Cambodia • College students killed by National Guard at Kent State and by local police at Jackson State • Environmentalists celebrate first Earth Day

1971 Pentagon Papers released • My Lai massacre is exposed

1972 President Nixon visits mainland China • Watergate break-in occurs • Nixon wins reelection in a landslide

1973 Congress investigates spreading Watergate scandals • Vice President Spiro Agnew resigns after pleading no contest to income tax evasion • Supreme Court legalizes abortion in *Roe v. Wade* • War in Middle East leads to Arab oil embargo and energy crisis

1974 Facing impeachment, President Nixon resigns • Gerald Ford becomes president, issues blanket pardon • Violent antibusing protests in Boston

1975 South Vietnam falls • United States and Soviet Union sign human rights pledge in Helsinki Accords

1976 Jimmy Carter elected president

1977 Carter signs Panama Canal treaties

1978 Israel and Egypt sign Camp David Accords • Supreme Court rules on affirmative action in *Bakke* case

1979 Crisis at Three Mile Island nuclear plant • Militant students storm American embassy in Iran, taking hostages • Soviet troops invade Afghanistan

1980 U.S. boycotts Olympic Games in Moscow • Ronald Reagan elected president

The Miracles of 1969

In the summer of 1969, NASA fulfilled John F. Kennedy's bold promise to land a man on the moon "before this decade is out." The lunar mission culminated eight years of extraordinary progress and awful failure, including the 1967 *Apollo 1* disaster in which three astronauts died on the launch pad when their capsule exploded in flames. On July 16, astronauts Neil Armstrong, Edwin "Buzz" Aldrin, and Michael Collins began their 286,000-mile lunar mission—*Apollo 11*—from Cape Kennedy aboard the command vessel *Columbia*. As they neared their destination, Armstrong and Aldrin entered the *Eagle*, a fragile moon module, for the final descent. On July 20, before a television audience of 500 million people, Neil Armstrong put his foot on the lunar surface and said: "That's one small step for man, one giant leap for mankind."

Armstrong and Aldrin spent twenty-one hours on the moon. A television camera beamed back pictures of the men gathering samples, measuring temperature (234 degrees Fahrenheit in sunlight, 279 below zero in darkness), and planting a small American flag. What struck viewers was the sight of two space-suited figures leaping from place to place in the light gravity against a background of perfect desolation. As they rocketed back to Earth, the astronauts provided breathtaking pictures of the world from 175,000 miles away. "No matter where you travel," Armstrong joked, "it's nice to get home."

More than 400,000 revelers enjoyed the sounds of Jimi Hendrix, Joan Baez, Jefferson Airplane, and others at the Woodstock festival north of New York City in the summer of 1969.
© Bettmann/Amalie Rothschild/Corbis

Other moon missions followed, including the dramatic rescue of *Apollo 13* in 1970. Americans marveled at the skill and bravery of these astronauts without fully understanding the scientific value of their missions. By studying lunar rocks and photographs, geologists learned that the earth and the moon were formed at the same time—about 4.6 billion years ago—and that both had been pounded for millions of years by a hail of comets, asteroids, and meteorites that helped reshape their outer crust. The moon missions spurred the growth of computer technology and led to numerous product advancements, from fireproof clothing to better navigation systems for jetliners.

A month after the moon landing, national attention shifted to an earthly extravaganza, the Woodstock Art and Music Fair, on a 600-acre dairy farm in the Catskill Mountains northwest of New York City. Billed as an "Aquarian Exposition," Woodstock fused rock music, hard drugs, free love, and antiwar protest into three days of mud-splattered revelry. Expecting a crowd of perhaps 100,000—a ridiculously low estimate for a pageant that included Janis Joplin, Jimi Hendrix, Joan Baez, The Grateful Dead, and Jefferson Airplane, among others—the organizers were overwhelmed by the response. More than 400,000 people showed up, knocking down the fences and ticket windows, creating mammoth traffic jams, gobbling up the available food and water, pitching tents in the fields, bathing nude in cattle ponds, and sharing marijuana and LSD.

Some news reports breathlessly portrayed the event as a cultural watershed. One magazine called Woodstock "an art form and social structure unique to our time." Another saw it as "the model of how good we will all feel after the revolution." In truth, however, the long weekend at Max Yasgur's farm was far less than that. The vast majority at Woodstock were middle-class students and workers, not cultural dropouts or political revolutionaries. "They would always keep something of Woodstock in their hearts," wrote one perceptive observer, "but that would be while they were making it in the system, not overthrowing it."

What survived Woodstock were the new attitudes of young people toward self-fulfillment, personal expression, political activism, and, in some cases, dangerous excess. These things did not die out in the 1970s, though they took rather different forms. The mellow portrait of Woodstock soon gave way to the ugly spectacle of Altamont, near San Francisco, where a rock concert featuring the Rolling Stones turned into a bloodbath, with one man beaten to death. In 1970, drug and alcohol addiction claimed the

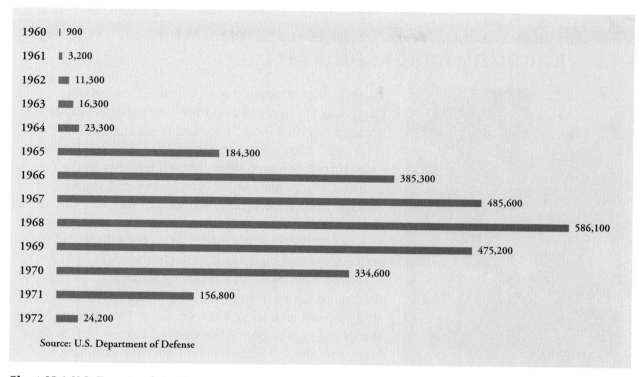

Chart 30.1 *U.S. Troop Levels in Vietnam, 1960–1972*
American troop levels increased dramatically in 1965, following the Gulf of Tonkin incident and the Viet Cong attack on U.S. Marines at Pleiku. As the chart shows, troop levels began to decrease significantly in 1969, as newly elected President Richard Nixon began his policy of Vietnamization.
Source: U.S. Department of Defense

lives of Janis Joplin and Jimi Hendrix. For many young people, the age of innocence was over.

Vietnamization

In order to bring America together, Richard Nixon realized, he had to end its military involvement in Vietnam. During his inaugural parade on January 20, 1969, Nixon heard the chants of antiwar protesters as his limousine made its way from the Capitol to the White House. The next morning he was handed the weekly American casualty figures from Vietnam: eighty-five killed, 1,237 wounded—a chilling reminder, he wrote, of the war's "tragic cost."

Within weeks, Nixon unveiled a plan, known as Vietnamization, to end America's participation in the war. It called for the gradual replacement of U.S. troops by well-trained and supplied South Vietnamese soldiers—a process that included the deployment of American air power and the intensification of peace efforts aimed at getting American and North Vietnamese troops out of South Vietnam. From Nixon's perspective, Vietnamization represented the best solution to a dreadful dilemma. He refused to abandon Vietnam. "I will not," he repeated, "be the first President of the United States to lose a war." Yet he could not continue a conflict that cost 14,600 American lives and $30 billion in 1968 alone.

Vietnamization did not work well on the battlefield, as time would show. But it did have the advantage of substituting Asian casualties for American ones, which made it popular in the United States. In June 1969, President Nixon announced that 25,000 American combat troops were being withdrawn from Vietnam—the first stage of a pull-out to be completed by late 1972. At the same time, the U.S. Air Force stepped up its missions over North and South Vietnam, and Cambodia as well.

Confrontation at Home

Despite Vietnamization and troop withdrawals, the antiwar movement retained considerable force. On

ICTURING THE PAST ✦ SOCIAL & CULTURAL EVENTS

TRAGEDY AT JACKSON STATE

© Bettmann/UPI/Corbis

In May 1970, news of the American incursion into Cambodia led to massive protests on college campuses. Six students died in separate incidents at Kent State in Ohio and Jackson State in Mississippi. The incidents, though very different, were lumped together in the press as disturbances against the war. In fact, the troubles at Jackson State were racially motivated. Jackson, the capital of Mississippi, was rigidly segregated, and students at the all-black college had clashed repeatedly with the all-white police force and highway patrol. On the night of May 14, following a series of rock-throwing episodes, the police fired more than 150 rounds into a dormitory, killing two students and wounding a dozen more. This chilling photo shows the violent police reaction. In comparison to Kent State, the Jackson State incident got little publicity, leading some to conclude that the death of black students was less important to mainstream America than the death of whites.

November 15, 1969—"Mobilization Day"—hundreds of thousands of people attended rallies in New York, Boston, San Francisco, Washington, and other cities to demand the immediate removal of all American troops from Vietnam. Some considered the war immoral; others viewed it as a lost cause that was ripping the nation apart. To show his contempt for the protests, President Nixon made a point of listing his schedule that afternoon, which included several hours of watching the Washington Redskins on television.

In March 1970, the White House announced the withdrawal of 150,000 more combat troops over the coming year. The nation's leading antiwar group, the Vietnam Moratorium Committee, responded by closing its national office. But a month later, in a startling development, the president told the nation that American troops had just invaded Cambodia to disrupt enemy supply lines which ran through that country along the so-called Ho Chi Minh Trail. The very success of Vietnamization depended on the elimination of these North Vietnamese sanctuaries, he declared, adding: "We are a strong people and we shall not be defeated in Vietnam."

Nixon misjudged the public reaction. The idea of expanding the war under any circumstances brought protesters back into the streets. At Kent State University in Ohio, several thousand students rampaged through the business district and clashed with local police. That evening, Kent State's ROTC building went up in flames, leading the governor to send in the National Guard. The troops were ordered to prevent students from gathering in large blocs—an ironic twist, since a noontime rally was planned to protest the guard's presence. On May 4, the guardsmen confronted 500 students at the rally, where rocks and bottles were thrown from a distance and tear gas was lobbed in return. Suddenly, without warning, a group of guardsmen fired their rifles at the crowd, killing four and wounding nine others.

Word of the shootings touched off campus protests nationwide. ROTC buildings were attacked, and governors in sixteen more states called out the National Guard. Many colleges simply shut down for the semester, canceling final exams and mailing diplomas to the graduates. Surveys showed a clear majority of

Americans approving of the National Guard's response at Kent State and supporting forceful measures against those who challenged government authority through unlawful, or even disrespectful, behavior. Many blue-collar workers fumed at the sight of draft-deferred, middle-class students protesting the war from the safety of a college campus while their own sons and brothers were slogging through the jungles of Vietnam. That rage turned to violence in New York City, when several hundred construction workers charged into an antiwar rally and severely beat the demonstrators and onlookers with hammers, pipes, and fists. A week later, President Nixon invited the leader of New York's construction workers' union to the White House, where the two men exchanged gifts and compliments. Nixon described his "honorary hard hat" as a symbol of "patriotism to our beloved country."

The violence continued in fits and spurts. Left-wing radicals bombed the headquarters of Mobil Oil, IBM, and other pillars of the "imperialist war machine." At the University of Wisconsin, the late-night bombing of a science center that housed a military research laboratory left one graduate student dead. In New York City, three radicals accidentally blew themselves to bits while mixing explosives. And in Chicago, a splinter group of the dormant Students for a Democratic Society attempted to "trash" the downtown business district in a final assault upon the "ruling class." Three hundred looters and window-smashers were arrested.

My Lai and the Pentagon Papers

The news from Vietnam was equally grim. Reports surfaced about a massacre of civilians by U.S. troops at the village of My Lai, a suspected Vietcong stronghold, in 1968. Encountering no resistance, an infantry unit led by Lieutenant William Calley methodically executed the villagers and dumped their bodies into a mass grave. A number of the women were raped; at least 200 people, many of them children, were murdered. Evidence of these atrocities was ignored by field commanders until a soldier not connected with the incident sent letters to the Pentagon and the press.

Most Americans considered My Lai an aberration. Yet the public reaction to Lieutenant Calley's court-martial verdict (guilty) and sentence (life imprisonment) in 1971 raised the very issues that had divided Americans since the war began. Some believed that government policy in Vietnam made such tragedies inevitable. Others insisted that Calley acted out of frustration after seeing so many of his fellow soldiers killed. Still others blamed a society—as one GI

put it—that "forced these kids to die in a foreign land for a cause it refused to defend at home." Congress and the White House were flooded with letters opposing the conviction. "Free Calley" signs appeared on car bumpers, in store windows, even in churches. Following numerous appeals and a personal case review by President Nixon, Calley was paroled in 1974.

The My Lai incident raised nagging questions about the fitness of American troops as the war dragged on. By all accounts, U.S. soldiers had fought superbly under trying circumstances until 1969. But the process of Vietnamization, the stepped-up troop withdrawals, the rising antiwar protests—all served to isolate those who remained in Vietnam. Drug use increased dangerously, with many soldiers turning from marijuana to heroin. Racial tensions flared, as did violent attacks on officers, known as "fraggings," in which disgruntled soldiers used hand grenades as weapons. Some men ignored direct orders to fight. They were reluctant to risk their lives for a cause that appeared all but lost.

Within weeks of Calley's court-martial, another crisis appeared with publication of the Pentagon Papers, a secret report of the decision-making process that led to American involvement in Vietnam. Commissioned in 1967, and containing numerous classified documents within its 7,000 pages, the report was made public by Daniel Ellsberg, a former intelligence officer who had turned against the war. Ellsberg gave a copy to the *New York Times,* which printed the first installment on June 13, 1971.

The report focused mainly on the Kennedy-Johnson years. From a political standpoint, President Nixon welcomed the embarrassment it caused his Democratic opponents. "This is about their administrations," he told his aides. "Let them argue about it." Yet Nixon soon viewed Ellsberg's behavior as a threat to his own presidency as well. He feared that continued leaks of classified material might reveal damaging information about current policies, such as the secret bombing of Cambodia. As a result, the White House sought a court injunction to halt further publication of the Pentagon Papers on grounds that national security was at stake. The Supreme Court rejected this argument, however, ruling six to three that suppression violated First Amendment guarantees.

Nixon did not give up the fight. Obsessed by the Ellsberg incident, he authorized the creation of a special White house unit, known as the "Plumbers," to "stop security leaks and investigate other sensitive matters." In a tape-recorded conversation on September 18, 1971, Nixon demanded that "the roughest, toughest people [get] to work on this." A few weeks

PICTURING THE PAST◆SOCIAL & CULTURAL EVENTS

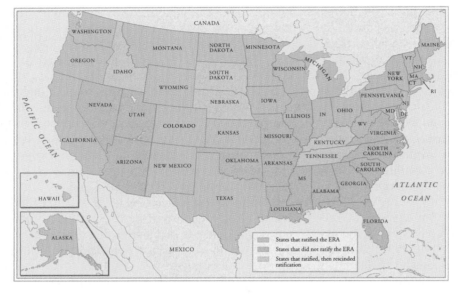

Map 30.1 *The Struggle for the Equal Rights Amendment*

Few issues proved more divisive in the 1970s than the Equal Rights Amendment. Written by feminist Alice Paul (see Chapter 21) a half century earlier, it declared that "equality of rights under the law shall not be denied or abridged . . . on account of sex." In 1972, following a powerful new lobbying effort by women's groups, Congress passed the ERA and sent it to the states for ratification. But a powerful countermovement arose, led by a conservative activist named Phyllis Schlafly, who condemned the ERA as "a total assault on the family" and an insult to God's plan for the sexes. The map clearly shows the regional and cultural divisions over the ERA, with much of the opposition coming from rural and/or southern states. Only thirty of the needed thirty-eight states voted in the end for ratification, and the amendment died.

---

later, the Plumbers carried out their first assignment, burglarizing the office of Ellsberg's psychiatrist in an attempt to gather embarrassing information. Nixon's top domestic advisor, John Ehrlichman, casually informed the president that other "little operations" were planned. "We've got some dirty tricks underway," he said. "It may pay off."

ACTIVISM, RIGHTS, AND REFORM

Political and social activism did not end with the 1960s, as the environmental movement and the antiwar protests clearly showed. While the angry, media-centered radicalism of groups like SDS and the Black Panthers largely disappeared, the movements for women's rights and minority rights remained very much alive, bringing progress and backlash in their wake.

Expanding Women's Rights

On August 26, 1970, feminist leaders organized a nationwide rally to mark the fiftieth anniversary of the Nineteenth Amendment, which had given women the right to vote. Thousands showed up with signs ranging from "Sisterhood is Powerful" to "Don't Cook Dinner—Starve a Rat Today." The speeches focused on equality for women in education and employment, the need for reproductive freedom, and passage of the Equal Rights Amendment (ERA), an idea first proposed in 1923.

The revived women's movement was already making strides. In 1969, feminist protests forced a number of the nation's best colleges, including Yale and Princeton, to end their all-male admissions policy, and the military academies soon followed suit. Between 1970 and 1974, the number of women attending law school and medical school more than doubled. During the 1970s as a whole, female graduates from the nation's law schools rose from 5 to 30 percent of each class; and at medical schools from 8 to 23 percent. Yet the number of women elected to public office or promoted to high management positions lagged far behind, and the wages of full-time working women remained well below those of men.

The women's movement had many voices and a wide range of ideas. Nothing better illustrated this diversity than the outpouring of books and magazines that provided an alternative to older publications such as *Good Housekeeping* and *Ladies' Home Journal*, which focused on motherhood, domesticity, and consumerism as the primary female roles. Handbooks like *Our Bodies, Ourselves* (1971) and *The New Woman's Survival Catalogue* (1972) sold millions of copies by combining a new feminist ideology, based on professional achievement and personal freedom, with medical and psychological strategies for good health. A flood of best-sellers emerged—Kate Millett's *Sexual Politics* (1969), Shulamith Firestone's *The Dialectic of Sex* (1970), and Germaine Greer's *The Female Eunuch* (1970) among them—contending that women could never experience fulfillment within the traditional confines of marriage and family life. In 1972, three scholarly journals devoted to women's studies appeared, as did the Berkshire Conference on the History of Women. That same year marked the publication of *Ms,* the first feminist magazine to attract a mass circulation. A sampling of its articles showed how dramatically times had changed: "Raising Kids Without Sex Roles," "Women Tell the Truth About Their Abortions," and "Do Feminists Do It Better?"

Minority Power

The political and cultural upheavals of the 1960s had produced a "rights consciousness" that spread from group to group, and movement to movement, as the decade progressed. For many such groups, 1969 was a pivotal year, marking their emergence on the national scene. That summer, for example, a routine police assault against homosexuals at the Stonewall Inn in Manhattan's Greenwich Village produced a most uncommon response. For the first time the patrons fought back, triggering several days of rioting and

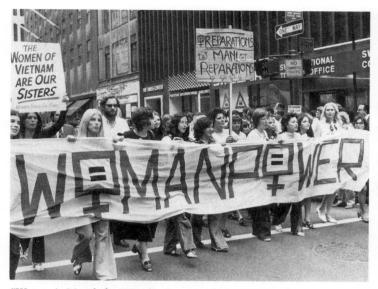

"Women's March for Equality" moves down New York's Fifth Avenue.
AP/Wide World Photos

Sparked by Manhattan's Stonewall Riot of 1969, in which homosexuals confronted police harassment with force, organizations like the Gay Liberation Front emerged to encourage group solidarity in the struggle for equal rights.
© Bettmann/Richard C. Wandel/Corbis

protest against the harassment of homosexuals. The "Stonewall Riot" led to the formation of the Gay Liberation Front, which, in turn, began the movement to encourage group solidarity within the homosexual community and to confront openly the prejudice that gay men and women had suffered, in fearful silence,

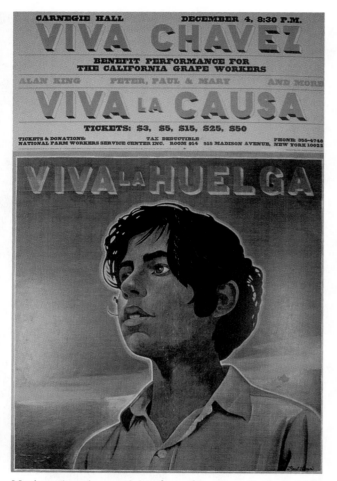

Mexican American activists formed La Raza Unida in 1969 to further "Chicano" causes. This poster advertises a benefit for striking grape workers in California.
Sally Andersen-Bruce, Museum of American Political Life, University of Hartford, West Hartford, CT

for so many years. "We reject society's attempt to impose sexual roles and definitions of our nature," announced the Gay Liberation Front. "We are stepping outside these roles and simplistic myths. We are going to be who we are."

In 1969, Mexican American activists in Texas formed La Raza Unida, a political party devoted to furthering "Chicano" causes and candidates through the ballot. This new party, which spread to several southwestern states, reflected the growing demand for political power and cultural self-determination within the Hispanic community, which had grown from 3 million in 1960 to more than 9 million a decade later. The increase, consisting mainly of Cuban Americans and Puerto Ricans on the nation's East Coast, and Mexican Americans throughout the West, provided unique opportunities for change.

On September 16, 1969, Mexican American students across the Southwest boycotted classes to celebrate ethnic pride (or "Chicanismo") on Mexico's Independence Day, while a group at Cal-Berkeley, shouting "Brown Power," staged a sit-in to demand a program in Chicano Studies. (Within a few years, more than fifty universities would have such a program.) Furthermore, political leverage by Hispanic groups spurred Congress to improve conditions for migrant farm workers, many of whom were Mexican American, and to provide federal funding for bilingual education, a much-debated concept that soon included the right of non-English-speaking students to schooling in their native language. Mexican Americans were also elected to the U.S. House of Representatives in Texas and California, to the U.S. Senate in New Mexico, and to the governorships of Arizona and New Mexico.

In the fall of 1969, several dozen Native Americans took over Alcatraz Island, an unoccupied former federal penitentiary in San Francisco Bay, to publicize the claims and grievances of a younger, more militant generation. "It has no running water; it has inadequate sanitation facilities; there is no industry; there are no health care facilities," said one protest leader, comparing the rocky island to a typical Indian reservation. The group spent nineteen months on Alcatraz, symbolically offering to buy it for "$24 in glass beads and red cloth."

The protest signaled a change in the American Indian community. By any measure, Native Americans were the most deprived single group in the United States, with an unemployment rate ten times higher, and a life expectancy twenty years lower, than the national average. In the late 1960s, a new group known as American Indian Movement (AIM), inspired by the black freedom struggles, began to preach a philosophy of "Red Power" that rejected the "assimilationist" policies of their elders. In 1972, AIM supported a march on Washington—named the Trail of Broken Treaties—that ended with a group of protesters barricading themselves inside the Bureau of Indian Affairs and wrecking much of the building. A year later, AIM militants seized the South Dakota village of Wounded Knee on the Pine Ridge Sioux Reservation, site of an infamous massacre by federal troops in 1890, to highlight both the squalid conditions there and the "broken promises" that stripped Native Americans of their independence and their land. Two Indians were killed in the seventy-one-day standoff with federal agents.

This pressure took political and legislative forms as well. In 1970, the federal government returned 48,000 acres of sacred land to the Taos Pueblo of New

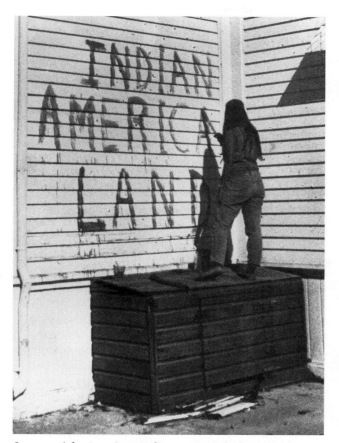

Seventy-eight American Indians occupied Alcatraz Island, site of an abandoned federal prison, in 1969.
© Bettmann/UPI/Corbis

Mexico, beginning a cautious policy of negotiation that grew significantly in the coming years. In addition, the Nixon administration targeted minority aid programs for Native Americans living in urban areas, while Congress added funding through the Indian Education Act of 1972. Nevertheless, the alarming rates of suicide, alcoholism, and illiteracy among Native American children continued throughout the 1970s and beyond—a clear warning of how much remained to be done.

Black Capitalism and Civil Rights

Richard Nixon took office at a crucial juncture in the campaign for civil rights. The epic struggles of the 1950s and early 1960s had formally abolished *de jure* (legal) segregation in public schools and public accommodations—a remarkable achievement—yet serious problems remained. The vast majority of southern children still attended all-white or all-black schools in defiance of *Brown v. Board of Education,* and the situ-

ation was little better in the North and West, where *de facto* segregation in housing and employment kept most neighborhood schools rigidly segregated by race. Furthermore, while the percentage of "middle-class" African Americans increased substantially in the 1960s, the rate of black unemployment remained twice the national average, and male joblessness in urban areas sometimes reached 40 percent. This meant a deepening economic split within the African American community, with almost half the black families enjoying middle-class status, and an equal percentage living below the poverty line in run-down, unsafe, segregated neighborhoods where jobs were scarce and single women, increasingly, raised children on their own.

Civil rights did not rank high on Nixon's domestic agenda. Because most blacks voted Democratic—Hubert Humphrey got 95 percent of their votes in 1968—the president owed them no political debt. On the contrary, he hoped to create a "new Republican majority" by winning over white working-class Democrats, north and south, who feared that minorities were getting too much attention from the federal government. Choosing his words carefully, Nixon described racial integration as a process that demanded a slow but steady pace. "There are those who want instant integration and those who want segregation forever," he said. "I believe that we need to have a middle course between those two extremes."

Nixon's boldest civil rights initiatives related to business and employment. In 1969, he created the Office of Minority Business Enterprise, noting that "people who own their own homes and property do not burn their neighborhoods." Over the next three years, the federal government tripled its assistance to minority enterprises through grants and low-interest loans. More controversial was the administration's proposal to bring black workers into the high-wage, "lily-white" construction industry. Known as the Philadelphia Plan, it required the construction unions—carpenters, masons, electricians, and the like—to set up "goals" and "timetables" for hiring black apprentices on government-sponsored projects. Some civil rights leaders praised the Philadelphia Plan as a major step toward economic equality; others condemned it as a cynical ploy to woo black voters away from the Democratic party. Everyone agreed, however, that the plan went far beyond the intent of the 1964 Civil Rights Act, which simply banned job discrimination on the basis of race, religion, sex, or national origin.

On the emotional issue of public school integration, the president took a more cautious approach. Hoping to win white political converts in the South, he supported the efforts of Mississippi officials in 1969 to

Roe v. Wade, 1973

In 1973, the Supreme Court heard the case of Jane Roe, pseudonym for an unmarried, pregnant Texas woman who challenged the state's century-old criminal abortion law. Writing for the majority, Justice Harry A. Blackmun struck down state statutes banning abortion in the first and second trimesters of a pregnancy on the ground that they violated a woman's right to privacy under the due process clause of the Fourteenth Amendment. Hailed by "pro-choice" advocates, and condemned by "pro-life" groups, the decision remains controversial to this day.

The principal thrust of appellant's attack on the Texas statutes is that they improperly invade a right, said to be possessed by the pregnant woman, to choose to terminate her pregnancy. Appellant would discover this right in the concept of personal "liberty" embodied in the Fourteenth Amendment's Due Process Clause; or in personal, marital, familial, and sexual privacy said to be protected by the Bill of Rights. . . .

This right of privacy, whether it be founded in the Fourteenth Amendment's concept of personal liberty and restrictions upon state action, as we feel it is, or, as the District Court determined, in the Ninth Amendment's reservation of rights to the people, is broad enough to encompass a woman's decision whether or not to terminate her pregnancy. The detriment that the State would impose upon the pregnant woman by denying this choice altogether is apparent. Specific and direct harm medically diagnosable even in early pregnancy may be involved. Maternity, or additional offspring, may force upon the woman a distressful life and future. Psychological harm may be imminent. Mental and physical health may be taxed by child care. There is also the distress, for all concerned, associated with the unwanted child, and there is the problem of bringing a child into a family already unable, psychologically and otherwise, to care for it. In other cases, as in this one, the additional difficulties and continuing stigma of unwed motherhood may be involved. All these are factors the woman and her responsible physician necessarily will consider in consultation. . . .

On the basis of elements such as these, appellants argue that the woman's right is absolute and that she is entitled to terminate her pregnancy at whatever time, in whatever way, and for whatever reason she alone chooses. With this we do not agree. Appellant's arguments that Texas either has no valid interest at all in regulating the abortion decision, or no interest strong enough to support any limitation upon the woman's sole determination, is unpersuasive. The Court's decisions recognizing a right of privacy also acknowledge that some state regulation in areas protected by that right is appropriate. As noted above, a State may properly assert important interests in safeguarding health, in maintaining medical standards, and in protecting potential life. At some point in pregnancy, these respective interests become sufficiently compelling to sustain regulation of the factors that govern the abortion decision. The privacy right involved, therefore, cannot be said to be absolute. In fact, it is not clear to us that the claim . . . that one has an unlimited right to do with one's body as one pleases bears a close relationship to the right of privacy previously articulated in the Court's decisions. The Court has refused to recognize an unlimited right of this kind in the past.

We therefore conclude that the right of personal privacy includes the abortion decision, but that this right is not unqualified and must be considered against state interests in regulation. . . .

Measured against these standards, the Texas Penal Code, in restricting legal abortions to those "procured or attempted by medical advice for the purpose of saving the life of the mother," sweeps too broadly.

To summarize and to repeat:

A state criminal abortion statute of the current Texas type, that excepts from criminality only a *life saving* procedure on behalf of the mother, without regard to pregnancy stage and without recognition of the other interests involved, is violative of the Due Process Clause of the Fourteenth Amendment.

(a) For the stage prior to approximately the end of the first trimester, the abortion decision and its effectuation must be left to the medical judgment of the pregnant woman's attending physician.

(b) For the stage subsequent to approximately the end of the first trimester, the State, in promoting its interest in the health of the mother, may, if it chooses, regulate the abortion procedure in ways that are reasonably related to maternal health.

(c) For the stage subsequent to viability the State, in promoting its interest in the potentiality of human life, may, if it chooses, regulate, and even prescribe, abortion except where it is necessary, in appropriate medical judgment, for the preservation of the life or health of the mother.

Source: *Roe v. Wade*, 410 U.S. 113, 1973.

---

postpone court-ordered school integration, while firmly opposing efforts to deny federal funding to segregated schools. When told that Justice Department officials were planning to speed up school integration, the president warned them to "knock off this crap," adding: "Do what the law allows you and not one bit more." As a result, the battle shifted back to the courts, especially the U.S. Supreme Court, where major changes were now underway.

The Burger Court

In 1969, Chief Justice Earl Warren stepped down from the bench. The seventy-seven-year-old Warren had submitted his resignation in 1968, expecting President Johnson to choose a suitably liberal replacement. But problems arose when Johnson nominated his close friend Associate Supreme Court Justice Abe Fortas to become the new chief justice. Senate conservatives, charging "cronyism," organized a filibuster to deny Fortas the post; then a brewing scandal over his finances forced Fortas to resign from the Court. This gave incoming President Nixon the luxury of appointing two Supreme Court justices at once.

The first choice went smoothly. The Senate quickly confirmed Judge Warren E. Burger, a moderate northern Republican, to replace Warren as chief justice. But Nixon's other nominee, Judge Clement Haynsworth, a conservative from South Carolina, ran into trouble when Senate liberals raised questions about his antagonism toward civil rights and organized labor. Fifteen Republicans joined forty Democrats to reject Haynsworth—a rare event for the Senate, which had not defeated a Supreme Court nominee since the days of Herbert Hoover.

Stung by the vote, President Nixon nominated another southerner, Judge G. Harrold Carswell, whose general qualifications and civil rights record were far inferior to Haynsworth's. The Senate rejected him as well. Nixon angrily blamed "hypocritical" northern liberals for the defeats of Haynsworth and Carswell, claiming that "the real reasons for their rejection [were] their legal philosophies . . . and the fact that they were born in the South." A few weeks later, the Senate unanimously confirmed Nixon's third choice, Judge Harry Blackmun of Minnesota. Ironically, the president got to make two more Supreme Court nominations the following year when Justices Hugo Black and John Marshall Harlan retired. His selections—William Rehnquist, a prominent Arizona conservative, and Lewis Powell, a distinguished Virginia attorney—were easily confirmed.

The Burger Court proved more independent than most people, including Nixon, had expected. Among other decisions, it upheld publication of the Pentagon Papers, struck down "capricious" state laws imposing the death penalty for rape and murder, thereby halting capital punishment for almost two decades (*Furman v. Georgia*, 1972); and ruled against President Nixon's claims of executive privilege in the Watergate scandals. In addition, the Burger Court held that state laws prohibiting abortion were unconstitutional because they violated a woman's "right to privacy" under the Fourteenth Amendment (*Roe v. Wade*, 1973). Justice Blackmun's majority opinion permitted a state to outlaw abortion in the final three months of pregnancy, noting, however, that the life and health of the mother must be considered at all times. The following year, almost 1 million legal abortions were performed in the United States.

The Burger Court also confronted segregation in the public schools. Its unanimous ruling in *Swann v. Charlotte–Mecklenburg Board of Education* (1971) served notice that controversial methods like "forced" busing could be used as legal remedies to achieve racial balance. Though millions of youngsters rode buses to school each day, the idea of transporting children to different neighborhoods in the name of racial integration fueled parental anger and fear. Opinion polls showed that whites overwhelmingly opposed forced busing, and that African Americans, by a smaller margin, also disapproved. For many black parents, busing simply obscured the problems of neglect and underfunding that had plagued their school districts for years.

Violence sometimes followed. In Boston, a court-ordered plan in 1974 to bus white schoolchildren to Roxbury, a poor black neighborhood, and black children to South Boston, a poor white neighborhood, led to mob action reminiscent of Little Rock, Arkansas, in 1957. Buses were stoned, black students were beaten, and federal marshals rushed in to protect them. Ironically, the schools in both neighborhoods were in awful condition, unlike the wealthy suburban Boston schools, which were not included in the desegregation plan. All too often, forced busing became a class issue, involving poorer people of all races.

NEW DIRECTIONS AT HOME AND ABROAD

Like John F. Kennedy, President Nixon cared more about foreign policy than about domestic affairs. "I've always thought the [United States] could run itself without a president," Nixon mused. "All you need is a competent Cabinet to run the country at home." As a moderate Republican in the Eisenhower mold, Nixon endorsed the basic outlines of the modern welfare state, which included social security, unemployment insurance, a minimum wage, the right to unionize, and health care for the elderly. Yet Nixon also understood—and exploited—the public's growing concern that the Great Society era had tilted too far in favor of poor people and minority groups. Convinced that Americans were fed up with wasteful government programs and angry street demonstrations, he tried to find, in his words, a domestic "middle ground."

Rethinking Welfare

President Nixon moved cautiously on the domestic front. His immediate goals were to implement a revenue-sharing plan that sent more tax dollars back to the states and localities, and to simplify the welfare system, making it more efficient and less expensive. Revenue sharing, designed to limit the power of the national government, was a modest success. Congress passed legislation transferring $30 billion in federal revenue over five years—less than Nixon wanted, but more than state and local governments had received in the past. Welfare reform proved a much harder sell. Here the president looked to domestic advisor Daniel P. Moynihan, a social scientist whose controversial writings on poverty and family breakup in the African American community reflected a shifting emphasis from equal rights, which focused on constitutional guarantees, to equal opportunity, which stressed socioeconomic gains. Everyone agreed that the current welfare system—Aid to Families with Dependent Children (AFDC)—was seriously flawed. Its programs lacked accountability, and the payments varied widely from state to state. At Moynihan's urging, President Nixon offered an alternative to AFDC, known as the Family Assistance Plan (FAP).

The new plan proposed a national standard for welfare designed to reduce the number of recipients—and bureaucrats—over time. Instead of providing a host of costly welfare services, the government would guarantee a minimum annual income to the poor, beginning at $1,600 for a family of four, with additional funding for food stamps. The individual states were expected to subsidize this income, and able-bodied parents (excepting mothers of preschool children) were required to seek employment or job training. Not surprisingly, FAP ran into withering criticism from all sides. Liberals complained that $1,600 was unreasonably low, while conservatives opposed the very concept of a guaranteed annual income. The National Welfare Rights Organization resisted the work requirement for women with school-age children, while community leaders and social workers worried about the elimination of vital services (and perhaps their own jobs).

To his credit, Nixon did not trim needed programs as his own plan went down to defeat. On the contrary, he supported Democratic-sponsored measures in Congress to increase food stamp expenditures, ensure better medical care for low-income families, and provide automatic cost-of-living adjustments (COLAs) for social security recipients to help them keep up with inflation. Although Nixon did not care to publicize this achievement, he became the first president since Franklin Roosevelt to propose a federal budget with more spending for social services than for national defense.

Protecting the Environment

On April 22, 1970, millions of Americans gathered in schools, churches, and parks to celebrate Earth Day, an event sponsored by environmental groups like the Sierra Club to educate people about the ecological problems afflicting the modern world. Begun a few years earlier, following the appearance of Rachel Carson's *Silent Spring,* the environmental movement gained strength after a series of well-publicized disasters, such as the chemical fire that ignited Cleveland's Cuyahoga River, the giant oil spill that fouled the beaches of Santa Barbara, and the "death" of Lake Erie by farm runoff and factory waste. The dire predictions of scientists about population growth, poisoned food and water, endangered species, and air pollution added fuel to the cause. As biologist Barry Commoner noted in his best-selling 1971 book, *The Closing Circle,* "our present course, if continued, will destroy the capability of the environment to support a reasonably civilized human society."

At first, President Nixon showed little interest in environmental problems. Indeed, his administration accidentally marked Earth Day by approving a project that raised serious ecological concerns, the 800-mile Alaskan oil pipeline. Yet Nixon soon considered environmentalism to be a powerful force—one which cut across class, racial, and political lines. Unlike many other issues, it gave the appearance of uniting Americans against a common foe.

Moving quickly, his administration banned the use of DDT in the United States, though not its sale to foreign countries; and stopped production of chemical and biological weapons, though not the plant defoliants or napalm used in Vietnam. More significantly, the White House supported a bipartisan congressional effort to establish the Environmental Protection Agency (EPA) and to pass the Clean Air Act of 1970 and the Endangered Species Act of 1973.

These were notable achievements. The Clean Air Act set strict national guidelines for the reduction of automobile and factory emissions, with fines and jail sentences for polluters. The Endangered Species Act protected rare plants and animals from extinction. The list included hundreds of categories above the microscopic level, from the spotted owl to the snail-darter, with the lone exemption being "pest insects." Congress also passed the Water Pollution Control Act over Nixon's veto in 1972. The law, mandating $25 billion

for the cleanup of America's neglected lakes and rivers, was too costly for the president, though it proved effective in bringing polluted waters back to life. The EPA, meanwhile, monitored the progress of these laws and required environmental "impact studies" for all future federal projects.

Though Americans readily agreed about the need for clean air, pure water, and protecting wildlife, the cost of doing these things did not fall equally on everyone's shoulders. Auto manufacturers warned that the expense of meeting the new emission standards would result in higher car prices and the layoff of production workers. Loggers in the Northwest angrily accused the EPA of being more interested in protecting a few forest birds than in allowing human beings to earn a living and feed their families. A common bumper sticker in Oregon read: "If You're Hungry And Out Of Work, Eat An Environmentalist." In response to pressure from labor unions and businesses about lost jobs, rising costs, and endless paperwork, the EPA modified some of its goals and deadlines for compliance with these new laws. Could strategies be devised to protect jobs and the environment simultaneously? Could American corporations effectively compete with foreign companies that did not face such restrictions? Should the United States abandon atomic power, offshore oil drilling, and other potential threats to the environment at a time when the demand for energy was rapidly increasing? Protecting the environment raised serious questions for the future.

A New World Order

Richard Nixon loved the challenge of foreign affairs. The secrecy, intrigue, and deal making fascinated him in ways that domestic matters never could. Determined to control foreign policy even more rigidly than previous presidents, Nixon bypassed the State Department in favor of the National Security Council, based in the White House itself. To direct the NSC, he chose Henry Kissinger, a German refugee and Harvard political scientist. In Kissinger, the president found the perfect match for his "realistic" view of foreign affairs in which hard assessments of the national interest took precedence over moral and ideological concerns.

Both men agreed that America's bipolar approach, based on the "containment" of Soviet Communism, no longer made sense. They wanted a more flexible policy that recognized not only the limits of American influence, but also the growing strength of Western Europe, Communist China, and Japan. They believed that the United States could no longer afford to play the world's police in every skirmish, or to finance an arms race that grew more dangerous—and expensive—with each passing year. The Nixon-Kissinger approach meant talking with old enemies, finding common ground through negotiation, and encouraging a more widespread balance of world power.

This innovative thinking, however, did not extend to all parts of the globe. The president still viewed Fidel Castro as a mortal enemy, and openly encouraged the CIA to undermine the democratically elected, left-wing government of Chilean President Salvadore Allende, who was overthrown and apparently murdered by right-wing military forces in 1973. "I don't see why we have to allow a country to go Marxist just because its people are irresponsible," Henry Kissinger argued. In Latin America, at least, the New World Order appeared strikingly similar to the old one.

The China Opening

In one sense, Richard Nixon seemed an odd choice to strip away years of rigid Cold War thinking in foreign affairs. He was, after all, a rough-and-tumble anti-Communist known for his bitter attacks on State Department officials during the McCarthy years. Yet that is what made his new initiatives all the more remarkable. Nixon's skill in foreign affairs lay in his ability to seize opportunities in a rapidly changing world. One of his first moves was to take advantage of the widening rift between Communist China and the Soviet Union.

The United States at this time did not even recognize Communist China. Since 1949, American policy considered the anti-Communist regime on Taiwan the legitimate government of mainland China. There were some who believed that only a politician with Nixon's Red-hunting credentials would dare to change this policy after so many years. No one could seriously accuse this president—as he had accused so many others—of being "soft on communism."

Nixon wanted a new relationship with China for several reasons. The trade possibilities were enormous. Better relations also increased the chances of a peace settlement in Vietnam, while strengthening America's bargaining position with the Soviet Union, which feared any alliance between Washington and Beijing. Most of all, Nixon realized that China must now be recognized as a legitimate world power. The United States could no longer afford to ignore this reality.

Nixon worked behind the scenes, knowing that Americans considered China the "most dangerous" nation on earth. The first public breakthrough came in 1971, when an American table tennis team was invited to China for an exhibition tour. This "Ping-Pong diplomacy" led both nations to ease trade and travel restrictions. Meanwhile, Henry Kissinger secretly visited Beijing to plan a summit meeting between Chinese and American leaders. President Nixon hinted at his future plans in a remarkable magazine interview. "If there is anything I want to do before I die," he said, "it is to go to China."

Nixon arrived there on February 22, 1972—the first American president ever to set foot on Chinese soil. For the next eight days, the world watched in amazement as he walked along the Great Wall and strolled through the Forbidden City. "The Chinese Army band played 'America the Beautiful' and 'Home on the Range,'" wrote the *New York Times*. "President Nixon quoted Chairman Mao Zedong approvingly, used his chopsticks skillfully, and clinked glasses with every Chinese official in sight."

The trip ended with a joint statement, known as the Shanghai Communiqué, that promised closer relations between the two countries in trade, travel, and cultural exchange. Each nation agreed to open a legation (not an embassy) in the other's capital city, beginning the process of diplomatic recognition that would take seven more years to complete. The most important issues, such as human rights and nuclear proliferation, were tactfully ignored. And the most controversial issue—the future of Taiwan—demonstrated the deep rift that still existed. Communist China asserted its claim to the island, demanding that American troops on Taiwan be removed. The United States called for a "peaceful solution" to the "Taiwan question" and promised to reduce its forces as "tensions" in the region declined. Still, the historic significance of Nixon's visit overshadowed the problems that lay ahead. "We have been here a week," he declared. "This was the week that changed the world."

Détente

Three months later, the president traveled to Moscow for a summit meeting with Soviet leader Leonid Brezhnev. A master of timing in foreign affairs, Nixon believed that his successful trip to China, coupled with a faltering Russian economy, would make the Soviets more likely to strike a serious deal with the United States. The key issues were arms control and increased trade. Both sides possessed huge atomic arsenals that cost billions of dollars and increased the chances of catastrophic war. The Russians desperately needed grain, heavy equipment, and technical assistance; American farmers and manufacturers saw new markets for their goods.

The Moscow Summit further enhanced the Nixon-Kissinger record in foreign affairs. On May 22,

1972, the United States and the Soviet Union signed a Strategic Arms Limitation Treaty (SALT) that limited the number of long-range offensive missiles (ICBMs), and an ABM agreement that froze the production of antiballistic missiles for the next five years. No one believed that the arms race was now over; both sides would continue to build long-range nuclear bombers and to develop the Multiple Independent Re-entry Vehicles (MIRVs), which permitted several warheads to be fired from a single missile. Yet these initial treaties, committing the superpowers to the principle of arms reduction, represented a stunning breakthrough in Soviet-American relations.

The economic agreements were less successful. Though U.S.-Soviet trade more than tripled over the next three years, the greatest increase came in a single wheat deal with American farmers and grain dealers that caused a temporary shortage in the United States. Not surprisingly, American consumers fumed at the idea of shipping low-priced wheat to a foreign country while bread prices rose dramatically at home.

Nevertheless, the Moscow Summit provided a solid foundation for détente, with both sides pledging to reduce world tensions and to coexist peacefully. As President Nixon left Moscow, he noted the differences between the Soviet leaders he faced in 1959, when he was vice president, and the ones who endorsed détente. The current leaders, he wrote, "do not have as much of an inferiority complex as was the case in Khrushchev's period. They do not have to brag about everything in Russia being better than anything anywhere else. But they still crave to be respected as equals, and on this point I think we made a good impression."

FOUR MORE YEARS?

After a full term in office, Richard Nixon could look back upon a record of notable achievement. Relations with Cold War opponents like the Soviet Union and Communist China had dramatically improved as détente replaced confrontation. Although the Vietnam War continued, the steady withdrawal of American troops meant fewer casualties and an end to the draft. Even the economy looked better, with unemployment and inflation presently under control.

The Landslide of 1972

Nixon's Democratic challengers faced an uphill battle. From the political right, Governor George Wallace of Alabama continued the presidential odyssey he began in 1968, when he captured five southern states as a third-party candidate. Campaigning this time as a Democrat, Wallace won wide support among white working-class voters for his opposition to forced busing and his attacks on "welfare cheats." After winning the Democratic presidential primary in Florida, and running a close second in Wisconsin, Wallace was shot and paralyzed by a would-be assassin, ending his presidential quest.

A few weeks later, on June 17, 1972, five men were arrested while burglarizing the Democratic National Headquarters at the Watergate complex in Washington, D.C. Four of them were Cubans who had worked previously for the CIA; they were led by James W. McCord, the security director for Richard Nixon's Committee to Re-Elect the President, known as CREEP. Supervising from a nearby hotel, and later arrested, were two presidential aides—Gordon Liddy and E. Howard Hunt—who belonged to the newly created "Plumbers" unit. Responding to the break-in, Nixon assured the public that no one "presently employed" in his administration was involved "in this very bizarre incident," adding: "What really hurts is if you try to cover it up."

At the Republican National Convention in Miami, the delegates enthusiastically renominated the Nixon-Agnew team. The Democratic race, however, proved far more contentious. The candidates included Hubert Humphrey, the 1968 presidential nominee; Senator George McGovern of South Dakota, the favorite of younger, more liberal Democrats; and Representative Shirley Chisholm of New York, the first African American to seek the presidential nomination of a major political party.

The Democratic National Convention, meeting in Miami Beach, reflected the party reforms that followed the bloody "siege of Chicago" in 1968. The changes were dramatic, with the percentage of female delegates increasing from 13 to 38 percent, blacks from 5 to 15 percent, and those under thirty years old from 3 to 23 percent. Moreover, these new delegates embraced the causes of numerous "out groups" in society, such as homosexuals, migrant workers, prisoners, and the urban poor. Deeply committed to the "rights revolution" of the 1960s, they proposed a major redistribution of political power and cultural authority in the United States.

The delegates chose George McGovern for president and Senator Thomas Eagleton of Missouri for vice president. But the campaign faced trouble from the start. Reporters learned that Senator Eagleton had been hospitalized in the past for mental depression and fatigue, twice undergoing electroshock therapy. At first, McGovern stood by his running mate, offering him "1,000 percent" support. As criticism mounted, however, McGovern replaced Eagleton with former Peace Corps Director Sargent Shriver, who accepted the position after six others turned it down. Appearing weak and opportunistic, McGovern dropped further in the polls.

Far more damaging was the lack of unity within Democratic ranks. Many of McGovern's key positions, such as amnesty for draft resisters, liberalization of marijuana laws, and greater welfare benefits for the poor, offended moderate and working-class Democrats who believed their party had moved too far to the left. On election day, Nixon overwhelmed McGovern, carrying every state but Massachusetts and winning 61 percent of the popular vote.

Yet Nixon's landslide victory was more limited than it appeared. Ticket splitting flourished in 1972, with the Democratic party easily retaining control of Congress. Thus, legions of Democratic voters rejected McGovern's message without deserting the party itself. Furthermore, the percentage of eligible voters who cast ballots in presidential elections continued to fall, from 62 percent in 1964, to 61 percent in 1968, to 56 percent in 1972. This suggested a growing alienation from the political process—and a hint of the protest to come.

Exit from Vietnam

Richard Nixon's impressive reelection victory seemed a sure sign that passions were cooling and better times lay ahead. The president's first task was to end the Vietnam conflict on honorable terms and secure the release of American prisoners of war. But the key to any settlement, Nixon understood, was the future security of South Vietnam. What would happen after U.S. troops left that country? Would the American sacrifice be in vain?

In the spring of 1972, North Vietnam had mounted a major offensive in the South, gambling that Nixon's concern about the coming presidential election would prevent the United States from responding. The offensive failed miserably, however, when Nixon ordered massive bombing raids against North Vietnam. That fall, secret negotiations between Henry Kissinger and North Vietnam's Le Duc To produced a temporary cease-fire. The United States agreed to withdraw its remaining troops from Vietnam in return for the release of its POWs. President Thieu would continue to govern South Vietnam, and North Vietnamese troops were allowed to remain there, until a final settlement was reached. A week before the 1972 presidential election, Kissinger declared that "peace is at hand."

The claim was premature. President Thieu opposed the cease-fire, demanding the removal of North Vietnamese troops from South Vietnam, while the North Vietnamese seemed intent on adding even more soldiers for a final assault. Following his reelection, President Nixon tried to force a settlement through a fierce air assault against North Vietnam. "These bastards," he said, "have never been bombed like they're going to be bombed this time." In late December 1972, American B-52s filled the skies over Hanoi and Haiphong, dropping more tonnage than all American planes had dropped in the previous two years. The damage done to North Vietnam was staggering: harbors, factories, railway lines, storage facilities, and sometimes adjoining neighborhoods, were destroyed. Moreover, where only one B-52 had been lost in combat throughout the entire war, fifteen were shot down in these so-called "Christmas bombings." North Vietnam's Communist allies did not strongly protest, even when a Soviet ship was damaged in Haiphong Harbor. Interested above all in continuing the process of détente with America, the Russians signaled North Vietnam to return to the bargaining table and make the best deal. On January 27, 1973, the United States and North Vietnam signed an agreement quite similar to the one that had fallen apart a few months before. President Nixon got Thieu's reluctant support by vowing to "respond in full force" if North Vietnam renewed the fighting in the South. The United States, he proclaimed, had achieved "peace with honor" at last.

What Nixon got, in reality, was an American exit from Vietnam that left the vulnerable Thieu government at the mercy of its Communist opponents. Despite his pledge, the United States could only respond to future treaty violations with air power; sending troops back into combat was now unthinkable. The agreement ended American involvement without guaranteeing South Vietnam's long-term survival.

The American public expressed relief at the settlement, but little jubilation. The war had divided the country, raised suspicions about government to dangerous levels, and drained billions of dollars from vital domestic programs. More than 50,000 U.S. soldiers were killed in Vietnam and 300,000 were wounded. At least 1 million Asians died, and more would perish in the coming years. As the *New York Times* noted, "There is no dancing in the streets, no honking of horns, no champagne."

Public attention soon shifted to the return of 587 American POWs. Many had spent up to seven years in North Vietnamese jails, and some had been tortured. "We are honored to have the opportunity to serve our country under difficult circumstances," said

The Nixon Tapes, 1973

Hundreds of pages of Richard Nixon's taped Oval Office transcripts have been made public. Among the most revealing is a late-night phone conversation between Nixon and his friend Hobart Lewis, editor-in-chief of *Reader's Digest,* on April 30, 1973, following the resignations of Nixon's closest advisors, Bob Haldeman and John Ehrlichman, who were deeply involved in the Watergate scandals.

President Nixon: You know, having to tell two men who didn't—who refused to resign, to tell them they had to was the toughest thing . . .

Lewis: Of course.

President Nixon: And they are great men.

Lewis: Of course they are.

President Nixon: But I had to do it.

Lewis: Well, you are going to miss them.

President Nixon: Oh, well, the hell with missing them. You can fill any position, Hobe.

The conversation then turns to the Watergate break-in. It shows a baffled Nixon, unable to comprehend that a burglary, a cover-up, and endless lying are grounds for serious criticism, much less an impeachment proceeding. The moral lessons of Watergate do not penetrate his world.

President Nixon: Isn't it a shame it's all about a crappy little thing that didn't work?

Lewis: No, of course.

President Nixon: Didn't work. Nobody ever got a Goddamn thing out of this damn bugging.

Source: Stanley Kutler, *Abuse of Power,* 1997, pp. 385–86.

---

their senior officer as his plane touched down on American soil. That very day, ex-President Lyndon Johnson died in his sleep. "His tragedy—and ours," Senator Edmund Muskie stated, "was the war."

Watergate and the Abuse of Power

As 1973 began, Richard Nixon's public approval rating stood at a remarkable 68 percent. With Vietnam behind him, the president appeared ready to launch a successful second term. Yet all that ended in April, when the Watergate burglars pleaded guilty to minor charges of theft and wiretapping in order to avoid a public trial. Suspecting a cover-up, federal judge John Sirica convinced the lead burglar, James McCord, to admit that high-ranking White House officials were involved in planning the break-in. This startling confession, combined with the investigative stories of *Washington Post* reporters Bob Woodward and Carl Bernstein, turned the Watergate affair into front-page news.

During the spring of 1973, President Nixon reluctantly appointed Harvard Law School professor Archibald Cox as an independent prosecutor in the Watergate case, while the Senate formed a special investigating committee chaired by seventy-three-year-old Sam Ervin of North Carolina, who modestly described himself as "a simple country lawyer." Under Ervin's careful direction, the committee heard sworn testimony from present and former Nixon aides about a "seamless web" of criminal activity designed to undermine the president's critics and political opponents. In meticulous detail, John Dean, the former White House counsel, implicated Nixon himself in a plan to ensure the silence of the imprisoned burglars by paying them "hush money."

Nixon, however, denied any involvement in Watergate. On national television, he took "responsibility" but no blame for the scandal, explaining that he had been too busy running the nation to bother with the day-to-day workings of his reelection campaign.

Former White House counsel John Dean documented President Nixon's role in the Watergate cover-up during his testimony before the Ervin committee in 1973.
© Fred Ward/Black Star

Facing certain impeachment and removal from office, President Nixon resigned on August 9, 1974.
© Bettmann/UPI/Corbis

Many Americans—and most Republican leaders—took Nixon at his word. As House minority leader Gerald R. Ford of Michigan declared, "I have the greatest confidence in the president and am absolutely positive he had nothing to do with this mess."

In July, White House aide Alexander Butterfield stunned the Ervin committee by revealing that Nixon had secretly recorded his Oval Office conversations since 1971. Sensing that the true story of presidential involvement in the Watergate scandal could now be uncovered, Judge Sirica, Special Prosecutor Cox, and

Chairman Ervin all demanded to hear the relevant tapes. But Nixon refused to release them, citing executive privilege and the separation of powers. When Cox persisted, Nixon ordered Attorney General Elliot Richardson to fire him. Richardson and his top deputy refused, leading to their swift removal. These dramatic developments, known as the "Saturday Night Massacre," produced angry calls for Nixon's impeachment.

There was trouble for the vice president as well. In 1973, a Baltimore grand jury looked into allegations that Spiro Agnew, as governor of Maryland, had accepted illegal payoffs from building contractors. After first denying these charges, the vice president resigned his office and pleaded *nolo contendere* (no contest) to one count of income tax evasion. He received three years' probation plus a $10,000 fine.

Under the Twenty-fifth Amendment, adopted in 1967, the president is obligated to nominate a vice president "who shall take the office upon confirmation by a majority vote of both houses of Congress." To bolster his declining fortunes, Nixon chose the well-respected Gerald Ford, who was quickly confirmed. But the president ran into more trouble when the Internal Revenue Service (IRS) disclosed that he owed $500,000 in back taxes from 1970 and 1971, having paid less than $1,000 in each of these years. Responding emotionally, Nixon told a press conference that "I am not a crook."

By this point, however, public confidence in Nixon had disappeared. The testimony of John Dean, the Saturday Night Massacre, the resignation of Spiro Agnew, the embarrassing IRS disclosures—all cast doubt on the president's morality and fitness to lead. A Gallup poll taken in November 1973 showed Nixon's public approval had dropped to 27 percent. In desperation, the president released transcripts of several Watergate-related conversations (but not the tapes themselves), claiming that they cleared him of wrongdoing. Many thought otherwise. The transcripts contained ethnic and racial slurs, vulgar language (with "expletives deleted"), and strong hints of presidential involvement in a cover-up.

Nixon's refusal to release the tapes reached a climax in July 1974, when the House Judiciary Committee debated charges of presidential impeachment before a national television audience. Led by Chairman Peter Rodino of New Jersey and the eloquent Barbara Jordan of Texas, the committee approved three charges—obstruction of justice, abuse of power, and contempt of Congress—at the very moment that a unanimous Supreme Court ordered Nixon to comply with Judge Sirica's subpoena for the Watergate tapes. On August 5, the president released the material that sealed his fate. While providing no evidence that Nixon knew about the Watergate burglary in advance, the tapes showed him playing an active role in the attempt to cover up White House involvement in the crime.

Faced with certain impeachment and removal, Richard Nixon became the first president to resign from office. In a tearful farewell to his staff on August 9, he preached the very advice that he, himself, was incapable of following. "Never get discouraged. Never be petty," he said. "Always remember. . . . Those who hate you don't win unless you hate them. And then you destroy yourself."

OPEC and the Oil Embargo

In the midst of the Watergate scandal, a serious crisis erupted over the nation's energy needs. On October 6, 1973—the Jewish high holiday of Yom Kippur—Egypt and Syria attacked Israel from two sides. After some hesitation, the United States backed Israel, a longtime ally, by airlifting vital military supplies. While American aid proved essential in helping Israel repel the attack, the Organization of Petroleum Exporting Countries (OPEC), led by Saudi Arabia and other Arab nations, responded by halting oil shipments to the United States, Western Europe, and Japan.

The oil embargo created an immediate panic, though the problem had been building for years. As the U.S. economy flourished after World War II, its energy consumption soared. Americans, barely 6 percent of the world's population in 1974, used over 30 percent of the world's energy. Furthermore, as the expense of exploring and drilling for domestic oil increased, the United States turned to foreign suppliers, especially in the Middle East. Between 1968 and 1973, America's consumption of imported oil tripled from 12 to 36 percent.

This reliance on foreign sources left the United States extremely vulnerable to the OPEC embargo. No nation was more dependent on fossil fuels, and no nation had been more wasteful. As the cold weather set in, President Nixon warned that "we are heading toward the most acute shortage of energy since World War II." In response, the government reduced highway speed limits to 55 miles per hour, lowered thermostats in office buildings to 68 degrees, approved daylight savings time in winter, eased environmental restrictions on coal mining, and pushed the development of nuclear power. Across the nation, stores and factories closed early, families dimmed their Christmas lighting, and northern colleges canceled their midwinter semesters. Long lines formed at the gas stations, which were closed on Sundays to conserve precious fuel.

The oil embargo ended in April 1974, but the impact lingered on. Energy costs rose dramatically, even

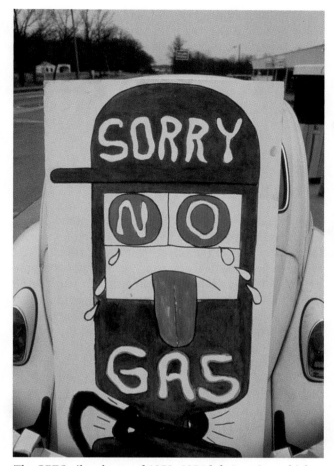

The OPEC oil embargo of 1973–1974 left Americans high and dry at the gas pumps.
© 1998 Dennis Brack/Black Star

as supplies returned to normal, because OPEC tripled its price. A gallon of gas in the United States rose from 30 cents (before the embargo) to 75 cents and more. Consumers faced soaring inflation, while manufacturers confronted higher production costs. Some regions, such as the automobile- and steel-producing Midwest, were particularly hard hit, while other areas, like the energy-producing Sunbelt, gained in population and political influence.

Above all, the energy crisis shook the foundations of the American dream. For three decades, a booming economy had produced a standard of living unparalleled in terms of material comfort, home ownership, and access to higher education. American culture thrived on the assumption of upward mobility—that the nation's children would do better than their parents had done. After 1973, that assumption was in peril.

Prosperity could no longer be taken for granted. Following the oil embargo, average weekly earnings in the United States (adjusted for inflation) stopped growing for the first time in thirty years. So, too, did worker productivity. The increased cost of energy, combined with spiraling federal deficits and aggressive foreign competition in manufacturing and technology, made the American economy more vulnerable than before. Some experts predicted a new age in which limits and sacrifice replaced abundance and expansion.

GERALD FORD IN THE WHITE HOUSE

Vice President Gerald Ford, a former football star at the University of Michigan who had served honorably for two decades in the U.S. House of Representatives, seemed like the ideal figure to restore public confidence in the presidency. As a Republican party loyalist, he had opposed most of Lyndon Johnson's Great Society legislation, while strongly supporting the war in Vietnam. Yet even Ford's political opponents praised his decency, his integrity, his humble, straightforward ways. After the charisma of John Kennedy, the explosive energy of Lyndon Johnson, and the divisive appeals of Richard Nixon, Americans were ready, it appeared, for a leader with common values and an ordinary touch. As the new president joked, "I'm a Ford, not a Lincoln."

The Watergate Legacy

Gerald Ford entered the White House at a pivotal time. Although not an activist by nature, he inherited a situation in which the legislative branch of government, emboldened by the disasters of Watergate and Vietnam, appeared anxious to restore its former authority by cutting the executive branch down to size. In 1973, for example, Congress passed the War Powers Act that required the president to notify Congress within forty-eight hours about the foreign deployment of American combat troops. If Congress did not formally endorse that action within sixty days, the troops would be withdrawn. In addition, Congress passed the Freedom of Information Act, which gave the American people unprecedented access to classified government material.

The Senate also held a series of spectacular hearings into the abuses, and criminal activity, of executive intelligence agencies such as the FBI and the CIA. The public learned that FBI agents had routinely harassed, blackmailed, and wiretapped prominent Americans such as Martin Luther King, Jr., while CIA operatives had engaged in illegal drug experiments, money laundering, and bungled assassinations of world leaders like

President Ford entered the White House after Watergate with the vow to "put Watergate behind us." His pardon of President Nixon, however, opened old wounds.
© Bettmann/UPI/Corbis

Fidel Castro. These revelations led President Ford to create a monitoring device known as the Intelligence Oversight Board. But Congress, with fresh memories of the Watergate cover-up, formed a permanent watchdog committee to investigate such behavior on its own.

Ford, too, fell victim to the Watergate morass. During his vice presidential confirmation hearing in 1973, he had gone on record against a possible presidential pardon for Richard Nixon. "I do not think the public would stand for it," he declared. Yet in September 1974, President Ford reversed his earlier position by granting Nixon a "full, free, and absolute pardon" for all crimes he "may have committed" during his term in office. Ford based his decision on a number of factors, including the impact of a criminal trial on Nixon's health. Above all, however, Ford hoped that a presidential pardon would finally put the "national nightmare" of Watergate to rest.

In fact, the opposite occurred. By appearing to place one man above the law, the pardon raised serious doubts about Gerald Ford's most cherished asset: his spotless character. Within days, the new president's public approval rating dropped from 72 to 49 percent. What bothered many Americans was the fact that Ford had granted the pardon without demanding contrition in return. Richard Nixon barely apologized for Watergate. He never admitted his crimes. For Gerald Ford, the pardon was an act of mercy, but others wanted justice as well.

The new president also tried to heal the internal wounds of the Vietnam War. Within days of taking office, he offered "conditional amnesty" to the 350,000 Americans of draft age who had refused service in the armed forces by leaving the country. Under Ford's plan, a draft resister might be permitted to reenter the United States in return for alternative service in a hospital or a charitable institution. Not surprisingly, the program met stiff resistance. Many who left the country believed they had performed an act of conscience, while veterans' groups viewed them as military deserters who should serve their time in jail. As a result, only 20,000 people took part in the program.

As South Vietnam fell to the Communists on April 29, 1975, people scrambled to board the final helicopters on the roof of the American embassy in Saigon.
© Bettmann/UPI/Corbis

The Fall of South Vietnam

In October 1974, at a secret conclave outside Hanoi, the leaders of Communist North Vietnam prepared their final plans for the conquest of South Vietnam. Their main concern was the United States. Would it respond "in full force" to Communist violations of the 1973 peace accords? The North Vietnamese did not think so. "Having already withdrawn from the South," they reasoned, "the United States could hardly jump back in."

Their assessment was correct. The North Vietnamese launched a massive assault in March 1975, overwhelming South Vietnamese forces near the Demilitarized Zone (DMZ). The Vietcong, still suffering from the frightful losses inflicted during the Tet offensive of 1968, played a minor role in the fighting. As North Vietnamese troops advanced, a mixture of chaos and panic gripped South Vietnam, with thousands of soldiers deserting their units and masses of civilians clogging the highways in desperate flight. Ignoring a plea from President Ford, Congress refused to extend emergency aid to South Vietnam. On April 23, Ford acknowledged the obvious. The Vietnam War, he said, "is finished as far as America is concerned."

Saigon fell to the Communists on April 29. The televised images of Americans desperately boarding the last helicopters from the embassy grounds seemed a painful yet fitting conclusion to our nation's longest war. "What we need now in this country," said a solemn Henry Kissinger, "is to put Vietnam behind us and to concentrate on problems of the future."

This was easier said than done. The humiliating collapse of South Vietnam raised serious questions about the soundness of America's foreign policy and the limits of its military power. Furthermore, for those most deeply affected—the veterans of Vietnam—the collapse raised personal questions about the meaning of their sacrifice to the nation and to themselves. With the exception of the POWs, these veterans received no public tributes, no outpouring of thanks. Congress passed no special "GI Bill" to pay for their college tuition, to help them find employment, or to finance their new homes. Some Americans condemned the veterans for serving in an "immoral war," while others blamed them for participating in the nation's first military defeat. "The left hated us for killing," said one dejected veteran, "and the right hated us for not killing enough."

The vast majority of Vietnam veterans expressed pride in their military service and a willingness to fight there again. Most of them adjusted well to civilian life, although a sizable minority (one out of six, according to the Veterans Administration) suffered from posttraumatic stress disorder, substance abuse, and sometimes both. In addition, some veterans claimed that their exposure to Agent Orange, a toxic herbicide used to defoliate the jungles of Vietnam, had produced high rates of cancer, lung disease, and even birth defects in their children. After more than a decade of controversy, Congress passed legislation that extended benefits to Vietnam veterans with medical conditions linked to Agent Orange.

Public sentiment softened over time. Opinion polls by the late 1970s showed that most Americans considered the Vietnam veteran to be both a dutiful soldier and the victim of a tragic war. In 1982, the Vietnam Veterans Memorial, a dramatic wall of black granite with the names of 58,000 Americans who died or are missing in that war, was unveiled on the Mall in Washington, D.C. Attracting large, respectful crowds, the memorial affords recognition for the sacrifices of all who served in Vietnam.

Stumbling Toward Defeat

The pardon of Richard Nixon and the fall of South Vietnam served to erode much of the goodwill that had accompanied Gerald Ford's early days in office. The president also faced a bleak economic picture, darkened by spiraling energy costs, in which unemployment and inflation reached their highest levels in years. "The state of the union," Ford admitted in 1975, "is not good."

The president and the Congress disagreed about the best medicine for the economic slump. The Republican Ford, believing that a balanced federal budget was the key to cutting inflation, proposed sizable cuts in government programs and a voluntary citizen's campaign to curb rising prices, which he called "Whip Inflation Now" (WIN). The Democratic Congress called for increased federal spending to spur the economy and to lower unemployment by creating new jobs. Although Ford vetoed more than sixty bills during his brief tenure in office, Congress overrode the president to increase social security benefits, fund public works projects, and raise the minimum wage.

In foreign affairs, Ford tried to maintain the policy of détente begun by Nixon and Kissinger, who remained as secretary of state. But unlike Nixon, the new president worried conservatives with his alleged weaknesses as a negotiator. Of particular concern was the Helsinki Accord of 1975, which pledged the United States and the Soviet Union, among other nations, to recognize the Cold War boundaries dividing Eastern and Western Europe and to respect human rights within their borders. Many Americans were dismayed by the formal acceptance of Soviet domination over nations such as Poland and East Germany; and many more were skeptical about any Russian promise regarding human rights. "I am against this agreement," said former Governor Ronald Reagan of California, "and I think all Americans should be against it."

Even Ford's occasional successes left controversy in their wake. In 1975, for example, communists in Cambodia seized the American merchant ship *Mayaguez* in international waters off the Cambodian coast. The president responded with a daring rescue mission in which forty-one U.S. Marines were killed and forty-nine were wounded, although it turned out that the Cambodians had already released the *Mayaguez* and its crew. Though Ford received some criticism for not consulting Congress before sending troops into action, most Americans, recalling the *Pueblo* incident and the fall of South Vietnam, applauded his decisive action. "It was wonderful," declared Senator Barry Goldwater. "It shows we've still got balls in this country."

The Election of 1976

Gerald Ford dreamed of winning the White House in his own right. Yet unlike previous incumbents, who normally breezed through the presidential nominating process, Ford faced a serious challenge in 1976 from Ronald Reagan and the Republican right. Reagan's polished presence and outspoken conservatism played well against Ford's reserved manner and middle-of-the-road approach. With great fanfare, Reagan portrayed Ford as a weak president, unable to tame a Democratic Congress or to confront the Russians at Helsinki. In his sharpest attack, Reagan blasted Ford for opening negotiations aimed at reducing American control of the Panama Canal. "We built it, we paid for it, it's ours," Reagan thundered, "and we should tell [Panama] that we are going to keep it."

Though Reagan battled Ford to a draw in the state primaries, the president won a narrow victory at the Republican National Convention in Kansas City by agreeing to support a party platform sympathetic to the Reagan forces. The platform condemned both the Helsinki agreement and the Panama Canal negotiations, while endorsing constitutional amendments to legalize school prayer and prohibit abortions. For vice president, the Republican delegates selected Senator Bob Dole of Kansas, a tough campaigner with conservative views.

Because Ford appeared so vulnerable in 1976, the Democratic race for president attracted a very large field. Among the candidates was a little known ex-governor of Georgia named James Earl ("Jimmy") Carter, Jr. Few observers took him seriously at the start, and the voters asked, "Jimmy who?" When Carter told his mother that he intended to run for president, she replied, "president of what?" Yet Carter ran an effective, well-financed campaign, portraying himself as a political outsider, untainted by the arrogance and corruption of Washington.

Carter struck the right pose for the post-Watergate era. A deeply religious man, who promised voters, "I will never lie to you," he combined the virtues of small town America with the skills of the modern corporate world. Born in Plains, Georgia, in

1924, Carter attended local schools, graduated with distinction from the U.S. Naval Academy, and spent seven years as a naval officer working on nuclear submarines. Following the death of his father in 1953, Carter returned to Plains to run the family's farm supply and peanut business. As the company prospered, he turned to politics, winning a state senate seat in 1962 and the Georgia governorship eight years later. Known as a "new South" politician, Carter supported progressive causes and reached out to black constituents through his concern for civil rights.

Meeting in New York City, the Democratic National Convention chose Carter for president and Senator Walter Mondale of Minnesota for vice president. Carter ran a safe campaign that fall, avoiding controversial issues while claiming that America was no longer "strong" or "respected" in the world. The media, meanwhile, caught Ford in a series of bumbling accidents—banging his head on a car door, tripping on the steps of an airplane, falling down on the ski slopes, whacking spectators on the golf course with his tee shots—that made him look clownish and inept. Before long, the comedian Chevy Chase was beginning almost every episode of *Saturday Night Live* by taking a terrible tumble in the role of Gerald Ford. And the president only made things worse for himself with a series of embarrassing verbal blunders, such as his insistence during the televised debate with Carter that "there [was] no Soviet domination of Eastern Europe." By election day, many Americans viewed Ford as a decent man, doing his best in a job that appeared to overwhelm him.

Still, the race was very close. Carter won 40.8 million votes, Ford 39.1. The electoral count was 297 to 240. Carter swept the entire South (except for Virginia) and the key industrial states of Ohio, Pennsylvania, and New York. Ford did well in the West, carrying every state but Texas. Polls showed Carter with large majorities among both minority voters and working-class whites who had rejected McGovern in 1972. In this election, at least, the New Deal coalition held firm.

Jimmy Carter became the first president from the Deep South in more than a century, signifying that region's increased strength—and acceptance—in the national arena. Furthermore, his election witnessed the growing importance of state primaries in the nominating process as well as the influence of the new Fair Campaign Practices Act of 1974. The law provided federal funds to the major candidates ($22 million each in this election), while establishing limits on personal contributions and a stricter accounting of how funds were disbursed. The result, as the 1976 election amply displayed, was a longer, more expensive presidential campaign season, with television advertising playing an ever larger role.

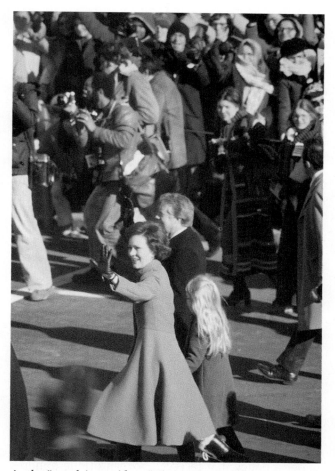

As the "people's president," Jimmy Carter led his inaugural parade on foot down Pennsylvania Avenue in 1977.
© Bettmann/UPI/Corbis

The Ford-Carter election continued the downward trend in voter turnout, from 55.7 percent in 1972 to 54.4 percent in 1976. Polls showed a growing sense of apathy and disillusionment among the American people, a loss of connection with politics as a positive force in their lives. As one bumper sticker put it, "Don't Vote. It Only Encourages Them!"

THE CARTER YEARS

The new Democratic administration began with promise and hope. President-elect Carter took the oath of office as Jimmy (not James Earl) Carter before leading the inaugural parade on foot down Pennsylvania Avenue dressed in a simple business suit. Determined to be a "people's president," Carter surrounded himself with populist symbolism—giving fireside chats in a sweater and blue jeans, attending town meetings from New Hampshire to New Mexico, and staying overnight in the homes of ordinary Americans. "We must have a new spirit," he declared. "We must once again have full faith in our country—and in one another."

Civil Rights in a New Era

As governor of Georgia, Jimmy Carter had opened the doors of government to minorities. As president, he did much the same thing. Women, African Americans, and Hispanics were appointed to federal positions in record numbers as judges, ambassadors, and White House aides. Women, for example, filled three of Carter's cabinet-level positions and numerous other policy-making roles. In addition, Carter's wife, Rosalyn, greatly expanded the role of first lady by serving as a key advisor to the president and representing him on diplomatic missions.

Though Carter strongly supported civil rights and gave special attention to the plight of minorities in the inner cities, the momentum for racial change in the 1970s had shifted from the executive branch to the federal courts. During Carter's term, the issue of affirmative action took center stage in *University of California Regents v. Bakke* (1978). Allan Bakke, a thirty-eight-year-old white man, was denied admission to the University of California medical school at Davis. He sued on the grounds that his test scores exceeded those of several black applicants who were admitted under a policy that reserved sixteen of one hundred spots for minorities in each entering class. The policy amounted to "reverse discrimination," Bakke charged, and thus violated his right to equal protection under the law. The case raised a fundamental conflict between the government's obligation to treat all citizens equally regardless of race, and its responsibility to help the long-suffering victims of racial discrimination enter the mainstream of American society. In a 5–4 ruling, the Supreme Court struck down the medical school's quota policy as a violation of Bakke's constitutional rights. But it held that universities might consider race as a factor in admission "to remedy disadvantages cast on minorities by past racial prejudice."

The *Bakke* decision began a passionate debate over affirmative action that continues to this day. Opponents considered it to be a racially divisive policy as well as a dangerous step away from the American tradition of individual rights. Why penalize innocent whites, they argued, for the sins of their ancestors? But supporters of affirmative action viewed it as the surest way to remedy discrimination, past and present. "In order to get beyond racism, we must take race into account," wrote Justice Thurgood Marshall. "There is no other way."

Human Rights and Global Realities

President Carter knew little about foreign affairs. His political career had been spent entirely on state and local concerns. Yet Carter viewed his inexperience as an asset, freeing him from worn-out thinking and stale ideas. He believed that a fresh approach to foreign affairs would move America beyond the "big power" rivalries of the Cold War era. What America needed, he thought, was a foreign policy that stressed democracy and human rights—in short, the idealism of the United States.

Carter chose a diverse foreign policy team. His U.N. ambassador, Andrew Young, was a black civil rights leader who emphasized better U.S. relations with the developing world, especially in Africa. His secretary of state, Cyrus Vance, was an experienced diplomat who worked tirelessly to keep détente alive. And his national security advisor, Zbigniew Brzezinski, was a Columbia University professor, born in Poland, who proposed a tough front against the Soviet Union, which he blamed for most of the world's ills. Their conflicting advice sometimes left the president confused.

Yet Carter scored some impressive foreign policy successes. Emphasizing human rights in Latin America, he withdrew American support for Chile, cut off aid to the repressive Somoza regime in Nicaragua, and encouraged the governments of Brazil and Argentina in their halting steps toward democracy. Carter also presented the Senate with a treaty that relinquished American control over the Panama Canal by the year 2000, and a second one that detailed American rights in the Canal Zone thereafter. Both treaties provoked fierce national debate; both passed the Senate by a single vote.

Carter's greatest triumph occurred in the Middle East. In 1977, Egyptian President Anwar Sadat stunned the Arab world by visiting Israel to explore peace negotiations with Prime Minister Menachem Begin. Their discussions were cordial but fruitless, for neither man seemed willing to take the risks that peace demanded. When the talks broke down, President Carter invited Sadat and Begin to his presidential retreat at Camp David in Maryland. For two full weeks in September 1978, Carter shuttled between the cabins of the two Middle Eastern leaders, patiently working out the details of a "peace process" between Egypt and Israel that other nations might later join.

The Camp David Accords led to a historic treaty the following year. Egypt agreed to recognize the state of Israel, which previously had been unthinkable for an Arab nation, while Israel pledged to return the captured Sinai Peninsula to Egypt. The treaty did not consider other vital issues, such as the fate of displaced Palestinians and the future of Israeli-held Arab territory in Gaza and the West Bank. Yet few could deny the enormity of what had transpired, or the pivotal role played by President Carter in bringing it about.

Economic Blues

Early success in foreign affairs, however, could not mask Carter's problems with the troubled economy. During the 1976 presidential campaign, candidate Carter had focused on high inflation (6 percent) and unemployment (8 percent) that gripped the United States. Combining these figures into a "misery index" of 14, he had promised the American people immediate relief.

Carter's program to stimulate the economy depended on a mixture of tax cuts, public works, and employment programs—a kind of "pump priming" reminiscent of Franklin Roosevelt's New Deal. The Democratic-controlled Congress responded sympathetically by funding large public works projects, reducing taxes by $30 billion, and raising the minimum wage from $2.30 to $3.35 over a five-year span. The good news was that unemployment dropped to 6 percent by 1978; the bad news was that inflation rose to 10 percent—and kept climbing.

Carter changed his approach. Creating jobs took a back seat to the problem of runaway inflation. Unlike Richard Nixon, who fought this problem by implementing wage and price controls, Carter tried to attack inflation by tightening the money supply (through higher interest rates) and by controlling the federal deficit. This meant reduced government spending, a turnabout that alienated the Democratic Congress. Moreover, Carter's new policies appeared to increase unemployment without curbing inflation—the worst of both worlds. Before long, the "misery index" stood at 21.

This was not all Carter's fault, of course. The decline of American productivity, the growth of foreign competition, and the surging cost of imported oil had plagued the nation for some time. In 1977, Carter offered a substantive plan for the energy crisis, which he described as "the moral equivalent of war." (Critics called it "meow.") The plan arrived on the heels of the worst winter in modern American history, a season of blizzards, record low temperatures, and Arctic winds. Based mainly on conservation—or reduced energy use—it ran into immediate opposition from oil companies, gas producers, the auto industry, and others who advocated the increased production of fossil fuels and the deregulation of prices. "This country didn't conserve its way to greatness," a Texas oil man complained. "It produced its way to greatness."

The National Energy Act, passed in November 1978, did little to reduce America's energy consumption or its reliance on foreign oil. Carter's original

Anwar Sadat (left) and Menachem Begin shake hands at Camp David, Maryland, as Jimmy Carter, who brought the men together, smiles in the background.
© Bettmann/UPI/Corbis

plans to stimulate conservation efforts were overshadowed by incentives to increase domestic energy production through tax breaks for exploration, an emphasis on alternative sources (solar, nuclear, coal), and the deregulation of natural gas. The law did not address, much less solve, the nation's fundamental energy problems—as Americans would soon discover.

The Persian Gulf

In January 1979, a chain of events unfolded that shook the nation's confidence and shattered Jimmy Carter's presidency. The year began with the overthrow of America's dependable ally, Shah Riza Pahlavi of Iran; it ended with the United States appearing helpless and dispirited in the face of mounting challenges at home and abroad.

On a visit to Iran in 1977, President Carter had described it as "an island of stability in one of the most troubled areas in the world." Iran was vital to American interests, both as an oil supplier and a bastion against Soviet influence in the Middle East. Thousands of American workers and their families lived in Iran, while thousands of Iranian students attended college in the United States. Ironically, President Carter's concern for human rights did not extend to Iran, where the army and secret police used widespread torture and repression to keep the shah and his ruling elite in power. Against all evidence, Carter even congratulated the shah for "the admiration and love your people give to you."

The Iranian Revolution was led by Ayatollah Ruhollah Khomeini, an exiled cleric, and his devoted followers. Their aim was not to set up a democracy, but

$\mathcal{P}$ICTURING THE PAST ✦ ECONOMICS & TECHNOLOGY

THREE MILE ISLAND

© Bettmann/UPI/Corbis

By the mid-1960s, nuclear power had emerged as a viable alternative to fossil fuels—a cheaper, cleaner, and virtually inexhaustible energy source for the future. As the number of commercial nuclear power plants increased, so, too, did their size. Among the largest was Three Mile Island (pictured) in the Susquehanna River near Harrisburg, Pennsylvania. Though a growing environmental movement in the 1970s had raised safety concerns regarding these huge facilities, and Hollywood had recently produced a box office smash, *The China Syndrome*, about a nuclear power plant disaster, the dangers still seemed remote. Then, in March 1979, a mechanical failure at Three Mile Island threatened to blanket the surrounding countryside with radioactive fallout, and thousands fled their homes. Though engineers were successful in stabilizing the damaged reactor, the looming white stacks of Three Mile Island came to symbolize the tremendous risks associated with nuclear power. There are just over 100 nuclear power plants in the United States today; almost all were constructed before the awful scare at Three Mile Island.

---

rather to form a fundamentalist Islamic state. When demonstrations paralyzed Iran, the shah fled his country, leaving the religious fundamentalists in control. One of Khomeini's first moves was to end oil shipments to "the Great Satan" America, thus allowing other OPEC countries to raise their prices even more. In the United States, long gas lines reappeared and the price reached an incredible one dollar per gallon.

With Americans reeling from months of bad news, President Carter went on national television to speak partly about the energy crisis, but mostly about a "crisis of confidence" that struck "at the very heart and soul and spirit of our national will." His address was remarkably candid. Rather than assuring anxious Americans that they had nothing to fear, or trying to rally

them with ringing phrases about honor and duty, the president spoke of a nation in trouble, struggling with the values of its cherished past. In place of "hard work, strong families, and close-knit communities," he said, too many Americans "now worship self-indulgence and consumption. Human identity is no longer defined by what one does but by what one owns."

Having passionately diagnosed the illness, Carter provided no cure. The "crisis of confidence" deepened. In October, the deposed shah of Iran, suffering from cancer, was allowed to enter the United States for medical treatment. This decision, which Carter viewed as a simple humanitarian gesture, produced an explosive backlash in Iran. On November 4, militant students stormed the American embassy in Tehran, taking dozens of

American hostages and parading them in blindfolds for the entire world to see. The militants demanded that the United States turn over the shah for trial in Iran. Otherwise, the Americans would remain as captives—and perhaps be tried, and executed, as spies.

Carter had almost no leverage with these militants, who were supported by Khomeini himself. His attempts to settle the crisis through the United Nations were ignored by Iran. His orders to embargo Iranian oil and suspend arms sales were empty gestures, since other nations refused to do the same. The remaining options—freezing Iran's assets in American banks or threatening to deport Iranian students from the United States—did nothing to change the fate of the hostages in Tehran.

For a time, the American people rallied behind their president. Carter's approval rating jumped from 30 to 61 percent in the first month of the crisis. Yet Carter grasped what many others did not: there was no easy solution to the hostage standoff. "It would not be possible, or even advisable," he warned, "to set a deadline about when, or if, I would take certain acts in the future." As the nation waited, public patience grew thin.

The year ended with yet another nasty surprise. In December, Russian soldiers invaded neighboring Afghanistan to quell a revolt led by Muslim fundamentalists against the faltering pro-Soviet regime. The invasion ultimately backfired; fanatical resistance from Afghan fighters turned the country into a graveyard for Russian troops. Determined to act boldly in light of the continuing Iran hostage crisis, Carter cut off grain shipments to the Soviet Union and cancelled America's participation at the upcoming Summer Olympic Games in Moscow—a boycott that many nations chose to ignore. More significantly, he announced a "Carter Doctrine" for the Persian Gulf, warning that "outside aggression" would "be repelled by any means necessary, including military force." For the first time since Vietnam, young men were ordered to register for the draft. In addition, Carter requested a major increase in defense spending, with $50 billion set aside for new weapons systems such as the multiple-warhead MX missile, which moved from place to place on secret railroad cars to prevent the enemy from tracking it. By 1980, the Cold War was heating up again. Afghanistan and its aftermath had dealt a serious blow to détente.

Death in the Desert

As President Carter and the American people staggered through the repeated shocks of 1979, one issue dominated the national agenda: the fate of the hostages in Iran. The crisis took on symbolic importance as an example of America's declining power in the world—its in-

ability to defend its citizens, its vital interests, its national honor. The television networks flashed nightly pictures of the hostages on humiliating public display in Tehran while frenzied crowds shouted "Death to Carter" and "Down with the United States." In Washington, meanwhile, the president met regularly with the families of the hostages and worked tirelessly to find a diplomatic solution. But this seemed all but impossible, because the Iranians, demanding both the shah and an American apology for supporting him, were not interested in a quick settlement. Reluctantly, Carter ordered a secret mission to free the hostages by force.

The result was disastrous. In April 1980, American commandos reached the Iranian desert, where two of their helicopters were disabled by mechanical problems. Another hit a U.S. cargo plane, killing eight members of the rescue mission. The commandos departed without ever getting close to the hostages in Tehran. To make matters worse, the Iranians proudly displayed the burned corpses for television crews. Most Americans blamed the president for the debacle. What little remained of Jimmy Carter's credibility disappeared that fateful day in the Iranian desert.

CONCLUSION

The United States in 1980 was an uneasy land. The social upheavals of the 1960s and 1970s had fostered anxiety as well as progress. The movement for civil rights, so certain in the era of bus boycotts, lunch counter sit-ins, and voting rights marches, was now

In 1979, student militants stormed the American embassy in Iran and took dozens of U.S. citizens hostage. Unable to negotiate their release, President Carter approved a secret rescue mission that ended in disaster.
© Bettmann/UPI/Corbis

By 1980, many Americans looked for someone to rescue the nation and restore its damaged prestige.
AP/Wide World Photo

deeply divided over issues such as forced busing and affirmative action. So, too, the struggle for women's rights generated fierce controversy over abortion, sex roles, workplace equality, and the ERA. On the economic front, Americans faced a world of new troubles—a world of stagnant incomes, rising unemployment, mounting trade deficits, and skyrocketing inflation. No longer were young people guaranteed the prospect of moving a rung or two above their parents on the ladder of success.

Above all, the nation appeared momentarily to lose confidence in its leaders and its goals. Watergate, OPEC, the fall of South Vietnam, Three Mile Island, the hostage crisis, the bungled rescue attempt—all seemed to reflect a loss of purpose, authority, and prestige. As the 1980 election approached, many Americans looked back into the past with a deep sense of nostalgia, hoping for someone to rescue the country and restore the American dream.

Recommended Readings

Carroll, Peter. *It Seemed Like Nothing Happened: America in the 1970s* (1982). A critical overview of American life in the new age of limits.

Chavez, Lydia. *The Color Bind* (1998). Analyzes the political battle surrounding affirmative action in California.

Hull, N. E. H., and Hoffer, Peter. *Roe v. Wade* (2001). Provides an excellent analysis of the abortion rights controversy in American history.

Isaacson, Walter. *Kissinger* (1992). A comprehensive biography of the man who helped shape America's foreign policy in the 1970s and beyond.

Kutler, Stanley. *Abuse of Power: The New Nixon Tapes* (1997). The story of a president's demise told through the secret tapes that brought him down.

Lukas, J. Anthony. *Common Ground: A Turbulent Decade in the Lives of Three American Families* (1986). Examines the busing crisis in Boston from several perspectives.

Rudenstine, David. *The Day the Presses Stopped: A History of the Pentagon Papers Case* (1996). Looks at the legal and political issues surrounding the decade's most heralded First Amendment crisis.

Schoenwald, Jonathan. *A Time for Choosing* (2001). Describes the rise of modern conservatism leading to Ronald Reagan's election.

Shilts, Randy. *And the Band Played On* (1987). A superb account of the spreading AIDS epidemic in the homosexual community.

Wandersee, Winifred. *On the Move: American Women in the 1970s* (1988). Highlights the political struggle of women in this decade and the changes that occurred.

American Journey Online and InfoTrac College Edition

Visit the source collections at http://ajaccess. wadsworth.com and infotrac.thomsonlearning.com and use the Search function with the following key terms to explore documents, images, audio and video clips, articles, and commentary related to the material in this chapter.

Kent State	Watergate
Roe v. Wade	Gerald R. Ford
Jimmy Carter	Camp David Accords
La Raza Unida	Henry Kissinger

Additional resources, exercises, and Internet links related to this chapter are available on the American Passages Web site: http://history.wadsworth.com/passages2e

31 THE REAGAN-BUSH YEARS 1981–1992

THE REAGAN REVOLUTION

REAGAN AND FOREIGN POLICY

SOCIAL TENSIONS AND STRAINS OF THE 1980s

THE 1984 PRESIDENTIAL ELECTION

REAGAN'S SECOND TERM

THE 1988 PRESIDENTIAL ELECTION

KINDER, GENTLER GEORGE HERBERT WALKER BUSH

Ronald Reagan captured the nation's attention with his friendly manner, rugged looks, and cowboy demeanor. His policies of building up defense and cutting taxes were controversial in the 1980s. His admirers see him as the architect of American victory in the Cold War.
© Evans Michael/Corbis Sygma

The presidency of Ronald Reagan defined the decade of the 1980s. His election in 1980 brought to office the most conservative president since Herbert Hoover, and his efforts to redirect the nation toward a smaller and less activist government aroused bitter controversy. After two decades of "failed presidencies," Reagan's ability to serve for two consecutive presidential terms contributed to a mood of renewed optimism that endured until he left office.

The actual achievements of Reagan and his successor George H. W. Bush remain in dispute. During these two administrations, the Cold War ended, the Berlin Wall toppled, and the Soviet Union collapsed. Reagan's partisans gave him the credit for ending the threat of what he had called "the evil empire." Yet victory in the Cold War did not result in a reduction of foreign policy issues and a safer world for the United States.

While the economy boomed during the 1980s, the federal government's budget deficit increased. Rich Americans became richer, while the gulf between the affluent and the poor widened. Under the pressures of global economic change, American businesses became more efficient and less unwieldy. The price, however, was a loss of jobs in many key industries as American workers faced the trauma of "downsizing." By the end of the 1980s, despite the prosperity of the Reagan era, apprehension about the economic future of the average American grew. For all the ebullience and optimism of the Reagan-Bush period, critical social questions remained unanswered.

CHRONOLOGY

1981 Ronald Reagan inaugurated as president • Iranian-held hostages freed from captivity • Sandra Day O'Connor appointed to the Supreme Court • President Reagan survives assassination attempt • AIDS outbreak begins in United States

1982 Severe economic recession grips nation • Democrats make gains in congressional elections

1983 President Reagan proposes Strategic Defense Initiative (SDI) • Social security reforms adopted • United States invades Grenada

1984 Geraldine Ferraro becomes first female vice presidential candidate of a major party • Macintosh computer introduced • Ronald Reagan reelected

1985 Rock Hudson dies of AIDS • Gramm-Rudman-Hollings Act adopted • Reagan administration begins negotiations with Iran that lead to Iran-Contra scandal

1986 Tax Reform Act passed • *Challenger* space shuttle explodes • Immigration Reform Act adopted • Democrats regain control of Senate in elections • Iran-Contra scandal erupts

1987 United States and Soviet Union pursue arms control • Iran-Contra hearings held

1988 Democrats nominate Michael Dukakis to run for president • Antidepressant drug Prozac introduced • George H. W. Bush elected president

1989 United States invades Panama to capture Manuel Noriega • Berlin Wall comes down • Chinese kill demonstrators in Tiananmen Square • In *Webster v. Reproductive Health Services,* Supreme Court upholds right of states to limit abortion access

1990 George H. W. Bush abandons "no new taxes" pledge • Iraq invades Kuwait • Americans with Disabilities Act passed

1991 Iraq defeated in Gulf War • Clarence Thomas nominated to and confirmed for Supreme Court • Soviet Union collapses

THE REAGAN REVOLUTION

When Ronald Wilson Reagan took the oath as president of the United States on January 20, 1981, he was the oldest man to assume the nation's highest office. Born in Illinois in 1911, he had been an actor and television personality. Disillusioned with the political liberalism of his youth, he became a Republican and ran for governor of California in 1966, promising to reduce spending and provide a leaner government.

It proved more difficult for Reagan to enact his conservative agenda than he had anticipated. Instead of reducing spending and shrinking government as he had promised, taxes rose and the California government bureaucracy grew. Nevertheless, his blend of conservative rhetoric and a sunny disposition made him a favorite among conservatives in the 1970s. He lost a race for the Republican nomination to Gerald Ford in 1976 but became the party's nominee four years later with George H. W. Bush as his running mate.

The problems of the Jimmy Carter administration gave Reagan his opportunity. He became the embodiment of the new national sentiment for lower taxes, restraints on government spending, and concern about inflation. At the same time, he promised increased spending on national defense and a stronger U.S. role overseas to meet the threat of Communism.

Carter Versus Reagan

The 1980 presidential election campaign took place in the shadow of an ongoing crisis involving fifty-two American hostages who had been seized in Iran during that country's revolution against the shah. Initially the plight of the hostages helped Jimmy Carter fend off the challenge of Senator Edward M. Kennedy of Massachusetts for the Democratic presidential nomination. A failed military attempt to rescue the hostages in April 1980 undercut Carter's standing with the voters and made his nomination a hollow prize. Still, most Democrats believed that the president could defeat Reagan. The White House attached little significance to the third-party candidacy of John Anderson, a Republican member of Congress, who ran as a moderate alternative to both major party nominees.

"Are You Better Off?"

During the campaign, Reagan assailed Carter's record on the economy and national defense. The president fired back that Reagan was a dangerous and unreliable political extremist. The election came down to a televised debate between the two men in late October 1980.

Polls indicated that the race was a dead heat. When Carter attacked Reagan's position on Medicare, the challenger responded with a wry remark: "There you go again," making Carter seem petulant and carping. In winding up the debate, Reagan asked the American people "Are you better off?" than four years earlier.

Reagan and the Republicans won the election by a substantial margin in the popular vote: 44 million ballots for Reagan to 35 million for Carter and 5.7 million for John Anderson. In the electoral college, Reagan garnered 489 votes and Carter forty-nine. The Republicans regained control of the Senate, picking up twelve seats from the Democrats.

The Rise of the Christian Right

A central element in Reagan's electoral victory was the votes of evangelical Christians. One manifestation of their political clout was the Moral Majority, an organization founded by the Reverend Jerry Falwell of Virginia in 1979. Falwell tapped into the expanding base of evangelicals in denominations such as the Southern Baptist Convention. The Moral Majority assailed abortion, homosexuality, rock music, and drugs.

Throughout the 1980s, evangelical Christianity permeated American politics. On cable television, viewers tuned in to Pat Robertson's *700 Club* on the Christian Broadcasting Network, which Robertson had founded. Other ministers such as Jim Bakker with his *PTL* (*Praise the Lord*) program and the fiery evangelist Jimmy Swaggart commanded sizable audiences. Though both Bakker and Swaggart eventually ran afoul of the law for fraud (Bakker) and sexual misadventures (Swaggart), their message resonated in many areas of the nation. Ronald Reagan never implemented the evangelical agenda, but he gave them a sympathetic hearing that enhanced their influence on American public life.

The divisive issue of abortion helped fuel the rise of the Christian Right. Following the Supreme Court decision in *Roe v. Wade* (1973), the number of abortions in the United States stood at 1.5 million per year. Foes of abortion, most notably in the Roman Catholic church and among evangelical Protestants, asserted that the unborn baby was a human being from the moment of conception and entitled to all the rights of a living person. To reduce the number of abortions and to overturn the *Roe* decision, the "right to life" forces, as they called themselves, pressured lawmakers to cut back on the right of abortion and to enact restrictive laws. The Hyde amendment, adopted in Congress in 1976, banned the use of Medicaid funds to pay for abortions for women on welfare.

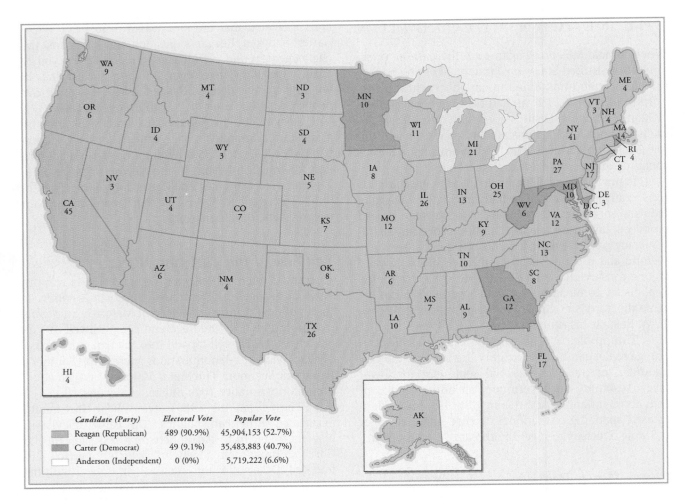

Candidate (Party)	Electoral Vote	Popular Vote
Reagan (Republican)	489 (90.9%)	45,904,153 (52.7%)
Carter (Democrat)	49 (9.1%)	35,483,883 (40.7%)
Anderson (Independent)	0 (0%)	5,719,222 (6.6%)

Map 31.1 *The Election of 1980*
> The election map reveals the repudiation of Jimmy Carter and his administration in 1980 and the swing to the right that put Ronald Reagan in the White House. Carter's economic record and the foreign policy problems of the late 1970s left him without an effective national political base.

The anti-abortion forces believed that more direct action was warranted. They conducted picketing and boycotts of abortion clinics in the 1980s and arranged for massive public demonstrations. Their tactics became more violent as the decade progressed. Operation Rescue tried to prevent patients from entering abortion clinics. Other protesters turned to bombing of buildings and assassination of doctors. The Republican party became largely anti-abortion in its policies and programs. The Democrats were equally committed to what was called "a woman's right to choose."

Reagan in Office

Reagan set out his goals in a single sentence: "We must balance the budget, reduce tax rates, and restore our defenses." The incoming president believed that it would

be possible to achieve all of these objectives at the same time. Reagan brought striking political gifts to the White House. His long career in Hollywood had given him a skill in conveying his views that won him the title of "The Great Communicator." When delivering a prepared speech with a teleprompter to guide him, Reagan could read a text with practiced artistry. His use of humor, especially when he stressed his own foibles, was deft; it reinforced his rapport with his fellow citizens. He exuded a degree of optimism about his country, sincerity about his positions, and confidence in the rightness of his views that made him a masterful politician during his first six years as president.

Yet Reagan had significant weaknesses, too. He knew very little about the actual operation of the federal government and displayed scant curiosity about such matters. He read very few of the documents that crossed his desk and watched movies when he should have been reading position papers. As a friend put it, "He lived life on the surface where the small waves are, not deep down where the heavy currents tug." Reagan believed that there were few hard choices in governance, and he did not inform the nation of the serious alternatives that had to be faced in reducing the deficits and curbing government spending.

The president was not a simple man. Many commentators said that Reagan played the role of president better than any other president since Franklin D. Roosevelt. But after the glow of the performance faded, there remained the question of whether he had done more than walk through the presidency.

The Reagan Team

Part of the success that Reagan achieved during his first term came about because of the effective staff that managed his daily activities. His chief of staff was James Baker, a Texas politician who had not been close to the Reagans before the election. Joining him were Michael Deaver, who directed media activities, and Edwin Meese—a longtime friend from California who tended to policy issues. These men "packaged" the president in settings that capitalized on his warm relationship with the American people. The gritty details of government went on out of the public's view. The approach worked well, partly because these aides allowed Reagan to deal with the large issues that interested him instead of the mundane details of governing, for which he had little aptitude or serious interest.

Another important player in the Reagan presidency was his wife Nancy. Criticized for her opulent lifestyle during her early days as first lady, she won over the Washington media with a deft blend of self-deprecating humor and commitment to a "Just Say No" campaign against drugs. Behind the scenes she managed the president's schedule with the help of an astrologer. She also fretted about Reagan's place in history and urged the president privately to promote some degree of détente with the Soviet Union over nuclear weapons.

The Early Months

As Reagan started his administration, the Republicans controlled the White House and the Senate, where they commanded a 53–46 majority. Democrats remained the majority in the House of Representatives, 242–190. In 1980, the inflation rate was over 12 percent, the unemployment rate was above 7 percent, and the prime interest rate had gone to almost 20 percent. The national debt had reached $908 billion. In Reagan's view, the responsibility for these ominous figures lay with the fed-

Nancy Reagan was a very controversial first lady because of her opulent lifestyle. She responded to criticism with the "Just Say No" campaign against drugs, and she played a very large role in all the decisions of her husband's administration.
Reproduced from the Collections of the Library of Congress

eral government. As he told Congress on February 18, 1981, "The most important cause of our economic problems has been the government itself."

To remedy the situation, the administration embraced a program that combined traditional Republican suspicion of government spending with an aggressive reduction in federal income taxes. The term "supply-side economics" became shorthand for what this program promised to do. The government should lower income and corporate tax rates to give private business and individual taxpayers more money to spend. The predicted surge in productive economic activity would result in an increase in tax revenues, which would prevent large budget deficits.

Defining the Reagan Presidency

In his first year Reagan implemented his policy agenda as promised. The release of U.S. hostages in Iran on January 20, 1981, removed that troublesome issue

The assassination attempt against Ronald Reagan on March 30, 1981, wounded the president more seriously than was revealed at the time. His optimism and high spirits in the face of his wound added to public confidence. This picture shows an unidentified Secret Service agent yelling instructions after shots were fired.
AP/Wide World Photo

from the public sphere. When Reagan was shot on March 30, 1981, the would-be assassin's bullet came closer to ending his life than the public knew. The president's courage and good humor in this moment of crisis increased his popularity and added to the reservoir of goodwill that he commanded.

A second event that raised Reagan even higher in the polls was his handling of a strike by the Professional Air Traffic Controllers Organization (PATCO). As government employees, the controllers could not legally strike, and the president fired them when they refused to heed a back-to-work order. The message for the nation was that the White House would be tough on organized labor.

The Economic Agenda

During the first half of 1981, a coalition of Republicans and "boll weevil Democrats" (southern and western conservatives) pushed through legislation that trimmed tax rates by 25 percent over three years. In tandem with the tax measure, the administration sought budget cuts for a number of discretionary social programs to advance the president's goal of a balanced budget by 1984. Although the budget act, passed in the House on June 25, 1981, promised future reductions in spending, during its first year it provided $16 billion in immediate cuts. That was $200 billion less than would have been required to achieve a real step toward a balanced budget.

The Limits of the Reagan Revolution

Two major policy commitments limited what the Reagan administration could accomplish. The president declined to make cuts in what he termed "the social safety net": social security, Medicare, veterans' benefits, Head Start, and school lunch programs. All of these spending policies had vocal and powerful supporters. The practical result was that almost half of the federal budget was placed beyond the reach of congressional budget-cutting efforts.

The other priority of the Reagan administration was a sharp increase in defense spending. Reagan believed that the nation's military establishment had been neglected during Carter's presidency. In 1979, however, the Democratic Congress and the administration had begun a long-range program to build up American military power, and the Reagan White House expanded on that initiative. During the Ford-Carter years, defense budgets had been less than $200 billion annually. Under Reagan, the Pentagon budget rose to nearly $300 billion per year by 1985.

A Growing Deficit

The outcome of modest cuts in social programs and entitlements, sharp hikes in defense spending, and a reduction in tax rates was a growth in the government deficit to $128 billion by 1982. The ballooning federal deficits continued throughout the Reagan era, producing a surge in the national debt. The goal of a balanced budget in 1984 vanished quickly, never to return while Reagan was in the White House. A dramatic change had occurred in the government's fiscal situation, with serious consequences for the future. The huge deficits drove economic policy for the decade that followed and future generations were left with a massive debt to fund and pay off.

Reagan's Domestic Policies

In his inaugural address, President Reagan proclaimed: "In this present crisis, government *is* not the solution to our problem; government *is* the problem." As part of his response to a large, intrusive government, Reagan advocated an extensive program of deregulation to lessen regulation of the private sector.

The Reagan administration pursued a new course in environmental policy. Secretary of the Interior James G. Watt, a conservative who disliked all restrictions on public lands in the West, sought to open new areas for oil drilling, cut back on the acquisition of land for national parks, and put in place other bureaucrats eager to reduce the amount of environmental regulation that the government con-

Table 31.1	Federal Government Deficits, 1980–1989 (In U.S. Dollars)
1980	73,808,000,000
1981	78,936,000,000
1982	127,940,000,000
1983	207,764,000,000
1984	185,324,000,000
1985	212,260,000,000
1986	221,140,000,000
1987	149,661,000,000
1988	155,151,000,000
1989	153,319,000,000

Source: *World Almanac*, 1995, p. 108.

One of the hotly disputed issues of the 1980s was the burgeoning federal budget deficit. Under Ronald Reagan, as this table shows, the annual deficit rose to as high as $221 billion in 1986 and stayed around $150 billion annually for the last six years of the Reagan presidency. Balanced budgets became an illusory goal. Republicans asserted that lower tax rates would produce more revenues, which did occur. At the same time, however, the White House and Congress engaged in more spending on defense and entitlement programs such as Medicare and social security with governmental red ink being the result. Interest on the federal debt became one of the major expenditures of the government. Both parties seemed quite willing to pass these debts on to future generations rather than confront the electorate with the unpleasant choices of higher taxes or lower spending. This simple table thus raises questions about the sense of responsibility in 1980s politics and the larger social health of the United States in that period.

---

ducted. Appointees in the Environmental Protection Agency (EPA) came under fire for having used regulations for political and personal gain.

The Savings and Loan Disaster

The most spectacular and disastrous example of deregulation occurred in 1982, when Congress and the White House agreed to lift restrictions from the savings and loan industry. During a time of high inflation and rising interest rates, savings and loan institutions had difficulty earning a profit because of the low rates of interest they were allowed by law to pay on their deposits. In 1980, Congress increased federal insurance coverage to $100,000 per account and allowed savings and loan companies to offer even higher interest rates. These measures did not, however, increase the profits on the money that the thrift institutions loaned. Partly in response to lobbying by the industry and the large campaign contributions that lawmakers received, Congress decided to deregulate these companies and allow them to invest in higher risk assets, including commercial real estate, fine art, and, in some instances, speculative or fraudulent ventures.

At the same time that lending practices were relaxed, the Reagan administration cut back on the number of banking and regulatory examiners. With federal deposit insurance guaranteeing that they would be bailed out, savings and loan operators plunged into ventures that were risky and often illegal. At first, there seemed to be few problems, but by 1983 and 1984 troubling signs of weakness appeared in the banking and savings and loan businesses.

The Social Security Crisis

By the early 1980s, social security, the most popular New Deal program, had reached a funding crisis. During the 1970s, Congress and the Nixon administration had established a system of cost-of-living-adjustments (COLAs) that raised benefits for social security recipients as the rate of inflation rose (known as indexing). Indexing of benefits caused the cost of social security to soar as the population

One of the most hotly debated foreign policy issues of the 1980s had to do with the Reagan administration's support for the rebels against the Sandinista government in Nicaragua. The "Contras," as they were known, are shown here training in a remote area of their country.
© Bettmann/Reuters/Corbis

aged and more people received social security checks. But efforts to trim COLAs seemed futile because of the political fact that tinkering with social security benefits guaranteed electoral defeat for anyone who tried it.

President Reagan learned that lesson in the spring of 1981 when the administration proposed a cut in benefits for early retirees (those who would begin receiving benefits at age sixty-two). When the initiative was announced, gleeful Democrats assailed it and Republicans in Congress deserted Reagan. Social security did not come up again until December 1981, when the president appointed a bipartisan panel to deal with long-range funding of the retirement program. The result, announced after the 1982 elections, was a compromise that raised payroll taxes to pay for social security, taxed some of the benefits of people over sixty-five who had high incomes, and put off providing for the long-term viability of the system. For the moment, the social security system seemed to be on solid ground once again.

REAGAN AND FOREIGN POLICY

In foreign affairs, the new administration came into office with what seemed to be a clear, simple agenda about the relationship of the United States to its principal adversary. In 1983, Reagan called the Soviet Union "an evil empire" and said that the Cold War was a struggle between "right and wrong and good and evil." In dealing with the Soviets, then, the president insisted arms agreements be based on the principle of "trust but verify." He was convinced that the United States could outspend the Soviet Union in an arms race. Faced with an aging and incompetent Soviet leadership between 1981 and 1985, the White House avoided any summit meetings during that period. As a result, Soviet-American relations experienced a distinct chill during Reagan's first term.

This stern language did not rule out flexibility in some areas. Early in the new administration the president lifted the grain embargo that President Carter had established when the Soviet Union invaded Afghanistan in 1980. It was an action that pleased American wheat farmers. Reagan also reiterated his view that a nuclear war could not be won and should never be fought. Although the new White House team did not like the SALT II Treaty that Carter had negotiated, it largely observed the pact's provisions. Increased tensions between East and West overshadowed these gestures of restraint.

One area where the rivalry between the two superpowers flared was Central America. The Reagan administration believed that the victory of the Sandinistas in Nicaragua in 1979 represented a serious threat to U.S. interests in the region, especially in neighboring El Salvador. By late 1981, the United States was underwriting a rebellion against the Sandinista regime led by a faction called the "Contras." Although President Reagan likened the anti-Sandinistas to the patriots of the American Revolution, in 1982 the Democratic House of Representatives adopted an amendment that sought to block funds from being used to oust the Sandinistas. In Latin America, suspicion about U.S. policy increased during 1982.

The 1982 Elections

Reagan and his administration paid a political price for the policies of the first two years. A severe recession continued until almost the end of 1982. Although Reagan argued that the recession would soon end, the Republicans suffered a setback at the polls in the congressional elections. The Democrats gained twenty-seven seats in the House while the Republicans maintained their dominance in the Senate. Nevertheless, President Reagan again urged his fellow Republicans to "stay the course."

A Rebounding Economy and Foreign Policy Success

Shortly after the election the economy picked up steam, stimulated by the Reagan tax cuts. The inflation rate declined and unemployment receded. As the recovery gained strength, so did Reagan and his party. Adding to the president's popularity was the U.S. invasion of the Caribbean island of Grenada in October 1983. Fearing that radicals close to Fidel Castro and Cuba were about to turn Grenada into a Soviet base, the administration launched a powerful invasion force that secured control of the island after a brief struggle. The episode was a public relations success and further enhanced Reagan's image as a decisive leader.

In fact, the foreign policy scene was more complex than the victory in Grenada indicated. The war in Nicaragua was not going well for the Contras, and El Salvador was experiencing atrocities from right-wing death squads that murdered their opponents and left-wing insurgents sympathetic to Nicaragua. In 1984, Congress adopted a second, more restrictive, amendment to prevent the government from aiding the Contras.

In the Middle East Reagan's hopes of producing a lasting peace between Israel and its neighbors were also frustrated. The administration did not stop Israel from invading Lebanon in June 1982, and U.S. Marines were sent into the region as part of a multinational peacekeeping force. American involvement in Lebanon's turbulent politics led to the death of 239 marines when a terrorist bomb blew up a barracks in 1983. The marines were withdrawn, and terrorists concluded that the United States would not stand firm in a crisis.

Star Wars: The Strategic Defense Initiative (SDI)

In March 1983, the most significant defense policy initiative of the first Reagan term came when the president announced what he called the Strategic Defense Initiative (SDI). Reagan envisioned a system of weapons, based in space, that would intercept and shoot down Soviet missiles before they could reach the United States. Influenced by memories of science fiction serials in which he had starred as a young man, as well as by advocates of an antimissile system, Reagan wanted "a defensive screen that could intercept those missiles when they came out of their silos."

An appealing vision on the drawing board or in animated versions for television, SDI confronted immense technical problems that made it unlikely that it could be deployed for years. Critics promptly dubbed it "Star Wars" after the hit movie and questioned its technical rationale. For Reagan, the program represented an answer to the problem of relying on nuclear deterrence to stave off war between the superpowers. He pressed forward with SDI over the objections of his political opponents and the displeasure of the Soviet Union, whose leaders knew that their faltering economy could never duplicate SDI if the Americans ever achieved it.

SOCIAL TENSIONS AND STRAINS OF THE 1980s

Nuclear war was not the only danger that Americans faced in the early 1980s. In the early Reagan years Americans learned of a new and deadly disease. Scientists called it AIDS (for acquired immune deficiency syndrome). The source of the virus was in Africa, and it first appeared in the United States in 1981. The virus ravaged the immune system of its victims, and there was no known cure. Most of those infected were doomed to an inevitable and painful death. By the end of Ronald Reagan's first term, the number of confirmed AIDS deaths had reached 3,700 in the U.S.

The major process by which the virus spread within the population was through the exchange of bodily fluids. Mothers who were infected passed the condition on to their children; infected blood was transferred during transfusions. The most vulnerable groups were drug addicts, bisexuals, and homosexuals. During the first half of the decade, the spread of AIDS and fears about the fatal prognosis for those who had the disease seemed to be confined to the homosexual community. Later, largely through the sharing of needles for drug injection and unsafe sexual practices, AIDS began spreading more rapidly among heterosexuals, especially in low-income communities.

The Intertwining of Technology and Culture

The sudden emergence of the AIDS epidemic was only one of the rash of new social and cultural developments that occurred during the early 1980s. The nation experienced the initial stages of a revolution in communications and culture that left American society dramatically altered by the time Reagan left office in 1989. The elements of this revolution included the development of the personal computer and the ability of individuals to use the new technology to improve their lives. At the same time the spread of cable television and the emergence of alternatives to then major television networks allowed news and entertainment to be shared with ever-increasing speed.

The emergence of the personal computer transformed the American economy in the 1980s. One of the most popular was the Macintosh, made by Apple Computer, shown here in its early version.
Courtesy of Apple Computer, Inc.

The Personal Computer

In 1981, International Business Machines (IBM) announced that it would market a computer for home use. Recognizing the potential impact of such a product, two young computer software writers proposed to develop the operating system for the new machine. Bill Gates and Paul Allen of Microsoft adapted an existing software program and transformed it into DOS (disk operating system), which ran the hardware created by IBM. Important changes followed throughout the decade, including the Lotus 1-2-3 spreadsheet program in 1982, Microsoft Windows in 1983, and the Apple Macintosh Computer in 1984. After January 1983, sales of personal computers rose from 20,000 annually to more than half a million per year.

The computer revolution gathered momentum over the course of the 1980s. People found that they could publish books from their desktops, trace financial accounts, make travel reservations, and play a wide assortment of computer games. Growing out of the Advanced Research Projects Agency of the Pentagon was a network of computers founded in 1969. As computer users and researchers exchanged messages over this and other networks in the late 1970s and early 1980s, the National Science Foundation promoted the Internet as an overall network bulletin board. Usenet groups and email became more common as the 1980s progressed.

The Cable Generation

In 1981, a new network appeared on cable television. Music Television (MTV) presented round-the-clock videos of rock performers aimed at a teenage audience. At about the same time, Ted Turner launched the Cable News Network (CNN) and a related programming service, Headline News, that presented the news in half-hour segments twenty-four hours a day. As cable television expanded during the 1980s, the dominance of the three major television networks (ABC, CBS, and NBC) gave way to a dizzying array of programming that offered viewers such all-sports channels as Entertainment Sports Programming Network (ESPN), all country music channels such as Country Music Television (CMT), and several services showing first-run movies.

MTV offered the most intriguing cultural development of the period. Its audience was the middle- and upper-middle-class adolescent and preteen market for rock music. MTV featured major performers in video versions of their hits or potential hits mouthing (or "lip-synching") the words to a prerecorded soundtrack. So successful was MTV that in 1985 it spawned a second network, VideoHits1 (VH1), with a similar format.

The American Family in the 1980s

The American people responded to new and troubling changes in the family and its place in society during Reagan's presidency. In 1981, the number of divorces stood at nearly 1.2 million annually, the highest rate ever. At the same time, the number of births to unmarried women rose dramatically during the 1970s. With these developments came a marked increase in the number of single-parent families, which rose from 3.8 million in 1970 to 10.5 million by 1992. The impact of this trend was especially evident among African Americans: by the end of the 1980s, more than 60 percent of all African American families were single-parent families.

The erosion of the traditional family translated into economic hardship for many children of single-parent homes. In 1983, the Bureau of the Census reported that 13 million children under age six were growing up in poverty. Much of the government's spending on efforts to alleviate poverty was directed at the elderly, so by the end of the 1980s, they received from the federal government eleven times the amount spent to address the needs of children.

One major area of concern for families was the state of the public schools. A series of high-profile national studies suggested that American education was "a disaster area." Students did not receive instruction in the skills needed if they were to succeed in a complex and competitive world. Parents complained that their children had to do little homework, were graded too easily, and often graduated without marketable skills. Conservatives blamed this state of affairs on the National Education Association (NEA), the teachers union, and government policies that "threw money" at schools. Liberals countered that government must spend even more to address the problems of the public schools. By 1983, another national survey, titled *A Nation at Risk*, said that the country faced dire consequences if public education did not undergo sweeping reform.

Responses to Change

As families felt the effects of these economic and social changes, Americans responded with contradictory approaches. On the one hand, sexual mores became more tolerant. On the other, efforts to recapture "traditional family values" animated many groups on the conservative end of the political spectrum. The boundaries that had governed the depiction of sexual behavior in the movies and on television relaxed in significant ways during the 1980s. On prime-time television, viewers could hear language and see sexual intimacy depicted in a fashion that would have been unthinkable a few years earlier. Materials that previous generations would have considered pornographic now seemed to be readily available, even to children and teenagers.

At the same time that some cultural taboos were relaxed, conservative groups struck back against what they saw as excessive permissiveness and laxity. Resolving the tension between the conservative social values of many Americans and the entertainment industry's efforts to maintain high ratings by meeting the demand for programming with violent or sexual content remained difficult throughout the 1980s.

THE 1984 PRESIDENTIAL ELECTION

At the beginning of 1984, Reagan's popularity rating stood at 55 percent, and the electoral map seemed to favor the Republicans. The Democratic base in the South was disappearing, and the president had made substantial gains among what were known as "Reagan Democrats," people who shared the president's social conservatism. Reagan's only apparent vulnerability was his age. At seventy-three, he was sometimes detached and vague, and he clearly lacked stamina. Unless something happened to emphasize his age, Reagan was the favorite to win another term.

Democrats experienced staggering problems in finding a plausible candidate to run against the incum-

Faced with a popular incumbent and a likely defeat, Democratic presidential candidate Walter Mondale took a chance and named Geraldine Ferraro, a New York congresswoman, as his vice presidential candidate. The gesture put Ferraro into history as the first woman chosen by a major political party for its national ticket, but it did not help Mondale avoid a decisive defeat at the hands of Ronald Reagan.
AP/Wide World Photo

bent president. In the initial stages the front-runner seemed to be former Vice President Walter Mondale of Minnesota. Mondale had strong ties to the traditional elements of the Democratic party—labor, women, and environmentalists. He was not a good public speaker and lacked a vibrant personality, yet it was widely expected that he would win the nomination.

Two challengers emerged to stop Mondale's bid for the nomination. The first was the Reverend Jesse Jackson, a veteran of the civil rights movement, who combined powerful oratory with espousal of radical causes. He became the first credible African American candidate to seek the nomination of a major party, but he proved unable to reach beyond black voters in the primaries. The other Democratic hopeful was Senator Gary Hart of Colorado, who styled himself a "new Democrat," which meant that he did not endorse the use of government power to regulate society to the extent that Mondale did. Although Hart won a surprise victory in the New Hampshire primary, Mondale countered with effective television ads and won a majority of the convention delegates before the Democrats gathered in San Francisco in July.

Mondale's chances of winning the election against Reagan were slim at best. Under those circumstances, the choice of the vice presidential nominee became largely symbolic. Mondale came under intense pressure to select a woman as his running mate, and in the week before the convention opened he agreed to the selection of Representative Geraldine Ferraro of New York. An intelligent, thoughtful politician, Ferraro did little for the Mondale campaign where it needed help the most, in the South and West.

The Republicans had all the best of the 1984 campaign. President Reagan's popularity crested during the celebrations of the fortieth anniversary of the D-Day invasions in June, and his appearance at the 1984 Olympic Games in Los Angeles identified him with an event in which American athletes dominated the competition. In a time of patriotic enthusiasm, Reagan seemed more in tune with the optimism and confidence of the moment.

Mondale Versus Reagan

The only stumble for Reagan came in the first of two televised debates. He showed his age and lack of a clear grasp of many issues. The consensus was that Mondale had won a clear victory over the president. Two weeks later, after much Republican soul-searching, however, Reagan rebounded. When a questioner asked him about his age, the president replied that he would not allow age to be an issue. "I am not going to exploit, for political purposes, my opponent's youth and inexperience," he said.

Reagan won by a landslide. He carried forty-nine of the fifty states; Mondale narrowly won his home state and swept the District of Columbia. The president collected 59 percent of the popular vote. The Republicans retained control of the Senate; the Democrats lost seats in the House but maintained their dominance of that chamber.

REAGAN'S SECOND TERM

Changes in the president's staff marked the transition from one administration to the other. The team that had initially guided Reagan's fortunes broke up. The White House chief of staff, James Baker, agreed to exchange jobs with the secretary of the treasury, Donald Regan. The president accepted the swap without much thought, a friendly gesture that had serious consequences. Regan lacked political skill and did not know how to showcase the president's better qualities to his advantage.

Tax Reform and Deficits

Despite Reagan's pledge to balance the federal budget by 1984, the combinations of tax cuts and increased spending on both defense and discretionary programs widened the budget deficit. Federal receipts reached $666 billion by 1984, but outlays stood at almost $852 billion, with a resulting deficit of $186 billion.

The administration did not have a strategy to trim the deficit, but the Senate devised a plan for doing so. Created by a new Republican senator, Phil Gramm of Texas, the measure required that federal spending programs be reduced by specified amounts or face across-the-board percentage reductions. Sponsored by Senators Warren Rudman of New Hampshire, one of Gramm's Republican colleagues, and Senator Ernest F. "Fritz" Hollings, a South Carolina Democrat, the scheme quickly became known as "Gramm-Rudman-Hollings." It promised to produce lower deficits without requiring lawmakers to choose among tough options. Congress embraced it enthusiastically, especially because the tough cuts in government spending would not be mandated until after the 1986 elections.

The AIDS Crisis: The Second Phase

In October 1985 the public's perception of the threat of AIDS intensified when the movie star Rock Hudson died of the disease. More than 6,700 other Americans succumbed to AIDS in 1985, and the death toll shot up to 15,504 annually two years later.

The administration's response to AIDS reflected the division between those who wanted to deal with the virus as a public health issue and those who viewed it in ideological terms. In October, Surgeon General C. Everett Koop issued a report that recommended three steps to control AIDS: "One, abstinence; two, monogamy; three, condoms." On the conservative side of the political spectrum, the mention of condoms aroused intense opposition that blocked further initiatives during the remainder of the president's second term.

Table 31.2	New AIDS Cases in the United States, 1988–1993
1988	30,648
1989	33,576
1990	41,642
1991	43,660
1992	45,883
1993	102,780

Source: *World Almanac*, 1997, p. 975.

Ronald Reagan's Second Inaugural Address, January 1985

This excerpt from Ronald Reagan's second inaugural address conveys the themes of optimism and smaller government that Reagan advanced throughout the 1980s.

. . . Four years ago I spoke to you of a new beginning, and we have accomplished that. But in another sense, our new beginning is a continuation of that beginning created two centuries ago when, for the first time in history, government, the people said, was not our master. It is our servant; its only power that which we, the people, allow it to have.

That system has never failed us. But for a time we failed the system. We asked things of government that government was not equipped to give. We yielded authority to the national government that properly belonged to states or to local governments or to the people themselves. We allowed taxes and inflation to rob us of our earnings and savings and watched the great industrial machine that had made us the most productive people on earth slow down and the number of unemployed increase.

By 1980 we knew it was time to renew our faith, to strive with all our strength toward the ultimate in individual freedom consistent with an orderly society.

We believed then and now there are no limits to growth and human progress when men and women are free to follow their dreams. And we were right. And we were right to believe that. Tax rates have been reduced, inflation cut dramatically, and more people are employed than ever before in our history.

We are creating a nation once again vibrant, robust and alive. But there are many mountains yet to climb. We will not rest until every American enjoys the fullness of freedom, dignity, and opportunity as our birthright. It is our birthright as citizens of this great republic.

And if we meet this challenge, these will be years when Americans have restored their confidence and tradition of progress; when our values of faith, family, work, and neighborhood, were restated for a modern age; when our economy was finally freed from government's grip; when we made sincere efforts at meaningful arms reductions by rebuilding our defenses, our economy, and developing new technologies helped preserve peace in a troubled world; when America courageously supported the struggle for individual liberty, self-government, and free enterprise throughout the world and turned the tide of history away from totalitarian darkness and into the warm sunlight of human freedom.

My fellow citizens, our nation is poised for greatness. We must do what we know is right and do it with all our might. Let history say of us, these were golden years—when the American Revolution was reborn, when freedom gained new life and America reached for her best. . .

The 1986 Tax Reform Battle

The administration did achieve one major domestic policy success, which the president embraced eagerly, even though he was not its primary sponsor. In 1986, Congress made significant reforms in the nation's tax laws.

After passing the House in late 1985, the tax bill faced uncertain prospects in the Senate. By April 1986, the Senate Finance Committee seemed likely to kill the bill or load it with special preferences. At that point, lawmakers devised a bill with a much lower top rate for all taxpayers and an end to many time-honored deductions. The proposed law was quickly approved by the Finance Committee, and sailed through the Senate by a vote of ninety-seven to three in June 1986. After a difficult passage through a Senate-House conference committee,

P

ICTURING THE PAST ✦ SOCIAL & CULTURAL EVENTS

THE *CHALLENGER* DISASTER

AP/Wide World Photo

In the 1980s, cable television brought live events into American homes on a twenty-four hour basis. Reality sometimes meant instant tragedy as happened with the explosion of the *Challenger* space shuttle on January 28, 1986, before a shocked audience at the scene and millions of television viewers. The immediate realization that the seven crew members had died was written on the faces of family members and other onlookers. Subsequent revelations about technological and management failures added to the gravity of the incident. At the time young people told interviewers that the explosion would long remain the defining moment of their lives. As years passed, however, and other calamities occurred, the *Challenger* incident receded in the popular consciousness until another shuttle accident destroyed *Columbia* in February 2003. Even that terrible event did not rekindle more than transitory memories of the *Challenger* calamity seventeen years earlier. Judgments about historical significance shift with the passage of time.

---

the tax reform law was approved and signed in September 1986.

The Age of the Yuppie

The economic boom of the mid-1980s fostered an atmosphere of moneymaking and social acquisitiveness. Wall Street traders like Michael Millken and Ivan Boesky promoted lucrative corporate mergers through high risk securities known as "junk bonds." Top executives received staggering annual salaries. The head of Walt Disney, for example, earned $40 million in 1987. Wall Street experienced a "merger mania" in which corporations acquired competitors through hostile takeovers.

The youth culture reflected the spirit of materialism that permeated the 1980s. Tennis star Andre Agassi appeared in ads asserting "image is everything." In the centers of technological change on the East and West

Coasts, the press proclaimed the emergence of the "young urban professionals," dubbed "yuppies" by the media. These individuals had cosmetic surgery to retain a young look, took expensive vacations, and purchased costly sports equipment. Self-indulgence seemed to be a hallmark of young people.

The Challenger *Disaster*

A sobering moment in the frenetic decade came on January 28, 1986, when the space shuttle *Challenger* exploded. All seven crew members perished in the disaster. The event happened live before a shocked audience that watched the spacecraft lift off normally and then explode a few seconds later into a mass of wreckage.

An official investigation followed while the shuttle fleet was grounded. Its proceedings revealed that the space program had grown overconfident about its procedures. Slipshod technology had contributed to the tragedy, but the incident did not undermine the public's faith in scientific progress and material abundance. By the end of the 1980s, the shuttle program had resumed its regular series of flights.

Foreign Policy in the Second Reagan Term

Soviet-American relations entered a new phase when Mikhail Gorbachev came to power in Moscow. Aware of the weaknesses in his society and its economy, Gorbachev pursued a more conciliatory policy toward the West while trying to implement a restructuring of Soviet society that came to be known as *perestroika* (broadly defined as "restructuring"). He announced reductions in the deployment of Soviet missiles and said that the Soviet Union wanted to be part of Europe, not an opposing ideology. He and Reagan agreed to hold a summit conference in Geneva in November 1985. Although not much was achieved at the meeting, the two leaders discovered that they liked each other. The two world leaders met again at Reykjavik, Iceland, in October 1986. There they attempted to outdo each other in calling for reductions in the number of nuclear weapons, with the president even offering to rid the world of all such weapons. Again there were no substantive results, but the experience indicated that a genuine arms agreement might be possible. Both the president and Nancy Reagan hoped to crown Reagan's second term with an arms control treaty that would establish his historical reputation as a peacemaker.

The Iran-Contra Affair

In November 1986 the American public first learned that the United States had sold arms to the Islamic regime in Iran that had sponsored terrorist activities for most of the 1980s against the United States. Within a month the revelation came that money obtained from the arms sales had been used to support the Nicaraguan Contras in violation of congressional amendments barring the practice. The Reagan administration had deceived Congress, broken the law, and lied to the American people.

In 1985, members of the National Security Council (NSC) became convinced that the release of American hostages held in Lebanon could be secured if the United States sold arms to Iran. National Security Advisor Robert McFarlane believed that "moderates" in Iran would use their political influence to free hostages if American weapons were forthcoming. The Iranians could use weapons in their bitter war with Iraq, which had been going on since 1982. Since disclosure of this new policy would have outraged Americans and provoked congressional investigations, the president's approval of arm sales was kept secret.

The actual shipment of weapons to Iran was carried out by Israel with the United States replacing the transferred munitions. Unfortunately, the Iranians accepted the antitank and antiaircraft missiles, but released only three hostages. The Iranian government had deceived the United States.

In the course of the arms deals, however, the transactions generated profits. A member of the NSC staff, Marine Colonel Oliver North, had what he later called a "neat idea." He proposed that profits from the sale of weapons to Iran be used to support the Contras in Nicaragua. Although North maintained that his actions did not break the law, they were in clear violation of congressional directives barring the provision of aid to the Contras. Moreover, the use of funds without legislative approval was against the law. In addition, a privately financed, unaccountable, and clandestine foreign policy operation was well outside constitutional limits.

News of the scandal leaked out in October 1986 when the Sandinistas shot down one of the planes taking weapons to the Contras. A captured crew member revealed the Central Intelligence Agency's links to the operation. Early in November news of the arms-for-hostages deal surfaced in the Middle East. The reports did not affect the congressional elections in which the Democrats regained control of the Senate for the first time in six years and retained their majority in the House as well.

For several weeks the Reagan White House tried to mislead Congress and the public about what had taken place. On November 13, 1986, the president told the American people: "We did not—repeat, did not—trade weapons or anything else for hostages, nor will we." He maintained this position even though it conflicted with the known facts.

Attorney General Edwin Meese conducted a slow, ineffective probe of what had happened. In late November conclusive proof of the diversion of money to the Contras came out. The president fired Oliver North and accepted the resignation of John Poindexter, McFarlane's successor as national security advisor and one of the central figures in the clandestine operation, which the press was now calling the Iran-Contra scandal.

Three separate probes of the scandal began in early 1987. Reagan appointed the Tower Commission, named after its chair, former Senator John Tower of Texas, to look into the White House's role in the scheme. The House and Senate created a joint

The Iran-Contra scandal produced a congressional investigation at which the star witness was Marine Colonel Oliver North. His appearance in his winter uniform in mid summer and his aggressive tactics toward his questioners made him a national hero to conservatives.
AP/Wide World Photo

committee to examine the policy and its execution. The lawmakers soon decided to grant many of those individuals involved immunity in exchange for their testimony. That decision hampered the task of the special counsel, Lawrence Walsh, who was named to consider whether specific laws had been violated.

While everyone concerned professed a desire to get to the bottom of the scandal, there was little inclination, even among Democrats, to see Ronald Reagan impeached for his role in it. His second term had only a year and a half to run, and many Washington insiders questioned whether it would be good for the country to have another president driven from office in disgrace.

The Tower Commission, for its part, chastised the president for an inept "management style" that allowed his subordinates to lead him into the scandal. On March 4, 1987, Reagan said that he accepted the commission's findings while reiterating that he had not intended to trade arms for hostages. His poll ratings rose and once again the public responded to his leadership.

For others involved in the scandal, the hearings brought a surge of notoriety that made North a subject of national debate and discredited the other Reagan aides involved. When North testified before the House-Senate Committee during the summer of 1987 in his winter marine uniform, he proved a compelling presence on television. He exaggerated his closeness to Reagan and made some inaccurate or misleading

statements. But his skill before the cameras deflected some of the blame from Reagan.

North and the other participants were indicted by Lawrence Walsh and convicted for some of their misdeeds, including perjury, mishandling government moneys, and other crimes. Because Congress had granted them immunity, however, higher courts overturned their convictions on the ground that the trials had been influenced by what had been heard in the congressional proceedings.

Whatever the legalities of the Iran-Contra affair, it demonstrated the weaknesses of Reagan's handling of foreign policy. Reagan had failed to ask hard questions about the arms-for-hostages proposals, and he had allowed erratic subordinates like North to mishandle the nation's foreign policy. The outcome discredited the American stance on terrorism and indicated that Reagan's command of his own government was weak and uncertain.

Remaking the Supreme Court: The Nomination of Robert Bork

One of the Reagan administration's major goals was to make the federal judiciary more conservative. The White House succeeded in doing so in the lower courts because, during eight years in office, Reagan nominated more than half the members of the federal judiciary.

In July 1981, Reagan named the first woman to be appointed to the Court, Sandra Day O'Connor of Arizona. The president did not have another opportunity to appoint a justice until Chief Justice Warren Burger resigned in 1986. Reagan elevated Justice William Rehnquist to replace Burger and named Antonin Scalia, a federal appeals court judge, to take the seat that Rehnquist vacated. Scalia was the first Italian American appointed to the court, and his intellectual brilliance appealed to conservatives.

In June 1987, after the Democrats had regained control of the Senate, Justice Lewis Powell resigned and President Reagan named Robert Bork, another federal appeals court jurist, to replace him. During a long career as a legal writer before becoming a judge, Bork had taken many controversial stands on divisive issues. He had opposed the decision in *Roe v. Wade* (1973) that established a woman's right to have an abortion, and he had questioned other decisions in the areas of privacy and civil rights. The nomination galvanized Democrats in the Senate, the civil rights movement, and women's groups in a campaign to defeat Bork.

The judge's admirers claimed that his enemies had distorted his record, but his foes were able to depict Bork as a conservative ideologue outside the mainstream of

A search for Soviet-American understanding was a notable feature of Ronald Reagan's second term. His friendship with the Soviet leader Mikhail Gorbachev resulted in a marked lessening of the Cold War tensions as the decade of the 1980s ended.
AP/Wide World Photos

American judicial thinking. Bork's performance before the Senate Judiciary Committee failed to counteract the negative public opinion that his opposition had generated. In October 1987, Bork was defeated when fifty-eight senators voted against him. Anthony Kennedy was nominated and confirmed to the Court early in 1988.

Reagan and Gorbachev: The Road to Understanding

The Iran-Contra affair produced changes in Reagan's administration that prepared the way for genuine foreign policy achievements. Former Senator Howard Baker became Reagan's chief of staff, Frank Carlucci was named secretary of defense, and Lieutenant General Colin Powell served as the national security advisor. By late 1987, negotiators for the two sides had agreed to remove from Europe intermediate range missiles with nuclear warheads. Gorbachev came to Washington in December 1987 for the formal signing

of the pact. Seven months later, Reagan went to Moscow to meet Gorbachev in an atmosphere of hope and reconciliation. Tensions between the two countries eased as the Soviets pulled out of Afghanistan and indicated that they no longer intended to stir up international problems. The improvement in the superpower rivalry helped Reagan regain some of his popularity with the American people as his administration neared its end.

THE 1988 PRESIDENTIAL ELECTION

With Ronald Reagan ineligible to seek a third term, the Republican party had to pick a successor to carry its banner against the Democrats. Vice President George Bush soon emerged as the front-runner.

George H. W. Bush came from an aristocratic New England background but had moved to Texas after combat service in the navy during World War II. Elected to the House of Representatives in 1966, he stayed for two terms and made a losing bid for the Senate in 1970. Service in the Ford administration as envoy to China and director of the Central Intelligence Agency added to his impressive roster of government posts. He ran against Reagan for the Republican nomination in 1980 and became the vice presidential choice despite doubts among conservatives about his allegiance to their cause. In the race for the nomination, Bush's superior organization and strength in the South enabled him to defeat Senator Robert Dole of Kansas.

At the Republican convention in New Orleans, Bush made two important decisions. For his running mate, he selected Senator J. Danforth Quayle of Indiana. Handsome and young, Quayle was generally regarded as a lightweight by his Senate colleagues, but he provided a contrast to Bush's age and experience. Quayle's candidacy got off to a shaky start when it was revealed that he had entered the Indiana National Guard at a time when enlistment there precluded active service in the Vietnam War.

Bush's other major decision involved the issue of deficits and taxes. In his acceptance speech, he predicted that Democrats in Congress would pressure him to raise taxes. He promised to reject all such proposals. "Read my lips," would be his answer to Democrats, "No new taxes!" Repeated and emphasized throughout the campaign, this pledge became identified with Bush as a solemn promise to the electorate.

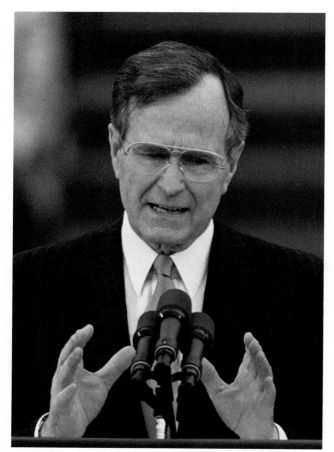

George H. W. Bush won the Republican nomination and the presidential election in 1988 on his promise to continue the legacy of Ronald Reagan and on his pledge of "no new taxes."
© Bettmann/UPI/Corbis

The Democratic Choice

As for the Democrats, with Reagan no longer a candidate, they believed that they now had a chance to retake the White House. The prospective front-runner for the nomination was Senator Gary Hart, but his candidacy collapsed amid charges of sexual misbehavior. Jesse Jackson ran again, but his strength remained concentrated among black voters. Out of the field of other candidates, Massachusetts Governor Michael Dukakis emerged as the best-financed and best-organized contender. He defeated Jackson in a series of primaries in the spring and came to the Democratic convention with the nomination locked up.

Dukakis emphasized his family's Greek immigrant background and stressed his success in stimulating the Massachusetts economy during the 1980s. Democrats paid less attention to his tepid personality and lackluster abilities as a campaigner. At the

convention, he selected Senator Lloyd M. Bentsen of Texas as his running mate. When the Democratic convention ended, Dukakis had a strong lead in the public opinion polls.

The Campaign

The campaign that followed was a nasty one. The Republicans raised questions about Dukakis that undermined his lead. The most penetrating of these issues had to do with prison furloughs that Massachusetts law granted to jailed criminals. In one case, a black convict named William Horton had been released on furlough, then fled Massachusetts, and committed a rape in another state. The Republicans and their surrogates used the "Willie" Horton case in powerful television commercials to demonstrate Dukakis's ineptitude as governor, but the racial dimensions of the incident were also evident. Bush won the election with a solid margin in the electoral vote, though the Democrats retained control of Congress.

The Reagan Legacy

Even before Ronald Reagan left office on January 20, 1989, the debate about the impact of his presidency was underway. His partisans proclaimed the "Reagan Revolution" had transformed American attitudes toward government. They also assigned him a major role in winning the Cold War. Critics pointed to the huge federal budget deficits that persisted throughout the 1980s, blamed Reagan for policies that had widened the gap between rich and poor, and pointed out that he had failed to address serious urban problems.

Both Reagan's admirers and his enemies overstated his influence on American history. By the early twenty-first century, the nation still seemed to want a smaller government in theory and more government services in practice. Reagan had halted the expansion of the welfare state, but that would probably have occurred in any event by the 1980s. Reagan certainly deserved some credit for the decline of the Soviet Union, though that nation's internal difficulties were more significant than the actions of the United States at the end of the Cold War. Reagan's most enduring legacy was the federal budget deficit. Although Congress appropriated the money, he set national priorities, and his spending for defense went well beyond affordable levels. Reagan proved that big spenders could come in conservative as well as liberal models.

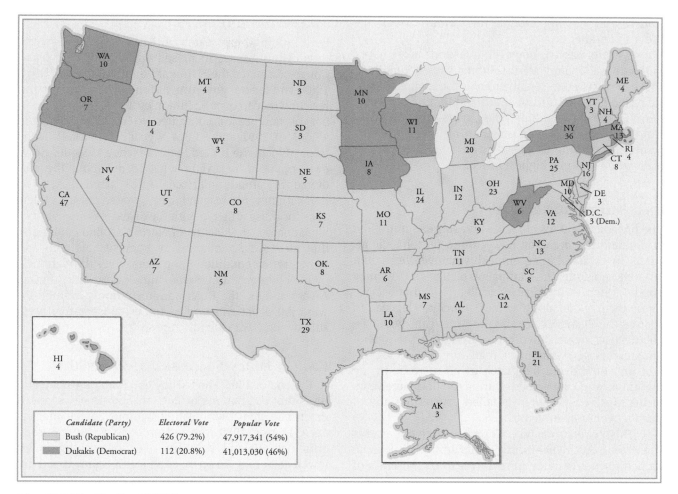

Map 31.2 *The Election of 1988*

Legend from map:

Candidate (Party)	Electoral Vote	Popular Vote
Bush (Republican)	426 (79.2%)	47,917,341 (54%)
Dukakis (Democrat)	112 (20.8%)	41,013,030 (46%)

KINDER, GENTLER GEORGE HERBERT WALKER BUSH

George H. W. Bush came into office pledging to carry on Reagan's policies, but promising to do so in a more humane and judicious manner. He spoke of a "kinder, gentler" nation and government that would carry out conservative programs with less harshness than had marked the Reagan years. He urged Americans to engage in charitable endeavors that would become "a thousand points of light" to inspire others to good works. Bush had no grand vision of what his administration should accomplish in the domestic arena.

Foreign affairs interested the new president much more than did shaping policy on health care, the environment, or social policy. Attuned to diplomacy because of his service as director of the CIA and ambas-

sador to China, he prized the personal contacts he had made around the world and used them to good effect at moments of crisis. He had an effective foreign policy team. His secretary of state, James A. Baker, was a close friend and an adroit power broker; the national security advisor, Brent Scowcroft, and the chair of the Joint Chiefs of Staff, General Colin Powell, executed the president's policies with skill and efficiency. The collapse of communism in 1989–1990, the challenge of Iraqi expansionism in the Middle East, and the shaping of a new role for the United States gave the Bush administration's foreign policy makers much to do.

The first half of the Bush administration went very well. The president relished the art of governing and he approached his job by engaging in a frenzy of activity. His press conferences demonstrated his command of information in a way that Reagan never displayed. The public became used to seeing Bush jogging, entertaining numerous visitors to the White

House, and rushing around the country from one event to another.

As time passed, however, questions arose about the purpose behind all this frenetic exertion. Bush spoke of the need to set larger goals for his presidency. He called it, in the abrupt shorthand that he often employed, "the vision thing." The phrase came into general use in discussions of whether Bush wanted to accomplish anything as president or simply wished to occupy the nation's highest office.

Bush's Domestic Policy

The president and his chief of staff, John Sununu, had no intention of breaking new ground in domestic affairs. They wanted to accomplish whatever they could without violating the campaign pledge of "no new taxes." Much to the dismay of Republican conservatives, Bush went along with Democratic legislation such as the Clean Air Act and the Americans with Disabilities Act, which involved a growth in the federal bureaucracy and expanded regulations. Any legislation that he did not like, such as an increase in the minimum wage, he vetoed. During the first three years of his presidency, Congress failed to override any of Bush's twenty-eight vetoes.

Bush's relations with Congress were not always successful. At the beginning of his administration he named former Senator John Tower to be secretary of defense. After a bitter struggle focusing on Tower's problems with alcoholism and other personal indiscretions, the Senate rejected their former colleague. To replace Tower, Bush picked Representative Richard Cheney.

On some domestic issues, Bush favored exhortation over government programs. He promised to be the "education president" but left most of the responsibility for changes in the system to the states and localities. The "war on drugs" was renewed, with emphasis on stopping the inflow of narcotics to the United States rather than reducing the demand for them among the population. An overall decline in drug use enabled the administration to claim victory for its strategy.

By 1989, however, the Bush administration had to deal with another major domestic issue. The deregulated savings and loan industry had a major collapse that left the taxpayers with a $500 billion cost to bail out depositors for the failed institutions. Congress established the Resolution Trust Corporation to sell off the assets of the failed banks and savings and loans and to obtain as much money as possible from their sale.

The Continuing AIDS Crisis

Both funding for research on AIDS and public awareness of the disease increased during the Bush years. Congress created the National Commission on AIDS in 1989, and federal government funds for treatment and research rose to over $2 billion by 1992. Still, the number of new cases continued to increase, reaching 45,603 in 1992 and 83,814 a year later. Total deaths from AIDS in the United States reached 198,000. However, opinions regarding what to do about the epidemic remained polarized. AIDS activists wanted more money for research and greater cultural tolerance for those afflicted with the disease. Conservatives like Senator Jesse Helms of North Carolina contended that most AIDS victims were homosexuals who had brought their condition upon themselves through their own behavior. After some initial sympathy toward AIDS patients, the Bush administration's attitude toward AIDS patients cooled under conservative pressure as the 1992 election approached.

Foreign Policy Successes, 1989–1990

At the end of 1988, Gorbachev had told the United Nations that the nations of Eastern Europe were free to determine their own destiny without Soviet interference. During 1989, the old order in Eastern Europe crumbled. Poland held free elections; Hungary allowed its borders to open; and East Germany eased the barriers to travel to West Germany. By the end of 1989, the Cold War seemed to be over with the United States the clear winner. In Nicaragua, voters ousted the unpopular Sandinista government in 1990.

The Bush administration handled these developments carefully. Mindful of the nuclear weapons in the hands of the Soviet military, the president avoided gloating over the success of the West. The trend in favor of the United States continued into 1990 as Gorbachev, in February, renounced the Communist party's monopoly over political power. The White House faced hard choices about which leader to support as rivals to Gorbachev emerged during 1990, particularly the new president of the Russian Republic, Boris Yeltsin.

One country where the administration's foreign policy encountered difficulty was China. Student protests during the spring of 1989 led to a brutal crackdown on demonstrators in Beijing's Tiananmen Square. The spectacle of students being killed and wounded, as well as the repressive policies of the Chinese government, produced an outcry in the United States. However, Bush believed that it was important to maintain good relations with the Chinese leaders, so

The mass protests in China in the spring of 1989 were part of the events that shook Communism during the end of the Cold War. On May 27, 1989, student leader Wang Den addressed a huge crowd in Tiananmen Square in Beijing. A week later Chinese troops crushed the uprising.
AP/Wide World Photo

the administration's response to the events of June 1989 was muted and cautious.

Closer to home, however, the Bush administration took more decisive action toward Panama's strongman ruler, Manuel Noriega. Corrupt and deeply involved in the international narcotics trade, Noriega had been on the United States's payroll for many years as an informant on drug matters. In 1989, his dictatorial regime refused to adhere to the results of national elections. The White House sent additional troops to Panama and called for an uprising against Noriega. For his part, Noriega declared a state of war on American military personnel and their families to be captured and tortured.

In late December, the United States launched an invasion that quickly overcame the Panamanian army.

Noriega eluded capture for a few embarrassing days until he sought refuge in a Vatican embassy. In early 1990, he surrendered to the Americans and in 1992 was tried and convicted of drug trafficking in a federal court in Florida. The episode raised Bush's standings in the polls.

The End of No New Taxes

By the spring of 1990, President Bush's pledge of "no new taxes" had become ingrained in the minds of the American people. Conservative Republicans expected him to adhere to the commitment in spite of the desire of the Democratic majorities in Congress to raise taxes. In 1989, the president worked out a strategy with Congress that provided for budget savings. Bush also wanted to lower the tax rate on capital gains, but that legislation became stalled in the Senate. With the budget deficit growing, however, the Democrats did not see how spending cuts alone could reduce it. Having suffered setbacks in the 1988 elections, the Democrats were not going to propose tax increases unless President Bush agreed to them. Meanwhile, the Gramm-Rudman-Hollings law provided for substantial reductions in spending by the fall of 1990 if the president and Congress did not reach a viable budget agreement.

By early 1990, there were signs that the economy had begun to slow down. The gross domestic product had grown slowly in 1989; there had been a slight loss in manufacturing jobs; and producer prices had risen. With a weakening economy, a budget stalemate posed dangers for both parties, and neither side really wanted to face the implications of the cuts that Gramm-Rudman-Hollings contemplated.

Negotiations between the president and congressional Democrats continued until, on June 26, 1990, Bush announced that dealing with the deficit problem might have to include "tax revenue increases." Republicans reacted with fury. Although the reversal of "no new taxes" may have made economic and political sense to those close to Bush, the president had squandered much of the trust that the American people had placed in him in 1988. Despite the foreign policy victories that lay ahead, he never fully regained it over the rest of his administration.

Iraq and Kuwait

Foreign policy events soon overshadowed the political fallout from the broken tax pledge. On August 2, 1990, the Iraqi army of Saddam Hussein invaded the oil-rich kingdom of Kuwait and seized it within a few days. Suddenly the oil supplies of the United States and the industrialized world faced a new and ominous threat from the Iraqi dictator. Bush's response and the war that followed restored his popularity temporarily and seemed at the time to make his reelection a certainty.

During the 1980s, Iran and Iraq had fought a brutal and costly war that had drained the human and material resources of both countries. The United States had not taken sides in the conflict, hoping that the two countries, both of which were hostile toward the United States, would exhaust each other. Once the war ended, however, the Bush administration had pursued a conciliatory policy, allowing Iraq to purchase heavy machinery and paying little attention to its efforts to build a nuclear bomb and acquire weapons of mass destruction. During the spring of 1990, the American ambassador in Baghdad had informed Hussein that the United States took "no position" on Iraq's dispute with Kuwait. In fact, the Iraqis regarded Kuwait as part of their nation.

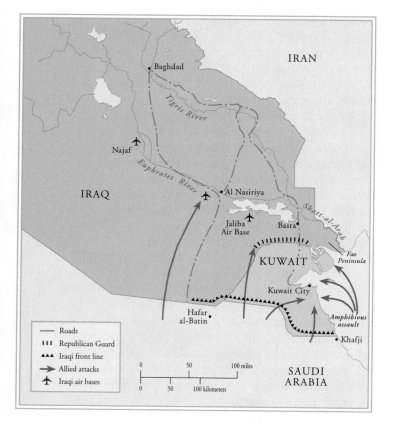

Map 31.3 *The War in the Persian Gulf*
This map reveals the strategy of the allies in 1991 against the Iraqi army. The long arrow to the west represents the sweep around the enemy's flanks to encircle the Iraqi army and destroy it. After 100 hours of combat, the Bush administration stopped the fighting, and the main remaining elements of the enemy escaped to reimpose Saddam Hussein's power on Iraq after the allied forces departed.
View an animated version of this map or related maps at http://history.wadsworth.com/ passages2e.

When Iraqi military units rolled into Kuwait, Bush decided that the takeover must be resisted. "Iraq will not be permitted to annex Kuwait," he told Congress. Heavy economic sanctions were put into effect. More important, in Operation Desert Shield the United States deployed American troops in Saudi Arabia to deter Hussein from attacking that country. Behind the scenes, the administration had already decided that if necessary it would use military force to oust the Iraqis from Kuwait.

For the remainder of 1990, the Bush administration moved military forces into Saudi Arabia. The end of the Cold War meant that the United States had the support of the Soviet Union in isolating Iraq from the rest of the world and therefore had much greater freedom of action than would have been the case even two years earlier. Bush displayed impressive diplomatic skill in assembling and holding together an international coalition to oppose Iraq.

The Budget Battle

On the domestic side, the budget issue remained unsettled until the president and the Democratic leadership worked out a deficit reduction plan in September 1990. Republicans in the House of Representatives lobbied against the plan, which was defeated a few days later. Intense negotiations between the White House and Capitol Hill produced a deficit reduction agreement at the end of October that involved both tax increases and spending cuts. Angry Republicans charged that Bush had capitulated to the opposition. The Republicans went into the fall elections in a divided and unhappy mood. Their losses were modest—eight seats in the House and one in the Senate—but the conservative faithful continued to smolder with anger against Bush. The president informed conservatives that the White House had fulfilled its legislative agenda for the presidency.

War in the Persian Gulf

After the elections, Bush stepped up the pressure on Saddam Hussein to leave Kuwait. The United Nations Security Council agreed to the use of armed force against Iraq if Kuwait had not been freed by January 15, 1991. As the diplomatic options faded, Congress insisted on a vote over whether American troops should go into combat in the Middle East. The result, on January 12, 1991, was a victory for the president, although the margin in the Senate was only five votes. Five days later, Operation Desert Storm began.

The military outcome was never in doubt. In a demoralizing series of strikes, the allied coalition bombed the Iraqi army into submission. The most that

*P*ICTURING THE PAST✦POLITICS & DIPLOMACY

VICTORY IN THE GULF WAR

AP/Wide World Photo

The war in the Persian Gulf produced striking images of victory such as this one of Iraqi prisoners captured by the First Marine Division on February 26, 1991. President George H. W. Bush and others proclaimed that the coalition triumph had erased "the Vietnam Syndrome" from American life. The 100-hour war played well on television, and Bush's popularity soared for a time. The failure to end the rule of Saddam Hussein, however, meant that the apparent military success was incomplete. In the dozen years that followed, Hussein reemerged as a threat and by 2003 the second war in the Persian Gulf occurred. A picture that seemed to mark an American victory when it was taken thus became a testament to a continuing problem with terrorism and nations such as Iraq that resisted the will of the international community.

Hussein could do in retaliation was to send Scud missiles against Israel in hopes of fracturing the coalition. The Iraqi ruler also set Kuwaiti oil wells on fire and dumped oil into the Persian Gulf. None of these actions, however, posed a serious threat to the build-up of the allied armies. Yet the use of air power alone did not compel Hussein to leave Kuwait.

The second phase of Desert Storm began on February 24, 1991, with a huge assault of American and allied troops against the weakened Iraqi defenders. A series of encircling maneuvers ousted the Iraqis from Kuwait with huge losses in troops and equipment. Estimates of the number of Iraqi soldiers killed ranged as high as 100,000. American deaths totaled 148, including eleven women. Within 100 hours, the ground phase of the war ended in a complete victory on the battlefield for the anti-Iraq forces. President Bush decided not to press for Hussein's removal from power, a decision that was later criticized, and key units of the Iraqi army were left intact to fight again against their own people.

Victory in the Gulf War sent Bush's popularity soaring to record levels; he received approval ratings of nearly 90 percent in some polls. The nation basked in the glow of military success, which seemed to end the sense of self-doubt that had persisted since the Vietnam War. The chairman of the Joint Chiefs of Staff, General Colin Powell, became a nationally respected military figure and a possible vice presidential or presidential candidate. Bush's own reelection seemed assured. Major figures in the Democratic party decided not to challenge Bush in 1992.

Yet the political dividends from Bush's military triumph did not last long. Hussein bounced back from his defeat to reassert his power in Iraq and, despite United Nations inspections, rebuilt his nation's economy and war-making capacity.

Other foreign policy problems troubled the White House during 1991. In Russia, Gorbachev faced a coup designed to bring hard-liners back into power. A rival of Gorbachev, Boris Yeltsin, led demonstrations

President George H. W. Bush meets with General Colin Powell, chairman of the Joint Chiefs of Staff, and General Norman Schwartzkopf in the wake of the allied victory in the Gulf War.
AP/Wide World Photos

against the plotters in Moscow and their coup, which then failed. Thereupon the Soviet Union collapsed and its component nations broke apart. Yeltsin consolidated his power with promises of economic reform and put himself in a position to succeed Gorbachev. With the demise of the Soviet Union, the major threat of the Cold War had ended, but the instability in Eastern Europe posed new threats to world peace.

One area of turmoil was Yugoslavia where the Communist government had long suppressed historic rivalries among Serbs, Croats, Bosnians, and other nationalities. Tensions between Christians and Muslims added to the dangerous potential of the situation. Civil war broke out in 1991 as Serbs battled Croats, Slovenes, and Bosnians. The Bush administration recognized Bosnia as an independent nation and thus became involved in a Balkan struggle whose problems spilled over into the next presidency.

The Battle over the Clarence Thomas Nomination

Like Ronald Reagan, George H. W. Bush wanted to continue the conservative trend that the Supreme Court had been following since the 1970s. That goal seemed even more important in light of the Court's ruling in *Webster v. Reproductive Health Services* (1989), whereby the justices decided in a 5–4 ruling

that states could set limits on the ability to obtain an abortion. Any change in the Court could affect that volatile controversy. When the liberal justice, William Brennan, retired in 1990, the president named David Souter of New Hampshire to succeed him. Confirmation by the Senate came easily because no one was quite sure where Souter stood on abortion.

The next nomination, in 1991, led to one of the most sensational confirmation struggles in the nation's history. When Justice Thurgood Marshall retired, many wondered whether Bush would name an African American to succeed him. The president selected Clarence Thomas, a Reagan appointee to the federal bench who had long opposed such programs as affirmative action.

Thomas's qualifications for the Supreme Court were modest, but he seemed to be on the way to easy confirmation until it was revealed that a black law professor at the University of Oklahoma, Anita Hill, had accused Thomas of sexual harassment when she had worked for him at the Equal Employment Opportunity Commission during the early 1980s. Her charges led to dramatic hearings in which Hill laid out her allegations and Thomas denied them. A national television audience watched the hearings in fascination. In the end, the Senate voted fifty-two to forty-eight to confirm Thomas, who proved to be an intense advocate of conservative positions. The controversy played a major role in alerting the public to the prevalence of sexual harassment in the workplace.

A Sense of Unease

When the controversy over the Thomas nomination ended, many observers believed that George H. W. Bush could expect easy reelection in 1992. No strong Democratic candidates had emerged to challenge him. Bush had the support of most Republicans, although there were rumblings of opposition among conservatives. It seemed probable, however, that Bush would be renominated and would then defeat whomever the Democrats put up against him. After twelve years of Bush and Reagan, the Republican coalition seemed in solid control of the nation's politics and its policy agenda.

When the Republicans made such optimistic assumptions, they failed to notice that the American people were anxious and fearful as the 1990s began. Major corporations had cut their payrolls to reduce costs in what became known as "downsizing." Large firms like IBM, Procter & Gamble, and Chrysler Corporation trimmed their payrolls dramatically. IBM reduced its workforce by 100,000. Other businesses moved production facilities overseas in search of lower labor costs. The economy created millions of jobs, but many of them were low-paying service jobs. Multinational corporations became a focus of voter anger, as did the specter of immigrants taking jobs away from native-born Americans.

In 1990, the press began commenting on "Generation X," the generation of Americans under age twenty-five, which accounted for some 75 million people. Following on the heels of the baby boomers of the 1960s and 1970s, Generation Xers were derided as a "generation of self-centered know-nothings" in search of personal gratification and quick riches. The offspring of broken marriages and single-parent homes, they had raised themselves while their parents were at work, spent endless time before television sets and computer games, and were sexually active at ever younger ages.

As 1992 began, there was a growing sense that the nation faced serious choices. One law student in North Carolina said, "For the first time I feel that a group of Americans is going to have to deal with the idea that they're not going to live as well as their parents." That fear of diminished possibility and reduced opportunity would seem odd later in the 1990s, but it was a genuine concern in the popular mind as the 1992 election approached.

CONCLUSION

The Reagan-Bush years began with a national mood of apprehension and fear about the future. Twelve years of Republican rule saw the end of Communism, the victory in the Gulf War, and the return of economic prosperity. Yet somehow, for all the rhetoric of "Morning in America" under Reagan and "a New World Order" under Bush, the reality did not add up to the sunny prospects that the triumph over Communism was supposed to bring. The nation looked for the new choices and new opportunities that a presidential election could provide.

Recommended Reading

Cannon, Lou. *President Reagan: The Role of a Lifetime* (1991). A biography of the president by a reporter who covered his entire career.

Draper, Theodore. *A Very Thin Line: The Iran-Contra Affair* (1991). A thorough review of the scandal and its effects.

Fitzgerald, Frances. *Way Out There in the Blue: Reagan, Star Wars, and the End of the Cold War* (2000). A critical look at the Strategic Defense Initiative

Greene, John Robert. *The Presidency of George Bush* (2000). Covers the George H. W. Bush presidency thoroughly.

Johnson, Haynes. *Sleepwalking Through History: America in the Reagan Years* (1991). Supplies the perspective of a Washington reporter on the 1980s.

Johnson, Haynes. *Divided We Fall: Gambling with History in the Nineties* (1994). Covers the Reagan-Bush transition and carries the story down to the outset of the Clinton presidency.

Mervin, David. *George Bush and the Guardianship Presidency* (1998). Provides the perspective of a British scholar on the George H. W. Bush administration.

Parmet, Herbert. *George Bush: The Life of a Lone Star Yankee* (1997). The best biography of the forty-first president.

Pemberton, William E. *Exit with Honor: The Life and Presidency of Ronald Reagan* (1997). A sound one-volume study of the man and his impact on the nation.

Sloan, John W. *The Reagan Effect: Economics and Presidential Leadership* (2000). Looks at the president's handling of the economy.

American Journey Online and InfoTrac College Edition

Visit the source collections at http://ajaccess. wadsworth.com and infotrac.thomsonlearning.com and use the Search function with the following key terms to explore documents, images, audio and video clips, articles, and commentary related to the material in this chapter.

Ronald Reagan	Strategic Defense Initiative
Iran-Contra	Oliver North
Sandra Day O'Connor	Mikhail Gorbachev
George H. W. Bush	Tiananmen Square
Clarence Thomas	Anita Hill

Additional resources, exercises, and Internet links related to this chapter are available on the American Passages Web site: http://history.wadsworth.com/passages2e

32 FROM PROSPERITY TO TERRORISM 1992–2003

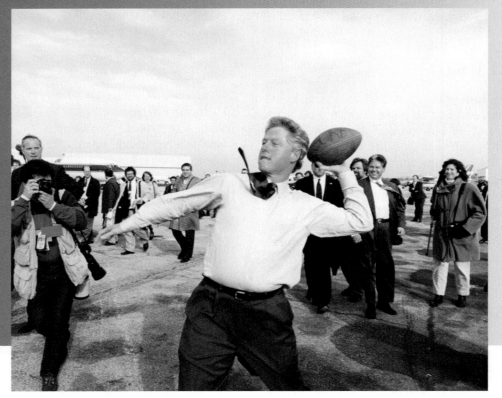

During his first race for the White House, Bill Clinton sought to convey an image of youthful energy and vigor. At an airport in 1992, he makes a long pass to his running mate, Al Gore, out of camera range.
AP/Wide World Photo

The 1992 presidential contest interrupted the pattern of Republican electoral victories that had, with the exception of Jimmy Carter in 1976, dominated American politics since 1968. William Jefferson ("Bill") Clinton of Arkansas defeated incumbent George H. W. Bush and billionaire independent candidate Ross Perot in a campaign that involved Americans in campaigning and voting in greater numbers than had occurred in many years.

Clinton's victory began a turbulent decade. The new president stumbled during his first year in office. Popular discontent with his performance helped the Republicans regain control of both houses of Congress in 1994 for the first time in four decades. Then, defying predictions that he was finished, Clinton rebounded to win a second term in 1996 and became the first Democrat since Franklin D. Roosevelt in 1936 to be reelected to a second term. Personal scandals led to his impeachment, trial, and acquittal. The Republicans won the disputed 2000 election behind George W. Bush. Then, in a sudden turn of events, the terrorist attacks of September 11, 2001, confronted the nation with new dangers, including a possible war with Iraq.

CHRONOLOGY

1992 Ross Perot becomes third-party candidate for president • William Jefferson Clinton and Al Gore form the Democratic presidential ticket • Clinton and Gore win the presidential contest

1993 Siege of Branch Davidians at Waco, Texas, ends in fiery incident • Congress narrowly passes Clinton's economic program

1994 Republicans regain control of House of Representatives for the first time in forty years

1995 Murrah Federal Building bombed in Oklahoma City • Dayton Peace Accords bring shaky peace to Bosnia • Federal government shutdown occurs

1996 Hillary Rodham Clinton is subpoenaed before grand jury • Robert Dole is Republican nominee for president • Clinton reelected president

1997 Federal budget deficit falls dramatically • Balanced budget agreement reached • Supreme Court rules that case of *Clinton v. Jones* can proceed while Clinton is president

1998 Scandal involving Monica Lewinsky and Clinton breaks • Clinton testifies before grand jury and admits to "inappropriate relationship" with Lewinsky • House starts impeachment inquiry against Clinton • Democrats make House gains in congressional elections

1999 Clinton acquitted after impeachment trial • War in Serbia launched by NATO

2000 Disputed election results in Florida end in Supreme Court ruling that George W. Bush is president

2000 Hillary Rodham Clinton elected to the U.S. Senate

2001 Congress passes Bush's tax cut • Terrorist attack occurs on September 11 • War in Afghanistan

2002 Republicans regain control of Senate and dominate all branches of government

2002 Former President Jimmy Carter receives Nobel Peace Prize

2003 *Columbia* space shuttle explodes, killing all seven astronauts • United States prepares for war against Iraq • Mister Rogers dies

AN ANGRY NATION: 1992

The onset of the 1992 presidential election found Americans fretful and anxious. The economy had slipped into a recession by mid-1991 with unemployment rising, consumer confidence waning, and corporations laying off large numbers of employees. Americans again feared that downsizing and restructuring meant that their jobs were disappearing overseas.

Outside Washington, unhappiness intensified about how officials in Congress and the White House conducted themselves. Speaker of the House of Representatives James Wright (D-Texas) had resigned under an ethical cloud in 1989 because he had accepted money from lobbyists and special interest groups. Other lawmakers of both parties had abused the procedures of the House bank to write checks for which there were not sufficient funds in their accounts. The House post office had been handled in a corrupt way as well. Campaign finance reform stalled as members continued to accept large contributions from corporations, labor unions, and special interest groups with a stake in the outcome of legislation. Voter anger surged during 1991.

The Embattled Bush Presidency

Political pundits expected George H. W. Bush to win the presidency again. His success in the Gulf War seemed to

For a season, Ross Perot brought fresh energy and new ideas into American politics. He captivated hordes of reporters when his campaign was still a novelty and his personality seemed attractive.
AP/Wide World Photo

assure his reelection. Still, the volatile nature of public opinion at the start of 1992 indicated that even Bush would not have an easy road back to the White House. His approval rating, once over 90 percent in 1991, had slipped, and conservatives assaulted his political leadership. The president seemed to many Americans to have little awareness of their problems and hopes.

President Bush overcame the challenge of conservative columnist Patrick Buchanan to lock up the Republican nomination. Meanwhile the Democrats saw their major contenders drop out of the race before it began. Into the vacuum stepped a political newcomer, Arkansas governor Bill Clinton.

Bill Clinton: A New Democrat

From the outset, Clinton aroused conflicting passions among Democrats and the voters in general. He was a young, attractive southern governor who campaigned as a "New Democrat" with a strong civil rights record. He had supported education and economic growth in Arkansas. On the negative side, however, critics charged that he had cheated on his wife Hillary Rodham Clinton with numerous women. During the Vietnam War, which he had opposed, he received special treatment to avoid the draft but never gave a full explanation about how he had behaved. There were also whispers about his business dealings, especially investments in a land development called Whitewater. An Arkansas columnist dubbed him "Slick Willie," and the tag stuck.

President Bush's trouble continued, however, when he responded slowly and without much effectiveness to racial rioting that erupted in Los Angeles during the spring of 1992. Neither Bush nor Clinton pleased a significant number of minority voters as the election progressed.

The Perot Insurgency

Many citizens, especially Republicans, looked for an alternative. The national spotlight turned to a Texas computer billionaire named Ross Perot. Plain-spoken and tough-talking, the feisty Perot argued that professional politicians lacked the will to deal with the country's problems. Faced with a losing football team, he said, "the best approach would be to get a new coach, a new quarterback, start with basics, clean it up." Announcing his candidacy on Larry King's national call-in television program, Perot stirred enthusiasm among citizens looking for an alternative to Bush and Clinton.

During the spring of 1992, Perot benefitted from a grassroots movement that put his name on the ballot in all of the states. He soon led Bush and Clinton in the

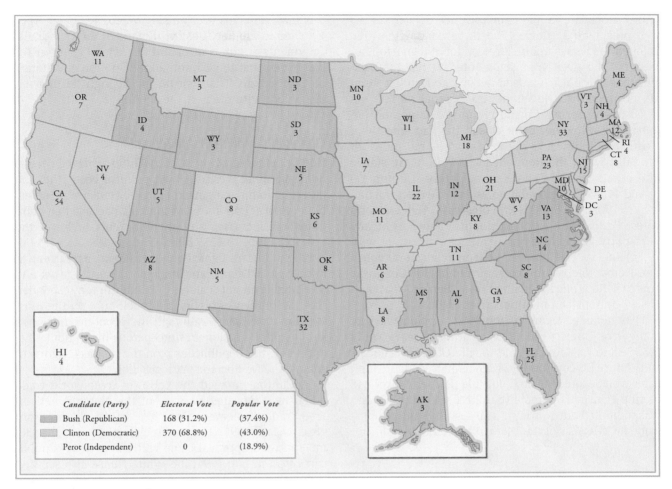

Map 32.1 *The Election of 1992*

This map shows the ability of Bill Clinton to capitalize on the discontent with George Bush and the Republicans to carve out a landslide electoral victory. Since Clinton only received 43 percent of the vote, however, questions about his legitimacy as president soon appeared from the Republicans.

polls. Without specifying just what he would do, he promised to grapple with the budget deficit and clean up Washington. As the media investigated his previous record in business and politics, evidence of erratic and silly behavior surfaced. He monitored the private lives of his employees, and some called him "Inspector Perot." His poll numbers sank. Just before the Democratic National Convention, Perot withdrew from the race.

THE 1992 ELECTION CAMPAIGN

Bill Clinton received an electoral boost when Perot left the race, and the Arkansas governor swept to the Democratic nomination. He selected Senator Albert Gore of Tennessee as his running mate. Although the presence of two southerners on the national ticket defied political wisdom, the Democratic team seemed youthful and energetic. A bus tour of the heartland of the country after the national convention attracted much favorable publicity. Clinton's lead in the polls widened before the Republicans held their convention in August.

The GOP delegates nominated Bush and Vice President Quayle amid an atmosphere in which the conservative social agenda dominated. In a fiery speech, Patrick Buchanan declared a cultural war to reclaim America from liberals, immigrants, and homosexuals. He assailed Hillary Rodham Clinton as well. The spectacle added to Bill Clinton's support, especially with women voters in the nation's suburbs.

In October 1992, Ross Perot changed his mind and reentered the presidential race, choosing Admiral

James Stockdale, a Vietnam prisoner of war, as his vice presidential choice. The three candidates then debated the issues before large national television audiences. The election engaged voter interest to an extent that had not been seen in several decades. Perot did not regain the levels of support that he had enjoyed in the spring, yet he retained a large and enthusiastic following. Bush closed the gap somewhat during the final weeks of the campaign, but the Perot candidacy split the Republican base in many states. The result was a Clinton-Gore victory. Clinton received 44,908,254 popular votes and 370 electoral ballots to Bush's 39,102,343 votes and 168 electoral votes. Perot made the best popular showing of any third-party candidate in American history with 19,741,065 votes. However, he won no electoral votes. The Democrats continued their control of Congress, but the Republicans gained one Senate seat and picked up fourteen members in the House.

A notable feature of the 1992 election was the number of women candidates who won seats in the U.S. Senate. In the aftermath of the Clarence Thomas and Anita Hill controversy, Democratic women candidates won Senate seats in California (Barbara Boxer and Dianne Feinstein), Illinois (Carol Moseley Braun), and Washington (Patti Murray). The results, said pundits, made it "The Year of the Woman" in national politics.

THE CLINTON PRESIDENCY

Clinton's presidency faltered even before he took office. As one of his first announced priorities, the president-elect indicated that he intended to lift the long-standing ban against declared homosexuals serving in the armed forces. After much debate within the military, the Clinton administration adopted a "Don't Ask, Don't Tell" approach in which gay personnel would not be asked about their sexual orientation and should not be openly homosexual. This stance contradicted Clinton's election appeal as a moderate rather than a liberal Democrat, and the religious right began an assault on the president and his wife that would continue throughout the next four years. Several embarrassing problems with the selection of women and minorities for cabinet and subcabinet positions caused an appearance of presidential disarray to form around Clinton that further impeded his ability to govern.

After Clinton was inaugurated, an armed confrontation between agents of the Bureau of Alcohol, Tobacco, and Firearms and members of the Branch Davidian religious sect outside Waco, Texas, in April 1993 led to the fiery deaths of many of the Davidians. Opponents of gun control and the federal government contended that the Clinton administration envisioned dictatorial rule. That fear on the far right further fed discontent with the new president.

Clinton's Domestic Agenda

During his first two years, Bill Clinton achieved several domestic objectives at a high political cost. With the barest of voting margins in both the House and Senate, he secured adoption of an economic package that combined tax increases and spending cuts to lower the deficit for 1993 to $255 billion and for 1994 to $203 billion. Republicans depicted the president as returning to a traditional Democratic strategy of raising taxes and predicted economic calamity ahead. Clinton responded that the burden of higher levies fell only on the most wealthy Americans. Although the economy remained strong and the nation was prosperous throughout 1993 and 1994, the Republicans won the political argument against the Democratic tax legislation.

Clinton pursued the cause of freer world trade when he advocated passage of the North American Free Trade Agreement (NAFTA), which cleared Congress in late 1993. The trade agreement split the Democrats, and approval came with the help of Republican votes. In late 1994, the White House also secured congressional endorsement of the General Agreement on Tariffs and Trade (GATT) in a lame-duck session of the Democratic Congress. Again, Republican votes were central to this administration victory.

Reforming Health Care

The major goal of the new administration was reform of the nation's system of health care. Nearly 40 million citizens did not have health insurance, and the costs of medical care were rising at an alarming rate. In a dramatic expansion of the responsibilities for first ladies, Clinton asked his wife to head the task force to prepare a health care plan within one hundred days. Working throughout 1993, Hillary Clinton's planners produced a health care blueprint in September. It envisioned health alliances to emphasize managed care, asked Americans to pay more to consult private physicians, and expanded coverage to include all citizens.

The plan soon became the target of attacks from Republicans and the insurance industry as too bureaucratic, complex, and costly. The insurance industry used effective television ads of a mythical couple named "Harry and Louise" discussing the alleged drawbacks of the Clinton plan. Despite the intense lobbying efforts that Hillary Clinton expended, the "Clinton Health Plan," as it was known, had few friends in Congress. Republicans denied that any serious health care reform was needed and refused to present alternatives of their own. The drumbeat of opposition from the insurance industry took its toll on public opinion. By 1994 the health care issue had become a major liability for the Clinton White House.

Clinton's Political Troubles

Despite his domestic accomplishments, President Clinton's popular approval ratings remained low, often under 50 percent of the electorate. From the political right, the president and his wife stirred dislike that bordered on outright hatred. Republicans charged that the Clintons were socialists bent on entrenching homosexuals, bureaucrats, and atheists in power in Washington. When an aide to the president, Vincent Foster, committed suicide during the summer of 1993, right-wing talk show hosts circulated wild and unfounded rumors that Foster had been murdered at the instructions of the president and his wife.

More serious were the charges of financial impropriety and ethical lapses that dogged the Clintons from their years in Arkansas. Investments that they had made in an Arkansas real estate venture on the Whitewater River became entangled with the failed savings and loan firm run by business associates of the Clintons, James and Susan McDougal. Federal regulators grew interested in these transactions, and in 1993 press reports disclosed that the Clintons could be named as potential witnesses and even targets of an investigation. Charges soon surfaced that an effort at a cover-up had been mounted from the White House. The all-purpose label for these and other related "scandals" was "Whitewater." Investigators also looked into Hillary Clinton's profitable trades in commodity futures in the 1970s.

The charges against the Clintons led to the appointment of an independent counsel, or special prosecutor, in 1994. The first counsel was a Republican named Robert Fiske. When he concluded that Vincent Foster's death was a suicide, angry conservatives had him replaced with another counsel, Kenneth Starr, a former federal judge and solicitor general during the Bush administration.

Personally embarrassing to President Clinton were allegations that he had sexually harassed an Arkansas state employee named Paula Corbin Jones in 1991. Jones filed a civil rights lawsuit in the spring of 1994 in which she claimed that then Governor Clinton had made unwanted sexual advances in a hotel room, including exposing himself to her. The president's lawyers attempted to have the suit delayed until after the end of his administration on the grounds that such litigation disrupted his ability to carry out his official duties.

Clinton and the World

Bill Clinton came into office with his mind concentrated on domestic issues, and, as a result, his foreign policy got off to a rocky start. He faced a complex set of circumstances in the world in early 1993. The United States was heavily involved in a number of places around the globe—Haiti, Bosnia, and Somalia—but the previous administration had not linked these commitments to any kind of coherent structure other than George H. W. Bush's vague references after the Gulf War to a "New World Order."

As a result, Clinton's first year produced a number of foreign policy problems and disasters that created an image of the president as out of his depth on the world stage. In October 1993, eighteen American servicemen died in a raid in Somalia that included television footage of crowds dragging the body of an American pilot through the streets. The White House also suffered a setback in Haiti after a peacekeeping force was repulsed by angry inhabitants of the island threatening violence.

The main foreign policy problem of these initial months was in Bosnia where Clinton had been so critical of the Bush administration and its policies during the 1992 campaign. In office, the proper course of action seemed less clear. With United Nations peacekeeping troops, predominantly British and French, on the ground, the military options for Clinton were limited since the first targets of retaliation from the Serbs would be the allied troops. Working through the United Nations also proved frustrating for the White House. Tensions rose between Washington and its allies throughout 1993 over the proper course of action in the Balkans.

In less publicized ways, the administration had some accomplishments. It succeeded in obtaining the withdrawal of Russian troops from the Baltic Republic of Estonia in 1994. Clinton also helped to broker peace negotiations among Ireland, Great Britain, and the Irish Republican army's political arm Sinn Fein ("Ourselves Alone"). In the Middle East, State Department negotiators facilitated talks between Yasir Arafat of the Palestine Liberation Organization and Prime Minister Yitzhak Rabin of Israel that led to a celebrated handshake on the White House lawn. The United States

In a troubled first year in office, a handshake between two Middle Eastern enemies at the White House represented one of the foreign policy successes for the Clinton administration.
AP/Wide World Photo

also intervened in Haiti in 1994 and produced the ouster of the military rulers as a prelude to more democratic government.

The perception that Clinton was weak in foreign policy exacerbated his political troubles at home. During his first two years in office, Clinton's popularity ratings fell, his hold on the country remained weak, and there was speculation that he would be another one-term president. On the right, the determination to oust Clinton in 1996 gathered momentum.

THE REPUBLICAN REVOLUTION: 1994

By 1994 the cumulative effect of the charges against the president and a Republican resurgence from the setback of 1992 transformed the political scene as the congressional elections approached. Several elements fed the Republican offensive. In the House of Representatives, the Republicans chose as their next leader their ideological champion, Representative Newton ("Newt") Gingrich of Georgia. A former historian, Gingrich saw himself as the embodiment of a fundamental revolution in American values that would sweep away the residue of the "Great Society" in favor of "The Opportunity Society." An adroit po-

litical tactician, the burly, rumpled Gingrich used the television coverage of Congress that began in the late 1970s (called C-SPAN) to broadcast his ideas to a national constituency. His militancy contributed to a partisan intensity in the House, and he saw his greatest initial triumph when he forced Speaker Jim Wright from office for financial misconduct in 1989. Gingrich continued his abrasive tactics into the early 1990s, and conservative members in the House rallied to his banner.

Aiding the Republican cause was the rise of conservative talk-radio, embodied in its most militant exponent, Rush Limbaugh. With his denunciation of "feminazis" and "environmentalist wackos," Limbaugh appealed to a growing audience of followers known as "Dittoheads" because they simply said "ditto" when conveying praise of the master rather than reiterating the specifics of their adulation. A stocky, articulate performer, Limbaugh had millions of daily listeners over his "Excellence in Broadcasting" network where he touted his "Talent on Loan from God." He and other conservatives on the radio assailed the Clintons and their program throughout 1993 and 1994.

To dramatize their appeal, Gingrich and the Republicans offered "A Contract with America" as their election platform. Composed of proposals tested in focus groups for their popularity with the voters, the Contract promised action on such items as a balanced budget amendment, term limits for Congress members, and making legislators obey the regulations they applied to society. All of these measures and others would be acted on within the first one hundred days of a Republican victory. As the elections began, the Republicans found their poll numbers rising, the Democrats in retreat, and the prospect of regaining control of Congress a real possibility for the first time in four decades.

The Democrats and President Clinton stumbled throughout the autumn of 1994. The failure to achieve reform of the health care system and a general weariness with big government underlined the apparent futility of the incumbents. Efforts to scare the voters about the prospect of a Republican takeover fell flat. On election night, the Republicans swept to victory. They had 235 seats in the House to 197 for the Democrats, and they controlled the Senate by a margin of fifty-three to forty-seven. Newt Gingrich became Speaker of the House and Robert Dole was the Senate majority leader. The elections immediately prompted predictions that President Clinton's prospects for regaining the White House in 1996 were bleak.

PICTURING THE PAST✦POLITICS & DIPLOMACY

THE REPUBLICAN REVOLUTION OF 1994

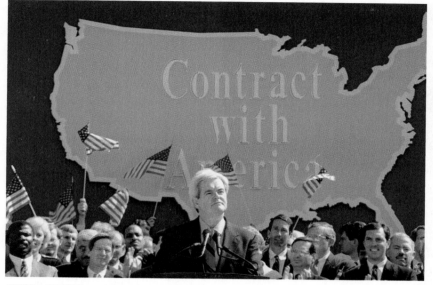

AP/Wide World Photo

The Republican takeover of Congress in 1994 was orchestrated by Newt Gingrich of Georgia, pictured here with his fellow GOP House candidates on September 27, 1994. The use of striking visuals such as the blue background for the "Contract with America" slogan and the American flags that the candidates wave attest to the influence of television on how political campaigns are marketed. The provisions of the "Contract" had also been poll-tested with focus groups to ensure the maximum electoral popularity.

This photograph shows how American politics in the 1990s had become a series of visually alluring, highly staged productions designed to address substantive issues but to evoke a desired response from viewers. The Republicans in 1994 proved far more adept at turning the techniques of show business and Hollywood to their advantage than did their Democratic rivals.

RACE IN THE 1990S

The O. J. Simpson Case

While Washington watched the 1994 elections with great intensity, Americans spent more time that autumn transfixed by what promised to be the last "Trial of the Century." In mid-June 1994, Nicole Brown Simpson, the estranged ex-wife of professional football star and Heisman Trophy winner Orenthal James "O. J." Simpson, was brutally murdered at her home. Nearby lay the corpse of Ronald Goldman, an acquaintance and restaurant employee. Police suspicions soon focused on O. J. Simpson, whose Ford Bronco had blood that could be traced to the crime scene and who had apparently left physical evidence of his presence there.

Although Simpson's playing career in the National Football League had ended some years earlier, he re-mained a national celebrity because of appearances in movies and television advertising. It soon became evident that the nation was polarized about Simpson's guilt or innocence. Most white Americans believed that the strong evidence pointed to Simpson as the killer. Many black Americans talked of a police conspiracy to frame the former football star and associated his prosecution with earlier examples of racial injustice.

These opinions solidified during the protracted trial that began during the fall of 1994 and stretched on into much of 1995. Televised daily and covered in excruciating detail, the trial played out as a racially charged drama that dominated talk shows, tabloids, and popular opinion in what became a national obsession. As the months of testimony and controversy stretched into 1995, the Simpson trial took on a life of its own as a forum where Americans confronted sensitive and explosive issues about how society dealt with minorities and race.

*P*ICTURING THE PAST✦SOCIAL & CULTURAL EVENTS

HISPANICS ENTER POLITICS

John Ledgard/The Economist

The shifting nature of the population in the United States began a slow but important change in the nation's politics in the 1990s as ethnic diversity became more pronounced. One of the most important groups in this process was Americans of Hispanic origin. In the states of the Southwest and the Far West, Hispanics made their presence felt at the polls, both as candidates and as voters. This picture, taken in California during the 1990s, offers visual evidence of the rising importance of Hispanic candidates in that state. A decade later, both major parties were competing vigorously for the expanding vote that Hispanics represented. In the initial phase the Democrats had an advantage over their Republican rivals. These election signs also attest to the ways in which the American political system accommodated to the tide of immigration that occurred in the 1990s. More than just advertisements for individual candidates, election posters and signs can, if watched carefully, measure subtle changes in the way Americans conduct their political activities.

The Immigration Backlash

Adding to the social tensions of 1994 was the issue of immigration, both illegal and legal. Voters in California adopted Proposition 187, a ballot initiative that barred illegal immigrants from receiving state benefits in education and health. Immigration into the United States had grown dramatically during the 1980s. By the early 1990s legal immigrants, most of whom were Hispanics and Asians, totaled almost 600,000 per year. Estimates of the number of illegal immigrants to settle in the United States ranged from 300,000 to half a million. The Immigration and Naturalization Service (INS) forecast that there might be as many as 13 million immigrants coming to the United States during the 1990s. That would be the largest amount in all of American history.

Debate about the value and cost of this wave of immigrants roiled American politics during the first half of the 1990s. Critics of immigration charged that "the racial and ethnic balance of America is being radically altered through public policy." Studies demonstrated that immigrants, both legal and illegal,

contributed more to society in taxes and productivity than they consumed from government services, but the mere increased presence of Hispanics and Asians, the so-called "browning of America," produced political conflict, especially in California. In 1994, the rising discontent about immigration in California led to a landslide election victory for Proposition 187. After its adoption, court challenges delayed its implementation, but by 1996 the governor ordered many of its provisions into effect. On the national level Congress debated immigration restrictions as it decided what to do about reform of the welfare system.

THE REPUBLICANS IN POWER

The new Republican majorities in Congress went to work in January 1995 with great energy to implement their "Contract with America." Laboring long hours at the start, they enacted a measure to make the regulations they imposed on Americans apply to Capitol Hill as well. The Republicans also pushed for a balanced budget amendment to the Constitution. Meanwhile, President Clinton accepted some of the Republican ideas in his State of the Union message and praised his own record on the economy. Speaker of the House Newt Gingrich was an effective leader of his Republican troops in this early phase of the session, but his propensity for colorful attacks on his opponents made him a center of controversy.

The pace of the "Republican Revolution" remained hectic into the spring of 1995. Although the balanced budget amendment failed by a single vote in the Senate, Congress did pass a law to restrict itself from making the states enforce regulations without supplying the necessary funds to do so. Clinton approved the "unfunded mandates" measure on March 22, 1995. The Republicans failed, however, to pass a constitutional amendment imposing term limits on members of Congress. By April, Republicans proclaimed that they had enacted most of the contract within the one hundred days they had set for themselves.

Tragedy in Oklahoma City

Then a national tragedy shifted the political landscape. On April 19, 1995, the Alfred P. Murrah Federal Building in Oklahoma City blew up, killing 168 people inside. Two suspects, Timothy McVeigh and Terry Nichols, were quickly arrested and identified as having links with an extremist "militia" movement that sought the violent overthrow of the government of the United States. The public learned that small groups of militia met secretly in the countryside to practice guerilla warfare tactics against the day when the ZOG (Zionist Occupation Government) in Washington would precipitate the final confrontation on behalf of the United Nations and the "New World Order." The glare of publicity revealed that the militia movement, while violent and dangerous, commanded only a small cadre of followers.

The aftermath of the bombing enabled President Clinton to regain a position of trust and confidence with the American people. He went out to Oklahoma City in the wake of the tragedy and participated in the ceremony of national mourning for the victims. Clinton's speech on that occasion struck a resonant note of national healing and identified the president with the broad political center of the country. The two suspects, McVeigh and Nichols, were both tried and convicted for their roles in the bombing.

The Republicans Falter

Republican overreaching also contributed to the president's rebound in the polls during the remainder of 1995. As the Republicans in Congress attacked environmental legislation and sought to remove government regulations on business, the White House assailed them for endangering the gains that the nation had made in clean air and clean water. Clinton threatened to veto legislation that cut back on environmental spending and money for education. He cast his first veto as president in June 1995 when he turned down a Republican spending measure that would have trimmed more than a billion dollars from education funding.

Troubles dogged Clinton during 1995, especially the long-running Whitewater saga, which saw congressional committees probe the scandal in detail. Despite the best efforts of Republican lawmakers, the inquiry did not turn up evidence that would incriminate the president or his wife in wrongdoing. The special prosecutor, Kenneth Starr, continued his investigations with indictments and convictions of several Arkansas political and business figures, but that effort also yielded nothing to embarrass the Clintons directly.

The Race for the Republican Nomination

With the perception after the 1994 elections that Clinton would be a one-term president, the Republicans had an abundance of potential challengers for their nomination in 1996. The most formidable candidate would be General Colin Powell whose service as Chairman of the Joint Chiefs of Staff in the Gulf War had made him a national military hero associated with military success. As the first African American to be a serious contender for the Republican prize, Powell would be an asset to the party's ticket if he would agree to run as vice president. Throughout most of 1995, Powell hinted that he was a Republican and thinking about running for president.

Beyond Powell, the Republican field for 1996 included Senator Robert Dole who began as the presumed front-runner. Since the party generally selected the leading candidate in the polls, Dole was likely to be nominated unless he stumbled badly. At seventy-two, Dole had to overcome the age problem, his reputation as a strident partisan, and a perception that he would be the easiest target for a resurgent Clinton.

Dole endeavored to tap into the cultural fears of the right wing of his party in May 1995 when he assailed what he called "nightmares of depravity" that peppered audiences of adolescents with images of grotesque violence and sexual activity. The senator also went after the variant of pop music known as "gangsta" rap, which he labeled as degrading to women and in favor of crime. The speech invigorated Dole's floundering candidacy during the summer of 1995.

Clinton Resurgent: Bosnia

The big political winner in the second half of 1995 continued to be President Clinton. Against all the critics who charged that his policy in Bosnia would lead to an American involvement and a military disaster, the president succeeded by the end of the year in producing a cease-fire in the conflict. The price was the presence of American ground troops in the Balkans, but even that risky commitment did not lead to the disaster that so many had anticipated. The opportunity for a cease-fire emerged out of a complex series of events during the summer and fall of 1995. In July, a Serb offensive imperiled several cities that were regarded as "safe havens" for refugees from the fighting. Helped by arms that had come in from Muslim countries, Croatian and Bosnian forces launched an offensive against the Serbs. At the end of August, Clinton authorized air strikes against the Bosnian Serbs. Within a week, a tentative peace agreement was declared, and a month later a cease-fire was reached. The United States then brokered peace negotiations in Dayton, Ohio, which produced a settlement. American troops were dispatched to help enforce the peace agreement.

THE SIMPSON VERDICT AND THE POLITICS OF RACE

While politics raged on during 1995, the O. J. Simpson trial plodded toward a conclusion. Popular interest in the proceedings remained high, especially as the end of the trial neared. The Simpson defense team associated its client with the oppression and injustice that blacks had received in the United States and put the Los Angeles Police Department on trial. The racial divisions about the trial had not lessened as the case went to the jury in September 1995. After very brief deliberations, Simpson was acquitted on all counts.

Black audiences cheered the verdict as it was announced. Whites watching on television expressed dismay. The national debate over the case intensified as commentators divided along racial lines over the significance of Simpson's acquittal. Some Simpson partisans asserted that the jury's decision represented an effort to make up for decades of biased white verdicts toward black defendants.

The Million Man March

In October 1995, the Nation of Islam and its controversial leader, Louis Farrakhan, organized "a holy day of atonement and reconciliation" for black men. Designed to bring 1 million black men to the nation's capital, the event became known as the "Million Man March." Estimates of the actual number of participants varied widely, but the more positive assessments said that Farrakhan and his organization had reached their goal. Commentators made comparisons with the March on Washington in August 1963 and the striking oratory of Martin Luther King, Jr. Because of Farrakhan's espousal of anti-Semitic sentiments and his expressed dislike for white Americans, the 1995 march did not have the moral resonance of the earlier occasion, but it galvanized the participants. Within the black community, debate raged about the role of Farrakhan and his value as a spokesman for African American aspirations.

Culture Wars: Multiculturalism and Political Correctness

The Simpson trial and the Million Man March took place in the context of a national debate about what the United States should do regarding the continuing question of racial injustice and the presence of diverse minority groups within the existing culture. One source of debate and tension was the related issues of "multiculturalism" and what came to be called "political correctness." Both terms had highly charged, controversial meanings.

Multiculturalism had emerged in the 1980s in academic institutions as a means of opening up the study of history and literature to a larger range of cultural and social experiences among groups not previously included in the American past. In gender, class, and racial concerns, multiculturalism sought to draw attention to such issues as the role of black soldiers in the Civil War, Japanese Americans in World War II internment camps, and women in the American Revolution, to pick among countless examples. In its positive aspects, multiculturalism was an effort to include groups, ideas, and experiences that had not been part of the mainstream. In history it meant depicting, according to historians, "the dignity of common people who quietly struggle under difficult conditions and who, in large and small ways, refuse to submit to abuse, discrimination, and exploitation."

By the early 1990s, however, multiculturalism had come under attack from its enemies on the right who accused its adherents of enforcing what was called "political correctness." The critics of multiculturalism said that the academic left was using the movement to balkanize American society into warring ethnic groups, was limiting free speech on campuses, and was repudiating the whole tradition of Western culture.

While some of the criticisms of multiculturalism did identify areas of exaggeration and overstatement from its proponents, the critics also overdramatized isolated incidents and blew small errors into larger trends. What was significant about these cultural divisions was the polarization of American society in the 1990s that they revealed. In 1994–1995, for example, an exhibition at the Smithsonian Institution to mark the fiftieth anniversary of the atomic bombing of Hiroshima became a flashpoint when veterans groups charged that the organizers of the show were adopting an anti-American, pro-Japanese point of view. The curators who mounted the show responded that they were trying to reflect the diversity of scholarly opinion about the event. The protest triumphed: the exhibition was canceled and the director of the Air and Space Museum forced to resign. By the end of the decade, passions about multiculturalism had cooled somewhat, but tensions in other areas of society remained volatile over such issues as affirmative action and gay rights.

The Battle over Gay Rights

The efforts of gays and lesbians to attain political and social equality within the United States were met with a strong counteroffensive from conservatives who regarded homosexuals as a threat to the nation's values. In the 1990s, homosexuals contended that they should have the right to marry (in what were called "same-sex" marriages) just as heterosexuals did. Identifying their campaign with the civil rights movement of the 1960s, gay groups wanted attacks on those who were openly homosexual to be classified as "hate crimes."

Conservative groups assailed homosexuality as a sin or a disease. Christian groups ran elaborate advertising campaigns to persuade homosexuals to abandon their lifestyle and seek religious treatment. Periodic acts of violence directed against gays spurred calls for federal legislation to prevent such actions. Passions on the issue remained intense in the first decade of the twenty-first century as efforts to ban same-sex marriages advanced in several states.

Affirmative Action and Civil Rights

Another issue that provoked serious divisions within society was the policy of affirmative action in industry, higher education, and government to provide minorities with greater opportunities for advancement. Al-

though the Supreme Court had ruled in the late 1970s that race could be employed in university admissions when the goal was to achieve diversity in the student body, the justices scaled back on that commitment in a number of cases involving such policies as minority set-aside programs or congressional districts drawn to produce heavily minority-populated districts.

Unhappiness with affirmative action as a policy led some states such as California to adopt Proposition 209 in a referendum that abolished programs to assist minorities. In the *Hopwood v. Texas* case (1996), a federal circuit court invalidated the affirmative action plan of the University of Texas Law School, noting that any effort by universities to promote affirmative action was unconstitutional. The issue remained unresolved in the courts by 2002 as some states adopted plans to admit the top ten percent of graduating high school students, irrespective of their race or ethnicity, to their state universities.

CLINTON WINS A SECOND TERM

As the budget negotiations between President Clinton and the Republican Congress produced no result toward the end of 1995, some of the more militant members of the GOP majority in the House called for a concerted effort to shut down the government as a way of pressuring the White House to agree to their position. Assuming that Clinton lacked the resolve to withstand a closing of the government, these Republicans foresaw a humiliating cave-in from a president they distrusted and hated.

The Republican strategy backfired. Two government shutdowns occurred, a brief one in November and a second that lasted for twenty-one days from mid-December 1995 into early January 1996. Rather than blaming the president for the deadlock, as the Republicans had anticipated, the public put the responsibility on the Republicans for the government closures that affected tourists in Washington and at popular national parks.

Clinton's Political Fortunes Improve

Speaker Gingrich proved to be a liability for his party. In November 1995, Israeli leader Yitzhak Rabin was assassinated. Gingrich flew with the president to the funeral and then complained that he had not had a chance to talk with Clinton about the budget during the flight. He also had to leave *Air Force One* through the rear door, an action that the Speaker took as a personal insult. He went public with his grievances. The ensuing flap left Gingrich looking petty and undercut his stature as a budget bargainer.

In early 1996, the Republicans realized that the prolonged shutdown was hurting their cause. Accordingly, they reached an accommodation with the White House that brought the crisis to an end. An interim measure to reopen the government passed both houses on January 5 and the government resumed official operations the next day.

The First Lady Under Fire

While President Clinton had the upper hand in the national political arena, the long-running Whitewater saga took an ugly turn for Hillary Rodham Clinton in the early days of January. Billing records from Hillary Clinton's former law firm in Arkansas, sought by the special prosecutor in 1994, turned up in the White House. Kenneth Starr, the Whitewater prosecutor, subpoenaed Mrs. Clinton to testify before his Washington grand jury. Her appearance marked the first time that a first lady had testified in a criminal proceeding while her husband was in office. She spent four hours before the grand jury panel, but no results followed from her testimony. In mid-1997, press reports said that the jury had ended its life without issuing indictments against her.

The long-running Whitewater investigation brought Hillary Clinton to the federal courthouse in Washington, the only first lady to be involved in a criminal proceeding as a possible target. No charges were ever filed against her and she was elected to the United States Senate in 2000.
The Washington Times/Daniel Rosenbaum

Running parallel with Starr's probe were several congressional inquiries into the Whitewater story, the most notable being the one that Senator Alphonse D'Amato of New York conducted through the Senate Banking Committee. D'Amato's probe covered a wide range of issues relating to the economic activities of the Clintons in Arkansas, but the hearings yielded very little tangible evidence that implicated the president and first lady in criminal activity. The failure of D'Amato's inquiry to turn up sensational revelations helped defuse the Whitewater story as the 1996 election got underway.

The Republicans Pick Dole

As the 1996 election approached, Robert Dole solidified his position at the head of the Republican party. A decorated World War II veteran and a gifted lawmaker, Dole had run in 1988 against George H. W. Bush for the GOP prize, but had lost badly. An indifferent speaker at best, Dole campaigned in a frenetic but often unfocused manner. He was not a good organizer, and friends worried about his ability to sustain a national presidential campaign.

Dole faced a number of challengers to his candidacy as 1996 began, but he won the key South Carolina primary on March 2. Successive victories brought the Kansas senator within sight of the nomination by April 1996. The early victory left the Dole campaign broke and unable to counter Clinton's advertising until after the Republican National Convention in late summer when Dole received federal matching funds as the official Republican nominee. To jump-start his lagging candidacy, Dole tried a sensational gesture and resigned his Senate seat in June to campaign as a man without office or Washington power. He remained behind in the polls.

The spring of 1996 did not mean undiluted triumphs for President Clinton. In late May, his onetime business partners, James and Susan McDougal, were found guilty of fraud and conspiracy in dealings in Whitewater-related transactions. One of the witnesses in the case alleged that then Governor Clinton had pressured him to make an illegal loan some years earlier. President Clinton denied the allegation under oath when he testified as a defense witness. The fallout from these episodes did not undermine Clinton's drive for reelection or his position in the public opinion polls.

The Rise of the Internet

While politicians and commentators focused on the 1996 presidential contests, another force was affecting the economy and American culture. The powerful

Senator Robert Dole of Kansas attained his long-held dream of winning the Republican presidential nomination in 1996, but he could not unseat a popular incumbent. His picture, taken at a rally in New Hampshire while he is being introduced, fails to show the war wounds to his right hand and the pencil that he always gripped.
©Bettmann/Corbis

Dominating the new field were such corporations as America Online which provided connections for 30 percent of all Internet users in the country in 1996. Other businesses sought consumers on the Web through specific Web pages or by purchasing advertising space on popular Web sites. Some new firms, such as the discount bookseller Amazon.com, saw their common stock soar in value in 1998 because of the potential growth of their markets. Popular movies such as *You've Got Mail* (1998) and the rise of news outlets on the Web that included "Salon," "Slate," and the "Drudge Report" (named after its host, conservative Matt Drudge) underscored how the Internet had permeated American life. Investments in Internet stocks helped fuel the economic boom of the late 1990s.

So important had computers and the Internet become by 1998 that the prospect of a computer breakdown in the year 2000 emerged as a major social problem. Y2K, as it was known, stemmed from the inability of older computers to read the year 2000 correctly and remain functioning. Finding and fixing imbedded computer codes cost business and government hundreds of billions of dollars in 1998 and 1999. Some Americans hoarded food and weapons in preparation for what they forecast as a breakdown of civilization on January 1, 2000. In any case the fate of the nation's economy was now tied to the operation and reliability of its computers.

Welfare and Other Reforms in Congress

With the election approaching and polls showing their standing with the public in jeopardy, the Republican majority on Capitol Hill saw cooperation with the White House as a political necessity. As a result, the president and Congress found common ground on reform of the nation's welfare system in the summer of 1996. A compromise measure came out of Congress at the end of July. The bill produced sweeping changes in caring for the poor. In place of the long-standing Aid for Dependent Children (AFDC) program, lawmakers established a system of block grants to the individual states. The federal responsibility to provide for the poverty-stricken, adopted during the New Deal and expanded in succeeding decades, ended. The measure also specified that legal immigrants into the United States would not be eligible for benefits during their first five years of residence. The legislation fulfilled Clinton's 1992 campaign promise to "end welfare as we know it," but it left many Democrats unhappy with the current direction of their party.

The waning days of the Congress saw other accomplishments that gave the president issues on which

growth of the Internet and the World Wide Web in the 1990s transformed the way Americans got their news and communicated with each other. The development of browsers that could read the Hyper Text Markup Language (HTML) facilitated this process during the first half of the decade. In 1996, 18 million people, or about 9 percent of the population, accessed the Internet on a regular basis. A year later the figure stood at 30 million adults. By 1998, 20 percent of all American households had Internet access, and the growth continued unabated into the twenty-first century. With more than 96 million computers in use in 1995, or 364.7 per 1,000 Americans, the United States led the world in its share of Internet usage.

to run and allowed the Republican Congress to rebut the charges that it was unable to act constructively. In August, lawmakers enacted a raise in the minimum wage in two steps to $5.15 per hour. It was the first hike since 1991 and came after intense Republican opposition. Responding to the continuing public unhappiness with immigration problems, Congress included in its spending legislation funds for new personnel for the Immigration and Naturalization Service, the hiring of additional Border Patrol agents, and more severe penalties for bringing in illegal aliens. Republicans failed to get language that would have barred public education to the children of illegal immigrants. The achievements of Congress undercut Dole's argument that Clinton was not an effective leader.

The National Conventions

Both parties struggled for the political advantage in their national conventions. These gatherings had now become television spectacles rather than deliberative events, and both Republicans and Democrats endeavored to display themselves in a favorable light before a national audience. The major networks abandoned earlier policies of "gavel-to-gavel" coverage, with programming focused on key moments in the proceedings. Everything was carefully scripted and choreographed.

Mindful of their public relations disaster in Houston in 1992, the Republicans sought to reassure voters that they were an acceptable and inclusive alternative to the Democrats. Their problem remained, however, one of making Senator Dole an exciting and charismatic figure who could compete with Clinton, an adroit and skilled campaigner. Dole launched his preconvention offensive with the promise of a 15 percent tax cut over a three-year period. Reflecting the sentiment within the party for what was known as a "flat tax," an income tax at a low rate for all citizens, he advocated a "fairer, flatter tax." To Democratic charges that his proposal would "blow a hole in the deficit," Dole responded by saying that he would propose prudent spending cuts to find the $548 billion needed to offset his tax reductions. For Dole, long a champion of a balanced budget, the tax cut proposal represented an eleventh-hour conversion to the supply-side ideology of the Reagan wing of his party. The second daring maneuver came when Dole announced that he had asked former Congressman Jack Kemp of New York to be his running mate. A favorite of the conservatives, Kemp had long endorsed tax cuts and was popular among African American voters. In many respects, the choice was an odd one. Kemp brought little electoral strength to the ticket. The Re-

publicans had no hopes of carrying New York State, for example. Kemp was also an indifferent campaigner, but at the convention his selection lifted the spirits of the Republican delegates who saw Dole trailing badly in the polls to the incumbent president.

Perot Again

Midway between the conventions of the major parties came the meeting of the Reform party that Ross Perot had established as the vehicle for his second presidential candidacy. Perot won the nomination easily. Yet he had not captured the public's imagination as had happened in 1992. Perot's hope was to elbow his way into the presidential debates against Clinton and Dole, but, despite efforts to use the federal courts to gain access, Perot had to watch from the sidelines.

With a commanding lead in the public opinion polls, President Clinton enjoyed a harmonious convention when the Democrats met in Chicago in late August. The platform stressed centrist themes and spoke of a "New Democratic party." Clinton and Vice President Gore were renominated, and the president promised four more years of prosperity and moderate reform in what he called his last election campaign.

During September 1996, the campaign unfolded as though Clinton and the Democrats were certain winners. Despite some fluctuations, the lead over Dole in the polls remained strong. The two presidential debates did not attract the attention that had characterized the 1992 debates, and Dole failed to crack Clinton's armor with attacks on his character and administration scandals. By the middle of October, optimistic Democrats predicted a landslide for the president and a good chance that the party might recapture the House and Senate from the Republicans.

Campaign Scandals

Then newspaper reports appeared about improprieties and possible crimes in the fund-raising for the Democratic party and the Clinton campaign. Money had flowed into the president's campaign war chest from Asian sources, and possible links to Communist China and Indonesian businesses emerged. Every day as the campaign wound down, new revelations of questionable campaign contributors and dubious funding sources followed. The lead for the Democratic congressional candidates eroded and even some slippage occurred for President Clinton. Rather than a triumphal march, the waning days of the 1996 election saw Clinton and his party staggering toward the finish line under a severe cloud of scandal.

A Mixed Result

Clinton's lead wavered a little as the election neared, largely because of the barrage of press coverage of the campaign finance issue. Although most news organizations predicted a double-digit presidential win, that did not happen. Nor did Clinton achieve the majority of the popular vote that he sought to overcome the Republican taunt that he was a minority president. The result over Dole was never really in doubt on election night, but the triumph was more limited than had seemed possible when the campaign started.

The Democratic ticket won 379 electoral votes and 49 percent of the popular vote to 41 percent (159 electoral votes) for Dole and Kemp. Ross Perot and the Reform party lagged with 8 percent of the popular vote and no electoral votes. Clinton's electoral coalition included California (to which he had devoted attention all during his first term), New York, Illinois, Michigan, and Ohio. The president also carried two staunchly Republican states—Florida and Arizona.

While Dole had lost badly, the Republicans gained some consolation out of the election results. Despite a heavy assault from organized labor and Democratic congressional candidates, the Republicans retained control of both houses of Congress. In the House the Republicans had a diminished majority of only ten seats. The Republicans picked up two Senate seats for a fifty-five to forty-five margin over the Democrats. Since they needed sixty votes to block a Democratic filibuster, the Republicans would have to compromise with their opponents to get any legislation passed. The stage was set for another scenario of divided government to which the nation had become accustomed since the late 1960s.

A New Cabinet

For his second term, President Clinton assembled a new cabinet. To succeed the outgoing secretary of state, Warren Christopher, the president selected the ambassador to the United Nations, Madeleine Albright. She became the first woman to serve as secretary of state, and she soon emerged as one of the most effective and popular members of the government. Her ability to work with the chairman of the Senate Foreign Relations Committee, Jesse Helms of North Carolina, smoothed the way for diplomatic initiatives in early 1997 on such issues as reforming the United Nations and the Bosnian policy.

In a gesture of bipartisanship, Clinton named former Maine Republican Senator William Cohen as his secretary of defense. Long interested in defense issues, Cohen was a moderate who could build coalitions with

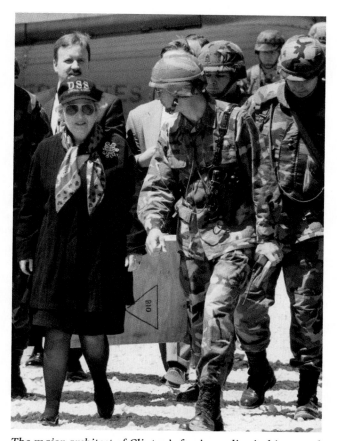

The major architect of Clinton's foreign policy in his second term was Secretary of State Madeleine Albright, shown in a 1997 visit to American troops in the Balkans.
AP/ Wide World Photos

his former colleagues in the Senate while enjoying good relations with Democrats as well. More inclined to end the Bosnian commitment than Madeleine Albright, Cohen was a cautious voice in the Pentagon. Few crises, however, disturbed his early months in office.

Modest Programs Modestly Advanced

For his second term, President Clinton avoided large initiatives that might put him at odds with the Republican Congress. During the winter of 1997, he worked out a budget agreement that promised a balance within a few years. The American economy proved so robust through the summer of 1997 that the deficit fell rapidly and forecasters projected that a budget surplus might emerge by the end of the year. The stock market soared throughout this period, reaching above 8,000 on the Dow Jones Industrial Average in July.

Clinton's goals for a second term seemed indistinct and modest well into 1997. Carrying forward the strategy of his reelection victory, he identified himself with small, incremental ideas such as a V-chip to enable parents to control the television programming that their children watched, a voluntary television ratings system, and greater computer training for schoolchildren.

An Ambitious Foreign Policy

For a president who had come into office promoting domestic issues, Clinton seemed to relish the international stage during his fifth year in office. He pushed hard for the North Atlantic Treaty Organization to add members from former Communist states in Eastern Europe and saw his vision fulfilled when Poland, Hungary, and the Czech Republic were added to the alliance. To overcome Russian opposition to expansion of NATO, the United States and its allies told Moscow in May 1997 that neither nuclear weapons nor large numbers of combat forces would be placed on the soil of the new member states. That publicly placated the Russians.

In other areas of foreign policy, the world's trouble spots remained volatile. The situation in Bosnia, while improved since the Dayton agreement, still pitted Serbs, Croats, and Bosnians against each other despite the uneasy peace that American troops in NATO helped maintain. As for the Middle East, tensions between Palestinians and Israelis worsened amid sporadic terrorist violence. The Clinton administration pressed both sides for more movement to implement

peace, but progress was elusive. Throughout the world there were rumblings about Islamic terrorism, but that seemed to most Americans, in and out of government, an improbable threat.

An Economic Boom

Throughout 1997, the American economy roared into high gear. Unemployment fell to 4.8 percent and inflation no longer seemed a problem. With jobs plentiful and prices stable, a sense of economic optimism pervaded the nation and kept Clinton's job approval ratings around the 60 percent mark.

Adding to the euphoria was the apparent end of the budget deficit problem that had shaped politics for so many years. Surging tax revenues meant that red ink started to disappear. The 1997 budget deficit was only $25 billion, the lowest since 1974, and 1998 promised the unheard of—a budget surplus. As a result of these trends, Congress and the president worked out a balanced budget agreement in May that was signed into law on August 5. Clinton proclaimed: "The sun is rising on America again." Politicians could suddenly believe they could look forward to budget surpluses for years to come. This success relied on using the money in the Social Security Trust Fund to offset other spending, but elected officials played down this budgetary sleight-of-hand in their public comments. Few realized at the time that many of the revenue statements of the corporations in the "New economy" were fraudulent. Major examples of this practice were the energy giant ENRON and the communications company Worldcom, both of which were largely crooked schemes by the late 1990s.

CLINTON EMBATTLED

The political result of these favorable economic events was a good year for President Clinton that left him popular and Democrats optimistic about regaining control of the House in 1998. The major setback of the year came when the Supreme Court ruled 9–0 on May 27, 1997, in *Clinton v. Jones* that the sexual harassment lawsuit against the president could go forward while he was in office. Other problems dogged Clinton. Congressional probes on the 1996 campaign scandal indicated that the president and Vice President Al Gore had played a larger role in raising money than they had earlier admitted. Kenneth Starr's Whitewater investigation moved along without major indictments but still posed a potential threat to the White House.

Each month brought new products to introduce consumers to the wonders of the digital age. Here a salesman in an electronics store demonstrates the high definition television that was forecast to replace older television sets by the year 2000.

© 1998, The Washington Post. Photo by Michael Williamson. Reprinted with permission

President Clinton's admissions of his sexual intimacy with Monica Lewinsky proved abundant source material for cartoonists. Jules Feiffer in the New York Times *offers one interpretation of the president's misbehavior.*
© Jules Feiffer

The Monica Lewinsky Scandal

Then, in mid-January 1998, a stunned nation learned that a former White House intern named Monica Lewinsky had been involved in a sexual relationship with President Clinton during her employment. Once the news broke, Clinton asserted that he had not had sex with Lewinsky. For seven months he reiterated that version of events. Meanwhile, Kenneth Starr investigated whether Clinton had lied under oath in the

Independent Counsel Kenneth Star pressed Congress to impeach President Bill Clinton in 1998.
© Getty Images

Paula Jones case when he said he had not had sex with Lewinsky, whether he had obstructed justice, and whether he had asked others to lie on his behalf. This sordid spectacle absorbed vast amounts of television news coverage throughout 1998.

Clinton's strategy of delay worked in the short run. His poll numbers remained high, and Starr's popularity sagged. In the end, however, abundant evidence emerged that Clinton and Lewinsky had been physically intimate. On August 17, 1998, Clinton acknowledged "inappropriate" conduct with Lewinsky when he testified before Starr's Washington grand jury from the White House. That night he told the nation the same thing in a four-and-a-half-minute speech that was widely regarded as a low point of his presidency.

A few weeks later Starr sent a report to the House of Representatives alleging that there were grounds for impeaching Clinton for lying under oath, obstruction of justice, abuse of power, and other offenses. The House Judiciary Committee recommended that an impeachment inquiry commence, and the House voted to authorize a probe after the 1998 elections.

The Monica Lewinsky scandal and its fallout left Clinton a wounded president. He retained the ability to achieve foreign policy successes such as a deal he brokered between Israelis and Palestinians in October 1998. With Clinton's resiliency as a politician, a rebound during his last two years was possible. But his tactics and conduct in handling the Lewinsky matter had cost him dearly in terms of his political capital with the American people by the end of 1998.

The 1998 Elections

The Republicans entered the 1998 election season with high ambitions to build on their majorities in the House and Senate. In the Senate, they hoped to reach a total of sixty Republicans which would enable them to end Democratic filibusters. After Clinton's speech on August 17, it seemed as if a Republican rout was in the offing. Alienated Democrats were predicted to stay home and energized Republicans would flock to the polls to rebuke Clinton. With the Monica Lewinsky scandal working for them, the Republicans had only to run out the clock for a big victory.

Instead, the Republicans overplayed their hand. Their moves to impeach Clinton awakened the Democrats and produced a backlash. By the time the Republicans figured out what was going on, it was too late. On November 3, 1998, the Democrats in the House actually gained five seats, not enough to regain control, but an amazing feat in the sixth year of a two-term presidency. Republican control of the House narrowed to 223–211, a very thin majority. In the Senate, the two parties battled to a draw, with the Republicans holding the same 55–45 edge that existed when election day dawned. Two significant Republican victories came in Florida and Texas, where the two sons of George H. W. Bush, Jeb Bush in Florida and George W. Bush in Texas, were elected governor. For George W. Bush, his reelection made him the prospective front-runner for the Republican presidential nomination in 2000.

Clinton Impeached and Acquitted

Despite the results of the congressional elections, Republican leaders in Congress pressed ahead with the impeachment of President Clinton. In December the House Judiciary Committee, on a nearly party-line breakdown sent four articles of impeachment to the full House. That body adopted two articles of impeachment charging President Clinton with perjury in his grand jury testimony in August 1998, and with obstruction of justice in his relationship with Monica Lewinsky, members of his staff, and other individuals. The Senate opened its trial in mid-January. By the end of the month, it became evident that the forty-five Democrats would not vote for conviction and a two-thirds majority to convict and remove the president did not exist.

President Clinton's popularity with the public remained high, and his State of the Union address on January 19, 1999, drove his poll ratings still higher. He was acquitted on both counts when the Senate voted on February 12, 1999. On the perjury count, the total was 45 Republican senators voting to convict the president while all 45 Democrats and 10 Republicans voted for acquittal. On the second article involving obstruction of justice, the Senate split evenly with 50 Republican votes for conviction and 45 Democrats and 5 Republicans voting for acquittal. William Jefferson Clinton remained in office, a wounded chief executive with two years left on his second term.

The impeachment episode reflected the intense emotions that Clinton had provoked during his time in the White House. To the Republicans and Americans on the right, he was an illegitimate president who had committed crimes in office that warranted his removal. To the remainder of the country, some 65 percent according to most polls, he was a president who, while probably guilty of the offenses with which he was charged, was performing well in office and should not be removed.

During the weeks following the end of the impeachment trial, pundits forecast that Clinton's poll ratings would drop once the crisis was over. That did not happen as the economy remained prosperous and the Dow Jones Industrial Average hovered around 10,000. In late March 1999, NATO began airstrikes against the Serbian government to stop "ethnic cleansing" of the Albanians near the city of Kosovo. Despite the warning of Clinton's critics, the air campaign ended in success for the NATO forces.

The much feared Y2K crisis proved to be largely a nonevent, though the government did report having foiled several terrorist plots set for January 2000. Once the date had passed without major incident amid worldwide celebrations of the calendar change, Americans turned to the onset of the presidential election season.

The 2000 Presidential Campaign: Bush Versus Gore

The Republican front-runner was Governor George W. Bush of Texas, the son of the former president. Elected in 1994 and reelected in 1998, the Texan announced for president in mid-1999 and soon amassed a campaign treasury that ultimately reached more than $100 million. Bush promised that he would be "a compassionate conservative" who would "change the tone" in Washington after the partisan discord of the Clinton era. He advocated a $1.6 trillion tax cut and promised to reform the educational system.

Bush lost the New Hampshire primary to Senator John McCain of Arizona, but then won a number of primaries to lock up the delegates needed to control

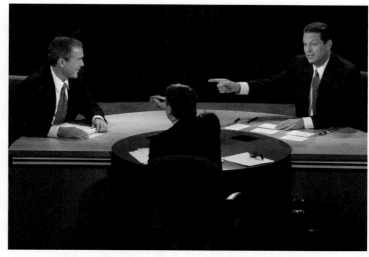

The three televised debates between George W. Bush and Albert Gore proved unusually important in deciding the outcome of the 2000 presidential election.
© Reuters NewMedia Inc./Corbis

	Electoral Vote		Popular Vote	
	Number	%	Number	%
Gore (Democrat)	267	49.6	50,996,582	48.4
Bush (Republican)	271	50.4	50,456,062	47.8
Nader (Green)	----	----	2,858,843	2.7
Buchanan (Reform)	----	----	483,760	.4

Map 32.2 *The Election of 2000*

The map of the 2000 election reflects the closeness of the electoral vote. Note the extent to which the voters were distributed into a pro-Gore coalition on the coasts and a pro-Bush coalition in the interior of the nation, with some key exceptions in the Middle West and Far West. A comparison with the presidential election of 1896 (see page 545) gives an interesting sense of how partisan alignments changed during the twentieth century.

the national convention in Philadelphia. With Richard "Dick" Cheney as his running mate, Bush had a double-digit lead over his Democratic opponent, Vice President Al Gore.

Gore had easily won his party's nomination but had problems separating himself from the scandals of the Clinton years. He also faced a hostile press corps that focused on every lapse to paint Gore as indecisive and opportunistic. Gore emerged from the Democratic convention behind Bush but closed the gap during September 2000. The election hinged on the three presidential debates.

Although neither candidate did well, Bush exceeded the low expectations that media pundits set for him. Gore was better on substance but was labeled arrogant and condescending. As a result, the race remained tight down to the election. As the votes were counted, the Republicans retained control of the

House of Representatives, and the Senate split evenly with 50 Democrats and 50 Republicans. Gore led in the presidential popular vote, but the electoral vote produced a dead heat. It became clear that the state of Florida would determine the result since its 25 electoral votes would push either of the two candidates past the 271 electoral votes needed. State officials put Florida in the Bush column by fewer than 600 ballots after going over the official returns that came in during the week after the election. Gore's forces noted irregularities and flawed ballots in several Democratic counties and sought a recount in those areas.

The Bush camp insisted that the result favoring its man should be final, and charges of fraud, manipulation, and political pressure flashed back and forth throughout November. Finally, the case of *Bush v. Gore* reached the United States Supreme Court in mid-December. On the key issue of whether a recount should occur, the Court ruled 5–4 in favor of Bush in a decision that many commentators dubbed both hasty and partisan. Gore accepted the outcome as final and conceded the election.

TERRORISM AND THE BUSH PRESIDENCY

In office, Bush governed as a conservative who opposed abortion, rolled back environmental regulations, and pursued foreign policy initiatives that

The scandal over the failed corporation Enron produced pain for its investors and employees but little public outrage.
© Cagle Cartoons

placed less reliance on working with the nation's overseas allies. Congress enacted Bush's large tax cut, but the president saw control of the Senate slip out of Republican hands when Senator James Jeffords of Vermont left the GOP to become an independent. The economy was slowing and the stock market experienced substantial losses. Such corporations as ENRON and Worldcom led a wave of corporate failures based on corrupt accounting.

September 11, 2001, and After

One issue, international terrorism, had not been of central concern to most Americans during the 1990s. A bombing of the World Trade Center in New York City in 1993 had not shaken the nation out of its indifference to the threat. Other attacks on American embassies in Africa in 1998 and a similar assault on the destroyer USS *Cole* in Yemen in October 2000 had not brought the issue home. The name of the leader of one terrorist group—Osama bin Laden—was largely unknown to the average citizen, even though bin Laden, a fundamentalist Muslim of Saudi Arabian origin, sought the violent end of American influence in the Middle East from his base in Afghanistan. Even a frightening report from a prestigious commission in February 2001 warning of a likely terrorist attack on American soil did little to disturb the lack of alertness that pervaded the government and the mass media.

On the morning of September 11, 2001, two hijacked jetliners slammed into the twin towers of the World Trade Center in New York City. Both buildings collapsed into flames and rubble, and almost three thousand people died. A third airliner crashed into the Pentagon leaving another 200 people dead. A fourth plane fell to the ground in rural Pennsylvania after the passengers attacked the hijackers. All air traffic was grounded for several days, consumer spending slumped, and the weakened economy slipped into recession.

This devastating attack on American soil, which was quickly linked to bin Laden and his terrorist network, Al Qaeda, rattled the nation's morale as it became clear that the terrorists sought nothing less than the destruction of the United States itself. President Bush promised "war on terrorism" and launched air strikes and ground troops into Afghanistan and its Taliban regime that harbored bin Laden. Soon the Taliban government had been toppled and Al Qaeda disrupted but American forces remained in Afghanistan into 2003.

The Bush administration targeted Saddam Hussein and his government in Iraq as the other focus of the antiterrorist effort. Preparations for war accelerated during 2002 while the White House sought diplomatic support for efforts to curb Hussein and the weapons of mass destruction he possessed. By the autumn of 2002, a United Nations resolution calling on Hussein to admit inspectors had been passed. Hussein said that his government would agree to the resolution, but his previous flouting of the inspections process made the United States suspicious. War with Iraq remained a strong possibility as the year ended.

The terrorist threat validated George W. Bush as a national leader, and his popularity rose. In the congressional elections of 2002 the Republicans, using a strong organization and ample campaign contributions, rode Bush's campaigning and the public confidence in his leadership to victory. Security issues affected the voters more than did the faltering economy and the Democratic emphasis on domestic problems. The GOP regained control of the Senate and widened its majority in the House. As 2003 began, the president and his party seemed poised to enact their conservative agenda. A taped message from Osama bin Laden in November 2002 warned of fresh attacks and more American deaths. Meanwhile, a confrontation with Iraq loomed. The war on terrorism seemed likely to continue for years to come.

By the middle of March 2003, the war with Iraq had begun. Dissatisfied with the work of the United Nations weapons inspectors, the United States had failed to obtain a second United Nations resolution authorizing force. The strong opposition of the international community to an American invasion of Iraq, combined with diplomatic setbacks by the

ICTURING THE PAST ✦ POLITICS & DIPLOMACY

GROUND ZERO AFTER THE ATTACK OF SEPTEMBER 11, 2001

© AFP/Corbis

The terrorist attack of September 11, 2001, left many enduring images of the pain that Americans felt when the World Trade Center towers were hit and then collapsed. The area where the debris from the two buildings came down was quickly named Ground Zero as crews worked tirelessly to remove the rubble and look for the remains of the dead. The devastation of the site itself, within the buildings of Lower Manhattan, confirmed the impact of this calamitous event. Yet plans for reconstruction of the area and work to remove the effects of the terrorist assault began almost at once as society rebounded. This concluding image for the Picturing the Past section thus speaks to the continuity of American history and the resilience of the American people in moments of trial and danger. In time this picture, like all the others that have been discussed in this phase of the textbook, will slip into the past and become an artifact of a vanished era. For the moment, with the pain of September 11 still fresh, it reveals the dangers and hope that the country faces as the twenty-first century begins.

Bush White House, left Washington frustrated. The Bush administration, along with its only major ally, Great Britain, decided that an attack on Saddam Hussein's brutal regime could not be delayed. Expectations were for a swift resolution of the fighting on the order of what had occurred during the ground war in the Gulf in 1991. Vice President Cheney said that "significant elements" of Hussein's military force were "likely to step aside" once war began. In this mood of confidence about victory, President Bush told the military "let's go" on March 19, 2003 and the war commenced.

Once launched, the power offensive of the America coalition swept through Iraq in a dramatic three-week campaign that left the United States in military control of the nation. Saddam Hussein was either dead or in hiding, the major officials of Iraq were captured, and the symbols of Hussein's rule had been destroyed. After a month, the hunt for weapons of mass destruction had not turned up any major finds, and Bush administration figures suggested that the process of locating such weapons might take additional time. Religious fervor swept some members of the Iraqi population who had not been able to express their true feelings for decades. What kind of government would emerge in Iraq remained unclear. In the United States the victory bolstered the foreign policy credentials of President Bush who declared the major combat phase of the war over on May 1, 2003.

President George W. Bush Responds to Terrorism

Following the terrorist attacks of September 11, 2001, President George W. Bush addressed a joint session of Congress on September 20. The well-received speech lifted President Bush in the polls and began a period of unprecedented, sustained popularity for the new chief executive. This excerpt from his speech focuses on Bush's explanation of what had happened to the United States, the role of the Muslim religion in the crisis, and what the stricken nation was prepared to do to win the war. In the immediate aftermath of the attacks, the issue of Iraq and Saddam Hussein, so important in the months to come, had not yet emerged as a central concern of foreign policy for the United States.

. . . On September the 11th, enemies of freedom committed an act of war against our country. Americans have known wars—but for the past 136 years, they have been wars on foreign soil, except for one Sunday in 1941. Americans have known the casualties of war—but not at the center of a great city on a peaceful morning. Americans have known surprise attacks—but never before on thousands of civilians. All of this was brought upon us in a single day—and night fell on a different world, a world where freedom itself is under attack.

Americans have many questions tonight. Americans are asking: Who attacked our country? The evidence we have gathered all points to a collection of loosely affiliated terrorist organizations known as al Qaeda. They are the same murderers indicted for bombing American embassies in Tanzania and Kenya, and responsible for bombing the USS *Cole*.

Al Qaeda is to terror what the mafia is to crime. But its goal is not making money; its goal is remaking the world—and imposing its radical beliefs on people everywhere.

The terrorists practice a fringe form of Islamic extremism that has been rejected by Muslim scholars and the vast majority of Muslim clerics—a fringe movement that perverts the peaceful teachings of Islam. The terrorists' directive commands them to kill Christians and Jews, to kill all Americans, and make no distinction among military and civilians, including women and children.

This group and its leader—a person named Osama bin Laden—are linked to many other organizations in different countries, including the Egyptian Islamic Jihad and the Islamic Movement of Uzbekistan. There are thousands of these terrorists in more than 60 countries. They are recruited from their own nations and neighborhoods and brought to camps in places like Afghanistan, where they are trained in the tactics of terror. They are sent back to their homes or sent to hide in countries around the world to plot evil and destruction.

The leadership of al Qaeda has great influence in Afghanistan and supports the Taliban regime in controlling most of that country. In Afghanistan, we see al Qaeda's vision for the world.

Afghanistan's people have been brutalized— many are starving and many have fled. Women are not allowed to attend school. You can be jailed for owning a television. Religion can be practiced only as their leaders dictate. A man can be jailed in Afghanistan if his beard is not long enough.

The United States respects the people of Afghanistan—after all, we are currently its largest source of humanitarian aid—but we condemn the Taliban regime. (Applause.) It is not only repressing its own people, it is threatening people everywhere by sponsoring and sheltering and supplying terrorists. By aiding and abetting murder, the Taliban regime is committing murder.

And tonight, the United States of America makes the following demands on the Taliban: Deliver to United States authorities all the leaders of al Qaeda who hide in your land. (Applause.) Release all foreign nationals, including American citizens, you have unjustly imprisoned. Protect foreign journalists, diplomats and aid workers in your country. Close immediately and permanently every terrorist training camp in Afghanistan, and hand over every terrorist, and every person in their support structure, to appropriate authorities. (Applause.) Give the United States full access to terrorist training camps, so we can make sure they are no longer operating.

These demands are not open to negotiation or discussion. (Applause.) The Taliban must act, and act immediately. They will hand over the terrorists, or they will share in their fate.

I also want to speak tonight directly to Muslims throughout the world. We respect your faith. It's practiced freely by many millions of Americans, and by millions more in countries that America counts as friends. Its teachings are good and peaceful, and those who commit evil in the name of Allah blaspheme the name of Allah. (Applause.) The terrorists are traitors to their own faith, trying, in effect, to hijack Islam itself. The enemy of America is not our many Muslim friends; it is not our many Arab friends. Our enemy is a radical network of terrorists, and every government that supports them. (Applause.)

Our war on terror begins with al Qaeda, but it does not end there. It will not end until every terrorist group of global reach has been found, stopped and defeated. (Applause.)

Americans are asking, why do they hate us? They hate what we see right here in this chamber—a democratically elected government. Their leaders are self-appointed. They hate our freedoms—our freedom of religion, our freedom of speech, our freedom to vote and assemble and disagree with each other.

They want to overthrow existing governments in many Muslim countries, such as Egypt, Saudi Arabia, and Jordan. They want to drive Israel out of the Middle East. They want to drive Christians and Jews out of vast regions of Asia and Africa.

These terrorists kill not merely to end lives, but to disrupt and end a way of life. With every atrocity, they hope that America grows fearful, retreating from the world and forsaking our friends. They stand against us, because we stand in their way.

We are not deceived by their pretenses to piety. We have seen their kind before. They are the heirs of all the murderous ideologies of the 20th century. By sacrificing human life to serve their radical visions—by abandoning every value except the will to power—they follow in the path of fascism, and Nazism, and totalitarianism. And they will follow that path all the way, to where it ends: in history's unmarked grave of discarded lies. (Applause.)

Americans are asking: How will we fight and win this war? We will direct every resource at our command—every means of diplomacy, every tool of intelligence, every instrument of law enforcement, every financial influence, and every necessary weapon of war—to the disruption and to the defeat of the global terror network.

This war will not be like the war against Iraq a decade ago, with a decisive liberation of territory and a swift conclusion. It will not look like the air war above Kosovo two years ago, where no ground troops were used and not a single American was lost in combat.

Our response involves far more than instant retaliation and isolated strikes. Americans should not expect one battle, but a lengthy campaign, unlike any other we have ever seen. It may include dramatic strikes, visible on TV, and covert operations, secret even in success. We will starve terrorists of funding, turn them one against another, drive them from place to place, until there is no refuge or no rest. And we will pursue nations that provide aid or safe haven to terrorism. Every nation, in every region, now has a decision to make. Either you are with us, or you are with the terrorists. (Applause.) From this day forward, any nation that continues to harbor or support terrorism will be regarded by the United States as a hostile regime . . .

Source Excerpt from *Address to a Joint Session of Congress and the American People*, accessed February 11, 2003, on the White House Web site: www.whitehouse.gov/news/releases/2001/09/print/20010920-8.html.

CONCLUSION

As the twenty-first century began in January 2001, the United States seemed to be an optimistic and confident society with a strong economy, declining crime rates, and a powerful international position. By the end of the year, the future seemed darker. The terrorist threat posed the likelihood of a long, expensive conflict that might change the openness of American society into a more disciplined and less free nation.

Whether the people of the United States fully grasped the danger that they faced remained in doubt.

Beyond the immediate menace of terrorism lay other concerns. The issue of race amid an increasingly diverse population was still unresolved with the potential to disrupt the social fabric. The exploitation of the environment threatened the degradation of the natural world and the resources on which prosperity depended. Within national politics, there were signs that the public's commitment to democratic values could be fraying. The United States had made a significant historical journey from the time when Europeans first appeared on the North American continent down to the age of the Internet. But the future course of the American Passage was an unfolding story in which the optimism of the nation's history would be a precious asset in the dangerous times that lay ahead for the people of the United States.

Recommended Readings

Benjamin, Daniel, and Simon, Steven. *The Age of Sacred Terror* (2002). An excellent look at the roots of terrorism and the American response during the 1990s.

Berman, William C. *From the Center to the Edge: The Politics & Policies of the Clinton Presidency* (2001). A brief, analytic look at Clinton's record in office.

Conason, Joe, and Lyons, Gene. *The Hunting of the President* (2000). Looks at the anti-Clinton campaign and its development.

Drew, Elizabeth. *On the Edge: The Clinton Presidency* (1994). Provides a reporter's analysis of Clinton's first year in power.

Drew, Elizabeth. *Showdown: The Struggle Between the Gingrich Congress and the Clinton White House* (1996). Continues Drew's account of the internal politics of the Clinton White House in the struggle with Newt Gingrich and the Republicans.

Halberstam, David. *War in a Time of Peace: Bush, Clinton, and the Generals* (2001). Examines the nation's involvement in the Balkans.

Minutaglio, Bill. *First Son: George W. Bush and the Bush Family Dynasty* (1999). Offers biographical background on the future president.

Toobin, Jeffrey. *Too Close to Call* (2001). Considers the events of the disputed presidential election of 2000 in Florida.

Walker, Martin. *The President We Deserve* (1996). A perceptive look at Clinton from a British perspective.

Woodward, Bob. *Bush's War* (2002). Provides an inside look at the early phase of the struggle against terrorism.

American Journey Online and InfoTrac College Edition

Visit the source collections at http://ajaccess.wadsworth.com and infotrac.thomsonlearning.com and use the Search function with the following key terms to explore documents, images, audio and video clips, articles, and commentary related to the material in this chapter.

Branch Davidians	Oklahoma City bombing
Dayton Peace Accords	Monica Lewinsky
Kenneth Starr	Contract with America
Million Man March	Whitewater investigation
September 11, 2001	War against terrorism

🌐 **Additional resources, exercises, and Internet links related to this chapter are available on the American Passages Web site: http://history.wadsworth.com/passages2e**

The Declaration of Independence
The Unanimous Declaration of the Thirteen United States of America

When in the Course of human events it becomes necessary for one people to dissolve the political bands which have connected them with another, and to assume among the Powers of the earth, the separate and equal station to which the Laws of Nature and of Nature's God entitle them, a decent respect to the opinions of mankind requires that they should declare the causes which impel them to the separation.

We hold these truths to be self-evident, that all men are created equal, that they are endowed by their Creator with certain unalienable Rights, that among these are Life, Liberty and the pursuit of Happiness. That to secure these rights, Governments are instituted among Men, deriving their just Powers from the consent of the governed. That whenever any Form of Government becomes destructive of these ends, it is the Right of the People to alter or to abolish it, and to institute new Government, laying its foundation on such principles and organizing its Powers in such form, as to them shall seem most likely to effect their Safety and Happiness. Prudence, indeed, will dictate that Governments long established should not be changed for light and transient causes; and accordingly all experience hath shewn, that mankind are more disposed to suffer, while evils are sufferable, than to right themselves by abolishing the forms to which they are accustomed. But when a long train of abuses and usurpations, pursuing invariably the same Object evinces a design to reduce them under absolute Despotism, it is their right, it is their duty, to throw off such Government, and to provide new Guards for their future security. Such has been the patient sufferance of these Colonies; and such is now the necessity which constrains them to alter their former Systems of Government. The history of the present King of Great Britain is a history of repeated injuries and usurpations, all having in direct object the establishment of an absolute Tyranny over these States. To prove this, let Facts be submitted to a candid world.

Text is reprinted from the facsimile of the engrossed copy in the National Archives. The original spelling, capitalization, and punctuation have been retained. Paragraphing has been added.

He has refused his Assent to Laws, the most wholesome and necessary for the public good.

He has forbidden his Governors to pass Laws of immediate and pressing importance, unless suspended in their operation till his Assent should be obtained; and when so suspended, he has utterly neglected to attend to them.

He has refused to pass other Laws for the accommodation of large districts of people, unless those people would relinquish the right of Representation in the Legislature, a right inestimable to them and formidable to tyrants only.

He has called together legislative bodies at places unusual, uncomfortable, and distant from the depository of their Public Records, for the sole Purpose of fatiguing them into compliance with his measures.

He has dissolved Representative Houses repeatedly, for opposing with manly firmness his invasions on the rights of the People.

He has refused for a long time, after such dissolutions, to cause others to be elected; whereby the Legislative Powers, incapable of Annihilation, have returned to the People at large for their exercise; the State remaining in the mean time exposed to all the dangers of invasion from without, and convulsions within.

He has endeavoured to prevent the Population of these States; for that purpose obstructing the Laws for Naturalization of Foreigners; refusing to pass others to encourage their migrations hither, and raising the conditions of new Appropriations of Lands.

He has obstructed the Administration of Justice, by refusing his Assent to Laws for establishing Judiciary Powers.

He has made Judges dependent on his Will alone, for the tenure of their offices, and the amount and payment of their salaries.

He has erected a multitude of New Offices, and sent hither swarms of Officers to harass our People, and eat out their substance.

He has kept among us, in times of peace, Standing Armies without the Consent of our legislatures.

He has affected to render the Military independent of and superior to the Civil Power.

He has combined with others to subject us to a jurisdiction foreign to our constitution, and unacknowledged by our laws; giving his Assent to their Acts of pretended Legislation:

For Quartering large bodies of armed troops among us:

For protecting them, by a mock Trial, from Punishment for any Murders which they should commit on the Inhabitants of these States:

For cutting off our Trade with all parts of the world:

For imposing Taxes on us without our Consent:

For depriving us in many cases, of the benefits of Trial by Jury:

For transporting us beyond Seas to be tried for pretended offences:

For abolishing the free System of English Laws in a neighbouring Province, establishing therein an Arbitrary government, and enlarging its Boundaries so as to render it at once an example and fit instrument for introducing the same absolute rule into these Colonies:

For taking away our Charters, abolishing our most valuable Laws, and altering fundamentally the Forms of our Governments:

For suspending our own Legislatures, and declaring themselves invested with Power to legislate for us in all cases whatsoever.

He has abdicated Government here, by declaring us out of his Protection, and waging War against us.

He has plundered our seas, ravaged our Coasts, burnt our towns, and destroyed the lives of our people.

He is at this time transporting large Armies of foreign Mercenaries to compleat the works of death, desolation and tyranny, already begun with circumstances of Cruelty and perfidy scarcely paralleled in the most barbarous ages, and totally unworthy the Head of a civilized nation.

He has constrained our fellow Citizens taken Captive on the high Seas to bear Arms against their Country, to become the executioners of their friends and Brethren, or to fall themselves by their Hands.

He has excited domestic insurrections amongst us, and has endeavoured to bring on the inhabitants of our frontiers, the merciless Indian Savages, whose known rule of warfare, is an undistinguished destruction of all ages, sexes and conditions.

In every stage of these Oppressions We have Petitioned for Redress in the most humble terms: Our repeated Petitions have been answered only by repeated injury. A Prince, whose character is thus marked by every act which may define a Tyrant, is unfit to be the ruler of a free People.

Nor have We been wanting in attentions to our British brethren. We have warned them from time to time of attempts by their legislature to extend an unwarrantable jurisdiction over us. We have reminded them of the circumstances of our emigration and settlement here. We have appealed to their native justice and magnanimity, and we have conjured them by the ties of our common kindred to disavow thee usurpations, which, would inevitably interrupt our connections and correspondence. They too have been deaf to the voice of justice and of consanguinity. We must, therefore, acquiesce in the necessity, which denounces our Separation, and hold them, as we hold the rest of mankind, Enemies in War, in Peace Friends.

WE, THEREFORE, the Representatives of the UNITED STATES OF AMERICA, in General Congress, Assembled, appealing to the Supreme Judge of the world for the rectitude of our intentions, do, in the Name, and by Authority of the good People of these Colonies, solemnly publish and declare, That these United Colonies are, and of Right ought to be FREE AND INDEPENDENT STATES; that they are Absolved from all Allegiance to the British Crown, and that all political connection between them and the State of Great Britain, is and ought to be totally dissolved; and that, as Free and Independent States, they have full Power to levy War, conclude Peace, contract Alliances, establish Commerce, and to do all other Acts and Things which Independent States may of right do. And for the support of this Declaration, with a firm reliance on the protection of divine Providence, we mutually pledge to each other our Lives, our Fortunes and our sacred Honor.

The Constitution of the United States of America

We the People of the United States, in Order to form a more perfect Union, establish Justice, insure domestic Tranquility, provide for the common defence, promote the general Welfare, and secure the Blessings of Liberty to ourselves and our Posterity, do ordain and establish this Constitution for the United States of America.

ARTICLE I.

Section 1. All legislative Powers herein granted shall be vested in a Congress of the United States, which shall consist of a Senate and House of Representatives.

Section 2. The House of Representatives shall be composed of Members chosen every second Year by the People of the several States, and the Electors in each State shall have the Qualifications requisite for Electors of the most numerous Branch of the State Legislature.

No Person shall be a Representative who shall not have attained to the Age of twenty five Years, and been seven Years a Citizen of the United States, and who shall not, when elected, be an Inhabitant of that State in which he shall be chosen.

Representatives and direct Taxes[1] shall be apportioned among the several States which may be included within this Union, according to their respective Numbers, which shall be determined by adding to the whole Number of free Persons, including those bound to Service for a Term of Years, and excluding Indians not taxed, three fifths of all other Persons.[2] The actual Enumeration shall be made within three Years after the first Meeting of the Congress of the United States, and within every subsequent Term of ten Years, in such Manner as they shall by Law direct. The Number of Representatives shall not exceed one for every thirty Thousand, but each State shall have at Least one Representative; and until such enumeration shall be made, the State of New Hampshire shall be entitled to chuse three; Massachusetts eight; Rhode Island and Providence Plantations one; Connecticut five; New York six; New Jersey four; Pennsylvania eight; Delaware one; Maryland six; Virginia ten; North Carolina five; South Carolina five; and Georgia three.

When vacancies happen in the Representation from any State, the Executive Authority thereof shall issue Writs of Election to fill such Vacancies.

The House of Representatives shall chuse their Speaker and other Officers; and shall have the sole Power of Impeachment.

Section 3. The Senate of the United States shall be composed of two Senators from each State, chosen by the Legislature thereof, for six Years; and each Senator shall have one Vote.[3]

Immediately after they shall be assembled in Consequence of the first Election, they shall be divided as equally as may be into three Classes. The Seats of the Senators of the first Class shall be vacated at the Expiration of the second Year, of the second Class at the Expiration of the fourth Year, and of the third Class at the Expiration of the sixth Year, so that one third may be chosen every second Year; and if Vacancies happen by Resignation, or otherwise, during the Recess of the Legislature of any State, the Executive thereof may make temporary Appointments until the next Meeting of the Legislature, which shall then fill such Vacancies.[4]

No Person shall be a Senator who shall not have attained to the Age of thirty Years, and been nine Years a Citizen of the United States, and who shall not, when elected, be an Inhabitant of that State for which he shall be chosen.

The Vice President of the United States shall be President of the Senate, but shall have no Vote, unless they be equally divided.

The Senate shall chuse their other Officers, and also a President pro tempore, in the Absence of the Vice President, or when he shall exercise the Office of President of the United States.

The Senate shall have the sole Power to try all Impeachments. When sitting for that Purpose, they shall be on Oath or Affirmation. When the President of the United States is tried, the Chief Justice shall preside: And no Person shall be convicted without the Concurrence of two thirds of the Members present.

Judgment in Cases of Impeachment shall not extend further than to removal from Office, and disqualification to hold and enjoy any Office of honor, Trust or Profit under the United States: but the Party convicted shall nevertheless be liable and subject to Indictment, Trial, Judgment and Punishment, according to Law.

Text is from the engrossed copy in the National Archives. Original spelling, capitalization, and punctuation have been retained.

[1]Modified by the Sixteenth Amendment.

[2]Replaced by the Fourteenth Amendment.

[3]Superseded by the Seventeenth Amendment.

[4]Modified by the Seventeenth Amendment.

Section 4. The Times, Places and Manner of holding Elections for Senators and Representatives, shall be prescribed in each State by the Legislature thereof, but the Congress may at any time by Law make or alter such Regulation, except as to the Places of chusing Senators.

The Congress shall assemble at least once in every Year, and such Meeting shall be on the first Monday in December, unless they shall by Law appoint a different Day.[5]

Section 5. Each House shall be the Judge of the Elections, Returns and Qualifications of its own Members, and a Majority of each shall constitute a Quorum to do Business; but a smaller Number may adjourn from day to day, and may be authorized to compel the Attendance of absent Members, in such Manner, and under such Penalties as each House may provide.

Each House may determine the Rules of its Proceedings, punish its Members for disorderly Behaviour, and, with the Concurrence of two thirds, expel a Member.

Each House shall keep a Journal of its Proceedings, and from time to time publish the same, excepting such Parts as may in their Judgment require Secrecy; and the Yeas and Nays of the Members of either House on any question shall, at the Desire of one fifth of those Present, be entered on the Journal.

Neither House, during the Session of Congress, shall, without the Consent of the other, adjourn for more than three days, nor to any other Place than that in which the two Houses shall be sitting.

Section 6. The Senators and Representatives shall receive a Compensation for their Services, to be ascertained by Law, and paid out of the Treasury of the United States. They shall in all Cases, except Treason, Felony and Breach of the Peace, be privileged from Arrest during their Attendance at the Session of their respective Houses, and in going to and returning from the same; and for any Speech or Debate in either House, they shall not be questioned in any other Place.

No Senator or Representative shall, during the Time for which he was elected, be appointed to any civil Office under the Authority of the United States, which shall have been created, or the Emoluments whereof shall have been encreased during such time; and no Person holding any Office under the United States, shall be a Member of either House during his Continuance in Office.

Section 7. All Bills for raising Revenue shall originate in the House of Representatives; but the

Senate may propose or concur with Amendments as on other Bills.

Every Bill which shall have passed the House of Representatives and the Senate shall, before it become a Law, be presented to the President of the United States; If he approve he shall sign it, but if not he shall return it, with his Objections to that House in which it shall have originated, who shall enter the Objections at large on their Journal, and proceed to reconsider it. If after such Reconsideration two thirds of that House shall agree to pass the Bill, it shall be sent, together with the Objections, to the other House, by which it shall likewise be reconsidered, and if approved by two thirds of that House, it shall become a Law. But in all such Cases the Votes of both Houses shall be determined by yeas and Nays, and the Names of the Persons voting for and against the Bill shall be entered on the Journal of each House respectively. If any Bill shall not be returned by the President within ten Days (Sundays excepted) after it shall have been presented to him, the Same shall be a Law, in like Manner as if he had signed it, unless the Congress by their Adjournment prevent its Return, in which Case it shall not be a Law.

Every Order, Resolution, or Vote to which the Concurrence of the Senate and House of Representatives may be necessary (except on a question of Adjournment) shall be presented to the President of the United States; and before the Same shall take Effect, shall be approved by him, or being disapproved by him shall be repassed by two thirds of the Senate and House of Representatives, according to the Rules and Limitations prescribed in the Case of a Bill.

Section 8. The Congress shall have power To lay and collect Taxes, Duties, Imposts and Excises, to pay the Debts and provide for the common Defence and general Welfare of the United States; but all Duties, Imposts and Excises shall be uniform throughout the United States;

To borrow Money on the credit of the United States;

To regulate Commerce with foreign Nations, and among the several States, and with the Indian Tribes;

To establish an uniform Rule of Naturalization, and uniform Laws on the subject of Bankruptcies throughout the United States;

To coin Money, regulate the Value thereof, and of foreign Coin, and fix the Standard of Weights and Measures;

To provide for the Punishment of counterfeiting the Securities and current Coin of the United States;

To establish Post Offices and post Roads;

[5]Superseded by the Twentieth Amendment.

To promote the Progress of Science and useful Arts, by securing for limited Times to Authors and Inventors the exclusive Right to their respective Writings and Discoveries;

To constitute Tribunals inferior to the supreme Court;

To define and punish Piracies and Felonies committed on the high Seas, and Offences against the Law of Nations;

To declare War, grant Letters of Marque and Reprisal, and make Rules concerning Captures on Land and Water;

To raise and support Armies, but no Appropriation of Money to that Use shall be for a longer Term than two Years;

To provide and maintain a Navy;

To make Rules for the Government and Regulation of the land and naval Forces;

To provide for calling forth the Militia to execute the Laws of the Union, suppress Insurrections and repel Invasions;

To provide for organizing, arming, and disciplining, the Militia, and for governing such Part of them as may be employed in the Service of the United States, reserving to the States respectively, the Appointment of the Officers, and the Authority of training the Militia according to the discipline prescribed by Congress;

To exercise exclusive Legislation in all Cases whatsoever, over such District (not exceeding ten Miles square) as may, by Cession of particular States, and the Acceptance of Congress, become the Seat of the Government of the United States, and to exercise like Authority over all Places purchased by the Consent of the Legislature of the State in which the Same shall be, for the Erection of Forts, Magazines, Arsenals, dock-Yards, and other needful Buildings;—And

To make all Laws which shall be necessary and proper for carrying into Execution the foregoing Powers, and all other Powers vested by this Constitution in the Government of the United States, or in any Department or Officer thereof.

Section 9. The Migration or Importation of such Persons as any of the States now existing think proper to admit, shall not be prohibited by the Congress prior to the Year one thousand eight hundred and eight, but a Tax or duty may be imposed on such Importation, not exceeding ten dollars for each Person.

The Privilege of the Writ of Habeas Corpus shall not be suspended, unless when in Cases of Rebellion or Invasion the public Safety may require it.

No Bill of Attainder or ex post facto Law shall be passed.

No Capitation, or other direct, Tax shall be laid, unless in Proportion to the Census or Enumeration herein before directed to be taken.

No Tax or Duty shall be laid on Articles exported from any State.

No Preference shall be given by any Regulation of Commerce or Revenue to the Ports of one State over those of another: nor shall Vessels bound to, or from, one State, be obliged to enter, clear, or pay Duties in another.

No Money shall be drawn from the Treasury, but in Consequence of Appropriations made by Law, and a regular Statement and Account of the Receipts and Expenditures of all public Money shall be published from time to time.

No Title of Nobility shall be granted by the United States: And no Person holding any Office of Profit or Trust under them, shall, without the Consent of the Congress, accept of any present, Emolument, Office, or Title, of any kind whatever, from any King, Prince, or foreign State.

Section 10. No State shall enter into any Treaty, Alliance, or Confederation; grant Letters of Marque and Reprisal; coin Money; emit Bills of Credit; make any Thing but gold and silver Coin a Tender in Payment of Debts; pass any Bill of Attainder, ex post facto Law, or Law impairing the Obligation of Contracts, or grant any Title of Nobility.

No State shall, without the Consent of the Congress, lay any Imposts or Duties on Imports or Exports, except what may be absolutely necessary for executing its inspection Laws: and the net Produce of all Duties and Imposts, laid by any State on Imports or Exports, shall be for the Use of the Treasury of the United States; and all such Laws shall be subject to the Revision and Controul of the Congress.

No State shall, without the Consent of Congress, lay any Duty of Tonnage, keep Troops, or Ships of War in time of Peace, enter into any Agreement or Compact with another State, or with a foreign Power, or engage in War, unless actually invaded, or in such imminent Danger as will not admit of delay.

ARTICLE II.

Section 1. The executive Power shall be vested in a President of the United States of America. He shall hold his Office during the Term of four Years, and, together with the Vice President, chosen for the same Term, be elected, as follows:

Each State shall appoint, in such Manner as the Legislature thereof may direct, a Number of Electors, equal to the whole Number of Senators and

Representatives to which the State may be entitled in the Congress: but no Senator or Representative, or Person holding an Office of Trust or Profit under the United States, shall be appointed an Elector.

The Electors shall meet in their respective States, and vote by Ballot for two Persons, of whom one at least shall not be an Inhabitant of the same State with themselves. And they shall make a List of all the Persons voted for, and of the Number of Votes for each; which List they shall sign and certify, and transmit sealed to the Seat of the Government of the United States, directed to the President of the Senate. The President of the Senate shall, in the Presence of the Senate and House of Representatives, open all the Certificates, and the Votes shall then be counted. The Person having the greatest Number of Votes shall be the President, if such Number be a Majority of the whole Number of Electors appointed; and if there be more than one who have such Majority, and have an equal Number of Votes, then the House of Representatives shall immediately chuse by Ballot one of them for President; and if no Person have a Majority, then from the five highest on the List the said House shall in like Manner chuse the President. But in chusing the President, the Votes shall be taken by States, the Representation from each State having one Vote; A quorum for this Purpose shall consist of a Member or Members from two thirds of the States, and a Majority of all the States shall be necessary to a Choice. In every Case, after the Choice of the President, the Person having the greatest Number of Votes of the Electors shall be the Vice President. But if there should remain two or more who have equal Votes, the Senate shall chuse from them by Ballot the Vice President.[6]

The Congress may determine the Time of chusing the Electors, and the Day on which they shall give their Votes; which Day shall be the same throughout the United States.

No Person except a natural born Citizen, or a Citizen of the United States, at the time of the Adoption of this Constitution, shall be eligible to the Office of President, neither shall any Person be eligible to that Office who shall not have attained to the Age of thirty five Years, and been fourteen Years a Resident within the United States.

In Case of the Removal of the President from Office, or of his Death, Resignation, or Inability to discharge the Powers and Duties of the said Office, the Same shall devolve on the Vice President, and the Congress may by Law provide for the Case of

Removal, Death, Resignation or Inability, both of the President and Vice President, declaring what Officer shall then act as President, and such Officer shall act accordingly, until the Disability be removed, or a President shall be elected.[7]

The President shall, at stated Times, receive for his Services, a Compensation, which shall neither be encreased nor diminished during the Period for which he shall have been elected, and he shall not receive within that Period any other Emolument from the United States, or any of them.

Before he enter on the Execution of his Office, he shall take the following Oath or Affirmation:—"I do solemnly swear (or affirm) that I will faithfully execute the Office of President of the United States, and will to the best of my Ability, preserve, protect and defend the Constitution of the United States."

Section 2. The President shall be Commander in Chief of the Army and Navy of the United States, and of the Militia of the several States, when called into the actual Service of the United States; he may require the Opinion, in writing, of the principal Officer in each of the executive Departments, upon any Subject relating to the Duties of their respective Offices, and he shall have Power to grant Reprieves and Pardons for Offences against the United States, except in Cases of Impeachment.

He shall have Power, by and with the Advice and Consent of the Senate, to make Treaties, provided two thirds of the Senators present concur; and he shall nominate, and by and with the Advice and Consent of the Senate, shall appoint Ambassadors, other public Ministers and Consuls, Judges of the supreme Court, and all other Officers of the United States, whose Appointments are not herein otherwise provided for, and which shall be established by Law; but the Congress may by Law vest the Appointment of such inferior Officers, as they think proper, in the President alone, in the Courts of Law, or in the Heads of Departments.

The President shall have Power to fill up all Vacancies that may happen during the Recess of the Senate, by granting Commissions which shall expire at the End of their next Session.

Section 3. He shall from time to time give the Congress Information of the State of the Union, and recommend to their Consideration such Measures as he shall judge necessary and expedient; he may, on extraordinary Occasions, convene both Houses, or either of them, and in Case of Disagreement between them, with Respect to the Time of Adjournment, he

---

[6]Superseded by the Twelfth Amendment.

[7]Modified by the Twenty-fifth Amendment.

may adjourn them to such Time as he shall think proper; he shall receive Ambassadors and other public Ministers; he shall take Care that the Laws be faithfully executed, and shall Commission all the Officers of the United States.

Section 4. The President, Vice President and all civil Officers of the United States, shall be removed from Office on Impeachment for, and Conviction of, Treason, Bribery, or other high Crimes and Misdemeanors.

ARTICLE III.

Section 1. The judicial Power of the United States, shall be vested in one supreme Court, and in such inferior Courts as the Congress may from time to time ordain and establish. The Judges, both of the supreme and inferior Courts, shall hold their Offices during good Behaviour, and shall, at stated Times, receive for their Services, a Compensation, which shall not be diminished during their Continuance in Office.

Section 2. The judicial Power shall extend to all Cases, in Law and Equity, arising under this Constitution, the Laws of the United States, and Treaties made, or which shall be made, under their Authority;—to all Cases affecting Ambassadors, other public Ministers and Consuls;—to all Cases of admiralty and maritime Jurisdiction;—to Controversies to which the United States shall be a Party;—to Controversies between two or more States;—between a State and Citizens of another State;[8]—between Citizens of different States,—between Citizens of the same State claiming Lands under Grants of different States, and between a State, or the Citizens thereof, and foreign States, Citizens or Subjects.

In all Cases affecting Ambassadors, other public Ministers and Consuls, and those in which a State shall be Party, the supreme Court shall have original Jurisdiction. In all the other Cases before mentioned, the supreme Court shall have appellate Jurisdiction, both as to Law and Fact, with such Exceptions, and under such Regulations as the Congress shall make.

The Trial of all Crimes, except in Cases of Impeachment, shall be by Jury; and such Trial shall be held in the State where the said Crimes shall have been committed; but when not committed within any State, the Trial shall be at such Place or Places as the Congress may by Law have directed.

Section 3. Treason against the United States, shall consist only in levying War against them, or in adhering to their Enemies, giving them Aid and Comfort. No Person shall be convicted of Treason unless on the Testimony of two Witnesses to the same overt Act, or on Confession in open Court.

The Congress shall have Power to declare the Punishment of Treason, but no Attainder of Treason shall work Corruption of Blood, or Forfeiture except during the Life of the Person attainted.

ARTICLE IV.

Section 1. Full Faith and Credit shall be given in each State to the public Acts, Records, and judicial Proceedings of every other State. And the Congress may by general Laws prescribe the Manner in which such Acts, Records and Proceedings shall be proved, and the Effect thereof.

Section 2. The Citizens of each State shall be entitled to all Privileges and Immunities of Citizens in the several States.

A Person charged in any State with Treason, Felony, or other Crime, who shall flee from Justice, and be found in another State, shall on Demand of the executive Authority of the State from which he fled, be delivered up, to be removed to the State having Jurisdiction of the Crime.

No Person held to Service or Labour in one State, under the Laws thereof, escaping into another, shall, in Consequence of any Law or Regulation therein, be discharged from such Service or Labour, but shall be delivered up on Claim of the Party to whom such Service or Labour may be due.

Section 3. New States may be admitted by the Congress into this Union; but no new State shall be formed or erected within the Jurisdiction of any other State, nor any State be formed by the Junction of two or more States, or Parts of States, without the Consent of the Legislatures of the States concerned as well as of the Congress.

The Congress shall have Power to dispose of and make all needful Rules and Regulations respecting the Territory or other Property belonging to the United States; and nothing in this Constitution shall be so construed as to Prejudice any Claims of the United States, or of any particular State.

Section 4. The United States shall guarantee to every State in this Union a Republican Form of Government, and shall protect each of them against Invasion; and on Application of the Legislature, or of the Executive (when the Legislature cannot be convened) against domestic Violence.

ARTICLE V.

The Congress, whenever two thirds of both Houses shall deem it necessary, shall propose Amendments to this Constitution, or, on the Application of the

[8]Modified by the Eleventh Amendment.

Legislatures of two thirds of the several States, shall call a Convention for proposing Amendments, which, in either Case, shall be valid to all Intents and Purposes, as Part of this Constitution, when ratified by the Legislatures of three fourths of the several States, or by Conventions in three fourths thereof, as the one or the other Mode of Ratification may be proposed by the Congress; Provided that no Amendment which may be made prior to the Year One thousand eight hundred and eight shall in any Manner affect the first and fourth Clauses in the Ninth Section of the first Article; and that no State, without its Consent, shall be deprived of its equal Suffrage in the Senate.

ARTICLE VI.

All Debts contracted and Engagements entered into, before the Adoption of this Constitution, shall be as valid against the United States under this Constitution, as under the Confederation.

This Constitution, and the Laws of the United States which shall be made in Pursuance thereof; and all Treaties made, or which shall be made, under the Authority of the United States, shall be the supreme Law of the Land; and the Judges in every State shall be bound thereby, any Thing in the Constitution or Laws of any State to the Contrary notwithstanding.

The Senators and Representatives before mentioned, and the Members of the several State Legislatures, and all executive and judicial Officers, both of the United States and of the several States, shall be bound by Oath or Affirmation, to support this Constitution; but no religious Test shall ever be required as a Qualification to any Office or public Trust under the United States.

ARTICLE VII.

The Ratification of the Conventions of nine States, shall be sufficient for the Establishment of this Constitution between the States so ratifying the Same.

Done in Convention by the Unanimous Consent of the States present the Seventeenth Day of September in the Year of our Lord one thousand seven hundred and Eighty seven and of the Independence of the United States of America the Twelfth. In witness whereof We have hereunto subscribed our Names,

Articles in Addition to, and Amendment of, the Constitution of the United States of America, Proposed by Congress, and Ratified by the Legislatures of the Several States, Pursuant to the Fifth Article of the Original Constitution.

AMENDMENT I[9]

Congress shall make no law respecting an establishment of religion, or prohibiting the free exercise there-of; or abridging the freedom of speech, or of the press; or the right of the people peaceably to assemble, and to petition the Government for a redress of grievances.

AMENDMENT II

A well regulated Militia, being necessary to the security of a free State, the right of the people to keep and bear Arms shall not be infringed.

AMENDMENT III

No Soldier shall, in time of peace, be quartered in any house, without the consent of the Owner, nor in time of war, but in a manner to be prescribed by law.

AMENDMENT IV

The right of the people to be secure in their persons, houses, papers, and effects, against unreasonable searches and seizures, shall not be violated, and no Warrants shall issue, but upon probable cause, supported by Oath or affirmation, and particularly describing the place to be searched, and the persons or things to be seized.

AMENDMENT V

No person shall be held to answer for a capital or otherwise infamous crime, unless on a presentment or indictment of a Grand Jury, except in cases arising in the land or naval forces, or in the Militia, when in actual service in time of War or public danger; nor shall any person be subject for the same offence to be twice put in jeopardy of life or limb; nor shall be compelled in any criminal case to be a witness against himself, nor be deprived of life, liberty, or property, without due process of law; nor shall private property be taken for public use, without just compensation.

AMENDMENT VI

In all criminal prosecutions, the accused shall enjoy the right to a speedy and public trial, by an impartial jury of the State and district wherein the crime shall have been committed, which district shall have been previously ascertained by law, and to be informed of the nature and cause of the accusation; to be confronted with the witnesses against him; to have compulsory process for obtaining witnesses in his favor, and to have the Assistance of Counsel for his defence.

[9]The first ten amendments were passed by Congress September 25, 1789. They were ratified by three-fourths of the states December 15, 1791.

AMENDMENT VII

In suits at common law, where the value in controversy shall exceed twenty dollars, the right of trial by jury shall be preserved, and no fact tried by a jury, shall be otherwise reexamined in any Court of the United States, than according to the rules of the common law.

AMENDMENT VIII

Excessive bail shall not be required, nor excessive fines imposed, nor cruel and unusual punishments inflicted.

AMENDMENT IX

The enumeration in the Constitution, of certain rights, shall not be construed to deny or disparage others retained by the people.

AMENDMENT X

The powers not delegated to the United States by the Constitution; nor prohibited by it to the States, are reserved to the States respectively, or to the people.

AMENDMENT XI[10]

The Judicial power of the United States shall not be construed to extend to any suit in law or equity, commenced or prosecuted against one of the United States by Citizens of another State, or by Citizens or Subjects of any Foreign State.

AMENDMENT XII[11]

The Electors shall meet in their respective States and vote by ballot for President and Vice-President, one of whom, at least, shall not be an inhabitant of the same State with themselves; they shall name in their ballots the person voted for as President, and in distinct ballots the person voted for as Vice-President, and they shall make distinct lists of all persons voted for as President, and of all persons voted for as Vice-President, and of the number of votes for each, which lists they shall sign and certify, and transmit sealed to the seat of the government of the United States, directed to the President of the Senate;—The President of the Senate shall, in the presence of the Senate and House of Representatives, open all the certificates and the votes shall then be counted;—The person having the greatest number of votes for President, shall be the President, if such number be a majority of the whole number of Electors appointed; and if no person have such majority, then from the persons having the highest numbers not exceeding three on the list of those voted for as President, the House of Representatives shall choose immediately, by ballot,

the President. But in choosing the President, the votes shall be taken by states, the representation from each state having one vote; a quorum for this purpose shall consist of a member or members from two-thirds of the states, and a majority of all the states shall be necessary to a choice. And if the House of Representatives shall not choose a President whenever the right of choice shall devolve upon them, before the fourth day of March next following, then the Vice-President shall act as President, as in the case of the death or other constitutional disability of the President.—The person having the greatest number of votes as Vice-President, shall be the Vice-President, if such number be a majority of the whole number of Electors appointed, and if no person have a majority, then from the two highest numbers on the list, the Senate shall choose the Vice-President; a quorum for the purpose shall consist of two-thirds of the whole number of Senators, and a majority of the whole number shall be necessary to a choice. But no person constitutionally ineligible to the office of President shall be eligible to that of Vice-President of the United States.

AMENDMENT XIII[12]

Section 1. Neither slavery nor involuntary servitude, except as a punishment for crime whereof the party shall have been duly convicted, shall exist within the United States, or any place subject to their jurisdiction.

Section 2. Congress shall have power to enforce this article by appropriate legislation.

AMENDMENT XIV[13]

Section 1. All persons born or naturalized in the United States, and subject to the jurisdiction thereof, are citizens of the United States and of the State wherein they reside. No State shall make or enforce any law which shall abridge the privileges or immunities of citizens of the United States; nor shall any State deprive any person of life, liberty, or property, without due process of law; nor deny to any person within its jurisdiction the equal protection of the laws.

Section 2. Representatives shall be apportioned among the several States according to their respective numbers, counting the whole number of persons in each State, excluding Indians not taxed. But when the right to vote at any election for the choice of electors for President and Vice-President of the United States, Representatives in Congress, the Executive and Judicial officers of a State, or the

---

[10]Passed March 4, 1794. Ratified January 23, 1795.

[11]Passed December 9, 1803. Ratified June 15, 1804.

[12]Passed January 31, 1865. Ratified December 6, 1865.

[13]Passed June 13, 1866. Ratified July 9, 1868.

members of the Legislature thereof, is denied to any of the male inhabitants of such State, being twenty-one years of age, and citizens of the United States, or in any way abridged, except for participation in rebellion, or other crime, the basis of representation therein shall be reduced in the proportion which the number of such male citizens shall bear to the whole number of male citizens twenty-one years of age in such State.

Section 3. No person shall be a Senator or Representative in Congress, or elector of President and Vice-President, or hold any office, civil or military, under the United States, or under any State, who, having previously taken an oath, as a member of Congress, or as an officer of the United States, or as a member of any State legislature, or as an executive or judicial officer of any State, to support the Constitution of the United States, shall have engaged in insurrection or rebellion against the same, or given aid or comfort to the enemies thereof. But Congress may by a vote of two-thirds of each House, remove such disability.

Section 4. The validity of the public debt of the United States, authorized by law, including debts incurred for payment of pensions and bounties for services in suppressing insurrection or rebellion, shall not be questioned. But neither the United States nor any State shall assume or pay any debt or obligation incurred in aid of insurrection or rebellion against the United States, or any claim for the loss or emancipation of any slave; but all such debts, obligations, and claims shall be held illegal and void.

Section 5. The Congress shall have the power to enforce, by appropriate legislation, the provisions of this article.

AMENDMENT XV[14]

Section 1. The right of citizens of the United States to vote shall not be denied or abridged by the United States or by any State on account of race, color, or previous conditions of servitude—

Section 2. The Congress shall have power to enforce this article by appropriate legislation.

AMENDMENT XVI

The Congress shall have power to lay and collect taxes on incomes, from whatever source derived, without apportionment among the several States, and without regard to any census or enumeration.

AMENDMENT XVII[15]

The Senate of the United States shall be composed of two Senators from each State, elected by the people

thereof, for six years; and each Senator shall have one vote. The electors in each State shall have the qualifications requisite for electors of the most numerous branch of the State legislatures.

When vacancies happen in the representation of any State in the Senate, the executive authority of such State shall issue writs of election to fill such vacancies: *Provided,* That the legislature of any State may empower the executive thereof to make temporary appointments until the people fill the vacancies by election as the legislature may direct.

This amendment shall not be so construed as to affect the election or term of any Senator chosen before it becomes valid as part of the Constitution.

AMENDMENT XVIII[16]

Section 1. After one year from the ratification of this article the manufacture, sale, or transportation of intoxicating liquors within, the importation thereof into, or the exportation thereof from the United States and all territory subject to the jurisdiction thereof for beverage purposes is hereby prohibited.

Section 2. The Congress and the several States shall have concurrent power to enforce this article by appropriate legislation.

Section 3. This article shall be inoperative unless it shall have been ratified as an amendment to the Constitution by the legislatures of the several States, as provided in the Constitution, within seven years from the date of the submission hereof to the States by the Congress.

AMENDMENT XIX[17]

The right of citizens of the United States to vote shall not be denied or abridged by the United States or by any State on account of sex.

Congress shall have power to enforce this article by appropriate legislation.

AMENDMENT XX[18]

Section 1. The terms of the President and Vice-President shall end at noon on the 20th day of January, and the terms of Senators and Representatives at noon on the 3d day of January, of the years in which such terms would have ended if this article had not been ratified; and the terms of their successors shall then begin.

Section 2. The Congress shall assemble at least once in every year, and such meeting shall begin

---

[14]Passed February 26, 1869. Ratified February 2, 1870.

[15]Passed May 13, 1912. Ratified April 8, 1913.

[16]Passed December 18, 1917. Ratified January 16, 1919.

[17]Passed June 4, 1919. Ratified August 18, 1920.

[18]Passed March 2, 1932. Ratified January 23, 1933.

at noon on the 3d day of January, unless they shall by law appoint a different day.

Section 3. If, at the time fixed for the beginning of the term of the President, the President elect shall have died, the Vice-President elect shall become President. If a President shall not have been chosen before the time fixed for the beginning of his term, or if the President elect shall have failed to qualify, then the Vice-President elect shall act as President until a President shall have qualified; and the Congress may by law provide for the case wherein neither a President elect nor a Vice-President elect shall have qualified, declaring who shall then act as President, or the manner in which one who is to act shall be selected, and such person shall act accordingly until a President or Vice-President shall have qualified.

Section 4. The Congress may by law provide for the case of the death of any of the persons from whom the House of Representatives may choose a President whenever the right of choice shall have devolved upon them, and for the case of the death of any of the persons from whom the Senate may choose a Vice-President whenever the right of choice shall have devolved upon them.

Section 5. Sections 1 and 2 shall take effect on the 15th day of October following the ratification of this article.

Section 6. This article shall be inoperative unless it shall have been ratified as an amendment to the Constitution by the legislatures of three-fourths of the several States within seven years from the date of its submission.

AMENDMENT XXI[19]

Section 1. The eighteenth article of amendment to the Constitution of the United States is hereby repealed.

Section 2. The transportation or importation into any State, Territory, or possession of the United States for delivery or use therein of intoxicating liquors, in violation of the laws thereof, is hereby prohibited.

Section 3. This article shall be inoperative unless it shall have been ratified as an amendment to the Constitution by conventions in the several States, as provided in the Constitution, within seven years from the date of the submission hereof to the States by the Congress.

AMENDMENT XXII[20]

No person shall be elected to the office of the President more than twice, and no person who has held the office of President, or acted as President, for more than two years of a term to which some other person was elected President shall be elected to the office of the President more than once.

But this Article shall not apply to any person holding the office of President when this Article was proposed by the Congress, and shall not prevent any person who may be holding the office of President, or acting as President, during the term within which this Article becomes operative from holding the office of President or acting as President during the remainder of such term.

AMENDMENT XXIII[21]

Section 1. The District constituting the seat of Government of the United States shall appoint in such manner as the Congress may direct:

A number of electors of President and Vice President equal to the whole number of Senators and Representatives in Congress to which the District would be entitled if it were a State, but in no event more than the least populous State; they shall be in addition to those appointed by the States, but they shall be considered, for the purposes of the election of President and Vice President, to be electors appointed by the State; and they shall meet in the District and perform such duties as provided by the twelfth article of amendment.

Section 2. The Congress shall have power to enforce this article by appropriate legislation.

AMENDMENT XXIV[22]

Section 1. The right of citizens of the United States to vote in any primary or other election for President or Vice President, or for Senator or Representative in Congress, shall not be denied or abridged by the United States or any State by reason of failure to pay any poll tax or other tax.

Section 2. The Congress shall have power to enforce this article by appropriate legislation.

AMENDMENT XXV[23]

Section 1. In case of the removal of the President from office or of his death or resignation, the Vice President shall become President.

[20]Passed March 12, 1947. Ratified March 1, 1951.

[21]Passed June 16, 1960. Ratified April 3, 1961.

[22]Passed August 27, 1962. Ratified January 23, 1964.

[23]Passed July 6, 1965. Ratified February 11, 1967.

[19]Passed February 20, 1933. Ratified December 5, 1933.

Section 2. Whenever there is a vacancy in the office of the Vice-President, the President shall nominate a Vice President who shall take office upon confirmation by a majority vote of both Houses of Congress.

Section 3. Whenever the President transmits to the President pro tempore of the Senate and the Speaker of the House of Representatives his written declaration that he is unable to discharge the powers and duties of his office, and until he transmits them a written declaration to the contrary, such powers and duties shall be discharged by the Vice President as Acting President.

Section 4. Whenever the Vice President and a majority of either the principal officers of the executive department or of such other body as Congress may by law provide, transmit to the President pro tempore of the Senate and the Speaker of the House of Representatives their written declaration that the President is unable to discharge the powers and duties of his office, the Vice President shall immediately assume the powers and duties of the office of Acting President

Thereafter, when the President transmits to the President pro tempore of the Senate and the Speaker of the House of Representatives his written declaration that no inability exists, he shall resume the powers and duties of his office unless the Vice President and a majority of either the principal officers of the executive department or of such other body as Congress may by law provide, transmit within four days to the President pro tempore of the Senate and the Speaker of the House of Representatives their written declaration that the President is unable to discharge the powers and duties of his office. Thereupon Congress shall decide the issue, assembling within forty-eight hours for that purpose if not in session. If the Congress, within twenty-one days after receipt of the latter written declaration, or, if Congress is not in session, within twenty-one days after Congress is required to assemble, determines by two-thirds vote of both Houses that the President is unable to discharge the powers and duties of his office, the Vice-President shall continue to discharge the same as Acting President; otherwise, the President shall resume the powers and duties of his office.

AMENDMENT XXVI[24]

Section 1. The right of citizens of the United States, who are eighteen years of age or older, to vote shall not be denied or abridged by the United States or by any State on account of age.

Section 2. The Congress shall have power to enforce this article by appropriate legislation.

AMENDMENT XXVII[25]

No law, varying the compensation for the service of the Senators and Representatives, shall take effect, until an election of Representatives shall have intervened.

[24]Passed March 23, 1971. Ratified July 5, 1971.

[25]Passed September 25, 1789. Ratified May 7, 1992.

Admission of States

Order of admission	State	Date of admission	Order of admission	State	Date of admission
1	Delaware	December 7, 1787	26	Michigan	January 26, 1837
2	Pennsylvania	December 12, 1787	27	Florida	March 3, 1845
3	New Jersey	December 18, 1787	28	Texas	December 29, 1845
4	Georgia	January 2, 1788	29	Iowa	December 28, 1846
5	Connecticut	January 9, 1788	30	Wisconsin	May 29, 1848
6	Massachusetts	February 6, 1788	31	California	September 9, 1850
7	Maryland	April 28, 1788	32	Minnesota	May 11, 1858
8	South Carolina	May 23, 1788	33	Oregon	February 14, 1859
9	New Hampshire	June 21, 1788	34	Kansas	January 29, 1861
10	Virginia	June 25, 1788	35	West Virginia	June 20, 1863
11	New York	July 26, 1788	36	Nevada	October 31, 1864
12	North Carolina	November 21, 1789	37	Nebraska	March 1, 1867
13	Rhode Island	May 29, 1790	38	Colorado	August 1, 1876
14	Vermont	March 4, 1791	39	North Dakota	November 2, 1889
15	Kentucky	June 1, 1792	40	South Dakota	November 2, 1889
16	Tennessee	June 1, 1796	41	Montana	November 8, 1889
17	Ohio	March 1, 1803	42	Washington	November 11, 1889
18	Louisiana	April 30, 1812	43	Idaho	July 3, 1890
19	Indiana	December 11, 1816	44	Wyoming	July 10, 1890
20	Mississippi	December 10, 1817	45	Utah	January 4, 1896
21	Illinois	December 3, 1818	46	Oklahoma	November 16, 1907
22	Alabama	December 14, 1819	47	New Mexico	January 6, 1912
23	Maine	March 15, 1820	48	Arizona	February 14, 1912
24	Missouri	August 10, 1821	49	Alaska	January 3, 1959
25	Arkansas	June 15, 1836	50	Hawaii	August 21, 1959

Population of the United States

Year	Total population	Number per square mile	Year	Total population	Number per square mile	Year	Total population	Number per square mile
1790	3,929	4.5	1806	6,451		1822	10,268	
1791	4,056		1807	6,644		1823	10,596	
1792	4,194		1808	6,838		1824	10,924	
1793	4,332		1809	7,031		1825	11,252	
1794	4,469		1810	7,224	4.3	1826	11,580	
1795	4,607		1811	7,460		1827	11,909	
1796	4,745		1812	7,700		1828	12,237	
1797	4,883		1813	7,939		1829	12,565	
1798	5,021		1814	8,179		1830	12,901	7.4
1799	5,159		1815	8,419		1831	13,321	
1800	5,297	6.1	1816	8,659		1832	13,742	
1801	5,486		1817	8,899		1833	14,162	
1802	5,679		1818	9,139		1834	14,582	
1803	5,872		1819	9,379		1835	15,003	
1804	5,065		1820	9,618	5.6	1836	15,423	
1805	6,258		1821	9,939		1837	15,843	

Figures are from *Historical Statistics of the United States, Colonial Times to 1957* (1961), pp. 7, 8; *Statistical Abstract of the United States: 1974*, p. 5, Census Bureau for 1974 and 1975; and *Statistical Abstract of the United States: 1988*, p. 7.

Note: Population figures are in thousands. Density figures are for land area of continental United States.

Population of the United States, continued

Year	Total population	Number per square mile	Year	Total population[1]	Number per square mile	Year	Total population[1]	Number per square mile
1838	16,264		1884	55,379		1930	122,775	41.2
1839	16,684		1885	56,658		1931	124,040	
1840	17,120	9.8	1886	57,938		1932	124,840	
1841	17,733		1887	59,217		1933	125,579	
1842	18,345		1888	60,496		1934	126,374	
1843	18,957		1889	61,775		1935	127,250	
1844	19,569		1890	63,056	21.2	1936	128,053	
1845	20,182		1891	64,361		1937	128,825	
1846	20,794		1892	65,666		1938	129,825	
1847	21,406		1893	66,970		1939	130,880	
1848	22,018		1894	68,275		1940	131,669	44.2
1849	22,631		1895	69,580		1941	133,894	
1850	23,261	7.9	1896	70,885		1942	135,361	
1851	24,086		1897	72,189		1943	137,250	
1852	24,911		1898	73,494		1944	138,916	
1853	25,736		1899	74,799		1945	140,468	
1854	26,561		1900	76,094	25.6	1946	141,936	
1855	27,386		1901	77,585		1947	144,698	
1856	28,212		1902	79,160		1948	147,208	
1857	29,037		1903	80,632		1949	149,767	
1858	29,862		1904	82,165		1950	150,697	50.7
1859	30,687		1905	83,820		1951	154,878	
1860	31,513	10.6	1906	85,437		1952	157,553	
1861	32,351		1907	87,000		1953	160,184	
1862	33,188		1908	88,709		1954	163,026	
1863	34,026		1909	90,492		1955	165,931	
1864	34,863		1910	92,407	31.0	1956	168,903	
1865	35,701		1911	93,868		1957	171,984	
1866	36,538		1912	95,331		1958	174,882	
1867	37,376		1913	97,227		1959	177,830	
1868	38,213		1914	99,118		1960	178,464	60.1
1869	39,051		1915	100,549		1961	183,672	
1870	39,905	13.4	1916	101,966		1962	186,504	
1871	40,938		1917	103,414		1963	189,197	
1872	41,972		1918	104,550		1964	191,833	
1873	43,006		1919	105,063		1965	194,237	
1874	44,040		1920	106,466	35.6	1966	196,485	
1875	45,073		1921	108,541		1967	198,629	
1876	46,107		1922	110,055		1968	200,619	
1877	47,141		1923	111,950		1969	202,599	
1878	48,174		1924	114,113		1970	203,875	57.5[2]
1879	49,208		1925	115,832		1971	207,045	
1880	50,262	16.9	1926	117,399		1972	208,842	
1881	51,542		1927	119,038		1973	210,396	
1882	52,821		1928	120,501		1974	211,894	
1883	54,100		1929	121,700				

[1]Figures after 1940 represent total population including armed forces abroad, except in official census years.

[2] Figure includes Alaska and Hawaii.

Year	Total population[1]	Number per square mile	Year	Total population[1]	Number per square mile	Year	Total population[1]	Number per square mile
1975	213,631		1985	239,283		1995	263,434	
1976	215,152		1986	241,596		1996	266,096	
1977	216,880		1987	234,773		1997	267,901	
1978	218,717		1988	245,051		1998	269,501	
1979	220,584		1989	247,350		1999	272,700	
1980	226,546	64.0	1990	250,122	70.3	2000	281,400	79.6
1981	230,138		1991	254,521		2001	286,909	
1982	232,520		1992	245,908		2002	289,947	
1983	234,799		1993	257,908				
1984	237,001		1994	261,875				

[1]Figures after 1940 represent total population including armed forces abroad, except in official census years.

Presidential Elections

Year	Number of states	Candidates[1]	Parties	Popular vote	Electoral vote	Percentage of popular vote[2]
1789	11	**George Washington**	No party designations		69	
		John Adams			34	
		Minor Candidates			35	
1792	15	**George Washington**	No party designations		132	
		John Adams			77	
		George Clinton			50	
		Minor Candidates			5	
1796	16	**John Adams**	Federalist		71	
		Thomas Jefferson	Democratic-Republican		68	
		Thomas Pinckney	Federalist		59	
		Aaron Burr	Democratic-Republican		30	
		Minor Candidates			48	
1800	16	**Thomas Jefferson**	Democratic-Republican		73	
		Aaron Burr	Democratic-Republican		73	
		John Adams	Federalist		65	
		Charles C. Pinckney	Federalist		64	
		John Jay	Federalist		1	
1804	17	**Thomas Jefferson**	Democratic-Republican		162	
		Charles C. Pinckney	Federalist		14	
1808	17	**James Madison**	Democratic-Republican		122	
		Charles C. Pinckney	Federalist		47	
		George Clinton	Democratic-Republican		6	
1812	18	**James Madison**	Democratic-Republican		128	
		DeWitt Clinton	Federalist		89	
1816	19	**James Monroe**	Democratic-Republican		183	
		Rufus King	Federalist		34	
1820	24	**James Monroe**	Democratic-Republican		231	
		John Quincy Adams	Independent Republican		1	

[1]Before the passage of the Twelfth Amendment in 1804, the Electoral College voted for two presidential candidates; the runner-up became vice president. Figures are from *Historical Statistics of the United States, Colonial Times to 1957* (1961), pp. 682–83; and the U.S. Department of Justice.

[2]Candidates receiving less than 1 percent of the popular vote have been omitted. For that reason the percentage of popular vote given for any election year may not total 100 percent.

Presidential Elections, continued

Year	Number of states	Candidates[1]	Parties	Popular vote	Electoral vote	Percentage of popular vote[2]
1824	24	**John Quincy Adams**	Democratic-Republican	108,740	84	30.5
		Andrew Jackson	Democratic-Republican	153,544	99	43.1
		William H. Crawford	Democratic-Republican	46,618	41	13.1
		Henry Clay	Democratic-Republican	47,136	37	13.2
1828	24	**Andrew Jackson**	Democratic	647,286	178	56.0
		John Quincy Adams	National Republican	508,064	83	44.0
1832	24	**Andrew Jackson**	Democratic	687,502	219	55.0
		Henry Clay	National Republican	530,189	49	42.4
		William Wirt	Anti-Masonic	33,108	7	
		John Floyd	National Republican		11	2.6
1836	26	**Martin Van Buren**	Democratic	765,483	170	50.9
		William H. Harrison	Whig		73	
		Hugh L. White	Whig	739,795	26	
		Daniel Webster	Whig		14	
		W. P. Mangum	Whig		11	
1840	26	**William H. Harrison**	Whig	1,274,624	234	53.1
		Martin Van Buren	Democratic	1,127,781	60	46.9
1844	26	**James K. Polk**	Democratic	1,338,464	170	49.6
		Henry Clay	Whig	1,300,097	105	48.1
		James G. Birney	Liberty	62,300		2.3
1848	30	**Zachary Taylor**	Whig	1,360,967	163	47.4
		Lewis Cass	Democratic	1,222,342	127	42.5
		Martin Van Buren	Free Soil	291,263		10.1
1852	31	**Franklin Pierce**	Democratic	1,601,117	254	50.9
		Winfield Scott	Whig	1,385,453	42	44.1
		John P. Hale	Free Soil	155,825		5.0
1856	31	**James Buchanan**	Democratic	1,832,955	174	45.3
		John C. Frémont	Republican	1,339,932	114	33.1
		Millard Fillmore	American	871,731	8	21.6
1860	33	**Abraham Lincoln**	Republican	1,865,593	180	39.8
		Stephen A. Douglas	Democratic	1,382,713	12	29.5
		John C. Breckinridge	Democratic	848,356	72	18.1
		John Bell	Constitutional Union	592,906	39	12.6
1864	36	**Abraham Lincoln**	Republican	2,206,938	212	55.0
		George B. McClellan	Democratic	1,803,787	21	45.0
1868	37	**Ulysses S. Grant**	Republican	3,013,421	214	52.7
		Horatio Seymour	Democratic	2,706,829	80	47.3
1872	37	**Ulysses S. Grant**	Republican	3,596,745	286	55.6
		Horace Greeley	Democratic	2,843,446	[3]	43.9
1876	38	**Rutherford B. Hayes**	Republican	4,036,572	185	48.0
		Samuel J. Tilden	Democratic	4,284,020	184	51.0
1880	38	**James A. Garfield**	Republican	4,453,295	214	48.5
		Winfield S. Hancock	Democratic	4,414,082	155	48.1
		James B. Weaver	Greenback-Labor	308,578		3.4

[1]Before the passage of the Twelfth Amendment in 1804, the Electoral College voted for two presidential candidates; the runner-up became vice president. Figures are from *Historical Statistics of the United States, Colonial Times to 1957* (1961), pp. 682–83; and the U.S. Department of Justice.

[2]Candidates receiving less than 1 percent of the popular vote have been omitted. For that reason the percentage of popular vote given for any election year may not total 100 percent.

[3]Greeley died shortly after the election; the electors supporting him then divided their votes among minor candidates.

Year	Number of states	Candidates[1]	Parties	Popular vote	Electoral vote	Percentage of popular vote
1884	38	**Grover Cleveland**	Democratic	4,879,507	219	48.5
		James G. Blaine	Republican	4,850,293	182	48.2
		Benjamin F. Butler	Greenback-Labor	175,370		1.8
		John P. St. John	Prohibition	150,369		1.5
1888	38	**Benjamin Harrison**	Republican	5,477,129	233	47.9
		Grover Cleveland	Democratic	5,537,857	168	48.6
		Clinton B. Fisk	Prohibition	249,506		2.2
		Anson J. Streeter	Union Labor	146,935		1.3
1892	44	**Grover Cleveland**	Democratic	5,555,426	277	46.1
		Benjamin Harrison	Republican	5,182,690	145	43.0
		James B. Weaver	People's	1,029,846	22	8.5
		John Bidwell	Prohibition	264,133		2.2
1896	45	**William McKinley**	Republican	7,102,246	271	51.1
		William J. Bryan	Democratic	6,492,559	176	47.7
1900	45	**William McKinley**	Republican	7,218,491	292	51.7
		William J. Bryan	Democratic; Populist	6,356,734	155	45.5
		John C. Wooley	Prohibition	208,914		1.5
1904	45	**Theodore Roosevelt**	Republican	7,628,461	336	57.4
		Alton B. Parker	Democratic	5,084,223	140	37.6
		Eugene V. Debs	Socialist	402,283		3.0
		Silas C. Swallow	Prohibition	258,536		1.9
1908	46	**William H. Taft**	Republican	7,675,320	321	51.6
		William J. Bryan	Democratic	6,412,294	162	43.1
		Eugene V. Debs	Socialist	420,793		2.8
		Eugene W. Chafin	Prohibition	253,840		1.7
1912	48	**Woodrow Wilson**	Democratic	6,296,547	435	41.9
		Theodore Roosevelt	Progressive	4,118,571	88	27.4
		William H. Taft	Republican	3,486,720	8	23.2
		Eugene V. Debs	Socialist	900,672		6.0
		Eugene W. Chafin	Prohibition	206,275		1.4
1916	48	**Woodrow Wilson**	Democratic	9,127,695	277	49.4
		Charles E. Hughes	Republican	8,533,507	254	46.2
		A. L. Benson	Socialist	585,113		3.2
		J. Frank Hanly	Prohibition	220,506		1.2
1920	48	**Warren G. Harding**	Republican	16,143,407	404	60.4
		James N. Cox	Democratic	9,130,328	127	34.2
		Eugene V. Debs	Socialist	919,799		3.4
		P. P. Christensen	Farmer-Labor	265,411		1.0
1924	48	**Calvin Coolidge**	Republican	15,718,211	382	54.0
		John W. Davis	Democratic	8,385,283	136	28.8
		Robert M. La Follette	Progressive	4,831,289	13	16.6
1928	48	**Herbert C. Hoover**	Republican	21,391,993	444	58.2
		Alfred E. Smith	Democratic	15,016,169	87	40.9
1932	48	**Franklin D. Roosevelt**	Democratic	22,809,638	472	57.4
		Herbert C. Hoover	Republican	15,758,901	59	39.7
		Norman Thomas	Socialist	881,951		2.2
1936	48	**Franklin D. Roosevelt**	Democratic	27,752,869	523	60.8
		Alfred M. Landon	Republican	16,674,665	8	36.5
		William Lemke	Union	882,479		1.9

[1]Candidates receiving less than 1 percent of the popular vote have been omitted. For that reason the percentage of popular vote given for any election year may not total 100 percent.

Presidential Elections, continued

Year	Number of states	Candidates	Parties	Popular vote	Electoral vote	Percentage of popular vote[1]
1940	48	**Franklin D. Roosevelt**	Democratic	27,307,819	449	54.8
		Wendell L. Willkie	Republican	22,321,018	82	44.8
1944	48	**Franklin D. Roosevelt**	Democratic	25,606,585	432	53.5
		Thomas E. Dewey	Republican	22,014,745	99	46.0
1948	48	**Harry S. Truman**	Democratic	24,105,812	303	49.5
		Thomas E. Dewey	Republican	21,970,065	189	45.1
		J. Strom Thurmond	States' Rights	1,169,063	39	2.4
		Henry A. Wallace	Progressive	1,157,172		2.4
1952	48	**Dwight D. Eisenhower**	Republican	33,936,234	442	55.1
		Adlai E. Stevenson	Democratic	27,314,992	89	44.4
1956	48	**Dwight D. Eisenhower**	Republican	35,590,472	457	57.6
		Adlai E. Stevenson	Democratic	26,022,752	73	42.1
1960	50	**John F. Kennedy**	Democratic	34,227,096	303	49.9
		Richard M. Nixon	Republican	34,108,546	219	49.6
1964	50	**Lyndon B. Johnson**	Democratic	43,126,506	486	61.1
		Barry M. Goldwater	Republican	27,176,799	52	38.5
1968	50	**Richard M. Nixon**	Republican	31,785,480	301	43.4
		Hubert H. Humphrey	Democratic	31,275,165	191	42.7
		George C. Wallace	American Independent	9,906,473	46	13.5
1972	50	**Richard M. Nixon**	Republican	47,169,911	520	60.7
		George S. McGovern	Democratic	29,170,383	17	37.5
1976	50	**Jimmy Carter**	Democratic	40,827,394	297	50.0
		Gerald R. Ford	Republican	39,145,977	240	47.9
1980	50	**Ronald W. Reagan**	Republican	43,899,248	489	50.8
		Jimmy Carter	Democratic	35,481,435	49	41.0
		John B. Anderson	Independent	5,719,437		6.6
		Ed Clark	Libertarian	920,859		1.0
1984	50	**Ronald W. Reagan**	Republican	54,281,858	525	59.2
		Walter F. Mondale	Democratic	37,457,215	13	40.8
1988	50	**George H. Bush**	Republican	47,917,341	426	54
		Michael Dukakis	Democratic	41,013,030	112	46
1992	50	**William Clinton**	Democratic	44,908,254	370	43.0
		George H. Bush	Republican	39,102,343	168	37.4
		Ross Perot	Independent	19,741,065		18.9
1996	50	**William Clinton**	Democratic	45,628,667	379	49.2
		Robert Dole	Republican	37,869,435	159	40.8
		Ross Perot	Reform	7,874,283	0	8.5
2000	50	**George W. Bush**	Republican	50,456,062	271	47.9
		Albert Gore	Democratic	50,996,582	266	48.4
		Ralph Nader	Green	2,858,843	0	2.7

[1]Candidates receiving less than 1 percent of the popular vote have been omitted. For that reason the percentage of popular vote given for any election year may not total 100 percent.

Presidential Administrations

President	Vice President	Secretary of State	Secretary of Treasury	Secretary of War	Secretary of Navy	Postmaster General	Attorney General
George Washington 1789–1797	John Adams 1789–1797	Thomas Jefferson 1789–1794 Edmund Randolph 1794–1795 Timothy Pickering 1795–1797	Alexander Hamilton 1789–1795 Oliver Wolcott 1795–1797	Henry Knox 1789–1795 Timothy Pickering 1795–1796 James McHenry 1796–1797		Samuel Osgood 1789–1791 Timothy Pickering 1791–1795 Joseph Habersham 1795–1797	Edmund Randolph 1789–1794 William Bradford 1794–1795 Charles Lee 1795–1797
John Adams 1797–1801	Thomas Jefferson 1797–1801	Timothy Pickering 1797–1800 John Marshall 1800–1801	Oliver Wolcott 1797–1801 Samuel Dexter 1801	James McHenry 1797–1800 Samuel Dexter 1800–1801	Benjamin Stoddert 1798–1801	Joseph Habersham 1797–1801	Charles Lee 1797–1801
Thomas Jefferson 1801–1809	Aaron Burr 1801–1805 George Clinton 1805–1809	James Madison 1801–1809	Samuel Dexter 1801 Albert Gallatin 1801–1809	Henry Dearborn 1801–1809	Benjamin Stoddert 1801 Robert Smith 1801–1809	Joseph Habersham 1801 Gideon Granger 1801–1809	Levi Lincoln 1801–1805 John Breckinridge 1805–1807 Caesar Rodney 1807–1809
James Madison 1809–1817	George Clinton 1809–1813 Elbridge Gerry 1813–1817	Robert Smith 1809–1811 James Monroe 1811–1817	Albert Gallatin 1809–1814 George Campbell 1814 Alexander Dallas 1814–1816 William Crawford 1816–1817	William Eustis 1809–1813 John Armstrong 1813–1814 James Monroe 1814–1815 William Crawford 1815–1817	Paul Hamilton 1809–1813 William Jones 1813–1814 Benjamin Crowninshield 1814–1817	Gideon Granger 1809–1814 Return Meigs 1814–1817	Caesar Rodney 1809–1811 William Pinkney 1811–1814 Richard Rush 1814–1817
James Monroe 1817–1825	Daniel D. Tompkins 1817–1825	John Quincy Adams 1817–1825	William Crawford 1817–1825	George Graham 1817 John C. Calhoun 1817–1825	Benjamin Crowninshield 1817–1818 Smith Thompson 1818–1823 Samuel Southard 1823–1825	Return Meigs 1817–1823 John McLean 1823–1825	Richard Rush 1817 William Wirt 1817–1825
John Quincy Adams 1825–1829	John C. Calhoun 1825–1829	Henry Clay 1825–1829	Richard Rush 1825–1829	James Barbour 1825–1828 Peter B. Porter 1828–1829	Samuel Southard 1825–1829	John McLean 1825–1829	William Wirt 1825–1829
Andrew Jackson 1829–1837	John C. Calhoun 1829–1833 Martin Van Buren 1833–1837	Martin Van Buren 1829–1831 Edward Livingston 1831–1833 Louis McLane 1833–1834 John Forsyth 1834–1837	Samuel Ingham 1829–1831 Louis McLane 1831–1833 William Duane 1833 Roger B. Taney 1833–1834 Levi Woodbury 1834–1837	John H. Eaton 1829–1831 Lewis Cass 1831–1837 Benjamin Butler 1837	John Branch 1829–1831 Levi Woodbury 1831–1834 Mahlon Dickerson 1834–1837	William Barry 1829–1835 Amos Kendall 1835–1837	John M. Berrien 1829–1831 Roger B. Taney 1831–1833 Benjamin Butler 1833–1837
Martin Van Buren 1837–1841	Richard M. Johnson 1837–1841	John Forsyth 1837–1841	Levi Woodbury 1837–1841	Joel R. Poinsett 1837–1841	Mahlon Dickerson 1837–1838 James K. Paulding 1838–1841	Amos Kendall 1837–1840 John M. Niles 1840–1841	Benjamin Butler 1837–1838 Felix Grundy 1838–1840 Henry D. Gilpin 1840–1841
William H. Harrison 1841	John Tyler 1841	Daniel Webster 1841	Thomas Ewing 1841	John Bell 1841	George E. Badger 1841	Francis Granger 1841	John J. Crittenden 1841
John Tyler 1841–1845		Daniel Webster 1841–1843 Hugh S. Legaré 1843 Abel P. Upshur 1843–1844 John C. Calhoun 1844–1845	Thomas Ewing 1841 Walter Forward 1841–1843 John C. Spencer 1843–1844 George M. Bibb 1844–1845	John Bell 1841 John C. Spencer 1841–1843 James M. Porter 1843–1844 William Wilkins 1844–1845	George E. Badger 1841 Abel P. Upshur 1841–1843 David Henshaw 1843–1844 Thomas Gilmer 1844 John Y. Mason 1844–1845	Francis Granger 1841 Charles A. Wickliffe 1841–1845	John J. Crittenden 1841 Hugh S. Legaré 1841–1843 John Nelson 1843–1845
James K. Polk 1845–1849	George M. Dallas 1845–1849	James Buchanan 1845–1849	Robert J. Walker 1845–1849	William L. Marcy 1845–1849	George Bancroft 1845–1846 John Y. Mason 1846–1849	Cave Johnson 1845–1849	John Y. Mason 1845–1846 Nathan Clifford 1846–1848 Isaac Toucey 1848–1849

(continued)

President	Vice President	Secretary of State	Secretary of Treasury	Secretary of War	Secretary of Navy
Zachary Taylor 1849–1850	Millard Fillmore 1849–1850	John M. Clayton 1849–1850	William M. Meredith 1849–1850	George W. Crawford 1849–1850	William B. Preston 1849–1850
Millard Fillmore 1850–1853		Daniel Webster 1850–1852 Edward Everett 1852–1853	Thomas Corwin 1850–1853	Charles M. Conrad 1850–1853	William A. Graham 1850–1852 John P. Kennedy 1852–1853
Franklin Pierce 1853–1857	William R. King 1853–1857	William L. Marcy 1853–1857	James Guthrie 1853–1857	Jefferson Davis 1853–1857	James C. Dobbin 1853–1857
James Buchanan 1857–1861	John C. Breckinridge 1857–1861	Lewis Cass 1857–1860 Jeremiah S. Black 1860–1861	Howell Cobb 1857–1860 Philip F. Thomas 1860–1861 John A. Dix 1861	John B. Floyd 1857–1861 Joseph Holt 1861	Isaac Toucey 1857–1861
Abraham Lincoln 1861–1865	Hannibal Hamlin 1861–1865 Andrew Johnson 1865	William H. Seward 1861–1865	Salmon P. Chase 1861–1864 William P. Fessenden 1864–1865 Hugh McCulloch 1865	Simon Cameron 1861–1862 Edwin M. Stanton 1862–1865	Gideon Welles 1861–1865
Andrew Johnson 1865–1869		William H. Seward 1865–1869	Hugh McCulloch 1865–1869	Edwin M. Stanton 1865–1867 Ulysses S. Grant 1867–1868 John M. Schofield 1868–1869	Gideon Welles 1865–1869
Ulysses S. Grant 1869–1877	Schuyler Colfax 1869–1873 Henry Wilson 1873–1877	Elihu B. Washburne 1869 Hamilton Fish 1869–1877	George S. Boutwell 1869–1873 William A. Richardson 1873–1874 Benjamin H. Bristow 1874–1876 Lot M. Morrill 1876–1877	John A. Rawlins 1869 William T. Sherman 1869 William W. Belknap 1869–1876 Alphonso Taft 1876 James D. Cameron 1876–1877	Adolph E. Borie 1869 George M. Robeson 1869–1877
Rutherford B. Hayes 1877–1881	William A. Wheeler 1877–1881	William M. Evarts 1877–1881	John Sherman 1877–1881	George W. McCrary 1877–1879 Alexander Ramsey 1879–1881	R. W. Thompson 1877–1881 Nathan Goff, Jr. 1881
James A. Garfield 1881	Chester A. Arthur 1881	James G. Blaine 1881	William Windom 1881	Robert T. Lincoln 1881	William H. Hunt 1881
Chester A. Arthur 1881–1885		F. T. Frelinghuysen 1881–1885	Charles J. Folger 1881–1884 Walter Q. Gresham 1884 Hugh McCulloch 1884–1885	Robert T. Lincoln 1881–1885	William E. Chandler 1881–1885
Grover Cleveland 1885–1889	T. A. Hendricks 1885	Thomas F. Bayard 1885–1889 Daniel Manning 1885–1887 Charles S. Fairchild 1887–1889	William C. Endicott 1885–1889	William C. Whitney 1885–1889	William F. Vilas 1885–1888 Don M. Dickinson 1888–1889
Benjamin Harrison 1889–1893	Levi P. Morton 1889–1893	James G. Blaine 1889–1892 John W. Foster 1892–1893	William Windom 1889–1891 Charles Foster 1892–1893	Redfield Procter 1889–1891 Stephen B. Elkins 1891–1893	Benjamin F. Tracy 1889–1893
Grover Cleveland 1893–1897	Adlai E. Stevenson 1893–1897	Walter Q. Gresham 1893–1895 Richard Olney 1895–1897	John G. Carlisle 1893–1897	Daniel S. Lamont 1893–1897	Hilary A. Herbert 1893–1897
William McKinley 1897–1901	Garret A. Hobart 1897–1899 Theodore Roosevelt 1901	John Sherman 1897–1898 William R. Day 1898 John Hay 1898–1901	Lyman J. Gage 1897–1901	Russell A. Alger 1897–1899 Elihu Root 1899–1901	John D. Long 1897–1901

Postmaster General	Attorney General	Secretary of Interior	Secretary of Agriculture	Secretary of Commerce and Labor
Jacob Collamer 1849–1850	Reverdy Johnson 1849–1850	Thomas Ewing 1849–1850		
Nathan K. Hall 1850–1852 Sam D. Hubbard 1852–1853	John J. Crittenden 1850–1853	Thomas McKennan 1850 A. H. H. Stuart 1850–1853		
James Campbell 1853–1857	Caleb Cushing 1853–1857	Robert McClelland 1853–1857		
Aaron V. Brown 1857–1859 Joseph Holt 1859–1861 Horatio King 1861	Jeremiah S. Black 1857–1860 Edwin M. Stanton 1860–1861	Jacob Thompson 1857–1861		
Horatio King 1861 Montgomery Blair 1861–1864 William Dennison 1864–1865	Edward Bates 1861–1864 James Speed 1864–1865	Caleb B. Smith 1861–1863 John P. Usher 1863–1865		
William Dennison 1864–1866 Alexander Randall 1866–1869 William M. Evarts 1868–1869	James Speed 1865–1866 Henry Stanbery 1866–1868 O. H. Browning 1866–1869	John P. Usher 1865 James Harlan 1865–1866		
John A. J. Creswell 1869–1874 James W. Marshall 1874 Marshall Jewell 1874–1876 James N. Tyner 1876–1877	Ebenezer R. Hoar 1869–1870 Amos T. Akerman 1870–1871 G. H. Williams 1871–1875 Edwards Pierrepont 1875–1876 Alphonso Taft 1876–1877	Jacob D. Cox 1869–1870 Columbus Delano 1870–1875 Zachariah Chandler 1875–1877		
David M. Key 1877–1880 Horace Maynard 1880–1881	Charles Devens 1877–1881	Carl Schurz 1877–1881		
Thomas L. James 1881	Wayne MacVeagh 1881	S. J. Kirkwood 1881		
Thomas L. James 1881 Timothy O. Howe 1881–1883 Walter Q. Gresham 1883–1884 Frank Hatton 1884–1885	B. H. Brewster 1881–1885	Henry M. Teller 1881–1885		
A. H. Garland 1885–1889	L. Q. C. Lamar 1885–1888 William F. Vilas 1888–1889	Norman J. Colman 1889		
John Wanamaker 1889–1893	W. H. H. Miller 1889–1893	John W. Noble 1889–1893	Jeremiah M. Rusk 1889–1893	
Wilson S. Bissel 1893–1895 William L. Wilson 1895–1897	Richard Olney 1893–1895 Judson Harmon 1895–1897	Hoke Smith 1893–1896 David R. Francis 1896–1897	J. Sterling Morton 1893–1897	
James A. Gary 1897–1898 Charles E. Smith 1898–1901	Joseph McKenna 1897–1898 John W. Griggs 1898–1901 Philander C. Knox 1901	Cornelius N. Bliss 1897–1898 E. A. Hitchcock 1898–1901	James Wilson 1897–1901	

(continued)

President	Vice President	Secretary of State	Secretary of Treasury	Secretary of War	Secretary of Navy	Postmaster General	Attorney General
Theodore Roosevelt 1901–1909	Charles Fairbanks 1905–1909	John Hay 1901–1905 Elihu Root 1905–1909 Robert Bacon 1909	Lyman J. Gage 1901–1902 Leslie M. Shaw 1902–1907 George B. Cortelyou 1907–1909	Elihu Root 1901–1904 William H. Taft 1904–1908 Luke E. Wright 1908–1909	John D. Long 1901–1902 William H. Moody 1902–1904 Paul Morton 1904–1905 Charles J. Bonaparte 1905–1906 Victor H. Metcalf 1906–1908 T. H. Newberry 1908–1909	Charles E. Smith 1901–1902 Henry C. Payne 1902–1904 Robert J. Wynne 1904–1905 George B. Cortelyou 1905–1907 George von L. Meyer 1907–1909	Philander C. Knox 1901–1904 William H. Moody 1904–1906 Charles J. Bonaparte 1906–1909
William H. Taft 1909–1913	James S. Sherman 1909–1913	Philander C. Knox 1909–1913	Franklin MacVeagh 1909–1913	Jacob M. Dickinson 1909–1911 Henry L. Stimson 1911–1913	George von L. Meyer 1909–1913	Frank H. Hitchcock 1909–1913	G. W. Wickersham 1909–1913
Woodrow Wilson 1913–1921	Thomas R. Marshall 1913–1921	William J. Bryan 1913–1915 Robert Lansing 1915–1920 Bainbridge Colby 1920–1921	William G. McAdoo 1913–1918 Carter Glass 1918–1920 David F. Houston 1920–1921	Lindley M. Garrison 1913–1916 Newton D. Baker 1916–1921	Josephus Daniels 1913–1921	Albert S. Burleson 1913–1921	J. C. McReynolds 1913–1914 T. W. Gregory 1914–1919 A. Mitchell Palmer 1919–1921
Warren G. Harding 1921–1923	Calvin Coolidge 1921–1923	Charles E. Hughes 1921–1923	Andrew W. Mellon 1921–1923	John W. Weeks 1921–1923	Edwin Denby 1921–1923	Will H. Hays 1921–1922 Hubert Work 1922–1923 Harry S. New 1923	H. M. Daugherty 1921–1923
Calvin Coolidge 1923–1929	Charles G. Dawes 1925–1929	Charles E. Hughes 1923–1925 Frank B. Kellogg 1925–1929	Andrew W. Mellon 1923–1929	John W. Weeks 1923–1925 Dwight F. Davis 1925–1929	Edwin Denby 1923–1924 Curtis D. Wilbur 1924–1929	Harry S. New 1923–1929	H. M. Daugherty 1923–1924 Harlan F. Stone 1924–1925 John G. Sargent 1925–1929
Herbert C. Hoover 1929–1933	Charles Curtis 1929–1933	Henry L. Stimson 1929–1933	Andrew W. Mellon 1929–1932 Ogden L. Mills 1932–1933	James W. Good 1929 Patrick J. Hurley 1929–1933	Charles F. Adams 1929–1933	Walter F. Brown 1929–1933	J. D. Mitchell 1929–1933
Franklin Delano Roosevelt 1933–1945	John Nance Garner 1933–1941 Henry A. Wallace 1941–1945 Harry S. Truman 1945	Cordell Hull 1933–1944 E. R. Stettinius, Jr. 1944–1945	William H. Woodin 1933–1934 Henry Morgenthau, Jr. 1934–1945	George H. Dern 1933–1936 Harry H. Woodring 1936–1940 Henry L. Stimson 1940–1945	Claude A. Swanson 1933–1940 Charles Edison 1940 Frank Knox 1940–1944 James V. Forrestal 1944–1945	James A. Farley 1933–1940 Frank C. Walker 1940–1945	H. S. Cummings 1933–1939 Frank Murphy 1939–1940 Robert Jackson 1940–1941 Francis Biddel 1941–1945
Harry S Truman 1945–1953	Alben W. Barkley 1949–1953	James F. Byrnes 1945–1947 George C. Marshall 1947–1949 Dean G. Acheson 1949–1953	Fred M. Vinson 1945–1946 John W. Snyder 1946–1953	Robert P. Patterson 1945–1947 Kenneth C. Royall 1947	James V. Forrestal 1945–1947	R. E. Hannegan 1945–1947 Jesse M. Donaldson 1947–1953	Tom C. Clark 1945–1949 J. H. McGrath 1949–1952 James P. McGranery 1952–1953

Secretary of Defense

James V. Forrestal 1947–1949
Louis A. Johnson 1949–1950
George C. Marshall 1950–1951
Robert A. Lovett 1951–1953

President	Vice President	Secretary of State	Secretary of Treasury	Secretary of War	Secretary of Navy	Postmaster General	Attorney General
Dwight D. Eisenhower 1953–1961	Richard M. Nixon 1953–1961	John Foster Dulles 1953–1959 Christian A. Herter 1957–1961	George M. Humphrey 1953–1957 Robert B. Anderson 1957–1961		Charles E. Wilson 1953–1957 Neil H. McElroy 1957–1961 Thomas S. Gates 1959–1961	A. E. Summerfield 1953–1961	H. Brownell, Jr. 1953–1957 William P. Rogers 1957–1961

Secretary of Interior	Secretary of Agriculture	Secretary of Commerce	Secretary of Labor	Secretary of Health, Education and Welfare	Secretary of Housing and Urban Development	Secretary of Transportation
E. A. Hitchcock 1901–1907 James R. Garfield 1907–1909	James Wilson 1901–1909	George B. Cortelyou 1903–1904 Victor H. Metcalf 1904–1906 Oscar S. Straus 1906–1909				
R. A. Ballinger 1909–1911 Walter L. Fisher 1911–1913	James Wilson 1909–1913	Charles Nagel 1909–1913				
Franklin K. Lane 1913–1920 John B. Payne 1920–1921	David F. Houston 1913–1920 E. T. Meredith 1920–1921	Secretary of Commerce W. C. Redfield 1913–1919 J. W. Alexander 1919–1921	Secretary of Labor William B. Wilson 1913–1921			
Albert B. Fall 1921–1923 Hubert Work 1923	Henry C. Wallace 1921–1923	Herbert C. Hoover 1921–1923	James J. Davis 1921–1923			
Hubert Work 1923–1928 Roy O. West 1928–1929	Henry C. Wallace 1923–1924 Howard M. Gore 1924–1925 W. J. Jardine 1925–1929	Herbert C. Hoover 1923–1928 William F. Whiting 1928–1929	James J. Davis 1923–1929			
Ray L. Wilbur 1929–1933	Arthur M. Hyde 1929–1933 Roy D. Chapin 1932–1933	Robert P. Lamont 1929–1932 William N. Doak 1930–1933	James J. Davis 1929–1930			
Harold L. Ickes 1933–1945	Henry A. Wallace 1933–1940 Claude R. Wickard 1940–1945	Daniel C. Ropert 1933–1939 Harry L. Hopkins 1939–1940 Jesse Jones 1940–1945 Henry A. Wallace 1945	Frances Perkins 1933–1945			
Harold L. Ickes 1945–1946 Julius A. Krug 1946–1949 Oscar L. Chapman 1949–1953	C. P. Anderson 1945–1948 C. F. Brannan 1948–1953	W. A. Harriman 1946–1948 Charles Sawyer 1948–1953	L. B. Schwellenbach 1945–1948 Maurice J. Tobin 1948–1953			
Douglas McKay 1953–1956 Fred Seaton 1956–1961	Ezra T. Benson 1953–1961	Sinclair Weeks 1953–1958 Lewis L. Strauss 1958–1961	Martin P. Durkin 1953 James P. Mitchell 1953–1961	Oveta Culp Hobby 1953–1955 Marion B. Folsom 1955–1958 Arthur S. Flemming 1958–1961		

President	Vice President	Secretary of State	Secretary of Treasury	Secretary of Defense	Postmaster General[1]	Attorney General	Secretary of Interior	Secretary of Agriculture
John F. Kennedy 1961–1963	Lyndon B. Johnson 1961–1963	Dean Rusk 1961–1963	C. Douglas Dillon 1961–1963	Robert S. McNamara 1961–1963	J. Edward Day 1961–1963 John A. Gronouski 1961–1963	Robert F. Kennedy 1961–1963	Stewart L. Udalt 1961–1963	Orville L. Freeman 1961–1963
Lyndon B. Johnson 1963–1969	Hubert H. Humphrey 1965–1969	Dean Rusk 1963–1969	C. Douglas Dillon 1963–1965 Henry H. Fowler 1965–1968 Joseph W. Barr 1968–1969	Robert S. McNamara 1963–1968 Clark M. Clifford 1968–1969	John A. Gronouski 1963–1965 Lawrence F. O'Brien 1965–1968 W. Marvin Watson 1968–1969	Robert F. Kennedy 1963–1965 N. deB. Katzenbach 1965–1967 Ramsey Clark 1967–1969	Stewart L. Udalt 1963–1969	Orville L. Freeman 1963–1969
Richard M. Nixon 1969–1974	Spiro T. Agnew 1969–1973 Gerald R. Ford 1973–1974	William P. Rogers 1969–1973 Henry A. Kissinger 1973–1974	David M. Kennedy 1969–1970 John B. Connally 1970–1972 George P. Schultz 1972–1974 William E. Simon 1974	Melvin R. Laird 1969–1973 Elliot L. Richardson 1973 James R. Schlesinger 1973–1974	Winton M. Blount 1969–1971	John M. Mitchell 1969–1972 Richard G. Kleindienst 1972–1973 Elliot L. Richardson 1973 William B. Saxbe 1974	Walter J. Hickel 1969–1971 Rogers C. B. Morton 1971–1974	Clifford M. Hardin 1969–1971 Earl L. Butz 1971–1974
Gerald R. Ford 1974–1977	Nelson A. Rockefeller 1974–1977	Henry A. Kissinger 1974–1977	William E. Simon 1974–1977	James R. Schlesinger 1974–1975 Donald H. Rumsfeld 1975–1977		William B. Saxbe 1974–1975 Edward H. Levi 1975–1977	Rogers C. B. Morton 1974–1975 Stanley K. Hathaway 1975 Thomas D. Kleppe 1975–1977	Earl L. Butz 1974–1976
Jimmy Carter 1977–1981	Walter F. Mondale 1977–1981	Cyrus R. Vance 1977–1980 Edmund S. Muskie 1980–1981	W. Michael Blumenthal 1977–1979 G. William Miller 1979–1981	Harold Brown 1977–1981		Griffin Bell 1977–1979 Benjamin R. Civiletti 1979–1981	Cecil D. Andrus 1977–1981	Robert Bergland 1977–1981
Ronald W. Reagan 1981–1989	George H. Bush 1981–1989	Alexander M. Haig, Jr. 1981–1982 George P. Shultz 1982–1989	Donald T. Regan 1981–1985 James A. Baker 1985–1988 Nicholas F. Brady 1988–1989	Caspar W. Weinberger 1981–1987 Frank C. Carlucci 1987–1989		William French Smith 1981–1985 Edwin Meese 1985–1988 Richard Thornburgh 1988–1989	James G. Watt 1981–1983 William P. Clark 1983–1985 Donald P. Hodel 1985–1989	John R. Block 1981–1986 Richard E. Lyng 1986–1989
George H. Bush 1989–1993	J. Danforth Quayle 1989–1993	James A. Baker 1989–1992 Lawrence S. Eagleburger 1992–1993	Nicholas F. Brady 1989–1993	Richard Cheney 1989–1993		Richard Thornburgh 1989–1990 William Barr 1990–1993	Manuel Lujan 1989–1993	Clayton Yeutter 1989–1990 Edward Madigan 1990–1993
William Clinton 1993–2001	Albert Gore 1993–2001	Warren M. Christopher 1993–1996 Madeleine K. Albright 1997–2001	Lloyd Bentsen 1993–1994 Robert E. Rubin 1994–1999 Lawrence H. Summers 1999–2001	Les Aspin 1993–1994 William J. Perry 1994–1996 William S. Cohen 1997–2001		Janet Reno 1993–2001	Bruce Babbitt 1993–2001	Mike Espy 1993–1994 Dan Glickman 1995–2001
George W. Bush 2001–	Richard B. Cheney 2001–	Gen. Colin L. Powell 2001–	Paul H. O'Neil 2001–	Donald H. Rumsfeld 2001–		John Ashcroft 2001–	Gale A. Norton 2001–	Ann M. Veneman 2001–

[1]On July 1, 1971, the Post Office became an independent agency. After that date, the postmaster general was no longer a member of the Cabinet.

Secretary of Commerce	Secretary of Labor	Secretary of Health, Education and Welfare		Secretary of Housing and Urban Development	Secretary of Transportation	Secretary of Energy	Secretary of Veterans Affairs	Secretary of Homeland Security
Luther H. Hodges 1961–1963	Arthur J. Goldberg 1961–1963 W. Willard Wirtz 1962–1963	A. H. Ribicoff 1961–1963 Anthony J. Celebrezze 1962–1963						
Luther H. Hodges 1963–1965 John T. Connor 1965–1967 Alexander B. Trowbridge 1967–1968 C. R. Smith 1968–1969	W. Willard Wirtz 1963–1969	Anthony J. Celebrezze 1963–1965 John W. Gardner 1965–1968 Wilbur J. Cohen 1968–1969		Robert C. Weaver 1966–1968 Robert C. Wood 1968–1969	Alan S. Boyd 1966–1969			
Maurice H. Stans 1969–1972 Peter G. Peterson 1972 Frederick B. Dent 1972–1974	George P. Shultz 1969–1970 James D. Hodgson 1970–1973 Peter J. Brennan 1973–1974	Robert H. Finch 1969–1970 Elliot L. Richardson 1970–1973 Caspar W. Weinberger 1973–1974		George W. Romney 1969–1973 James T. Lynn 1973–1974	John A. Volpe 1969–1973 Claude S. Brinegar 1973–1974			
Frederick B. Dent 1974–1975 Rogers C. B. Morton 1975 Elliot L. Richardson 1975–1977	Peter J. Brennan 1974–1975 John T. Dunlop 1975–1976 W. J. Usery 1976–1977	Caspar W. Weinberger 1974–1975 Forrest D. Matthews 1975–1977		James T. Lynn 1974–1975 Carla A. Hills 1975–1977	Claude S. Brinegar 1974–1975 William T. Coleman 1975–1977			
Juanita Kreps 1977–1981	F. Ray Marshall 1977–1981	Joseph Califano 1977–1979 Patricia Roberts Harris 1979–1980		Patricia Roberts Harris 1977–1979 Moon Landrieu 1979–1981	Brock Adams 1977–1979 Neil E. Goldschmidt 1979–1981	James R. Schlesinger 1977–1979 Charles W. Duncan, Jr. 1979–1981		

		Secretary of Health and Human Services	Secretary of Education					
		Patricia Roberts Harris 1980–1981	Shirley M. Hufstedler 1980–1981					
Malcolm Baldridge 1981–1987 C. William Verity, Jr. 1987–1989	Raymond J. Donovan 1981–1985 William E. Brock 1985–1987 Ann Dore McLaughlin 1987–1989	Richard S. Schweiker 1981–1983 Margaret M. Heckler 1983–1985 Otis R. Bowen 1985–1989	Terrell H. Bell 1981–1985 William J. Bennett 1985–1988 Lauro Fred Cavazos 1988–1989	Samuel R. Pierce, jr. 1981–1989	Drew Lewis 1981–1983 Elizabeth H. Dole 1983–1987 James H. Burnley 1987–1989	James B. Edwards 1981–1982 Donald P. Hodel 1982–1985 John S. Harrington 1985–1989		
Robert Mosbacher 1989–1991 Barbars Franklin 1991–1993	Elizabeth Dole 1989–1990 Lynn Martin 1992–1993	Louis Sullivan 1989–1993	Lamar Alexander 1990–1993	Jack Kemp 1989–1993	Samuel Skinner 1989–1990 Andrew Card 1990–1993	James Watkins 1989–1993	Edward J. Derwinski 1989–1993	
Ronald H. Brown 1993–1996 William M. Daley 1997–2000 Norman Y. Mineta 2000–2001	Robert B. Reich 1993–1996 Alexis M. Herman 1997–2001	Donna E. Shalala 1993–2001	Richard W. Riley 1993–2001	Henry G. Cisneros 1993–1996 Andrew M. Cuomo 1997–2001	Federico F. Peña 1997–1998 Rodney E. Slater 1997–2001	Hazel O'Leary 1993–1996 Federico F. Peña 1997–1998 Bill Richardson 1998–2001	Jesse Brown 1993–1997 Togo D. West, Jr.[2] 1998–2001	
Donald L. Evans 2001–	Elaine L. Chao 2001–	Tommy G. Thompson 2001–	Roderick R. Paige 2001–	Melquiades R. Martinez 2001	Norman Y. Mineta 2001–	Spencer Abraham 2001–	Anthony Principi 2001–	Tom Ridge 2003–

[2]Acting secretary.

Justices of the U.S. Supreme Court

Name	Term of service	Years of service	Appointed by	Name	Term of service	Years of service	Appointed by
John Jay	1789–1795	5	Washington	Rufus W. Peckham	1895–1909	14	Cleveland
John Rutledge	1789–1791	1	Washington	Joseph McKenna	1898–1925	26	McKinley
William Cushing	1789–1810	20	Washington	Oliver W. Holmes, Jr.	1902–1932	30	T. Roosevelt
James Wilson	1789–1798	8	Washington	William R. Day	1903–1922	19	T. Roosevelt
John Blair	1789–1796	6	Washington	William H. Moody	1906–1910	3	T. Roosevelt
Robert H. Harrison	1789–1790	—	Washington	Horace H. Lurton	1910–1914	4	Taft
James Iredell	1790–1799	9	Washington	Charles E. Hughes	1910–1916	5	Taft
Thomas Johnson	1791–1793	1	Washington	Willis Van Devanter	1911–1937	26	Taft
William Paterson	1793–1806	13	Washington	Joseph R. Lamar	1911–1916	5	Taft
John Rutledge[1]	1795–	—	Washington	**Edward D. White**	1910–1921	11	Taft
Samuel Chase	1796–1811	15	Washington	Mahlon Pitney	1912–1922	10	Taft
Oliver Ellsworth	1796–1800	4	Washington	James C. McReynolds	1914–1941	26	Wilson
Bushrod Washington	1798–1829	31	J. Adams	Louis D. Brandeis	1916–1939	22	Wilson
Alfred Moore	1799–1804	4	J. Adams	John H. Clarke	1916–1922	6	Wilson
John Marshall	1801–1835	34	J. Adams	**William H. Taft**	1921–1930	8	Harding
William Johnson	1804–1834	30	Jefferson	George Sutherland	1922–1938	15	Harding
H. Brockholst Livingston	1806–1823	16	Jefferson	Pierce Butler	1922–1939	16	Harding
Thomas Todd	1807–1826	18	Jefferson	Edward T. Sanford	1923–1930	7	Harding
Joseph Story	1811–1845	33	Madison	Harlan F. Stone	1925–1941	16	Coolidge
Gabriel Duval	1811–1835	24	Madison	**Charles E. Hughes**	1930–1941	11	Hoover
Smith Thompson	1823–1843	20	Monroe	Owen J. Roberts	1930–1945	15	Hoover
Robert Trimble	1826–1828	2	J. Q. Adams	Benjamin N. Cardozo	1932–1938	6	Hoover
John McLean	1829–1861	32	Jackson	Hugo L. Black	1937–1971	34	F. Roosevelt
Henry Baldwin	1830–1844	14	Jackson	Stanley F. Reed	1938–1957	19	F. Roosevelt
James M. Wayne	1835–1867	32	Jackson	Felix Frankfurter	1939–1962	23	F. Roosevelt
Roger B. Taney	1836–1864	28	Jackson	William O. Douglas	1939–1975	36	F. Roosevelt
Philip P. Barbour	1836–1841	4	Jackson	Frank Murphy	1940–1949	9	F. Roosevelt
John Catron	1837–1865	28	Van Buren	**Harlan F. Stone**	1941–1946	5	F. Roosevelt
John McKinley	1837–1852	15	Van Buren	James F. Byrnes	1941–1942	1	F. Roosevelt
Peter V. Daniel	1841–1860	19	Van Buren	Robert H. Jackson	1941–1954	13	F. Roosevelt
Samuel Nelson	1845–1872	27	Tyler	Wiley B. Rutledge	1943–1949	6	F. Roosevelt
Levi Woodbury	1845–1851	5	Polk	Harold H. Burton	1945–1958	13	Truman
Robert C. Grier	1846–1870	23	Polk	**Fred M. Vinson**	1946–1953	7	Truman
Benjamin R. Curtis	1851–1857	6	Fillmore	Tom C. Clark	1949–1967	18	Truman
John A. Campbell	1853–1861	8	Pierce	Sherman Minton	1949–1956	7	Truman
Nathan Clifford	1858–1881	23	Buchanan	**Earl Warren**	1953–1969	16	Eisenhower
Noah H. Swayne	1862–1881	18	Lincoln	John Marshall Harlan	1955–1971	16	Eisenhower
Samuel F. Miller	1862–1890	28	Lincoln	William J. Brennan, Jr.	1956–1990	34	Eisenhower
David Davis	1862–1877	14	Lincoln	Charles E. Whittaker	1957–1962	5	Eisenhower
Stephen J. Field	1863–1897	34	Lincoln	Potter Stewart	1958–1981	23	Eisenhower
Salmon P. Chase	1864–1873	8	Lincoln	Byron R. White	1962–1993	31	Kennedy
William Strong	1870–1880	10	Grant	Arthur J. Goldberg	1962–1965	3	Kennedy
Joseph P. Bradley	1870–1892	22	Grant	Abe Fortas	1965–1969	4	Johnson
Ward Hunt	1873–1882	9	Grant	Thurgood Marshall	1967–1994	24	Johnson
Morrison R. Waite	1874–1888	14	Grant	**Warren E. Burger**	1969–1986	18	Nixon
John M. Harlan	1877–1911	34	Hayes	Harry A. Blackmun	1970–1994	24	Nixon
William B. Woods	1880–1887	7	Hayes	Lewis F. Powell, Jr.	1971–1987	15	Nixon
Stanley Matthews	1881–1889	7	Garfield	**William H. Rehnquist**[2]	1971–	—	Nixon
Horace Gray	1882–1902	20	Arthur	John P. Stevens III	1975–	—	Ford
Samuel Blatchford	1882–1893	11	Arthur	Sandra Day O'Connor	1981–	—	Reagan
Lucius Q. C. Lamar	1888–1893	5	Cleveland	Antonin Scalia	1986–	—	Reagan
Melville W. Fuller	1888–1910	21	Cleveland	Anthony M. Kennedy	1988–	—	Reagan
David J. Brewer	1890–1910	20	B. Harrison	David Souter	1990–	—	Bush
Henry B. Brown	1890–1906	16	B. Harrison	Clarence Thomas	1991–	—	Bush
George Shiras, Jr.	1892–1903	10	B. Harrison	Ruth Bader Ginsburg	1993–	—	Clinton
Howell E. Jackson	1893–1895	2	B. Harrison	Stephen G. Breyer	1994–	—	Clinton
Edward D. White	1894–1910	16	Cleveland				

Note: Chief Justices appear in bold type.

[1]Acting Chief Justice; Senate refused to confirm appointment.

[2]Chief Justice from 1986 on (Reagan administration).

CREDITS

Huntington Library, San Marine, California; **210,** Courtesy, Peabody Essex Museum, Salem, MA

Chapter 8
213, Collection of the New York Historical Society; **216,** North Wind Picture Archives; **217,** National Art Gallery, 1985.66, 279, Smithsonian Institution; **219,** Moorland-Spingarn Research Center, Howard University; **220,** The Historical Society of Pennsylvania (Bb 882 B756 44); **222,** From the Collections of The New Jersey Historical Society, Newark, New Jersey; **223,** The Granger Collection, New York; **225,** Courtesy of Duke University Archives; **227,** Courtesy, Archivo General de Indias, Seville, and the Spanish Colonial Research Center, University of New Mexico; **230,** Courtesy of Houghton Library, Harvard University; **232,** The Granger Collection, New York; **234,** Colonial Williamsburg Foundation; **234,** Copyrighted by the White House Historical Association; **235,** Smithsonian Institution, Bureau of American Ethnology; **237,** From the Director of the Vigo County Historical Society Collection; **237,** New York State Historical Association, Cooperstown; **238,** Anne S. K. Brown Military Collection, Brown University Library

Chapter 9
243, New York Public Library The Granger Collection, New York; **243,** The Granger Collection, New York; **246,** The Granger Collection, New York; **252,** The Granger Collection, New York; **253,** The Granger Collection, New York; **253,** The Granger Collection, New York; **255,** © Bettmann/Corbis; **256,** Cincinnati Historical Society; **259,** Abby Aldrich Rockefeller Folk Art Center, Williamsburg, VA; **263,** The Granger Collection, New York; **269,** The Granger Collection, New York; **270,** © Bettmann/Corbis

Chapter 10
273, 1942. 8 34(587)/ PA; Sully, Thomas, Andrew Jackson, Andrew W. Mellon Collection © 1998 Board of Trustees, National Gallery of Art, Washington, 1845, oil on canvas, 518, 438 (20 318 × 17 114); framed; 749 × 666 (29 112 × 26 114); **275,** The Granger Collection, New York; **276,** © Bettmann/Corbis; **277,** The Granger Collection, New York; **281,** The Granger Collection, New York; **283,** From "The Union," 1835, courtesy of The New York Public Library; **284,** The Granger Collection, New York; **288,** Woolaroc Museum, Bartlesville, Oklahoma; **290,** The Granger Collection, New York; **291,** Oberlin College Archives, Oberlin; **292,** © Bettmann/Corbis; **294,** Jermiah Pearson Hardy, "Catherine Wheeler Hardy and her Daughter Anna Eliza Hardy" 1842. Museum of Fine Arts, Boston, M. and M. Kavolik collection; **295,** David A. Schorsch Co.; **296,** The Granger Collection, New York

Chapter 11
299, Museum of the City of New York; **303,** Collection of the Albany Institute of History & Art. Photograph by Joseph Levy; **307,** The Historic New Orleans Collection, Accension #1975.931 & 2; **311,** Courtesy of Special Collections, University of Miami Libraries; **312,** From the Collections of the Library of Congress; **313,** North Wind Picture Archives; **314,** The Granger Collection, New York; **315,** From the Collections of the Library of Congress; **316,** The Granger Collection, New York; **317,** The Granger Collection, New York; **318,** The New York Museum/Art Resource, NY; **318,** Courtesy of the Edgar Allan Poe Museum, Richmond, Virginia; **318,** The Granger Collection, New York; **319,** Smithsonian Institution; **324,** Courtesy of the Massachusetts Historical Society

Chapter 12
327, © Shelburne Museum, Shelburne, Vermont; **333,** The Granger Collection, New York; **334,** California History Section, California State Library; **335,** The Granger Collection, New York; **336,** Mormon Panormana Eighteen/Crossing the Mississippi on the Ice, by C. C. A. Christensen © Courtesy Museum of Art, Brigham Young University, All rights reserved; **337,** The Granger Collection, New York; **338,** The Granger Collection, New York; **338,** The J. Paul Getty Museum, Los Angeles; **339,** Women's Rights National Historical Park, Courtesy of Seneca Falls Historical Society; **339,** The Granger Collection, New York; **341,** The Granger Collection, New York; **342,** © Bettmann/Corbis; **342,** The Granger Collection, New York; **345,** © Corbis; **346,** The Granger Collection, New York; **346,** © Bettmann/Corbis; **348,** © Bettmann/Corbis; **349,** From the Collections of the Library of Congress; **350,** Sketch of Honolulu, Oahu, 1840, by James Dwight Dana, Courtesy of Mission Houses Museum Library, Collections of the Hawaiian Mission Children's Society; **352,** © Corbis

Chapter 13
355, Winslow Horner, "Sunday Morning in Virginia" 1877 Cincinnati Art Museum, John M. Emerey Funds Acc. 1924. 247; **358,** The Granger Collection, New York; **361,** Painting of a block house in New Braunfels, by Carl G. von Iwonski. Courtesy of the Daughters of the Republic of Texas Library; **363,** The Kansas State Historical Society, Topeka, Kansas; **363,** The Granger Collection, New York; **364,** The Granger Collection, New York; **366,** The Granger Collection, New York; **372,** © Bettmann/Corbis; **375,** © Bettmann/Corbis; **376,** From the Collections of the Library of Congress; **378,** © Bettmann/Corbis; **380,** The Granger Collection, New York; **381,** The Granger Collection, New York

Chapter 14
383, Seventh Regiment Fund; **388,** North Wind Picture Archives; **390,** The Museum of the Confederacy, Richmond, Virginia. Copy Photography by Katherine Wetzel; **390,** The Granger Collection, New York; **390,** Courtesy Sidney King; **391,** Courtesy of the National Park Service, Kennesau Mountain National Park. Photo, Harpers Peng Conservation Center; **391,** Courtesy of the Carl Vinson Institute of Government—the University of Virginia. Photo by Ed Jackson; **393,** © Corbis; **394,** The Granger Collection, New York; **396,** © Bettmann/Corbis; **397,** Williamson Art Gallery & Museum, Birkenhead, England; **398,** The Granger Collection, New York; **400,** Museum of the city of New York, The Harry T. Peters Collection. 57-300-51; **400,** Collection of President Franklin P. Roosevelt U.S. Naval Historical Center Photograph; **403,** The Western Reserve Historical Society, Cleveland Ohio; **405,** Chicago Historical Society, P & S-1932.0027; **406,** Corbis-Bettmann; **409,** From the Tharpe Collection of American Military Art; **410,** © Stock Montage, Inc.

Chapter 15
412, © Bettmann/Corbis; **416,** © Bettmann/Corbis; **417,** © The Stock Montage; **420,** The Granger Collection, New York; **421,** © The Stock Montage; **424,** The Granger Collection, New York; **430,** Corbis; **430,** The Granger Collection, New York; **432,** North Wind Picture Archives; **433,** © Bettmann/Corbis; **433,** North Wind Picture Archives; **434,** © Corbis; **435,** © Bettman/Corbis; **437,** North Wind Picture Archives; **438,** Reproduced from the Collections of the Library of Congress; **438,** The Granger Collection, New York; **439,** The Granger Collection, New York

Chapter 16
442, From the Collections of the Library of Congress; **445,** The Granger Collection, New York; **446,** From the Collections of the Library of Congress; **447,** The Granger Collection, New York; **447,** California History Section, California State Library; **449,** The Granger Collection, New York; **449,** From the Collections of the

Library of Congress; **451,** The Granger Collection, New York; **452,** From the Collections of the Library of Congress; **453,** The Granger Collection, New York; **455,** From the Collections of the Library of Congress; **455,** No credit necessary; **457,** From the Collections of the Library of Congress; **460,** The Granger Collection, New York; **460,** The Granger Collection, New York; **464,** Kansas State Historical Society; **465,** From the Collections of the Library of Congress; **466,** From the Collections of the Library of Congress

Chapter 17
470, Reproduced from the Collections of the Library of Congress #LC-US261-449; **471,** Courtesy American Antiquarian Society; **471,** The Library Company of Philadelphia; **473,** Courtesy American Antiquarian Society; **476,** From the Collections of the Library of Congress; **481,** Courtesy of the Rockefeller Archive Center; **482,** From the Collections of the Library of Congress; **483,** The Granger Collection, New York; **484,** From the Collections of the Library of Congress; **486,** The Granger Collection, New York; **486,** The Granger Collection, New York; **487,** Reproduced from the Collections of the Library of Congress; **488,** © Bettmann/Corbis; **489,** The Granger Collection, New York; **490,** The Granger Collection, New York; **491,** Reproduced from the Collections of the Library of Congress; **494,** Kansas State Historical Society; **498,** © Bettmann / Corbis; **500,** Courtesy of the University of Pennsylvania Art Collection, Philadelphia, Pennsylvania; **503,** From the Collections of the Library of Congress

Chapter 18
505, The Granger Collection, New York; **507,** The Granger Collection, New York; **508,** W. Louis Sonntag, Jr., The Bowery at Night, 1895. Museum of the City of New York; **509,** The Granger Collection, New York; **511,** From the Collections of the Library of Congress; **515,** The Granger Collection, New York; **515,** © Collection of The New York Historical Society; **517,** Courtesy Northwestern University Archives; **519,** The Granger Collection, New York; **522,** The Granger Collection, New York; **523,** The Granger Collection, New York; **524,** © David J. & Janice L. Frent Collection/Corbis; **525,** Chicago Historical Society, #CHI-03590; **526,** © Bettmann/Corbis; **526,** Reproduced from the Collections of the Library of Congress; **528,** Chicago Historical Society

Chapter 19
529, From the Collections of the Library of Congress; **532,** No credit necessary; **532,** © Bettmann/Corbis; **534,** From the Collections of the Library of Congress; **535,** Brown Brothers, Sterling, PA; **536,** From the Collections of the Library of Congress; **538,** © Corbis; **539,** © UPI/Bettmann/Corbis; **541,** © Smithsonian Institution; **544,** Reproduced from the Collections of the Library of Congress; **544,** The Granger Collection, New York; **544,** The Granger Collection, New York; **548,** The Granger Collection, New York; **549,** Theodore Roosevelt Collection, Harvard College Library; **550,** Reproduced from the Collections of the Library of Congress; **551,** From the Collections of the Library of Congress; **553,** Culver Pictures, Inc.

Chapter 20
555, The Granger Collection, New York; **559,** The Granger Collection, New York; **562,** The Granger Collection, New York; **563,** © UPI/Bettmann/Corbis; **566,** From the Collections of the Library of Congress; **568,** The Granger Collection, New York; **570,** The Granger Collection, New York; **572,** The Granger Collection, New York; **572,** © Bettmann/Corbis; **573,** Reproduced from the Collections of the Library of Congress; **574,** The Granger Collection, New York; **575,** Albert Shaw, A Cartoon History of Roosevelt's Career (1910); **576,** By W. A. Rogers. From the Herald

(New York); **576,** By Homer Davenport. From the Evening Mail (New York); **578,** From the Bostwick-Frohardt Collections, owned by KMTV and on permanent loan to Western Heritage Museum, Omaha, Nebraska

Chapter 21
579, The Granger Collection, New York; **579,** © Bettmann/UPI/ Corbis; **580,** From the Collections of the Library of Congress; **581,** Reproduced from the Collections of the Library of Congress; **584,** From the Collections of the Library of Congress; **588,** Courtesy of the Theodore Roosevelt Coll., Widener Library, Harvard University; **589,** © Bettmann/UPI/Corbis; **589,** Reproduced from the Collections of the Library of Congress; **590,** The Granger Collection, New York; **594,** From the Collections of the Library of Congress; **595,** Courtesy, Clifford K. Berryman Collection, U.S. Senate, Center for Legislation Archives; **597,** The Granger Collection, New York; **600,** Reproduced from the Collections of the Library of Congress; **601,** From the Collections of Henry Ford Museum & Greenfield Village; **603,** © Bettmann/ UPI/Corbis; **604,** George Bellows, "The Cliff Dwellers" 1913. Los Angeles County Museum of Art, Los Angeles; **605,** Reproduced from the Collections of the Library of Congress

Chapter 22
609, From the Collections of the Library of Congress; **612,** The Granger Collection, New York; **613,** The Granger Collection, New York; **613,** Photographs and Print Division, Schomburg Center for Research in Black Culture, New York Public Library, Astor, Lenox, and Tilden Foundations; **614,** Photographs and Prints Division, Schomburg Center for Research in Black Culture, New York Public Library, Astor, Lenox and Tilden Foundations; **615,** Washington Evening Star, November, 1915; **620,** The Granger Collection, New York; **624,** Gift of Henry Colgate, Picker Art Gallery, Colgate University; **626,** © Bettmann/UPI/Corbis; **629,** U.S. Signal Corps. Photo No. 111-SC-26063 in the National Archives; **631,** U.S. Signal Corps. Photo No. 111-SC-62979 in the National Archives; **632,** © Bettmann/Corbis; **633,** National Archives #165-WW-269.c-7; **635,** Brown Brothers

Chapter 23
641, From the Collections of the Library of Congress; **644,** From the Collections of the Library of Congress; **645,** The Granger Collection, New York; **645,** No credit necessary; **648,** © Bettmann/Corbis; **649,** The Granger Collection, New York; **650,** © Frank Driggs/Corbis; **651,** © Bettmann/UPI/Corbis; **653,** The Granger Collection, New York; **654,** Chicago Historical Society; **657,** The Granger Collection, New York; **658,** From the Collections of the Library of Congress; **659,** © Bettmann/UPI/Corbis

Chapter 24
661, From the Collections of the Library of Congress; **663,** The Granger Collection, New York; **666,** From the Collections of the Library of Congress; **668,** © Bettmann/UPI/Corbis; **672,** © Bettmann/UPI/Corbis; **673,** © Bettmann/Corbis; **673,** © Bettmann/Corbis; **674,** © Bettmann/Corbis; **676,** The Granger Collection, New York; **676,** Reproduced from the Collections of the Library of Congress #USZ62 045911 903241; **680,** © Bettmann/UPI/Corbis; **680,** The Granger Collection, New York; **682,** © Bettmann/UPI/Corbis

Chapter 25
684, © Bettmann/UPI/Corbis; **684,** U.S. Coast Guard photo no. 26-WA-6J-14 in the National Archives; **685,** © Bettmann/UPI/Corbis; **685,** © Bettmann/UPI/Corbis; **688,** Franklin D. Roosevelt Library/The New Yorker; **690,** © Bettmann/UPI/Corbis; **691,**